Proceedings of the
J.R.R. Tolkien Centenary Conference
1992

Proceedings of the Conference held at Keble College, Oxford, England.
17th - 24th August 1992 to celebrate the centenary of the birth of
Professor J.R.R. Tolkien
Incorporating the 23rd Mythopoeic Conference (Mythcon XXIII) and Oxonmoot 1992.

edited by Patricia Reynolds and Glen GoodKnight

1995

Milton Keynes and Altadena

The Tolkien Society
The Mythopoeic Press

Mallorn 33
Mythlore 80

Published by the Mythopoeic Press, PO Box 6707, Altadena, California 91003-6707, USA. and The Tolkien Society, ℅ 16 Gibsons Green, Heelands, Milton Keynes, England, MK13 7NH. Printed in the United States of America.

The Mythopoeic Press is an imprint of The Mythopoeic Society which is a non-profit organisation incorporated in California USA. The Tolkien Society is a Charity registered in England No. 273809

First published 1995

Published as
Mythlore, Volume 21, Number 2 (Whole Number 80), Winter 1996
and
Mallorn 33

Copyright © The Tolkien Society and the Mythopoeic Society 1995
Copyright © of the individual papers remains with the authors
Quotations from the Works of J.R.R. Tolkien are printed by kind permission of the publishers HarperCollins*Publishers* and the Estate of J.R.R. Tolkien. Quotations published here for the first time are copyright © The Tolkien Trust 1995
The R.S. Thomas poem "The Kingdom" on page 20 first appeared in *H'm* and is printed by kind permission of R.S. Thomas and the publishers Macmillan Publishers Limited © R.S. Thomas 1972. The base maps on pages 399-408 are derived from maps by Karen Wynn Fonstad first published in *The Atlas of Middle-earth* and are reproduced by kind permission of the publishers Houghton Mifflin Co. and HarperCollins*Publishers* and are copyright © Karen Wynn Fonstad 1981. The conference logo, used on the cover and the section headings is © Marian Haas 1991. Tom Shippey's paper "Tolkien as a Post-War Writer" on pages 84-93 was first published in *Scholarship and Fantasy: Proceedings of The Tolkien Phenomenon May 1992 Turku, Finland* and is printed here by kind permission of the publishers The University of Turku, © Tom Shippey 1993. Jane Chance's paper "Power and Knowledge in Tolkien: The Problem of Difference in 'The Birthday Party'" on pages 115-120 was first published in *The Lord of the Rings: The Mythology of Power* and is printed here by kind permission of the publishers Twayne Publishers, © Twayne Publishers 1992. The illustrations on pages 410-414 are © Ruth Lacon 1995. The figures on pages 174, 176, 177, 182 and 184 are reproduced by kind permission of the Bodleian Library and Oxford University Press © Oxford University Press 1995. The figures on pages 178, 179, 180, 181 and 183 are reproduced by kind permission of Oxford University press copyright 1921. Previously unpublished quotations from work on *The Oxford English Dictionary* on pages 177, 179, 181, 182, 184 and 185 are reproduced by kind permission of Oxford University Press © Oxford University Press 1995. The photograph on page 303 is by and © The Royal Library, The Hague 1995, reproduced by kind permission. The photographs on pages 305, 307 (left hand side) and 308 are by and © C.M. Tholens 1995, reproduced by kind permission. Quotations from Robert Westall's article "Hunt for Evil" on pages 235 and 236 and his letter on pages 236 and 237 both of which first appeared in *Signal* are reproduced with the kind permission of Laura Cecil the literary executor for the author's estate and the publisher Thimble Press © Robert Westall 1981. Quotations from Robert Westall's previously unpublished letter on pages 237 and 238 are reproduced with the kind permission of Laura Cecil the literary executor for the author's estate © the estate of Robert Westall 1995. Quotations from the transcript of the BBC radio programme *Talking Books* by Arthur Calder Marshall on page 233 are reproduced by kind permission of the British Broadcasting Corporation and Elaine Greene, the author's agent © BBC 1955. Quotations from Philip Neil's letter on page 236 first published in *Signal* are reproduced with the kind permission of the author and the publisher Thimble Press © Neil Philip 1981. The text of the previously unpublished postcard from E.P. Thompson on page 239 is published with the kind permission of the author © E.P. Thompson 1995. Quotations from Rayner Unwin on page 227 are published with the kind permission of Rayner Unwin and HarperCollins. John Elison's paper "Baggins Remembered" on pages 394-395 was first published in *Oxonmoot 92 Programme Book* published by the Tolkien Society and the Mythopoeic Society © the publishers and John Ellison.

All rights reserved. No part of this publication may be reproduced, stored in any retrieval system, or transmitted in any form or by any means, electronic, mechanical, photocopying, recording, or otherwise without the prior permission of the publishers.

The right of the authors of individual papers in this volume to be identified as the authors of their papers has been asserted in accordance with sections 77 and 78 of the Copyright Designs and Patents Act 1988.

British Library Cataloguing in Publication Data. A catalogue record for this book is available from the British Library.

ISBN 0-905520-06-8 (The Tolkien Society – paperback)
ISBN 0-905520-09-2 (The Tolkien Society – hardback)
ISBN 1-887726-04-7 (The Mythopoeic Press – paperback)

Mythlore ISSN 0146-9339
Mallorn ISSN 0308-6674

The views and opinions expressed in this publication are those of the individual authors, and do not necessarily represent the views of either editor or either society.

MYTHLORE is published quarterly by The Mythopoeic Society at 386 E. Poppyfields, Altadena, CA 91001. Second Class postage paid at Altadena, CA, and at other mailing offices (Monterey Park, CA). *Mythlore* is published quarterly for $20 per year (4 issues; membership in The Mythopoeic Society is included) by The Mythopoeic Society. **POSTMASTER: Send address changes to *MYTHLORE*, P.O. Box 6707, Altadena CA 91003-6707.**

Contents

Contents	3
Unpublished contributions	6
Editorial	7
Opening Address	10

Section 1: Recollection and Remembrance

Vera Chapman	*Reminiscences: Oxford in 1920, Meeting Tolkien and Becoming an Author at 77*	12
Glen H. GoodKnight	*Tolkien Centenary Banquet Address*	15
Fr. Robert Murray	*Sermon at Thanksgiving Service, Keble College Chapel, 23rd August 1992*	17
George Sayer	*Recollections of J.R.R. Tolkien*	21
Rayner Unwin	*Publishing Tolkien*	26

Section 2: Sources and Influences

Nils Ivar Agøy	Quid Hinieldus cum Christo? – *New Perspectives on Tolkien's Theological Dilemma and his Sub-Creation Theory*	31
Verlyn Flieger	*Tolkien's Experiment with Time: The Lost Road, "The Notion Club Papers" and J.W. Dunne*	39
Deirdre Greene	*Higher Argument: Tolkien and the tradition of Vision, Epic and Prophecy*	45
Virginia Luling	*An Anthropologist in Middle-earth*	53
Charles E. Noad	*Frodo and his Spectre: Blakean Resonances in Tolkien*	58
Gloriana St. Clair	*An Overview of the Northern Influences on Tolkien's Works*	63
Gloriana St. Clair	*Volsunga Saga and Narn: Some Analogies*	68
Chris Seeman	*Tolkien's Revision of the Romantic Tradition*	73
Tom Shippey	*Tolkien as a Post-War Writer*	84
Norman Talbot	*Where do Elves go to? Tolkien and a Fantasy Tradition*	94

Section 3: *The Lord of the Rings*

Marjorie Burns	*Eating, Devouring, Sacrifice and Ultimate Just Desserts*	108
Jane Chance	*Power and Knowledge in Tolkien: The Problem of Difference in "The Birthday Party"*	115
Joe R. Christopher	*The Moral Epiphanies in* The Lord of the Rings	121

Patrick Curry	*"Less Noise and More Green": Tolkien's Ideology for England*	126
Gwenyth Hood	*The Earthly Paradise in Tolkien's* The Lord of the Rings	139
Gloriana St. Clair	*Tolkien as Reviser: A Case Study*	145
Christina Scull	*Open Minds, Closed Minds in* The Lord of the Rings	151

Section 4: *The Silmarillion*

Alex Lewis	*Historical Bias in the Making of* The Silmarillion	158
Eric Schweicher	*Aspects of the Fall in* The Silmarillion	167

Section 5: Linguistics and Lexicography

Peter M. Gilliver	*At the Wordface: J.R.R. Tolkien's Work on the* Oxford English Dictionary	173
Christopher Gilson and Patrick Wynne	*The Growth of Grammar in the Elven Tongues*	187
Deirdre Greene	*Tolkien's Dictionary Poetics: The Influence of the* OED's *Defining Style on Tolkien's Fiction*	195
Natalia Grigorieva	*Problems of Translating into Russian*	200
Bruce Mitchell	*J.R.R. Tolkien and Old English Studies: An Appreciation*	206
Tom Shippey	*Tolkien and the Gawain-poet*	213

Section 6: Response and Reaction

Vladimir Grushetskiy	*How Russians See Tolkien*	221
Wayne G. Hammond	*The Critical Response to Tolkien's Fiction*	226
Jessica Yates	*Tolkien the Anti-totalitarian*	233

Section 7: Tolkien Studies

Helen Armstrong	*Good Guys, Bad Guys, Fantasy and Reality*	247
Christine Barkley	*The Realm of Faërie*	253
Christine Barkley	*Point of View in Tolkien*	256
Joe R. Christopher	*J.R.R. Tolkien and the Clerihew*	263
Edith L. Crowe	*Power in Arda: Sources, Uses and Misuses*	272
Chris Hopkins	*Tolkien and Englishness*	278
Carl J. Hostetter and Arden R. Smith	*A Mythology for England*	281
Nancy Martsch	*A Tolkien Chronology*	291

Tadeusz Andrzej Olszański	*Evil and the Evil One in Tolkien's Theology*	298
René van Rossenberg	*Tolkien's Exceptional Visit to Holland: A Reconstruction*	301
Anders Stenström	*A Mythology? For England?*	310
Dwayne Thorpe	*Tolkien's Elvish Craft*	315

Section 8: Middle-earth Studies

Jenny Coombs and Marc Read	*A Physics of Middle-earth*	323
David A. Funk	*Explorations into the Psyche of Dwarves*	330
William Antony Swithin Sarjeant	*The Geology of Middle-earth*	334
Lester E. Simons	*Writing and Allied Technologies in Middle-earth*	340

Section 9: The Inklings

Charles A. Coulombe	*Hermetic Imagination: The Effect of The Golden Dawn on Fantasy Literature*	345
David Doughan	*Tolkien, Sayers, Sex and Gender*	356
Colin Duriez	*Tolkien and the Other Inklings*	360
Lisa Hopkins	*Female Authority Figures in the Works of Tolkien, C.S. Lewis and Charles Williams*	364
Diana Lynne Pavlac	*More than a Bandersnatch: Tolkien as a Collaborative Writer*	367
Stephen Yandell	*"A Pattern Which Our Nature Cries Out For": The Medieval Tradition of the Ordered Four in the Fiction of J.R.R. Tolkien*	375

Section 10: Flights of Fancy

John Ellison	*Baggins Remembered*	394
Hubert Sawa	*Short History of the Territorial Development of the Dwarves' Kingdoms in the Second and Third Ages of Middle-earth*	396
Angela Surtees and Steve Gardner	*The Mechanics of Dragons: An Introduction to The Study of their 'Ologies*	411

Section 11: Other Writers

Madawc Williams	*Tales of Wonder – Science Fiction and Fantasy in the Age of Jane Austen*	419
J.R. Wytenbroek	*Natural Mysticism in Kenneth Grahame's* The Wind in the Willows	431
J.R. Wytenbroek	*Cetacean Consciousness in Katz's* Whalesinger *and L'Engle's* A Ring of Endless Light	435

Index 439

Papers presented at the Conference and not submitted for publication

Helen Armstrong *How Dare You Call Me That!*

William Cater *Interviewing Tolkien*

Michael Foster *Easter in Middle-earth*

Paul Nolan Hyde *The Language of Children: A Vocabulary Contest Between* The Hobbit *and* The Lord of the Rings

Stephen Medcalf *The Language Learnt of Elves*

Ned Raggett *An Unread Classic? Tolkien and Today's Reading Audience*

John D. Rateliff *The Lost Road, The Dark Tower and "The Notion Club Papers" : Tolkien and Lewis' Time Travel Triad*

Brian Sibley *The Radio and the Ring: Thirty-seven Years of Broadcasting Tolkien*

Michael Tiedemann *Manwë's Mistake: An Approach to the Reasons for the Flight of the Noldor*

Panel discussions

Fantasy Role-playing and Tolkien's World Moderated by Chris Seeman, panelists: Andrew Butler, Glenn Kuring, Brian Murphy, Eric Rauscher, Madawc Williams

Illustrating Tolkien Moderated by Christina Scull, panelists: Denis Bridoux, Sylvia Hunnewell, Ted Nasmith, Susanne Stopfel, Patrick Wynne

Immortal Love? Moderated by Angela Surtees, panelists: Ruth Lacon, Jeremy Morgan, Catherine Thorn

Music and Tolkien's World Moderated by Alex Lewis, panelist: Alisdair Roberts

A Not-So-Secret Vice: Tolkienian Linguistics Moderated by Carl F. Hostetter, panelists: Jenny Coombs, David Doughan, Paul Nolan Hyde, Nancy Martsch, Arden Smith, Patrick Wynne

The Relationship between Tolkien's Academic and Middle-earth Works Moderated by Pat Reynolds, panelists: Verlyn Flieger, Deirdre Greene, Gloriana St. Claire, Tom Shippey

Tolkien and the Inklings Moderated by Glen H. GoodKnight, panelists: Joe Christopher, Colin Duriez, Verlyn Flieger, Diana Pavlac, John Rateliff

Tolkien and Oxford University Moderated by Christina Scull, panelists: Dierdre Greene, Stephen Medcalf, Bruce Mitchell, Tom Shippey

Tolkien's Precursors Moderated by John D. Rateliff, panelists: Rikki Breem, Marjorie Burns, Verlyn Flieger

The Value of "The History of Middle-earth" Series Moderated by Ned Raggett, panelists: Helen Armstrong, David Bratman, Paul Nolan Hyde, Brian Murphy

Slide presentations

Wayne Hammond *Pauline Baynes, Illustrator*

Joy Hill *Tolkien's Fan Mail* Presented by Christina Scull and Wayne Hammond

Gary Hunnewell *The Good, the Bad and the Ugly: The Commercialism of J.R.R. Tolkien*

Ted Nasmith *The Tolkien Art of Ted Nasmith: A Chronological Review*

Christina Scull *Illustrating Tolkien*

Philip Smith *Creative Bindings of Tolkien's Works*

Michael Underwood *Artwork Inspired by J.R.R. Tolkien*

Editorial

Glen H. GoodKnight

The dream that the Mythopoeic Society would one day hold a conference in Oxford is nearly as old as the Society itself. The Society originally began in Southern California, that near-mythical place, both so curiously and inordinately lionized and denigrated by those who live elsewhere. All groups must have a place for their beginnings, while ideas, visions, and friendships know no borders. Naturally the first Mythopoeic Conferences were held in California. Gradually as the interest and membership of the Society grew to national and international scope, we desired to hold Conferences in other areas. I always felt Oxford was the ideal and ultimately logical location. I spoke of this several times in the Society's early history of the 1970s. After our Conference in Wheaton, a suburb of Chicago, I ended my "Editorial Note" in *Mythlore* 43, Autumn 1985, with this statement:

> The center of the Society is not in one geographical place. It is . . . found anywhere where the vision is shared in the hearts and imaginations of the people involved. This was clearly proved in 1985. Now a milestone has been passed . . . I am confident that in the future we will see other Mythopoeic Conferences in other geographical centers . . . We need to be positive and progressive, and why not? Eventually, Onward to Oxford!

When in 1987 the Society celebrated the 50th anniversary of *The Hobbit* at Marquette University, with Christopher Tolkien as Guest of Honour, an announcement was made at the Banquet to celebrate the Tolkien Centenary with a Conference at Oxford. Immediately after the banquet it was learned that the Tolkien Society in Britain was also planning to hold a Centenary Conference as well. In brief, we negotiated to jointly hold a Conference for this occasion, and the long process of planning began.

The Conference spanned eight unforgettable days, August 17-24, 1992. Even though longer than previous Conferences, it followed the same pattern of making the papers the predominant feature of the programming. In the early days of The Mythopoeic Society, the first three Conferences published a separate *Proceedings*. Beginning with the fourth Mythopoeic Conference, papers have been published in *Mythlore*. Because the Conference was jointly sponsored, it was decided to publish the papers in a *Proceedings* that is a special issue of *Mythlore* and *Mallorn*.

How I regret that the *Proceedings* cannot capture the full panoply of exciting events, memorable experiences, and renowned locations that cannot be adequately expressed on paper: the wonderful international mix of people, the camaraderie at the dining hall, the crush of the Opening Ceremonies at Blackwell's, the sublimely perfect Memorial Service, the whimsical masquerade, the Banquet, the dramatic performances, Christopher Tolkien's reading of "The New Shadow" in the ancient and magnificent Sheldonian Theatre, and the city of Oxford itself, to name only a few.

Regardless, what we do have here is remarkable unto itself. In these pages you are able to read in full *and* in leisure nearly every paper given at the Centenary Conference — something that was rarely, if ever, possible for those attending, due to the multiple scheduling during the Conference.

The Tolkien Centenary Conference was meant to lovingly celebrate J.R.R. Tolkien's 100th birthday. It was intended for all who love this man and his works, regardless of their nationality or academic credentials. Thus those attending represented a wide spectrum of people, from academic scholars to homemakers, from young people to those wise with years, from those only having read some of his books once to those who have read everything he wrote and some works many, *many* times. The papers reflect, in part, this spectrum. The vast majority are written by serious scholars on Tolkien and his work, but there are other kinds of material here as well. There is the section that contains personal recollections and appreciations of J.R.R. Tolkien; there are those few papers that are on other topics, and a few that perhaps might be described as "tongue-in-cheek." Those who feel that a Proceedings should only contain serious scholarly papers, need to consider that, as significantly scholarly as this *Proceedings* is, it does also reflect other aspects of the Conference.

Getting this Proceedings to completion and in your hands has been a very great undertaking, requiring many, many details to be worked through. As in any production by more than one person, many compromises needed to be worked out. Sometimes certain aspects of these compromises may not please all concerned. If decisions were to be made by myself alone, a number of things would have come out differently. Nevertheless the overall product and its achievement speaks for itself.

For those who miss the usual artwork, reviews, letters, Inklings Bibliography, columns, and the other features, be assured they will resume with the next regular issue of *Mythlore*.

I hope that this *Proceedings* will prove to be the milestone in Tolkien scholarship that I believe it will. It is sure to provoke much new thoughts, insights and ideas in those that read it. Should this be true in your case, I hope you will consider writing a letter of comment or a paper for publication in *Mythlore*, whether you are a current subscriber or not. Critical responses to printed ideas is a long-standing tradition of *Mythlore*, and submissions of papers, letters, reviews and artwork are very welcome.

It was suggested by more than one at the Conference that there should be a Bicentenary Tolkien Conference held in 2092. If so, we must set to work at once to adequately prepare for a Conference that could possibly equal the one we experienced in 1992.

Patricia Reynolds

J.R.R. Tolkien, I believe, was a man who liked parties. No-one who wrote so entrancingly of "songs, dances, music, games, and, of course, food and drink" – not to mention presents and fireworks – could possibly hate them himself. When the 1992 Tolkien Centenary Committee came to one of it's least onerous tasks and chose a name for the conference, "A Long-Expected Party" leapt to the fore of someone's mind, and struck a chord with all of us.

The conference was many years in the planning stage. There were instances in which, individually or collectively, we doubted that it could happen. New Year's Day, 1990 dawned, and many of us felt that the new decade brought the conference uncomfortably close – but somehow more possible. Every member of the organizing committee can tell you of the moment when they personally knew it was happening, knew that it was *working*. As for some magician in a tower, the fog cleared, and the vision we had conjured appeared.

But, of course, it did not appear by magic. My fellow Chairman, Christina Scull, and I are thankful to our fellow organizing committee members, to the committee of the Tolkien Society and stewards of the Mythopoeic Society (both for pitching in, and for diverting the best energies of their society into this project for many years), to the writers and artists who contributed to publications, to the stewards and other volunteers, to those who presented papers, contributed to panels, or provided entertainments, and to those who were simply grabbed and did more than they were asked.

The conference was held at Keble College, Oxford, England. The conference could not have been held in any other city than Oxford, home for most of Tolkien's adult life. This caused a few problems (when Keble was built, for example, a bathroom was provided on each floor against opposition: why, some argued, did students need baths: they went home at the end of each term, didn't they?) but overall, the "city of dreaming spires" had no competition.

Songs, dances, music and games there were in plenty. Also plays and coach tours and slide-shows and exhibitions. Tolkien's works inspire great creativity in its readers: and so does seeing other's responses.

There were three streams of papers and panels running concurrently, focusing on a great diversity of subjects. Looking back, it is scarcely believable that so much was fitted into one week. I am very pleased that so many papers have been fitted into one volume: a very few were not available to us for one reason or another, and these are listed. I hope that there is at least one which has what Glen GoodKnight has termed the "what – you too!" factor, and at least one which makes you cry "what!!!", and produces a thoughtful letter or article in rebuttal. As editors of *Mythlore* and *Mallorn*, Glen and I await your responses.

The first section, **Recollection and Remembrance**, contains papers and presentations, mainly by people who knew J.R.R. Tolkien. The second section, **Sources and Influences** looks, conversely, at those Tolkien knew. The following two sections deal with specific works: ***The Lord of the Rings***, ***The Silmarillion***. A wide variety of approaches to the books are taken. The fifth section, **Linguistics and Lexicography** is not "just elvish" – although there *is* a paper on those languages: also here are papers on Tolkien's work on the languages and texts of our world, the effect his work had on his writings, and the effect his writings have on translators. The sixth section, **Response and Reaction** contains papers dealing with other effects of Tolkien's writing. The seventh section is the largest, covering as it does **Tolkien Studies**: papers concerned with more than one of Tolkien's books, or with his life. Section eight, **Middle-earth Studies** is titled after a distinction John Ellison and I drew in *Mallorn* 31 – while "Tolkien Studies" are comparable to the body of work surrounding any other author ("Shakespeare Studies" or "Dickens Studies", for example), "Middle-earth Studies" are serious examinations of Middle-earth, treating its history, geography and cultures as topics of study – comparable rather to "Pacific Rim Studies" or "European Studies". While the papers dealing with those Tolkien influenced and was influenced by are given sections of their own, one group of relationships is so special and complex, that section nine is set aside for **The Inklings** alone. Here there are overviews of those relationships, and comparisons between the works of various members of the group. The papers in Section ten **Flights of Fancy** take an imaginative approach to "Tolkien Studies" and "Middle-earth Studies". Finally, in the section titled: **Other Writers** the spotlight is turned from Tolkien to 18th century authors, Kenneth Grahame, Welwyn Wilton Katz and Madeleine L'Engle.

While the conference took place in England, and was jointly organized by a British and American society, conference attendees came from across the world. We were especially pleased to welcome scholars from Russia, Poland and the Czech Republic. The changes in world politics in the late 80s and early 90s became close to our hearts through these people. It is hard to explain the atmosphere: knowing that whoever you sat down with at a meal, or next to in a lecture was as enthusiastic about Tolkien as you are is a unique experience. My own personal "this is going to work" moment came at a Bardic Circle. This is a traditional Mythcon event, where a circle of people take turns to read, or recite, sing or play. Inspiration is usually something "fantasy", not necessarily Tolkien, and on this night the songs and stories came from across the world, and the fellowship was tangible.

The appearance of these, the *Proceedings* of that conference has been to me no less of a marvel than that of the conference itself. The contributors have all been very patient – with my own slowness, and especially after the joint catastrophe of having my computer stolen and misplacing the most recent back up discs. Like the Conference itself, it is a joint production of the Mythopoeic Society and the Tolkien Society. Like the Conference itself, it is the product of many hands: principally, Glen and I have to thank Charles Noad for a Herculean proof-reading task and Trevor Reynolds for typing, re-typing, indexing, translating computer manuals into English and being positive. Helen Armstrong for additional typing. Secondary proof readers; Amanda Campbell, Christine Crawshaw, Richard Crawshaw, Anthony Dumas, John Ellison, Angela Gardner, Christina Hammond, Mr R. Heaton, Sarah Sturch and Andrew Wells also deserve our thanks. Design advice was given by Wayne Hammond and Lester Simons. Richard Crawshaw and Mark Sapey redrew maps and diagrams. General support and encouragement came from many people – for quality and quantity Lynn Maudlin, David Bratman and members of the Tolkien Society Committee 1992-5, under its chairman Amanda Campbell must be honoured. Of course, all errors and omissions are due to the editors alone.

Tolkien once described the elves in an interview with Denis Guerolt, who asked "Did you intend, in the *Lord of the Rings* that certain races should embody certain principles: the Elves wisdom, the Dwarves craftsmanship ...?"

After explaining he had to differentiate them somehow, and only having humanity to work with, the characteristics are taken from humanity, Tolkien continued:

> the elves are simply in a sense an expression of certain, not really wholly legitimate, desires the human race has about itself. We should all, or at least large parts of the human race would like to have greater power of mind, greater power of art (by which I mean that the gap between the conception and the power of execution should be shortened), we should like that, and we should like, of course, longer time, if not indefinite time to go on knowing more and making more. Therefore we make the elves immortal, in a sense . . .
> (Tolkien, 1980)

This volume deserves to have been edited by elves: but I am comforted by the thought that it will contribute to the desire of many to know more and make more.

I hope that something of the spirit of the conference comes to you through these papers. This may be for you a happy recollection of those times, or a foreshadowing of some future meeting with Tolkien scholars, who like their mentor, are undoubtably people who like parties.

Reference

Tolkien, J.R.R. 1980. *Tolkien and Basil Bunting*. London: BBC Cassettes. Transcribed by author.

Opening Address

Christina Scull

"I shall not keep you long", as Bilbo said on another occasion. At *his* Long-expected Party the were ONE GROSS guests coming from all parts of the Shire at the special supper. At *our* Long-expected Party we have more than twice that number coming from all parts of the world. One regret I have for the Conference is that my Argentinian correspondent was unable to come and South America is unrepresented. Mentioning *Argentina* brings me to one of Tolkien's great achievements: love and appreciation of his works bring people together, overriding national boundaries and differences. Here it is no longer relevant that we are British, Norwegian, Swedish, Finnish, Russian, Polish, Czech, Austrian, German, Belgian, Dutch, Nigerian, Japanese or from the United States, Canada, Australia or New Zealand, or even that we are members of this or that national or international Tolkien Society; but that we all enjoy reading Tolkien's works and feel that something special has been added to our lives thereby.

I hope that during the Conference many new friendships will be made and in future a face and personality can be visualised when you see a name in a magazine or journal.

By the time you read the above it will be over three years since I made that speech in Blackwell's Bookshop in Oxford on Monday 17 August 1992, at the Opening Ceremony of the Tolkien Centenary Conference. The hopes I expressed were fully realised and I think that those who attended will remember, among other things, the pervading feeling of friendship and the pleasure experienced in listening to papers and discussions and exchanging ideas about Tolkien and his works. Although the Centenary Conference was a unique event, many Tolkien Societies world-wide hold their own smaller festivals, and the number of these has increased with the founding of new Tolkien Societies. Such gatherings usually have an international element, small or large, and provide opportunities to meet old friends and make new ones. Since 1992 I have attended two Mythcons in the U.S.A., two "Hobbitons" organised by the Socièta Tolkieniana Italiana, and "The Celebration of the Destruction of the Ring" in Prague organised by the Czech Tolkien Society. I was sorry not to have been able to attend the Northern Tolkien Festival organised jointly in 1994 by all the Nordic Tolkien Societies. In Britain the Tolkien Society's Oxonmoot has continued to attract many devotees of Tolkien from abroad. Our enjoyment of Tolkien has led to a fellowship which encircles the globe.

Perhaps I might be permitted to introduce a personal note into this celebration of the international fellowship of Tolkien. At the Closing Ceremony of the Centenary Conference the announcement was made of my engagement to Wayne Hammond from the U.S.A. whom I had met through our shared interest in Tolkien. We were married in December 1994 and I am moving to the U.S.A. Tolkien certainly unites us across oceans and boundaries and cultural differences.

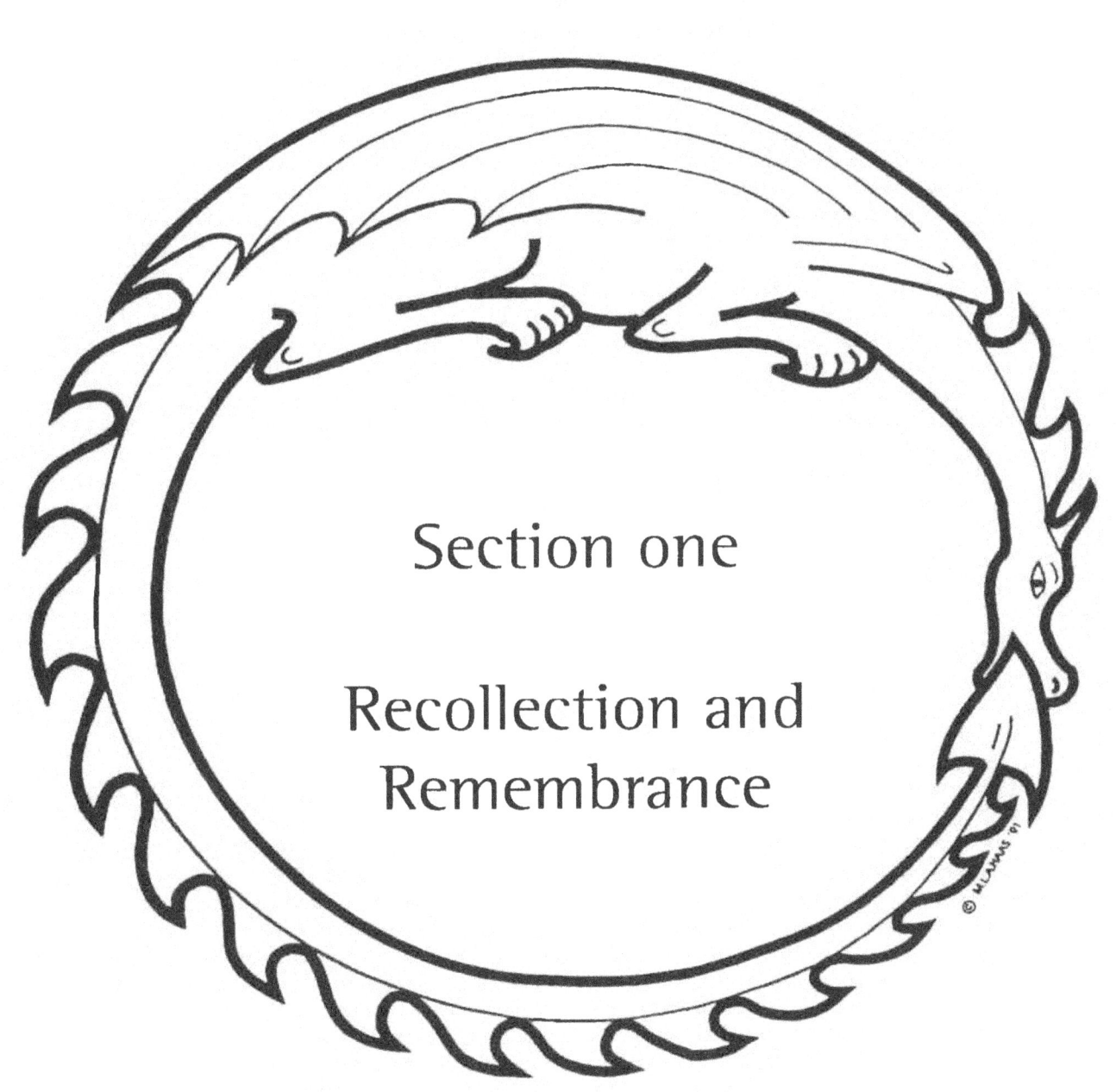

Section one

Recollection and Remembrance

Reminiscences: Oxford in 1920, Meeting Tolkien and Becoming an Author at 77

Vera Chapman

Abstract: Reminiscences of Vera Chapman's life, including going up to Oxford just after the First World War (between the time when Tolkien was an undergraduate and his return as a Professor).

Keywords: Sir Hugh Allen, Holst, Oxford, Gilbert Murray, Walter Raleigh, Joseph Wright

I came to Oxford in October 1918, but before that I had seen it as a vision of Quietness – first in a dream, as the quietest town on earth, all cream-coloured classic porticoes, bathed in autumn sunshine – then when I paid a brief visit there in the summer of 1918, and saw it rather as I had dreamt it. I came up (we always speak of "Coming Up", or "Going Down", to or from Oxford) to sit for yet another examination, I think to qualify me for entrance, and as an attempt to win a scholarship. I remember sitting for one at least of the papers in the old Divinity School, somewhere in that great complex of buildings between the Sheldonian and the Bodleian – a very ancient place, with a marvellous fan-vaulted ceiling to look at for inspiration. Being successful, I finally "Came Up" at the commencement of the autumn (or Michaelmas) term of 1918. Arrived at the station – in those days we had two railway-stations, to make travelling more difficult – and with another Bournemouth girl, took a *hansom-cab* – there were two still plying, mostly used, I am told, in the mock funeral processions accorded to those who were "Sent Down", a thing which I am glad to say never occurred in my time. So, marvelling at the continued quietness of Oxford, I came to Lady Margaret Hall in a hansom-cab.

Almost the first experience that met us was the Spanish Flu. We all found ourselves laid in bed with high temperatures, and all the senior members of the college (called Dons) immediately volunteered to act as nurses to us. This was, of course, somewhat embarrassing, when we hardly knew them. But they did indeed nurse us devotedly, forgetting all else. This was no slight influenza-cold. One afternoon I lay in my bed and heard the plaintive sounds, from the chapel immediately below my room, of a memorial service being held for one of us who had succumbed to it. Not a very encouraging beginning to one's Oxford life! But I am glad to say the rest of us survived, and were sent for convalescence in threes and fours for a couple of weeks to Headington and other bracing places, where we ate and smoked a great deal. Then as soon as we settled back in, came the great excitement of *The Armistice* – it felt like the beginning of a new world. No matter if there were still problems – the slaughter had ceased, and the men were coming back. Better still, the women, having kept the University alive all those four years, were now to be admitted as members of the University – with the titles of B.A. and M.A. and the rest – and with the Cap and Gown.

That Cap and Gown! We were all ceremonially matriculated in 1919, in an impressive gathering in the Sheldonian. Dress was important – that Cap and Gown was to be worn worthily and not disgraced. Conventional coat, skirt and blouse was the usual wear, and this must be "subfusc" in colour, that is, navy-blue, black, dark grey, brown, possibly dark violet, not green, and certainly *not* the deep claret red which my mother had selected for me. No, it would not do, and I must wear my old workaday blue suit. Likewise shoes – I had a good new pair, but alas! being new, they *squeaked* – "No, Miss Fogerty, that won't do. You must go up and change them", and so there was I hurrying for my life, to put on my old shoes while they all waited for me . . . such was my matriculation into Oxford.

After that excitement not much remained of the first term – I got a very bad report on my work, and I daresay others did the same. However, the world was before us.

We went to lectures in some of the great old colleges, though most of them had been made into hospitals for the war-wounded. But we had to behave ourselves, being marked out by our new Caps and Gowns. Scholarship holders wore well-shaped flowing gowns, but others wore a ridiculous garment over their coats – not long enough to reach half-way down the back, and decorated with rudiments of sleeves – these are still worn, and you may notice them when term starts. The caps were to be worn soberly – not pushed to the back of the head with the point aspiring upward (as often seen now) but straight upon the head, with the point modestly lowered between the eyebrows. Nor must we give any cause for disapproval – we must sit together, apart from the men, and, if we had any acquaintances among them, not greet them or give any sign of recognition – coming out of the lecture we must not converse, or claim any friendship in the street – above all, no *new* friendships were to be formed – that was the very thing that was to be rigidly avoided.

Our colleges were rigidly cloistered. One man, and one man only, stood as guardian at our door – the porter – and he might admit fathers, or uncles, or brothers, but not, *not* cousins. We were bidden to remember that our small bed-sitters were "technically our bedrooms" (I do not think any of our women's colleges had suites of rooms, as the men always had). If one of us wished to entertain a young man, to tea, she required first a letter from a parent to the Principal – then a public sitting-room in the college must be booked, and then a senior member (or "Don") must be engaged to join the party and act as chaperone. For we were still slowly emerging from the "chaperone age". We might go shopping in the town on our own, with one notable exception: Buol's in the "High", the only place where chocolates could be bought (sweet rationing did not come in till the Second World War). The place had a dreadful reputation. Bump Suppers – that is, celebration of victories in the early spring Boat Races – were held there, and were understood to be Shameless Orgies, and young women who were not nice were said to frequent there – so unless you had a bona-fide boy-friend who could go in and buy for you – no chocolates. For the theatre, a chaperone was always necessary, though one for the whole house was enough, only *not* the gallery – but when the d'Oyly Carte Company came to Oxford, and everyone went to the gallery – why, most official eyes were winked, and chaperone or no we were all there!

So passed our three years – our college has a beautiful outlook to the river, and we had our boats. One direction, that is, downstream, we could not follow very far, for there were barriers – so there were if you tried to go upstream from Magdalen Bridge – for between these barriers was "Parson's Pleasure", where the men used to dive and swim, in the . . . in the *summer*, of course! I am told that this Garden of Eden is now to be thrown open to all comers as just another nice part of the river!

And, river pleasures apart, you will be asking me: did you encounter any Great Men? Who were your Idols of the time?

Well, some of them have left a name beyond the University walls – there was Gilbert Murray, not only a translator from the Greek but a poet in his own right. He opened to us the romance and tragedy of the Greek playwrights – but, sadly, the sands of his life were already running out and I only remember one lecture of his.

It was our custom for those of us who had been admitted during each year to produce a play to entertain the others – and that produced by my "year" was a modern Greek drama: *Perseus Pertinax*, with lyrics by Gilbert and Murray. The Great Man himself came to a performance of this, and enjoyed the frightful parodies we perpetrated.

Next was Walter Raleigh – at last made *Sir* Walter. He claimed collateral descent from the famous Sir Walter Raleigh – there was one son, who died on one of his father's expeditions to Virginia, but I understand there must have been siblings, from one of whom he claimed descent. He bore a remarkable (and perhaps cultivated) resemblance to the Great Elizabethan – a pale and well-shaped face, gleaming white hair, neat white "imperial" – A great personality, and a lively guide to the romantic treasures of the past. I remember him remarking that the Wife of Bath was a woman whom any man would be proud to have known – that stuck in my mind, and grew in later years to my own book.

We had come to Oxford, most of us, to partake of the literary treasures of the past – but the Powers That Were decided to make it less easy for us – English was a language, and we must study Early English or Anglo-Saxon. I don't know what good this did to our literary style, but we swallowed it with the rest. We studied under Joseph Wright, and that is the nearest that I ever got to Tolkien himself, for Tolkien studied under Joseph Wright. I have my own memory of Joseph Wright (rough old character that he was, raised by his own efforts from the mill-benches of the Midlands) looming over me like a thundercloud: "*Madam – that was a Howler!*" I must explain that a "howler" was much worse than a bloomer – it was a mistake so remarkable as to be preserved for posterity. I don't know what mine was – I never was interested in Anglo-Saxon enough to find out.

For the rest I confess to idolizing Sir Hugh Allen, of the Oxford Bach Choir. To sing under his baton was both a discipline and an experience. We used to practise in a little circular "Theatre" in the Natural History Museum (just across the way from Keble), which I very much suspect of being a surgical and anatomical "theatre" in the bad old days. We were greatly honoured in having Mrs. Farnell, wife of the Vice-Chancellor and a much respected lady, as our practise pianist. Sir Hugh was no respecter of persons. He dropped upon her, hairy and coatless, in a peculiarly difficult part of Holst – "What the devil are you doing?" She looked up at him with a sweet smile, and retorted, "I'm damned if I know."

But mostly he was on the side of the angels – the powerful ones. On one famous occasion he led us through *The Dream of Gerontius* and also Holst's strange and mystical *Hymn of Jesus*. Holst himself conducted this, the second time it had ever been produced – it was at that time something of a landmark in modern music. Its strange assonances and rhythms took some getting used to. But *Gerontius* was already a favourite, but had Gervase Elwes, the perfect voice, and the perfect presence for so very spiritual a part. Almost his last performance – for that winter Elwes went on a tour of America, and a stupid accident on a railway platform robbed the world of the one and only Gerontius.

My last term came, with exams and all the excitement – I did the best I could, and passed with Second Class Honours – only one of my year (about one hundred women) secured a First. And so I left Oxford, and went to join my parents and sisters in South Africa, where it was hoped I should become a lecturer. But no lectureships were then vacant, so inevitably I became a teacher – no other of the various careers seemed to be open to me – but I'll confess now that I was a dismal failure at the job. After two years I married a Clergyman of the Church of England, attached to the missionary Diocese of Lebombo – but as my husband's health broke down in the tropics, we returned to England, and the next part of my life was in country vicarages. I had always wanted to write, but life was too busy, neither had I any clear idea of what I should write about. I wrote various quite impossible novels, all very naïve, and none of them acceptable to publishers. Only after the commencement of the Second War, I by then being a widow and pursuing various jobs in London, I recalled the images of romance in the old stories cherished in the classics, and secured a publisher for my dream version of *The Green Knight*; not very long before Tolkien produced his modern version of that ancient romance. I did not copy Tolkien's version, which had not yet appeared. When this book appeared I thought I was an author at last! – and the small firm of Rex Collings brought out two more Arthurian stories of mine (*The King's Damosel* and *King Arthur's Daughter*) and then *The Wife of Bath* (remembering Raleigh's approval of that lady) and *Blaedud the Birdman*, founded on the traditions of the City of Bath – then a story for children about Romans in Britain, called *Judy and Julia*. All these were put on the market, and mildly commented on – but they did not sell. Rex Collings would accept no more – in spite of an American version of *The Wife of Bath* which was advertised in terms which made it seem positively pornographic – which it isn't, or I might have made more money! I tried another book for children, *Miranty and the Alchemist*, which was published by André Deutsch, but that, again, did not sell. Only one reader did appreciate it and firmly asked for a sequel – that was my great-granddaughter!

So far I cannot claim to have taken my place among writers. I continue to try, and still have an array of manuscripts waiting like unborn children. Who knows? I might yet be lucky.

Meantime I took in hand to found the Tolkien Society – but that is another story.

Tolkien Centenary Banquet Address

Glen H. GoodKnight

As someone we all know, Bilbo Baggins, once said: "I hope you are all enjoying yourselves as much as I am . . . I don't know half of you half as well as I should like; and I like less than half of you half as well as you deserve." Sincere compliments to the Conference Committee for making it all possible for us all to come to this "little party," so long-expected and so well executed, and for having made dreams tangible for those here today. Intelligence, creativity, and good will know no borders. While we each may pronounce our English slightly differently, we each also speak the language of Tolkien, and in our diversity *here* we find unity. Sharing this experience together here with all of you from so many countries is a personal dream come true. I have held it almost as long as The Mythopoeic Society has been in existence – twenty-five years this autumn. For all these years I have dreamed that one day we would be here, in this noble city, seeing the places, and walking the very streets where John Ronald Reuel Tolkien and the other Inklings met, sharing ideas and fellowship, and shaping their greatest works.

In producing the Tolkien Centenary Issue of *Mythlore*, I had the pleasure of receiving and reading the many tributes to Tolkien that poured in. Each person's comments were unique and yet there was a common bond that ran through all of them – the same bond that has brought us together here. We are all grateful to Tolkien for making our lives richer, more appreciative of good things great and small, for opening many new doors in our imaginations, recovering the sense of wonder, and for showing us that a transcending hope is possible. At those times when our lives become strongly intimidated by the daunting negative challenges presented to us, we can pause to recall:

> Far above the Ephel Dúath in the West the night-sky was still dim and pale. There, peeping among the cloud-wrack above a dark tor high up in the mountains, Sam saw a white star twinkle for a while. The beauty of it smote his heart, as he looked up out of the forsaken land, and hope returned to him. For like a shaft, clear and cold, the thought pierced him that in the end the Shadow was only a small and passing thing: there was light and high beauty for ever beyond its reach.

For Tolkien to have given all these gifts, and more, is no small accomplishment, and we are here to celebrate the genius of the man who had such clarity of vision.

One of the ways I have tried to honour Tolkien this year, and in the process create great pleasure for others and myself, was to organize weekly readings of his masterpiece: *The Lord of the Rings*. Since March a small group of about ten to fifteen people have met in my home every Sunday afternoon, to take turns reading aloud from the book. These readings have been a reaffirmation for myself. Even though I am reading passages all the time, mainly as I edit *Mythlore*, it has been some years since I have read the story all the way though from beginning to end. We have made a wonderful discovery: in the act of reading *aloud*, Tolkien's humour jumps out from the pages, mostly from the mouths and actions of the hobbits. Frequently the whole room will be filled with laughter as a certain passage is read. The latest incident was in the chapter "The Houses of Healing." We see the healing hands of Aragorn bring back Faramir from near death. When Faramir awakes he says, "My lord, you called me. I come. What does the King command?" Then we see Aragorn bring back Éowyn from her dark dreams of despair. She opens her eyes to her brother, and says: "Éomer! What joy is this? For they said that you were slain. Nay, but that was only the dark voices in my dream. How long have I been dreaming?" When lastly Aragorn calls Merry by name:

> And when the fragrance of *athelas* stole through the room, like the scent of orchards, and of heather in the sunshine full of bees, suddenly Merry awoke, and he said:
> "I am hungry. What is the time?"

Tolkien takes us to the depths of fear and the heights of joy, and yet keeps us humble with smiles, knowing nods, and outright laughter.

A week ago, Sunday, in the readings we reached the point where Sam and Frodo escape from the Tower of Cirith Ungol. Those who were unable to come here are taking a two-week break, preparing a mailing for the Mythopoeic Society's 25th Anniversary. We will resume a week from Sunday with three weeks more to read the climax and bitter-sweet denouement. What a rich six months this has been.

Twenty-five years ago, unwilling to abide the frustrating isolation any longer, I organized a picnic in a public park to celebrate Bilbo and Frodo's Birthday. I was looking for people who might say "What? You too? I thought I was the only one." I was *not* disappointed. We had games, a lore contest, a costume judging, a mathom exchange, birthday cake and plenty of mushrooms. The first discussion meeting was announced for the following month, and we then entered upon a long road, with many twists and turns, that brings us here today. That picnic twenty-five years ago has made the Mythopoeic Society the oldest on-going Tolkien-related organization and the very first devoted to either C.S. Lewis or Charles Williams.

Next month in September, twenty-five years later, we will again celebrate Bilbo and Frodo's birthday, with costumes, birthday cake, mathoms, and mushrooms. This time¹ will be very special as we will also have a slide show of highlights of these twenty-five years, and to crown the event, we will read the "Epilogue" to *The Lord of the Rings*. Those of you who have a seen a copy of *Sauron Defeated*, know the bitter-sweet passage it is.

Over the years, as we all know, Tolkien has suffered literary and media detractors. Frequently they have described Tolkien and we his readers as Escapists. We know from his essay "On Fairy-Stories" he made a sharp distinction between the Escape of the Prisoner and the Flight of the Deserter. He asks the burning question, "Why should a man be scorned, if, finding himself in prison, he tries to get out and go home?"

But I am thinking about a different kind of escape, or actually a different kind of "no escaping." An inescapable feeling that has brought us here together; has kept us reading and re-reading Tolkien many times across many years. To slightly adapt a page from C.S. Lewis' excellent short book, *An Experiment in Criticism*, will put it well.

> If you find two people reading their fantasy, you must not conclude that they are having the same experience. Where one finds only danger for the heroes, the other may feel the "aweful." When one races ahead in curiosity, the other may pause in wonder. Reading a particular story, one will ask "will the hero escape?" The other feels "I shall never escape this. This will never escape me. These images have struck roots far below the surface of my mind."

Tolkien's genius is that he, as sub-creator, creates a world where the reader is invited and permitted to let the power of his or her own imagination intermingle and effoliate the realm of Arda, in a way suggestively parallel to that in which the Valar contributed to the creation of the World. Tolkien sets the roots of subcreation in our own minds, and we also become through this participatory process myth-makers ourselves.

What a wonderful gift he received and then shared with us. I am unceasingly impressed by his life-long loyalty to his gift of vision – a vision of affirmation and "hope unlooked for."

Thank you Professor Tolkien.

Thank you to the Tolkien family for continuing, enriching and expanding this vision for we his readers.

Thank you all.

August 20, 1992

---

[1] The 25th Anniversary Celebration was held in September of 1992, at the stately South Pasadena Public Library, in Southern California. The highlight of this festive event was the Reading of the "Epilogue" to *The Lord of the Rings*, which is a very poignant passage.

Sermon at Thanksgiving Service, Keble College Chapel, 23rd August 1992

Fr. Robert Murray

With many such parables he spoke the word to them, as they were able to hear it; he did not speak to them without a parable (Mark 3:33-34).

It is with feelings of deep gratitude that I stand before you this morning: gratitude to God for the life and gifts of J.R.R. Tolkien, to himself for his friendship, and to his family for wishing that I should preach at this memorial service.

I do not know of Tolkien's ever being asked to preach a sermon, but he had a high ideal of what a good sermon should be.

> Good sermons require some art, some virtue, some knowledge. Real sermons require some special grace which does not transcend art but arrives at it by instinct or "inspiration"; indeed the Holy Spirit seems sometimes to speak through a human mouth providing art, virtue and insight he does not himself possess: but the occasions are rare.
>
> (Tolkien, 1981, p. 75).

Tolkien recognised this gift in his parish priest, Douglas Carter, one of whose sermons inspired a long and theologically rich letter to his son Christopher (Tolkien, 1981, pp. 99-102). That was in October 1944, just about the time that I, newly arrived in Oxford, was discovering the joy of friendship with the Tolkiens. Less than eighteen months later, when they realised that I was being drawn to share their faith, they introduced me to Father Carter, which led to a lasting friendship with that wonderful man and preacher.

But sermons should not be overburdened with reminiscences; and Tolkien, though he enjoyed being honoured, would not have wanted a sermon to be focused on him, but only on the things of God. Yet it seemed right to choose a text on which we can usefully bring some of Tolkien's ideas to bear. As far as I know, he left few if any writings directly on the Bible; yet if we consider the text I have chosen, about how Jesus taught through parables, we can find in Tolkien's writings not only many passages bearing on the nature and power of this art in which Jesus excelled, but also wonderful examples of the art itself, though Tolkien never claimed the term parable for any of his own stories.

"With many such parables", says Mark, "[Jesus] spoke the word to them, as they were able to hear it." In this sentence, clearly, "the word" stands for what Jesus intended to communicate, while "parables" are the means which he adopted. "The word", of course, means the Gospel, the Good News. As for "parable", today it is probably often thought of as a kind of story implying a meaning, but this is rather *allegory*, which is only one of the many verbal arts covered by the biblical terms (Hebrew and Greek) which we translate by "parable". The primary sense is "comparison", but also included are allegory, proverb, satire and almost any verbal image, metaphor or paradoxical saying. Starting from the modern sense we might wonder if it is true that Jesus never taught except in parables; but if we realise that the term includes all his vivid images – "the lilies of the field [which] neither toil nor spin", or "blind guides" – then the statement is seen to be more broadly true.

Why did Jesus use parables? Mark says that Jesus spoke the Word to the people "as they were able to hear it", implying that he chose the medium of parable so as to temper his message to their capacity. But the question can be looked at in two ways: parable can be viewed in its attractive and stimulating power, or in its comparative obscurity as a mode of communication. The evangelists take the second viewpoint, and connect Jesus' use of parable with the fact which deeply troubled them, as it did Paul, namely that a large proportion of the Jews had not accepted Jesus as the Messiah and his teaching as the Word of God. Today, however, I would like to consider Jesus' parables rather in their art, as the method used by a wonderful teacher.

Mark's phrase "as they were able to hear it", though only a brief hint, is relevant to both aspects of the question why Jesus used parables. Mark implies that Jesus took account of the capacity of his audiences, realising how they varied both in education and in openness to him; he therefore chose not to confront them all immediately with a challenge for which many might not be ready, but rather to use a medium which could first attract and then fascinate and tease the mind, even for a long time, till the hearers might form their own response.

Parable, in its biblical range of meaning, is a skilful use of the arts of speech so as not to impose or compel, but to invite a response in which the hearer is personally active. One of the most instructive examples in the Bible is the parable by which the prophet Nathan brought David to repentance for his adultery and virtual murder (2 Sam 12). He tells the king a touching little story of a powerful rich man who forced a poor man to give up his one beloved ewe lamb. David erupts with a rage which betrays his inward turmoil, for his reaction is out of proportion to the circumstances in the story, but much more appropriate to his own sin. In itself the parable expressed no personal accusation; yet it so played on David's imagination and feelings that it awakened his benumbed conscience and prepared him to discover and face the truth about himself. Only when the parable had done its work did Nathan turn the naked light of reality on David: "You are the man . . ." Since then, for every reader, this whole episode in the story of David has itself become a parable – for the power of stories to act as parables depends not on whether they are fictitious or factually true, but on whether they possess that potential universality which makes others find them applicable, through an imaginative perception of analogy, to other situations.

At this point you will all have picked up one of Tolkien's memorable words, "applicable". He used it often when discussing the power of stories to suggest more to the reader than they say, without their being artificial allegories. He always insisted, of course, on the autonomy of story as an art in itself, which needs no other justification than to arouse delight. A good story need not have a "message", yet Tolkien often acknowledged that most great stories, whether as wholes or in many particulars, abound in morally significant features which are applicable to the experience of readers far removed in time and place from the story-teller. In other words (though I do not think he ever said so), many stories partake of the nature of parable. There is, however, one species within the genus parable which Tolkien did discuss explicitly, and with an ambivalent attitude to it, namely allegory. He often expressed dislike of it, both in general and in C.S. Lewis's use of it. In his Foreword to *The Lord of the Rings* he said about allegory:

> I much prefer history, true or feigned, with its varied applicability to the thought and experience of readers. I think that many confuse "applicability" with "allegory"; but the one resides in the freedom of the reader, and the other in the purposed domination of the author
>
> (Tolkien, 1968, p. 9).

Tolkien could not, however, refuse allegory some place, provided it were kept in it. It could serve in an argument; there he was quite prepared to make up allegories and call them such, as he did twice in two pages of his great lecture on *Beowulf* (Tolkien, 1983, pp. 6-8). But even when discussing story he could be more tolerant of allegory, and allow that

> any attempt to explain the purport of myth or fairytale must use allegorical language. (And, of course, the more "life" a story has the more readily will it be susceptible of allegorical interpretations: while the better a deliberate allegory is made the more nearly will it be acceptable just as a story.)
>
> (Tolkien, 1981, p. 145)

All this is relevant to the interpretation of Jesus' parables, for it has long been a critical dogma that none of them is an allegory or may legitimately be interpreted as one. Yet allegory was part of the biblical parable genre; the prophetic books contain many examples, especially as a way of meditating on the history of Israel and other nations. Must Jesus be protected from the imputation that he ever told a story as an allegory, or that this may be among the possible modes of "applicability"? Let us look at an example or two.

Mathew, Mark and Luke all begin their presentation of Jesus' parables with the Sower. This starts with a simple picture from ordinary life. It could have remained just that, a natural symbol, the potency of which to produce metaphor Jesus might have released poetically by a few hints. But he goes on, describing the kinds of place where the seed might fall and its fate in each, ranging from frustrated germination to the greatest fruitfulness. There Jesus stops, with his habitual call: "He who has ears to hear, let him hear". (Even this is metaphor, for physical hearing has ended; "hearing" now means inward perception and response.)

Now the disciples ask for an explanation. (Here the evangelists insert their discussion about why Jesus' teaching was not accepted by so many of his own people.) The interpretation which is then presented as Jesus' own is fully allegorical, in terms of different human responses to the Word. Now modern scholars are almost all agreed that this comes from early Christian reflection, not from Jesus. They may well be right in their linguistic arguments; but if an interpretation is given in the words of a hearer, that need not mean that he misunderstood the speaker's drift or imposed his own ideas. What shall we conclude? It is clear that Jesus left the people with an open-ended picture of seed sown with various results; but he and his audience shared a tradition of teaching through images, and he was a preacher proclaiming a radical message about God of which many of them must have heard rumours. They could hardly fail to see in the sower an image of Jesus himself.

As for the meaning of the rest, he left them free, but he had baited a whole string of hooks. Allegory is woven into the fabric of the parable, but with a delicacy which does not spoil the joy of working it out for oneself. And for *that* reason I believe that the interpretation which is given is not precisely from Jesus. Not that it says what he did not mean, but that it says less than he may have meant. It focuses the application on many kinds of hearers in their various situations. But the parable can be applied by *an individual* to his or her varying situations or states. On another occasion Luke tells us that, when Jesus was picturing some scenes of servants behaving responsibly or not during their master's absence, Peter asked him "Lord, are you telling this parable for us or for all?" (Lk 12:41). A perceptive question; but Jesus answered only by another question, still within the imagery of his parable, which could lead Peter and every reader to realise that the answer is "both".

Tolkien's "applicability" is a better, because more flexible, key to understanding Jesus' parables than any rigidly-defined set of categories. Let us look at the Good Samaritan. In its context the story is spoken to help an inquirer, who has shown good will, to answer his own question "who is my neighbour?" Jesus provocatively pictures a most hated kind of neighbour who does a most truly neighbourly action. The inquirer is forced to realise this. But then Jesus turns the question round: it is now no longer "how should I define (that is, limit) the category of neighbour?", but "how should I behave, now that I have had to recognize that *anyone* can be my neighbour?" Now in its own context this is a story which seems to function not allegorically, but by virtue of what each character actually does or suffers. It is an invented story, not history, but it *could* have happened. Each character is significant in himself, not by symbolising someone else. What the story suggests is applicable to many other situations, but by the force of the good and bad examples it contains, not by allegory.

And yet it has been read allegorically. The church fathers developed an interpretation which makes the whole story and every detail into an allegory of the drama of sin and redemption. To give only some main points, "he fell among robbers" refers to the Fall caused by Satan. The Samaritan, interpreted as meaning "guardian", symbolizes Christ; his mount, the incarnation; the inn is the Church, and so on. The whole thing is amazingly ingenious; it edified generations of Christians. But beside a straightforward reading of the parable in its own context, it seems simply perverse. And yet. . . ? Is there not something about the Samaritan's compassion and taking trouble which almost irresistibly makes a Christian reader think of Jesus? This thought can then easily lead the reader to identify with the wounded man, and then to universalise him. And there you have the germ of a reading which is allegorical. In fact we find a simple form of this kind within a century after Luke.[1] Is *this* perverse, or is it another possible aspect of the story's "applicability"?

Once again I cannot do better than quote Tolkien:

> Of course, Allegory and Story converge, meeting somewhere in Truth. So that the only perfectly consistent allegory is a real life; and the only fully intelligible story is an allegory. And one finds, even in imperfect human "literature", that the better and more consistent an allegory is the more easily can it be read "just as a story"; and the better and more closely woven a story is the more easily can those so minded find allegory in it. But the two start out from opposite ends. (Tolkien, 1981, p. 121)

"From opposite ends". This exactly expresses the difference between, on the one hand, the development of natural symbolism by metaphor, simile or parable and, on the other, the artificiality of allegory. The one starts from things and human life in the actual world, seeing them as charged with natural symbolic potency; a flash of imaginative insight perceives how this potency can engender new meaning in another context, and so *meta-phora* occurs, the transference of a symbol's power so as to illuminate something else; but it is offered freely to whoever can respond. Jesus' greatest parables work as complex forms of this way of "sub-creation", which we might call "nature-based"; and so, of course, do Tolkien's own stories – though we must note that the material on which his imagination worked was as much human languages and words as the world and nature.

On the other side is allegory (of which poetic riddles may be regarded as singular specimens). The functioning of allegory is powered not so much by the symbolic potency latent in things or in human life as by a plan or message which the author conceals under artificially constructed symbols, with clues to lead the reader to discover what is the intended solution in the actual world. All this, I believe, is implicit in those short phrases in which Tolkien says that story and allegory "start out from opposite ends", and that [the applicability of] "the one resides in the freedom of the reader and the other in the purposed domination of the author".[2] But it is also important that he recognised that, in the greatest stories and allegorical narratives, the qualities of both modes of sub-creation may overlap and mingle. And so they do in at least some of the parables of Jesus.

One more feature of Jesus' parables, and a very important one, is signally illuminated by Tolkien's literary insight. Many of the parables represent persons coming to a moment of decision, the outcome of which has all-important consequences. Undoubtedly Jesus intended, by picturing vivid examples, to confront people with a challenge to realise the reality of God in a new way, and to change their values and way of life. Everything would depend on how they took this turning-point. You can guess what, among Tolkien's ideas, I see as bearing on this feature of the parables: it is his focus on the climax and outcome to which a "fairy-story" leads. In Greek literary theory this was called *katastrophe*, but to designate the diversity of outcomes, happy or unhappy, he coined the pair of terms *eucatastrophe* and *dyscatastrophe*. As a Christian, Tolkien saw "the *eucatastrophic* tale" as "the true form of fairy-tale, and its highest function" (Tolkien, 1988, p. 62).[3] At this point the human sub-creative art of story becomes the "far-off gleam or echo of *evangelium* in the real world" (Tolkien, 1988, p. 64), the supreme Good News in human history. As well as in the essay *On Fairy-Stories*, Tolkien expressed this relationship powerfully in the poem *Mythopoeia* (Tolkien, 1988, pp. 97-101).

Time allows me to allude only briefly to examples of Tolkien's own "sub-creation" which (though he would have been embarrassed by the suggestion) could be compared with biblical stories. The Bible contains traces of various poetic creation myths besides the accounts in Genesis, especially in Job and the Psalms. But in all literatures since the formation of the sacred books of humankind, surely there is hardly a creation myth to equal, in beauty and imaginative power, the one with which *The Silmarillion* begins (Tolkien, 1977, pp. 15-22).[4]

---

[1] The simple allegorical hints come in Irenaeus, *Adv. Haer.* III, 17, 3. The complicated development was chiefly due to Origen (*Hom. on Luke* 34), and was summed up by Augustine (*Quaest. Evang.* II, 19). There is a brief summary of this at the beginning of C.H. Dodd, *The Parables of the Kingdom* (1935; Fontana Books 1961).
[2] Cf. note 1.
[3] and cf. Tolkien (1981, pp. 101-2). Tolkien's formations from the Greek *katastrophe* were a useful (as well as elegant) development because, whereas the Greek word was ambivalent, in English it has only a "bad" sense.
[4] Cf. Tolkien (1981, p. 195): "So in this myth, it is 'feigned' (legitimately whether that is a feature of the real world or not) that He gave special 'sub-creative' powers to certain of His highest created beings: that is a guarantee that what they devised and made should be given

I will say little here about *The Lord of the Rings*. Two of my quotations from Tolkien refer to his wish that it should not be read as an allegory. It is, of course, a monumental example of sub-creation of a Secondary World; its plot is woven with strands of *dyscatastrophe* and *eucatastrophe*. That he hoped it could stand as "a far-off gleam or echo of *evangelium*" is revealed in his published letter to myself, who had spoken of the concealed "order of Grace" (Tolkien, 1981, p. 172), and by the deep feeling of his reply to another correspondent, who had sensed in *The Lord of the Rings* "a sanity and sanctity which is a power in itself" (Tolkien, 1981, p. 413). How could he have dreamed that, within thirty years of its publication, readers in Russia would be drawn to the Christian faith by reading it?

Two stories of Tolkien's, however, stand out as so rich in "applicability" that it is not improper to call them parables, though entirely in the form of pure creations of fantasy: I mean, of course, *Leaf by Niggle* and *Smith of Wootton Major*. Both of them abound in those qualities of parable, of *eucatastrophe* and *evangelium*, which we have been considering. But we must remember the words of Roger Lancelyn Green about *Smith of Wootton Major* which pleased Tolkien: "To seek for the meaning is to cut open the ball in search of its bounce" (Tolkien, 1981, p. 388). In place of comment, I would like to let play on them some lines from two poets, utterly unlike each other and unlike Tolkien. The first passage is a stanza near the end of Browning's "Abt Vogler" (1864, stanza 10); it is more exalted than the simplicity of *Leaf by Niggle*, but I think that it says what the story hints at:

> All that we have willed or hoped or dreamed of good shall exist;
> Not its semblance, but itself; no beauty, nor good, nor power
> Whose voice has gone forth, but each survives for the melodist
> When eternity affirms the conception of an hour.
> The high that proved too high, the heroic for earth too hard,
> The passion that left the ground to lose itself in the sky,
> Are music sent up to God by the lover and the Bard,
> Enough that he heard it once: we shall hear it by-and-by.

My other choice is a short poem by R.S. Thomas (1972). Though Tolkien held that a product of creative fantasy could reflect "a far-off gleam or echo of *evangelium*", he never went so far as to suggest that "Faërie" could be an image of the Kingdom preached by Jesus. Perhaps he was too conscious of its unbaptised roots. And yet . . . Just listen:

> THE KINGDOM
> It's a long way off but inside it
> There are quite different things going on:
> Festivals at which the poor man
> Is King and the consumptive is
> Healed; mirrors in which the blind look
> At themselves and love looks at them
> Back; and industry is for mending
> The bent bones and minds fractured
> By life. It's a long way off, but to get
> There takes no time and admission
> Is free, if you will purge yourself
> Of desire, and present yourself with
> Your need only and the simple offering
> Of your faith, green as a leaf.

References

Browning, Robert. 1684. "Abt Vogler" in *Dramatis Personae*.

Thomas, R.S. 1972. "The Kingdom" in *H'm* (1972), reprinted in *Later Poems: A Selection*. London: Macmillan, 1983.

Tolkien, J.R.R. 1981. *Letters of J.R.R.Tolkien* ed. Humphrey Carpenter. London: George Allen & Unwin.

Tolkien, J.R.R. 1968. *The Lord of the Rings*. London: George Allen & Unwin.

Tolkien, J.R.R. 1983. *The Monsters and the Critics and Other Essays*. London: George Allen & Unwin.

Tolkien, J.R.R. 1988. *Tree and Leaf*, second edition. London: Unwin Hyman.

---

the reality of Creation." Tolkien once told me that he liked to believe that God had given the angels some part in the work of creation. I took him to be expressing a theological speculation, since at that time I had not yet seen *The Silmarillion*.

Recollections of J.R.R. Tolkien

George Sayer

Abstract: Reminiscences of walking with Tolkien around Malvern and of visits to his house in Sandfield Road. What he said and what our mutual friend, C.S. Lewis, said about him.

Keywords: C.S. Lewis, Warnie Lewis, *The Lord of the Rings*: production, Malvern Hills, tape-recording, Edith Tolkien, Tolkien: biography, and Catholic Church, gardening, lecturing

On earth Ronald Tolkien loved parties, so I think he'll be there among the immortals enjoying this imaginative and beautifully organized centenary party. One or two items on the menu may surprise him – for instance why should mushrooms or morels, homely English things, be translated into French, not at all his favourite language? But that's a detail. I hope nothing I say will offend him if he bothers to listen, that all I say about him will be worthy of the great courtesy and kindness he always showed me.

I got to know him through C.S. Lewis, who was my tutor when I read English at Magdalen. Lewis took a low view of the standard of lecturing in Oxford – a view that was I think, correct. He advised me to go only to two-and-a-half series of lectures in first year. The two were his own lectures and those of Nevill Coghill. The half was Tolkien's. "I don't know what to say about Tolkien," was how he put it.

> He is scholarly, and he can be brilliant though perhaps rather recondite for most undergraduates. But unfortunately you may not be able to hear what he says. He is a bad lecturer. All the same I advise you to go. If you do, arrive early, sit near the front and pay particular attention to the extempore remarks and comments he often makes. These are usually the best things in the lecture. In fact one could call him an inspired speaker of footnotes.

"An inspired speaker of footnotes." INSPIRED. The word stuck in my mind, but it was not until many years later that I realised that Lewis was saying something profoundly true about Tolkien's writing as well as his lecturing. He really is an inspired writer. The general level of his work is high and every now and then one comes across passages and whole incidents of real inspiration. The Ents are an example. They are a wonderful invention that owes, as far as I know, nothing to previous writing. They are like nothing else that has ever been. They are charming and loveable with, also, the sadness characteristic of the author, a sadness that underlies much of his humour. Another example is the ride to Gondor where the prose narrative rises to the truly heroic, the rarest thing in modern literature and perhaps the literary quality that its author admired most. What one could call very good footnotes sometimes occurred in his private conversation. If he was with several other people and not very interested in what they were talking about, he might mutter to whoever sat nearest him a comment that was, as far as one could hear it, of real interest.

But in spite of the footnotes, I was disappointed in Tolkien's lectures. Unlike Lewis, who had a fine resonant voice, he had a poor voice and made things worse by mumbling. I did try arriving early and sitting in the front. I then found myself sitting in the midst of a small group of young women who knew each other rather well. At least some of them must have gone to him for tutorials. I think that in the early days the women's colleges sent him pupils because he was a married man. If he had not been, a woman undergraduate would not have been allowed to go to a tutorial with him alone. She would have had to be chaperoned by another woman. I think he retained this connection with women's colleges after the demise or neglect of the chaperoning rule.

I noticed that some of them spoke of him with affection, as "rather sweet". The more homely enjoyed going to his North Oxford house and meeting the little Tolkiens, as I heard them called, presumably Christopher and Priscilla. I followed the good example of those around me and tried to take notes. This wasn't easy for he went quite fast. The footnotes were for me certainly the best part but there were not enough of them and I enjoyed them for wrong or quite unintellectual reasons, because in them Tolkien showed a rather pleasant sense of humour. But in spite of these I foolishly soon gave up going. Since this may shock those of you who do not know Oxford and Cambridge, I had better explain that going to lectures was entirely voluntary at these ancient universities. It still is, and is unnecessary too for success in Schools. My step-daughter, Sheena, who was recently up at St. John's, never went to a single lecture all the time she was up. Yet she got a first.

My real relationship with Tolkien did not begin until about thirteen years later. It was during the school holidays at Malvern where I was teaching. Quite near the college I came across C.S. Lewis and his brother Warren apparently setting out for a hike. They were wearing open-neck shirts, very old clothes, had stout walking sticks, and one of them was carrying a very ancient looking rucksack. It was the fact that they were doing it in Malvern that surprised me because I know that C.S. Lewis was certainly not the old-boy type, even though his brother was. They explained that they had swopped houses with Maureen, Mrs. Moore's daughter, who had married Leonard Blake, the Director of Music at Malvern College. She had gone to Lewis's house, The Kilns, to be with her mother, who was ill. With them was Tolkien and a man whom they introduced to me as Humphrey Havard, "our friend and doctor". Lewis invited me to have some beer with them at the pub called The Unicorn. There he asked me which were the best walks in the area, and then if I could join them for the next few days, acting as their guide. Lewis then drew me on one side and said that they would be extremely grateful if I would be willing to walk much of the time with Tolkien, while they went on ahead.

> He's a great man, but not our sort of walker. He doesn't seem able to talk and walk at the same time. He dawdles and then stops completely when he has something interesting to say. Warnie finds this particularly irritating.

I soon found that the brothers liked to walk hard and fast for half an hour, a period which Warnie would time, for Jack never wore or, as far as I know, owned a watch. Then they would have what they called a "soak". This meant sitting or lying down for the time it took to have a cigarette. Then the other man would shoulder the pack, which was their name for the rucksack, and they would go on walking hard for another half-hour. Humphrey Havard had been most kind in walking some of the time with Tolkien but he had to go back to Oxford the following day.

It worked really well. Tolkien seemed glad to be left behind by the Lewis brothers, whom he described to me as "ruthless walkers, very ruthless indeed". Certainly he was not used to their sort of walking, and got quickly out of breath when we walked uphill. Just as C.S. Lewis said, he tended to stop walking, certainly walking fast, whenever he had something interesting to say. He also liked to stop to look at the trees, flowers, birds and insects that we passed. He would not have suited anyone who, like the Lewis brothers, walked partly for health, in order to get vigorous exercise. But it delighted me. He talked so well that I was happy to do nothing but listen, though even if one was by his side, it was not always easy to hear all that he said. He talked faster than anyone of his age that I have known, and in a curious fluttering way. Then he would often spring from one topic to another, or interpolate remarks that didn't seem to have much connection with what we were talking about. He knew more natural history than I did, certainly far more than the Lewises, and kept coming out with pieces of curious information about the plants that we came across. I can remember one or two examples. Thus on the common wood avens:

> This is Herb Bennet, in Latin *Herba Benedicta*. What do you think that means?
>
> The Blessed Plant.
>
> Yes, though the English form wants it to be *St. Benedict's Herb*. It is blessed because it is a protection from the devil. If it is put into a house "the devil can do nothing, and if a man carries it about with him no venomous beast will come within scent of it."

And upon the celandine:

> Did you know that when picking celandine various combinations of *Aves* and *Paternosters* have to be said? This was one of the many cases of Christian prayers supplanting pagan ones, for in ancient times there were runes to be spoken before it was picked.

Though he was generally interested in birds and insects, his greatest love seemed to be for trees. He had loved trees ever since childhood. He would often place his hand on the trunks of ones that we passed. He felt their wanton or unnecessary felling almost as murder. The first time I heard him say "ORCS" was when we heard not far off the savage sound of a petrol-driven chain saw. "That machine," he said, "is one of the greatest horrors of our age." He said that he had sometimes imagined an uprising of the trees against their human tormentors. "Think of the power of a forest on the march. Of what it would be like if Birnam Wood really came to Dunsinane."

I had the impression that he had never walked the hills before though he had often admired the distant view of them from the Avon valley near Evesham. Some of the names of the places we saw from the hills produced philological or etymological footnotes. *Malvern* was a corruption of two Welsh words, "moel" meaning *bear*, and "vern" derived from *bryn* or *fryn* meaning *hill*. This of course told us that the area was in early times heavily wooded, though the ten-mile ridge of the hills was not. The main pass over the hills is called the Wyche. This gave him an opportunity of talking about the various meanings of the word "Wyc".

It was the custom of the Lewis brothers to eat the bread and cheese they brought with them in a pub and to drink with it a couple of pints of beer, always bitter. They liked the beer to be drawn from the wood and the pub to be simple, primitive and above all without a radio. Tolkien agreed strongly with this taste. I can think of a pub he wouldn't enter because there was a radio on. But he was happy drinking beer, or smoking his pipe in a pub among friends.

Usually he was genial and relaxed, as if liberated from the worries of ordinary life. As I sat with him and the Lewis brothers in the pub, I remember being fascinated by the expressions on his face, the way they changed to suit what he was saying. Often he was smiling, genial, or wore a pixy look. A few seconds later he might burst into savage scathing criticism, looking fierce and menacing. Then he might soon become genial again. There was an element of acting about this gesturing, but much that he said was extremely serious.

Except at Inklings meetings I saw nothing of Tolkien for perhaps two years after this. Lewis gave me bulletins about him, and talked quite a lot about *The Lord of the Rings*, its greatness and the difficulty of getting it published. He thought this was largely Tolkien's fault because he insisted that it should be published with a lengthy appendix of largely philological interest. In negotiation with Collins he had even gone so far as to insist that it should be published with the earlier work, *The Silmarillion*, a book that Lewis had tried to read in typescript, but found very heavy going. The two together would make a volume of over a million words. Even alone *The Lord of the Rings* would, Lewis thought, be the better for pruning. There was a large section that in his opinion weakened the book.

Of course Lewis's enthusiasm made my wife and me most eager to read the book. Lewis said that he would try and get a copy for us, but he did not see how. Then on one of my visits to Magdalen he told me that Tolkien had given up hope of ever having it published. This was a real calamity, but it brought great good to me. "Look," he said, "at what I have here for you!" There on his table was the typescript of *The Lord of the Rings*. Of course I must take the greatest care of it, read it in a month or less, and return it personally to the author, 'phoning him first to make sure that he would be there to receive it. It was far too precious to be entrusted even to the more reliable post of forty years ago.

Of course my wife and I had the thrilling experience that all of you remember vividly. Well before the month was up, I turned up with it at Tolkien's house, then in Holywell. I found him obviously unhappy and dishevelled. He explained that his wife had gone to Bournemouth and that all his friends were out of Oxford. He eagerly accepted my invitation to come to Malvern for a few days. "But what shall I do with the other book? I can't leave it here." So I drove Tolkien to Malvern with the typescripts of *The Lord of the Rings* and *The Silmarillion* on the back seat. What a precious cargo!

His talk now was mainly of his books. He had worked for fourteen years on *The Lord of the Rings* and before that for many years on *The Silmarillion*. They really were his life work. He had in a sense planned them before he went to school, and actually written one or two of the poems while he was still at school, I think the Tom Bombadil poems. He had now nothing to look forward to except a life of broken health, making do on an inadequate pension. He was so miserable and so little interested in anything except his own troubles that we were seriously worried. What could we do to alleviate his depression? I could walk with him and drive him around during the day, but how were we to get through the evenings? Then I had an idea. I would take the risk of introducing him to a new machine that I had in the house and was trying out because it seemed that it should have some valuable educational applications. It was a large black box, a Ferrograph, an early-model tape recorder. To confront him with it was a risk because he had made it clear that he disliked all machinery. He might curse it and curse me with it, but there was a chance that he would be interested in recording on it, in hearing his own voice.

He was certainly interested. First he recorded the Lord's Prayer in Gothic to cast out the devil that was sure to be in it since it was a machine. This was not just whimsey. All of life for him was part of a cosmic conflict between the forces of good and evil, God and the devil. I played it back to him. He was surprised and very pleased. He sounded much better than he had expected. He went on to record some of the poems in *The Lord of the Rings*. Some he sang to the tunes that were in his head when writing them. He was delighted with the result. It was striking how much better his voice sounded recorded and amplified. The more he recorded, and the more often he played back the recordings, the more his confidence grew. He asked to record the great riddle scene from *The Hobbit*. He read it magnificently and was especially pleased with his impersonation of Gollum. Then I suggested he should read one or two of the best prose passages from *The Lord of the Rings*, say, the "Ride of the Rohirrim", and part of the account of the events on Mount Doom. He listened carefully and, I thought, nervously, to the play-back. "You know," he said, "they are all wrong. The publishers are wrong, and I am wrong to have lost my faith in my own work. I am sure this is good, really good. But how am I to get it published?"

Of course I had no idea. But I had to say something, so I said, "Haven't you an old pupil in the publishing business?" After a pause he said: "There's only Rayner." "Then send it to him and ask for his help."

I won't tell you what happened after that because you will have heard it from Rayner Unwin himself.

He went on recording until I ran out of tape.

Of course compared with this nothing in my relationship with Tolkien is of much importance, but I will tell you a few other things. I don't think he much liked the food he had while staying with us, because my wife was then working through a French cookery book, and he seemed to detest everything French – I don't know why. We thought he had a bad appetite. Nevertheless he thanked her with a charming bread-and-butter letter written in Elvish and complete with English translation.

While with us he asked if he could do something to help in the house or garden. He was quite domesticated, not at all an impractical academic. We thought, in the garden, for our garden has never been a tidy or weed-free one. He chose an area of about two square yards, part flower border and part lawn and cultivated it perfectly: the border meticulously weeded and the soil made level and exceedingly fine; the grass cut with scissors closely and evenly. It took him quite a long time to do the job, but it was beautifully done. He was in all things a perfectionist. I think his training in domesticity, in housework, gardening, and looking after chickens and other creatures gave to his writing a homely and earthy quality. On Sunday we took him to Mass at the Church to which we always go ourselves. Before we left the house he asked if confessions were heard before Mass. I told him they were. He said he always liked to go to confession before receiving communion. I do not think that this was because he had on his conscience any sin that most people would regard as serious. True, he was what spiritual directors call "scrupulous", that is, inclined to exaggerate the evil of the undisciplined and erring thoughts that plague most of us. But he was above all a devout and strict old-fashioned Catholic, who had been brought up to think that if possible one should go to confession first. This was the usual nineteenth-century attitude. It lingered in backward parts. Thus my wife tells me that in her village in County Kerry in the nineteen-thirties, no one would have thought of going to communion without going to confession first. In the pew in front of us there were two or three children who were trying to follow the service in a simple picture book missal. He seemed to be more interested in them than in events at the altar. He lent over and helped them. When we came out of the church we found that he was not with us. I went back and found him kneeling in front of the Lady Altar with the young children and their mother, talking happily and I think telling stories about Our Lady. I knew the mother and found out later that they were enthralled. This again was typical; he loved children and had the gift of getting on well with them. "Mummy, can we always go to church with that nice man?" The story also illustrates one of the most important things about him, his great devotion to Our Lady. He wrote to me years later a letter in which he stated that he attributed anything that was good or beautiful in his writing to the influence of Our Lady, "the greatest influence in my life." He meant it. An obvious example is the character of Galadriel.

The few days he spent in Malvern with that early model Ferrograph tape recorder at a time when he was "in the doldrums" as he put it in a letter, made me one of his friends. He invited me to call on him whenever I was in Oxford and with remarkable frankness talked to me not merely about *The Lord of the Rings* and his other writings but about his private worries about things such as money, religion and family.

In the spring of 1953 he moved to Sandfield Road, a turning on Headington Hill off the London Road. I think that when I called, it was always Mrs. Tolkien who answered the door. One of her jobs was to protect her husband from people who would interfere with his work. She would then go upstairs to tell him that I, an admissible visitor, was there. I always found him seated at a large desk or table with many papers in front of him in a room full of books and piles of papers. I was told that there was also a bookstore and a sort of office in what would have been the garage if he had had a car. Until *The Lord of the Rings* was a success he talked a good deal about his misfortunes. He had much to complain about. The expenses of the move had made him rather short of money, and yet he would have to contribute more than he could afford towards publication of *The Lord of the Rings*. Perhaps the best way of conveying his state of mind will be to read a few sentences about his anxieties from a letter he wrote to me at the end of August, 1953. It also shows that he had taken with enthusiasm to the use of a tape recorder:

> When I got your letter I was altogether played out. Not that I have been able to relax, beyond one morning's long sleep.
>
> Life has been most complicated and laborious with domestic comings and goings and difficulties arranging for Father John and anxieties about my daughter lost in France. Amidst all this I have had to work day and (especially) night at the seemingly endless galleys of the Great Work that had piled up during Vivas, at drawings and runes and maps; and now at the copy of Vol. II. Also at Sir Gawain.
>
> Immediately after Vivas Newby of the Talks Department descended on me. The upshot is that my translation is being taken in toto, uncut, as the basis of six broadcasts at Christmas. But they do not take equally kindly to me as the actual performer. However I go to London tomorrow for an audition. This is where a tape-recorder would have been so helpful. I had to hire a horrid old sound Mirror, the best I could get locally, but it was very helpful in matters of timing and speed. With the help of Christopher and Faith, I made some three voice experiments and recordings of the temptation scenes. An enormous improvement – and assistance to the listener. Chris was making an extremely good (if slightly Oxonian) Gawain, before we had to break off.
>
> I got as near to Malvern as Evesham on August 23rd. The wedding of my nephew Gabriel Tolkien, at which John officiated. I thought not without longing of the Dark Hills in the distance, but I had to rush straight back.

He doubted if many people would buy the book at the high price of 25 shillings a volume. He feared too that the few people who read it would treat it as an allegory or morality about the nuclear bomb or the horrors of the machine age. He insisted over and over again that his book was essentially a story, without any further meaning. "Tales of Faerie," he said, "should be told only for their own sake."

One of the advantages of the house in Sandfield Road was that Tolkien's doctor, Humphrey Havard, lived in the same street, only a few doors away. He sometimes took him to church. I once asked him how he was and had the answer:

> All right now, but I've been in a very bad state. Humphrey came here and told me that I must go to confession and that he would come early on Sunday morning to take me to confession and communion. That's the sort of doctor to have.

This story shows his humility. He had a very low opinion of his own merits, and fairly easily got into a depressed state when thinking of his faults and deficiencies. Life was a war between good and evil. He thought the sacraments freed one from enthralment to Sauron. Once he spoke to me of Ireland after he had spent part of a summer vacation working there as an examiner: "It is as if the earth there is cursed. It exudes an evil that is held in check only by Christian practice and the power of prayer." Even the soil, the earth, played a part in the cosmic struggle between forces of good and evil.

He thought hatred of Catholics was common in Britain. His mother, to whom he was most deeply devoted, was a martyr because of her loyalty to the Catholic Faith, and his wife, Edith, was turned out of her guardian's house when she was received into the Church. In 1963 he wrote in a letter:

> And it still goes on. I have a friend who walked in procession in the Eucharistic Congress held in Edinburgh, and who reached the end with a face drenched with the spittle of the populace which lined the road and were only restrained by mounted police from tearing the garments and faces of the Catholics.

He found little or nothing wrong with the pre-Vatican II Church, and therefore thought the reforms of the 1960s misguided and unnecessary. He frequently complained about the new English translations of the Latin texts used in Catholic services, because they were inaccurate or in bad or clumsy English.

Lewis told Tolkien that of all his friends he was "the only one impervious to influence". This was largely true. It was no defect. Combined with his belief in all the traditional virtues such as courage, loyalty, chastity, integrity and kindness, it gave to him as a man and to *The Lord of the Rings* tremendous moral strength. He was unswervingly loyal to the Christian Faith as taught him by his guardian and benefactor, Father Francis Morgan.

Our mutual friend, C.S. Lewis, was a frequent topic of conversation. Their relationship before the war had been very close, so close that Edith Tolkien had resented the time that her husband spent with him. Lewis who was aware of this for his part found it impossible to see as much as he would have liked of Tolkien, whom he described as "the most married man he knew". But apart from the fact that one of them was married, the two had different concepts of friendship. Tolkien wanted to be first among Lewis's friends. Lewis may have loved Tolkien as much but he wanted him to be one among several friends. Tolkien was jealous of the position that Charles Williams, of whom he did not entirely approve, occupied in Lewis's affections. They were separated also by the success of the Narnia stories, the first of which appeared when he was struggling to get *The Lord of the Rings* through the press. He described it to be "about as bad as can be". It was written superficially and far too quickly (I think that perhaps he envied Lewis his fluency), had an obvious message, but above all was a mix-up of characters from dissimilar and incompatible imaginative worlds. Dr. Cornelius, Father Time, The White Witch, Father Christmas and Dryads should not be included in the same story. I never saw the force of this criticism.

At long last, after the three volumes were successfully launched, he became what Lewis called "cock-a-hoop" and talked with great enthusiasm of the fate of the pirated paperback version and the astonishing growth of the Tolkien cult. He enjoyed receiving letters in Elvish from boys at Winchester and from knowing that they were using it as a secret language. He was overwhelmed by his fan mail and would-be visitors. It was wonderful to have at long last plenty of money, more than he knew what to do with. He once began a meeting with me by saying: "I've been a poor man all my life, but now for the first time I've a lot of money. Would you like some?"

In my later visits he was nominally hard at work getting *The Silmarillion* into a form suitable for publication. But after a time I began to wonder how much he really did. I can think of two visits at an interval of a month. On the second I am almost sure that he had the same page open as on the first. I have been told that he spent much of his time reading detective stores. I don't blame him. His life work was complete.

I once asked him about the origin of *The Silmarillion* and *The Lord of the Rings*. It seemed to be more than anything else philological. Then just as I was leaving to go on a walk with C.S. Lewis he handed me a pile of papers. "If you're interested, have a look at these."

Lewis and I took them to a pub and looked at them over bread and cheese. "Good Heavens!" he exclaimed, "he seems to have invented not one but three languages complete with their dialects. He must be the cleverest man in Oxford. But we can't keep them. Take them straight back to him while I have another pint."

If I was there at the right time in the afternoon he would take me to have tea in the drawing room on the floor below, Edith Tolkien's room. The atmosphere was quite different, with hardly any papers and few books. She did most of the talking and it was not at all literary. Frequent subjects were the doings of the children, especially Christopher, the grandchildren, the garden in which I think Ronald enjoyed working, the iniquities of the Labour Party, the rising price of food, the changes for the worse in the Oxford shops and the difficulty of buying certain groceries. The road had deteriorated since they had moved there. It used to be a quiet cul-de-sac. Now the lower end had been opened up and lorries and cars rushed through on their way to a building site or to Oxford United's football ground. There were also some very noisy people in the road. They even had as near neighbours an aspiring pop group.

Ronald (I call him Ronald in talking to you, but I always addressed him by his Inklings nickname, "Tollers") told me that when she was younger Edith had been a fine pianist. Some of the conversation was about music. On one occasion she played to us on a very simple old-fashioned gramophone a record that she had just bought. Her husband was relaxed and happy with this domesticity. Anyway, it was an important part of his life. Without a liking for the homely and domestic, he could not have written *The Hobbit*, or invented Frodo and Sam Gamgee, characters that sustain quite convincingly the story of *The Lord of the Rings*, and link the high romance to the everyday and the ordinary.

He told me that he was moving to Bournemouth because the house was too big and too much work for Edith, and in order to escape the fan mail and the fans. I did not go there. The last time I met him was after his return to Oxford. He was with children (perhaps great-grandchildren), playing trains: "I'm Thomas the Tank Engine. Puff. Puff. Puff." That sort of thing. I was conscripted as a signal. This love for children and delight in childlike play and simple pleasures was yet another thing that contributed to his wholeness as a man and the success of his books.

Publishing Tolkien

Rayner Unwin

Abstract: During the last thirty years of the Professor's life, but especially towards the end, Rayner Unwin met, talked with, and worked for, J.R.R. Tolkien. It was a business relationship between author and publisher, but increasingly it became a trusting friendship as well. In an ideal world authors and publishers should always act in partnership. This certainly happened between Professor Tolkien and George Allen & Unwin, but in some respects, the speaker explains, the collaboration had very unusual features.

Keywords: *Beowulf*, *Farmer Giles of Ham*, *The Father Christmas Letters*, *The Hobbit*, illness, illustrations, letters, *The Lost Road*, maps, *Mr. Bliss*, *The Silmarillion*, typesetting

I have thought for a long time about what I could say this morning that might be either original or interesting. Alas, I have used up most of the personal anecdotes that I could remember after twenty or thirty years in various recent articles and talks. And I am acutely aware that all of you, who have come so far to this conference, are much better informed about Tolkienian matters than I shall ever be.

Publishing Tolkien is the title of my talk, and it covers the only subject that gives me any justification for being here. But what, I have to ask myself, was so different (apart from the actual contents of the books) about publishing Tolkien and publishing anybody else?

I thought it might be easier if I concentrated on a period when I was myself only indirectly involved, and by carefully examining the correspondence of a single year try to isolate those peculiarities that made the relationship between Tolkien and his publisher special. I have chosen 1937 – the year during which *The Hobbit* was actually published. By the beginning of this year the single-spaced typescript had already been read by a precocious ten-year-old, a contract had been signed, and copy had gone to the printer for setting.

Most of you will have read the highlights of the 1937 correspondence in the book of *Letters*. Indeed, if you're like me, it is more and more to that book that I turn in order to recapture the true flavour of the man. Eleven letters to his publishers are reproduced in whole or in part in *Letters*. But this is only the tip of the iceberg.

In the publishing file for 1937 there are 26 letters from Tolkien to Allen and Unwin, and 31 letters from Allen and Unwin to Tolkien. In addition there is evidence that other notes were exchanged when routine packets were posted between the author and the Production Dept. There is no evidence that either side telephoned each other during the year. Telephones were regarded as an intrusion, and anyway, at a distance of 60 miles, wildly extravagant. On one or two occasions a cable was sent across the Atlantic, and when, in December, a reprint of *The Hobbit* was called for, Tolkien was told: "the last minute crisis was so acute that we fetched part of the reprint from our printers at Woking in a private car in order to avoid delay." On one occasion Charles Furth called on Tolkien in Oxford, and twice in the autumn Tolkien came to London by train where he met my father for the first time and was "overwhelmed" by his kindness.

But the vast majority of all communication was by letter. On Tolkien's part these were all in handwriting, often up to five pages long, detailed, fluent, often pungent, but infinitely polite and exasperatingly precise.

The first point that struck me as I read through the file was the sheer quantity of patience and time that was spent on preparing a children's book by an unknown author for press in exactly the way the author wanted. I doubt very much if any author today would get or exchange such leisurely courtesies as passed between Tolkien and his principal correspondents at Allen and Unwin. They were Charles Furth, the senior editor, and Susan Dagnall, the editorial Jill-of-all-trades who had "found" *The Hobbit* for the publisher she had recently come to work for. Towards the end of the year my father also entered into the correspondence.

The text should have been a straightforward typesetting job. When the first batch of proofs came through in February Tolkien found "some minor discrepancies that come out in print and make it desirable to have the whole story together before passing for press." But after the proofs had all arrived he wrote, "the type-setting throughout was guilty of very few divergences from copy and in general proof-corrections are light. But I ought to have given the MS. a revision." Later on it became apparent that it was not just the odd letter or word that needed correction: blocks of text needed to be replaced, but "I have calculated the space line by line as carefully as possible."

With admirable calm Charles Furth replied at the end of March: "it is not improbable that the printers will prefer to send revises of the whole book, because your author's corrections are pretty heavy." Revised proofs were produced and quickly dealt with. But Tolkien wrote a fortnight later, "I have (I fear) again altered 8 words to rectify narrative errors that escaped my previous care; and I have also corrected necessarily about 7 errors that descended from copy and also escaped. I have marked in red a few new errors, and one or two others that were overlooked."

No-one had lost their cool – indeed Susan Dagnall at one point went out of her way to report that "our Production Dept has not felt that you have at any time been in the least troublesome."

But it was apparent that the "free" allowance for author's corrections provided under the contract (10% of the actual cost of typesetting) was going to be exceeded. Charles Furth hinted at this, and Tolkien acknowledged the hint. "I must pay what is just, if required, though I shall naturally be grateful for clemency."

As we know, even corrected revised proofs were not enough to make perfect copy. In October Tolkien was acknowledging "a piece of private bad grammar, rather shocking in a philologist", when he used the incorrect plural of "dwarf" and wished he had substituted the archaic word "dwarrow". And early next year Christopher, ill in bed, was earning tuppence a time for spotting mistakes in the printed text.

Probably the greatest part of the voluminous correspondence concerned maps, illustrations and embellishments. Tolkien was always apologetic about his skills as a draughtsman or as an artist. "I discovered (as I anticipated) that it was rather beyond my craft and experience" he said when he sent his first draft of *The Hobbit* jacket. Charles Furth was quick to reassure him: "the only feature about which we were not entirely happy in the cover is the flush on the central mountain, which makes it look to our eyes just a trifle like a cake."

The maps were equally worrying. "I have small skill, and no experience of preparing such things for reproduction," he protested. But the pictures were worst of all. When Houghton Mifflin asked to see some of his colour pictures he felt "even greater hesitation in posing further as an illustrator, or as one to be preferred to good American artists". As to *Mr. Bliss*, "the pictures seem to me mostly only to prove that the author cannot draw."

Now we would all of us agree that he protested too much, and his publishers certainly were very happy to encourage him to do all the embellishments himself. It was cheaper, too, not to have to employ a cartographer, designer or jacket artist. Indeed Tolkien realised this and managed to extract $100 from Houghton Mifflin for the use of the four colour pictures that they chose. And just before publication my father produced an ex-gratia advance of £25 in appreciation of all Tolkien had done to make *The Hobbit* look an attractive book.

But once the publisher decided to use his work he became a total perfectionist. In January he examined his art-work proofs microscopically. "In Mirkwood . . . a spot of grease, which I removed with the finger, has been reproduced as a black dot . . . In the Wilderland map the t in Hobbiton has a defect not in copy". In February "the thin white outline of one of the background trees is slightly broken: some of the tiny dots outlining a flame have failed to come out . . . In the 'Hall at Bag-End' I misguidedly put in a wash shadow reaching right up to the side beam. This has of course come out black . . ."

In April, "I am sorry it proved impossible to substitute the better drawn runes in the space on the map. Those now shown are ill-done (and not quite upright)!"

As late as July (21 September was the actual publication date) Tolkien, who had taken a hand in the blocking on the binding-case, was writing "I still hanker after a dragon, or at least some sort of rune-formula." Charles Furth, having conceded central, upright lettering rather than italic tried to dig his heels in about the lines at top and bottom, "because without them we feel the binding will be bare, and that if they are made straight lines it will look too much like a Macmillan textbook."

I marvel (but am not entirely surprised) that Allen and Unwin really thought they were economising by using the author as an amateur designer-cum-illustrator. But in those happy days cost-benefit analysis had scarcely been invented. I know that Charles Furth was probably responsible for seeing 50 or 60 other books through the press that year, on a wide spectrum of subjects, not all as complicated as this children's book.

I believe that the overall standards of editing and production were probably higher then than now; and I know that no senior editor in any publishing company today would dream of indulging an author to the extent that the author of *The Hobbit* was indulged. I say this with gratitude because it laid the foundation for a relationship of trust that I inherited. And although at times it nearly drove one mad, it meant that the life-long partnership that existed between Tolkien and his publisher, rare even in its time, would be a total anachronism today.

Another major difference between pre-war and post-war life concerns health. Authors and publishers alike were constantly falling ill, and not just for a day or two. Nothing emphasises more vividly the pre-antibiotic world than the correspondence of 1937.

On 4 January Tolkien was "faced by a family laid low one by one by influenza, brought back from school for the entire ruin of Christmas. I succumbed myself on New Year's Eve." Four days later we learn that Miss Dagnall had been laid low by the prevailing 'flu.

In February an ingenious method of printing the moon-runes on Thrór's map so that they would seem to be "both there and not there" went wrong. First "the magic was left out through a misunderstanding" and fresh blocks were promised. Then (I quote Charles Furth), "unfortunately both the responsible member of the Production Dpt. and the blockmaker's representative who had worked out the scheme went down with, 'flu simultaneously."

In March Charles Furth reported that "we have again been afflicted by illness here and are therefore short-handed." All went well until July when Tolkien wrote, "I attempted something about the cover but could not bring it off – mainly owing to my ill-health and to the serious illness of one of my children."

In the autumn it was my father's turn to collapse. Tolkien

wrote, "it was very good of you to answer me from your bed. I hope your cold is now better, though mine always cling." A little later the reason why Arthur Ransome, who thought *The Hobbit* was "great fun", had not responded earlier was because he was "temporarily laid up in a nursing home in Norwich." At the end of the year the wheel comes full circle and we learn that Tolkien had been "working under difficulties of all kinds, including ill-health, since the beginning of December." It is, I think you will agree, a miracle that anything ever got accomplished against such a blizzard of infection.

Another of the peculiarities of the year when *The Hobbit* was published was the surge of other projects that Tolkien produced, which largely confused his publisher and led to nothing for at least twelve years.

Mr. Bliss had been submitted at much the same time as *The Hobbit* (though I have no recollection of earning my shilling from it). Charles Furth wrote very positively in January saying: "it should be hardly necessary to state that we should very much indeed like to publish this little book which is in a class which it shares with *Alice in Wonderland* and the extremely few comparable books. The difficulty is solely a technical one, but it seems at the moment serious." It remained a serious technical problem for the next 40 years or so; but it should not be forgotten that colour photolithography was in its infancy before the last world war, and no other technique could have dealt with the book in its unique original form. Throughout the year Tolkien half-heartedly offered to re-design it in such a way that it could be produced, but Allen and Unwin, after their initial enthusiasm – and with increasing first-hand experience of trying to satisfy Tolkien's high standards for reproducing illustrations – began to put it on the back burner.

Farmer Giles of Ham (which I did earn a shilling by reporting on) was then much shorter than the version that was eventually published in 1949, but in the end my father sent it back, saying that if there was enough material of a like character to put with it it would make an excellent book. There were, as we know, no other tales of the Little Kingdom available, and for lack of them *Farmer Giles* too went onto the back burner.

Then, after *The Hobbit* had been published, and the reviews and sales had turned out to be everything that could be desired, my father wrote to warn Tolkien that "a large public" would be "clamouring next year to hear more from you about Hobbits,"

Soon afterwards Tolkien came to London, met my father, and over lunch totally confused him with a mass of projects, mostly half-completed, seldom suitable for children, and often deriving from the unexplained matter of Middle-earth. All of which were offered for publication. My father's typed note of this bombardment is worth quoting in its entirety.

1. He has a volume of fairy stories in various styles practically ready for publication. [Then a pencil note: "only 3 or 4 ready. Sil Marillion"]
2. He has a typescript of a History of the Gnomes, and stories arising from it.
3. Mr. Bliss.
4. The Lost Road, a partly written novel of which we could see the opening chapters.
5. A great deal of verse of one kind and another which would probably be worth looking at.
6. Beowulf upon which he has done as yet very little.
7. He spoke enthusiastically of a children's book called The Marvellous Land of Snergs, illustrated by George Morrow and published by Benns some years ago. He mentioned that The Hobbit took him 2 or 3 years to write because he works very slowly.

Lastly in pencil, he added "The Father Christmas Letters".

My father was obviously completely at a loss. What he really wanted was another book about Hobbits. What Tolkien was offering was everything but. The material was farmed out to various readers. Susan Dagnall was given *The Lost Road* and confessed it to be "a hopeless proposition." I seem to have been given a bit of the "great deal of verse" in the form of Tom Bombadil, which I thought was "quite a good story", but suggested that he should write something quite different.

The worst gaffe of all was to send Edward Crankshaw, one of the firm's outside readers, *The Geste of Beren and Lúthien* in both prose and verse versions, without mentioning its provenance or the name of the author. Crankshaw said: "I don't know whether this is a famous geste or not, or, for that matter, whether it is authentic. I presume it is, as the unspecified versifier has included some pages of a prose version (which is far superior)." Crankshaw went on to complain of "eye-splitting Celtic names" and "something of the mad, bright-eyed beauty that perplexes all Anglo-Saxons in the face of Celtic Art." But his conclusion was damning. "The tinkling verses go on – and on, conveying almost nothing. On that count alone I am afraid this is not worth considering."

Charles Furth pencilled "what do we do?" on the report, and passed it to my father who spent much of the latter part of the year returning Tolkien's rejected offerings one by one, with conciliatory letters – usually asking for more about Hobbits to publish next year. Despite my father's unfortunate habit of quoting parts of reader's reports back to Tolkien (he did it with Crankshaw, and much later did it with me) Tolkien was remarkably resilient at the bad news. "I did not think any of the stuff I dropped on you filled the bill", and although he doubted if he had anything more to say about Hobbits he resolved to try.

But, as he remarked a little later, "my mind on the story side is really preoccupied with the 'pure' fairy stories or mythologies of the Silmarillion, into which even Mr. Baggins got dragged against my original will, and I do not think I shall be able to move much outside it – unless it's finished (and perhaps published) – which has a releasing effect." All the same, on 19 December Tolkien told Charles Furth, "I have written the first chapter of a new story about Hobbits – 'A long-expected party'."

It is interesting to see how almost all the elements of Tolkien's posthumous publications surfaced in 1937, and subsequently became submerged to await the "releasing effect" of the publication of *The Silmarillion*. Only the much-urged sequel to *The Hobbit*, which was absorbed by, but ultimately not subdued by, the unfinished *Silmarillion*, escaped into print in his lifetime, together with the enlarged History of the Little Kingdom, which had always staunchly resisted the drag to integrate it with Middle-earth.

The year 1937 covered the whole publication of *The Hobbit*, and you have heard some of the minutely detailed problems that afflicted the production and design of the book. It is surprising, therefore, to see how trustingly Tolkien allowed his publisher to promote and market the finished product. He became involved with the American edition only because of their desire for pictures. But he neither criticised nor interfered with sales, though he was appreciative of good news when it reached him.

When Miss Dagnall proposed a series of small advertisements saying "What is a Hobbit?" he replied "my youngest boy hopes Miss Dagnall's 'teasers' will appear on lines of sandwichmen, ending up with gaudy pictorial explanation." I wonder if Christopher would still feel that way today?

When asked for useful contacts or reviewers he was unusually vague. "*The Catholic Herald* takes a mild interest in me, and would certainly review any work of mine, though I cannot guarantee the tone: it is apt to be rather highbrow in spots." C.S. Lewis – who Tolkien thought had been disgruntled when June publication proved impossible – produced splendid (anonymous) reviews in both *The Times* and the *TLS*, on the strength of which my father persuaded Bumpus, the prestigious Oxford Street bookshop, to order 50 copies. Richard Hughes, whom he had never met, wrote appreciatively. All these happenings interested Tolkien, but once the book had been made to his satisfaction he was happy to let his publishers get on with it. He noted that Parkers was the only bookshop in Oxford that displayed it; he reckoned his own college was good for half-a-dozen copies "in order to find material for teasing me"; but he never initiated enquiries about sales outside Oxford, or likely earnings, though he had every reason to wish to know.

He was also unnaturally resigned when the reprint that was rushed through before Christmas allowed no time for corrections. It was, perhaps, another example of the act of publication having a releasing effect.

Many of the characteristics that I have tried to identify from the details of a single year may also be discovered in the correspondence and recollections of subsequent decades. I believe that Tolkien changed very little. Circumstances and people changed around him, but he had pondered so long and so hard on what he wished to achieve; he was so humble yet so certain of his goals; so instinctively courteous and so unpretentious in his manner; so prone to the distractions of ill-health and domestic misfortune, yet so remorseful at his failure to overcome them; that those who worked with him – people like his publishers – were not irritated by the trail of disasters and confusions that seemed to accumulate around his, and their, well-intentioned actions; but rather were spurred to achieve that impossible perfection that Tolkien always strove towards himself, and by example made his exasperated publishers wish to achieve it too.

Section two

Sources and Influences

Quid Hinieldus cum Christo? – New Perspectives on Tolkien's Theological Dilemma and his Sub-Creation Theory

Nils Ivar Agøy

Abstract: In the 1920s and 1930s Tolkien's developing, and to all appearances pagan, *legendarium* posed a theological dilemma to its devoutly Christian author. How could it be reconciled with his faith? There are striking parallels with the Danish theologian, poet and philologist N.F.S. Grundtvig (1783-1872). This paper will try to establish whether Tolkien's answer, which is only partly to be found in "On Fairy-Stories", was directly influenced by Grundtvig's attempts at reconciling Norse myths and Christendom.

Keywords: N.F.S. Grundtvig, Christian Myth, Norse Myth, Tolkien: *legendarium*, sub-creation, theology

This paper takes as its point of departure Tolkien's "sub-creation theory" as presented in his 1939 essay "On Fairy-Stories". The theory is interpreted partly as an answer to a theological dilemma that had confronted Tolkien in the 1920s and early 1930s. Tolkien's ambitious project of writing a "mythology for England", which he had begun during the First World War, soon ran into trouble. With precious little old mythological material related specifically to England to work from, Tolkien eventually had to write most of the *legendarium* from his own imagination, only occasionally able to weave in strands of authentic myths and traditions from the "North-West of the Old World". As we know, he nevertheless had the sense of "discovering", not "inventing". But what he discovered did not seem to mix at all well with his orthodox brand of Catholic Christianity. The grand mythological themes he wanted to address inevitably trespassed on to the territory of Theology. To the limited extent that he was able to work from ancient material, what he was transmitting were indubitably Pagan traditions. In the first versions of his *legendarium*, so-called "Gods" figured strongly. They were limited, intriguing and impulsive like the Norse Gods, and even counted a couple of ethically very shady war-gods in their midst. The questions inevitably arose: Should a Christian be writing this sort of thing at all? Would not a Christian spend his time more fruitfully, and to the greater glory of God, doing something else? Could he justify placing Pagan mythology in a favourable light?

Tolkien dealt with these difficulties in two distinct ways. One was to experiment and re-write; he changed his "Gods" to "gods" and later to "Valar", he deleted references to Thor and Njord, he put in the Catholic Purgatory only to take it out again – and gradually he was left with a structure fundamentally consonant with Christianity.[1] The other was to make a three-fold statement – in "Mythopoeia", "On Fairy-Stories" and "Leaf by Niggle" (one could also include "Beowulf: The Monsters and the Critics") – to the effect that writings such as his were not only not contrary to Christianity, but had a value of their own in helping us to see

---

[1] The specifically Christian character of the later versions of the *legendarium* (including *The Lord of the Rings*) has been frequently overlooked despite the wealth of theological clues. Middle-earth is strictly monotheistic, God is all-powerful and good, and He has created the universe from nothing (*creatio ex nihilo*). A sharp distinction is drawn between the Creator and His Creation. The Creation is not eternal, its history is linear, with a beginning and an end. This combination of features is unique to Judeo-Christian beliefs. Tolkien does not describe the initial Fall of Man, but presupposes it (Tolkien, 1977b, p. 141, cf. Tolkien, 1981, p. 147 ff. p. 203 ff.). This contradicts Lobdell's theory (1981, chapter III) that not all humans in Middle-earth were affected by original sin). Many other testimonies to the underlying Christianity may be found in the less lofty levels of the *legendarium*.

Of course, the Christianity of the *legendarium* is not complete, nor is it intended to be. Set in a pre-Christian age, it lacks the Incarnation, "an *infinitely* greater thing than anything I would dare to write" in Tolkien's words (1981, p. 237). What he wanted was a story that could be "accepted . . . shall we say baldly, by a mind that believes in the Blessed Trinity" (Tolkien, 1981, p. 146).

the world as it really is, and giving consolation in that they affirm the Christian hope, sometimes even giving far-off glimpses of God's fairy-story for Man, the *Evangelium* itself. In using his imagination to make fairy-tales and myths, Man was exercising his God-given power of "sub-creation". When God made Man in His, the Creator's image (Genesis 1, 26-27), He intended that Man, too, should create.[2]

In the view taken here – that the "sub-creation theory" was in part a response to a strongly felt personal dilemma – it is not surprising that this theory has usually been regarded as original, as a unified statement. As for the separate elements in it, however, most may be found somewhere or other within the vast reaches of European philosophy and theology. Christian theology has always theorized on the exact nature of the Image of God in Man; and to identify it with human creativity in some form was an early suggestion, eagerly taken up by nineteenth century Romantic philosophers.[3] The view that non-Biblical myths may contain glimpses of truth is also ancient. Among certain influences close to Tolkien in time and space are George MacDonald, G. K. Chesterton and Owen Barfield, with Ernst Cassirer and Dorothy L. Sayers as strong additional possibilities.[4] In the following, we will explore the possibility that Tolkien's "sub-creation theory" was fundamentally and decisively influenced by the writings of the Danish theologian, poet, historian, mythographer and educationalist, Nikolaj Frederik Severin Grundtvig (1783-1872).

Grundtvig is a towering figure in Danish and Norwegian cultural history, with – especially in Denmark – an influence so permeating that he has become part of the cultural wallpaper. He was an untiring advocate of freedom: of expression, in education and in religious life. He started a theological movement that was to change both the Danish and the Norwegian church in important ways. He was also Scandinavia's greatest hymn-writer – more than one third of the hymns in the current Danish hymn-book are his. And he is remembered for his lifelong efforts to actualize and transmit Old Scandinavian mythology and history to new generations. Together with his beloved Danish mother tongue, the old mythology, rather than imported culture and school Latin and German, should form the basis of education and cultural life. This strong emphasis on national traditions and language is perhaps one reason why Grundtvig is so little known outside Scandinavia. Very little of his enormous and thematically diverse literary production has ever been translated into other languages.

In effect, Grundtvig did for the Danes what Tolkien wanted to do for the English: he wrote a mythology for his people. In the heyday of Romanticism and national awakenings his undertaking was by no means unique. It was not qualitatively different from Lönnroth's better-known work to shape the *runos* preserved in Finnish popular tradition into the national epic *Kalevala*, or Wilhelm Grimm's attempt "to fit together all the bits and pieces of Germanic heroic literature" (Shippey, cited in Agøy, 1992, p. 28). Out of the historically disparate, often defaced and ill-fitting shards of Norse mythology, folklore and history, Grundtvig built a single dramatic structure, spanning all the ages of the world. Although the structure was artificial, Grundtvig believed that he was not inventing anything new, but rather poetically restoring the "image-language" (*Billedsprog*) of his forebears to its original unity and splendour. Like Tolkien a century later, Grundtvig believed in the incalculable intrinsic value for a people of its own mythology. In Grundtvig's view, myths were the repository of a people's specific understanding of reality, and were in a sense prophetic. From its myths one could read the people's destiny.[5]

When Grundtvig was first overcome by *Asarusen*, "the intoxication of the Aesir", as a young man, he did not regard it as incompatible with his Christian faith, although some of his contemporaries regarded him as more Pagan than Christian at the time. Grundtvig, by then a full-fledged Lutheran theologian, in 1808 wrote that he "prostrated himself" at the altar of the old Norse Gods (Rønning, 1907-14, II, 1, p. 89).[6] He believed that Christianity was a further development of Paganism and that there was actually no fundamental conflict between the two. To him, Christ was simply "a purer son of the All-father than Odin".[7] This syncretist view is vividly illustrated in some famous lines from an 1808 poem:

Høje Odin! Hvide Krist!
Slettet ud er Eders Tvist,
Begge Sønner af Alfader.
Mighty Odin! Christ the White!
Your feud has now been wiped away,
[ye are] both sons of the All-father.

In 1810, all that was to change. In an intense personal crisis, Grundtvig was converted to "serious Christianity" and remained an orthodox Lutheran for the rest of his life. Now, for the first time, the relationship between Christianity and Norse mythology came to constitute an existential problem

---

[2] Tolkien's theory will not be presented in full format here. References to the four works mentioned in this paragraph will only be given occasionally.

[3] Some parallels and useful further references are given in Vink (1990).

[4] Of Chesterton's books, *The Everlasting Man* and *Orthodoxy* are the most interesting ones here. Chesterton believed that, as it was objectively true that God had created the world, the Christian truth must necessarily "break through" into it continually, independent of the direct Revelation in Christ. He also suggested that History is God's fairy-tale for humanity. George MacDonald believed that the Cross and Resurrection experience is constantly re-created in the human imagination, which he saw as an "image of the imagination of God": see Duriez, 1992, p. 127, cf. p. 170. On influence from Barfield and Sayers, see Flieger, 1983, chapters III and IV and Vink, respectively. See also Grant, 1979, p. 94, Bergmann, 1977, and Hidal, 1986.

[5] The value of myth is forcefully argued in Grundtvig, 1832, especially pp. 65 ff. Cf. Aronson, 1960, p. 199 ff.

[6] Cf. Rønning, 1907-14, II, 1, p. 85 and p. 159. Cf. Thaning, 1983, pp. 20 ff.

[7] ". . . en renere søn af Alfader end Odin". Cited in Rønning, 1907-14, II, 1, p. 159. Cf. Grell, 1980, p. 22.

for him. He never forgot with what anguish he finally affirmed, in 1810, that Christ was the only way to salvation "for those who know of his birth" (Rønning, 1907-14, II, 1, p. 202).

This religious about-face initially lead him to renounce his earlier decision to "devote his life and his power to raising a speaking stone on the grave mound of Pagan antiquity": "a Christian had more important things to do".[8] In Aulë-like desperation, he even considered burning the all-but-finished manuscript of a large cycle of poems based on the Volsung and Nivlung traditions. He eventually published the poems, but he did add last-minute Christianizing conclusions, and repented in the foreword his previous "harmful and irresponsible" (*daarlig og letsindig*) words about the wild and blood-stained "idols and heroes of antiquity" (Grundtvig, 1904-9, I, p. 553).[9] However, he could not for long resist the call of the North. He fought desperately to find safe passage over the slippery theological slopes that lead thither.[10] And gradually, he seemed to discern a way. In opposition to the philosophical and theological Establishment, Grundtvig stressed the Creation as a fundamental theme of theology.[11] This led to a position on Natural Theology that was rare for that day and age. He emphasized God's creation as an on-going process, rejecting the Enlightenment view that it was an act completed long ago. Created Man always searched for his Creator, and struggled to define what being human meant. Among Pagans – defined as people cut off by time or space from the revelation of Christ – the search and the struggle had to take Pagan forms, resulting in mythologies which were therefore not necessarily objectionable. Before his religious crisis Grundtvig had regarded Christianity as the perfect, original myth, a myth that had actualized itself in History.[12] This view survived 1810, nor did Grundtvig ever have any difficulties in admitting that Pagan mythologies contained glimpses of the Truth that "in the fullness of Time descended corporeally and lit a Light in the Dark, that threw its radiance backwards to the beginnings of the world and shot its rays out to its end."[13] It followed that even Pagans could have visions that, although confused, also contained elements of truth.

Pagans who, in the cosmic struggle between Good and Evil, chose Good, deserved "admiration and lenient judgement in a sinful world".[14] Pagans were merely people who had not yet become Christians.

Grundtvig found that Norse mythology, in particular, contained so much of the truth as to constitute a "separate expression of the Mosaic-Christian view of Man, his conditions and history." (Grell, 1980, note 49, p. 195).[15] In Grundtvig's terminology, it had "universal-historic" importance, an importance to be rivalled only by the Old Testament. The same Spirit that spoke to the prophets of the Hebrews also spoke to the scalds of the North, though his voice was for them harder to discern. Where the revelation in Christ offers mankind a true expression of its relationship to the eternal things, Norse mythology explains humanity's relationship to the temporal, to the world.[16] Thus it affirms and complements Christianity, and studying it is a praiseworthy, indeed necessary enterprise. To become a true Christian, Man must first learn to know himself as Man: "*Menneske først og Christen saa*", in a famous phrase. This was simply not possible without knowledge of the spirit and philosophy of one's own people – in the case of Scandinavia embedded in Norse mythology.[17]

Grundtvig's very positive evaluation of mythology presupposed a sharp division between "paganism" (or "mythology") on the one hand and "idolatry", the actual worship of Pagan deities, on the other. Grundtvig believed that while Norse mythology was "the Northern Pagans" natural philosophy and image-language, the "*idolatry*, the *worship* of Odin, Thor and Frey and their images instead of the only invisible God, Creator of Heaven and Earth, was . . . an uninspired *distortion* of the original Paganism".[18]

---

[8] ". . . ofre sit Liv og sin Kraft til at rejse paa Hedenolds Gravhøj en talende Sten", cited in Grundtvig, 1904-1909, I, p. 546.

[9] The prevailing critical view is that Grundtvig seriously flawed his work by introducing the changes. Some critics have felt that Tolkien, too, damaged his *legendarium* by making it conform with Christianity. They feel that it lost some of its original freshness, vigour and ambiguity in the process.

[10] On the central position of this dilemma for Grundtvig, see for instance the quote in Thaning, 1963, p. 48.

[11] See Grell, 1980, pp. 31, 36; cf. Aronson, 1960, p. 167.

[12] Cf. Grundtvig, 1983, pp. 99 ff.

[13] ". . . i Tidens Fylde legemlig nedsteeg og tændte et Lys i Mørket, der kastede sit Skin tilbage mot Verdens Begyndelse og udskiød sine Straaler til dens Ende" (Grundtvig, 1983, p. 81). Cf. Grundtvig, 1832, pp. 370 ff., p. 384; Grell, 1980, p. 114; Rønning, 1907-14, III, 1, p. 45.

[14] "Beundring of skaasom Bedømmelse i en syndig Verden" (Grundtvig, 1832, pp. 98 ff.). Cf. Thaning, 1963, p. 48.

[15] Cf. Grundtvig, 1983, p. 184, "Nordens Mytologi er Verdenshistoriens Billedsprog" in Grell, 1988, pp. 91, 157; and Thaning, 1963, p. 451.

[16] It should be noted that this does not reflect any division of human life into a "spiritual" and a "temporal" sphere. Such a separation was wholly foreign to Grundtvig's theology. Cf. Grundtvig, 1832, pp. 65 ff., Thaning, 1983, pp. 51 ff. For a poetical defence of Norse mythology as valuable to Christians, see "Gylden-Aaret" [The Golden Year] (1834) and especially "Nordens Aand" [The Spirit of the North] (1834) in Grundtvig, 1904-1909, VIII.

[17] See for instance Grundtvig, 1832, pp. 65 ff., Thaning, 1963, p. 52, pp. 630 ff., p. 705; Thaning, 1983, p. 95.

[18] ". . . som de nordiske Hedningers naturlige tankegang og Billedsprog, men *Afguderiet*, *Dyrkelsen* af Odin, Thor og Frey og deres Billeder istedenfor den eneste usynlige Gud, Himmelens og Jordens Skaber, det var ligesaavel en aandløs *Forvanskning* af det oprindelige Hedenskab" (Grundtvig, 1983, p. 199). Grundtvig goes on to explain that the Christian faith underwent a similar distortion in that Christians started to worship saints and their relics "som Helgen-Tilbedelsen og Billed-Dyrkelsen i Pavedømmet var og er en *aandløs Forvanskning* af den oprindelige Christendom. Derfor følde ogsaa vore Nordiske Fædre, da de første lærde at kiende *Christendommen* og den *Bibelske*

Grundtvig's "Sub-Creation Theory"

Another crucial feature of Grundtvig's theology were his views regarding the nature of human creativity that led to mythology. Mythology was a result of Man's poetic ability, which itself was the Image of God in Man. Man the creator was both creation and image of God the Creator. Even after the Fall, Man has retained a remnant of Fantasy (*indbildningskraft Fantasi*) which is the form in which the poetic ability manifests itself, and thereby the possibility to glimpse at the higher truth about Man and God; but now the ability can also be put to ill uses.[19] Without God's help, Fallen Man can no longer distinguish between Truth and Lie.

The function of the poetic ability is not to *invent*, but to *uncover*: It is derivative, albeit not passive. The poet (*skjalden*) is "the Lord's fellow worker" (*Herrens medarbejder*) (Rønning, 1907-14, IV, 2, p. 162). When correctly used, the poetic ability will of its nature express truth, whether the user intends it or not (Grell, 1980, pp. 49 ff.).[20] And the ability should be used. Only by "imitating [God's] Creation" (*efterligne Skabelsen*, a possible translation might be "sub-creating") can Man realize the Image of God that he carries within him and become aware of his own true nature (Grundtvig, 1983, p. 79).[21]

Like God, also for Man the instrument of creation is the word. The fundamental importance of "Man's word" (*Menneskeordet*) is constantly emphasized in Grundtvig's writings. It is an integral part of the Image of God in Man, and the sole channel of knowledge about Man's relationship to his Maker.[22] The medium of the poetic ability, and the symbol of Man's lordship over the rest of creation, is language (Grell, 1980, p. 116). Man's word echoes God's word in that it re-creates in images the things which God's word has made reality. Man is created; therefore his word, his "image-language", contains an image of God's Word of Creation (Grell, 1980, pp. 128, 154, Grell, 1988, p. 96, Grell, 1980 pp. 66, 71).

Tolkien and Grundtvig: Influence or Coincidence?

Grundtvig's thoughts on mythology, Christianity and human creativity show striking similarities to Tolkien's "sub-creation theory". Tolkien, too, drew a sharp distinction between religion and mythology, which he found "almost devoid of religious significance" (Tolkien, 1988, p. 27, Tolkien, 1977a, p. 20, and cf. p. 22). Tolkien, too, regarded non-Christian mythologies not necessarily as lies, but as humanity's attempts – reading God's creation, but without the revelation in Christ – at explaining man's position in the world. They both rejected the view that myths were to be understood primarily as primitive attempts at explaining natural or social phenomena (Garde, 1897, p. 6. Cf. Tolkien, 1988, pp. 25-27). Both men were firm believers in Natural Theology, but, as pointed out in Tolkien's case by Colin Duriez, they held it to be founded on Fantasy (i.e. imagination) rather than Reason (Duriez, 1992, p. 186, cf. p. 61). For both men, Christianity was the true mythology, the one fusion of History and Myth, throwing reflections and shadows backwards and forwards in time. Both men believed that Man, made in the image and likeness of a Maker, fulfilled that Maker's will by creating with words, thereby helping him to gain a better understanding of his existence and uncovering underlying truth. Both men referred to Man's gift of Fantasy as his symbol of kingship over the rest of creation. Both agreed that the gift was used most effectively when describing those things that could not be directly observed in the primary world.[23] Both believed that language and myth were inextricably entwined. And both men, finally, hoped that the fruits of Man's creativity would be redeemed in God's new creation.[24]

In short, all the central elements in Tolkien's sub-creation theory can be found in Grundtvig and are expressed in very similar terms. The point is not that these elements, taken singly, are so original. We have seen that several of them are

---

Historie, at disse vel stred imod al *Afguds-Dyrkelse*, men at de godt lot sig rime sammen med deres hedenske Forestillinger om Livets Kræfter Kamp og Udvikling i Tidens Løb, saa de to Ting var som Alvor og Gammen, der altid i Norden kan godt sammen . . . " Cf. Thaning, 1963, p. 142 and Thaning, 1983, p. 95.

[19] See Grell, 1980, pp. 41-44, cf. pp. 74 ff. See also Grundtvig, 1832, pp. 70 ff.

[20] Cf. Grundtvig, 1904-1909, VIII, p. 351, from "Skjalde-Blik paa Danmarks Stjerne" (1840): "Billed-Sproget er dobbelt Sandt,/Og tænker end Thrym, det er kun Tant,/Thor siger: løft kun Sløret!" see also Thaning, 1963, p. 451.

[21] Cf. Aronson, 1960, p. 190.

[22] Grell, 1980, pp. 59-63. Cf. Grell, 1988, p. 93; Aronson, 1980, p. 206; and Thaning, 1963, pp. 675 ff. Grundtvig believed that only one's cradle tongue could function as "image-language" and convey adequately the truth about God and Man. The position of the straightforward popular language was therefore a measure of the cultural status of the people/nation. An important point in this connection is that because this language, *Modersmaalet*, was inherited from Pagan forebears and shaped by their imagination, its "natural, Pagan Character and Form" must necessarily be used even when conveying Christianity: Thaning, 1983, p. 95, cf. Aronson, 1980, p. 178. See also Haarder, 1983, pp. 76 ff. Aronson has pointed out that Grundtvig did not derive his idea of the Image of God in Man only from Genesis, but also from the nature of language: Aronson, 1980, pp. 38, 13, cf. p. 41.

[23] Tolkien, 1988, pp. 24 ff; Grundtvig, 1983, p. 158: ". . . det er langt fra, at vort Ord er stærkest, naar det nærvner og beskriver hvad Man kan see for sine Øine og tage paa med Hænder, men det er netop i sin Kraft, naar det udtrykker det usynlige og Ubegripelige, som lever i os, eller svæver over os, og skaber saaledes en heel usynlig Verden, som vi Mennesker har for os selv og see kun Skygger og Billeder af i den synlige Verden" ["it is not by far so, that our word is strongest when it mentions and describes what a man may see with his eyes and touch with his hands; it is precisely when it gives expression to the invisible and unfathomable that it gains its full power, [the things] that live in us, or hover above us, and creates in this fashion a whole invisible world, which we humans have to ourselves [as opposed to animals – NIA] and of which we can only see shadows and images in the visible world"].

[24] Grell, 1980, p. 67, cf. Aronson, 1960, p. 50; Tolkien, 1988, p. 66. Grundtvig believed that there was room for development and improvement even in Paradise (i.e. Man can contribute): Aronson, 1960, p. 48.

not. The point is, rather, that almost exactly the same elements were offered in defence by these two men who came from very different backgrounds but were faced with very much the same kind of problem: how to reconcile mythology, including self-made mythology, with orthodox Christianity; and: why Christians should spend time on mythologies and fairy-stories at all.[25]

Our next question must obviously be: was Tolkien directly influenced by Grundtvig? Had Tolkien even heard about Grundtvig, the untranslated Danish theologian?

The last question is easy enough. Tolkien must have had *some* knowledge of Grundtvig because Grundtvig was one of the pioneers in Tolkien's professional field: Anglo-Saxon studies. When Thorkelin published the first modern edition of *Beowulf* in Copenhagen in 1815, it was Grundtvig who pointed out the very serious deficiencies in it. With his *Bjovulf's Drape* in 1820, Grundtvig was himself the first to translate the poem into a modern language, and was also "the first to understand the story of *Beowulf*", according to one authority (Tinker, 1974, p. 23. Cf. Chambers, 1932, p. 515).. The discovery that king Hygelac in the poem was actually identical with a historical person mentioned by Martin of Tours – to Tolkien one of the "most important facts . . . that research has discovered" – was Grundtvig's.[26] On the basis of his intimate knowledge of Norse mythology he was also the first to trace the links between the Eddic and the Anglo-Saxon literatures.[27] In 1829-31, at a time when there was almost no interest in Anglo-Saxon in Britain, Grundtvig made repeated visits to British libraries, collections and places of learning to study the old manuscripts – and also to try and rouse the British scholars of the day from their indifference regarding their Old English heritage. In this he was successful – so much so that he eventually discovered to his sorrow that not all his British colleagues welcomed what they regarded as foreign interference.[28]

Professionally, Tolkien probably knew Grundtvig best as a critic and editor of *Beowulf*. Grundtvig's name figures in most of the standard works on *Beowulf* that Tolkien used, and, as Tom Shippey has pointed out, it is likely that Grundtvig is present in Tolkien's famous 1936 lecture on *Beowulf* as one of the very old voices, not as far out as some of the newer ones, crying that the poem was a "mythical allegory" (Tolkien, 1977a, p. 5, cf. Shippey, 1982, p. 223). What Grundtvig had to say about *Beowulf* was in fact very similar to what Tolkien stated in his lecture. Grundtvig regarded *Beowulf* as a portrayal of "Man's struggle against the Force of Darkness" (*Menneske-Kampen mod hin Mørkets Magt*), possessing a measure of "poetic truth" (1983, p. 96); Tolkien's words were "man at war with the hostile world, and his inevitable overthrow in Time" (1977a, p. 16).[29] They agreed on the nature of the fundamental conflict: the monsters were the enemies of both God and Man, and should be fought even without hope of final victory.

Beowulf, which occupied both Tolkien and Grundtvig intensely, is thus the most certain link between them. Intriguingly, Tolkien used part of his lecture to argue that the *Beowulf* poet confronted exactly the same problem as he himself (and Grundtvig) struggled with: "shall we or shall we not consign the heathen ancestors to perdition? [. . .] *Quid Hinieldus cum Christo?*" He then gave his (and Grundtvig's) answer at once, echoing his poem "Mythopoeia" (then unpublished): "The author of *Beowulf* showed forth the permanent value of that *pietas* which treasures the memory of man's struggles in the dark past, man fallen and not yet saved, disgraced but not dethroned" (Tolkien, 1977a, p. 22).[30]

Whether Tolkien knew other parts of Grundtvig's vast and wide-spanning literary production is more difficult to decide. There are many reasons why Grundtvig would have appealed to Tolkien, other than their burning love of the same traditions. Their basic outlook was in many respects very similar. Tolkien loved the "noble northern spirit" and felt a measure of distaste for the East. Grundtvig regarded the Anglo-Saxon/Scandinavian culture as a high civilization in its own right. It was neither peripheral, barbaric, nor a mere derivation of more southerly or easterly cultures (inferior except for the Hebrews and the Greeks). Where Tolkien talked about the "fundamentally similar heroic temper of ancient England and Scandinavia" (Tolkien, 1977a, p. 19. Cf. p. 23), Grundtvig never tired of pointing out that the ancient northern civilization had comprised Scandinavia and England both; in his *Høinorden*, England was always enthusiastically included. For both men, England was the blessed land where the northern spirit had first been "sanctified and Christianized".[31] Grundtvig's hope for the future of civilization was that the "Heroic Spirit of the North" would rise anew when England and Scandinavia discovered their ancient bonds and joined forces once again – not politically,

---

[25] Of course, this is not to say that there are no significant differences between Grundtvig's and Tolkien's theories. For instance, Grundtvig lack's Tolkien's "Eucatastrophe" (but on the other hand often points to the way the real "Eucatastrophe", the Gospel, is reflected in the imagination).

[26] Tolkien, 1977a, p. 3. Grundtvig's influence in the field of Anglo-Saxon studies is explored in detail in Rønning, 1885. See also Garde, 1897, and Haarder, 1983.

[27] Garde, 1897, pp. 18, 21. Grundtvig believed that the Eddic poems had at one stage survived only in Anglo-Saxon form.

[28] In 1830 he was asked by a London firm of booksellers to edit a series of editions of Anglo-Saxon works, starting with *Beowulf*, only to see the idea taken over by the British scholar Benjamin Thorpe, who launched a competing series with the backing of the Antiquarian Society. Because of this, Grundtvig's series never progressed beyond the planning stage.

[29] Cf. Tolkien, 1977a, p. 25; "Man alien in a hostile world, engaged in a struggle which he cannot win while the world lasts". On further similarities (and differences!) between Tolkien's and Grundtvig's interpretations and evaluations of the poem see also Haarder, 1975, chapter 4 (including many relevant quotes from Grundtvig); and Haarder, 1983, pp. 74 ff.

[30] Cf. p. 27. The parallel to "Mythopoeia" is not only to stanza 5, but also to 6-11.

[31] Tolkien's words in Tolkien, 1981, p. 56, cf. Grundtvig, 1832, pp. 107 ff.

but culturally.³² (One of the many places where this wish was formulated was in an Anglo-Saxon poem introducing Grundtvig's 1861 *Beowulf* edition, which Tolkien had no doubt read.) Like Tolkien, Grundtvig lamented the fact that the English had lost sight of their mythological and cultural roots. As *The History of Middle-earth* has shown, Tolkien, too, was intensely interested in uncovering and revitalizing those roots. He may have seen Grundtvig's 1831 prospectus to a proposed "Anglo-Saxon library", written in English and proclaiming, with characteristic zeal, the immense historical significance of Anglo-Saxon civilization and the concomitant importance of studying it.

But for Tolkien to have assimilated more than broad outlines of Grundtvig's thought he would have had to either have read him in Danish or received his information indirectly.

The last-mentioned possibility is not so far-fetched as it might seem. Grundtvig's writings were read by many German scholars, and constantly reviewed and referred to in German philological, historical and theological literature. When he visited Cambridge in 1831, Grundtvig found that his name was well known through German academic journals (Rønning, 1885, V, pp. 138, 144). Tolkien certainly kept up with the most important German-language publications in his field, and may, if his reading was wide enough, have become acquainted with the main features of Grundtvig's way of thought through them. And of course Tolkien may have learnt about Grundtvig from colleagues who specialized in fields which required familiarity with Scandinavian academic literature.³³

If Tolkien's sub-creation theory was directly influenced by Grundtvig, it is nevertheless more probable that he read him in the original. The book he is most likely to have been influenced by is Grundtvig's central work on mythology, *Nordens Mythologi* from 1832, re-issued in 1870 (and not to be confused with a book of the same title published in 1808). Although they are found in different places, this book contains most of the elements of what I have called Grundtvig's "sub-creation theory". It also discusses why myths are so vitally important for a people, and the "universal-historic" value of North-West-European traditions. But could Tolkien read modern Danish? This is a debatable point. Unlike some of his colleagues, Tolkien very seldom referred to Scandinavian-language academic literature in his published works, which may be an indication that he did not read much of it.³⁴ It is not possible to deduce any intimate knowledge of modern Scandinavian from the few references he does make. They do show, however, that he could penetrate a text if he really wanted to. This is borne out by Tolkien's controversy with the Swedish translator of *The Lord of the Rings*: Tolkien wrote, in 1957, that his knowledge of Swedish was "inadequate", but he was nevertheless able, with the aid of a dictionary and motivated by strong personal interest, to make his way through some pages of text in that language.³⁵ He may of course have had a better command of it in earlier years. There are only five Scandinavian-language books among the 320 or so Tolkien donated to the Bodleian Library and the British Faculty Library in Oxford, and they do not change the picture.³⁶

---

³² See for instance Grundtvig, 1832, pp. 3 ff., Rønning, 1885, V, p. 183, Bang, 1932.

³³ For instance, both R.W. Chambers, author of a classic *Beowulf* introduction, and Fr. Klaeber, the man behind the standard *Beowulf* text edition, were familiar with even rather obscure articles in Scandinavian languages, and knew Grundtvig not only as a *Beowulf* scholar, but also as the author of *Nordens Mythologi* (1832).

The possibility that some account of the learned Dane with the grand and stimulating views survived somehow in academic circles in Britain cannot be entirely ruled out. Grundtvig travelled to England four times, in 1829, 1830, 1831 and 1843. He talked to many of the most distinguished scholars in England and was invited to both Oxford and Cambridge for extended stays. The visits may have left marks of some sort in annual reports, correspondence, lecture notes, publications with limited circulation or the like. However, it is of course unlikely that any such accounts could, on their own, have given more than the vaguest intimations of Grundtvig's interests and philosophy.

³⁴ A cursory check shows that he referred to Torp's *Nynorsk etymologisk ordbog* and to Finnur Jónsson's *Den Norsk-Islandske Skjaldedigtning* (1912-15) in "Sigelwara Land" (Tolkien, 1932 and 1934). Jónsson's book pops up again in *Finn and Hengest: The Fragment and the Episode* (edited by Alan Bliss on the basis of Tolkien's lecture notes, 1982). In his chapters on "Philology: General Works" in *The Year's Work in English Studies 1923-25* (1924, 26 & 27), Tolkien mentions an unexamined Swedish-language book in 1923 (p. 33) and accords Professor Otto Jespersen's *Menneskehed, Nasjon, og Individ i Sproget* (1925) high marks, but only eight lines, in 1925. According to the back cover of Jespersen's book, the work was also available in English, but Tolkien does not seem to have exerted himself to get hold of that edition, which would seem to indicate that he could read Jespersen's Danish. Cf. Shippey, 1982, p. 223. – The fact that Tolkien, when referring to Norwegian fairy-tales in "On Fairy-Stories", used Dasent's *Popular Tales from the Norse* rather than Asbjørnsen and Moe's landmark collection of Norwegian fairy-tales may be an indication that he did not easily read modern Norwegian. Admittedly, Tolkien also quoted from Dasent's introduction.

There are some scraps of Danish in the privately published *Songs for the Philologists* (Tolkien, Gordon *et al*, 1936), to which Tolkien was the major contributor. Bodil Kragh (1985, p. 120, note 9) thinks that these were written by Tolkien, but according to Tolkien's own notes to the collection this is not correct.

³⁵ Tolkien, 1981, p. 263, cf. pp. 304-7. Cf. Ohlmarks, 1978, p. 23: "Han trodde sig förstå svenskan flytande, men saknade i själva verket även mycket elementära begrepp om språket . . .", and p. 143: "Han kunde möjligen begripa huvudinnehållet i en enklare svensk text". Ohlmarks' book is generally unreliable, however.

³⁶ According to lists given to me in June 1992 by Anders Stenström. Two of them are relatively uninteresting in that they mainly contain texts in ancient languages. Two others, *Færøske Folkesagn og æventyr* by Jakob Jakobsen (ed.) (1898-1901) and *Færøiske Qvæder om Sigurd Fofnersbane og hans Æt* by Hans Christian Lyngbye (ed.) (1822) are also text editions, but of greater interest to us because the Faeroese language in them can be said to be a kind of intermediate stage between South-West Norwegian and Icelandic, but is much closer to modern Scandinavian languages than the latter. If Tolkien could read Faeroese fluently, Grundtvig's Danish would probably not have daunted him.

On the basis of the striking parallels between the two, it seems probable that Grundtvig's philosophy was one of the major sources Tolkien drew on when forming his "sub-creation theory". Polygenesis – that the two men, both deeply religious and faced with similar dilemmas, should independently have formed very similar theories – cannot so far be categorically ruled out, but it does seem to me to be less likely.

But if Grundtvig was so important, would not Tolkien have mentioned him explicitly somewhere? Not necessarily. In writing about "Tolkien's Sources: the True Tradition" (mentioning Grundtvig!), Tom Shippey has made the point that Tolkien's sources of inspiration are not always evident in his published writings, including his letters. For instance, it is indisputable that Tolkien, when writing "On Fairy-Stories", was deeply influenced by Owen Barfield's *Poetic Diction*. Yet we would never guess this solely from what Tolkien published.

Tracing Tolkien's sources is a risky business. He himself had no great sympathy for those who, when savouring a plate of soup, wished to examine the bones of the ox out of which it had been boiled. Part of what he meant was that tracking down the sources and influences on a story does not necessarily help you appreciate the story as such – a position very few of his critics have adopted. To a certain extent, the same is applicable to non-fiction, such as "On Fairy-Stories". Tolkien's theory should stand or fall on its own merits. I believe, nevertheless, that further study of the relationship between Grundtvig and Tolkien may enable us to reach a deeper understanding not only of what Tolkien did and did not mean with his "sub-creation theory", but of the character of his *legendarium* as well.

References

Agøy, Nils Ivar. 1992. "An interview with Tom Shippey", *Angerthas in English* 2 (1992), pp. 27-49.

Aronson, Harry. 1960. *Mänskligt och kristet. En studie i Grundtvig's teologi*. Stockholm: Scandinavian University Books.

Bang, J. P. 1932. *Grundtvig og England*. Copenhagen: Kirkeligt samfund.

Bergmann, Frank. 1977. "The Roots of Tolkien's Tree. The Influence of George MacDonald and German Romanticism upon Tolkien's Essay 'On Fairy-Stories'" *Mosaic*, X, 2., 1977, pp. 5-14.

Chambers, R. W. 1932. *Beowulf. An Introduction to the Study of the Poem with a Discussion of the Stories of Offa and Finn*, second edition. Cambridge: Cambridge University Press.

Duriez, Colin. 1992. *The Tolkien and Middle-earth Handbook*. Speldhurst, U.K.: Monarch Books.

Flieger, Verlyn. 1983. *Splintered Light: Logos and Language in Tolkien's World*. Grand Rapids, MI: Eerdmans.

Garde, Axel. 1897. *Grundtvigs mytologi*. Studier fra sprog- og oldtidsforskning nr. 33. Copenhagen.

Grant, Patrick. 1979. *Six Modern Authors and Problems of Belief*. London: Macmillan.

Grell, Helge. 1980. *Skaberordet og billedordet: Studier over Grundtvigs teologi om ordet*. Copenhagen: privately printed.

Grell, Helge. 1988. *Skaberånd og folkeånd: En undersøgelse af Grundtvigs tanker om folk og folkelighed og deres forhold til hans kristendomssyn*. Århus: privately printed.

Grundtvig, N. F. S. 1832. *Nordens Mythologi eller Sindbilled-Sprog historisk-peotisk udviklet og oplyst*, second edition. Copenhagen: Schûbothe.

Grundtvig, N. F. S. 1904-1909. *Grundtvigs Udvalgte Skrifter I-X*. Ed. Holger Begtrup. Copenhagen: Gyldendal.

Grundtvig, N. F. S. 1983. *Historie og kristendom: en Grundtvig-antologi*. Haarby: Forlaget i Haarby.

Haarder, Andreas. 1975. *Beowulf: The Appeal of a Poem*. Copenhagen: Akademisk Forlag.

Haarder, Andreas. 1983. "Grundtvig and the Old Norse Cultural Heritage", pp. 72-86 in Christian Thodberg and Anders Pontoppidan Thyssen eds. *N. FF. S. Grundtvig. Tradition and Renewal*. Copenhagen: The Danish Institute.

Hidal, Sten. 1986. *Kelter, dystre domprosten och Tolkien*. Vejbystrand: Catholica.

Jakobsen, Jakob (ed.). 1898-1901. *Færøske Folkesagn og æventyr*. Copenhagen: S. L. Møller.

Jespersen, Otto. 1922. *Modersmålet fonetik*. Kristiana/Copenhagen: Gyldendal.

Jespersen, Otto. 1925. *Menneskehed, Nasjon, og Individ i Sproget*. Oslo: Aschehoug.

Jónsson, Finnur. 1912-15. *Den Norsk-Islandske Skjaldedigtning*. Copenhagen: Gyldendal-Nordisk folag.

Kragh, Bodil. 1985. *»Heorot Revisited« Håbløshed og heltemod: Brugen af Beowulf – som litteratur og i litteratur – i det tyvende århundrede, med hovedvægt på J. R. R. Tolkiens forfatterskab*. Odense.

Lobdell, Jared. 1981. *England and Always: Tolkien's World of the Rings*. Grand Rapids, MI: Eerdmans.

The remaining work was the above-mentioned Otto Jespersen's textbook of (Danish) phonetics, *Modersmålet fonetik* (1922).

Lyngbye, Hans Christian (ed.). 1822. *Færøiske Qvæder om Sigurd Fofnerbane og hans Æt*. Randers: G. Elmenhoff.

Ohlmarks, Åke. 1978. *Tolkiens arv*. Stockholm: Plus.

Rønning, Frederik. 1885. "N. FF. S. Grundtvig og den oldengelske literatur", pp. 321-366 in *Historisk Månedsskrift* vol. IV, 1885, pp. 1-41 and pp. 129-187 in vol. V, 1885.

Rønning, Frederik. 1907-1914. *N. FF. S. Grundtvig I-IV*. Copenhagen: Schønbergske forlag.

Shippey, T. A. 1982. *The Road to Middle-earth*. London: Allen and Unwin.

Thaning, Kaj. 1963. *Menneske først – Grundtvigs opgør med sig selv* I – III. Copenhagen: Gyldendal.

Thaning, Kaj. 1983. *Grundtvig*. Oslo: Gyldendal.

Tinker, Chauncey. 1974. *The Translations of* Beowulf *A Critical Bibliography*. Hamden, CT: Archon Books.

Tolkien, J. R. R. 1924. "Philology: General Works" in eds. Sir Sidney Lee and F. S. Boas *The Year's Work in English Studies 1923*, pp. 20-37. London: Humphrey Milford.

Tolkien, J. R. R. 1926. "Philology: General Works" in eds. F. S. Boas and C. H. Herford *The Year's Work in English Studies 1924*, pp. 26-65. London: Humphrey Milford.

Tolkien, J. R. R. 1927. "Philology: General Works" in eds. F. S. Boas and C. H. Herford *The Year's Work in English Studies 1925*, pp. 32-66. London: Humphrey Milford.

Tolkien, J. R. R. 1932. "Sigelwara Land", part one in *Medium Ævum* 1, pp. 183-196.

Tolkien, J. R. R. 1934. "Sigelwara Land", part two in *Medium Ævum* 3, pp. 95-111.

Tolkien, J. R. R. 1977a. *Beowulf: The Monsters and the Critics*. Norwood, PA: Norwood Editions.

Tolkien, J. R. R. 1977b. *The Silmarillion*. London: Allen & Unwin.

Tolkien, J. R. R. 1981. *Letters of J. R. R. Tolkien*. Ed. Humphrey Carpenter. London: Allen & Unwin.

Tolkien, J. R. R. 1982. *Finn and Hengest: The Fragment and the Episode* ed. Alan Bliss. London: George Allen & Unwin.

Tolkien, J. R. R. 1988.*Tree and Leaf*, second edition. London: Unwin Hyman.

Tolkien, J. R. R., and Gordon, E. V. *et al.* 1936. *Songs for the Philologists*. London: privately published.

Vink, Renée. 1990. "The Image of the Maker", pp. 43-59 in *Elrond's Holy Round Table. Essays on Tolkien, Sayers and the Arthur Saga*. Leiden: Tolkien Genootschap Unquendor.

Tolkien's Experiment with Time: *The Lost Road*, "The Notion Club Papers" and J. W. Dunne

Verlyn Flieger

Abstract: Tolkien's two time-travel stories, *The Lost Road* and "The Notion Club Papers", derive their mode of operation from a theory of time as a field proposed in 1927 by J.W. Dunne. This paper explores the relationship between Dunne's theory and the fictive psychology of dream and memory that provides a working basis for Tolkien's time travel.

Keywords: J.W. Dunne, *The Lost Road*, "The Notion Club Papers"

"When C.S. Lewis and I tossed up," Tolkien wrote in 1964, "and he was to write on space-travel and I on time-travel, I began an abortive book of time-travel of which the end was to be the presence of my hero in the drowning of Atlantis" (Tolkien, 1981, p. 347). That "abortive book" was *The Lost Road*, which Tolkien left unfinished to begin *The Lord of the Rings*. It was one of only two efforts at time-travel, the other being the also abortive "The Notion Club Papers", also in its time abandoned in favour of *The Lord of the Rings*. Both are stories of twentieth-century men who travel back in time through their dreams. This treatment of dream and time qualifies them as both science fiction, after the manner of H.G. Well's *The Time Machine*, and dream-vision, after the manner of Dante and Mark Twain and Lewis Carroll.

What differentiates Tolkien's stories from their predecessors in both genres is the principle by which he turned dream into a time-machine. This was derived from a theory of time proposed by J.W. Dunne, an aeronautical engineer who in 1927 published a book called *An Experiment with Time*. Tolkien read the third edition of Dunne's book around about Christmas of 1934, and submitted an unfinished draft of *The Lost Road* to Allen & Unwin in November of 1937.

Like Tolkien's fiction, Dunne's *Experiment* combined time and dream to make a totality greater than the sum of its parts. He based his work on his own dreams, specifically on his experience of dreaming events which to his waking mind had not yet happened, but which did happen soon afterward. To explain the phenomenon, Dunne suggested that time is not the inevitable forward flow which our human senses perceive, but is instead a constant, ever-present totality, like space. We move through time as we move through space, and it is our movement, not time's, which creates the illusion of forward progress. If all time, like all space, is always present, Dunne postulated that human consciousness can – and does, in dreams – extend its field of observation to travel through time in any direction.

Like the convention of dream vision, this is not in itself an especially new concept. It has been a subject for physicists and philosophers from Einstein to Ouspensky, and was the playing-field for the imaginations of writers as disparate as Henry James and E.R. Eddison. It was Dunne's particular model for the process which Tolkien found useful. Dunne envisioned a world of time-and-space wider than that perceivable to the conscious, waking mind, which he called Observer 1. Observer 1, he suggested, exists within the wider-perceiving, broader-ranging sleeping and dreaming mind which he called Observer 2. Observer 1's limited, waking experience is confined to its immediate field of attention, the so-called present, which Dunne named Field 1, or Time 1. But this larger Observer 2, containing (therefore exceeding the scope of), Observer 1, must then have access to a larger field of attention – Field 2 or Time 2 – which is not confined to the observable present.

To visualise the distinction, imagine someone watching a watcher, or picture a double set of parentheses, one set enclosing the other. If you want to carry on the conceit you can frame these parentheses with a third set, or add a third watcher to watch the second watcher watch the first watcher. Each successive parenthesis, or watcher, will encompass a larger awareness, a wider field of time. Dunne's theory, which for obvious reasons he called Serialism, went all the way to what he called "the observer at infinity," or "the ultimate observer".

Tolkien found in *An Experiment With Time* a principle through whose operation the mind could dream through time in any direction. This psychic principle he combined with Carl Jung's wholly compatible psychological theory of the collective unconscious, the commonly shared, unconscious memories of the human community, and used both to effect a mode of travel through dreamed serial identities. As he described *The Lost Road*:

> The thread was to be the occurrence time and again in human families . . . of a father and son called by names that could be interpreted as Bliss-friend and Elf-friend . . . It started with a father-son affinity between Edwin and Elwin of the present, and was supposed to go back into legendary time by way of an Eädwine and Ælfwine of circa A.D. 918, and Audoin and Alboin of Lombardic legend and so [to] the traditions of the North Sea concerning the coming of corn and culture heroes . . . In my tale we were to come at last to Amandil and Elendil leaders of the loyal party in Númenor.
>
> (Tolkien, 1981, p. 347)

One of Tolkien's earliest inventions was the traveller Ælfwine – called by the elves Eriol – who functions as the auditor in *The Book of Lost Tales*. It is Ælfwine through whose consciousness the stories of the Ainur and Valar, and the chaining of Melkor, are transmitted. As Christopher Tolkien has pointed out, the surname "Errol" of the twentieth-century heroes of *The Lost Road* is close enough to Eriol to imply an association between the two. Moreover, the meaning of Eriol, "one who dreams alone", suggests the dreams through which the hero of *The Lost Road* accomplishes his time-travel. Thus the Anglo-Saxon *Ælfwine*, "Elf-friend" – of which *Elwin* and *Alboin* are the modern British and Lombardic forms – provides both the story's encompassing concept and all its characters' encompassing identity.

Ælfwine may have been a formative as well as a connective element in Tolkien's story. Christopher Tolkien comments that with:

> the thought of a "time-travel" story in which the very significant figure of the Anglo-Saxon Ælfwine would be both "extended" into the future, into the twentieth century, and "extended" also into a many-layered past, my father was envisaging a massive and explicit linking of his own legends with those of many other places and times: all concerned with the stories and the dreams of peoples who dwelt by the coasts of the great Western Sea.
>
> (Tolkien, 1987, p. 98)

This seems to suggest that the "very significant" figure of the Anglo-Saxon Ælfwine was to be the flax from which Tolkien spun his "thread", that this character's extension into the many-layered past and the twentieth-century future would make all the Elf-friends, all the Elwins and Alboins, avatars of Ælfwine. In Dunne's terms he would be the ultimate observer, the encompassing consciousness which carried within it the whole scheme.

This expansive concept was not to be realised, however, for Tolkien never got round to filling in the outline he had made, and the story survives only as a fragment. As published it is shorter and simpler than the story Tolkien described, and contains only two of the many father-son pairs he envisioned. The fragment is worth attention, however, for it illustrates Tolkien's own theories about how dreams work and how they should be used in fiction. As anyone who has read his essay "On Fairy-Stories" knows, Tolkien had decided opinions about the use of dream in narrative. He was comfortable with dream as vision, or as revelation of the unconscious, but not with the use of dream as narrative frame. The problem as he sees it is not with the dream itself, but with the awakening, with the sharp disjuncture between dream and reality.

> It is true [he says] that . . . in dreams strange powers of the mind may be unlocked . . . But if a waking writer tells you that his tale is only a thing imagined in his sleep, he cheats deliberately the primal desire . . . the realisation, independent of the conceiving mind, of imagined wonder.
>
> (Tolkien, 1983, p. 116)

Tolkien wanted to unlock these strange powers of the mind, but he didn't want the effect achieved by dream-vision stories, the rude return to waking reality that calls the dream into question. He wanted something subtler, a dream that would call reality into question. The quietness with which Tolkien eases *The Lost Road* into dream without ever identifying it as such, makes the dream-state both the narrative technique and the basic fabric of the story, blurring the distinctions between sleep and waking, and blurring past and future into a seamless present.

You have to read *The Lost Road* carefully to see how he does it. The first chapter begins in Cornwall in the present time, and introduces the hero of *The Lost Road*, Alboin Errol, and his father Oswin. Calling in search of his son, Oswin is answered by "a young voice" which sounds like "someone asleep or just awakened." Alboin is stretched out on a wall overlooking the sea, and Oswin remarks that he "must be deaf or dreaming." This early in the narrative the comment seems no more than a mild parental complaint, a throwaway line. But at the opening of Chapter III the same scene and lines are repeated with only slight variation by another father-son pair, Elendil and his son Herendil. The names have altered slightly from the "Amandil and Elendil" of Tolkien's first description to Elendil and Herendil, but the plan is the same, and it is clear that we are no longer in present England, but in the past and in Númenor.

And now both fathers' comments that their sons are dreaming takes on new significance. Both boys are of an age, both stretched out on sea walls, and the similarity of character and situation suggests a link. Both boys insist that they are *not* dreaming, but are awake. The similarity in the episodes is clearly no accident, and the re-echoes of dialogue convey the impression of two events occurring simultaneously, of parallel or overlapping time-schemes. Beyond the repetition of scene and character and dialogue, the emphases in both episodes on the boys as dreamers suggests that each may be dreaming the other. And if that is the case, then we have been in dream from the very opening of the story, and the whole of the narrative is to be understood as a dreamed reality.

From here it is only a small step to see it as the sort of dream experience described by Dunne, an experience in which Observer 2 (the connected ancestral consciousness of both boys) ranges freely through past and future while Observer 1 (each temporal, individual boy) sleeps. Though only two identities are here connected, the extended list of father-son pairs that Tolkien envisioned would merely have lengthened the thread, but would not have materially altered it. It must be admitted that the shape of the story never really jelled, for Tolkien never filled in his outline, and the ideas often overlap or compete with one another. The one consistency, the one thing to remember, is that all the names are the same, all variations on Ælfwine and Eädwine, and therefore all the identities are serial recurrences, incarnations of one another.

Evidence for this lies in the titles which Tolkien gave his chapters. Chapter I, in which Alboin is stretched out on the wall, was to be called "A Step Forward. Young Alboin". In the context of the chapter by itself this title makes very little sense. No journey into the future is described, so in what sense and for whom is it a step forward? Certainly not for Oswin calling to his son, or to Alboin sleeping on a wall. But if both title and chapter foreshadow the dreaming Herendil, if his is a step forward through time and dream into Alboin's present consciousness (though not revealed as such until Chapter III) the title is pregnant with meaning. It becomes, indeed, a key to the whole design.

The title of Chapter III, "A Step Backward: Ælfwine and Eädwine", suggests a reverse process, the modern consciousness dreaming backward into the past. Tolkien did in fact start (though he never finished or inserted into the narrative) an Anglo-Saxon episode in which a character named Ælfwine awakens stretched out on a bench in an Anglo-Saxon hall. It seems probable that the awakening of this Ælfwine was to be coincident with the falling asleep of his Alboin counterpart, and that dream, as before, was to be the means of transition from one time to another.

Alboin's falling asleep is in fact, the transition, though in the text as published this occurs in Chapter II, "Alboin and Audoin". Alboin Errol, no longer "young Alboin", but the father of a son Audoin, falls asleep in his chair. It is not said that he dreams, only that he passes "out of the waking world". In this sleeping state he hears a voice and sees a figure whose face reminds him of his father. "I am with you," says the voice. "I was of Númenor, the father of many fathers before you. I am Elendil, that is in Eressëan 'Elf-friend', and many have been called so since." The name makes the connection clear, but in what sense is Elendil "with" Alboin?

I suggest that in Alboin's sleeping state the figure of Elendil operates as Dunne's "ultimate observer", an ultimate consciousness free to move through time in any direction, within whom the other observing consciousnesses – including Alboin's – are contained. Both Dunne and Tolkien went to some length to explain how this is possible. Their rationales are remarkably similar. Dunne writes:

> It is not surprising that [analysis] has brought to light no law which *compels* the ultimate observer to direct his attention to any particular phenomena in any particular field. That such attention is, as a matter of plain fact, habitually directed during waking moments to phenomena in Field 1 is obvious enough; but the theory leaves us with habit as the only compulsion in the matter . . . Nevertheless, the habit was no *law*. It could be overcome . . . And in the rare instances when this was successfully effected, attention in Field 2 was free to slip away . . .
> (Dunne, pp. 195-6)

Listen now to Tolkien's dialogue between the dreaming Alboin and what I will call his Elendil-self – Dunne's ultimate observer. Elendil speaks first, addressing Alboin:

> "You may have your desire."
> "What desire?"
> "The long-hidden and half-spoken: to go back."
> "But that cannot be, even if I wish it. It is against the law."
> "It is against the *rule*. Laws are commands upon the will . . . Rules are conditions; they may have exceptions . . . I ask if you would have your desire?"
> "I would."
> "You ask not how: or upon what conditions."
> "I do not suppose I should understand how, and it does not seem to me necessary. We go forward as a rule, but we do not know how."
> (Tolkien, 1987, p. 48)

Except for the fact that Dunne uses the word *habit* where Tolkien uses *rule* it is clear that both are talking abut the same thing. A point of importance is that in both texts the conventional perception of the forward movement of time is reduced from a law to a custom, whether developed from within, as in Dunne's "habit", or imposed from without, as with Tolkien's "rule".

As Tolkien left it, the Cornwall portion of the story breaks off in Chapter II at a point where Audoin, returning from a walk with the intention of telling his father about his own dreams, sees his father sitting by the fire apparently asleep.

> Audoin was creeping out of the room, heavy with disappointment . . . As he reached the door, he thought he heard . . . his father's voice . . . murmuring something: it sounded like *herendil* . . . He turned back hopefully.
> "Good night!" said Alboin. "Sleep well, Herendil! We start when the summons comes." Then his head fell back against the chair.
> "Dreaming," thought Audoin. "Good night!"
> And he went out, and stepped into sudden darkness.
> (Tolkien, 1987, pp. 52-3)

Since this is followed immediately by the first Númenórean chapter, the obvious intent of the episode is to show that Audoin has stepped into another time. Alboin's "We start when the summons comes", coupled with Audoin's step into darkness, is clearly intended as the transition from one world and time into another.

A note by Christopher Tolkien gives a revealing sidelight on the transition and its implications.

> Since the Númenórean episode was left unfinished, this is a convenient point to mention an interesting note that my father presumably wrote while it was in progress. This says that when the first "adventure" (i.e.

Númenor) is over "Alboin is still precisely in his chair and Audoin just shutting the door."
(Tolkien, 1987, p. 57)

This is very much the way dreams do operate; the dream stretches out over seemingly endless time and space within the unconscious process of the dreamer, during what to the conscious observer are the documentably brief intervals of dreaming sleep. This is precisely the operational principle of Dunne's theory. The dream frees the dreamer's awareness, enabling it to move freely over the field of time. Observer 2 can go anywhere for any length of time, while Observer 1 sleeps on, fixed in one place and one time.

How successful the story would have been had Tolkien finished it, we shall never know, for the project was dropped when it was scarcely more than well-begun, and that was the end of the idea for some time. All his creative powers for the next seven years were focused on *The Lord of the Rings*. Nevertheless, the idea lay fallow at the back of his mind, and when he came to a halting-place in the new book, it sprouted again.

On July 21, 1946, Tolkien wrote to Stanley Unwin:
I have in a fortnight of comparative leisure round about last Christmas written three parts of another book, taking up in an entirely different frame and setting what little had any value in the inchoate *Lost Road* . . .
(Tolkien, 1981, p. 118)

Tolkien's dismissal of *The Lost Road* as "inchoate" may say more about the story's unfinished state than about its guiding concept. And though he was also to leave "The Notion Club Papers" unfinished, this next effort shows a considerable advance in technical sophistication over *The Lost Road*. Tolkien's handling of his material is surer, and his sense of story better developed. There is an increase in narrative tension through a carefully-orchestrated sequence of psychological aberrations, a judicious sprinkling of plot-teasers in the first part of the story, and a gothic use of weather, culminating in the story's violent climax in a night of storm. The tone of this second narrative is more energetic and its setting more clearly contemporary, more conspicuously grounded in time and place, than that of the earlier story. The characters, too, are better imagined. The argumentative, rumbustious members of the Notion Club are a distinct improvement over the rather quiet Errols, while Tolkien's earliest drafts make it clear that the wit, rough badinage, and often heated exchanges were drawn from life – specifically the Inklings.

Focus on the past is still paramount, but there is a venture into the future as well, for the story's fictive present is postdated forty or so years beyond the time of its composition, from the forties to the eighties of the twentieth century, and the narrative frame of the story pushed still farther ahead. This projected future is mere prologue, however. The past is still the focus, a section of time more immediate and more exciting than either the narrative present or its future. In addition, the plot and situation are framed by elaborate pseudo-editorial commentary describing the finding of the papers on a trash heap in a College basement, and their identification as minutes of meetings of some past, unknown Oxford club. Then comes an account of the conflicting opinions of experts about dating and provenance – are the *Papers* a hoax? could the dating be a deliberate red herring? This is followed by a list of the members – again with editorial comment; all this before we come to the story itself.

Since he had jettisoned the Errol fathers and sons in favour of the Notion Club, and replaced Cornwall with Oxford, Tolkien's comment that he intended to retain "what little had any value" from *The Lost Road* clearly meant the time-travel idea itself. But it also meant the concept of a static field of time to which dreams give access, as well as the idea of collective or ancestral memory. Though these elements gave him a basis on which to build, the progress of the new narrative went through even more stops and starts than *The Lost Road*. As it stands, it falls into two sections, Part One being "The Ramblings of Ramer" and Part Two "The Strange Case of Arundel Lowdham", but both parts were subject to extensive revision. Part One consists of manuscripts A, B, C, and a final typescript D, while Part Two has a manuscript E and typescripts F1 and F2, with F2 continuing to the place where the narrative breaks off.

Part One sets up the theory. Largely a discussion of competing principles and techniques, it is all talk and little action, while Part Two noticeably increases the pace and tension. The history of composition suggests that between Tolkien's original conception of Part One and his development of Part Two the focus and perhaps the direction of the story underwent a change. The titles themselves suggest a shift of emphasis from Ramer to Lowdham. Thus, not just the editorial introduction, but also "The Ramblings of Ramer", constitute a long preamble to the tale, which is "The Strange Case of Arundel Lowdham" and his travel through time.

The preamble is important, however, for it shows Tolkien's concern with both the technique and the aesthetic of time-travel as a mode of fiction. Once his narrative frame has simultaneously established the setting and called its time into question, his story itself begins with a heated discussion of exactly those parameters of science fiction. The question before the Notion Club is whether the means of entry into other space or time can legitimately be a mere device, an arbitrary "frame" around the narrative, or whether it must be an integral component of the story. Readers of Tolkien's essay "On Fairy-Stories" already know the answer. An arbitrary frame will not satisfy, indeed it will undermine the intended effect of the story, the "realization, independent of the conceiving mind, of imagined wonder". In "The Notion Club Papers" the chief defender of this position is the Club's recorder Nicholas Guildford, who here speaks for Tolkien:

An author's way of getting to Mars (say) is part of *his* story of *his* Mars; and of *his* universe, as far as that particular tale goes. It's part of the picture, even if it's only in a marginal position; and it may seriously affect all that's inside.
(Tolkien, 1992, p. 163)

In this respect the first part of the *Papers* is self-reflexive, for the whole frame-embedded discussion of frame is itself a frame. It is designed to present the credentials for Tolkien's way of getting to "*his* Mars", that is, Númenor, which is, of course, by dreams. Here he frankly uses a kind of Inklings-argumentation, setting up the question, discussing and dismissing all previous attempts, and then producing his own solution. Again he uses the voice of Guildford:

> "No! For landing on a new planet, you've got your choice: miracle; magic; or sticking to normal probability, the only known or likely way in which anyone has ever landed on a world."
> "Oh! So you've got a private recipe all the time, have you?" said Ramer sharply.
> "No, it's not private, though I've used it once."
> "Well? Come on! What is it?"
> "Incarnation. By being born", said Guildford.
> (Tolkien, 1981, p. 170)

Having thus carefully introduced and integrated his time-travel principle, Tolkien proceeds to introduce the device itself, the dreaming minds of his characters. But where *The Lost Road* eased its story and characters into dream presented as waking reality, "The Notion Club Papers" allows the dream-state to dramatically erupt into and momentarily displace the present reality of his protagonist, Lowdham. Like Alboin Errol, but more dramatically, Lowdham dreams a reality and eventually comes to live it. Once again, the name is the clue to Tolkien's intent, and to his use of Dunne's theory. Lowdham's full name is Alwin Arundel Lowdham. The attentive reader will recognise Alwin as a variant spelling of Elwin and both as forms of Ælfwine, making it clear that Tolkien had not strayed far from his original design, and that the Ælfwine consciousness was once again to be the ultimate observer, that encompassing consciousness with whose awareness other, lesser observers would move across the field of time. To underscore the significance of the name, Lowdham is explicitly referred to by one member of the club as "Elf-friend".

But with the character of Lowdham the narrative takes a sharp departure from the scheme of *The Lost Road*. No ghostly dream-visitor appears to Lowdham, or invites him to journey into the past. Simply, his waking experience begins to be bizarrely punctuated by sudden flashbacks into an unremembered past, moments when he clearly takes on another personality, and expresses emotions untypical of his ordinary, waking self. Such an unpremeditated shift of consciousness, a flashback without warning to a forgotten, earlier state, is a recognised psychological phenomenon involving the involuntary eruption into present consciousness of some memory — usually repressed and often violent — whose return is triggered by some present event. It is not so much a remembering as a re-experiencing of the past, of any moment too powerful to be immediately processed by the receiving psyche.

In Tolkien's hands this becomes not so much a psychological as a psychic gateway into locked-off areas of the soul. He has extended the concept beyond past experience to encompass past lives. This recalls Guildford's speech about the only way to land on a new world, and his word *incarnation* with its implied corollary, *re-incarnation*. Lowdham is increasingly — and apparently involuntarily — regressing into some previous life and identity, a past identity which gains increasing power over the present until, in a climactic scene of storm and memory, it possesses him altogether and sweeps him wholly into another time.

In its handling of the transition from present to past, "The Notion Club Papers" displays considerably more dramatic tension than its predecessor. Where the Errols were to move into the past as Alboin sat quietly asleep in his chair and Audoin stepped into "sudden darkness", the comparable episode in the "Papers" has the past come storming directly into the present in a night of psychological and meteorological tumult. For this scene, Tolkien has gathered the club in Ramer's rooms, all present except Lowdham, who arrives late, waving a sheaf of papers. He has been dreaming intensively, and has written down what he can remember. The record of his dreams proves to be actual texts in two unknown languages which seem to be paired accounts of the destruction by storm and flood of *Atalantë*, the Downfallen. Atalantë, of course, is Númenor.

The Oxford weather matches the mood of the texts, and the Club's discussion proceeds in the thundery oppressiveness of an approaching storm. The discussion of Lowdham's dream-texts has the immediate effect of increasing the intensity and duration of his flashbacks. I have called these "flashbacks", but they could as well be called "flashforwards", or better yet "co-incidents" in the most literal sense. For they are neither backward not forward but concurrent, both apparent directions being simply options in the always present, static field of time. A new manifestation of this is that the power of these eruptive memories begins to engulf another member of the Club as well as Lowdham, Wilfrid Jeremy, who also begins to take on another identity. Suddenly, and to the complete bewilderment of the Notion Club, both Lowdham and Jeremy undergo a complete regression into past identity. While fully present in body, both men pass mentally and emotionally out of present-day Oxford and into the time-consciousness of Númenor, wherein they begin to address one another as Nimruzīr and Abrazān. As familiar to one another in that time frame as in their ordinary one, they share not only a history but common knowledge of some anticipated, impending catastrophe.

Bizarre as the scene is, however, the groundwork has been laid for it in a previous meeting's debate about the power of myth to transcend both history and fiction, to establish a life of its own. "The daimonic force that the great myths and legends have," is compared to an explosive which "may slowly yield a steady warmth to living minds, but if suddenly detonated . . . might go off with a crash . . . might produce a disturbance in the real primary world." This is precisely what happens on the night of the storm. Discussion of the content of Lowdham's dream-texts detonates the daimonic force of the Atalantë/Númenor myth, and it does indeed go off with a crash, as the cataclysm that drowns Númenor produces a disturbance in the primary world of Oxford. While the Notion Club watches in bewilderment, and the dark clouds come up over Oxford, Lowdham and Jeremy, together in their past world, stand at the window staring into the storm and speaking apprehensively of the Lords of the West, of Eru and the Valar.

A significant detail here is Guildford's irresistible visual impression of "two people hanging over the side of a ship", conveying in one phrase the obvious but important fact that, in another time, they are necessarily in another place. That the place is a ship makes the shift even clearer, for it is one of the ships that ride out the destruction of Númenor. I must emphasise that this is not a simple case of the present's return to the past, or of the past coming into the present, but of both impinging on one another. For a little space the two times overlap, and the storm is a synchronous event in both, yet with its deepest meaning and most profound effect in the past. Suddenly the two men fall to their knees and cover their eyes, crying out to one another of "glory fallen into deep waters", of wind like "the end of the world", of huge waves "like mountains moving". As the gathering storm sweeps over Oxford, inundating Ramer's rooms, soaking and scaring the daylights out of the hapless Notion Club, so also and in another time-frame it sweeps Lowdham and Jeremy into the destruction of Númenor.

This glimpse of the past is quickly replaced by the present, for the next meeting records the Notion Club's anxiety over Lowdham and Jeremy, who have not been seen since they stumbled out of Ramer's rooms at the height of the storm. When they do return they bring fresh news of both dream and time-travel, for Lowdham, out-topping Dunne, reports that "Jeremy and I seem to have got into the same dream together, even before we were asleep." The dream is the Anglo-Saxon episode which Tolkien originally wrote for inclusion in *The Lost Road*. Narrated by Lowdham in the identity of Ælfwine, an Anglo-Saxon of the early tenth century, this first real adventure is framed as the memory of a dream narrated by the dreamer to his audience. Tolkien takes care to keep the dream-quality alive, for when "with a sudden change of tone and voice" Lowdham finishes his story, his hearers "jump like men waked suddenly from a dream." Momentarily caught up in this collective dreaming, the Club agrees to meet again in a week to hear further tales of Ælfwine.

But there were to be no further tales, for there, most frustratingly, the story breaks off, though Tolkien had made notes and sketches for its continuation. Why he never finished it is anybody's guess. In Christopher Tolkien's judgement the whole concept had become too elaborate and complex to be sustainable. In any case, *The Lord of the Rings* was still a work-in-progress at that time, and its completion was more important, both for Tolkien and for the enrichment of his mythology. Nevertheless, the unfinished works are provocative in their implications. Had either *The Lost Road* or "The Notion Club Papers" come to completion, we would have had a dream of time-travel through actual history and recorded myth which would have functioned as both introduction and epilogue to Tolkien's own invented mythology. The result would have been time-travel not on the scale of ordinary science fiction but of epic, a dream of myth and history and fiction interlocking as Tolkien wanted them to, as they might well once have done.

References

Tolkien, J. R. R. 1981. *The Letters of J.R.R. Tolkien*, ed. Humphrey Carpenter. Boston: Houghton Mifflin.

Tolkien, J.R.R. 1983. *The Monsters and the Critics and Other Essays*, ed. Christopher Tolkien. London: Allen & Unwin.

Tolkien, J.R.R. 1987. *The Lost Road*, ed. Christopher Tolkien. Boston: Houghton Mifflin.

Tolkien, J.R.R. 1992. "The Notion Club Papers" in ed. Christopher Tolkien *Sauron Defeated*, pp. 145-327. London: HarperCollins.

Higher Argument: Tolkien and the tradition of Vision, Epic and Prophecy

Deirdre Greene

Abstract: This paper attempts to place Tolkien's fiction in a distinctively English literary context: a tradition of visionary writing which strives toward national epic, existing from Spenser through Milton (and in certain respects, Blake) to Tolkien.

Keywords: Arthur, Blake, creation, divine inspiration, epic, inspiration, Milton, prophecy, Spenser, vision

> Very few visionary poets can be called classical. That is because visions and revelations occur mostly on the outer limits of a given culture, they belong to the deprived and the unrecognized and to those who cultivate secret wisdom . . . Our own culture rests on reason and on science, our morality is practical and our philosophy is distrustful of visions. If we are still hungry for visions we seek them in the realm of poetry. There, on the outer limits of our culture, we allow them to exist.
> (Levi, 1986, p. 27)

Peter Levi's observations on visionary poetry are equally applicable to all visionary writing. Indeed, they easily and usefully transfer to fantastic and mythopoeic literature, which partakes of the visionary impulse. The fiction of J.R.R. Tolkien shares much with the poetry Levi describes: it exists on the edges of the literary canon; it ignores or denies value to the empirical precepts of our culture; it defies the pragmatic morality and philosophy on which our culture rests; it is turned to, though often sheepishly or covertly, by a huge readership – hungry for something, not knowing what they seek. I do not hope to explain what Tolkien's readers search for, or why; however, a significant part of what they find is an alternative to the conventional vision of our culture, and, through that vision, access to threads of English literary tradition which weave far back into our cultural history.

Owing to the relatively recent appearance of prose fiction, the tradition of visionary literature is largely a poetic tradition. Therefore, connections between Tolkien and his predecessors in the "line of vision" are necessarily made across kind; for the purposes of this study, the differences between poetry and prose are less important than the similarities that arise in literary expressions of the visionary impulse.

Literary criticism in this century has been inhospitable to vision, preferring mimesis or empiricism. This representational aesthetic is a recent development in European literary history by comparison with the long tradition of mythic, symbolic, and romantic writing in our culture. It arose with the novel in the eighteenth century. Although the evolution of what would become realism and naturalism ran concurrently with the romantic movement in the eighteenth and nineteenth centuries, in the twentieth century (during the lifetimes of T.S. Eliot and F.R. Leavis) literary taste turned against romanticism in its various forms in favour of empirical literature. Literary practice tended toward recording the truth of sensation and experience, observation of the present, psychological reality, and ordinary human behaviour. In the latter half of the century, however, the "new" critical dogmatism receded before the emergence of a variety of alternative critical approaches and a flexible scholarly attitude to their application; access to slipped threads of the English literary history could be regained.

Of particular interest has been the discernment of a tradition of visionary writing extending from Spenser through Milton (and, in a somewhat different form, Blake) into this century (Wittreich, 1975, p. 98), where it must be seen to include Tolkien. Although Tolkien's best achievements were in prose and the great works of the others were poetic, these writers are united by their narrative mode, their concern with myth and symbol, and their illuminating interior vision. Indeed, Tolkien might be said to have significantly developed the visionary tradition by translating what had been poetic concerns into prose form, and to have developed the tradition of the English novel by injecting it with strains of visionary, romantic and mythic literary practice. While other novelists of this century, not least James Joyce and Virginia Woolf, have written visionary fiction, Tolkien's accomplishment is distinctive and warrants a separate examination.[1]

---

[1] For a study of Tolkien's contribution to the development of the novel through his incorporation of earlier literary practices, see D.M.

The line of visionary poets has its roots, significantly, in Tolkien's scholarly province: in the fourteenth century with Chaucer, Langland, and the *Pearl* poet. Dryden describes this succession in his "Preface to the Fables":

> Milton was the poetical son of Spenser . . . Spenser more than once insinuates, that the soul of Chaucer was transfus'd into his body; and that he was begotten by him Two hundred years after his Decease . . . Milton has acknowledg'd to me, that Spenser was his Original.
> (Dryden, 1963, p. 630)

The line of visionary poets does not end with Milton. Blake in his poem *Milton* claimed that the soul of the dead poet in a beam of light had entered the tarsus of his left foot. Less exotic expressions of admiration for Spenser and Milton were made by other Romantic poets. In this century the tradition of "prophetic" verse is exemplified in the work of W.B. Yeats and David Jones, among others. Although Tolkien made no claims on the souls of his predecessors, he saw himself as inspired, saw his writing as sub-creation under God, and observed that his fiction seemed to come from outside himself. This artistic posture is, of course, neither singular nor new. Whereas for Aristotle the poet was chiefly a "maker" or craftsman, for Plato "all good poets epic as well as lyric compose their beautiful poems not by art, but because they are inspired and possessed" (Plato, 1971, p. 1142). This paper examines the works of Spenser, Milton, and Tolkien (with some reference to Blake) in terms of the operation of a visionary aesthetic and the Platonic understanding of the literary artist as inspired. That is not to say that these are visionary writers in quite the same way or to the same degree. Specifically, they are considered in terms of two elements common to the works of all: the influence of the apocalyptic books of *The Bible*, particularly *Revelation*, and the tension between the epic and the prophetic impulse.

Contrary to the long-standing belief that the most important influence on the epics of Spenser and Milton was the classical poets, more recent scholarship has shown that the influence of the classics was, in fact, secondary to that of the *Bible*, especially the apocalyptic books. Gabriel Harvey, Spenser's teacher and literary intimate, expressed this opinion of *Revelation*: it is "the verie notablest and moste wonderful Propheticall or Poeticall vision" (Wittreich, 1979, p. 8). The nexus of prophecy and poetry was apparent to Milton as well. He writes in "The Reason of Church Government" that the Hebrew prophets surpass the classical poets "in the very critical art of composition" (Milton, 1951, p. 424). In *Paradise Regained* this position is reiterated in the figure of Christ:

> All our Law and Story strew'd
> With Hymns, our Psalms with artful terms inscrib'd,
> Our Hebrew Songs with Harps in *Babylon*,
> That pleased so well our Victor's ear, declare
> That rather *Greece* these Arts from us deriv'd . . .
> (Milton, 1938, p. 393)

While Milton here makes a very doubtful historical claim, this passage expresses Milton's belief in the artistic primacy of the Hebrews and his regard for *The Bible* as an artistic model. Tolkien's reliance on *The Bible* as a chief source of creative inspiration, then, assumes stylistic as well as thematic significance for discussions of his prose fiction.[2]

An observation common to criticism of Spenser, Milton, and Tolkien is that their works are remarkably pictorial. This quality suggests the influence of the apocalyptic books of *The Bible*, in which messages are conveyed not through direct statement but through clusters of complex visual symbols. An example from *Revelation* may demonstrate the pitch this visual complexity can reach:

> . . . I saw seven lampstands of gold and among them: One like the Son of Man wearing an ankle-length robe, with a sash of gold about his breast. The hair of his head was as white as snow-white wool and his eyes blazed like fire. His feet gleamed like polished brass refined in a furnace, and his voice sounded like the roar of rushing waters. In his right hand he held seven stars. A sharp, two-edged sword came out of his mouth, and his face shone like the sun at its brightest.
> (*Revelation* 1:12-16)

In terms of ordinary verisimilitude, this passage is simply bizarre. Scripture scholars, however, mining near-forgotten iconographies, dissect such passages to extract their meanings. One may identify at least some of the symbols through the most common conventions of European Christian culture, as conveyed in the literary tradition: gold indicates both purity and sovereignty; white emphasizes purity again; fire suggests spiritual power; a two-edged sword denotes truth; the shining face speaks of divinity. These are but the most accessible elements of the symbolic picture: other meanings may be guessed and a complex exegesis produced.

Allegorical literature of the medieval period imitated this verbal iconography. Peter Levi in his essay on "Visionary Poets" emphasizes the interdependence of allegory and vision in the work of Dante, the "great example of a visionary poet central to European and Christian culture". Levi writes of the surrealistic quality of visionary writing, traceable through the period from John of the Cross to Spenser (Levi, 1986, pp. 31-32). Spenser's *Faerie Queene* in particular is characterised by complex visual descriptions laden with symbolic meaning:

> A louely Ladie rode him faire beside,
> Vpon a lowly Asse more white then snow,
> Yet she much whiter, but the same did hide
> Vnder a vele, that wimpled was full low,
> And ouer all a black stole she did throw,
> As one that inly mournd: so was she sad,
> And heauie sat vpon her palfrey slow:
> Seemed in heart some hidden care she had,
>   And by her in a line a milke white lamb she lad.
> (Spenser, 1980, p. 30)

This depiction of Una is visual and external. Perception of

Greene, 1989, chapters 3 and 5.
[2] Tolkien's reliance on *The Bible* as a poetic model is addressed in Shippey, 1982, p. 151.

her sadness, for example, is based strictly on her deportment. Nevertheless, careful reading of the iconographic symbols in this portrait allows the reader to make certain moral judgements. She rides a white ass, the colour of which indicates sexual purity as its image evokes the humility of Christ's entrance into Jerusalem. Una, the personification of truth, is more white than the ass; truth is thereby shown to be supported by humility, but also to be subtly more fine a virtue. Una's garments clearly indicate modest sobriety. The lamb she leads is another symbol of purity, as well as of Christ's sacrifice. This lamb is commonly associated with St. George in religious art.[3] The whole picture, of course, is impossible in terms of nature, but like the images from *Revelation*, some of which it borrows, it is dense with meaning.

Milton is less startling in his deviations from nature, but he too operates outside the bounds of empirical representation:

> But see the Virgin blest,
> Hath laid her Babe to rest.
> Time is our tedious song should here have ending;
> Heavn's youngest teemed Star,
> Hath fixt her polish't Car,
> Her sleeping Lord with Handmaid Lamp attending:
> And all about the Courtly Stable,
> Bright-harnest Angels sit in order serviceable.
> (Milton, 1951, p. 315)

The Gospel descriptions of Christ's nativity, the visitation of the angels, and the appearance of the star are combined with images of a court, and more significantly, with the image of a heavenly chariot. This chariot is an evocation of Elijah's miraculous passage from Earth to Heaven. It has some relation also to the classical mythologies which portray the heavenly bodies as chariots of light or fire. This dense fusion of imagistic reference sets Milton, like Spenser, outside the narrowly mimetic practice we have come to know as realism.

Tolkien's images are closer again to primary reality; they are dreamlike, though not simply dreams. In his writings on the mythological First and Second Ages of Arda, the pictures are appropriately fantastic, though they have a blurred or shadowed quality, as if seen through a glass, darkly. Tuor's encounter with Ulmo, the Water god, exemplifies this:

> . . . as he went he saw that the sun was sinking low into a great black cloud that came up over the rim of the darkening sea; and it grew cold, and there was a stirring and murmur as of a storm to come. And Tuor stood upon the shore, and the sun was like a smoky fire behind the menace of the sky; and it seemed to him that a great wave rose far off and rolled towards the land, but wonder held him, and he remained there unmoved. And the wave came towards him, and upon it lay a mist of shadow. Then suddenly as it drew near it curled, and broke, and rushed forward in long arms of foam; but where it had broken there stood dark against the rising storm a living shape of great height and majesty.
> Then Tuor bowed in reverence, for it seemed to him that he beheld a mighty king. A tall crown he wore like silver, from which his long hair fell down as foam glimmering in the dusk; and as he cast back the grey mantle that hung about him like a mist, behold! he was clad in a gleaming coat, close-fitted as the mail of a mighty fish, and in a kirtle of deep green that flashed and flickered with sea-fire as he strode slowly towards the land . . . and then for the light of his eyes and for the sound of his deep voice that came as it seemed from the foundations of the world, fear fell upon Tuor and he cast himself down upon the sand.
> (Tolkien, 1980, p. 28)

This passage exhibits the iconographic features seen in Spenser and Milton: the dark cloud to signal danger, the moving sun to indicate the work of a divinity, the great wave to represent awesome power, a silver crown for sovereignty, shadowy mist for mystery, fire and light for spiritual power, and a mighty voice for prophecy. The dreamlike quality is achieved through the presence of shadows and mists, as well as peculiar grammatical constructions that suggest Tuor is unsure of what he is seeing: "it seemed to him", "A tall crown he wore like silver", and "his long hair fell down as foam". Also, Tuor experiences a common dream terror: transfixed in the face of an overwhelming danger, he cannot turn to run.

In Tolkien's writings about the legendary Third Age, his images retain this complexity of visual structure but become more romantic, less mythopoeic. They are possible in terms of nature, but strange and burdened with symbolic meaning. Frodo's first sight of Goldberry in the house of Tom Bombadil tells the reader a great deal about the woman and, by association, her mate:

> They were in a long low room, filled with the light of lamps swinging from the beams of the roof; and on the table of dark polished wood stood many candles, tall and yellow, burning brightly.
> In a chair, at the far side of the room facing the outer door, sat a woman. Her long yellow hair rippled down her shoulders; her gown was green, green as young reeds, shot with silver like beads of dew; and her belt was of gold, shaped like a chain of flag-lilies set with the pale-blue eyes of forget-me-nots. About her feet in wide vessels of green and brown earthenware, white water-lilies were floating, so that she seemed to be enthroned in the midst of a pool.
> (Tolkien, 1983a, p. 138)

The dwelling has low roofs, indicating simple humility; it is filled with light, suggesting spiritual good; the furnishings and the candles are of natural materials, connoting rural closeness to nature. Goldberry's chair, far opposite the door, suggests a throne in a reception hall. Her yellow hair suggests innocence and goodness; it is yellow rather than gold, emphasizing her unassuming nature. Her gown associates her with lush, young vegetation. Her belt is the gold of purity and sovereignty, but it celebrates in its floral design the eternal, cyclical triumph of nature. She is encircled by water and flowers, symbols of purity and

---

[3] Hamilton's notes on the iconographic content of *The Faerie Queene* (Spenser, 1980) are copious and enlightening.

fertility. As a whole, the image asserts Goldberry as a queen or a local deity, whose power derives from nature; she is associated with water, morning, and spring, and so belongs to the germinating, birthing, and burgeoning segment of the nature cycle. The reader is left with the impression that her power is so fundamental that there is no need for any display of sovereignty; Goldberry's power is that of earth, water, and warmth. Tolkien has combined the complex symbolism of the elaborate pictorial images of Spenser and Milton with observation of real things found in this world to produce a plausible image of great illustrative significance; again he has taken the effects of older literature and shaped them to more modern literary taste.

This sort of warmth and humanity has been intimately associated with the visionary tradition, a point Levi makes with respect to Dante:

> Visionary poetry always has its roots in personal earthly experience . . . The visions that make the best poetry are very often tranquil and serene, like the contemplation of the stars, from which in part they may arise. But in whatever visionary state Dante may have conceived or even composed his final cantos, poetry is a mortal terrestrial thing, and all our languages are earthly and mortal.
> (Levi, 1986, p. 33)

The same, of course, may be said of prose. However inspired Tolkien was in his sub-creation, and whatever the lofty themes he expressed, the form he gave them was human and comprehensible — though full of the resonance of more romantic and mythic literary ages.

This pictorial style is closely connected with the search for spiritual enlightenment. It is an attempt to externalize interior vision. The difficulty of this enterprise is clear from the prayer that ends the *Faerie Queene*:

> For, all that moueth, doth in *Change* delight:
> But thence-forth all shall rest eternally
> With Him that is the God of Sabbaoth hight:
>   O that great Sabbaoth God, graunt me that Sabbaoth's sight.
> (Spenser, 1980, p. 735)

Likewise, Milton's Samson at the end of his life finds a purpose in suffering and an opportunity provided by God for him to defeat the enemies of Israel. This Biblical story obviously parallels Milton's sense of his own life: sightless and anathematized, he too found opportunity at the close of his life to fulfil the promise of his youth.

Tolkien attempted in two long short stories to articulate his disappointment and his hope of expressing his interior vision. In *Smith of Wootton Major* he suggests that he has been blessed by God with rare insight into the Perilous Realm, a symbol for Tolkien of the spiritual world of archetypes and ideals, but that his penetrating vision has been taken away. This was written at a low ebb in Tolkien's creative life, when he felt that what he had written was flawed or imperfectly conceived and that his creative energies were sapped so he would write no more. He called it "an old man's book, already weighted with the presage of bereavement" (Tolkien, 1981, p. 389). According to Humphrey Carpenter (1978, pp. 133-134), Tolkien was often subject to despair about his writing. A more hopeful and more representative statement of his feelings on the subject is "Leaf by Niggle". Allegorical readings of this story are numerous, equating Niggle with Tolkien, his wonderful imagined tree with the unfinished mythopoeic *Silmarillion*, and his one canvas of a single detailed leaf with *The Lord of the Rings*. Although he characterizes himself as a procrastinating, "niggling", unfulfilled artist, he suggests through Niggle's one perfect leaf that he has fully and clearly expressed at least a small part of his interior vision. "Leaf by Niggle" also intimates Tolkien's resignation to his mortality, expressed as inability to realize in his lifetime his vast sub-created history; as an author Tolkien ultimately rested in the belief that his work partook of the divine Creation.

The question remains, however, to what extent Tolkien, like Milton and Spenser, felt his work to be literally inspired. E.K., writing the argument to the "October" eclogue of *The Shepherdes Calender*, is supposedly faithful to Spenser's own ideas when he asserts that poetry is

> . . . no arte, but a diuine gift and heauenly instinct not to bee gotten by laboure and learning, but adorned with both: and poured into the witte by a certaine (enthusiasm) and celestial inspiration . . .
> (Spenser, 1912, p. 456)

The poet is not simply a "maker", but a channel for divine communication. As for Milton, the supreme confidence with which he acts as an amanuensis to God is simply startling:

> If answerable style I can obtaine
> Of my Celestial Patroness, who deignes
> Her nightly visitation unimplor'd,
> And dictates to me slumbring, or inspires
> Easie my unpremeditated verse:
> Since first this Subject for Heroic Song
> Pleas'd me, long choosing, and beginning late . . .
> (Milton, 1951, p. 198)

Milton's lifelong preparation for the writing of some great work is clear, for example, in the opening to "Lycidas". His steadfast commitment to the Christian muse, the Holy Spirit who is said to be the female aspect of the Trinity, indicates an attitude that the true poet, like the true prophet, has an actual vocation from God.

Tolkien's ontological and literary theory of *sub-creation* articulates most completely Tolkien's belief that man's creative impulse derives from his having been made in the image and likeness of the Creator. Further, he stated that true sub-creation, as opposed to realistic representation, involves the making of things that do not occur in God's creation:

> . . . we may cause woods to spring with silver leaves and rams to wear fleeces of gold, and put hot fire into the belly of the cold worm. But in such "fantasy", as it is called, new form is made; Faërie begins; Man becomes a sub-creator.
> (Tolkien, 1983b, p. 122)

Clearly Tolkien held his fiction to be of a higher kind than the realistic fiction that dominated his generation; to some degree he was rebuking writers for their obsession with realism. He felt that he was contributing to the effoliation of

Creation by making things that were possible to God but not actually made by him (Tolkien, 1981, pp. 188-189). By logical association, if inclination and ability to create are given by an omniscient and omnipotent God, then whatever proceeds from that faculty proceeds from God. In this context, Tolkien's attitude to his writings as independent of himself supports the assumption that he saw them as in some way inspired by God. Certainly his view of divine participation in his creative acts is not as exaggerated as that of authors from more innocent, less rationalizing religious ages, yet the sense of inspiration – and of sacrality – remains.

Out of this sense of a writer as spokesman for God – as prophet – Spenser, Milton, and Tolkien all display an angry distrust of the making of heterodox images. In *The Faerie Queene*, Archimago summons spirits out of Hell to delude the Red Cross Knight as he sleeps, giving him dreams of Una's impurity. In *Paradise Regained* Christ rejects the pagan oracles as diabolical:

> No more shalt thou by oracling abuse
> The Gentiles; henceforth Oracles are ceast . . .
> God hath now sent his living Oracle
> Into the World, to teach his final will,
> And sends his Spirit of Truth henceforth to dwell
> In pious Hearts, an inward Oracle
> To all truth requisite for men to know.
> (Milton, 1951, p. 361)

Another important visionary poet, William Blake, distrusts settled religious images altogether, emphasizing the personal nature of such images and the danger of attempting to universalize them:

> The Vision of Christ that thou dost see
> Is my Vision's Greatest Enemy:
> Thine has a great hook nose like thine,
> Mine has a snub nose like to mine:
> Thine is the friend of All Mankind,
> Mine speaks in parables to the Blind:
> Thine loves the same world that mine hates,
> Thy Heaven doors are my Hell Gates.
> (Blake, 1979, p. 748)

Tolkien gives his evil characters the power to create false images in the minds of men, or to cause men to perceive true images in a false structure. Sauron bends the mind of Denethor so that he interprets the visions in the Palantír as signs of the undeniable victory of Mordor (Tolkien, 1983a, pp. 887, 889). Saruman, through the enchantment of his voice, conjures false images of his own character, the roles of his listeners, and his relation with Gandalf:

> So great was the power that Saruman exerted in this last effort that none that stood within hearing were unmoved. But now the spell was wholly different. They heard the gentle remonstrance of a kindly king with an erring but much-loved minister. But they were shut out, listening at a door to words not meant for them: ill-mannered children or stupid servants overhearing the elusive discourse of their elders, and wondering how it would affect their lot. Of loftier mould these two were made: reverend and wise. It was inevitable that they should make alliance. Gandalf would ascend into the tower, to discuss deep things beyond their comprehension in the high chambers of Orthanc. The door would be closed, and they would be left outside, dismissed to await allotted work or punishment. Even in the mind of Théoden the thought took shape, like a shadow of doubt: "He will betray us; he will go – we shall be lost."
>
> Then Gandalf laughed. The fantasy vanished like a puff of smoke.
> (Tolkien, 1983a, p. 605)

The quality of Saruman's voice gradually turns into a visual scenario showing Gandalf's betrayal, until the sound of Gandalf's laughter disperses Saruman's unwholesome images. Villains and tempters in the work of Spenser, Milton, Blake, and Tolkien are generally protean figures, who by hypocrisy delude the innocent or ignorant and lead them into sin.

The struggle for vision, clarity, and certitude which characterizes the post-lapsarian worlds of these writers is counterpointed in the psychological landscapes they create. In Spenser, the landscape as well as the characters can have allegorical significance. In Milton and Tolkien, the inner life of the characters is realized in the surrounding landscape. Confusion is rendered as a labyrinth or a forest. Wisdom and virtue have specific loci which have been described as "temples"; these are usually gardens or houses, where the sojourner discovers absolute values (Williams, 1975, p. 31). In this regard one observes the contrast in Book III of *The Faerie Queene* between the Garden of Adonis, an illustration of fruitful sexuality, and the dense forest through which the knights pursue a false ideal of beauty. In *Comus*, Milton's most Spenserian work, the virgin's temptation is illustrated in her wanderings through a dark forest where she is abducted by Comus and held till rescued by her brothers who bring her safe to her father's house. In *The Hobbit*, Bilbo's moral confusion is acted out in his blind groping through the Goblin caves of the Misty Mountains; the confusion of the dwarves when deprived of Gandalf's leadership is displayed through their hopeless disorientation in Mirkwood. In *The Lord of the Rings*, the hobbits' misadventures in Midgewater and the Old Forest illustrate their struggle toward their destinies as quest heroes; the benighted passage of Frodo and Sam through Cirith Ungol demonstrates their faith and resourcefulness despite ignorance, confusion, and lack of hope. In contrast to these "labyrinths", Bilbo finds refuge in the House of Beorn and in Rivendell, while Frodo and his companions rest in the "temples" of the house of Tom Bombadil, Rivendell, Lothlórien, and Ithilien. It must be observed that there are false "temples", *loci* of infernal values, such as the Bower of Bliss, Pandemonium, Orthanc, and Orodruin; these must be rejected, escaped, purged, or destroyed. The temple-labyrinth archetype is, of course, common throughout English literature, and we need look no further for examples than to the comedies of Shakespeare or to *Pilgrim's Progress*.

The essence of prophetic writing, however, lies not simply in its representation of man's quest for abiding values; rather it rests in a spiritual perspective on history (Fletcher, 1971, p. 5). In its debased sense, *"prophet"* is applied to a prognosticator of events. In a more narrowly defined sense (appropriate to these writers who were deeply concerned with words *per se* and with theology) a prophet is one who discerns in history the movements of God, leading to a final revelation. So, with the long genealogies found in Books II and III of *The Faerie Queene*, facts are submerged in myths and symbols which attempt to soften the hard line between the temporal and the eternal. Human history is traced symbolically to its supernatural source:

> It told, how first *Prometheus* did create
> A man, of many partes from heartes deriued,
> And then stole fire from heauen to animate
> His worke, for which he was by Ioue depriued
>   Of life him selfe, and hart-strings of an Ægle riued.
>   (Spenser, 1980, p. 270)

Spenser's weaving of a mythical lineage for Elizabeth is an attempt to transform English history into a sort of spiritual fable. In *Paradise Lost*, Milton recreates the history of Satan's rebellion in a long narrative by the archangel Raphael; at the end of the poem another archangel, Michael, grants Adam a vision of the future of man after the expulsion from the Garden. In *The Lord of the Rings*, references are made that tie the events of this legendary (though clearly temporal) history to the primordial, mythological powers of that world. Elrond says, as he tells the Tale of the Ring, "Eärendil was my sire" (Tolkien, 1983a, p. 260), the same Eärendil that we know from Bilbo's song to be the evening star. This draws mythological time (or eternity) into the temporal world of the War of the Ring.[4] The reunion of the two branches of the descendants of Eärendil through the wedding of Aragorn and Arwen stands at the beginning of the Fourth Age, our Age, the Age of Men, drawing eternity into primary temporal history. It has been asserted that in Spenser and Milton temporal reality is always viewed in the context of eternity (Wittreich, 1975, pp. 105-106); can this observation extend also to Tolkien? This would, in part, explain his contention that *The Lord of the Rings* is a profoundly Christian work, though it contains no specific religious references (Tolkien, 1981, pp. 172-173).[5] The grand struggles of heroic figures within history, legendary or real, are significant chiefly in terms of what exists outside time. For Spenser, Milton, and Tolkien, epic is subordinate to prophecy as the temporal is subordinate to the eternal.

Thus, there is in the marriage of epic and prophecy a certain incompatibility. Whereas an epic is the utterance of a given culture in celebration of itself, prophecy, grounded in a providential view of history, reproaches the present age and calls it to repentance (Wittreich, 1975, pp. 105-106). Spenser, Milton, and Tolkien attempted to write great national works, English epics. Yet all three were consciously, if not explicitly, Christian in their writings. Christian values and the *virtu* of heroic narrative are often contradictory; therefore, all three display some discomfort with epic conventions. For these writers, military victory, the very stuff of national epic, is itself worth little. Observe the particularly unsanguinary Spenserian hero Sir Guyon, who triumphs over his enemy Acrasia by capturing and leading her away. It is difficult to transfer such an attitude to the classical epics and still more to the Northern Sagas; Achilles would not merely bind the hands of Hector, and Kullervo could not restrain his hand from wholesale slaughter. Milton, like Spenser, abjures the standard epic practice in refusing to sing only "of arms and the man":

> Wars, hitherto the only argument
> Heroic deemed, chief mastery to dissect
> With long and tedious havoc fabled knights
> In battles feigned (the better fortitude
> Of patience, and heroic martyrdom
> Unsung) . . .
>   (Milton, 1951, p. 198)

Whereas Spenser used physical combat as an allegory for the ongoing struggle of the Christian to overcome sin, Milton expanded this symbol to treat the cosmic struggle between good and evil. Combat in *Paradise Lost* is absolutely spiritual — in that it is conducted by spirits. Even in *Samson Agonistes* physical conflict is only valuable in so far as it shows the workings of providence.

Tolkien effects a curious blend of conventional heroism and Christian values. Although he celebrates the martial skill of his heroes and evokes the "bloody battle-mood" of the Rohirrim with frank admiration, skill at arms is only praised when it is used to defeat evil, non-human characters. Also, such heroic episodes are brief in contrast with his solemn, minutely observed telling of the covert quest of Mount Doom, of the painful endurance of Frodo and the loving, patient loyalty of Sam, who are the central heroes of that expansive work. Theirs is a song of "patience, and heroic martyrdom". When Frodo engages in physical combat, it is with his dark self, Gollum; their frenzied wrestling at the Cracks of Doom is at once "real" and an external rendering of Frodo's spiritual conflict over his desire for the Ring. Tolkien's comment on heroism in "Ofermod" recalls the opening passage of *Paradise Lost*, cited above: "It is the heroism of obedience and love not of pride or wilfulness that is the most heroic and the most moving . . ." (Tolkien, 1966, p. 22). Although Tolkien discouraged readings of his work as historical allegory, one must remember that in the First World War Tolkien served in the trenches and that in the Second World War, while he was writing a large part of *The Lord of the Rings*, two of his sons and scores of his former students bore arms. Once again, there is an ideal common to Spenser, Milton, and Tolkien: the refusal to glorify military exploits can be seen as a refusal to glorify, for its own sake, the history of man. In other words, the prophet triumphs over the national author.

Tension between prophecy and epic is seen in the works of all three authors. *The Faerie Queene* is certainly an attempt to write an epic on the matter of England: Gloriana, the

---

[4] For a study of Eärendil and how he connects the world of *The Lord of the Rings* with the mythological phase of Arda's history, see David Harvey, 1985, pp. 94-99.
[5] For a broad discussion of Christianity in Tolkien's fiction, see D.M. Greene, 1989, chapter 2.

symbolic centre of the poem, is a representation of Spenser's monarch. The dedicatory sonnets of the work betray a hope that the poet's influential readers will be moved to grant him some advancement. The exploits of Arthur and his fellow English heroes and heroines seem not only the rewriting of traditional tales, but also an expression of the peculiar patriotic ebullience of the reign of Elizabeth. In all this, Spenser the secular and national poet seems a least a match for Spenser the prophet.

Yet the problem is not solved by finding a balance or a simple contrast of values in *The Faerie Queene*. Spenser's erstwhile epic moves further and further from the celebration of temporal reality in the history of England. His disappointment with Burleigh, or the depredations of the "Blatant Beast", or some brooding sense of his own mortality, edges Spenser toward more otherworldly concerns as the poem progresses:

> I well consider all that ye have sayd,
> And find that all things stedfastnes doe hate
> And changed be: Yet being rightly wayd
> They are not changed from their first estate;
> But by their change their being do dilate:
> And turning to themselues at length againe,
> Doe work their owne perfection so by fate:
> Then ouer them Change doth not rule and raigne;
>> But they raigne ouer change, and doe their states maintaine.
>
> (Spenser, 1980, p. 734)

The Mutability Cantos represent, to some degree, a shift in the focus of the poem from ethical considerations bearing on Christian life in this world to a meditation on the transience of this world in light of the permanence of the next. While it is commonly judged that *The Faerie Queene* is structurally incomplete, thematically it is complete – or rather it can go no further. Spenser comes to a point at which he loses enthusiasm for the temporal order. His original epic intention is no longer viable, and it is subsumed into the religious vision.

Milton, early in his career, decided against writing his own Arthuriad. In doing so he pressed further along the path on which Spenser had begun. Except in certain of his sonnets, Milton was not the nationalistic poet Spenser had been. While the earlier poet could assume to write a national epic, the Puritan Revolution and the subsequent Restoration had deeply divided England; a single vast work could not even hope to give voice to a fragmented national spirit (Kerrigan, 1974, p. 263). *Paradise Lost* could no more pretend to achieve this end than could explicitly Royalist poems such as "Absalom and Achitophel". Milton appears to have sensed the end of that era in which national epic was possible for an English author. Having eschewed temporal power as a theme for his composition, he expresses doubt about his undertaking:

> Me, of these
> Nor skilled nor studious, higher argument
> Remains, sufficient of itself to raise
> That name, unless an age too late, or cold
> Climate, or years, damp my intended wing
> Depressed . . .
>
> (Milton, 1951, p. 198)

It was, in fact, "an age too late" for national poetry. However, in Milton's work this handicap is liberating. In a way that Spenser is not, Milton is free to rebuke his age for losing sight of divine purpose: it must have seemed to many that England had missed an opportunity to build the New Jerusalem. Milton, a political outsider, can adopt the true prophetic role of a voice crying in the wilderness (Kerrigan, 1974, p. 263). In another sense, the poet stands in the place of the archangel Michael, unfolding a vision of the future to the fallen nation:

> So shall the world go on,
> To good malignant, to evil men benign,
> Under her own weight groaning till the day
> Appear of respiration to the just
> And vengeance to the wicked, at return
> Of him so lately promised to thy aid,
> The woman's seed – obscurely then foretold,
> Now amplier known thy saviour and thy Lord;
> Last in the clouds from Heaven to be revealed
> In glory of the Father, to dissolve
> Satan with his perverted world, then raise
> From the conflagrant mass, purged and refined,
> New heavens, new Earth, ages of endless date
> Founded in righteousness and peace and love,
> To bring forth fruits, joy and eternal bliss.
>
> (Milton, 1951, p. 301)

Milton's terrible warning, founded in the social and religious climate of his time and place, becomes a vision of apocalypse and a new Eden.

Although very early in his career Tolkien contemplated and even began work on an Arthuriad (Carpenter, 1978, p. 171) his nationalistic sense that the Arthur cycle was Welsh in origin and appeared in English literature only through French influence spoiled his pleasure in the thing, and he abandoned it. What he most desired was truly English matter to work with – which, if it had ever existed, was long since lost or totally obscured by the cultural upheaval of successive invasions. Therefore he thought to recreate the "true" matter of England, using his philological expertise to do so.

Tolkien constructed a cosmogony and a long mythological history based on residual indications in medieval literature of the ancient beliefs of the people of Britain and on aspects of various European myths and legends which he believed were compatible with English character.[6] This mythology reflects Christian values and beliefs, so it is to a degree anomalous. The anomaly is compatible, however, with his belief that all myths apprehend some eternal truth (Carpenter, 1978, p. 99), and he held that eternal truth was most completely apprehended by Christianity. In a curious way, his scrupulous avoidance of explicitly Christian reference in his mythology follows Milton's movement in epic away from temporal concerns to eternal questions. In an age of

---

[6] T.A. Shippey's *The Road to Middle-earth* (1982) is the most enlightening study of Tolkien's reconstruction of his "asterisk mythology".

fragmented world and religious views, Tolkien could not appeal to a fundamental national consensus or body of beliefs; to be heard, his work had to be syncretistic, imaginative, and unifying. Therefore, over decades he constructed his own mythology, seeking internal cohesion and fidelity to what he perceived as eternal truth.

The central work of his *legendarium* focuses on the transitional period between the mythological phase of the history and the earliest beginnings of our recorded history. *The Lord of the Rings* may be read as a prose epic celebrating English history and culture while quietly demonstrating the superior, implicitly Christian, "heroism of obedience and love". Tolkien's own version of the Mutability Cantos is expressed in the "cheerfully sad" speeches of Elrond and Galadriel, who delineate the perennial threat of evil in the fallen world: "I have seen three ages in the West of the world, and many defeats, and many fruitless victories" (Tolkien, 1983a, p. 260); ". . . through ages of the world we have fought the long defeat." (Tolkien, 1983a, p. 376). Though he did not attempt to allegorize the national and international events of his lifetime, Tolkien's implicit argument in *The Lord of the Rings* (indeed in much of his other fiction also) is that power, technological and political, is entangled in the fallen state of the world and is therefore both dangerous and transitory, and that the Christian virtues of faith, hope, and love are necessary to man's survival in this world and into the next. The elegiac aspect of the work, mourning the loss of the green countryside, or myth and mystery, or innocence, is equally an admonishing cry to preserve and renew these things. The interlaced structure and its concomitant theme of the governance of providence appeals to the reader to observe the working of God in history. Though Tolkien did not proselytise in his fiction, he seems truly to be a voice crying in the wilderness

References

Blake, William. 1979. *Blake: Complete Writings*, ed. Geoffrey Keynes. Oxford: Oxford University Press.

Carpenter, Humphrey. 1978. *J.R.R. Tolkien: A biography*. London: Unwin Paperbacks.

Cullen, Patrick. 1974. *Infernal Triad: The Flesh, the World, and the Devil in Spenser and Milton*. Princeton, NJ: Princeton University Press.

Dryden, John. 1963. "Preface to the Fables" in *Seventeenth Century Prose and Poetry*, eds. A.M. Witherspoon and F.J. Warnke. New York: Harcourt Brace & World.

Fletcher, Angus. 1971. *The Prophetic Moment: An Essay on Spenser*. Chicago: The University of Chicago Press.

Greene, D.M. 1989. "A Study of J.R.R. Tolkien's Fiction." M.Litt. thesis, Oxford University.

Harvey, David. 1985. *The Song of Middle-earth: J.R.R. Tolkien's Themes, Symbols, and Myths*. London: George Allen and Unwin.

Kerrigan, William. 1974. *The Prophetic Milton*. Charlottesville: University Press of Virginia.

Levi, Peter. 1986. "Visionary Poets" in *Agenda* XXIV, 3 (Autumn 1986).

Miller, David M. 1978. *John Milton: Poetry*. Boston: Twayne.

Milton, John. 1938. "Paradise Regained" in *Milton. Complete Poetry and selected Prose*, ed. E.H. Visiak. London: Nonesuch Press.

Milton, John. 1951. *Paradise Lost and Selected Poetry and Prose*, ed. Northrop Frye. Toronto: Holt, Rinehart, and Winston.

Plato. 1971. "Ion" in *Critical Theory Since Plato*, ed. Hazard Adams. New York: Harcourt, Brace, Jovanovich.

Shippey, T.A. 1982. *The Road to Middle-earth*. London: George Allen and Unwin.

Spenser, Edmund. 1912. *Poetical Works*, eds. J.C. Smith and E. De Selincourt. London: Oxford University Press.

Spenser, Edmund. 1980. *The Faerie Queene*, ed. A.C. Hamilton. New York: Longman.

Tolkien, J.R.R. 1966. "Ofermod" in *The Tolkien Reader*. New York: Ballantine Books.

Tolkien, J.R.R. 1978. *The Hobbit*. London: George Allen and Unwin.

Tolkien, J.R.R. 1981. *The Letters of J.R.R. Tolkien*, ed. Humphrey Carpenter. Boston: Houghton Mifflin.

Tolkien, J.R.R. 1980. *Unfinished Tales*, ed. Christopher Tolkien. London: George Allen and Unwin.

Tolkien, J.R.R. 1983a. *The Lord of the Rings*. London: Unwin Paperbacks.

Tolkien, J.R.R. 1983b. "On Fairy-Stories" in *The Monsters and the Critics and Other Essays*, ed. Christopher Tolkien. London: George Allen and Unwin, pp. 109-161.

Williams, Kathleen. 1975. "Milton, Greatest Spenserian" in *Milton and the Line of Vision*, ed. J.A. Wittreich. Madison: University of Wisconsin Press.

Wittreich, Joseph Anthony. 1975. "'A Poet Amongst Poets': Milton and the Tradition of Prophecy", *Milton and the Line of Vision*, ed. J.A. Wittreich. Madison: University of Wisconsin Press.

Wittreich, Joseph Anthony. 1979. *Visionary Poetics: Milton's Tradition and his Legacy*. San Marino, California: Huntington Library.

An Anthropologist in Middle-earth

Virginia Luling

Abstract: The author is an anthropologist who works as a campaigner for indigenous people's rights. From this perspective she has some thoughts about Tolkien's work as a vision of an unwesternized Europe, and on the re-enchantment of the world.

Keywords: anthropology, disenchantment, Drúedain, Drûg, Easterlings, re-enchantment, Southrons, wild men, Woodwose

> We are all human beings, but the fact of our being human does not manifest itself in abstraction but in the particularity of real living human beings in different climes and races. We can talk of the human capacity for language, but the capacity manifests itself in real concrete languages as spoken by different peoples of the earth.
>
> (Ngugi Wa Thiongo, 1993, p. 26)

I

An African tribesman, many years ago, discussing with a British anthropologist the idea that particular clans among his people were specially related to certain plants, animals or objects, jokingly suggested that his guest's symbols should be "paper" and "lorry", since it was these things that had always chiefly helped his people. ("Paper" to this man would have meant not literature but official forms – probably tax forms – or accounts.) He was summarising the view of most people in the modern world of what it means to be "European" – in the sense that includes American, and Western culture generally. Bureaucracy and the machine. "Europeanisation", "westernisation" and "modernisation" are synonymous. "Sarumanisation" would be a fair enough term.

This is often linked with the "rationalisation" which sees the world more and more in terms of impersonal cause and effect rather than personal forces – what the wise and melancholy sociologist Max Weber, quoting Schiller, liked to call the "disenchantment of the world" (*das Entzauberung der Welt*).[1] The gods and fairies disappear, and with them a way of experience. "They are sailing, sailing westward over the sea and leaving us . . ." In Tolkien's work it is the elves who have departed, leaving only scattered and incoherent traditions behind them as clues in the disenchanted present day, the time of "the dominion of Men". What Tolkien audaciously embarked upon was the "re-enchantment of the world". (I nearly wrote "embarked single-handed", and indeed he clearly often felt desperately alone in his work. But of course his was not the only attempt, and this indeed is one of the recurrent themes in European literature over the last two hundred years.)

The re-enchantment, not just of any part of the world, but his own part, "the north-west corner of the old world", and that simply because it *was* his own: ". . . if you want to write a tale of this sort you must consult your roots, and a man of the North-west of the Old World will set his heart and the action of his tale in an imaginary world of that air, and that situation" (Tolkien, 1981, p. 212). In his earliest conceptions, it was the island of Britain itself that had once been the elves' country, and it was from there that they took ship. His work is, as Tom Shippey rightly, says, "ethnic". He wanted to celebrate his native country, not as the birthplace of science, commerce and the industrial revolution, but as the final home of enchantment. He stands, so to speak, for a Europe that has not been "Europeanised".

His England, the country that he loved and for whose origins his imagination groped among the clues of legend and language, was not the England that became a commercial Empire, not a conquering but a conquered nation – conquered by "1066 and all that". ("All that" being the "Whig view of history" that is cheerfully mocked in the Sellars and Yeatman book.) So with that other island nation, Númenor: the time when its people became conquerors of "lesser men", the age of their greatest outward power and wealth, was also the time of their inward corruption when they began to worship Sauron.[2]

But such is the identification of Europe with modernity, that people today who look for a not-yet-disenchanted world generally find it, or think they find it, among the peoples of the "third world", or even more in that "fourth world" of indigenous minorities who have been called the "victims of progress" (Bradley, 1975). As an anthropologist by training, I have studied peoples of that kind, and my job at present is

---

[1] Weber, placed by fate in the opposite camp to Tolkien in more than one sense, believed that this emptiness and impersonality was a destiny that had to be faced, and that only cowardice would make one deny it.

[2] The relation between this and Tolkien's English Catholicism – the embattled faith of a minority with memories of persecution – is naturally obscure both to the mainstream English, who still tend to see the Roman Church as foreign and somewhat creepy, and to people from other countries where it is synonymous with power and establishment.

with an organisation that campaigns on their behalf when, as frequently happens, they are dispossessed or persecuted. My hope is that by bringing these two preoccupations of mine together, I can provide a slightly unusual angle on Tolkien's work.

I suggest that Tolkien's imagination brings him close to such peoples, even though they are geographically distant and different in "temper" from those whom he created. An alternative way of approaching this theme would be to recall another centenary that was commemorated in 1992, that of Columbus' discovery of America, and the clash between those who glorify that event and what it symbolises, and those who mourn it. I claim that Tolkien's work puts him among the mourners, though some of the latter might not readily recognise him as an ally. This is not the place even to touch on the tortuous issues of actual power in the primary world – I am concerned only with the imperialism of the imagination.

For instance, it is a common experience in such traditional societies, that old people fear to tell their legends to the Western investigator or the young man who has been to school, for fear of being snubbed or laughed at. When I was doing research in a small town in Somalia, there were those who did not want me to write down legends like the one about how their town was covered in mist which hid the sun, until a miraculous boy was made their ruler, and became the ancestor of a dynasty which still continues, or the one about another ancestor who became the unwilling guest of a water-spirit at the bottom of the river, and then was set free with magical gifts – for fear I would publish them and so make their community look ridiculous.

Then again, the thing that often seems to separate such peoples from "western" society is their intense closeness to and love of the earth, of their land. Take, for instance these words of *Datu* (leader) Mampadayag of the Banwaon tribe in the Philippines:

> For us, the earth is the Creator's gift. We see it as connected to our own lives, physically part of our bodies. we live on the earth and return home to it at death . . . the earth is our parent, it is our father and mother who helps us grow and wakes us from our sleep. The earth is dear to our bodies. When our bodies are pinched it hurts; when the land is ravaged, it hurts in the same way. The earth is filled with life: bees, pigs, birds, monkeys, trees, fish and wild chickens. This is the milk of the Creator that we take from her breasts. This gives abundance to our lives.
> (Survival International, 1991, p. 2)

Not so far from this is the closeness to the earth and love of it that is a theme of Tolkien's work, embodied especially in the Elves, whose lives are part of the life of the Earth, and who cannot leave it. The tension between the earth-bound Elves, and Men, whose destiny lies "beyond the circles of the world", is an aspect of Tolkien's wrestling with the relation of Christianity to "paganism", both in its light and in its dark and malign aspects. He responded to the struggle which he saw going on in the mind of the poet of *Beowulf*, between his faith on the one hand, and his loyalty and reverence for his native tradition on the other – the same struggle that still goes on in many consciences all over the world today.

Tolkien, the sincere Christian who decided that what his nation needed was a "pagan" mythology, stood with the *Beowulf* poet in defending the old heroic tales against their narrow and fanatical suppressors (narrowness and fanaticism are perennial and come in many forms). So, too, his work by implication stands with the Filipino *Datu*, and the old men who fear their stories will be laughed at by the school-educated young.

Also, perhaps, as a celebrator of trees, with one small and not yet articulate representative of an unassuming people:

> ". . . As he came to a towering, smooth tree, he placed his hands against the trunk to steady himself, drew back his head, and stared up at the tree, all the way up to the leafy kingdom of its crown spread out against the sky. He stood that way for ten minutes, now and again gently patting the tree." This was Baja, a motherless toddler from the Aka Pygmies in central Africa, whose community was being wiped out by disease until they moved back into their forest. "I carried Baja out to his tree every day for a week . . . At first I had no hope that he would live, but like the rest of us he had been through the worst. He, too, was a survivor."

(Sarno, 1993)

II

So far I have looked at the general stance of Tolkien's work; now I want to enter Middle-earth and look at some of its inhabitants, and consider how he treats the equivalent of the non-European peoples that anthropologists generally study – first the "wild men" of Druadan forest, or as they become in his later writings, the Drûgs; and then the peoples of the South and East of Middle-earth. In fact, it was some time in the development of Tolkien's world before these peoples became distinct. In the early versions of the Helm's Deep chapter, the "Wild Men" are fighting for Saruman; these later became the Dunlendings (Tolkien, 1990, pp. 16, 18).

The phrase "wild men" first occurs, in the final version of *The Lord of the Rings*, when Faramir, explaining the Gondorian theory of anthropology to Frodo and Sam says, ". . . so we reckon Men in our lore, calling them the High, or Men of the West, which were Númenoreans; and the Middle Peoples, Men of the Twilight, such as are the Rohirrim and their kin that dwell still far in the North; and the Wild, the Men of Darkness" (Tolkien, 1987a, p. 287). Here the phrase does not seem to refer to the Drúedain, but to the peoples under Sauron's domination. Now this sounds very like the classic Victorian evolutionary sequence of Savagery – Barbarism – Civilisation, which was around in Tolkien's youth, and has still not disappeared from the public mind though anthropologists dropped it long ago.

But if we look closer, we see that the resemblance is only superficial; the whole structure of assumption underlying the two schemes is quite different. For the anthropology of Middle-earth is not evolutionary at all. The "high" civilisations of Gondor and its predecessor Númenor have not developed by their own interior dynamic out of societies like that of the Rohirrim; they owe their arts and wisdom to their contact with the Elves, their teachers. And the "high" cultures are not about to lead on to something else even higher and better – Saruman is not an improvement except in certain aspects of technology. The Rohirrim, too, owe their "twilight" status to being descended from the Elf-friends of old. The "Men of Darkness" are those who have not enjoyed the influence of the Elves, and thus fall an easy prey to Sauron. "Sauron dominates all the multiplying hordes of Men that have had no contact with the Elves and so indirectly with the true and unfallen Valar" (Tolkien, 1981, p.153). The Elves, though not free from corruption themselves, are transmitters of the knowledge – I think one can fairly say the faith – of Aman, by which they and their allies resist Sauron. They are also the teachers of the arts of life – building, writing, and all that is generally summed up as "civilization" – but this is by virtue of their own innate gifts. In evolutionary thinking the advance of civilisation is also a progressive "disenchantment" as people grow more rational (whatever exactly that means). But here civilisation and enchantment are not opposed but go together.

As for the Drúedain, the way they develop is typical of Tolkien's method of work, which was to start from certain hints or suggestions already given – either in outside sources or in his own work – and grow and elaborate them into something new. We first meet them in *The Lord of the Rings*, when they show the Rohirrim the hidden road to Minas Tirith. There they are very much the stereotype of the "savage". Indeed their appellation "woodwoses" derives from the sort of folkloric traditions from which that stereotype partly derives; for Europeans when they crossed the oceans saw what their traditions predisposed them to see, the embodiments of their own fantasies of "wild men". They are gnarled and strange in appearance, almost naked, communicate by beating drums, are "woodcrafty beyond compare" (Tolkien, 1987b, p. 105), and hunt with poisoned arrows. One may add that they are constantly hunted and persecuted by other sorts of men, including the Rohirrim. They are also somehow connected with the ancient, huge, Polynesian-looking figures of the Stonewain Valley. The only thing they are not is black, which would be incongruous in supposed ancient inhabitants at this latitude.

So far the Drúedain are a sort of identikit Savage, but Tolkien later elaborated on the rather perfunctory hints contained in *The Lord of the Rings*, as he so often let random hints in his work grow and develop, and the more attention he paid to the Drúedain, the further they moved from the stereotype that seems to underlie the earlier descriptions. They are shown to have a past in the First Age, and are a highly idiosyncratic breed of their own, "a wholly different kind" so different from other men that Tolkien has to take pains to distinguish them from Hobbits or Dwarves. Not only are they not the same as the "men of darkness" – they have throughout the ages been harried and persecuted by them (Tolkien, 1980a).

The notable thing about these earlier Drúedain or Drûgs – who are not called Wild Men – is their symbiotic relationship with the forest-dwelling People of Haleth. The tie between them was such that they actually migrated together (unlike the Men and Hobbits of Bree, to whom they are compared, who had simply landed up by different routes in the same place). The Haladrim and the Drûgs evidently needed each other.

When you find such a link between human groups in our world, one people is always in some sort of servant or client relationship to the other – not necessarily a grossly exploitative one. Something of the sort would be possible here, and fits in with Tolkien's intention to turn the old serving man in the "Tale of Túrin", Sador, into a Drûg (Tolkien, 1980a, p. 386 note 8). I think the tie between them was something like that between the "Pygmies" of the African forests and the taller, farming villagers in the same forests. The Pygmies, as hunters, provide meat and honey to the villagers, and sometimes work on their farms. In exchange they get food crops and other goods (at least that was how it was until recently). I assume that the People of Haleth were farmers growing crops in the forest clearings, and that the Drûgs as hunters similarly provided them with the products of the forest, and with their skill as healers and other uncanny gifts (this is a very common attribute of "separate" people of inferior status), and also did odd jobs, getting their bread and butter in return. We may assume that they were content with the arrangement, since there was limitless forest for them to escape into if they found their conditions unacceptable. In such a situation the only way that unwilling workers can be kept on the job is by physical force, i.e. as slaves – as we are told the Easterlings did in fact keep their thralls.

Part of this reconsideration of the Drúedain is a new look at their representative Ghân-buri-Ghân as he appears in *The Return of the King*, talking pidgin-Westron, and using the name "Wild Men" for his people. Now it turns out he did so as a concession to his hearers – "not without irony" (Tolkien, 1980a, p. 384). A person who can look with irony at others' labelling of him has become a three-dimensional being with a point of view of his own.

I suggest that this reworking of the nature of the Drúedain was deliberate, almost a retraction; that Tolkien recognised that the Drúedain as they appear in *The Lord of the Rings* are not properly accounted for, since they belong to a different world of thought, and that some way had to be found to explain their characteristics in terms of his world, not that of early twentieth-century popular anthropology. At the same time he made his second attempt (after the dual society of Bree) to draw a situation where two different peoples live side by side in amity.[3]

---

[3] The Drûgs/Drúedain present some interesting ethnographic problems. There is a remaining puzzle about the Púkel-men of Stonewain Valley – since it was evidently ancestors of the Drúedain who made them. Were they a hunting and gathering or "foraging" people? It seems likely, but hunter-gatherers generally have to keep on the move to live, and people on the move do not carve large monumental statues. There are occasional exceptions to the first of those statements, where there is sufficient abundance of wild foods for a people to

The difference between the men of Rhûn and Harad and the Drúedain is that Tolkien never gave the former the kind of loving attention he gave the latter. We know them only as enemies, Sauron's cannon-fodder. There is only one moment where one of them becomes an individual, the passage where Sam looks at the dead Southron warrior, with "his scarlet robes . . . tattered . . . his black plaits of hair braided with gold . . . drenched with blood"; and "his brown hand" clutching "the hilt of a broken sword", and wonders "what the man's name was and where he came from; and if he was really evil of heart, or what lies or threats had led him on the long march from his home; and if he would not really rather have stayed there in peace" (Tolkien, 1987a, p. 269). The attitude of the Gondor men-at-arms to the people they have been fighting for centuries is straightforward: "Curse the Southrons!" It is the outsider with an innocent eye who asks himself these questions, including, significantly, "what the man's name was".

Apart from this moment they remain vague, undeveloped figures, swarthy, in scarlet, and waving scimitars, or bearded and axe-wielding, never moving beyond the derived stereotype.

If we have something here that looks outwardly like what in our world we know as "racism", we can dismiss that appearance, not only because Tolkien in his non-fictional writing several times repudiated racist ideas, but because – once again – in his sub-creation the whole intellectual underpinning of racism is absent.[4] The Haradrim and the Variags of Khand are corrupt not because they are biologically inferior but because they are human and therefore corruptible. In any case, though they are politically subject to Sauron it is uncertain – as Sam perceives – how far they are corrupt as individuals (unlike Orcs, who are a separate problem, and one that Tolkien himself never really solved).[5] The men of Gondor and their allies are "nobler", not by their intrinsic nature but because they have had the luck to inherit from their ancestors the mediated tradition – the faith – of Aman, and more or less held onto it – though they are constantly in danger of letting go. (As far as actual descent goes, they are ultimately the same as the Rohirrim.) There is moreover no question here of "level" of culture – the Variags are clearly the counterparts of the Rohirrim in this respect.

But was there no opposition, no resistance to Sauron among the peoples of the South and East? We are getting, after all, an entirely Gondorian historical view. By definition this would be aware only of those Southrons and Easterlings who marched in Sauron's armies, not those – if any – who refused to do so. Were there any who refused?

Tolkien appears to have thought not. In the conception of the work, the men of those regions were all servants of the Enemy, whether corrupted or deluded. (One thing we are told is that the other two Wizards of the Five, the Blue Wizards, went to the East; we do not know what happened to them or whether they fulfilled their mission. Tolkien himself (1981, p. 280) suggested that they abandoned it and themselves became the centre of "magical" cults, which later survived). What seems to underlie this is a deeply pessimistic assumption about Men in general – that unless touched by Aman, mediated by the Elves, they are bound to become corrupt. This willingness to condemn Men in the lump arises out of a dark and despairing undercurrent in Tolkien's work, and balances his at times almost excessive readiness to go easy on the individual (as Tom Shippey has noted – 1992, pp. 138-9). But at the same time one feels that he just was not particularly interested in the Southrons and Easterlings.

Partly I think this is because in a sense they do not belong in the mythical framework at all. All mythologies are necessarily both universal and local: universal in their scope, because they deal with the nature of things; local in point of view and "temper", because they arise out of particular cultures. This tension is present in the mythology[6] devised by Tolkien, since it is both about the human condition in general, and deliberately made specific to a certain part of the world.

In the cosmology of the early work, much of the world seems to be uninhabited. In the legends of the First Age, the action is firmly confined to the north-west, and men of other regions do not enter into consideration, except as coming into the projected tale of Eärendil's voyages, and that never did get off the ground. With the Second and Third Ages, however, the geography shifts south-east, with the Enemy's fortress in that quarter, and it is natural that his armies are recruited from those regions, and that they draw on inherited

---

form permanent settlements. One such people were the Indians of the Northwest American coast, the Kwakiutl and others, who enjoyed such abundance of fish in their rivers that they had no need to move around, and they did indeed produce large and impressive carvings – not in stone, but in wood, the famous "totem poles". So what was the Drúedain equivalent of the Kwakiutl's salmon? Or had they actually taken up farming or herding at one time, and developed a more complex society, before they were driven back into the forests and a hunting and hunted existence? Another problem is how many people the Druadan Forest could actually have supported by this way of life, which needs large areas of country per person. The forest seems to have been only about 60 by 20 miles. Ghân-buri-Ghân's band was probably quite small. But I prefer to leave this question unanswered, and let the Púkel-men keep their mystery.

[4] The intellectual basis of much modern anti-racism is also absent. Opposition to racism since World War II has been backed by the scientific dismantling of the whole concept of "races" as permanent, distinct entities, and with the scientifically more debatable tendency to minimize or even deny altogether the importance of heredity of any kind. But in Tolkien's world heredity – descent – is clearly very important, together with an emphasis on hierarchy, understood as opposed to tyranny, not synonymous with it.

[5] A note on racial characteristics of Orcs: they are (a) "swart", i.e. black or brown, (b) slant-eyed, and (c) extremely hairy. So take your pick.

[6] It has been questioned whether "mythology" is really the appropriate term for Tolkien's work. Tolkien himself hardly ever used it; instead, he uses a number of different words, as though he, like his commentators since, could never find quite the right term to describe what he had invented. *Legendarium* (or connected body of legend) is perhaps the nearest to the mark. Yet since it does start off with a "cosmogonic myth", and includes a pantheon of god-like beings, the word seems unavoidable.

images of "paynims" and other enemies.

Moreover, it is essential to the mythical vision that was in Tolkien's work from the beginning that there should be one, and only one, source of resistance, and that is situated in the North-west. "These legends are North-centred – because it is represented as an historical fact that the struggle against Morgoth and his servants occurred mainly in the North, and especially in the North-west, of Middle-earth, and that was so because the movement of Elves, and of Men afterwards escaping from Morgoth, had been inevitably *westward*, towards the Blessed Realm, and *north-westward* because at that point the shores of Middle-earth were nearest to Aman" (Tolkien, 1980b, p. 398). To have shown many sources of rebellion would confuse the picture; besides, it is also essential to the myth that the resisters should be greatly outnumbered.

So there was no resistance among the Haradrim. If this was Tolkien's view of the matter I must accept it; since it is his sub-creation, not mine. (In any case, as we have seen, it was not a question that concerned him much.) However, it concerns me, and when a work is put into the public domain it becomes available to other imaginations, and it is I think legitimate to give one's fantasy a little play in the world Tolkien made available to us. I have another idea of what happened in these regions, which, following his own method, draws on hints in the work itself.

Just because there was no large scale and successful resistance to Sauron outside the North-west, need this mean no resistance at all? Perhaps the two Wizards who went to the East did not altogether fail in their mission. Perhaps Gandalf's undercover activities in Near Harad (Tolkien, 1980b, p. 398) were not fruitless. Did the Valar not have ways of letting their influence reach these peoples, or appear among them, even in strange forms? Are there unwritten chapters in the history of Middle-earth? If there are, they would have to be written in other languages, and belong to another "earth and air". (What *was* the name of the strange warrior?)

There was at least one person from the North-west, we know, who had travelled far into those regions and had more than the ordinary Gondorian knowledge of them. In my imagination I like to add a paragraph to the great tale (found in only one manuscript of the Red Book, it clearly represents a tradition from Gondor, but its authenticity is disputed), telling how when King Elessar, after his crowning "sat on his throne in the Hall of the Kings and pronounced his judgements" and "embassies came from many lands and peoples", and he "pardoned the Easterlings that had given themselves up, and sent them away free, and he made peace with the peoples of Harad; and the slaves of Mordor he released" (Tolkien, 1987b, p.246-7) – that among the swarthy envoys from the South, was a face that he recognised. Then, to the amazement of all (and the displeasure of some), the King and the Southron embraced one another – for, long before, this man had saved the life of a hunted stranger from the followers of the Serpent, and they had broken their bread together in an outlaws' camp under the strange stars.

References

Bradley, John H. 1975. *Victims of Progress*, second edition. California: Cummings Publishing Company.

Sarno, Louis. 1993. *Song from the Forest*. London and New York: Bantam Press.

Sellars, W.C. and Yeatman, R.J. 1930. *1066 and all That*. London: Methuen.

Shippey, T.A. 1992. *The Road to Middle-earth*, second edition. London: Grafton Paperbacks.

Survival International. 1991. *Survival News* 29.

Thiongo, Ngugi Wa. 1993. "The Universality of Local Knowledge" in *Moving the Centre; the Struggle for Cultural Freedoms*, ed. James Currey. London: Heinemann.

Tolkien, J.R.R. 1980a. "The Drúedain" in *Unfinished Tales*, J.R.R. Tolkien, ed. Christopher Tolkien. George Allen & Unwin, pp. 377-87.

Tolkien, J.R.R. 1980b. "The Istari" in *Unfinished Tales*, J.R.R. Tolkien, ed. Christopher Tolkien. George Allen & Unwin, pp. 388-402.

Tolkien, J.R.R. 1981. *Letters of J.R.R. Tolkien*, ed. Humphrey Carpenter with Christopher Tolkien. London: George Allen & Unwin.

Tolkien, J.R.R. 1987a. *The Two Towers*, second edition. London: George Allen & Unwin.

Tolkien, J.R.R. 1987b. *The Return of the King*, second edition. London: George Allen & Unwin.

Tolkien, J.R.R. 1990. *The War of the Ring*, ed. Christopher Tolkien. London: Unwin Hyman.

Frodo and his Spectre: Blakean Resonances in Tolkien

Charles E. Noad

Abstract: Comparisons between Blake and Tolkien are tempting, not least because of superficial resemblances, but more valid comparisons can be made in their treatment of similar underlying themes. One such is that shown in the opposition of Los and his Spectre (Blake) and of Frodo and Gollum (Tolkien), where a comparison points up the outlooks and limitations of both writers.

Keywords: William Blake, Frodo, Gollum, *Jerusalem*, language, Los, mythology, Spectre

I hope I am not doing any great violence to anyone's sense of the appropriate by seeming to yoke together William Blake and J.R.R. Tolkien. That the differences, both in personality and in the kind of work they produced, between the radical Swedenborgian proto-Romantic and the conservative Catholic scholar, were many and profound, scarcely needs to be emphasised, and this ramble through a few instances where their thoughts have parallels of a kind shall not seek to minimise those differences. And let me note here that neither shall I attempt any sort of overall comparison between Blake and Tolkien. Genius is characteristically intensely personal and ultimately incommensurable. Blake and Tolkien had each his own genius; neither could have achieved exactly what the other did.

And yet there are resemblances in certain aspects of their creative work which are at least superficial and which may sometimes point to deeper common concerns. Quite apart from the most general fact that each wrote some peculiar books, both were preoccupied with language and the way in which it affects one's perceptions of the world. To Blake, the English language was the "rough basement" (*Jerusalem* 36:58; Erdman, 1988, p. 183)[1] upon which was erected the symbolic system of the way his compatriots comprehended the world. And, as his idealised self proclaimed:

> "I must Create a System, or be enslav'd by another Mans"
>
> (*Jerusalem* 10:20; Erdman, 1988, p. 153)

A good deal of Blake's writing could be described as an attempt to make the reader rub up against the net of language which binds his perceptions, and so perhaps to help wake him from the single vision of Newtonian sleep. His purpose was not so much to create his own system, as to "Strive[e] with Systems to deliver Individuals from those Systems" (*Jerusalem* 11:5; Erdman, 1988, p. 154).

Tolkien's attitude to language was different. If Blake, once he had come to perceive the part that language plays in moulding our perception of the world, was in a constant struggle against it, then Tolkien was enamoured of it, having been fascinated by it from the earliest age, and, not least because of his technical competence in that field, was able to adopt a far more positive view of it than Blake was ever able to attain. I have no doubt that Tolkien was aware of the way that language can mould thought, but he expressed this awareness by actually inventing languages other than his own, and by exploring the concept of each person having his own unique "native language" which perfectly expressed his linguistic sensibilities; a perfect system to be created, perhaps. Thus, in this instance, they have a common concern, but they approach it with markedly different attitudes.

They are also concerned with, and make use of, the form of myth. In the modern world we don't have myths, at least not myths in the sense in which we consider the ancient world to have had them. True, in the most general sense, a myth can simply mean a widespread belief about some important aspect of humanity or of the universe at large or of the relationship between them. But "myth" has rather more specific meanings to us in that it can refer to form as well as to content. A nature-myth can sum up an antique culture's beliefs about seed-time and harvest, about thunder and lightning; but the modern eye is more likely to be held by the narratives about the gods and goddesses, about the superhuman, and sometimes subhuman (if that is a real distinction), personalities who embody or control such phenomena. In the ancient mind there may have been no easy distinction between the form and the content, between the gods and the thunder; but this distinction is what most strikes us, and we consequently associate myth with the accounts of the superhuman beings, and not with the phenomena it seeks to explain. This distinction is characteristic of the modern world, and the functions which

---

[1] References to Blake's writings in the text take the form (plate number):(line number), followed by a page reference to the standard scholarly Blake text (Erdman, 1988). Thus "*Jerusalem* 36:58; Erdman, 1988, p. 183" refers to plate 36, line 58 of *Jerusalem*, which can be found on page 183 of the Erdman edition.

myth once performed have separated into science and storytelling.

Yet, if we no longer explain the World in terms of superhuman personalities (excepting those who would hold that one Great Personality underlies all things), accounts of such beings may still have a function in the modern world. If they can no longer be used to describe those aspects of existence amenable to scientific endeavour, perhaps they can be used to explore, if not to explain, other things which are not easily – if at all – quantifiable, indeed to "say things which cannot be said in any other way."

In that sense, then, two of the foremost modern mythologisers are William Blake and J.R.R. Tolkien. The "Prophetic Books" of the former are crowded with the actions and the speeches of the strange persons, at once both superhuman and human, which he uses to expound his concerns about the human soul and its perceptions of the world, and which might very loosely be termed "emblematic personages". However, we should note that it was not Blake's purpose to create a pseudo-mythology. To Blake, "All deities reside in the human breast" (*The Marriage of Heaven and Hell* 11; Erdman, 1988, p. 38), and if he found himself writing of persons who seem to perform actions in a mythic dimension, then that was because that was the only way he could express his ideas.

Tolkien's invented mythology was partly a conscious attempt at one time to create a kind of homegrown grand mythology for his native country – which was perhaps, in a way, also Blake's purpose in his Prophetic Books – and partly a way of creating a world in which his invented languages could undergo complex historical evolutions; but it was also a way of expressing some very profound things which he could not do in any other way. This is of course a very large subject which would require another conference in itself, and I hesitate to provide any kind of sound-bite definition. I shall just limit myself here to suggesting that the world which Tolkien made for his mythology is very much bound up with the languages for which it was meant to provide a background; that that world is in a sense a manifestation of the linguistic preferences which underlie it, in the same way – I suppose that this was a metaphor of which Tolkien was conscious – that the material world is a manifestation of the Music of the Ainur. His personal linguistic preferences resulted in his creating a world, or system, nearer to his heart's desire.

So much for a glance at language and myth and how they were used by Blake and by Tolkien. And yet, any attempt to summarize Blake must give anyone who has actually read him all the way through a moment's pause, at the least. A moment ago I attempted to summarize Blake's mythology in terms of "emblematic personages". While it is (probably) not untrue to describe it thus, it scarcely touches the surface; the attempt is absurd. Blake's work is complex indeed, to put it very mildly, and I shall not attempt at all to exhaust that complexity, even supposing I were capable of doing so. Even if the claim could be advanced that Blake's work was well-understood, any one-sentence summary would have to be so generalized as to be meaningless. This is not to belittle the researches that have been made into his writings, but can we really say we understand Blake? Not so very long ago, a prominent Blake scholar declared:

> . . . compared to what we know about [Byron's] *Don Juan*, we know nothing whatever about [Blake's] *Jerusalem*. When I read an article about *The Four Zoas*, I end up feeling like a sensationalist whose special form of self-abuse is the shock that comes from moving off the cool, stable surfaces of scholarly explanations into the molten grid of the work that needs explaining . . . But I refuse to pretend to believe that even the wisest of Blake scholars feel confident in their understanding of *The Marriage of Heaven and Hell*, much less the strange poems in the Pickering manuscript, and less still *Europe*, *The Four Zoas*, *Milton*, or *Jerusalem*.
> (Eaves, 1982, p. 389)

Well, I shall not really be attempting to describe Blake's myth, and even if I sometimes seem to, it will be more a form of hand-waving in the hope that the general direction will be sensed, rather than a carefully printed signpost.

It isn't too difficult to draw attention to parallels between details of the myths of Blake and Tolkien. There is the structural aspect. It would take little effort, for example, to "map" Blake's "Four Zoas" and their emanations (of which more anon) onto certain of the Great Valar, male and female. They both seem to form sets of Jungian quarternaries. If we use the elements with which they are associated, then we get: Fire – Luvah and Melkor; Air – Urizen and Manwë; Water – Tharmas and Ulmo; Earth – Urthona and Aulë. Geographically, Blake's Eden, Beulah, Generation and Ulro could be equated with Valinor, Eressëa, Middle-earth and Mordor: all, in one sense, different states of being. But such comparisons are, I think, of little real significance: myths have to have some sort of structure, and the fourfold structure has its own appeal and will do as well as any.

Of possibly greater significance are a few of the names. To Tolkien, "Vala" and "Orc" are the names of types of creature; to Blake, they are the names of individuals, Vala having the function of being (again, very roughly) the alluring, visible Nature which we see in ordinary waking consciousness, or "Newtonian sleep". Orc is the spirit of revolution. He features strongly in Blake's "prophecies", as his non-lyrical poems came to be called, of the revolutionary last decades of the eighteenth century, but he had faded to little more than a name by the time we reach *Jerusalem*, well into the nineteenth. The two Orcs have been discussed elsewhere, by Randel Helms (1970, pp. 31-5). (Oddly enough, Orc is the manifestation in the material world of Luvah, the Zoa corresponding to Melkor; but that is just happenstance.) To Blake, "Tiriel" was the King of the Western Plains in the early, heavily allegorical poem of that name; to Tolkien, "Fíriel" was the mortal maiden who is denied passage to the western lands in "The Last Ship."

Why Blake chose the names he did has been the subject of a good deal of scholarly exploration. Certainly they were not derived from an imaginary language or languages, but rather seem to have been coined for the occasion, sometimes almost by accident. For example, the name "Urizen", the "Zoa" of reason, and so of laws and of oppressive political and religious orthodoxy, could well have been inspired in part by the phrase "or reason", as in: "Those who restrain desire, do so because theirs is weak enough to be restrained; and the restrainer or reason usurps its place & governs the unwilling." This is a pretty typical passage from the early *The Marriage of Heaven and Hell*.

Whatever their origins, and however they are pronounced, Blake could invent beautiful, if sometimes grotesque, names; for example: Palamabron, Urthona, Myratana, Enitharmon, Luvah, Urizen, Golgonooza, Dranthon, Ahania, Tharmas, Entuthon Benython, Palamabron, Ulro. A few of the names in his earlier prophecies were, as it happens, derived fairly directly from someone who might just about be called a proto-fantasist, though whether he could be regarded as any kind of literary ancestor of Tolkien I shall leave to other minds to decide. For instance, "Oothoon" in *Visions of the Daughters of Albion* almost certainly comes from the heroine "Oithona" in the tale of that name by James Macpherson, who published that and much else as the authentic works of the ancient Scottish bard "Ossian". The poems of "Ossian", as translated by Macpherson, although subject to doubts about their authenticity from the likes of Macpherson's contemporary, Samuel Johnson, nevertheless enjoyed an extraordinary popularity throughout Britain and Europe, even Goethe joining in the praises, as well as, very likely, the young Blake; certainly he always professed a belief in their authenticity. Perhaps "Ossian's" popularity goes to show that there has always been some sort of thirst in modern society for writing of a fantastical nature. However, since I personally find "Ossian" virtually unreadable, I shall not use him to try to prove that particular point. I certainly do not think that "Ossian"/Macpherson had the slightest direct influence on Tolkien.

Of much greater significance are those aspects of Blake's and Tolkien's myths not where they have a surface resemblance, but where they are used to explore the same kind of underlying truth. In one of those fascinating sections where Tolkien, with unique and unquestionable authority, discusses "what might have been" had *The Lord of the Rings* taken a different turn, he considers what would have happened had Gandalf taken the Ring and fallen to its temptation: "Gandalf as Ring-Lord would have been far worse than Sauron. He would have remained 'righteous', but self-righteous. He would have continued to rule and order things for 'good', and the benefit of his subjects according to his wisdom (which was and would have remained great)." It is this cycle of history which Blake was so concerned that we should break out of, where revolutionary ardour, once it has triumphed, apes the tyranny it has overthrown, where Orc has in effect become Urizen. Any Blakean reading the foregoing description of a Gandalf fallen to the Ring will instantly recognise Urizen. Take a look at the last plate of *The Book of Urizen*. There's Gandalf, Gandalf corrupted that is, glaring out at the reader.

As regards the subject of this paper's title, I should emphasise that I shall be dealing with just a part of Blake's myth, and then only with an aspect of that part. Blake saw Man as a fourfold being, comprising the power of reason, the imagination, the emotions, and the body. In the beginning, these were simply aspects of a single, harmonious whole. But since the Fall they have become separated and no longer work in harmony one with another. On a superhuman scale, these aspects are the Four Zoas: Urizen, Urthona, Luvah, and Tharmas, who are the disunited parts of the Eternal Man, sometimes called Albion, a kind of collective person representing either England or the whole human race. But on the scale of the divided individual – even if that individual is one of the Zoas themselves – the division is slightly different in kind. This too comprises a fourfold scheme, in which a person consists of the Emanation, the Humanity, the Spectre and the Shadow. However, Blake paid much more attention to the Emanation and the Spectre, which he appeared to consider much more important, or at least more interesting, than the others. There is no direct correspondence as such with the fourfold Zoas, although the Spectre seems most associated with the reasoning power.

The Emanation represents, according to one critic, the "total form of all the things a man loves and creates" (Frye, 1947, p. 73). But when separated, it can be a source of torment as well as inspiration. It is characteristically female, and it is the counterpart of the male spectre.

The spectre – what is a spectre? I suppose spectres need some description nowadays. Insofar as the spectre is a separated part of the human unity it might be said to represent that unity when viewed from the outside and considered as an object, especially as an object for the calculating, reasoning power to work on: in a sense, humanity reflected in a mirror and viewed as an object – a selfhood. This is a rather reflexive definition, but you find yourself doing that with Blake. In a way, the spectre is like a kind of *döppelganger*. This separated selfhood is an indication of the absence of individual unity or integration.

And in order to gain the desired unity, the spectre must be put off:

> Each man is in Spectre's power
> Until the arrival of that hour,
> When his Humanity awake
> And cast his Spectre into the Lake
> (*Jerusalem* 37:32-5;Erdman, 1988, pp. 184, 810)
> The Negation is the Spectre; the Reasoning Power in Man
> This is a false Body: an Incrustation over my Immortal
> Spirit; a Selfhood, which must be put off & annihilated alway
> To cleanse the Face of my Spirit by Self-examination.
> (*Milton* 40:34-7; Erdman, 1988, p. 142)

But given that it exists, the spectre has its uses, principally to assist in its own annihilation. In a world of fallen humanity, there will indeed be a spectre in each individual; and on the quasi-allegorical level at which the "action" of the Prophetic Books takes place, the Spectre can be made to work for the redemption of the Eternal Man. *Jerusalem* is concerned with this theme, the recovery of Paradise. In this poem (again, greatly to oversimplify), Los, the spirit of Poetic Inspiration, who is himself the manifestation in time of Urthona, the Zoa of the Imagination, compels his Spectre to assist him in his work of "building Golgonooza / Compelling his Spectre to labours mighty; trembling in fear / The Spectre weeps, but Los unmoved by tears or threats remains" (*Jerusalem* 10:17-19; Erdman, 1988, p. 153). The initial products of Los's spectre-assisted labours at his furnaces are the Spaces of Erin and the city of Golgonooza, which seem to represent the purity of the body and the city of art, respectively, both concepts necessary for the salvation of the fallen Albion. It is of course no coincidence that the poet, Blake, sees poetry as essential for the saving of Albion, and that it is Los, the very Genius of the poetic spirit, who carries out this work in the poem. The relationship of Los and his Spectre can be found in Blake's own life in that, not too surprisingly, it reflects impulses within Blake himself: Los is the part of him that wants to write poetry, to print his "illuminated" books, to open the worlds of Eternity to his fellow men, but the Spectre is the more mundane, cynical, self-centred, watch-the-expenses part of him, which makes him keep his nose to the grindstone of the immediate, material world; perhaps even a necessity in a fallen world, but he still must not be allowed to gain the upper hand. (Does this remind anyone of Barfield's "Burgeon" and "Burden"?)

Blake is quite explicit on the matter in a letter of late 1804 to his sometime patron, the otherwise now completely forgotten minor Augustan poet, William Hayley: "For now! O Glory! and O Delight! I have entirely reduced that spectrous Fiend to his station, whose annoyance has been the ruin of my labours for the last passed twenty years of my life . . . he is become my servant who domineered over me, he is even as a brother who was my enemy" (Erdman, 1988, pp. 756-7). This spiritual release was occasioned by a visit to a new art gallery which displayed copies of several hundred old masters, causing him to escape from the shadow of classicism in art and to re-experience and regain the artistic perceptions of his youth.

The point here is that Blake saw some aspects of his mythology in very personal terms, in particular he was able to see the Spectre as a part of himself which needed to be struggled against unceasingly. The "spectrous Fiend" was what he himself could easily become were he to give up his calling and cease to be a true poet. The ferocity of this struggle is reflected in that between Los and his Spectre in *Jerusalem*. The former threatens the latter with all manner of harm:

> I know thy deceit & thy revenges, and unless thou desist
> I will certainly create an eternal Hell for thee. Listen!
> Be attentive! be obedient! Lo the Furnaces are ready to receive thee.
> I will break thee into shivers! & melt thee in the furnaces of death;
> I will cast thee into forms of abhorrence & torment if thou
> Desist not from thine own will, & obey not my stern command!
>
> (*Jerusalem* 8:7-12; Erdman, 1988, p. 151)

Los cries, Obey my voice & never deviate from my will

> And I will be merciful to thee . . .
> If thou refuse, thy present torments will seem southern breezes
> To what thou shalt endure if thou obey not my great will.
>
> (*Jerusalem* 10:29-36; Erdman, 1988, p. 153)

Now it might cogently be argued that this kind of thing should not be interpreted in human terms. We are dealing not with human beings but with abstractions, with symbols; and in any case, his spectre is a part of Los himself. This is largely true, but whatever else Blake's characters are or symbolize, they are still presented in human form: they do not speak as bloodless symbols. And although in other parts of his works, the symbolic aspect is indeed very apparent, and we need not suppose for a moment that Blake is describing the actions and situations of ordinary human beings, when we come to Los and his Spectre we really have got a human situation, an interaction – a series of dialogues – between two persons. One of these persons is the Poetic Genius, the good guy, and the other is his total negation, the bad guy. And the good guy, because he knows he is fighting for a good cause, in effect the salvation of the world, uses any means necessary to pursue that cause, including threatening the bad guy with infinitely dreadful punishments.

This might make some of us uneasy. Certainly it makes one wonder about Blake. He indeed saw Pity as an attribute of the divine, but one cannot help but feel that he understood it as something to be indulged in only after victory of a sort had been achieved. Possibly this is to misjudge Blake. As I noted earlier, any claim really to understand him must be regarded as dubious. In the present case, it could very well be that Los is himself far from perfect, and that perfection and pity are both bound up with the result of the work he forces his Spectre to achieve.

So to sum up, Blake saw the Spectre as a divided part of the self, but one which in a fallen world could be ruthlessly bullied into serving the Imagination and redeeming the individual through Art.

Gollum first entered Tolkien's writings as a minor character in *The Hobbit*. Originally he seems to have been no more than a kind of bogeyman, something of a Mewlip, perhaps; but if so a rather hobbitified Mewlip: he does not seem to be greatly different from Bilbo in size, and he knows the ancient and venerable Riddle Game. It is even implied that he was himself hobbitlike – ". . . ages before, when he lived with his grandmother in a hole in a bank by a river" (Tolkien, 1966a, p. 86) – but when Bilbo meets him he is the very opposite of the bucolic normality of a hobbit, and someone the sooner got away from the better.

It was when he began to work on the sequel to *The Hobbit* that Tolkien began to explore who Gollum really was. He was obviously intimately connected with the main link between the books, the magic ring of invisibility which Bilbo had obtained from him in the course of their brief acquaintance. And Frodo's initial impressions of Gollum come of course entirely through Bilbo's eyes: he wonders why Bilbo didn't kill such a loathsome creature at the time, and so prevent all the trouble, which Gandalf has just been telling him about, that he has caused since. Gandalf has to remind him that Pity stayed his hand at the time, and implies that Pity, far from being a luxury one can have when it costs its giver nothing, is bound up with the fate of the Ring. Besides, to kill without Pity would have been the first step to making Bilbo into another little Gollum himself.

Frodo (as well as the reader) learns a good deal more about Gollum after he intercepts Frodo and Sam at the edge of the Emyn Muil. It might have been thought expedient to kill Gollum there and then, but Frodo has grown somewhat: they can't kill him outright, "not as things are." But Gollum is also preserved for another reason than Pity: he knows the way into Mordor. And since getting into Mordor by a secret way is fundamental to the task of destroying the One Ring, Gollum's assistance is essential. In fact, since the salvation of the world now depends on it, it must, if necessary, be compelled.

This is a paradoxical situation: Frodo, steadfastly resisting the ever-present lure of the Ring, compelling another hobbit, one who long ago gave himself entirely over to that lure, to guide him to the Ring's destruction. Perhaps Gollum's presence made it easier for Frodo to resist the Ring, as he was able constantly to see in front of him exactly what he would become were he to give in to it. Their positions regarding the Ring formed a kind of symmetry: the real Frodo making a potential Frodo, his own possible self – his Spectre – guide him. And sometimes Gollum had to be forced to his task: "In the last need, Sméagol, I should put on the Precious; and the Precious mastered you long ago. If I, wearing it, were to command you, you would obey, even if it were to leap from a precipice or to cast yourself into the fire. And such would be my command. So have a care, Sméagol!" (Tolkien, 1966b, p. 248).

Thus, there is this parallel between Blake and Tolkien: Frodo, like Los, has to threaten a person who is his *alter ego* to help him in his work for the salvation of the world. But, even allowing for the fact that Frodo and Gollum are set within a realistic situation and Los and his Spectre aren't, there are some significant differences in the matter. We do not doubt that Los means exactly what he says; but we doubt if Frodo does. He has to utter dire threats against Gollum which the latter will believe; but the reader has room to doubt whether Frodo would ever carry out his threats. Apart from the fact that Frodo would lose his only guide into Mordor, we have by now read enough to understand that in Tolkien's world the side of good must be consistently good: coercion and force, although sometimes necessary, must be kept to the minimum; free will must be truly free; pity is bound up with ultimate victory.

This is a real difference, and does not merely hinge upon an interpretation of necessity. Tolkien's world was one where, ultimately, good would finally prevail, even if evil had its temporary, if insufferable, triumphs. But Blake's world seems to have been one where, at least in limited areas, evil really could triumph for ever. In the former, using evil to fight evil merely postponed the final victory; in the latter, salvation was uncertain and so anything necessary had to be done to achieve victory.

In the end, this difference seems to resolve itself into a difference of faith: having faith in the ultimate victory of good allows that good to be fully integrated into the means of its triumph; but if you do not have that faith, then the best you can hope for is a not too tarnished victory. Tolkien, though sometimes pessimistic and full of doubts, had that faith; Blake, although he hoped that the Fall could one day be reversed in the World, in the end, I think, lacked it.

To sum up, we have seen that there are some superficial resemblances between the invented mythologies of Blake and Tolkien, and that there are some parallels, some resonances, which are much more significant, where their use of aspects of their myths allows them to explore common concerns, even if they come to differing conclusions. Even so, I do not think that Tolkien was actually influenced by Blake in any way. He undoubtedly knew of Blake, even if no more than someone that should be "read" as part of one's basic "Eng. Lit." background. Even so, Blake's reputation did not stand very high when Tolkien began his academic career in the early 1920s, and his subsequent professional activities would not have involved him having to read anyone so modern as Blake. Others of the "Inklings", including Charles Williams and C.S. Lewis, had some appreciation of the poet, so Tolkien may well have picked up some points on the subject from them, but I do not know of any particular ideas that impressed themselves upon Tolkien.

Since the essence of myth, ancient or modern, "real" or invented, is to say something about matters of universal concern, it is hardly surprising that Blake and Tolkien should sometimes run on parallel lines. And perhaps it is this very concern with matters of real importance which distinguishes the true maker of myths from the mere inventor.

References

Eaves, Morris. 1982. "Introduction" to "Inside the Blake Industry" in *Studies in Romanticism*, Vol. 21, No. 3, Fall 1982. p. 389.

Erdman, David V. (ed.) 1988. *The Complete Poetry and Prose of William Blake* (Newly Revised Edition). New York: Anchor-Doubleday.

Frye, Northrop. 1947. *Fearful Symmetry: A Study of William Blake*. Princeton: Princeton University Press, (1970 reprint).

Helms, Randel. 1970. "Orc: the Id in Blake and Tolkien" in *Literature and Psychology*, Vol. 20, No. 1, 1970. pp. 31-5.

Tolkien, J.R.R. 1966a. *The Hobbit* (third edition). London: George Allen & Unwin.

Tolkien, J.R.R. 1966b. *The Two Towers* (second edition). London: George Allen & Unwin.

An Overview Of the Northern Influences on Tolkien's Works

Gloriana St. Clair

Abstract: J.R.R. Tolkien studied the Old Norse literature and mythology thoroughly. While knowing Northern literature does not provide a key to unlock the meanings of his major works, his characters, creatures, implements, customs, incidents, and themes do have antecedents in the Eddas and sagas. This paper assesses the extent and impact of those antecedents.

Keywords: Eddas, Northern literature, J.R.R. Tolkien: influences upon, mythology, sagas

In a 1966 essay entitled "The Shire, Mordor, and Minas Tirith," Charles Moorman concluded, "The greatest single influence upon Tolkien is the Eddas and sagas of the North." The purpose of this talk is to provide an overview of the influence of Northern literature on Tolkien's master work, *The Lord of the Rings*. First, I will define Northern literature and provide a brief description of Tolkien's knowledge of it. Then I will discuss creatures, customs, personalities, and themes that show a Northern influence.

Northern literature

At Oxford, Tolkien taught Old English language and literature. Old English or Anglo-Saxon is the language spoken in England from 450 to 1150; it has an extraordinarily rich literature, including the Old English poem *Beowulf*. Towards the end of the Old English period, the Scandinavian countries – Norway, Sweden, and Denmark – flourished. Iceland, Greenland, and North America were discovered; the former two were colonized. The literature produced during this period had mythological underpinnings collected in works called the Eddas with an older *Poetic Edda* and a later, more literary *Prose Edda*.

In addition, many anonymous authors wrote several kinds of prose works called sagas. Sagas were written in the Old Norse language, the parent language for Norwegian, Swedish, Danish, and Icelandic. Many types of sagas were written: historical sagas, such as the *Heimskringla* (history of the kings of Norway), the Faeroe and Orkney islands sagas, and the *Saga of the Jomsvikings*. Sagas of olden times concerned themselves with the legends and myths of former times. *The Volsunga Saga* and the *Saga of King Heidrek*, which Christopher Tolkien translated, are two examples. Lying sagas were stories about far away places and creatures – genii, dragons, magic carpets; Tolkien did not seem much interested in these. Most successful artistically and most influential on Tolkien and all others who have read them are the family sagas. These Icelandic sagas give an amazingly clear and vivid picture of the society of Iceland in the tenth and eleventh centuries. Five sagas stand out for their excellence – the *Eyrbyggia Saga*, *Egil's Saga*, *Laxdale Saga*, the *Saga of Grettir the Strong*, and *Njal's Saga*. While each of these offered raw material for the creation of *The Lord of the Rings*, I have selected many examples from the *Njal's Saga*.

Tolkien's knowledge

Tolkien began studying Old English at age sixteen when his schoolmaster George Brewerton lent him an Anglo-Saxon primer. He moved on to read the Old English poem *Beowulf*. He studied Middle English and then began to read Old Norse, reading the *Volsunga Saga*, the Old Norse version of the story of Sigurd and the dragon Fafnir, in the original language (Carpenter, 1977, pp. 34, 37). He delighted his friends in the Tea Club, subsequently renamed the Barrovian Society, with tales from Volsunga, and he read a paper to the school literary society on Norse Sagas (Carpenter, 1977, pp. 46, 49).

Here at Oxford Old Norse was his special or secondary subject, and he learned from the well-known scholar W.A. Craigie. He probably read most of the sagas discussed in Craigie's *Icelandic Sagas* (1913, *passim*). Tolkien's biographer Humphrey Carpenter comments that Old Norse literature and mythology "had a profound appeal to Tolkien's imagination" (Carpenter, 1977, p. 65).

Tolkien continued his interest in Northern literature throughout his life. He and his colleague E.V. Gordon, the editor of an Old Norse text, founded a Viking Club for undergraduates to drink beer and read sagas (Gordon, 1957, pp. vii-x, Carpenter, 1977, p. 105). At Oxford, he formed a club called the Coalbiters to encourage the reading and discussion of Icelandic sagas in the original language (Carpenter, 1977, pp. 119-20). The Inklings supplanted the Coalbiters in the 1930s, but only after all the principal Icelandic sagas and the *Poetic Edda* had been covered (Carpenter, 1977, p. 149). Tolkien, who had read these works in their original language and discussed them with a succession of professional colleagues, had a profound knowledge of this body of literature.

Nature of the influences

Tolkien's interest in Northern literature manifests itself in many ways. In a 1979 article in *Mythlore*, I argued that the most proper genre for *The Lord of the Rings* is the saga. In spite of intimations by the critics that the darker landscapes are Northern, I think the landscapes of *The Lord of the Rings* are not greatly inspired by the volcanoes, glaciers, and hot springs of the sagas. The Ring and other implements do have some interesting parallels in Northern literature, but on balance they are more medieval in their inspiration than exclusively Northern.

Creatures

The hobbits are Tolkien's unique contribution to the people of Middle-earth. Hobbits share many characteristics of the Icelanders of the famous family sagas. Both have an exaggerated sense of hospitality; Bilbo's concern about the adequacy of food for the dwarves is an example. In the *Njal's Saga*, Gunnar's wife the ignoble Hallgerd steals to maintain her table. That act begins a blood feud which eventually kills off all the major characters (Bayerschmidt and Hollander, 1955, pp. 107-61). Both hobbits and Icelanders love to reckon their ancestors: the heritage of the Tooks is clear in Frodo and his cousins. Icelanders often divide themselves along lines of kinship in a feud. Both hobbits and Icelanders like fancy clothes. Hobbits dress in bright colours – green and yellow – and Icelanders have blue and black silk gowns, elaborate fur cloaks, silver and gold outfits, and ornate armours. Even hobbit timidness has a Viking antecedent. Thorin's account of the dangerous adventure ahead reduces Bilbo to shaking like a melting jelly. This whole scene may relate to an account of a hero named Hott who is cured of his fear by the hero Bothvar in the saga of King Hrolf (Gordon, 1957, p. 32).

The Elves of Northern literature are man-sized and intermarry with humans. In both Northern literature and *The Lord of the Rings*, elves have traditions of healing and of being capable smiths. The Eddas mention Dark Elves, perhaps some suggestion for orcs, but their main inspiration must come from elsewhere.

The catalogue of dwarves in the Poetic Edda provides the names for sixteen dwarves in *The Hobbit*, and two more names come from the *Prose Edda*. J.S. Ryan pulled all of this together in 1965 (pp. 50-51). Many dwarf characteristics – short stature with long beards, love for treasure, skill as smiths, and bad temper – derive from the Eddas and sagas.

In a letter to his son Christopher, Tolkien called Gandalf his "Odinic wanderer" (1981, p. 119). The wizards seem to have their inspiration in the gods of Old Norse mythology: Gandalf from Odin, the all-father; Saruman from the wicked god Loki, Radagast perhaps from the fertility God Frey. The other two Istari who were sent but played no part in the affairs of Middle-earth might have been patterned after Balder, Heimdall, or Thor.

Norse cosmography reveals the world as a circular disk held by the roots of Yggdrasil, the world Ash. Ents derive from this conception. The Old Willow's attempt to ingest Pippin parallels a story of a magician who is regenerated by being pulled into a tree and subsequently kicked out in the Magnus saga (Schlauch, 1916, pp. 137-38). Trolls, like those who capture Bilbo and the dwarves, play little part in Icelandic saga except as a common term of insult.

In "On Fairy-Stories," Tolkien says that as a child he "desired dragons with a profound desire." Although dragons are scattered through medieval literature, they are particularly interesting in Northern literature and in the Old English poem *Beowulf*. In the *Volsunga Saga*, Fafnir is a human brother of Regin and Otr. Otr shape-shifts into an otter whom the God Loki kills in a moment of senseless violence. The father demands that the skin be covered with gold as a weregild or blood payment. The gods comply by stealing the gold from the dwarf Andvari who curses it. Covering a remaining whisker with a cursed ring was a detail of the story that tickled Tolkien's imagination. The brother Fafnir turns into the talking, greedy dragon who is eventually slain by the hero Sigurd. But this dragon and the one in *Beowulf* pale beside the magnificence of Tolkien's Smaug.

Other parallels with Northern connections would include some birds, wargs, horses, the eye of Sauron, Bombadil and Goldberry, the balrog, and Shelob. The creatures of *The Lord of the Rings* have many antecedents in the creatures of Northern mythology and literature.

Customs

Northern customs do not appear equally distributed among the creatures of Middle-earth. While I have noted that hobbits share some customs with Icelanders, the peoples of Rohan and Gondor are the closest in the patterns of their society.

Noel, Green, and I have all explored the relationship between the riddle game between Bilbo and Gollum and the one between the King and Gestumblindi, who is Odin in disguise (Noel, 1977, p. 33; Green, 1970, pp. 112-18; St. Clair, 1979, pp. 11-16). Many of the riddles are alike, and both contests end with the same kind of singular question.

Runes and spells are also common to both worlds. Christopher Tolkien notes that the runes of *The Lord of the Rings* are Old English ones, but they were used in Old Norse language and society, too. Odin hanged himself on the world tree to gain a knowledge of the runes. They were the basis of his power to heal, to break metal, to thwart evil, to quench flames, to seduce, to destroy witches, and to speak to hanged men (Crossley-Holland, 1980, p. 188).

The patronymic style for names – Thorin son of Thráin son of Thrór King under the Mountain; Frodo son of Drogo – follows Northern styles such as Leif Erikson. These high and formal names fit in with a tradition of courtesy. The entrance of Aragorn, Legolas, Gimli, and Gandalf into King Théoden's court runs in close parallel to the entry of Beowulf and his companions into King Hrothgar's presence. Traditions of woman rulers (Éowyn's stewardship), of required service in war, and of a ruling steward are also common to Middle-earth and Northern lands.

Burial customs of Gondor and the North Sea are similar.

Denethor speaks of the funeral pyre as a barbaric custom, but the history of the kings of Norway notes that Odin instituted it. Both cultures also built barrows to shelter their dead kings. The funeral pyre of Denethor offers an ironic commentary on the pyres described in the poem *Beowulf* – one for Beowulf himself and one for Hnaef in an interpolated narrative.

Subterranean descents appear often in Northern literature and in *The Lord of the Rings*. The hobbits' encounter with the Barrow-wight early in *The Fellowship of the Ring* has many parallels to a scene in the *Saga of Grettir the Strong*. In both, the hero is warned not to go near the barrow, a long arm gropes for and seizes the hero, the hero strikes back, the hero gets out of the barrow, treasure is hauled up, and the hero goes away with a sword. Bilbo's subterranean descent into the goblin cavern may also be closely compared with Beowulf's adventures with Grendel and Grendel's mother.

The underpinning of Norse ethics was a system of *comitatus* (loyalty to friends, to lord), kinship, and revenge. The Fellowship setting out from Rivendell is not bound by a formal oath but by this unspoken commitment to the leader, to the Ringbearer, to the mission. Both Merry and Pippin enter into formal retainer relationships with King Théoden and the steward Denethor. The effect of *comitatus* is to make the bond of friendship as close as that of kinship. The code demanded revenge for the death of a friend or a kinsman. Revenge motivates many saga actions, but plays only a minor role in *The Lord of the Rings*. One example, the dwarves' long war to avenge the killing and humiliation of Thrór, has some close parallels with *Njal's Saga*. Weregild, the paying of money or a service, as an alternative to revenge is common in the sagas. In *The Lord of the Rings*, Pippin takes service with Denethor, and the horse Felaróf comes into service of Eorl of Rohan as service weregild. Thus, particularly among the men of Rohan and Gondor, customs practised in Northern countries are present.

Personalities

In *The Lord of the Rings*, eight characters (Beorn, Denethor, Boromir, Faramir, Aragorn, Théoden, Éowyn, and Galadriel) have significant sources in specific individuals or types of individuals in Northern literature. Today, I'm going to sketch antecedents for Denethor and Galadriel.

Denethor is part of a tradition of Norse heroes who prefer suicide to the shame of being unable to revenge the death of a son or a close friend. The *Eyrbyggja Saga*, the *Vatnsdale Saga*, *Egil's Saga*, and *Saga of the Jomsvikings* all have stories about an Icelander who shuts himself up to die because he cannot accomplish a revenge. The *Beowulf* poet, writing about third-century Danes, chronicles a father's grief for his dead son in a beautifully written passage. Like Hrethel in *Beowulf*, Denethor has two sons – Boromir dead, Faramir dying. This passage about Hrethel also echoes through Théoden's exchange with Saruman before Orthanc (Tolkien, 1966b, pp. 185-6).

Further, the character of Denethor also draws specifically on Njal from the *Saga of Burnt Njal*. Both are good-looking men with the gift of foresight. Each loses his favourite son. Both complain that their sons will not follow their advice any longer. Both refuse to go on without their honour while they might be saved if they chose. Both die on a blazing funeral pyre. This comparison adds dimension to the character of Denethor. The intelligent, courageous, perceptive, witty Njal is what Denethor might have been if Denethor had not come under Sauron's influence through use of the palantír.

Galadriel's tale is an unfinished one. Unlike other characters in *The Lord of the Rings*, Tolkien was still evolving her nature and her adventures. In the *Unfinished Tales*, Christopher Tolkien observes that the story of Galadriel and Celeborn has more problems than any other story of Middle-earth. He concludes that "the role and importance of Galadriel only emerged slowly, and that her story underwent continual refashionings" (Tolkien, 1980, p. 228). I believe that Tolkien had two women in Northern literature in his subconscious when he created Galadriel. Between them, they account for some of her contradictions and for the unsatisfactory nature of her story.

One of these women is Unn the Deep-minded whose adventures occur in the *Laxdale Saga*, the *Sturlunga Saga*, and the *Landnamabok*. Unn has several characteristics that Tolkien might have drawn upon as he was creating Galadriel. After Unn's son who has become ruler over half of Scotland is killed, she builds a ship in secret and escapes to Iceland with her family and her wealth. She settles land, providing for those nobles accompanying her. She is a generous woman who governs well. At the end of her life she arranges for the marriage of her favourite grandson, prepares a great feast, entertains her guests well, and retires to her bedcloset, where she dies. She is buried in a ship under a mound. Like her, Galadriel is also a paragon among women. Her name from her mother is Nerwen (man-maiden) reflecting her height and prowess as a leader. She was strong, brilliant, learned, and swift in action. Both she and Unn had intelligence and second sight. Galadriel also builds a ship and sails away. She does so without permission and thus violates a ban against departure and is forbidden to return.

Galadriel has two characteristics not shared with Unn the Deep-minded: golden hair and pride. Hallgerd, the wicked wife of Gunnar in *Njal's Saga*, has most remarkable hair: "long silken hair that fell to her waist." In *Njal's Saga*, Gunnar, who is defending himself against his enemies, asks Hallgerd for two strands of her hair to fashion a bowstring. Hallgerd wants to know if anything depends on it. Gunnar says that his life does; she reminds him of a slap he gave her and refuses. Gunnar dies overcome by many wounds. This scene must surely be an inspiration for the dwarf Gimli's request for a strand of Galadriel's hair.

Hallgerd's pride may also have contributed to the character of Galadriel. Hallgerd and Njal's wife battle over who will have the seat of honour at high table, killing several men in their feud. Galadriel's pride results in a long exile from the West. Although forgiveness is offered, she does not accept it until she believes she has earned it through her rejection of the Ring. The mixture of these two influences makes Galadriel a more interesting character. These two personalities indicate some of the ways in which both individuals and types of characters in Northern literature provided materials for Tolkien's imagination.

Themes

Tolkien's friend and colleague C.S. Lewis said, "If we insist on asking for the moral of the story, that is its moral: a recall from facile optimism and wailing pessimism alike, to that hard, yet not quite desperate, insight into Man's unchanging predicament by which heroic ages have lived. It is here that the Norse affinity is strongest: hammer-strokes but with compassion" (Lewis, 1968, p. 15). The concept of fate in Northern works, the need for courage, a conception of evil, the tragedy of mortality, the doom of the immortals, and the paradox of defeat are themes common to Northern literature and *The Lord of the Rings*.

Fate is a complex subject in literature. Beowulf finishes a speech about how he would want his famous mail-shirt disposed if Grendel were to eat him with the statement, "Fate goes ever as it must" (Crossley-Holland, 1968, p. 44). As a warrior, he believes that Fate controls events. Numerous characters from the sagas share his beliefs and his statement of them. In *The Lord of the Rings*, Gandalf expresses this concept when he notes that Bilbo was meant to find the Ring. Gandalf also declares that Gollum "is bound up with the fate of the Ring." He continues, "My heart tells me that he has some part to play yet, for good or ill, before the end; and when that comes, the pity of Bilbo may rule the fate of many – yours not least" (Tolkien, 1966a, p. 69). The rule of God, which wars with the concept of Fate in *Beowulf*, is absent from *The Lord of the Rings*. The One has intervened by sending the Istari to aid Middle-earth in this battle, but no further actions are taken. The other idea frequently expressed in *Beowulf* and in the sagas is that "Fate often saves an undoomed man when his courage is good." The warrior's personal courage may mitigate against an evil fate.

Heroic ages have lived through courage, and courage is one of the great lessons of *The Lord of the Rings*. In *Beowulf*, courage is a quality of the hero. In his battle with Grendel, Beowulf fights alone. When he dives into Grendel's mother's mere, his companions sit around the edge of the vile lake. When he faces the dragon, most desert, leaving him with only his kinsman Wiglaf. In the sagas, many more characters exhibit courageous behaviour. Njal's wife and grandson die with him; women, servants, and dogs all behave in an admirable manner. Likewise in *The Lord of the Rings*, all characters are called to courageous behaviour. Sam overcomes his multitude of fears to stay with Frodo beyond the end, Théoden is raised from despair to heroism, Éowyn and Merry stand against a Ringwraith – all are tried and find the courage to face their worst fears. Just as Elrond has composed the Fellowship to represent the free peoples of Middle-earth; so all these peoples demonstrate their worthiness to be free through their courage.

Evil in *The Lord of the Rings* is just as complex as courage is. The monsters are a great feature of the poem *Beowulf* and of the Northern eddas. A brief list shows variety: Sackville-Baggins, Old Man Willow, Mirkwood forest, Bill Ferny, the mountain Caradhras, Ringwraiths, wargs, orcs, the Balrog, Southern men, Saruman, Boromir, Shelob, and Sauron. Sauron himself is a corrupted Maia – an angelic figure who has fallen into evil.

In Northern literature, evil remains. The promise of Ragnarök or the Twilight of the Gods is the promise of one more battle, for the gods and heroes in Valhalla remain there for yet another battle with the monsters. Similarly in *The Lord of the Rings*, Gandalf warns that the Shadow will come again. In a letter, Tolkien describes the ending of the *Silmarillion*: "This legendarium ends with a vision of the end of the world, its breaking and remaking, and the recovery of the Silmarilli and the 'light before the Sun' – after a final battle which owes, I suppose, more to the Norse vision of Ragnarök than to anything else, though it is not much like it" (Tolkien, 1981, p. 149). Courage may prevail today but tomorrow evil arises again.

Because the wages of heroism is death in time, each character must in the end render up life in Middle-earth or leave Middle-earth forever. In spite of the facile report of a critic that all the good boys came home alive, by the end of the appendices all are dead or gone. What Tolkien says of Beowulf applies equally to Aragorn and others: "He is a man, and that for him and many is sufficient tragedy . . . It is the theme in its deadly seriousness that begets the dignity of tone: *lif is læne: eal scæceð leoht and lif somod* [Life is transitory: light and life together hasten away]" (Tolkien, 1937, p. 18). The tragedy of the *Laxdale Saga* and many others is that Iceland has too few men of promise to have them engaging in blood feuds with each other. When the heroes die in a saga, their small society is bereft of leadership.

The fate of the immortals is equally bleak. In Norse mythology, the old gods became more and more closely associated with humans until they were no more than larger-than-life ancestral heroes of men. Many battled against the monsters at Ragnarök and were slain. In *The Lord of the Rings*, the Elves flee from Middle-earth taking with them their high artistic, aesthetic, and scientific aspects. As the dwarf Gimli observes: "If all the fair folk take to the Havens, it will be a duller world for those who are doomed to stay" (Tolkien, 1966c, p. 150). The verb doomed summarizes the situation: the world will be less lovely, less enchanting, less exciting, yet man's fate is to remain in it.

The mortality of man and the departure of the immortals create an atmosphere of hopelessness. A variety of characters express this sentiment: "the doom of Gondor is drawing nigh," "many hopes will wither in this bitter spring," "our hope dwindles." Yet, in Tolkien's view and in the view of the saga writer, their courage is more worthy because they believe their cause is hopeless. Thus, in *Njal's Saga*, the author values Njal's sons' decision to go into the house even though he knows that the attackers will burn them there.

Lewis notes "Northern hammer-strokes but with compassion." The Northern hammer-strokes occur in the heroic battles, the instances of courage, and the death of mortals. Compassion is not common in the hard, cold world of Northern sagas and Eddas. Compassion is Tolkien's addition to the heroic form, and I believe that he primarily achieves it through the creation of hobbits. In a letter, Tolkien makes another important statement about the moral: "A moral of the whole . . . is the obvious one that without the high and noble the simple and vulgar is utterly mean; and without the simple and ordinary the noble and heroic is meaningless" (Tolkien, 1981, p. 160). Even in the historically-inspired Icelandic family sagas, the emphasis is on the actions of the high and noble. In *The Lord of the Rings*, the existence of the hobbits helps readers participate in those actions.

Conclusions

This overview reveals that Tolkien fused many elements of Northern literature together into his creation of Middle-earth and its stories. The term "influence" is perhaps a more descriptive one than "borrowing." Tolkien knew *Beowulf* and *Njal's Saga*, two works with some clear antecedents, extremely well. Throughout his life, he had filled his imagination with these and other Northern tales. More extraordinary than finding their influence in his work would have been not to find it there. Certainly, other literatures and mythologies also influenced his creation, but an analysis of all influences would probably reveal that "the greatest single influence upon Tolkien is the eddas and sagas of the North."

References

Bayerschmidt, Carl and Hollander, Lee M. (trans.). 1955. *Njal's saga* (Njál's Saga). New York: New York University Press.

Carpenter, Humphrey. 1977. *Tolkien: A biography*. Boston: Houghton Mifflin.

Craigie, W.A. 1913. *The Icelandic Sagas*. Cambridge: Cambridge University Press.

Crossley-Holland, Kevin (trans.). 1968. *Beowulf*. New York: Farrar, Straus & Giroux.

Crossley-Holland, Kevin. 1980. *The Norse Myths*. New York: Pantheon.

Gordon, E.V., ed. 1957. "Hrolfs saga Kraka" in *An Introduction to Old Norse*. Oxford: Clarendon, pp vii-x.

Green, William Howard. 1970. The Hobbit *and Other Fiction by J.R.R. Tolkien: Their Roots in Medieval Heroic Literature and Language*. (Ph.D. diss., Louisiana State University, 1970).

Lewis, C.S. "The Dethronement of Power" 1968. *Tolkien and the Critics*. Eds. Neil D. Isaacs and Rose A. Zimbardo. Notre Dame: Notre Dame University Press.

Noel, Ruth M. 1977. *The Mythology of Middle-earth* Boston: Houghton Mifflin.

Ryan, J.S. 1965. "German Mythology Applied – The Extension of the Literary Folk Memory" in *Folklore* LXXVII (1965), pp. 45-59.

St. Clair, Gloriana. 1979. "*The Lord of the Rings* as Saga," in *Mythlore* 6, no. 2 (Spring 1979), pp. 11-16.

Schlauch, Margaret. 1916. *The Romance in Iceland*. Princeton: Princeton University Press.

Tolkien, J.R.R. 1937. *Beowulf: The Monsters and the Critics*. London: British Academy.

Tolkien, J.R.R. 1964. "On Fairy-Stories" in *Tree and Leaf*. London: Unwin Books.

Tolkien, J.R.R. 1966a. *The Fellowship of the Ring*. London: George Allen & Unwin.

Tolkien, J.R.R. 1966b. *The Two Towers*. London: George Allen & Unwin.

Tolkien, J.R.R. 1966c. *The Return of the King*. London: George Allen & Unwin.

Tolkien, J.R.R. 1980. *Unfinished Tales*. London: George Allen & Unwin.

Tolkien, J.R.R. 1981. *The Letters of J.R.R. Tolkien* ed. Humphrey Carpenter. Boston: Houghton Mifflin Company.

Volsunga Saga and Narn: Some Analogies

Gloriana St. Clair

Abstract: "Narn", one of the works in the *Unfinished Tales*, has many parallels with the thirteenth-century Old Norse *Volsunga Saga*, which Tolkien read and studied. This paper will assess comparisons between the heroes, women, dragons, plots, and tokens for their contribution to understanding Tolkien's relationship to his sources, and will note Tolkien's craft in source-assimilation.

Keywords: Aerin, *Beowulf*, completeness, dragons, dwarves, Fafnir, girdles, Glaurung, helms, mythology, "Narn", Sigfried, Sigurd, swords, Tolkien: influences upon, Túrin, *Volsunga Saga*, Richard Wagner

In a letter to Milton Waldman, a potential publisher of a combined *Silmarillion* and *The Lord of the Rings*, Tolkien says, "There is the *Children of Húrin*, the tragic tale of Túrin Turambar and his sister Níniel – of which Túrin is the hero: a figure that might be said (by people who like that sort of thing, though it is not very useful) to be derived from elements in Sigurd the Volsung, Oedipus and the Finnish Kullervo [*Kalevala*]" (Tolkien, 1981, p. 150). This paper discusses the relationship between the "Narn i Hîn Húrin" and the *Volsunga Saga*, the story of Sigurd the Volsung. My thesis is that the "Narn", an Unfinished Work, shows less polish and craft than *The Lord of the Rings*, revealing its debts to the originating work more clearly. Tolkien pulled his works out of the cauldron of his imagination. This study investigates what was in that cauldron and how it was served up in this tale. While Tolkien did not find such studies particularly useful, I believe this one does offer a glimpse into his relationship with his materials and his craft. First, I'm going to outline the versions for the two stories, then discuss the characters, survey some similar tokens, note some peculiar unfinished aspects, and draw some conclusions.

Versions of the Stories

Tolkien's story about the Children of Húrin exists in several versions: "The Lay of the Children of Húrin" is an alliterative poem written in 1918 and existing in two separate manuscripts, combined by Christopher Tolkien and published in *The Lays of Beleriand* (Tolkien, 1985, pp. 3-130). "Turambar and the Foalókë" is a prose version of the story apparently written by the middle of 1919 while Tolkien was working on the *Oxford English Dictionary* (Tolkien, 1984, pp. 69-143). The dating is derived from Humphrey Carpenter's discovery of a passage written on a scrap of proof for the Dictionary in one of Tolkien's early alphabets (Tolkien, 1984, p. 69). Another version of the tale appears as "Of Túrin Turambar" in *The Silmarillion*. "Narn i Hîn Húrin" in *Unfinished Tales* provides the most comprehensive telling of the story.

"Sigurd the Volsung" has a number of versions – four may be important here: the *Eddas*, the *Volsunga Saga*, *Beowulf*, and the *Nibelungenlied*. The *Poetic Edda* (800-1050 AD) is the oldest repository of poems telling the Northern Myths. *The Prose Edda*, written by Snorri Sturluson in the thirteenth-century, tells these stories more fully from an educated point of view. Snorri also wrote the history of the kings of Norway and several sagas. Written by an unknown Icelandic author in the thirteenth-century, the *Volsunga Saga* recreates in prose the stories from the poetic *Elder Edda* in order to glorify the heroic past of the Norse people in their golden age on the Rhine (*Volsunga Saga*, 1971, p. 18). The *Volsunga* author makes heavy use of his copy of the *Elder Edda* in the same way that Tolkien handily employed the materials he had written already about Middle-earth. Tolkien's interest in creating a mythology for England paralleled the *Volsunga Saga* author's purpose.

The eighth-century Old English poem *Beowulf* uses material from the *Volsunga* legend as one of seven interpolated narratives. However, the *Volsunga Saga* lacks the craft that makes *Beowulf* notable. *Volsunga*'s author does not bring to his task the level of genius in the moulding of scenes, the construction of story, the portraying of details, or the creation of character that the *Beowulf* poet does. The *Volsunga Saga* does not catch and hold our interest or suspend our disbelief with the power of the most exalted pieces of literature.

Written at about the same time as the *Volsunga Saga*, the *Nibelungenlied* is a long German poem composed in a complicated rhymed strophe. The poem was apparently designed to be performed by a bard in a princely court. The medieval manuscript had been forgotten until it was rediscovered in the eighteenth-century, in the same way that the *Kalevala* and the *Elder Edda* were (*The Nibelungenlied*, 1961, pp. xi-xiii).

The contrast between the German poem and the Norse saga is stark. Like *The Lord of the Rings*, the *Volsunga Saga* is filled with action while *The Nibelungenlied* dwells at length on descriptions of costumes, arms, and feasts. So pronounced is the interest in clothing that the reader might imagine the author to be a cloth merchant's wife. The hardihood, individual strength, and fearlessness of the *Volsunga Saga* are replaced with courtliness, vast armies, and treacheries. The earlier tales of the Volsunga kin, the revenge for King Volsung, and the winning of the gold are foregone in favour of expanded telling of the revenge for Sigfried (Sigurd). The love story, which provides an uncomfortable motivation in the *Volsunga Saga*, is refined and magnified in *Nibelungenlied*.

Because Wagner's Ring cycle was being used by the Nazis for propaganda, Tolkien makes a number of disparaging remarks about it in the *Letters*. Wagner made active use of the same sources Tolkien did. Elizabeth Magee, in *Richard Wagner and the Nibelungs*, notes that Wagner based the first version, "Der Nibelungen-Mythus," on the *Eddas*, *Nibelungenlied*, *Thidreks Saga*, and *Das Lied vom Hürnen Seyfrid*. In 1848, Wagner had not yet read the *Volsunga Saga* itself and knew it only through other works derived from it, such as the *Amelungenlied* and Wilhelm Grimm's *Deutsche Heldensage*. Between 21 October 1848 and 1 January 1849, Wagner borrowed von der Hagen's translation of *Volsunga Saga* from the Royal Library at Dresden. His particular debts to it include Siegfried's ancestors, history of the sword, the conception of Odin the Wanderer, much material in the second version of *Die Walküre*, and the wolf motif. Much other Volsung material came through Fouqué's dramatic poem "Sigurd der Schlangentödter" (Magee, 1990, pp. 67, 124, 154, 160, and 214). Tolkien may have known Wagner's *Ring* but he did know Wagner's primary sources and perhaps also his German works based on Nibelung matter. Wagner's interpretation of all these materials does not seem to have specifically influenced the "Narn".

Characters

Several characters in the "Narn" seem to have antecedents in the *Volsunga* materials. I'm going to discuss the heroes (Túrin and Sigurd), Sigurd's mother Signy and Túrin's aunt Aerin, the dragons Glaurung and Fafnir, and the dwarves. In both plots, a sister and brother are involved (Sigmund and Signy; Túrin and Nienor); a highborn maiden (Brynhild is a Valkyrie daughter of Odin; Finduilas, an elf) loves a mortal hero; a compromise solution (Brynhild's marriage to Gunnar; Nienor's possible marriage to Brandir) fails because the hero demonstrates hubris.

Túrin and Sigurd: The heroes of these tales are not very admirable; it is fairly difficult for the reader to care whether they triumph or not. Neither of them has ever earned my sighs or tears. Túrin is prideful and stiff-necked. He rushes from justice even though he is innocent of the murder of Saeros. He refuses to return to King Thingol's court even though a great deal has been sacrificed to bring him news of his pardon. He ignores his commitment to Finduilas and Gwindor even though he has been warned of negative consequences. Repeatedly, he attempts to start over by putting everything behind him and taking a new name. Successively, he calls himself Túrin, Neithan, Agarwaen, Thurin, Mormegil, Wildman of the Woods, and Turambar. Had he acknowledged his unlucky fate and attempted to cope with it, he would not have brought so much woe to so many. As in the sagas, where character development is sketchy, Túrin's character is described when he is a child; he never grows beyond it. Several times Tolkien mentions his fatal pride and that of his mother, who would not humble herself to be an alms-guest even of the King. In pronouncing judgment in the death of Saeros, King Thingol says that Túrin is too proud for his state (Tolkien, 1980, p. 83). Pride as a motivating force has one of its greatest expressions in the Greek play *Oedipus*, which Tolkien acknowledges as an inspiration for this work (Tolkien, 1981, p. 150). However, Oedipus is an appealing character while Túrin is not.

These same criticisms can be levelled at the *Volsunga Saga*. Sigurd is equally unwilling to face up to his problems. He remembers finally that he had plighted troth to Brynhild, but instead of making some provisions for the eventual unmasking of that secret, he goes ahead with his regimen of hunting and combat. His pride leads him to give that same troth ring Brynhild had had to his wife Gudrun. When he knows that Brynhild has discovered that he disguised himself as Gunnar, he merely suggests that Gudrun not taunt her about it. Thus, Sigurd dies at the hands of his brother-in-law Gutthorm, but not before the hero can cast his sword Gram into his slayer[1] (*Volsunga Saga*, 1971, p. 189). Like Túrin, Brynhild kills herself with her own sword and is laid on Sigurd's funeral pyre with him.

It is clear that Túrin is an apprenticeship character for Tolkien. Motivations in the work are diverse: the curse on the family of Húrin; the curse on the sword; the evil of Morgoth and his creatures Glaurung and the orcs. These externals and Túrin's own pride provide some complexity of motivation in the story. In the "Turambar and the Foalókë" version Melko (Morgoth) tells Túrin's father that his son's career will bring both Elves and Men to grief as a punishment for Húrin's steadfastness against evil. Tolkien apparently abandoned this statement of motivation in order to balance fate with pride (Tolkien, 1984, p. 71). Túrin is consistently unwilling to face up to his fate and to turn and fight against it. He gets into a bad situation, makes a mistake like chasing Saeros to the brink of a cliff, and is too proud to explain the circumstances of his actions.

Aerin and Signy: The theme of a woman with divided loyalty is a recurring one in Northern literature, and it does provide an interesting and dramatic situation, which is only incidental in the "Narn". The characters of Lady Aerin in the "Narn" and of Signy, Sigmund's sister and Sigurd's aunt in the *Volsunga Saga*, provide another parallel between the

---

[1] After Gunnar eggs Gutthorm on to kill Sigurd, the dead hero, his three-year-old son, and his killer Gutthorm are laid upon a blazing pyre. In a missed dramatic moment, the author narrates: "thereto was Brynhild borne out, when she had spoken with her bower-maidens, and bid them take the gold that she would give; and then died Brynhild, and was burned there by the side of Sigurd, and thus their life days ended" (*Volsunga Saga*, 1971, p. 201). Compared with the death of Denethor, this scene lacks narrative building, descriptive adornment, and dramatic power.

tales. Although Túrin urges Aerin to accompany him as he goes in search of his mother and sister, she refuses in characteristic Norse fashion. She chooses the fate of burning in the house with her husband as Signy does in the saga. In *Volsunga Saga*, after Sigmund her brother and Sinfjotli her son begin to burn her husband's hall, they beg Signy to come out. She reminds them of her sacrifices to bring about the revenge on her husband for having killed her father and her brothers. She has killed her weakling sons, made herself into a witch woman to seduce her brother, and thus bred a son worthy to be Sigmund's partner in revenge. But she is loyal to her husband, too, and chooses not to live long after his death but to die in the burning house with him. In the "Narn", Túrin looks back in his flight from his old home, sees the hall ablaze, and learns from his companions that Lady Aerin has courageously burned herself in the house with her husband. The companion makes this epitaph for Aerin: "She did much good among us at much cost. Her heart was not faint, and patience will break at the last" (Tolkien, 1980, p. 109). Aerin shares her nobility and the dual call on her loyalties with Signy.

Dwarves: The dwarf Mîm from the "Narn" story is the most caricatured of Tolkien's dwarves. The incident could be lifted out of the tale and inserted into a Norse saga without the reader's adverse notice. In the "Narn", the dwarf Mîm is particularly stiff-necked; caught by Túrin's outlaw bands, he wishes to go home but refuses to leave his sack as surety. The outlaws have killed Mîm's son, for whom weregild is offered and accepted. Mîm curses the killer and is cursed in return.

Mîm's reluctance to leave his sack recalls the dwarf Andvari who is connected with the treasure in the *Volsunga Saga*. In the story, Hreidmar has three sons – Regin, Otter, and Fafnir. Regin tells Sigurd that his brother shifted into the shape of an otter. While the otter was eating fish from the river near the dwarf Andvari's gold, the god Loki, in company with Odin and Honir, kills Otter with a stone. The gods carry off the otter skin to Hreidmar's house, where Hreidmar recognizes his son's skin and demands weregild for his death. Loki returns to the river, casts a net, and catches the dwarf Andvari in the shape of a pike. Loki requires a ransom – the entirety of the dwarf's great golden treasure. When Loki demands a final gold ring as part of the ransom, the saga-writer says, "then the dwarf went into a hollow of the rocks and cried out, that the gold-ring, yea and all the gold withal should be the bane of every man who should own it thereafter" (*Volsunga Saga*, 1971, p. 130). When the gold is spread over the otter's hide, Hreidmar notices that one whisker is uncovered. Odin draws the ring Andvari's Loom from his finger and covers the whisker. Tolkien found this detail of the story fascinating and mentions it twice in his 1962 letters about the publication of *The Adventures of Tom Bombadil*. In the poem "Bombadil goes Boating", a reference, "Your mother if she saw you, / she'd never know her son, unless 'twas by a whisker," involves identification by a whisker. In a letter, Tolkien says, "I am afraid it [a second poem about Tom Bombadil] largely tickles my pedantic fancy, because of its echo of the Norse Niblung matter (the otter's whisker)" (Tolkien, 1981, p. 315), and "the otter's whisker sticking out of the gold, from the Norse Nibelung legends" (Tolkien, 1981, p. 319). That Tolkien makes no use of this favourite detail – the whisker itself – in the "Narn" is typical of his relationship with his material. His pattern of borrowing was unpredictable and elements borrowed were changed to meet his own purposes.

Dragons: Each of these sets of stories also employs a dragon. In *Volsunga Saga*, Fafnir, the brother of the smith Regin, has become a dragon because he has brooded too long over the gold treasure the gods paid as weregild for the wrongful death of Otter. In the "Narn", the dragon's genesis is less interesting; he is the first of the fire-drakes of Morgoth (Tolkien, 1977, p. 116). Fafnir warns Sigurd that the treasure will be his downfall, but Sigurd replies that he would lose all his wealth if that meant he would never die, but all men must die (*Volsunga Saga*, 1971, p. 147). The dragon Glaurung's power to put humans into trances reduces their retorts to his conversations. Tolkien uses this device several times in the "Narn". Túrin is in a trance while the dragon redirects his energies from the rescue of Finduilas to a vain solicitude for his mother's safety. Glaurung then creates the mist that Morwen disappears into; at the same time casting a spell of forgetfulness on Nienor. Fafnir also reminds Sigurd that many times each will be the other's bane. While Sigurd escapes Fafnir himself, the ring is his undoing and that of many others. Glaurung plays with Túrin in a like manner.

The plans for the dragon's demise are similar in the "Narn" and the *Volsunga Saga*. In the saga, Regin has suggested that Sigurd should dig a pit and stab the dragon in his soft underbelly as he passes over. Regin plans for Sigurd to kill the dragon whose venomous blood will at the same time destroy Sigurd, leaving the treasure for Regin's use. Fortunately, Odin in the disguise of an old man advises Sigurd to dig several connected pits and thus escape drowning in dragon blood (*Volsunga Saga*, 1971, pp. 141-142). Túrin chooses a narrow ravine for his attack upon the dragon. As Glaurung crosses the perilous river, Túrin can shove his sword into the dragon's soft underside. This approach from the underside also occurs in *Beowulf*. With traditional understatement, the *Beowulf*-poet describes Wiglaf's stroke as "a little lower down." Then Beowulf and Wiglaf cut the worm in half. In the *Volsunga Saga*, Sigurd thrusts under the left shoulder (*Volsunga Saga*, 1971, p. 142). Further, the heroes have boasted to kill the dragon or die. Túrin says: "The die is cast. Now comes the test, in which my boast shall be made good, or fail utterly. I will flee no more. Turambar indeed I will be, and by my own will and prowess I will surmount my doom – or fall. But falling or riding, Glaurung at least I will slay" (Tolkien, 1980, p. 126). Beowulf's speech is much more eloquent.

In addition, Tolkien turned to the *Beowulf* poet to treat the fate of the coward in a dragon encounter. In the "Narn", Brandir kills the cowardly Dorlas who has feared to bring news that would have saved Nienor's life. In *Beowulf*, ten companions who fear to meet the dragon are ostracized. Later in *The Lord of the Rings*, Tolkien will have Aragorn set the fearful to less daunting tasks – a more compassionate alternative to cowardice.

Glaurung is much more anthropomorphic than *Beowulf*'s dragon or even Fafnir, who is, of course, a man whose greed has turned him into a dragon. Glaurung's commanding ability to collect orcs to him and to direct them in battle makes the dragon seem more a part of an organized pattern of evil. In *The Hobbit*, Smaug is an entrepreneur for evil; he is independent from the evils of Sauron. Smaug is content in guarding his treasure hoard and has not been regularly ravaging the countryside until Bilbo steals his cup. While Glaurung is more clearly tied into the evils emanating from Morgoth, Smaug operates more like the Balrog and Shelob, who are entirely or mainly independent from Sauron. In a letter to Naomi Mitchison, who had written in praise of *Farmer Giles of Ham*, Tolkien acknowledges the relationships among the dragons of Northern literature: "I find 'dragons' a fascinating product of imagination. But I don't think the *Beowulf* one is frightfully good. But the whole problem of the intrusion of the 'dragon' into northern imagination and its transformation there is one I do not know enough about. Fáfnir in the late Norse versions of the Sigurd-story is better; and Smaug and his conversation obviously is in debt there" (Tolkien, 1981, p. 134). Glaurung seems to have been a good start for Tolkien's quest for a greater dragon. Glaurung carries on better conversations than Fafnir but his range of emotions is limited. Glaurung's persecution of the Children of Húrin derives from his kinship with the evil being Morgoth, who despises Húrin's courage in the face of his overwhelming evil power. Glaurung's powers are limited to casting spells on Húrin's children, making Túrin's natural hubris more effective, and threatening to kill them outright. The urbanity and emotional range of the worldly but wicked Smaug are yet to be realized.

Tokens

Generally, the argument can be made that the tokens are medieval in nature rather than peculiarly Northern or particularly from the *Volsunga Saga*. However, a number of the more important devices do have recognizable and important antecedents in the story of the Volsungs. I'll mention three: the Helm, the embroidered girdle, and the broken sword. The troublesome ring from *Volsunga* has its impact on *The Lord of the Rings*.

The idea for the Helm of Hador may have come from the Helm of Awe, which Sigurd wins from the dragon in the *Volsunga Saga*. No particular use is made of this token in that story, but a dragon-helm and its attendant invisibility do play a significant role in Wagner's Ring. Tolkien apparently liked the idea and began to play with it in the "Narn". The image on the dragon-helm is to be that of Glaurung, who was supposed to taunt Túrin about the mastery implied by wearing the helmet. Túrin's reply points out that the helmet represented scorn rather than allegiance to the dragon. As the story exists in *The Silmarillion* and the *Unfinished Tales*, Túrin receives the helm from King Thingol, wears it in battles until the orcs capture him, and does not use it again.

Christopher Tolkien conjectures from remaining notes that Tolkien intended for the helm to reappear during Túrin's adventures. Túrin would not wear the Helm, then, "lest it reveal him," but he was to wear it in confrontation with Glaurung. While the Helm serves to protect Túrin from the dragon's deadly gaze, the worm's taunting has its effect: "But being thus taunted, in pride and rashness he [Túrin] thrust up the visor and looked Glaurung in the eye" (Tolkien, 1980, p. 155). The Helm was also to figure in the denouement with Glaurung when Túrin would reverse the dragon's words about mastery.

The concept of a peaceful zone created by the power of an elven queen is well-defined in *The Lord of the Rings*. There, Galadriel has created the beautiful realm of Lórien by the power of her ring; however, she warns that when the One Ring is destroyed, Lórien will also fail. In the "Narn", Tolkien tries, not very successfully, to arrange some dramatic tension from concepts of entering and exiting from this zone. Túrin and Morwen both complain to King Thingol that they were reluctant to enter into the Girdle of Melian because they did not want to have to remain there forever. Queen Melian explains twice that the Girdle is open and the relatives of Húrin may leave or stay at their will. While some intimations of this concept also appear in *The Lord of the Rings*, Tolkien does not elaborate on it. The idea of calling this zone the Girdle may have been suggested by Brynhild's embroidered girdle in the *Nibelungenlied*. However, the more famous girdle in works that Tolkien knew well is the green girdle in *Sir Gawain and the Green Knight*. There, the hero Gawain is given the girdle to protect him against an axe blow from a green giant (Tolkien and Gordon, 1967). The idea of protection is clearer from the *Sir Gawain* story than from the *Nibelungenlied*.

The unlucky sword used in the killing is a key implement in the "Narn". Beleg has received the sword as a gift from King Thingol for his delivery of the King's pardon to Túrin. Beleg, who wants a sword of worth against increasing orc attacks, chooses the sword Anglachel, which was made by the smith Eöl the Dark Elf. The sword has been given unwillingly as bride-payment for the elf's wife. Eöl's counterpart may be Regin, the smith-tutor whose machinations set in motion the multiple curses and adventures in the *Volsunga Saga*. As Thingol starts to give the sword to Beleg, Queen Melian remarks that the sword still has the malice of its smith's dark heart in it (Tolkien, 1977, p. 202). After Beleg is buried, they notice that the blade of the sword has turned black, dull, and blunt, as if it mourns for Beleg. Just as the broken sword Gram is reforged for Sigurd's use in the *Volsunga Saga*, this sword takes on a new identity: "The sword Anglachel was forged anew for him by cunning smiths of Nargothrond, and though ever black its edges shone with pale fire; and he [Túrin] named it Gurthang, Iron of Death" (Tolkien, 1977, p. 210). The sword partakes of the characteristics of heroic-literature swords which cannot be sheathed without first drinking blood.

At the end of his tale, Túrin realizes that he has hated Brandir, who loved Túrin's sister-wife Nienor, unjustly. Túrin addresses the sword and asks if it will slay him swiftly.

The sword replies: "Yea, I will drink thy blood gladly, that so I may forget the blood of Beleg my master, and the blood of Brandir slain unjustly. I will slay thee swiftly" (Tolkien, 1977, p. 225). The evil, perceived in the sword by good Queen Melian, has indeed played a pervasive role in the tales of the Children of Húrin. Although the dragon has perished from the sword, many others have also been lost: Mîm, Beleg, and Brandir were slain by the sword; Nienor and Finduilas have died because Túrin was involved in matters relating to the sword; and Túrin himself dies on its dark edge. Fortunately, talking swords are not common in Northern literature, and, again fortunately, Tolkien did not repeat this transparent, didactic device.

Unfinished Aspects

What is particularly worthy of critical attention about the "Narn" is its unfinished aspects. In incident after incident, details are unresolved and left dangling. One of the greatest joys of *The Lord of the Rings* is its completeness. Questions are answered, fates are revealed, pieces are pulled together. I believe that Tolkien's repeated inspired revisions of *The Lord of the Rings* gave that work cohesion. I wish he had had the opportunity to do the same for this work because the potential for another great masterpiece lies within it.

Here are some of the pieces that he could have pulled together:

- The knife given as a gift to the boy Túrin could have played a significant role when Túrin returned to his home.
- Mîm's curse doesn't get fully carried out.
- Túrin's proclivity for falling into trances is difficult to understand and justify as a plot device. His trancelike state recalls Brynhild's sleep on the magic mountain, but her trance is a punishment for disobedience to Odin.
- Túrin's character flaw is not well enough defined. He suffers from hubris but also from a kind of unbecoming fecklessness, which is not quite of tragic quality. All of this is equally true of Sigurd.
- Fate and character as the operators in the story are not so well handled as in *The Lord of the Rings*, in *Oedipus*, or in *Beowulf*.
- Brandir's lameness serves no plot purpose and duplicates Sador's lameness. Neither seems to provide a significant insight into character.
- The incest theme seems underused; its plot significance in the *Volsunga Saga* is much more compelling.

Conclusions

Comparisons between the stories of Sigurd the Volsung and that of Túrin son of Húrin do seem to have some value. Seeing characters and tokens in their original settings shows the basic materials that went into Tolkien's cauldron of story. Little went through that cauldron unchanged. At every opportunity, Tolkien's own imagination and creativity moulded, shaped, and sculpted elements from earlier stories to fit the needs of his own tales. In the instance of an early and never-finished work, such as the "Narn", the pieces borrowed are much more recognizable than those found in the later, polished master work, *The Lord of the Rings*. In a comparison of the "Narn" with Sigurd the Volsung, the reader has an unusual opportunity to observe the process of Tolkien's creativity. And people who like that sort of thing can see the elements of Sigurd the Volsung.

References

Magee, Elizabeth. 1990. *Richard Wagner and the Nibelungs*. Oxford: Clarendon Press.

The Nibelungenlied. 1961. Trans. Margaret Armour. New York: Heritage Press.

Tolkien, J.R.R. 1977. *The Silmarillion*, ed. Christopher Tolkien. Boston: Houghton Mifflin.

Tolkien, J.R.R. 1980. *Unfinished Tales*, ed. Christopher Tolkien. London: George Allen & Unwin.

Tolkien, J.R.R. 1981. *The Letters of J.R.R. Tolkien*, ed. Humphrey Carpenter. Boston: Houghton Mifflin.

Tolkien, J.R.R. 1985. *The Lays of Beleriand*, ed. Christopher Tolkien. Boston: Houghton Mifflin.

Tolkien, J.R.R. 1984. *The Book of Lost Tales*, part II, ed. Christopher Tolkien. Boston: Houghton Mifflin.

Tolkien, J.R.R. and Gordon, E.V. (eds.). 1967. *Sir Gawain and the Green Knight*, second edition, ed. Norman Davis. Oxford: Clarendon.

Volsunga Saga: The Story of the Volsungs and Niblungs. 1971. Trans. William Morris. New York: Collier Books.

Tolkien's Revision of the Romantic Tradition

Chris Seeman

Abstract: This paper explores Tolkien's vision of fantasy within the broader historical context of Romanticism, clarifying the ways in which he inherits and revises Romantic views of the creative imagination via the concept of "sub-creation". Possible links with Coleridge's thought are considered, especially with respect to the uses of Romanticism in the context of Christianity.

Keywords: Owen Barfield, Samuel Taylor Coleridge, creative imagination, fantasy, imagination, Romantic thought

Introduction

In the continuing debate over the genre of Tolkien's writings, the appreciation of his life and work as a whole, and his relationship to the other Inklings, the term "Romanticism" has enjoyed some currency. In characterizing Tolkien in this way, recourse has often been made to the now well-trodden essay "On Fairy-Stories". The invocation of such concepts as *sub-creation*, *secondary belief*, and *eucatastrophe* have inevitably led to comparisons of Tolkien's views on artistic creation with the traditional conventions of Romantic thought; in particular, with those of Samuel Taylor Coleridge. But while a handful of commentators have explored these connections in some depth, as yet no one (to my knowledge) has advanced a clear or convincing analysis of Tolkien's place within the Romantic tradition. No one, for example, has addressed in a straightforward manner the question of whether Tolkien has made any significant contribution to Romantic thought, or if his views are merely idiosyncratic. Many have carefully taken note of Tolkien's apparent disagreements with Coleridge, but few (it seems) have given much thought to what those discrepancies might mean as part of a larger picture.

My purpose here is to explore the use of Romanticism as a way of characterizing Tolkien's self-understanding in the context of Romanticism. Specifically, I want to examine more closely his relationship to Coleridge's views in order to clarify what makes Tolkien's understanding of fantasy distinctive within the tradition of Romantic thought. Central to my evaluation is the conclusion that sub-creation (surely Tolkien's most celebrated expression) is *not*, in fact, the most crucial facet of his theory of the fairy story. Instead, what emerges as the most distinctive feature of his aesthetic is the *restriction* of sub-creation to the narrative mode, and the exclusion of the visual as a vehicle of authentic fantasy. My argument, simply put, is that Tolkien's seemingly minor disputes with Coleridge in reality form the necessary basis for his claim that drama – and indeed all visual modes of art – are essentially hostile to fantasy (Tolkien, 1989a, pp. 47-48).

The absoluteness of Tolkien's position demands explanation – not only in its own right but because, unlike the concept of sub-creation itself (which enjoys a central place in Romantic thought), its restriction to narrative stands out as an anomaly[1]. I offer that Tolkien is being neither facetious nor idiosyncratic in his rejection of these artistic modes. Accordingly, the logic of this rejection is to be deduced from the differing concerns which narrative and the visual signify for him. To summarize briefly my argument, Tolkien revises the Romantic tradition by asserting the validity of fantasy as a distinct mode of art. He differentiates fantasy from other art forms by restricting it to narrative, thereby highlighting its non-visual or non-representational character. For Tolkien, non-visual art implies:

1) a particular relationship between the artist and the hearer, which demands an active use of the imagination from the latter,

2) an ambivalence within the human desire to realize fantasy in the primary world, hindered by the Fall but anticipating the *evangelium*, and

3) the ongoing role of humanity as sub-creator, embodied in the continual recovery of authentic vision through fantasy.

Ultimately, this will lead us beyond the Romantic tradition to Tolkien's deeply-held religious convictions. In the last analysis, it is the contours of Tolkien's theology which account for the shape of his Romanticism. None of this should be surprising to anyone acquainted with Tolkien's writings, but for the most part this understanding has been applied only to the more obvious aspects of "On Fairy-

---

[1] Since its beginnings in the eighteenth-century, Romanticism has freely included both the dramatic and the visual within its aesthetic canon. For examples of this, see Engell, 1981.

Stories"; and since these suggest continuity with the tenets of Romantic thought, they tend to neglect this crucial revision.

Tolkien, Coleridge, and the Romantic Tradition

Attempts to identify possible Romantic links to Tolkien's thought have focused either upon the essay or upon his relationships with the other Inklings; in particular, with Owen Barfield. This latter possibility has most recently been advocated by Gareth Knight, whose introduction to the writings of the Inklings posits Barfield as a common denominator connecting the work of Tolkien, Lewis and Williams to a more or less explicit Coleridgian hermeneutic:

> It is in the psychological and philosophical thought of Coleridge, on the subject of the imagination, that the secret of the power of the creative work of the other Inklings is to be found . . . This was less a conscious following after Coleridge than a deliberate choice to cultivate the "mythopoeic" in their writing . . . Their common purpose had its roots in a unity of spiritual intention or compatibility . . . Barfield, through his intellectual influence, both orally and as expressed in *Poetic Diction* provided an intellectual stimulus to much of this.
> (Knight, 1990, pp. 10, 11, 13-14)

In his analysis of the nature and extent of the Inklings' association, Humphrey Carpenter has made reference to *Poetic Diction* as expressive of Barfield's views on language, and confirms that Tolkien had indeed read and approved of the book (Carpenter, 1979, p. 42). Carpenter is quick to remind us, however, of the major differences in Tolkien and Barfield's religious outlooks and how those differences do have a significant impact on their respective understandings of myth (Carpenter, 1979, pp. 153-157). The mere fact of Barfield's discipleship to Coleridge may, therefore, not be sufficient warrant for Knight's view of Barfield as the principal mediator of the Romantic tradition to Tolkien. As an heuristic convenience, Coleridge's thought may be a useful lens for highlighting and accounting for some of the commonalities of the Inklings as a group; but his views can neither explain – nor explain away – the differences in the self-understandings of Tolkien, Lewis, Williams, and Barfield. Nor does the invocation of Coleridge alone provide an adequate framework for assessing the relative significance of those differences.[2]

There are no explicit references to Coleridge by name in "On Fairy-Stories".[3] Commentators on the essay have pointed out at least two passages where they believe Tolkien to have been consciously engaging Coleridge's views:
1) Tolkien's objection to the phrase "willing suspension of disbelief"[4] as an accurate description of the subjectivity induced by an effective narrative (Tolkien, 1989a, p. 36), and
2) Tolkien's redefinition of "fantasy" in relation to what he calls the technical use of the term "imagination" (Tolkien, 1989a, pp. 44ff). What follows is a brief survey of the remarks and observations which have been made on these possible connections to Coleridge's thought.

Considering Tolkien's substitution of his own expression "secondary belief" (Tolkien, 1989a, p. 37) for Coleridge's willing suspension of disbelief, Randel Helms (1974, pp. 11, 77-78), Frank Bergmann (1977, p. 13), and Henry Parks (1981, p. 142) argue that Tolkien is here strengthening Coleridge's words by giving them an affirmative rather than a negative sense, or by shifting attention from the passive acceptance of the reader to the active role of the author. Ann Swinfen concurs with this view (Swinfen, 1984, p. 7), but suggests that it points to a much deeper philosophical gap between the two writers:

> Coleridge evolved his theory of imagination in reaction to the associationist theories of Locke and Hartley, but despite his reading of neo-Platonists like Cudworth or such earlier writers as Plotinus and Proclus, he never fully subscribed to the Platonic view that the primary world is a world of shadows cast by ideal realities. Tolkien can be seen as essentially a Christian Neo-Platonist . . . while Tolkien probably took the term "secondary" from Coleridge, Tolkien's sub-creative art which creates secondary worlds is also capable of affording glimpses of joy and eternal truth. Coleridge did not feel that imagination could grasp truths which were beyond the scope of reason, although he believed that religious faith might do so.
> (Swinfen, 1984, pp. 8-9)

A dissenting voice to the view that more than mere terminology is at stake is that of Jan Wojcik, who downplays the significance of this semantic distinction in order to affirm that Tolkien and Coleridge are in basic agreement as to "the functioning of the imagination in art, the nature of the artistic product, and the motives behind creation" (Wojcik, 1968, p. 134).

Regardless of how one views this matter, it is important to note that (subsidiary to his main thesis) Wojcik commits a significant error in his reading of Tolkien. In his framing of the issue of secondary belief and the willing suspension of disbelief, Wojcik claims that Tolkien "labors over words rather than meaning" (Wojcik, 1968, p. 137); for, he reasons, if these two expressions were to be taken literally, it would imply that Tolkien was arguing "as if there were an ontological difference in the kind of art inducing each state" (Wojcik, 1968, p. 136). Wojcik is absolutely correct in his reasoning on this point; what seems to escape him is the fact that this is exactly what Tolkien is arguing.

---

[2] This difficulty is compounded by Knight's own conflicting motivations for invoking Coleridge. On the one hand, he wants simply to highlight the similarities of the Inklings from a particular angle; on the other hand, he sees their differences as divisive to his attempt to "rescue" them from the appropriation of their writings in the cause of religious "orthodoxy". Knight's usage of Coleridge's ideas thus serves as a normative (rather than a merely heuristic) counter-framework of interpretation.
[3] By contrast, Tolkien does make explicit reference to George MacDonald and to G.K. Chesterton. For a useful analysis of the similarities between Tolkien's and MacDonald's views of fairy story, see Bergmann's 1977 article.
[4] Used by Coleridge in Chapter XIV of the *Biographia Literaria*, 1907.

My own view is that Tolkien's decision to take issue with Coleridge's expression is both conscious and intentional. Tolkien, it must be remembered, is speaking not of artistic creation in general but of a particular mode of art as distinct from others. Hence, Tolkien is not seeking to replace Coleridge's critical vocabulary as generally applicable to certain kinds of aesthetic experience; rather, he is asserting that there is a radical difference between the fairy story mode and all others. For so complete a distinction as Tolkien is attempting, a precise and substantive difference in terminology is called for.

Both secondary belief and the willing suspension of disbelief concern the reception of art; this, however, is ancillary to Tolkien's and Coleridge's differences regarding the nature and purpose of artistic creation itself. It is here that the true extent of Tolkien's revision of Romantic thought becomes apparent. In the essay, Tolkien identifies the fairy story mode with the term "fantasy" (Tolkien, 1989a, p. 45). This he does in reaction to what he characterizes as a misapplication of the meaning − "in technical not normal language" (Tolkien, 1989a, p. 44) − of the term "imagination". Tolkien is here striking for the very heart of the Romantic tradition − that is to say, the role and status of the creative imagination. But while the terms "fancy" − which Tolkien views as "a reduced and depreciatory form of the older word Fantasy" (Tolkien, 1989a, p. 45) − and "imagination" play a central role in Coleridge's aesthetic thought, he did not invent them; nor is Tolkien, for that matter, justified in asserting their distinction to be one of "technical use" only:

> Coleridge's famous distinction between "fancy" and "imagination" used to be thought either to have originated with him or to have had an obscure German source. But actually a growing distinction between the terms took place in English usage throughout the eighteenth century, and in much the same direction in which Coleridge developed or ramified it.
> (Engell, 1981, p. 172)

Before reviewing the commentators on Tolkien's usage of these two terms, therefore, some background is needed to appreciate fully the weight of associations bound up with this pair. The term "imagination"

> had not, by 1700, become connotative in a broad sense. It meant a fairly limited power connected, in the main, with the simple formation of images . . . By the 1720s and 1730s the imagination begins to acquire a distinctly positive character. It becomes the power not only to invent images but also to animate and excite, providing what Dryden called the "life-touches" and "secret graces" of art . . . it acquired a moral, aesthetic, and even religious value that was almost exclusively positive . . . As the idea evolved . . . it became a vital principle for an expanding network of concepts and values. The understanding of genius, poetic power, and originality, of sympathy, individuality, knowledge, and even of ethics grew and took lifeblood from the idea of the imagination.
> (Engell, 1981, pp. 34, 41, 47)

This, in brief, is the background within which Tolkien is working in "On Fairy-Stories."

But it is also necessary to explain why the uses of fancy and imagination underwent the transformations that they did: we must ask why these more or less synonymous ideas became distinguished in the first place, why people came to insist on maintaining the distinction and, finally, why Tolkien found it necessary to revise it. James Engell, in his historical survey of Romanticism, remarks that Thomas Hobbes was apparently the last major writer to speak of fantasy or fancy in the non-depreciative sense:

> As this distinction developed, it involved a reversal of the traditional distinction between the two terms. Coming from the Greek, *phantasia* carried with it the suggestion of creativity and play of mind, with the possible implication of license and illusion as a by-product of that freedom. The Latin *imaginatio*, on the contrary, had a block-like, Roman solidity derived from the primary word "image," which referred to a mental concept as much as a visual "image". It was akin to the word "imitation" and carried with it a sense of fidelity and accuracy. But precisely because *phantasia* suggested a greater freedom of mind, whether for creative insight, for perception, or for illusion, the word "fancy" began to bear the brunt of suspicion or distrust thrown by seventeenth century rationalism and, above all, by the fashionable colloquial speech that echoed it . . . In the search for a new or different word to express what . . . rationalism seemed to leave out, the more solid word "imagination," with its implication of being firmly rooted in the concrete, was at hand.
> (Engell, 1981, p. 173)

The usage of *phantasia* and *imaginatio*, then, begins to shift as these ideas become caught up in other distinctions and concerns.

Tolkien's first move in "On Fairy-Stories" is to restrict the meaning of imagination to its pre-Romantic sense as the mental faculty of forming images of objects no longer present to the senses (Tolkien, 1989a, p. 44). In this he agrees with Hobbes' view of imagination as "decaying sense" (Engell, 1981, p. 14). It is also notable that many Romantic definitions of fancy agree with Tolkien's characterisation of the image-making faculty. What Tolkien has done, then, is to return imagination from its enlarged meaning and to recover its literal sense. "In the new hierarchy of terms," observes Wojcik,

> Imagination would occupy its previous position in the Thomistic system which describes it as the image making function, and a new word, Fantasy (a word that Thomas held to be synonymous with imagination), would be the term which described [what Coleridge called] the "secondary" or "intellectualized" imagination.
> (Wojcik, 1968, p. 135)

But why was it necessary to invent a categorical distinction where no such distinction had previously existed?

Tolkien's quarrel over the kind of "belief" induced by sub-creation already hints at a solution to this problem. What seems to be at stake is the truth value of art in its various forms, particularly those forms which do not merely seek to "reproduce" or "imitate" empirical reality. This concern, in turn, addresses the question of the value and validity of art, which for Romantic thought comes to be signified by the image of the artistic process as analogous to God's creative activity. While this vision of humanity as "sub-creative" has many precedents in both Classical and Renaissance thought (Engell, 1981, pp. 44, 50), it is only with the Romanticism of the eighteenth and nineteenth centuries that it becomes wholly identified with the term "imagination" (Engell, 1981, p. 138). The inevitable semantic consequence of this amplification of meaning, as Tolkien himself observed (Tolkien, 1989a, p. 44), is that "imagination" must now stand for more than one thing; that is, both its literal meaning as the image-making faculty and its broader designation for the creative process as a whole. In assessing Tolkien's remarks on this point, then, it will be helpful to consider whether his views about fantasy are best characterized as being Romantic or Classical.

Tolkien's attempt at recovering a Classical (or Thomistic) sense of imagination is clear enough; but his treatment of fantasy is rather more nuanced and does not fit neatly into either category. Robert Reilly characterizes Tolkien as "elaborating" and "slightly qualifying" the Romantic view (1971, pp. 203-204). With respect to Coleridge, he sees Tolkien to be "defending," "reviving," and "making explicit and Christian Coleridge's claim for the worth of the creative imagination" (Reilly, 1971, pp. 205, 210). Swinfen, on the other hand, once more emphasizing philosophical differences as the root of their semantic manoeuvring, sees Tolkien "to all intents and purposes" as consciously reversing Coleridge's position (Swinfen, 1984, p. 8). Wojcik, viewing Tolkien's apparent disagreements as red herrings, asserts that he is fundamentally in agreement with Coleridge (Wojcik, 1968, p. 134).

One reason for the wide divergence in judgement over this point is certainly the differing interests and concerns each commentator is addressing; yet just as central to their disagreement is a shared failure to identify the different concerns which Tolkien *himself* is addressing in his definition of fantasy as a distinct artistic mode. This failure to clarify his remarks leads Reilly to make a confusing and partially erroneous statement which Wojcik fails to correct in his own critique of Reilly's argument. In his book *Romantic Religion*, Reilly states that Coleridge "thought of the two capacities [that is, fancy and imagination] as wholly distinct faculties". "Tolkien," he then goes on to claim, "would re-combine them because he believes 'the verbal distinction philologically inappropriate, and the analysis inaccurate'" (Reilly, 1971, p. 204). Wojcik, accepting Reilly's characterisation of Tolkien's position, suggests that "Coleridge would combine them also; and Tolkien is closer to Coleridge in his thinking than either he or Reilly think" (Wojcik, 1968, p. 135).

Wojcik and Reilly's confusion derives from their conflation of two connected statements made by Tolkien which seem to be identical, but are in fact distinct in meaning. I quote these here in full:

[1] For my present purpose I require a word which shall *embrace* both the Sub-creative Art in itself and a quality of strangeness and wonder in the Expression, derived from the Image: a quality essential to fairy-story.

[2] I propose, therefore, to arrogate to myself the powers of Humpty-Dumpty, and to use Fantasy for this purpose: in a sense, that is, which *combines* with its older and higher use as an equivalent of Imagination the derived notions of "unreality" (that is, of unlikeness to the Primary World), of freedom from the domination of observed "fact", in short of the fantastic.

(Tolkien, 1989a, p. 45, my emphasis)

If Tolkien does indeed speak of fantasy as "combining," he also speaks of it as "embracing". Beyond the obvious difference in the meaning of these two words, it must be noted that Tolkien is here using their nuance to clarify two separate aspects of his definition of fantasy. When he uses the expression "combining," Tolkien is referring to the senses of meaning which he intends the word itself to evoke (as over against its conventional, depreciative sense). By contrast, when Tolkien speaks of fantasy as "embracing" he refers not to the semantic associations of the word, but rather to its referent, which is for him both the artistic process itself and the finished product.

What needs to be emphasized here is that Reilly is incorrect when he claims that Tolkien is combining the Coleridgian faculties of fancy and imagination. On the contrary, Tolkien insists that the two be categorically separated, "imagination" being restricted to its descriptive meaning as image-making, and "fantasy" elevated to replace the Romantic faculty of the creative imagination. In preserving this categorical distinction between fantasy and imagination, then, Tolkien is best characterized as Romantic rather than Classical. But Swinfen, too, is not wholly accurate in her claim that Tolkien simply "reverses" the terms of the distinction, for as we have already shown, Tolkien is not defining fantasy as a general mental faculty but as a distinct mode of art. In this, perhaps, he is unique to the Romantic tradition.

This cohabitation of both Romantic and Classical elements in Tolkien's definition is also perceptible in the double sense which he attaches to the word "fantasy". In Tolkien's own words, he wishes the term to resonate with both "its older and higher use as an equivalent of Imagination" – that is, the Thomistic sense described by Wojcik – and "the derived notions of 'unreality' . . . of freedom from the domination of observed fact . . . of the fantastic" (in other words, its "depreciative" Romantic sense)[5]. "But while admitting that," he continues, "I do not assent to the depreciative tone. That the images are of things not in the primary world (if that

---

[5] I take the Romantic-Classical model from Alex Lewis, whose article on the interplay of these elements in Tolkien's own fiction concurs that Tolkien cannot be fit into either category (narrowly understood). See especially Lewis, 1988, p. 11.

indeed is possible) is a virtue not a vice. Fantasy (in this sense) is, I think, not a lower but a higher form of Art, indeed the most nearly pure form, and so (when achieved) the most potent" (Tolkien, 1989a, p. 45). With these words it becomes clear that Tolkien is not (as Reilly would characterize him) only "slightly qualifying" Romantic conventions; he is in fact overhauling the entire framework of Romantic sensibilities by privileging fantasy as the very paradigm of all art. The keynote of Tolkien's revisionist view pivots on his refusal to assent to the depreciative usage of "fantasy," the origins of which we now turn to in more detail.

Behind the diminution of *phantasia* into fancy "lies the eighteenth-century tradition of empirical psychology" (Engell, 1981, p. 130). John Locke's famous distinction between simple and complex ideas generated reflection on the active and passive dimensions of human perception, ascribing to the mind both "productive" and "reproductive" powers (Engell, 1981, pp. 18, 20). It is into this cluster of related distinctions that the heretofore synonymous terms "fancy" and "imagination" were cast.

As with the Classical sense of *imaginatio*, the mind was capable of reproducing sense impressions as they were received from the empirical world. In addition to this, the mind could also actively alter, rearrange, and connect these impressions in a conscious, purposeful and productive way. The eighteenth-century expression for this latter power was "association," and the framework of associationist psychology was soon adopted into the critical vocabulary of Romantic aesthetics as a principle of artistic creation.

But not without modifications. From the preceding psychological distinction between the "reproduction" of images and their "productive" association, we might expect *phantasia* to designate the latter faculty as a positive foundation for the artistic process; but in fact what takes place is a further Romantic fracturing of the associative principle into a greater and a lesser degree, "almost every discussion of the imagination during the last third of the century," writes Engell:

> contains either a direct or an implied distinction between "fancy" and "imagination". Although there is no clear-cut correspondence in all these distinctions, at least one generalization can be made. Most of them assume fancy . . . to be mainly an associative power that supplies the mind or the inner eye with numerous images . . . But the imagination fuses, combines, transforms, and orders images so that they produce an artistic or aesthetic unity.
> (Engell, 1981, p. 176)

A three-fold understanding of perception as it pertains to art thus develops in Romantic thought. This may be summarized as a distinction between *memory* (the simple reproduction of sense-impressions, coextensive with human consciousness), *fancy* (the associative faculty of productively combining and rearranging sense-impressions), and *imagination* (the power of transforming these associations into art). There were several reasons for introducing this tripartite distinction, and a consideration of why fancy was systematically excluded from the fold of genuine art will aid us in understanding Tolkien's motives for altering its conventional meaning.

Tolkien himself speaks of fancy as the "enchanter's power" and views the association of ideas in terms of the "the powers of generalisation and abstraction":

> The human mind . . . sees not only *green-grass*, discriminating it from other things (and finding it fair to look upon), but sees that it is *green* as well as being *grass*. But how powerful, how stimulating to the very faculty that produced it, was the invention of the adjective: no spell or incantation in Faerie is more potent. And that is not surprising: such incantations might indeed be said to be only another view of adjectives, a part of speech in a mythical grammar. The mind that thought of *light*, *heavy*, *grey*, *yellow*, *still*, *swift*, also conceived of magic that would make heavy things light and able to fly, turn grey lead into yellow gold, and the still rock into swift water. If it could do the one, it could do the other; it inevitably did both. When we can take green from grass, blue from heaven, and red from blood, we have already an enchanter's power – upon one plane; and the desire to wield that power in the world external to our minds awakes. It does not follow that we shall use that power well up on any plane . . . But in such "fantasy", as it is called, new form is made; Faerie begins; Man becomes a sub-creator.
> (Tolkien, 1989a, pp. 24-25)

But Tolkien, too, sees association as a lesser or subsidiary power, and so distinguishes it with his definition of imagination:

> The mental power of image-making is one thing, or aspect; and it should appropriately be called Imagination. The perception of the image, the grasp of its implications, and the control, which are necessary to a successful expression, may vary in vividness and strength: but this is a difference of degree in Imagination, not a difference in kind. The achievement of the expression, which gives (or seems to give) "the inner consistency of reality" (That is: which commands or induces Secondary Belief.), is indeed another thing, or aspect, needing another name: Art, the operative link between Imagination and the final result, Sub-creation.
> (Tolkien, 1989a, pp. 44-45)

Again, it must be recalled that while the sense of Tolkien's term "fantasy" combines both the Classical definition of *imaginatio* with the associative, Romantic definition of fancy, what it *embraces* are not the faculties of *phantasia* and *imaginatio*, but rather two *moments* in the aesthetic act. This is perhaps best exemplified in "Leaf by Niggle", where Tolkien's artist, looking upon his realized art, calls it a gift: "He was referring to his art, *and also to the result*; but he was using the word quite literally" (Tolkien, 1989b, p. 88, my emphasis). For Tolkien, then, "the result" includes both the artefact itself and the act of beholding it.

Why Tolkien makes this distinction between the sense and referent of the word will be explored later; what is important to note at present is that Tolkien is in fundamental agreement with the Romantic tradition as to the general character of association and its subsidiary status within the artistic process as a whole. Disagreement emerges only over the issue of where "fantasy" belongs within this framework. The tradition simply equates it with association, and so restricts it; Tolkien acknowledges its associative dimension, but then asserts that this is "a virtue not a vice". More specifically, there are two aspects of Tolkien's definition of fantasy which Romantic thought denies to associative fancy. These are 1) its inability to achieve aesthetic unity ("the inner consistency of reality"), and 2) its lack of connection to reality (its truth value).

These two aspects are in fact quite closely related. By definition it would be impossible for something without any relationship to reality whatsoever to be possessed of the "inner consistency" of the latter. Moreover, the lack of any reality-referent can also signify a lack of purpose, which in turn could make the goal of aesthetic unity unrealisable. Tolkien, of course, argues against such a view of fantasy. "Fantasy," he says, "is a rational not an irrational activity" (Tolkien, 1989a, p. 45). If it is indeed "rational" – that is, motivated and controlled by the faculty of reason – then it must involve (for Tolkien) both conscious will and purpose. At some level, it must also engage reason, as expressed by the question: "Is it true?" (Tolkien, 1989a, p. 36).

Because one of the effects of successful fantasy is its inducement of a kind of subjectivity distinct from that produced by our perception of empirical reality – that is, of an affirming "secondary belief" – Tolkien must defend his assertion of the rationality of fantasy on two levels. The first of these concerns us with Tolkien's disagreement with the Romantic tradition over the relation between fantasy and the associative faculty; the second moves us finally to Tolkien's novel claim that narrative alone is the only proper mode of the fantastic. These two levels cannot be understood independently, for they rely upon one another for their coherence – if Tolkien had accepted the associative definition of fantasy, his subsequent restriction of fantasy to narrative would have been quite unnecessary. Before moving on to our evaluation of the significance of narrative for Tolkien, then, we must dwell for a little longer on Tolkien's response to the "depreciation" of fantasy by Romantic thought.

One of the limitations ascribed to fancy as association is that it is "mechanistic," and thus incapable of aesthetic unity. "This association can be spontaneous or willed, ordered or random, yet it is 'mechanical' because the images associated are not transformed; they appear in the bits and pieces in which they were first experienced" (Engell, 1981, p. 179). One of the limitations to such fancy is its apparent arbitrariness – the parading of its artifice of dissonant images which appear to lack any natural relationship to each other. Tolkien recognises this problem, but sees it as distinct from the issue of secondary belief:

> Fantasy has . . . an essential drawback: it is difficult to achieve. Fantasy may be, as I think, not less but more sub-creative; but at any rate it is found in practice that "the inner consistency of reality" is more difficult to produce, the more unlike are the images and the rearrangements of primary material to the actual arrangements of the Primary World. It is easier to produce this kind of "reality" with more "sober" material. Fantasy thus, too often, remains undeveloped; it is and has been used frivolously, or only half-seriously, or merely for decoration: it remains merely "fanciful". Anyone inheriting the fantastic device of human language can say *the green sun*. Many can then imagine or picture it. But that is not enough – though it may already be a more potent thing than many a "thumbnail sketch" or "transcript of life" that receives literary praise.
>
> To make a Secondary World inside which the green sun will be credible, commanding Secondary Belief, will probably require labour and thought, and will certainly demand a special skill.
> (Tolkien, 1989a, p. 46)

But here again Tolkien is simply arguing over whether the term "fantasy" ought to designate both association and the achievement of aesthetic unity.

Where he really comes into conflict with Romantic sensibilities is when he debunks the notion that the primary world is the only criterion from which to judge the aesthetic value of patently imaginative creations. For many Romantic thinkers, fantastic associations are merely fanciful because their existence is impossible in the primary world (Engell, 1981, p. 120). For Tolkien, by contrast:

> Fairy-stories were plainly not primarily concerned with possibility, but with desirability. If they awakened *desire*, satisfying it while often whetting it unbearably, they succeeded . . . Fantasy is made out of the Primary World, but a good craftsman loves his material, and has a knowledge and feeling for clay, stone and wood which only the art of making can give. By the forging of Gram, cold iron was revealed; by the making of Pegasus horses were ennobled; in the Trees of the Sun and Moon root and stock, flower and fruit are manifested in glory.
> (Tolkien, 1989a, pp. 39, 54-55).

Tolkien's vocabulary of "revealing," "ennobling," and "manifesting" clearly evokes the Romantic sense that human imagination is ultimately creative as God is creative. For Tolkien, then, purely fantastic creations (like the Pegasus) do constitute an aesthetic unity because the human desire from which they arise is natural rather than contrived. Their truth value rests not in their fidelity to the primary world but in their capacity to signify desire. This argument, however, simply transfers the question of validity from the signifier to the signified, and so Tolkien's defence of fantasy must ultimately be a defence of the legitimacy of human desire. It is this which leads Tolkien from the Romantic philosophy of art to his own convictions about humanity as a Catholic Christian. In this, his theory of fantasy undergoes significant departures from Romantic thought; and it is to these departures which we now turn.

Drama and Narrative

For Tolkien, fantasy is a thing "best left to words, to true literature":

> It is a misfortune that Drama, an art fundamentally distinct from Literature, should so commonly be considered together with it, or as a branch of it. Among these misfortunes we may reckon the depreciation of Fantasy. For in part at least this depreciation is due to the natural desire of critics to cry up the forms of literature or "imagination" that they themselves, innately or by training, prefer. And criticism in a country that has produced so great a Drama, and possesses the works of William Shakespeare, tends to be far too dramatic. But Drama is naturally hostile to Fantasy. Fantasy, even of the simplest kind, hardly ever succeeds in Drama, when that is presented as it should be, visibly and audibly acted.
> (Tolkien, 1989a, pp. 46-47)

To some, Tolkien's judgement may appear unnecessarily polemical, particularly when one recalls the intensely "dramatic" character of much of his own creative writing[6], and perhaps it is for this reason that less attention has been paid to this aspect of "On Fairy-Stories". But Tolkien's emphasis on the "hostility" of drama to fantasy, as I have been insisting and will now demonstrate, is an integral element to what makes him distinctive in the context of Romanticism.

Tolkien has basically two qualms about drama's attempting to be a medium of fantasy: 1) it necessarily relies on visual representation, and 2) it is necessarily anthropocentric in both its form and content. Beginning with the first problem, I will show that Tolkien's two revisions of the Romantic tradition already discussed – that is, his preference for the expression "secondary belief" over Coleridge's willing suspension of disbelief, and his refusal to restrict the meaning of "fantasy" to its depreciatory sense as a mechanical, associative faculty – are identical in spirit and motive to his polemic against drama. Interestingly, we will find that Tolkien's criticism of the limitations of drama in many ways resonates with the conventional Romantic view of "fancy" as a lesser form of imagination.

A principal defect in dramatic attempts at achieving the fantastic, in Tolkien's view, is that: "the producers of drama have to, or try to, work with mechanism to represent either Fantasy or Magic" (Tolkien, 1989a, p. 47). If fantasy is difficult to achieve through words, how much more difficult is it to effect before the naked eye? These are good grounds for disqualifying drama in Tolkien's view since, for him, fantasy must be capable of producing secondary belief. Because drama is rarely able to conceal its own artifice it can, like Romantic fancy, hope to achieve little more than a willing suspension of disbelief.

If Tolkien's criticism were directed merely against this technical ineptitude of mechanism for producing visual fantasy, we might hold some doubts as to its continuing validity; for today, over half a century after the essay was written, we do possess a cinematic art (certainly both visual and dramatic) with the power of giving the inner consistency of reality to fantastic images with great facility. But Tolkien's reasoning is, in fact, much more comprehensive:

> A reason, more important, I think, than the inadequacy of stage-effects, is this: Drama has, of its very nature, already attempted a kind of bogus, or shall I say at least substitute, magic: *the visible and audible presentation of imaginary men in a story*. That is in itself an attempt to counterfeit the magician's wand. To introduce, even with mechanical success, into this quasi-magical secondary world a further fantasy or magic is to demand, as it were, an inner or tertiary world. It is a world too much. To make such a thing may not be impossible. I have never seen it done with success. But at least it cannot be claimed as the proper mode of drama . . . For this precise reason – that the characters, and even the scenes, are in Drama not imagined but actually beheld – Drama is . . . an art fundamentally different from narrative art.
> (Tolkien, 1989a, p. 48)

With drama the eye of the beholder must inevitably be focused upon the human condition – it is human beings who make up the primary content of dramatic performance. "Very little about trees as trees can be got into a play" (Tolkien, 1989a, p. 48). Moreover, Tolkien's claim that drama's difference from narrative lies in the fact of its being beheld rather than imagined is surely linked to literature's capacity to circumvent the dramatic focus on the humane.

In other words, it seems that we have here stumbled upon the beginnings of an understanding of the motive behind Tolkien's definition of fantasy as narrative art embracing both the act of artistic creation itself and the experience of the finished product. The principal content of fantasy or the fairy story (that is to say, the absence of a limited dramatic focus on the human condition as such) is somehow related in Tolkien's mind to the form in which the finished product is experienced (that is, through the exercise of the imaginative faculty rather then being "beheld" by the human eye). These two aspects of Tolkien's aesthetic (the non-anthropocentric and the non-visual) ultimately join forces to lay the foundation for his vision of fantasy as a narrative of alterity – of otherness, of transcendence. Taken together, these three dimensions of the visual form the mediating link between Tolkien's terminological disputes with Coleridge and his unique theology of the eucatastrophe as the highest function of fantasy. We examine each of these dimensions in turn.

---

[6] The "drama" of Tolkien's writing lies as much in the aurality of reading and hearing it as it does in the narrated story itself. In this respect, John Ellison observes that Tolkien's sub-creation "is a world of sound as much as it is a world of sense and specific meaning. Sound, that is, expressed not only through the medium of his languages, real and invented, but also in the wealth of sound images in the text, with all their consequentially evoked sensations of light and darkness, colour and space. This is the dimension of reality that Tolkien found to be lacking in spoken drama . . . LotR plays itself out as an immense drama against a scenic panorama which each reader creates and paints in his or her own mind, and which no literal stage representation could even begin to rival" (Ellison, 1988, p. 18).

1. Imagination and the Visual

We begin by recalling that Tolkien's criticism of drama as fantasy extends beyond the incidental ineptitude of mechanism to the *fact* of its representing the fantastic visually:

> The radical distinction between all art (including drama) that offers a *visible* presentation and true literature is that it imposes one visible form. Literature works from mind to mind and is thus more progenitive. It is at once more universal and more poignantly particular. If it speaks of *bread* or *wine* or *stone* or *tree*, it appeals to the whole of these things, to their ideas; yet each hearer will give to them a peculiar personal embodiment in his imagination. Should the story say "he ate bread", the dramatic producer or painter can only show "a piece of bread" according to his taste or fancy, but the hearer of the story will think of bread in general and picture it in some form of his own. If a story says "he climbed a hill and saw a river in the valley below", the illustrator may catch, or nearly catch, his own vision of such a scene; but every hearer of the words will have his own picture, and it will be made out of all the hills and rivers and dales he has ever seen, but specially out of The Hill, The River, The Valley which were for him the first embodiment of the word.
>
> (Tolkien, 1989a, p. 70)

In the above-quoted passage we get a glimpse of Tolkien the Neo-Platonist (cf. Swinfen's remark, 1984, p. 9); but we also discover another important facet of his idea of secondary belief. We affirm here with the commentators that Tolkien seeks a stronger, more positive expression than Coleridge's "willing suspension of disbelief;" but *pace* Parks' view (cf. Parks, 1981) that Tolkien's intention is to strengthen the voice of the *narrator*, what he is in fact doing is expanding the role of the *hearer*. Just as in his art the artist actively participates in God's primary creative activity, so too in his or her hearing of the artist's narrative the hearer actively participates in the act of imagination induced (indeed, necessitated) by its non-visual character. In Tolkien's own words, such narrative makes it possible for artist and hearer to become "partners in making and delight" (Tolkien, 1989a, p. 50)[7].

This understanding aids us in further clarifying Tolkien's definition of fantasy as an artistic mode. Rather than speaking of a unity in the process of creation with the finished, sub-creative product, we might more accurately speak of a collaboration between the work of the author and the work of the reader/hearer; for the implication of Tolkien's remarks about narrative force us to view the artistic product as unfinished until the hearer has actively "completed" it by way of imaginative effort. This, I believe, is the logic behind Tolkien's claim that fantasy must "embrace both the Sub-creative Art in itself and a quality of strangeness and wonder in the Expression, derived from the Image" (Tolkien, 1989a, p. 45).

All forms of art, to use Tolkien's vocabulary, involve the possession and use of the imaginative faculty, the artistic process itself, and the artistic product; within this schema, the fantastic narrative is distinguished by the particular character of the relationship between the author and hearer (or, alternately, between the two moments of artistic creation and reception). This can be illustrated by the following diagram:

"ART" "THE EXPRESSION"
(the work of the artist)   (the imaginative work of the hearer)

"THE IMAGE"
(the imaginative faculty common to both artist and hearer)

The visual, then, is hostile to Tolkien's aesthetic because it destroys this special relationship between author and hearer which is necessary for the operation of fantasy[8].

2. Identity and Difference

Tolkien's second reason for the exclusion of drama as fantasy — its necessarily limited focus on the human condition — concerns not so much the means or operation of fantasy as its ultimate purpose or goal which, as we have already suggested, looks toward that which is other and transcendent to human experience. In this sense it is the limitations of the human condition itself which constitute a kind of visual presence needing to be transcended in order for fantasy to begin. This is the "quality of strangeness and wonder in the Expression, derived from the Image" of which Tolkien speaks — the quality which awakens our desire and invites us to participate in its operations.

The claim that fantasy is not properly "about" the human condition raises the thorny question of its value and validity as a product of human imagination. Despite Tolkien's assertion of its virtue (Tolkien, 1989a, p. 45), this question has served as a central rallying point in attacks levelled against the fantastic from many quarters, notably in the criticism of Tolkien's own work on the part of the literary establishment. If fantasy were "about" nothing other than itself, totally unconnected with reality, then it would indeed be legitimate to regard it as little more than an exercise in depreciative fancy. But as we have already seen, Tolkien

---

[7] In her unpublished thesis, Deirdre Greene (1989) has explored this dimension of Tolkien's aesthetic from the very fruitful perspective of reception theory. Her study of Tolkien's fictional writings provides insightful examples of how this "providential" relationship between the artist and the reader/hearer outlined at the philosophical level in "On Fairy-Stories" manifests itself in the very texture and event structure of his narrative at the literary level.

[8] One of Coleridge's motivations in insisting on the fancy-imagination distinction was the need to separate artistic genius from the unwashed masses, who are at best only capable of mechanical fancy (*Biographia Literaria* Chapter VI). Tolkien, by contrast, uses this distinction to *unite* the activity of the artist with the reader/hearer. The operation of fantasy is, indeed, impossible without the active, participatory role of the reader/hearer's imaginative faculty. It is the imagination which facilitates partnership in making and delight.

views fantasy as generated by *legitimate* human desires. Fantasy remains a valid art form because, for him, those desires refer to or anticipate something which itself possesses an "underlying reality" (Tolkien, 1989a, p. 64), though a reality distinct from that which we now experience.

As we have seen, part of the self-referentiality of fantasy's being "about" itself stems from the unity of the form and content necessary to its operation: its non-visual mode of presentation offers us images of things which are themselves not to be seen within the world as we know it. It now appears that this correlation is intentional, and that Tolkien's insistence that fantasy embrace the activity of both artist and hearer is extended to its final goal as well as its operations. Tolkien expresses this view not only at the philosophical level, but in the content of his own creative writings. This is best seen in the role played by the Elves:

> At the heart of many . . . stories of the elves lies, open or concealed, pure or alloyed, the desire for a living, realized sub-creative art . . . Of this desire the elves, in their better (but still perilous) part, are largely made; and it is from them that we may learn what is the central desire and aspiration of human Fantasy – even if the elves are, all the more in so far as they are, only a product of Fantasy itself.
> (Tolkien, 1989a, p. 50)

The central desire of fantasy, then, is that our sub-creations be granted primary existence – that they become a part of reality. Tolkien's Elves signify this desire because (unlike us) they *do* possess the power (in the secondary world) of giving primary reality to their artistic creations. The Elves are "about" themselves because they are only a product of our imagination – once again, the forms which our imagination invents or "discovers" are identical or organically related to the content of our desires.

It would be accurate to say that, in this sense, Tolkien holds to an autotelic or self-generating view of fantasy (hence his claim for its validity), but only in the larger context of his Romantic belief in humanity as sub-creative – made, that is, "in the image and likeness of a Maker" (Tolkien, 1989a, p. 52); for not all human desires are equally legitimate, and for this reason the Elves signify not only the identity of our desire, but the peril of difference – that which we cannot and should not seek to realize in this world. Tolkien therefore distinguishes genuine artistic desire (signified by Elvish "enchantment") from its counterfeit (which he calls "magic"):

> Enchantment produces a Secondary World into which both designer and spectator can enter, to the satisfaction of their senses while they are inside; but in its purity it is artistic in desire and purpose. Magic produces, or pretends to produce, an alteration in the Primary World . . . it is not an art but a technique; its desire is *power* in this world, domination of things and wills.
> (Tolkien, 1989a, pp. 49-50)

Tolkien also identifies magic with "the machine" (that is, technology):

> Unlike art which is content to create a secondary world in the mind, [machinery] attempts to actualize desire, and so to create power in this World; and that cannot really be done with any real satisfaction . . . And in addition to this fundamental disability of a creature, is added the Fall, which makes our devices not only fail of their desire but turn to new and horrible evil.
> (Tolkien, 1981, pp. 87-88)

Another aspect of visuality for Tolkien, then, is that it can suggest an illicit attempt to realize desire in this world – to display something visually becomes a metaphor of coercion.

It is for this reason that our desires, for Tolkien, must not only be expressed, but *contained* by the boundaries which separate art from the primary world[9]. Because the primary world is, for him, a fallen world, our sub-creative desire cannot help but be fraught with ambivalence and danger. Hence, the rejection of visuality constitutes one element in Tolkien's larger moral resistance to the perils and temptations of humanity's fallen nature. But if our desires are corruptible, so too they are in Tolkien's mind redeemable. Indeed, if the central desire of fallen humanity is the realization of its imaginative creations, then just as central must be the desire to escape our fallen state itself.

Romantic thought had made art the analogy of divine creation, but it is Tolkien who brings fantasy into a unique relationship with salvation history. Whereas tragedy is, for Tolkien, the highest function of drama, eucatastrophe is the highest function of fantasy, which he describes as

> a sudden and miraculous grace: never to be counted on to recur. It does not deny the existence of *dyscatastrophe*, of sorrow and failure: the possibility of these is necessary to the joy of deliverance; it denies (in the face of much evidence, if you will) universal final defeat and in so far is *evangelium*, giving a fleeting glimpse of Joy, Joy beyond the walls of the world, poignant as grief.
> (Tolkien, 1989a, p. 62)

"The Birth of Christ," writes Tolkien, "is the eucatastrophe of Man's history. The Resurrection is the eucatastrophe of the story of the Incarnation . . . It is not difficult to imagine," he continues,

> the peculiar excitement and joy that one would feel, if any specially beautiful fairy-story were found to be "primarily" true, its narrative to be history, without thereby necessarily losing the mythical or allegorical significance that it had possessed. It is not difficult, for one is not called upon to try and conceive anything of a quality unknown. The joy would have exactly the same quality, if not the same degree, as the joy which the "turn" in a fairy-story gives . . . It looks forward (or backward: the direction in this regard is unimportant) to the Great Eucatastrophe. The Christian joy, the *Gloria*,

---

[9] In her important structural study of the genre, Rosemary Jackson sees the representation of desire and its containment as two principal strategies deployed by fantastic literature to achieve its effects (Jackson, 1988, p. 3).

is of the same kind; but . . . this story is supreme, and it is true. Art has been verified.
(Tolkien, 1989a, pp. 65-66)

Tolkien's view of the Incarnation as "verifying" art is the key thought in the above-quoted passage which links it to the theme of visuality as realisation. Unlike most Romantic christologies which tend to focus on Christ as the prototype of artistic creation alone, Tolkien focuses not on the mediatory aspect of the person of Christ, but on the *fact* of incarnation itself – that desire has in fact been fulfilled in the primary world and, hence, becomes the prototype not of creation but of future fulfilment.

Unlike much Romantic thought, which came to ascribe a saving character to the exercise of the imagination, Tolkien viewed salvation as strictly the province of the *evangelium* itself. In characterising the eucatastrophe of human fantasy as "looking forward or backward" toward the primary eucatastrophe, however, he nevertheless grants it a special status – not only verifying the *evangelium* and being verified by it in turn, narrative fantasy also comes to confirm our continued nature as sub-creators. It looks not only backward to the Incarnation; it looks forward to the Parousia and final redemption. In this latter function it becomes not so much the analogy to salvation, but prophetic in character. This moves us to the final (and in this case positive) sense which the visual signifies for Tolkien, which he calls "recovery."

3. Recovery as the Redemption of the Visual

Tolkien describes recovery as the "regaining of a clear view":

> I do not say "seeing things as they are" and involve myself with the philosophers, though I might venture to say "seeing things as we are (or were) meant to see them" – as things apart from ourselves. We need, in any case, to clean our windows; so that the things seen clearly may be freed from the drab blur of triteness or familiarity – from possessiveness.
> (Tolkien, 1989a, p. 53)

This rediscovery of difference is crucial to Tolkien's defence of fantasy because it gives a rationale for its independent value apart from the anticipation of the *evangelium*. Like the many leaves of a single tree, each new story "is a *unique* embodiment of the pattern" (Tolkien, 1989a, p. 52, my emphasis). "No assumptions about the nature of reality, even purely supernaturalist or acausal beliefs held absolutely, release the storyteller from the *task* of *making* a story" (Parks, p. 147). In this respect, the unrealisability of human desire as signified by the non-visual character of fantasy refers as much to a positive aspect of our nature as it does to the negative consequences of the Fall – if desire were absolutely satisfied, it would imply that our role as sub-creators was at an end. But this is surely not the case: "Redeemed Man," writes Tolkien, "is still man":

> Story, fantasy, still go on, and should go on . . . So great is the bounty with which he has been treated that he may now, perhaps, fairly dare to guess that in Fantasy he may actually assist in the effoliation and multiple enrichment of creation. All tales may come true; and yet, at the last, redeemed, they may be as like and as unlike the forms that we give them as Man, finally redeemed, will be like and unlike the fallen that we know.
> (Tolkien, 1989a, p. 66)

Conclusion

Two general conclusions may be drawn from this analysis of Tolkien's thinking. Firstly, Tolkien's revisions of Romantic thought are necessary components to his defence of literary fantasy as a genre in its own right. Secondly, while eucatastrophe remains Tolkien's unique contribution to Christian Romanticism, it is his insistence upon the non-visual character of fantasy (rather than the idea of sub-creation as such) which structurally links Tolkien's aesthetics to his theology, and it is an appreciation of this link which allows us to view Tolkien's Romanticism as an integral dimension to his life and work as a whole.

References

Bergmann, Frank. 1977. "The Roots of Tolkien's Tree: The Influence of George MacDonald and German Romanticism upon Tolkien's Essay 'On Fairy-Stories'" in *Mosaic: A Journal for the Comparative Study of Literature and Ideas*, 10/2, pp. 5-14.

Carpenter, Humphrey. 1979. *The Inklings: C.S. Lewis, J.R.R. Tolkien, Charles Williams, and their friends*. Boston: Houghton Mifflin Company.

Coleridge, Samuel Taylor. 1907. *Biographia Literaria* (2 volumes). Oxford: Oxford University Press.

Ellison, John. 1988. "Tolkien, Wagner, and the End of the Romantic Age" in Iwan Rhys Morus *et al.* (eds.) *Tolkien and Romanticism: Proceedings of the Cambridge Tolkien Workshop 1988*. Cambridge: The Cambridge Tolkien Workshop, pp. 14-20.

Engell, James. 1981. *The Creative Imagination: Enlightenment to Romanticism*. Cambridge, Massachusetts: Harvard University Press.

Greene, Deirdre. 1989. *A Study of the Fictional Works of J.R.R. Tolkien*, M. Litt. thesis: Christ Church, Oxford.

Helms, Randel. 1974. *Tolkien's World*. Boston: Houghton Mifflin Company.

Jackson, Rosemary. 1988. *Fantasy: The Literature of Subversion*. London: Routledge.

Knight, Gareth. 1990. *The Magical World of the Inklings: JRR Tolkien, CS Lewis, Charles Williams, Owen Barfield*. Longmead: Element Books Limited.

Lewis, Alex. 1988. "Tolkien and the Development of Romance" in Iwan Rhys Morus *et al.* (eds.), *Tolkien and Romanticism: Proceedings of the Cambridge Tolkien Workshop 1988*. Cambridge: The Cambridge Tolkien Workshop, pp. 8-13.

Parks, Henry B. 1981. "Tolkien and the Critical Approach to Story" in Neil B. Isaacs and Rose A. Zimbardo (eds.), *Tolkien: New Critical Perspectives*. Lexington, Kentucky: The University Press of Kentucky, pp 122-149.

Reilly, R.J. 1971. *Romantic Religion: A Study of Barfield, Lewis, Williams, and Tolkien*. Athens, Georgia: University of Georgia Press.

Swinfen, Ann. 1984. *In Defence of Fantasy: A Study of the Genre in English and American Literature since 1945*. London: Routledge and Kegan Paul.

Tolkien, J.R.R. 1981. *Letters of J.R.R. Tolkien*, ed. Humphrey Carpenter. London: George Allen & Unwin.

Tolkien, J.R.R. 1989a. "On Fairy-Stories" in *Tree and Leaf*. Boston: Houghton Mifflin Company, pp. 9-73.

Tolkien, J.R.R. 1989b. "Leaf by Niggle" in *Tree and Leaf*. Boston: Houghton Mifflin Company, pp. 75-95.

Wojcik, Jan. 1968. "Tolkien and Coleridge: Remaking of the 'Green Earth'" in *Renascence*, 20/3, pp.134-139, 146.

Tolkien as a Post-War Writer[1]

Tom Shippey

Abstract: *The Lord of the Rings*, though unique in many ways, is only one of a series of fantasies published by English authors before, during, and just after World War II, works united in their deep concern with the nature of evil and their authors' belief that politics had given them a novel understanding of this ancient concept. This paper sets Tolkien in this contemporary context and considers what has been unique in his understanding of the modern world.

Keywords: evil, William Golding, C.S. Lewis, George Orwell, post-War writers, T.H. White, World War II

In my book *The Road to Middle-earth* I attempted to set Tolkien in a professional context. Among that book's theses were the assertions that the major influence on Tolkien's fiction was his job as a professor of English language; that his creativity drew insistently on the texts and techniques he studied and taught lifelong; that viewed in this light he belonged to a long tradition of philologists who tried to work out from the history of often dead languages to a recreation of the lost literatures of those languages; that just as the philologist used the asterisk as a mark of the "reconstructed" word, and moved on from it to the reconstructed story or poem, so Tolkien had gone on from the *-word to the "lost tale" and eventually to a kind of "asterisk-reality"; and so on. The drive of these arguments was insistently historical. Not only did I try to set Tolkien within the history of his profession, that profession itself was also overwhelmingly concerned with history and with change. Overwhelmingly, but not quite entirely. Ever since Saussure it has been a commonplace that languages can be considered not only "diachronically", in the manner of the old philologists, but also "synchronically", i.e. as functioning systems existing at a particular moment. I believe then that in spite of the intention of my book mentioned above, there is a logic also in considering Tolkien's work, and especially his major work *The Lord of the Rings*, not just against the context of his life and learned inheritance, but also against the (at first sight perhaps adventitious) context of its moment of publication: in the case of *The Lord of the Rings*, 1954-55.

At that particular moment it is clear enough that Allen & Unwin, Tolkien's publishers, felt that they were taking a commercial risk and bringing out a work with few or no parallels (see Carpenter, 1977, pp. 214-16). In a sense they were absolutely correct. Yet looking back from what is now nearly a forty-year perspective, one can see that Tolkien and *The Lord of the Rings* were not quite as isolated in their nature and appeal as they must have seemed at the time. Indeed, from that perspective, it seems arguable that the major works of English fiction in the post-war decade were more like each other, and more like Tolkien, than critical orthodoxy would then or now accept. Among the unquestioned landmarks of the period were George Orwell's *Nineteen Eighty-Four* (published in 1949), together with his *Animal Farm* (1945); and William Golding's *Lord of the Flies*, published the same year as the first volume of *The Lord of the Rings*. Less unquestioned as a landmark, but still a work whose importance and popularity have grown steadily, was T.H. White's *The Once and Future King*, published as a tetralogy with that title only in 1958, but with a more complex history than that single date suggests (see further below). To this I would add C.S. Lewis's *That Hideous Strength*, published in 1945. The named works by these five authors, Lewis, Orwell, Tolkien, Golding and White, seem to me to hang together in unexpected ways: they are all non-realistic works, whether one regards them as science fiction, fantasy, fable or parable (all descriptions which have been applied); and they are all books insistently marked by war, all works by writers who are "post-war" in more than an accidental or chronological sense.

One might ask, post-*which* war? It is often thought – and naturally so, when one considers such passages as the description of the Dead Marshes in *The Lord of the Rings* IV/2,[2] with its strong reminiscences of the destroyed landscapes and half-buried dead of the Flanders battlefields – that Tolkien is in essence a post-World War I writer. Before accepting this, one should consider a few dates and places. Of the five writers I have mentioned, Tolkien was the eldest: he was born in 1892, in Bloemfontein, South Africa. Lewis came next: 1898, Belfast. Orwell was born in 1903 in

---

[1] First published in *Scholarship & Fantasy: Proceedings of* The Tolkien Phenomenon *May 1992 Turku, Finland*, edited by K.J. Battarbee, *Anglicana Turkuensia*, 12 (1993). Turku, Finland: University of Turku, 1993, pp. 217-236.
[2] Since there are so many editions in circulation, references to *The Lord of the Rings* are given where useful by book and chapter number. It will be remembered that there are two books in each of the three volumes of *The Lord of the Rings*.

Bengal, White in 1906 in Bombay, and Golding in 1911 in Cornwall – the only one of these often self-consciously English writers to be native-born.[3] They were all in short quite old enough for one to expect the current of their novelistic careers to have shown itself by the outbreak of World War II, and perhaps for major works to have appeared. Actually all of them seem to have been either slow starters or slow finishers. Orwell did write and publish novels from 1935 on, but their interest for us now is mostly retrospective: we read back from *Nineteen Eighty-Four* because of that work almost alone. Lewis's first novel was *Out of the Silent Planet*, of 1938: it is the start of the trilogy completed by *That Hideous Strength*. Golding's first novel was *Lord of the Flies*, published when he was in his forties. White's career, meanwhile, is the most similar to Tolkien's. Like Tolkien, he had published a successful children's book, *The Sword in the Stone* of 1938, compare *The Hobbit* of 1937. Like Tolkien, he had gone on with a continuation of it, the tone of which turned increasingly more adult, more serious, and less immediately acceptable to his publishers. The second and third volumes of what was to become *The Once and Future King* came out in 1939 and 1940, but White's publishers (Collins) declined in 1941 to print the fourth and fifth volumes.[4] What eventually appeared as *The Once and Future King* in 1958 was a complex compromise, with the fifth volume omitted (eventually to appear posthumously as *The Book of Merlyn* from the University of Texas Press in 1977), but much of its contents subsumed into a new version of the first. Just as *The Lord of the Rings* took eighteen years to be written and appear (and still left room for posthumous additions), so White's work took twenty, with nearly twenty more before it appeared in full, if not as its author intended.

One could say then that all these writers of fiction became novelists relatively late (most obviously Tolkien and Golding, with no major creative works till they were in their forties). They were also perhaps not all natural writers, or writers to whom their craft came easily. Bernard Crick, Orwell's biographer, quotes a friend as saying of the young Orwell, "He wrote so badly. He had to teach himself writing . . . I remember one story that never saw the light of day . . . it began 'Inside the park, the crocuses were out . . .' Oh dear, I'm afraid we did laugh" (Crick, 1980, p. 179). They all made their greatest achievements (with the exception here of Golding) as fabulists or writers of fantasy.

And while they were all pre-World War I by birth, they were all effectively or as regards their major impact post-World War II by publication date. Finally, all five authors share a theme which explains many of the connections mentioned above. That theme is the nature of evil, a subject handled by all five with extreme originality, deep reluctance to accept prior opinion, however authoritative, and sometimes a degree of obsession.

The reason why these authors should be fascinated by that theme is apparent. All (except this time White) had been shot, or at least seriously shot at. Orwell was shot through the throat in the Spanish Civil War on 20th May 1937. He is said to have been a millimetre from death (Crick, 1980, p. 335). Lewis was hit by shell splinters in the leg, hand, face and lung on 15th April 1917; for a moment he thought he was dead already (Wilson, 1990, p. 56). Little is known of Golding's life, because of his dislike of biography, but he saw no less than five years' active service in the Royal Navy, 1940-45, was present at the sinking of the *Bismarck* and as an officer on a rocket-launching craft on D-Day, the invasion of Normandy. He has written eloquently, in *Pincher Martin* (1956), of the horror and pathos of drowned corpses. Tolkien went "over the top" with the Lancashire Fusiliers on 14th July 1917 and saw three months service in the trenches before being invalided out.[5] Only White did not have actual battle experience, spending most of World War II, out of conviction, in the neutral Irish Republic; yet White was in a sense the most obsessed of all with the topic, declaring openly if not quite convincingly that "the central theme of [his own?] Morte d'Arthur is to find an antidote for War",[6] and stating in the final colophon to *The Book of Merlyn* that he wrote *nationibus certantibus diro in bello* [while the nations were striving in fearful war], and had broken off *ut pro specie pugnet* [so that he could fight for his species] – not, that is, for his nation, but for a wider cause, but warfare just the same.

My suggestion is that in spite of the many differences between these writers there is an overriding similarity linking the facts presented above. In essence I am saying that these five writers all have as their major theme the nature of evil; that this theme was forced upon them by their life-experience, which I would say furthermore was a characteristically British life-experience, not shared for

---

[3] George Orwell chose his pen-name because he felt his real name, Eric Arthur Blair, did not sound English enough; Blair is a Scottish name, the Orwell a river in Suffolk. Tolkien's name is German by derivation, but from generations back; Tolkien felt deeply wedded to the landscape of the English Midlands, see Carpenter, *Biography*, pp. 18-19. Lewis was Irish by birth, but almost entirely English by education and connections. His Irishness was in any case that of the Northern Irish Protestant, frequently *plus royaliste que le roi*.

[4] For detailed information see Warner, 1967, and Shippey, 1983.

[5] There is a little doubt here as to how much action Tolkien saw. Carpenter's *Biography*, pp. 82-5, gives the impression that Tolkien took part only in one attack, and that a failure. This may be an understatement, caused on the one side by Tolkien's English reluctance to dramatise, and on the other by the now-established myth that all World War I attacks were failures. In so far as I have been able to trace Tolkien's battalion in official historical sources, it seems to have taken part in a highly successful attack not in terms of "breaking through", but in terms of "writing down" enemy units. Its activities during the period Tolkien was present include some of the bitterest fighting of the war, round the Schwaben Redoubt and against the Prussian Guard (units of which were annihilated). Tolkien remained deeply proud of the Lancashire Fusiliers, which won more Victoria Crosses during World War I than any other regiment in the Army.

[6] See his letter of 6th December 1940 (Gallix, 1984, p. 117).

instance by Americans or by most Europeans;[7] that they became writers of fiction to some extent to articulate this theme; and finally that all five authors turned to fantasy, or fable, or science fiction, however one likes to label their genres, because they felt that the theme of human evil was not one which could be rendered adequately or confronted directly through the medium of realistic fiction alone. These authors then were not "escapist" in their turn away from realism, though the accusation has often been levelled at Tolkien, Lewis and White, at least (see Shippey, 1992, pp. 285-7). If they avoided, as they did, the directly political issues of their time and place, such as class-distinction, they did so not out of cowardice or irresponsibility, but because they felt that there were far more critical issues lying beneath those, which those authors directly concerned with politics were in their turn trying to evade, escape from, or turn a blind eye to. There can be little doubt, certainly, that compared with many authors and genres of the mainstream English novel – thirties novels, campus novels, Virginia Woolf or E.M. Forster – the group of post-war fantasists I have identified was remarkably strongly affected by the major issue of British politics 1900-1950, which was war; and remarkably determined to concentrate on the problem which for them it raised above all: I repeat, the nature and origin of evil.

All succeeded in rendering this with uncommon and memorable force. Yet on it they all held different, sometimes totally different opinions. The most famous image of evil which they were to produce is perhaps the one in *Nineteen Eighty-Four* (Part III/3), in which O'Brien explains the future of humanity to his helpless and broken prisoner, Winston Smith. Speaking of the Party, O'Brien declares:

> We have cut the links between child and parent, and between man and man, and between man and woman. No one dares trust a wife or a child or a friend any longer. But in the future there will be no wives and no friends. Children will be taken from their mothers at birth, as one takes eggs from a hen. The sex instinct will be eradicated. Procreation will be an annual formality like the renewal of a ration card. We shall abolish the orgasm. Our neurologists are at work upon it now. There will be no loyalty, except towards the Party. There will be no love, except the love of Big Brother. There will be no laughter, except the laugh of triumph over a defeated enemy . . . All competing pleasures will be destroyed. But always – do not forget this, Winston – always there will be the intoxication of power, constantly increasing and constantly growing subtler. Always, at every moment, there will be the thrill of victory, the sensation of trampling upon an enemy who is helpless. If you want a picture of the future, imagine a boot stamping on a human face – for ever.

This picture of the future has proved unforgettable ever since. Yet it is remarkable that however accurately he "extrapolated" from the real experience of his own life,[8] Orwell had literally no idea or theory to offer of the *cause* of the behaviour he recorded. Another of the striking moments in *Nineteen Eighty-Four* is the one in which Winston, having finally obtained (from O'Brien) the famous banned book by the traitor Goldstein, starts to read its cogent account of how the Party got and holds its power. Orwell expends some thirty-five pages, more than a tenth of the total work, on excerpts from this book. It seems obvious to me at least that he does so in a genuine attempt to explain to the reader how a situation like that of *Nineteen Eighty-Four* could in reality come about. Goldstein, in this view, is merely a "disguised narrator" for Orwell, his book an equivalent of the well-known science fiction device of the "captain's log", by which real past and imagined future are connected. Yet when Winston comes at last and at length to the question one cannot help asking, the "central secret", the "original motive", the question of *why* the Party behaves like this – he stops reading! Orwell covers up the gap by having Julia fall asleep. Winston is sure he can finish the book another day. But neither he nor we ever get the chance to read on. It is hard not to see this strange break as a confession of inability on Orwell's part. He felt he could see how evil in his world was organised and supported. What he could not explain, either via O'Brien explaining the pleasures of power to Winston, or through the medium of the Goldstein book, was why people felt impelled to it. As evil existed in his experience, it seemed to lack even the perverse pleasures of sadism.

Lewis, by contrast, has an elaborate thesis about the origins of evil in the twentieth century, which one can pick out of his fiction with little difficulty. It is noticeable that he tends to locate his images of evil in rather trivial, if gruesome actions; and that (like Golding below) he sometimes specifically excepts war from the category of the truly horrific. Thus, in chapter 9 of *Voyage to Venus*, or *Perelandra* (1943), Lewis spends nearly a thousand words on the maiming by the Un-man (or Devil) of a frog, and on the hero's attempts to put it out of its misery. At the end the hero is "sick and shaken", and Lewis remarks that "It seems odd to say this of a man who had been on the Somme". Nevertheless, he insists, that is the case. Evil is not to be measured by the force used or the size of the result, but by motive as well. Meanwhile in *That Hideous Strength* two years later Lewis seems struck like Orwell by the pointlessness and joylessness in the visions of the future his plotters present. At one moment (in chapter 8/III) the members of N.I.C.E. (the National Institute for Co-ordinated Experiments) are talking among themselves, and so frankly, about their intentions. They vary

---

[7] Obviously, only Britain and her major enemies Germany and Austria were at war for the maximum ten years between 1914 and 1945: other nations had periods of neutrality or defeat. War was particularly traumatic to British society because it had been unusually un-military beforehand, having for instance no system of conscription until well into both wars. See further Paul Fussell, *The Great War and Modern Memory*. One American author who does resemble this group of Britons in several ways, life-experience included, is Kurt Vonnegut: his *Slaughterhouse-Five, or The Children's Crusade* (1969) is based on personal war experience.

[8] I discuss the real-life bases for Orwell's opinions in Shippey, 1987.

a good deal – some being fools, some villains and some devil-possessed, and it is admittedly a fool speaking. But what he says is that the N.I.C.E. ideal is to destroy life in favour of what he calls Mind:

> "We must get rid of it. By little and little, of course. Slowly we learn how. Learn to make our brains live with less and less body: learn to build our bodies directly with chemicals, no longer have to stuff them full of dead brutes and weeds. Learn to reproduce ourselves without copulation."
>
> "I don't think that would be much fun," said Winter.
>
> "My friend, you have already separated the Fun, as you call it, from the fertility. The Fun itself begins to pass away. Bah! I know that is not what you think. But look at your English women. Six out of ten are frigid, are they not? You see? Nature herself begins to throw away the anachronism."

Like O'Brien, the speaker here[9] focuses on a rejection of sexuality for power. Yet there is little doubt as to why he and his colleagues pursue their plan. They are the end-product of an anti-religious and pro-scientific attitude which Lewis linked strongly with H.G. Wells and his followers, producing a parody of their dreams of scientific expansion and pseudo-Darwinian evolution at the end of *Out of the Silent Planet*, in 1938; and introducing an easily-recognisable Wells caricature in the figure of Horace Jules, Director of N.I.C.E., near the end of *That Hideous Strength*. In essence Lewis accepted George Bernard Shaw's thesis about the theory of evolution leading on, via loss of faith and erosion of morality, to the two World Wars (see Shaw, 1921). This view was shared by none of the other authors considered here, not even Tolkien. Yet some of its components are present in the others; and there is a distinct similarity between the joyless, pointless visions of O'Brien and Filostrato.

Evolution is once again a key concept in the work of T.H. White, though as with Lewis his attitude to it is a complex and not entirely approving one. In *The Sword in the Stone* the Wart (later to become King Arthur) is repeatedly metamorphosed into one animal or another. From each species he learns something, whether good or ill. What comes over with particular strength, though, is White's bitter rejection of the notion that humanity is in some way at the pinnacle of evolution. Far from it, he insists. In *The Book of Merlyn* (chapter 5), the enchanter – it might be noted that he is a major character in Lewis's *That Hideous Strength* as well – argues that even the traditional classification of humanity as *homo sapiens* is totally wrong. The distinguishing quality of humanity is not ability to reason but ferocity. He is:

> *Homo ferox*, the Inventor of Cruelty to Animals, who will rear pheasants at enormous expense for the pleasure of killing them; who will go to the trouble of training other animals to kill; who will burn living rats, as I have seen done in Eriu, in order that their shrieks may intimidate the local rodents; who will forcibly degenerate the livers of domestic geese, in order to make himself a tasty food; who will saw the growing horns of cattle, for convenience in transport; who will blind goldfinches with a needle, to make them sing; who will boil lobsters and shrimps alive, although he hears their piping screams; who will turn on his own species in war, and kill nineteen million every hundred years; who will publicly murder his fellow men when he has adjudged them to be criminals; and who has invented a way of torturing his own children with a stick, or of exporting them to concentration camps called Schools, where the torture can be applied by proxy . . .
>
> Yes, you are right to ask whether man can properly be called *ferox*, for certainly the word in its natural meaning of wild life among decent animals ought never to be applied to such a creature.

Just as with Orwell's Goldstein, there can be little doubt that Merlyn here is just White speaking through a "disguised narrator". When Merlyn says "as I have seen done in Eriu", White is referring to his own wartime stay in Ireland. When Merlyn rebukes those who train animals to kill, and beat children in schools, one should remember that White too had been a master in an English public school, where corporal punishment was routine, and had taken a passionate interest in training hawks. He is including himself firmly in the criticism made here; and the reason he does so shines not only from everything Merlyn says, but also from the entire frame of *The Once and Future King*. Loaded though his fiction is with kindly, decent, well-meaning characters, White says repeatedly that the source of evil in humanity is neither born of politics nor the result of nineteenth-century loss of faith: instead, it is genetic, inborn. Revealingly, White rewrites the whole traditional Arthurian legend at critical points to make his case. Since the thirteenth century, writers have had to find different answers to the question of why Sir Lancelot killed Sir Gareth, his friend and ally, standing by unarmed precisely because he did not wish to oppose Lancelot's rescue of Guenevere. Since the twelfth it has been an established fact that the Last Battle of Camlann was caused, against the wishes of everyone present, when a knight drew his sword to kill an adder, provoking instant fears of treachery. But White altered the last incident to make it even more totally pointless: in his version the snake was not a poisonous adder but a harmless grass-snake (one of the sympathetic beasts of *The Sword in the Stone*). The knight cut at it not because it was in any way a danger but because people are like that. In the same way Lancelot lashed out at the unarmed Gareth, as White makes Lancelot say himself, because humans are "horrible creatures . . . If we see a flower as we walk through the fields, we lop off its head with a stick. That is how Gareth has gone." Like Lewis,

---

[9] His name is Filostrato, "the one destroyed by love". Lewis obviously knew this perfectly well, see his essay "What Chaucer really did to [Boccaccio's poem] *Il Filostrato*", first printed in *Essays and Studies for the English Association* 17 (1932), pp. 56-75. Lewis perhaps means to convey by this contradiction that Filostrato is a principled fanatic, genuinely in love with his own warped vision, though eager to destroy human love.

White is capable of locating his worst images of evil in the trivial – in *pâté de foie gras*, or in the boy Kay out shooting birds for sport. His view of the problem of war, of concentration camps and liquidations, is that they are all part of a continuum which begins in daily life and has its root in human genetics.

My final example of post-war visions of evil is the most directly stated and obvious of all. It comes from Golding's 1965 essay "Fable" – a piece written in part because of the pressure of continual requests from students to explain to them what the author had meant by *Lord of the Flies*, whence its directness and lack of camouflage. His "overall intention", Golding replied (not without a certain exasperation) had been this:

> Before the second world war I believed in the perfectibility of social man; that a correct structure of society would produce goodwill; and that you could remove all social ills by a reorganization of society. It is possible that today I believe something of the same again; but after the war I did not because I was unable to. I had discovered what one man could do to another. I am not talking of one man killing another with a gun, or dropping a bomb on him or blowing him up or torpedoing him. I am thinking of the vileness beyond all words that went on, year after year, in the totalitarian states. It is bad enough to say that so many Jews were exterminated in this way and that, so many people liquidated – lovely, elegant word – but there were things done during that period from which I still have to avert my mind lest I should be physically sick . . . I do not want to elaborate this. I would like to pass on; but I must say that anyone who passed through those years without understanding that man produces evil as a bee produces honey, must have been blind or wrong in the head.
>
> (Golding, 1965, pp. 86-7)

In this view, very much as in White's, evil is simply genetic. In people, producing evil is an instinct or a reflex. Golding recognises that his opinion may in a sense be a prejudiced or conditioned one, created by the experience of a particular time; he even hints that he may be getting ready to modify or reverse it. At the same time he insists that anyone with his experience who did not share his opinion "must have been blind or wrong in the head". One might paraphrase by saying that Golding is prepared to accept that there might be a larger view of humanity than the one he put in *Lord of the Flies*; but that any larger view would be incomplete if it did not at least contain his. There is meanwhile in Golding's mental state a strong element of disillusionment, shared both by Orwell and by Lewis. Golding says he had once believed in "the perfectibility of social man", i.e. before World War II. War jolted him out of that belief. It did the same to Orwell, as one can see from *Animal Farm*, an allegory of disillusion, though admittedly Orwell's disillusionment had started earlier than Golding's, perhaps with the treatment he received after return from Spain in 1937. Meanwhile Golding shared with Lewis a strong interest in, and even stronger rejection of the works of H.G. Wells. He produced a relatively affectionate Wellsian parody in his novelette "Envoy Extraordinary", from 1956, reprinted in *The Scorpion God* (1971) (see Shippey, 1973). His second novel *The Inheritors* (1955) is a more serious and damning refutation of the Wells story "The Grisly Folk". The case has yet to be argued, but one explanation of the structure of *Lord of the Flies* is to say that it follows in some detail the explanation of how religions arose in Wells's once well-known, now virtually forgotten work *The Outline of History* (1920); to which one is partially guided by the entries under Baal, or Baal-zebub, the "lord of the flies" himself, in the index of that work. Part of Golding's disillusionment, in other words, was with the promises of science and rationality; he however did not follow Lewis into a return to Christianity, a belief that evil was or could be genuinely diabolic.

Summing up the above, one might say that Orwell had no explanation for the origin of evil in his day; Lewis was trying to revive a traditional religious one; White preferred a genetic one; and Golding was poised somewhere between White and Orwell, though with significant agreements even with Lewis. All four however were observing much the same phenomena; all were capable of writing with a genuine bitterness and horror, which far outstrips anything in the recent genre of "horror fiction"; and none of them paid any attention at all to the official explanations of their time and culture, as promulgated by politicians, church leaders, literary critics, or even the "great tradition" of their predecessors as English novelists.

I now come to the question of how Tolkien fitted in to the group outlined above: and in some ways the answer must be, not too well. He was certainly like them in his rejection (or ignorance) of recent literary tradition, as in his overall pattern of life-experience. On the other hand he had less apparent interest than any of them in politics, or genetics, or science and the loss of faith, or H.G. Wells, all replaced in his case by an overriding professional interest in philology.[10] More significantly, it is hard to find in Tolkien a passage which equals in horror and degradation the excerpts from Orwell or White above, or anything like the disembowelling of the frog in Lewis or the killing of Piggy in Golding. In Tolkien, horror tends to take place "off-stage", as with the "place of dreadful feast and slaughter" in *The Lord of the Rings* IV/4; Shelob, the Ringwraiths and the Uruk-hai, while imaginatively threatening, do not make the same accusations about humanity that O'Brien, Filostrato and Merlyn do. Indeed it is significant that when I asked (at the presentation of this paper at "The Tolkien Phenomenon" in Turku) for examples from Tolkien's work of ultimate evil, the most penetrating example I was given, by Professor Verlyn Flieger, was Frodo's claiming of the Ring in the chambers of the Sammath Naur in *The Lord of the Rings* VI/3. This runs as follows:

---

[10] Though one has to say that this interest in its turn was shared by Lewis, another professional medievalist, and by White, a passionate amateur.

Then Frodo stirred and spoke with a clear voice, indeed with a voice clearer and more powerful than Sam had ever heard him use, and it rose above the throb and turmoil of Mount Doom, ringing in the roof and walls.

"I have come," he said. "But I do not choose now to do what I came to do. I will not do this deed. The Ring is mine!" And suddenly, as he set it on his finger, he vanished from Sam's sight.

In the context of *The Lord of the Rings*, this is certainly a most ominous and potentially disastrous moment. Putting on the Ring means going over to the other side, the side of evil. In the future it will lead to a destroyed and enslaved Middle-earth, and to Frodo as a wraith, or as a new Sauron. The moment negates everything that has been achieved so far, by men, elves or wizards. Yet at the same time putting on a ring is hardly in itself an image of evil. Nor is it self-evidently clear what it is that Frodo is doing wrong. When he says, "the Ring is mine", he has a case, at least in terms of ordinary legality. After all, he never stole it; it was given to him honestly; even Bilbo can only just be called a thief. None of this refutes what has been said above about the critical nature of the moment in terms of the special circumstances of *The Lord of the Rings*. But one could say that readers of that work are not made to feel the pointless, sterile, self-willed cruelty of evil as are readers of the other works discussed above.

Yet Tolkien certainly had a theory of evil, and took as deep an interest in the subject as any of the authors mentioned above. I have discussed his theory in historical/philological terms in *The Road to Middle-earth*,[11] and will not repeat the argument here. My conclusions were that Tolkien's theory was in a sense a distinctively modern one, centring on the idea that evil is an addiction; that Tolkien also kept up a balance between two old and apparently contradictory views of evil, (a) the Christian/Boethian one that evil is an absence, essentially internal, a temptation or a delusion, and (b) the Northern/heroic one that evil is an outside force to be fought physically; and that the weaving or "interlacing" of these views through the narrative presents a clear, individual, even idiosyncratic image of the nature of life in this world, which has contributed a great deal (whether consciously-realised or not) to the success of Tolkien's work.

A further point repeatedly made in my book, however, was that no matter how clearly Tolkien might express himself, to many of his readers, and most especially to professional readers like reviewers and literary critics, his views were unacceptable and often literally invisible.[12] It is this phenomenon which can perhaps best be approached "synchronically", in the context of the time. One of Tolkien's most hostile (though at the same time most involved) commentators was Edwin Muir. He reviewed each volume of *The Lord of the Rings* as it came out, in reviews for *The Observer* dated 22nd August 1954, 21st November 1954, and 27th November 1955. I cannot confirm that the assertion is true, but if it *is* true (as has been said) that the anonymous review for the *Times Literary Supplement* of 25th November 1955 was also Muir's work, then Muir had four tries at Tolkien – five if one counts also the letter in *TLS* of 9th December, in which the anonymous reviewer replied to demonstrations of his own inaccuracy. One thing that these four (or five) pieces share is their evident anxiety to do Tolkien down, and on the principle that "any stick will do to beat a dog" Tolkien is attacked on many counts: childishness, inadequate style, etc. However, a recurrent worry in all of them is failure to present evil in an acceptable (I would say, for the reviewer(s) a *recognisable*) way. The first *Observer* review complains that "[Tolkien's] good people are consistently good, his evil figures immutably evil; and he has no room in his world for a Satan both evil and tragic". The third *Observer* review resists the comparison with Malory offered by Naomi Mitchison, and says: "The heroes of the Round Table did not end happily. They were as brave as the heroes of the Ring, but they knew temptation, were sometimes unfaithful to their vows, or torn between the opposing claims of love and duty." The *TLS* review complains again that the evil characters in Tolkien are not sufficiently analysed: "save for their cruelty in war (and the Good do not as a rule grant quarter) we are never told exactly in what their wickedness consists", while as for the other side "there seems to be nothing outstandingly virtuous in their character". The assertions being consistently made are: evil characters are not sufficiently explained; good characters are not sufficiently mixed; and while the two sides are kept unrealistically apart (pure good and pure evil), they nevertheless behave in much the same way, especially as regards the use of force. To make the point even clearer, when a former colleague of mine, Mr. David Masson, wrote to the *TLS* on 9th December 1955, pointing out moderately that the reviewer had made a string of factual errors, and was as far at fault in his lack of perception over good and evil, the reviewer replied: "Throughout the book the good try to kill the bad, and the bad try to kill the good. We never see them doing anything else. Both sides are brave. Morally there seems nothing to choose between them."

Some of these complaints are as factually wrong as the repeated inability of reviewers (Muir included) to get the characters' names right: the notion that Tolkien's good people are "consistently good" for instance ignores a string of characters including Boromir, and the scene where Frodo claims the Ring; while the belief that evil is immutable is contradicted by open statements that even Sauron "was not always so", and the whole idea of the Ringwraiths. Yet to advance, one has to try to see what lies behind these reviews' evident anxiety (the cause, in my opinion, of their wilful lack of perception). One sees for instance more than once in Muir the feeling that *The Lord of the Rings* does not conform to literary pattern. Why can't it be more like *Paradise Lost*, have a Satan "both evil and tragic"? One answer to that was given by C.S. Lewis, whose *Voyage to Venus* is in effect a long

---

[11] See chapter 5 in both editions, and esp. pp. 123-33 in the 2nd edition.
[12] I write "literally" here because of the evidence that several of his critics simply could not take in elementary data like the names of the characters (see Shippey, 1992, pp. 1-5, 123-4, 156-7, 283-4).

commentary on *Paradise Lost*: in chapters 9 and 10 of that work Lewis makes it clear that he thinks that the "sombre tragic Satan out of *Paradise Lost*" (as well as the "suave and subtle Mephistopheles" of the Faustian tradition) are simply false as images of what evil is really like. In the same way Muir asks why Tolkien's heroes couldn't be more like the traditional Arthurian ones, especially (Muir is evidently thinking) Sir Lancelot and Queen Guinevere, with their adulterous and destructive passion? An answer to that was given by T.H. White (see above) with his rejection of the standard Arthurian interpretations and his insistence that evil in the real world is not individual and exciting at all, but a mere reflex action. Muir in short is trying to impose a literary pattern on Tolkien, and resenting the fact that Tolkien rejects that pattern; but the pattern was rejected by other authors as well, and always for the same reason: they felt that old literary patterns were unable to cope with the twentieth-century experience of evil (of which they, N.B., had first-hand and non-literary experience).

And then there are the linked issues of cruelty, mercy and violence. Tolkien very much resented the accusation of mercilessness, writing to his defender David Masson on 12th December 1955 (see Shippey, 1992, fn. p. 132) that "Surely how often 'quarter' is given is off the point in a book that breathes Mercy from start to finish: in which the central hero is at last divested of all arms, except his will?" Other defenders made similar replies, Masson for instance arguing that the great contrast was not Good and Evil but "love and hatred" (the *TLS* letter already cited), and W.H. Auden even more tellingly pointing out that a contrast between good and evil lies in the very structure of the book, in that good can imagine evil (which is why neither Gandalf nor Galadriel nor Faramir nor Frodo till the very end will take the Ring), but that evil "defiantly chosen . . . can no longer imagine anything but itself" (which is why Sauron takes no precautions at all against the attempt to reach the Sammath Naur) (see Auden, 1956, and Shippey, 1992, p. 156). But once again, viewing the matter "synchronically", it is not enough to argue these reviews down. One has to try to see what particular anxieties caused them, what challenge Tolkien's view of good and evil (like those of his fellow "fabulists") was presenting to the moral pieties of official culture.

Here it seems to me once again that life-experience is the clue. Tolkien's critics in the mid-1950s were frequently unhappy with the violence habitually used by the forces of good in his story. In the context of the heroic literature of earlier periods – the literature of Tolkien's professional life – this criticism is simply weird. There is never any possibility of Beowulf reasoning with Grendel, for instance, or Sir Gawain refusing to decapitate the Green Knight when challenged to do so. During the twentieth century, though, a lesson bitterly learnt is that "violence breeds violence", that (to go back to British experience) victory in World War I bred only the desire for vengeance which erupted in World War II. The whole British experience of World War I moreover tended to show that there was no clear indication of right and wrong as between the two sides, no matter what official propaganda might say. One common reaction to these and similar realisations was then to decide that "Violence is always wrong", that "the end never justifies the means". It was in this spirit that the Oxford Union in 1937 passed its famous resolution that "This House will in no circumstances fight for King and country"; it is this spirit that animates the *TLS* reviewer's "Morally there seems nothing to choose between them", and the *Observer* reviews' repeated calls for a blurring of the lines between good and evil (as regards motivation), and a simultaneous sharpening of them (as regards behaviour). Good and evil are seen as defined by attitudes to force.

This belief was quite clearly not shared by several of the writers here discussed. Golding, one notes, specifically excepts acts of war from his definition of evil: "I am not talking of one man killing another with a gun . . .", see above. In the same way one climax of *Voyage to Venus* (published in 1943, I repeat) is the realisation by the academic and pacific hero that it is his duty not just to reason with the Un-man in defence of the Lady's innocence but to attack him physically; *That Hideous Strength* also ends in a slaughter, of innocent (or at least semi-innocent) as well as guilty. Orwell never wavered in his belief that World War II had to be fought to a finish, calling on all resources of patriotism, however seemingly discredited. While White's attitude to force wavers continually, he insists on presenting the very idea of the Round Table as an attempt (unsuccessful, but perhaps not ultimately unsuccessful)[13] to civilise the human genetic urge to violence. In this context, Tolkien's good, violent, kindly, bloodthirsty characters – the adjectives just used fit particularly well for Théoden King – seem much less eccentric, paradoxical or thoughtless than so many reviewers indicated. The "postwar fabulists" I am discussing were all without exception highly conscious of the way in which good intentions could be perverted into evil, whether in Sauron or in Napoleon the pig in *Animal Farm*. Where they parted company with the very common academic view of Muir or a dozen later critics was in their refusal to accept that the danger of perversion excused inaction. It is very tempting to add that this joint refusal had its root in their own experience. Four of them had seen battle, all had lost friends, two of them had been shot: they were not prepared to accept that it had all been a mistake. By contrast many of their critics came from the most sheltered classes of British society. It is easy to believe that evil will go away if you ignore it, if you have never left an academic environment.

The question of civilising or legitimising violence also seems to me to be a highly realistic and critically important one, especially in the context of Tolkien's or Golding's lifetimes. To put the matter personally, I myself, though born

---

[13] At the end of *The Once and Future King*: "The cannons of his adversary were thundering in the morning when the Majesty of England drew himself up to face the future with a peaceful heart." Three lines above, King Arthur is sure that "Mordred must be slain". The very last words of the tetralogy – White is relying on the belief that Arthur is not dead but will come again in England's need – are "THE BEGINNING".

in 1943, have met Englishmen who have to my certain knowledge shot surrendered prisoners; burned men alive with petrol; killed unarmed women and children: all of them, I have to say, in normal life kindly, decent men who would never think of doing such things *except in wartime*. The latter fact, they thought (with exceptions and with different degrees of conscience) excused the former ones. The problem such men create – and I have no doubt that all the "fabulists" were much more aware of such things happening than I am – is how one resists evil without becoming it. It seems to me that much of *The Lord of the Rings*, as of *Lord of the Flies* or *The Once and Future King*, is dedicated to dramatising this particular problem. But it is emphatically *not* a solution to it to say, with Muir, that there is no need for violent resistance at all, or that evil is all in the mind.

A final perspective on Tolkien may be provided by considering the literary world of England in the between-wars period. This was characterised by intense post-war irony, cynicism, and rejection of authority. The thesis of Martin Green, in his book *Children of the Sun: a narrative of "decadence" in England after 1918* (1977), is that from 1918 onwards English literature was dominated for a while by *Sonnenkinder* – privileged young men, often homosexuals, often Old Etonians, deeply contemptuous of the older generation, and classifiable as Naifs, Dandies or Rogues. Green gives examples of each of these groups from both life and literature, for instance and respectively: Waugh's Sebastian, from *Brideshead Revisited*; the Burgess-MacLean-Philby group of traitors from Cambridge; Waugh's Basil Seal from *Put Out More Flags*. He sees this domination as essentially disastrous in both life and literature, leading to both national and literary decline. I can again report from personal experience with what fury this thesis was greeted, even in 1977, by the heirs and descendants of the group Green identified: at least one reviewer for a national newspaper was approached personally and told in all seriousness that this book *had to be squashed*, and that failure to join in the squashing would have unpleasant consequences. The reviewer, a colleague, wrote a highly laudatory review. There were no unpleasant consequences. But forty years earlier, when Tolkien was writing *The Hobbit*, or twenty years earlier, when *The Lord of the Rings* was meeting its reviewers, the *Sonnenkinder* were more firmly in control.

It is striking that Green is quite unable to fit Tolkien into the literary scene he presents so thoroughly. He mentions him only twice, puts him in a "Christians" group with Lewis,[14] and sees him via his Catholicism as a literary descendant of G.K. Chesterton :

> Chesterton's most direct descendants were C.S. Lewis, Dorothy Sayers, Charles Williams and J.R.R. Tolkien [*sic*] – the Oxford "Inklings". These people escaped dandyism and aestheticism – to which they all felt some attraction – but without confronting it. They provided themselves with a handsomer dialectical enemy, the forces of evil as defined by orthodox Christian theology, which they located on the contemporary scene most often in the misuse of science and social science . . . Most aspects of their ideological and imaginative behaviour strike me as more generous, intelligent, and dignified than those of either Leavis or Waugh – or Orwell, for that matter – if considered in the abstract. But considered in the concrete, the ideas of the last three have at various times meant everything to me, while the others *mean*, in that sense, nothing. I approve what they did, but theoretically; I read the books it resulted in approvingly, but I am not really engaged by them at all.
>
> And one reason surely is that these writers removed themselves from the cultural dialectic. Undignified as that often was, both personally and intellectually, that was where the action was . . .

And Green goes on to say that for all his awareness of their personal qualities, he is "no more attracted to Auden and Lewis and Tolkein [*sic*, again]" than he ever was (1977, pp. 495-7).

It is perhaps significant that for all his general benevolence, Green is still unable to spell Tolkien's name correctly. Just like Muir, Edmund Wilson and the other critics who consistently misspelled the names of the characters, there is a suspicion that some non- or pre-literary antipathy prevents Green from looking closely and sharply at what he is criticising (though Green of course has the honesty to admit openly his inability to take an interest). One can see this antipathy two ways. What was it like for Tolkien, or Lewis, to find themselves in an Oxford whose literary circles were dominated by the kind of young man Green describes, and for whom they would quite certainly feel the deepest distaste? The answer is clear enough: they dropped out (as many must have done), creating a cult of self-conscious simplicity, heartiness, even Philistinism, as a kind of protection. That cult may seem rather ridiculous now.[15] But if you did not wish to collaborate, like Waugh, or oppose, like Orwell, what other option was there? Meanwhile both Lewis and Tolkien made their plan to go "over the heads" of the literary Establishment and appeal to a mass market where they believed, or hoped, that they would still find unprejudiced readers. Lewis was successful in this from an early stage, using radio as well as print to make his mark; Tolkien struck later and cut deeper. Neither has ever been forgiven for it.

But one can see the antipathy between critics and "fabulists" in another way. I commented in the "Afterword" to *Road* how very strange I found it that a critic like Philip Toynbee should be able to write such a perfect description of Tolkien under the heading of the "Good Writer" – someone private and lonely, "shocking and amazing", excessively knowledgeable and (N.B.) deeply dissatisfied with "modern

---

[14] White and Golding do not figure in Green's index at all. Orwell is seen persuasively as (though an Etonian) a rejector of the ethos, an "anti-dandy"

[15] See for instance the accounts in Carpenter, 1977, pp. 53-4, or Wilson, 1990, pp. 129-32. Wilson also remarks on the ethos of 1920s Oxford in pp. 71-2.

English"! — and still fail completely to see how well Tolkien's work fitted his own description, when it appeared. Yet Toynbee is a perfect product of the "decadent" environment Green describes, labelled unhesitatingly by Green as one of the naifs, "all limpid sensitiveness and generous responsiveness". The sensitivity and responsiveness were in the end just an act; but put in this context one can see how threatening the public success of writers like Tolkien was to the *Sonnenkinder* and their heirs. It told them their time was over. They had controlled literature in the post-World War I period. No doubt they had looked forward to substantial reinforcement for their cynical, irreverent and irresponsible beliefs in the post-World War II period. Instead the beliefs and the control were challenged, though I do not believe (remembering 1977 and the *furore* over Green's book) that they have by any means been overthrown.

I would argue, then, that Tolkien can be seen as in essence a post-World War II writer; one of a group of English writers whose subjects were war and evil; who drew their subjects from their own life-experience, little affected or assisted by the views of official culture, whether literary or political; and who wrote in non-realistic modes essentially because they felt they were writing about subjects too great and too general to tie down to particular and recognisable settings. The views of this group about evil, widely different though they were, were similar in that they challenged the comfortable opinions of sheltered contemporaries, which is why none of the group (except Golding) has *both* been accepted into the unstated but well-known "canon" of academic texts *and* had his works receive a reading of the kind "which its author may be supposed to have desired", to use a Tolkienian phrase.[16] I hope this paper has suggested a way in which Tolkien can be set in a contemporary as well as a historical context, and has pointed to the importance — political as well as literary — of the group in which I place him, and of the themes which that group felt impelled to treat.

References

Anon. 1955a. "The Saga of Middle Earth" in *Times Literary Supplement*, 25th November 1955, p. 704.

Anon. 1955b. Letter in *Times Literary Supplement*, 9th December 1955, p. 743.

Auden, W.H. 1956. "At the End of the Quest, Victory" in *The New York Review of Books*, 22nd January 1956, p. 5.

Carpenter, Humphrey. 1977. *J. R. R. Tolkien: A biography*. London: George Allen & Unwin.

Crick, Bernard. 1980. *George Orwell: A Life*. Harmondsworth: Penguin Books.

Fussell, Paul. 1975. *The Great War and Modern Memory*. London & New York: Oxford University Press.

Gallix, François (ed.). 1984. *T. H. White, Letters to a Friend: the correspondence between T. H. White and L. J. Potts*. London: Alan Sutton.

Golding, William. 1954. *Lord of the Flies*. London: Faber & Faber.

Golding, William. 1955. *The Inheritors*. London: Faber & Faber.

Golding, William. 1956a. *Pincher Martin*. London: Faber & Faber.

Golding, William. 1956b. "Envoy Extraordinary", reprinted in *The Scorpion God*. London: Faber & Faber.

Golding, William. 1965. *The Hot Gates*. London: Faber & Faber.

Green, Martin. 1977. *Children of the Sun: a narrative of "decadence" in England after 1918*. London: Constable.

Lewis, C.S. 1932. "What Chaucer really did to *Il Filostrato*", in *Essays and Studies for the English Association* 17 (1932), pp. 56-75.

Lewis, C.S. 1938. *Out of the Silent Planet*. London: Bodley Head.

Lewis, C.S. 1943. *Voyage to Venus*, or *Perelandra*. London: Bodley Head.

Lewis, C.S. 1945. *That Hideous Strength*. London: Bodley Head.

Masson, David. 1955. Letter in *Times Literary Supplement*, 9th December 1955, p. 743.

Muir, Edwin. 1954a. "Strange Epic" in *The Observer*, 22nd August 1954, p. 7.

Muir, Edwin. 1954b. "The Ring" in *The Observer*, 21st November 1954, p. 9.

Muir, Edwin. 1955. "A Boy's World" in *The Observer*, 27th November 1955, p. 11.

Orwell, George. 1945. *Animal Farm*. London: Secker & Warburg.

Orwell, George. 1949. *Nineteen Eighty-Four*. London: Secker & Warburg.

Shaw, George Bernard. 1921. "Preface" to *Back to Methuselah* (1921) in *Prefaces by Bernard Shaw*. London: Constable.

Shippey, T.A. 1973. "Science Fiction and the Idea of History" in *Foundation* 4 (1973), pp. 4-19.

---

[16] In my article on Orwell (Shippey, 1987) above I give reasons for my belief that *Nineteen Eighty-Four*, for all its "canonical" status, still frequently provokes only "averted-eye" or emasculating responses from post-"decadent" literary critics.

Shippey, T.A. 1982. *The Road to Middle-earth*, first edition. London: George Allen & Unwin.

Shippey, T.A. 1983. "*The Once and Future King*" in *The Survey of Fantasy Literature*, ed. Frank N. Magill. Englewood Cliffs, NJ: Salem Press. Volume 3, pp. 1149-57.

Shippey, T.A. 1987. "Variations on Newspeak: the Open Question of *Nineteen Eighty-Four*", in *Storm Warnings: Science Fiction Confronts the Future*, ed. George Slusser *et al*. Carbondale, IL: Southern Illinois University Press, pp. 72-93.

Shippey, T.A. 1992. *The Road to Middle-earth*, second enlarged edition. London: HarperCollins.

Tolkien, J.R.R. 1937. *The Hobbit*. London: George Allen & Unwin.

Vonnegut, Kurt. 1969. *Slaughterhouse-Five, or The Children's Crusade*. New York: Delacorte.

Warner, Sylvia Townsend. 1967. *T.H. White: a Biography*. London: Jonathan Cape.

Wells, H.G. 1920. *The Outline of History*. London: Cassell.

White, T.H. 1938. *The Sword in the Stone*. London: Collins.

White, T.H. 1958. *The Once and Future King*. London: Collins.

White, T.H. 1977. *The Book of Merlyn*. Austin: University of Texas Press.

Wilson, A.N. 1990. *C.S. Lewis: a Biography*. New York and London: Norton.

Where do Elves go to? Tolkien and a Fantasy Tradition

Norman Talbot

Abstract: The departure of the Elves from Middle-earth haunted Tolkien's imagination, but it has also fascinated many other writers before and since. After Kipling and Tolkien, the twin pivots in recent literary ideas about Elves, the destiny of the Elves is being treated in more and more diverse ways. But Hy Braseal is so hard to imagine, given the Americas in this century: how can the people of the starlight still "go west"? Most go "in" instead, into humanity or into places (and computer programs) with that special Elf-friendly charge.

Keywords: Anderson, Arnold, Ballads, Barrie, Baudino, Beagle, Blake, Boyer, Bradley, Brooks, Charrette, Cherryh, Corbet, Dean, de la Mare, de Lint, Drayton, Duane, Elves, Fairies, Frost, Goethe, Hogg, Holdstock, Housman, Jones, Kay, Keats, Kerr, Kipling, La Motte Fouqué, Lewis, Lyly, Macdonald, Milton, Moon, Morris, Pope, Rossetti C, Rossetti D G, Shakespeare, Shelley, Spenser, Swinburne, Tennyson, Tolkien, T.H.White, Wolfe, Wrede.

> They were a race high and beautiful, the older Children of the world, and among them the Eldar were as kings, who now are gone: the People of the Great Journey, the people of the Stars.
>
> J.R.R. Tolkien (1955, p. 415)

All mythologies, cultural traditions and substantial bodies of folklore contain stories about at least one other race than the human. Long-lived if not "immortal", and associated with phenomenal nature, especially deep forests, this is normally an Elder Race, wiser and more in touch with both natural powers and magical Power. In North-Western Europe, the most satisfactory term for this fictional race is Elf, since "fairy" has become degraded and miniaturised. If Tolkien's commentator in Appendix F of *The Lord of the Rings* laments of "Elves",

> This old word . . . has been diminished, and to many it may now suggest fancies either pretty or silly, as unlike the Quendi of old as are butterflies to the swift falcon . . .
>
> (Tolkien, 1955, p. 415)

What would he say of "fairies"? Precisely what Kipling, with the same metaphor, had said a half-century earlier (see p. 98 below).

Other "Other races" are identified with mountains and caves and hence with working metal and stone, as with dwarfs, or with oceans, lakes and streams, as with mermaids and naiads. Others are associated with the will of an all-powerful creator divinity, like angels, cherubim and seraphim, or with a menacing opponent to that divine power, like devils, demons and efreet. None of these, not even angels, have Elven glamour or Elven gramary – and these two words, cognate with "grammar", remind us of the poetic eloquence of that race.

Elves and similar Other races have their own other world, within or contingent with ours, reached by mortals only through a mysterious and dangerous process (usually a journey, perhaps underground or undersea, or even by flight) though sometimes a ritual or a simple invitation will suffice. Oriental, Classical and Celtic traditions, more than the Teutonic, emphasise that the heterocosm is a garden paradise: fountains, birdsong, flowers and great trees, starshine and twilight are appropriate. A palace or high tower, feasting, song, music, jewels, an assured (often hierarchical) social structure and a protected atmosphere, identify the Other-world as cultured, not a bucolic Arcadia.

Elves of the kind that interested Tolkien are humaniform or humanoid, highly cultured but by no means effeminate or decadent, more or less magical, and either immortal or apparently immune to aging. Generally they are both more beautiful and wiser, more spiritually intense, than human beings. This study offers some comments on Tolkien's relationship to the various traditions of elven portrayal, and gives some examples of later variants, more or less "anxiously" influenced by his work.

I

> I could say "elves" to him,
> But it's not elves, exactly, and I'd rather
> He said it for himself.
>
> Robert Frost, "Mending Wall"

It is first worth asking why human tale-tellers and audiences feel a need for Elves; after all, even those who believe in the literal reality of angels, devils or ghosts are unlikely to claim the same factual status for Elves. Nor, in the way that kindly sceptics explain away Thor as an superstitious attempt to account for thunder, can Elven activity explicate many phenomena either of the external world of nature or of human experience and destiny. Rather, they represent an admirable, unattainable mode of life, a blessed interaction between the self and "unspoiled" nature, such as trees, river, stars, an existence distanced from the mortal and yet similar enough for our minds willingly to suspend disbelief in it. Our present stage of ecological consciousness and conscience welcomes and needs such a fiction.

Second, Elves represent, along with this attunement to nature, a less "earthy" mode of experience, wilder and more inspired than dull, predictable humanity. Because "immortal", more liberated in both time and physical nature, they perceive a world and live a life unpolluted by most of our deadly sins, especially economic rationalism. Elven values, unlike human certitudes, are not held with any expectation of future (or renewed) global domination, and can thus be justified only by their intrinsic qualities. Again, because Elves are "soulless", accepting no definition of self at variance with their bodily experience, their criteria of conduct cannot privilege spiritual over physical being. They are at one with themselves, present where they are.

Temporally, Elves are not in a hurry, having many lifetimes of men in which to understand – and complete – the projects they conceive. They do not fear death or have any doubt of their destiny in the Undying Realms, whether in the Halls of Mandos or as living migrants. They have therefore developed an aesthetic, a code of conduct, and a readiness to value nobility and beauty which humans cannot equal. Our limitations are well expressed by two of the condensed, clarified humans called hobbits:

". . . we can't live long on the heights."

"No . . . Not yet, at any rate. But at least, Pippin, we can now see them, and honour them. It Is best to love first what you are fitted to love, I suppose: you must start somewhere and have some roots, and the soil of the Shire is deep. Still, there are things deeper and higher . . ."

(Tolkien, 1955, p. 146)

This passage, taken ruthlessly out of context, indicates the shift in perspective that stories with Elves in them, like some other aspects of "High Fantasy", can offer. Elves are best evoked from the outside, through focalisation characters not themselves at all Elvish, whose expectations are more like our own.

Third, to have Elves in a story defamiliarises that story. They are not only different from us, their difference is itself a narrative instrument, expressed in everything from music, poetry, languages and ethical values to artifacts and social conventions. Defamiliarisation, Viktor Shklovsky's "ostranenie", is a more celebratory distancing than Brecht's "Verfremdung", alienation; however, both Marxists emphasise the need for fictions that deconstruct the smug bourgeois ideology of "realism". Such a deconstruction is, they felt, not only aesthetically pleasing but morally right because a major obstacle to revolution is the bourgeois assumption that empirical normality is necessarily, reassuringly true, and totally confirmatory of the status quo.

Tolkien wanted no revolution, of course, but aimed to estrange us from our habit-ridden mental routines and self-indulgent unresponsiveness so that we might recover our sense of wonder, our spiritual – and physical – mindfulness of the world. In a pleasant twist, we are brought to realise two contrary facts. On the one hand, we have always longed to communicate with some Other, intelligent non-human life in our universe; on the other, our parochial habits of mind have always tempted us to pretend that the Other is evil, to abjure the different or unfamiliar because of its otherness, yet knowing the Other is an essential step to knowing the Self.

Fourth, responsive readers, having deconstructed the "normal", can thrill appropriately to narrative clues that enable them to construct the Other. Tolkien delights in encyclopedias of philological and cultural wealth, both implied within the narrative and assembled in appendices. The most complex history and the most splendid range of linguistic and orthographic invention by far belong to the Elves, marvellously unlike humanity in so many details. Their history and values are glorious, glamorous and poignant as they fight "the long defeat" against Morgoth and Sauron. Even their past faults intrigue, especially pride, as in their domineering benevolence towards human cultures in earlier ages of Middle-earth; admittedly, the Noldor bias of *The Silmarillion* probably exaggerates this dominance.

The Elves of the Third Age are surrounded and outnumbered, but their attachment to their own culture and languages is the more intense. Their elegiac pride is at least part of the reason why Elf/human marriages are so difficult and ennobling, and why the mortal man that achieves such a marriage must himself become distant from the rest of us.

II

Pinch him, pinch him, black and blue;
Saucy mortals must not view
What the queen of stars is doing,
Nor pry into our fairy wooing.

John Lyly, song from *Endimion*

The name "elf" comes from the Norse alfr (plural alfar). Two kinds of Elf inhabit and fight over a magical heterocosm, coextensive with but not easily accessible from our own Middle Earth. The lios-alfar, light-elves, are "good", though not much interested in or respectful of clumsy mortals like us. The svart-alfar, dark-elves, are wicked. They hate light-elves, humans, and most other things; orc-like, when there is no-one else around they pass the time by hating each other. Both races are soulless, so the Christian Norse at least assure us, but they are long-lived and immune to aging, if not actually immortal. They are smaller than humans, and use some kinds of magic, including magical weapons; worse, knowing of certain "gates" between our world and theirs, they can (if they wish) steal human babies and leave changelings in their place. Norse

Christians felt that the alfar should go to either their own world, safely sealed off, or Hell.

An accomplished contemporary narrative, using the changeling motif and Elves (as well as other creatures) taken direct from Norse tradition rather than, from Tolkien, is Poul Anderson's *The Broken Sword* (1954, revised 1973). Equally Nordic and vigorously, inventive is the Iceland-and-Elfland series by Elizabeth Boyer that begins with *The Sword and the Satchel* (1984). These may be compared with the consciously post-Tolkien works discussed in parts V and VI of this study, most of which pursue Celtic rather than Nordic otherworlds.

Since Tolkien produced his most influential scholarly work on the Old English "Beowulf" and the Middle English "Sir Gawain and the Green Knight", it is significant that both refer only briefly to Elves and that neither sounds much like the Norse tradition. In Beowulf "ylfe" are children of Cain, as Grendel is; a grim and ominous descent, implying a direct kinship with mortal men. The Green Knight is himself described as an "aluish mon", which implies personal and integral magical powers, though it seems to be Morgan le Fay's magic that allows him to survive beheading.

Tolkien shows very keen awareness of the alfar tradition, but adapts it to a very different world-view. The distinction between his "light" and "dark" Elves is historical, not moral: the callaquendi are so called because they lived in the West in the light of the Two Trees, whereas the moriquendi, in the East, never experienced that light. There are no bad Elves in Tolkien's stories; however proud, unforgiving or impulsive, all are devoted enemies of evil. Any who are caught up with the works of Morgoth, or later of Sauron, have been so irreparably marred that the term Elf can no longer apply. The frenetically fighting and breeding hordes of Orcs that serve the two Enemies were made by Morgoth as a parody of Elves, probably from the bodies and minds of horribly misguided, viciously tortured Elves he had entrapped.

Tolkien's Elves are tall, courtly and graceful, wise if somewhat enigmatic, and by no means wholly alien to humans: three major intermarriages are crucial to the history of Middle-earth. In their music and song, their healing and archery, their beauty, wisdom and self-possessed grace, they are strikingly Apollonian figures, if one ignores their delight in laughter. They were once great artificers and artists, but as their hold on Middle-earth comes to an end they prefer only to "make" in the evanescent forms of music and poetry. As the first-born of Ilúvatar the creator, so long-lived as to be almost immortal, and carrying with them always the knowledge of their true home beyond the Western Seas, they understand time and the ironies of success and failure as humans never will. They cannot be expected to revere their short-lived human neighbours; still, in *The Lord of the Rings* if not in *The Hobbit*, they alloy their amusement at us with a scrupulous grave respect.

There are no woods in Iceland, Elizabeth Boyer's frame environment, and her Norse Elfland naturally reflects this in being not in the least arboreal; her grim Elves live in fortified farms. The wood-elves in *The Hobbit*, like Anderson's Elves, live in a hill, with prisons, implying a harsh judicial system, still farther underground. However, their forest-dwelling aspect is crucial. Their keen eyes and pointed ears may be like the alfar, but their love of trees, and that supple woodcrafty elusiveness that is only partly to do with magic, connects them with the higher Elves.

The complex glamour of Galadriel is also emphatically unlike any figure of the Norse tradition. The true ruler of the hidden and time-forgetful dreamwood of Lórien, she really does carry about her some of the menace of the stories that have sprung up among the Rohirrim:

> Then there is a Lady in the Golden Wood, as old tales tell! . . . Few escape her nets, they say. These are strange days! But if you have her favour, then you also are net-weavers and sorcerers, maybe.
> (Tolkien, 1954b, p. 35)

Tolkien was well aware of the superb British ballads of the Elf-Queen, "Thomas the Rhymer" and "Tam Lin", and also, in spite of his well-known mistrust of Shakespeare, of the ambiguous Faery royalty of *A Midsummer Night's Dream*. Titania and Oberon will not mitigate a quarrel that has disastrous consequences for all those anywhere near them; both Oberon's attitude to Titania's sexuality during the feud and her own cool reaction at its denouement are markedly at variance with human morality.

As for the Elf-Queen ballads, Thomas the Rhymer cannot utter even a word of protest at the Lady's commands, but must simply submit. Explicitly the ruler of a world that Christian Heaven/Hell oppositions cannot begin to describe, she is all-powerful within that realm. She has presumably sealed her secret ways into Elfland, to emerge no more (unless an equally charming poet attracts her). Tam Lin's Elf-Queen lives closer to evil, and though he has been her special pet she is about to hand him over to the Devil to pay the "tiend to Hell" when Janet rescues him. To defy the Queen's will is very dangerous, for her enmity cannot ever be adulterated with pity. Where so cruel and fatal an Elf-Lady should go is of course Hell, since she has no Tam to hand over – after all, she has sought to enthral a baptised Christian boy. Janet's ordeal evokes laws that the Elf-Queen dare not transgress, but had she foreseen the frustration of her plan, she says, she would have plucked out Tam's eyes and set wooden ones there instead. Diana Wynne Jones has presented an admirably rich and subtle modern reworking of the story in *Fire and Hemlock* (1985); a somewhat less adroit but still memorable version is Pamela Dean's college romance *Tam Lin* (1991).

Galadriel knows the potential in herself for an Elf-Queen's role and rule, were she to accept the One Ring:

> I shall not be dark, but beautiful and terrible as the Morning and the Night! Fair as the Sea and the Sun and the Snow upon the Mountain! Dreadful as the Storm and the Lightning! Stronger than the foundations of the earth. All shall love me and despair!
> (Tolkien, 1954a, p. 381)

As Christianity and human love checked Tam Lin's Elf-Queen, Galadriel checks herself, and since the ring's coming implies the end of the Elves in Middle-earth, whether by the defeat of Sauron or his victory, she accepts her own ending: "I will diminish, and go into the West, and remain Galadriel" (Tolkien, 1954a, p. 381). In the ballads, the tall and awe-inspiring Queens give a sinister and voluptuous edge to the mysteries of Elfland: the twilight they rule is erotic as well as frightening and potentially cruel. Presumably because the sex-drive in male Elves is very low, Elven ladies are perennially interested in innocent mortal males; Nick Bottom and Tam Lin escape, but their stories exist because they are not typical. The Belle Dame sans Merci role that Galadriel rejects is obscenely parodied by Shelob's incestuous tyranny as the Terrible Mother to her broods (Tolkien, 1954b, p. 332).

Galadriel is not, of course, the Queen of all Elves. Where Thomas the Rhymer's captor differentiates her realm entirely from the Christian Heaven and Hell, and Tam Lin's mistress pays a tax to Hell, Galadriel and her elven subjects have a theology that is reconcilable with Christianity. They worship the one true God, but through an intermediary High Goddess, Elbereth or Varda, whose symbology and intercessory role markedly resemble the Blessed Virgin Mary (who was, incidentally, the object of Tolkien's special reverence). Virtual queen of the Valar, she is especially associated with starlight, and Galadriel uses her powerful elven-ring not to take power over others but to testify to her devotion to Elbereth. She also identifies herself with the memory of Eärendil, and this celestial mariner, father of her son-in-law Elrond, is Venus, the evening star, sometimes called Stella Maris or Star of the Sea, that Catholic sailors regard as an emblem of Mary.

It is important to add that though Tolkien's Elves have the same declining birthrate as Elves in the ballads, and also regularly lose population as more of them heed the lure of the Sea and of Valimar beyond, Elven-ladies like Galadriel are no more obsessed with sex than are their lords. If few children are born, it is partly because all Elves know they are not long, in their time-scale, for Middle-earth.

III

Farewell rewards and Fairies,
 Good housewives now may say,
For now foule sluts in Dairies
 Doe fare as well as they.
  Richard Corbet, "The Fairies' Farewell"

The reference to *A Midsummer Night's Dream* above should remind us of the regrettable degradation of Elves in some late Renaissance texts. The tiny servants Titania set to serve Bottom are suitably trivial, but Tolkien complains in "On Fairy Stories", referring mainly to Drayton, of the assumption that all fairies were so. Ariel, in *The Tempest*, is a wind-elemental of power and shape-shifting ability, but his famous song about lying in a cowslip's bell has also contributed to the idea of the minuscule fairy. Shakespeare's central fairies were of course human-size, and not only because played by humans: at the narrative level, in view of the sexual commerce between mortal and fairy freely evoked by Titania and Oberon, "little people" would seem as grotesque as with Elf-Queens and Elven seducers in the ballads, and Spenser's often amorous (and highly pugnacious) elven knights. Yet in the seventeenth century, Puritan and Arminian alike adopted the pretence that all fairies were only the size of Mustardseed, Peaseblossom, Cobweb and Moth (who was probably "Mote").

Fays, fairies and other Others were made safely decorative and essentially impotent by this late Renaissance diminution. From flower-haunting, wand-wagging, insect-duelling absurdities like Drayton's Pigwiggen descend Pope's Sylphs and Barrie's Tinkerbell. Shakespeare's – or Oberon's – Puck, that arrogant earthy, formidable trickster, had been contemptuous of all human mortals, even the ruling classes; over-civilised imaginations found it all too easy to shrink even Puck to a mere brownie or lob allowed to bully only slatternly servants and reward only obedient ones. The culture that considered itself "Augustan", "The Enlightenment", knew where they wanted Elves to go: into cowslips – or at least into absurdity, tinsel and lower-class rural superstition.

Milton's "L'Allegro" evokes the Elves of this kind, degraded to small country magics, but Richard Corbet's "The Fairies' Farewell" has a more direct relevance, because of its use in one of Tolkien's major influences, the Sussex stories of Kipling, *Puck of Pook's Hill* (1906) and *Rewards and Fairies* (1910). Fairy rings prove to the high-church bishop that the fairies had been happy in England until the Reformation and the expulsion of the Roman Catholic faith:

Witness those rings and roundelays
 Of theirs, which yet remaine,
Were footed in Queene Maries dayes
 On many a grassy playne;
But since of late, Elizabeth,
 And later James, came in,
They never daunc'd on any heath
 As when the time bath bin.

They have all fled the country. Far from being indifferent about or cruel to mortals, these miniature aliens are vulnerable to any change in human affairs.

My complaint against the trivialising late Renaissance writers may have a weak spot. Walter de la Mare cites a passage in Chaucer in which the Elves have not only forsaken England but also speech, and become sinister in the extreme. According to de la Mare's quotation in the first volume of his *Come Hither* anthology, the diabolised Prince Oberon "is of heyght but of III fote, and crokyed shulderyd . . . And yf ye speke to hym, ye are lost for ever." (de la Mare, 1923, p. 391) Squat and misshapen these Silent People may be; they are certainly not trivialised. This is what comes of paying too many "tiends" to Hell! However, I cannot find the Chaucer passage itself.

Puck, producer of Kipling's excellent stories (he tells three), scorns the tinselly creatures spawned by a disempowered tradition and sentenced to hard labour by didactic Victorian children's authors. His own narration of "Dymchurch Flit" agrees to some extent with Corbet's; it evokes a pathetic gathering of enfeebled "people of the Hills", made sick by the human hatred that pervaded the Civil War, and other dogma-based cruelty of human to human, and begging Mrs Whitgift to help them to flee to France. Puck still has a soft spot for Romney Marsh families;

though a trickster, he seems in general a friend to man rather than a cruel or indifferent spirit. Noticeably, halfwits are more on the wavelength of fairies than other, more rational people.

The second book begins with Puck's other major story of the People of the Hills, "Cold Iron", where King Huon and Queen Esclairmonde of Elfland, alien to iron, salt and roofs, raise a protege (not precisely a changeling), to take power as a ruler, wise-man or healer among "folk in housen". However, when a grown boy, by what cannot be chance, the lad picks up and puts on the iron ring of servitude that Thor had cast down long before. Thus he enters our mortal world as a serf and the begetter of a whole powerless, hard-working peasantry. Old Hobden, the children's special working-class friend, who has, incidentally, married into the Whitgifts, is typical of this earthy, shrewd inheritance of cold iron and its divorce from conscious association with magic.

Both these stories, and the self-metamorphic nature of Puck himself, can only be understood as the Grey Havens of the Elves' response to Middle Earth. Puck begins his immersion of Dan and Una into Sussex by eloquently establishing what "the People of the Hills" were, as opposed to "fairies". In British prehistory, when every corner of the wild landscape resonated with power, things were different:

> Butterfly wings indeed! I've seen Sir Huon and a troop of his people setting off from Tintagel Castle for Hy-Brasil in the teeth of a sou'-westerly gale, with the spray flying all over the Castle, and the Horses of the Hills wild with fright. Out they'd go in a lull, screaming like gulls, and back they'd be driven five good miles inland before they could come head to wind again. Butterfly-wings! It was Magic – Magic as black as Merlin could make it, and the whole sea was green fire and white foam with singing mermaids in it. And the Horses of the Hills picked their way from one wave to another by the lightning flashes! That was how it was in the old days!
> (Kipling, 1905, p. 12)

Kipling's stories directly influenced Tolkien, and not only in that he echoes Puck's scorn of Tinkerbells and presents tall, fierce Elves who are prepared to ride a storm. First, the name Hobson is not unlike "hobbit-son", and both connote small, resilient, dexterous English countryfolk, with a peasant relish for good rich food and drink. Specifically, the grandfather of Samwise Gamgee, the most intrinsically hobbit of Tolkien's heroes, was Hobson Gamgee (Tolkien, 1955, p. 383).

More curiously still, Puck resembles a hobbit. He has tough, hairy bare feet, a short broad stature, elusiveness in the fields and woods and a keen, disinterested observation of Big People. Puck has separated himself off from the vanished Faerie as a genius loci, identified with the country around "Pook's Hill". There he can be summoned only by an odd threefold ritual which mortal learning could not hit upon, but children's luck can:

> You've done something that Kings and Knights and scholars in old days would have given their crowns and swords and books to find out. If Merlin himself had helped you, you couldn't have managed better! You've broken the Hills – you've broken the Hills! It hasn't happened in a thousand years . . .
>
> Unluckily the Hills are empty now, and all the People of the Hills are gone. I'm the only one left. I'm Puck, the oldest Old Thing in England . . .
> (Kipling, 1906, pp. 6-7)

Since in "Dymchurch Flit" Puck can, when somewhat enlarged, pass for an old friend of Hobson, his Sussex has strong claims to be an inspirational parallel to the Shire, especially Buckland and the Marish as seen by the genius loci of the Old Forest, Tom Bombadil. The most obvious evidence for this is in his interest in Frodo and his companions, with whom he discusses Shire folk and affairs, history and prehistory (Tolkien, 1954a, p.143), but it is confirmed by "Bombadil Goes Boating", the second poem of *The Adventures of Tom Bombadil* (Tolkien, 1962), where the jovial silliness of Tolkien's narration contrasts Puck-like with the subtlety of its physical contexting. Among other intriguing connections between Puck and Tolkien is, in his explanation of why People of the Hills don't like being called "fairies", the apt sardonic question, "How would you like to be spoken to as 'Son of Adam' and 'Daughter of Eve' all the time?" Tolkien may well have recalled this with relish when he first read *The Lion, the Witch and the Wardrobe* (Lewis, 1950)!

Interestingly, Kipling's stories also influenced the finest creation of what might be called "magic historicism" from the Matter of Britain, T.H. White's *The Once and Future King* (1958). Tolkien's heterocosm has a joyous, purposeful integrity; White's Arthurian tetralogy swirls together narrative, historical and stylistic registers just as playfully and purposefully. Kipling's authentic historicism, made charming for Dan and Una, is brilliantly plundered in chapter X of the first book, "The Sword in the Stone", as Robin Wood tells the two boys he thinks Morgan the Fay is a "fairy". Kay asks if she is "one of those people with bluebells for hats, who spend the time sitting on toadstools." (p. 98) After the laughter, Robin repeats that she is probably a real fairy (though the word is unlucky), one of the Oldest Ones that were driven underground, into the hills, as Gaels, Romans and Saxons conquered the surface of Britain. Robin accounts for the Renaissance diminution and ruralisation of the Good Folk by this retreat, and adds that their unfeeling ferocity towards humans is because they have, literally, no hearts. To call one is to give it power to take you into its eerie world. White's impudent presentation of Elfland as the Castle of Fat, in a pastiche of the Irish "Vision of Mac Conglinne", disappoints many readers, retaining the alien feel but sacrificing the lofty beauty.

IV

> Adieu! The Fancy cannot cheat so well
> As she is famed to do, deceiving Elf!
> John Keats, "Ode to a Nightingale"

In the wild rhapsodic assortment of quasi-elvish characters re-discovered or re-invented by Gothic, Romantic and Victorian writers before Kipling, some, like Goethe's

Erl-König, are dark, cruel and treacherous indeed. The ancient Elf-Queen, especially, reappears in such beguilers as the superficially beautiful Geraldine in Coleridge's "Christabel", Keats' spell-weaving Circe in "Endymion", MacDonald's shapeshifting and D.G. Rossetti's heart-entwining Liliths, Tennyson's subtle wizard-beguiling Vivien, and Swinburne's sadistically passionate Dolores, "Our Lady of Pain". Fear and Victorian misogyny chime well with the erotic frisson of horror in such poets as the last three named.

But it is easy to mislead oneself about male presentations of female power and beauty, especially when associated with elvish magic, in the Romantic period. Keats is the master of withheld moral judgments of female protagonists like Lamia and "La Belle Dame Sans Merci". What is sure is that they are not immortal, soulless seducers who set out cruelly to entrap and destroy the men who respond to them, whatever the assertions of other, deeply neurotic males in those narratives. In "Ode on Melancholy", similarly, it would be foolish to blame either the mistress or Beauty, Joy and Pleasure, or even the Goddess Delight, for the desires of the male who is determined actively to seek "the Melancholy" through them.

Although the word "witch" is usually worth dissociating from the Elf-Queen, Shelley's "The Witch of Atlas" presents her as the outward and visible form of the muse, like Keats' Psyche, playing elaborate games with perception and common-sense. The magic of the Elven world in which James Hogg's Kilmeny finds herself is unmenacing, even paradisal, except that she longs for it ever after, and cannot live long in a mortal world that lacks all meaning, sundered from so passionate an experience. That no one intended to beguile her heart away become clear when "Kilmeny" is compared to Christina Rossetti's "Goblin Market".

La Motte Fouqué's "Undine" and Matthew Arnold's "Forsaken Merman" provide excellent examples of the Elf as markedly superior in both morality and ethics to humans of Middle Earth that both desire and betray their Other-world lovers. William Morris, very much later, offers a *Wood Beyond the World* ruled by a cruel Elf-Queen, but her servant and rival defeats her and briefly becomes the good Elf-Queen, aiding with her benevolent magic both her mortal lover and the Bear Tribe that worships her. She loses her Elven powers by marrying Walter; in effect, this is Arwen's choice, although Tolkien never refers to sexual magic, or Arwen's virginity.

Tolkien knew most of these narratives, in all probability, well enough to avoid direct resemblances. A more seductive Faery for him was that of the Celtic Sidhe, an Other-world with temporal defences more complex than those of Keats' Lamia and "faery's child", situated beyond or beneath the waves or within the hollow hills. In their timeless proud glamour, passion and freedom they are contemptuous of as well as horrified by church Christianity. The great women of the Sidhe like Fand are fiercely and erotically attracted to male mortals of a certain nobility. Far less moral and ethical than the Elves of *The Silmarillion*, the Sidhe resemble them physically. They are twilight and starlight people, obsessed by music and song, horses and the sea, war and love. Alienated from their country by the virtuous disaster of Christianity, they flee westward to the Isles of the Blest, Tir Nan Og, Odain Saker or Hy Braseal. Since one of his Elvish languages was Welsh-based, Tolkien is also aware of *The Mabinogion*'s rather more disguised Underworld Elves.

Authors influenced by Tolkien now often aim at far more overtly Celtic effects. Incidentally, in Irish tradition sex between mortal and Sidhe was rarely progenitive, but Tolkien has interrogated that probability. Narratives discussed in part VI include many cross-breeds, and some, like Katherine Kerr's, depend primarily upon half-elf characters.

V

The Good are attracted by Mens perception
And think not for themselves
Till experience teaches them to catch
And to cage the Fairies & Elves.
   William Blake, "Motto to the Songs of Innocence & Experience"

Tolkien's influence upon later fantasy fiction is too vast to be quantified, and this applies to his extraordinarily detailed sub-creation of Elves as much as to any part of his oeuvre. When a writer looms so inescapably over two generations of successors, the anxiety of influence, to use Harold Bloom's apt term, must affect even the most bare-faced of imitators and purloiners. The unforgettable Elves of Middle-earth are echoed, borrowed, pastiched, misremembered, misunderstood, degraded, betrayed and subverted, in hundreds of fantasies, space operas, science fantasies and role-playing scenarios and modules. As this range of verbs implies, there is nothing wrong with being influenced; it all depends on how the influence is deconstructed and the material re-earned.

Although it may seem injudicious to begin by discussing bad books, Terry Brooks provides an extraordinary example of what Bloom calls "clinamen", metamorphic theft. His Shannara series is a shameful formulaic rehash of major aspects of *The Lord of the Rings*, but his Elves suffer even more from the comparison than the rest of the turgid, dull, ill-expressed and adverb-ridden concoctions. I should add that my comments are derived only from the first three books; there are more, but life is too short.

Why are Brooks' Elves so especially weak? From the evidence of the first book, *The Sword of Shannara* (1983), it is clear that they have no magic, no special skills (a very young "highlander" human called Menion Leah is already superior at both tracking and archery), and give no impression of otherness or distance at all. They are differentiated from the other races only by a slightly prettier appearance and mild good intentions towards nature. When something of their history is eventually revealed, it emerges that they are not Elves at all, but merely humans who would have liked to be Elves! These pseudelves cannot detect or face the book's Absolutely Evil Dark Lord, but merely contribute one of the armies decimated in the dreary climactic battle.

Since all true Elves have been killed off, the hereditary magic elven-sword of the title, and some curious "elfstones", can only be wielded by the last descendant, a hobbit-sized half-elf called Shea (as in Sidhe, perhaps). He is himself Elven only in having high cheekbones and pointed ears, and uses his Elvish weapons confusedly and with reluctance. The sword works, though: when it inoculates Absolute Evil with self-knowledge, He evaporates!

In the sequel, *Elfstones of Shannara* (1987), Shea's grandson Wil, a one-eighth-elf protagonist, wields the stones (but no sword). Reluctant and unbelieving, he does so seldom, and only to protect Amberle, a pseudelven princess, ex-handmaid of the one indubitably magical object in the pseudelves' kingdom, a spirit-tree called the Elcryss. The tree has been keeping demons locked up in other dimensions for millennia, but is dying, so while Wil and Amberle follow their quest many pseudelves massacre and are massacred by the demons. In a spectacular testament to how little magic the pseudelves have, Amberle must be metamorphosed into a new Elcryss, not a true Elf, to shut up the demons again.

The third book, *Wishsong of Shannara* (1988), has two quests: Wil's daughter and son, both one-sixteenth Elven, use spell-songs instead of magic artifacts to defeat another Absolute Evil in two simultaneous climaxes. This seems to imply that Elven-magic has become genetically imprinted to their family, so that Elves will now manifest themselves in humanity, but there is no indication as to how or why this has happened. Formula fiction is perhaps too wedded to the commoner denominators of audience expectation to cope with such questions.

In Patricia Wrede's semi-formulaic *Shadow Magic* (1987), the magic-wielding Shee (again Sidhe?) have long ago retreated, like a lost race, from an almost forgotten alliance of four sentient races into a forbidden mountain city. They supply a few woodland Wardens, but most forest work is done by small agile Wyrds, the second of the four peoples; the others are water-dwelling Neisa, who specialise in healing, and Men, plains-dwelling farmers and fighters. Urban and rigidly governed, with a taste for trim white stonework and strict formal gardens, the Shee teach and respect magic. However, supreme power comes with the rediscovery of the peoples' four emblems, sword, cup, shield and staff, and the single crown that rules them. A young half-elf maiden uses all these to wipe out an invading army controlled by shadowmen, and becomes queen of the renewed alliance. The Shee have returned, both in themselves and within Men, rejuvenated by interbreeding.

A richer work, Marion Bradley's Arthurian fantasy *The Mists of Avalon* (1983), focuses upon a female magical order in Avalon, ruled by the Holy Mother Vivien and including a striking Morgan le Fay, here Morgaine. Its power is based on natural cycles, visionary enlightenment and various forms of priestly dedication ranging from chastity to ritual sex. However, Avalon is becoming inaccessible, receding farther into the mists as Britain and its court come more and more under the influence of a malevolent, sin-based Christianity: Avalon is geographically coincident with the Christian Glastonbury, whose buildings and fields are now the place's primary reality. Mysteries are claimed in Glastonbury and demonstrably active in Avalon, but a third, older Elfland or Faery, totally magical, occupies the same physical space as both.

This Elfland, an earlier, time-misted reality, is only occasionally present. Though the word Elf is avoided, it is an unmistakable Elven Other-world, perhaps the proto-Avalon, but certainly almost timeless. Morgaine is attracted to this realm, either by its Elf-Queen or by her own spiritual temperament, at crucial moments, and advised there, lucidly if not morally. Morgaine is "of the fairies" because of her resemblance to the "little people" who served this lost magical other-world and still row through the mists for the present, equally fated priestesses. By the book's end, Morgaine has fulfilled her own and Arthurian Britain's fate, by her own good deeds and bad, courage and fear, wisdom and folly. The Elves have already left Morgaine's world, not to go into the West but into a past which is still, though almost inaccessible, physically "here", still Britain. Avalon, already decimated of priestesses, will follow.

Of the many dashing Celtiads that have brandished their Irish orthography in recent years, one of the most indicative of the retreat of the Sidhe is the unpretentious Young Adult story by Diane Duane, *A Wizard Abroad* (1993). Duane's smart young American wizards find their Irish counterparts have, for the time being anyway, something no other wizards can claim, a wary understanding with the ancient powers of their land. But the Sidhe have been alienated from the country they loved most, that has bound them more than any, and cost them more than the others. Their ancient and elaborate realm within the hill does not often allow human contact, even when the bargains are expressed in their own terms – and the terms of any human bargain with the Sidhe are precarious. Except in emergencies, Eire has become more like the secular human USA than Hy Braseal.

The ferocious relationship between the human protagonists of C.J. Cherryh's *Faery in Shadow* (1993) and his Sidhe contacts stems partly from his own heroic guilt as a patricide, and partly from the fact that he is therefore bound to the Sidhe's mixture of the whimsical and the vicious. He sees his role of service to the noble silver-handed Nuallan, of the high Daoine Sidhe, as that of causing murder and mayhem wherever he goes among men. His one constant (but madly inconstant) companion is of the dark Sidhe, a shape-changing pooka called Dubhain, prone to whisky and fond of wickedness, and other powers he meets seem equally liable to lacerate his body and soul, whether they are beautifully innocent half-selkie twins or coldly wicked witches that set on monsters of the lock to do their hunting for them. It is no wonder that Caith spends most of his time cursing, suffering and barely managing to keep battered body and guilty soul together. The Sidhe will not even let him lose his cursed sword, or his memory, and when he becomes their liberating hero no spot of triumph remains upon his imagination. Caith knows the world is changing around the Sidhe, and he would, if he could, build a ship with his bare hands if it would only take them forever oversea.

Any story in which Elf-like beings are thoroughly

menacing, cruel or indifferent to human ethics is almost forced to avoid both the term "Elf" and any hint of direct influence from Tolkien, so much are good Elves now identified with his work. This is especially true of homocosmic fantasy, that which is set in our contemporary world. Two excellent, very independent fantasies provide useful examples, In Gene Wolfe's teasing Arthurian thriller *Castleview* (1990), Morgan has a travelling castle, a little like the Welsh mythological Caer Sidi, that haunts a small Illinois town. Except when making a specific demand on mortal humanity it keeps aloof, and only the occasional halfwit (like the "Dymchurch Flit" Bee Boy) can enter uninvited. Morgan le Fay's marvellous, arbitrary, sinister Elf-like people and sub-people are alien to human virtue but rather fascinated by it. Defying the common sense of modern North American life, their challenge evokes from it a hero; like Arthur, Will E. Shields will be struck down and defeated, then taken to the Avalon-castle in all honour, for healing, as a sort of "tiend" to Elfland.

Peter S. Beagle's *The Folk of the Air* (1987) is equally inventive in presenting an Elven invader of contemporary American society. The unforgettably beautiful and sinister "boy", Nicholas Bonner, is called out of atemporal imprisonment by a teenage witch. As well as playing murderous tricks on a medieval role-playing society, he works with the witch to destroy his mother, a timeless earth-goddess in human aspect. Though the term is never used, Nicholas is far more Elf than demon, a totally amoral and alien force loose among the humans, who, as with all Elvishness, good or evil, try not to notice, and usually succeed. As Hamid says,

> I have also seen more than a hundred intelligent people steadily denying something . . . right in front of their eyes. Unmaking it, you hear what I'm saying? . . . You ever want to see the real witchcraft, you watch people protecting their comfort, their beliefs. That's where it is.
> (Beagle, 1987, p. 237)

VI

> And see ye not that braid, braid road
>   That winds about the fernie brae?
> That is the road to fair Elfland,
>   Where thou and I this night maun gae.
>   Anon., "Thomas the Rhymer"

The author best-read in Tolkien, most intensely aware of and intimately subversive of his major works, is Guy Gavriel Kay. His *Fionavar Tapestry* (1985-6), a genuine trilogy as *The Lord of the Rings* is not, offers a multiverse, focused on a rich heterocosm, the proto-world Fionavar, but including legendary Arthurian Britain as well as our contemporary homocosm. The lios-alfar of Fionavar are, as usual, few in number and dwindling. A thousand years ago, after sharing with Men and Dwarves a great and grievous victory, they converted their radiant country, Daniloth, into a misted and shadowy time-labyrinth. When the Dark Enemy, Rakoth Maugrim, is again set free, his most intense hatred is still reserved for the Elves of Light, as his orcs and wolves well know. Elves love the physical world's beauty, music and spirit but, being almost ageless, they can weary of time. Each Elf will ultimately be called by a personal song to sail alone across the Western ocean to a mystic Other-world only Elves can attain. When the trilogy begins, the last veteran of the great war has just, in the lovely Elven euphemism, "heard his song".

The twist to this charmingly sentimental reprise of the longing Tolkien's Elves feel for Valimar is correspondingly shocking. The song that calls each lios alfar is a fake: Rakoth has set a vast sea-monster, the Soulmonger, far out in the Western Ocean, to sing poignant Elvish melodies as bait for them. When each little boat approaches, its occupant is swallowed and incorporated into the lyric seduction for the rest of the doomed Elven race. Just as Sam laments naively in the second chapter of *The Lord of the Rings*, "They are sailing, sailing, sailing over the Sea, they are going into the West and leaving us" (Tolkien, 1954a, p. 54), but in a savagely parodic sense.

In the second book of the trilogy, *The Wandering Fire* (1986a), when this dreadful discovery is made, Soulmonger is destroyed. However, the truth about Elven destiny must still be revealed to the remaining lios alfar, removing the mystic consolation for all their heroic dedication to the cause of the Light. Yet this irony too is not the end: with the Soulmonger silenced, the befouled dream of the Elven West is cleansed. In the third book, *The Darkest Road* (1986b), Leyse, the Lady of the Swan Mark (in our world's version of the story Elaine, the Lily Maid of Astolat, the Lady of Shalott), meets Lancelot and knows her love for him will never be requited. Ready to leave her life, she "hears her song", not from the hideous maw of the monster but from the authentic mystery her people have been so viciously denied. Leyse's solitary renunciation takes her beyond the physical West to a newly accessible Elvish mystery, distinct from that heterocosm to which the other Arthurian characters in Kay's vigorously post-Tolkien romance are apparently bound.

Even more than *The Mists of Avalon*, Katharine Kerr's Deverry series is based on Celtic material. The texts are *Daggerspell* (1986), *Darkspell* (1987), *Dawnspell: The Bristling Wood* (1990a), and *Dragonspell: The Southern Sea* (1990b). Her narrative, as it relates to mortals, pivots upon the rebirth of spirits in a series of identities, subtly overlapping,

Though Tolkien's Elves are aware of patterns of rebirth, the matter does not become crucial to their conduct, while the souls of his mortal men are taken beyond Middle-earth, so cannot be reborn. Gandalf is a very special case, since he is sent back from death immediately, not in a new being but as himself again – repeated, as Keats put it, in a finer tone. Kerr's Gandalf-like wisdom-character Nevyn, who wields good dweomer (the term used for magic) at the core of most of the opposition to evil, is a special case too: he has lived out many normal lifetimes in this one form, in fulfilling a sacred vow.

The Elves of Deverry, the Elcyion Lacar, live far from most human habitations. They have typical Elven longevity, so the reasons for this are still fresh in their minds. Many centuries back, they had dwelt in Deverry proper, in seven beautiful cities, but had been driven (West, of course) into the grasslands by iron-wielding, wainriding human invaders. Eschewing literacy and "civilisation", the Elves are in effect pointy-eared Plains Indians, fierce and proud, unsurpassed archers and horsemen, with some dweomer. Those invaders, destroyed by virulent plagues, have no connection with the mortals now inhabiting Deverry, but the Elcyion Lacer still mostly prefer to have no truck with "round-ears". Most humans who trade with them mistrust and despise them in turn. There is no physical barrier between Elf and human, just distance, mutual incomprehension – and often violent dislike.

Nonetheless, there are half-elves; indeed, they play crucial roles in each book of the Deverry series. They are more or less pointy-eared, long-lived, dexterous, ethically responsive, and endowed with dweomer; most humans who meet dweomer fear and deny it. Some half-elves, like all Elcyion Lacer, can see the "wild-folk", grotesque elementals invisible to dweomerless humans, and Elven tradition has it that God created Elves from wildfolk just as He created humans from forest beasts.

The Elcyion Lacar are more complex than their theology because, as with Bradley's Avalon, a further time-level exists. On some etheric or astral plane, still and forever live lordly proto-elves, lethally glamorous to and contemptuous of their degenerate, iron-using descendants. By their wills and within a separate time-state they maintain an etheric version of their seven cities; a living Elf entering this "world" is lost to time and sometimes to sanity, sometimes to life. These proto-elves do precisely what they wish, or so they believe, but their ethical judgment has atrophied and they are unable to take seriously the affairs of the living, even direct conflicts between good and evil. Half-elves, our heroes, are the abomination of the proto-elven Faery.

The same implacability and amorality characterises the quasi-mythical or archetypal denizens of Robert Holdstock's *Mythago Wood* (1986) and its sequel *Lavondyss* (1988). As they become more and more divorced from the "normal" world of mortal humanity, suffering becomes a matter of course rather than of concern. The more archetypal the hero, the more able he is to approach the world beyond the fire, "where time has no meaning"; but to become the almost invincible legendary Outsider seems to entail becoming vilely brutal, and to take on the role of his equal and opposite Kinsman may produce the same degradation. To attain Elflike awareness of story and freedom within time seems to alienate all human bonds.

In "Cold Iron", Puck offhandedly cites the last Elf-Queen, the Lady Esclairmonde, as having been "a woman once, till she followed Sir Huon across the fern, as we say." (Kipling, 1910, p. 9) In Gael Baudino's *Strands of Starlight* (1989), the core of the story is how a mortal female becomes an Elf. Baudino's whole story focuses on Miriam's transformation, set in a shrewdly deconstructed South of France just after the massacre of the Cathars. Archbishop Cranby, sweepingly ambitious, finds fun and profit in persecuting "witches" and other non-approved peoples, including Elves. Since he wants to lead a crusade against the prosperous and reprehensibly cheerful Free Towns, their cordial relations with the woodland Elves make a good excuse. Elves are, after all, heretics: their theology omits reference to Original Sin and its Supreme Being is female: a star-goddess very like Elbereth. Her worshippers learn to trace the possibilities of the future, the strands of starlight, and act, by and large, wisely.

Though they are called "unnatural", Elves can intermarry with humans. A friend of Miriam's has a child by an Elf-lord, and not just because she is herself a witch. Significantly, the Elves themselves rarely breed; quietist lovers of the world, they have also become too wise to wish to fight, even for survival or vengeance, and whatever the provocation. At least, that is what they think they think. With the passionate Miriam and Cranby's villainy as catalysts, they have to change.

A small, frail teenager, Miriam is imprisoned and tortured by Cranby's clerics because she has healing powers. When she heals an aristocratic hunter, Cranby's ally, of terrible wounds, and he promptly rapes her, her anger suddenly changes her life. She forces the Elves to transform her into a warrior-maid so that she can kill him. The transformation succeeds, but during her weapons training she actually turns into an elf, so her values change too, against physical revenge. Radiant Superwomen, Elf-Queens, do not do murder, and wrath is not the only guide of the spirit. She becomes a noble and discerning Elf, and enters the greenwood with no regrets for her lost human identity. However, Elves are becoming rarer, and there are no young pure-blooded Elves.

Elizabeth Moon's slow-moving and circumstantial trilogy about a female warrior, *The Deed of Paksenarrion* (1982), only reluctantly concedes the possibility of magic, or Elves, and only late in the last book of the trilogy does their history become clear. In the distant past, before ordinary humans arrived, Elves had done great harm in the south of the continent and retreated, shamed, into upland forest areas north of the mountains. Their guilty past involved a civil war in which the Light-Elves, the Sinyi or singers, expelled the Dark-Elves, the Iynisin or unsingers, who worship the Anti-God Nayda, unnamer. The Sinyi's name for themselves and for their High King of Heaven, Adyan, Namer of Names, both closely resemble Quendi, "the Speakers". Not that they always speak or sing truth: they are tempted to pretend that the Iynisin are extinct, which is far from true. These demonic dark-elves follow an intellectual Shelob, the spider-goddess Achyra, deceiver and binder of all virtue, though she hates Light-Elves and paladins most.

The Elder Race here is more neglectful and evasive than in Tolkien, but there are strong similarities to Elves of Lórien. They "own" no land, but Elflands are almost inaccessible to unguided humans; within them times and seasons are quite distinct from those of neighbouring human areas. When the queen moves, her place and time move with her! True Elves are associated with music, light and beauty, especially stars and woodland, while the Iynisin are also called Kuaknom, "tree-haters", and live in caverns. The Elven civil War between the celebratory Sinyi and the jealous Iynisin began, it emerges, when proto-humans (tree-worshippers, kuakkganni) came to worship the sacred First Tree, and It responded to their worship.

The last book of the trilogy focuses on the one kingdom, Lyonya, traditionally ruled by half-elves. The Elven half of its royal family has been lost, and with it the necessary sensitivity to the "taig" or spirit of the natural environment. Elves have longevity, of course, and a very low birthrate; they are, as might be expected, desperately committed to the cherishing of their few children. Humans are, by comparison, flourishing, and Elves overtly resent this; true Elves also resent half-elves. Of course it is not easy for even the pious among humans to love Elves either. Imbued with intrinsic grace and harmony, they hate and despise – and seek instinctively to avoid – conflict and turmoil that humans can readily endure. They will not long have realms of their own, but will fade away into the deepest woods, leaving subtle, invaluable traces of themselves to glamorise humanity's busy gene-pool.

With all their limitations, Moon's Elves will fight gladly against evil when they are shown unequivocal evidence of it. They end the trilogy with a decisive charge against orcs, various monsters and a wide range of human evildoers:

> All at once the piercing sweet call of an elvenhorn lifted her heart, the sound she had heard in Kolobia, and never forgotten. She looked east. A wave of silver light rolled down the forested slope, as if the starlight had taken form. Out of the trees rode what none there had ever seen. Tall, fair, mounted on horses as pale as starlit foam, they cried aloud in ringing voices that made music of battle. Rank after rank they came, bringing with them the scent of spring, and the light of elvenhome kingdoms that is neither sun nor star.
> (Moon, p. 1015)

This not only powerful in itself, but eloquent of Tolkien's continued influence. His Elves do not use cavalry, in the last years of the Third Age at any rate, but an Eldar version of the Ride of the Rohirrim, led by cavalier Elf-Lords like Glorfindel, may very well have been In Elizabeth Moon's mind.

VII

Comrade, look not on the west:
'Twill have your heart out of your breast;
'Twill take your thoughts and sink them far,
Leagues beyond the sunset bar.
                A.E. Housman, "The West"

Well, where do Elves go to? According to many writers, to whom Tolkien's challenging ecological ethic has become self-evident truth, they have retreated, disgusted by human crowds, ecological stupidity and our noisy, relatively high-technology urban life. Until recently they would have gone, like weary Noldor gathering at the Grey Havens, on a Celtic-twilit voyage westward over the sea. American writers, in particular, conscious of a largely American readership, can nowadays rarely accept this convention; an honourable exception is the Canadian Charles de Lint, with *Moonheart* (1984) and its sequel *Spiritwalk* (1992), but his migrants left Celtic Europe in the days of Merlin. Some Elves, like Tolkien's laiquendi or green-elves, still seek a haven in deeper and deeper woods, but in proportion as their reasons become better this retreat has become less convincing: our homocosm is limited in scope, and humans are an expansionist race. The Brazilian rain-forest that might have seemed an obvious choice a little while ago is being destroyed apace. A similar limitation of environmental choice faces mer-people, clearly a related species. They too cannot travel much farther into nature.

Our round world offers no Uttermost West, Hy Braseal or Tir Nan Og to go to; Europeans do not go West to the United States, or New Yorkers West to California, in the expectation of Elfland. Elves alienated by our moral world-time, our religious practices (mostly Christian, though Islam must be at least as inimical) or by our allied and equally depressing secular certitudes, may find their magic ebbs or deteriorates like their birthrate. The image of the Last Elf is likely to be of Arwen, bereft of her mortal husband and forever separated from her Elven kin, lying under the withered trees of Cerin Amroth. But there are other, more or less imponderable destinations. In proportion as Tolkien is more influential than Lewis, authors are more wary of the mystical direction "higher up and further back"; it is as hard to write a convincing "deeper time" as a good heaven. However, some writers do present intriguing unheavenly destinations through Nature.

Cyberpunk Elves might seem unlikely to fantasists who avoid contemporary science fiction, but the rapid development of role-playing games and the continuing prosperity of computer games has produced many miscegenations between science, especially of the virtual reality kind, and magic. Indeed, proverbial among SF readers is the reflection that any phenomenon of whose scientific or technological basis the observer is totally ignorant must be indistinguishable from magic. Whether the guidelines and conventions of fantasy role-playing games invite players to confect Elves as sweetly-pretty herbalist heroines or discipline them as spell-wielding valkyries may not much matter, in that it is the players who eventually make such decisions, but there is little either elvishly beautiful or elvishly alien about those presented by authors like Weis and Hickman who "novelise" such games. Perhaps surprisingly, the cyberpunk end of the market is more Elf-nourishing than the TSR Trademark end.

Cyberpunk Elves star in FASA's role-playing game Shadowrun, set in a highly-urbanised future world dominated by giant corporations and more openly criminal organisations that have easily outlasted orthodox government and civil power. But this tough context is not "hard SF" in the old sense, because only a little while after our present day, the magic that has been blocked from most human experience comes back into the world again and, to quote the blurb, "Elves, Trolls & Ogres shed their human aspects & assumed their true forms". Mere humans are, alas, called norms; and orcs are, even more alas, spelled Orks. The trilogy called *Secrets of Power* (1990-1) by Robert N. Charrette, has an excellent range of Elves; this is how the first one in the first volume is introduced:

> Darkness had covered the land for some hours when the Elf stepped out under the sky to relieve himself. The forest was full of soft sounds, its life undisturbed by the presence of the lone Elf. A slight breeze meandered among the great dark boles of the trees, tickling their leaves into a soft rustle. The same wayward air played with the strands of his white hair and caressed his skin, making the Elf smile with pleasure.
>
> *Never Deal with a Dragon* (1990, p. 11)

Not very good writing, admittedly, but the naturalistic emphasis of the first sentence is lucidly developed by the revelation that the Elf does not live in the forest but actually works in the highest of hi-tech. His communion with the stars is broken off:

> He snugged the surgical steel jack into the socket at his temple and his fingers flew across the keyboard of his Fuchi 7 cyberdeck, launching him into the Matrix. His vision shifted to that dazzling electronic world of analog space . . .

Yes, he's a criminally-employed database decker, and his name is not Dorethuriel but Dodger. And the hero has to dig pretty deep to discover Dodger's long-buried ethics.

The ruler and "paladin" defenders of Tir Tairngire, or Elfland, loosely equivalent to the old state of Oregon, are far more lethal, and perhaps have no long-buried ethics. The scholarly Professor Laverty has much to recommend him, but little inclination to mix it with the bad guys, and certainly not with his ruler, Erhan. In the second volume we find that English Elves are just as tricky, though they have the merit of hating the pseudo-Arthurian renegade druids. But the most remarkable Elf is the Australian Aboriginal Urdli. Nobly anti-urban, unswerving, implacable, he stands out among his Caucasian elvish colleagues. However, he is also corruptible, not through the influence of others, but through his own pride and certitude, a veritable Fëanor of absolutist temperament. His destruction, and the fated love the Elf Dodger feels for Morgan le Fay, here presented as the spirit of Cyberspace, darken and mute the triumph of ancient magical integrity over the loathsome corporation. Elven happy endings are always poignant.

Among contemporary writers the most popular destination for the departing Elves is undoubtedly into humanity, especially in the compromise form of half-elves. The magical skills associated with Elves, such as telepathy, communication with trees, birds and other creatures, and spiritual healing, chime in perfectly with the dreams, and sometimes the claims, of New Age rhetoric about human potential. It is therefore no surprise that writers should find a responsive audience for stories in which Elven traits surface in mortals, even if only certain particularly noble or wise mortals. To recognise our Selves we have always needed the Other, and the Human Other is the most immediately rewarding form it can take. Fantasy by its nature invites audience expectation of a revivifying if not always a happy ending; it is inevitable that writers should seek to mitigate the dark wisdom of Elrond, who saw "a bitter parting beyond the end of the world" (Tolkien, 1956, p. 340), and celebrate the Elf within, wonderfully defamiliarising our fellow mortals.

Note

In recent years many more elves have established their various degrees of eerie disdain or fey mockery in fantasy fiction, role-playing games and computer-generated narratives. Dave Duncan's ebullient tetralogies *A Man of His Word* (1990-91) and *A Handful of Men* (1992-94) create a world in which Elves are simply one of the more unapproachable of many races, all capable of wielding magical words of power. The sky trees they dwell in are mountain-high, and their bird-like beauty and aesthetic detachment are just as rarefied and chilling.

Esther Friesner's Welfies (obviously from the jeer Elfy-welfy) seem even sillier than the other species in her *Majyk By Accident* (1993), *Majyk By Hook Or Crook* and *Majyk By Design* (both 1994):

> Pointed ears and huge, slanted leaf-green eyes peeked out through golden hair so long and flossy I was amazed they could see to aim their weapons . . .
>
> "And how the hell did they hide in the trees when they're all wearing bright pink leotards . . . With sequins, yet."
>
> (Friesner, 1993, pp. 97-98)

These male Welfies are high-camp parodies of High Elves. However, the anti-hero's first female Welfie is tiny, with multi-coloured shimmery wings, so Friesner can mock the boutique flitting-and-sipping fairy as well as the tall, glamorous sylvan archers. Yet the story's central Welfie, Mysti, fleeing the fairy image, turns into a cross-dressing, swashbuckling, wrong-righting hero, whose comic passion and panache defy the spangled absurdity of her people. Welfitude must be forgiven an estranged wife who would win a duel with D'Artagnan! At the end of the trilogy Mysti enters humanity by her renewed, consummatable marriage to the protagonist Kendar, a buffoon mage.

The most brilliant sustained attack upon the prestige, morality and personal hygiene of the High Elves is Terry Pratchett's *Lords and Ladies* (1992). With a wittily eclectic extravagance incomparable among writers of comic fantasy, he presents lethally vicious Elves, ultimate aristocrats that dominate and despise the mortal world they use as toybox, prey, and forced-labour pool:

> . . . When they get into a world, everyone else is on the bottom. Slaves. Worse than slaves. Worse than animals, even. They take what they want, and they want everything. But worst of all, the worst bit is . . . they read your mind. They hear what you think, and in self-defence you think what they want. *Glamour*. And it's barred windows at night, and food out for the fairies, and turning around three times before you talks about 'em, and horseshoes over the door.
>
> (Pratchett, 1992, p. 163)

No wonder they have to be sealed Beyond The Fields We Know by a stone circle Gateway (a highly magnetic one, necessarily) by the power of Cold Iron and the heroic rebellion of witches, dwarves, trolls, orang-utans and other sensible species.

Are Pratchett's vile elves are still trying to get out? Hear them sniffing behind the sentimental cracks in New Age Occultism, clawing at the nightmare underside of folklore-psychic Cultism? Brr.

References

Anderson, Poul. 1954. *The Broken Sword*. London: Sphere, revised 1973.

Anderson, Poul. 1979. *The Merman's Children*. New York: Berkley.

Arnold, Matthew. 1849. "The Forsaken Merman" in *The Strayed Reveller and other Poems*. London.

Barrie, J.M. 1904. *Peter Pan*. London.

Baudino, Gael. 1989. *Strands of Starlight*. London: Orbit.

Baudino, Gael. 1993. *Maze of Moonlight*. New York: Roc.

Beagle, Peter S. 1987. *The Folk of the Air*. London: Headline.

Blake, William. 1793. *Songs of Innocence and of Experience*. London.

Boyer, Elizabeth. 1980. *The Sword and the Satchel*. New York: Del Rey.

Boyer, Elizabeth. 1981. *The Elves and the Otterskin*. New York: Del Rey.

Boyer, Elizabeth. 1982. *The Thrall and the Dragon's Heart*. New York: Del Rey.

Boyer, Elizabeth. 1983. *The Wizard and the Warlord*. New York: Del Rey.

Boyer, Elizabeth. 1986. *The Troll's Grindstone*. New York: Del Rey.

Bradley, Marion. 1983. *The Mists of Avalon*. London: Michael Joseph.

Brooks, Terry. 1983. *The Sword of Shannara*. New York: Del Rey.

Brooks, Terry. 1987. *The Elfstones of Shannara*. New York: Del Rey.

Brooks, Terry. 1988. *Wishsong of Shannara*. New York: Del Rey.

Charrette, Robert N. 1990. *Never Deal with a Dragon*. New York: Roc.

Charrette, Robert N. 1991. *Choose Your Enemies Carefully*. New York: Roc.

Charrette, Robert N. 1991. *Find Your Own Truth*. New York: Roc.

Cherryh, C.J. 1993. *Shadow of Faery*. New York: Random House.

Coleridge, Samuel Taylor. 1798. *Christabel*. London.

Corbet, Richard. 1628. "The Fairies' Farewell". London.

Dean, Pamela. 1991. *Tam Lin*. New York: Tor.

de la Mare, Walter. 1923. *Come Hither*. London: Constable.

de Lint, Charles. 1984. *Moonheart*. London: Pan.

de Lint, Charles. 1992. *Spiritwalk*. New York: Tor.

Drayton, Michael. 1627. *Nymphidia*. London.

Duane, Diane. 1993. *A Wizard Abroad*. London: Corgi.

Duncan, Dave. 1990-91. *A Man of His Word*. (*Magic Casement*. New York: Ballantine Books, 1990; *Faery Lands Forlorn*. New York: Ballantine Books, 1991; *Perilous Seas*. New York: Ballantine Books, 1991; *Emperor and Clown*. New York: Ballantine Books, 1991).

Duncan, Dave. 1992-94. *A Handful of Men*. (*The Cutting Edge*. New York: Ballantine Books, 1992; *Upland Outlaws*. New York: Ballantine Books, 1993; *The Stricken Field*. New York: Ballantine Books, 1993; *The Living God*. New York: Ballantine Books, 1994).

Friesner, Esther M. 1993. *Majyk By Accident*. New York: Ace Books.

Friesner, Esther M. 1994. *Majyk By Hook Or Crook*. New York: Ace Books.

Friesner, Esther M. 1994. *Majyk By Design*. New York: Ace Books.

Frost, Robert. 1914. "Mending Well" in *North of Boston*. Boston: G.K. Hall.

Goethe, Johannes Wolfgang von. 1892?. "Der Erl-König", Köln. Set by Schubert 1816.

Hogg, James. 1813. *The Queen's Wake*. Edinburgh.

Holdstock, Robert. 1984. *Mythago Wood*. London: Gollancz.

Holdstock, Robert. 1988. *Lavondyss*. London: Gollancz.

Housman, A.E. 1922. *Last Poems*. London: G. Richards Ltd.

Jones, Diana Wynne. 1985. *Fire and Hemlock*. London: Methuen.

Kay, Guy Gavriel. 1985. *The Summer Tree*. London: George Allen & Unwin.

Kay, Guy Gavriel. 1986a. *The Wandering Fire*. London: George Allen & Unwin.

Kay, Guy Gavriel. 1986b. *The Darkest Road*. London: George Allen & Unwin.

Keats, John. 1818. *Endymion*. London.

Keats, John. 1820. *Lamia*. London: Taylor and Hessey.

Keats, John. 1847. "La Belle Dame Sans Merci". London.

Kerr, Katherine. 1986. *Daggerspell*. London: Grafton.

Kerr, Katherine. 1987. *Darkspell*. London: Grafton.

Kerr, Katherine. 1990a. *Dawnspell: The Bristling Wood*. London: Grafton.

Kerr, Katherine. 1990b. *Dragonspell: The Southern Sea*. London: Grafton.

Kipling, Rudyard. 1906. *Puck of Pook's Hill*. London: Macmillan.

Kipling, Rudyard. 1910. *Rewards and Fairies*. London: Macmillan.

La Motte Fouqué, Friedrich. 1811. *Undine*. Berlin.

Lewis, C.S. 1950. *The Lion, the Witch, and the Wardrobe*. London: Geoffrey Bles.

Lyly, John. 1591. *Endimion*. London.

MacDonald, George. 1895. *Lilith*. London: Chatto & Windus.

Milton, John. 1637. *Comus*. London: Humphrey Robinson.

Milton, John. 1645. "L'Allegro" and "Il Penseroso" in *Poems of Mr. John Milton*. London: Ruth Raworth.

Moon, Elizabeth. 1992. *The Deed of Paksennarion*. New York: Baen.

Morris, William. 1894. *The Wood Beyond the World*. London: Kelmscott Press.

Pope, Alexander. 1714. *The Rape of the Lock*. London.

Pratchett, Terry. 1992. *Lords and Ladies*. London: Gollancz.

Rossetti, Christina. 1862. *Goblin Market*. London.

Rossetti, D.G. 1868. *The House of Life*. London.

Shakespeare, William. 1596. *A Midsummer Night's Dream*. London: Thomas Fisher.

Shakespeare, William. 1611. *The Tempest*. London.

Shelley, P.B. 1820. "The Witch of Atlas". London.

Spenser, Edmund. 1589. *The Faerie Queene*. London.

Swinburne, A.C. 1866. "Dolores" in *Poems and Ballads*. London: E. Moxon & Co.

Tennyson, Alfred. 1859. "Merlin and Vivien" in *Idylls of the King*. London: E. Moxon & Co.

Tolkien, J.R.R. 1937. *The Hobbit*. London: George Allen & Unwin.

Tolkien, J.R.R. 1954a. *The Fellowship of the Ring*. London: George Allen & Unwin.

Tolkien, J.R.R. 1954b. *The Two Towers*. London: George Allen & Unwin.

Tolkien, J.R.R. 1955. *The Return of the King*. London: George Allen & Unwin.

Tolkien, J.R.R. 1977. *The Silmarillion*. London: George Allen & Unwin.

White, T.H. 1958. *The Once and Future King*. London: Collins.

Wolfe, Gene. 1990. *Castleview*. New York: Tor.

Wrede, Patricia. 1987. *Shadow Magic*. New York: Ace.

Section three

The Lord of the Rings

Eating, Devouring, Sacrifice and Ultimate Just Desserts

Marjorie Burns

Abstract: Bilbo's fear of being eaten is expanded in *The Lord of the Rings* to include the Dark Lord's "devouring". In both the nursery sense of being "eaten up" and in the more sophisticated sense of enslavement, Tolkien uses this theme to discuss selfhood and free will, and to separate those who serve from those who consume and possess.

Keywords: cannibalism, communion, death, food, *The Hobbit*, *The Lord of the Rings*, morality, sacrifice

Twenty-eight days after conception, before we have gained features or limbs or any indication of lungs, while we are still only half a centimeter in length, our embryonic selves – in anticipation of a lifetime of eating – have already developed a beginner's digestive tract. It will lie there for eight more months before we face the world, a clear indication that we are, in essence, creatures of appetite almost from the first: little Shelobs and Gollums, waiting for a meal.

There are few matters in life more elementary than food and few that so neatly cut both ways. We are eaters or we are eaten; we are feeders or we are food, and our simplest, earliest stories are based on these twin concerns. Little Red Riding Hood carries a basket of goodies and meets a devouring wolf. The wisest of the three little pigs (in the more daring versions of the story) dines on the wolf that previously ate his brothers. Hansel and Gretel nibble on the house of a child-devouring witch, a "cannibal witch," to borrow Tolkien's expression (Tolkien, 1964, p. 32). And, as Goldilocks learns, it may be splendid to indulge in porridge but not at all so pleasing to be found by three hungry, vandalized bears.

It is hardly necessary to point out the extent to which Tolkien was aware of this basic narrative concept and the extent to which eating permeates his Middle-earth stories. The greatest pleasures in Middle-earth are the pleasures of food and drink, just as the greatest risks are the risks of being devoured. But Tolkien's writing, on any topic, works on multiple levels; and his references to food reach far beyond the pleasures associated with eating or the terrors associated with being eaten, to include a complex range of ethical issues and themes.

Food as a means of alluding to moral issues is hardly unique to Tolkien; it is a device as old as the story of the Fall. But, where the Eden story is concerned primarily with the concept of obedience and the consequences of breaking rules, Tolkien's stories focus more on the nature of excess, on the ways in which the misuse of ambition or of appetite destroys the very self it seeks to embellish or feed. It is the term *misuse* that is important here, since, in Tolkien's moral scheme, appetite and selfhood are not in themselves objectionable and even extravagance has its place.

Appetite, selfhood – and large doses of both – are, in fact, inseparable from life. They are, as well, our greatest sources of pleasure, and it is clear that Tolkien, for all his sense of morality, is by no means opposed to pleasure. Though *consuming* and *possessiveness* are, for him, negative terms (most applicable to dragons), Tolkien nonetheless understands both the pleasures of consuming and the pleasures of possessing. We see this in his celebration of food, drink, and pipe-weed, and in his obvious appreciation of decorative items, clothing, crafts, and well wrought swords and armor. And just as he believes in pleasure, he believes as well in the value of desire and the satisfaction of desire. This is why he gives highest praise, in his essay, "On Fairy-Stories," to those stories that succeed in both awakening and satisfying desire. There are risks, of course; desire, appetite, and self-promoting ambition, like the Land of Faerie itself, are highly "perilous." They can lead, all too easily, to excess; they can lead to dissipation and rabidity, to covetousness and voracity; and excesses of this sort, in Tolkien's world, are the primary sources of conflict and misery.

And just as the fault lies not in our longings, nor our physical natures, nor in the awakening and satisfying of desire, but rather in our own failure to avoid excess, so too the solution belongs to us individually and alone. It is the self that matters here, the self, of its own volition, choosing for good or ill. It is the self – swayed by narcissism, ambition, and greed – that causes abuse, insurrection, and sin. It is the self – tempered by fellowship, commitment, and kindly consideration – that allows for moral good.

It is for this reason that the citizens of Bree can belong "to nobody but themselves" (Tolkien, 1954, p. 161) or that Beorn can be "under no enchantment but his own" (Tolkien, 1987, p. 103) and still be admirable. Independence of this sort does not preclude consideration of others or loyalty to others. Aragorn, Faramir, Galadriel, Beorn: each has his or her own individual preferences, thoughts, and desires; and yet each is capable of foregoing pleasure or security for the sake and safety of others. They belong, then, fully to themselves but serve – by choice – a larger order as well. In Tolkien's world, these are the individuals who ultimately succeed or who ultimately become fulfilled. But those others, the ones who consistently seek more than their due, those who demand more and more for the self and for the self alone, are the ones whose reward is – paradoxically – only an emptiness, a hungering, endless negation. "Lost, lost" (in Gollum's own words): "No name, no business, no Precious, nothing. Only empty. Only hungry; yes, we are hungry" (Tolkien, 1965a, p. 298).

This weighing of greed and generosity, of selfishness and sacrifice, appears again and again throughout *The Hobbit* and *The Lord of the Rings*. Greed (with its failure to acknowledge the rights or existence of others) shows itself not only in Smaug's hoard, the lusts of Shelob, or the nihilistic corruptions of Sauron but also in the simple excesses of hobbit nature, young Frodo's passion for mushrooms, for example, or Lobelia's propensity for acquiring Bilbo's spoons. So too sacrifice (expressly undertaken for others) appears in a variety of forms, from Bilbo's "painful" recognition that he, as host, "might have to go without" cake (Tolkien, 1987, p. 16), or Fatty Bolger's Crickhollow stand, on up to those wrenching oblations of self, those sacrifices that risk life, limb, or peace of mind, sacrifices that Gandalf, Frodo, or Aragorn most clearly exemplify.

Not all of this – not high-level sacrifice at least – may appear overtly related to the theme of food and consumption, and yet the connection is there. In matters of moral choice, we are takers or we are givers, and our words for expressing these concepts are rich with metaphor. In the act of taking or taking over, we *assimilate*, *incorporate*, or *absorb*, terms that are perhaps most appropriate to business, *corporate* business in particular, with its Latin root *corpus* completing the image of a body that feeds. So too, when we lust, when we long excessively for something, we are *consumed* by the desire to possess.

This particular form of overindulgence, indulgence that *consumes*, is most apparent in Tolkien in all those confrontations with beings or beasts that seize, devour and so possess those they come upon – for consuming, in its most negative sense, is nothing more than possessiveness, the extreme of isolating, self-indulgence that Shelob embodies, desiring "death for all others . . . and for herself a glut of life, alone" (Tolkien, 1965a, p. 333). But when we deny the urgings of ego or flesh and choose instead to give to others, when we give up our own needs to serve the needs or lives of others, we *nourish*, *nurture*, *sustain*, and *preserve*.

These moral issues and the imagery that supports these issues are the same in *The Hobbit* as they are in *The Lord of the Rings*, in spite of obvious differences in emphasis and tone. We see Bilbo, after his escape from the Misty Mountains, deciding it is "his duty" to go back into "the horrible, horrible, tunnels and look for his friends" (Tolkien, 1987, p. 83); we see him among the spiders, fighting, taunting, throwing stones, in order to save the dwarves. Again and again Bilbo endangers himself to benefit or rescue others, and danger in *The Hobbit* is, with very few exceptions, the danger of being eaten.

In *The Hobbit*, in fact, the fear of being eaten is presented far more blatantly and far more frequently than it is in *The Lord of the Rings*. At the same time, however, our apprehension is considerably less. We know Bilbo will escape. We know something or someone will surely turn up in time. This is, of course, entirely appropriate. *The Hobbit*'s lighter, nursery-tale tone, its more open reference to being eaten, as well as its stronger emphasis on food in general, are what we expect in a book aimed mainly at children. Tolkien understood the thrill that comes from games or stories that tease about "gobbling up," and he was well aware of the ways in which food and eating specifically fascinate children. Like Kenneth Grahame and Lewis Carroll, he understood the particular pleasure children find in descriptions of plentiful, frequent meals: breakfasts, dinners and teas, complete with cakes, scones, tarts, pies, and those intriguing wines and ales that belong to the world of adults.

The book opens with images of almost excessive and certainly improbable plenty. Bilbo has not only one kitchen, one dining-room, one pantry but "kitchens, dining-rooms," and "pantries (lots of these)" (Tolkien, 1987, p. 11). The very roundness of hobbits, and even the roundness of their tunnels and doors, adds to this image of secure and well-fed comfort. Tolkien, however, is quick to insert a high level of danger into this comfortable Shire world. Bilbo's hobbit peace and habitual indulgence are soon replaced by privation and anxiety, by the fear of both doing without food and the fear of ending up as someone else's meal. Kenneth Grahame's Mole may experience the terror of the Wild Wood, Lewis Carroll's Alice may hear the fate of oysters or find herself chided by the pudding she begins to slice, but only Tolkien, of these three writers, addresses the threat of being eaten quite so frequently and with such explicitness.

Bilbo, the champion of second breakfasts, the one who dreams again and again, on the long weary trail, of buttered toast, bacon and eggs, and "the kettle just beginning to sing" (Tolkien, 1987, p. 35), faces the threat of being eaten at nearly every turn. He confronts, in order of appearance: trolls and goblins and Gollum and wolves and spiders and Smaug, every one of them perpetually hungry, and every one of them eager to remedy that condition.

There is a certain basic pattern to these fear-of-being-eaten scenes. When the dwarves and Gandalf and Bilbo are troubled or weary or suffering most acutely from hunger themselves, the threat of being eaten is most likely to occur. "We must just tighten our belts and trudge on – or we shall be made into supper, and that will be much worse than having none ourselves," says Gandalf to the desperately hungry Bilbo after the goblin caves (Tolkien, 1987, p. 87). In incident after incident, misery leads to carelessness, and carelessness leads to their nearly being devoured.

Chronologically, the first fear-of-being-eaten incident is the troll adventure – and to borrow from a thirteenth-century Icelandic text, "not much is worse than trolls" (Jónsson,

1912-15, vol. BII, pp. 141-42). The pattern of temptation that leads to adversity is presented through the trolls' alluring fire and the "toothsome" smell of their roast mutton, which brings about the dwarves' captivity and the prolonged possibility of being roasted, boiled, or squashed into jelly.

This is followed by the Misty Mountains, where the cave that should have sheltered them from cold and wind and weather opens the way to goblins, a nasty, "always hungry" breed. For Bilbo, there is Gollum as well and Gollum's increasing hunger. Not only does Bilbo's fate – to be eaten or escorted out – depend on the riddle game that Gollum instigates, but the nature of the riddles themselves accentuates the theme. Of the nine riddles asked (discounting Bilbo's dubious pocket question) three, the egg and the two fish riddles, deal directly with food; three others speak of teeth and biting and devouring. Equally suggestive are the contents of Gollum's pockets: "fish-bones, goblins' teeth, wet shells, a bit of bat-wing, a sharp stone to sharpen his fangs on" (Tolkien, 1987, p. 73). And Gollum's very name comes from the "horrible swallowing noise" he frequently makes in his throat (Tolkien, 1987, p. 68). Throughout all of this, Bilbo is terribly hungry himself. Nor does his ultimate escape from Gollum and the goblin tunnels offer much relief. Wolves are soon on their trail, as are a second installment of goblins, gleefully singing about roasting them "alive" or stewing "them in a pot" (Tolkien, 1987, p. 95).

The pattern continues in Mirkwood, where the rapid depletion of their stores is contrasted both by Bombur's sumptuous dreams and the increasingly more lavish feasts that tempt them, finally, off the trail and into the spiders' domain. And after the spiders comes Smaug, a devourer of maidens and ponies, "the Chiefest and Greatest of Calamities," who knows "the smell (and taste) of dwarf – no one better" (Tolkien, 1987, p. 190-1).

In *The Hobbit*, in fact, the threat of being eaten is so dominant that even the eagles and Beorn, decent folk who give the Company food and shelter and fellowship, are likely to be touched with carnivorous possibility. The eagles, Bilbo learns to his relief, do not intend to tear him up "for supper like a rabbit" after all (Tolkien, 1987, p. 97). But rabbit is precisely what the eagles do bring them for supper, and the notion that rabbits and hobbits have something in common is one that appears repeatedly throughout the books. This rabbit association and the vulnerability it implies are nicely reinforced by the-not-entirely-safe Beorn, who pokes Bilbo in the stomach and comments that "little bunny is getting nice and fat" (Tolkien, 1987, p. 115).

The threat of being eaten appears in other less obvious ways as well. In *The Hobbit*, where it is clearly best to maintain a lighter tone, Tolkien twice shows us the dwarves engulfed in bags or comically enveloped in webbing, a sort of symbolic, pre-ingestion indicative of what nearly does occur. The "jaws" of Old Man Willow, closing tightly on Merry, work in a similar way to prepare us for the greater engulfing and the considerably more ominous spell that occurs on the Barrow-downs. But most intriguing are Tolkien's threatening entrances and his underground passageways. In both *The Hobbit* and *The Lord of the Rings*, they invariably suggest a form of devouring. In a world of living landscapes, where mountains have "shoulders," "feet," and "limbs" and where caves, tunnels, entrances, and gullies have "mouths" or are described as "gaping" or "yawning," Tolkien's journeys through dark, winding passages and through gateways into dangerous realms seem very ingestive indeed. Within the darkest reaches of these inner worlds lie villains and beasts, most of whom subsist on whatever comes their way. Tolkien's exits (rather appropriately referred to as the "back door" and the "lower gate" in the Misty Mountains adventure) further add to the impression of digestive tract journeys made through the earth itself. Even Mirkwood, with its tunnel-like entrance, and the Wood-elves' cavern produce something of this effect. And when Tolkien describes the "green gums" and the "jagged teeth" of the Barrow-down episode, the image of a living, devouring, underworld spirit is unmistakable.

Particularly intriguing in this context is the word *Mordor*, a word meaning "black land" in Tolkien's elvish language, Sindarin, but a word that is also highly suggestive (through Latin roots) of both devouring and death. (*Mordant* and *mortuary* are perhaps our closest English words.) As Sam and Frodo approach the boundaries of Mordor at Cirith Gorgor, these Latin-based images are strongly reinforced. The "mouth" of the pass itself is guarded on each side by the Towers of the Teeth; here lies the iron gate, Morannon (the Teeth of Mordor). No one, unless summoned by Sauron, can pass this gate without feeling "their bite" (Tolkien, 1965a, p. 244).

Names of this sort are far more suggestive of horror and risk than are comparable place-names in *The Hobbit*, with its Misty Mountains or Lonely Mountain or even its Desolation of Smaug. We are now in a world that is at once more hostile and disturbing and more noble and significant than the one Bilbo journeyed through, and impending danger is no longer presented in conversational or offhanded ways. This is certainly true of the threat of being eaten. In *The Lord of the Rings* direct references to the possibility of being eaten, to the possibility of being literally ingested, are considerably less frequent than they were in *The Hobbit*, but the threat, when it does occur, is a far more serious one. In *The Hobbit*, for example, we are told that goblins eat "horses and ponies and donkeys (and other much more dreadful things")" (Tolkien, 1987, p. 60). And it is easy enough to guess what those "much more dreadful things" might be, but it is only in *The Lord of the Rings* that Tolkien moves beyond comic/horror threats or hints and speaks directly of Saruman awarding "man's-flesh to eat" to the fighting Uruk-hai (Tolkien, 1965a, p. 49).

Cannibalism – defined here as any Middle-earth race devouring another – represents the ultimate betrayal, the ultimate failure to acknowledge the value and rights of others. It is a practice we hear of mostly among the orcs, a breed whose speech is packed with cannibal reference and threat. "You're cooked," the Isengarder orcs jeer to their rivals. "The Whiteskins will catch you and eat you" (Tolkien, 1965a, p. 56). And this cannibalistic note is intensified by certain suggestions that orcs eat not just other races but possibly other orcs as well. Even if Tolkien's allusions to orc-eat-orc behaviour are only intended as metaphor, as orcish ways of referring to death or defeat, the level of horror is increased. "Go, or I'll eat you," Shagrat threatens Snaga (Tolkien, 1965b, p. 182). "It's orc-flesh they eat," the evil-voiced Grishnákh says of the Uruk-hai, a derisive comment as much as an accusation, likely enough, but one appropriate to the breed (Tolkien, 1965a, p. 49). Finally, however, the most vivid intimation of orcs eating orcs comes not so much from threat and speech as from the image of Shagrat stabbing again the already wounded Gorbag and then pausing to lick the blade.

Orcs have been fittingly intensified over the goblins we knew in *The Hobbit*, but Gollum/Sméagol, on the other hand, has to some extent and in certain ways been softened by the time we meet him again. In *The Lord of the Rings* he no longer appears to be actively seeking hobbit flesh or even orc for that matter, though there are rumours of a blood-drinking ghost that clearly apply to him, and Sam suspects him of being "not too dainty to try what hobbit tastes like" (Tolkien, 1965a, p. 228). For the most part, however, and from what we actually see, he now lives mostly off lower life forms (beetles, snakes, fish, and worms), things snared in the water or dug from the earth, particularly wet earth, and possibly out of the grave, as his comments on not being able to touch the dead forms in the marshes indicate to Sam. Gollum has become less of an eater of fresh meats and something more of a grubber in marshes and pools, something more of a ghoul. In part this shift is indicative of a slow degeneration, but his apparent (and perhaps only temporary) willingness to forego hobbit flesh also makes sense in another way. Tolkien intends us to gain a certain sympathy for Sméagol. He is not yet fully lost, and he is tied to Frodo through more than simply the Ring. Hobbits, we learn, are the closest remaining links to Sméagol's own lost, "hobbit-like" race (making him a "Proto-Frodo," to quote a student of mine); and it is not until he is balancing at the edge of the chasm of Mount Doom that he bites and maims his hobbit counterpart.

Like the orcs, Sméagol also uses the term "eating" to suggest defeat or extermination, but only in connection with the Dark Lord and his destruction of other lives and other individual wills. "He'll eat us all, if He gets it [the Ring], eat all the world" is Sméagol's cry to Frodo (Tolkien, 1965a, p. 245), an opinion that is by no means Sméagol's alone but which is nowhere else expressed with such simplicity. References to Sauron's "devouring" occur throughout the books. Faramir, for example, closely echoes Sméagol when he speaks of the "destroyer who would devour all" (Tolkien, 1965a, p. 280). But Sméagol's reduction, his description of the Dark Lord's intentions as mere "eating", neatly reveals the basic similarity that exists between goblin/orc voracity and the more abstract cravings that the Dark Lord represents. That the sins of this now mostly disembodied but still formidable being can be reduced to a display of excessive appetite, to something rather like greed at table, places Sauron, for a moment, in the same category as any mortal who contrives to gain more than his or her fair share. From the Sackville-Bagginses' yearning for Bag End to the Dark Lord's lonely, raging hunger, the drive is essentially the same – the drive, that is, but not the degree.

However much Tolkien may wish us to see the ultimate cheapness of soul that binds all those who sin by acquisition or by an excessive yearning for power, he is also highly aware of position and the difference position makes. Lobelia and Gollum; Wormtongue, Saruman, Denethor: each is capable of rising only so far. Each has a limit, a glass ceiling (to borrow from present-day terminology) in ambition, influence or even in ill intent. For this reason, Gandalf explains, the One Ring could not give Gollum unlimited power but only "power according to his stature" (Tolkien, 1954, p. 63). At most he sees himself as "Gollum the Great," "*The* Gollum," and eating fish every day (Tolkien, 1965a, p. 241).

Just as Sméagol's reduction of the Dark Lord's devastation to a simple act of eating reveals both the elemental nature and the baseness of Sauron's transgressions, so too Shelob's role as a lesser but parallel figure accentuates His essential pettiness. She is, in fact, almost a parody of Sauron in certain of His aspects. Though Shelob, unlike Sauron, has no desire for slaves, willing or otherwise, and though there are hints of sexual appetite in Tolkien's presentation of Shelob, hints that appear in no other character, nonetheless the Dark Lord and Shelob both serve to represent the far extreme of a single negative urge. The swollen, engulfing existence that Shelob desires is little different from the expanding reaches of Mordor that the Dark Lord's destruction creates. Each brings darkness. Each brings death. Each wishes for no other power than his or hers alone. Each is an example of appetite run amuck. "All living things" are Shelob's "food" (Tolkien, 1965a, p. 332), and Sauron, we are told, "would devour all."

What is emphasized by such statements is the sheer extent of Shelob's and Sauron's appetites, the insatiability each exemplifies. But in Tolkien's world it is not simply appetite that serves as a moral gauge. Virtue or corruption can also be measured through the particulars of diet alone. To put it simply, the baddies eat bad and the goodies eat good. We see this first in *The Hobbit*, where food taken from the trolls' larder must be examined and chosen with care. Similarly, Pippin in *The Two Towers* wisely rejects the "flesh flung to him by an Orc, the flesh of he dared not guess what creature" (Tolkien, 1965a, p. 54). More telling yet are Sméagol's inability to tolerate elvish food, his disgust for cooked rabbit and herbs, and his preference instead for things raw, for cold fish, worms, or "something slimy out of holes" – all of which indicate his regression, his devolution back to a primordial world of "black mud," wetness, and a "chewing and slavering" existence (Tolkien, 1965a, pp. 231-2).

For certain of his negative characters, Tolkien adds yet another element of horror. For the orcs and Shelob (and for Sauron, the devourer of souls), the repulsion we feel over what they eat is magnified by the pleasure each takes in the willful infliction of pain. This, above all, is what gives spice to orc or Shelob meals. In a chapter full of cannibalistic hints, we hear the orcs' regret that the hobbits are to be delivered alive, that there will be no chance for "play"; so too Shelob and the Dark Lord both desire the consciousness of those they torture and consume. Shelob, though she may wish for no other existence but her own, does not "eat dead meat, nor suck cold blood" (Tolkien, 1965a, p. 350). She wants her victims alive and "plays" like a cat with those who become her food. There is little difference between this and Sauron's desire for unwilling, agonized slaves; and when Sauron's emissary, the Mouth of Sauron, is sent to mislead and demoralize the Army of the West, to "play these mice cruelly" before they are to be struck and killed, the comparison with Shelob again is evident (Tolkien, 1965b, p. 164).

Tolkien's decent and idealized characters are, of course, equally defined by what it is they eat. Their foods, which they share with others, and the warm fellowship which accompanies their meals, all serve to place them clearly on the side of the good. The inn at Bree has "good plain food, as good as the Shire could show, and homelike" (Tolkien, 1954, p. 166). Beorn, for all the danger he exudes, eats no meat but lives "most on cream and honey" (Tolkien, 1987, p. 103). Tom Bombadil's table, laden with "yellow cream, honeycomb, and white bread and butter" (Tolkien, 1954, p. 132), the meal eaten with Faramir in the "Window on the West," and even Treebeard's rich, woodsy, invigorating water, are really much the same.

Each of these individuals shares similar, fleshless (or nearly fleshless) diets. We hear only now and then of hobbits eating meat; Strider speaks of "berry, root, and herb" to be found along the way and mentions only as a secondary possibility his "skill as a hunter at need" (Tolkien, 1954, p. 203). The highest and the best eat no meat at all; and the Elves, we are told, have an "appetite for music and poetry and tales," which they seem to like "as much as food, or more" (Tolkien, 1954, p. 250). Their drinks (and Tom Bombadil's) have the qualities of wine, while the less ethereal hobbits serve mostly ale or beer.

But the value of elven food goes beyond what might be called simple dietary correctness. The elven *lembas* (or waybread), carried by the Fellowship, has a symbolic meaning as well. *Lembas* feeds both the will and the body and is touched with eucharistic elements. It is "given to serve . . . when all else fails" (Tolkien, 1954, p. 386) and in the elvish language, Quenya, means "bread of life." In the shadow of Cirith Ungol, before their journey "down into the Nameless Land," Frodo and Sam share what Tolkien twice refers to as a "last meal," the last perhaps they will "ever eat together." It consists of some food from Gondor, but more telling are the "wafers of the waybread of the Elves" and the water they sparingly drink (Tolkien, 1965a, p. 320). Above all it is the *lembas* that gives Frodo the strength to continue on his march to death, burdened like Christ with the object of his own torture. Later, in "The Land of Shadow," communion is suggested again. Though it is Mordor water they drink this time, not clear, wine-like water, it comes to them comes through Sam's call to the Lady for "clean water and plain daylight" (Tolkien, 1965b, p. 195), a call that is virtually a prayer. It becomes, then, a form of elven water after all; and taken along the way with the remaining fragments of elf wafer and – perhaps most important – with memories of the Lady herself, it constitutes communion.

Thoughts or memories of this sort, linking us to others (as Sam is linked to Galadriel) are themselves a form of communion. Repeatedly, throughout the grim and seemingly hopeless chapters of *The Return of the King*, it is compassionate thoughts of others that confer the strength to endeavor and persevere. It is, for example, the combination of "understanding" and "pity" that Bilbo feels for Gollum that allows him, "quite suddenly" to achieve his leap in the dark (Tolkien, 1987, pp. 79-80). After the Fellowship is separated, we hear repeatedly that they think of one another. Merry thrusts down "his own dread" through thoughts of Pippin's ordeal (Tolkien, 1965b, p. 107). At the Tower of Cirith Ungol, Sam forces "himself to think of Frodo, lying bound or in pain or dead" (Tolkien, 1965b, p. 180). And with this he goes on. Each kind and unselfish thought brings stamina and greater resolve. In a similar way Sam gains heart from the thought that he and Frodo are part of the great story, that they too are part of the Ring's history and on the side of the good; others have been brave before them, and brave for the sake of others; so they must be as well.

Even Gandalf's gentle chiding to Bilbo, not to disbelieve prophecies he helped to bring about, and not to imagine it all had occurred for his benefit alone, makes the same point. In our own small way, Tolkien believes, each of us inexorably belongs to the story and can play a hero's or a villain's part. And if we accept the discrete and appropriately veiled connections to Christ's sacrifice and our own roles in a world that calls for relinquishing, sharing, and freely given service, we become part of the Christian body and have taken of the body of Christ. We are a fellowship and a community, and we share in a communion that nurtures us even when we believe ourselves alone.

It is all there in Gandalf facing the Balrog, in his falling and rising from death; it is there in the Rangers, who, unacknowledged, continue to protect the Shire; in Faramir remaining at his lonely outpost; in Galadriel choosing for the benefit of Middle-earth rather than for glory; even Butterbur – though only "on the edge of very great troubles" (Tolkien, 1965b, p. 272) – contributes to the cause. "I also am a steward," Gandalf says (Tolkien, 1965b, p. 31); and, in truth, we are all stewards, those of us who serve the good and give of ourselves through willing service and aid.

The contrast with Shelob's blubbering over the wound Sam gives to her "beloved flesh" or Gollum's "whistling and gurgling" self pity, "horrible to listen to" (Tolkien, 1987, pp. 77-8), are highly indicative. The "beloved" in Shelob's reference to her own flesh (like Gollum's evoking of "Precious") has almost a religious ring, a Biblical and devotional tone; she is her own deity, a goddess of self. "Her Ladyship," says one of the Mordor orcs, quite appropriately, for Shelob is a distorted queen, a ruler of darkness and death, the antithesis of the "Lady" Galadriel, whose demeanor carries its own religious associations and who is a bestower of light and life and who willingly accepts her own and her people's diminishing for the sake of a greater good.

Sacrifices, such as the one Galadriel makes in rejecting the Ring and relinquishing her position in Lothlórien and

Middle-earth, are invariably freely given. Circumstances may urge an undertaking or a renunciation, but the choice must always remain one's own. But relinquishings of this sort, though they entail loss, though they may require sacrifices of life or limb or rejections of power and glory, do not mean failure, ruin, or permanent deprivation. When Galadriel, rejecting the Ring, speaks of diminishing, this is not a diminishing of self or soul. Like Milton's Eve, she has been tempted by the title of "Queen"; but she – unlike Eve – passes the test; and, in rejecting the Ring's invitation, she will, in her own words, "remain Galadriel" (Tolkien, 1954, p. 381). Her better self has grown, and she may now return to the West. It is only Pippin and Merry who grow in actuality, whose service and hardship for others are marked by a representative increase in size, but all those who give and serve and nourish others gain or grow in one sense or another. Gandalf is now Gandalf the White. Aragorn is king. Faramir is the Steward of Gondor and marries Éowyn; and Frodo, who has suffered the most, who has lost his easy hobbit joy and who has been outwardly (and almost ritualistically) marked by the loss of a finger, has grown too, as Saruman knows and bitterly resents. Frodo will have his reward; he has gained something of an elvish nature and will go to the West and heal.

Those who give, then, gain; those who take less for the sake of others ultimately become more. They gain in fellowship as well; and it is through fellowship that we find earth's finest rewards. It is this that the dying Thorin has learned when he speaks of valuing "food and cheer and song above hoarded gold" (Tolkien, 1987, p. 243). And what Thorin learns is what Tolkien wants us to learn as well; he wants us to look closely at our choices and our commitments and to consider where they lead. Thorin, like Boromir, chooses a path that seems to offer appropriate and warranted power but which leads instead to disruption, to early death and defeat. In Thorin and Boromir, then, Tolkien shows us the soul in balance, the soul that falters and fails, but he shows us as well that the soul – at the moment of death – can turn again to the good, as both of these characters do.

This sense of a soul in balance also applies to Gollum and greatly increases the significance of his character. For all his slow degeneration, he too is not fully lost; he too may yet be redeemed. He is, as well, an indication of what Frodo may become, of what Frodo nearly does become; and he serves, then, as a warning to us, a reminder that we are capable of good but that the drive to seize and consume is ever with us, that the possibility of failure or sin or moral deterioration is therefore ever with us as well. We cannot have it otherwise, as Tolkien fully understands. We are of the body; we live by consuming, and consuming has its inevitable, orcish side. It is for this reason that Tolkien speculates in "The New Shadow," about the orc within us all, about the ways in which we must inevitably appear as destroyers and adversaries to those other forms of life we consume or feed upon. To trees, whose wood we cut and whose fruit we take and devour, we wear (at least in part) the face of enemies.

This mixture of innocence and rapacity, innate to the human/hobbit condition, is neatly suggested at the conclusion of *The Lord of the Rings*. In the midst of Tolkien's exhilarating description of the regenerated Shire, one brief but faintly chilling picture stands out in contrast to the otherwise idyllic scene, the picture of hobbit children sitting – surrounded by abundance – eating countless plums and piling up the stones like "the heaped skulls of a conqueror" (Tolkien, 1965b, p. 303). Certainly, a hobbit child, amassing the skulls of vanquished plums, is a long way from becoming a Sauron, but the instincts of a conqueror and devourer are there just the same.

And Tolkien wants us to recognize this; he wants us to recognize that we are creatures of appetite and ego and that simple, instinctive gratification can lead to overstepping, to excess, to claiming as our own whatever comes our way. But he wants us to remember as well that we are capable of becoming more than egos and appetites. We can choose to give as well as to receive; we can learn to relinquish as well as to possess. And if we stretch ourselves beyond our earthly natures, if we serve and share and sacrifice in small ways and in great, we, like Tolkien's small and larger heroes, shall received our rewards and be more than we were before.

But those who take, those who seize, hoard, and consume and consider only the self will be served otherwise. Their reward will be a hollowness and a void; they wished for distinction and singularity, a power theirs *alone*, and they end with singular loneliness; they end – often enough and most dramatically – by wasting or fading away, by a dispatching by fire or a dispersing by wind. We see this first with the envying, hungering Barrow-wight, whom Tom orders to shrivel like "cold mist" and whose "long trailing shriek" fades away "into an unguessable distance" (Tolkien, 1954, pp. 153-4).

At the end of *The Return of the King*, Tolkien replays this scene in a number of ways. In a passage highly reminiscent of the demise of Orgoglio (Pride) in *The Faerie Queene*, the Nazgûl Lord, who threatens Éowyn that her "flesh shall be devoured" and whose "great shoulders" rise over her moments before his defeat, falls into instant nothingness. His cry, which fades to a "shrill wailing, passing with the wind," becomes "bodiless and thin," dies and is "swallowed up" (Tolkien, 1965b, pp. 116-7). Later, as Mordor itself steams, crumbles and melts, the last of the Nazgûls tear "like flaming bolts" through the sky, utter a piercing cry, and then crackle, wither, and go out (Tolkien, 1965b, p. 224); the spirit of Sauron, rises into "a vast threatening" but impotent shadow that fills "all the sky" before it is taken by the wind and "all blown away" (Tolkien, 1965b, pp. 227). Even Gollum, with his final "shriek" and "wail" fading into the fiery depths of Mount Doom, comes to a similar end. And, finally, Saruman – in imitation of Sauron to the last – gathers into a grey mist that rises "like smoke from a fire," then bends away in the wind, with a "sigh" that dissolves "into nothing" (Tolkien, 1965b, p. 300).

These are the just desserts. The eaters are unbodied; the eaters are eaten. Those who would have more and everlastingly more end by becoming less; those who serve none but themselves end by being alone. This is as true of the Master of Dale, deserted by his companions and starving in the wilderness, as it is of the Dark Lord himself. But those who follow the path of true service and loyal fellowship move through pain and loss and misery to peace and reunion and grace, to that ultimate blessing which, in Tolkien's own words, is a joy as "poignant as grief", an echo and vision of *"evangelium"* (Tolkien, 1964, pp. 60 and 62).

References:

Jónsson, Finnur (ed.). 1912-15. *Den norsk-islandske skjaldedigtning*. Copenhagen: Gyldendal-Nordisk forlag.

Tolkien, J. R. R. 1954. *The Fellowship of the Ring*. Boston: Houghton Mifflin.

Tolkien, J. R. R. 1964. "On Fairy-Stories," *Tree and Leaf*. London: Allen & Unwin.

Tolkien, J. R. R. 1965a. *The Two Towers*. Boston: Houghton Mifflin.

Tolkien, J. R. R. 1965b. *The Return of the King*. Boston: Houghton Mifflin.

Tolkien, J. R. R. 1987. *The Hobbit, or There and Back Again*. London: Unwin Hyman.

Power and Knowledge in Tolkien: The Problem of Difference in "The Birthday Party"[1]

Jane Chance

Abstract: It is not altogether clear from reading *The Lord of the Rings* for the first time how political the hobbits Bilbo and Frodo are, even in the introductory chapter "A Long-expected Party". For there exist power struggles among the different hobbit families in the Shire, absurd in some cases, significant in others. One mark of the ability of Bilbo and Frodo is their sensitivity to the politics of the Shire, a faculty born of nurture and nature that will enable Frodo's mission and attract followers. This paper will reveal how Tolkien's understanding of leadership rests upon what might be termed a Post-modernist relationship between power and knowledge.

Keywords: Foucault, *The Hobbit*, leadership, *The Lord of the Rings*, politics, power

Tolkien shares with the social philosopher and theorist Michel Foucault similar concerns relating to the question of power and knowledge. Although Tolkien's major fictional writings did not emerge in response to the political and academic events in France during the late sixties, as did Foucault's essays, nevertheless he spent most of his mature life as a professor working within the British equivalent of the academy, and his greatest popularity coincided with a similar historical phenomenon – the rise of student power during the late sixties and early seventies. To provide this context for the study of Tolkien, then, is to invite comparison with a thinker whose views on the question of power and knowledge share a remarkable likeness.

Most important, both thinkers question power as sovereignty, power as substance. In *Power/Knowledge: Selected Interviews and Other Writings*, Foucault notes that, "Power in the substantive sense, '*le' pouvoir*, doesn't exist . . . In reality power means relations, a more-or-less organised, hierarchical, co-ordinated cluster of relations" (Foucault, 1980, p. 198). This concept of a power grid implies constant change and flux and therefore by definition a "complex domain" of particular powers and many issues (Foucault, 1980, p. 188). To analyse this network requires attention to the whole interworking rather than to the responsibility of the individual alone, requires attention, that is, to what might be termed the domain of the political: "Every relation of force implies at each moment a relation of power (which is in a sense its momentary expression) and every power relation makes a reference, as its effect but also as its condition of possibility, to a political field of which it forms a part" (Foucault, 1980, p. 189). Tolkien, as we shall see, might well agree with this politicization of power – and of knowledge.

Like Foucault, both Tolkien and his fellow Inkling C.S. Lewis question the validity of the human sciences to represent the rationality of the age. Foucault focuses upon the institutional matrices of hospital and asylum at a time when the working class was in revolt against the power of institutions, whether schools, hospitals, or prisons, and therefore against the knowledge they claimed as their province. Tolkien fictionalizes this institutional matrix through the creation of the Dark Lord Sauron and his imitators linked with the land of death, Mordor, that he ruled so tyrannously. Both thinkers object to the importance of post-Enlightenment technologies in the governance of peoples.

In "The Eye of Power", Foucault defines the essential institutional model as Bentham's eighteenth-century architectural device of the "Panopticon," a ring-shaped building enclosing a tower that oversees cells that might contain a convict – or a lunatic, a patient, a worker, or a student (Foucault, 1980, p. 147). It is the same model used by Tolkien to locate the nature of Sauron's power, Saruman's power, Shelob's power, even the Sackville-Bagginses' power. Visibility – the searching Eye of Sauron – is necessary to ensure access to all individuals; it is this same visibility which insists upon a rigorous and universal power. The ultimate form of visibility locates within the individual, or what Foucault describes as "the gaze" – "An inspecting gaze, a gaze which each individual under its weight will end

---

[1] This paper was first published as part of Jane Chance's *The Lord of the Rings: The Mythology of Power* (1992, pp. 19-35).

by interiorising to the point that he is his own overseer, each individual thus exercising this surveillance over, and against, himself. A superb formula: power exercised continuously and for what turns out to be a minimal cost. When Bentham realizes what he has discovered, he calls it the Colombus's egg of political thought, a formula exactly the opposite of monarchical power" (Foucault, 1980, p. 155). Through this structure power becomes what Foucault terms a "machinery that no one owns" (Foucault, 1980, p. 156). For this reason there is no point in the prisoners taking over the tower in Bentham's Panopticon: in echo of one of Frodo's central points about "ownership" of the Ring (a type of Panopticon), Foucault asks rhetorically, "Do you think it would be much better to have the prisoners operating the Panoptic apparatus and sitting in the central tower, instead of the guards?" (Foucault, 1980, pp. 164-5).

Like Tolkien, Foucault has criticized the concept of power as formulated through the repressive speech-act of the "interdict," or the "enunciation of law, discourse of prohibition" (Foucault, 1980, p. 140). Instead Foucault has identified a positive desire for productive power running through the social body (Foucault, 1980, p. 119), making necessary an "in*corpo*ration" of power in order to have access to individuals' bodies (Foucault, 1980, p. 125). And it is the intellectual as free subject ("the clear, individual figure of a universality whose obscure, collective form is *embodied* in the proletariat," my italics, p. 126), especially within the university, who has become most aware of specific struggles in the precise arenas where work or life has engaged him or her. An example of the "specific" intellectual in the post-World War Two period, Oppenheimer suggests the scientific knowledge available in making the atomic bomb which posed a political threat because of a "universal" discourse, in that the nuclear threat affected the entire world (Foucault, 1980, p. 128). If we substitute "Saruman," "Gandalf," or even "Bilbo" and "Frodo" for J. Robert Oppenheimer, we begin to understand how Tolkien's concept of the wizard, or the scholar-historian who bears the Ring, functions analogously to the figure of the specific intellectual embodying the "proletariat." Like Foucault, Tolkien is concerned with the political problem of the intellectual, one not of "science" or "ideology," but of "truth" and "power." So Foucault concludes his essay, "Truth and Power," "It's not a matter of emancipating truth from every system of power (which would be a chimera, for truth is already power) but of detaching the power of truth from the forms of hegemony, social, economic and cultural, within which it operates at the present time . . . The political question, to sum up, is not error, illusion, alienated consciousness, or ideology; it is truth itself" (Foucault, 1980, p. 133).

The context, then, from which Tolkien derives his vision of power is institutional and political, like that of Foucault – meaning the university, academia. And the philosophy he propounds accordingly is constructed by means of the tools of the specific intellectual in attaining the primary goal – the power of language in the pursuit of truth. Both the context and the philosophy are concealed by the fictional veil of the heroic narrative, whose singular structure, repeated in its various books, assumes its own power.

The power of truth and its liberation from hegemony is indeed the great theme of *The Lord of the Rings*. A novel that mythologizes power and the problem of individual difference (as theoretically defined), *The Lord of the Rings* in its three volumes focuses first, in *The Fellowship of the Ring*, upon the problem of individual and class difference within the social body or construct, second, in *The Two Towers*, on the heroic power of knowledge and language in the political power struggle, and third, in *The Return of the King*, on the ideal of kingship as healing and service, in a unique inversion of master-servant roles and the domination of one by the other.

The introduction to this mythology of power begins with the role of the individual within society as symbolized by "A Long-expected Party", or what might be termed "The Birthday Party," the first and most important chapter of *The Fellowship of the Ring* and thus of *The Lord of the Rings*. Here, this conventional celebration of the individual, the self (Bilbo, in this case) is marked by his gift-giving to others (liberality) and climaxes in his disappearance. That is, intellectual heroism, in Tolkien's world, is achieved through social involvement, service to others, the disappearance of self-indulgence. The "gift" of the Ring by Bilbo to his nephew Frodo is the gift of invisibility, because wearing it "stretches" the self: that is, resisting the desire to submit to the authority of its maker, Sauron, wears out any individual, but the resistance paradoxically, over time, strengthens the determination to resist.

In the three volumes of *The Lord of the Rings*, the individual uses this gift to test resistance to institutionalized power and the power of others within the community. In *The Fellowship of the Ring*, language as the articulation of knowledge and desire serves as moral and political weaponry against threats to survival and community (which threats often take the form of subversive language and its concomitant power). In *The Two Towers*, knowledge, as reflected in the power of language, can be used or misused as an effective and manipulative weapon by the powerful, or those who aspire to power – Wormtongue and Saruman, chiefly. The adversaries in this volume also include the inarticulate and dumb (Gollum, Shelob) whose rage leads to murder, or Mordor: a greater evil than the cunning manipulation of words is wordless and mindless violence, untameable by communication or rational discourse.

But this second volume also reveals the civilizing power of service to others – Gollum, serving Master Frodo, becomes Sméagol. Similarly, in the third volume, *The Return of the King*, the leader's true power emerges from wise and healing service to the community. The maintenance of society is best advanced by the caretaker and the gardener, those who take care, nurture others, and continue the work of the family or nation. In their role of understanding and tolerating individual differences within the community, indeed, using those differences productively, the caretakers empower both the individual and society, or, together, the social network.

For it is not altogether clear from reading *The Fellowship of the Ring* and *The Lord of the Rings* the first time (much less the fifth or the tenth) how political are the hobbits Bilbo and his nephew Frodo, even in the introductory chapter, "A Long-expected Party". This lack of clarity arises because the Shire in which they live exudes a pastoral innocence that masks the seeds of its potential destruction. We recall the "charming, absurd, helpless hobbits" (Tolkien, 1965, p. 79) in the Shire, whom Gandalf worries might become enslaved by Sauron, the "kind, jolly, stupid Bolgers, Hornblowers, Boffins, Bracegirdles . . . not to mention the ridiculous Bagginses" (Tolkien, 1965, p. 79). For the moment they are protected because Sauron has "more useful" servants, but there is always a threat from him because of his "malice and revenge." And yet the difference between the isolated, safe, jolly Shire and the distant, evil Dark Power is not as marked as it might seem. For there exist power struggles among the different hobbit families in the Shire region, absurd in some cases, significant in others. One mark of the ability of Bilbo and Frodo – their power – is their sensitivity to the politics of the Shire, a faculty born of nurture and nature that will enable Frodo's mission and attract followers.

The political problems in the Shire grow out of its deceptively "safe" isolation from the rest of Middle-earth. Its inhabitants suspect those who come from outside, who are different from them in ways they do not understand. A stranger – initially and more familiarly, a Brandybuck, later and more ominously, a Dark Rider – arouses mistrust, and the inhabitants band closer together. Sandyman the Miller, from the beginning, creates a problem for Frodo through his suspicious notice of the queerness of the visitors to Bag End (among whom are the strange dwarves and the magical Gandalf). This queerness extends also therefore to Bag End itself and ultimately, by association, to its owners, Bilbo and then Frodo (Tolkien, 1965, p. 47). Sameness is familiar and secure, and sameness means hobbitlike. The hobbits relish what is natural for them, which involves physical activities, living close to nature – living in holes, eating, smoking tobacco. To do otherwise is unhobbitlike. "Hobbits", Tolkien once acknowledged, "have what you might call universal morals. I should say they are examples of natural philosophy and natural religion" (Norman, 1967, p. 100). Marks of distinction – wealth, education, even leadership – can set a hobbit apart, make him different. The major political problem for any potential leader, then, is to maintain the trust of those led – to make leadership seem "natural," and to diminish "queerness."

Bilbo is "very rich and very peculiar," largely because of his perpetual youth (Tolkien, 1965, p. 43), both of which make him seem different, queer: "It isn't natural, and trouble will come of it!" (Tolkien, 1965, p. 43). Part of this "trouble" results from social inequities that his wealth and good physical fortune exacerbate. But in addition Bilbo is "queer" to the other inhabitants of the Shire (Tolkien, 1965, p. 77) because he has been changed by his travels – his knowledge of the world – and his possession of the Ring, which has stretched him thin (that is, his awareness of moral issues – his knowledge of good and evil – has been expanded by having carried the Ring for so long). The tug between the desire of the self for the Ring (the "Precious," or for what the self wishes to incorporate into the self) and the hobbit's desire to think of others beyond himself – to protect the Shire and the world by keeping the Ring hidden from Sauron's eye – has made him thin; it is no accident that the natural wearing of the Ring on the finger renders its wearer invisible – when the Ring masters its wearer, it totally erases the *identity* of the wearer, that is, he becomes without a self. Bilbo never connected the "life" of the Ring with the Ring. "He took all the credit for that to himself, and he was very proud of it. Though he was getting restless and uneasy. *Thin and stretched* he said. A sign that the ring was getting control" (Tolkien, 1965, p. 77). Ironically, the Ring appeals to the desires of the self for gold, power, love, as a means of mastering that individual.

The anticipated "trouble" is, however, averted in part by Baggins' generosity. He shares his money with his friends and relatives: "He had many devoted admirers among the hobbits of poor and unimportant families" (Tolkien, 1965, p. 43). Again, generously sharing his fortune allays the fears of difference among the less fortunate hobbits. He is considered "well-spoken," polite, gentle, largely because, as well-off as he is, he treats his servant the Gaffer (Sam Gamgee's father) with great deference for his knowledge – reversing the usual master-servant relationship: "Bilbo was very polite to him, calling him 'Master Hamfast', and consulting him constantly upon the growing of vegetables – in the matter of 'roots', especially potatoes, the Gaffer was recognized as the leading authority by all in the neighbourhood (including himself)" (Tolkien, 1965, pp. 44-5). Bilbo's sensitivity to the lower social class of his servant allows him to balance out their relationship through his genteel deference to the authority that his servant does demonstrate, knowledge of vegetable-growing. Bilbo has also taught the gardener's son Sam to read (Tolkien, 1965, p. 47) – a Middle-earth reflection of the Victorian ideal of educating the poor. The mutual respect of the hobbit "aristocrat" and the gardening servant-authority makes Bilbo politically correct and an astute politician.

Two major social problems engage the political skills of Bilbo. First is the arrival of Frodo, an orphan and his heir, which causes the Sackville-Bagginses (Bilbo's other close heirs) consternation because their expected inheritance will presumably be reduced. Second is the necessary inheritance of Bag End (and its "treasure") by Frodo, predicated upon the disappearance of Bilbo at the advanced age of 111 after a magnificent Birthday Party. Because of the continued enmity of the detested Sackville-Bagginses after the disappearance, Frodo will inherit these same familial problems requiring *his* political skills.

The Birthday Party, in the Shire, represents a symbolic paradigm for the ideal relationship between master and servant, wealthy aristocrat and members of the populace. As a site for potential self-aggrandizement and indulgence – which would not have been tolerated by the inhabitants within if they had been either not invited, or invited, but expected to bring gifts – its signification for the political hobbit Bilbo is to mark the abundance of self-confidence, largesse of the self, by *giving away* gifts to all who attend and by offering the splendour of fireworks, songs, dances, music, games, and fine and abundant food for all. It is, then, the perfect symbolic and political moment for Bilbo to disappear – that is, his largesse signifies the disappearance of *selfishness*, and masks his literal individual disappearance. At this party, no one is not invited, and every guest is given presents, in the hobbit fashion (Tolkien, 1965, p. 50). Indeed, the liberality of Bilbo in inviting everyone to his Birthday Party is, as the Gaffer reminds the suspicious and manipulative Sandyman, another, more positive aspect of Bilbo's "queerness." The party thus also symbolizes Bilbo's long political concern for others – he is a noble man, a true gentleman, *because* he thinks only of others. And hobbits, in general, who have the practice of giving presents to others on their own birthdays, are the least acquisitive of beings. The Sackville-Bagginses – Otho and his wife Lobelia – attend even though they "disliked Bilbo and detested Frodo" (Tolkien, 1965, p. 53), largely because of the magnificence of the invitation.

Politic Bilbo in his speech to the hobbits expresses his fondness for all of them and praises them as "excellent and admirable" (Tolkien, 1965, p. 54). This speech is important, because the occasion also honours his heir-nephew's birthday, which means Frodo will come of age, and therefore Bilbo must make his disappearance. But even generous Bilbo, as a natural aristocrat, has difficulty in ridding himself entirely of the Ring – hobbit that he is, he is still related to the Sackville-Bagginses, and thus shares in their (even for hobbits) excessive greed. Desire is a part of what the Ring represents.

The Ring of course works its power – illustrating the nature of the novel as a work about power – because more than anything it wishes to return to its maker-master and therefore wants to be put on (to make the wearer *naturally* invisible but supernaturally visible to the Eye of Sauron). In relation to the individual, then, possessing it means the individual loses sense of who he is and what he truly wants.

Bilbo initially has difficulty giving up the Ring – he wants to keep it, or the Ring wants him to – and he loses sight of that facility of the Ring, which makes him mistrust others as different, and therefore (as with Sandyman) not with-me, for-me:

> "'Now it comes to it, I don't like parting with it at all, I may say. And I don't really see why I should. Why do you want me to?' he asked, and a curious change came over his voice. It was sharp with suspicion and annoyance. 'You are always badgering me about my ring; but you have never bothered me about the other things that I got on my journey'" (Tolkien, 1965, p. 59).

Bilbo wants to keep the Ring because it is his – he found it: "It is my own. I found it. It came to me" (Tolkien, 1965, p. 59). The specialness of the Ring – and therefore the specialness it confers upon its owner – enhances the self, fills him with the illusion of power. And perhaps that specialness is what has made him "queer" to others. It is the last gift, the one he most has to give away – to Gandalf first, and then to his heir Frodo. As with Frodo on Mount Doom, however, fighting first with himself and then with Gollum, Bilbo resists Gandalf as an adversary, using the same language as Gollum: "It is mine, I tell you. My own. My precious. Yes, my precious" (Tolkien, 1965, p. 59).

To free himself Bilbo has to let it go – which he finds difficult. Gandalf's demand for the Ring (as it lies on the mantel) arouses Bilbo's suspicions and fear that the wizard is a thief. Gandalf wins him over by saying, "I am not trying to rob you, but to help you. I wish you would trust me, as you used" (Tolkien, 1965, p. 60). Bilbo apologizes, "But I felt so *queer* . . . And I don't seem able to make up my mind" (Tolkien, 1965, pp. 60-61, my italics).

What does the queerness represent, if not Bilbo's power in the Shire, which he regrets giving up – his power as "lord"? His specialness as an individual, the reason he is young perpetually, wealthy, generous? It is an enabler. For this reason it is difficult for Bilbo to give up the Ring, and yet death – another way the "disappearance" signifies – is what we all must pass through, to give up ourselves. Renunciation is the final gift – to allow the self to grow and mature, one must learn to be selfless. Thus, the "presents" given to Bilbo's relatives are all "corrective" gifts, intended to change vices in the relatives (a pen and ink bottle to a relative who never answers letters, for example): "The poorer hobbits, and especially those of Bagshot Row, did very well" (Tolkien, 1965, p. 65).

The present Bilbo gives his nephew Frodo is similar in function – the Ring. With this possession comes the necessity for the quest – no "gift" at all, but an unequalled opportunity for maturation. Frodo at the age of fifty (when Gandalf pronounces the need for the quest to return the Ring) "comes of age," becomes himself, an individual – but in the narrative, unlike the normal *bildungsroman* on which this work is modelled, he must *return* his "gift" to its maker, at Mount Doom – such a return, the ultimate hobbit birthday gift – to its "mother" source rather than its "father" owner Sauron. Instead of going on a quest to obtain some knowledge or thing, he goes instead to divest himself (and the world) of this power. In life, maturity means the loss of the child into adulthood. This quest reverses this – the adult Frodo (at fifty) must attempt to recuperate the child – as the Ring returns to its origin.

What does this quest signify? We have established that the political hobbit we see in Bilbo "rules" his Shire through self-abnegation and generosity; but the rule implied by the Ring is entirely different. As the inscription testifies, it allows for differences – Elves, Dwarves, Men – but only because there is One Ring intended to align their differences. "One Ring to rule them all, One Ring to find them, / One Ring to bring them all and in the darkness bind them, / In the Land of Mordor where the Shadows lie" (Tolkien, 1965, p. 81). Returning the Ring to its origin means refusal of power as domination of the One – of sameness – and acceptance of power as respect for difference and diversity. It is Frodo, more different even than his unnatural uncle Bilbo, who is better suited to this quest.

Different from Bilbo because of his mother's dark familial roots in the Old Forest, Frodo may be acceptable to the Shire only because of his uncle Bilbo's wealth and favour. Like his uncle Bilbo Baggins, Frodo is "queer." Most interestingly of all, Frodo Baggins begins his fictive life (as does his creator his maturity) as an orphan, and an orphan from "across the river" (also like his creator). He is a Baggins (from Hobbiton) but his mother was a Brandybuck, from Buckland "where folks are so queer," says Old Noakes (Tolkien, 1965, p. 45). Their "queerness" is caused by living on the wrong side of the Brandywine River, next to the Old Forest, and also because they use boats on the big river, which "isn't natural," says the Gaffer, at least for hobbits (Tolkien, 1965, p. 45).

Indeed, his father, Drogo Baggins, was a "decent respectable hobbit" until he drowned in an uncustomary outing on the water. It was because he and Miss Primula Brandybuck (Bilbo's first cousin on his mother's side) took out a boat on the river one night after a grand dinner at the home of his father-in-law Old Gorbadoc that either his weight sank the boat or she pushed him in (Tolkien, 1965, pp. 45-46).

After Bilbo's disappearance – or rather, his successful self-renunciation – Frodo's first test as Lord of the Manor comes of course from the Sackville-Bagginses (who offer him low prices for other things not given away and who spread rumours that Gandalf and Frodo conspired to get Bilbo's wealth). That he can tolerate difference is symbolically clear to the reader (if not to Lobelia Sackville-Baggins) because he is accompanied by his cousin Merry *Brandybuck* – like Frodo's mother, from Buckland near the Old Forest. But Frodo mistakenly assumes at first that Bag End is his "inheritance" – his for keeping.

As time passes, Frodo perpetuates Bilbo's reputation for "oddity" (Tolkien, 1965, p. 70) by continuing to give Birthday Parties for his uncle. His closest friends are Merry Brandybuck (from the queer Brandybucks) and Peregrin Took and other younger hobbits who had descended from the Old Took and had been fond of Bilbo (Tolkien, 1965, p. 71) (we remember that *Bilbo's* mother was a Took). Like Bilbo, Frodo preserves his youth, and at fifty the Shire inhabitants begin to think him "queer."

This tension between the "normal" and the "queer" hobbit blossoms into the ethical drama of *The Lord of the Rings* in later chapters and books. The question Tolkien addresses is this: how can individuals (and nations) so different from another coexist in harmony? The danger is clear: the Brandybucks will be forever stigmatized by the Shire inhabitants because they choose to live beyond the river in unhobbitlike fashion. And what is to prevent a Dark Hobbit Lord from then using this Shire fear of difference to separate the Brandybucks from the Bagginses? To divide one family branch from another, to insist that all must be the same and live within the Shire? To act and to think and to dress as all the Shire inhabitants?

Difference, for Tolkien, leads to recklessness (the unusual youthful Frodo stealing mushrooms and venturing into others' lands), adventure (Bilbo, Frodo, going off on their respective journeys), and ultimately, wisdom and understanding. Difference can also be social – the difference between a Baggins and a Gamgee, which is artificial and serves no valid purpose if used to separate the two. The validity of manual labour (for example, gardening, domestic service) is ultimately certified by Sam's heroism, as he carries Frodo up Mount Doom, just as Gollum's moral deficiency is validated by his final contribution to civilization and cosmic Good when he disobeys his Master and steals the Ring. The servant – Sam or Gollum – ultimately contributes as much or more to Middle-earth than the Master Frodo. For Tolkien, it is the generosity of the Master, but also his obverse chief weaknesses, pride and avarice, that depend upon and demand the unflagging support and dedicated valour of the humble servant, whose chief strength is his humility and his chief weakness, lack of self-assertion. Tolkien's point is that each serves the other; where the difference of one ends the complementary difference of the other begins. The relationship is circular and yet based on both need and desire, necessity and obligation, the dance of Self and Other, until the music ends.

Despite his initial difference-seeming, Gollum, in a sense, is a type of distant hobbit, an *alter ego* for Bilbo-Frodo (just as the Cain-and-Abel parable of Déagol-Sméagol emphasizes family-murder and cousin-hate). So Gollum, like Frodo, regards the Ring as his Birthday Present because he acquires it on that special day. For Frodo, Gollum is the Shire equivalent of a Brandybuck, and the hobbit reacts to the idea of Gollum as did Sandyman to him – by suspecting Gollum's strangeness, his "queerness." Frodo wishes Gollum had been killed long ago (Tolkien, 1965, p. 92), not understanding the mercy or pity that stayed Bilbo's hand – and therefore (ironically), the same mercy or pity that will save **him** ultimately on the lip of Mount Doom. Even more ironically, it is Gollum's disobedience toward his "Master" Frodo at Mount Doom – only in a greater and providential sense to be construed as mercy, pity – that saves Frodo. And it is not that Gollum's (or Frodo's) *hand* is stayed – ironically, it is his *finger* that is bitten off with the Ring still attached – that saves Frodo – and Middle-earth.

If we look more closely at the role of minor characters in the novel, the tension of difference between self and other, familiar and unlike, becomes more clear-cut. Tolkien's joy in creating characters is to reverse suspicious expectation in his "heroes" and in his readers. For example, it is not clear to Frodo whether Farmer *Maggot* is friend or foe (Tolkien, 1965, p. 132): his name suggests a disgusting creature associated with the eggs of flies and decaying organic matter, death, the earth. And to adult Frodo whose youthful memories recall the anger of Maggot and his dogs over the theft of mushrooms the Farmer looms as an adversary. Maggot, however, provides a different point of view for Frodo when he recalls Frodo as "reckless," one of the "worst young rascals" (Tolkien, 1965, pp. 135-136). The truth is that a protective Maggot has shielded the hobbits from the inquiries of a hooded Black Rider, and also that the recklessness of youthful Frodo represented an harbinger of his present heroics and venture into Mordor. Nevertheless, Farmer Maggot remains a hobbit whose advice to Frodo now reflects the typical suspiciousness of the Shire: "You should never have gone mixing yourself up with Hobbiton folk, Mr.

Frodo. Folk are *queer* up there" (Tolkien, 1965, p. 136, my italics).

Further, Frodo's fellow hobbits Merry and Pippin and his servant Sam have "conspired" (Tolkien's word) behind Frodo's back to accompany him on his journey. This "conspiracy," normally a pejorative term, occurs despite Frodo's protective attempts to keep the purpose of his mission (and the existence of the Ring) a secret from them. His misguided attempts to shield them from danger seriously underestimate their own "queerness" (for Brandybucks and Tooks live beyond the River next to the Old Forest) and thus their own potential for heroism and adventure (to say nothing of their common hobbit desire to serve, epitomized in the Gardener Sam Gamgee, the most modest, socially and personally, of them all). Difference, and the power of words to empower or else end that difference, polarizes the forces of good and evil, social class, and political group in *The Lord of the Rings*.

References

Chance, Jane. 1992. *The Lord of the RIngs: The Mythology of Power*. Boston: Twayne.

Foucault, Michael. 1980. *Power/Knowledge: Selected Interviews and Other Writings*. Trans. Colin Wilson et al. Brighton, Sussex: Harvester Press.

Norman, Philip. 1967. "The Prevalence of Hobbits" in *The New York Times Magazine*, 15 January 1967, pp. 30-31, 97, 100, 102.

Tolkien, J.R.R. 1965. *The Fellowship of the Ring*. New York: Ballantine Books.

The Moral Epiphanies in *The Lord of the Rings*

Joe R. Christopher

Abstract: The topic of this study is not entirely new – other critics have written about the visionary moments in *The Lord of the Rings* that show various types of insights – but the author is interested in a modern context for those which are most psychologically orientated, suggested by Ashton Nichols' *Poetics of Epiphany*, and also in their use in the genre of the prose romance.

Keywords: Aragorn, Bilbo, Tom Bombadil, *Dubliners*, epiphany, Frodo, Galadriel, Gandalf, Gollum, James Joyce, *The Lord of the Rings*, naturalism, Ashton Nichols, *The Poetics of Epiphany*, romance (prose romance), Sam, Saruman, J.R.R. Tolkien, the Transfiguration

As a romance, *The Lord of the Rings* is filled with marvels of various sorts. There are dream visions and a variety of magic. But in this paper I would like to concentrate on one particular type of vision which seems somewhere between magic and psychology, but closer to the latter.

However, let me begin with two examples which are not what I am discussing. They will set up a contrast that will clarify the later illustrations. First, when Tom Bombadil tells Frodo, Pippin, Merry, and Sam the history of the daggers he gives them from the Barrow-wight's treasure,

> [t]he hobbits did not understand his words, but as he spoke they had a vision as it were of a great expanse of years behind them, like a vast shadowy plain over which there strode shapes of Men, tall and grim with bright swords, and last came one with a star on his brow. Then the vision faded, and they were back in the sunlit world.
> (Tolkien, 1991, p. 161, 1:8)[1]

In this case, I am not certain if this "vision as it were" is simply an imaginative response to Tom's history or if it is a magical vision due to some of Tom's power. Perhaps it is due to nothing more than Tolkien's desire to be as imagistic as possible, not to bog his narrative down in straight historical summaries. But, at any rate, this is a type of historical vision, and I am interested in visions revealing the psychology of a person – usually in this romance an almost archetypal aspect of the person.

My second example, also from *The Fellowship of the Ring*, is closer to my psychological concern. This occurs at Rivendell when Bilbo asks Frodo first to show him the Ring and then indicated he would like to hold the Ring:

> . . . Frodo quickly drew back the Ring. To his distress and amazement he found that he was no longer looking at Bilbo; a shadow seemed to have fallen between them, and through it he found himself eyeing a little wrinkled creature with a hungry face and bony groping hands.
> (Tolkien, 1991, p. 248, 2:1)

Obviously this vision does not show Bilbo's true nature. It is psychological revelation, assuredly, but one of Frodo's tie to the Ring. It is close to the borderline of my concerns.

I am going to print three examples of what I am concerned with, cite some more evidence, and then give two more contrasting examples, not from Tolkien, before I reach my conclusion. The first of my basic examples is close to what I have just read. It occurs when Frodo and Galadriel are talking in Lothlórien; he offers her the Ring, and she responds to the temptation by saying, "In place of the Dark Lord you will set up a Queen." And then she demonstrates her point:

> She lifted up her hand and from the ring that she wore there issued a great light that illumined her alone and left all else dark. She stood before Frodo seeming now tall beyond measurement, and beautiful beyond enduring, terrible and worshipful.
> (Tolkien, 1991, p. 385, 2:7)

I said when I began that these revelations of character seemed somewhere between magic and psychology. Obviously Galadriel's is at the magical side of the scale; it is also the only one of my examples which reveals a *potential* character. If she were given the Ring, she would become the evil queen – beautiful but deadly. It is clearly an archetypal role.

Let me move to *The Two Towers* and give an example at the opposite extreme: purely psychological. This is the episode in which, as Gollum leads Frodo and Sam near the gates of Minas Morgul, he returns one time to find them asleep.

---

[1] References to *The Lord of the Rings* include book and chapter after the page number.

Gollum looked at them. A strange expression passed over his lean hungry face . . . [his eyes] went dim and grey, old and tired . . . slowly putting out a trembling hand, very cautiously he touched Frodo's knee – but almost the touch was a caress. For a fleeting moment, could one of the sleepers have seen him, they would have thought that they beheld an old weary hobbit, shrunken by the years that had carried him far beyond his time, beyond friends and kin, and the fields and streams of youth, an old starved pitiable thing.
(Tolkien, 1991, p. 742, 4:8)

Tolkien is so orientated to one person seeing another in these visions that he has to imagine what Gollum would have looked like if Frodo or Sam were awake. But, despite the rhetorical framework, what is depicted is a psychological moment in which Gollum's original hobbit nature resurfaces. It has parallels in, I assume, all of our psyches when we respond to some stimulus as we would have years earlier. A rekindled romance at a high-school reunion is one example. This most psychological of these moments in *The Lord of the Rings* – when Gollum's long-buried, better nature is in the ascendency – is also the least archetypal, as one might expect.

Finally, let me consider what I think is a typical example. This occurs earlier in *The Two Towers*. At this point, in the presence of Gimli and Legolas, Aragorn announces his name and titles to Éomer, produces the Broken Sword that has been reforged, and charges Éomer to choose quickly to aid him or not:

Gimli and Legolas looked at their companion in amazement, for they had not seen him in this mood before. He seemed to have grown in stature while Éomer had shrunk; and in his living face they caught a brief vision of the power and majesty of the kings of stone. For a moment it seemed to the eyes of Legolas that a white flame flickered on the brows of Aragorn like a shining crown.
(Tolkien, 1991, p. 454, 3:2)

The reference to "the kings of stone" is to two stone statues of Aragorn's ancestors seen earlier, on the companions' journey down the river Anduin (Tolkien, 1991, p. 413, 2:9). Both Gimli and Legolas here observe their friend's growth in stature, and it is the elf – usually in Tolkien the elves are of a higher spiritual nature than the other rational beings – it is the elf Legolas who observes the crown-like flame on Aragorn's head. Aragorn's kingly grandeur is being revealed, his archetypal kingly qualities, so to speak.

A reader also notices the word *seemed*. "He *seemed* to have grown . . .", ". . . it *seemed* to the eyes of Legolas that a white flame flickered . . ." This is typical of Tolkien's handling of these moments: in Galadriel's rejection of the Ring, she stands, "*seeming* now tall beyond measurement"; in Gollum's moment of *caritas*, if the sleepers had "seen him, they *would have thought* [him] an old weary hobbit . . ." (stresses added). Whatever the cause of Tolkien's impulse toward these Hawthornean ambiguities, they seem appropriate in a romance published in a naturalistic milieu. They allow a reader to intellectually deny the vision that, nevertheless, affects his or her emotional response to the book.

At this point, I imagine a reader of this paper complaining, "This is it? These are your three examples? Do you expect to reach a conclusion on the basis of such limited evidence? The flaw here is that of the hasty generalization." Let me, therefore, make a list of what I take to be examples of this sort of psychological revelation. The first example is my final one from *The Fellowship of the Ring*:

(1) When Gandalf leaves Frodo after Bilbo's farewell party, "the old wizard looked unusually bent, almost as if he was carrying a great weight" (Tolkien, 1991, p. 54, 1:1). A minor example, obviously, but the "almost as if" suggests the *seeming* of the above instances.

There are three more examples from *The Two Towers*:

(2) When Gandalf returns from Moria, he reveals himself to Gimli, Aragorn, and Legolas when

[h]e . . . leaped to the top of a large rock. There he stood, grown suddenly tall, towering above them. His hood and his grey rags were flung away. His white garments shone.
(Tolkien, 1991, pp. 515-16, 3:5)

There is something of a "resurrection body", in Christian terminology, about Gandalf's appearance here; but the essential point is that his tallness suggests his power, or his greatness in general, and his white garments suggest his goodness.

(3) When King Théoden rejects Saruman's offer of peace, Saruman reacts with anger, leaning

over the rail as if he would smite the King with his staff. To some suddenly it seemed that they saw a snake coiling itself to strike.
(Tolkien, 1991, p. 604, 3:10)

In the western tradition, at least, the snake is an archetypal image of evil.

(4) When Frodo swears Gollum by the Ring to be good,

[f]or a moment it appeared to Sam that his master had grown and Gollum had shrunk: a tall stern shadow, a mighty lord who hid his brightness in grey cloud [the elven cloak], and at his feet a little whining dog.
(Tolkien, 1991, p. 643, 4:1)

It is difficult to say whether this should be described as archetypal or as metaphoric.

And, finally, there are three examples from *The Return of the King*; I pass over Frodo's vision of Sam as an orc, when he discovers Sam is wearing the Ring (Tolkien, 1991, p. 946, 6:1) – it is the same type of vision as his distorted view of Bilbo, discussed earlier. Here, then, are the three:

(5) When Sam looks across the plain of Mordor toward Mount Doom,

Sam's plain hobbit-face grew stern, almost grim, as the will hardened in him, and he felt through all his limbs a thrill, as if he was turning into some creature of stone and steel that neither despair nor weariness nor endless barren miles could subdue.
(Tolkien, 1991, p. 969, 6:3)

Is this visionary at all? It is certainly close to being

simply a psychological description with a semi-simile introduced by "as if". And certainly it is the only one of these instances when a focal character is aware of his own change. But the word *thrill* – "he felt through all his limbs a thrill" – suggests that something is happening to Sam beyond his control.

(6) Perhaps the most elaborate of these visions is that given to Sam after Gollum has attacked Frodo on the way up Mount Doom:

> Then suddenly . . . Sam saw these two rivals with other vision. A crouching shape, scarcely more than the shadow of a living thing . . . ; and before it stood stern . . . a figure robed in white, but at its breast it held a wheel of fire.
> (Tolkien, 1991, p. 979, 6:3)

I have cut that passage some and I omit the speech from the fire, not *per se* from the figure in white. But what I have quoted is archetypal enough, and the phrase "other vision" is basically what these passages are about.

(7) The final passage is parallel to the earlier one about Aragorn's kingship; when he is proclaimed king and is about to enter Minas Tirith, this is his description:

> . . . when Aragorn arose all that beheld him gazed in silence, for it seemed to them that he was revealed to them now for the first time. Tall as the sea-kings of old, he stood above all that were near; ancient of days he seemed and yet in the flower of manhood; and wisdom sat upon his brow, and strength and healing were in his hands, and a light was about him.
> (Tolkien, 1991, p. 1004, 6:5)

This might be taken as a mere description, yet one notices the double use of *seemed*, the emphasis on his tallness, and the final, presumably non-literal clause, "a light was about him".

I offer these seven instances, and the earlier three, as my evidence of a type of revelation in *The Lord of the Rings* that involves the characters; typically they are shown to be moral or immoral; their archetypal aspects are normally revealed.

I said at this point that I wanted to give two more contrasting examples, neither from Tolkien. I do, but they are very different contrasts and will support different points. First, I want to contrast what Tolkien is doing with religious visions. Let me go to one of the basic ones in the western traditions – the Transfiguration in the New Testament. All three of the Synoptic Gospels have versions of this (Mark 9:2-9; Matthew 17:1-8; Luke 9:28-36). I will use a condensation of St. Matthew's:

> . . . Jesus took Peter, James and his brother John, and led them up a high hill by themselves; in their presence he was transfigured, his face shone like the sun, and his clothes turned white as light. There appeared to them Moses and Elijah, who conversed with Jesus . . . a bright cloud overshadowed them, and from the cloud a voice said,
> "This is my Son, the Beloved,
> in him is my delight:
> listen to him."
> When the disciples heard the voice, they fell on their faces in terror . . .
> (Moffatt, 1950, *NT* p. 23)

Jesus' association with light and his white clothes may suggest some of the figures in Tolkien, such as Gandalf the White; but most of the details are unlike Tolkien. The Bible does not use the word *seem*; the incident is asserted to *be*, not to *seem*. The usual interpretation of Moses and Elijah is that they are symbolic, standing for the Law and the Prophets, the two parts of the Jewish Scriptures that were canonized in Jesus' day. (The third division of the Jewish canon, the Writings, was not completely accepted until about AD 100.) Implicitly, the vision is claiming that Jesus and his teachings are equal to the Jewish tradition. *This* sort of didacticism, a type of allegorical presentation, is alien to Tolkien. The theophanic speech from the cloud is also alien to Tolkien's emphasis on the revelation of the inner nature of the individual. And, of course, the disciples falling on their faces may be typical of the Middle East, but it is not appropriate for Tolkien's non-theophanies.

My purpose in this contrast of *The Lord of the Rings* and the Bible is not to depreciate either work, of course. After all, Tolkien wrote the former and believed the latter. My only point is that the visionary moments I have pointed to may be archetypal but they are not religious in any ordinary sense.

My second contrast will be with a work, *Dubliners*, by James Joyce. But here I need to explain part of my title. Joyce, as is generally known in literary circles, used the term *epiphany* to mean two things: (1) a "moment of revelation in which an object (often a person) or an experience reveals" its inner essence, its quiddity, its whatness; or, somewhat later in Joyce's development, (2) "a verbal strategy by which numerous details in a poem or story are coalesced into a sudden disclosure of meaning" (Nichols, 1987, p. 10). The second of these is not what concerns me, but only the first. The first suggests the type of revelation I have traced in Tolkien's work in which a person reveals his or her inner essence. Joyce, however, inhabits a naturalistic world, not an archetypal one, so his revelations do not have the same dimensions as Tolkien's.

I suppose I should immediately give an example from Joyce, but let me digress for two paragraphs. What suggested this topic to me was a book of criticism I was reading – Ashton Nichols' *The Poetics of Epiphany: Nineteenth-Century Origins of the Modern Literary Movement*. It was not ideal for my purpose, as it is mainly concerned with the use of the secular epiphany in poetry – from Wordsworth's "spots of time", through Coleridge, Shelley, Browning, Tennyson, Yeats, Wallace Stevens, down to Seamus Heaney; it even gives part of chapters over to Hopkins' and T.S. Eliot's revival of the religious epiphany. It would take this paper far from its topic to discuss these writers, but what I found interesting in the book was the attempt by secular writers to find a basis for meaning. But my phrasing is probably not fair to them: it is better to say that they have momentary experiences which seem fraught with meaning, probably for psychological reasons, and they then recount these moments in their poems.

It does not work the same way for fiction writers, obviously, unless their works are autobiographical. But many modern writers do create epiphanies for their characters. An embittered teacher of commercial fiction from whom I once took a course claimed there were only two types of stories: one began with the hero having a problem and ended with him happy; the other began with the hero happy and ended with him having a problem. The first was the type of story that sold and that people liked to read; the second was the type that did not sell and that English majors liked to read. As I said, he was embittered. It would be fairer to say that the traditional-story plot is problem, complication, solution. The solution does not have to be happy — although it often is — so long as it develops logically from the problem and complication. The other type of story — of which Joyce is one of the founders — has a plot that goes problem, complication, realization. Joyce's term for that realization is *epiphany*.

Let me give a couple of simple examples from Joyce's book of short stories. First, let me use the end of the short story "Araby". This is one of the first-person narratives in the book. In it, a boy goes to a special type of sale and social event in Dublin, called a bazaar, planning to buy a gift for the older sister of a friend of his, being infatuated with the young woman; but, when he finally gets there, as the bazaar is closing, he cannot decide quickly what to buy, being perhaps also intimidated by the English accents of some of the people. This is the way the story ends:

> . . . I turned away slowly and walked down the middle of the bazaar. I allowed the two pennies to fall against the sixpence in my pocket. I heard a voice call from one end of the gallery that the light was out. The upper part of the hall was now completely dark.
>
> Gazing up into the darkness I saw myself as a creature driven and derided by vanity; and my eyes burned with anguish and anger.

I assume this is a naturalistic story; the voice calling that the light is out is someone reporting a fact to someone else. But the light of the boy's infatuation, so to speak, is also out, and it is the narrator himself that sees the significance of the epiphanic words, sees what they reveal to him about him. Earlier, I referred to Sam's hardening as he looks at the plain of Mordor as the single example in which the focal character at any one point in *The Lord of the Rings* experiences, rather than observes, an epiphany. Here, in the first person, is the same sort of experiencing. But the difference between a heroic romance and a naturalistic short story lies between the tone of the fictions and what the characters learn — Sam gains strength, the boy realizes his folly.

The conclusion of another story will show an example of the other strategy, in which an onlooker realizes the significance of an epiphany — in this case, of course, a naturalistic epiphany. This story, titled "Clay", tells of an elderly woman, Maria, who works in a laundry and who, on an All Hallows' Eve — what Americans would call Hallowe'en — goes to visit friends. Evidently she was a nursemaid years ago to the man of the house, and she is still treated like a relative of sorts. As the story closes, she sings "I Dreamt I Dwelt", repeating the first verse by accident instead of singing the second. Some critics make a point of what is omitted, but I assume the one stanza Joyce prints provides the ironic epiphany. She sings of dreaming she dwells in marble halls, but actually she works in a laundry; she has no "vassals and serfs at [her] side", and so on through the stanza, ending with someone loving her, which is also not true. This is the way the story ends:

> . . . when she had ended her song Joe [her foster son, in some sense] was very much moved. He said that there was no time like the long ago and no music for him like poor old Balfe, whatever other people might say; and his eyes filled up so much with tears that he could not find what he was looking for and in the end he had to ask his wife to tell him where the corkscrew was.

There are two ways to read this conclusion, I believe. One way is to assume that Joe has missed the irony — what I have called the ironic epiphany, which reveals the complete barrenness of Maria's life — and he does indeed get sentimental over the old music. This is to treat Joe as part of the irony and the reader is the only perceptor. The other way of reading this is to see him as reacting to the ironic revelation, making excuses in terms of music to cover up his tears. Since this is a realistic fiction, and the conclusion is handled objectively, there is no way to decide between these readings, although I prefer the latter.

However, my basic point is how different this is from anything Tolkien is doing. Can both Joyce and Tolkien be said to be using the epiphanic technique? I believe so. I said that *The Lord of the Rings* is a romance, and *Dubliners*, to slightly simplify, is naturalistic fiction. Naturalism has nothing to show beyond this world, unless it is a dream or a daydream. The epiphany has to be without a visionary aspect. In the simple instances I have used, the naturalistic revelations are of one's own folly and of one's limited life; the means are a shout about the light being out and a sentimental song.

Tolkien's examples I have already given, but I should make it clear that I do not suggest that he was consciously influenced by the other writers of the nineteenth and twentieth centuries. Indeed, if he had known he was doing anything similar to James Joyce, he probably would have cut every epiphany in *The Lord of the Rings*. But sometimes ideas or artistic techniques simply seem to be "in the air", to be part of the temporal milieu.

Tolkien's problem was an artistic one, of course. How could he show moral qualities — particularly potential ones or developing ones — in his fiction? He could, of course, directly comment to his reader, and he does some of that, perhaps influenced by the *Beowulf*-poet who moralizes directly in his poem. Tolkien would have known, if he ever considered Hemingway's attempt to remove all moral reflections from the authorial voice, that the weight of tradition was against Hemingway.

But Tolkien was not satisfied with telling his reader; he wanted, in Joseph Conrad's term, to make his reader *see*. This was shown in the first quotation I used, in the historic vision that accompanied Tom Bombadil's account. For this purpose, Tolkien developed the visionary epiphany – the use of "other vision", as he calls it – which reveals the moral and archetypal qualities of characters.

So far as I am aware, it is not a technique used extensively, nor in most instances at all, by other writers of romances. But it seems a technique very appropriate for a romance. Forgive me for introducing another critical name, in this case that of a pure critic, not an involved writer; but this point *is* one of critical significance. Northrop Frye has created a chart of narrative types running from myth at the top; through romance next; down to high mimesis, such as in tragedies, and low mimesis, such as in comedies; to a form on the bottom which he called irony but logically should have been called naturalism and some related forms that most often deal with people below average in one way or another (Frye, 1957, pp. 33-34). I use Frye simply as typical of the common feeling that the romance is close to myth. As such, the vision of the archetypal characteristic of the individual – the mythic characteristics, so to speak – is *not* surprising; and the use of a vision is as appropriate for the romance as it would be out of place in a low mimetic and in a naturalistic work. The genres call for very different types of epiphanies.

In his use of the epiphanic moment, then, I find Tolkien to be doing something that is typical of modern literature; but he is doing it in an artistically appropriate way for his genre and in a way to make as concrete as possible the morality of his characters. This is only one aspect of his artistry out of many, but it is one which reveals Tolkien both as an unconsciously modern author and, more importantly, as a consciously moral author, as most great authors have been.

References

Frye, Northrop. 1957. *Anatomy of Criticism: Four Essays*. Princeton, NJ: Princeton University Press.

Joyce, James. 1914. *Dubliners*. London: Grant Richards.

Moffatt, James (trans.). 1950. *A New Translation of* The Bible *Containing the Old and New Testaments*. New York: Harper and Brothers. [The Old and New Testaments have separate pagination in this edition.]

Nichols, Ashton. 1987. *The Poetics of Epiphany: Nineteenth-Century Origins of the Modern Literary Movement*. Tuscaloosa: The University of Alabama Press.

Tolkien, J.R.R. 1991. *The Lord of the Rings*, illus. Alan Lee. Boston: Houghton Mifflin. [Citations by book and chapter should allow the use of any edition.]

"Less Noise and More Green": Tolkien's Ideology for England[1]

Patrick Curry

Abstract: This essay explores Tolkien's work (especially *The Lord of the Rings*) in terms of what I identify as his three central concerns, described here as English culture, nature and ethics. I also defend the work against its detractors, especially cultural materialists. I am more concerned with the reception of the work (e.g. its contemporary meanings) than its production.

Keywords: culture, Englishness, ethics, nature, social and political criticism

I

What I am trying to do here is take a serious social and political look at *The Hobbit* and *The Lord of the Rings* that respects both the works as books, as literary artefacts, AND my own subjective experience of them. My title takes its cue from Tolkien's well-known desire "to restore to the English an epic tradition and present them with a mythology of their own". By ideology, all I mean is that his particular view of Englishness, is not, of course, socially neutral, but selective in a way that emphasises some aspects at the expense of others. That's all — nothing more or less.

Sociological literary criticism has a reputation, often richly deserved, of practising a gross or subtle reductionism that sometimes leaves its subject little more than a collection of elements representing something else. In that, of course, it is hardly alone; for example, there are Freudian, feminist, structuralist, Jungian, anthroposophical, and Marxist interpretations of fairy tales, of which the same could said with varying amounts of justice. (Jack Zipes (1979), with a degree of seriousness that is hard to determine, has pointed out of *The Hobbit* that it clearly involves an alliance between the lower-middle class (Bilbo) and working-class miners and skilled workers (the dwarves) in order to overcome a parasitic capitalist exploiter who "lives off the hard work of small people and accumulates wealth without being able to appreciate its value" (the dragon). This is fun, but it says as much about Marxism as a fairy tale as it does about the capaciousness of *The Hobbit*.)

I have tried hard to avoid such a practice, my chief motive being an abiding love of Tolkien's work and respect for its integrity. But I have also benefited from some excellent warnings if ever tempted. There is his own, of course: "he that breaks a thing to find out what it is has left the path of wisdom". But also Professor Shippey's: "Adventure in Middle-earth embodies a modern meaning, but does not exist to propagate it" (1982).

Thus armed, I settled down to a little non-reductionist *ideologiekritik* of *The Hobbit* and *The Lord of the Rings*. However I quickly encountered trolls, if not Black Riders, because although the role of hobbits – who chiefly embody Tolkien's ideological Englishness – is crucial, it became apparent that they are so to speak nested within a larger and more weighty matter, just as the Shire is within Middle-earth: namely nature, the natural world. Following this up, then, I found myself at the edge of this second circle too, but still within my remit. In Tolkien's terms, I had been brought up short by the Sea. This third sphere proved to be the most encompassing of all: the spiritual, or, in this context, what is essentially the same, ethical. What has made trying to analyse Tolkien's project daunting is the way its heart lies in the overlap of these three concerns: the cultural (Englishness), the natural (nature) and the spiritual (ethics). It seems to me that any meaning found in or derived from his work that does not inseparably embody all three concerns is inessential. But each one exerts enormous centrifugal force as a subject in its own right. Thus, despite my best efforts to exert some editorial control, this tale too has grown in the telling.

I should emphasise that my chief critical interest is the meaning, especially the wider social significance, of the work, not the man. Of course there is a relationship between the two. But it is complex, and the one simply cannot be deduced from the other. And as Tolkien himself reminded us, "when we have done all that research . . . can do . . . there remains a point too often forgotten: that is the effect produced *now* by these old things in the stories as they are." Besides, it is both boring and pointless to spill ink establishing whether Tolkien was "reactionary" or "progressive". Neither can the work itself be pigeonholed in such a way – as if its meaning was forever fixed, and not whatever it presents itself as, in ways that cannot be

---

[1] This paper has been culled from a book which Floris Books will publish in 1996.

predetermined. I am going to argue that the *The Lord of the Rings* has a life of its own in ways beyond what Tolkien himself could have anticipated, and which are a part of the explanation of its enduring appeal.

Let us look at that appeal for a moment. English-language sales for *The Hobbit* total 29 million (ahead of my other single work of fiction this century); for *The Lord of the Rings*, 18.5 million. And that only covers up till 1989. Tolkien's global popularity is well-known, from the "Middle-earth Libre" graffiti in Quebec to the adoption of his work (I am told) by an Italian anarchist group. It is also attested to by the 30-odd translations, an early and possibly fabulous example being that into Vietnamese in 1969. (A South Vietnamese army division immediately, and rather perceptively, adopted the Eye of Sauron as their emblem.) There is even an area of submarine features off the South-West coast of Ireland named after Tolkien characters (hence "Gollum's Channel", and so on). So no one could argue that all this was a flash-in-the-pan phenomenon, riding on the heels of the 60s counter-culture; sales in the 90s remain brisk.

Yet this extraordinary popular success has been accompanied by relentless critical hostility. Beginning with Philip Toynbee's sneers and Edmund Wilson's rant in the 1950s, it has never flagged. The general view was perhaps best summed up by the poet John Heath-Stubbs: "A combination of Wagner and Winnie-the-Pooh".

Given that criticism from the left tends to be more social and political, that's what I intend to concentrate on here. Amid all the critical rubbish, there are a few serious points. First, however, let's get the rest of it out of the way.

Catherine R. Stimpson brought up several common refrains in 1969. "An incorrigible nationalist," she wrote, Tolkien "celebrates the English bourgeois pastoral idyll. Its characters, tranquil and well fed, live best in placid, philistine, provincial rural cosiness" (or would prefer to). His language reveals "class snobbery" (both trollism and orcism, in fact). His characters are cleanly divided into "good and evil, nice and nasty" (notwithstanding the fact, which she notes, that almost all the races are a collection of good, bad and indifferent individuals; and completely overlooking the inner struggles of Gollum, Boromir, Denethor and Frodo himself. This is *not* a serious point).

Finally, "Behind the moral structure is a regressive emotional pattern. For Tolkien is irritatingly, blandly, traditionally masculine . . . He makes his women characters, no matter what their rank, the most hackneyed of stereotypes. They are either beautiful and distant, simply distant, or simply simple". Here it is tempting to reply, guilty as charged. Even with the characters of Galadriel, Éowyn and Shelob – without whom *The Lord of the Rings* would be seriously impoverished, and who are more complex than Stimpson allows – Tolkien's paternalism if not patriarchy is unmissable. Yet it is too easy to ask a work to be something it isn't, or its author to do something he or she didn't set out to do. Indeed, maybe we should be grateful that Tolkien *didn't* attempt a more feminist Middle-earth. Consider the ghastly results, for example, when two otherwise superb writers, John Fowles and Dennis Potter, tried to place female characters centre-stage in *The Mantissa* and *Blackeyes* respectively. Just imagine what Tolkien might have wrought!

Some of these points were recently recycled in the *New Statesman and Society* (Kaveney, 1992): Tolkien's emphasis on social hierarchies (no mention however of "the hour of the Shire-folk, when they arise from their quiet fields to shake the towers and counsels of the great"); the fact that "praise of Tolkien has often been the cover for a broadside attack on modernism and even on realism" (is nothing sacred?); and a putative link between Tolkien's cult following and "the authoritarian direction taken by much American commercial fantasy and science fiction". (He really should have anticipated that, back in 1937.) The author concludes that Tolkien is "worth intelligent reading, but not passionate attention". Clearly, this town isn't big enough for both of us.

It is true that Tolkien's evil creatures are frequently "swart, slant-eyed", foul-mouthed and apparently poorly educated, and tend to come from the south ("the cruel Haradrim") and east ("the wild Easterlings") – both threatening directions in Tolkien's "moral cartography". It is also true that black is a terrible colour, especially when contrasted with white. It must be admitted that Tolkien is drawing on centuries of such moral valuation (not unrelated to historical experience) attached to his chosen setting, in order to convey something immediately recognisable in the context of his story, without attempting to mitigate the possibility of a racist interpretation. (I say "possibility"; it is grossly insulting to his readers to assume they automatically transfer their feelings about orcs to all the swart or slant-eyed people they encounter in the street.) Thus as Clyde Kilby (1977) recounts, when Tolkien was once asked what lay east and south of the Middle-earth of *The Lord of the Rings*, he replied:

> "Rhûn is the Elvish word for east. Asia, China, Japan, and all the things which people in the West regard as far away. And south of Harad is Africa, the hot countries." Then Mr. Resnick asked, "That makes Middle-earth Europe, doesn't it?" To which Tolkien replied, "Yes, of course – Northwestern Europe . . . where my imagination comes from."

(In which case, as Tolkien also admitted, Mordor "would be roughly in the Balkans.")

However, he reacted sharply to reading a description of Middle-earth as *Nordic*:

> Not *Nordic*, please! A word I personally dislike; it is associated, though of French origin, with racialist theories . . . The North-west of Europe, where I (and most of my ancestors) have lived, has my affection, as a man's home should; but it is not "sacred", nor does it exhaust my affections.

It is also, I believe, more Tolkien's material than his message. Consider that the races in Middle-earth are most striking in their variety and autonomy. Without suggesting that a clear-cut choice exists, is this an instance of ethnocentrism, or multiculturalism? Or even, given that most of the races are closely tied to a particular geography and ecology, and manage to live there without exploiting it to the point of destruction – bioregionalism? Again, one of the subplots of *The Lord of the Rings* concerns an enduring friendship between members of races traditionally estranged (Gimli and Legolas); and the most important wedding in the book, between Aragorn and Arwen, is an interracial marriage. As usual, the picture is a great deal more complex than the critics perceive.

It is also true that Tolkien was deeply hostile to "modernity". I am as grateful as anyone for the benefits of modernity, but it is becoming very hard to celebrate their undiluted beneficence; to that extent, Tolkien's diagnosis, at least, is starting to look increasingly prescient. In any case, there is certainly no reason whatsoever to automatically associate modernity with progressive politics.

So let's turn now to some more serious charges, beginning with Tolkien's central and most unique characters: the hobbits.

II

With this audience, of all people, I don't need to catalogue the traits of hobbits: their fondness of food and drink, closeness to the land, hostility to machines, anti-intellectualism and inarticulateness. Though I will remind you of what one famous hobbit almost replied, when asked, "What is finer than flying?" Bilbo only allowed his native tact, not to mention caution, to overrule suggesting, "A warm bath and late breakfast on the lawn afterwards". "Nonetheless," their chronicler notes, "ease and peace had left this people still curiously tough". This being, in Shippey's words, "the notorious Anglo-hobbitic inability to know when they're beaten".

As Tolkien notes, Bilbo and Frodo were exceptional in many ways: their wealth, bachelorhood, and aestheticism. Sam, as a recently and exceptionally lettered gardener, was far more typical, or as Tolkien put it, "the genuine hobbit". But your behaviour had to be extreme to land you in any real trouble; for "The Shire had hardly any 'government'". The only real officials were the Mayor of Michel Delving, Postmaster and First Shirriff, plus various hereditary heads of clans.

Now it doesn't take any great perceptiveness to see in "these charming, absurd, helpless" (and not-so helpless) hobbits a self-portrait of the English, something which Tolkien even admitted, in an unguarded moment, to Clyde Kilby. Take the view in 1940 by George Orwell, and still instantly recognizable (albeit sadly altered in some respects), of a conservative people neither artistically nor intellectually inclined, though with "a certain power of acting without thought"; taciturn, preferring tacit understandings to explication; endowed with a love of flowers and animals, valuing privateness and the liberty of the individual, and respecting legality; not puritanical and without definite religious belief, but strangely gentle (and here we feel our losses in the 1980s), with a hatred of war and militarism that coexists with a strong unconscious patriotism. Orwell sums up English society as "a strange mixture of reality and illusion, democracy and privilege, humbug and decency".

With apologies to Tolkien, *plus ça change*. True, these attributes are inextricably mingled with ones (some) English have *wanted* to find in the mirror; none are eternal and immutable. Because they constitute a national fantasy, however, it does not follow that they have no social reality. Also, if I may be so bold, Tolkien's portrait is not altogether a flattering one; it includes greed, small-mindedness and philistinism.

But the kind of Englishness the hobbits embody is more particular than that. Although identifiably modern in many respects – and as several commentators have noticed, it is crucial that Bilbo and Frodo *be* modern, in order to mediate between ourselves and the ancient and therefore somewhat foreign world they inhabit – they also represent, as David Harvey (1985, p.114) puts it, "the archetypal pre-Industrial Revolution English yeomen", but even more specifically pre-the Conquest of 1066, before the hated Norman Yoke imposed centralized autocratic government, a foreign language and an alien cultural tradition, and the rootless cosmopolitanism of an elite Latin education – which, as Shippey has pointed out, culminated in among other things the creation of a "distinctive literary caste": the same caste that harried Tolkien throughout his life and after.

But whether Anglo-Saxon, feudal or modern, the hobbits' bucolic and organic "naturalness" clearly falls within the long tradition in English letters of nostalgic pastoralism or ruralism, celebrating a time "long ago in the quiet of the world, when there was less noise and more green". Listen to some of these titles and remarks, from the nineteenth and early twentieth century: Tennyson's *English Idylls* – William Morris's "fair green garden of Northern Europe" – the Poet Laureate Alfred Austin's *Haunts of Ancient Peace* (1902) (that could easily be a song by Van Morrison today: no coincidence) – Ford Madox Ford's *The Heart of the Country* – Henry Newbolt's *The Old Country* – Kipling's "Our England is a garden" – Maurice Hewlett's *Song of the Plough* – and there are many more, but you get the idea. In other words, there has long been a deep cultural gulf between England's (southern) "green and pleasant land" and her (northern) "dark satanic mills"; or as Martin Weiner (1985) puts it with an aptness all the better for my case because it is (presumably) unintentional, "The power of the machine was invading and blighting the Shire".

Of course the irony here is that by 1851 England was already the world's first urban nation, with over half the population living in towns. This has led many critics to see ruralism as *simply* a fantasy (in the unkind sense) – "a psychic balance wheel", in Weiner's words. But nothing, I'm afraid, is that simple.

The fount for social criticism of this sort is *The Country and the City*, by Raymond Williams (1985). It is an important and influential book, but one which I dislike. Let's try to put it to work in understanding Tolkien. Williams says that nostalgic "celebrations of a feudal or aristocratic order" embody values that "spring to the defence of certain kinds of order, certain social hierarchies and moral stabilities", which he implies act in defence of social injustices, and even blood-&-soil fascism. Perhaps this is the place, therefore, to consider the politics (in the narrow sense) of Middle-earth.

Tolkien described his own political opinions as leaning to "Anarchy (philosophically understood, meaning abolition of control, not whiskered men with bombs) – or to 'unconstitutional' Monarchy." "I am not a 'socialist' in any sense", he wrote, "because the 'planners', when they acquire power, become so bad . . . the spirit of 'Isengard', if not of Mordor, is of course always cropping up. The present design of destroying Oxford in order to accommodate motor-cars is a case. But our chief adversary is a member of a 'Tory' Government." (The proposal referred to was a so-called relief road through Christ Church meadow – a very contemporary ring to that.)

Anarchism or libertarianism has a left/right instability that has always irritated both those wings, who like to have these matters cut-and-dried. No socialist, nor even democrat then, but neither in Tolkien is there a whiff of "blood and soil" fascism. And that is what we find in Middle-earth. One might say "subsidiarity rules OK" – that is, decisions seem indeed to be taken at the lowest possible level, closest to those who are most affected by them. Indeed, the Shire functions by a sort of municipal democracy. None of this, of course, applies to Mordor – an utterly authoritarian regime with a slave-based economy featuring intensive industrialism and agribusiness.

Raymond Williams continues:
> In Britain, there is a precarious but persistent rural-intellectual radicalism: genuinely and actively hostile to industrialism and capitalism; opposed to commercialism and the exploitation of the environment; attached to country ways and feelings, the literature and the lore.

This sounds generous, but here comes the big Reservation:
> in every kind of radicalism the moment comes when any critique must choose its bearings, between past and future . . .

Furthermore, "We must begin not in the idealisations of one order or another, but in the actual history to which they are only partial and misleading responses". Thus myth and revolution are *alternative*, not complementary responses to crisis.

This is nonsense: positivist about "history", essentialist in holding the political character of traditions to be inherent and fixed, and intellectualist in thinking that ideological and factual criticism is a sufficient basis for a political programme. Most unforgivably, it ignores the massive lesson that the left, by now, should have learned from Gramsci (or, failing him, Mrs. Thatcher): that people do not live by factual and historical bread alone, but also by ideas, values and visions of alternatives. The past feeds the future, as *myth* does revolution: something that Orwell understood better than many who have patronized him since.

What really matters now about the image of pre-Conquest England "as a free and equal rural community" benefiting from "a primitive freedom" and "the perpetual impulse of 'Nature'" (in Williams's excellent description) is not the extent to which things were actually otherwise – which is itself an interpretation rather than a fact, and may become mobilised as a resource in one political direction or another – but rather the *use* of such an image in the present. Within his own remit, Tolkien himself – old reactionary though he undoubtedly was, in the true meaning of the word – saw this very clearly. Indeed, his anti-positivism is bizarrely in tune with the best and most refreshing aspects of postmodern philosophy. "History often resembles 'Myth'", he wrote, "because they are both ultimately of the same stuff".

Of course, it is true that the defence of the "vanishing countryside" can become deeply confused with the defence of the old rural order. But it certainly *need* not. As Weiner notes, there have been "variants of ruralism to suit all political inclinations . . . Conservatives and Imperialists, anti-Imperialists, Liberals and Radicals." The meaning of such a myth is not written on stone. Today it is standing up to the bulldozers in Twyford Down and Oxleas Wood, while simultaneously encouraging defenders of the corrupt and undemocratic "Mother of Parliaments" that has sent them in; in the struggle between landowners and ramblers, it is claimed on both sides.

One contemporary writer, Fraser Harrison, goes straight to the heart of the matter:
> While it is easy to scoff at the whimsicality and commercialism of rural nostalgia, it is also vital to acknowledge that this reaching-out to the countryside is an expression, however distorted, of a healthy desire to find some sense of meaning and relief in a world that seems increasingly bent on mindless annihilation.

Accordingly, says Harrison, "it becomes meaningful to talk of 'radical nostalgia'". (The word itself means precisely *homesickness*.) It does express a truth of its own, which reflects an authentic and deeply felt emotion. The pastoral fantasy nostalgia invented is after all an image of a world in which men and women feel at home with themselves, with each other and with nature, a world in which harmony reigns. It is an ideal.

Tolkien himself listed as a primary function of fantasy *Recovery*, which he defined as the "regaining of a clear view". In a nice twist, his wonderful discussion of *escapism* in "On Fairy-Stories" even turns the tables on his "progressive" critics, who are confusing, he writes, and
> not always by sincere error, the Escape of the Prisoner with the Flight of the Deserter. Just so a Party-spokesman might have labelled departure from the misery of the Führer's or any other Reich and even criticism of it as treachery . . .
>
> For a trifling instance: not to mention electric street-lamps of mass-produced pattern in your tale is Escape (in that sense) . . . out comes the big stick: "Electric lamps have come to stay," they say . . . "The march of Science, its tempo quickened by the needs of war, goes inexorably on . . . making some things obsolete, and foreshadowing new developments in the utilization of electricity": an advertisement. This says the same thing only more menacingly.

Tolkien has put his finger here on the deep complicity of *social realists*, and socialist thought in general, with the scientific/technological/managerial state and its ideology which it professes to be contesting. And given the nature of this monster, is it any surprise that by way of metaphoric contrast, Tolkien and so many other people have turned to nature?

III

That point brings me to the borders of the Shire. But we are still in Middle-earth. As Gildor said to Frodo, "it is not your own Shire. Others dwelt here before hobbits were; and others will dwell here again when hobbits are no more. The wide world is all about you: you can fence yourselves in, but you cannot for ever fence it out." And as Tolkien himself commented, "hobbits are not a Utopian vision, or recommended as an ideal in their own or any age. They, as all peoples and their situations, are an historical accident – as the Elves point out to Frodo – and an impermanent one in the long view."

What is most striking about this larger world, that notwithstanding the ignorance of the hobbits about its reality and importance, encloses and sustains the Shire in space, as well as precedes and follows it in time? Certainly the variety, richness and consistency of its sense of place is extraordinary. The fact is that Middle-earth is more real to me (and I am certainly not alone in this) than many "real" places; and if I should suddenly find myself there (which would of course astound me – but not utterly) I would have a better idea of how to find my way about than if I had been dropped in, say, central Asia or South America.

But what is most striking about Tolkien's world – and this has been noticed by many readers, and even some literary critics – is its profound feeling for the natural world: geography and geology, ecologies, flora and fauna, the seasons, weather, the night-sky, and the Moon in all its phases. The experience of these phenomena as comprising a living and meaningful cosmos saturates his entire story. Even the various races of people are rooted to, and unimaginable (both to themselves and us) without, their natural contexts. As Sam said of the Elves in Lothlórien, "Whether they've made the land, or the land's made them, it's hard to say . . ."

Tolkien obviously had a particular affection for flora. I counted 64 species of non-cultivated plants specifically mentioned in *The Hobbit* and *The Lord of the Rings* – surely an unusual number for any work of fiction – in addition to his own nine invented (or discovered) kinds. But pride of place, obviously, goes to trees. Every forest in Middle-earth has its own unique personality. And none more memorably than the green city of Caras Galadhon in Lothlórien.

Tolkien does not romanticize nature, however. Angela Carter points out in another connection that the wood in Shakespeare's *A Midsummer Night's Dream* is

> *the* English wood. The English wood is nothing like the dark, necromantic forest in which the Northern European imagination begins and ends, where its dead and the witches live . . . For example an English wood, however marvellous, however metamorphic, cannot, by definition, be trackless . . . But to be lost in the forest is to be lost to *this* world, to be abandoned by the light, to lose yourself utterly, an existential catastrophe . . . Nineteenth-century nostalgia disinfected the wood, cleansing it of the grave, hideous and elemental beings with which the superstition of an earlier age had filled it. Or rather, denaturing those beings until they came to look like those photographs of fairy folk that so enraptured Conan Doyle.

All good stuff, but its interest here lies in how it *doesn't* apply to Middle-earth. In fact, such "denaturing" of Elves was exactly what Tolkien held against Shakespeare. The hobbits may go rambling through an English wood of a day's outing, but as any reader of *The Hobbit* could tell you, wandering off the path in Mirkwood definitely amounts to an "existential catastrophe". Tolkien made no attempt to prettify "the hearts of trees and their thoughts, which were often dark and strange, and filled with a hatred of things that go free upon the earth."

Individual trees figure importantly too: the Party Tree, Old Man Willow, the White Tree in Minas Tirith – to say nothing of the two cosmogonic trees of Telperion and Laurelin. And, of course, hobbits were not Tolkien's only unique creation; he also gave us Ents, and Treebeard.

When asked the cardinal question in any kind of war – in fact, the question that is itself (however discreet) the first act of war (however polite): "Whose side are you on?" – Treebeard replies,

> I am not altogether on anybody's *side*, because nobody is altogether on my *side*, if you understand me: nobody cares for the woods as I care for them, not even Elves nowadays.

It is easy to hear the voice of Tolkien himself here. He freely acknowledged his own "tree-love", writing – perhaps in view of his own "totem tree", a birch in his front yard – to the *Daily Telegraph*, not long before his death, that "In all my works I take the part of trees as against all their enemies".

He even referred to *The Lord of the Rings* as "my own internal Tree". But not the only one. "I have among my 'papers'," he once wrote, "more than one version of a mythical 'tree'". The reference, or application, to his Niggle's surviving painting "Leaf", but a tiny fragment of the Great Tree of his ambition, is obvious.

He was well aware, of course, of the hallowed place of trees in mythology and folk-lore everywhere. But his personal involvement with trees, combined with their mythic resonance, produced an extraordinarily vivid depiction. Tolkien's trees are too vulnerable ever to be *just* symbols.

And there was an historical dimension too. He would have well aware that (as W.G. Hoskins put it), "From rising ground England must have seemed one great forest before the fifteenth century, an almost unbroken sea of tree-tops with a thin blue spiral of smoke rising here and there at long intervals". Middle-earth's own Old Forest was itself already only a survivor of vast forgotten woods . . . And at the opening of the story in *The Lord of the Rings*, even such remnants are on the edge of doom. Fangorn is threatened by Saruman, who "has a mind of metal and wheels, and does not care for growing things". And if that were not enough, "it seems that the wind is setting East, and the withering of all woods may be drawing near". For in what remains of the green garden of Middle-earth, has re-appeared the Ring of Power. "The Ring! What shall we do with the Ring, the least of rings, the trifle that Sauron fancies?" Elrond alone permits himself any irony, even as he too, as do all the good and great, acknowledges his helplessness.

Here we must tread carefully, for Tolkien has warned us repeatedly against an allegorical or topical reading of his story. (I'm sure you all know his words well. He also once wonderfully complained, "To ask if the Orcs 'are' Communists is to me as sensible as asking if Communists are Orcs".) And he is right. He had worked hard to create a literary artefact that precisely *isn't* "allegorical or topical" – and very wisely, as we shall see. Without suggesting that the meaning of the Ring is thereby exhausted, however, I shall avail myself of my right as a reader to perceive "applicability" – a particular application that is, I believe, forcing itself upon us daily.

Consider that the Ring epitomises the strongest economic and political form of power in Middle-earth, which threatens to dominate all others in one vast autocratic realm. There are apparently no limits to its power in the material realm; true, it cannot create beauty or understanding or healing, but it rules over the three Elven Rings that can. And from *their* point of view, its transformative power is entirely destructive. Furthermore, this potential will be realised to the full once the Ring is entirely under the control of Sauron.

Needless to say, if "the Ring is taken, then the Shire will be no refuge." Indeed, in the first book of *The Lord of the Rings*, it becomes apparent that Tom Bombadil alone is unaffected by it. Although not (in my opinion) Tolkien's most felicitous character, Tom Bombadil clearly represents, in Tolkien's own words, "the spirit of the (vanishing) Oxford and Berkshire countryside". But the point about him here is that as Galdor says, "Power to defy our Enemy is not in him, unless such power is in the earth itself. *And yet we see that Sauron can torture and destroy the very hills.*" That fact becomes brutally clear in Frodo and Sam's agonizing journey to Mordor. I will spare you the full description of the desolation before Mordor: "a land defiled, diseased beyond all healing", where, in Frodo's words "Earth, air and water all seem accursed".

Do we not see just this blighted industrial wasteland today in Eastern Europe and Russia? And could we not find its equivalents elsewhere: in poisoned rivers and even whole seas; clear-cut and slashed and burned acres that were once rainforest, richest in life anywhere on the planet; smoking, reeking cities where life, by contrast, is cheap? This process has a name, by the way. The Greek *oikos*, which gives us *eco*, means house or abode; the Latin *caedere*, to kill. Hence, *ecocide*. (And the combination of Greek and Latin only confirms that no good can come of it.)

Professor Shippey (1982) has observed of the Ring that "it is a dull mind which does not reflect, 'Power corrupts, and absolute power corrupts absolutely'." And he shrewdly reminds us that the Ring is addictive in a very modern way. But this interpretation can be further tightened up with no loss of meaning, indeed with some gain. It needs no allegorical special pleading or stretch of the imagination to see that our Ring is that malevolent contemporary amalgam of three things: the power of the nation-state – capitalism in the form of transnational economic muscle – and scientism, or the monopoly of knowledge by modern technological science. Like Tolkien's Ring, there are apparently no limits to its potential mastery of nature (certainly not those of Mercy); and once it is on the finger of its collective principal servants – that is, completely removed from any democratic accountability – there will be no way to control it at all. (Those servants have no wish to control it; rather, to feed it.)

There is precious little control as things are, of course. Sporadic public protest and non-governmental organisations worry away at its edges and fight "the long defeat", but always under the shadow of "that vast fortress, armoury, prison, furnace of great power, Barad-dur . . . secure in its pride and its immeasurable strength". (And not the least because, in a twist even Sauron never thought of, almost everybody – even those who will suffer the most by its adoption, even those who are already living in ways that constitute the solution to its terrible problems – seems so seduced by the monster's hand-maidens in advertising and the media that they can hardly wait to sign up. Addictive indeed.)

Tolkien has been accused of a simple-minded moral Manicheism, simply pitting good against evil. This charge is bizarrely wide of the mark. One of the glories of Middle-earth is its messy pluralism; the alliance against Mordor is only just cobbled together (thanks mainly to Gandalf) among people with drastically different agenda. *The Lord of the Rings* celebrates difference and defends neutrality. These are precisely the things that are jeopardised by Sauron, who seeks to turn all Middle-earth into one vast and homogenous entity, under his all-seeing Eye that might remind us not only of " single vision", in Blake's words, but Foucault's alarm-call about the insidious growth of institutionalised knowledge-as-power: "Where religions once demanded the sacrifice of bodies, knowledge now calls for experimentation on ourselves, calls us to the sacrifice of the subject of knowledge". (And let us recall that Saruman's thirst for knowledge at all costs was precisely what baited Sauron's trap in which he was caught.)

The social and human brutalization this entails absolutely cannot be separated from the ecological. Sauron's own strategy recognises this fact: be sure to destroy your victims' natural habitat, and with it their way of life, before remaking it and them in your own terrible image. Such deprivation is of course proceeding apace. At home, it's true, our rivers haven't yet started catching fire, like the pitiable Cuyahoga in Cleveland; but "They're always a-hammering and a-letting out a smoke and a stench, and there isn't no peace even at night in Hobbiton. And they pour out filth a purpose; they've fouled all the lower Water, and it's getting down into Brandywine." When, that is, rivers and streams aren't disappearing altogether, due to overabstraction (an apt word for it!) by the water companies newly privatised and protected by the government.

Given that trees were Tolkien's special concern, however, I

will merely note that whereas forests once covered sixty percent of the earth's land surface, they now cover less than six – and in England, roughly *half* of the already decimated ancient woodlands still present in 1945 have since been destroyed. But for anyone who knows hobbits reasonably well, I think I can bring it still closer to home. There was an obscure report last year, tucked away in one of the Sunday broadsheets, entitled "Wild fungi face extinction as pollution threat increases". It seems that wild mushrooms are dying out across Europe; in Holland 91 species have disappeared and another 182 are on the verge of extinction; in Germany the number of chanterelles taken annually has dropped from several thousand pounds to a few hundred, while in Britain the once common cep can now only be found in remote parts; ditto the wood blewits. The cause? Increased levels of nitrogen and sulphur in the air, and heavy metals leaching into the soil. One ecologist said "mass extinctions" were now imminent, and that the consequences for trees, vital symbiotes for fungi, were unknown, but he feared the worst.

Given that the New World Order can apparently dispense with the material attributes of nature, what hope for moral or aesthetic arguments? As Richard Mabey writes (1984, pp. ix-x), these "are now seen as, at their best, sentimental and impractical, and at their worst – it is a favourite phrase – 'purely subjective preferences'. Somewhere along the line many deep and widely shared human feelings have become regarded as a devalued currency". Or as Fraser Harrison powerfully puts it (1984, pp. 170-1),

> throughout these years, nature has nevertheless prevailed as the richest source of metaphor concerning the human condition. It is in this sense that I believe we can claim to have our own indispensable *cultural* need of conservation . . . Apart from all other consequences, the loss of each species or habitat from the countryside amounts to a blow struck at our own identity.

Yet such a position continues to be the target of critical cynicism. Keith Thomas (1983), for example, has written that "the cult of the countryside" beginning in the eighteenth century was "in many ways a mystification and an evasion of reality . . . The irony was that the educated tastes of the aesthetes had themselves been paid for by the developments which they affected to deplore". And the historian Ludmilla Jordanova goes farther (1987). Western capitalist society, she argues, sentimentalises animals and plants in order to systematically destroy them without facing the fact. "'Man' never left centre stage; nature has never been, and will never be, recognised as autonomous".

A gloomy outlook indeed! But it should be possible, without being branded a traitor, to reply, "It ain't necessarily so". That is, cultural conservationists are *not* necessarily cultural conservatives (in the pejorative sense). In fact, not even cultural conservatives are. Tolkien's position, for example, has acquired a new and distinctly radical meaning – or at the very least, potential meaning – as the crisis which partly motivated its writing has deepened and widened.

So a little humility seems in order. Can one really comfortably speak for *reality*, and dismiss all outrage at the desecration of nature by those of middle-class provenance as necessarily *affectation*? (I myself cannot deny such origins; nor that I never feel so sane and reverential as when I am in the company of broad-leaved trees, the taller and older the better. But I would utterly deny anyone else's right or ability to infallibly disqualify my experience in such a way.) And in any case, wasn't the overall social *reality* one of all-too human inconsistency, paradox and confusion, as well as (rather than simply) unadulterated hypocrisy? I would also question (except of course as a bold rhetorical move) the use of the word *never*. If "never has been" is already debatable, how much more so is "never will be"!

Ironically, the permanent human possession of centre stage is increasingly coming under question. In the struggle over the fate of irreplaceable primary old-growth forests in North America, for example, the contestants are increasingly polarised between "humanists" (in this case the logging industry and its supporters) and "deep ecologists" (often under the aegis of the organisation Earth First!). For the former, as Robert Pogue Harrison so elegantly writes (1992) – rather belying the messiness of the fight: two activists for Earth First! have already been blown up by a car bomb, apparently planted by a Christian fundamentalist pro-logger –

> there can be no question of the forest as a consecrated place; as a place of strange or enchanting or monstrous epiphanies; as a natural sanctuary. There can be only the claims of human mastery and possession of nature – the reduction of forests to utility . . .

John Fowles has put it more bluntly:

> We shall never fully understand nature (or ourselves), and certainly never respect it, until we dissociate the wild from the notion of usability – however innocent or harmless the use.

(And even more certainly, I would add, never revere it.) Nor is Tolkien wanting here, for that is just what Frodo experienced in Lórien: "He felt a delight in wood and the touch of it, neither as forester nor as carpenter; it was the delight of the living tree itself". Or as Gimli rhetorically asked Legolas, "Do you cut down groves of blossoming trees in the spring-time for fire-wood?" Sadly, we do.

Such an insight or plea is a hard one to make, in the face of more obvious, powerful and immediate considerations. One is easily accused of "indulging in fatuous romanticism". But the survival of anything worth the name "nature" – and therefore of whatever it means to be human in relation to nature – looks increasingly likely to depend on the success of just such a case. With the entry of this dimension, however, we are at the very edge of Middle-earth. To be precise, we are still in Tolkien's world, but we have been brought up short by the Sea.

IV

This shore marks the literal and symbolic limit of both the natural world – itself enfolding the Shire, of course – and the domination, actual or potential, of the Ring. Thus, as Legolas recalled when he first heard the gulls at Pelargir, "The Sea! . . . Alas! for the gulls. No peace shall I have again under beech or under elm". Or as Frodo replies, when Sam comments of Rivendell that "There's something of everything here", "Yes, something of everything, Sam, except the Sea". As Tolkien himself said:

> There are other things more grim and terrible to fly from than the noise, stench, ruthlessness, and extravagance of the internal-combustion engine. There are hunger, thirst, poverty, pain, sorrow, injustice . . . And lastly there is the oldest and deepest desire, the Great Escape: the Escape from Death.

And in a letter:

> I suppose there is applicability in my story to present times. But I should say, if asked, the tale is not really about power and Dominion: that only sets the wheels going; it is about Death and the desire for deathlessness. Which is hardly more than to say it is a tale written by a man!

Part of his "message", he once added, was "the hideous peril of confusing true 'immortality' with limitless serial longevity. Freedom from Time, and clinging to Time . . . Compare the death of Aragorn with a Ringwraith." "Endless serial living" – what a wonderful phrase! especially in its chilling kinship, unforeseen by Tolkien, with the "serial killing" of our own day. And from the same land comes its perfect embodiment, the practice of cryogenics – that is, freezing the body immediately after physical death, in the morbid hope of subsequent revival, thanks to the literally unstoppable "progress" of science. (As someone who shares with Tolkien "a heartfelt loathing" for Disney and all his works – but also because the point would have been useful, as a marker of the vast difference between their works – I recently learned with regret that the tale of Walt Disney's frozen head is apocryphal.)

Of course, it is one thing to assert and appreciate the profound value of limits (as unfashionable in this century as it is prescient), and quite another to do so when faced with the ultimate personal Limit (so far as most of us know). Tolkien was very well aware of this, and in fact saw it as one of the keys to his beloved *Beowulf*. He called it

> the theory of courage, which is the great contribution of early Northern literature . . . It is the strength of the northern mythological imagination that it faced this problem, put the monsters in the centre, gave them victory but no honour, and found a potent but terrible solution in naked will and courage . . .

As a Christian, of course, Tolkien believed that the victory of the monsters was illusory, or at least, not final. *The Lord of the Rings* contains repeated hints about "more than one power at work", beyond even that of the greatest in Middle-earth, namely Sauron; that Bilbo was *meant* to find the Ring; about "chance-meetings", and "luck". But as Shippey says, "Mordor and 'the Shadow' are nearer and more visible." There is no question of luck or chance interfering with the exercise of free will, and at almost any point in *The Lord of the Rings*, things could have gone disastrously wrong. Indeed, what finally gave this power the opportunity to intervene at the crucial last hurdle, when Frodo is standing at the Crack of Doom, was his and Sam's stubborn persistence;, plus their free exercise (and Bilbo's before them) of "Pity, and Mercy". Without that, there would have been no Gollum, and Frodo would have claimed the Ring.

"Pity and Mercy" sum up why I have chosen to call this third sphere (after culture and nature) ethics. They also bring us to the question of the Christian (or otherwise) nature of *The Lord of the Rings*. Of Tolkien's own Christianity there is no doubt, but the uncomfortable relationship between that religion and nature – no time for that. The important differences between Catholicism and Protestantism – nor that. Only what Tolkien described as the "monotheistic world of natural theology" of Middle-earth. He maintained that *The Lord of the Rings*

> is of course a fundamentally religious and Catholic work; unconsciously so at first, but consciously in the revision. That is why I have not put in, or have cut out, practically all references to anything like "religion", to cults or practices, in the imaginary world. For the religious element is absorbed into the story and the symbolism.

Now it is a curious and important question why Tolkien should have *wanted* to cut out all references to religion in "a fundamentally religious work"; we shall return to it. First, and at the risk of impertinence, I want to contest this description of *The Lord of the Rings* as economical with the truth; or at least, seriously inadequate.

True, it is nominally monotheistic. At the top is God, called "the One". But as Tolkien admits, He "indeed remains remote, outside the World, and only directly accessible to the Valar or Rulers. These take the place of the 'gods', but are created spirits . . ." The One only directly intervened in history once, and that was in the momentous reshaping of the world in the Second Age. There is never the slightest suggestion that He would do so again.

The Valar, also described as "the Guardians of the World" and (interestingly) as "powers", are somewhat more present. They have at least visited Middle-earth, and one in particular – Elbereth – is the object of song, prayer and supplication in *The Lord of the Rings*. This, it seems to me, introduces a real element of polytheism into the picture, which therefore cannot, by definition, be *fundamentally* Christian.

Other aspects of *The Lord of the Rings* point to the same conclusion. For example, there is evidence of an active animism: the manifestation of the mountain Caradhras's displeasure in snow; the herb *athelas*, that makes the air sparkle with joy; the reflection of Sauron's attack in a great engulfing cloud, and the subsequent change in the winds prefiguring the turn of the tide in the battle for Minas Tirith . . . This, and much else, is contained in one of Tolkien's most marvellous passages, when the Captain of the Nazgûl confronts Gandalf before the ruined gates of Minas Tirith, in the moment when the cock crows, welcoming only the morning, and "as if in answer there came from far away another note. Horns, horns, horns. In dark Mindolliun's sides they dimly echoed. Great horns of the North wildly blowing". And after the battle, "A great rain came out of the Sea, and it seemed that all things wept for Théoden and Éowyn, quenching the fires in the City with grey tears". The "as if" and "it seemed" here are plainly a sop to rationalists. When Tolkien writes that "Tree and stone, blade and leaf were listening", he does *not* mean it metaphorically.

Polytheism and animism are, of course, pagan by (Christian) definition, and the celebrations of 1420 are a veritable pagan feast. (One could almost say "orgy".) On Midsummer eve – not just any old day in the year – "the sky was blue as sapphire and white stars opened in the East, but the West was still golden, and the air was cool and fragrant . . ." This is the setting for the symbolic marriage (and its subsequent consummation) of the King and his bride, Arwen Evenstar. It comes as no surprise that 1420 became famous for its weddings, and in an inverse "wasteland" effect the land too is restored to fertility. Young hobbits, you will recall, sat on the lawns under the plum-trees and ate, "until they had made piles of stones like small pyramids, or the heaped skulls of a conqueror, and then they moved on."

There are other interesting complications I can't go into: the practice of reincarnation among the Dwarves, for example, which Tolkien defended in reply to a Christian reader who felt he had "overstepped the mark". True, quasi-Christian grace and prophecy appear in *The Lord of the Rings*, along with tantalising traces of Christ-like attributes on the part of Gandalf and Frodo. But divination, long a *bête noir* of the Church, figures too; and in any case, all these things have far older lineages than their relatively recent Christian versions. That also applies to Eärendil. As the Morning and Evening Star, the brightest *star* in the heavens – namely, Venus – and the emblem and icon of Elbereth, his goddess of feminine compassion, Eärendil has antecedents considerably older and more precise than either angels or Mary.

It could even be said that Tolkien's religious mythology is, in one major respect, not supernatural at all, but humanistic. As Zipes has pointed out (1979), "Tolkien raises the small person, the Hobbit, to the position of God, that is, he stands at the centre of the universe . . . The spiritual world manifests itself through the actions of the redeemed small person".

None of this is intended to denigrate the Christian elements in Tolkien's work. Indeed, none of the elements I have found should be taken as somehow trumping or cancelling out the others. (I am not suggesting, for example, that *The Lord of the Rings* is either "really" or "unconsciously" pagan.) The point is the extraordinary richness and complexity of the work. And when we turn to how and why Tolkien wrote what he did, the point emerges clearly that its syncretism, including (indeed requiring) the elimination of "practically all references to anything like religion" (as we now understand it) was a conscious and deliberate decision.

The clue to this lies in Tolkien's old exemplar, the author of *Beowulf*. In his British Academy lecture (1936), Tolkien characterised the poem as "a fusion that has occurred at a given point of contact between old and new, a product of thought and deep emotion". Living in such a time, when paganism (including its "Northern courage") was succumbing to the new religion – but unevenly, and unpredictably – its author had responded to this dilemma by suppressing the specifically Christian. Is it surprising, then, that Tolkien should decide to emulate the Beowulf-poet, and see to it that "the religious element is absorbed into the story and the symbolism"? For he was undoubtedly keenly aware that he too lived at a given point – the other end of the same historical epoch, the "post-Christian" to *Beowulf*'s "pre-", when once again there was no single clear and over-arching set of values. Christian, pagan, humanist and many other values mix and collide; there is no single criterion by which to judge between them that is even nearly universally accepted, yet none of them is unaffected by the others. (For that reason one cannot meaningfully speak of a "return" to any of them.) And the same applies politically, socially, philosophically . . . If there is one dictum that sums up this situation – and incidentally suggests a positive response – it must be Joseph Schumpeter's: "To realize the relative validity of one's convictions and yet stand for them unflinchingly is what distinguishes a civilised man from a barbarian". And it is entirely fitting, if ironic, that it is Schumpeter's civilised man, not his barbarian, who now embodies the pagan virtue of "Northern courage" that Tolkien so admired. As part of the same process, the green of leaves which used to signify barbarism is now well on its way to becoming the sign of a society sufficiently civilised to value nature.

Tolkien "realized the absurdity in post-Christian days", in Richard L. Purtill's words (1984), "of attempting original myth". His solution was to attempt a re-creation through literary myth. In some remarks in a letter about the Arthurian myth, he finds it (he says) not only "imperfectly naturalised" (more British than English) and over-generous with *faerie*, but

> For another and more important thing: it is involved in, and explicitly contains the Christian religion.
>
> For reasons which I will not elaborate, *that seems to me fatal* . . . (I am speaking, of course, of our present situation, not of ancient pagan, pre-Christian days . . .)

Thus Tolkien needed Frodo and the hobbits not only to give his disabused modern readers access to the ancient heroic world of Middle-earth but also as a mediation, like *The Lord of the Rings* as a whole, "between pagan myth and Christian truth" – and between that Truth and modern myth.

Actually, with his usual extraordinary attention to detail and consistency, he even implied this point within *The Lord of the Rings*. For already in Frodo's day, "Gone was the *mythological* time when Valinor (or Valimar), the Land of the Valar (gods if you will) existed physically in the Uttermost West, or the Eldaic (Elvish) immortal Isle of Eressëa; or the Great Isle of Westernesse (Númenor-Atlantis)." The gods, whose judgement was (effectively) perfect and final, were no longer available; the seas were now bent, and anyone setting sail in search of the "ancient or True West" will simply return to their starting-point. The old "straight way" was gone, and with it all "straight sight".

V

With that, I have come to the edge of the "third sphere" in

Tolkien's world (if one can speak so of something so vast and open-ended). There are of course endless loose ends. (Is Tom Shippey, for example, soft on Orcs?) But what really remains is to emphasise the overlap, or rather synthesis, of the three nested considerations – culture, nature and spirit – that I have identified. That synthesis, I believe, is what guided Tolkien himself, and still embodies the modern meaning of his work.

Out of the mirror of Englishness, for example, Tolkien picked not only the obviously appropriate – a love of nature in general and flora in particular – but native traditions of frugality, self-sufficiency and community. And it could be argued that the strongly implicit and tacit sense of the sacred that Tolkien conveys is peculiarly English.

But the interaction of "nature" and "spirit" is particularly potent. As Sam says deep in Mordor, recalling Galadriel's seemingly fantastic offers earlier, "If only the Lady could see us or hear us, I'd say to her: 'Your ladyship, all we want is light and water: just clean water and plain daylight, better than any jewels, begging your pardon.'" What haunts his thoughts is "the memory of water; and every brook or stream or fount that he had ever seen, under green willow-shades or twinkling in the sun . . ." Meanwhile, the growing ravages of the Ring on Frodo are having precisely the reverse effect: "No taste of food, no feel of water, no sound of wind, no memory of tree or grass or flower, no image of moon or star are left to me. I am naked in the dark, Sam, and there is no veil between me and the wheel of fire." So much for the supposed other-worldliness (and tweeness) of *The Lord of the Rings*. It is in fact a work in which a deeply sensual appreciation of this world is interfused with an equally powerful sense of its ineffability. This is actually a movement within the story of *The Lord of the Rings*: from the simple, sensual appreciation of Pippin's bath song – "Oh! Water hot is a noble thing!" – to a deeper and truer appreciation of these things, in which their aesthetic, spiritual and (literally) vital dimensions are indissolubly one.

The vision at the heart of *The Lord of the Rings* is therefore indeed one of "The cosmos as a whole . . . an organism at once *real*, *living* and *sacred*" (Mircea Eliade). But it goes farther, because *while* we live, the sacred – although it extends "beyond the limits of the world", via death – is meaningless without its natural embodiment. (Or worse! since Tolkien identified the obscenity of "endless serial living" as one such attempt.)

Finally, this world-view is not simply opposed to "a positivist, mechanist, urbanized, and rationalist culture", but grafted onto some native cultural traditions whose survival-value has been (sorely) tried and tested. Without that, *The Lord of the Rings* would have remained a fantasy indeed. But just as Frodo and (in the end) Sam are no ordinary hobbits, so Tolkien envisages not a passive acceptance of English society as it is, but its rather radical transformation. (And note too that the efforts of the aristocratic and artistic Elves to merely preserve are explicitly doomed to failure.)

In short, Tolkien's work urges *a new ethic, based on the resacralisation of life, and the lineaments of life* – good earth, clean water, plain daylight – *that is deeply rooted in the local culture*. Nothing less will enable us to destroy the power of the Ring.

Such an ethic is no substitute, of course, for a political programme and determined local action; but then again, without it they will certainly fail. Nor is it all as ambitious as it perhaps sounds; all that is needed is for the "resacralisation" to become sufficiently widespread and powerful – *whatever* its class (or other) origins – for its effects to make a difference. A new church is not required.

Richard Mabey has seen this point clearly (1984). In response to the crises of industrial society, he writes:

> increasingly the shape of the most promising alternatives is emerging out of what we loosely call "the rural tradition". That . . . may begin to succeed as a movement in the real world if we recognise that the experience of nature is not exclusive to a particular place or moment, a way of life or position of privilege, but is an aspect of all our individual lives and of our collective history.

And "collective" here means just that: everybody, even (potentially) your city-dwellers whose direct experience of nature is minimal, and whose "yearning for a relationship with nature and the land [is] based, not on ownership or labour, but on simple delight and sensual and spiritual renewal". For they too – despite their hopelessly middle-class, inchoately nostalgic, inauthentically "suburban and half-educated" character – are in search not only "for a modern role for the countryside", but for themselves. As Fraser Harrison puts it, recalling a remark of Hazlitt's that Nature is a kind of universal Home, "what must be conserved before anything else is the desire in ourselves for Home – for harmony, peace and love, for growth in nature and in our imaginative powers – because unless we keep this alive, we shall lose everything."

Just so, and that brings us (finally) back to *The Hobbit* and *The Lord of the Rings* as the literary artefacts with which we started out. For here is the answer to the charge that Tolkien was writing for or on behalf of a cosy elite; that his work was ideological in a strict and pejorative sense. The "desire for Home" may cut out many, but it certainly does so in no simple way that follows from class, race or gender. True, those principally feeling and actually acting on behalf of such a desire may be middle-class in origin; but the same may be said of those leading virtually every modern revolutionary movement (including those identified as Marxist). It does not follow that the benefits will be confined to people like themselves – or do others not need, let alone appreciate, clean water, good air and healthy food? And that applies to more "frivolous" things too. It is those who sneer at the middle-classness of ecologism who most patronise the masses.

In fact, as we have seen, any bias built into Tolkien's books works against a highly educated or literate, and to that extent privileged readership; if they have an "average" or "typical" reader, it is just such an object of critical scorn as the humble city-dweller I have just described. So what is he or she getting from these books, and how, while the loremasters are engaged on weightier matters?

Let us recall Tolkien's belief that fairy-stories offer, "in a peculiar degree or mode, these things: Fantasy, Recovery, Escape, Consolation . . ." When I first read *The Lord of the Rings* at the age of sixteen, after an unwitting preparation thanks to *The Hobbit*, seven years earlier, I was overcome with the unmistakable sense of having encountered a world that was more real than the one I lived in; or one, at least, whose reality was much more concentrated. Accompanying this feeling was the equally odd one of inexplicable familiarity with that world. And finally, there was a definite sense of loss when I had finished, which (combined with delight and curiosity) impelled me to immediately recommence reading it. None of this was a unique experience on my part; to a greater or lesser degree, *The Lord of the Rings* has affected many readers in just this way, and it deserves some attempt at understanding.

Let's look at the "sense of loss" first. It is actually well-described within the book itself, at the point where the Company is setting off in their boats on the Silverlode, when it seemed to them that "Lórien was slipping backward, like a bright ship masted with enchanted trees, sailing on to forgotten shores, while they sat helpless upon the margin of the grey and leafless world." This deprivation, with its unwilling return to a "grey and leafless world", can actually be hard to bear. Or again – and it is no coincidence that this incident also involves Lothlórien, "the heart of Elvendom on earth" – when Frodo was walking up Cerin Amroth, he felt that "When he had gone and passed again into the outer world, still Frodo the wanderer from the Shire would walk there . . ."

That passage ought to remind us of another one, from the glory days of Edwardian children's literature: ". . . wherever they go, and whatever happens to them on the way, in that enchanted place on the top of the Forest a little boy and his bear will always be playing". If, Dear Reader, that sort of thing makes you want (like Dorothy Parker) to fwow up, Tolkien's is less likely to for a number of reasons. First, it is less important in the context of the book as a whole. Second, it is embedded in a much more sombre (and distinctly adult) view of life, with the monsters very nearly if not quite dead-centre. Third, it is important to notice that at the end of his tale, and various hints about other worlds notwithstanding, Tolkien returns us firmly to *this* one: at the Grey Havens, after the departure of Frodo and Gandalf, Sam "stood far into the night, hearing only the sigh and murmur of the waves on the shores of Middle-earth, and the sound of them sank deep into his heart". We stand with him. As his own definition of Recovery implies, Tolkien's "*evangelium*" permits only a "fleeting glimpse of Joy" in *this* world, not permanent transportation to the next. The nostalgia he engenders, therefore, is finally redirected back into our own lives here.

In my view, Tolkien's work awakes precisely that longing for Home, in which "pain and delight flow together and tears are the very wine of blessedness". And being a boy (or girl) is not a necessary prerequisite.

What about the sense of hyper-reality? And how could one feel it to be almost intimately familiar, upon the first reading of a book supposedly about a very different place and/or time? Here I think the word "mythology", so over-used in connection with Tolkien, is actually useful. Carl Kerenyi (1951) defined the stuff of mythology as:

> an immemorial and traditional body of material contained in tales about gods and god-like beings, heroic battles and journeys to the Underworld – tales already well-known but not unamenable to further reshaping. Myth is the *movement* of this material . . .

Furthermore, "Myth gives a ground, lays a foundation. It does not answer the question 'why?' but 'whence?'" All this fits Tolkien like a fine glove, and he could have supplied a clear answer to Kerenyi's rhetorical (and slightly plaintive) question, "is an immediate experience and enjoyment of mythology still in any sense possible?"

His incorporation into *The Lord of the Rings* of English and "Northern" cultural traditions, including the mythological, was not just a calculated strategy; it was unavoidable for a man so thoroughly steeped in them. But they give his work a tremendous advantage over that of others, possibly otherwise similar, because those traditions still live. Thus, if I had been able to articulate my early experience of familiarity adequately at the time, I would have said it felt not so much like a discovery as a *re*-discovery, a reconnection with something that I now see is a *living* tradition. It does not just embrace the myths attached to England as somehow a preternaturally "green and pleasant land" (although that counts too).

The result, it seems to me, is the same sense of wonder that Keats experienced upon encountering Chapman's *Homer*, for the same kind of reason in relation to our Greek cultural heritage; only Tolkien has performed this service (with infinitely less thanks), in relation to that of "North-west Europe", for later, larger and less "literary" generations. And again, none the less or worse for that! Amanda Craig recently quoted *Private Eye* to the effect that *The Lord of the Rings* appeals only to "computer programmers, hippies and most Americans" (1992). She nicely puts this to work, observing that "The fact that Tolkien's world appeals to computer programmers is possibly less a sign that it is infantile than that he developed a hypnotic style and narrative which quickens the reluctantly literate as well as the devoutly bookish. Few writers in any century can claim the same."

As for the hyper-reality of Middle-earth, one would have to be a pretty unreconstructed positivist to say that such things as mythologies, let alone cultural traditions, are somehow less real than say, the proverbial table; or even to say that they did not contain, however coded, a great deal of *emotion* in the form of accumulated human experience: hopes, wishes, fears . . . Tolkien's books present a highly distilled and concentrated (albeit also highly selective) version of just that.

This analysis accords with Tolkien's own experience of writing *The Lord of the Rings*, in which it "grew", he "was drawn irresistibly" toward certain things, and "discovery" felt much more the case than "invention". If one reacts as reader in the manner I have described, it is impossible to feel that this was mere rhetoric designed to enhance his creation. And Middle-earth was emphatically not "created": certainly not, at least, in the fashionable modern sense of creation *ex nihilo*. It was a *co-creation*, in partnership with some very old and durable cultural materials. It would be unduly extravagant – or worse, fundamentalist – to say that he literally discovered Middle-earth. But neither did he simply invent it.

Whether his books are defined as quest or fairy-story or "myth" and "low mimesis" and "irony" all embedded deeply in romance, they are certainly story-telling of a kind long unfashionable as an adult genre. But giving "mythic" its full cultural and historical due due allows us to see Tolkien's uniqueness more clearly. Within the baggy genre of "fantasy", for example, it is what raises *The Lord of the Rings* above even well-written books that however embody a more purely personal mythology, like David Lindsay's *Voyage to Arcturus* and Mervyn Peake's Gothic "Gormenghast" trilogy, and Freudian-fantastic fables by Angela Carter (1985); let alone meretricious fiction like Lindsay Clarke's *The Chymical Wedding*, a kind of literary "Twin Peaks".

The only books I can think of that seem strictly comparable to *The Lord of the Rings*, in the terms in which I have analysed it here, are Herman Melville's *Moby Dick*, Mikhail Bulgakov's *The Master and Margarita*, and Russell Hoban's *Riddley Walker*. They too draw their power from a profound and startlingly fresh connection with mythic aspects of the Judaeo-Christian cultural tradition (though not of course Tolkien's unique "Northern" contribution). And they have also presented literary critics with intractable problems, who are usually obliged to treat them, in the end, as *sui generis*. Except maybe for Hoban's, they could also all be described as life-works.

This is Tolkien's true company of peers. He is saved by his deep and tough roots in a particular cultural soil from the extraordinarily deracinated (and therefore shallow) universalism of *Star Wars*, with its bargain-basement Jungian archetypes, eulogised by Joseph Campbell; and by his brilliant re-creation of myth from the ghastly death-in-life of Disney's imitation, with its plastic grass and "genuine replica" fairy castles.

His books, and along with it his many readers, are fully deserving of critical respect – even a little passionate attention. They are not only a cry (as Marx said of religion) from "the heart of a heartless world, the soul of soulless conditions", but a plea for what I have called the resacralisation of life. That plea gleams with an ancient hope: peace within and among people, and between people and nature. Indeed, Tolkien's own personal epitaph might be the parting words to Aragorn or *Estel* from his mother: "I gave Hope to the Dúnedain, I have kept no hope for myself."

References

Carter, Angela. 1985. *Black Venus*. London: Chatto and Windus.

Craig, Amanda. 1992. "Lord of all he conveyed, despite his fans" in *The Independent*, 25 January 1992.

Harrison, Fraser. 1984. "England, Home and Beauty" in Richard Mabey with Susan Clifford and Angela Kind (eds.) *Second Nature*, pp. 162-72. London: Jonathan Cape.

Harrison, Robert Pogue. 1992. *Forests: The Shadow of Civilization*. Chicago: University of Chicago Press.

Harvey, David. 1985. *The Song of Middle-earth*. London: George Allen and Unwin.

Jordanova, Ludmilla. 1987. "The Interpretation of Nature: A Review Article", in *Comparative Studies in Society and Nature*, XXIX:1 (January 1987), pp. 195-200.

Kaveney, Roz. 1992. "The Ring Recycled", in *New Statesman and Society*, 20/27 December 1992, p. 47.

Kerenyi, Carl. 1951. "Prolegomena", in C. G. Jung and C. Kerenyi, *Introduction to a Science of Mythology: The Myth of the Divine Child and the Mysteries of Eleusis*, pp. 1-32. London: Routledge and Kegan Paul.

Kilby, Clyde. 1977. *Tolkien and the Silmarillion*. Berkhamstead: Lion Publishing.

Mabey, Richard. 1984. "Introduction: Entitled to a View?" in Richard Mabey with Susan Clifford and Angela Kind (eds.) *Second Nature*, pp. ix-xix. London: Jonathan Cape.

Orwell, George. 1940. "The Lion and the Unicorn: Socialism and the English Genius".

Purtill, Richard L. 1984. *J.R.R. Tolkien: Myth, Morality, and Religion*. San Francisco: Harper Row.

Shippey, T.A. 1982. *The Road to Middle-Earth*. London: George Allen and Unwin.

Stimpson, Catherine R. 1969. *J.R.R. Tolkien* (Columbia Essays on Modern Writers, no. 41). New York: Columbia University Press.

Thomas, Keith. 1983. *Man and the Natural World: Changing Attitudes in England 1500-1800*. London: Allen Lane.

Tolkien, J. R. R. 1936. *Beowulf: The Monsters and the Critics*. London: The British Academy.

Tolkien, J. R. R. 1964. "On Fairy-stories" in *Tree and Leaf*. London: George Allen and Unwin.

Tolkien, J. R. R. 1966. *The Lord of the Rings*, second edition, three volumes. London: George Allen and Unwin.

Tolkien, J. R. R. 1978. *The Hobbit*, fourth edition. London: George Allen and Unwin.

Tolkien, J. R. R. 1981. *Letters of J.R.R. Tolkien* ed. Humphrey Carpenter. London: George Allen and Unwin.

Weiner, Martin J. 1985. *English Culture and the Decline of the Industrial Spirit 1850-1980*. Harmondsworth: Penguin.

Williams, Raymond. 1985. *The Country and the City*. London: Hogarth Press.

Zipes, Jack. 1979. *Breaking the Magic Spell*. London: Heinemann.

The Earthly Paradise in Tolkien's *The Lord of the Rings*

Gwenyth Hood

Abstract: Valinor, modelled on the Earthly Paradise, is described more fully in Tolkien's posthumously published works than in *The Lord of the Rings*. Yet the fleeting Valinorean images within the trilogy have a powerful impact, heightening and simultaneously providing consolation for the horrors of Mordor.

Keywords: Ainulindalë, Earthly Paradise, Elves, innocence, Lórien, *The Lord of the Rings*, Valinor

Throughout all the grim and harrowing ordeals which dominate the action of *The Lord of the Rings*, a lovely but fleeting vision haunts the background. This is the vision of the Earthly Paradise, which enters some of the darkest moments of the trilogy. This vision gives the trilogy much of its power, both heightening the contrasting horrors and providing consolation for them.

The Earthly Paradise appears in many guises, most of them bound up with the image of Valinor. The relationship between Valinor and Middle-earth in Tolkien's mythology is best delineated in the Ainulindalë or Music of the Ainur, which was published with *The Silmarillion*.[1]

As the Ainulindalë tells the story, Ilúvatar creates the Ainur or holy ones (paralleling pagan gods as well as Biblical angels), teaches them music, and encourages them to sing before him. All the Ainur join in this great symphony, until Melkor decides that he can do better and makes his own discordant song. This creates confusion, but Ilúvatar, being an artist, cannot triumph simply by destroying Melkor, for that would ruin his pattern. Hence, he makes two attempts to reharmonize the symphony. First, he devises a "second theme," later associated with Manwë, chief of the Valar, which is "like and unlike" the first theme. But "the discord of Melkor rose in uproar and contended with it . . . until many of the Ainur were dismayed and sang no longer" (Tolkien, 1977, p. 16). Then Ilúvatar begins a "third theme," which is "unlike the others" (Tolkien, 1977, p. 16) and of haunting sweetness and subtlety. Somehow this new theme takes up the "most triumphant notes" of Melkor's discords, and in relation to the first and second themes, makes the whole symphony beautiful again (Tolkien, 1977, p. 17). This third theme is later identified with "the Children of Ilúvatar . . . Elves and Men" (Tolkien, 1977, p. 18).

Having made a victorious end to the music, Ilúvatar gives, first visual, then physical, reality to the symphony and it becomes the known universe with all its history (Tolkien, 1977, p. 19). Part of this is Middle-earth in the Third Age, in which the action of the trilogy takes place.

From all this, we see that Ilúvatar's first theme, the primal harmony, embodies the pattern of nature as the One intended it to be, uncorrupted and without need of redemption. Of this harmony, the Valar, or Powers of the World, are instruments, and Valinor, the land which they have moulded to their liking and kept (mostly) free from the assaults of Morgoth and his allies, embodies it. Of course, during Tolkien's Third Age, when *The Lord of the Rings* takes place, Valinor must partly express the "second theme" rather than the first one. Manwë is its "Elder King," and to some extent it is affected by, and must resist, evil. Valinor's first bloom ended (along with the unmarred first theme) when the Two Trees were destroyed long ago. Now the Valar are, as the Appendices relate, "Guardians of the World," and their guardianship involves some military action since it was the "Host of Valinor" which "broke Thangorodrim and overthrew Morgoth," in the first age (Tolkien, 1965a, p. 319; Tolkien, 1965c, p. 452).

In the Third Age, however, Valinor has become more remote from the lives of the human characters. Like the Medieval idea of the Earthly Paradise, it is neither attainable by them (ordinarily), nor yet the height of their desires. It is not attainable, since as the Appendices of the trilogy tell us, Valinor was "removed forever from the circles of the world" (Tolkien, 1965c, p. 392) when the Númenórean Ar-Pharazôn strove to invade it and take by force the immortality which was not intended for man. In this it resembles the Biblical Eden, which is guarded from the fallen Adam and Eve to prevent them from eating the fruit of the Tree of Life and living forever (Genesis 3:22-24).

Valinor is not the proper fulfilment of human desire; Tolkien's humans dream of something greater, as Aragorn

---

[1] The Ainulindalë seems, indeed, to be the part of Tolkien's mythology which he worked out with the greatest care, for in *The Book of Lost Tales*, Part I, Christopher Tolkien states that with this short masterpiece there is an unbroken manuscript tradition from the earliest to the latest versions, which is not the case with many of Tolkien's other stories (Tolkien, 1983, p. 62).

suggests when he tells the grieving Arwen that he thinks it is better to die and leave "the circles of the world" beyond which "there is more than memory" (Tolkien, 1965c, p. 428) than to cross the sea to Valinor. In this, Valinor resembles the Earthly Paradise as Dante portrays it, perched on top of Mount Purgatory, where human souls experience it briefly after they are cleansed of sin, only to abandon it quickly for the Heavenly Paradise.

Still, despite this, Valinor, as the Earthly Paradise within Tolkien's trilogy, remains the model of perfection most perceptible to the human imagination, since the fullness of Ilúvatar's symphony, embodied in the third theme, has not yet been played out. The human (and hobbit) characters must have some conception of the original harmony in order to grasp, even fleetingly, the nature of the whole symphony which their third theme will have made beautiful when the Music is completed.

For Valinor in Tolkien's work is, of course, not truly permanent or complete; it will be destroyed in the end, along with the world whose first pattern it embodied, to make way for the creation of a new world, free from the corruption of the old. Though expectations of this cataclysm, incorporating elements of the Apocalypse as well as the Northern mythology of Ragnarǫk, are much more explicit in *The Silmarillion* and *Unfinished Tales*, there are some cryptic references to it in the trilogy. Faramir, son of Denethor, Steward of Gondor, shows a consciousness of it when he says that his men give homage to "Númenor that was, and . . . to the Elvenhome that is, and to that which is beyond Elvenhome and will ever be" (Tolkien, 1965b, p. 361). The idea of the renewal of the world (correlating both to Tolkien's mysterious Second Music of the Ainur, and to the Christian idea of the New Heaven and the New Earth) is suggested briefly a few times. Galadriel seems to be referring to it when she says to Fangorn that they will meet, "Not in Middle-earth, nor until the lands that lie under the wave are lifted up again. Then in the willow-meads of Tasarinan we may meet in the Spring" (Tolkien, 1965c, p. 321).[2]

Meanwhile, in the ages before this cataclysm, the vitality of Middle-earth fades slowly but surely, and the High Elves, being bound to the deteriorating structure, live virtually endless lives watching their world slowly die. From some perspectives the life of the mortal creatures would be preferable, as Tolkien has his creator Ilúvatar say in *The Silmarillion*:

> It is one with this gift of freedom that the children of Men dwell only a short space in the world alive, and are not bound to it, and depart soon whither the Elves know not . . . wherefore they are called the Guests or the Strangers. Death is their fate, the gift of Ilúvatar, which as Time wears even the Powers [Valar] shall envy.
>
> (Tolkien, 1977, p. 42)

But in the Third Age, when this last battle is still far off, the humans and hobbits are more likely to envy the Elves for their access to Valinor. During the War of the Rings itself, Valinor appears blessedly unaffected by the struggle. The Valar will not receive the Ring of Power if it is brought to them, because it is bound up with difficulties that do not concern them. Meanwhile, no one can reach Valinor without permission, which is not readily granted; to fend off unwelcome visitors, Elbereth (Varda) appears in Galadriel's second poem, "holy and queenly," imposing separation:

> For now the Kindler, Varda, the Queen of the Stars, from Mount Everwhite has uplifted her hands like clouds, and all paths are drowned deep in shadow . . . Now lost, lost to those from the East is Valimar!
>
> (Tolkien, 1965a, p. 489)

Only those can reach Valinor who partake of its consecration and purity, and these, if they choose to seek Valinor, may not return to Middle-earth. Thus Eärendil found, upon attaining Valinor, that while he was accepted and allowed to assume the purity of the land (they clothe him in "elven white") in doing so the inhabitants initiate him in wisdom beyond Middle-earth, preventing his return. As Bilbo's poem describes it:

> and words unheard were spoken then
> of folk of Men and Elven-kin,
> beyond the world were visions showed
> forbid to those that dwell therein.
>
> (Tolkien, 1965a, p. 310)

Similarly the Elves, who are evidently permitted to return to Valinor when they choose, seem unable to come back to Middle-earth once they go. They must depart, "never to return," or, as Samwise says, "They are sailing, sailing, sailing over the Sea, they are going into the West and leaving us" (Tolkien, 1965a, p. 74).

Yet although it is forbidden to all but a few, humans must know something of Valinor, since it embodies Ilúvatar's original harmony. Hence, images of this distant and forbidden Paradise haunts the trilogy, evoked by many names, some referring to it as a whole and some to places within it: Valinor (Tolkien, 1965a, p. 309;), Valimar (Tolkien, 1965a, p. 489), Eldamar (Tolkien, 1965a, p. 309), Elvenhome (Tolkien, 1965a, p. 309), the Uttermost West (Tolkien, 1965a, p. 321), Ilmarin (Tolkien, 1965a, p. 309), Eressëa (Tolkien, 1965a, p. 321)[3] and the Blessed Realm

---

[2] Since Tasarinan is one of the lands of Middle-earth which Fangorn mentions in his poem (Tolkien, 1965b, p. 90), all of which now "lie under the wave," and Galadriel speaks of meeting there again, but not "in Middle-earth," it would seem that she hopes for a meeting when both Middle-earth and Valinor will be under a new dispensation after the Second Music.

[3] Eressëa's claim to be part of Valinor may be disputed. Though there are Elves in Valinor (which justifies its title "Elvenhome"), Tolkien distinguishes the island Eressëa, to which the Elves of Middle-earth will ultimately repair, from Valinor proper, since it is not on the mainland (Tolkien, 1965c, p. 452). Tolkien's motivation for making Eressëa separate in *The Lord of the Rings* and *The Silmarillion* is now obscure, but Christopher Tolkien reports that in the earliest versions, Eressëa was eventually to be moved back to Middle-earth, where it would become England (Tolkien, 1983, pp. 22-27). However, both places are vaguely called "the West" throughout the work, and no separation is imposed between the inhabitants; hence, it seems proper to class them together as far as their relationship with Middle-earth is

(Tolkien, 1965a, pp. 294, 313). The names of the powers of Valinor are also invoked repeatedly: the Valar in general (upon whom Faramir's men call to turn back the Mûmak, Tolkien, 1965b, p. 341); Elbereth, who is most characteristically named by High Elves (Frodo recognizes Gildor and his company as High Elves because "they spoke the name of Elbereth," Tolkien, 1965a, p. 117); the Elder King (Tolkien, 1965a, p. 310); Oromë (to whom Théoden upon Snowmane is compared, (Tolkien, 1965c, p. 138)).

Physically speaking, Valinor is only glimpsed from afar in the trilogy, as we are permitted to follow Frodo's progress at the end almost to its shores and he perceives "a sweet fragrance" and "the sound of singing," and sees "a far green country under a swift sunrise," (Tolkien, 1965c, p. 384). Like the physical glimpse, images of the Blessed Realm in the poetry of the trilogy are also fleeting and remote, but they do attribute some distinctive qualities to Valinor. They suggest a Valinor distant from Middle-earth, free of evil, and marked by beauty, grandeur and (relative to Middle-earth) permanence. That Valinor is distant from the inhabitants of Middle-earth in both time and space is a recurring theme. Valinor is "where ends the world" (Tolkien, 1965a, p. 309), and Galadriel sings mournfully of the distance "across so wide a Sea" (Tolkien, 1965a, p. 483). The seas of Middle-earth once flowed "straight to the western shore" but have been "bent" (Tolkien, 1965a, p. 182; Tolkien, 1965c, p. 392). This physical separation correlates with a separation in consciousness. Valinor's life is at a higher level of mind and cannot be comprehended by minds accustomed to the lesser powers of Middle-earth. Gildor's company sings, "We still remember, we who dwell,/ In this far land beneath the trees", apparently exercising the memory in preparation for a return. Galadriel indicates that were the Elves to remain in Middle-earth after the powers of the Elven Rings had passed away, they would "forget and be forgotten." They would "forget" perhaps not only Valinor itself but their own relationship with nature which it epitomizes (Tolkien, 1965a, p. 472).

Valinor's richness, grandeur, concord, beauty, communion, and permanence are suggested in a series of interwoven images in which separate elements are difficult to isolate. There is grandeur in the lofty mountain ("Everwhite" in Galadriel's second poem). Shores full of pearls and jewels suggest beauty and romantic distance all at once: "strands of pearl," (Tolkien, 1965a, p. 309); "jewels of Calacirya" (Tolkien, 1965a, p. 489). All these things are repeatedly suggested in Bilbo's poem on Eärendil's journey to Valinor:

> He tarried there from errantry,
> and melodies they taught to him,
> and sages old him marvels told,
> and harps of gold they brought to him . . .
> He came unto the timeless halls
> where shining fall the countless years,
> and endless reigns the Elder King
> in Ilmarin on Mountain sheer; . . .
> (Tolkien, 1965a, pp. 309-10)[4]

But Valinor remains in the distance and it is through the Elves that the human characters experience the Earthly Paradise most vividly in the context of the trilogy. Though both Elves and Men belong to Ilúvatar's third theme, Tolkien records "Ilúvatar made [the Elves] more like in nature to the Ainur, though less in might and stature" (Tolkien, 1977, p.41). That Elves (or Fairies, as he called them in *The Book of Lost Tales*) are more closely bound than man with the original harmony of nature is an idea that Tolkien presents not merely in *The Silmarillion* but in his famous essay "On Fairy-Stories," where he challenges the notion that fairies are "supernatural."

> *Supernatural* is a dangerous and difficult word in any of its senses, looser or stricter. But to fairies it can hardly be applied, unless *super* is taken merely as a superlative prefix. For it is man who is, in contrast to fairies, supernatural . . . whereas they are natural, far more natural than he.
> (Tolkien, 1966, p. 39)

Tolkien's elves on Middle-earth thus represent superlative nature – that is, nature as Ilúvatar intended it to be – rather than the supernatural. Elves do not represent the state of human prelapsarian innocence, but they come very close. Though the Silvan Elves have never been to Valinor, and the High Elves (or Noldor) left that place in disobedience to the commands of the Valar, at this point in the trilogy they seem to have patched up whatever differences they had, since the way to Valinor is once more open to them. T. A. Shippey relates Tolkien's treatment of the Elves and the Earthly Paradise to the conception of the Middle English author of the legend of St. Michael in *The Early South English Legendary* that Elves were neutral angels. Even among the neutrals, however, some inclined to God without entering the fray, and these were confined to earth or the Earthly Paradise until Judgment Day, at which time they would be allowed to return to Heaven (Shippey, 1983, p. 178). This Medieval vision, oddly enough, corresponds to all the varieties of Elves mentioned in *The Lord of the Rings* and *The Silmarillion* – the ones who remained obedient to the Valar, those who seemed to rebel (against the Valar, but perhaps not truly against Ilúvatar) and desired to return afterwards, and those who became evil and joined the side of Morgoth.

Elves, within the trilogy, are more "natural" than Men because they are intended to find fulfilment in nature, and they "die not until the world dies" (Tolkien, 1977, p.42).

---

concerned.

[4] Tolkien, in his mythology, makes the Christian distinction between time and eternity, and Valinor, he states plainly in one of his letters (Tolkien, 1981, p. 203), is not in eternity, but is part of the created world and also bound in time. "Timeless" in Bilbo's poem about Eärendil apparently means merely "unharmed by time," since time passes there in "shining years," instead of being marred by violence and blight as on Middle-earth. Time is clearly not absent, since Galadriel also refers to the accumulating years in Valinor, twice using the image of growing and falling leaves to emphasize the steady continuity as well as the enduring vigour: "There long the golden leaves have grown upon the branching years" (Tolkien, 1965a, p. 482); and "[L]ike gold fall the leaves in the wind, long years numberless as the wings of trees!" (Tolkien, 1965a, p. 489).

Men are supernatural because they hunger for eternity, and "have a virtue to shape their life . . . beyond the Music of the Ainur, which is as fate to all things else" (Tolkien, 1977, p. 41). The Elves more precisely embody the original harmony of nature; Men carry within them the potential for creating the Second Music.

In his essay, Tolkien states that one of the "operations" of fairy stories is "satisfaction of certain primordial human desires," among them that desire, "ancient as the Fall," to "converse with other living things" (Tolkien, 1966, pp. 44, 80). In the trilogy, it is the Elves who enjoy many of these Edenic pleasures. In complete harmony with their natural or physical being, they are immortal and they never age. They also never completely lose dominion over themselves, even in imagination or sleep. Legolas can "sleep" by "resting his mind in the strange paths of elvish dreams, even as he walked open-eyed in the light of this world" (Tolkien, 1965b, p. 37). Besides being at one with themselves, Elves are also at harmony with the natural world around them and yet in a position to lead and guide it. Elrond causes the flood which sweeps away the Black Riders at the Fords of Bruinen, but Gandalf describes the event thus: "The river of this valley is under [Elrond's] power, and it will rise in anger when he has great need to bar the Ford" (Tolkien, 1965a, p. 296).[5] Elvish harmony with nature demands listening as well as speaking. "They always wished to talk to everything, the old Elves did" (Tolkien, 1965b, p. 90), Fangorn remarks, when he credits the Elves with having aroused in the Ents the desire to speak. The three Elven rings, which make Rivendell and Lórien what they are, also reveal Elvish benevolence, being made by elves who "did not desire strength or domination . . . but understanding, making, and healing, to preserve all things unstained" (Tolkien, 1965a, p. 352). Even without use of the three rings, nature responds to Elvish love and becomes especially beautiful and resistant to evil in places where they live or have lived. "Much evil must befall a country," Gandalf says, "before it wholly forgets the Elves, if once they dwelt there" (Tolkien, 1965a, p. 371). Legolas notes that when he brings some of his people to Ithilien, the land will be "blessed" (Tolkien, 1965c, p. 289).

Besides their affinity for landscapes, rivers and plants, the Elves also have a bond with animals. They ride horses without rein or bridle for "such was the elvish way with all good beasts" (Tolkien, 1965b, p. 51). Around Elves, animals develop unusual wisdom. Glorfindel's horse "will not let any rider fall that [Glorfindel] command[s] him to bear" (Tolkien, 1965a, p. 281). Gandalf says that Sam's favourite pony, Bill, has learned so much at Rivendell that he is able to make his way back from Moria to Bree in safety (Tolkien, 1965a, p. 396; Tolkien, 1965c, p. 338). In their role as instructors and guides for sentient beings, the Elves tend to overflow with compassion for all living things which are not wholly evil, even for Gollum, who finds in their attempts to heal him an opportunity for escape (Tolkien, 1965a, pp. 334-5). They are dedicated healers, sensitive in spotting harms and blights. Gildor perceives the moment he meets Frodo that there is "a shadow of fear" on him (Tolkien, 1965a, p. 118). Glorfindel perceives the serious nature of Frodo's Morgul wound, and comforts him with his touch, though it is left to Elrond, the greatest healer (and of human descent), to find and remove the inward-working shard (Tolkien, 1965a, pp. 281, 292). But the Elves are not only able to perceive, understand and heal; they also "make." What they make, however, harmonizes so well with the natural world that it is sometimes difficult to tell where one leaves off and the other begins. "[W]e put the thought of all that we love into all that we make" (Tolkien, 1965a, p. 479), says an Elf of Lórien, and therefore the garments which Galadriel gives the Fellowship carry with them the hues of Lórien and render their wearers practically indistinguishable from their environment.

It is in the Elven environments that we get our most vivid glimpse of what Valinor must be like. Most vivid of all is the experience of Lothlórien, which is ruled by Galadriel. Of all the lands in Middle-earth, Valinor is mirrored most closely in Lórien, whose realm is, as Aragorn says, "the heart of Elvendom on earth" (Tolkien, 1965a, p. 456).

Frodo experiences his entrance to the central part or "naith" of Lórien almost as if it were an Earthly Paradise in its newness and flawlessness:

> It seemed to him that he had stepped through a high window that looked on a vanished world . . . All that he saw was shapely, but the shapes seemed at once clear cut, as if they had been first conceived and drawn at the uncovering of his eyes, and ancient as if they had endured for ever. He saw no colour but those he knew, gold and white and blue and green, but they were fresh and poignant, as if he had at that moment first perceived them and made for them names new and wonderful . . . No blemish or sickness or deformity could be seen in anything that grew upon the earth. On the land of Lórien there was no stain."

(Tolkien, 1965a, pp. 454-5).

Indeed, Aragorn goes so far as to claim that Lórien is, like Valinor, pure of evil; rebuking Boromir's suspicions of Galadriel, he declares: "There is . . . in this land no evil, unless a man bring it hither himself" (Tolkien, 1965a, p. 464). Repeatedly Tolkien emphasizes the differences between Lórien and the outside world; the characters there are hardly aware of time going by: "For the Elves the world moves, and it moves both very swift and very slow. Swift, because they themselves change little, and all else fleets by . . . Slow, because they do not count the running years, not for themselves" (Tolkien, 1977, p. 503). This, too, likens Lórien to Valinor, where "like gold fall the leaves in the wind, long years numberless as the wings of trees!" (Tolkien, 1965a, p. 489). Lórien seems, relative to the rest of Middle-earth, a timeless land.

Yet, vivid though their glimpse of the Earthly Paradise is in Lórien, the Fellowship do not have to wait

---

[5] The initiative for flooding comes from Elrond, but the anger is genuinely the river's, and once aroused it is not completely under the Elves' control. As Gandalf says, "For a moment I was afraid that we had let loose too fierce a wrath, and the flood would get out of hand and wash you all away" (Tolkien, 1965a, p.296).

until they reach Lórien to get a sense of it. They are prepared, in a fashion, to understand and appreciate Lórien before they get there, and they are reminded of Lórien throughout the rest of the quest. Indeed, images of Valinor, and Lórien suggesting Valinor, appear frequently throughout the trilogy, often in the midst, or immediately after, its darkest moments.

It is, after all, just when Frodo and his companions are leaving the Shire pursued by Black Riders that the Elvish music of Gildor and his companions floats over the air and they hear the song of "Elbereth" and the "starlight on the Western Seas" (Tolkien, 1965a, p. 117). Frodo immediately realizes that it is a "strange chance" (Tolkien, 1965a, p. 118) to meet Elves who once lived in Valinor and will soon return to it. In the Old Forest, after the encounter with the malicious willow, the hobbits are rescued by Tom Bombadil, oldest and fatherless, who "knew the dark under the stars when it was fearless – before the Dark Lord came from the Outside" (Tolkien, 1965a, p. 182). In Bombadil's house, Frodo has a vision of Valinor as he is to see it at the end of his quest, "a far green country . . . under a swift sunrise" (Tolkien, 1965a, p. 187).

On the road once more, when they are again threatened by Nazgûl, this time upon Weathertop, Aragorn seeks to comfort and strengthen the Fellowship with his story of Lúthien and Beren, who loved each other and fought with Morgoth on Middle-earth, and met beyond the Sundering Seas in Valinor. Undoubtedly, this is part of what inspires Frodo to call, "Elbereth!" in the crisis of the witch-king's attack (Tolkien, 1965a, p. 263), and once more, at the Ford of Bruinen, to cry in desperation, "By Elbereth and Lúthien the Fair, you shall have neither the Ring nor me!" (Tolkien, 1965a, p. 286). These cries were marks of the loyalty which helped preserve Frodo from domination by evil; Gandalf later tells him that the Morgul blade failed to transform him into a wraith because he "resisted to the last" (Tolkien, 1965a, p. 293).

The Fellowship visits Lórien, of course, immediately after the disastrous journey through Moria. After their departure, all members of the Fellowship have cause to remember their stay there, as their Elven apparel is mentioned by everyone who meets them and Gandalf returns to them by Galadriel's agency, bearing messages from her.

But it is Frodo and Sam, upon the darkest and loneliest journey of all, who remember Lórien most deeply and who draw from it the Valinorean imagery most vividly. They are the most dependant on the Elvish provisions – clothing, *lembas*, and rope which comes when called. But Galadriel's phial with the light of Eärendil's star in it turns out to be of crucial importance in lighting their way, both physically and spiritually, through the land of Mordor. When they uncover it in Shelob's lair it "kindled to a silver flame . . . as though Eärendil had himself come down from the high sunset paths with the last Silmaril upon his brow" (Tolkien, 1965b, p. 418). This reminds the hobbits, once more, of the Powers which are on their side, and Frodo is inspired to cry *Aiya Eärendil Elenion Ancalima!* ("Hail, Eärendil, brightest of stars!") not knowing what he says (Tolkien, 1965b, p. 418.)

The same phial's light breaks the spell of the watchers at the tower of Cirith Ungol, and, as Samwise puts it, rings "the front-door bell" (Tolkien, 1965c, p. 218), making possible Frodo's rescue. While passing through the watchers the second time, Frodo and Sam take to crying out upon Eärendil and Elbereth respectively (Tolkien, 1965c, pp. 231, 234-5). Perhaps it is significant that Samwise, who will be able to live a normal life in Middle-earth, blessed by Galadriel's gift, is the one who consistently thinks to call upon Elbereth, a power of the Earthly Paradise, whereas Frodo, who will completely sacrifice his earthly happiness for the good of others, has been led to call upon those names which are entangled with the suffering and sacrifice implied in the Third theme: Lúthien and Eärendil.

The events of the trilogy take place within the final phase of the Music when there seem to be two themes struggling, the sweet, subtle, profound but soft third theme, and Morgoth's "vain," harsh, blaring music, whose triumphant moments are, however, stolen and taken up into the third theme. It should have been a triumphant moment for Sauron's side when Frodo, having travelled so long and with so much suffering and patience, to destroy the Ring, finds that he cannot do so, and claims the ring for himself. But then the hidden power of the third theme – Bilbo's and Frodo's pity and patience, which left Gollum alive to track Frodo in his own obsessive lust for the Ring – overthrows the hopes of Sauron, and the Ringbearers survive to enjoy a Middle-earth cleansed from Sauron's woes for a while. Though Middle-earth will proceed on through all the bitterness of the third theme, for the moment, there is an interlude where the second theme is heard more loudly, and imagery of the Earthly Paradise appears everywhere. A shoot of Nimloth, the White Tree of Gondor, is found to herald the new age; after the King is crowned, Arwen Undómiel comes to Gondor and sings of Valinor with the two trees in bloom. The Shire is revived with Galadriel's gift of soil from her orchards, and for a time mirrors Lórien, which mirrors Valinor. Legolas comes with his friends to make Gondor "blessed" (Tolkien, 1965c, p. 289).

Of course, this is just a respite before the end; the Earthly Paradise is in the past and will continue to fade; Galadriel and Elrond are shortly to depart over the Sea to wait their time in Valinor, and Frodo will go with them, still suffering from his wounds. Yet, though faded, the Elves leave resonances of the primal harmony behind them, while the third theme becomes more prominent in the symphony.

In Tolkien's *The Lord of the Rings* Frodo and Sam are embarked upon a journey which is a descent into physical and spiritual hell. We know it is not a pointless journey, however, because it is done for the sake of others in a world whose highest hopes are expressed in the imagery of the Earthly Paradise of Valinor and Lórien. Samwise, finding himself "at journey's end . . . / in darkness buried deep" only needs to remind himself that "above all shadows rides the Sun/ and Stars for ever dwell." The imagery of Valinor throughout the story not only provides this hope, but also gives the characters reasons to pay attention to the horrors around them, because, after all, they must heed them in order to overcome them. Without hope, it would be natural to close one's eyes to both the beauty and the horror; without hope, Frodo's sufferings would simply be another aspect of Mordor. Hence, the imagery of the Earthly Paradise throughout *The Lord of the Rings* makes the characters' gallant struggle both poignant and imaginatively believable.

References

Shippey, T. A. 1983. *The Road to Middle-Earth*. Boston: Houghton Mifflin Co.

Tolkien, J. R. R. 1965a. *The Fellowship of the Ring*. New York: Ballantine Books.

Tolkien, J. R. R. 1965b. *The Two Towers*. New York: Ballantine Books.

Tolkien, J. R. R. 1965c. *The Return of the King*. New York: Ballantine Books.

Tolkien, J. R. R. 1966. "On Fairy Stories." in *Essays Presented to Charles Williams*, ed. C. S. Lewis. Grand Rapids, MI: Eerdmans. pp. 38-89.

Tolkien, J. R. R. 1977. *The Silmarillion*. Ed. Christopher Tolkien. Boston: Houghton Mifflin.

Tolkien, J. R. R. 1981. *The Letters of J.R.R. Tolkien*, ed. Humphrey Carpenter. Boston: Houghton Mifflin.

Tolkien, J. R. R. 1983. *The Book of Lost Tales*, Part 1 ed. Christopher Tolkien. Boston: Houghton Mifflin.

Tolkien as Reviser: A Case Study

Gloriana St. Clair

Abstract: The publication of drafts of *The Lord of the Rings* allows scholars to assess Tolkien as a reviser. A comparison of the early presentations of Gondor in *The History of "The Lord of the Rings"*, with the finished scenes indicates the nature and direction of Tolkien's changes. This paper will discuss how the process of revision contributed to the overall effect of the work.

Keywords: Aragorn, Gandalf, heroism, ring, Strider, J.R.R. Tolkien: reviser, Trotter

"It was begun in 1936, and every part has been written many times. Hardly a word in its 600,000 or more has been unconsidered. And the placing, size, style, and contribution to the whole of all the features, incidents, and chapters has been laboriously pondered," wrote Tolkien to Milton Waldman in 1951 (Tolkien, 1981, p. 160). The publication of *The History of "The Lord of the Rings"* in 1988, 1989, and 1990 makes it possible for scholars to begin to see how extensive and important Tolkien's continuing revision of the work was to its final effect. The purpose of this paper is to touch on three of those revisions. I believe their overall effect was a darkening one. Through revision, Tolkien moved from a sequel to his children's story *The Hobbit* to the dark power of *The Lord of the Rings*. A great number of topics might be discussed relating to this thesis; the three I've selected are: Trotter appears and becomes Strider, the King of Númenor; the King of the Golden Hall; and minor revisions in "The Shadow of the Past."

Trotter becomes Strider and the King of Númenor

"Suddenly Bingo [Frodo] noticed that a queer-looking, brown-faced hobbit, sitting in the shadows behind the others, was also listening intently. He had an enormous mug (more like a jug) in front of him, and was smoking a broken-stemmed pipe right under his rather long nose. He was dressed in dark rough brown cloth, and had a hood on, in spite of the warmth, –and, very remarkably, he had wooden shoes!" (Tolkien, 1988, p. 137). This quotation is from the 1938 version of the manuscript; the story at that time was called simply the sequel to *The Hobbit*; this particular hobbit was named Trotter. Tolkien confesses in a 1955 letter to W.H. Auden that he had no clearer idea who this new character was than Frodo did (Tolkien, 1981, p. 216).

Many authors find that the circulation of manuscripts is a key to highly creative work. It seems that this particular change may have been engendered in this way. In a 1938 letter to Charles Furth, Tolkien says, "I am personally immensely amused by hobbits as such, and can contemplate them eating and making their rather fatuous jokes indefinitely; but I find that is not the case with even my most devoted fans (such as Mr Lewis and ? Rayner Unwin). Mr Lewis says hobbits are only amusing when in unhobbitlike situations" (Tolkien, 1981, p. 38). However, I suspect that Lewis and Unwin provided only criticisms, not suggestions for solutions. Tolkien, Lewis, and Unwin were all focusing on an amusing tale; a proper sequel for *The Hobbit*.

The idea for the change from a larger-than-average-sized hobbit into one of the Kings of Men is recorded on a scrap of paper dated October 1939. Tolkien next conceived of Trotter as an elf but then almost immediately made him a real ranger and a descendent of the ancient men of the north (Tolkien, 1989, p. 7). But as Tolkien made the change from a hobbit as quest-assistant to a serious and committed man who will be king, the whole tenor of the story changed. It ceased to be an amusing tramp through the woods with the adventures of very lovable hobbits and took on the formal epic duties of saving mankind from the rise of evil.

This one change reflected itself in other ways. The company was to have been composed entirely of hobbits travelling with Gandalf. It now came to represent a coalition of all the free creatures of Middle-earth. That allowed Tolkien to introduce the theme of the importance of difference and variety. In the United States, we would say that Tolkien established the importance of cultural diversity to the survival of the world. This theme plays itself out in a number of serious ways, but one of the most enjoyable results is the continued bantering between Gimli and Legolas.

This change also set in place the moral of the work as Tolkien states it in a letter to Milton Waldman: ". . . without the high and noble the simple and vulgar is utterly mean; and without the simple and ordinary the noble and heroic is meaningless" (Tolkien, 1981, p. 160). Tolkien began with the mighty – the tales of *The Silmarillion* reflect an Elvish point of view. In *The Hobbit*, he invented hobbits, a foil for the mighty, but he found limitations to that as he began to compose another story. All who have read *The Lord of the Rings* recognize the value of hobbits, whose timid natures have almost eradicated any heroic spark. That creatures of their nature should have the courage to engage in the War of the Ring opens participation to every reader. The unique view of the doings of heroes through the eyes of a patent stay-at-home is an important element in the overall effect of the work. However, to add another hobbit would be superfluous. To introduce the King of Numenor in a tavern near the Shire was brilliant.

While the effects of this change were major in the creation of themes and in the opportunities for future action, the continuity between the scene featuring Trotter and the one featuring Strider is great. Some parts of the plot remain the same: Frodo sees the stranger, is warned to curb his companion's loose lips, creates a greater stir by singing a comic song and vanishing, and has a serious conversation with the new character in his room. Other parts change: The whole timing changes from a few months to several years (see Tolkien, 1989, pp. 5-14), Tolkien goes through several ideas about who has the letter, whether there are one or two letters, and what the letter will say. Trotter's act of eavesdropping on the conversation of the travelling hobbits moves around a good bit and is finally omitted entirely.

The speeches assigned to the characters are more homologous than I would have expected. Because the whole text is expanding enormously, it is difficult to assess whether the hobbit ranger was more garrulous than his kingly successor.

Some levels of diction are changed to suit the new importance of the speaker. The initial conversation in the common room is virtually identical, and continues very much in line for a few pages. In the room, Trotter uses the phrase, "and give you what I've got, and what's more I'll keep your secret under my hood (which is closer than you or your friends keep it)" (Tolkien, 1988, p. 148). These remarks are gone. Later in the scene when Strider is talking about the process of their accepting him, the earlier character says, "Also, if you want to know, it amused me to see if I could induce you to take me on – just by my gifts of persuasion. It would have been nice (though quite wrong) if you had accepted me for my manners without testimonial! But there, I suppose my looks are against me!" In the final version, Strider says, "'But I must admit,' he added with a queer laugh, 'that I hoped you would take to me for my own sake. A hunted man sometimes wearies of distrust and longs for friendship. But there, I believe my looks are against me.'" This new conception of the speech appears in the 1939 Fourth Phase draft but the sentence is not yet perfectly formed. The revised sentence is epigrammatic in quality and typical of a remark that might have been made by a Norse hero in similar circumstances. The effect of such phrases, and of new dark additions, such as "The Enemy has set traps for me before now", greatly increase the perceived danger in the scene. "More alarming," Tolkien remarked in his letter to Stanley Unwin (Tolkien, 1981, p. 58).

Trotter's wooden shoes are now replaced with Strider's "high boots of supple leather that fitted him well, but had seen much wear and were now caked with mud." The cloak is more fully described as being travel-stained and made of heavy dark-green cloth. The hood still shades his face, but now Tolkien mentions that the "gleam of his eyes could be seen." This detail fits into a pervasive pattern of eye imagery culminating in the Eye of Sauron. After the introduction of the letter, Tolkien notes "In his [Strider's] eyes gleamed a light, keen and commanding." At this point, Strider throws back his cloak, puts his hand on the hilt of Andúril, and declares, "I am Aragorn son of Arathorn; and if by life or death I can save you, I will." – a dark but compelling statement (Tolkien, 1967a, p. 183).

Two other good pieces are introduced in the Fourth Phase. Trotter tells Frodo that the Ring does not belong to either of them but that Frodo is ordained to guard it for a time. This idea is moved to the Council of Elrond chapter. When Sam challenges Trotter, he suddenly seems to grow taller. This detail remains and is replicated with Gandalf and Bilbo and in an encounter between Frodo and Galadriel in the finished version.

A general darkening of the work occurs through the addition of key descriptions and actions:

- Strider now says, "I have hunted many wild and wary things" (Tolkien, 1967a, p. 175).
- "They [the Black Riders] will come on you in the wild, in some dark place where there is no help. Do you wish them to find you? They are terrible!" (Tolkien, 1967a, p. 177).
- Butterbur says, "Though I don't know what the likes of me can do against, against –" and Strider finishes, "Against the Shadow in the East" (Tolkien, 1967a, p. 181).

Thus, in the course of the chapter "Strider," Tolkien moves the reader from the amusing antics of Frodo's rendition of "The Cat and the Fiddle" in the Prancing Pony chapter to Merry's frightening account of seeing the Black Riders just outside the Inn. Changes in Strider's nature, in plot incidents, in speech, and in description all darken.

The King of the Golden Hall

In *The Road to Middle-earth*, T.A. Shippey says that this chapter is straightforwardly calqued on *Beowulf* (1982, p. 94). Editor Christopher Tolkien also labels various portions as "Beowulfian" or notes that portions of *Beowulf* are "very distinctly echoed" (Tolkien, 1989, p. 449). Readers of Tolkien's essay "Beowulf: the Monsters and the Critics" know a little bit about what he thought the meanings of that poem are. Two important themes are these. In the eternal battle against Chaos and Unreason, men join with the gods; their resistance becomes more perfect because it lacks hope (Tolkien, 1984, pp. 19-21).

And that great theme of "*man on earth*, rehandling in a new perspective an ancient theme: that man, each man and all men, and all their works shall die" (Tolkien, 1984, p. 23). In *Beowulf*, Tolkien thought the nearness of a pagan time lent a "shadow of its despair" (Tolkien, 1984, p. 23). I believe that some of Tolkien's debts to *Beowulf* were rather conscious ones because he knew the poem so intimately.

The imaginative spark for this particular adventure seems to have come from the horse Shadowfax, previously called Halbarad and Greyfax. In one outline, Tolkien has Gandalf riding an eagle to do battle with the Black Riders; had that conception materialized, these incidents might have been lost to the story. In 1939 outlines, Tolkien projects horsemen riding behind Gandalf to Gorgoroth and in another draft Gandalf calls in at Isengard riding horses from Rohan. Boromir's fate was not yet determined, but one plan was to have him flee to Saruman. Christopher Tolkien notes that the structure of the narrative in the west would be wholly changed by the "emergence of the Kingdom of Rohan into the full light of the story" (Tolkien, 1989, p. 215).

Because this chapter had a connection with *Beowulf*, its preliminary drafts were dark indeed. Gandalf says, "For behold! the storm comes, and now all friends should gather together, lest each singly be destroyed" (Tolkien, 1967b, p. 117). And Théoden says, "For I fear that already you have come too late, only to see the last days of my house. Not long now shall stand the high hall which Brego son of Eorl built. Fire shall devour the high seat" (Tolkien, 1967b, p. 120). Although Brego is originally the son of Brytta, the remainder of the text remains exactly the same. Yet, in the process of revision, Tolkien makes the story even darker. He had originally intended for Gimli and Gandalf to arrive separately from Aragorn and Legolas. The latter two were to enter the hall and walk up to Théoden. Then he conceived the Beowulfian entry in which the guard challenges the hero and his companions and demands their story. The challenge came in Old English, which Aragorn understood and answered. The addition of the challenge establishes the land as one in such a state of turmoil that security is tight and courtesies have been put aside. In revision, the Old English text was abandoned, except for two phrases.

The original tableau of Théoden includes two fair women and the "wizened figure of a man with a pale wise face" (Tolkien, 1989, p. 444). Théoden speaks the speeches recounting the death of the Second Master of the Mark and the accusations that Gandalf brings only bad news and should be called "Láthspell" (Tolkien, 1989, p. 444). Wormtongue's role emerges only slowly as the drafting proceeds. His enmity to Éomer is not present in the earliest drafts. When Gandalf and Théoden look out from the porch, Gandalf asks Théoden to send for Éomer. At that point, Tolkien conceived the story of the imprisonment; Wormtongue now receives his name Frána, which was not replaced by Gríma until much later.

Tolkien originally intended for Gandalf to update Théoden on the disposition of the original fellowship members. At this stage of the composition, many of their stories were still evolving. In the final version, Gandalf speaks secretly to Théoden and concludes with a reference to the Ringbearer and his fate. Reflecting *Beowulf*'s themes, the idea of hopelessness, finally expressed as "How thin indeed was the thread upon which doom still hung" (Tolkien 1967b, p. 121), persists through all drafts.

With the connection to *Beowulf*, Tolkien now was on firm and familiar ground. Christopher Tolkien notes, "the story as known from *The Two Towers* of the unmasking of Wormtongue, the rehabilitation of Eomer, the meal before departure, the gift of Shadowfax, was achieved almost unhesitatingly" (Tolkien, 1989, p. 446). One major change, however, was the deletion of that second woman standing on the dais.

The second woman was Idis, the daughter of Théoden. In the earlier drafts, actions which might have been hers – serving wine and serving as the governor in the King's absence – seemed to fall to Éowyn. What function Tolkien might have intended for her is unclear, but Éowyn overshadows her in every way. Undoubtedly, the darkness of the tale deepens when Théoden rides off to final battle saying "I have no child. Théodred my son is slain" rather than, "Behold I go forth. I have no son. I name Eomer my sister-son to be my heir" (Tolkien, 1989, p. 451). Indeed, Théodred was slain only five days before; his recent death in a battle against Saruman is poignant indeed, and somewhat underutilized. Tolkien did not really need two women in the story at this point. Éowyn and her brother made a more appealing team for use in the scenes ahead than the daughter Idis did.

In one early draft, Tolkien planned, "Aragorn weds Eowyn sister of Eomer (who becomes Lord of Rohan) and becomes King of Gondor." In another set of undated notes, Tolkien mentions cutting out the love-story of Aragorn and Éowyn because Aragorn is too old and grim. He considers making Éowyn the twin sister of Éomund, a stern amazon woman; this would have made her Théoden's age and not a generation younger. The stern amazon woman idea, though, he maintained from this point on. These notes further forecast that she should die to avenge or save Théoden. Indeed, she does almost die to avenge Théoden, but the appearance of Faramir saves her, for Tolkien now has some plot purpose for her.

The composition of the company riding forth from Rohan to war changed a good bit as the process of revision progressed. In some earlier versions, Merry rides with King Théoden; Éomer and Éowyn as stern amazon accompany him openly. These versions also support the theme of the diversity of peoples required in the fight against evil, but in the end Tolkien selected the device of having Éowyn disguise herself and surreptitiously take Merry along with her to the coming battle. That allows him the effective dramatic surprise of having her reveal herself before the Ringwraith, whose destruction occurs at the hand of a woman and a hobbit, rather than a more traditional hero.

Numerous critics have lambasted *The Lord of the Rings* for the paucity of its love interests, even though love stories have traditionally received little attention in heroic works. Tolkien says, "this tale does not deal with a period of 'Courtly Love' and its pretences; but with a culture more primitive (sc. less corrupt) and nobler" (Tolkien, 1981, p. 324). Those primarily interested in love stories should look elsewhere. Galadriel offered Tolkien an opportunity to make a small sortie into courtly love with Gimli's devotion to the elven woman. Éowyn offers some other avenues for exploration. One of Wormtongue's motives for destroying Théoden is Wormtongue's disgusting lust for Éowyn, but that motive receives much less attention than the betrayal brought about by Saruman's power over Théoden's counsellor.

Even though Tolkien thought Aragorn "too old and lordly and grim" to marry Éowyn, the addition of the love story clearly appealed to him. While he considered letting Éowyn die, he moved ahead with the story and later in 1944 created the character of Faramir. That allowed him to bring the issue of unrequited love into the story, for while Éowyn pines for Aragorn, Faramir pines for her. While this love story is a fairly simple one, it does provide a much needed counterbalance for the dark events of the battles at hand. Later in that year, Tolkien also identified an old and serious mate for Aragorn. He introduces Arwen in the chapter "Dunharrow", in which the elf-lords deliver messages to Aragorn from Elrond and Arwen (the "Lady of Rivendell"). This match is a much higher one, again increasing Aragorn's stature and importance in the story. Further, it allows Tolkien to touch again briefly on two favourite themes from *The Silmarillion* – the love of an immortal for a mortal, and the renunciation of immortality.

Thus, in the revisions to the content of "The King of the Golden Hall" Tolkien continued his practice of making the story darker and more complex. Even though the initial content reflected themes from that dark masterpiece *Beowulf*, the story as it developed became even more sombre. The creation of Wormtongue had the most profound effect. In it, Tolkien illustrated human duplicity, for while Saruman's evil relates back to Sauron, it is also independent from Sauron. Saruman has made evil choices for selfish reasons; he would set himself up as the dark lord if he could. Wormtongue as his pawn engages in evil not out of allegiance to Sauron but out of an inappropriate lust for power. Tolkien quite brilliantly uses these two characters to translate evil right back into the hobbits' own home – the Shire.

Minor Revisions in "The Shadow of the Past"

So far I have looked at passages in which major changes occurred in the direction of the story, but now I want to move to a more confined section and to look at the kinds of minor revisions that were occurring. For this purpose, I have selected a portion of the chapter "The Shadow of the Past," that section in which Gandalf tells Frodo Gollum's story. In *The Fellowship of the Ring*, this passage begins after a space in the text with Frodo saying, "'Gollum!' cried Frodo. 'Gollum? Do you mean that this is the very Gollum-creature that Bilbo met? How loathsome!'", and ends at a text break with Gandalf saying, "But I am afraid there is no possible doubt: he had made his slow, sneaking way, step by step, mile by mile, south, down at last to the Land of Mordor" (Tolkien, 1967a, pp. 63-68).

The text history of this passage is as follows:

- In a note written early in 1938, Tolkien sketches the story ahead saying, "Ring must eventually go back to Maker, or draw you towards it. Rather a dirty trick handing it on?" (Tolkien, 1988, p. 43).
- First version: Also in 1938, Tolkien had three chapters prepared. These chapters included a two-page version of the passage.
- Between the first and second versions of this text, Tolkien wrote a page of "Queries and Alterations." In that exercise, he conceived the idea that this ring was the ruling ring. The text established in the first version is repeated with only minor alterations and two-and-a-half pages of new text are added (Tolkien, 1988, pp. 261-264).
- A third phase seems to have been completed by February 1939 with only few details altered in this passage. However, Tolkien had now changed Bingo's name to Frodo (Tolkien, 1988, pp. 320-321).
- From the end of 1942 until sometime in 1944, Tolkien did not work on the manuscript; he says in the "Foreword" to the second edition, "Foresight had failed and there was no time for thought." Christopher Tolkien labels this fourth phase as a "very substantial rewriting" of Gandalf's discussion of Gollum's motives.

The elements in this four-page passage are divided into these more or less arbitrary several paragraph sections for further discussion:

- Discussion of Gollum as a hobbit and the riddle game
- Gollum's toughness
- The Ring itself
- Gandalf's knowledge
- Gandalf sees Gollum
- Gollum leaves the mountain
- Elves track Gollum East
- Aragorn tracks Gollum

Discussion of Gollum as a hobbit and the riddle game

This nineteen-line passage had its origins in nine lines in the first phase. In it, Bingo's reaction to the idea of Gollum being a hobbit is established. Gandalf argues, as he will continue to do through the phases, that their backgrounds were similar. Bingo's original assessment of Gollum's story is, "How very horrible and sad." By the fourth phase, this has been amended to "How loathsome!" and in a rejoinder Frodo says, "What an abominable idea!" By the fourth phase, the beginning of this passage is almost exactly the same as the published text. Sometime between the fourth phase and the publication, Tolkien reinforced the idea of Frodo's chauvinistic response to Gandalf's assertion that Gollum was a hobbit. He gives Frodo a whole paragraph about hobbits not being the only creatures who do riddles, hobbits not cheating, and Gollum's own evil motives. This addition underlined the expanding theme of the need for all the creatures of Middle-earth to cooperate against the power of Sauron.

Gollum's toughness

Phase one devotes twenty-one lines to this discussion. In Phase two, Gandalf comments to Bingo, "Frightfully wearisome, Bingo, in fact finally tormenting (even if you do not become a Wraith). Only Elves can stand it, and even they fade." The last sentence about the Elves enduring the Ring but fading is removed in the next revision as Tolkien's exploration of the nature of the Ring grew. The final text in *The Fellowship of the Ring* is twenty-eight lines long. Gandalf's explanation of Gollum's state of mind becomes much more fulsome with the wizard exploring more fully Gollum's hobbitness and speculating on Gollum's reaction to

Bilbo. Gandalf retains hope for Gollum's cure. Gollum's internal struggle against the power of the Ring is presented poignantly. The simple description of Gollum's wretchedness has been transformed into a thoughtful discussion of the influence of great evil on a wretched but redeemable creature.

The Ring itself

In the first draft, the next section of text focuses around Bingo's suggestion that Gollum might have given the Ring to the goblins; Gandalf rejects this on the practical grounds that the goblins were already beastly and miserable enough and that it would have been difficult to have an invisible goblin on the loose. This whole discussion will later be reduced to Frodo's line, "Wouldn't an Orc have suited it better?" (Tolkien, 1967a, p. 65).

Already in the first phase the text carries the idea that agency played a part in the Ring's removal from Gollum to Bilbo. In the second phase, that idea becomes clearer with Gandalf uttering the justly famous speech, "I can put it no clearer than by saying that *Bilbo was 'meant' to have the Ring*, and that he perhaps got involved in the Quest of the treasure mainly for that reason." The original ending line of the speech in this version is, "In which case you were meant to have it. Which may (or may not) be a comforting thought" (Tolkien, 1988, p. 262). In the final version, this idea is even more clearly stated, for Tolkien replaces the discussion of Bilbo's involvement with the quest with the simple but expressive phrase, "and *not* by its maker", in phase four. The word "meant" receives the emphasis of italics and the equivocation over Frodo's having the Ring is resolved by the final draft. Gandalf says, "And that may be an encouraging thought" (Tolkien, 1967a, p. 65).

Christopher Tolkien reports that this section was expanded in the third version; at some point before the final publication, Tolkien described the power of the Ring in determining its own fate more clearly in a paragraph beginning, "A Ring of Power looks after itself, Frodo." This addition is excellent in clarifying the situation and fits with Professor Shippey's interpretation of the Ring as a sentient being (Shippey, 1982, p.108).

A paragraph dealing with another power was added to this section at the fourth phase – a Ring trying to return to its master now appears. Between the fourth phase and the final one, Tolkien rearranged the sentences in this area, made them much more succinct, and tied the ideas into concrete examples from the history of the Ring. I suspect that "Of the Rings of Power and the Third Age" might have been composed between phase four and the final version.

Gandalf's knowledge

Frodo questions the source and certainty of Gandalf's knowledge about the Ring beginning in the second phase of the story where many essential elements of this section – the fire writing, the knowledge of the Wise, and the reference to Elven history (Gilgalad and Isildor, not Elendil and Isildur) already appear. In phase two, Gandalf urges Bingo to recall Gollum's first riddle, which he does. Christopher Tolkien remarks in the notes, "It is not very evident what Gandalf had deduced from Gollum's first riddle" (Tolkien, 1988, p. 271). Apparently, J.R.R. Tolkien also found the reference obscure, for in phase four, Gandalf does not ask about it but rather discusses how he pieced the story together from Gollum, from the minds and histories of the creatures of Middle-earth, and from his own logic. In the final version, Gollum's story and Gandalf's logic suffice. All the early versions end with Frodo/Bingo trying to reconcile the account just given with Bilbo's original account. That concern is subsumed into later discussion about why the differences exist.

Gandalf sees Gollum

"You have seen Gollum?" Seeing Gollum illustrates Tolkien's phrase, "This tale grew in the telling" (Tolkien, 1967a, p. 5). Phase two provides the first text for Gandalf's extended forty-four-line account of Gollum's movements between his meeting with Bilbo and his eventual entry into Mordor. In this early account, Gollum thinks he has been misunderstood and ill-treated; he is unwilling to say anything after the Riddle Game. Gollum now believes that he has powerful friends and he knows Bilbo's name. Gandalf quotes his answers to the question about how he came to know Bilbo's name[1]. His cunning, his creeping into Mirkwood, his trail of horrors, and his tracking by the Wood-elves are all present in the original presentation of the story. In fact several lines are precisely the same. In phase three, Frodo's question changes to, "You have seen Gollum!" Tolkien continues to wrestle with the problem of how Gollum came to have the Ring. Sometime after work on the fourth phase, he conceived the idea that the Ring had been associated with a birthday and wrote that across the manuscript. The development of that idea then resolved many of the problems in this section of the manuscript.

The revisions after phase four continued with refinements of words and phrases. Gollum's quotations now refer to his encounter with Bilbo rather than to how he knew Bilbo's name. The account of Gollum's travels is more detailed. We know that he followed Bilbo's trail to Esgaroth and then on towards the Shire, but he turned aside; as Tolkien notes in the final draft, "No, something else drew him away" (Tolkien, 1967a, p. 67).

Only in the final version does Gandalf discuss his mistake in abandoning the search for Gollum because Gandalf still trusted the lore of Saruman. Aragorn, now introduced as "the greatest traveller and huntsman of this age of the world," finds Gollum. The scene ends with the sentence in the first draft, "I have in fact a horrible fancy that he made his slow sneaking way bit by bit to the dark tower, to the Necromancer, the Lord of the Rings. I think that Gollum is very likely the beginning of our present trouble; and that through him the Lord found out where to look for this last and most precious and potent of his Rings." This passage

---

[1] Christopher Tolkien points out that Bilbo tells him in *The Hobbit*.

underwent considerable expansion that allowed it to explain the details of this new interest by the Lord. In the finished version, the section ends dramatically, "But I am afraid there is no possible doubt: he had made his slow, sneaking way, step by step, mile by mile, south, down at last to the Land of Mordor" (Tolkien, 1967a, p. 68). In the following section, the heavy silence includes "no sound of Sam's shears."

In the Foreword to *The Fellowship of the Ring*, Tolkien stated, "this tale grew in the telling" (Tolkien, 1967a, p. 5). This comparison of passages from versions of *The Lord of the Rings* illustrates that statement thoroughly. In instance after instance, ideas are sketched forth only to be filled in and expanded as the tale developed more fully.

References

Shippey, T. A. 1982. *The Road to Middle-earth*. London: George Allen & Unwin.

Tolkien, J. R. R. 1967a. *The Fellowship of the Ring*, second edition. Boston: Houghton Mifflin.

Tolkien, J. R. R. 1967b. *The Two Towers*, second edition. Boston, Houghton Mifflin.

Tolkien, J. R. R. 1981. *The Letters of J.R.R. Tolkien*, ed. Humphrey Carpenter. Boston: Houghton Mifflin.

Tolkien, J. R. R. 1984. "Beowulf: The Monsters and the Critics." *The Monsters and the Critics and Other Essays*, ed. Christopher Tolkien. Boston: Houghton Mifflin.

Tolkien, J. R. R. 1988. *The Return of the Shadow* (*The History of "The Lord Of The Rings"*, part one), ed. Christopher Tolkien. oston: Houghton Mifflin.

Tolkien, J. R. R. 1989. *The Treason of Isengard* (*The History of "The Lord of the Rings"*, part two), ed. Christopher Tolkien. Boston: Houghton Mifflin.

Open Minds, Closed Minds in *The Lord of the Rings*

Christina Scull

Abstract: A study of prejudice and tolerance, from the insularity of the Hobbits of the Shire to the mistrust between the Elves and Dwarves and the very nationalistic outlook of Denethor. This paper will show how some characters grew and became more tolerant, and that Tolkien was sensible enough to realize that only small steps can be taken at a time. It will also consider the unwillingness of some to believe in anything not witnessed with their own senses, thus leading them to discard as legendary much of the wonder of Middle-earth.

Keywords: belief, nationalism, power, prejudice, tolerance

Some time ago I planned a grandiose paper about the importance of the theme of not holding on to power, possessions, preconceived ideas, and so forth, in *The Lord of the Rings*. While reading and making notes I began to realize the importance of open-mindedness as a recurrent theme, coming to the surface again and again in several ways. Tolkien shows many of his characters prejudiced against other races, or having preconceived ideas about them. Some feel the same about others of their own race who live a distance away; and some are so predisposed to consider their own people or city more important than any other, or their own powers and abilities greater than any other person's, that they hardly value others and do not see the need to take other opinions into account. These are common human failings which are as rife as ever today, and Tolkien's underlying plea for more tolerance, for more open-mindedness, is still relevant. We should adopt Treebeard's motto, "Do not be hasty", in forming opinions of others; we should not immediately reject the unknown or alien, but equally we should not assume that all that outwardly seems fair is so. Another aspect of closed minds is the rejection of much ancestral knowledge as legend or as tales fit only for children. Some of Tolkien's characters learn from experience how wrong and stupid these prejudices are, and grow in stature; others refuse to widen their limited vision and have to accept the consequences. Tolkien is not so idealistic as to believe that attitudes in general can be changed overnight, but he does suggest that the example of a few may lead to the gradual erosion of barriers and a greater willingness to question commonly held ideas and values.

Much of the prejudice is only underlying and not active, especially with the Hobbits. In the days before they came to the Shire, the three breeds of Hobbits had contact with other races: the Harfoots with the Dwarves, the Stoors with Men, and the Fallohides with Elves. They learnt much from the Dúnedain who had granted them the Shire, but they always kept to themselves, and after the fall of the North Kingdom they had little contact with anyone outside their own land. They came to distrust the Elves and those who had dealings with them. The miller called the Dwarves who visited Bilbo "outlandish" and referred to Gandalf as "that old wandering conjuror" (Tolkien, 1967a, p. 32). The job of the Bounders was to keep undesirable strangers outside the Shire, and though genuine travellers could use the Great Road, the Hobbits were not interested in hearing news of other places from them.

The Hobbits were equally doubtful about other hobbits, not those of a different breed, but those who lived in a different part of the Shire. In this Tolkien probably intended to reflect the attitudes of inhabitants of the English countryside in the days before travel was common, when areas beyond the next village or market town were considered "foreign" and the people "different". The hobbits in the Ivy Bush thought that those who lived in Buckland were "queer" because they lived on the wrong side of the river, near the Old Forest, and messed about in boats. Lobelia Sackville-Baggins calls Frodo a "Brandybuck" and means it as an insult. The Gaffer tells the Black Rider that "they're queer folks in Buckland" (Tolkien, 1967a, p. 79). We are told that Sam had a natural mistrust of inhabitants of other parts of the Shire. The Shire hobbits referred to those of Bree as Outsiders and considered them dull and uncouth.

Farmer Maggot says that Frodo should not have got himself mixed up with Hobbiton folk: they're queer. Frodo had been caught as a young hobbit, by Maggot, stealing his mushrooms, and had built him up into a figure of fear and avoided him. When Frodo meets him again he realizes that he has been stupid, and that his false picture had led to him missing a good friend.

The hobbits of the Shire, though they do not know it, have long been protected from the outside world by the Rangers. This has enabled them to develop their own peaceful culture but left them with little resource to protect themselves from the ambition of Lotho Sackville-Baggins and the machinations of Saruman and the depredations of the ruffians they imported. The trouble started when Lotho, thinking only of his personal ambition and wanting to dominate the Shire, brought in Men to aid him. He may genuinely have thought the Shire would benefit but he did not consult anyone else. In the same way, Vortigern brought the Anglo-Saxons into Britain, and both Vortigern and Lotho suffered disaster when they could not control those they had invited. The hobbits do little to protect themselves until the four members of the Fellowship return. They need the leadership of those who have grown in wisdom and character through their contacts with the wider world to recover the freedom of the Shire. Even when the intruders are ejected the hobbits are not really interested in what has been happening outside their boundaries. The Cottons are typical: they "asked a few polite questions about their travels, but hardly listened to the answers: they were far more concerned with events in the Shire" (Tolkien, 1967c, p. 291). But since Sam, Merry, and Pippin eventually occupied the three offices in the Shire of Mayor, Master, and Thain, and were also Counsellors of the Northern Kingdom and continued to travel outside the Shire visiting the Northern and Southern capitals of the restored Kingdom, the Shire could not but become gradually more involved in the affairs of the wider world.

The growth in understanding of Merry and Pippin is shown by their conversation in the Houses of Healing:

"We Tooks and Brandybucks, we can't live long on the heights" [said Pippin].

"No," said Merry. "I can't. Not yet, at any rate. But at least, Pippin, we can now see them, and honour them. It is best to love first what you are fitted to love, I suppose: you must start somewhere and have some roots, and the soil of the Shire is deep. Still there are things deeper and higher; and not a gaffer could tend his garden in what he calls peace but for them, whether he knows about them or not. I am glad that I know about them, a little."
(Tolkien, 1967c, p. 146)

Merry and Pippin choose to leave the Shire in their old age and return to Rohan and to Gondor, where they die and their bodies are placed beside that of the King. Frodo, who has mixed Hobbit blood, is aware of Hobbit prejudices. When Lobelia says to him "you're no Baggins – you – you're a Brandybuck!", he says either tactlessly or jokingly to Merry Brandybuck: "That was an insult, if you like" (Tolkien, 1967a, p. 48). There are times when he thinks that the inhabitants of the Shire are too stupid and dull for words, but nonetheless he is willing to leave the Shire and all he loves to save it for them. His words to Gandalf at Rivendell show his prejudice against other races:

We should never have done it without Strider . . . it was Strider that saved us. Yet I was afraid of him at first. Sam never quite trusted him, I think, not at any rate until we met Glorfindel . . . I have become very fond of Strider. Well, *fond* is not the right word. I mean he is dear to me; though he is strange, and grim at times. In fact, he reminds me often of you. I didn't know that any of the Big People were like that. I thought, well, that they were just big, and rather stupid: kind and stupid like Butterbur; or stupid and wicked like Bill Ferny. But then we don't know much about Men in the Shire, except perhaps the Breelanders.
(Tolkien, 1967a, pp. 232-3)

Frodo here is beginning to think for himself, and indeed had made the right decision at Bree to trust Strider when almost everyone else advised against it. But he can still misjudge: Gandalf says that Frodo does not know much about the Breelanders if he thinks old Barliman is stupid.

Both Sam and Frodo learn to be less prejudiced and even to feel pity for their enemies. It is easy to make simplistic judgements, but a greater knowledge of the person or race involved can lead to an understanding of the other's viewpoint and can change attitudes. When he is first told about Gollum, Frodo cannot believe that such a creature is really a Hobbit, and thinks it a pity that Bilbo did not kill him. He does not understand why Gandalf and the Elves have also spared Gollum's life, for he deserves death. He, Frodo, does not pity him. Gandalf says that that is because he has not seen him. Much later, when Frodo meets Gollum, he does pity him and spares him again and again. It takes Sam a long time to feel any sympathy, and his suspicious mind spoils the possibility of Gollum repenting at the Pass of Cirith Ungol; but Sam too spares his life, on Mount Doom, because Sam has himself borne the burden of the Ring, even though only for a short time, and now understands Gollum's suffering. Knowledge leads to understanding and tolerance. And the pity of Frodo and Sam ensures the success of the quest, since Frodo is unable at the last to throw the Ring into the Fire.

Later Frodo also feels pity for Lotho, spares Saruman, and tries to prevent the hobbits from taking vengeance and shedding more blood than is necessary. Sam is less sympathetic to those who had done so much to destroy the Shire, but it was he who felt some empathy for the slain Southron in Ithilien. "He wondered what the man's name was and where he came from; and if he was really evil of heart, or what lies or threats had led him on the long march from his home; and if he would not really rather have stayed there in peace" (Tolkien, 1967b, p. 269). Were his feelings perhaps inspired by the Christmas truces of the First World War, when men discovered that their enemies in the opposing trench were only other humans, with problems and feelings like their own?

Moving out of the Shire we come to Bree where, unusually, two races, Men and Hobbits, lived together amicably, "minding their own affairs in their own ways, but both rightly regarding themselves as necessary parts of the Bree-folk" (Tolkien, 1967a, pp. 161-2). It would appear from this that neither race tried to impose its culture on the other. Tolkien calls the situation at Bree an excellent arrangement. But the Breelanders still see those who are not native to Bree as "other" and "different". Butterbur refers to hobbits from the Shire as "Outsiders" and then corrects himself. He has very little opinion of Strider and no real interest in what he does: "He is one of the wandering folk – Rangers we call them . . . What his right name is I've never heard: but he's known round here as Strider. Goes about at a great pace on his long shanks; though he don't tell nobody what cause he has to hurry. But there's no accounting for East and West, as we say in Bree, meaning the Rangers and the Shire-folk, begging your pardon" (Tolkien, 1967a, pp. 168-9). When the hobbits of the Fellowship return to Bree at the end of the war they find events there have given Butterbur a better appreciation of how the Rangers have protected Bree and of what the Breelanders owe them. Butterbur welcomes the idea of decent respectable folk on the roads – but he does not want them settling nearby: ". . . we don't want no outsiders at Bree, nor near Bree at all. We want to be let alone. I don't want a whole crowd o' strangers camping here and settling there and tearing up the wild country" (Tolkien, 1967c, p. 272). Tolkien is realistic: individuals may grow greatly in understanding, but attitudes of the population in general change only slowly.

The Elves also hold themselves apart. Gildor says that "the Elves have their own labours and their own sorrows, and they are little concerned with the ways of hobbits, or of any other creatures upon earth" (Tolkien, 1967a, p. 94). Lindir in Rivendell does not see much difference between Hobbits and Men: "It is not easy for us to tell the difference between two mortals . . . To sheep other sheep no doubt appear different . . . Or to shepherds. But Mortals have not been our study. We have other business" (Tolkien, 1967a, p. 249). The Elven realm of Lórien is closely guarded, and few from outside, of any race, are allowed to enter. Yet Elves, especially Gildor, Glorfindel, and Galadriel, do help the hobbits and the Fellowship. Great help is also given by Elrond, who is a descendant of alliances of Elf and Man which played such a significant part in the History of the First Age. Rivendell is a place where all races are made to feel welcome. It is not that the Elves do not care about other races, but that they work on a different level, on a different time-scale because of their immortality. But they are willing to sacrifice much that they love if the power of Sauron may be ended.

Perhaps the greatest reconciliation theme in the book is the growing friendship of Legolas the Elf and Gimli the Dwarf, whose races had mistrusted each other since the Dwarves sacked the Elvish stronghold of Menegroth in the First Age. Again Tolkien is realistic and does not suggest a miraculous rapprochement of the two races, but that through the friendship of Legolas and Gimli their peoples may begin to understand each other better. We can also see that Elven attitudes differ, even before their friendship grows, in the contrast of the welcomes given by Galadriel and by Celeborn. At the Council of Elrond, Gimli's father Glóin is annoyed to hear that the Wood-elves have shown more tenderness to Gollum than they did to the Dwarves. Gimli and Legolas do not show any open hostility to each other as they travel with the Fellowship but there is tension under the surface. When Gandalf refers to the "happier days, when there was still close friendship at times between folk of different race, even between Dwarves and Elves" (Tolkien, 1967a, p. 316), each is quick to declare that it was not the fault of his race that the friendship waned. Again, when Legolas refers to sorrow coming to Lothlórien when Dwarves awoke evil under the mountain, Gimli quickly defends his people. They find that Dwarves are not welcome in Lórien, and Gimli objects to being blindfolded. Legolas comments: "A plague on Dwarves and their stiff necks!" (Tolkien, 1967a, p. 362). Gimli says, a little maliciously, that he is willing to be blindfolded if Legolas shares his fate, and the dispute is solved only when Aragorn, showing good judgement, suggests that the whole company be blindfolded. Legolas sums up the sadness of the situation: "Alas for the folly of these days! Here all are enemies of the one Enemy, and yet I must walk blind, while the sun is merry in the woodland under leaves of gold!" (Tolkien, 1967a, p. 362). Haldir comments: "Indeed in nothing is the power of the Dark Lord more clearly shown than in the estrangement that divides all those who still oppose him" (Tolkien, 1967a, p. 362).

Celeborn welcomes Gimli as the first Dwarf to be allowed into Lórien for many years, and hopes that it is a sign that in the present darkness of the world better days are at hand. He repents his welcome when he hears of the Balrog, but Galadriel, who is a Noldorin Elf with a greater understanding and appreciation of Dwarves, intervenes and welcomes Gimli with words that change his attitudes forever. She smiles at him, and he "looked up and met her eyes; and it seemed to him that he looked suddenly into the heart of an enemy and saw there love and understanding" (Tolkien, 1967a, p. 371). From that moment he gave his heart to her and loved her in a way that echoes the courtly love of the Middle Ages. And because he loves her, he loves her people and wants to bring reconciliation between Dwarves and Elves. When she asks him what he would do with the strand of her hair that he had requested, he says: "Treasure it, Lady, in memory of your words to me at our first meeting. And if ever I return to the smithies of my home, it shall be set in imperishable crystal to be an heirloom of my house, and a pledge of good will between the Mountain and the Wood until the end of days" (Tolkien, 1967a, p. 392). The gift that Galadriel grants to him is one that she had refused Fëanor, the greatest of the Noldor.

From that time on, friendship grows between Gimli and Legolas, and they become almost inseparable, praising each other and having a friendly rivalry during the battle of Helm's Deep. Their friendship is greater than their prejudices and fears, for each agrees to visit places of interest to the other, even though he fears them. Legolas even concedes that for the first time, a Dwarf had won a contest for words, for he cannot match Gimli in describing the Caves of Aglarond as well as they deserve. It is Gimli, rather than Legolas, who defends Galadriel from the aspersions cast on her by the Rohirrim. Yet he shows that he realizes that others are entitled to their opinions when he accepts Éomer's preference of the beauty of Arwen to that of Galadriel. When Legolas departs over the Sea, Gimli goes with him because of their great friendship and because he wishes once more to see the beauty of Galadriel.

An example of a persecuted race is the Woses. The

Rohirrim call them the Wild Men of the Woods, and it seems that at times they have been hunted and treated as animals, since they reject rich rewards for their aid in the War of the Ring and ask only that if the Rohirrim are victorious they leave them alone and no longer hunt them like beasts. After the war, Aragorn confirms the promise by giving Druadan Forest to Ghân-buri-Ghân and his folk forever and forbidding Men to enter it without their leave.

Aragorn, a Man with some Elvish blood who was fostered by Elrond Half-elven and taught by Elves, and who has travelled widely in Middle-earth and served both in Rohan and Gondor, has few prejudices, but for good reasons takes his time to decide about the hobbits. Even when he has decided that they are friends, he at first underestimates them – though that is not entirely surprising, considering their unwise behaviour at the Inn. He is surprised by Merry's courage in following the Black Rider, even though he comments that the action was foolish. At Weathertop he admits that Frodo is made of sterner stuff than he had guessed. His final love and appreciation of the hobbits is evident in his remark as Merry rides away with Théoden and Éomer: "There go three that I love, and the smallest not the least. He knows not to what end he rides; yet if he knew, he still would go on" (Tolkien, 1967c, p. 53). And his real understanding of them is shown in the fraught atmosphere of the Houses of Healing, when he realizes that light words such as hobbits would use themselves would be more suitable than solemn speeches.

At the Council of Elrond, when Boromir lauds the part played by Gondor in protecting the rest of Middle-earth and remarks on the grudging thanks they get, Aragorn points out that the Rangers, his people, do as much but do not expect praise and thanks, and accept that their care must be kept secret if simple folk are to remain simple. Aragorn and his folk do have a pride in their race, but they do not carry it to excess, and they accept the obligations that go with it as a duty to be carried out regardless of thanks or praise. Nationalism seems far less developed in the North than it is in the South. Théoden shows how nationalism can lead to suspicion and rejection of those from outside in times of tension. The companions are told: "It is the will of Théoden King that none should enter his gates, save those who know our tongue and are our friends. None are welcome here in days of war but our own folk, and those that come from Mundburg in the land of Gondor" (Tolkien, 1967b, pp. 112-13). When Théoden has been cured by Gandalf of his suspicion and hostility, he changes dramatically and becomes courteous and welcoming to all he meets, including Ents, Hobbits, and Woses, and real affection grows between him and Merry, leading to firm links between the Mark and the Shire. His mind which had been closed is now open.

Treebeard seems to be one of the most fair-minded of the characters in *The Lord of the Rings*. He thinks deeply and avoids making hasty decisions. Yet after he has sung the Elven song about the Ents and Entwives, which seems to present each side equally, he can't resist saying: "I daresay it is fair enough. But the Ents could say more on their side, if they had time!" (Tolkien, 1967b, p. 81). I wonder, if the Ents and the Entwives had met again, if they would have had any more success living together.

An interesting comparison can be made of the attitudes of Faramir, Boromir, and Denethor to personal power and to their native city. Faramir has always yielded place to his elder brother and has no great personal ambitions. He quite happily yields the Stewardship to the returning King. He easily avoids the temptation of the Ring and realizes that the ends achieved by using the Enemy's weapon will not be worth it. He wants the city he loves to be free, but has no ambitions for her to have world dominion:

> For myself, I would see the White Tree in flower again in the courts of the kings, and the Silver Crown return, and Minas Tirith in peace: Minas Anor again as of old, full of light, high and fair, beautiful as a queen among other queens: not a mistress of many slaves, nay, not even a kind mistress of willing slaves . . . I would have her loved for her memory, her ancientry, her beauty, and her present wisdom. Not feared, save as men may fear the dignity of a man, old and wise.
> (Tolkien, 1967b, p. 280)

Boromir also loves Minas Tirith, but admires her mainly for her role in the forefront of the battle against the Enemy. Unlike Faramir, he seems to enjoy fighting for its own sake and the glory he earns by it. Faramir judges his brother well: "If it were a thing that gave advantage in battle, I can well believe that Boromir, the proud and fearless, often rash, ever anxious for the victory of Minas Tirith (and his own glory therein), might desire such a thing and be allured by it" (Tolkien, 1967b, pp. 279-80). Boromir shows his feelings clearly at the Council of Elrond, saying that Minas Tirith alone holds back the Dark Lord and does not get the praise and help it deserves. He interprets everything in relation to Minas Tirith. "Is then the doom of Minas Tirith come at last?" he asks (Tolkien, 1967a, p. 260). It is he who suggests using the Ring against Sauron, and although he seems to accept the decision of the Council, he never really understands, and is tempted by the Ring. He is convinced that he would not succumb to its evil, and his words to Frodo on Amon Hen show his underlying prejudice in favour of the Men of Gondor. "These elves and half-elves and wizards, they would come to grief perhaps. Yet often I doubt if they are wise and not merely timid . . . True-hearted Men, they will not be corrupted" (Tolkien, 1967a, p. 414). He never outgrows his early suspicions of Galadriel. When he cannot persuade Frodo, he tries to use force. Nonetheless he is a loyal comrade for most of the journey south, repents his attack on Frodo, and dies defending Merry and Pippin. His love of Minas Tirith and desire to save her were the main causes of his fall, and his desire for personal glory only a contributory factor. He does not seem to have resented Aragorn, and Faramir judges that he would have reverenced him if he were convinced of his claim, though he might have seen him as a rival as war leader. The implication is that Boromir might not have minded giving up the Stewardship but would have resented losing the supreme command of the armies. But I think that if Boromir could have saved Minas Tirith only by giving up everything he would have made that sacrifice.

Denethor equates himself with Minas Tirith. He is not willing to surrender the Stewardship to a returning king and justifies his decision by denigrating the line of Isildur. He is not a man to consider his allies as equals or to be able to appreciate a wider policy, or to see that anything beyond Minas Tirith is worth saving. This should be contrasted with the willingness of the Elves to consider the greater good, and with Gandalf's statement that he too is a steward and will not utterly have failed in his task if anything fair survives. Denethor's view is: "Yet the Lord of Gondor is not to be made the tool of other men's purposes, however worthy. And to him there is no purpose higher in the world as it now stands than the good of Gondor" (Tolkien, 1967c, p. 30). Love of native land or city, the desire to defend it against an aggressor, is not of itself bad, but for Denethor it seems to be as much because Gondor belongs to him as because he really loves it. When it seems likely that no heir will survive him to continue his house, he abandons the defence of the city and thinks only of his own grief. He seeks death, and not a death useful to Minas Tirith, defending it on the battlefield, but a wasted death also killing his son. His mind is so taken up with self-love and love of the power of his office that he can see nothing else, and if he cannot have what he wants he will have nothing. We also know that as a young man he had resented the military success of the disguised Aragorn. His vision is so much narrower than that of Beregond, who says that "Gondor shall not perish yet. Not though the walls be taken by a reckless foe that will build a hill of carrion before them. There are still other fastnesses, and secret ways of escape into the mountains. Hope and memory shall live still in some hidden valley where the grass is green" (Tolkien, 1967c, p. 39).

Three times in the story a very important theme occurs, of judging for oneself and not obeying orders blindly. These passages were written well before the end of the Second World War and the trials for war crimes when the defence was often that the accused was just obeying orders. But they show Tolkien's interest in the important issue of whether blind obedience should prevail over personal responsibility. Éomer goes without his king's leave to waylay the orcs, and he should have taken the Three Hunters back to Meduseld since the law of Rohan forbade strangers to wander in the land without permission from the king. Éomer chooses to put his own life at risk and not only lets them go freely but lends them horses. Aragorn's reply to his query as to how men should judge in such times makes Tolkien's own feeling plain: "As he ever has judged. Good and ill have not changed since yesteryear; nor are they one thing among Elves and Dwarves and another among Men. It is a man's part to discern them, as much in the Golden Wood as in his own house" (Tolkien, 1967b, p. 41). Similarly, Faramir decides to judge for himself and not obey orders to slay all he finds in Ithilien without the leave of the Lord of Gondor. He spares and helps Frodo, Sam, and Gollum. How might the quest have fared if Éomer or Faramir had not acted so? Pippin and Beregond disobey Denethor and save the life of Faramir. The blind obedience of Denethor's other servants who would have burnt Faramir is not a virtue.

A very unfortunate example of racial prejudice led to the first decline of Gondor. The kinstrife that resulted when Valacar took a wife not of Númenórean descent led to bitter fighting and the destruction of Osgiliath and the lasting enmity of Umbar. The marriage came about because Valacar's father had sought greater friendship with other races of Men and sent his son to live in the North for some years. Later, after the failing of the royal house, the earlier Stewards also sought alliances with non-Númenóreans. This strengthened Gondor even if the Númenórean blood ran less true in Gondor thereafter. It did show that they had learnt from the past. The Dúnedain of the North did not make such alliances and preserved their racial purity, but at the cost of becoming very diminished in numbers.

Tolkien depicts his "good" leaders showing mercy to all but Orcs. The Rohirrim spare the Dunlendings on condition they take an oath not to pass the Fords of Isen. The Dunlendings are amazed, for they have been told that the Rohirrim were cruel and would burn them alive. Aragorn pardons those who surrendered and made peace, and gives the lands about Lake Núrnen to the slaves of Mordor that he has released. The only exception, one that has worried many readers of Tolkien and has been much criticized, is that no mercy is ever shown to Orcs. Indeed, killing Orcs seems to be regarded as good in itself, whereas regret is shown on occasion for enemies of other races who are slain. Tolkien was aware of possible criticism, but nothing has been published which satisfactorily accounts for a race that seems to be considered irredeemably evil.[1] Tolkien wrote in a letter to Naomi Mitchison that Elves "represent really Men with greatly enhanced aesthetic and creative faculties" (Tolkien, 1981, p. 176). Perhaps, without approaching too near to allegory, Orcs might be considered to represent the evil aspects of human nature which have to be destroyed if the Good is to prevail. But I do not want to press that, and I admit that the Orcs remain an exception to Tolkien's usual pleas for mercy and tolerance and sympathy for others, whether of one's own race or not.

Another way in which narrowness of mind can be shown is a refusal to believe in anything that lies outside one's personal experience, often denigrating it by calling it not true, just a legend or tale for children, or mistrusting it if its existence can no longer be denied. Ted Sandyman does not believe in dragons or walking trees, though we know that they do exist in Tolkien's world. It is probably his lack of wonder that leads to Ted actually welcoming the industrialization of the Shire. Sam has his fair share of Hobbit prejudices, but he thinks that there is something in legends, and he wants to meet Elves. The Men in the South who have little contact with Elves seem to distrust them: Boromir does not want to enter Lórien; Éomer remarks, "Then there is a Lady in the Golden Wood, as old tales tell! Few escape her nets, they say" (Tolkien, 1967b, p. 35);

---

[1] But see *Morgoth's Ring* (1993), published subsequent to the first presentation of this paper.

Wormtongue refers to Galadriel as the Sorceress of the Golden Wood and says that "webs of deceit were ever woven in Dwimordene" (Tolkien, 1967b, p. 118). But Éomer later asks pardon for his rash words, thus showing that when he has thought, he realizes that he has no real knowledge. Faramir says that "in Middle-earth Men and Elves became estranged in the days of darkness, by the arts of the Enemy, and by the slow changes of time in which each kind walked further down their sundered roads. Men now fear and misdoubt the Elves, and yet know little of them" (Tolkien, 1967b, p. 288). Again mistrust is seen as the result of evil and fostered by lack of contact. We should be more outward-looking and not turn inwards. Yet even Faramir says that it is perilous to have dealings with the Golden Wood.

Elves also know less as they have less contact. Celeborn warns the Fellowship against Fangorn Forest, and Treebeard says that Celeborn must be "falling rather behind the world" (Tolkien, 1967b, p. 70); yet he admits that had they been going the other way he would probably have warned them against Lórien. Boromir dismisses Ents as old wives' tales, and even Aragorn is surprised to find that they really exist: "Then there is truth in the old legends about the dwellers in the deep forests and the giant shepherds of the trees? Are there still Ents in the world? I thought they were only a memory of ancient days, if indeed they were ever more than a legend of Rohan" (Tolkien, 1967b, p. 102). Théoden is also surprised to see the Ents and to realize how narrow has been the perspective of the Rohirrim:

> Ents! Out of the shadows of legend I begin a little to understand the marvel of the trees, I think. I have lived to see strange days. Long we have tended our beasts and our fields, built our houses, wrought our tools, or ridden away to help in the wars of Minas Tirith. And that we called the life of Men, the way of the world. We cared little for what lay beyond the borders of our land. Songs we have that tell of these things, but we are forgetting them, teaching them only to children, as a careless custom.
> (Tolkien, 1967b, p. 155)

Halflings are also only a little people in old songs and children's tales for the Rohirrim. Théoden welcomes all these races new to him and establishes good and warm relations. In Minas Tirith the healers have also forgotten much lore and think the rhyme about *athelas* only doggerel.

In "On Fairy-Stories" Tolkien regretted the relegation of legends and fairy tales to the attic and to the nursery. In *The Lord of the Rings* he shows how foolish this is. As a philologist he would have known how much of human history can be deduced from the evolution of language and that various studies were proving that some aspects of many legends could be authenticated. The late nineteenth century was also a time of archaeological discovery which often showed that there were some true elements in old poems and tales. Since Schliemann's finds at Troy and Mycenae, no longer are the poems of Homer thought entirely false to the period they claim to describe. We still have no real proof that King Arthur ever existed, but archaeology does show that the Saxon advance was stopped and reversed for some time, and it may be that the leader who achieved this provided the foundation for the stories of Arthur.

Tolkien shows Evil as having a very narrow outlook. Saruman seeks his own aggrandizement and will overlook any evil that is necessary to achieve what he wants. He will not repent even when a prisoner in Orthanc. As Gandalf says, he has withered altogether. Sauron in his search for world domination has an even narrower outlook: "the only measure that he knows is desire, desire for power; and so he judges all hearts. Into his heart the thought will not enter that any will refuse it, that having the Ring we may seek to destroy it" (Tolkien, 1967a, pp. 282-3). Galadriel says that she perceives the Dark Lord's mind but that he cannot see her thought. The quest succeeds because Sauron, even when he knows that the Ring is being brought south, assumes that it is being taken to Minas Tirith so that the new Ring Lord can challenge him. "That we should wish to cast him down and have *no* one in his place is not a thought that occurs to his mind", says Gandalf. "That we should try to destroy the Ring itself has not yet entered into his darkest dream" (Tolkien, 1967b, p. 100). So Sauron takes no special measures to prevent anyone entering Mordor, and the Ring is eventually destroyed.

Open-mindedness is as relevant in our world as it is in Tolkien's Middle-earth. So many of our problems have their source in intolerance, nationalism, and closed minds. But the popularity of Tolkien's writings in so many countries has contributed to breaking barriers and uniting his devotees across international boundaries.

References

Tolkien, J.R.R. 1981. *Letters of J. R. R. Tolkien*, ed. Humphrey Carpenter with the assistance of Christopher Tolkien. London: George Allen & Unwin.

Tolkien, J.R.R. 1967a. *The Fellowship of the Ring*, Second edition, revised second printing. London: George Allen & Unwin.

Tolkien, J.R.R. 1967b. *The Two Towers*, Second edition, revised second printing. London: George Allen & Unwin.

Tolkien, J.R.R. 1967c. *The Return of the King*, Second edition, revised second printing. London: George Allen & Unwin.

Tolkien, J.R.R. 1993. *Morgoth's Ring*, ed. Christopher Tolkien. London: HarperCollinsPublishers.

Section four

The Silmarillion

Historical Bias in the Making of *The Silmarillion*

Alex Lewis

Abstract: Biases due to the point of view from which *The Silmarillion* is narrated are discussed. These biases are compared with those found in primary world histories.

Keywords: bias, histories, *The Silmarillion*

The Silmarillion, published some four years after the death of its author J.R.R. Tolkien, was the piecing together of tales that spanned half a century of single-minded writing effort (Tolkien, 1979a, pp. 7-9). Critics have hailed the achievement as the creative equivalent of a whole people (Ezard, 1977, p.16), and indeed it is a complex and many stranded work spanning a vast timescale whose complexity has baffled fans and sometimes thwarted some readers' attempts to penetrate it. But always it has proven itself worth the effort as it contains some of Tolkien's greatest writings and his most powerful tales and descriptions.

However, being as complex and long-viewed as this means that we can regard it in much the same way as a "history book". Indeed, it is written as a history book, and – as the saying goes – history is always written by the victors. In this sense I believe that Tolkien incorporated into *The Silmarillion* – either intuitively or on purpose – the kinds of bias and one-sided reporting of events that occurs naturally within the course of real history. It is perhaps for this reason that *The Silmarillion* is such a powerful and compelling work, because it approximates "real history" in subtle ways rather than merely telling a catalogue of events in shopping-list fashion. Within *The Silmarillion*, Tolkien does give us a clue that perhaps he intended this bias to exist all along, for (Tolkien, 1979b, p. 123) it is admitted that *The Silmarillion* is incomplete and "only a part is here told of the deeds of those days, and most is said of the Noldor, and the Silmarils, and the mortals that became entangled in their fate."

In this paper I wish to examine the internal biases within the story framework and try and uncover the nature of this "political bias" in *The Silmarillion* – that is to say "political" merely within the confines of the world *in which the work is set*, and not within the primary world context. I believe this to be a worthwhile exercise since just as with real history, there are characters who are portrayed as being essentially just and good, on whose side the reader would ally himself, and there are also characters who are portrayed as essentially unreliable or even evil and whom the reader is expected to have little if any sympathy with. To have some idea for the reasons behind the portrayals and which characters fit into this will give us a glimpse into the political dynamics within the intricate world that Tolkien created in *The Silmarillion*.

The first question that must be asked is: who wrote *The Silmarillion*? By this I do not mean the primary world author, but instead the internal authorship of the work as we read it and as Tolkien intended it. Christopher Tolkien explains in *The Book of Lost Tales, part 1* that the three volumes bound in red leather that Bilbo carried back to the Shire and which were his "translations from the elvish" must have been *The Silmarillion*, and was possibly the device that J.R.R. Tolkien might have used to introduce the reader familiar with Middle-earth and the Third Age into the vast expanse of the earlier years and histories (Tolkien, 1985, pp. 5-6).

So the physical chronicler of *The Silmarillion* within the tale is Bilbo Baggins. It is said that Frodo did not use these writings much as they did not concern the events of the War of the Ring. Bilbo is said to have used all the authorities both written and living within Rivendell to write his work. Let us examine what these sources might have been and their possible affiliations in the context of Middle-earth.

Most obviously there is Elrond. Looking into Elrond's family tree, we know that his mother and father were Elwing and Eärendil (see table 1). Eärendil's parents were Tuor and Idril and Idril's parent who appears within the tales is Turgon of Gondolin. Turgon's father was Fingolfin whose mother was Indis, a Vanya. It is interesting to note that none of the elvish side of the family are Fëanorians and that Fëanor had a different mother to his two half-brothers Fingolfin and Finarfin. Lúthien's parents were Thingol and Melian. At Melian we stop, but with Thingol we once more have someone who is not a Noldo and more significantly not connected to the Fëanorians. The first strand of possible bias thus comes into play: Fëanorians are not very closely related to Elrond and therefore would tend to receive little sympathetic treatment from him. It is to be seen whether one can trace a correlation of any sort between the treatment of characters and their relationship to Elrond through bloodlines.

Then we have Glorfindel who was in Rivendell during Bilbo's stay (Tolkien, 1974a, p. 218). All we know of him is that he was once of Gondolin but he died and returned in the Third Age to Rivendell. He too has no known connection

Table 1: Elrond's Family Tree

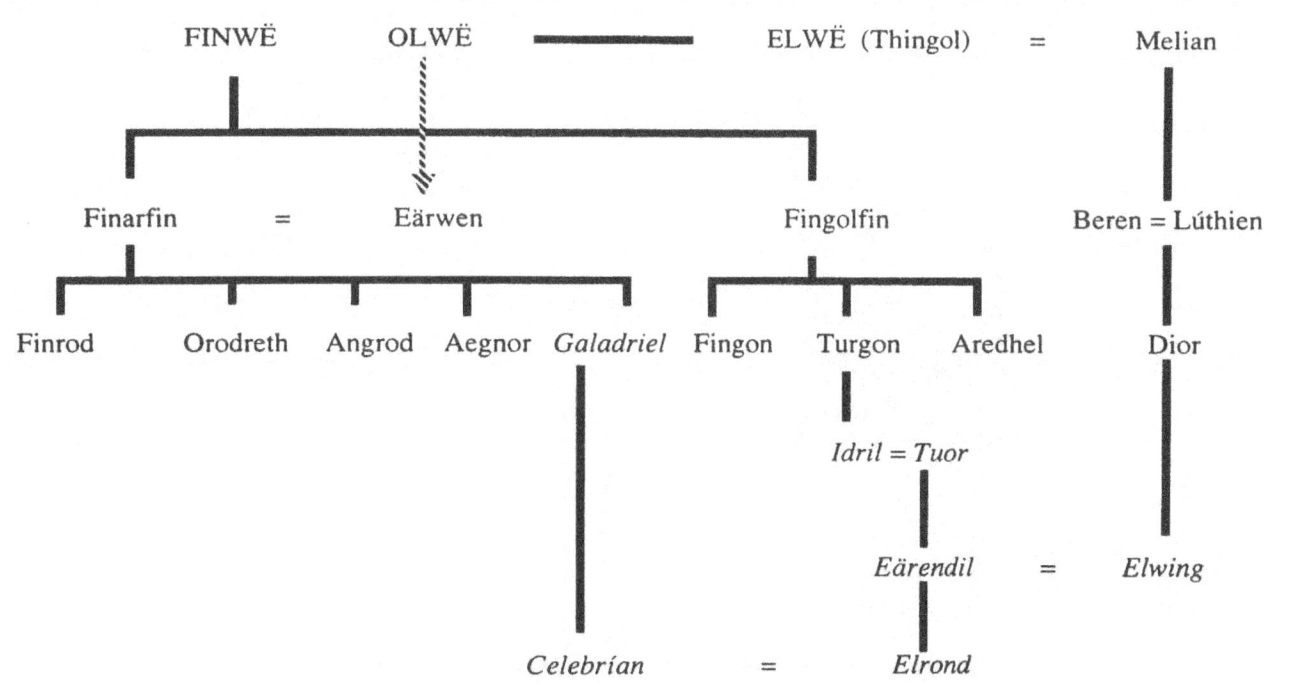

Those in italics would have been known personally by Elrond

with the Fëanorians, belonging as he does to Turgon's people who marched from Vinyamar to Gondolin and built the hidden city.

Erestor we know little about other than that he is one of Elrond's people. Being a loremaster he is most likely to be a Noldo, and he would be expected to follow Elrond's "political leanings" as he was closely influenced by his lord.

Galadriel may also have been a source – though not a very strong one from Bilbo's viewpoint. *The Silmarillion* betrays a singular paucity of information regarding her. She lived in Lórien and seldom came to Rivendell, and Bilbo met her rarely. She was also not of the Fëanorians and is said to have been at odds with Fëanor (Tolkien, 1982b, p. 230).

Elrond's daughter Arwen may have been a source of information for Bilbo's writings. She would have been in Rivendell during some of the time that Bilbo lived there. He knew her, from what he says to Frodo on his arrival (Tolkien, 1974a, p. 224). Again it can be reasonably assumed that she too would follow her father's views in historical/political matters.

Non-elvish sources are more difficult to determine. For mortals we probably can suspect only Aragorn whom Bilbo knew very well and who it would be guessed might follow the thoughts of Elrond since he was in love with Elrond's daughter and was brought up in Rivendell and taught by him too. Gandalf the wizard may have been a source for Bilbo, though I would imagine that he was not a very important one. He was close and did not speak much about important things and usually treated Bilbo in a kind though patronising way; for he was not the more worldly-wise Hobbit that Frodo turned into and to whom Gandalf would make statements of a deeper nature.[1] Also Gandalf's time was that of the Third Age – as he himself tells us (Tolkien, 1974c, p. 220). His knowledge of the earlier times would have been second-hand as he did not become involved with Middle-earth history in earlier Ages. However, his influence may have been crucial in one respect for giving a balance to Fëanor's case, since Gandalf obviously demonstrated a high regard for Fëanor's creativity as he spoke of the Palantír of Orthanc and how through it he might see Fëanor at work (Tolkien, 1974b, p. 181).

So *The Silmarillion* as we receive it is at least third-hand information, usually fourth- and sometimes even more (see table 2) – from the original person who experienced events or some intermediary, to one of the above and then to Bilbo, who was either good at shorthand or had a phenomenal memory. The only parts that can be said to be more closely reported are those told by Elrond concerning his own adventures (see table 2), and the brief telling of the Gondolin tale that Glorfindel might have talked to Bilbo about, though the bareness of that tale as told would indicate that Glorfindel spoke little to Bilbo about Gondolin. Perhaps it was too painful for him to recall it.

I would hypothesise that much as Galadriel was under a ban of exile but passed her test by refusing the One Ring and was allowed to go to the West (Tolkien, 1981, p. 386), Elrond's task was to pass on his knowledge to others so that it would not die out when he left Middle-earth. He had chosen to be of the Firstborn and yet remained in Middle-earth when elves were returning to the West. It is not clear

---

[1] Gandalf says, "You are old enough, and perhaps wise enough" (Tolkien, 1974a, p. 42).

Table 2: Handing down of story to Bilbo

Ch. 1 and 2	Story of Valar	nth hand
Ch. 3 and 4	Elwë Thingol and Melian	6th hand
Ch. 5 and 6	Princes of Noldor and Chaining Melkor	5th hand
Ch. 7	Fëanor banned	5th hand
Ch. 8	Melkor and Ungoliant	nth hand
Ch. 9	Darkening of Valinor	5th hand
Ch. 10	The Sindar	5th hand
Ch. 11 and 12	Sun and Moon, Men awaken	nth hand
Ch. 13	Noldor return, Battle under Stars	5th hand
Ch. 14	Beleriand and realms	5th hand
Ch. 15	Turgon and Ulmo, Gondolin built, Melian and Galadriel	nth, 4th and 3rd hand
Ch. 16 and 17	Maeglin, Of Men	4th hand
Ch. 18	Battle of Sudden flame, Fingolfin's death	nth and 4th hand
Ch. 19	Beren and Lúthien	5th and nth hand
Ch. 20	Fifth Battle: Nirnaeth	5th and nth hand
Ch. 21	Túrin's Tale including Mîm's story	5th and nth hand
Ch. 22	Húrin's journey, Thingol's death, Dior's death	nth and 3rd hand
Ch. 23	Tuor's story	4th and 3rd hand
Ch. 24	Eärendil's journeys and War of Wrath	nth, 2nd & 3rd hand

just how far his actions were sanctioned and whether the ban covered him too. His family line contains people who did fall under that ban (Tolkien, 1981, p. 407).

Therefore it can be concluded that *The Silmarillion* is essentially an elvish viewpoint of the world and its history, and of the kindred of the elves it is essentially Noldorin but distinctly anti-Fëanorian. I shall give examples that support this conclusion below.

Looking to the text of *The Silmarillion* and the events described there, we can see an immediate drawing up of camps of good/light versus evil/darkness (Tolkien, 1979b, p. 41). This is quite classical practice in historical texts and has been carried out by peoples from the earliest days (see for instance David and Goliath in *The Old Testament*, Shakespeare's treatment of *Richard the Third* and historical texts concerning the War of the Roses, and even today propaganda directed at Saddam Hussein during the Gulf War that has been proved false, such as the babies in the hospital incubators story (BBC, 1992)). This is not to suggest that a fictional history should seek to do anything other than what real life does – quite the opposite – nor to suggest that Melkor was not the "Black Foe of the World" as he was dubbed, but that the mechanism for polarisation is already established in the first pages of the work, and that colours the reader's attitude towards each party thereafter.

Melkor's inability to create but only mimic is something that needs to be looked at in the context of what the Valar as a whole were capable of. The Valar may create *if their actions are sanctioned by Eru*. Yavanna made the Ents and growing things and Aulë made the dwarves. Melkor was said to be the most powerful of the Valar (Tolkien, 1979b, p. 28) and that even his contribution is "part of the whole and tributary to its glory" (Tolkien, 1979b, p. 18). Eru explains to Ulmo that without Melkor's influence snow and ice and steam and clouds might not have come to pass (Tolkien, 1979b, p. 20). Therefore Melkor represents a balance or dynamic that allows Arda to work and develop. He is essential to the genesis of the whole story of the Noldorin elves as are his "creations": orcs, dragons, trolls and so on. It is *The Silmarillion* that tells us that orcs are elves that were stolen and twisted; it is something the reader takes as a given fact. Melkor and the Orcs might have told a different story.

Of course elves would not have viewed Melkor's role in Arda in a positive way as needed balance, and thus their portrayal of Melkor is as an evil to be got rid of. Tolkien has the elves possessing limited knowledge within his sub-created world and therefore the decisions they take and conclusions they come to are subject to those restrictions. This is a normal mechanism for an author to use for characters within a book.

There are three themes of Eru. Men are a necessary part of Arda, the second-comers. But during the Ages of the Trees only Valinor had light. Middle-earth was dark and the Firstborn came into being seeing only stars. The Valar persuaded them to come and live in the light of Valinor; they did not instead spread the light beyond their realm to all of Middle-earth. They were in effect acting *possessively* to the light. The elves who didn't heed the call to go to Valinor are dismissed from consideration as "Moriquendi". Yet we know from when the Noldor returned to Middle-earth that those elves that had remained behind were well organised and lived in peace for much of the time (Tolkien, 1979b, p. 107). Even the Teleri are mildly reprimanded for their lack of steadfastness (Tolkien, 1979b, p. 71) whereas the Vanyar (Elrond's ancestry contains Vanyar blood from Indis) are exalted as being elvish perfection (Tolkien, 1979b, p. 69). When Melkor was imprisoned elves lived in bliss in Valinor, but beyond, it was not possible for mortal men to arise since the sun and moon had not yet risen (Tolkien, 1979b, p. 122). These lights that shone equally upon all the lands of Arda were needed by mortal men. Therefore it can be said that the demise of the Two Trees was a necessary part of Eru's plans in order to allow light to reach all of Arda for the arising of the Second-comers. Indeed, Fëanor's words (Tolkien, 1979b, p. 97) are as follows: "Here once was light, that the Valar begrudged to Middle-earth, but now dark levels all . . ." In this there is the germ of truth about the Valar's use of light in Arda, but it is presented as Fëanor's folly of the darkness of his heart speaking. Once more, we have evidence of a political slant to events that give *The Silmarillion* a realism far removed from mere contrivance.

The elvish centricity of *The Silmarillion* can be seen in the description of death as the "gift of Ilúvatar". Elves do not understand death; it does not affect them, therefore they can be philosophical about it. Men have not the same viewpoint and are always described as being coarse and imperfect. Yet at the last Arwen describes death as she sees Aragorn die:[2] Now at last an understanding of death comes to the deathless.

With the enslavement of Melkor by the Valar we have the first political statement. *The Silmarillion* is at pains to point out that elves had no part in the battle to enslave Melkor and thus his blame of them for causing his downfall is unjust (Tolkien, 1979b, p. 59). Thereafter, propaganda against Fëanor and his sons begins, showing Fingolfin and Finarfin to be reasonable sons of Finwë, and Fëanor to be hot-headed and impetuous. Finwë is painted as a fairly neutral character, misguided perhaps in his love for his eldest son (Tolkien, 1979b, p. 75). This fits in with the pattern of Elrond's ancestry, Finwë being a direct ancestor of his as are Fingolfin and Finarfin, but Fëanor is less directly related. Even though Elrond through Bilbo has to admit that Fëanor was the greatest of the Noldor, there is a definite attempt to show that even his greatest creations were not his own – the Silmarils were jewels made with the light of the Two Trees, i.e. they came of Yavanna, a point driven home at the time of their darkening by Tulkas: "And did not the light of the Silmarils come from her work in the beginning?" (Tolkien, 1979b, p. 91). The argument between Fëanor and his half-brothers is shown as a completely black and white situation, with Fëanor entirely in the wrong and the two half-brothers acting with extreme forbearance and showing mercy towards him. This is the kind of event that may well contain the "seeds" of political bias – though as with all of these events, there is no other source to which we can turn to obtain alternative accounts; all there is for the discerning reader is a steady body of evidence pointing in one way. The disagreements culminate in the taking of the Oath and the Kinslaying at Alqualondë; other Noldor took their part in that battle, but it is the Fëanorians who are said to shoulder the principal guilt and blame (Tolkien, 1979b, p. 103).

Fëanor and his kin cannot give us the benefit of their viewpoint as they are not writing *The Silmarillion*, the kin of Fingolfin are. It is noteworthy that of the other Noldor present at the time of the Oathtaking it is said, "Fingolfin and Turgon his son therefore spoke against Fëanor, and fierce words awoke, so that once again wrath came near to the edge of swords." Fingolfin and Turgon are Elrond's paternal antecedents and they are skilfully cleared of blame, more so than others (Tolkien, 1979b, p. 98).

Leaving for Middle-earth, Fingolfin and his people are left behind on the shores of Aman, and Fëanor's words to his son are reported; how could Elrond or Fingolfin's people know these words? They were told to Maedhros and it would seem unlikely he would wish to admit such sentiments to any. The followers of Fingolfin were on the western shore and would only have seen the light of the burning ships at Losgar (Tolkien, 1979b, p. 106). Yet the departure of the Fëanorians almost seems to occur at the wish of the powers of the West or rather of Ilúvatar (Tolkien, 1979b, p. 105): "And as though it came at his call, there sprang up a wind from the north-west, and Fëanor slipped away secretly." Later, it says (Tolkien, 1979b, p. 129), "many of Fëanor's people indeed repented of the burning . . . and they would have welcomed them [Fingolfin's folk], but they dared not, for shame." Again this is a distinctly pro-Fingolfin camp stance that Tolkien casts events in, thus lending the partisan nature of Noldorin politics to the enrichment of *The Silmarillion*.

Once in Middle-earth, we are given detailed and lavish descriptions of the dwellings of Fingolfin's children and of Thingol; Gondolin, Nargothrond and Doriath, but we are left with bare bones of areas where the seven sons of Fëanor live.[3] Maedhros and his brothers live "east beyond Aros" and this important sector is dismissed in thirteen lines of text! Yet the Fëanorians and Thingol between them "bore the brunt of Morgoth's attacks"! This is another instance of the political bias skilfully built into *The Silmarillion*; once more, this could be intentional on the part of Tolkien to create the "feel" of real history as in the real world.

Another instance of the essentially elf-centred nature of *The Silmarillion* is the treatment of dwarves in the histories (Tolkien, 1979b, p. 108): "Ever cool was the friendship between the Naugrim and the Eldar, though much profit they had one of the other." The treatment of Mîm's people is given brief mention in Túrin's tale – they seem to have been hunted down like animals by the elves, and even the elf-biased *Silmarillion* can do little to ease the wrongness of this act, though it is not dwelt upon very much (Tolkien, 1979b, p. 245) as one comes to expect, skilfully mirroring real history once more.

In Beleriand Thingol is given a high profile – a whole chapter to himself (Chapter 10) – and the fact that he did not go to Valinor is played down. The only other leader of elves who is mentioned is Denethor, who led the Green-elves, and even he is glossed over. Why is Thingol raised in prominence? Possibly because Thingol is the father of Lúthien, who bore Dior, whose daughter was Elwing – Elrond's mother.

A clear indication of the anti-Fëanorian bias in *The Silmarillion* is given by the account of the Battle-under-Stars (Tolkien, 1979b, p. 126). This was a real victory for the elves, but of course it was achieved by the Fëanorians alone. How is it described? Is it given a chapter to itself? No, it is dismissed in seventeen lines. Compare with the Battle of Sudden Flame which takes up the whole of a chapter (Chapter 18) and which was a defeat. Similarly, Fëanor's demise is given a caveat: he is extremely courageous: "Nothing did he know of Angband or the great strength of defence that Morgoth had so swiftly prepared; but even had he known it would not have deterred him . . .", but it *adds*: "for he was fey, consumed by the flame of his own wrath" (Tolkien, 1979b, p. 126). This subtlety devalues Fëanor's courage by insinuating that it was a fit of battle fever or beserker action. Fëanor fought with many Balrogs (unlike Ecthelion who fought only one) but this battle is dismissed in six lines (Tolkien, 1979b, p. 126). How skilfully the method of bias is woven into the story-line to make it seem closer to real history than to contrived events.

When first contact is made with Thingol, Angrod is sent to talk to the king in Doriath (Tolkien, 1979b, p. 132). It is said: "but being true, and wisehearted, and thinking all griefs now forgiven, he spoke no word concerning the kinslaying." How could he possibly have thought all was forgiven? The words of the messenger from Mandos were quite clear. Indeed, the fact is mentioned in passing by Melian in one brief line much later on (Tolkien, 1979b, p. 155). So, Angrod was deceiving Thingol whose kin were Olwë's, Lord of the Teleri. But this deception is glossed over – because he is not of the Fëanorian camp. Angrod is the son of Finarfin and so related more directly to Elrond. Thingol also is treated very sympathetically at this point, seeing as he all but excluded any elves to come to his halls other than as guests: "King Thingol welcomed not with a full heart the coming of so many princes in might out of the West, eager for new realms . . ." (Tolkien, 1979b, p. 131). This is a cool welcome and he is not overly criticised for this and other worse actions. But then Thingol was directly related to Elrond. Thingol sends only Mablung and Daeron (Tolkien, 1979b, p. 134) to the Mereth Aderthad, Feast of Reuniting. He was granted twenty years of peace from Morgoth by the actions of those Princes who invited him to that feast, so this seems more than a little ungrateful of him.

Fingon for some reason seems to be played down as regards his valour; he saved Maedhros single-handed and was friendly with the son of Fëanor (was this why, perhaps?), and he routed the Orcs and wounded Glaurung and made him retreat (Tolkien, 1979b, p. 138). Yet his brave act was not made as much of as Fingolfin's. Once more, an intricate web of subtle bias is being built up and it is hard to think that this was not done on purpose to simulate a "real world" history full of political dynamics.

Ulmo comes to speak to Turgon and tells him to prepare armour and leave it in Vinyamar. He tells him (Tolkien, 1979b, p. 150): ". . . the curse of the Noldor shall find thee too ere the end . . ." But how was Turgon implicated in the quest of the Silmarils? We can tell how some elves were drawn into it; Thingol desired a Silmaril and Finrod was drawn by his promise to Beregond into Beren's quest. Turgon as far as we know never desired the jewels. This is probably one of the most puzzling parts of the tale. It is only the coming of Maeglin and Eöl to Gondolin that bring about its demise. Could it be that Eöl was somehow connected to the Fëanorians or he or his son had nurtured a desire of the Silmarils? We shall never know. For a further discussion of bias against Eöl and Maeglin, see Appendix A of this paper.

The Silmarillion's view of men is decidedly elf-centred (Tolkien, 1979b, p. 169): "Now the Eldar were beyond all other peoples skilled in tongues . . . Men had long had dealings with the Dark Elves east of the mountains, and from them had learned much of their speech." This is certainly a distinct bias towards elves.

The tale of the awakening of mortal men has a strong parallel with the fall of Adam and Eve, thus mirroring "original sin" (Tolkien, 1979b, p. 170): "when men awoke in Hildórien . . . spies of Morgoth were watchful . . . tidings were soon brought to him; and this seemed to him so great a matter that secretly under shadow he himself departed from Angband and went forth into Middle-earth, leaving to Sauron the command of the War." But: "Of his dealings with Men the Eldar indeed knew nothing . . . a darkness lay upon the hearts of Men . . . even in the people of the Elf-friends whom they first knew." So Morgoth was essentially playing the role of the serpent in Eden (Hildórien). Therefore according to elves, all men are untrustworthy. This is a very skilful biasing of the history by the author towards the elvish peoples, the Noldor in particular.

Indeed, with men, it seems that the Fëanorians were more helpful to them than the others (Tolkien, 1979b, pp. 171-2). See where men dwelt: Bëor and Baran went to Estolad – the lands of Amrod and Amras. Haladin went to Thargelion in the north – the lands of Caranthir. Caranthir looked kindly on men (Tolkien, 1979b, pp. 175) and did Haleth great honour – which proves that he was capable of kindness, unlike the bad press he is given earlier in *The Silmarillion*.

Amlach sought service with Maedhros after Morgoth's deceit was uncovered (Tolkien, 1979b, p. 174). But Thingol simply banned men from Doriath and was excused for doing so (Tolkien, 1979b, pp. 172-3): "he was ill pleased . . . because he was troubled by dreams concerning the coming of Men, ere ever the first tidings of them were heard. Therefore he commanded . . . [etc.]". A skilful biasing in his favour by the author.

The puzzle of Galadriel is the most interesting, for here we can see Tolkien constructing a "political" statement on a character. She is said to depart from Valinor at the same time as the Fëanorians in *The Silmarillion* (Tolkien, 1979b, p. 98), and yet in *Unfinished Tales* we have a possible reconstruction of the story to show that she left Valinor independently of the others (Tolkien, 1982b, p. 232). This is as Christopher Tolkien says an attempt to elevate her in status above that originally intended. More discussion of Galadriel's role in *The Silmarillion* and how it closely follows this pattern of bias towards certain elvish families is given in Appendix B of the paper. It shows that the pattern Tolkien established (whether consciously or not) is maintained with Galadriel as with the other characters.

At the Dagor Bragollach, we have another clear indication

of bias against the Fëanorians (Tolkien, 1979b, p. 180). The text tells us that Fingolfin was ill at ease and wanted to attack Morgoth, but that the other Noldor "were little disposed to hearken to Fingolfin, and the sons of Fëanor at that time least of all." But what of their Oath?[4] Surely any plan to attack Morgoth should have elicited their immediate help? It does not fit. And yet, we are told that the Fëanorians in the Dagor Bragollach were the hardest hit by Morgoth (Tolkien, 1979b, p. 183): "war had gone ill with the sons of Fëanor, and well nigh all the east marches were taken by the assault. The Pass of Aglon was forced, though with great cost to the hosts of Morgoth." So they fought, and they fought well. But it is not given much good press. Indeed, of all the elves, Maedhros was probably the most successful of them during this battle (Tolkien, 1979b, p. 183): "Maedhros did deeds of surpassing valour, and the Orcs fled before his face . . . for . . . his spirit burned like a white fire within, and he was as one that returns from the dead." It is told simply that the Fortress of Himring could not be taken. This is dismissed in seven lines.

Compare now if you will the description of Fingolfin's battle with Morgoth (Tolkien, 1979b, pp. 184-5): We are given sixty-eight glorious lines of vivid description – yet no one else was there to witness the duel! This is all hearsay and legendry. Yet the detail is incredible: Ringil the sword of the High King glittered like ice and Fingolfin inflicted seven wounds on his foe. Morgoth bore down Fingolfin three times to the ground and the High King hewed at Morgoth's foot before he died. But this ties in well with Elrond's family connection to Fingolfin, and so the bias reinforces the "historicity" of the work.

We see the same threads of bias in another tale: When Huor and Húrin are brought to Gondolin, Maeglin is given an extremely bad press for being against allowing them to leave. But Turgon the King had made his rule and he was breaking it (Tolkien, 1979b, p. 191), and it is precisely because Turgon allows them to leave that Morgoth learns vital information: "the strange fortune of Húrin and Huor reached the ears of the servants of Morgoth." Therefore Morgoth takes Húrin alive to find out more (Tolkien, 1979b, p. 235) and he betrays Gondolin by going to the Fen of Serech (Tolkien, 1979b, p. 276): "and Morgoth smiled, for he knew now clearly in what region Turgon dwelt . . . This was the first evil that the freedom of Húrin achieved." Morgoth had his spies draw closer to where he now guessed Gondolin to lie (Tolkien, 1979b, p. 291): ". . . none knew [in Gondolin] that the region wherein the Hidden Kingdom lay had been at last revealed to Morgoth by the cries of Húrin . . ." Thus was Maeglin taken. The differences between the full account given in *The Book of Lost Tales* and the short version in *The Silmarillion* are marked. Here we see Maeglin in the worst light (Tolkien, 1986, p. 178). But Turgon was a direct antecedent of Elrond and Maeglin was not, and so he is blamed entirely for the fall of Gondolin (Tolkien, 1986, p. 178). Tolkien began revising this tale (Tolkien, 1982a, pp. 5-6) but never finished it: how would he have treated Maeglin the second time around? We shall unfortunately never know.

If any character is likely to be favoured then it is without doubt Beren who will be treated kindly by *The Silmarillion*. He is a great-grandfather of Elrond. Thingol acts abominably towards him and towards his own daughter – imprisoning her in a tree and setting Beren on a quest that he believes will lead to his death (Tolkien, 1979b, pp. 201-2): ". . . if there were hope or fear that Beren should come ever back alive to Menegroth, he should not have looked again upon the light of heaven, though I had sworn it." Beren is essentially defeated in the dungeons of Sauron (Tolkien, 1979b, p. 211) until Lúthien comes to save him, and once again it is Lúthien's power that allows them to reach Angband and gives Beren a chance to cut a Silmaril from the iron crown (Tolkien, 1979b, p. 217), and it is Beren's lack of power that allows Carcharoth to bite off his hand with the jewel (Tolkien, 1979b, p. 218) and eventually to kill Beren in the woods. Yet he is honoured as a great hero; it was actually Lúthien who was the truly heroic figure in the tale, but he is the one credited in *The Lord of the Rings* by Elrond with the bravery of gaining the Silmaril (Tolkien, 1974a, p. 259).

The Union of Maedhros (Tolkien, 1979b, p. 226) is a master stroke of tactics that might have worked. But critically Thingol would not cooperate or help (Tolkien, 1979b, p. 227). Yet he is not criticised for his lack of cooperation, rather Celegorm and Curufin are held to blame (Tolkien, 1979b, p. 227). And in this Fifth Battle we begin to see the elvish bias of *The Silmarillion* working against men. Húrin was a far better tactician than Fingon or Turgon. He had the best idea of keeping the high-ground advantage (Tolkien, 1979b, p. 230) – a fact that is overlooked in the eulogising of Fingon: Indeed, Fingon's forces break ranks and without orders! This shambles is portrayed as "glorious" -- much as the charge of the Light Brigade might be, and *for much the same reasons* (i.e. that particular version of history is told by the British in Crimea). Indeed elvish bias against men in this battle is pinpointed by one telling sentence (Tolkien, 1979b, p. 232): "Yet neither by wolf, nor by Balrog, nor by Dragon, would Morgoth have achieved his end, but for the treachery of Men." Yet tactically it does not seem such a fatal blow to the elvish alliance. The damage was already done (a) by the uncoordinated attack of Fingon's forces and (b) by Maedhros's delayed arrival, and (c) by Glaurung. The bias against dwarves is even greater perhaps, for Azaghâl's valour in wounding Glaurung is dismissed in one paragraph (Tolkien, 1979b, p. 233)! This was a great deed and one can see the subtle skill of the author in giving it this lesser level of attention. To have done more would have altered the balance of the work and made it less elf-centred. And again of the sons of Fëanor, there is but one small paragraph (Tolkien, 1979b, p. 232): "though all were wounded none were slain." So they fought valiantly and skilfully it seems – but history passes them over: for this history, like real history, is written by those who see it in a particular way: Elrond's way.

---

[4] Compare with an earlier scene where the six brothers risked Maedhros's life because: "they were constrained also by their oath, and might not for any cause forsake the war against their Enemy" (Tolkien, 1979b, p. 128).

Túrin's tale is covered extremely carefully (it is no coincidence, perhaps, that it was one of the tales with the largest number of versions) – and it seems to be so since it casts Thingol in a good light. For about the only time in his whole life he seems to have acted charitably. He succours Túrin, forgives his slaying of Saeros, allows Beleg to seek him, succours Morwen and Nienna and even allows Húrin to enter Doriath and cast the Nauglamír at his feet and accuse him of deeds that he had not committed. Had it been Beren instead of Húrin, he would surely have been slain on the spot, but Thingol stays his hand. Celegorm and Curufin are criticised for turning the people of Nargothrond against their king (Tolkien, 1979b, p. 204): the years of secrecy had actually served them well. When Túrin persuaded them to build a bridge and to go out openly against their foes, their downfall came swiftly (Tolkien, 1979b, p. 254). So were the sons of Fëanor not in fact being wise to suggest secrecy? In this we see a differential bias, the order being that Túrin is treated better than the Fëanorians. Túrin is shown as an ill-fated person, while Tuor (being more closely related to Elrond) is cast in quite a different light and always seems to be right about everything; of course they were different characters, but it is interesting to note the family connections, all the same. It fits the political bias of everything that precedes it, too. We have the line of bias: Tuor – Túrin – Fëanorians.

The extant versions of the role of the dwarves in the slaying of Thingol and the taking of the Silmaril and Nauglamír are interesting. In *The Silmarillion* (Tolkien, 1979b, p. 281) the dwarves are shown in a very bad light: ". . . and they were filled with a great lust to possess them [Nauglamír and Silmaril], and carry them off to their far homes in the mountains. But they dissembled their mind, and consented to the task." But in *The Book of Lost Tales* (Tolkien, 1986, p. 227): "they knew nonetheless that they were prisoners, and trying the exits privily found them strongly warded." Tolkien here I feel intentionally builds up the elvish bias against dwarves in the final versions of the work. It is these tensions that give *The Silmarillion* its dynamics and realism.

Coming to Eärendil, Elrond's father, we see him forsaking their mother Elwing for a long time to go to sea. She grieved for him and yet he is not reprimanded by history for that (Tolkien, 1979b, p. 296): "and she sat in sorrow by the mouths of Sirion." And had he remained behind, would the Fëanorians have attacked Elwing's folk? It is difficult to determine such a thing, of course.

The final act in Beleriand's history, the capture of the two remaining Silmarils by Maedhros and Maglor, appears to be far too simple. Eönwë would surely have taken more care, since Maedhros and Maglor had demanded the jewels from him (Tolkien, 1979b, p. 304): "And they sent a message therefore to Eönwë, bidding him yield up now those jewels which of old Fëanor their father made and Morgoth stole from him." Could this be the will of Ilúvatar working to ensure that the Silmarils did not return to Valinor and perhaps be used in an attempt to rekindle the Two Trees? For Eönwë tells the two brothers (Tolkien, 1979b, p. 304): "The light of the Silmarils should go now into the West, *whence it came in the beginning . . .*" This seems to indicate they are planned to be kept exclusively by the Valar in the West and that this may be contrary to Ilúvatar's designs.

To compare the writing of *The Silmarillion*, which is elf-written, to man-written narrative, we can look to the section "Of the Rings of Power and the Third Age." Here, history as told by men is put into its context. The whole of *The Lord of the Rings* and its major appendices are summarised in two pages (Tolkien, 1979b, pp. 365-6); this is Elrond's version, as opposed to *The Lord of the Rings*, the history told by Frodo and corrected by Aragorn.

So the political slant to events is what gives *The Silmarillion* a realism far removed from mere contrivance. The incidences of narrative bias throughout the text towards certain characters and against others seem to suggest that they were placed there on purpose by the author, rather than a natural development, reinforcing in my belief the enormous skill of the author by which the work gains such credibility and realism for the reader.

As a final word, I shall give the floor to the words of Professor Tolkien himself, as expressing views on the subject of war and the victors, written to Christopher on 30th January 1945. This (Tolkien, 1981, p. 111) indicates that he was more aware than many of his time of the perils of victory and biases of history: "I have just heard the news. . . . . Russians 60 miles from Berlin. It does look as if something decisive might happen soon. The appalling destruction and misery of this war mount hourly: destruction of what should be (indeed is) the common wealth of Europe, and the world, if mankind were not so besotted, wealth the loss of which will affect us all, victors or not. Yet people gloat to hear of the endless lines, 40 miles long, of miserable refugees, women and children pouring West, dying on the way. There seem no bowels of mercy or compassion, no imagination, left in this dark diabolic hour. By which I do not mean that it may not all, in the present situation, mainly (not solely) created by Germany, be necessary and inevitable. But why gloat! We were supposed to have reached a stage of civilization in which it might still be necessary to execute a criminal, but not to gloat, or hang his wife and child by him while the orc-crowd hooted. The destruction of Germany, be it 100 times merited, is one of the most appalling world-catastrophes."

Appendix A: A more detailed discussion of Eöl and Maeglin

Of Eöl we have few facts. He is said to be "of the kin of Thingol" (Tolkien, 1979b, p. 159) and is named the Dark Elf. But this is a derogatory term used of Thingol too (Tolkien, 1979b, p. 132). Eöl says to Maeglin: "You are of the house of Eöl, Maeglin, my son, and not of the Golodhrim. All this land is the land of the Teleri" (Tolkien, 1979b, p. 161). But we have no idea who related this information to Elrond. Certainly Eöl and Aredhel died within a short time of arriving in Gondolin and must hardly have been able to talk to anyone, and Maeglin would hardly have admitted such words to Turgon, for he was trying to curry favour with his uncle (Tolkien, 1979b, p. 166). Also, a sharp conversation between Curufin son of Fëanor and Eöl in the deep woods is related – but by whom? Eöl can hardly have lived long enough to sit and tell this tale. Eöl "thanks" Curufin for helping him (Tolkien, 1979b, p. 163): "It is good, Lord Curufin, to find a kinsman thus kindly at need. I will remember it when I return."

Curufin: "Do not flaunt the title of your wife before me. For those who steal the daughters of the Noldor and wed them without gift or leave do not gain kinship with their kin." This skilfully casts both speakers in a bad light – Eöl as a grudge-holder and Curufin as a hothead. It has to be remembered: who was the witness to this conversation? Nobody.

It is interesting to see how Maeglin (Tolkien, 1979b, p. 160) is described in terms very much like those for Fëanor himself! "Then he called him Maeglin, which is Sharp Glance, for he perceived that the eyes of his son were more piercing than his own, and his thought could read the secrets of hearts beyond the mist of words." Also (Tolkien, 1979b, p. 160): "His words were few save in matters that touched him near, and then his voice had a power to move those that heard him and to overthrow those that withstood him."

Compare that with what is said of Fëanor (Tolkien, 1979b, p. 74): "He was tall, and fair of face, and masterful, his *eyes piercingly bright* and his hair raven-dark; in the pursuit of all his purposes eager and steadfast. Few ever changed his courses by counsel, none by force." And (Tolkien, 1979b, p. 96): "Fëanor was a master of words, and *his tongue had great power over hearts* when he would use it . . ." This is somewhat uncanny and there seems to be an echo of Fëanor within Maeglin; both bring about destruction to peoples by various ways. This can be traced even further and into creativity. The craft of Eöl and Maeglin is mighty. Indeed, only Fëanor or Celebrimbor created things in such abundance apart from them. Eöl made the magical dark swords Anglachel and Anguirel, and the dark metal *galvorn* (Tolkien, 1979b, p. 159). Maeglin fashioned the seventh gate of Gondolin according to the last writings on Gondolin (Tolkien, 1982b, p. 49). Oddly, there is a glimpse of another thread that enters the tale (Tolkien, 1979b, p. 163). Turgon had a liking for Maeglin: "and he looked with liking upon Maeglin his sister-son, seeing in him one worthy to be accounted among the princes of the Noldor." And Maeglin was not unvaliant. At the Nirnaeth (Tolkien, 1979b, p. 166): "Wise in counsel was Maeglin and wary, and yet hardy and valiant at need. And that was seen in after days: for when in the dread year of the Nirnaeth . . . Maeglin would not remain in Gondolin as regent of the King but went to the war and fought beside Turgon, and proved fell and fearless in battle." Yet he is then portrayed as a craven who betrayed Gondolin to save his life and to gain Idril (Tolkien, 1979b, p. 292) – even though it is said he loved the beauty of Idril and desired her without hope (Tolkien, 1979b, p. 167). If he had no hope in this, why should he bother to insist?

Of Aredhel (Tolkien, 1979b, p. 160): "It is not said that Aredhel was wholly unwilling (to marry Eöl)." Indeed, there seems to have been a deep rift between the King and the White Lady of the Noldor which *The Silmarillion* seems to play down. She "wearied of the guarded city" – but only after staying there for 200 years. On her departure, bitter words were spoken by her to Turgon her brother: "I am your sister and not your servant, and beyond your bounds I will go as seems good to me. And if you begrudge me an escort, then I will go alone" (Tolkien, 1979b, p. 157). Was it Idril that did not see eye to eye with Aredhel, perhaps? Such "family matters" are kept beyond the remit of *The Silmarillion* when it comes to Elrond's immediate kin. The same is not the case with either the Fëanorians or mortals such as Túrin.

Appendix B: More on Galadriel's treatment

Galadriel's reported actions in Beleriand in the First Age are few, suggesting that perhaps she was not a significant source of information for Bilbo's scholarship, but she did play a key part in bringing Thingol's wrath upon the Fëanorians. It is Galadriel who first tells Melian of the Silmarils and Finwë's death (Tolkien, 1979b, p. 152). But she does nothing more than raise Melian's suspicions concerning the Noldor. After this Melian is against the Fëanorians (Tolkien, 1979b, p. 152) but Thingol is still ambivalent. Then a short while later on hearing from Círdan, Thingol turns against the Fëanorians and the Noldor and bans Quenya from being spoken in his realm (Tolkien, 1979b, pp. 153, 155). Thingol's banning of Quenya is by Tolkien's standards a heinous crime; forcing a language out of existence, the elvish mode of communication that was closest to the Valar. Yet Thingol is not castigated for this as much as one might expect – because of his connection to Elrond; another example of the bias built into the story as it is told in *The Silmarillion*.

Galadriel also does not return to Valinor after the War of Wrath – she is rather glossed over at this juncture in preference to the acts of the sons of Fëanor (Tolkien, 1979b, p. 306). This is of course to be expected as the story is of those events connected with the Silmarils, but it also adds to the slant of events reported. Thus Galadriel is shown to be close to Elrond – they are both Ringbearers, but, more than that, they are related by the marriage of Elrond to Celebrían, Galadriel's daughter. Therefore Galadriel is treated well.

References

BBC. 1992. *Outlook*, BBC World Service programme, 16 January 1992.

Ezard, John. 1977. "Tolkien's Paradise Lost" in *The Guardian*, 15 Sept. 1977. p. 16.

Tolkien, Christopher. 1979a. "Foreword" in J.R.R. Tolkien, ed. Christopher Tolkien, *The Silmarillion*. London: Unwin Paperbacks. pp. 7-9.

Tolkien, Christopher. 1982a. "Introduction" in J.R.R. Tolkien, ed. Christopher Tolkien, *Unfinished Tales of Númenor and Middle-earth*. London: Unwin Paperbacks (Unicorn). pp. 1-14.

Tolkien, Christopher. 1985. "Foreword" in J.R.R. Tolkien, ed. Christopher Tolkien, *The Book of Lost Tales, part one*. London: Unwin Paperbacks (Unicorn). pp. 1-11.

Tolkien, J.R.R. 1974a. *The Fellowship of the Ring*. London: Unwin Books.

Tolkien, J.R.R. 1974b. *The Two Towers*. London: Unwin Books.

Tolkien, J.R.R. 1974c. *The Return of the King*. London: Unwin Books.

Tolkien, J.R.R. 1979b. *The Silmarillion*, ed. Christopher Tolkien. London: Unwin Paperbacks.

Tolkien, J.R.R. 1981. *Letters of J.R.R. Tolkien*, ed. Humphrey Carpenter. London: George Allen & Unwin.

Tolkien, J.R.R. 1982b. *Unfinished Tales of Númenor and Middle-earth*, ed. Christopher Tolkien. London: Unwin Paperbacks (Unicorn).

Tolkien, J.R.R. 1986. *The Book of Lost Tales, part two*, ed. Christopher Tolkien. London: Unwin Paperbacks (Unicorn).

Aspects of the Fall in *The Silmarillion*

Eric Schweicher

Abstract: This paper begins with an analysis of the evolution of the Fall in the Western tradition, which will be compared with its image in Middle-earth. The *Ainulindalë* and the *Quenta Silmarillion* will be examined to show how Vala, Elf, Dwarf, and Man fall into corruption, and the consequences of this fall.

Keywords: creation, Eden, eucatastrophe, evil, the Fall, sin, sub-creation

> There cannot be any "story" without a fall – all stories are ultimately about the fall – at least not for human minds as we know them and have them.
> (Tolkien, 1981, p. 147)

This statement by J.R.R. Tolkien has given me much to think about. It seems to imply that Tolkien felt compelled to refer to "a fall" somewhere in his works. On close scrutiny, I soon discovered that *The Silmarillion* did not contain one fall, but a whole panoply of them, hinting at a cosmological complexity unattained in any other piece of writing. This paper aims at exposing the different versions of the Fall we find in J.R.R. Tolkien's *The Silmarillion*, mythologically speaking his most significant work.

In the Judaeo-Christian tradition, the Fall was the occasion when Adam and Eve disobeyed God and were expelled from the Garden of Eden. The serpent's most effective beguiling affected humanity in that from the Fall came the knowledge of – and thus the existence of – good and evil.

In the Christian tradition, the Fall is linked with temptation, sin, revolt and punishment. The Incarnation and Death of Christ repair the damage caused by the Fall.[1] The Incarnation, Crucifixion and Resurrection thus make salvation possible. But the Middle-earth versions are not always so "eucatastrophic" (Tolkien, 1988, p. 62), to use Tolkien's own adjective; that is to say they do not offer many clues about salvation, if any. Only the Elves are allowed to cross into Eden, and Men remain stuck in Middle-earth (except for the chosen few), which they inherit from the Elves.

The original Fall in Middle-earth described in the account of Creation, the Ainulindalë, is the Fall of Melkor, "mightiest among the Ainur" (Tolkien, 1986, p. 17), one of the Creator's close servants, angels, or semi-gods in a sense. During the Great Music which gave shape to the world, Melkor started a tune of his own, thereby rebelling against God, Ilúvatar. This situation echoes that of the traditional "Schöpfungsdrama", as alluded to by Paul Ricoeur in his *Symbolik des Bösen*:

> der Ursprung des Bösen . . . ist das "Chaos", mit dem der Schöpferakt Gottes kämpft . . .
> (Ricoeur, 1971, p. 197)
> the origin of evil . . . is chaos, against which God's creative act fights . . .[2]

Melkor fell because he became more interested in himself, in his own "creation", than in God. Melkor then became the source of uttermost evil, the dark power against which good fought throughout Middle-earth's history. Melkor's rebellion marks the birth of evil in Tolkien's cosmology. Original sin entered the world well before the first Man, or in this case the first Elf, ever set foot on Earth, which Tolkien seems to confirm when he says in one of his letters:

> the rebellion of created free-will precedes the creation of the World (Eä); and Eä has in it, *subcreatively* introduced, evil, rebellions, discordant elements of its nature already when the Let it Be was spoken. The Fall or corruption, therefore, of all things in it and all inhabitants of it, was a possibility if not inevitable.
> (Tolkien, 1981, pp. 286-7; italics mine)

First to be engulfed in the waves of Melkor's Fall were his brethren, the Valar. Among them Aulë fell, "for he so desired to see the Children [Elves and Men], that he became impatient and tried to anticipate the will of the Creator" (Tolkien, 1981, p. 287) by creating his own children, the Dwarves. Again we are facing a sub-creative rebellion against God, which this time is incorporated into his creation by Ilúvatar Himself, since He allowed Aulë's sub-creation to join His own Children in Middle-earth.[3] Aulë's Fall came from a well-intended act, namely the desire to accelerate the inhabiting of Earth, so that Aulë's skills could be taught and used by the "Children". Even Melkor's Fall came from a good intention, if we consider that Melkor only wanted to do a better job as God's angel by increasing his own power. God's intervention in Aulë's favour transforms the potential evil of Aulë's rebellion into something positive, namely the

---

[1] One could object that Men still die, though Christ has conquered death through resurrection, and thus has not completely reversed the consequences of the Fall.
[2] Translation by the author.
[3] It is amusing to note in contrast that the Norse Dwarves are created from the "maggots" delving under the earth, almost as an afterthought to the creation of Man (see Kevin Crossley-Holland, 1980, p. 6).

creation of Dwarves[4] that completed God's own creation. After all, Ilúvatar said that

> no theme may be played that hath not its uttermost source in me . . . [and] he that attempteth this shall prove but mine instrument in the devising of things more wonderful, which he himself hath not imagined.
> (Tolkien, 1986, pp. 17-18)

This is what happened in Aulë's case, but it is obviously far more complex with Melkor, as it should be!

Other angels fell as well, not as victims of their own rebellion, but rather swept away as a result of Melkor's Fall, because they became his followers and servants. They were also drawn into darkness by their own weakness, by their aspiration to taste of the forbidden fruit of power in Middle-earth. They were Maiar, angelic figures of lesser power, and the Fall worked on them a terrible transformation, for most of them became creatures of fire and destruction, the Balrogs.[5] Melkor's soul fell at the very instant of his rebellion, but in appearance he remained fair, a tool of corruption that brought the Fall of others. Sauron's appearance served the same ends, when it succeeded in binding to him the Nazgûl, and Ar-Pharazôn, among others, before he became terrifying to look upon as the Red Eye.

The Fall of the Elves, contrary to the biblical Fall of Man, does not affect all Elves, at least not directly. It was mainly the Fall of the Noldor, "the most gifted kindred of the Elves" (Tolkien, 1981, p. 148), who found themselves in Valinor at the time when Melkor, who had been defeated and captured by the other Valar, was being freed to roam in Valinor. In Melkor's eyes the Elves were "the representatives of sub-creation par excellence" (Tolkien, 1981, p. 146), that for which he had rebelled but which he would never be able to achieve, and they became "the special object of his desire and hate" (Tolkien, 1981, p. 146). As with the Maiar, Melkor tried to subdue the Noldor, lying to them, and slowly preparing their rebellion against the Valar. But the Noldor's Fall, as opposed to that of the Maiar, is "into possessiveness and . . . into perversion of their art to power" (Tolkien, 1981, p. 146). According to T.A. Shippey, however, the Noldor's Fall is due to a

> variety of pride . . . not quite . . . "possessiveness" or wanting to own things, but rather a restless desire to *make* things which will forever reflect or incarnate their own personality.
> (Shippey, 1982, p. 180)

I think the possibility of "clean" sub-creation existed for the Noldor, but it is soon marred by Melkor, who manages to turn the sub-creative desire of the Noldor into a self-oriented quest. This echoes the Bible: the trap is set, and Lucifer has awakened the Noldor's temptation. Unfortunately for the Elves, the Noldor succumbed, and created the Silmarils at the worst possible moment. Out of those jewels of power came the Noldor's pride but also their sorrow, a Fall that took them into destruction, and with them all those that became involved in one way or another with the Silmarils. Sub-creation, Rebellion and Kinslaying sealed off the Noldor's doom by bringing upon them the curse of the Valar. Thus was Sub-creation perverted and Eden lost to the most powerful of the Elves. Tolkien said that

> [*The Silmarillion*] is . . . fundamentally concerned with the problem of the relation of Art (and Sub-creation) and Primary Reality.
> (Tolkien, 1981, p. 145)

Sub-creation was born from a strong feeling of love for that "Primary Reality", from the knowledge that life means also death, and that the world as it appears to the sub-creator's senses must pass one day. Thus the sub-creative desire is "filled with the sense of mortality, and yet unsatisfied by it" (Tolkien, 1981, p. 145). And the expression of that very dissatisfaction gives birth to art. Yet it also means a rebellion against the laws of the universe, and this is where Sub-creation may provoke the sub-creator's Fall. This raises the problem of "Primary Reality", and mortality applied to the Elves.

One cannot help speaking of a *memento mori* motive while referring to Man. Yet *The Silmarillion*, as stated before, is primarily concerned with Elves, who are immortal and thus cannot yearn for a state of being where death does not exist. Humphrey Carpenter points out that

> Old age, disease, and death do not bring [the Elves'] work to an end while it is still unfinished or imperfect. They are therefore the ideal of every artist.
> (Carpenter, 1978, p. 101)

But because their work reaches uttermost perfection, they may fall into possessiveness. Elves do not experience death, even when they are slain in battle, but they are confined to Valinor. They witness the death of Man, and with him that of all living things in the world. This causes the Elves to desire to keep alive the memories of the past and of things that were by putting them into works of art. The Silmarils themselves, though they soon become the instruments of the Noldor's Fall, are meant to preserve the light of the Two Trees of Valinor, the symbol of a pure, prelapsarian world.

In fact, one could even argue that immortality sharpens the sense of brevity and mortality, as all things in the world seem to whirl still swifter into the abyss of Time. Tolkien seems to confirm this by putting the following words into the mouth of Legolas:

> For the Elves the world moves, and it moves both very swift and very slow. Swift, because they themselves change little, and all else fleets by: it is a grief to them. Slow, because they do not count the running years, not for themselves. The passing seasons are but ripples ever repeated in the long stream. Yet beneath the Sun all

---

[4] Of course, one could argue that the Dwarves themselves are not the friendliest people and the epitome of good in Middle-earth. For this one need only look at the war which tore apart the Kingdom of Doriath and that of the Dwarves, or at some extracts from *The Hobbit*, particularly those involving Thorin Oakenshield, in which the Dwarves appear as some greedy, overproud and easily-angered creatures who would sooner hack your head off than give you a scrap of bread.

[5] Incidentally, Saruman's Fall is related to the Fall of the Maiar, being himself one of them (though no physical transformation takes place in this instance. This offers us yet another facet of the Fall).

things must wear to an end at last.
(Tolkien, 1969, pp. 408-9)

Yet it is true that, though Elvish Sub-creation may express dissatisfaction with the state of things in the universe, the rebellion that that dissatisfaction presupposes cannot reach the intensity of human rebellion, since Man also yearns to leave something in time, to scratch the marble of eternity before death takes him. This is made clear by the story of the Númenóreans.

The Noldor's punishment (and that of all those entangled in the quest for the Silmarils) could not be death, for the Elves are immortal, as I have already mentioned. "Weariness of life" (Shippey, 1982, p. 179) was their punishment, sorrow and grief in Middle-earth under the shadow of Lucifer. The fact that the Elves do not die is not something which has any parallel in Judaeo-Christian ideas about the Fall. "Accordingly," says Shippey, "they do not have to be rescued from death by a Saviour" (1982, p. 177), which, of course, makes their sorrow and punishment all the more unbearable. To achieve some sort of Redemption, the Elves need to overcome their pride and to be able to surrender the object of their pride to the Valar, namely the Silmarils. With the jewels they have to give up supra-human or indeed supra-elvish power. In the *Quenta Silmarillion*, Eärendil whose blood is both human and Elvish assumes by right, and some would say by fate, the difficult task of bearing not the Red Arrow to the Valar, but one Silmaril (with much the same effect!). But Eärendil is not a Saviour, rather a messenger. Thus with the Fall of Elves Tolkien has introduced a new dimension into the question of the Fall. The *Quenta Silmarillion* is primarily concerned with the Fall of Elves, but we should still ask ourselves what happens to Man in that world. As stated before, Man also appears in the story, yet of his Fall in Middle-earth not much is said.[6]

As a matter of fact, Man "does not originate 'on stage' in Beleriand, but drifts into it, already sundered in speech, from the East" (Shippey, 1982, p. 176). In a longer version of the Tale of Túrin we are told of Men in Beleriand that

> a darkness lies behind [them], and out of it few tales have come. The fathers of [their] fathers may have had things to tell, but they did not . . . The Mountains stand between [Men in Beleriand] and the life they came from, flying from no man now knows what.
> (Tolkien, 1980, p. 61)

As Shippey rightly suggests, one could assume that

> the exploit of Morgoth of which the Eldar never learnt was the traditional seduction of Adam and Eve by the serpent, while the incoming [Men] are all sons of Adam flying from Eden.
> (Shippey, 1982, p. 176)

This seems to be attested by the fact that some Men who arrived later in Beleriand, when their predecessors and kindred had already established themselves as friends and allies of the Elves, were mostly servants of Morgoth, fallen men who betrayed the league of good forces in their greatest battle, the Nirnaeth Arnoediad. Man seems to have a Fall in Middle-earth. Tolkien does not deny its existence, and he does not try to replace the Fall of Man by the Fall of Elves. Men are human in the *Quenta Silmarillion*, and accordingly they are mortal. But death is neither a punishment, nor a direct consequence of their Fall. The condition of Man, like that of the Elves, was determined long before the world was created, in the Great Music of the Ainur. Man's fate is not clear in the Elves' minds, nor is it really clear to the Valar. Only Mandos, Lord of the Dead, knows what happens to Men once they die, but not much is said of that; it is as if Tolkien went thus far in the telling of a cosmology that might appear pagan from more than one perspective, and did not want to tell us more, or to go beyond a specific point.

The brief span of human life on Middle-earth is considered as a wonder by the Elves, for whom life has no limits in time. In that sense, one should ponder over Lúthien's decision, when offered to choose between the Elven or the human condition for her second life, to join the daughters of Eve. Of course, her love for Beren, who remains mortal, has influenced her decision. But there is more to it than appears to the eye: would she not prefer to share the wonder of death rather than experiencing weariness of life, as some among the Elves did?

As indicated by the Music of the Ainur, immortality and death seem to be tokens given respectively to Elves and Men. Yet there is a fear of death on Middle-earth, which is paradoxical if one considers death as a gift. Sador, for example, one of Húrin's servants, leaves the walls of an Elven fortress to escape a more than probable death at the hands of the enemy, and becomes a woodcutter (Tolkien, 1980, p. 60). This example, associated with a secondary character, shows that the fear of death is common among Men. Yet, as I said earlier, death cannot be seen as a punishment for the Fall of Man. The Fall must have had an influence on the attitude of Man towards death, and there one must see Melkor's influence, which lures Men into believing that what they have been given as a gift is but a bitter fruit. Hence also the envy of Men, and sometimes their jealousy and hate, for the immortality of the Elves.

When I say that the Fall of Man in Middle-earth is not shown explicitly by Tolkien, that is only a half-truth. Of course, there is the suggestion that the Edain who arrived in Beleriand in the First Age were flying from the growing shadow in the East, where something terrible had happened to their people. However, there is also a tale about the Fall of Man in Middle-earth, perhaps a second Fall; the *Akallabêth*, or *The Downfall of Númenor*. Tolkien does not explicitly tell us what happened to Man in the East. But the Downfall of Númenor is developed in detail as the story of the second Fall of Man in Middle-earth. Tolkien said that:

> *The Downfall* is partly the result of an inner weakness in Men — consequent, if you will, upon the first Fall (unrecorded in these tales), repented but not finally healed . . . Its central theme is (inevitably, I think, in a

---

[6] If it is true, and it is sometimes acknowledged to be so even by Tolkien himself, that the Elves are a reflection of humanity, they are also Elves. The difficulty consists precisely in distinguishing their "elvishness" from their humanity.

story of Men) a Ban, or Prohibition.
(Tolkien, 1981, p. 154)

In *The Silmarillion*, "the Lords of Valinor forbade [the Númenóreans] to sail so far westward that the coasts of Númenor could no longer be seen" (Tolkien, 1986, p. 315), and the land where once the Two Trees had stood should come into view. Here, as in the Bible, the Ban is soon defied, as "the Númenóreans began to murmur, at first in their hearts, and then in open words, against the doom of Men" (Tolkien, 1986, p. 317); for though they had been given a longer life span than other Men in the world, the Númenóreans still had to die one day, and where the serpent was not (at least in the beginning of their bliss), its shadow still lingered until it took shape again with Sauron's coming. This prompts Tolkien to say that

> Reward on earth is more dangerous for men than punishment!
> (Tolkien, 1981, p. 154)

And later:

> Their reward is their undoing – or the means of their temptation. Their long life aids their achievements in art and wisdom, but breeds a possessive attitude to these things, and desire awakes for more *time* for their enjoyment.
> (Tolkien, 1981, p. 154)

Possessiveness is something I have already alluded to in the case of the Elves. But the motives of Men are obviously quite different. Possessiveness declares itself in works of Númenórean art, and in the accumulation of riches, as the former "helpers and teachers" (Tolkien, 1986, p. 320) to the Men of Middle-earth become "lords and masters and gatherers of tribute" (Tolkien, 1986, p. 320). Possessiveness expresses itself mainly in a desperate attempt to escape death. Death is thus far from being seen as a divine gift, and signifies rather the passage into a very dark and frightening unknown. The attack against Valinor attempted by the glorious fleet of Ar-Pharazôn is then nothing more than the last convulsion of an old man enraged by the approach of death. In this, as in much of the evil that afflicted Middle-earth, the work of Lucifer is clearly revealed, and more precisely Sauron's beguiling lies. According to Tolkien, "a good Númenórean died of free will when he felt it to be time to do so" (Tolkien, 1981, p. 205). That is exactly what Aragorn did, having been given "not only a span thrice that of Men of Middle-earth, but also the grace to go at [his] will, and give back the gift" (Tolkien, 1969, p. 1100), bitter though it may seem to Queen Arwen. Yet Aragorn also added:

> Behold! we are not bound for ever to the circles of the world, and beyond them is more than memory.
> (Tolkien, 1969, p. 1100)

With Aragorn's death the gift is given back, and the example set for Man. Reward has disappeared, only hope remains, and the Fourth Age.

Beside Elves and Men, there are also Dwarves in Middle-earth. The Dwarves appear before Man, at the same time as the Elves, and yet we know nothing of their Fall. If a Fall there was, then it must have been their creation itself, the sub-creative rebellion of Aulë. We know very little of their fate, but "the Elves [say] that [the Dwarves have] no life beyond Arda and the death of their bodies" (Foster, 1978, p. 100) which would seem logical. They are not considered to be God's Children, and thus were given neither death nor immortality.

However, the Dwarves "themselves claimed that Aulë would bring them to the halls of Mandos, whence they will join the Children of Ilúvatar" (Foster, 1978, p. 100). This indicates that Aulë tries to imitate God not only in giving life but in giving death as well. Yet since the Dwarves live longer than Men in Middle-earth (about 250 years, according to Foster (1978, p. 100)), we might consider that this was their gift, their *ersatz* for the lack of salvation after their death. For this reason it is uncertain whether they fell.[7]

Finally, and rather illogically, I admit, let us turn our attention back to the main culprit, namely Lucifer. The Archvillain personified by Morgoth (and later by Sauron) has a grand design that exemplifies the purpose of evil in general: to corrupt and destroy the land and its creatures, and to rule over the whole world. Yet this has not always been his intention. Melkor's Fall was essentially an attempt to increase his own power, by doing better than the other angels in the tending and embellishing of Earth. It was an action which complemented rather than challenged God. The Fall transforms this ambition into a will to fight and destroy what God has created and what the Valar have made fair. It is prompted by the realization that he cannot match the beauty of their works. As Tolkien writes:

> The Enemy in successive forms is always "naturally" concerned with sheer Domination . . . but the problem: that this frightful evil can and does arise from an apparently good root, the desire to benefit the world and others – speedily and according to the benefactor's own plans – is a recurrent motive.
> (Tolkien, 1981, p. 146)

This would explain why the Fall is a recurrent motive throughout *The Silmarillion*. But repetitive Falls do not lessen the gravity of their consequences. Let us recognize that though it is all too easy for good to become evil through a Fall, it is impossible for evil to regain a prelapsarian condition. However, I am not saying that it is impossible for Elves or Men, who have suffered the Fall, to be redeemed (which is something true evil cannot imagine let alone understand). The Fall of Man has not automatically turned Adam into an evil creature, for only Melkor became utterly evil when he fell. The sin of Men was allegedly a rebellion against God, but that did not make Orcs out of them. Men were simply thrown out of the Garden of Eden, free to wander on Earth where some may fall prey to evil. The Fall

---

[7] One could argue that the Dwarves in Middle-earth are not really a paragon of virtue. They spend their lives digging for precious ores and gems, creating powerful kingdoms under mountains, and establishing commercial links with Elves and Men, gathering more and more riches, and power. They always stand at the edge of the chasm, and it would not take much to push them down. Somehow, they themselves never really fall, though their realms often do. Their very creation made them a living paradox.

of the Elves does not make them Lucifer's minions either, since their sole desire once in Middle-earth is to oppose and to eradicate evil. Nevertheless the Fall brings woe and suffering among the peoples of Middle-earth.

I started this paper with a quotation by Tolkien insisting on the fact that all stories written or made up by humans had to have a Fall in them. After reading his work, we have reasons to believe, I think, that Tolkien remained true to that principle: though he carefully avoids mentioning directly the first Fall of Man (perhaps because he takes "as read" the myth of Adam and Eve), he tells us about *five* other Falls, which affect all inhabitants of Middle-earth, and even angels.[8]

We do not know if there ever was a tree of knowledge in Middle-earth of which Man sinfully tasted. We know at least of two other trees that might fit the image, but they were cut down before Man could dream of setting foot on the lands where they used to grow. When the idea of landing in Valinor did come to his mind, it was already too late; nevertheless Man was punished for daring to do so.

If there is a Fall in Middle-earth, is it really because of Man, or of his neighbours and sometimes representations, Elves and Dwarves? It would be too easy to say that Man alone has the potential for a new Fall. There must always be a Dark Lord prowling around.[9] There has been a Dark Lord since long before the Children of Ilúvatar ever "awoke" on Arda. In other words, evil has always existed "without" Man in and around Arda. It has designs of its own that are not those of Man, and though evil can, and will, use Man in its designs, it does not need Man. Evil could simply have destroyed Man. But it prefers to corrupt slowly for its own pleasure.

The Silmarillion is thus a far cry from the Bible, in that it is, in my opinion, far richer in possibilities and scope. But, like the Bible, it tells us that all things must pass, though some hope always remains, whatever the consequences of the fall, and the might of evil.

References

Carpenter, Humphrey. 1978. *J.R.R. Tolkien: A biography*. London: Unwin Paperbacks.

Crossley-Holland, Kevin. 1980. *The Norse Myths: A Retelling*. London: Deutsch.

Foster, Robert. 1978. *The Complete Guide to Middle-earth: An A-Z guide to the Names and Events in the Fantasy World of J.R.R. Tolkien, from* The Hobbit *to* The Silmarillion. London: Allen and Unwin.

Ricoeur, Paul. 1971. *Die Symbolik des Bösen. Phänomenologie der Schuld II*, trans. M. Otto. Freiburg and München: Verlag K.A.

Shippey, T.A. 1982. *The Road to Middle-earth*. London: Allen & Unwin.

Tolkien, J.R.R. 1969. *The Lord of the Rings*. London: Allen & Unwin.

Tolkien, J.R.R. 1986. *The Silmarillion*, ed. Christopher Tolkien. London: Unwin Paperbacks.

Tolkien, J.R.R. 1980. *Unfinished Tales of Númenor and Middle-earth*, ed. Christopher Tolkien. London: Allen & Unwin.

Tolkien, J.R.R. 1981. *Letters of J.R.R. Tolkien*, ed. Humphrey Carpenter with Christopher Tolkien. London: Allen & Unwin.

Tolkien, J.R.R. 1988. "On Fairy-Stories", in *Tree and Leaf*, J.R.R. Tolkien. London: Unwin Hyman.

---

[8] One might argue that there can only be one Fall, followed by a series of chain reactions. But it is difficult to find a fact that could explain or justify such a theory. The only link between those events is the influence of Morgoth, and the pattern of the Falls (a "good" intention, temptation, and some part of possessiveness). The only way, in my opinion, in which those repetitive Falls might be regarded as a one and only event is to see them as a deliberate arrangement by Tolkien to look at the traditional image of the Fall from different angles.

[9] And thus the Fall is *not* a biological flaw in human nature!

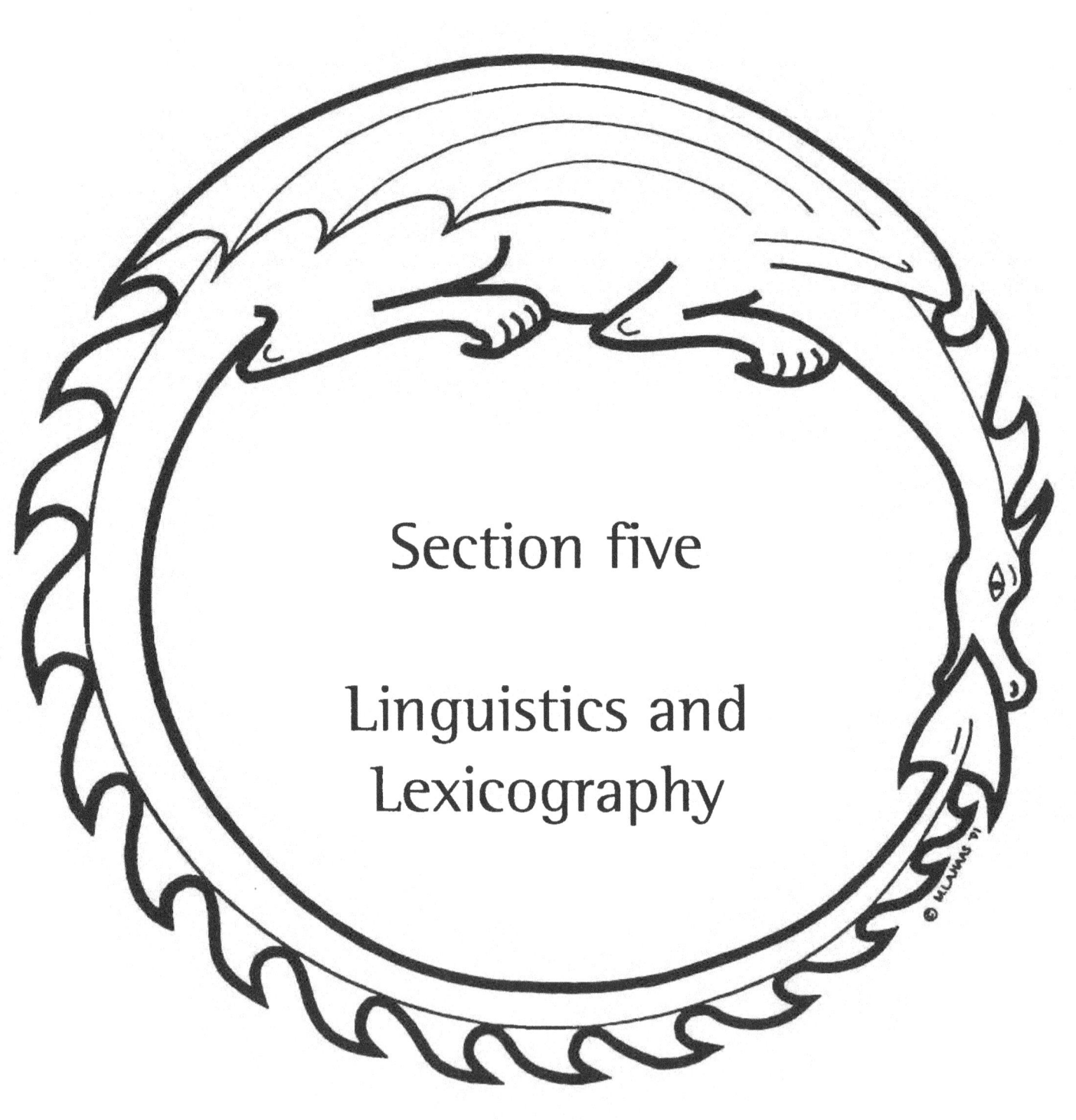

Section five

Linguistics and Lexicography

At the Wordface: J.R.R. Tolkien's Work on the *Oxford English Dictionary*

Peter M. Gilliver

Abstract: A description of J.R.R. Tolkien's time working on the *Oxford English Dictionary* together with a detailed analysis of the evidence for his contribution to the entries for individual words.

Keywords: lexicographer, *Oxford English Dictionary*

That Tolkien considered his involvement in the compiling of the *Oxford English Dictionary* in 1919-20 to have been time well spent is shown by his observation that he "learned more in those two years than in any other equal period of my life" (quoted in Carpenter, 1977, p. 101). That he also conceived an abiding affection for the Dictionary is evident from the episode in *Farmer Giles of Ham* where "Four Wise Clerks of Oxenford", consulted as to the meaning of *blunderbuss*, reply with the *OED* definition (the Clerkes being of course the four original Editors of the *OED*).[1] As a lexicographer at work on the same dictionary some seventy years later, I was interested to learn what I could about Tolkien's tasks and working methods.

Long before the completion of its first edition in 1928, the *Oxford English Dictionary* was already justly famous as the largest survey of the English language ever undertaken.[2] Work began in the 1850s under the auspices of the Philological Society, and publication began in 1884 with the first instalment, or fascicle, under the editorship of its first and most famous Editor, James Murray. To increase the rate of progress Henry Bradley was appointed as a second Editor in 1887; he was later joined by William Craigie and Charles Onions. Sir James Murray died in 1915, so that when Tolkien arrived there remained three teams of lexicographers proceeding through separate swathes of the alphabet, each headed by an Editor. At the beginning of 1919 the letters U-Z and parts of S had not yet appeared in print: Tolkien was assigned to Henry Bradley's team, which had just begun work at the beginning of W. Tolkien's background and philological training suited him particularly well for work on vocabulary of Germanic origin, in which W was probably the richest of the remaining letters.

Having been unable to consult the diary which, uncharacteristically, Tolkien kept from the beginning of 1919, I have had to rely instead on the available *OED* working papers. The Dictionary was passed to press in the form of bundles of slips, each bearing either illustrative quotations (most of which were sent in by members of the public) or portions of editorial text. Much of this copy was donated to the Bodleian Library, along with some slips discarded in the course of the editorial process, but not before the extraction and dispersal of three components of the text: materials relating to Scottish, Middle English, and early Modern English were (somewhat haphazardly) separated out and dispatched to the historical dictionary projects concerned. Various other contemporaneous bodies of material still reside in the archives of Oxford Dictionaries, including slips intended for use in the preparation of the 1933 *Supplement*. The standard "Dictionary slip" was a quarter-sheet of foolscap, but some contributors sent in quotations on more or less any similarly-sized piece of paper that came to hand, and many of the lexicographers did likewise: in their case this included torn-up proofs of earlier *OED* fascicles and, crucially, discarded earlier drafts of editorial material.[3] (Of course, a slip of paper discarded by Tolkien might not be re-used until it was picked up years later by another lexicographer.) Some slips must have been destroyed altogether, and many others are presently unavailable because of the aforementioned dispersal of the slips; but by examining the remaining material for the letter W, I hope that I have managed to reconstruct a reasonably full picture of Tolkien's involvement in the creation of Dictionary text. (Although he could conceivably have been involved in the coverage of words beginning with other letters, the manuscript evidence available to me suggests otherwise, at least as far as the first edition of the *OED* is concerned.)

Precise dating of most of Tolkien's lexicographical work is difficult, since very few slips (and none of Tolkien's) bear

---

[1] Another passage in Tolkien's creative writing which contains a concealed reference to the *OED* occurs in the *Notion Club Papers*, where "Michael Ramer" ponders the implications of an 1877 definition of the word *crystal* by Thomas Huxley, which is cited in the *OED* entry for the word (Tolkien, 1992, p. 208).
[2] For a more comprehensive account of the history of the *OED* see Murray, 1977.
[3] Tolkien also made use of these for other purposes: parts of a revision of *The Fall of Gondolin* were written on drafts of the etymology of *wariangle* (Tolkien, 1984, p. 147). The versos of slips are also informative about other *OED* workers: see Dutton, 1987.

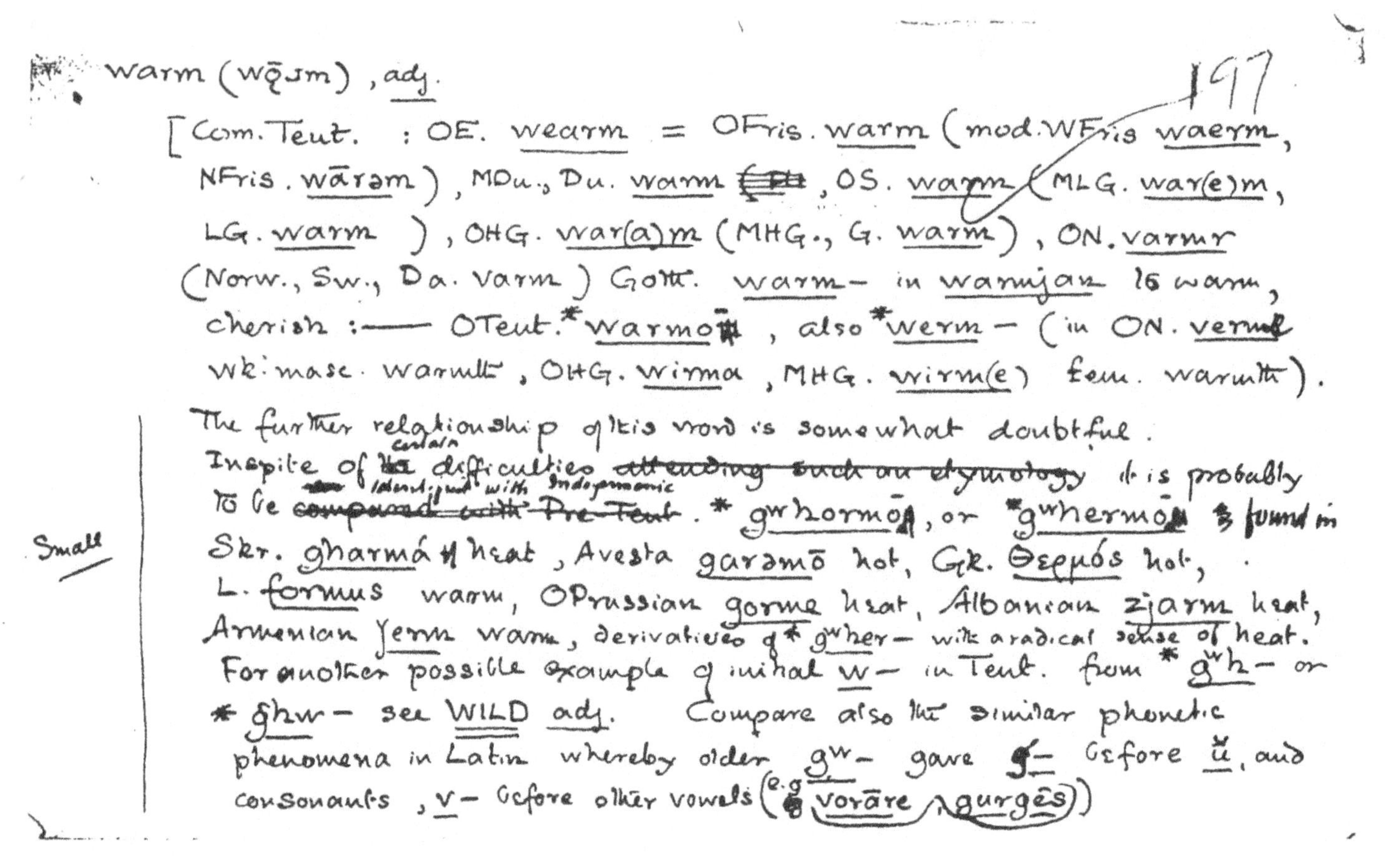
warm (wǭɹm), adj. 197

[Com. Teut.: OE. wearm = OFris. warm (mod. WFris. waerm, NFris. wāram), MDu., Du. warm, OS. warm (MLG. war(e)m, LG. warm), OHG. war(a)m (MHG., G. warm), ON. varmr (Norw., Sw., Da. varm) Goth. warm- in warmjan to warm, cherish :— OTeut. *warmo-, also *werm- (in ON. verm- wk. masc. warmth, OHG. wirma, MHG. wirm(e) fem. warmth).

Small

The further relationship of this word is somewhat doubtful. In spite of ~~the~~ certain difficulties ~~attending such an etymology~~ it is probably to be ~~compared with Pre-Teut.~~ identified with Indogermanic *gʷhormo-, or *gʷhermo- found in Skr. gharmá heat, Avesta garəmō hot, Gk. θερμός hot, L. formus warm, OPrussian gorme heat, Albanian zjarm heat, Armenian jerm warm, derivatives of *gʷher- with a radical sense of heat. For another possible example of initial w- in Teut. from *gʷh- or *ghw- see WILD adj. Compare also the similar phonetic phenomena in Latin whereby older gʷ- gave g- before ŭ and consonants, v- before other vowels (e.g. vorāre, gurgēs))

Figure 1: *OED* slips, headword *Warm*, etymology. (*Reproduced by permission of the Bodleian Library*)

any indication of when they were written. A certain amount can be deduced from the dates stamped on bundles of slips when they were sent for typesetting: for example, Tolkien must have started writing definitions before 3 April 1919, which is when the first bundle to which he contributed was sent to press. Beyond this, all that is certain regarding the start of his work is that by the end of March 1919, according to Oxford University Press accounts, he had been paid one-and-a-half months' salary, although this may have been for work begun late in 1918 and carried out part-time. (Humphrey Carpenter's biography states that Tolkien joined the staff of the Dictionary in November, soon after the Armistice.) The OUP accounts also show that he ceased to be paid out of Dictionary funds at the end of June 1920, but that for the last month he was engaged in work connected with an anthology of Middle English texts (Sisam, 1921)[4] rather than the *OED* – although, as we shall see, this work did in fact continue to benefit the Dictionary. Tolkien remained in touch with Henry Bradley after ceasing to work for OUP, as is shown by a postcard from Leeds, dated 26 June 1922, in which he quotes an Anglo-Saxon riddle (which he describes as *enigma saxonicum nuper inventum*), but it seems unlikely that the contact was more than social.[5] As for the order in which Tolkien performed the main body of his lexicographical work – the drafting of Dictionary entries – I have had to assume that work proceeded through the alphabetical sequence, as it does in Oxford Dictionaries today, and have therefore described it in alphabetical order by headword, except where there is good reason to do otherwise.

According to Humphrey Carpenter, in his first weeks Tolkien "was given the job of researching the etymology of

[4] Tolkien's contribution was the preparation of a glossary, which appeared separately as *A Middle English Vocabulary* (1922) – his first published book.

[5] Later in 1923 Tolkien's riddle was published in the anthology *A Northern Venture* (Leeds University English School Association, 1923) under the heading "Enigmata Saxonica Nuper Inventa Duo". The cordiality of Tolkien's relations with Bradley are vividly conveyed in the heartfelt obituary (signed "J.R.R.T."): "To see him working in the Dictionary Room at the Old Ashmolean and to work for a time under his wise and kindly hand was a privilege not at that time looked for. [. . .] The Memory of more recent years recalls with a sense of great loss his piled table in the Dictionary Room; and many, whether occasional visitors, or workers in that great dusty workshop, that brownest of brown studies, preserve a picture of him as he sat writing there, glimpses of him momentarily held in thought, with eyes looking into the grey shadows of the roof, pen poised in the air to descend at last and fix a sentence or a paragraph complete and rounded, without blot or erasure, on the paper before him" (Tolkien, 1923). The obituary ends with an alliterative verse tribute to Bradley, once again in Anglo-Saxon.

warm, wasp, water, wick (lamp), and *winter*" (Carpenter, 1977, p. 101). The extent to which Tolkien's work on these etymologies was made use of by later editors is, unfortunately, uncertain, since many of the relevant slips are missing: however, most of the etymology of *warm* at least is in Tolkien's hand, and although it is completed in Henry Bradley's hand, it is likely that this is based on an earlier draft by Tolkien (see figure 1).

Probably even before this etymological research, and certainly before he began to draft entries on a substantial scale, Tolkien embarked on an ancillary task which drew upon his thorough knowledge of Old English, and whose results were made use of long after he had given up work on the Dictionary. At some stage during the collection of quotation evidence, numerous important Old and Middle English texts had been examined by readers who copied out illustrative quotations but were unable to lemmatize the words illustrated, that is, to convert the form occurring in the text to the form with which a dictionary entry would be headed. Tolkien was one of a small number of people who lemmatized these slips by writing the correct lemmas alongside the cited forms noted by the less able readers, thereby allowing the slips for each lemma to be placed together. Quotations of this type exist for words in the range *waedle* to *wursien*.

Somewhat surprisingly, I have found very little evidence that Tolkien habitually wrote out quotations encountered during his everyday reading, as his colleagues certainly did: slips sent in by readers from all over the English-speaking world were, of course, still flooding in – as they do to this day – and it must surely have been as automatic for lexicographers in Tolkien's time as it is now for myself and my colleagues to contribute quotations from their own reading in the same way. However, apart from a single quotation for the word *smirkle*, taken from Lewis Carroll's *Sylvie and Bruno*, no quotations in Tolkien's handwriting for words outside the letter W have come to light. The existence of one slip, nevertheless, does suggest that there were others which simply cannot be found; which is a pity, since they would have provided an interesting glimpse of Tolkien's recreational reading habits.

After some little time spent in learning his job, then, Tolkien at last started work on the drafting of Dictionary entries. This central task seems to have been organized much as it is today: each assistant was allocated an alphabetical range by his or her Editor, and would deal with all aspects of the final text – pronunciation, spelling variants, and etymology, as well as the defining of the various senses and the selection and copy-editing of illustrative quotations. The text prepared in this way would eventually be revised by the Editor, who frequently made substantial changes such as re-classifying the senses (and rewriting the definitions accordingly), choosing different quotations, and even deciding to reject a word entirely, often because of a paucity of quotation evidence. Variations to this routine were made when some assistants were not competent to deal with certain aspects of particular entries, such as the etymology of a word derived from an unusual language (in some cases these were even left to be added in proof).

The raw material for the creation of Dictionary text, namely the quotation slips, would have already undergone some initial processing by the time an assistant such as Tolkien came to work on it: this included sorting into alphabetical order (no small task) and, in the case of more complex words, preliminary arrangement of slips approximately by sense. Some of the sub-editors who carried out this work went further, and wrote first drafts of definitions.[6] A great many of these editorial slips were, however, rejected by the "official" lexicographers, including Tolkien, as is shown by the fact that definitions by these later workers are frequently written on the backs of the earlier drafts.

Tolkien's first editorial range appears to have been a short one consisting of the verb *waggle* and its cognates. Quite what training he will have received is not at all clear: it seems most likely to me that once embarked on drafting proper, assistants would be expected to learn from their mistakes. Certainly these early slips show an incomplete grasp of "house style", as can be seen from the number of corrections made by Bradley, who also rewrote the etymology of *waggle v.* completely (see figure 2). This initial range (*waggle* to *waggly*) was evidently returned with annotations to Tolkien, who made some further corrections. Tolkien also wrote out two quotations for an unrelated word (dealt with for the most part by Bradley), *wag(g)el* "a name for the Black-backed Gull, *Larus marinus*, in its immature state", probably through finding misfiled references to them among the evidence for *waggle*.

His next task, alphabetically, was to work on parts of the entry for the noun *wain* (wagon). He may have dealt with the whole entry, but all slips relating to the three main published senses show evidence only of Bradley's hand, and it seems more likely that Tolkien was assigned only the etymology and the end of the entry (where combinations such as *wain-house* and *wain-trees* are dealt with). Characteristically, the long etymological note contains a speculation about the ultimate derivation of the word, which Bradley felt obliged to tone down (see figures 3a and 3b).

The same division of labour between Tolkien and Bradley is observed in the case of *waist*: here, however, several of the *waist-* combinations require entries of their own, and in some cases division into senses. Thus having organized the final paragraphs of the entry for the main noun, Tolkien proceeded to write full entries for *waistband* (two senses), *waist-cloth* (three senses), and – after considerable deliberation (surely to be expected of a future connoisseur of the garment) – *waistcoat* (see figure 4). In fact Tolkien identified no less than four distinct varieties of garment denoted by this word, two of which he further subdivided into several subsenses (including at least three senses omitted from the published

---

[6] For a full account of the various stages of the editorial process, see the article "The history of the Oxford English Dictionary" which appears in the prefatory matter to the Second Edition of the *OED*. See also Murray, 1977.

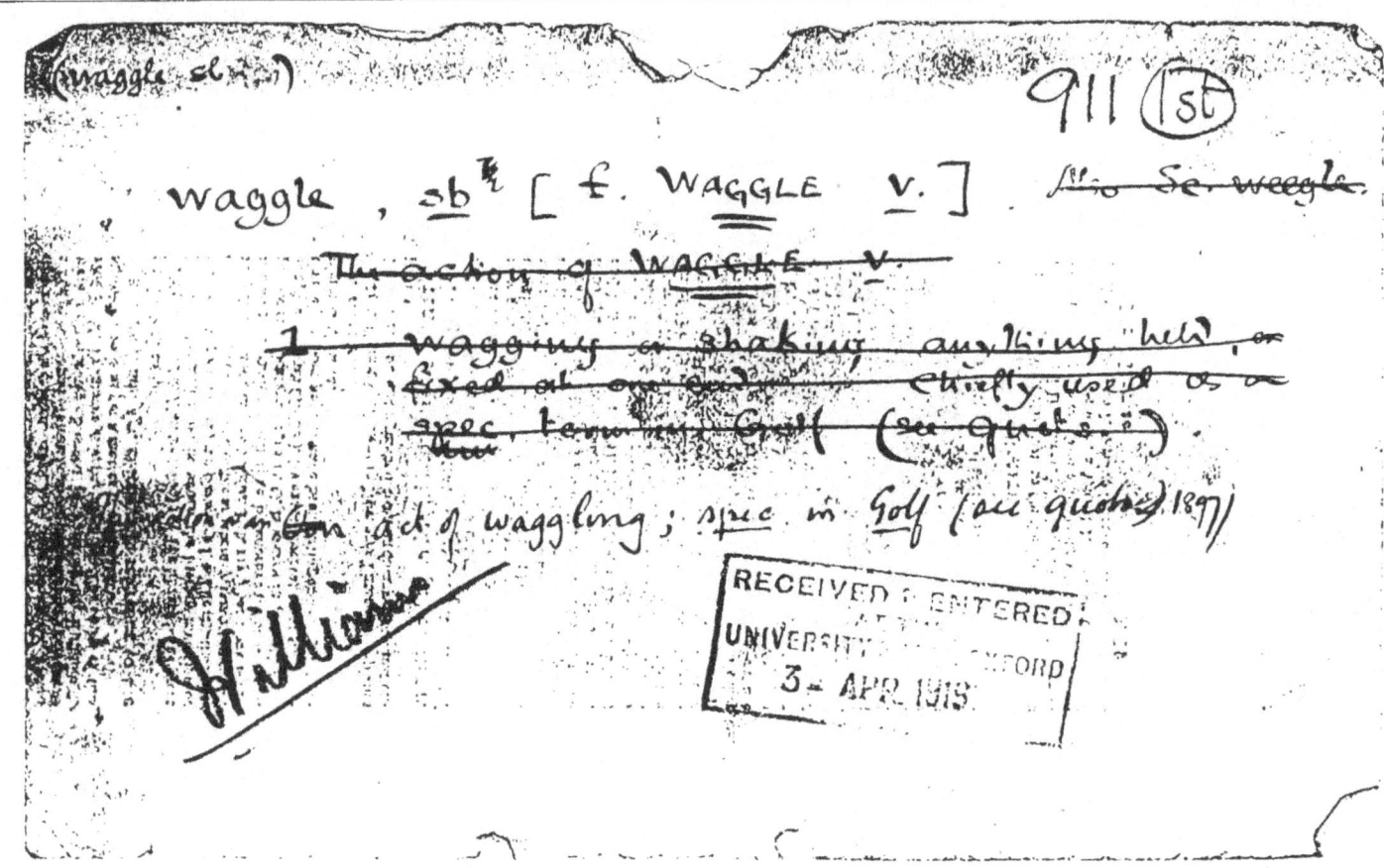

Figure 2: *OED* slips, headword *Waggle*, *(a)* noun (start); *(b)* verb (first sense). *(Reproduced by permission of the Bodleian Library)*

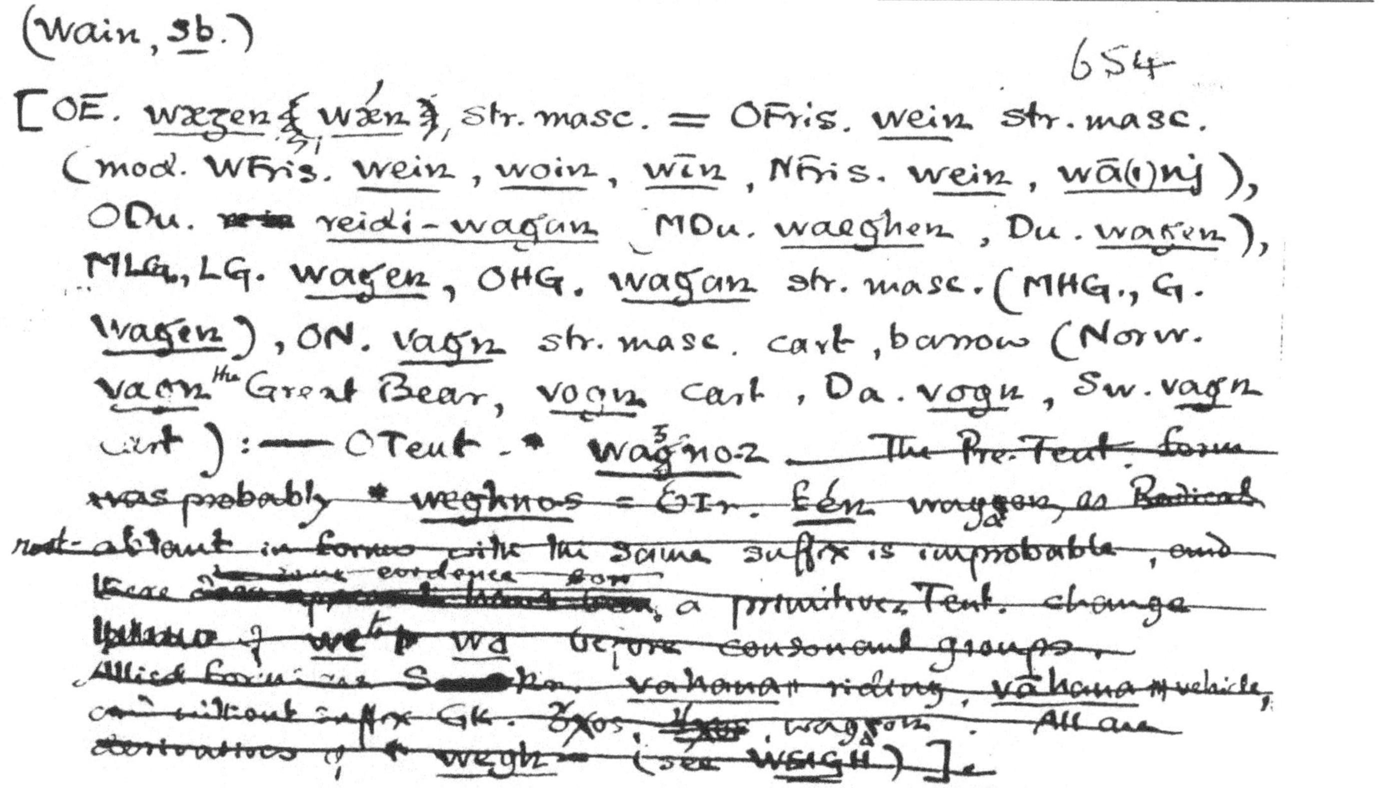

Figure 3a: *OED* slips, headword *Wain*, etymology. *(Reproduced by permission of the Bodleian Library)*

entry), with two historical notes in small type completing the thorough description. (The note attached to sense 1a is in Bradley's hand, but is probably based on a first draft by Tolkien.)

After *waistcoat* follow several other *waist-* compounds and derivatives (*waisted*, *waist-rail* and the like). The complex word *wait* was dealt with by Bradley, but he once again allowed Tolkien to "mop up" the related words, including *waiting* (together with combinations such as *waiting-room* and *waiting-woman*), *wait-a-bit* (a South African plant, whose diversity of spelling received comprehensive treatment before the simplifying touch of Bradley's pen) and *waiter*, whose eleven senses were left much as Tolkien drafted them. In a dictionary the size of the *OED* even nonce-words can find room; however, at this stage in the project the Editors were under considerable pressure to keep the volume of text down as much as possible, and so Tolkien's original full-scale entries for *waiterage* ("the performance of a waiter's duties"), *waiterdom* ("waiters considered as a class, or collectively"), *waiterhood* ("the state or condition of a waiter") and *waitering* ("the occupation of a waiter") were subsequently condensed into a subentry under *waiter*, and his definition of *waiterful* ("as much of anything as can be carried on a waiter, or tray") was omitted entirely.

With the exception of *waith* and *waive* and their cognates, the next five pages of the published Dictionary are closely based on Tolkien's work, including entries for the various kinds of *wake* – the nouns, that is: Bradley apparently considered the main verb too important or difficult for Tolkien at this stage, wrote the etymology himself and left the senses to be defined by another assistant. The nouns were, in any case, something of a handful, there being possibly as many as five etymologically distinct words, of which three were eventually included. It may be worth examining some of the evidence left by Tolkien of his deliberations about two of these (see figure 5). The senses to do with vigils and wakefulness go back to Middle English, although now surviving only in connection with funerals (especially in Irish contexts) and some rural English merrymaking. Once again Tolkien's impulse was to say more about the history of the word and its connotations than Bradley could allow space for: the final draft of the published sense 3 carried a small-type note in which Tolkien observed, "This custom (cf. next sense) appears never to have been free from frivolous or disorderly tendencies. It now survives most vigorously in Ireland, or colonies of Irish." This (deleted) note represents the last stage in a long struggle to convey a sense of the word's overtones: earlier drafts of sense 4b (originally further subdivided into two subsenses by Tolkien) show a whole succession of attempts to capture aspects of a rural English wake:

> very frequently mentioned with disapproval as characterised by riot, drunkenness, and dissolute conduct
>
> a typical scene of uncultured excess or of unsophisticated simple speech
>
> associated with the preservation of certain rustic sports as wrestling, single-sticks etc. [. . .] also used as a typical scene of boorish, sometimes unsophisticated or simple, speech and manners
>
> the holiday-making marked by fairs, sports and often riot and drunkenness incident to such annual local

feasts.

The second etymologically distinct noun *wake* gave Tolkien problems of a different kind, to do with the arrangement of the senses. At one point he copied out the *OED* definitions of several senses of the words *rear* and *train* onto separate slips, presumably as models on which to base his own treatment of the corresponding senses: indeed his final draft of the preamble to the phrase "in the wake of" suggested that "in these expressions WAKE is often practically synonymous with TRAIN" – a remark deleted by Bradley as not in keeping with the usually self-contained style of *OED* entries, with minimal cross-referencing. Tolkien was clearly still learning.

The words following *wake* (except for an entry for *wake-robin*) belonged to the ranges of other assistants. Tolkien's next word was *wallop*: both the relatively straightforward noun, and the verb, concerning the etymology of which Tolkien provides no less than five paragraphs of scholarly speculation, hardly altered at all by Bradley, who by this stage clearly had considerable confidence in him (see figure 6) – sufficient confidence to entrust him with the Old English word *walm* (synonymous in some senses with *wallop*, which is perhaps why Tolkien was given both to do). Incidentally, Tolkien apparently had sufficient evidence for the bizarre expression "the right to wallop one's own nigger" to draft a slip for it, but must have excised it from his entry at a fairly early stage, judging from its provisional sense number.

In the next few pages of the Dictionary, most of which is the work of others, Tolkien contributed to three other isolated words: *walnut*, *walrus* and *wampum*. I am sure that the reason for this departure from the usual assignment of a continuous alphabetical range is that all three words turned out to have unusually tricky etymologies. Frustratingly, the entire entry for *wampumpeag* (the Algonquian word from which *wampum* derives) is missing; but Tolkien's deliberations over *walnut* and *walrus* have certainly left their mark.[7] In the case of *walrus* at least six neatly written versions (of which figure 7 is probably one of the earliest) of the etymology precede the final printed form, all attempting to reconstruct the route by which Old Norse *rosmhvalr* or *rosmall* arrived in Dutch (from which it was borrowed into English in the seventeenth century) as *walrus*. Bradley was obviously pleased with the result since when the fascicle *W–Wash* was published in October 1921, *walnut*, *walrus* and *wampum* were amongst the few entries singled out in its Introduction as containing "etymological facts or suggestions not given in other dictionaries".

Tolkien seems next to have been assigned the whole of the range containing the challenging words *wan*, *wander* and *wane*. Whether or not there is any truth in the suggestion, often made, that in his creative writing Tolkien brings particular enthusiasm to his descriptions of "bad things", he certainly relished the task of working out the sense-development of *wan* and *wane*. In particular he was intrigued that *wan*, which in Old English had meant "dark, gloomy,

WAIN.

† **Waiming.** *Obs.* Also 4 **wamming,** 5 **waymynge.** [Perh. a corruption of WAYMENT *sb.* or WAYMENTING *vbl. sb.*, perh. an alteration of *waining*, WONING *vbl. sb.*] Lamentation.

a 1300 *Cursor M.* 5721 He herd þair waiming and vn-quert. *Ibid.* 14314 Iesus þair wamming [*Gott.* waining] vnderstod. *c* 1420 *Anturs of Arth.* 87 (Douce MS.), Hit ȝaules, hit ȝameres, with waymynges wete.

Waimto, obs. form of WAME-TOW.

Wain (wēⁱn), *sb.*[1] Forms: 1 **wæȝn, (weȝn), wæȝen, wǽn,** 2–3 *Orm.* **waȝȝn,** 3–7 **wayne, waine,** 4–7 **wayn,** (5 **wayen,** 6 **waayne,** 4 *Sc.* **vayn**), 4–5 **weyne,** (5 **wene,** 6 **weene, weane,** 7 **wean, whene**), 5–7 **wane,** 3– **wain.** [OE. *wæȝen, wǽn*, str. masc. = OFris. *wein* str. masc. (mod. WFris. *wein, woin, wīn*, NFris. *wein, wā(i)nj*), OLow Frankish *reidi-wagan* (MDu. *waeghen*, Du. *wagen*), MLG., LG. *wagen*. OHG. *wagan* str. masc. (MHG., G. *wagen*), ON. *vagn* str. masc. cart, barrow (Norw. *vagn* the Great Bear, *vogn* cart, Da. *vogn*, Sw. *vagn* cart) :—OTeut. **wagno-z* :—pre-Teut. **woghno-s* f. Indogermanic root **wegh-*, **wogh-* to carry, etc.: cf. WEIGH, WAW *vbs.*, WAY *sb.* Outside Teut. cognate words of similar meaning are Irish *fén* (:— pre-Celtic **weghno-s*) wagon, Gr. ὄχος (ϝόχος :— **wogho-s*), chariot, Skr. *vahana* neut., *vāhana* neut., chariot.

The pre-Teut. form may possibly have been **weghno-s*, corresponding with the pre-Celtic form; there is some evidence of an OTeut. change of *we-* to *wa-* before consonant groups.]

1. A large open vehicle, drawn by horses or oxen, for carrying heavy loads, esp. of agricultural produce; usually four-wheeled (but see 1 b); a wagon.

The word does not occur in the Bible of 1611, though Wyclif and the 16th c. translators use it. As a colloquial word it survives only in dialects, but in poetry it is commonly used instead of *wagon*.

Beowulf 3134 þær wæs wunden gold on wæn hladen. *c* 725 *Corpus Gl.* (Hessels) U 143 *Ueniculum* [read *Uehiculum*], wæȝn. *c* 1250 *Gen. & Ex.* 2362 He bad cartes and waines nimen, And fechen wiues, and childre, and men, And gaf hem ðor al lond gersen. 1297 R. GLOUC. (Rolls) 8596 Þat þer nas non so heuy charge of wayn ne of oþer þinge þat me ne miȝte ouer grete wateres boþe lede & bringe. *a* 1300 *Cursor M.* 5229 His suns all and þair flitting..In weynis war þai don to lede. 1375 BARBOUR *Bruce* x. 164 That apon his cowyn gat he Men that mycht [ane] enbuschement ma, Quhill that he vith his vayn suld ga Till lede thaim hay in-to the peill. *Ibid.* xi. 24 A litill stane oft, as men sayis, May ger weltir ane mekill wane. 1398 TREVISA *Barth. De P. R.* xvii. lxxii. (1495) 646 And at the laste heye is led home in cartes and in waynes and broughte in to bernes for dyuers vse and nedes. 1432–50 tr. *Higden* (Rolls) I. 137 Thei haue noo howses, caryenge theire wyfes and children in waynes [L. *in plaustris*]. 1449 *Yatton Churchw. Acc.* (Somerset Rec. Soc.) 92 For custom for our wene to Bristowe warde comyng and goyng, iiij d. 1473 *Rental Bk. Cupar-Angus* (1879) I. 182 The said tenandis..sal led to the abbay viii score of fuderis of petis the abbai fyndand wanis meit and drink to the ledaris. 1521 *Lincoln Wills* (1914) I. 88 To William my son my bonden wane, ij oxen that cam from Hornecastell, [etc.]. 1523–34 FITZHERB. *Husb.* § 5 And or he shall lode his corne, he muste haue a wayne, a copyoke, [etc.]. 1576 *Act* 18 *Eliz.* c. 10 § 1 Everye person..shalbe charged to finde..one Carte Wayne Tumbrell..Carres or Dragges furnished for thamendment..of the Highe wayes within the severall Parishes. 1588 in *Archæologia* LXIV. 366 For viij weanes of Pilleseley which ladd Timber from Penttridge, xvj d. 1617 MORYSON *Itin.* III. 19 Alexander the great set on fier with his owne hands the wanes of carriage taken from Darius. 1627 MAY *Lucan* v. I i, The horses trample ore Safely where ships haue saild; the Bessians Furrow Mæotis frozen backe with waines. 1641 BEST *Farm. Bks.* (Surtees) 46 Wee leade in our winter corne usually with three waines. 1688 W. SCOT *Hist. Name Scot* I. (1894) 35 According to the old Proverb, They but fell from the Wains tail. 1731 T. BOSTON *Mem.* vii. (1899) 106 On Thursday..came the wains with the household-furniture from Dunse. 1784 COWPER *Task*

Figure 3b: *OED*, fascicle *W–Wash*, p. 19 (part).

[7] Tolkien's daughter Priscilla has kindly informed me that he was sufficiently exercised by these two words in particular to discuss them at home.

Figure 4: *OED*, fascicle *W–Wash*, p. 23.

Wake (wēɪk), *sb.*[1] Forms: 4 **wak, woke,** *Sc.* **walk,** 6 **waoke,** also *pl.* (sense 4) **waakes, wakesses, waks,** 2– **wake.** [In form the word corresponds to OE. **wacu* str. fem., occurring once in *nihtwaco* night-watch. Compare also the wk. fem. forms, MDu. *wake* (Du. *waak*), MLG. *wake*, OHG. *wacha* (MHG., modG. *wache*), wakefulness, watching, watch, ON. *vaka* (MSw., Sw. *vaka*, Norw. *voka*) watch, vigil, eve of a feast; related to WAKE *v.* In the sense 'state of wakefulness', the sb. is prob. in part a new formation in ME. on the stem of WAKE *v.*, on the analogy of *sleep* vb. and sb. In sense 4 adoption from ON. is possible; the sense 'merry-making' is found in ON. and Norw.; cf. ON. *Jónsvaka*, Norw. *Jóns(v)oka* St. John's Eve, Midsummer festivities.]

1. The state of wakefulness *esp.* during normal hours of sleep. *Obs.* exc. in *sleep and* (*or*) *wake*, *wake and dream.*

a 1250 *Owl & Night.* 1590 Al for hire louerdes sake Haneþ daies kare and niȝtes wake. 1596 SHAKS. 1 *Hen. IV*, III. i. 219 Making such difference betwixt Wake and Sleepe, As is the difference betwixt Day and Night. 1823 'JON BEE' *Dict. Turf* s. v., At Bristol one eye is ever upon the wake while the other nappeth. 1844 MRS. BROWNING *Brown Rosary* II, Repeat the vow—declare its cause and kind Which, not to break, in sleep or wake, thou bearest on thy mind. 1898 J. B. CROZIER *My Inner Life* I. iv. 33 In that half-conscious state between sleep and wake. 1913 *Edin. Rev.* Jan. 194 Their beauty is the beauty of a kind of mirage that haunts the borders between wake and dream.

†**b.** A state or period of wakefulness. *Obs.*

1611 BEAUM. & FL. *Philaster* II. (1620) 22 What thinke you of a pleasing dreame to last till morning? *Gal.* I shall chose

Church of Westminster. *a* 1641 BP. MOUNTAGU *Acts & Mon.* (1642) 434 After this Supper ended followes [among the Essenes] a sacred wake, or vigill, kept in this manner.

3. The watching (*esp.* by night) of relatives and friends beside the body of a dead person from death to burial, or during a part of that time; the drinking, feasting, and other observances incidental to this. Now chiefly *Anglo-Irish* or with reference to Irish custom. Also applied to similar funeral customs in other times or among pagan peoples.

1412–20 LYDG. *Chron. Troy* IV. 3261 What shulde I now any lenger dwelle..for to telle..of þe pleies called palestral, Nor þe wrastelyng þat was at þe wake? *a* 1529 SKELTON *P. Sparowe* 437 The gose and the gander, The ducke and the drake, Shall watche at this wake. 1572 *Inv. Ketshange* (Somerset Ho.), Her wacke and buriall xiiijs. 1700 DRYDEN *Pal. & Arc.* III. 998 The warlike Wakes continu'd all the Night, And Fun'ral Games were played at new-returning Light. 1724 SWIFT *Acc. Wood's Exec.* Misc. (1735) V. 317 When he was cut down, the Body was carried through the whole City to gather Contributions for his Wake. 1726–31 WALDRON *Descr. Isle of Man* (1865) 60 When a person dies, several of his acquaintance come to sit up with him, which they call the Wake. 1778 *Phil. Surv. S. Irel.* 210 The series of ceremonies used on the night,..that the corpse remains unburied, is what they call a wake. 1814 W. S. MASON *Statist. Acc. Irel.* I. 596 The Presbyterian wake is conducted with profound silence and great decorum... The wakes of the members of the established church differ little from those in other parts of Ireland. 1857 LIVINGSTONE *Trav.* xxiii. 468 A poor man and his wife were accused of having bewitched the man, whose wake was now held in the village. 1874 C. E. NORTON *Lett.* (1913) II. 42 Summer is dead. We have had a great wake over him, and the echoes of it have scarcely yet died away. 1894 GLADSTONE *Odes Hor.* II. xviii. 18 New contracts for new marbles thou dost make, But thou art near thy wake.

4. The vigil of a festival (and senses thence derived).

In this use *wake* is a translation of Eccl. L. *vigilia*, primarily referring to the rule of the early church that certain feast-days should be preceded by services lasting through the night. When this rule had ceased to exist, the vigil continued to be a pretext for nocturnal festivity, and the use of the word *wake* was extended to denote not only the eve but also the feast-day itself, and the whole period during which festivities continued.

a. The vigil or eve of a festival, and the observances belonging to this. Also, a festival. *Obs.* exc. *dial.*

15.. *Part of a Register* (1593) 64 Their Saints dayes and their prescript seruice. Their waakes, and idolatrous bankets. 1523 BERNERS *Froiss.* (1812) I. clxix. 207 Great solemnytes were made in all churches, and great fyers and wakes, throughout all Englande. 1600 SURFLET *Country Farm* II. xliii. 276, I knowe well that the common sort doe verily thinke and auerre, that this seede cannot be gathered but on the night of the wakes of S. Iohn in sommer. *a* 1629 HINDE *J. Bruen* xxix. (1641) 89 Their Wakes and Vigils, in all riot and excesse of eating and drinking. *a* 1806 H. K. WHITE *Poems* (1837) 136 Such is the jocund wake of Whitsuntide. 1876 *Mid-Yorks. Gloss.*, *Wake*, casually employed in Mid-Yorks. and the north, for vigils, or the superstitious rites performed on the eves of St. Agnes and St. Mark.

b. The local annual festival of an English (now chiefly rural) parish, observed (originally on the feast of the patron saint of the church, but now usually on some particular Sunday and the two or three days following) as an occasion for making holiday, entertainment of friends, and often for village sports, dancing, and other amusements.

In modern rustic use chiefly *pl.* in sing. sense and often with sing. construction (cf. the double pl. *wakeses*, in 16th c. *wakesses*). The word is now current only in certain districts, mainly northern and west midland; elsewhere the equivalent term is *feast* or *revels*.

a 1225 *Ancr. R.* 314 Heo hefde ileaned one wummone to one wake on of hore weaden. *c* 1290 *S. Eng. Leg.* 413/381

Wake (wēɪk), *sb.*[2] Also 6 ?**walk,** 7 **wack.** [Not found before the 16th c., but possibly much older; either directly or mediately a. ON. (**vaku*) *vǫk* str. fem., *vaka* wk. fem., hole or opening in ice. The ON. word was probably applied to the path made for itself by a vessel through ice, and from this use the sense 'trace or track of a vessel in the water' may have been developed by Scandinavian navigators in British seas. Sense 5, 'line of hay', if it really belongs to the same word, may be a transferred use of the nautical sense.

The word is represented in all the Scandinavian dialects, and has been adopted in Du., Fris., and Ger. The sense 'track of a vessel' is found, outside Eng., only in Norw. *vok* (dial. *vaak*), NFris. (Sylt) *waak*; the older sense, 'hole or channel in ice' (sometimes, 'a piece of water kept unfrozen by wind or current') belongs to MSw. *vaak*, *vak*, Sw. *vak* (cf. Sw. *väcka* to cut a hole in ice), Norw. *vok*, Da. *vaage*, WFris. *wek*, *wjekke*, Du. *wak* neut., MLG., LG. (whence mod.G.) *wake* fem.

The word is commonly supposed to be connected with ON. *vǫk-r*, Du. *wak*, moist, damp: see WAK *a.* This view involves some difficulty, as the ON. adj. has the stem *vǫkv-*, while the sb. has genit. *vakar*, pl. *vakar*, *-ir*. Connexion with WAKE *a.* and *v.* seems not impossible: the freeing of the water from ice may have been regarded as an awakening.]

I. 1. The track left on the water's surface by a ship (in the sea often marked by a smooth appearance).

[*a* 1547: see 4 a.] 1627 CAPT. J. SMITH *Sea Gram.* ix. 42 The wake of a ship is the smooth water a sterne shewing the way shee hath gone in the sea. 1703 DAMPIER *Voy.* III. I. 97 In the Wake of the Ship (as 'tis call'd) or the Smoothness which the Ship's passing has made on the Sea. 1768–74 TUCKER *Lt. Nat.* (1834) I. 412 The wake of a ship (by which, I think, the sailors understand the stream drawn after the stern by its motion,) follows the ship throughout her voyage. 1820 W. SCORESBY *Acc. Arctic Regions* II. 240 An 'eddy' having somewhat the resemblance of the 'wake' or track of a ship. 1852 CLOUGH *Poems*, '*Where lies the land*' 8 Or, o'er the stern reclining, watch below The foaming wake far widening as we go. 1861 DICKENS *Gt. Expect.* liv, Both steamers were drifting away from us, and we were rising and falling in a troubled wake of water. 1882 W. H. WHITE *Naval Archit.* (ed. 2) 553 The actual wake of a ship combines the stream line motions with those due to the frictional drag of the skin upon the water. 1913 *Engl. Rev.* Nov. 506 Her wake was without foam and closed sluggishly behind her.

attrib. 1865 MACGREGOR '*Rob Roy*' *Baltic* 229 A canoe was pulled at a rapid pace in the two wake waves astern of this great smack. 1909 BRIDGES *Paraphr. Virg. Æn.* VI 342 What God..Pluckt you away and drown'd i' the swift wake-water abandon'd?

†**b.** Phrases. *To fetch* (*get, get into, have*) *the wake of* (a pursued vessel): to get so close to her

II. 5. A line of hay prepared for carting. *dial.*

1847 HALLIWELL, *Wake*, hay placed in large rolls for the convenience of being carried. *West.* *Ibid.*, *Wakes*, rows of green damp grass. 1872–4 JEFFERIES *Toilers of Field* (1892) 259 The waggon safely jolted over the furrow, and on between the wakes of light-brown hay. 1879 — *Wild Life in S. Co.* vii. 143 Watching that the 'wallows' may be turned over properly, and the 'wakes' made at a just distance from each other.

III. 6. An open hole, or unfrozen place in the ice. *dial.* (East Anglia.)

1895 P. H. EMERSON *Birds* etc. *Norf. Broadland* II. xiii. 379. I passed a 'wake'—or open space in the ice—where the swans were swimming like sentries on duty.

†**Wake,** *sb.*[3] *Obs. rare*$^{-1}$. [Possibly a. some native African word, but evidently regarded by Jobson as onomatopœic.] A North African bird.

1623 JOBSON *Golden Trade* 155 The next [bird] in greatnesse, is called a Wake, in regard of the great noyse hee makes when hee flyeth, which resembleth what he is called by:..[it] is a bird of great stature, hauing the vpper part of his head carrying a beautifull shew, with a pleasing tuft on his Crowne, which I haue seene worne by great personages here at home.

Figure 5: *OED*, fascicle *W–Wash*, pp. 31-2 (part).

black", should have come to be applied to pale or faint things: the published entry represents his final conclusions (see figure 8), and is once again largely unchanged by Bradley, but it does not suggest the welter of different versions Tolkien considered, some of which are barely more than strings of near-synonymous words, apparently jotted down in an attempt to clarify his thinking (e.g. "with connot[ations] of fading foulness unnatural pallor"; "anaemic emaciated"): the various versions between them contain approximately forty "bad" adjectives and nouns, and even the final form of the entry is unusually plentiful in these. The verb *wane* may not have been all Tolkien's work, although the etymology is in his handwriting (a number of the senses are defined in Bradley's hand, and I could find no rejected versions by Tolkien): he did, however, deal with the archaic and obsolete nouns and adjective. By far the largest component of this range, however, was the work required on the verb *wander* and its cluster of related words. Once again Tolkien's final versions reach the printed page with little or no alteration. (On the back of one quotation for *wandering* are some rather curious jottings in Tolkien's hand, which appear to be rapidly-noted examples of some consonantal changes occurring in Indo-European languages (see figure 9). I regret to say that I cannot connect this philological doodle with either his lexicographical work or the invented languages he was working on at this time: it more probably relates to an incidental rumination or discussion with a colleague. Some of the Greek jottings appear to be an illustration of the philological rule known as Grassmann's Law.) Two of Tolkien's other entries in this range reflect his awareness of the poetical qualities of words: early draft entries for the obsolete nouns *wan* "bruise" and *wandreth* "adversity" include a note of the other *w-* words which frequently co-occur with each of them in alliterative writing – something not often commented on in *OED* definitions (and in fact deleted from *wan* by Bradley). In the case of *wandreth* Tolkien perceived in these co-occurring words (grouped as *woe/wrake/wer* and *wele/welthe/worldes riches*) a basis for distinguishing two senses, denoting respectively "evil circumstances, affliction, misery" and "embarrassment of circumstances, poverty": once again this was too expansive for the *OED*, and Bradley collapsed them into one definition, although a brief comment on the word's alliterative companions remains.

Tolkien's next word was *want* – one of the twenty or so commonest verbs in English, and surely ample evidence of Bradley's willingness to let him tackle even the most significant entries more or less without intervention or correction. Of the twenty-eight separate definitions for the verb, nineteen of Tolkien's slips went to press, including those for most of the main senses, and at least two more formed the basis of revised slips by Bradley. The early part of the entry for the noun is missing, but most of what remains in the manuscript is also Tolkien's largely unaltered text.

Isolated words, rather than alphabetical ranges, make up the rest of Tolkien's contribution to the first edition of the *OED*. He dealt with the etymologically troublesome

Figure 6: *OED*, fascicle W–Wash, p. 53 (part).

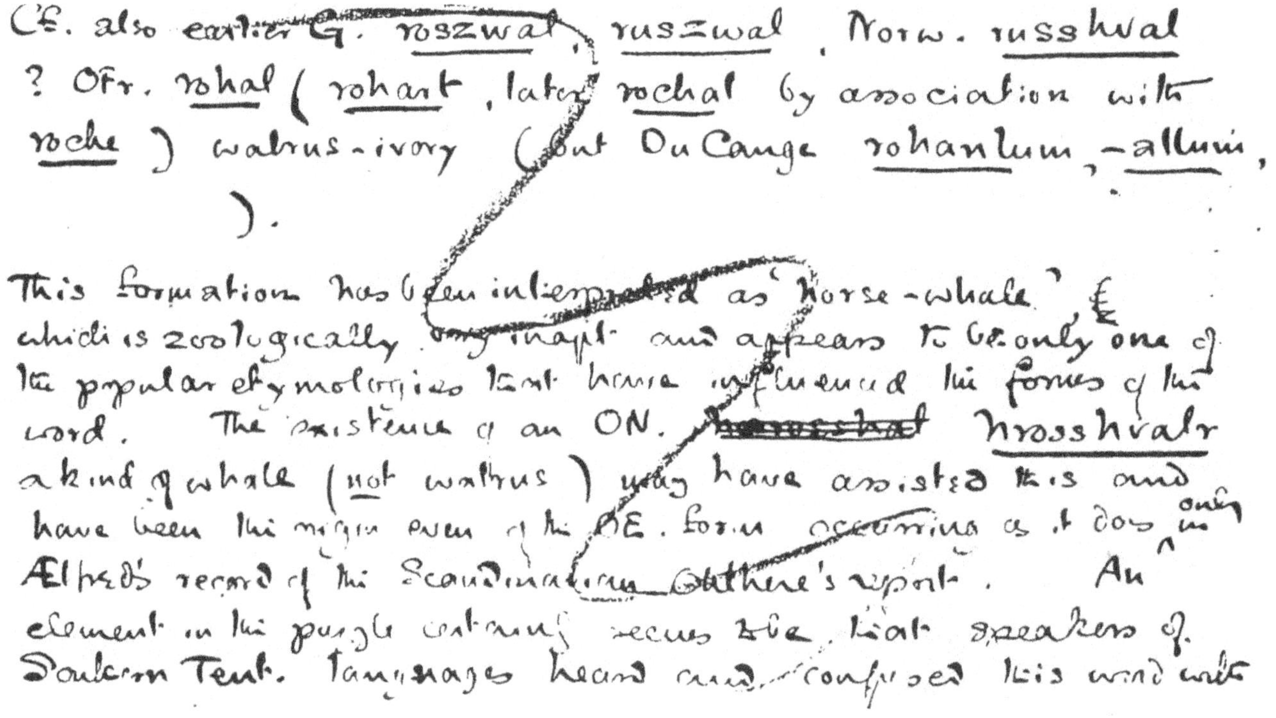

> Cf. also earlier G. roszwal, ruszwal, Norw. russhval
> ? OFr. rohal (rohart, later rochal by association with
> roche) walrus-ivory (but Du Cange rohanlum, -allum,
>).
>
> This formation has been interpreted as 'horse-whale' &
> which is zoologically inapt and appears to be only one of
> the popular etymologies that have influenced the forms of the
> word. The existence of an ON. [struck through] hrosshvalr
> a kind of whale (not walrus) may have assisted this and
> have been the origin even of the OE. form occurring as it does only in
> Ælfred's record of the Scandinavian Ohthere's report. An
> element in the puzzle containing seems to be that speakers of
> Southern Teut. languages heard and 'confused' this word with

Figure 7: *OED* reject slips, headword *Walrus*. *(Reproduced by permission of the Bodleian Library)*

wariangle (a name for the shrike, found in Chaucer), and with the once almost obsolete word *warlock*, which seems to have been revived by its use in the novels of Walter Scott: unfortunately many slips for this entry are missing, but from what remains it is clear that the etymology and sense-division, and most of the definition text, are Tolkien's work. Finally there are a small number of words which, while scattered across the letter W, are sufficiently similar in form for their early spellings to coincide, thus making it sensible for someone to work on them as a group. The main members of the group are *Weald*, *wield*, *wild* and *wold*: apart from *Weald* (much of which is missing, although the word itself and several derivatives were at least started by Tolkien), all of these lie in ranges edited not by Bradley but by his colleague C.T. Onions, who seems to have preferred rewriting a slip to attempting to annotate it with his corrections – thus leaving frustratingly few of Tolkien's own slips. However, discarded slips for most of the entry for *wold* have survived, as has Tolkien's etymology for *wild*, and I suspect that he in fact dealt with these words in their entirety, although to judge from the example of *wold* the definitions in the printed text are probably mainly the work of Onions: very little of Tolkien's definitions of *wold*, or even of his division of it into senses, escaped alteration. The etymologies, however, are vintage Tolkien, complete with long lists of cognates in other European languages living and dead, speculations about the ulterior origins of Old Teutonic *wilþijaz* and *walþuz*, and some general remarks about the sense-development of *wold* which are unusually chatty even for Tolkien:

> The primitive meaning of this word was probably "wild, unexplored, or untilled land; wilderness". In early Northern Europe these senses would easily interchange with the sense "forest". In OE. this later is the only evidenced meaning, and the occasional application of the word to mountainous districts appears to be a translation of L. *saltus* (e.g. *Pireni weald*). Some of the senses that appear later in English seem more easily derivable from an original meaning "wilderness", but this development is probably connected solely with the historical deforestation of England, which has produced districts of very varying character in place of former woodlands.
>
> WOLD (and its different forms) appears generally speaking to have become obsolete during the 15th., or early in the 16th., century, except locally or dialectally (especially as applied as a fixed name to certain definite localities). From the seventeenth century onwards its use is largely artificial, and its senses apparently due either to the changed character of the localities where the name had become fixed, or to knowledge of the word in OE. or ME. The distinction drawn in quot[ation] 1577 (Sense 1) between the forms *Wald* and *Wold*, and so by implication between Northern and

61

a Shell Fish..; whose Shell has the tincture of Pearl colour, flame colour, and white, some part thereof being taken out, the Indians make of it their Wampam Pieg; which Shell is a staple Commodity. 1605 Locke *Further Consid. Value Money* 27 Among the Indians, when it [*sc.* Corn] will sell for more yards of Wampompeal, which is their Money. 1705 T. M. *Bacon's Rebellion* (1835) 14 The Queen of Pamunky ..having round her head a plat of black and white wampum peage three inches broad in imitation of a crown. 1760 T. Hutchinson *Hist. Col. Mass. Bay* v. (ed. 2) 472 Good store of wampompag to purchase some peculiar favors or privileges. 1875 Jevons *Money* iv. 24 The wampumpeag of the North American Indians is a case in point, as it certainly served as jewellery.

Wamtow, Wamtye, obs. ff. Wame-tow, Wanty.

Wamus (wæ·məs). *U.S.* Also **waumus, wammus.** [a. Du. *wammes*, contracted f. *wambuis*, a. OF. *wambois, -eis*: see Wambais, Gambeson. Cf. G. *wams, wammus*, woollen jacket (MHG. *wambes, -eis*, jacket worn under the armour).] In southern and western U.S., a warm knitted jacket resembling a cardigan.

1805 in Thornton *Amer. Gloss.* 934, I got up, and found that my waumus was bloody. 1854 H. H. Riley *Puddleford* 14 (Thornton) He was attired with a red flannel 'wamus'. 1887 *Philadelphia Telegraph* 6 July 6/6 His attire was characterized by a long linsey 'wamus'. 1888 E. Eggleston *Graysons* xxviii. 309 This [wagon-spoke] he put into the baggy part of his 'wamus', or hunting-jacket.

Wamylle, obs. form of Wamble.

† **Wan,** *sb.*[1] *Sc. Obs.* 6 *pl.* **wannis, wannys.** [Perh. a subst. use of Wan *a.*[1] But cf. Wen.] A dark or livid mark produced by a blow; a bruise.

1533 Bellenden *Livy* (S.T.S.) I. 167 He..had done grete vassalege baith for þe honoure & defence of þe ciete, as weil apperit be sindri wannys & markis in his face and vther partis of his body. 1560 Rolland *Seven Sages* 59 The knicht..fand his sone withouttin wan or wound. 1567 *Gude & Godlie Ballads* (S.T.S.) 32 He it is, quhilk geuis wan and wound, And suddanlie he will mak haill and sound.

† **Wan,** *sb.*[2] *Obs.* Also 7 **wanne,** 8–9 *erron.* **wand.** [? a. Du. *wanne* (now *wan*): see Van *sb.*[1]]

1. A winnowing fan: = Van *sb.*[1] 1.

1615 Chapman *Odyss.* xi. 163 What dost thou with that wanne [Gr. ἀθηρηλοιγόν, winnowing fan], vpon thy necke?

2. The sail of a windmill: = Van *sb.*[1] 5.

Commonly spelt *wand*, the word being wrongly supposed to be a corruption of Wand *sb.*

1766 *Ann. Reg.* 77 The sails or wands of the mill..struck her so violently on the head, as to fracture her skull. 1825 Brockett *N. C. Gloss.*, *Wan*, a corruption of wand. '*A yard-wan.*'—'A *mill-wan.*' 1846 M. A. Richardson *Borderer's Table-bk.* V. 97 The wands of the..wind mill..were forced round with such velocity, that by the friction of the machinery, the mill was set on fire. 1876 *Whitby Gloss.*, *Wands* pl., long flexible rods. The sail frames of a windmill.

Wan (wǫn), *a.* Forms: 1 **wan(n, won(n,** 3– **wan,** 3–4 **won,** 4–5 **wane, wonn,** 4–6 **wann(e,** 5 **wonne.** [OE. *wann* (*wonn*), dark, gloomy, black. Not found in any of the other Teut. languages. Its original sense appears to have been 'dark in hue', with especially frequent application to things of gloomy unpleasant associations.

Relationships to Win *v.* (OTeut. **winnan* to strive, toil, suffer, etc.), or to Wound *sb.*, or Wen, present difficulties of sense-development or form. Relationship to Wane etc. is possible (cf. Celtic **wanno-*, OIr. *fann*, Welsh *gwan* faint, weak, feeble), but association of the two words in later (ME. and ModE.) periods is more probable than ultimate connexion.

In addition to this association the application to heavenly bodies, when obscured, or when compared to others more bright, possibly aided the general application to pale things. The application to the human face etc., when of unwholesome or unusual colour (through various emotions, disease, or death), also provided a possible occasion of sense-change. The senses 'livid,' 'sallow', and 'pale, sickly' are often indistinguishable.]

† **1.** Lacking light, or lustre; dark-hued, dusky, gloomy, dark. *Obs.* Chiefly *poet.*

Beowulf 702 Com on wanre niht scriðan sceadugenga. *a* 1000 *Boeth. Metr.* xi. 61 Hwæt, þa wonnan niht mona onlihteð. *c* 1230 *Hali Meid.* 43 Ant tah is betere a briht iacinct þen a charbucle won. *a* 1300 *Signs bef. Judgm.* 43 in *E.E.P.* (1862) 8 As fair and briȝte as þou seest ham hi worþ be-com as blak as cole and be of hiwe durke and wan for man-is sin þat hi sul þole. *c* 1400 *Destr. Troy* 303 So dang he þat dog with dynt of his wappon, Þat þe warlag was wete of his wan atter. *Ibid.* 6000 Mony chivalrous Achilles choppit to dethe: All his wedis were wete of þaire wan blode. *c* 1470 Henry *Wallace* vii. 488 In the furd weill, that was bath wan and depe, Feyll off thaim fell. *c* 1480 Henryson *Cock & Fox* 62 In froist, in snaw, in wedder wan and weit. *a* 1529 Skelton *P. Sparowe* 910 With vysage wan As swarte as tan. 1591 Savile *Tacitus, Agricola* 244 The Ocean bringeth forth pearle also, not orient, but duskish and wanne.

b. *esp.* in conventional application in poetry to the sea (waves, etc.) or other waters.

The original significance was perh. that of 'dark-hued', but the sense often approaches, or is blended with, the next.

In more recent poetry the word is probably (exc. by conscious archaism) to be understood rather as 'grey, pale', but the gloomy connotation remains.

Beowulf 1374 Þonon yðgeblond up astigeð won to wolcnum. *c* 1386 Chaucer *Knt.'s T.* 1598 Myn is the drenchyng in the see so wan. ? *a* 1400 *Morte Arth.* 492 Wery to the wane see they went alle att ones. *c* 1400 *Destr. Troy* 4633 The storme..walt vp the wilde se vppon wan hilles. *c* 1470 Henry *Wallace* vii. 814 Her is na gait to fle yone peple can, Bot rochis heich, and wattir depe and wan. 1501 Douglas *Pal. Hon.* ii. liii, Ouir waters wan, throw worthie woddis grene. 1535 Stewart *Cron. Scot.* I. 9 Quhair that tyme almost tha had all bene lost, Throw wan tydis so stark ran by the land. *a* 1780 *Johnie Cock* xvii. in Child *Ballads* III. 4/1 She'd ha wet her foot ith wan water, And sprinkled it oer my brae. 1865 Swinburne *Chastelard* i. ii. 32 Do you yet mind at landing how the quay Looked like a blind wet face in waste of wind And washing of wan waves? 1866 Kingsley *Herew.* xviii, Looking outside across the wan water for the sails which never came.

WAN.

† **c.** Applied to lead, or things compared to it (in colour). *Obs.*

1398 Trevisa *Barth. De P. R.* xix. xx. (1495) 876 Leed is whyte by kynde though it be wan wythout. 1477 Norton *Ord. Alch.* v. in Ashmole (1652) 56 Colour wan as Lead. 1520 Whitinton *Vulg.* (1527) 2 His lyppes be as wanne as lede. 1653 R. Sanders *Physiogn.* 183 A wan leadish colour.

† **2.** *transf.* or *fig.* Sad, dismal; also awful, fearful, deadly, cruel, wicked, etc. (Cf. uses of *dark, gloomy.*) *Obs. poet.*

c 1400 *Destr. Troy* 3602 There is no worship in weping, ne in wan teres! *c* 1440 *York Myst.* vii. 38 Me for to were fro warkes wanne. 1535 Stewart *Cron. Scot.* II. 407 Gratius God that hes all thing in erd, At his weilding to weill or ȝit wan werd.

† **3.** Of an unhealthy, unwholesome colour; livid, leaden-hued. Applied *esp.* to wounds, to the human face discoloured by disease, and to corpses. *Obs.*

c 700 *Epinal Gloss.* 576 *Livida toxica*: tha uuannan aetrinan. *c* 1375 *Cursor M.* 24470 (Fairf.) Þi bodi is wanne as þou ware dede. 1388 Wyclif 1 *Pet.* ii. 24 And he hym silf bar oure synnes in his bodi on a tre, that we be deed to synnes, and lyue to riȝtwisnesse, bi whos wan wounde ȝe ben heelid. 1398 Trevisa *Barth. De P. R.* xvii. xxxviii. (1495) 625 Powder of comyn wel medlyd wyth wexe dooth away wanne colour that comyth of smytynge. *Ibid.* xix. xxi. 876 Wanne colour betokenyth angwysshe and passion of the herte whyche drawyth inwarde the hete of blood. 1483 *Cath. Angl.* 408/1 Wann.., *cerulus, ceruleus, pallidus, liuidus.* 15.. Dunbar *Poems* lxxxvi. 35 Thy sone Jhesu, with his woundis wan, Quhilk deinȝeit him for our trespass to de. 1526 *Pilgr. Perf.* (W. de W. 1531) 257 And those moost beautyfull & fayre chekes, all bloo & wanne, with buffettes & beatynges. *c* 1560 A. Scott *Poems* xxxiii. 16 Evill lyfe, and langour but releif Off woundis wan. 1570 Levins *Manip.* 20/21 Wan.., *liuidus.* 1615 Sylvester tr. *H. Smith's Micro-cosm.* 72 The Nobler states with Enuy wan, Without end are torne and tost. 1655 Culpepper etc. *Riverius* ix. ix. 273 If..the wan and deadly color of the Face..be restored, there is hope of Health.

4. Pallid, faded, sickly; unusually or unhealthily pale. Most frequently applied to the human face (or to things with conscious metaphor from this application).

a 1300 *Cursor M.* 4547 For lene he was, and wan þe face. *Ibid.* 24471 Þi face es wan as ros vnrede. *a* 1310 in Wright *Lyric P.* vi. 28 Nihtes when y wende ant wake, for-thi myn wonges waxeth won. 1393 Langl. *P. Pl.* C. vii. 419 Thenne awakyde he wel wan and wolde haue ydronke. *c* 1400 *Destr. Troy* 8034 All wan was the weghe for his wete teres. *c* 1450 in *Retrosp. Rev.* (1853) Nov. 104 On a greene hylle he sawe a tree,..Pale hyt was and wanne of blee. 1530 Palsgr. 328/2 Wanne of coloure, *palle, yndeux, blesmie.* 1542 Udall *Erasm. Apoph.* 120 One..opposed Diogenes with this question, for what cause golde looked to the yie somewhat pale and wanne of coloure? 1561 T. Hoby tr. *Castiglione's Courtyer* iii. (1577) O j, In like manner where shee is somewhat fatter or leaner than reasonable sise, or wanner, or browner, to helpe it with garmentes. 1582 Stanyhurst *Æneis* iii. (Arb.) 77 Theire face wan withred in hunger. 1599 Marston *Antonio's Rev.* Prol. 3 The wan bleak cheek of the numd earth. 1628 Gaule *Pract. Th.* (1629) 360 His Body was now cold, and wanne, stiffe, and still. 1697 Dryden *Æneis* iii. 773 So thin, so ghastly meagre, and so wan, So bare of flesh, he scarce resembled Man. 1748 *Anson's Voy.* ii. xiii. 275 The wan and meager countenances of the crew. 1800 Coleridge *Christabel* ii. 621 Why is thy cheek so wan and wild, Sir Leoline? 1803 Scott *Cadyow Castle* xxiii, There, wan from her maternal throes, His Margaret, beautiful and mild, Sate in her bower, a pallid rose. 1829 Lytton *Devereux* ii. v, The hangings were wan and colourless. 1837 Dickens *Pickw.* xlvii, The crowd of wan, emaciated faces. 1863 Baring-Gould *Iceland* 120 Dawn broke at last, wan and blear in the south. 1897 *Allbutt's Syst. Med.* III. 329 The thickening of the blood in cholera is sufficient to account for the fall of arterial pressure, the diminished size of the pulse,..and the wan appearance of the patient.

fig. 1742 Gray *Eton* 68 Envy wan, and faded care. 1747 Collins *Passions* 25 With woful Measures wan Despair Low sullen Sounds his Grief beguil'd. 1883 R. W. Dixon *Mano* i. viii. 23 Why failed his thoughts to pierce the wan regret Of love within that look?

b. *esp.* in phr. *pale and wan* (*wan and pale*).

c 1374 Chaucer *Troylus* ii. 551 He for wo was pale and wan. 1447 Bokenham *Seyntys, St. Faith* 375 Bryht of ble He was & of colour neþir pale ne wan. 1513 Douglas *Æneis* ix. xiii. 4 Thar feris fleand pail and wan haue thai sene, And thar cheif ennemy closyt in thar wallis. 1588 Shaks. *Tit. A.* ii. iii. 90 Why doth your Highnes looke so pale and wan? 1590 Spenser *F. Q.* ii. xi. 22 As pale and wan as ashes was his looke. 1601 Holland *Pliny* xxviii. ix. II. 321 Drusus sometimes a Tribune of the Commons in Rome, dranke (as it is reported) Goats bloud, to make himselfe look pale and wan in the face. 1679 in *Verney Mem.* (1907) II. 333 He was grown pale, wan, lean and long-visaged. 1726 Ainsworth *Eng.-Lat. Dict.*, Blank (pale and wan), *pallens, pallidus.* 1812 J. Wilson *Isle of Palms* i. 675 Yea, many a visage wan and pale, Will hang at midnight o'er my tale. 1867 Miss Braddon *Rupert Godwin* i, Clara Westford's noble face is pale and wan this sunny morning.

c. *A wan smile*, a faint or forced smile (as of one sick or unhappy).

1877 Mrs. Forrester *Mignon* I. 217 With a wan smile as she sees her friend's grieved face. 1806 Conan Doyle *Exploits Gerard* v. (1903) 190 'But,' he added, with a wan smile, 'my Lenten fare is always somewhat meagre'.

d. Applied to the (light of) heavenly bodies, etc.: Faint, sickly, partially obscured. Also, of white objects, etc.: Dull, lustreless.

1601 Holland *Pliny* ii. xxx. I. 17 In the warres of Antonie, the Sunne continued almost a yeere long with a pale and wan colour. 1633 P. Fletcher *Purple Isl.* xi. i, The Moon grows wanne, and starres flie all away, Whom Lucifer locks up in wonted folds. 1667 Milton *P. L.* x. 412 The blasted Starrs lookt wan. 1771 Beattie *Minstr.* i. xxv, Ye mildews wan. 1798 Wordsw. *Night-piece* 2 The sky is overcast..Heavy and wan, all whitened by the Moon. 1881 J. Thomson *Ladies of Death* xxii, Moonless nights when stars are few and wan. 1873 W. Black *Pr. Thule* xxv, There were wan glimmerings of sunshine across the sea. 1889 Bridges *Sonn.* lvii, In autumn moonlight, when the white air wan Is fragrant in the wake of summer.

† **e.** Of colour: ? Pale, light. *Obs.*

1567 Maplet *Gr. Forest* 3 b, Whose interchanged greene colour resembleth almost the wan and yelow colour of Golde.

5. *absol.* (quasi-*sb.*) Wan hue, wanness. *poet.*

1821 Joanna Baillie *Metr. Leg.*, *Lady G. Baillie* iv, She saw a faint glow tinge the sickly wan. 1847 Tennyson *Princess* iii. 9 Melissa, tinged with wan from lack of sleep.

6. *Comb.*: chiefly parasynthetic, as *wan-coloured, -faced, visaged*; also complementary and advb., with pples., as *wan-looking, -silvering, -worn*; rarely qualifying other adjs. descriptive of colour, as *wan-sallow*, † *-white.*

1820 Wodarch *Introd. Conchol.* 12 Which..seldom exhibits any other appearance than that of a livid or *wan-colored surface. 1881 'Rita' *My Lady Coquette* x, It is a sorrowful, *wan-faced girl. 1913 *Blackw. Mag.* Aug. 281/1 Wan-faced men and towsel-haired women. 1882 'Ouida' *Maremma* I. 58 Wasted and *wan-looking folks. 1872 Tennyson *Gareth & Lynette* 443 A man of mien *Wan-sallow as the plant that feels itself Root-bitten by white lichen. 1849 Lytton *K. Arthur* v. i, *Wan-silvering through the bush, the cresset shone O'er the arch seer. 1508 Dunbar *Flyting* 101 *Wan wisaged widdefow, out of thy wit gane wyld. *c* 1530 *Judic. Urines* iii. xix. 61 And sume Auctours saye that *wan-whyte colour in vryn..sheweth begynnyng of digestyon. 1609 W. Barlow *Answ. Nameless Cath.* 141 To haue her painting wiped from her riueld browes and *wan-worn cheeks.

Wan (wǫn), *v.* Inflected **wanned, wanning.** Also 3 **wonne.** [OE. *wannian*, f. Wan *a.*]

† **1.** *intr.* To become dark, discoloured, or livid.

c 1000 *Vercelli MS.* 23 b/7 Þonne wannað he & doxaþ; oðre hwile he bið blæc & æniwe. *c* 1230 *Hali Meid.* 35 Þine ehnen schulen doskin & under þon wonnen. *a* 1400–50 *Wars Alex.* 4142 Þe son wadis, þe werd wannes at a wap & þe wedire gloumes. *Ibid.* 4627 Quen it [gold] walowes & wannes all oure thestres, ȝet ere we toghid to & fra be turnyng of eldris.

2. To grow pale. *poet.*

1582 Stanyhurst *Æneis* iv. (Arb.) 118 Al her visage waning with murder aproching [L. *pallida morte futura*]. 1599 Marston *Ant. & Mel.* iii. (1602) E 4, I haue a good head of haire, a cheeke Not as yet wan'd. 1602 Shaks. *Ham.* ii. ii. 580 (Q 1604) Is it not monstrous that this player heere.. Could force his soule so to his owne conceit That from her working all the visage wand [*Folio* warm'd]. 1847 Tennyson *Princess* iv. 142 Psyche flush'd and wann'd and shook. 1855 — *Maud* i. i. iii, And ever he mutter'd and madden'd, and ever wann'd with despair. 1866 Conington *Æneid* iv. p. 128 The queen,..wanning o'er with death foreseen. 1901 Henley *Hawthorn & Lavender* xlvi. 62 And by and by The wide-winged sunset wanned and waned. 1906 F. Thompson *To English Martyrs* 18 The troubled heavens do wan with care.

Hence **Wanned** *ppl. a.*, **Wa·nning** *vbl. sb.*

a 1513 Fabyan *Chron.* vii. 683 Whoom deth soo stern wyth his wannyd hewe Hath now purueyd. 1606 Shaks. *Ant. & Cl.* ii. i. 21 All the charmes of Loue, Salt Cleopatra soften thy wand lip. [1818: see Waned *ppl. a.*] 1888 *Longman's Mag.* Feb. 392 Many [actors] assert that the 'wanning' of the visage is a common..accompaniment of imagined terror.

Wan: see One, Wand *sb.*, When, Whenne, Whom, Win *v.*, Wone *sb.*

Wan- (wǫn), a prefix expressing privation or negation (approximately equivalent to Un-[1] or Mis-), repr. OE. *wan-, won-*, corresponding to OFris. *wan-, won-*, OS. *wan-* (only in *wanskefti* misfortune = OE. *wansceaft*), MLG., MDu. *wan-* (mod.Du. in many new formations, esp. in the sense 'wrong', 'mis-', as in *wanbestuur* misgovernment, *wanluid* discordant sound), OHG. *wan-, wana* (only in *wanwâfan* unarmed, *wanaheil* unhealthy, infirm, *wanawizzi* lacking wit, insane), MHG. *wan-* (only in *wanwitze* inherited from OHG.), mod.G. *wahn-* (in *wahnwitz, wahnsinn* insanity, commonly apprehended as compounds of *wahn* sb., delusion; also in some dialect words, chiefly adopted from LG.); ON., Sw., Da. *van-* (in many old formations, to which mod.Sw. and Da. have added many more, chiefly adopted from LG.). The prefix is in origin identical with Wane *a.*

In OE. the number of words formed with the prefix is considerable, but none of them has survived into modern English, and only one (*wanspêd*, ill-success) into ME. Of the many new formations that arose in ME., only *wantogen*, undisciplined, Wanton, still survives in use (with no consciousness of its etymological meaning); *wanhope* and *wantrust* may have been suggested by the equivalent MDu. forms. It was in the north that the prefix was most prolific, and it probably continued to be productive far into the modern period. The following words, peculiar to the Scottish and northern dialects, are recorded in the *Eng. Dial. Dict.*, mostly with examples (or references to glossaries etc.) from the 18th c., but few if any of them are now in current use:—*wancanny* adj., Wanchancy *a.*, *wanchear* grief, sadness, *wancouth* adj. = uncouth, *wandeidy* adj., mischievous, Wandought *a.* and *sb.*

Figure 8: *OED*, fascicle *W–Wash*, pp. 61-2 (part).

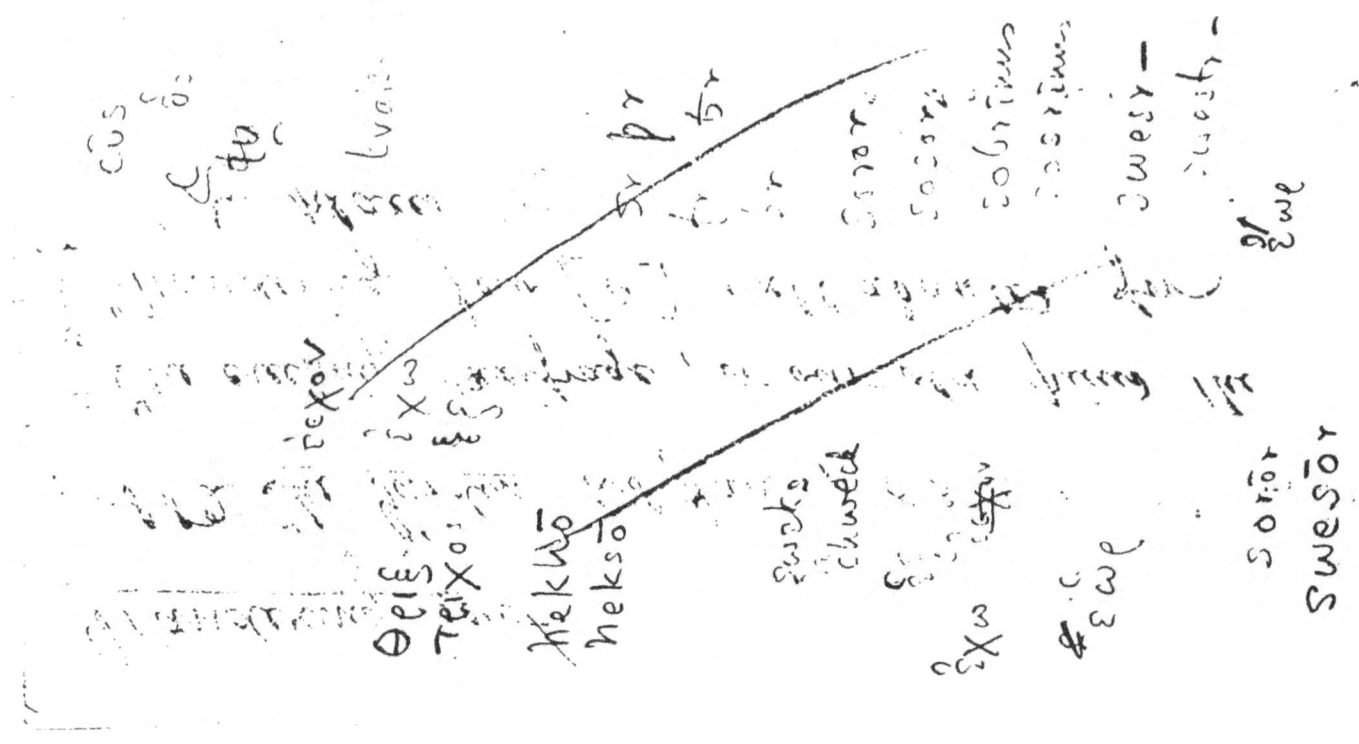

Figure 9: *OED* slips, headword *Wandering*, verso of quotation for *wandering Jew*. (Reproduced by permission of the Bodleian Library)

Midland or Southern usage, is not consistently borne out by the rest of the material.[8]

This brings us to the end of Tolkien's work on those fascicles of the *OED* on which he was directly engaged; but there is also a significant body of work left by him specifically for use in revising, expanding and updating the Dictionary, the necessity of which had long been recognised. Materials for the preparation of a *Supplement* had been accumulating for some time; and when this supplementary volume was published in 1933, the *OED* was re-issued in twelve volumes (it had until then only been available in the form of fascicles) which incorporated a number of minor corrections and revisions. Some material intended for the *Supplement* was written on slips and filed; much more was written into the margins of the various working copies of the Dictionary which the lexicographers consulted, and it is here that, thanks once again to Tolkien's highly distinctive handwriting, I have been able to identify a number of his suggestions.

Often work on a word towards the end of the alphabet would cast light on words nearer the beginning, which had already been dealt with in print. Thus, for example, in the course of his struggle with the derivation of *walrus* Tolkien discovered the etymology of the obscure word *rossome* "redness". He wrote a slip for the *Supplement* file suggesting that the published etymology "Obscure" be replaced by

a. early mod. G. *roseme* :– OHG. *rosamo* rubor, lentigo, MHG. *roseme*. (See Diefenbach s.v. *Lentigo*)

which Bradley subsequently approved and wrote in as marginalia, and which was incorporated in the corrected re-issue of 1933 (although drastically shortened to "G. †*roseme*", to allow it to be added to the entry without causing it to spill over onto a new line). Similarly, his work on the *wild/wold* group brought to light some errors and omissions, such as the interpretation of one Middle English passage as evidence for a supposed compound noun *rood-wold* whereas it was in fact an instance of a variant form of the past tense of *quell* "to kill", and the absence of cross-references to *wold* under its variant spellings. He would also make comments on the etymologies of (mainly) Germanic words, often adducing further evidence in support of etymological hypotheses described by the *OED* as unlikely; and occasionally he would make observations on modern English, as in his suggestions for updating the definition of

---

[8] In fact Tolkien was later able to have his say about the interrelatedness of these words: in *The Year's Work in English Studies* for 1924, the chapter on "Philology: General Works" (which Tolkien compiled for three years after moving to Leeds) includes a review of the newly-published *OED* fascicle *Whisking-Wilfulness* in which, as well as noting one or two errors and discussing the word *whole* at some length, Tolkien complains that in the etymology of *wild* "the connexion with *walþus* (*wold*, *weald*, forest) is rejected" (Tolkien, 1926, p. 48) — a connection which his own earlier draft etymologies had asserted.

brigade ("now a subdivision (usually a 3rd or 4th part) of a 'division', and consisting of 3-6 battalions" – obviously based on his own recent experiences), and his observation that, in addition to the entry for the Middle English diminutive *-kin*, the suffix *-kins* should be included because of its modern colloquial use "in endearing forms of address" (an entry along these lines did indeed appear in the 1933 *Supplement*).

But the vast majority of Tolkien's marginal annotations originate in the work he did on a number of fourteenth-century texts for Kenneth Sisam during the spring of 1920. The publication of "Sisam's 14th Cent[ur]y reader" (as it appears in the OUP ledger) entailed the careful examination of many important texts of the period, which are excerpted or given in their entirety in the book: in the course of this scrutiny Tolkien came across several dozen antedatings (instances of particular words being used earlier than their first date as given in the *OED*). So, for example, whereas in the *OED* the verb *hem* "to edge or border (a garment or cloth); to decorate with a border, fringe, or the like" is recorded no earlier than 1440, Tolkien noted the phrase "þe gurdel þat is golde-hemmed" in *Sir Gawain and the Green Knight*, which constitutes an antedating of at least forty years: in a few cases words were antedated by over a century.

Perhaps surprisingly, most of these marginalia have not been acted on: thus the second edition (1989) of the *OED* contains entries for *brigade* and *hem* which are unchanged as far as Tolkien's comments are concerned. The explanation of this lies in the two decades following the publication of the 1933 *Supplement*, during which OUP disbanded the *OED* team and work on maintaining the Dictionary ceased completely. Operations recommenced in 1957 with the appointment of Robert Burchfield to oversee the expansion of the 1933 *Supplement* into what eventually became four volumes, later to be combined with the original twelve together with about 5000 new entries to form the twenty-volume second edition of 1989; but this expanded edition is not a comprehensive revision of the original work, and many of the materials assembled for the task of revision have yet to be taken into account. In consequence, these handwritten notes by Tolkien may be made use of well into the next century, as work proceeds toward the third edition of the *OED*.

Conclusion

The significance of Tolkien's work on the *OED* at the beginning of his academic career is not easy to assess. His publications in the years immediately following 1920 include much in terms of philology that follows on directly from his work with Henry Bradley and Kenneth Sisam,[9] and his own statements indicate the value he himself placed on what he learnt while at work on the Dictionary. It is perhaps sufficient to say that without such an early and extensive opportunity to nurture his native fascination with words as individuals to be studied, the course of his subsequent academic career might have been very different. Certainly there are clear early signs of familiar tendencies in Tolkien's approach to writing of any kind: repeated and increasingly hasty re-drafting, a desire to say more than practical constraints allow, and an acute sensitivity to the impact words can have in addition to their apparent meanings.

I have not attempted to trace in detail the influence of Tolkien's lexicography on the vocabulary he used in his creative writing, but I would suggest that such research has the potential to cast considerable light on his creative processes. To take an obvious example, his use of the word *wold* – a fairly unusual word in modern English – to denote the grassy uplands of Rohan becomes more significant when we know how thoroughly he studied and puzzled over its origins and meanings. His writings of the 1920s, in particular the fragmentary *Lay of the Fall of Gondolin* and the various alliterative poems of that period, may contain evidence that other words assigned to him by Bradley continued to loom large in his vocabulary. I hope that by mapping out the extent of his work on the *OED* I have made available the raw materials on which such further research may be conducted.

Appendix: Entries in the *OED* worked on by Tolkien

(Wag(g)el)
Waggle sb., v.; Waggly
Wain sb.
Waist; Waistband, Waist-cloth, Waistcoat, Waistcoated, Waistcoateer, Waist-rail, Waist-tree; Waisted, Waister, Waistless
Wait-a-bit
Waiter; Waitership
Waiting sb., a.; Waiting-maid, Waiting-man, Waiting-room, Waiting-woman
Waitress
Wake sb., v.; Wake-robin, Wake-wort
Waldend
Wallop sb., v.; Walloper, Walloping sb., a.
Walm sb., v.; Walming
Walnut

---

[9] Indeed, with the exception of the edition of *Sir Gawain and the Green Knight* (1925), which he prepared with E.V. Gordon, all of his scholarly output up to 1932 can be described as philological: see Hammond, 1993.

Walrus
Wampum (?Wampumpeag?)
Wan sb., a., v.
Wander sb., v.; Wanderable, Wandered, Wanderer, Wandering sb., a., Wanderment; Wander-year
Wandreth
Wane sb., a., v.
Want sb., v; Want-louse
Wariangle
Warlock sb., v.; Warlockry
Warm a.
(?Wasp, Water?)
Weald; Wealden, Wealding
(?Wick?)
Wield
Wild
(?Winter?)
Wold

References:

Carpenter, Humphrey. 1977. *J.R.R. Tolkien: a biography*. London: George Allen and Unwin.

Dutton, M.L. 1987. "Lexicography and popular history: readers and their slips for the *New English Dictionary*" in *Dictionaries*, **9** (1987), pp. 196-210.

Hammond, Wayne G. 1993. *J.R.R. Tolkien: a descriptive bibliography*. Winchester: St Paul's Bibliographies.

Leeds University English School Association. 1923. *A Northern Venture*. Leeds: At the Swan Press.

Murray, K.M.E. 1977. *Caught in the web of words: James A.H. Murray and the Oxford English Dictionary*. Oxford: Oxford University Press.

Sisam, K. (ed.). 1921. *Fourteenth century verse and prose*. Oxford: Oxford University Press.

Tolkien, J.R.R. 1922. *A Middle English vocabulary*. Oxford: Oxford University Press.

Tolkien, J.R.R. 1923. "Henry Bradley, 3 Dec., 1845-23 May, 1923" in *Bulletin of the Modern Humanities Research Association*, no. 20 (October 1923), pp. 4-5.

Tolkien, J.R.R. 1926. "Philology: General Works" in *The Year's Work in English Studies* for 1924 (1926), pp. 26-65.

Tolkien, J.R.R. 1984. *The Book of Lost Tales, part two*, ed. Christopher Tolkien. London: George Allen & Unwin.

Tolkien, J.R.R. 1992. *Sauron Defeated*, ed. Christopher Tolkien. London: HarperCollins.

Tolkien, J.R.R. and Gordon, E.V. (eds.). 1925. *Sir Gawain and the Green Knight*. Oxford: Oxford University Press.

The Growth of Grammar in the Elven Tongues

Christopher Gilson and Patrick Wynne

Abstract: While some features of Elven grammar go back to the earliest records, such as the "Qenya Lexicon", others are unique to later works such as the "Secret Vice" poems and the *Etymologies*, and some do not emerge until after *The Lord of the Rings*. The Elven languages form an expanding canvas (like Niggle's), and many of the individual poems and sentences can be examined in terms of how they elaborate or enhance the overall grammar of Elvish.

Keywords: cases, grammar, Quenya, suffixes, tree of languages

In J.R.R. Tolkien's "latest philological writings," as noted in *Unfinished Tales* (p. 266), he said that in the ancient language of the Elves the word for a stout tree with many spreading branches was **galadā*, literally meaning "great growth". It is appropriate, then, that in *Leaf by Niggle* Tolkien used the image of a Tree as an allegorical representation of the "great growth" of his mythology of Middle-earth:

> It had begun with a leaf caught in the wind, and it became a tree; and the tree grew, sending out innumerable branches, and thrusting out the most fantastic roots. Strange birds came and settled on the twigs and had to be attended to . . .

Tolkien also described the Elven languages themselves in terms of several versions of a "Tree of Tongues" drafted to accompany the *Lhammas* and *Lammasethen*, works describing the development of the languages within the history of Middle-earth. This image of a tree, constantly branching out in increasing complexity, also serves as a suitable metaphor for the process by which Tolkien invented languages. The Elven tongues did not spring into existence fully formed; rather they grew and developed over the course of Tolkien's entire lifetime. Sometimes their development was as gradual as the slow growth of an oak; at other times there were sudden flowerings of new forms and grammatical features, or even new languages. It is this process of growth in Tolkien's creation of Elvish, the sending out of its innumerable branches and fantastic roots, that will be our concern today.

Of course, a full account of the creation of the Elven tongues might produce a book rivalling the size of the *Oxford English Dictionary*. For now we must limit ourselves to examining a single branch on the Tree of Tongues: Quenya, the High-elven speech of Valinor. Specifically, we will examine the growth of Quenya *grammar*, the means by which words in this language relate with one another to form meaningful sentences. There are, admittedly, gaps in our knowledge of Tolkien's development of Quenya grammar; not all of the material has been published, and not all of what has is fully understood. But insofar as the grammar of a language can be observed by examining actual sentences in that language, a sufficient number of High-elven sentences have been published from throughout the nearly sixty-year period Tolkien worked on Quenya to enable us to observe with some clarity the general course of its development throughout his life, as well as to understand the grammar as Tolkien might have conceived it at any given period.

In order to fully appreciate Quenya grammar as it appears in the earliest material, from the period of *The Book of Lost Tales*, we should first take a brief look at the grammar in its latest stage of development. In *The Lord of the Rings* and subsequent writings, Quenya is a highly inflected language, meaning that the grammatical relationships in a Quenya sentence are for the most part indicated by different endings added to the words. Nouns in particular are elaborately declined, and they provide our best example of the principle of inflection. Our understanding of the noun is very clear, thanks to a chart Tolkien made in 1966 or 1967 of the complete declensions of two Quenya nouns, *cirya* "ship" and *lasse* "leaf", which he sent to Richard Plotz of the Tolkien Society of America along with a page of explanatory notes. This chart of paradigms in "Book Quenya", the written form of the language, includes seven labelled cases: nominative, accusative, genitive, instrumental, allative, locative and ablative. Tolkien's notes state that the accusative was lost in "Spoken Quenya", having merged with the nominative. Each case occurs in four numbers: the singular, *lasse* "a leaf", two kinds of plural, *lassi* "all leaves" vs. *lasselī* "some leaves", and the dual, *lasset* "a pair of leaves".

In *The Lord of the Rings* Galadriel's Lament illustrates the use of all these cases. There are many examples of the nominative or uninflected case with singulars such as *yulma* "cup", and plurals *rámar* "wings", *eleni* "stars", and so on. There are genitive forms, such as *Vardo* "of Varda" and *aldaron* "of trees"; instrumental case forms like *súrinen* "in the wind"; allative *falmalinnar* "on the foaming waves"; a locative pronoun *yassen* "wherein"; and ablatives such as *sinda-nóriello* "out of a grey country". The dual number occurs in *máryat* "her hands", and we should also note that in a letter written to Richard Jeffery in 1972 (Tolkien, 1981, p. 427), Tolkien mentions that Quenya also has a dual marked by *-ú*, as in *Aldúya* the week-day named for the Two Trees.

The Book Quenya chart contains one unlabelled case at the end of each declension, as well as a set of shorter forms in parentheses for both the allative and locative cases. The unlabelled case – an example is *ciryava* – we will term *associative* for the sake of convenience. This is represented in Galadriel's Lament by *lisse-miruvóreva* "of the sweet mead", "swift draughts" of which Galadriel compares to the passing of her long exile. Finally the alternative forms of the allative case, such as *ciryan* for longer *ciryanna*, seem to have the same suffix as the dative pronoun *nin* "for me" used in the Lament.

When we look back to the earliest Quenya material, that associated with *The Book of Lost Tales*, we see that Quenya grammar, like Niggle's Tree, also began "with a leaf caught in the wind":

> *N·alalmino lalantila*
> *"Beneath the elms forever fall
> *Ne·súme lasser pínea . . .*
> The leaves upon a breeze so small . . ."

These are the opening lines of the earliest poem in Quenya: *Narqelion*, dated November 1915/March 1916, contemporary with the *Lost Tales* and the Qenya Lexicon, Tolkien's earliest dictionary of the High-elven tongue. The translation just given is our own, since none by Tolkien survives. Still, the meaning of much of the vocabulary is clear, and it is noteworthy that many nouns in this early poem endure without change into *The Lord of the Rings*, for example *alda* "tree", *Eldamar* "Elvenhome", and *ráma* "wing". Even the title, *Narqelion* "Autumn", reappears in 1962 as the title of the second section of another poem, *The Trees of Kortirion*. A large number of words in the Qenya Lexicon are identical with words in the late writings, and this continuity of conception is also apparent in Quenya names in the *Lost Tales* themselves, Christopher Tolkien noting that "it is remarkable how many of the names of the Valar in the earliest writings were never afterwards displaced or reshaped" (Tolkien, 1984a, p. 79). In general then, Tolkien seems to have arrived at his preferred phonetic style for Quenya words at a very early stage, and nouns in the early material appear to be derived from many of the same roots and formative suffixes seen in the late material.

Narqelion provides us with the only substantial record of grammatical usage in Quenya at its earliest stage, for Christopher Tolkien has said that he does not believe that any other Quenya poems survive from this period (Hyde, 1989, p. 49). Despite our inability to confidently translate every word or phrase in *Narqelion*, in a poem of this length we should still be able to discern evidence of the Quenya case system as it then stood. We saw that this is certainly true of *Namárië*, in which all of the cases laid out in the noun paradigms occur in some form in the poem, and these poems are of about the same length. This makes it rather surprising that so few cases seem to appear in *Narqelion*. The form *lintuilindova*, which seems to mean "having many swallows", may be the same associative case as *miruvóreva* "of mead", and the final *-r* in *pior* could be the same ending seen later in *vear* "in the sea", though *-r* is also a plural noun ending.

Most nouns in the poem, in fact, appear to be in the nominative, which in Quenya is the uninflected case, and grammatical relationships typically expressed by case inflections in later Quenya are indicated by other means, such as word order – for example, a genitive relationship is apparently expressed by simple apposition in *sinqi Eldamar* *"jewels of Elvenhome". Prepositions occur, as in *ter i·aldar* *"through the trees", and instead of the instrumental inflection so common in later writings, *Narqelion* has what looks like an instrumental prefix *ne·* in *ne·súme* *"in the wind". One word, *nierme* in the final line, appears to contain the plural noun *nier* "tears" plus a suffix *-me*. This suffix might be the same ending seen in *lenéme* "with assent" in *The Notion Club Papers* in 1946, and in *sinome* "in this place" in *The Lord of the Rings*. Thus *nierme* could mean "in tears" or "with tears". In the later material this suffix is not a case ending for nouns and does not appear on the Plotz chart. It is possible that the case system is so different in *Narqelion* that there are case endings here that we don't recognize as such. At any rate, suffixes like *-me* in *nierme* are probably the seeds from which the complex system of case-endings in the later grammar grew.

In contrast to the rarity of case endings in the *Lost Tales* material, the plural system as given in the Plotz declensions appears to have dated back to the very beginning. This is in fact one of the earliest grammatical patterns displayed in Tolkien's invented languages. Many of the names in the *Lost Tales*, especially those of kindreds, are plural nouns in Quenya, and these are listed in the Quenya Lexicon in their singular forms. There are three basic plural markers in early Quenya: an r-suffix, an i-suffix and a li-suffix. The r-suffix is used with nouns whose singular ends in a vowel, such as *ainu* "a pagan god", plural *Ainur* (Tolkien, 1984a, pp. 52, 248), or *fúmella* "poppy", plural *fúmellar* (pp. 74, 253). The li-suffix is also added to nouns ending in a vowel, as in *Noldo* "Gnome", plural *Noldoli* (pp. 48, 262). Beside numerous occurrences of *Noldoli* there is one instance of *Noldor* in the text of the *Lost Tales* (p. 162), showing a degree of interchangeability between the r-suffix and li-suffix.

The i-suffix has a slightly more complex pattern. It is used mostly with nouns whose singular ends in a consonant, such as *nandin* "dryad", plural *Nandini* (pp. 66, 261), or *Teler*, plural *Teleri*, one of the kindreds of the Elves (pp. 48, 267). The i-suffix is also used for some nouns ending in a vowel, with the final vowel of the singular replaced with the i-suffix in the plural. Thus *Solosimpe* "shore-piper" has the plural *Solosimpi* (pp. 16, 251), and *Angamandu* has the plural *Angamandi* "Hells of Iron" (p. 249). The noun *Vala* has both forms of plural; as Rúmil the Elvish philologist says to Eriol concerning the Gods, "these are they whom we now call the

Valar (or the *Vali*, it matters not)" (p. 58). This shows that the r-suffix and i-suffix are essentially equivalent in function. The fact that i-suffix plurals can be used with both consonant-stems and vowel-stems leads eventually to variation in the singular. Thus the plural noun *Silmarilli* is given with variant singular forms *Silmaril* and *Silmarille* in the *Etymologies* (Tolkien, 1987, p. 383).

The potential for such variability allowed Tolkien great leeway for changing the forms of names actually used in the *Lost Tales*, while still building an enduring grammatical structure within which the names fit. We find similar variation in word-formation, with numerous alternatives listed in the Qenya Lexicon, such as *koi* or *koire* "life", *taran* or *tarambo* "buffet", and so on. How far grammatical variation extends was determined by Tolkien in the process of inventing the forms that display it. In the case of plurals, it seems that while writing the *Lost Tales* Tolkien was still attempting to determine the extent to which the plural suffixes would be applied. Or so we might infer from the fact that in the very earliest layer of the texts of "The Cottage of Lost Play" and "The Music of the Ainur" there are examples of the singular noun *Ainu* used as a plural, instead of the usual form *Ainur* (see pp. 53, 60 n. 3), and singular forms *Telelle* and *Solosimpe* also appear in these earliest texts as plurals, only subsequently emended to the typical plural forms *Telelli* and *Solosimpi*. Alongside these singular forms with a plural sense, the familiar plural forms *Eldar* and *Noldoli* and *Teleri* already occur in the earliest drafts. So the suffixes had been established, but their full scope of application had not, nor whether all nouns would have or always employ distinct plural forms. When Tolkien set aside the *Tales*, the pattern of i-plural nouns like *lasse*, plural *lassi*, was firmly established, and the range of the r-plural type like *cirya*, plural *ciryar*, was further defined, with such examples as *Ainur*, *Noldor* and *Valar* all added to the grammatical picture.

Concurrent with the development of plural nouns, we can trace the emerging grammar of plural adjectives both in *Narqelion* and in another document associated with the *Lost Tales*, a drawing entitled *I Vene Kemen* "the Vessel of Earth", which depicts the land mass of the World as a great ship floating on the Outer Sea (Tolkien, 1984a, pp. 84-5). Many of the geographical names on this "World-Ship" drawing have the typical Quenya phrase structure of a noun followed by an adjective, for example *Tol Eressea* "the Lonely Isle". In several names on the drawing the noun is plural, and the adjective is also pluralized by the addition of an r-suffix, as in *I Nori Landar* "The Great Lands", *I·Tolli Kuruvar* "The Magic Isles", and *Neni Erumear* "Outermost Waters". The contrast between singular names like *Tol Eressea* and plurals like *Neni Erumear* demonstrates that Quenya has a rule of number agreement, meaning the adjective in a phrase is marked with a plural suffix if the noun is plural.

Further examples of r-plural adjectives appear only much later, in the story "The Lost Road", c. 1937. There in the Quenya song sung by Fíriel, a singular adjective *irima* "lovely" occurs in *Irima ye Númenor* "Lovely is Númenor", and the plural form appears in *Toi irimar* "which are beautiful", referring to the Sun and Moon (Tolkien, 1987, p. 72). These are *predicate adjective* constructions, where the adjective is equated with the subject of the sentence by means of the verb "to be".

A natural outgrowth of these equations of adjective with noun is the *substantive* use of the adjective, that is, where the adjective takes the place of a noun in the sentence. Thus Treebeard addresses Celeborn and Galadriel, *A vanimar, vanimálion nostari!* (Tolkien, 1969c, p. 259), which Tolkien translated in a letter, "O beautiful ones, parents of beautiful children" (Tolkien, 1981, p. 308). *Vanimar* "beautiful ones" is the plural form of the adjective *vanima* "beautiful, fair" (see Tolkien, 1987, p. 351) used with a generic noun understood. This usage is closely connected with the derivation of various names from adjectives. For example the adjective *sinda* "grey", as in *Sindacollo* "Grey-cloak" (Tolkien, 1977, pp. 348, 365), is also used as a noun meaning "a Grey-elf", so in effect *sinda* has the substantive plural *Sindar* "the Grey-elves". Other examples are *Fírimar* "Mortals" from the adjective *fírima* "mortal"; and *Vanyar* "the Fair Elves" from the adjective *vanya* "fair" (Tolkien, 1977, pp. 103, 53).

All of these scattered examples of r-plural adjectives have two things in common. Firstly, the singular of each one ends in *-a*. Secondly, all of the various ways in which they are used – that is, to modify or stand in for a noun mentioned in isolation, or used in direct address, or used as a predicate after the verb "to be" – all these are functions expressed by the nominative case in languages that distinguish between nominative and accusative. As we have said, the Plotz declension makes a distinction between nominative and accusative forms in Book Quenya, and for the noun *cirya*, which ends in *-a*, the nominative plural is *ciryar* while the accusative plural is *ciryai*. The implication may be that while the distinction between nominative and accusative *nouns* was lost in Spoken Quenya, with a nominative form like *ciryar* serving both functions, the distinction between nominative and accusative *adjectives* was retained, with forms like *erumear* and *vanimar* functioning only as nominative forms.

If this is so, then we might expect to find distinctive accusative forms of adjectives. It seems rather remarkable, then, that alongside the early evidence of plural adjectives like *erumear* and *landar* we can place five words in the poem *Narqelion* that end in the same diphthong *ai* that accusative *ciryai* does: *úmeai, malinai, kuluvai, sildai,* and *karneambarai*. The form and context of these words suggests that they are all adjectives. With *malinai* and *sildai* this is virtually certain, for an adjective *malina* "yellow" is given in the *Etymologies* (Tolkien, 1987, p. 386), and an adjective *silda* "gleaming" occurs in one of the "Secret Vice" poems in the phrase *sildaránar* "in the moon gleaming" (Tolkien, 1984c, p. 213). The grammatical suffix *-i* added to these adjectives in *Narqelion* appears to be the same plural marker *-i* we have seen in certain nouns, but added to the vowel-stem instead of replacing it. In other words, *malinai* derives from *malina* in the same way that accusative *ciryai* derives from nominative *cirya*.

This leaves us with a question: Do these adjectives in *Narqelion* have plurals formed with an i-suffix because they are accusative? The syntax of *Narqelion* may supply an answer. The third line of the poem contains our first plural adjective: *Ve sangar voro úmeai*. We know *ve* is "like" or "as" (OM2[1], ll. 4, 19, *Namárië* ll. 3, 10), and *sangar* "throngs" and *voro* "ever" (Tolkien, 1984b, p. 342, Tolkien, 1984a, p. 250). The adjective *úmea* may be related to the superlative ending of *erúmëa* "outermost" (Tolkien, 1984a, p. 262), and to *úvea* "abundant, in very great number, very large" (Tolkien, 1987, p. 396). If there is a comparison between the nouns *lasser* "leaves" and *sangar* "throngs" then the meaning is comparable to "leaves falling in the wind like ever numerous throngs". So *úmeai* may be accusative here, to agree with the function of the noun *sangar*, if Quenya puts the object of a comparison into the accusative case.

A second instance of *úmeai* occurs later in the poem in *Tukalia sangar úmeai* which we suggest means *"luring the numerous throngs" with *sangar* the direct object of the verbal form *tukalia*, possibly from the root *tuk-* "draw, bring". The adjective *úmeai* may have an accusative form to reflect the function of the phrase *sangar úmeai* "numerous throngs" as the direct object of the verb. The other examples of plural adjectives in *-ai* are even more difficult to interpret. But given the hypothesis that the Quenya adjective agrees in both number and case with the noun it modifies, or the noun it stands for, it seems quite plausible that the contrast between the plural adjectives in final *-i* in *Narqelion* and the plural adjectives in final *-r* on the "World-Ship" drawing is based on grammatical function. While we cannot recover all the details, it seems clear that in these two early documents we have the first budding of adjective syntax.

In the late material the adjective plural in *-ai* has undergone change in form, which is best exemplified in the final version of the poem *The Last Ark*, written in the last decade of Tolkien's life. This poem contains many plural adjectives whose singular forms are given in the accompanying "glossarial commentary", and there is a consistent pattern of plural adjectives formed by a shift in the final vowel. For example, singular *néka* "vague" in the glossary occurs in the poem in the plural form *néke* (l. 3), with a shift of final *-a* to *-e*. Similarly, the adjective *morna* "dark" (Tolkien, 1981, p. 382) appears in the poem in the plural form *morne* (l. 33). It is probable that this vowel shift was caused by addition of an original plural marker *-i*; that is, the original plurals of *néka* and *morna* were probably *nékai* and *mornai*, with the final diphthong *-ai* eventually reduced to *-e*. This is supported by Tolkien's notes to the Plotz declensions, in which he specifically mentions that reduction of final *ai* to short *e* was an historical phonetic development in Quenya.

Other forms in the poem and glossary demonstrate the pattern of plural formation in adjectives ending in *-e* and *-ea*. Thus singulars ending in *-e* shift to *-i* in the plural, as in *ninque* "white", plural *ninqui*, which is identical to the pattern of nouns like *lasse* "leaf" pl. *lassi*. Singulars ending in *-ea* shift to *-ie* in the plural, as in *elvea* "starlike", plural *elvie*; and *atalantea* "downfallen", plural *atalantie*, in effect a combination of the other two patterns. This bears out the impression we have begun to feel that the adjective is closely related to the noun in syntax, and that the Book Quenya declensions are the underlying source for the forms of both noun and adjective.

This brings us to the second dimension in the grammatical pattern of the noun and adjective, the growth of case-endings, which have only begun to emerge in the *Lost Tales* period. The simplest structure for combining two nouns into a single name is to treat one as though it were an adjective, and place it before the other noun, as in *Olóre Malle* "the Path of Dreams" (Tolkien, 1984a, p. 18), literally "Dream Path", or place it after, as in *Kópas Alqalunte* "Haven of the Swanships" (p. 164), literally "Haven Swanship". This structure is very versatile but also ambiguous, and becomes even more so if an adjective modifies one of the nouns. Within this grammatical context it seems quite natural that there should evolve a way to indicate which of two nouns is the modifier. In the name *Mar Vanwa Tyaliéva* "the Cottage of Lost Play" (p. 14), a suffix *-va* has been added to the noun *tyalie* "play" (p. 260) to indicate that it modifies the noun *mar* "dwelling" (p. 251).

This is the case we have termed associative, but which Tolkien himself leaves unlabelled in the Book Quenya declension. The Qenya Lexicon has several adjectives that end in *-va*, such as *kanuva* "leaden" or *tereva* "piercing" (pp. 268, 255). Since *tyaliéva* serves as an adjectival equivalent to the noun *tyalie* "play", it seems probable that the case-suffix *-va* grew out of the adjective ending. This would explain why the case has no label in the chart, since it does not correspond to any traditional case category, though usually it is translated by the English preposition "of".

One other rudimentary case-ending can be found in the *Lost Tales*, in connection with this same pattern of nouns modifying nouns. A variation on *Kópas Alqalunte* appears in the episode title "The Battle of *Kópas Alqalunten*". The suffix *-n* in *alqalunten* "of the swan-ships" is the same as the ending of the dative pronoun *nin* "for me" in Galadriel's Lament, and we can see that "haven for a swanship" is an apt translation of *Kópas Alqalunten*. The suffix also appears in the elements of a few compound names, such as *Harwalin* "near the Valar". This contains the word *har(e)* "near" (p. 253) and refers to the region just outside of Valinor. The name was later changed in the *Lost Tales* to *Arvalin* (p. 22) with similar form and equivalent meaning. These names each contain a form of the word *Vali* "Gods", found also in *Valinor* "Land of the Gods". So *Harwalin* and *Arvalin* seem to show our dative *-n* suffix added to the plural form of a noun, and indicating location, in conjunction with the adverbial prefix.

The next stage in the development of Elven grammar is displayed in the poems Tolkien presented as examples of the "Secret Vice" of language invention in his essay on the

---

[1] For convenience references to *Oilima Markirya* 1 (Tolkien, 1984c, p. 220-221) are given as OM1 and to *Oilima Markirya* 2 (Tolkien, 1984c, pp. 213-215) are given as OM2.

subject, which he read in 1931 about 15 years after composing *Narqelion* and compiling the Qenya Lexicon and related stories. We can point to a good deal of grammar here that is "newer" than the *Lost Tales*. First we can point to concepts that are clearly outgrowths of what has come before.

We find examples of the familiar plural i-suffix and li-suffix in the poem *Oilima Markirya* "The Last Ark" (Tolkien, 1984c, pp. 213-15), such as *tinwi* "stars" (l. 27) or *rámali* "wings" (l. 11). Parallel to these plural nouns we find new developments of plural adjectives. For example, in the phrase *laiqali linqi falmari* "the green wet waves" in the poem *Earendel* (l. 3), the adjective *laiqa* "green" (Tolkien, 1984a, p. 267) forms its plural *laiqali* using the same li-suffix seen in plural nouns such as *Noldoli*. Another way in which the adjective develops in parallel with the noun is in the use of certain case markers, such as the n-suffix. Thus in *Earendel* there also occurs the phrase *tyulmin talalínen aiqalin kautáron*, translated "the tall masts bent with the sails". The form *tyulmin* is a dative plural form of *tyulma* "mast" (Tolkien, 1987, p. 395), in the same way that the second element of *Arvalin* is the dative plural of *Vala*. The adjective *aiqalin* "tall" has the same plural suffix as *laiqali* "green", with the addition of the n-suffix. So it agrees in plurality with *tyulmin* and also in case. Notwithstanding the poetic word order separating *aiqalin* from *tyulmin*, there is probably a close association here of noun and modifier, as in the translation "tall masts", and parallel to the construction *laiqali linqi falmari* "green wet waves".

There are also two examples in an earlier version of *Oilima Markirya* of adjectives that have the plural ending *-ai* in combination with the n-suffix, *oilimain* "last" (l. 25) and *alkarain* "shining". The latter occurs at the very end of the poem: *ala fuin oilimaite / ailinisse alkarain* "after the last night upon the shining shore" (ll. 26-7). If *alkarain* is plural then it does not directly modify *ailinisse* "upon the shore" which is singular, but means something like "for the shining things", where a plural noun is understood but not expressed. The overall theme of the poem is the ultimate extinguishment of light in its passage westward, with the moon setting like "a corpse into the grave" and the "white ship . . . with wings like stars" finally foundered on the rocks that were once "white shining in the silver moon". It is these lights and white objects that make the shore shine, so in this context *ailinisse alkarain* means "upon the shore of the shining things", and metaphorically it is the foundering-place *for* the ship and the setting-place *for* the moon, in much the same way that the *Kópas Alqalunten* is a haven for ships.

While this explanation of *alkarain* as a dative form of the plural adjective remains tentative, the direction of the growth of this branch of the grammar is later confirmed. The first line of Fíriel's Song in "The Lost Road" (Tolkien, 1987, p. 63) contains the phrase *eldain a fírimoin* "for elves and mortals", clearly containing two dative plural nouns. *Eldain* "for elves" has the very same ending as *alkarain*, while *fírimoin* "for mortals" shows an equivalent formation presumably based on an o-stem noun **fírimo*. The latest recorded examples of dative nouns or adjectives predate *The Lord of the Rings*, which illustrates only the dative pronoun. But comparable to datives like *eldain*, *alkarain*, *aiqalin*, and *tyulmin*, we do have in the Book Quenya declension, shorter allatives *ciryan* and *lassen*, whose plurals *ciryain* and *ciryalin*, *lassin* and *lasselin*, surely constitute a late continuation of this same growth.

Several new case-forms of the noun appear in the "Secret Vice" poems. In fact the basic pattern of the cases familiar from late examples of Quenya begins to appear here in its essentials. Though some details are slightly different or lacking, we can point to examples of the genitive, instrumental, allative, locative and ablative cases. And there are many examples displaying various features of form and function.

Perhaps most fully represented at this stage is the locative case. In the earlier version of *Oilima Markirya* the phrase *veasse lúnelinqe* "upon the blue streams of the sea" (l. 3) exhibits the basic structure of the locative singular. It consists of the stem of the noun as seen in the nominative singular, here *vea* "sea" (OM2, l. 9), plus the suffix *-sse*. Similarly in the second version of the poem there is *óresse oilima* "in the last morning" (l. 34), with *óresse* from *óre* "the dawn" (Tolkien, 1984a, p. 264), which shows by the way that location in time as well as space can be expressed this way. The poem *Earendel* has *kiryasse* "upon a ship" (l. 2), with the precise form of the much later Book Quenya declension already achieved.

The locative plural has three forms, partly reflecting the nominative plural in two of its three endings. The form *alkarissen* "in the rays of light" (OM1, l. 25) corresponds to a nominative **alkari* "light-rays", plural of *alkar* or *alkare* "radiance" (Tolkien, 1987, p. 348). In the second version of *Oilima Markirya*, *ondolissen* "on the rocks" (l. 30) is based on the nominative plural *ondoli* "rocks" found in the earlier poem (l. 15). These two examples share the same pattern, the locative plural consisting of the nominative plural plus the suffix *-ssen*. The third type of locative plural is actually the first to occur. In the earlier version of the poem the form is *ondoisen* "on the rocks" (l. 19). This ends with the same syllable *-sen* as the other forms, but differs in lacking the double *s*. This is probably more striking in print than it is in speech, and may be due to euphonic reduction of **ondoissen* with its exceptionally long middle syllable.

The other example of this ending is in the same earlier version of the poem, in the phrase *ailissen oilimaisen* "upon the last beaches", where *oilimaisen* is the locative plural of adjective *oilima* "last", here closely associated with locative noun *ailissen* and therefore agreeing with it in case and number. The structure of this ending *-isen* seems to derive from the final *i* in adjective plurals like *malinai*, combined with a reduced form of the locative plural ending *-sen*. There is an obvious parallel between dative plural *oilimain* with its structure, adjective stem + *i* + case suffix, and locative plural *oilimaisen*, with stem + *i* + case marker *-sen*. Remarkably, if we follow the same lead that took us from dative adjective *alkarain* to dative noun *eldain* to shorter allative *ciryain* in the Plotz declension, we find no later forms just like *oilimaisen*, but in the declension chart we do find the shorter locative plural *ciryais*, and within the corpus of Quenya the form *ciryais* is closer to *oilimaisen* than to anything else.

The "Secret Vice" poems also feature a somewhat different form of the locative singular, its parallel function most clear in the rephrasing of *veasse lúnelinqe* "in the flowing sea" in the earlier *Oilima Markirya* as *lúnelinqe vear* in the second version (OM2, l. 7). This -*r* locative also occurs in *ringa ambar* "in her cold bosom" (l. 3), and the lines *silda-ránar, minga-ránar, lanta-ránar* "in the moon gleaming, in the moon waning, in the moon falling" (ll. 16-18). The last three parallel examples contain the word *Rána* "Moon", and the locative *ránar* is used figuratively to mean "in the light of the moon". The ending is found in no other nouns outside of this poem, but in the poem *Nieninque* we do have *yar i vilya anta miqilis* "to whom the air gives kisses" (l. 4). The pronoun *yar* "to whom" is locative in a dynamic rather than static sense, and its relation to other locatives can be understood by a paraphrase, *"upon whom the wind places kisses". The image of the line is metaphorical, and Tolkien seems to be exploring the potentials of Quenya idiom. The pronominal use of this locative ending -*r* takes on a life of its own, and shows up in the *Etymologies* in *tar* "thither" (Tolkien, 1987, p. 389), and *mir* "into" (p. 373). The r-locative can be associated with the s-locatives on the phonetic level, because *s* sometimes shifts to *r* in the history of Quenya. In the Qenya Lexicon, for example, there are variant noun-forms *solor, solosse* "surf" (Tolkien, 1984a, p. 266).

Another case that emerges in the "Secret Vice" poems is the instrumental, with suffix -*nen*. The examples at this stage are all plural. There is *lótefalmarínen* "with waves crowned with flowers" (OM1, l. 6), which derives from the i-plural form *falmari* "waves". There are also li-plural forms, such as *kulukalmalínen* "with golden lights" (l. 8), from *kalmali pl. of *kalma* "light" (cf. *kalma* "daylight", Tolkien, 1984a, p. 254, *calma* "lamp", Tolkien, 1969c, p. 401). The latter shows why this case is labelled instrumental. The full phrase is *kirya kalliére kulukalmalínen* "the ship shone with golden lights", that is the lights are the means or instrument by which the ship was shining. In a somewhat looser sense this is true of the "waves" in *lótefalmarínen* "with waves crowned with flowers", if we relate them to the preceding verb *falastanéro* "was loud with surf", since the waves produce the noise of the sea. The third type, the ai-plural, is represented for the same noun *kalma* "light" in the phrase *úrio kalmainen* "in the lights of the sun" (*Earendel* ll. 6-7).

There is no hint of any singular forms, and in their absence we might be tempted to speculate on a connection with locative plural *oilimaisen*, with the same diphthong *ai* and final *en*. But from this point of surface similarity these forms grew apart from each other in their later associations. As we saw, the final *en* in *oilimaisen* is treated as a redundancy, in the sense that when an archaic Book Quenya form of the ai-plural locative is devised, namely *ciryais*, it lacks this final *en*. On the other hand, these instrumental plurals have achieved their ultimate formation already, as can be seen from *ciryainen, ciryalínen* and *lassínen, lasselínen* on the declension chart. The singulars, when they emerge, contain the same form of the case ending -*nen* with its final consonant, as seen from *ciryanen* and *lassenen*, and also *súrinen* "in the wind" and *lírinen* "in the song", in the poem *Namárië*.

One example of the ablative case appears already in the "Secret Vice" poems, the phrase *oilima ailinello lúte* "leave the last shore" (OM2, l. 2), where the ablative singular *ailinello* derived from *ailin* indicates that the motion of the ship is away from the shore. We can compare Elendil's words repeated by Aragorn in *The Lord of the Rings, Et Eärello Endorenna utúlien* "Out of the Great Sea to Middle-earth I am come" (Tolkien, 1969c, pp. 245-6), where *Eärello* is "from the Great Sea". This case also develops a sense of direction without motion, as in *Rómello vanwa* "lost to those from the East" in *Namárië*.

The allative case, both singular and plural, appears in the first and second versions of *Oilima Markirya*, but with a slightly different form than it later acquires. The examples are singular in *Kaivo i sapsanta* "As a corpse into the grave" (OM1, l. 13), and plural in *tollalinta ruste* "upon crumbling hills" (OM2, l. 24). The latter is accompanied by the verb *lungane* "bending", and alludes to the sky touching the hilltops on the horizon. Whether referring to motion or extension, the allative means "towards" as opposed to the ablative "away from". The endings of *sapsanta* and *tollalinta* are parallel to the Book Quenya forms *ciryanna* and *ciryalinna*, except for the difference in consonant cluster, *nt* vs. *nn*. This change of the suffix -*nta* to -*nna*, whereby it acquires a double consonant parallel to locative -*sse* and ablative -*llo*, first emerges a few years later in the story "The Lost Road". There Alboin's dream-fragments of "Eressean" include such Quenya forms as *kilyanna* "into-Chasm" and *númenna* "westward" (Tolkien, 1987, p. 56).

A final case to mention is the genitive. The history of this case is complicated by the diversity of its functions. In broadest terms a construction is genitive if one noun defines the *genus* or subgroup to which another noun belongs. Its particular uses may vary from language to language. We have already seen that in *Mar Vanwa Tyaliéva* "Cottage of Lost Play", *Kópas Alqalunten* "Haven of the Swanships", and *úrio kalmainen* "in the lights of the sun", the same English preposition *of* is equivalent to three different case-endings in Quenya: -*va*, -*n*, and -*o*. We also saw *miruvóreva* "of sweet mead" and *aldaron* "of trees" in Galadriel's Lament, where this lack of a one-to-one correspondence between English prepositions and Quenya suffixes continues.

Since the purpose of the *Kópas* is to harbour ships, we suggested that *Alqalunten* in the sense "for swan-ships" ultimately connects with datives like *eldain* "for elves". But in the function of describing the kind of haven in terms of an attribute, we might compare *úri kilde hísen nie nienaite* "the Sun with wet eyes dropped tears of mist" in *Oilima Markirya* (OM1, ll. 21-2). Here *hísen* "of mist" describes the kind of weeping (cf. *híse* s.v. KHIS- "mist, fog", Tolkien, 1987, p. 364). In both these examples the suffix -*n* is added to final *e* of the nominatives, *alqalunte* and *híse*. But the *Etymologies* lists several consonant-stem nouns that have their genitive singular ("g.sg.") formed with suffix -*en*, such as *Valatar* "Vala-king", genitive *Valatáren* (Tolkien, 1987, p. 350). This genitive singular suffix -*en* seems to have developed by analogy from the final -*en* in genitives like *hísen*. For as we have mentioned, some Quenya nouns have alternative singular forms, and one such noun is *ambaron* "uprising, Orient" (p. 348). This is given in the *Etymologies* with g.sg. *ambarónen* and also with longer nominative *Ambaróne* whose final *e* is apparently the source for the *e* in *ambarónen*. The suffix has presumably spread from such nouns to other consonant-stems, like *Ilúvatáren*, genitive of *Ilúvatar* (Tolkien, 1987, p. 72) where the *e* has no etymological basis.

Meanwhile the o-genitive has developed alongside this n-genitive. They occur side by side for the same name in the *Etymologies*, where *Tulkas* is listed with genitives *Tulkatho*, *Tulkassen*. We saw the o-suffix in *úrio* "of the sun", derived from nominative *úri*. The earliest example seems to be *Silmeráno tindon* "shining in the silver moon" (OM1, l. 12), where genitive -*ráno* shows that the suffix replaces the final *a* of *Rána* "the moon" (l. 14). In both of these examples the kind of light is expressed in terms of its source, the Sun or the Moon. This genitive form also describes the relation of the whole object to one of its parts, as in *langon veakiryo* "the throat of the sea-ship" in the poem *Earendel* (l. 4). Here -*kiryo* achieves the same form as the genitive singular *ciryō* in the Plotz declension.

These functions are also seen in Galadriel's Lament, for example *rámar aldaron* "wings of trees", and also the related function of possession, as in *Vardo tellumar* "the domes of Varda". The genitive *aldaron* illustrates one of the plural forms of the genitive, the only case with a plural based on the nominative r-form, probably because it is the only case-suffix that begins with a vowel. There are also li-plural and i-plural genitives, such as *Valion* "of the Lords" in *Fíriel's Song*, derived from i-plural *Vali*. The genitive plural forms all post-date the "Secret Vice" poems, although remarkably enough their phonetic shapes occur in very early derivatives, like *Narqelion* "Autumn". The form *Aldaron* occurs in the *Lost Tales* as the name of a Vala interpreted as "king of forests" (Tolkien, 1984a, p. 66), which, granted the element of personification, is not so very far in meaning from *aldaron* "of trees". This word *alda* would in its plural *aldar* include the idea of a few trees or a very large number, even a forest. And this brings us back to where we began, for *alda* is the word whose primitive form is **galadā* "great growth", and this meaning encompasses vast forests as well as individual trees.

* * *

Although Quenya is but a single branch on the Tree of Tongues, we have not been able to examine more than a few of its leaves in an hour's time. We have looked briefly at three representative periods of its growth: in the earliest stage, that of the *Lost Tales*, the phonetic shape of Quenya words and the ways of forming plurals were already close to their final form, but the case system appears to have been rudimentary. Some 15 years later in the "Secret Vice" poems, the basic pattern of cases familiar from the late material began to appear in its essentials, though some cases had not achieved their final shapes. By the time of *The Lord of the Rings*, the case system had reached its full flower, culminating in the carefully arranged complexity of the Book Quenya declensions, with a paradigm of interrelated endings, and even indications of their development within the history of Quenya as a written and spoken language of Elves and Men.

In looking at the full sweep of Quenya's development as an invention, it is remarkable that Tolkien seemed to work mainly by a process of augmentation rather than replacement. The earliest cases in the *Lost Tales* material, such as the dative in final -*n* and the associative in -*va*, were not replaced by the new cases that arose later; rather the old cases continued to coexist alongside the new, developing increasingly complex functions and interrelationships. Thus the early Quenya material remains largely in accord with the very latest material. The sixty-year development of the grammar of the Quenya noun and adjective seems to have been a long process by which Tolkien slowly filled in the blanks of a grammatical paradigm, leading ultimately to the full Plotz declensions. It is interesting to note what Tolkien said about this process of invention, at a time that may not have seemed, but turned out to be, the middle of that process:

> Of course, if you construct your art-language on chosen principles, and in so far as you fix it, and courageously abide by your own rules, resisting the temptation of the supreme despot to alter them for the assistance of this or that technical object on any given occasion, so far you may write poetry of a sort. Of a sort, I would maintain, no further, or very little further, removed from real poetry in full, than is your appreciation of ancient poetry (especially of a fragmentarily recorded poetry such as that of Iceland or ancient England), or your writing of "verse" in such a foreign idiom.

(Tolkien, 1984c, pp. 218-9)

This courage to "abide by your own rules" is another way of looking at what we perceive as filling in the paradigm, for each rule that Tolkien continues to abide by ends up as a piece of the final pattern. It is significant that the criterion of success is that "you may write poetry of a sort." From the very beginning, with *Narqelion*, Quenya found its most vital means of grammatical development through poetry. The poems cited by Tolkien as examples of his favourite invented language have been our richest source for describing the growth of its grammar. In his conclusion to "A Secret Vice", Tolkien wrote of the power of poetry to free the creative mind of one devising an "art-language":

> But, none the less, as soon as you have fixed even a vague general sense for your words, many of the less subtle but most moving and permanently important of the strokes of poetry are open to you. For you are the heir of the ages. You have not to grope after the dazzling brilliance of invention of the free adjective, to which all human language has not yet fully attained. You may say
>
> > *green sun*
> > or *dead life*
>
> and set the imagination leaping.

Chart of the declensions of Book Quenya nouns;
sent by J.R.R. Tolkien to Richard Plotz c. 1966-67

		S	Pl 1	2	Dual
(a)	N	cirya	ciryar	ciryalī	ciryat
	A	ciryā	ciryai	"	"
	G	ciryō	-aron	-alion	ciryato
	I	ciryanen	-ainen	-alínen	ciryanten
(b)	All	ciryanna	-annar	-alinna(r)	ciryanta
		(ciryan)	(-ain)	(-alin)	(ciryant)
	Loc	ciryasse	-assen	-alisse(n)	ciryatse
		(ciryas)	(-ais)	(-alis)	
	Abl	ciryallo	-allon	-alillo(n)	ciryalto
(c)		ciryava	-	-alíva	
(a)		lasse	lassī	lasselī	lasset
		-ē	"	as for	as for
		lasseo	lassion	kiryalī	kiryat
		-enen	-ínen		
(b)		-enna	-ennar		
		(-en)	(-in)		
		-esse	-essen		
		(-es)	(-is)		
		-ello	-ellon		
(c)		-eva	—		

Chart © 1989 The Tolkien Trust

References

Hyde, Paul Nolan. 1988. "Narqelion: A Single, Falling Leaf at Sun-fading." in *Mythlore* 56, 1988. pp. 47-52.

Hyde, Paul Nolan. 1989. "Among the Trees: Seeking the Spirit of Narqelion." in *Mythlore* 60, 1989. pp. 48-53.

Martsch, Nancy. 1989. "The Dick Plotz Letter Declension of the Quenya Noun." in *Beyond Bree*, March 1989. p. 7.

Quiñónez, Jorge. 1989. "A brief note on the background of the letter from J.R.R. Tolkien to Dick Plotz concerning the Declension of the High-elvish Noun." in *Vinyar Tengwar* 6, July 1989. pp. 13-14.

Tolkien, J.R.R. 1966. "Leaf by Niggle." in *The Tolkien Reader*. New York: Ballantine Books.

Tolkien, J.R.R. 1969a. *The Fellowship of the Ring*. Boston: Houghton Mifflin.

Tolkien, J.R.R. 1969b. *The Two Towers*. Boston: Houghton Mifflin.

Tolkien, J.R.R. 1969c. *The Return of the King*. Boston: Houghton Mifflin.

Tolkien, J.R.R. 1977. *The Silmarillion*. Ed. Christopher Tolkien. Boston: Houghton Mifflin.

Tolkien, J.R.R. 1980. *Unfinished Tales*. Ed. Christopher Tolkien. Boston: Houghton Mifflin.

Tolkien, J.R.R. 1981. *The Letters of J.R.R. Tolkien*. Ed. Humphrey Carpenter, Boston: Houghton Mifflin.

Tolkien, J.R.R. 1984a. *The Book of Lost Tales, Part I*. Ed. Christopher Tolkien. Boston: Houghton Mifflin.

Tolkien, J.R.R. 1984b. *The Book of Lost Tales, Part II*. Ed. Christopher Tolkien. Boston: Houghton Mifflin.

Tolkien, J.R.R. 1984c. "A Secret Vice." *The Monsters and the Critics and Other Essays*. Ed. Christopher Tolkien. Boston: Houghton Mifflin.

Tolkien, J.R.R. 1987. *The Lost Road and Other Writings*. Ed. Christopher Tolkien. Boston: Houghton Mifflin.

Tolkien, J.R.R. 1992. *Sauron Defeated*. Ed. Christopher Tolkien, London: HarperCollins.

Wynne, Patrick and Christopher Gilson. 1990. "Bird and Leaf: Image and Structure in *Narqelion*." in *Parma Eldalamberon* 9, 1990. pp. 6-32.

Tolkien's Dictionary Poetics: The Influence of the *OED*'s Defining Style on Tolkien's Fiction

Deirdre Greene

Abstract: This paper examines the connections between Tolkien's writing of fiction and his work as a lexicographer on the *Oxford English Dictionary*. Some of Tolkien's most characteristic stylistic flourishes show the influence of the distinctive, charming defining style of the first edition of the O.E.D.

Keywords: definition, dictionary, lexicography, narrative, plot, structure, style

Tolkien was, as this Centenary Conference acknowledges through its breadth of papers and panel discussions, a man of many parts – so many and so varied that it is sometimes difficult to reconcile them in a theory of the evolution of his fiction. His roles as son, husband, father, friend, teacher, and scholar have been repeatedly scrutinized, though he himself doubted the value of biographical criticism and resented intrusions into his private life. Perhaps he would not object strongly to my study of his early work as a lexicographer, however, since there is an objective relation between the products, whether scholarly or artistic, of a single mind.

It is known by most informed readers that Tolkien worked as a lexicographer on the *Oxford English Dictionary*, but little has been written about his experience there. Aside from Humphrey Carpenter's (necessarily) cursory account, Peter Gilliver has done interesting (and I hope *seminal*) research on the entries Tolkien drafted for the *OED*, identifying what he worked on and explaining how he worked.[1] I will address how the process of historical lexicography and of writing entries for the *Oxford English Dictionary* may have affected his writing of fiction.

It would seem obvious that an experience which Tolkien described as the most instructive two years of his life should have had some perceptible impact on his writing. Tolkien said that in 1919 to 1920, drafting in **W** on the *OED* under the editorship of Henry Bradley, he "learned more . . . than in any other equal period" of his life (Carpenter, 1977, p. 101). If a writer must, according to the old dictum, "write what he knows", and the compilation and content of the *Oxford English Dictionary* accounts for a significant part of what Tolkien knew, then it follows that, in some form or other, Tolkien wrote about the *OED*.

It would also seem obvious that the *OED*, as the foremost scholarly project and most useful tool for research on the history of English, would continue to figure heavily among his interests – as indeed it did. As a scholar of language and literature Tolkien would have consulted it frequently, perhaps daily. He also maintained connections with the *OED* project for many years after leaving his position there as a lexicographer; throughout the 1960s and 1970s he was consulted by Robert Burchfield on material for the *OED* Supplements.[2] Moreover, beyond these points of contact, Tolkien admitted that his great scholarly love was historical lexicography, and at least once speculated on what his life might have been like had the work been more remunerative and he had been able to continue in the occupation of "harmless drudge".[3] His playful reference in *Farmer Giles of Ham* to the *OED*'s definition of **blunderbuss** (which includes the comment that this weapon is "Now superseded in civilized countries by other fire-arms") bespeaks a fond interest, some thirty years after his tenure at the *OED*, at least in the straightfaced humour of the dictionary's defining style.

Such easy access to the humour buried in the *Oxford English Dictionary* is gained only through intimate contact: much close consultation of its entries, or even (an experience I share with Professor Tolkien, much to my delight) drafting entries within its editorial conventions. While editing my M.Litt. thesis on Tolkien's fiction, I began also to work as an historical lexicographer on the fourth edition of the *Shorter*

---

[1] Peter Gilliver's paper, "At the Wordface: J.R.R. Tolkien's work on the *Oxford English Dictionary*" was presented at the Centenary Conference in Oxford, 1992 and is published in this volume.
[2] Many letters exchanged between Tolkien and the editors of the *OED* on particular lexicographical points are preserved in the dictionary archives at Oxford University Press in Oxford.
[3] Conversation with Priscilla Tolkien, Oxford, April 1990. The designation of a lexicographer as a "harmless drudge" originates in Samuel Johnson's wry definition in his English dictionary.

Oxford English Dictionary – and from 1988 to 1990 I learned more than in any equal period in my life. A large part of my work was to compress or conflate the information offered in the *OED* for incorporation into my smaller-format dictionary. To do so, I had to study the *OED*'s defining style very closely. With such study it quickly becomes clear that the *OED* has a character, a personality almost – a feature typically unknown and certainly unwelcome in a dictionary. This character owes, in large part, to the sheer scale of the project and the room available for definition: writing, like speech, betrays the author's character and context more clearly with every word. For those unfamiliar with the *OED*, I suggest Anthony Burgess's approach: take it to bed with you, like a "weighty mistress". Failing that, I direct you to the comprehensively, subtly, and elegantly defined entry for the word **language** noun²: it has five major senses, each with an average of two transferred or narrowed (subject specific) senses, and a section for attributive and combined uses. Also, the entry group for **out** is an exercise in grammatical distinctions too subtle even for most writers and illustrates this dictionary's attempt at minute precision: it accounts for **out** as a noun, verb, adjective, preposition, interjection, and combining form. Even an idle perusal of the *OED* reveals unexpected though completely characteristic biases: the first edition of this monument to English finds space for close and beautiful definitions for arcane scholarly terms (prosody, literary stylistics, grammar, theology, and philosophy are particularly rewarding fields of search, yielding **apharesis**, **senecdoche, subjunctive, parousia,** and **teleology**), while passing in complete silence over a basic and absolutely common word (**fuck** is the notable example) and dismissing the humble **manat** as "some kind of fish". In these entries, one imagines the tongues of the editors ("the Four Wise Clerks of Oxenford" of whom Tolkien writes in *Farmer Giles of Ham*) firmly in their cheeks, as in the **blunderbuss** entry.

And so, after a year or more steeped in the attitudes, conventions, and language of the *OED*, one evening I found myself again reading *The Lord of the Rings* (as one is wont to do for solace in this hard world). Wallowing in the high morality of Sam's sparing Gollum at the base of Mount Doom, I was suddenly struck by a shock of recognition:

"Oh, curse you, you stinking thing!" he said. "Go away! Be off! I don't trust you, not as far as I could kick you; but be off . . ."

(Tolkien, 1983, p. 980)

"Go away!"? "Be off!"?? This, from the Sam Gamgee of stout farming stock, so fierce, so rural, so determinedly salt-of-the-earth? The Sam Gamgee who told Bill Ferny he had an ugly face and then threw an apple at it? Who fought trolls and killed Shelob for love of Mr. Frodo? Who was described by the narrator moments before as inarticulate with "wrath and the memory of evil". Framed by the heated, colloquial "you stinking thing" and "not as far as I could kick you", "Go away! Be off!" stands out as formal – and rather unlikely. Suddenly, all the *OED* entries for expletives that had ever crossed my desk leapt to mind:

bugger verb, sense 2c. *coarse slang.*
With off: go away, depart.
sod verb ³, sense 2. *slang.*
With off: to go away, depart.
truss verb, sense 4. *obsolete.*
To take oneself off, be off, go away, depart.
wag verb, sense 7. To go, depart, be off.
Now *colloquial.*

It was clear that Sam, in the coded language of Tolkien's dictionary, was not only cursing, but **swearing at** Gollum, as well he might.

Thence, I ranged further for evidence that Tolkien's fiction drew on his experience specifically as a lexicographer as distinct from or at least in addition to his medieval scholarship. The old chestnuts, already commented on by other scholars, were there: in *Farmer Giles of Ham*, the reference to the *OED* entry for **blunderbuss** and the pun on **grammar** and **glamour**, and in *The Hobbit*, the "low philological jest" of naming the dragon **Smaug** (Shippey, 1982, pp. 40-41; Tolkien, 1981, p. 31). Yet there is a broader influence than these pointed jokes suggest: an attitude toward the use of language and to narrative construction that pervades Tolkien's work, from time to time breaching on the surface of tales like a whale showing part of its submerged bulk.

Most obviously, Tolkien foregrounds the lexicographer's concern with the semantic possibilities of words and phrases. In *The Hobbit*, Bilbo's initial conversation with Gandalf shows Bilbo using the same phrase as both a greeting and a farewell; Gandalf calls attention to the difference, not only of broad denotation (or basic meaning) but also of connotation (or subtle suggestion), between Bilbo's uses:

"Good morning!" said Bilbo, and he meant it. The sun was shining, and the grass was very green . . .
"What do you mean?" [Gandalf] said. "Do you wish me a good morning, or mean that it is a good morning whether I want it or not; or that you feel good this morning; or that it is a morning to be good on?"
"All of them at once," said Bilbo . . .

After Gandalf alarms the hobbit with talk of adventure, Bilbo changes his tone:

"Good morning!" he said at last. "We don't want any adventures here, thank you! You might try over The Hill or across The Water." By this he meant that the conversation was at an end.
"What a lot of things you use **Good morning** for!" said Gandalf. "Now you mean that you want to get rid of me, and that it won't be good till I move off."

(Tolkien, 1979, pp. 15-16)

For good measure, Gandalf then turns the noun phrase of salutation into a verb phrase which emphasizes the second, peremptory sense: "To think that I should live to be good-morninged by Belladonna Took's son, as if I was selling buttons at the door!" (Tolkien, 1979, p. 17)

Also clearly to be seen in *The Hobbit* is a self-conscious concern with styles of language, the effect created by particular syntactic structures, grammatical constructions, and a restricted lexicon. This parallels the *OED*'s practice of identifying typical usages according to geographical occurrence, register, or style. In *The Hobbit* Tolkien repeatedly contrasts the verbal styles of the dwarves with Bilbo's, and even distinguishes among the dwarves by verbal style and register of language. Compare the high-flown speech of Thorin:

> "Gandalf, dwarves and Mr. Baggins! We are met together in the house of our friend and fellow conspirator, this most excellent and audacious hobbit . . . We are met to discuss our plans, our ways, means, policy and devices. We shall soon before the break of day start on our long journey . . . It is a solemn moment . . ."
>
> This was Thorin's style. He was an important dwarf.
>
> (Tolkien, 1979, pp. 26-27)

with the pragmatic, businesslike expression of Gloin:

> "Yes, yes, but that was long ago . . . I was talking about *you*. And I assure you there is a mark on this door – the usual one in the trade, or used to be. *Burglar wants a good job, plenty of Excitement and reasonable Reward*, that's how it is usually read. You can say *Expert Treasure-Hunter* instead of *Burglar* if you like. Some of them do. It's all the same to us."
>
> (Tolkien, 1979, p. 28)

To characterize the trolls, Tolkien chooses a lexicon and accent which set them very quickly in a tradition of literary and dramatic villains. Words like **blighter, blinking**, and **blimey** place the trolls in their social hierarchy by register, and orthographic renditions of pronunciations ("'Ere, 'oo are you?", "yer", "et", "tomorrer", "'ell", and "a-thinkin") place them by accent. These are popularly perceived features of a working-class London dialect – stage cockney. To achieve his narrative ends, Tolkien, is not above exploiting a language stereotype.

In "Riddles in the Dark", Gollum is characterized through grotesque physical description, but even more so through his language. His sibilant "Preciousss" echoes in every reader's memory. Perhaps the most telling of his verbal peculiarities, however, is his use of the first person plural (*we, us*) to refer to himself but the third person neuter singular (*it*) to refer to Bilbo: it suggests Gollum's self-absorption and thorough identification with his Ring, as well as his objectifying of the hobbit as a potential meal.

The narrator's glossing of the speech of Dain's dwarves as they approach the Mountain calls attention not merely to the difference between their verbal style and the reader's own ordinary speech, but foregrounds their cultural character as it is expressed through that speech:

> "We are sent from Dain son of Nain," they said when questioned. "We are hastening to our kinsmen in the Mountain, since we learn that the kingdom of old is renewed. But who are you that sit in the plain as foes before defended walls?" This, of course, in the polite and rather old-fashioned language of such occasions, meant simply: "You have no business here. We are going on, so make way or we shall fight you!"
>
> (Tolkien, 1979, p. 261)

Bilbo's speech contrasts with that of most of the other characters throughout the novel. Two exchanges highlight his style especially well. With Smaug, Bilbo engages in a verbal duel, gradually penetrating and adopting (as best he can) the dragon's style of language. This passage demonstrates not only the difference between Bilbo's usual speech and the inflated style employed by Smaug, but also the difficulty with which Bilbo struggles toward the state of mind that produces this style (Tolkien, 1979, pp. 212-213). In the exchange of farewells between Bilbo and Balin, the verbal styles of hobbits and dwarves are contrasted yet again, but this time the contrast serves the further purpose of revealing how Bilbo, having experienced and learned much, remains essentially a hobbit in character:

> "Good-bye and good luck, wherever you fare!" said Balin at last. "If ever you visit us again, when our halls are made fair once more, then the feast shall indeed be splendid!"
>
> "If ever you are passing my way," said Bilbo, "don't wait to knock! Tea is at four; but any of you are welcome at any time!"
>
> (Tolkien, 1979, p. 274)

In *The Lord of the Rings*, this concern with appropriate or characteristic verbal style manifests chiefly in Tolkien's stringent avoidance of the dual voice. He rarely allows the narrator to lend his articulacy to a character in order to express that character's complex thoughts. Notwithstanding that I have already used a part to show how Tolkien encoded Sam's swearing, the passage in which Sam's sophisticated understanding of Gollum contrasts so sharply with his inability to express his thoughts stands out as Tolkien's most faithful expression of any of his characters through language:

> Sam's hand wavered. His mind was hot with wrath and the memory of evil. It would be just to slay this treacherous, murderous creature, just and many times deserved; and also it seemed the only safe thing to do. But deep in his heart there was something that restrained him: he could not strike this thing lying in the dust, forlorn, ruinous, utterly wretched. He himself, though only for a little while, had borne the Ring, and now dimly he guessed the agony of Gollum's shrivelled mind and body, enslaved to that Ring, unable to find peace or relief ever in life again. But Sam had no words to express what he felt.
>
> "Oh, curse you, you stinking thing!" he said. "Go away! Be off! . . ."
>
> (Tolkien, 1983, pp. 979-80)

Tolkien is at pains to show the differences between the languages of the peoples of Middle-earth through repeated references to their differing personal and place names. This is first seen in the names given to the swords of Westernesse found in the troll cave: what is **Orcrist** for elves is **Goblin-cleaver** for men and **Biter** for goblins; what is **Glamdring** for elves is **Foe-hammer** for men and **Beater** for goblins (Tolkien, 1979, p. 59). This attention to providing the right names of things in a particular lexicon carries over into *The Lord of the Rings* and becomes, as so many of Tolkien's stylistic devices, more sophisticated. The names of people and places are multiplied by the number of societies they are known to. Even the names of generic things are glossed in many Middle-earth languages:

> Thereupon the herb-master entered. "Your lordship asked for **kingsfoil**, as the rustics name it," he said; "or **athelas** in the noble tongue, or to those who know somewhat of the Valinorean . . ."
>
> "I do so," said Aragorn, 'and I care not whether you say now **asëa aranion** or **kingsfoil**, so long as you have some."
>
> (Tolkien, 1983, p. 899)

This gently comical vignette exposes the co-dependent sides of the lexicographer's approach to language: the herb-master is indulging in pedantry of the most tiresome kind, while Aragorn is insisting on grounding words in relation to external reality.

Finally, there are parallels between the *OED*'s characteristic definition structures and their underlying logic and Tolkien's narrative structures (in terms of plot structure and descriptive logic). This area of influence is perhaps the least easily pinpointed and defined, but the most pervasive.

The *Oxford English Dictionary* seeks to define in two ways: delineating distinctions between particular uses (identified as senses) while establishing connections between uses according to their semantic and grammatical development in a historical framework. Again, I direct readers to the entry for **language** n.².

Tolkien's plot-structures at their most complex show this tension between the clarifying separation out of an event from its narrative context in order to delineate its characteristics as an event, and the establishing of connections between events to illustrate the historical or causal developments which form the narrative pattern of the text. In *The Road to Middle-earth*, T.A. Shippey identifies the basic structural mode of *The Lord of the Rings* as *entrelacement*. This designation is, perhaps, not perfect – as Shippey states, this structural device is pre-novelistic (1982, p. 120); also, medieval and early modern models of *entrelacement* (such as Mallory's *Morte d'Arthur* and Spenser's *Faerie Queene*) are disjointed, unfulfilled, or incomplete, so that the final relation of all the narrative components is difficult to perceive; their plots are sometimes more labyrinthine than interlacing. I suggest that a useful model for Tolkien's interlaced narrative structure is the historical dictionary entry: lines of development separate and are followed, and then perhaps converge again, as in senses 1 and 2 of **language** n.².

An excellent example of the way in which Tolkien's plot-structure and development parallels the *OED*'s characteristic sense-structure is the plot line that centres on Pippin's theft of the Palantír of Orthanc. His action emerges from a complex set of events, beginning with Boromir's attempt to take the Ring from Frodo, which sends the hobbit into hiding and Pippin and Merry out alone to search for him. The younger hobbits are captured by orcs and brought inadvertently to Fangorn Forest, where they rouse Treebeard to attack Saruman at Isengard. Saruman is defeated and Pippin is nearby to recover the **palantír** that is thrown from the tower. It arouses his intense curiosity so that he steals it, looks into it, and sets in motion another chain of events with far-reaching effects in the War of the Ring. Gandalf takes Pippin into his own care, so that he is brought to Gondor where he eventually saves the life of Faramir; Merry is transferred to the care of Aragorn, who takes him to Rohan where he enters the service of Théoden, eventually following him to the Battle of the Pelennor Fields in which he helps Éowyn destroy the Lord of the Nazgûl. The **palantír** itself is given to Aragorn, whose use of it provokes Sauron to ignore his own land and attack Gondor, allowing Frodo to get to Mount Doom where the Ring is destroyed. The straight line of causality or plot development is clear; the offshoots of connection to other plotlines are also easily seen.

Yet the passage dealing with the event (the theft itself) stands out with almost surreal clarity against the events surrounding it. The moment, separate from the cumulative events leading into and out of it, is defined as an independent, coherent event by the clarity of its terse narrative, purely descriptive except for Pippin's sudden talking to himself:

> At last he could stand it no longer. He got up and looked round. It was chilly, and he wrapped his cloak about him. The moon was shining cold and white, down into the dell, and the shadows of the bushes were black. All about lay sleeping shapes. The two guards were not in view: they were up on the hill, perhaps, or hidden in the bracken. Driven by some impulse that he did not understand, Pippin walked softly to where Gandalf lay. He looked down at him . . .
>
> Hardly breathing, Pippin crept nearer, foot by foot. At last he knelt down. Then he put his hands out stealthily, and slowly lifted the lump up . . .
>
> "You idiotic fool!" Pippin muttered to himself. "You're going to get yourself into frightful trouble . . ."
>
> (Tolkien, 1983, p. 614-5)

Tolkien illustrates through his interwoven plots that causal development is the basis of history. In *The Lord of the Rings* the close interdependence of events, the relentless development of lines of causality, and the frequent use of retrospective narration (notably by Gandalf at Bag End and by all speakers at the Council of Elrond) blurs the beginnings and ends of the various stories told in the novel; the movement or process of history is the thing most clearly communicated. In the *OED* the logic of the entries, including the etymologies (which may trace a word from its earliest postulated origins in the mists of unrecorded time) and combinations or collocations (which represent the marriage of one word with another to produce a new lexical entity), demonstrates the ceaseless process of a word's development. The parallels are clear; Tolkien's own practice as a lexicographer and a writer of fiction provides the connection.

Henry James wrote that plot construction in the writing of a novel is like arbitrarily drawing a line around a body of events and showing that the things inside the line are connected to one another though not to anything outside. The General Introduction to the *OED* states that words and senses are "linked on every side" with other words and senses, and that "the circle of English has a well-defined centre but no discernible circumference. Yet practical utility has some bounds, and a dictionary has definite limits: the lexicographer must, like the naturalist, 'draw the line' somewhere." Tolkien, as a novelist closely attuned to historical lexicography, drew his line around tales plucked out of his "compendious history" of Middle-earth and drew the threads into tight connection between those tales, producing perhaps the most truly "historical" novel ever written.

References

Carpenter, Humphrey. 1977. *J.R.R. Tolkien: A biography*. London: George Allen & Unwin.

Oxford English Dictionary. Oxford: Oxford University Press, 1884-1921, 1933.

Shippey, T. A. 1982. *The Road to Middle-earth*. London: George Allen & Unwin.

Tolkien, J. R. R. 1979. *The Hobbit*. London: Unwin Paperbacks.

Tolkien, J. R. R. 1981. *The Letters of J.R.R. Tolkien*. Ed. Humphrey Carpenter. Boston: Houghton Mifflin.

Tolkien, J. R. R. 1983. *The Lord of the Rings*. London: Unwin Paperbacks.

Problems of Translating into Russian[1]

Natalia Grigorieva

Abstract: The general traditions of Russian literature has been based on the requirement that any literary translation should be good literature in itself as well as preserving the author's manner of writing. It seems that understanding of J.R.R. Tolkien and his books is growing very slowly in Russia. There have never been any professional literary works on Tolkien or the problems of translating his works. A number of approaches to translating are connected with this fact. A short history of this subject shows that both the author's attitude and fairy-story reality should be reproduced correctly and with care. I am going to compare Russian published versions of *The Lord of the Rings* (by V. Murav'ĕv & A. Kistyakovskiĭ, by V. Matorina, by N. Grigorieva & V. Grushetskiy, and by Z. Bobir). The following are discussed:
• The author's and translator's attitudes to the story they tell (horror and humour, fairies and dragons)
• Reliability of Middle-earth elements – how this is achieved by different approaches (hobbits' names and manner of speech, Elvish languages and so on)
• Folklore and the nature of the hero: ways to find analogies
• The laws of Faerie must not be changed!
  A fully adequate version should find solutions for all these problems; but really the more is done the better the translation.

Keywords: fairy-tales, reality, Russian literary and folklore tradition, Russian translations

Tolkien became known here among a small group of translators and philologists in the middle of the 70s. From the very beginning it has been clear that this outstanding author made an appreciable contribution to English and world literature. His works were dedicated "simply to England; to my country" (Tolkien, 1990, p. 144), but the stories about Middle-earth were founded on folklore materials including all the rich folklore of the European North-West, and the philosophical and moral problems of his works were of great human importance. It is a tradition of Russian literature that a literary translation should re-create the original's forms and content using the artistic means of another language to achieve adequate comprehension of the literary work under other cultural circumstances. *The Lord of the Rings* was closely connected with the mythological, heroical, historical and literary tradition of Western Europe so it was natural to suppose it would be hard to translate.

So it's not surprising that *The Lord of the Rings* was mentioned for the first time in 1976 in a review "Tolkien i kritiki" written by translator V. Murav'ĕv. It considered *A Tolkien Compass* (Lobdell, 1975) and works by Robley Evans and Randel Helms. He saw sources of Tolkien's creative work in the fact that

our age is an age to make decisions, an age when good and evil are directly opposed . . . This feeling has inspired Tolkien's book. And the fact that his understanding of the demands of the time was expressed through fairy-story, myth, heroic *epos*, didn't harm his purpose . . . His fantasy is definitely earth-grown. Based on folklore and mythology he tried to get a synthesis of a centuries-old collective imagination . . . Tolkien's epic has an invisible basis, that is, its magical-faery, historical-linguistic support . . .[2]
(Murav'ĕv, 1976, p. 110)

V. Murav'ĕv regards Middle-earth as a "faery-ordinary" world existing in four dimensions: in geography, history, morality and linguistics.

The genre of *The Lord of the Rings* was considered in papers and a thesis by another famous translator, S. Koshelev (1981). He defined the book as a philosophical fantasy romance with elements of a fairy-tale and heroic *epos*.

The way Russian readers comprehend Tolkien and his books at present depends partly on the way Tolkien became known here. So I'd like to present a short history of translations of Tolkien into Russian. I think it would be better to do no more than to explain in brief how and why certain names have been translated by different translators. Any translation has many more difficulties and problems

---
[1] Editors' note: some revisions to this paper have been made by the editors.
[2] All Russian quotations are translated by Natalia Grigorieva.

than just those connected with the names. The merits or defects of a translation partly depend on the way the names were translated I don't think it can describe translation by itself. Nevertheless they are significant, sometimes showing the method used by translator.

The first of Tolkien's books in Russian was *The Hobbit* (Tolkien/Rakhmanova, 1976) published in 1976. N. Rakhmanova's method was the traditional one for literary translations of fairy-tales. The names and places were simply transcribed for the most part, such as "Baggins" – *Вэггинс*, "Rivendell" – *Райвенделл*, Dale – *Дэйл*.

A slightly abridged version of "Leaf by Niggle", translated by S. Koshelev, was published in the popular magazine *Khimiya i zhizn* in 1980. The epilogue by Yu. Shreider called the story "a parable about creative work" (Shreider, 1980, p. 92) which is connected with the author's ordinary life. That is the reason why names with meanings were translated here. For example, Niggle was reproduced as *Мелкин*. In Russian it is associated with the word *Мелкий* (it means "small, modest, simple person") or with the word *Мел* (chalk) indicating that he is an artist. Moreover, *Мелкин* is phonetically close to the author's own name. So an autobiographical element of the story is stressed.

It is interesting that both translations and articles didn't get any attention from general readers or publishers or even literary critics, though they were done by professional translators and were really good. The first attempt to present *The Lord of the Rings* for Russian readers was done in 1982 by V. Murav'ev and A. Kistyakovskiĭ (Tolkien/Murav'ev & Kistyakovskiĭ, 1982). In those years the totalitarian state was still strong. It was impossible to publish the original exactly as it was, and a lot of changes were made to satisfy the censor's demands. For example, nearly everything connected with tobacco, strong drinks, and love adventures was cut out. I suppose the only reason to abridge "The Story of Beren and Lúthien" was the fact that Beren had to bring the bride-price of Lúthien to Thingol, and that was incompatible with socialistic ideology. It sounds funny now, but it was very serious in 1982!

Nevertheless this edition revealed Tolkien to general readers. Since then enthusiastic groups of young people have began to be interested in Middle-earth and its history. They were remarkably persistent in getting information. Tolkien became a kind of "secret knowledge" for some young intellectuals.

In 1986 *Farmer Giles of Ham*, translated by Usova, appeared (Tolkien/Usova, 1986). This fairy-tale, constructed as a witty literary game and full of numerous historical and pseudo-historical allusions, presents certain difficulties for translation. Some of them seem insuperable. Even the word "farmer" itself cannot be conveyed completely. The word "Фермер" is connected in Russian with "the capitalistic agricultural practice" and is definitely understood as a "new" word, no older than the nineteenth century. So Farmer Giles and a knight meeting has a kind of comical effect, but I am not quite sure the author would have planned it that way.

In 1987 *Smith of Wootton Major*, translated by E. Gippius and Yu. Nagibin, was published. The foreword by Yu. Nagibin declared that

> this is a fairy-story for grown-up children who are on the threshold of manhood. Those readers are endowed with a gift of understanding everything. This small story is amazingly rich in sense and the children for whom it was written would read much more in it and would get into depths that adults don't dream of.
> (Nagibin, 1987, p. 43)

A fairy-story is as real as a "Secondary World". The translators are as serious and respectful to it as the author himself.

This difference in the methods of translation depends on the difference between the stories themselves. Moreover, it's closely connected with the translator's personality and his individual understanding. I think that a translation's quality may be indirectly estimated by the number of other versions which appear after its publication. It is significant that no one serious attempt was made "to improve" or "to correct" these versions. It means for me that in spite of all their differences, every one of them answers the main Russian literary requirements for translated works. Any literary translation should convey the content and sense of the original and it should be appreciated by readers as a good literary work.

Thus nearly all the "small prose" of Tolkien had been satisfactorily translated and published before 1988. Nevertheless general readers remained hardly any more familiar with Tolkien than ten years before. Those who were carried away by Tolkien reading the first Russian version of *The Fellowship of the Ring* had been concentrating on studying *The Lord of the Rings*. It was accessible for a limited circle of people who were more or less familiar with English and luckily lived in large cities where it was easier to get the necessary information. When it became clear that the two other volumes of the book wouldn't be appearing in the near future, "home-made" translations appeared. It's difficult to ascertain their number exactly. We know of about ten of them, though I'm sure there have been many more. They were made by enthusiasts who hadn't expected to see their works legally published. Most of them were made in accordance with the translator's own way of understanding, sometimes even for their own liking. But they have never kept them to themselves. Actually these "home-made" translations were distributed widely among close and distant relatives and friends. For these purposes typewriters and photocopiers were used; when personal computers and discs appeared vast horizons opened for "samizdat" or "independent (of the political system) publishing". It's impossible to count the number of people who heard about Tolkien in this way. I suppose there were about twenty thousand of them.

This "underground" dissemination of *The Lord of the Rings* coincided with the process of "perestroika". For the first time in Soviet history there was no need to take censorship into account. Public consciousness was changing slowly towards spiritual freedom. These factors brought about a significant peculiarity in the "home-made" translations. Though literarily weak, they attempted to imitate a fairy-story reality as if it were "reality", not as a kind of convention invented by the author or borrowed from folklore to incarnate his own ideas.

The "Tolkien boom" reached Russia twenty-five years late. The present situation, when millions of copies of *The Lord of the Rings* and *The Hobbit* are being published, a lot of "Tolkien Societies" are arising and "Hobbit Role-Playing Games" are taking place is, I suppose, similar to yours between 1965 and 1968. For twelve years, from 1976 to 1988, no more than 200,000 copies of *The Fellowship* and *The Hobbit* were sold. Since 1989 millions of copies have been sold. All Tolkien's works which were published before 1973 and are therefore free of author's royalty payments have been published here except *The Adventures of Tom Bombadil* and the scholarly works of Tolkien. Unfortunately on the back of the wave of deep interest undisguised hackwork has appeared. Such is the translation by Z. Bobir named *The Lords of the Rings* (sic). It looks like an incompetent compilation of the old "home-made" translations. Another is one of the "pirate" *Silmarillions* which is abridged and literarily weak. The name of the translator isn't shown at all! "Pirate" editions are becoming a real nuisance. There are two of them now, and nobody knows what will follow!

Three versions of *The Lord of the Rings* translations are now legally published. Ours is the one published completely in 1991 (Tolkien/Grigorieva & Grushetskiy, 1991). It includes three volumes and nearly all the "Appendices". It was reprinted twice in 1992 in four books (including *The Hobbit*) and in three hardback volumes. The original version of *The Fellowship of the Ring – Khraniteli –* was radically revised by V. Murav'ëv after the death of A. Kistyakovskiĭ. It appeared in 1988 (Tolkien/Murav'ëv & Kistyakovskiĭ, 1988), the second volume, *Dve tverdini*, appeared in 1991 (Tolkien/Murav'ëv, 1991). The third volume still hasn't been published[3]. The translation of V. Matorina has just been completed in Khabarovsk (Tolkien/Matorina, 1991, and Tolkien/Matorina, 1992).

I'm now going to discuss these three Russian versions of *The Lord of the Rings*. But first of all I ought to note that as I'm a translator myself I'm afraid I'm not impartial, though I will attempt to be more or less objective.

In the "afterword" to the *Khraniteli* version of 1982, the translators see the idea of the strife between Good and Evil in the book as a traditional fairy-tale motif. Folklore elements drawn into the author's fantasy helped him to invent a wonderfully bright and coloured magic world. His personal experience of life, including two world wars, brought moral sense into this world. "A wealth of fantasy is displayed especially in the invention of Elvish languages and, for example, in such a hero as Tom Bombadil . . ." (Murav'ëv & Kistyakovskiĭ, 1982, p. 330). So it was only natural for translators to continue "the author's wonderful game of fairy world invention" (Murav'ëv & Kistyakovskiĭ, 1982, p. 328). By the way, *Alice in Wonderland* by Lewis Carroll has been translated in a similar way, when the word-play of the original was created anew by means of the Russian language.

The brightness and expressiveness of that translation by V. Murav'ëv and A. Kistyakovskiĭ still remains matchless. For example, their translation of Gollum's appeal to himself is worth a lot! "My precious" – *Моя Прелесть*. The word *прелесть* has two meanings in Russian. One of them is "beauty, charm", another (church) – "temptation". *Торбинсы из Торбы-на-Круче* ("Bagginses from Bag End"), *Скромби* for "Gamgee", *невысоклики* for "halflings" (unexpectedly it is very hard to find the proper word: most of them sound unpleasant in Russian), and *Лихолесье* for "Mirkwood" naturally entered Russian "tolkienistics". Some translators prefer to retain them in their versions (as V. Matorina does). But "wealth of fantasy" leads the translators too far, it seems. They've gone beyond the author's fantasy. The translators' activity is especially noticeable in the fragments that have no visible folklore antecedents. So the Shire was turned into *Хоббитания*, and Hobbits find themselves in close relation with rabbits or hares. "A Hare" is as traditional a hero of Russian nursery-tales as "a Rabbit" is of English. The process of "rabbitisation" has turned "Took" to *Крол*, "Brandy Hall" to *Зайгород* (from *заяч* – "a hare"), "Crickhollow" into *Кроличья Балка*.

The elvish language, as it was supposed to have been "invented by the author", underwent material changes. The Elvish name "Glorfindel" has been understood possibly as an English word and has been translated *Всеславур*, converting an Elf into a Russian knight. "Galdor" became *Гаральд*. I don't know the reasons for this conversion. "Lothlórien" was translated partly. So Elvish "loth", "a flower", was translated by *квет*, phonetically close to Russian *цвет*, *цветок* and Ukrainian *квиток*.

The fabulous world allows liberties with distances, and the legendarium, too. So, 20 miles changes to 20 leagues(!) which tired hobbits travel in a single day; the unfortunate Amroth is at the same time lying buried under Cerin Amroth and travelling over the Sea.

Any translation will have some mistakes, but here they form a system which definitely destroys the special style and soul of the book. That is inadmissible. I'd like to show one more inaccuracy which has been noticed by a few readers. It remains in the corrected version of 1988. It is typical. I am speaking about the fragment in which Orcs attack the Fellowship at Moria. In the original there is:

> Legolas shot two through the throat. Gimli hewed the legs from under another that had sprung up on Balin's tomb. Boromir and Aragorn slew many. When thirteen had fallen the rest fled shrieking, leaving the defenders unharmed . . .
> (Tolkien, 1991, p. 343)

In the translation (translated back) it is:

> Legolas shot two with his bow. Gimli hewed the legs from under another that had sprung up on Balin's tomb. Boromir slew three orcs and Aragorn five and Gandalf slew one[!]. The orcs wavered, draw back to the door

---
[3] It appeared in September, 1992.

and fled shrieking . . ."
(Tolkien/Murav'ëv & Kistyakovskiĭ, 1988, p. 400)

That is definitely impossible for Gandalf the Maia who was sent to Middle-earth by the Valar and was forbidden to kill, as is clear from *Unfinished Tales*.

In the revised version published in 1988 most of the errors and abridged fragments were corrected. Unfortunately, it didn't reverse the process of "rabbitization". V. Murav'ëv explains in his foreword to the book that "Hobbit" was constructed from two words – "homo" and "a rabbit" – and even names of hobbit-races were derived from images of the Hare in Russian folklore. Thus there appear *Струсы* for Stoors (derived from "coward", *трусишка* – that's the traditional nick-name for a Hare in children's stories), *лапитупы* for "Harfoots" and *беляки* for "Fallowhides". The last is one breed of hare in Russian. The translator explains that "the Hobbits came from a fairy-tale – an improvised home-made nursery-tale, in which a plush rabbit is taken from a toy-box and is placed into a doll's house . . ." (Murav'ëv, 1988, p.19). When the narration was growing in some sense of "reality", it's main hero-Hare grew in significance and "humanity", but he didn't turn into a man. So the manner of the *Khraniteli* version swings between drama and farce, and it is immutably "unreal" and far-fetched. Tom Bombadil talks in silly rhymes and behaves like Petrushka – a Russian folk farce-hero, like the English "Mister Punch". He reminds one of a jester or a trickster. I don't think it's a proper analogy.

It seems that the second volume was translated by V. Murav'ëv alone. *Dve Tverdini* was done in a more "naturalistic" manner, at any rate the fragment about orcs and battles. But the translator's desire for a "realistic" tone sometimes leads him to rudeness and abuse. The author himself recommended avoiding them, and if curses would be more or less comprehensible in the orcish manner of speech, then Elves, I suppose, are well-mannered people. But in Murav'ëv's translation even Legolas talks roughly without any need, like this: "– That's all, Aragorn! Black *svoloch'* close up! Let's go!" (Tolkien/Murav'ëv, 1991, p. 162). The English "bastard" is similar by expression to Russian *svoloch*. By the way, the original text is: "'All who can have now got safe within, Aragorn,' he called. 'Come back!'" (Tolkien, 1991, p. 561). I dare not show you examples of "orcish" vocabulary.

Sometimes this manner of speech changes to a high style hardly natural in ordinary speech. It's usual for Gandalf in this version, but it looks really funny when the Rohan guards speak no less imposingly.

Inaccuracy with the Elvish language began in "Khraniteli" and spreads here to the other languages, too. "Rohan" is translated *Ристания* (from Old Slavic *ристати* – to gallop) and *Мустангрим* (though *мустанг* is understood in Russian as an "American" word).

As for Rohan, a lot of historical analogies were used in the text. Some of them have a west-European origin and are understood as "foreign" by Russian readers. For example, "King of Rohan" turns to Scandinavian *конунг*. "Marshal of Riddermark" turns to French *сенешаль*. But some of the Rohan names and place-names were left untranslated. Mostly they are understood as "English", but sometimes transliteration plays a bad joke. For example, "Hornburg" turned into *Горнбург* which sounds German. So the translator's will mixes up in Rohan different countries, languages, centuries, etc.

I don't mean that it's a wrong approach to find analogies, including historical ones. Sometimes neutral terms need to be made concrete, such as the title "King" used in countries with different social systems. In my opinion, it is necessary to do this, but it is really difficult to avoid wrong or contradictory analogies. V. Murav'ëv has noted that Tolkien's books don't have any accidental events or arbitrary motives. Nevertheless V. Murav'ëv doesn't succeed in saving this wonderful integrity of the original. I think, it depends on the fact that the translator disbelieves in the very genre of fairy-story. This translation breaks one of the fairy-story principles which are discussed by Tolkien in his essay "On Fairy-Stories". This principle is the serious attitude of the story-teller to the "wonders" of his faery world. This attitude implies knowledge of the laws of Faerie and the translator's "inner" confidence in them.

We have tried to do just that with our translation. The essence of our method may be illustrated by an analogy. Imagine that you are going to copy a painting using coloured pencils only. There are two options. You could re-draw the picture accurately reproducing every colour and every detail. Or you could attempt to see this landscape "as it was seen by the artist" trying to understand why it has been so dear to him and to draw the picture anew. We've done more or less the same with Tolkien's books as far as our poor artistic abilities allow.

Thus we've been forced to answer: why is it written this way and what is the sense of it? For example, what is the role of the Shire and Hobbits in the total narrative structure? From our point of view, the Shire is the "threshold" which opens the way to Middle-earth. Our attitude to the fairy-story is formed here. We are familiar with many things in this place or at least we can recognize them. The Hobbits, our guides to the Fairy Land, are psychologically close to, and understandable by, us. The author underlines that they "are relations of ours: far nearer than Elves, or even than Dwarves" at the very beginning, not without reason. It is acceptable to consider Sam Gamgee as "an ordinary Englishman". I think it would be more exact to say "an ordinary man". At any rate, the favourite hero of Russian folk-tales who is usually third son of a King or a farmer and is named accordingly "Ivan-tsarevich" or "Ivan-durak", is as honest, direct, faithful, good-hearted, cunning and simple, thrifty and generous as Master Samwise.

That is the reason why hobbit's names and places should be translated. If you leave them unchanged, you automatically move your story to a very distant, unfamiliar and alien land. Moreover you lose some "speaking" (and humorous) names. I'd like to mention that all three Russian versions of *The Lord of the Rings* are similar here. But the effect of "familiarity" and "reality" was of especial meaning for us, so in achieving them we preferred to choose names already existing in folk toponymics. *Торба-на-Круче* by V. Murav'ëv sounds splendid, but no one place in Russia could be called so, and *Сумкина Горка* in ours is nearly possible. Different *горы* and *горки* ("hills") are usual for us.

V. Murav'ëv translates "Bree" as *Пригорье*, reproducing the dialect "a hill" with an invented literary word. We've found in a west-Russian dialect the word *Брыль* with the same meaning as the Celtic word and were pleased to discover how close phonetically they are! Prefixes *при* – "near, by" and *за* – "behind" – are typical for word-formation in Russian, but V. Murav'ëv over-uses them. *Пригорье, Приречье, Приречное Взгорье* or *Привражье*. The last two don't belong to the Shire, they are used for Emyn Muil, but it is difficult to guess this. As for us, we'd like to preserve the Hobbits' speech as a dialect of Common Speech and so we use for their names old or dialect words or construct something similar, as *Засумки* ("Bag-End") or *Скоцка* ("Buckhill").

I think misunderstandings with Common Speech and words related to it arise mostly if a translator doesn't follow as carefully as the author which language is really used and by whom.

As for the Elvish languages, the main problem may be defined this way: it's impossible to reproduce Elvish sounds exactly for two reasons. The first is the phonetic difference between the languages. Certain sounds don't exist in Russian (i.e. diphthongs and the *TH* combination). Some combinations of sounds can't be pronounced (i.e. the voiced consonants *V* or *B* at the end of the word). So even if you write *Гэндалв* in Russian letters, nevertheless it would be pronounced as *Гэндальф*.

The other side of this problem is that some words spelled "exactly" sound crude for Russian readers or produce some undesirable associations. So, "Durin" is so close phonetically to *дурень* (a fool) that it should be changed to *Дарин* or *Дьюрин*. The spelling of the name "Lúthien" was a subject for long discussion too. *Лутиэн* or *Лютиэн* are close phonetically, but both of them I consider unfitting. *Лютиэн* has unpleasant associations. It is similar to *лютость* (ferocity) and with *лютик* (a buttercup – it's a small yellow poisonous flower). *Лутиэн* is difficult for phonetic reasons. *Лучиэнь* changes hard consonant *т* for soft *ч* and finds a splendid association with the word *луч* – "a ray". For me, that is a better decision.

So it's clear that if you are intending to learn Elvish, you'd better use the original. Any translation may be counted satisfactory if it preserves the integrity of Elvish languages.

The next set of problems is concerned with the understanding of the hero in different cultures. There are three possibilities.

Supposing another culture has a similar image already, as in the case of Sam Gamgee. Then it is easy to achieve similarity in understanding. It is more difficult if a hero is unknown to another culture. I think we could consider Merlin as a prototype for Gandalf in English culture. But there is nobody resembling Gandalf in Russian culture. And there are no creatures like Elves or Dwarves. We are naturally familiar with dragons, werewolves or Beorn through our own folklore, but we know about Elves "at second hand". So our "Secondary Belief" in them is more weak. But you should be especially careful if an image exists in another culture but has another sense. "Old Willow-Man" V. Murav'ëv translates *Вяз* ("an Elm"), V. Matorina – as *Старуха Ива* ("Willow" is a female in Russian, so it would be "Old Willow-Woman"), we – as *Старый Лох*. In Russian folklore a Willow is a young tenderhearted sad girl. She is usually named "weeping". It's very hard for us to imagine she would be evil and black. So V.Murav'ëv changes a tree. An Elm is a man but it never has grown by the water! We found a dialect word *лох* for this type of tree which is a masculine noun and has no association with the folklore willow.

In conclusion, the subject is very large and I have shown you only a few of its problems. I don't think any Russian translations we have at our disposal are wholly adequate compared to the original. I don't even think that such a translation could be done at all, but I see two possibilities which give me a hope. Maybe some translator of genius will come. Or, more realistically, we'll get a number of translations which taken together could express all the variety of Tolkien's genius.

References

Koshelev, S. 1981. С. Кошелев. Жанровая природа «Повелителя Колец» Дж.Р.Р. Толкина. «Проблемы метода и жанра в зарубежной литературе», Сб. науч. трудов, Вып. 4. М. (МГПИ).

Lobdell, Jared. ed. 1975.*A Tolkien Compass*. La Salle, Illinois: Open Court.

Murav'ëv, V. 1976. "Tolkien i kritiki". 1976. В. Муравьев. Толкиен и критики. Обзор. «Современная художественная литература за рубежом», М., 1976, № 3, с. 110-114.

Murav'ëv, V. 1988. "foreword" in Tolkien, J.R.R. Translated by V. Murav'ëv and A. Kistyakovskiĭ. *Khraniteli*.

Murav'ëv, V. and Kistyakovskiĭ, A. 1982. "afterword" in Tolkien, J.R.R. Translated by V. Murav'ëv and A. Kistyakovskiĭ. *Khraniteli*.

Nagibin, Yu. 1987. "foreword" in Tolkien, J.R.R. trans. E. Gippius and Yu. Nagibin. "Smith of Wootton Major".

Shreider, Yu. 1980. "epilogue" in Tolkien, J.R.R. trans. S. Koshelev. "Leaf by Niggle".

Tolkien, J.R.R. 1990. *Letters of J.R.R. Tolkien*. London: Unwin Hyman.

Tolkien, J.R.R. 1991. *The Lord of the Rings*. London: HarperCollins Publishers.

Russian translations are given in chronological order:

Tolkien, J.R.R. Translated by N. Rakhmanova. 1976. *The Hobbit*. Джон Рональд Руэл Толкин. *Хоббит, или туда и обратно. Сказочная повесть*. Перевод с англ. Н. Рахмановой. Л., «Детская литература».

Tolkien, J.R.R. Translated by S. Koshelev. 1980. "Leaf by Niggle" in *Khimiya i zhizn*. No 7, pp. 84-92. 1980. Дж.Р. Toккин. «Лист работы Мелкина». Перевод с англ. С. Кошелева. *Химия и жизнь*, 1980, № 7, с. 84-92.

Tolkien, J.R.R. Translated by V. Murav'ev and A. Kistyakovskiĭ. 1982. *Khraniteli* [*The Fellowship of the Ring*]. Джон Рональд Руэл Толкиен. *Хранители. Летопись первая из эпопеи «Властелин Колец»*. Сокр. перевод с англ. А. Кистяковского и В. Муравьева. М., «Детская литература».

Tolkien, J.R.R. Translated by Usova. 1986. *Farmer Giles of Ham*. Д. Толкин. *Фермер Джайлс из Хэма, или, на простонародном языке, Возвышение и удивительные приключения фермера Джайлса, господина Ручного Ящера, графа Ящерного и короля Малого Королевства*. Перевод с англ. Г. Усовой. В сб. «Сказки английских писателей», Л., «Лениздат».

Tolkien, J.R.R. Translated by E. Gippius and Yu. Nagibin. 1987. "Smith of Wootton Major". Джон Р. Р. Толкиен. *Кузнец из Большого Вуттона. Сказка*. Перевод с англ. Ю. Нагибин, Е. Гиппиус. «Пионер», 1987, № 2, с. 43-54.

Tolkien, J.R.R. Translated by V. Murav'ev and A. Kistyakovskiĭ. 1988. *Khraniteli* [*The Fellowship of the Ring*]. revised edition. Джон Рональд Рузл Толкиен. Хранители. Летопись первая из эпопеи «Властелин Колец». Перевод с англ. В. Муравьева (Пролог и Книга первая) и А. Кистяковского (Книга вторая и все стихотворения) М., «Радуга».

Tolkien, J.R.R. Translated by V. Matoina. 1990. *The Hobbit*. Джон Рональд Роэл Толкин. *Хоббит, или Туда и Обратно*. Перевод с англ. В.А. М[аториной]. Хабаровск, «Амур».

Tolkien, J.R.R. Translated by V. Murav'ev. 1991. *Dve tverdini* [*The Two Towers*]. Джон Рональд Руэл Толкиен. *Две твердыни. Летопись вторая из эпопеи «Властелин Колец»*. Перевод с англ. В. Муравьева М., «Радуга».

Tolkien, J.R.R. Translated by Natalia Grigorieva and V Grushetskiy. 1991. *The Lord of the Rings*. Джон Рональд Руэл Толкиен. *Властелин Колец. Часть I. Братство Кольца. Часть II. Две крепости. Часть III. Возвращение короля*. Перевод с англ. Н. Григорьевой, В. Грушецкого. Перевод стихов И. Гриншпун. Л., «Северо-Запад».

Tolkien, J.R.R. Translated by V. Matorina. 1991. *The Lord of the Rings* part 1. Джон Рональд Розл Толкин. *Властелин Колец. Летопись первая. Содружество Кольца*. Перевод с англ. В.А. М[аториной]. Хабаровск, «Амур».

Tolkien, J.R.R. Translated by V. Matorina. 1992. *The Lord of the Rings* part 2. Джон Рональд Розл Толкин. *Властелин Колец. Летопись вторая. Две твердыни*. Перевод с англ. В.А. М[аториной]. Хабаровск, «Амур».

J. R. R. Tolkien and Old English Studies: An Appreciation

Bruce Mitchell

Abstract: Some scholars argue that Tolkien did not fulfil some of his responsibilities during his thirty-four years as an Oxford Professor, in that he spent the bulk of his research time on his imaginative writings, thereby depriving scholarship of valuable works he – or other holders of his Chairs – might have produced. This paper leaves posterity to judge this issue, but in assessing Tolkien's contribution to Old English studies, it will argue that one of them – his 1936 British Academy lecture, "Beowulf: The Monsters and the Critics" – has had more influence than most of the products of his critics, and that many Old English scholars owe much to his inspiration.

Keywords: Anglo-Saxon, *Beowulf*, Simone d'Ardenne, Middle English, Old English, Oxford, scholarship

"He smoked at me." This, Ladies and Gentlemen, was the reply of an Oxford graduate to a questioner who asked him how his tutor had taught him. "He smoked at me." J.R.R. Tolkien – Rawlinson and Bosworth Professor of Anglo-Saxon at Oxford University 1925-45, Merton Professor of English Language and Literature 1945-59, lover of pipe-weed – did indeed smoke at his pupils. But he did more than that. He helped us to resolve our difficulties. He stimulated us generously with his knowledge and his ideas. He inspired us with a love of our subject. He brought to his teaching the "humanity . . . revealed in so many aspects of him". (The words are those of Simone d'Ardenne of Liége, one of his best-known pupils, in Salu and Farrell, 1979, p. 33.) How fortunate we were to be in the genial presence of that formidable yet humane intellect.

Professor d'Ardenne rightly spoke of his "extraordinary knowledge of languages", noting that he "belonged to that very rare class of linguists, now becoming extinct, who like the Grimm brothers could understand and recapture the glamour of 'the word'" (d'Ardenne, 1979, pp. 36 and 35). The writer of *The Times* obituary (3rd September 1973) related that "Tolkien used to to describe himself as 'one of the idlest boys Gilson (the Headmaster [of King Edward's School, Birmingham]) ever had.'" "But", he went on, "'idleness' in his case meant private and unaided studies in Gothic, Anglo-Saxon and Welsh, and the first attempt at inventing a language . . ." Typical examples of his power as a philologist are his papers "Chaucer as a Philologist: The Reeve's Tale" (Tolkien, 1934a), in which he demonstrated how accurately Chaucer represented the language of the two Cambridge undergraduates John and Alleyn, who hailed from "Strother, fer in the north", and "Sigelwara Land" (Tolkien, 1932 & 1934b), which is an exhaustive investigation of the difficult word *Sigelhearwan* "Ethiopians", which appears in various forms in Old English. Both his humanity and his philological power are manifest in *The Lord of the Rings*. But these are topics I leave to other speakers at this Conference.

J.R.R. Tolkien had strong views about the place of Old English in English syllabuses:

> So-called Anglo-Saxon cannot be regarded merely as a root, it is already in flower. But it is a root, for it exhibits qualities and characteristics that have remained ever since a steadfast ingredient in English; and it demands therefore at least some first-hand acquaintance from every serious student of English speech and English letters. This demand the Oxford School has up to now always recognized, and has tried to meet.
>
> (Tolkien, 1979, p. 22)

I am in complete agreement with this and with the following observation about philology:

> Philology was part of my job, and I enjoyed it. I have always found it amusing. But I have never had strong views about it. I do not think it necessary to salvation. I do not think it should be thrust down the throats of the young, as a pill, the more efficacious the nastier it tastes.
>
> (Tolkien, 1979, pp. 17)

But I am puzzled by what followed:

> I do not think that it should be thrust down throats as a pill, because I think that if such a process seems needed, the sufferers should not be here, at least not studying or teaching English letters. Philology is the foundation of humane letters; "misology" is a disqualifying defect or disease.
>
> (Tolkien, 1979, p. 17)

My puzzlement arises from the fact that the English

syllabuses in operation in Oxford in the 1950s and 1960s, in whose creation J.R.R. Tolkien played a leading role, demanded a knowledge of Old English sound changes which did in fact require tutors to thrust the pill of philology – in the pejorative sense of the word – down their pupils' throats when there was no need to do so. It is not misology to oppose the unnecessary teaching of sound changes to first year undergraduates. It is common sense. In 1941, H. M. Chadwick of Cambridge, opposing such syllabuses, rhetorically asked:

> What would be thought of a Latin course which took no account of ancient Rome, or indeed of any question except the phonetic process by which – in later times – the word "homo" became "uomo" or "homme"?
>
> (Chadwick, 1941, p. ix)

As I said in the other place, "this was to be sure somewhat below the belt. But it was not a complete caricature of the atmosphere which prevailed at Oxford when I came up to Merton in 1952" (Mitchell, 1992, p. 13). This atmosphere, I am glad to say, no longer prevails.

The part played by J.R.R. Tolkien in the development of the English School is to be discussed in this morning's panel "Tolkien and Oxford University". Three things of importance, however, demand mention here. The first, his attitude to Old English, has already received it. The second is his continuing and justified opposition to the still prevailing hostility between what he described as "the bogeys *Lang* and *Lit*". He saw this division as false and dangerous, a smouldering fire of which he said: "It would have been better if it had never been kindled" (Tolkien, 1979, pp. 23-24). The third is research. To older generations of academics like myself, it seems that teaching now counts for nothing, that research is increasingly the only criterion of success, and that the good teacher without publications is damned. J.R.R. Tolkien saw the writing on this wall well before his retirement. He had met people who "took to research like otters to swimming" and recognised the existence of "natural researchers . . . [who] knew what they wanted to do" (Tolkien, 1979, p. 21). But he expressed more than disquiet about the general run of research in the Oxford English School, referring to

> activities, which have in recent years shown such rapid growth, forming what one might call our "hydroponic" department. A term which, I fear, I only know from science-fiction, in which it seems to refer to the cultivation of plants without soil in enclosed vehicles far removed from this world.
>
> (Tolkien, 1979, p. 19)

How right he was! He would have approved the verdict of a Texan scholar that "the average PhD thesis is nothing but the transference of bones from one graveyard to another". Fortunately, he did not live to see the time when the jibe could be extended to much of the work churned out by academics in English Schools or Departments throughout the world. It may have been this doubt about the value of research which resulted in the one act of academic casualness on his part of which I am personally aware: his failure in 1952 to send me to the scholar most fitted to supervise my DPhil. But it was more probably a momentary aberration. He never adopted the cavalier attitude shown by his predecessor in the Merton Chair who, after being told by the young New Zealander who was to be J.R.R. Tolkien's successor in that Chair of his intention to read Schools rather than to do research, replied (the story goes) along these lines: "Young man, what makes you think that your decision is of any conceivable interest to me?"

On the contrary, he exuded warm friendliness to all he met, a characteristic pleasantly revealed in the story of how he moved into 21 Merton Street in March 1972, "typically", as Humphrey Carpenter put it, "making friends with the three removal men and riding with them in their pantechnicon from Bournemouth to Oxford" (Carpenter, 1977, p.253). His pupils all felt this friendliness. I have always thought it strange that the editors of the *Studies* presented to him on his seventieth birthday did not include any reference to his qualities as a man; the book starts with W.H. Auden's poem "A Short Ode to a Philologist" and moves from there to an article on "The Old English Epic Style" (Davis and Wrenn, 1962). Those who know Oxford will perhaps be less surprised at this reticence than those who do not. But I am sure that I wrote for many in the letter of 8 September 1989 in which I accepted Christina Scull's invitation to give this talk:

> I am indeed conscious of the debt I owe to Professor Tolkien for the stimulus of seminal ideas which I received from his writings, his lectures, and in personal correspondence and conversation. I am also aware that I am not alone in this, for Tolkien was very generous with his ideas to those who sat at his feet. If I am in Oxford in August 1992 (and I hope to be), I would be very willing to acknowledge this in a brief contribution to your Conference.

Let me now fulfil this promise on behalf of myself and all those interested in Old English.

First, there is the elusive question of what J.R.R. Tolkien did by personal contact. Here I cannot speak for others; I can merely point to the many scholars who acknowledge a personal debt to him and from there go on to relate the story of how one of his successors in the Rawlinson and Bosworth Chair of Anglo-Saxon was wont to tell his audience to read a certain book and then to say, "This much-used and praised work bears on its title-page the name of X. But everybody knows that it was dictated by Tolkien." This was, no doubt, an exaggeration. But it does underline how generous Tolkien was with his ideas.

Second, I consider what J.R.R. Tolkien did by his Oxford lectures for undergraduates and graduates; in his day, there were no formal classes in research methods and resources for graduate students working in Old and Middle English. He himself, in his Valedictory Address, confessed his "ineffectiveness as a lecturer" (Tolkien, 1979, p. 16). He spoke quickly and was not always audible; connoisseurs of what he had to say soon learnt to arrive early and get seats in the first few rows. He sometimes spoke above his audience. He was apt to veer into enthusiastic discussion of points not central to his theme. But his love of the subject was always apparent and those who listened attentively gleaned much. Rapid delivery, however, was not apparent in one particular area, for he was wont to repeat the very necessary warning that most people today read Old English poetry too fast, thereby concealing the subtle semantic links and losing the music. (In this, they are not helped by the prevailing use of modern punctuation by editors of Old English poetry.) To hear J.R.R. Tolkien recite – or better, perform – Old English poetry was an unforgettable experience. The point is tellingly made in two tributes quoted by Carpenter:

> As one former pupil, the writer J.I.M. Stewart, expressed it: "He could turn a lecture room into a mead hall in which he was the bard and we were the feasting, listening guests." Another who sat in the audience at these lectures was W. H. Auden, who wrote to Tolkien many years later: "I don't think I have ever told you what an unforgettable experience it was for me as an under-graduate, hearing you recite *Beowulf*. The voice was the voice of Gandalf."
>
> (Carpenter, 1977, p. 133)

He also had a gift for the vivid and evocatory phrase. He characterised a Victorian rendering of a line of *Beowulf* – "ten timorous trothbreakers together" – as reminiscent of "the two tired toads that tried to trot to Tetbury". He pictured the Anglo-Saxon poet as a man filling in the half-lines of his poem with blocks of different colours, repeating himself with variation and advance. He saw, in the words of the *Exodus* poet (l. 43), *hleahtorsmiðum handa* "the hands of the laughter-smith" fashioning a pattern with his hands on the harp as he recited a poem, just as a blacksmith fashions a delicate piece of metalwork. Inspirational remarks – and sometimes valuable pearls – regularly dropped from his lips for those who were alert enough, and near enough, to catch them. Recently, when discussing a book by Daniel Donoghue (Donoghue, 1987), I recalled one such example:

> Even more exciting to me was his [Donoghue's] verdict on *Exodus*: "It may not be too fanciful to see these features in *Exodus* as a fossilized, literary preservation of a poem originally composed orally and transmitted by word of mouth" (p. 103). This carried me back thirty-five years to a room in the Examination Schools at Oxford where I strained to hear Tolkien, whose lectures were like a badly presented and served Cordon Bleu meal, and scribbled what I could catch about the *Exodus* poet:
>
>> If we have anything left by Cædmon apart from the *Hymn*, it is *Exodus* . . . marvellous word pictures . . . too excitable . . . at the Red Sea he just foams . . . if he'd only stood back, heard it from the top of the hill, he'd have done better . . . great scene . . . he's there . . . what happens? . . . blows up like a bullfrog!
>
> (Mitchell, 1988, p. 340)

On a larger scale, J.R.R. Tolkien's own lecture notes (and sometimes those taken by his pupils) have resulted in the production of two posthumous books which bear his name – *The Old English Exodus: Text, Translation, and Commentary*, edited by Joan Turville-Petre, and *Finn and Hengest: The Fragment and the Episode*, edited by Alan Bliss.

Third, I ask what J.R.R. Tolkien did for Old English studies by his publications and public lectures. I have already spoken of the article entitled *Sigelwara Land*. He contributed the section on "Philology: General Works" to *The Year's Work in English Studies* for 1923, 1924, and 1925. In these he showed the grasp of a master. One illustration, which contains a cautionary tale, must suffice: his comments on Eduard Sievers' article "Ziele und Wege der Schallanalyse" [Aims and Methods of Sound Analysis], published in 1924 (Tolkien, 1926, p. 34 fn. 3 & pp. 40-4). Here Sievers' thesis was that "motorics" – those who possessed the necessary qualities in their motor nerves – were capable of distinguishing the "personal curves" (*Personalkurve*) and the "voice quality or style" (*Stimmart*) of different authors and that these characteristics enabled Sievers to detect that certain lines in the poem *Genesis A* were composed by Cædmon. The problem was that, while no other scholar was able to claim that he possessed these qualities and was therefore able to test Sievers' conclusion, there was great reluctance to condemn him out of hand because some thirty years earlier he had dramatically been proved right in a controversy about the poem *Genesis B*. In 1887, Henry Bradley wrote thus:

> Professor Sievers, who was the first to call attention to the facts, has endeavoured to prove that this portion of the "Genesis" is a translation of an Old-Saxon poem by the author of the "Heliand". His principle argument is that several words and idioms characteristic of this passage are good Old-Saxon, but are found nowhere else in Anglo-Saxon. It is needless to say that the judgement of this distinguished scholar is deserving of the highest respect; but his conclusion appears to be open to grave objection. We must remember that the continental Saxons were evangelised by English missionaries; and, as Professor Stephens has forcibly urged, it is highly improbable that an ancient and cultured church like that of England should have adopted into its literature a poem written by a barbarian convert of its own missions. Moreover, Professor Sievers' linguistic arguments are not of overwhelming force.
>
> (Bradley in Stephen and Lee, 1908, p. 651)

Later, however, he was forced to recant:

> Several distinguished scholars endeavoured, by various complicated hypotheses, to account for the peculiar features of the passage without accepting the seemingly paradoxical theory of Sievers. The matter might have remained till this day in dispute, but in 1894 Professor Zangemeister of Heidelberg discovered among the manuscripts of the Vatican some leaves of parchment containing not only some portions of the *Heliand*, but fragments of an Old Low German poetical version of the story of Genesis, among which were twenty-five lines of the original postulated by Sievers for the Old English poem. After this discovery, it was no longer possible to doubt that the interpolated passage

of the Old English paraphrase was of continental origin. (Bradley, 1920, p. 12)

So scholars were understandably reluctant to condemn too readily what C. L. Wrenn called "the *soi-disant* scientific work of one of the very greatest of philologists" (Wrenn, 1946, p. 3). Working within this inevitable limitation and stressing that "a non-motoric, and even a potential but uninstructed motoric, can clearly not successfully criticise this work" (Tolkien, 1926, p. 42), J.R.R. Tolkien described "with diffidence" as he put it, "what appears to be the kernel of the matter" (Tolkien, 1926, p. 41). Many will wish that they could crystallize a difficult argument in difficult German with such lucid diffidence. He then perceptively drew attention to a major weakness:

> None the less, and possibly through lack of comprehension, one cannot help feeling doubts as to the view of the manner in which, say, poems are composed, which appears implicit in the argument . . . Indeed, the assumption which appears to be made throughout that written composition is virtually identical with unpremeditated speech, and is patient of the same analysis, causes one much uneasiness. This uneasiness increases when these methods are applied to other languages than the investigator's own, and to the monuments of dead languages, or the past stages of living ones.
> (Tolkien, 1926, pp. 42-3)

His conclusion was a brilliant warning which ought to be heeded today by many practitioners of modern linguistics:

> A suspension of judgement is inevitable until we can have opportunity of instruction in a more direct manner; condemnation out of hand merely because these two lectures read at first as nonsense is not called for by the desert of Sievers, or of his only less distinguished following. But neither is submission without understanding. The attitude, frequently to be observed in current German philological writings, that allows Sievers to be quoted as to the light his methods throw upon this or that form, while the quoter seems to remain unable to follow the process or to check the results, can only be called unhealthy; a dictatorship of this esoteric sort is not good, even if it dictate the truth.
> (Tolkien, 1926, pp. 43-4)

Turning now to more specifically literary publications and letters, I salute in passing, because of the pressure of time, two items. First, his memorable Prefatory Remarks to C. L. Wrenn's revision of John R. Clark Hall's prose translation of *Beowulf*, which discusses both "Translation and Words" and "Metre" and ends with this verdict on *Beowulf*: "It may not be, at large or in detail, fluid or musical, but it is strong to stand: tough builder's work of true stone" (Tolkien, 1950, p. xliii). Second, "The Homecoming of Beorhtnoth, Beorhthelm's son" (Tolkien, 1953, pp. 1-18), which – along with discussions of the issues involved in interpreting the Old English poem *The Battle of Maldon* and of the keyword *ofermod* – offers us a dramatic poem in Modern English in which we are told how the body of the dead leader Beorhtnoth was found among the slain and brought from the battlefield to the monastery of Ely. But our loudest notes of praise must be for his 1936 British Academy Lecture "*Beowulf*: the Monsters and the Critics" (Tolkien, 1937). In all three of these, we see J.R.R. Tolkien, in his own Valedictory words, trying "to awake *liking*, to communicate delight in those things that I find enjoyable" (Tolkien, 1979, p. 18).

Trying – and succeeding. The Greenfield and Robinson *Bibliography* records seventy items on "Literary Interpretations" of *Beowulf* before J.R.R. Tolkien's lecture and two-hundred-and-fifty between its publication and the end of 1972 (Greenfield and Robinson, 1980, pp. 176-89). I dare not guess how many items have appeared in the twenty years since then. But that lecture was seminal. J.R.R. Tolkien may not have produced "the first effective defense of the structure of the poem as a whole" as one critic argued.[1] However, I have no hesitation in repeating what I wrote in 1963 in a "withered nosegay of an article . . . my personal Festschrift" for J.R.R. Tolkien entitled "'Until the Dragon Comes . . .': Some Thoughts on *Beowulf*' (1963, p. 126):

> . . . that *Beowulf* is now viewed rather more as a poem and rather less as a museum for the antiquarian, a sourcebook for the historian, or a gymnasium for the philologist, is due in large measure to Professor Tolkien's famous British Academy Lecture of 1936 "*Beowulf*: The Monsters and the Critics".

It is fun to read. It is also a stylistic education, an intellectual challenge, a literary experience, and (for those who have ears to hear) a moral lesson. It ends with this verdict on the poem *Beowulf*:

> Yet it is in fact written in a language that after many centuries has still essential kinship with our own, it was made in this land, and moves in our northern world beneath our northern sky, and for those who are native to that tongue and land, it must ever call with a profound appeal – until the dragon comes.
> (Tolkien, 1937, p. 36)

He expanded this in 1963 in a treasured private letter:

> [Beowulf] died in sorrow, fearing God's anger. But God is merciful. And to you, now young and eager, death will also come one day; but you have hope of Heaven. If you use your gifts as God wills. *Bruc ealles well!*
> (Mitchell, 1988, p. 53)

All this does not mean that I agree with every opinion he expressed. I do not agree that Beorhtnoth's action in allowing the Danes to cross the causeway was an "act of pride and misplaced chivalry" (Tolkien, 1953, p. 1); a good case can be made out for the view that it was his duty to bring the Danes to battle. I do not agree that Beowulf, in his fight with the dragon, was similarly guilty of excessive pride and chivalry (Tolkien, 1953, pp. 13-18 and Mitchell 1988, pp. 8-9). I am inclined to detect what I describe as "a tendency towards over-sentimental identification" in his

---

[1] Jerome Mandel; see Stanley, 1990, pp. 379-80.

view that the Hengest of *Beowulf* is "very probably the Hengest who led the first Germanic invasion of Britain" (Mitchell, 1988, p. 338). And I find it hard to subscribe wholeheartedly to his view that lines 180a-88 of *Beowulf* are suspect as altered or interpolated (Tolkien, 1937, pp. 45-7; see Stanley, 1975, pp. 44-7 & 51-2). However, I do not think such disagreements would have worried J.R.R. Tolkien. He made me think and deepened my enjoyment. The same tribute would, I think, be paid even by the most severe critics of the views on the structure of *Beowulf* he expressed in the British Academy lecture; these included his sometime tutor Kenneth Sisam, who, however, wrote that the lecture gave "a general view of *Beowulf* as poetry, with a fineness of perception and elegance of expression that are rare in this field" (Sisam, 1965, p. 20).

Such then were the contributions to Old English studies of a man who, in them, displays the qualities which he himself praised in his poem on W.H. Auden:

> Woruldbúendra sum bið wóðbora,
> giedda giffæst; sum bið gearuwyrdig,
> tyhtend getynge torhte mæðleð;
> sum bið bóca gléaw, on bréosthorde
> wísdóm haldeð, worn fela geman
> ealdgesægena þæra þe úðwitan
> fróde gefrugnon on fyrndagum;
>
> . . .
>
> Among the people of earth one has poetry in him,
> fashions verses with art; one is fluent in words,
> has persuasive eloquence sound and lucid;
> one is a reader of books and richly stores
> his mind with memory of much wisdom
> and legends of old that long ago
> were learned and related by loremasters;
>
> . . .
>
> (Tolkien, 1967, pp. 96-7)

But one question remains to be asked: What could he have done if his attention had not been fixed elsewhere? Anyone who was actually taught by him or taught at Oxford while he was a professor there cannot avoid thinking of the intuitive hints he did not follow up, of the ideas to which he alone could have done justice, of the books and articles he planned but did not write. The edition of *Exodus* published posthumously under the editorship of Joan Turville-Petre (Tolkien, 1981) gives a glimpse of what we have lost. His edition of *The Wanderer* never came out; it would have been greatly different from but not necessarily superior to that produced by his friends and pupils Tom Dunning and Alan Bliss. His verse translation of *Beowulf* was never published . . . The catalogue could be extended even without reference to Middle English. Contributory factors to his failure to publish such works have been adduced. They include the administrative work expected of a professor (Carpenter, 1977, pp. 135-7), the tedious burden of examining (d'Ardenne, 1979, p. 34 and Carpenter, 1977, pp. 136 and 138) – neither of these was his alone – and the fact that he was a perfectionist (Salu & Farrell, 1979, pp. 14-15 and Carpenter, 1977, p. 138). But the major factor was that revealed in Carpenter's description of Professor Simone d'Ardenne's 1951 dilemma: "She realised sadly that collaboration with him was now impossible, for his mind was entirely on his stories" (Carpenter, 1977, pp. 140-1).

There are or have been those who think that J.R.R. Tolkien did not fulfil his research responsibilities during his thirty-four years as an Oxford professor and who argue that, since he could have achieved so much more than lesser mortals, Anglo-Saxon and Middle English studies would have been more in his debt if he had stuck to his scholarly last instead of writing *The Hobbit*, *The Lord of the Rings*, and the other works, which have made him admired by so many throughout the world. One such was the colleague who, when I asked him outside Blackwells in 1954 whether he had read the newly-published *The Fellowship of the Ring*, replied savagely, "No! When he writes a book on Old or Middle English, I'll read it." Such men challenge or have challenged the wisdom of electing him. J.R.R. Tolkien himself signalled his own awareness of such challenges. With his habitual generosity, he spoke in his Valedictory Address of his astonishment "at the time of my first election . . . a feeling that has never quite left me" (Tolkien, 1979, p. 16); of "1925 when I was untimely elevated to the *stól* of Anglo-Saxon" (Tolkien, 1979, p. 32); and said:

> If we consider what Merton College and what the Oxford School of English owes to the Antipodes, to the Southern Hemisphere, especially to scholars born in Australia and New Zealand, it may well be felt that it is only just that one of them should now ascend an Oxford chair of English. Indeed it may be thought that justice has been delayed since 1925.
> (Tolkien, 1979, p. 31)

This was a reference to the controversial election of 1925 to the Anglo-Saxon chair, in which J.R.R. Tolkien defeated his sometime tutor the New Zealander Kenneth Sisam – on, persistent rumour has it, the casting vote of the Vice-Chancellor. There are those who think or have thought that, if the decision had gone the other way, Old and Middle English scholarship might have been able to have its cake and eat it, to have not only the works of scholarship Sisam could not produce because of his full-time commitment to the Oxford University Press but also J.R.R. Tolkien's imaginative writings.

Here two points must be made. First, J.R.R. Tolkien's scholarly output, even excluding the posthumous work, exceeds that of at least some of his critics in quality and sometimes indeed in quantity. His 1936 British Academy Lecture has had more influence than most of their products. His stimulating influence on his pupils cannot be measured. (Nor, to be fair, can that which Sisam would have excercised.) Second it is only right to say that this dispute is not just one of ACADEMICS v. LITERARY ENTHUSIASTS. Jessica Yates, in discussing the relationship between J.I.M. Stewart's Dr. Timbermill and J.R.R. Tolkien, writes:

> At a party, a Professor gives Patullo his opinion of Timbermill: "A sad case . . . A notable scholar, it seems. Unchallenged in his field. But he ran off the rails somehow and produced a long mad book – a kind

of apocalyptic romance." Sounds familar?
(Yates, 1992, p. 25²)

It certainly does. But there are literary as well as academic unenthusiasts; they include or have included Edmund Wilson, Edwin Muir, Philip Toynbee, and Michael Moorcock.³

I leave posterity to adjudicate on the election issue and to decide on the abiding value of J.R.R. Tolkien's works of imagination. Like Beowulf, he lived a good life, doing what he felt compelled to do, choosing not to do what some critics thought he should do, achieving fame. Various epitaphs can be adduced:

> Oxford is as much the richer for having produced Tolkien as for having produced Lewis Carroll
> (Grassi, 1973);
> ... a lot of us are grateful for
> What J. R. R. Tolkien has done
> As bard to Anglo-Saxon
> (Auden, 1962, p. 12);
> Scholar and Storyteller
> (Salu and Farrell, 1979, title);
> I am afraid that what I would do is what I have usually done
> (Tolkien, 1979, p. 17);
>   þū þē self hafast
>   dædum gefremed, þæt þīn dōm lyfað
>   āwa tō aldre. Alwalda þec
>   gōde forgylde ... !
> You yourself have accomplished by your deeds that your fame will live for ever. May the Ruler of All requite you with good ... !
> (*Beowulf*, ll. 953b-95)

In 1992, the centenary of his birth, we leave him and his wife to the *sōdfæstra dōm* "the judgement [reserved] for the righteous" (*Beowulf* l. 2820b):

REQUIESCANT IN PACE

References

Auden, W.H. 1962. "A Short Ode to a Philologist" in Davis and Wrenn, 1962, pp. 11-12.

Bradley, Henry. 1920. "The 'Cædmonian' Genesis" in *Essays and Studies* Vol 6.

Carpenter, Humphrey. 1977. *J. R. R. Tolkien: A biography*. London: George Allen and Unwin.

Chadwick, H.M. 1941. *The Study of Anglo-Saxon*. Cambridge: Heffer.

d'Ardenne, S.R.T.O. 1979. "The Man and the Scholar" in Salu and Farrell, pp. 33-37.

Davis, Norman and Wrenn, C.L. (eds.). 1962. *English and Medieval Studies Presented to J. R. R. Tolkien on the Occasion of his Seventieth Birthday*. London: George Allen and Unwin.

Donoghue, Daniel. 1987. *Style in Old English Poetry: The Test of the Auxiliary*. New Haven and London: Yale University Press.

Dunning T.P. and Bliss, A.J. (eds.). 1969. *The Wanderer*. London: Methuen.

Grassi, John. 1973. "Professor J.R.R. Tolkien" in *The Oxford Times*, 7 September 1973.

Greenfield, Stanley B. and Robinson, Fred C. 1980. *A Bibliography of Publications on Old English Literature to the end of 1972*. Toronto, Buffalo, and London: Toronto University Press; Manchester: Manchester University Press.

Hall, John R. Clark (ed.). 1950. *Beowulf and the Finnesburg Fragment: A Translation into Modern English Prose*. New Edition, Completely Revised with Notes and an Introduction by C. L. Wrenn ... With Prefatory Remarks by J. R. R. Tolkien. London: George Allen & Unwin.

Mitchell, Bruce. 1963. "'Until the Dragon Comes': Some Thoughts on *Beowulf*" in *Neophilologus* 47 (1963), pp. 126-38, reprinted in Bruce Mitchell, 1988, pp. 3-15.

Mitchell, Bruce. 1988. *On Old English: Selected Papers*. Oxford, Basil Blackwell.

Mitchell, Bruce. 1992. *H. M. Chadwick,* The Study of Anglo-Saxon: *Fifty Years On*, (H. M. Chadwick Memorial Lectures 2). Cambridge: Department of Anglo-Saxon, Norse, and Celtic.

Salu, Mary and Farrell, Robert T. (eds.). 1979. *J. R. R. Tolkien, Scholar and Storyteller: Essays in Memoriam*. Ithaca and London: Cornell University Press.

Sisam, Kenneth. 1965. *The Structure of "Beowulf"*. Oxford: Clarendon Press.

Stanley, E.G. 1975. *The Search for Anglo-Saxon Paganism*. Cambridge: D. S. Brewer; Totowa, NJ: Rowman and Littlefield.

Stanley, E.G. 1990. Review, in *Review of English Studies* 41 (1990), pp. 379-80.

Stephen, Leslie and Lee, Sydney. eds. *Dictionary of National Biography*. Vol III. London: Smith and Elder. ⁴

Stewart, J.I.M. 1976. *A Memorial Service: A Novel*. London: Gollancz.

---

² The quotation is from Stewart, 1976.

³ See *The Times Saturday Review*, December 28 1991, pp. 30-3.

⁴ This volume was a re-issue of volumes first published in 1886 and 1887.

The Times Saturday Review. 28 December 1991. pp. 30-3.

Tolkien, J.R.R. 1926. "Philology: General Works" in *The Year's Work in English Studies*, 5 (1926 for 1924), pp. 26-65.

Tolkien, J.R.R. 1932. "Sigelwara Land" in *Medium Ævum* 1 (1932), pp. 183-96.

Tolkien, J.R.R. 1934a. "Chaucer as a Philologist" in *Transactions of the Philological Society* 1934, pp. 1-70.

Tolkien, J.R.R. 1934b. "Sigelwara Land" in *Medium Ævum* 3 (1934), pp. 95-111.

Tolkien, J.R.R. 1937. "Beowulf: the Monsters and the Critics" (Sir Israel Gollancz Memorial Lecture 1936), in *Proceedings of the British Academy* XXII (1937).

Tolkien, J.R.R. 1950. "Prefatory Remarks" in Hall, 1950, pp. ix-xliii.

Tolkien, J.R.R. 1953. "The Homecoming of Beorhtnoth, Beorhthelm's Son" in *Essays and Studies* 6 (1953), pp. 1-18.

Tolkien, J.R.R. 1967. "For W.H.A." in *Shenandoah: The Washington and Lee University Review* 18.2 (Winter 1967) pp. 96-7.

Tolkien, J.R.R. 1979. "Valedictory Address to the University of Oxford, 5 June 1959" in Salu and Farrell, 1979, pp. 16-32.

Tolkien, J.R.R. 1981. *The Old English Exodus: Text, Translation, and Commentary*, edited by Joan Turville-Petre. Oxford: Clarendon Press.

Tolkien, J.R.R. 1982. *Finn and Hengest: The Fragment and the Episode*, edited by Alan Bliss. London: George Allen & Unwin.

Wrenn, C. L. 1946. "The Poetry of Caedmon" (Sir Israel Gollancz Memorial Lecture 1946), in *Proceedings of the British Academy*, XXXIII.

Yates, Jessica. 1992. "Appetizers" in Gwyneth Morgan (ed.). *A Long-Expected Party, Progress Report 6*. Milton Keynes: The Tolkien Society and The Mythopoeic Society. pp. 23-26.

Tolkien and the *Gawain*-poet

Tom Shippey

Abstract: One of Tolkien's major academic works was the edition he prepared, with E.V. Gordon, of *Sir Gawain and the Green Knight*. Yet this poem is only one of four in identical dialect (an important point to Tolkien) and in the same manuscript. This paper considers the philological issues these poems raise, and shows how the theories, eccentricities and linguistics of the *Gawain*-poet were read and used by Tolkien.

Keywords: accent, Arthur, dialect, "etayn", linguistic transmission, literary transmission, philology, *Sir Gawain and the Green Knight*, Woses

Tolkien's involvement with the *Gawain*-poet lasted almost the whole of his professional or writing life. Before proceeding, I should explain that by "the *Gawain*-poet" I mean not only "the man who wrote *Sir Gawain and the Green Knight*", but also "the man who wrote the four anonymous poems now preserved in Cotton MS. Nero A.X, i.e. *Sir Gawain*, *Pearl*, *Purity* and *Patience*"[1]. All four are written in the same distinctive dialect. It is true that this need not mean they were written by the same hand, for the person who copied them all might for instance have "translated" poems in different dialects into his own; while, as Tolkien himself showed in his 1929 essay on "*Ancrene Wisse* and *Hali Meiðhad*", even in the Middle Ages, different people could under some circumstances have been taught at school to write the same English, no matter where they came from. So the four poems *could* all have had different authors. There has at least been a suggestion that a fifth poem, *St. Erkenwald*, in a closely similar dialect but a different manuscript, is also by "the *Gawain*-poet". I do not propose however to consider these issues. It is clear from note 13 of his 1953 essay (Tolkien, 1983b; see below) that Tolkien thought it "beyond any real doubt" that the man who wrote *Sir Gawain* "also wrote *Pearl*, not to mention *Purity* and *Patience*", while he offered no view on *St. Erkenwald*. "The *Gawain*-poet", then, meant to Tolkien the unknown author of the four late fourteenth-century poems in MS. Nero A.X.

As said at the start of this essay, Tolkien had the *Gawain*-poet in mind for at least fifty years. His first work on him was the joint edition of *Sir Gawain and the Green Knight* produced by Tolkien and his Leeds colleague E.V. Gordon, published by the Clarendon Press in 1925. It was an enormously successful book, which altered the whole current of English medieval studies – till then heavily Southern and Chaucerian in bias, at least at non-specialist level – and which is still in 1993 the standard edition (as revised and updated in 1967 by Tolkien's pupil Norman Davis). Its success led to an immediate suggestion that the same pair should go on and edit *Pearl* from the same manuscript. Almost as soon as the first edition appeared, however, Tolkien and Gordon ceased to live close together, as Tolkien went off to Oxford while Gordon took over Tolkien's Leeds chair. In Humphrey Carpenter's *Biography* (p.105), Tolkien is cited as referring rather ruefully to Gordon as "an industrious little devil"; it seems likely that Gordon wanted to press on with *Pearl* in the late 1920s while Tolkien (whose fears about his own lack of discipline can be glimpsed in "Leaf by Niggle") had turned much of his attention to other things. Time went by. Gordon died prematurely, in 1938; and when the edition of *Pearl* eventually appeared in 1953 it was signalled on the title page as "Edited by E.V. Gordon", but actually brought out by his widow Ida L. Gordon, a considerable medieval scholar in her own right. In her "Preface" to that work Mrs. Gordon records the original start as a joint product; mentions Tolkien's withdrawal from the project "when he found himself unable to give sufficient time to it"; and goes on to give "warmest thanks . . . to Professor Tolkien, who had the original typescript for some time and added valuable notes and corrections". One can probably conclude in the end that while the edition of *Pearl* is indeed largely E.V. Gordon's work, there are also substantial contributions by Ida Gordon, with in all probability both an initial input and later additions by Tolkien: some of the notes in the edition (as I indicate below) do seem resonantly Tolkienian.

In addition to these two works Tolkien also devoted the W.P. Ker Memorial Lecture of 1953 to "Sir Gawain and the Green Knight": this essay appears in the posthumous publication of 1983, *The Monsters and the Critics and Other Essays*, edited by Christopher Tolkien. The "Foreword" to that volume makes it clear that Tolkien had in 1953 just completed his alliterative verse translation of *Sir Gawain* into modern English, but that the version existing then was

---

[1] I say "the man" not only because of restricted female education in the Middle Ages, but also because of the poet's clear self-portrayal as feudal servant (in *Patience*) and as a father (in *Pearl*).

repeatedly altered and emended. It came out in final form in 1975, along with the translations of *Pearl* and *Sir Orfeo*. The publishing history of Tolkien on the *Gawain*-poet then runs from 1925 to 1983, while Tolkien, as far as we know, did not cease to think and comment on the poet's works from the 1920s till his own death in 1973. References to the *Gawain*-poet in fact crop up in unexpected places in Tolkien's scholarly works; the poet's influence on Tolkien's fiction is considered further below.

Why did Tolkien feel this attraction to the poems of Nero A.X? Since I have said repeatedly in my book *The Road to Middle-earth* that philology is "the only proper guide to a view of Middle-earth 'of the sort which its author may be supposed to have desired'" (Shippey, 1992, p. 7)[2] it is not surprising that I see Tolkien's interest in the *Gawain*-poet as primarily philological. I would separate it into three strands, those of class, place and tradition.

To deal with class first: it is obvious that the dialect of the *Gawain*-poet was in no way an ancestor of modern Standard English. All the poems are full (much fuller than Chaucer) of words now found only, if at all, in non-standard dialects. One could say indeed that the modern descendants of the *Gawain*-poet's dialect are among the least-regarded and lowest-status dialects of modern England. At one point in *Sir Gawain* the Lady, flirting with Sir Gawain, tells him he ought to be eager to teach "a ȝonke þynk" about love. The addition of an extra "g/k" sound in words like "young, thing, ring, finger" is still common in areas of the North-West Midlands; it is however a feature which ambitious parents and schoolteachers try hard to stamp out.

Yet in spite of these and other marks of modern low-status, the *Gawain*-poet, most surprisingly to a modern ear, betrays not the slightest sign of linguistic self-consciousness or inferiority. His language is indeed in other areas almost haughtily high-status, as in his careful and zestful descriptions (full of technical vocabulary) of the upper-class sport of hunting. Tolkien certainly appreciated this clash of linguistic indicators. In 1928 he wrote a "Foreword" to Walter E. Haigh's *Glossary of the Dialect of the Huddersfield District*, in which he said that Haigh's work was valuable "not only to local patriotism, but to English philology" generally. He picked out words showing sound-changes dating back to Old Germanic; noted also the way in which learned words were naturalised in a powerful local speech[3]; and went on to say that there was particular interest in the study of dialects of the North-West because of the signs in them of competition and cohabitation between Old English and Old Norse. Furthermore, he remarks, in the fourteenth century this north-west area was to become:

the centre of a revival of writings in vernacular speech, of which the most interesting examples preserved are poems in an alliterative metre descended from the old verse of Anglo-Saxon times, though clothed in a language now difficult to read because of its strong Scandinavian element and its many other peculiar and obscure dialectal words. These texts do not all come from the same part of the North-West, and where each was written is still in debate, but their connexion with the modern dialects, of which that of Huddersfield is an interesting example, is immediately apparent to any one glancing at this glossary. Indeed, such books as this one sometimes throw valuable light on the meanings or forms of words in these old poems, such poems as the romance *Sir Gawain and the Green Knight*, [and] the beautiful elegiac sermon known as *The Pearl* . . .
(Tolkien, 1928, p. xvi)

On the next page Tolkien picks out a particularly unexpected case of close resemblance between the aristocratic medieval *Gawain*-poet and Haigh's working-class modern informants. The *Gawain*-poet appears at one point to make a "mistake" in English, when the Green Knight, their challenge settled, asks Sir Gawain "to com to þy naunt", i.e. "to come to thine aunt". It looks as if someone, poet or scribe, has mixed up "þyn aunt" (used at line 2464) with "þy naunt" (line 2467), both forms deriving properly from Old French *aunte* (as the Tolkien-Gordon glossary says). But was this a "mistake"? Mr. Haigh's informants made it spectacularly clear that they used both words, in their pronunciation *ænt* and *nont*. However they regarded *nont* as normal, and *ænt* as affected. Haigh cites a man saying teasingly to his daughter, thought to be trying to ingratiate herself with her (rich) aunt Sally by talking a form of standard English:

"Thæ thinks thi nont Sally'll bau thi e niu frok if thæ toks faun (polite) to er – imitating her – 'ænt Sarah are yo goin' out? au'll mind th'ouse for yo waul yo kum back'. It's '*ænt* Sarah' this en '*ænt* Sarah' t'tuther; bet thi nont Sally'll maund er bræss muer ner tha maunds other *or*, er *er ees*."[4]

The *Gawain*-text was not mistaken, in other words (Tolkien always liked theories which corroborated old poems instead of correcting them); it offered a good rendition of actual speech, confirmed by observation in the present day; the fact that *ænt* and *nont* are no longer casually interchangeable bears witness only to the baleful effects of (Tolkien's phrase) "the powerful southern rival, literary English"; in happier days class had not been a linguistic issue, at least in poetry in English.

---

[2] The phrase in single inverted commas comes from the "Preface" to the Tolkien and Gordon edition of *Sir Gawain*, where the editors use it to describe their own intentions as regards the poet.

[3] As for instance the word "auction". I have commented on Tolkien's playing with the two meanings of this in *The Road to Middle-earth* (1992, p. 85).

[4] In this quotation I have not reproduced several of the marks used by Haigh to indicate pronunciation. It should be noted that in this dialect the dipthong "ai" is changed to "au". It is part of the father's teasing imitation of his daughter's accent that he has her say "mind" for "maund" – though not "I" or "while". A translation would run: "You think your aunt Sally'll buy you a new frock if you talk fine to her. "Aunt Sarah, are you going out? I'll mind the house for you till you come back." It's "Aunt Sarah" this and "Aunt Sarah" the other; but your Aunt Sally'll look after her money more than you look after either her or her house."

Tolkien would I am sure have preferred it if a West Midlands form of English had become standard, instead of the South-East Midlands form which actually did so. He was probably attracted on one level to the *Gawain*-poet's works by their demonstration that great poetry could be written without strain in what would now be regarded as a "vulgar" or "ugly" dialect. But which dialect is it, exactly? In the "Foreword" to Haigh Tolkien suggested that *Sir Gawain* was probably written "to the west of Huddersfield" (p. xvii n.), while he and Gordon declared in their 1925 edition that "the Lancashire character of the language is perfectly preserved" (p. viii). Tolkien himself was mistaken here, though in a way which I am sure he would be glad to have demonstrated. Later research since 1925 – of course conducted with the advantage of many more located texts than were available to Tolkien – puts the *Gawain*-poet a county and a half further south, in the valley of the River Dane, on the boundary between Cheshire and Staffordshire, and indeed (one can see there is no needless shilly-shallying among philologists) at map-reference 393364 on the Ordnance Survey charts, a location reckoned as correct to within a hundred yards[5]. Further corollaries of this very precise location[6] are that the poet was probably connected with Dieulacres Abbey near Leek in Staffordshire, that he may have imagined the castle of Sir Bertilak as being located at Knight's Low in Swythamley Park, and most relevantly for Tolkien that – writing in a local dialect for a local audience – he encouraged his hearers to imagine his Arthurian romance as set in a landscape they knew, and which they could name. Thus, as the huntsmen set out to hunt the wild boar (perhaps at Wildboarclough, just above the Dane), the poet says:

> Þenne such a glauer ande glam of gedered rachcheȝ
> Ros, þat þe rochereȝ rungen aboute
> (ll.1426-7)

Tolkien and Gordon in 1925 gloss "rocher" as "rock [Old French *roch(i)er*]" – one of the strong points of their edition was that it showed immediately which language words in the poem were derived from, Old English, Old Norse or Old French – and Tolkien's translation of 1975 accordingly reads:

> Then such a baying and babel of bloodhounds together arose, that the rock-wall rang all about them.

But if one is gathering hounds at Swythamley or Wildboarclough in the Dane valley, the rock-wall that is likely to be resounding is not "the rocheres", but "the Roaches" – the steep jagged hills overlooking the valley, still called "the Roaches", and with a name which derives from the Old French root *rocher* just as certainly as Tolkien and Gordon's proposed reading. I have remarked in *The Road to Middle-Earth* (1992, p. 87) how Tolkien liked in *The Hobbit* "to make names out of capital letters" – turning "the hill" into "The Hill", the stream at its foot into "The Water", and so on. I am sure Tolkien would have been delighted to see the *Gawain*-poet doing in a sense the opposite – turning "the Roaches" into "þe rochereȝ", the Flash brook three lines later into "a flasche" – but in the secure knowledge that his local audience would very probably as it were insert their own capital letters once more, and feel sure that they were living (as Tolkien thought we all do) on the site of ancient legend and romance.

This close equation by the *Gawain*-poet of legendary past and real present, of which Tolkien was not aware, is nevertheless corroborated by features of the *Gawain*-poet's dialect of which Tolkien was very well aware, namely its deep tap-root into old and largely forgotten tradition. Tolkien comments on this quality in the poem at the start of his 1953 essay, regrettably going on to say he is at present concerned with other matters (see Shippey, 1992, pp. 272-3). I do not think, though, that there is any difficulty in tracing what Tolkien meant, providing always that one looks at the *Gawain*-poet with a philological eye. Consider for instance lines 720-5 of the poem, describing Sir Gawain's adventurous ride from Camelot (evidently somewhere down South) into the wilderlands of the Pennines:

> Sumwhyle wyth wormeȝ he werreȝ, and with wolues als,
> Sumwhyle wyth wodwos, þat woned in þe knarreȝ,
> Boþe wyth bulleȝ and bereȝ, and boreȝ oþerquyle,
> And etayneȝ, þat hym anelede of þe heȝe felle;
> Nade he ben duȝty and dryȝe, and dryȝtyn had serued,
> Douteles he hade ben ded and dreped ful ofte.

Tolkien translated this passage as follows:

> At whiles with worms he wars, and with wolves also,
> at whiles with wood-trolls that wandered in the crags,
> and with bulls and with bears and boars too, at times;
> and with ogres that hounded him from the heights of the fells.
> Had he not been stalwart and staunch and steadfast in God,
> he doubtless would have died and death had met often.

But it is essential for a philological understanding to go back to the original, or indeed to go back and forward between original and translation, for (to quote Tolkien again):

> a good translation is a good companion of honest labour, while a "crib" is a (vain) substitute for the essential work with grammar and glossary, by which alone can be won genuine appreciation of a noble idiom and a lofty art.
> (Tolkien, 1983a, pp. 50-51)

If one looks at the original poem, and then at the Tolkien/Gordon glossary, several words in these six lines should catch the eye: for instance, "dreped". The Tolkien and Gordon glossary says "dreped, *pp.* slain, killed, 725. [OE. *drepan*, smite; ON. *drepa*, kill.]". So is the word an Old English or an Old Norse one? As one can see from his 1975 translation, Tolkien definitely took the word in its Old Norse sense, not its Old English one. "Ded and dreped" to him was a tautology, the line meaning "he would have been dead and killed time and time again". Why then give both etymologies (if the Old English one is irrelevant), and why convict the

---
[5] See McIntosh *et al.* (1986) especially vol. 1 p. 178 and vol. 3 p. 37 (where a misprint has crept in over the map-reference).
[6] The points below are made by R.W.V. Elliot in *The Gawain Country* (1984). Elliot's location of the poem was strikingly confirmed by McIntosh *et al.* in the 1986 study cited in note 5.

poet of repeating himself? The answer as usual is a philological one: I have no doubt that yet another of the points which drew Tolkien to the *Gawain*-poet was his dialect's unusual fusion of the two languages Tolkien studied most, Old English and Old Norse – a fusion so intimate that one could have an Old English past participle form (the Old Norse form would have given "drepen" not "dreped") with an Old Norse meaning. Even modern Standard English is to an extent not often realised a mixture of English and Norse. For the *Gawain*-poet's ancestors that mixture had been even deeper and more thorough. Though the poet was also extremely familiar with French, his language showed clearly an old and stubborn resistance to Latinate forms, southern influence, and Standard English. The point about "ded and dreped" is (in a way) a trivial one. But Tolkien thought such points could not be faked. They were the linguistic guarantors of true literary tradition: part of "this flavour, this atmosphere, this virtue that such *rooted* works have", as he says on the first page of his 1953 essay.

In any case there are more significant details in lines 720-5. The word "etayneȝ" certainly caught Tolkien's eye. It is glossed "ogre, giant . . . [OE. *eoten*]". Tolkien and Gordon obviously knew that the parallel word *iötunn* is extremely common in Old Norse – Tolkien uses it freely in his scholarly work. But the point here is first, that this time the form "etayn" *must* come from Old English, not Old Norse; and second, extremely significantly, that while *iötnar* are common in Norse literature, *eotenas* or "etayneȝ" are extremely rare in English. The word is found some half-dozen times in Middle English (see *OED* under "eten"), and just once in Old English: indeed, in *Beowulf* (not cited by the *OED*). Had the *Gawain*-poet got the word from *Beowulf*? Almost certainly not[7]. To him, as to the *Beowulf*-poet, it was not an antiquarian word to be snuffled out of a library, but a word from living speech, preserved (like the *ænt/nont* distinction) over centuries innocent of books. The fact that we rarely encounter the word only shows that in the Middle Ages the best stories were rarely written down. Nevertheless the survival of such words indicates a true tradition of giant-stories lasting from *Beowulf* to *Sir Gawain*, or to use Tolkien's dates, from about 725 AD to about 1375 – a longer interval than that which separates the *Gawain*-poet from us.

And then there are the "wodwos" of line 721. I have discussed the survival of this word up to the present day, indeed to the address of Tolkien's Leeds office and my own, in *The Road to Middle-Earth*, see p. 60 n., so I will say here only that it repeats the pattern of true tradition surviving in altered and in this case genuinely "mistaken" form. "Wodwos" is here clearly plural; its singular (in the *Gawain*-poet's mind) would presumably be "wodwo"; but the Old English word from which it should be derived, as Tolkien and Gordon record, would be *wudu-wása*, whose plural would be *wudu-wásan*. The *Gawain*-poet ought to have written "wodwosen" (and maybe he did). But somewhere down the line the true historical form was forgotten, except in place and personal names, no doubt because the stories and the concept of the "trolls of the forest" were being forgotten – till revived, of course, in the Woses (NB plural form), the "Wild Men of the Woods" of Druadan Forest in *The Lord of the Rings* 5/V, "The Ride of the Rohirrim".

Even the "mistakes" of the *Gawain*-poet, it will be seen, tell a story to the philological mind, of which Tolkien was the twentieth century's most prominent example. "Þy (n) aunt" bears witness to the naturalisation of French and the survival of living speech. "Dreped" and "etayneȝ" in their different ways tell us about the relations of Englishmen and Norsemen off the normal historical map; "etayneȝ" and "wodwos" between them hint at a great but lost tradition of story-telling, again off the normal literary and critical map. Yet more details could be picked out of the same six lines. A common "vulgarism" much reproved by schoolteachers is "dropping your aitches". Did the *Gawain*-poet drop his aitches? In line 723 "Etayneȝ" alliterates with "anElede" and is obviously meant to alliterate with "Heȝe". Should the latter then not be pronounced "Eȝe"?[8] One cannot be sure, but in his translation Tolkien scrupulously follows the "error" of his original: the only way to get the traditional and correct three alliterations out of Tolkien's line is to read it as: "and with Ogres that 'Ounded 'im from the 'Eights of the fells" – a perfectly plausible pronunciation in the area, just as good as Standard, and backed up not only by the *Gawain*-poet but once more by the *Beowulf*-poet, whose aitches are not above suspicion either.

Nevertheless, one may say in the end, words, etymologies and glossaries apart, what did Tolkien make of the *Gawain*-poet as a thinker, a poet, a story-teller: not just a language-user, a "set text", and a subject for budding philologists to cut their teeth on? We have substantial evidence here in the 1953 essay to which I have already referred. This is no easier to paraphrase than any other of Tolkien's scholarly works. But one conclusion I would venture to draw from it is that Tolkien saw the *Gawain*-poet – as he had earlier presented the *Beowulf*-poet – as an artist in vital respects much like himself: someone deeply embedded in a Christian and Catholic tradition, but nevertheless (if in definitely subordinate fashion) ready to make use of the lost, popular, monster-creating, "fairy-tale" traditions which we can infer fron his very vocabulary.

Tolkien's main point about *Sir Gawain* is thus that in it "the temptations of Sir Gawain, his behaviour under them, and criticism of his code, were for our author his story, to which all else was subservient" (Tolkien, 1983b, p. 83). "All else", one should remember, includes many of the most dramatic and mythically-suggestive scenes in the poem: the appearance of the fearsome Green Knight with axe and holly-branch at Arthur's court, his beheading by Sir Gawain, his instant resurrection, the long journey of the knight into the wilderness as quoted above, and the "trial-and-

---

[7] Though I am sure Tolkien would like to have it pointed out that the first person known to have owned *Beowulf* was Lawrence Nowell, Dean of Lichfield, the traditional heart of the West Midlands, and less than fifty miles from the River Dane. See (more explicitly) Sisam, 1953, pp. 61-4.

[8] One of the rules of alliterative verse is that all vowels may alliterate with each other.

repayment" scene in the midwinter snow at the eerie Green Chapel. All interesting, says Tolkien, but "subservient", even (1983b, p. 74) by comparison "perfunctory". Rather than expanding on any or all of these, Tolkien prefers to spend a high proportion of his essay discussing a scene so seemingly underweighted in the poem as to have received almost no critical discussion, and that discussion entirely mistaken; i.e., stanza 75 of the poem, in which Sir Gawain (having resisted the Lady's sexual temptations, but accepted from her a girdle as a gift) goes to confession and is absolved. On this stanza, Tolkien says, "the whole interpretation and valuation [of the poem] depends". Either the poet meant it, in which case it is to be taken seriously, or he was "just a muddler" and his story "just a fairy-story for adults, and not a very good one" (1983b, p. 87).

Tolkien's opposition here is a highly aggressive one, showing how very much he wanted to see the poet not only as an orthodox Catholic with strong awareness of the sacraments, but as a conscious ethical thinker. If one takes this scene Tolkien's way, then the poet makes his character go to confession and *either* not mention his retention of the girdle *or* be told by his confessor that retaining it, against the compact he has made with the Lady's husband, is not a sin. Tolkien prefers the second option, which involves him conceding that much of the action of the poem in the Beheading Game and the Exchange of Winnings compact is in a way not serious – though potentially fatal – but just "a game with rules". It is these rules Gawain is breaking by retaining the girdle, not a moral commandment. The moral code *would* have been broken, however, if Gawain had stooped to adultery with the Lady, and that is why the temptation scenes are the centre. One might sum up by saying that Tolkien views the poem as bringing two systems into conflict with each other, a Christian moral code and an aristocratic code of honour: the conflict being decided very definitely, by such scenes as the "confession" stanza, in favour of the former.

I am bound to say at this point that I disagree with Tolkien over some though not most of his interpretation[9]. I agree about the conflict of codes, but feel that the poet exerts his energies to reconcile them, rather than subordinating one to the other: in which case, to take up Tolkien's dilemma over the nature of Gawain's confession, the poet's intention was to suggest the former, not the latter, of Tolkien's alternatives – Gawain did not mention retention of the girdle any more than a modern would feel obliged to confess a foul at football or perhaps a post-dated cheque in business. It is true that I am not a Catholic, and so may underrate the force of what the poet shared with Tolkien. On the other hand, when Tolkien at the end puts the poem into elaborately but not ironically modern terms of "the Old School Tie" and "the colours of the First Eleven", I can perhaps speak as one who shared an Old School Tie with Tolkien, and deep interest in the same First Elevens and Fifteens, and so may stress only to a greater degree than he does the real importance of "games with rules" and "codes of honour".

It seems to me, indeed, that by stressing the poet's moral Catholicity Tolkien put himself into a difficult position, which he himself recognised, over the very nature of the temptation. For if the castle is "a courteous and Christian hall" (as I agree it is), what are we to think of the Lady's repeated temptations to adultery? What would have happened if Gawain had succumbed? Would his only problem then, in the Exchange of Winnings plot, have been keeping to the letter of his compact with the castle Lord? Surely not. Tolkien in fact refuses to pursue this line of thought, urging that all this is unthinkable, and not to be explained away by any of those "ancient and barbaric customs" (i.e. wife-swapping) against which C.S. Lewis also reacted[10], or by "tales in which memory of them is still enshrined". In saying this Tolkien once again abjured a whole tradition of ancient story of a kind he himself, in fiction, repeatedly used: a whole *legendarium* of ettens and woodwoses and soulless, dangerous elf-maidens. Yet despite abjuring it with the words "we are not in that world", Tolkien nevertheless finds suggestions of that world indispensable. The reason we do not wonder about the chances of a "successful" temptation, Tolkien says, lies in the menacing suggestions left over in the poem of "fairy story". If Gawain did respond to the Lady, he would meet something terrible, like the heroine of "Bluebeard" opening a forbidden door: "hanging in the background, for those able to receive the air of 'faerie' in a romance, is a terrible threat of disaster and destruction" (1983b, p. 83).

The interesting thing for those who, forty years later, are reading Tolkien's fiction is the careful and perhaps compulsive way in which Tolkien presents an image of an artist wholly dedicated to one tradition (the Christian and Catholic one), nevertheless employing echoes of another (the long and originally pre-Christian tradition of native fairy-tale and monster-story), and using both to create a critique of a third (an essentially secular code based on humour, etiquette and good manners). It is hard to resist the thought that Tolkien read the *Gawain*-poet this way because it resembled his own experience: though one might well put Tolkien a good deal closer to fairy-tale than his predecessor, if at the same time no further away from Catholicity. Perhaps the vital point, however, is that even in his strong advocacy of the one tradition Tolkien is unable to do without the other. Just as I see Tolkien's fiction as in several senses a "mediation" between a Christian world and a heroic pagan one (see Shippey, 1992, pp. 188, 198-200 etc.), so Tolkien sees the *Gawain*-poet as understanding and drawing on both those worlds, while in this case "subordinating" one to the other. And, just as I argue that this "mediation" between two worlds gives *The Lord of the Rings* a moral force which would be lacking if it were just "a saint's life, all about temptation [or] a complicated wargame, all about tactics" (Shippey, 1992, p. 133), so Tolkien says firmly, leading straight on from the quotation above about "the air of

---

[9] My views are explained in Shippey, 1971.
[10] Lewis's essay "The Anthropological Approach", first published in Tolkien's 1962 *festchrift* and reprinted in Lewis 1969, is in large part a reaction to interpretations of *Sir Gawain* such as Tolkien is here rejecting.

'faerie'", that in the mixed mode of *Sir Gawain*:
> The struggle becomes intense to a degree which a merely realistic story of how a pious knight resisted a temptation to adultery (when a guest) could hardly attain. It is one of the properties of Fairy Story thus to enlarge the scene and the actors; or rather it is one of the properties that are distilled by literary alchemy when old deep-rooted stories are rehandled by a real poet with an imagination of his own.
>
> (Tolkien, 1983b, p. 83)

De te narratur fabula, one might say: Tolkien describes himself. Nor would he, I feel, view it as anything but a compliment to be fitted into literary tradition in a place similar to that of the *Gawain*-poet. There is furthermore one typically, even pedantically philological point from the passage already cited which once more associates Tolkien with his predecessor. The poet says that Sir Gawain fought many dangerous ventures before he ever got to his temptation:

> Nade he ben duȝty and dryȝe, and dryȝtyn had serued,
> Douteles he hade ben ded and dreped ful ofte.

The first line of these two is, grammatically speaking, a double subordinate clause, if with its doubleness obscured by ellipsis. It means, in full expanded form: "If he had not been stalwart and staunch, *and* if he had not served the Lord", then he would doubtless have been dead and killed many times over. Put that way, one might wonder: "Well – what if he had been one but not the other? What if he had been stalwart and staunch, but not a servant of God? Or what if he had been a servant of God, but a timid and feeble one?" Gandalf would say perhaps that this is a problem best not thought about; but something like it seems to me a major part of the structure of *The Lord of the Rings* (see Shippey, 1992, pp. 128-38). And whether that is so or not, it is certainly interesting to see Tolkien himself repeating just such alternative but undecidable conditions. The *Gawain*-poet leaves it uncertain whether it is Gawain's ability or his piety which saves him; the *Beowulf*-poet has his hero similarly leave it undecided whether it is *wyrd* or "courage" that saves a warrior; and in exactly the same mode Gimli says to Merry and Pippin at *The Lord of The Rings* II, p. 169, that "luck served you there; *but* (my italics) you seized your chance with both hands, one might say." In other words luck would *not* have saved Merry and Pippin any more than serving God would have saved Gawain – *on its own!* In all these traditional stories courage and fortitude are as important as morality, piety, or the intervention of higher powers. That is what keeps them stories rather than allegories.

There are other aspects of the *Gawain*-poet's work to which Tolkien would, I am sure, have liked to pay tribute. It should not escape notice, for instance, that the poem *Purity* pays such particular attention to questions of secular good manners (seen at times as superior even to morality, or at least as more irritating when absent) that modern criticism has on the whole preferred to turn as blind an eye to them as to the issue of Gawain's confession. Tolkien would certainly also have responded powerfully to the clash of parental grief and Catholic consolation in *Pearl*, a clash perhaps even more powerful emotionally and even harder to "mediate" than that between knightly manners and Christian duty in *Sir Gawain*. Nevertheless I feel yet once more that the deepest appeal of the *Gawain*-poet to Tolkien lay in the innumerable problems he set for philologists, all of them full of suggestion for the "philological mind". At line 115 of *Pearl* the dreaming narrator finds himself in a land by a strange stream where dazzling stones shine:

> As stremande sterneȝ, quen stroþe-men slepe,

or as Tolkien translates it:

> As streaming stars when on earth men sleep.

"Stroþe" however does not mean "on earth". The note in Gordon's edition reads:

> 115 *stroþe-men*: of uncertain meaning and derivation. *Strothe* in *Sir Gawain* 1710 appears to be derived from ON. *storð* "stalks of herbage", but the North-West place-names containing Stroth, Strother . . . point to a native OE. **stroð, *stroðor* . . . **Stroð* appears to have had the meaning "marshy land (overgrown with brushwood)", and probably influenced the development of the imported ON. *storð*. Here *stroþe-men* is probably used in a generalized poetic sense to mean "men of this world" . . . , but *stroþe* would probably carry with it also, pictorially, a suggestion of the dark, low earth onto which the high stars look down.

One wonders how far credit for this note should be shared between E.V. Gordon, I.L. Gordon, and Tolkien. The philological point about Old English and Old Norse is only a reversal of what is said above about "dreped", and could have come from any of the three. The image of the men in the brushwood, asleep and in the dark, yet looked down on by the high, streaming stars *which they cannot see* seems however a perfect image of life in Middle-earth as portrayed by Tolkien and as remarked by Gildor or Galadriel. The marshy scrubland where the "stroþe-men" sleep is the same as *galadhremmin ennorath*, "tree-tangled" Middle-earth itself, and the "stremande sterneȝ" are the sign of Elbereth Gilthoniel, "Elbereth Star-kindler". In this as in many other ways the images of the *Gawain*-poet have been received and transmitted by Tolkien back into living literary tradition.

References

Elliott, R.W.V. 1984. *The Gawain Country*. Leeds: Leeds School of English.

Gordon, E.V. (ed.) 1953. *Pearl*. Oxford: Clarendon Press.

Lewis, C.S. 1969 "The Anthropological Approach" in *Selected Literary Essays*. Ed. Walter Hooper. Cambridge: Cambridge University Press, pp. 301-11.

McIntosh, Angus, Samuels, M.L. and Benskin, Michael. 1986. *A Linguistic Atlas of Late Medieval English*. 4. vols, Aberdeen: Aberdeen University Press.

Shippey, T. 1971. "The Uses of Chivalry: *Erec* and *Gawain*" in *Modern Language Review*. 66 (1971), pp. 241-50.

Sisam, K. 1953. "The Beowulf Manuscript" in *Studies in the History of Old English Literature*. Ed Kenneth Sisam. Oxford: Clarendon Press.

Tolkien, J.R.R. and Gordon, E.V. (eds.) 1925. *Sir Gawain and the Green Knight*. Oxford: Clarendon Press.

Tolkien, J.R.R. 1928. "Foreword" to Walter E Haigh, *A New Glossary of the Dialect of the Huddersfield District*. London: Oxford University Press.

Tolkien, J.R.R. (trans.) 1975. *Sir Gawain, Pearl and Sir Orfeo*. Ed. Christopher Tolkien. London: George Allen & Unwin.

Tolkien, J.R.R. 1983a. "On Translating Beowulf" in *The Monsters and the Critics and Other Essays*. Ed. Christopher Tolkien. London: George Allen & Unwin, pp. 49-71.

Tolkien, J.R.R. 1983b. "Sir Gawain and the Green Knight" in *The Monsters and the Critics and Other Essays*. Ed. Christopher Tolkien. London: George Allen & Unwin, pp. 72-108.

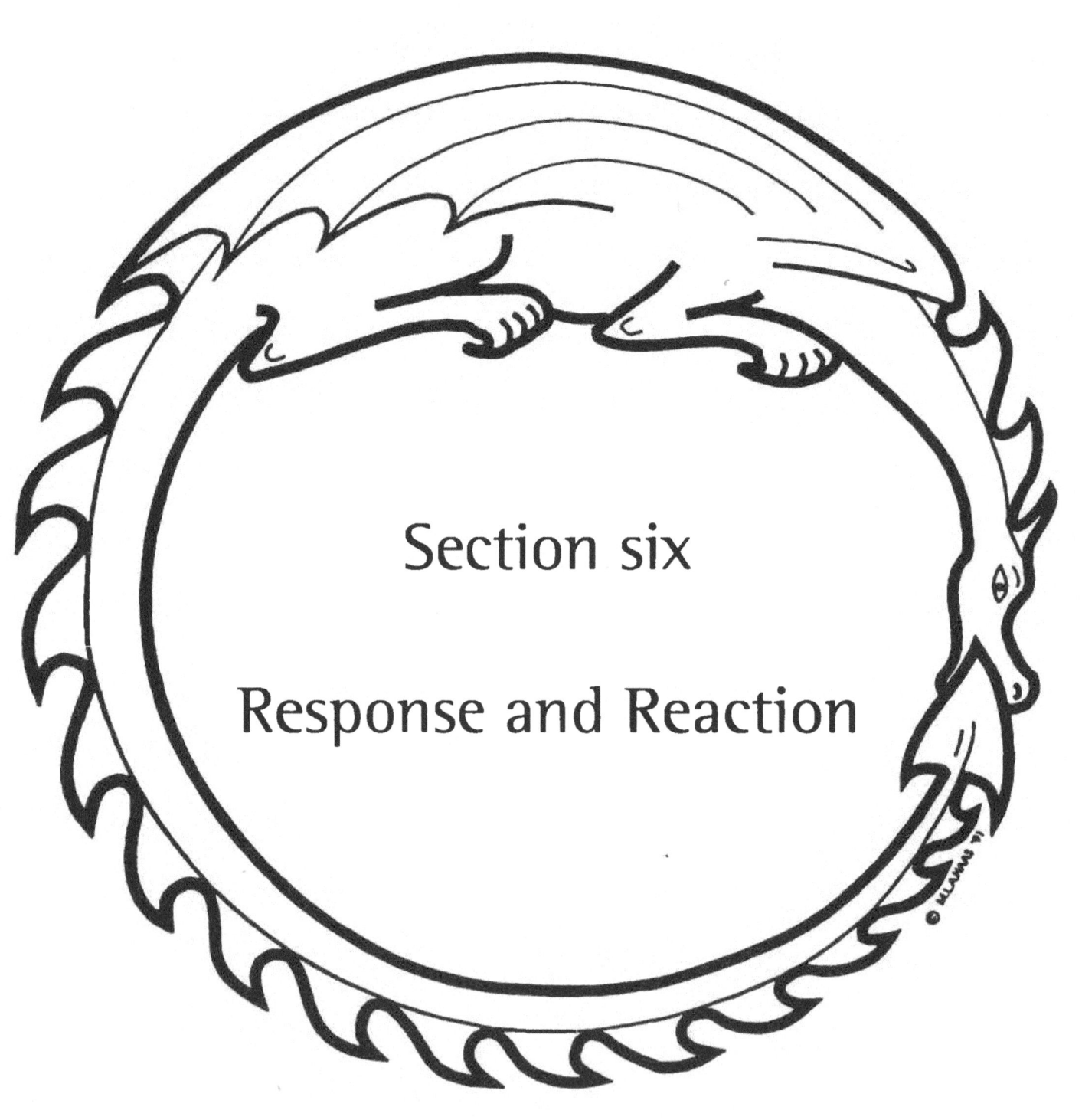

Section six

Response and Reaction

How Russians See Tolkien[1]

Vladimir Grushetskiy

Abstract: The understanding of J.R.R. Tolkien in Russia is affected by two circumstances. One is that the general public is only familiar with *The Hobbit* and *The Lord of the Rings*. The other fact is that for the last 75 years cultural values and ethical rules have been methodically changed and replaced with communist ideology. So I'd like to divide readers of Tolkien into four groups: children, youth, general readers and the intellectual elite.

J.R.R. Tolkien is of extremely great interest for children from 7 to 13. It seems that they enjoy their first meeting with true and really good fairy-story and explore this genre with care.

The teenager's perception is superficial. It depends on their increasing political and social apathy and is usually connected with escapism. Passions for war role-playing games and for writing imitations are typical for this group.

The general public is bewildered if in touch with Tolkien at all. Social consciousness doesn't have any scale of values fitting for *The Lord of the Rings*. Even literary criticism is extremely poor.

Elite readers are familiar with other books by J.R.R. Tolkien together with Russian culture and world cultural traditions. So this group is interested mostly in Tolkien's linguistics, philosophy, theology, etc.

Keywords: D. Andreev, Russian culture, Russian literature, visions

We are extremely obliged to everyone whose care has helped us to get here. We are gathered here by the call of the Force that constantly sounds in our world. Its call was heard and strengthened by J.R.R. Tolkien. Our work on *The Lord of the Rings* and *The Silmarillion* translations from 1984 to 1991 have became a part of our lives. It has changed them, and we would like to think not only ours. It is nearly impossible to imagine that anybody could read *The Lord of the Rings* and be left unchanged.

The Russian audience understands Tolkien in a rather special way. First of all, fairy-stories as a literary genre have always been rare in Russia. I mean novels corresponding to the demands of Tolkien's "On Fairy-Stories" essay. These few were absorbed and lost in the large mass of folk-tales. So *The Lord of the Rings* immediately attracted attention for its novelty and brightness. Secondly, Tolkien remains known by general readers only as the author of *The Hobbit* and *The Lord of the Rings*. His other books appeared in various issues of a rather small number of copies and are not widely known.

At first sight it's easy to find three different modes of readers' perception and accordingly three types of readers. The first group of readers includes people with a fresh perception whose abilities to connect with the "Secondary World" haven't been lost. They hear an echo of this "Secondary World" in *The Lord of the Rings* and enjoy it. This group is made up of children from 7 to 13. We have met them in schools, youth libraries and so on. We have seen a lot of children who have read and re-read the books many times, children living inside Middle-earth and exploring it closely. I think some of them are skilled in its history, languages, geography, heroes' biographies possibly better then we are. It is clear that Tolkien's books mean more to them than ordinary fairy-tales. Numerous pictures and dolls show that. The deep influence of the book is revealed by the innumerable questions they ask. I don't know a better way to instil human ethical norms into children's consciousness. It depends on the fact that only a few authors were able to find the right tone for speaking to children about human duty, honour, generosity and dignity. For the last 70 years they were usually influenced by corporate or communist ideology.

As Tolkien himself remarked, the main question for children is, "Is he good or is he bad?", and the book never avoids this question. But, of course, they are interested in other things too. For example, we were asked a question which we were unable to answer. A 12-year-old girl asked us, what is the reason that two such different heroes as Sauron and Frodo had their fingers cut off with the Ring. I'll be very pleased if anybody knows the answer.

Teenagers from 12 to 19 have certain peculiarities of perception. Younger children are usually introduced to Tolkien by adults. If teenagers encounter Tolkien it is usually a result of their conscious decision. This choice is fully their own. Typically this kind of reader has broad views and heightened interests in intellectual studies. They are usually high-school or college students interested in the humanities though often enough they specialize in education studies,

---

[1] Editors' note: some revisions to this paper have been made by the editors.

mathematics or programming. Since 1982, when the first translation of *The Fellowship of the Ring* was published, more than one hundred Tolkien-clubs have been formed in Russia. Before the mid-80s they had not had any information about each other, and they had poor information about Tolkien himself. Since then there has been more or less regular contacts between Russian fan-clubs in the various cities and regions. Some fanzines have been published and a kind of specialized information network has been created. A number of conferences have been held and a strange thing named "Khobbitskie Igrishcha" ["Hobbit Games"] appeared. So it is possible to say that these groups of youth exist in "Tolkien's World" and spend considerable effort to be there. It is an extraordinary phenomenon. Until recently societies of this sort were only created in Russia under the control of the official authorities.

As we are talking about Russia we should remember that generations lived in an all-embracing ideological atmosphere and were restricted to an extremely undistinguished literary production, because it belonged to the official "sacred" genre of "socialist realism". The appearance of *The Lord of the Rings* itself broke down the ethical norms that were passed by the ruling Party. This exceptional work based on the Christian ethics of its author was very timely although partly unexpected.

Certainly young people's passion for Tolkien contains elements of escapism, but I don't think this is a fault, as the author refutes this charge himself. Because Russia has existed until recently as a totalitarian state, Tolkien's words about a prisoner escaping from the walls of his prison have a special relevance here. The essence of escapism isn't so simple. It means the existence of "another" reality preferred by those who escape. From my point of view there are three possible forms of interaction between this "other reality" and "escapism". The first type is that the "escapist" is forced to attain to his "other reality" and so "his soul rises". The second is where a person tries to find a more comfortable place to live, that he tries to change his ordinary reality for something else which is placed "on the same level" and doesn't demand any inner work. The third type attempts to make a person worse.

There is no need to explain that *The Lord of the Rings* belongs to the first type and assumes higher norms of life than "primary" reality. So the word "escapism" does not have its abusive sense.

But I should say that most of the young audience is looking for action, and Tolkien's vast linguistic, philological and mythological background is rather difficult or boring for them. The depths of meaning are beyond their power of comprehension. "Khobbitskie Igrishcha", referred to above demonstrates that.

"Khobbitskie Igrishcha" is a role-playing game which continues over four or five days. Teams from various regions and cities gather together. The usual number of participants is between fifty and three hundred. Roles are chosen beforehand, but usually the war for the Ring becomes a main theme and organizers are forced to work hard to prevent evil from winning. Often the course of play breaks from the outline of the book's plot. Hobbits are forgotten. Their place is filled by knights, kings, wizards, nazgûl and so on. The translator S. Koshelev, who was seriously interested in the "Inklings", noted in his foreword to the *Chronicles of Narnia* by C.S. Lewis that

> ... the organizers of "Khobbitskie Igrishcha" have used Tolkien's profound philosophical epic ... as a basis for an orienteering competition. I wouldn't wonder if some years later teams of boy- and girl-scouts find in the Siberian woods a way from the Fords-of-Beruna to Cair-Paravel ..."
> (Koshelev, 1991, p. 19)[2]

Apparently, decades of a totalitarian regime have influenced people's minds so greatly that even those who caught only its fall have certain difficulties in understanding a fundamental theme of *The Lord of the Rings* – an idea that any power contains primary evil.

So the young participants of "Khobbitskie Igrishcha" strive to establish by force their own ideas of justice. Certainly it leads to some troubling effects on the players' minds. They put down noble and generous impulses and stress physical strength, tricks and unscrupulousness in realizing their roles. Usually they turn to cruelty in "battles". Player's injuries are increasing steadily. It looks as though the aggression of the participants will increase if the very principles of such games aren't changed by their organizers, and if they don't get rid of the temptation of Power and the symbol of the Ring.

Tolkien's popularity in Russia depends on the fact that general readers gained access to his works when the social system of the whole country had been swept away, when old cultural values were being devalued and new cultural values were in short supply. Young people accept Tolkien's world because it's completely honest. The intentional contrast between Good and Evil makes it clear. It is easy to recognize Tolkien's world because it contains true elements of "another" reality. I believe this larger world exists at the same time as our ordinary world and parallels it. Some aspects of this "other world" are retained in human mythologies. It seems to me that the word "Faerie" is closely connected with a certain kind of "other reality". Authors of mythologies have only "reflected" it, as Tolkien has.

Familiarity with "another world" demands some special knowledge. Usually young people are poorly informed about such matters. Explaining their feelings about the book, they prefer to say: "It's my sort of book", or "The book isn't for me". Those for whom an echo of "another world" has an importance make their choice automatically, never troubling to think about their reasons.

Often there isn't any visible influence on a person's outlook on the world, but sometimes a deep interest in *The Lord of the Rings* leads to serious studies in linguistics and mythology, and so considerably influences their way of life.

The second type of audience consists of "experienced readers". They are used to reading but they have generally

---

[2] Russian quotations are translated by Vladimir Grushetskiy.

been trained in the "socialist realist" literary tradition. Usually they admit that Tolkien's works are significant, but when they are reading them they feel an unaccountable irritation. Its source is clear enough. As I have said, fairy-story as a literary genre isn't well known in Russia. Hence there's no label to put on the text which defines a reader's expectation. The book is discouragingly straightforward. The depths of sense haven't been based on allegories, as was typical for Russian literature for half a century. Here, true significance returns to moral categories and the reader's attention is turned to ontological aspects of Being almost by force. It is difficult to analyse and to discuss this kind of text, and it's slowly producing a strange reaction. Literary critics (these are few, by the way) and reviewers and even some researchers and translators of Tolkien are tending to force their own ideas upon the author. His books are usually considered as allegories. So, Zerkalov explains that Tolkien has been forbidden in Russia for long years because of "the Darkness coming from the East" (1989, p. 81). Zerkalov asserts that the censors regarded this as a clear reference to the totalitarian system in the USSR.

Certainly the situation will improve if Tolkien's books are published. They cannot be published legally because of the lack of hard currency for rights payments. That is our common problem with modern foreign literature. As a result, some "pirate" editions, as a rule badly translated, have appeared and a lot of information is unreachable for general readers. *The Biography* by H. Carpenter, *Letters of J.R.R. Tolkien* and *The History of Middle-earth* are more or less known to a limited circle of researchers. The perceptions of the author's intentions are fully dependent on his critic's point of view. And the critics tend to declare: "Tolkien means that . . ." or "Tolkien hardly realized what he had written . . ." or even "though the author has asserted that, it's quite different . . ." V. Murav'ĕv explains in his foreword for his own translation of *The Lord of the Rings*:

> Though Tolkien denied it, the word "hobbit" grew from two words: "ho(mo)" [Latin] – "a man" and "(a ra)bbit"- English.
> (Murav'ĕv, 1988, p. 14)

A few pages later we can find in the "Prologue" the author's words that "Hobbits are relatives of ours". Book 4 chapter IV is entitled "Of Herbs and Stewed Rabbit", so possibly we should think that hobbits are cannibals. But a more important factor is that the translator finds a kind of baseless approach suitable for "a story for children". This approach is typical of a reader limiting Tolkien's work by a particular theme or genre. Nearly all reviews, papers, forewords are similar in one point. Each of them relates in detail WHAT is written but never explains WHY.

The Ring of Power is an extraordinary symbol for Russia. Our present struggle for power is too far from the ethical base of the book, so if you want to be listened to it's better to choose another subject.

Knowing how important *The Silmarillion* is for understanding *The Lord of the Rings* we were trying to publish *The Silmarillion* in Russian legally. It is a pity that our negotiations with HarperCollins were not successful. As a result there have been two "pirate" editions and two more are in preparation. The evil of the Ring is distorting intentions. These translations are hardly fit for literary Russians and need serious editing. One of these versions is drastically abridged, and another contains some passages from *Unfinished Tales*. Remembering the troubles the author had with "pirate" editions in the U.S.A. in the 60s the Russian *Silmarillion* published in the same way cannot be counted as a good centenary present for the author.

But it has happened now, and the readers' attitude to the author and *The Lord of the Rings* is changing. It is now becoming impossible to look on the books as a simple "fairy-story" or even a philosophical fairy-story. As the author himself maintained, *The Lord of the Rings* and *The Silmarillion* were planned as a duology. It's my opinion that taken as a whole they show the evolutionary ways of mankind through the idea of Transmyth. Tolkien's desire to create "a mythology for England" based on Christianity leads to more significant results. For example, Jung's archetypes are traced clearly in his narration.

I'm now going to discuss a comparatively small group of readers whose wide knowledge and deep comprehension are sufficient to distinguish several levels of understanding.

The plot of the narrative is not new. A story where a journey leads a hero to wonderful adventures has been a favourite plot for Chinese authors since the Middle ages.

Christian moral norms determining a hero's behaviour are nothing strange either.

The distinction between Good and Evil is traditional for fairy-stories.

The real wonder is the true sub-creative activity of Tolkien himself. Middle-earth is a brilliant example of "sub-created reality" which can be developed successfully only in the space of mythical existence. It demands a person knowing the very roots of mythological worlds, a person with the mythologically-oriented consciousness peculiar to visionaries.

I dare say that Russian readers have some advantage over other readers. It's significant, I suppose, that we had in 1991 a book by another visionary (he's Russian) at the same time that the complete translation of *The Lord of the Rings* appeared in Russian for the first time. It is more interesting that both books were written at the same time. The books have much in common, though any contact between the authors was quite impossible. The Russian visionary Daniil Andreev wrote his book in one of Stalin's prisons in 1950-1956. The book I'm speaking of is named *Roza Mira* – "The Rose of the World" (1991). It is not fiction, not fantasy nor a philosophical system. It presents the author's vision of the spiritual space of mankind. This large work is aimed against two evils – one of them is a world war, another is a world-wide tyranny, as the author himself expressed them. Andreev introduces the term "metaculture". It's a two-pointed pyramid which consists of a number of worlds with "other realities". On the one point of it is a demiurge – the white leader of his people; on the opposite is a dark demon who keeps his own country – but he is an eternal usurper of other countries and people. The author's point of view on metahistory is significant too. The term "metahistory" means that human history observed in ordinary reality depends on historical motions developing in other dimensions of planetary space inhabited by other races. Among these beings there is a level inhabited by a race remarkably similar to Tolkien's Elves. Andreev considers those beings are "older brothers of Men". They are our teachers, inspiring human fantasy. The Elven world has passed into the human unconsciousness but it hasn't become unreal. Tolkien's point of view on Elves declared in his essay "On Fairy-Stories" is wonderfully close to that of Andreev.

There are a lot of other coincidences. Some fragments from *The Rose of the World* are nearly word-for-word the same as in *The Silmarillion*, especially those concerning gods and angelic powers. Sometimes it seems that some words have not been invented, but have been "heard" from "another world". Elvish "Ennorath" – "Middle-earth" is phonetically similar to a term "Enrof" or "Enroth" used by Andreev for our Earth and all its spiritual planes.

Both authors agree about the nature of Power. Andreev believes that any Power is demonized by its origin. So any form of Power – totalitarian state or democracy – contains evil. An idea that the roots of evil would grow anew in this world if human power is not limited by ethical control is a repeated theme of Andreev. I think that has much in common with Tolkien's fundamental ideas. Let's reflect on the fact that two rather dissimilar authors have been so deeply interested in fundamental questions of human existence at the same time and have proposed such similar solutions.

Tolkien wrote:
> The peculiar quality of "joy" in successful Fantasy can ... be explained as a sudden glimpse of the underlying reality or truth ... But in the "eucatastrophe" we see in a brief vision that ... may be a far-off gleam or echo of *evangelium* in the real world ...
> (Tolkien, 1988b, p. 64)

Artists (or writers) who bring a gleam of "another reality" into our world were named "messengers" by Andreev. His definition is:
> "A messenger" is an artist in the wide meaning of the word who shows for others the highest Truth and the Light gleaming from supreme worlds.
> (Andreev, 1991, p. 174)

Tolkien and Andreev spent their lives reclaiming for myth its former significance. Myth arises and grows during human history as a reflection in human minds of "another reality", the reality of many-dimensioned planetary space in the form of a "Secondary World". So a harmonical non-contradictory picture of the world wouldn't be reached by adding national mythologies.

It also includes some key principles of esoteric doctrine of special meaning for Tolkien as they are corroborated by the plot reiterations in *The Silmarillion*.

So, Morgoth declares Arda his own kingdom and world harmony is broken by wars. Fëanor takes the Silmarils for his own and the straight ways of Elven evolution are bent.

Beren refuses the possession of the Silmaril, overcoming Death itself. Eärendil returning the Silmaril redeems the sin of the whole people.

Elendil dies looking for the Ring. Boromir falls holding out his hand for the Ring. Frodo refuses to possess the Ring, saving the World.

The simple idea that the world's troubles and evils have their sources in selfish motives is older than Christian precepts. However, it frightened Tolkien no more than the abyss of time which opened for him behind the words of "Eärendil, brightest of Angels". Our world has many dimensions – or, possibly, it would be better to say "many mansions". "Other realities" interconnect and interact with our ordinary world; Primary Evil in human history is a search for Power – these fundamental ideas allow us to put Tolkien into the rare and glorious fellowship of "messengers" whose names forever remain in the history of human culture. They constantly come into the world to restrain evil once more when darkness and perils are growing. Lewis's words about a person who has always felt Logres inside Britain and the complicated nets connecting the worlds could be applied to Tolkien.

The English theologian Blackmoor said that the twentieth century is bringing back the Devil for authority. If he was right then inevitably Tolkien, Lewis or Williams came to unmask Evil and return true values to the World.

Andreev, naming the different Gifts of "a messenger", said that one of them is an ability to contemplate "another world's" views. Could we guess that Tolkien's views of Middle-earth grew as a result of such an ability? Andreev declares that a true artist, beginning his creation here, in our ordinary world, continues his work "after death" in "another world". I think we can see that remarkable idea in Tolkien's *Leaf by Niggle*.

It's a pity that Tolkien's "small prose" isn't known to Russian general readers. Possibly this is because they are difficult for the public to understand. The literary critic Gopman wrote in his afterword to an edition of Tolkien's "small prose":
> And only a person who understands the necessity to strive [with evil], even not by himself possibly, in spite of its likely tragic result, for a person himself, that person only may win ...
> (Gopman, 1991, p. 299)

Here Gopman named one more group of Tolkien's readers who definitely accepted him immediately. That is, people who began their struggle with the socialistic totalitarian state in the USSR in the 70s despite the possibility of disastrous results for themselves personally and who were later called "dissidents". For such people, working in the spiritual underground, Tolkien's books were (and still are) a remarkable way to influence a person's mind, training an individual in certain ethical ideas. They saw two key ideas in *The Lord of the Rings*: that any ordinary farmer can work in his small garden in peace while he's guarded by Rangers – Dúnedain; that Good and Evil are the same at all times, and a man should find his own side in distinguishing between them.

As a rule, these ideas aren't articulated after reading the

book for the first or even second time, although they are especially significant for the present situation in Russia. The ordinary farmer is definitely forgotten in the larger scale of economical or geopolitical events. In turn, an ordinary farmer often loses his moral compass, and is unable to decide what is Good for him and what he ought to do. Tolkien's books provide a clear moral and ethical standard.

Russian readers need a fairy-story because, in Tolkien's own words, "it is one of the lessons of fairy-stories that on callow, lumpish, and selfish youth peril, sorrow, and the shadow of death can bestow dignity, and even sometimes wisdom."

References

Andreev, Daniil. 1991. *Roza mira* [*Rose of the World*]. Moscow: Prometei. Андреев, Даниил. *Роза мира*. Москва: Прометей.

Gopman, V. 1991. "Afterword" in J.R.R. Tolkien *List raboty Melkina i drugie volshebnye skazki*.

Koshelev, S. 1991. "Foreword" in C.S. Lewis *Khroniki Narnii*.

Lewis, Clive Staples. 1991. Translated with foreword by S. Koshelev. *Khroniki Narnii* [*Chronicles of Narnia*]. Moscow: Kosmopolis. Льюис, Клайв Стейплз. Предисловие, перевод: С Кошелев. *Хроники Нарнии*. Москва: Космополис.

Murav'ëv, V. 1988. "Foreword" in J.R.R. Tolkien. *Khraniteli*.

Tolkien, John Ronald Reuel. 1988a. Translated by V. Murav'ëv and A. Kistyakovskiĭ. *Khraniteli* [*The Fellowship of the Ring*]. Moscow: Raduga. Толкиен, Джон Рональд Руэл. Перевод: Муравьев, В. и Кистяковский, А. *Хранители: летопись первая из эпопеи «Властелин Колец»*. Москва: Радуга.

Tolkien, J.R.R. 1988b. *Tree and Leaf*. London: Unwin Hyman Ltd.

Tolkien, J.R.R. 1991. Translated and afterword by V. Gopman. *List raboty Melkina i drugie volshebnye skazki*. [*Leaf by Niggle and other fairy stories*]. Moscow: RIF. Толкин, Джон Рональд Руэл. Перевод, послесловие: Гопман, В. *Лист работы Мелкина и другие волшебные сказки*. Москва: РИФ.

Zerkalov, A. 1989. "Tri tsveta Dzhona Tolkina" ["The three colours of John Tolkien"] in *Znanie – sila* No. 11, 1989 p. 79-81. Moscow: Znanie. Зеркалов, А. «Три цвета Джона Толкина», *Знание – сила* № 11, 1989 с. 78-81. Москва: Знание.

The Critical Response to Tolkien's Fiction

Wayne G. Hammond

Abstract: This paper illustrates, primarily by reviewing reviews from *The Hobbit* to "The History of Middle-earth", how Tolkien's critics have approached his works and popularity. The paper also briefly comments on the state of Tolkien criticism in its second half-century.

Keywords: *The Hobbit*, *The Lord of the Rings*, Tolkien criticism, *The Silmarillion*, *Unfinished Tales*

In 1961 the critic Philip Toynbee wrote in the London *Observer*:

> There was a time when the Hobbit fantasies of Professor Tolkien were being taken very seriously indeed by a great many distinguished literary figures. Mr. Auden is even reported to have claimed that these books were as good as *War and Peace*; Edwin Muir and many others were almost equally enthusiastic. I had a sense that one side or other must be mad, for it seemed to me that these books were dull, ill-written, whimsical and childish. And for me this had a reassuring outcome, for most of his more ardent supporters were soon beginning to sell out their shares in Professor Tolkien, and to-day those books have passed into a merciful oblivion.[1]

Toynbee's dismissal of *The Lord of the Rings* was, of course, premature. Today the works of J.R.R. Tolkien are still read ardently, not only in Britain and America but around the world. *The Lord of the Rings* in fact was very popular at the time of Toynbee's remark, and more than thirty years and many thousands of readers later, it is a modern classic. To be fair, in 1961 the flurry of first reviews of *The Lord of the Rings* had ended, and almost nothing was being written about Tolkien. His fan movement had only just been born (in America), and the present great river of literature about him was not yet even a trickle. In that moment of critical calm, anyone might have misread the signs. But Toynbee clearly was inclined to do so, driven by (in Edmund Fuller's words) "an apparent total temperamental antipathy" (1968, p. 36) and by a need to convince himself, at least in the case of Tolkien, of the accuracy of his critical judgement. Later in his article Toynbee admitted that on several occasions he had "grossly misjudged a book, either to its advantage or to its detriment", and that the opinions of other critics now and then had led him to change his own; but he felt sure that he was right about "the Hobbits". Indeed, we find him in 1978, in a review of *The Inklings* by Humphrey Carpenter, still remarking on the "immaturity" of *The Lord of the Rings*, and on Tolkien, C.S. Lewis, and Charles Williams as "childish" in their devotion to "make-believe" (1978, p. 31). Some opinions are formed in steel and weather the years.

Toynbee's remarks are a good illustration, on the negative side, of the degree to which Tolkien's works often provoke a response more emotional than intellectual. Equally illustrative, on the positive side, would be the adulatory writings of some of Tolkien's fans, those who (as is their right) choose to love Middle-earth for its own sake and to give little or no thought to analysis. In between these poles is a vast territory of comments, opinions, and serious criticism about Tolkien. It is an ever-expanding country with many camps. It is, perhaps, necessarily vast: as Neil D. Isaacs has written, "in contemplating the artistry of Tolkien, one must broaden not only one's horizons but also one's definitions. Prose fiction has taken new turns or even jumps with Tolkien, and the critics must try to keep up" (1968, p. 11). And it is an interesting place to explore: to trace, one hundred years after his birth and more than fifty since the publication of *The Hobbit*, Tolkien's phenomenal popularity and influence, to better appreciate the varied effects he has had on his readers, and in the process even to shed further light, by reflection, on his works themselves.

An interesting place to explore – but so far, little described, though well mapped. In the September 1986 issue of *Beyond Bree* I put on my own critic's hat to review the annotated bibliography of Tolkien by Judith A. Johnson (Hammond, 1986, pp. 7-8), and noted that the book was not yet the properly critical analysis of Tolkien criticism that needs to be written. This was, I now think, an unfair comment. The criticism of Tolkien's fiction alone is the stuff of which long dissertations are made. It could not be, and was not meant to be, fully covered by Johnson in her book. But she, and Richard West, and Åke Bertenstam, and George Thomson, and other bibliographers of Tolkieniana have laid the groundwork for such a study. It remains only for someone to

---

[1] A letter by one C.D. Fettes, disputing Toynbee's remarks, was published in the *Observer* of 11 Feb. 1962. George Watson attempted to explain the dissension over *The Lord of the Rings* by describing Tolkien as the last Victorian: see "The Roots of Romance" [review of T.A. Shippey, *The Road to Middle-earth*], *Times Literary Supplement*, 8 Oct. 1982: 1098. Watson himself was a "dissenter" in the manner of Toynbee. He labelled *The Silmarillion* "flatulent and pretentious" and *The Lord of the Rings* "more of a phenomenon . . . than a work of literature, and more of an addiction than either . . ."

follow their guides. I cannot myself, in the space of this paper, write that important book; but I would like at least to contribute a chapter, or an introduction to a chapter, and to suggest a few directions to the ultimate author.

An account of the criticism of Tolkien's writings might begin with J.R.R. Tolkien himself. He was, as he once wrote, his "most critical reader of all" (Tolkien, 1966, p. 6). His letters are filled with self-analysis and second thoughts. He took note of his reviews, and was dismayed when he was misunderstood. He was concerned that his works should speak to a wider public, beyond his "inner circle" of readers. The latter included his wife and children, especially his son Christopher; and his "two chief (and most well-disposed) critics", C.S. Lewis and Rayner Unwin (Tolkien, 1981, p. 36). Lewis's criticism has been, or is being, well documented. Rayner Unwin's opinions were privately given to Tolkien, and for the most part are unpublished. Only his report on *The Hobbit* is widely known:

> Bilbo Baggins was a hobbit who lived in his hobbit-hole and *never* went for adventures, at last Gandalf the wizard and his dwarves perswaded him to go. He had a very exiting time fighting goblins and wargs. at last they got to the lonley mountain; Smaug, the dragon who gawreds it is killed and after a terrific battle with the goblins he returned home -- rich!
>
> This book, with the help of maps, does not need any illustrations it is good and should appeal to all children between the ages of 5 and 9.[2]

Rayner Unwin himself likes to point out, with regard to his final comment, that he wrote the report at age ten. While still young, he also reported on *Farmer Giles of Ham* in manuscript, and he wrote a very astute response to the poem "The Adventures of Tom Bombadil", which Tolkien had put forward as a successor to *The Hobbit*:

> I think that *Tom Bombadil* would make quite a good story, but as *The Hobbit* has already been very successful I think the story of Old Took's great grand-uncle, Bullroarer, who rode a horse and charged the goblins of Mount Gram in the battle of the Green Fields and knocked King Golfimbil's [sic] head off with a wooden club would be better. This story could be a continuation of *The Hobbit*, for Bilbo could tell it to Gandalf and Balin in his hobbit hole when they visited him.[3]

Boy or man, Unwin was found by Tolkien to be "a critic worth listening to" (1981, p. 120).

Professional critics began to take note of Tolkien's fiction in 1937, beginning with the reviewers of *The Hobbit*. As Åke Bertenstam (1988, p. 17) has written, these critics had among them a strong feeling of bewilderment. In their attempt to define *The Hobbit* they compared it to the *Alice* books, to *The Wind in the Willows* and other works by Kenneth Grahame, to the geometrical fantasy *Flatland*, and to works by William Morris and George MacDonald. Not all of these comparisons were apt. The reviewer in the *Times Literary Supplement* was the most perceptive in this regard:

> To define the world of "The Hobbit" is, of course, impossible, because it is new. You cannot anticipate it before you go there, as you cannot forget it once you have gone. The author's admirable illustrations and maps of Mirkwood and Goblingate and Esgaroth give one an inkling – and so do the names of dwarf and dragon that catch our eyes as we first ruffle the pages. But there are dwarfs and dwarfs, and no common recipe for children's stories will give you creatures so rooted in their own soil and history as those of Professor Tolkien – who obviously knows much more about them than he needs for this tale.
> (Lewis, 1937, p. 714)

Obviously, indeed, for the reviewer was C.S. Lewis, who had read *The Hobbit* in typescript and knew something of Tolkien's unpublished mythology.

Since *The Hobbit* was a children's book, many of its reviewers noted elements that would appeal to children, and many classified the book by age. Anne T. Eaton, in a slightly confused article in the *New York Times Book Review*, wrote that "the tale is packed with valuable hints for the dragon killer and adventurer in Faerie. Plenty of scaly monsters have been slain in legend and folktale, but never for modern readers has so complete a guide to dragon ways been provided." She specified ages eight to twelve as the appropriate readers for *The Hobbit* – but then wrote, in the same review, that the book was suitable for "ages from 8 years on", and finally called it "a book with no age limit" (1938, p. 12). C.S. Lewis again was on the mark in the *Times Literary Supplement*, with his statement that *The Hobbit* is "a children's book only in the sense that the first of many readings can be undertaken in the nursery" (1937, p. 714).

Having written a children's book, Tolkien was categorized as an author for children – at least, by the reviewers. His second book of fiction, *Farmer Giles of Ham* (1949), confirmed that label. *Farmer Giles* was published for children, though it had long before grown from a family game into a sophisticated tale combining fairy-story characters with references to medieval history, Oxford University, and the *OED*. Unlike *The Hobbit*, it went largely unremarked by the reviewers, a fact Tolkien ruefully noted (1981, pp. 138-9). But it too was received generally with favour.

The critics' mood and approach changed dramatically with the publication of *The Lord of the Rings* (1954-5). If Tolkien was a writer for children, what was this? A three-volume book, largely serious, compared by advance readers to Spenser, Malory, and Ariosto. The reviewers were put on their mettle. Some responded with the first serious analysis of Tolkien's fiction; others did not rise to the occasion.

The anonymous *Times Literary Supplement* reviewer of the first volume, describing hobbits, wrote that "it is as though

---

[2] From the manuscript reproduced in *The Annotated Hobbit*, ed. Douglas A. Anderson (1988) p. 2, quoted here with permission of Rayner Unwin.

[3] Rayner Unwin, report contained in an unpublished letter from Stanley Unwin to J. R. R. Tolkien, 16 Dec. 1937, quoted here with permission of Rayner Unwin and HarperCollins.

these Light Programme types had intruded into the domain of the Nibelungs." He noted Frodo's development "from a greedy young hobbledehobbit" to "a noble paladin", and remarked:

> Only considerable skill in narrative can surmount the difficulty of this complete change of key within the limits of one book. It is a near thing, but Professor Tolkien just pulls it off . . . Yet the plot lacks balance. All right-thinking hobbits, dwarfs, elves and men can combine against Sauron, Lord of Evil; but their only code is the warrior's code of courage, and the author never explains what it is they consider the Good . . .
> (Anon., 1954a, p. 541)

"Perhaps, after all," the reviewer thought, "this is the point of a subtle allegory", of the West against the Communist East. But "whether this is its meaning, or whether it has no meaning, *The Fellowship of the Ring* is a book to be read for sound prose and rare imagination."

W.H. Auden (1954, p. 37), writing in the *New York Times Book Review*, noted that *The Lord of the Rings*, unlike *The Hobbit*, was written in a manner suited to adults, "to those, that is, between the ages of 12 and 70" – a very odd range. He called *The Fellowship of the Ring* an adventure story, and compared it to John Buchan's *The Thirty-nine Steps*. Donald Barr, reviewing the second volume of *The Lord of the Rings*, also noted that it was not for children (a fact which still eludes some critics), and that it was "not metaphysical like E.R. Eddison's [fantasies], nor theological like George MacDonald's". He thought that the work would appeal to "readers of the most austere tastes" who "now long for the old, forthright, virile kind of narrative", and that it had "a kind of echoing depth behind it, wherein we hear Snorri Sturluson and Beowulf, the sagas and the Nibelungenlied, but civilized by the gentler genius of modern England" (1955, p. 4).

With the publication of *The Two Towers*, the *Times Literary Supplement* proclaimed the work to be "a prose epic in praise of courage", and noted that "within his imagined world the author continually unveils fresh countries of the mind, convincingly imagined and delightful to dwell in." However, "large sectors of this mythic world are completely omitted; women play no part [a frequent comment by critics, not fully warranted]; no one does anything to get money [!]; oddly enough, no one uses the sea, though that may come in the final volume. And though the allegory is now plainer there is still no explanation of wherein lies the wickedness of Sauron." (Anon., 1954b, p. 817). The *Times Literary Supplement* reviewer of *The Return of the King* also praised Tolkien's work, at length and with poetry: "At last the great edifice shines forth in all its splendour, with colonnades stretching beyond the ken of mortal eye, dome rising behind dome to hint at further spacious halls as yet unvisited." With foresight he found *The Lord of the Rings* "not a work that many adults will read right through more than once; though even a single reading will not be quickly forgotten. In the schoolroom it may be read more avidly, perhaps again and again. If that comes to pass its influence will be immeasurable. As with Kai Lung and *The Wind in the Willows*, posterity may identify not direct quotation, but half-hidden reference, which assumes that every well-rounded and book-loving undergraduate is familiar with the adventures of Frodo Baggins among the evil mountains of Mordor." (Anon., 1955, p. 704). But he thought that Tolkien could have distinguished Good and Evil better. In response to a reader's letter, the reviewer wrote, now with an astounding lack of perception, that "throughout the book the good try to kill the bad, and the bad try to kill the good. We never see them doing anything else. Both sides are brave. Morally there seems nothing to choose between them."[4]

By now the critical climate was such that W.H. Auden could write: "I rarely remember a book about which I have had such violent arguments. Nobody seems to have a moderate opinion; either, like myself, people find it a masterpiece of its genre or they cannot abide it . . ." (1956, p. 5).[5] Foremost among the latter group was the critic Edmund Wilson. In "Oo, Those Awful Orcs!" in the *Nation*, he wrote that "there is little in *The Lord of the Rings* over the head of a seven-year-old child. It is essentially . . . a children's book which has somehow got out of hand . . . an overgrown fairy story, a philological curiosity". It dealt with, he said, "a simple confrontation – of the Forces of Evil with the Forces of Good, the remote and alien villain with the plucky little home-grown hero. There are streaks of imagination" – Ents and Elves – "but even these are rather clumsily handled . . . The characters talk a story-book language that might have come out of Howard Pyle, and as personalities they do not impose themselves." Tolkien's "poverty of imagination", Wilson felt, was "almost pathetic". How is it, he asked, "that these long-winded volumes of what looks to this reviewer like balderdash have elicited such tributes" from C.S. Lewis, Naomi Mitchison, and Richard Hughes, among others? The answer, he believed, was "that certain people – especially, perhaps, in Britain – have a lifelong appetite for juvenile trash" (1956, pp. 312-13). Wilson's review was immediately notorious and provoked a counter-response, most notably "Hwaet We Holbytla . . ." by Douglass Parker in the *Hudson Review* (1956-7).[6] Parker's review of *The Lord of the Rings* not only provided balance to Wilson, it was one of the first lengthy comments on Tolkien's epic, and remains one of the most literate essays to deal with Tolkien and his fiction.

The most interesting series of reviews of *The Lord of the Rings* appeared in the *New Statesman and Nation*. Naomi Mitchison liked *The Fellowship of the Ring* for its details of

---

[4] Reply to letter to the editor from David I. Masson, *Times Literary Supplement*, 9 Dec. 1955: 743. Anthony Bailey made a similar comment in his "Power in the Third Age of the [*sic*] Middle Earth" (1956, p. 154). C.S. Lewis replied to all such readers who saw only black and white and no grey in *The Lord of the Rings*, in his "The Dethronement of Power" (1955).

[5] This review of *The Return of the King* provoked Tolkien to write an extensive private comment on his critics, published in *Letters of J.R.R. Tolkien* (pp. 238-44).

[6] Another good reply to Wilson, and to Philip Toynbee, is Shippey, 1982, pp. [1]-3.

geography and language. It was not, she wrote, an allegory but "a bigger bit of creation altogether: perhaps a mythology." She regretted only that "certain aspects of this mythic world are not completely worked out. Professor Tolkien is not an economist; there are uncertainties on the scientific side. But on the fully human side, from the standpoint of history and semantics, everything is there" (1954, p. 331). Maurice Richardson, the reviewer of *The Two Towers*, on the other hand, thought that the work would "do quite nicely as an allegorical adventure story for very leisured boys, but as anything else . . . it has been widely overpraised." The work, he said, had begun as "a charming children's book" but "proliferated into an endless worm". He thought its fantasy "thin and pale". He liked the battle scenes and the "atmosphere of doom and danger and perilous night-riding", and he thought that the allegory (as he perceived it to be) raised "interesting speculations": does the Ring relate to the atomic nucleus, and are Orcs at all equated with materialist scientists (1954, pp. 835-6)?

Francis Huxley, in reviewing *The Return of the King* in the *New Statesman and Nation* (1955, 587-8), also reviewed Richardson's review. "When what is really a mythological story is criticised for being childish," he wrote, "I, for one, immediately suspect Mr. Richardson of having missed the point." He thought Richardson's remark that the book was "an endless worm" inspired, though not in the way it was meant.

> Professor Tolkien has, indeed, used all his ingenuity in inventing the various languages of elfs [sic], orcs, hobbits and dwarfs, together with their histories and family trees which . . . form an appendix of a hundred pages; and perhaps one has to be a "very leisured boy" to appreciate them, or, of course, to invent them. The action of the history, however, has nothing in common with such mechanical inventions: it has not been contrived, it has arisen, like all true mythology. Small wonder, then, that the story is like a worm, throwing its coils about the reader: for is it not Frodo's blessed and unhappy fate to let himself be swallowed by the dragon of evil, the Dark Power, so that he may conquer it? He walks into its mouth, bearing the Ring that can make its wearer invisible, and also compel the dragon to his will: for the ring is the image of the dragon itself, endless because its tail is in its mouth (as a smattering of mythology will tell one); and the ring must be destroyed and not used for fear that Man will turn into a dragon, instead of the dragon turning into man.

After *The Lord of the Rings* was complete and its initial reviews had been published, the serious criticism of Tolkien began to pass for the most part from newspapers and wide-circulation magazines to specialist journals and to books and dissertations. But except for a lull in (roughly) 1957-1961, Tolkien has remained (for better or worse) in the public eye. *The Adventures of Tom Bombadil* (1962) and *Tree and Leaf* (incorporating "Leaf by Niggle", 1964) drew a modest critical response, and then the competition in the United States between the "pirate" Ace Books paperback edition of *The Lord of the Rings* and the authorized Ballantine Books edition changed the tone of Tolkien criticism once more. This publishers' "war over Middle-earth" and its root question of the validity of Tolkien's American copyright generated enormous publicity, which put a spotlight not only on the central issue but on the fan movement that had quietly grown around *The Hobbit* and *The Lord of the Rings* and was now in the thick of the controversy, roused in support of a favourite author against the injustice of an unauthorized publisher. The publicity also sold books, which was itself newsworthy. The general media took note of Tolkien's growing popularity, and of the "Tolkien cult", and became often more interested in his fame and phenomenal sales than in his texts.

Edmund Fuller observed in 1962 that the critical acclaim with which *The Lord of the Rings* was received was so great as to carry in it "an inevitable counterreaction – a natural hazard of any work unique in its time that kindles a joy by its very freshness" (p. 36). He was referring to early dissenters such as Edmund Wilson and Philip Toynbee; but their remarks were polite compared to some of the criticism that erupted in 1977 upon the long-anticipated (posthumous) publication of *The Silmarillion*, and that later was directed against *Unfinished Tales* and "The History of Middle-earth". Its force was strong, and is not yet spent.

Tolkien's publisher, Rayner Unwin, has said that the reviews of *The Silmarillion* were among the most unfair he had ever seen (Yates, 1978, p. 14). Not all were negative: Anthony Burgess, for one, wrote favourably in the *Observer* (1977); and John Gardner, in the *New York Times Book Review*, though he found faults, thought that the central part of the book had "a wealth of vivid and interesting characters, and all of the tales are lifted above the ordinary" (1977, p. 1). But these were in the minority. In contrast, Eric Korn in the *Times Literary Supplement* dismissed *The Silmarillion* as "unreadable" and found that "what is admirable or enjoyable" in *The Lord of the Rings* is absent in the later work, and that "what is bad is magnified. Most lamentable is the absence of landscape . . . no pubs or pipe-smoking Rangers or Wizards [are] in the world of *The Silmarillion*, no hobbits, or ents or Gollum . . . still [as in *The Lord of the Rings*] no women, but lots of female personages, all either Pallas Athene or Brunnhilde or Yseult, unnervingly large, healthy and clear-eyed, like John Buchan heroines." Korn also criticized Tolkien's language, which he said had "crossed the boundary between mythology and scripture, and lost its head entirely . . . [There are] too many exotic names for pleasure: not the Horns of Elfland faintly blowing but a garrulous station announcer for Finnish State Railways" (1977, p. 1097). Francis King, writing in the *Sunday Telegraph*, struck much the same note by comparing *The Silmarillion* to an "overlong and rather indigestible meal" and noting that though his writings have "indisputable grandeur and power . . . Tolkien forged no style of his own . . . but instead fell back on a late-Victorian archaism, reminiscent of George MacDonald and William Morris." King, too, found no women in *The Silmarillion* "worthy of the name", only a cast of males the majority of which "behave as though they had never reached puberty" (1977, p. 14). L.J. Davis in the

New Republic, perhaps the most caustic of the reviewers, compared *The Silmarillion* to the Book of Mormon and remarked that all of its characters "are 37 feet tall and live for a million years". He found Tolkien's book to be "a weak gloss" on *The Lord of the Rings* and likely to lead many of his admirers to "grave disappointment" (1977, pp. 38-40). Richard Brookhiser, in the *National Review* (1977), was more charitable but still negative on balance: *The Silmarillion* was "no discredit" to Tolkien but was less successful for its lack of hobbits.

Such responses were perhaps to be expected. *The Lord of the Rings* was a hard act to follow, and *The Silmarillion*, as many critics pointed out at length, was a very different book; and if instead it had been like its predecessor, Tolkien still would have been criticized, for repeating himself. That *The Silmarillion* sold well despite its many unfavourable critics is (depending upon one's point of view) either evidence of its true quality or a deplorable indication of the sheeplike nature of Tolkien fans who blindly practice "brand loyalty".[7] In any case, it still (unfairly) bears the stigma of a "difficult book", and has received less than its share of serious consideration.

Unfinished Tales, published in 1980, fared no better. Brian Sibley, writing in the *Listener*, called it "an expensive, 500-page postscript that adds little to its author's reputation or to the appreciation of his other work", though he added that it "also, mercifully, takes nothing from them" (1980, pp. 443-4). And Guy Gavriel Kay, who assisted Christopher Tolkien in editing *The Silmarillion*, wrote in a Canadian magazine that "for someone innocently seeking a good read, *Unfinished Tales* emerges as inaccessible, pedantic and perhaps ultimately saddening. Where has the magic gone? One feels at times like an archeologist, digging amongst the dusty rubble of a once-glorious civilization . . . Broken shards of pottery . . . the dry dust of scholarly footnotes replacing the gleam of enchanted swords." (undated, p. 16).

As for "The History of Middle-earth" (1983-), its reviewers have divided between those who find the series a tribute to Tolkien's imagination, and those who merely ask *Why?* I need not quote extensively from the reviews to suggest their flavour. Valerie Housden's remark in *Vector* on *The Lost Road and Other Writings* is typical: "A must for Tolkien freaks and those preparing doctorates, my cat and I agreed this book was a good excuse for a snooze on a rainy afternoon" (1988).[8] Of course, these books, analysing the development of Tolkien's works through a scholarly presentation of his manuscripts, *are* primarily for Tolkien specialists, and the careful buyer will recognize them as such. Reviewers may justifiably warn prospective readers that "The History of Middle-earth" is not necessarily for those "seeking more of the joy and excitement of the Hobbit stories" – but the critics protest too much, and many readers do not agree with them. The generally good sales of the series, the fan response to the four volumes that deal with the history of *The Lord of the Rings*, and the recent appearance in mass-market paperback of the two volumes of *The Book of Lost Tales* suggest that "The History of Middle-earth" appeals to more of Tolkien's public than his critics acknowledge.

From reviews an account of Tolkien criticism must pass to more formal scholarship, which I cannot begin to cover here. But I would like to make a few remarks about where Tolkien studies have been and where they might go. Looking at the first Isaacs and Zimbardo collection of essays about Tolkien, published nearly a quarter of a century ago, some of the comments it contains now seem simplistic. Our body of knowledge is so much greater today. Humphrey Carpenter's biography, and Tolkien's published letters, and "The History of Middle-earth" all inform and colour our views of Tolkien and his works – or should. Neil D. Isaacs twice over the years has made the irritating remark that he was concerned with Tolkien criticism aimed at the serious student of literature, not at the Tolkien fan. This is an artificial and even insulting distinction. Most good Tolkien criticism is being produced today by fans, many of whom are also professional academics, and the fan journals are the backbone of Tolkien studies, certainly its most ready outlet, and increasingly sophisticated. It is there, I think, that new ground is most likely to be broken.

Tolkien's readers may never catch up to his later books. I once spoke with a woman who said, with great enthusiasm, that she *loved* Tolkien's books, but when I mentioned *The Silmarillion* she gave me a blank stare. She knew only *The Hobbit* and *The Lord of the Rings*. Tolkien scholarship has had much the same blindness. Though Neil Isaacs, in the second Isaacs and Zimbardo collection, *New Critical Perspectives*, admitted that *The Lord of the Rings* is not Tolkien's only work worthy of attention, "still [there is] a general understanding that the trilogy [*sic*] is, if not the heart of Tolkien's work, at least head and shoulders above the rest of his creative corpus" (1981, p. [1]). He also remarked that "the publication of *The Silmarillion* should . . . stimulate some reexamination of certain critical issues regarding the trilogy" (p. 7). This is far too narrow a view.

Much can be said about *The Lord of the Rings*, and much remains to be said. But it is disappointing to see so little written on *Farmer Giles of Ham*, and *Smith of Wootton Major*, even *The Hobbit* after all these years. And now we have Tolkien's drafts: *Unfinished Tales*, currently nine volumes of "The History of Middle-earth", and John Rateliff's history of the *Hobbit* manuscripts yet to come. All of these need to be taken into account, if we are to see the span of Tolkien's creativity, the body of his works as a whole rather than just its individual parts. And new critical roads need to be taken: the study, for example, of Tolkien's

---

[7] See Auberon Waugh, "Some Useful Things to Do with Books", *Literary Review*, Apr. 1992: 1.
[8] Gillian Somerville-Large, who "reviewed" *The Lays of Beleriand* in the *Irish Times*, 28 Sept. 1985, could not even bring herself to read the book, "because Tolkien makes me queasy in the stomach". "You could read this stuff," she wrote, "or you could use the time to learn shorthand typing, computer studies or flower arranging." Only a handful of reviewers outside the fan literature have given "The History of Middle-earth" the consideration it deserves, e.g. Stephen Medcalf, "Elven Evolutions" (review of *The Book of Lost Tales*), *Times Literary Supplement*, 19 July 1985: 802.

language and languages – not just his invented tongues, but his English prose and poetic styles – and of his paintings and drawings, which also reflect his vision and are directly related to the development of his texts. Tolkien's critics, I say again, often have taken a narrow view. I am hopeful, however, that their eyes are now opening wider. The range and quality of papers presented at the Tolkien Centenary Conference are proof that this is so. The land Tolkien made is rich, and the paths to its heart are many. The critical response to Tolkien's works must follow all these roads, as far as they will lead.

References[9]

Anon. 1954a. "Heroic Endeavour", in *Times Literary Supplement*, 27 Aug. 1954, p. 541.

Anon. 1954b. "The Epic of Westernesse", in *Times Literary Supplement*, 17 Dec. 1954, p. 817.

Anon. 1955. "The Saga of Middle Earth", in *Times Literary Supplement*, 25 Nov. 1955, p. 704.

Anderson, Douglas A (ed.). 1988. *The Annotated Hobbit*. Boston: Houghton Mifflin.

Auden, W.H. 1954. "The Hero is a Hobbit", in *New York Times Book Review*, 31 Oct. 1954, p. 37.

Auden, W.H. 1956. "At the End of the Quest, Victory", in *New York Times Book Review*, 22 Jan. 1956, p. 5.

Bailey, Anthony. 1956. "Power in the Third Age of the Middle Earth", in *Commonweal*, 11 May 1956, p. 154.

Barr, Donald. 1955. "Shadowy World of Men and Hobbits", in *New York Times Book Review*, 1 May 1955, p. 4.

Bertenstam, Åke. 1988. "Some Notes on the Reception of *The Hobbit*", in *Angerthas* (publication of the Arthedain-Norges Tolkienforening, Oslo) 23 (16 Aug. 1988), pp. 16-17, 20-25.

Brookhiser, Richard. 1977. "Kicking the Hobbit", in *National Review*, 9 Dec. 1977, pp. 1439-40.

Burgess, Anthony. 1977. "Hobbit Forming", in *Observer*, 18 Sept. 1977, p. 25.

Davis, L.J. 1977. "Books Considered", in *New Republic*, 1 Oct. 1977, pp. 38-40.

Eaton, Anne T. 1938. Review of *The Hobbit*, in *New York Times Book Review*, 13 Mar. 1938, p. 12.

Fettes, C.D. 1962. Letter, in *Observer*, 11 Feb. 1962.

Fuller, Edmund. 1968. "The Lord of the Hobbits: J.R.R. Tolkien", in *Tolkien and the Critics: Essays on J.R.R. Tolkien's* The Lord of the Rings, eds. Neil D. Isaacs and Rose A. Zimbardo. Notre Dame: University of Notre Dame Press, pp. 17-39.

Gardner, John. 1977. "The World of Tolkien", in *New York Times Book Review*, 23 Oct. 1977, pp.1, 39-40.

Hammond, Wayne G. 1986. Review of Johnson, in *Beyond Bree* (newsletter of the American Mensa Tolkien Special Interest Group), Sept. 1986, pp. 7-8.

Housden, Valerie. 1988. Review of *The Lost Road and Other Writings*, in *Vector*, Feb./Mar. 1988.

Huxley, Francis. 1955. "The Endless Worm", in *New Statesman and Nation*, 5 Nov. 1955, pp. 587-8.

Isaacs, Neil D. 1968. "On the Possibilities of Writing Tolkien Criticism" in *Tolkien and the Critics: Essays on J.R.R. Tolkien's* The Lord of the Rings, eds. Neil D. Isaacs and Rose A. Zimbardo. Notre Dame: University of Notre Dame Press. pp. 1-11.

Isaacs, Neil D. 1981. "On the Need for Writing Tolkien Criticism", in *Tolkien: New Critical Perspectives*, eds. Neil D. Isaacs and Rose A. Zimbardo. Lexington: University Press of Kentucky, pp. 1-7.

Kay, Guy Gavriel. 1980. "Dug Out of the Dust of Middle-earth". [Source unknown, but published in Canada, 1980?], p. 16.

King, Francis. 1977. "Down among the Dwarves", in *Sunday Telegraph*, 18 Sept. 1977, p. 14.

Korn, Eric. 1977. "Doing Things by Elves", in *Times Literary Supplement*, 30 Sept. 1977, p. 1097.

Lewis, C.S. 1937. "A World for Children", in *Times Literary Supplement*, 2 Oct. 1937, p. 714.

Lewis, C.S. 1955. "The Dethronement of Power", in *Time and Tide*, 22 Oct. 1955, pp. 1373-4.

Masson, David I. 1955. Letter, in *Times Literary Supplement*, 9 Dec. 1955, p. 743.

Medcalf, Stephen. 1985. "Elven Evolutions", in *Times Literary Supplement*, 19 July 1985, p. 802.

Mitchison, Naomi. 1954. "One Ring to Bind Them", in *New Statesman and Nation*, 18 Sept. 1954, p. 331.

Parker, Douglass. 1956-7. "Hwaet We Holbytla . . .", in *Hudson Review* 9.4 (Winter 1956-7), pp. [598]-609.

Richardson, Maurice. 1954. "New Novels", in *New Statesman and Nation*, 18 Dec. 1954, pp. 835-6.

---

[9] My thanks to Åke Bertenstam, Jeffrey Drefke, Edwin Gilcher, Christina Scull, and Jessica Yates for supplying copies of some of the critical works discussed in this essay.

Shippey, T.A. 1982. *The Road to Middle-earth*. London: George Allen & Unwin.

Sibley, Brian. 1980. "History for Hobbits", in *Listener*, 2 Oct. 1980, pp. 443-4.

Somerville-Large, Gillian. 1985. Review of *The Lays of Beleriand*, in *Irish Times*, 28 Sept. 1985.

Tolkien, J.R.R. 1966. *The Fellowship of the Ring*, second edition. London: George Allen & Unwin.

Tolkien, J.R.R. 1981. *Letters of J.R.R. Tolkien*, ed. Humphrey Carpenter with the assistance of Christopher Tolkien. London: George Allen & Unwin.

Toynbee, Philip. 1961. "Dissension among the Judges", in *Observer*, 6 Aug. 1961.

Toynbee, Philip. 1978. "A Whimsical Trio", in *Observer*, 5 Nov. 1978, p. 31.

Watson, George. 1982. "The Roots of Romance", in *Times Literary Supplement*, 8 Oct. 1982, p. 1098.

Waugh, Auberon. 1992. "Some Useful Things to Do with Books", in *Literary Review*, Apr. 1992, p. 1.

Wilson, Edmund. 1956. "Oo, Those Awful Orcs", in *Nation*, 14 Apr. 1956, pp. 312-13.

Yates, Jessica. 1978. "Brummoot 1978", in *Amon Hen* (bulletin of The Tolkien Society) 32 (1978), pp. 11-14.

Tolkien the Anti-totalitarian

Jessica Yates

Abstract: A number of critics have looked for a political message in *The Lord of the Rings*, their dislike of the work, in some cases, apparently leading them to accuse Tolkien of holding extreme, usually right-wing, political views and making *The Lord of the Rings* a vehicle for them. These critics are particularly vehement about the danger of young people emerging from a reading of Tolkien's book with extreme right-wing views. I select some examples from my collection of political views, including the opinions of Robert Westall, E.P. Thompson, and Fred Inglis, together with a viewpoint from a member of the Communist Party.

Keywords: Communism, Fascism, Robert Giddings, Fred Inglis, intolerance, left-wing politics, literary criticism, racism, right-wing politics, E.P. Thompson, totalitarian states, war, Robert Westall

From the first publication of *The Lord of the Rings*, critics have not only judged it lacking in literary merit, but simplistic, even dangerous, in the political attitudes it is supposed to enshrine. I illustrate this aspect of Tolkien criticism with examples from 1955, 1973, 1980, 1981, and a debate about Tolkien and fascism which ran in several British Tolkien-related fanzines in the mid-80s.

There are two features of these attacks which I would emphasise: one, their superficial nature, which would often be refuted by a close study of the text, and by reading Tolkien's *Letters* (which were not, of course, available until late 1981); and two, the possibility by private correspondence or letters to an editor, of negotiating with these critics and modifying their attitudes, sometimes with a follow-up letter or article published in the same magazine.

As I may only present here a selection of critical arguments about Tolkien's politics, I have searched for rare material from newspapers, journals and fanzines, rather than give you extracts from material you are well-acquainted with, such as C.S. Lewis's reviews of *The Lord of the Rings* and Tom Shippey's detailed analysis in *The Road to Middle-earth*. So I begin with a very rare item indeed, discovered by me in the archives of Allen and Unwin, the transcript of the BBC Home Service review of *The Lord of the Rings* by Arthur Calder-Marshall in his *Talking of Books* programme, broadcast on 30th October 1955. This is an enthusiastic review by a writer who had a long literary career and died in 1992 aged 83 – it is a pity he did not give us some more permanent appreciation of Tolkien.

> . . . it is possible without falsification to interpret the allegory of *The Lord of the Rings*; its subject is exactly what one would expect a modern magical romance's subject to be, the nature of power. The One Ring is power. Power corrupts and absolute power corrupts absolutely. If you want to make a crude simplification: Sauron, the Lord of Darkness, is the Dictator and the Black Riders his secret police.
>
> But that would be an oversimplification. It is rather that in the land of Romance and Faerie, which lies in the magical Department of our mental State, there are enacted dramas which are similar to those of our daily lives in their emotional content . . .
>
> Each age has its contemporary myth, reflecting the dominant moods of the period; and *The Lord of the Rings* is as contemporary in its concern with the nature of power as *Animal Farm* or *Darkness at Noon*. It is a deliberate and successful attempt to use the fairy story as a literary form in order to say something about a contemporary problem without the complication of actual people, places and political systems. There is no attempt at any parallelism between the story and actual events. The parallelism is of a much subtler type; as when Frodo, for example, pursued by the Black Riders, is so frightened that to escape them, he puts on the Ring. But instead of becoming invisible, he becomes plainer to the Black Riders, the Ring having the same nature of evil as they have. I do not think Tolkien himself would object to my concluding that the parallel to this in the modern world is when one nation, convinced of the justice of its cause, employs a weapon of terror against its enemy, and in doing so becomes possessed by the very evil that it is fighting to destroy in the enemy.

A rare item of Tolkien criticism, and if you know Tom Shippey's book you'll recognise several of his points, made some twenty-five years earlier by the late Arthur Calder-Marshall.

My next example is an extremely hostile one. To commemorate Tolkien's death, several periodicals published tributes, among these being one in *The Listener*, the now-defunct magazine of the British Broadcasting Corporation. The academic J.W. Burrow's appreciation of *The Lord of the*

Rings (1973) was followed by an attack on the book by Tom Davis of Birmingham University (Davis, 1973a).

Regarding Burrow's exoneration of Tolkien from the need to portray complex characters in the manner of the modern novel, Davis writes:

> Literary critics don't demand that books written now should contain "inner conflicts and complex emotional interactions", only that they should not simplify dishonestly or be simple-minded, that they should say something of use to those who read them: us, now. It is not that Tolkien doesn't speak to the needs of a modern audience, or describe a modern world: he does (he couldn't do otherwise), but he pretends not to, and they are the wrong needs. For instance, Burrow notices that the book is about a confrontation between East and West, and that the "moral geography is decidedly European". To stop there is to compound the dishonesty or the simple-mindedness. In the East, says Tolkien, lives a race alchemically-created: androids. They are rather like ants. They have no souls. Oddly enough, they have lower-class urban (Cockney) accents. And this soulless urban proletarian collective Eastern society must be wiped out, without mercy to individuals or even recognition of them as individuals. As a statement about the modern world, this is, to put it nicely, simple-minded, and the needs it speaks to are not admirable . . .
>
> Good fairy-tales are about another world and this one: the interaction appeals to and encourages the child's maturity. Tolkien's novel is about arrested development. It appeals to the childish in adults. The hobbits are patronised as children, but allowed to wave "real" swords and do their share of slaughtering the orcs. These underdeveloped adults were among the heroes and models of the hippy movement, that impressive tribute to the concept of oral fixation. It is rare for literary criticism to have its judgements so massively validated.

When a critic of Tolkien adopts such an unpleasant, personal tone, it is difficult to pen an effective refutation which does not bring further attacks in its train. And so it happened. Three letters appeared disagreeing with Mr. Davis, including one by Burrow. One correspondent, Diana Reed, wrote that as the orcs had been corrupted beyond redemption, and were "a threat to other sentient life, why should killing them be considered morally wrong?" and that Davis had simply demonstrated his own "ignorance and intolerance" in his attack on *The Lord of the Rings*.

Yet another correspondent ridiculed Davis's use of "urban", "proletarian" and "collective" to describe the social structure in Mordor, where there were no towns or cities, no urban proletariat – instead orcs were soldiers, slaves or overseers, and far from being collective, it was a "class-conscious, super-feudal society" (Broomhead, 1973).

Tom Davis responded to his critics in pugnacious mood, determined to win the argument. He asserted that one kind of childishness he had in mind was "the feeling that the problems of the world can be solved by bombing one's enemies back into the Stone Age, (which is roughly what happens when the Ring is incinerated)". He insisted that Tolkien's portrait of Mordor was influenced by the Cold War attitude to Eastern Europe – moreover with

> interesting analogies with *1984*: hideous punishments (Shelob), a debased language and a central power that has his Eye on you. However, Orwell's depiction is painfully realisable, and he doesn't suggest that the solution lies in "Onward Christian Soldiers". But he was writing for adults . . . Those who think that my letter depicted the novel as an allegory, or who want me to explain why Tolkien could write as he did when C.S. Lewis didn't, have put themselves beyond the reach of reasonable controversy.

(Davis, 1973b).

A crushing conclusion indeed, which is, I believe, an unfair way of winning the argument.

We cannot be sure whether Tom Davis thinks that Stalin's Russia has been unfairly treated by cold warriors, but that is the impression I receive. He detests *The Lord of the Rings* because he thinks it might encourage the Cold War between the USA and USSR, or even World War III, but of course he completely misreads the book when he equates the destruction of the Ring with "bombing one's enemies back into the Stone Age". Having destroyed the Ring, the Western Allies may fight or make peace with the other races of Men in Middle-earth on an equal footing; and of course, Tolkien hated aerial bombing and denounced the atom bomb as soon as he heard of Hiroshima.

I need to make another point about George Orwell, apart from the insult that Orwell was writing for adults, which implies that Tolkien wasn't: Orwell was also writing about Eastern Europe, but Davis does not seem to mind *his* criticism of the Soviet Union in *Nineteen Eighty-Four*, which includes the pessimism of "a boot stamping on a human face – for ever" and concludes with Winston Smith's capitulation to Big Brother.

The Burrow-Davis controversy illustrates that there are some critics who are impervious to negotiation and possible compromise. I would like now to cite briefly a case where I felt confident enough to intervene, where I had a long letter published which disputed the critic's arguments, and eventually, I believe, won his respect. I am not going to quote extensively from his article or mine, because my letter was eventually expanded into an article for *Mallorn*, with his blessing.

In *Use of English* for Autumn 1980, Andrew Stibbs, a lecturer in education at Leeds University, published an article, "For Realism in Children's Fiction", in which he complained about a fashion which I too regretted – for using ghost stories as teaching material in secondary schools (which educate British children between the ages of 11 and 16). Stibbs advocated using children's fiction written in the realistic mode: novels like *Carrie's War* by Nina Bawden or Alan Garner's *Stone Book Quartet*. Stibbs then moved on to wonder if the popularity of children's fantasy was the result of the Tolkien cult, and chose for examination the chapter

"The Scouring of the Shire" which he found snobbish in its view of Sharkey's ruffians.

My response, published in *Use of English*, Summer 1981, followed up Stibbs's argument that books which teachers recommend should be books which improve their readers' personal development, with first a look at the healing qualities of fantasies by Ursula Le Guin and Diana Wynne Jones, and then a more detailed analysis of how *The Lord of the Rings* might be used to alert young readers to political and international evils such as the arms race or the police state. Finally, a pleasant letter from Stibbs in the Autumn 1981 issue accepted some of my points, and we had an occasional correspondence until I published my article "In Defence of Fantasy" in *Mallorn* 21 (Yates, 1984), when he gave us his blessing for quotations, thanked us for his complimentary copy, and did not even claim a right of reply.

Now I move to Robert Westall, whose criticism I shall examine in more detail. In January 1981 *Signal*, a thrice-yearly British children's literature magazine, published "The Hunt for Evil" by Robert Westall, who was then, and has remained, one of our leading novelists for older children and teenagers. Sadly, the news of his death reached me the very day that I typed these words for the editors of the *Proceedings*.

Westall's theme was: stereotyping in children's fiction, television and cinema, and the danger of influencing young people to stereotype other people whom they might see as enemies, as irredeemably evil. Examples from popular literature were Dracula – and the shark in *Jaws*. Examples from real life were Robert Mugabe and his guerilla soldiers in Zimbabwe; and concentration camp guards who loved their children. Based on a talk given to teachers, the article is vigorous, not intended to be scholarly. Westall criticises the "hunt for evil" theme in some of his own novels, asking, "How much am *I* doing to blind children to the fact that there is evil in the best of us, and good in the worst?", and then turns to *The Lord of the Rings* (mistakenly calling it a children's book), which, he says, is one of his favourite books, especially soothing when he falls ill.

> . . . when I look at it from the hunt-for-evil angle, it becomes the worst book of all. No wonder it is so soothing. Good and evil are separated like oil and water; utterly polarized. From the Dark Lord of Mordor to his humblest orc, the enemy are totally evil. The Dark Lord's only emotion, apart from rootless, reasonless hate, is fear for his own safety. He is much worse than Hitler . . .
>
> The orcs do not weep or bleed; Tolkien does not even allow them the virtue of courage . . . In all of *The Lord of the Rings* you will not find one halfway praiseworthy deed by the enemy. The orcs are simply hero-bait, to be slaughtered ad infinitum, piled in heaps and burnt. They are given a lower status than rats, although they are human in shape, think and talk like humans . . . A child brought up on a non-stop diet of Tolkien would be very inclined to see Robert Mugabe as the Dark Lord and the boys-in-the-bush as orcs.
>
> Nor do we find any evil within the goodies. If they do stray off the straight and narrow, it is not their own fault; they are under the spell of the Dark Lord's Ring. Even so, even when repentant, death is their only possible end. Either a heroic end, like Boromir, shot full of orc arrows, or a dreadful end like Denethor in the flames. Nobody is allowed to live on, a sadder and wiser being; a subtler and more enlightened mixture of good and evil. Tolkien's world is a world without mercy: Be ye perfect or go into the flames. The only compassion I can find in the whole book is in the treatment of the baddy Gollum. Only in Gollum do we see good and evil striving inside the same soul. But the moment passes, and Gollum goes down into the eternal flames as well . . .
>
> To sum up I think that, on the whole, *The Machine-Gunners* [Westall's first published novel, Macmillan, 1975] was a helpful, Jungian kind of book. And I think *The Devil on the Road* [Macmillan, 1978] was a destructive, intolerant, racialist kind of book. Like *The Lord of the Rings*. In the 1930s we had many such books, in which the villains were always inscrutable Chinese or blacks or evil dagoes. That is no longer possible. But it is still possible if you change "dago" into "orc". The message is the same: hate the alien; destroy the deviant. That is the evil message of the Hunt for Evil.

Westall went on to vent his anger at so much T.V. science fiction which seemed, according to him, to parade a series of "execrable monsters . . . always dealt with by total annihilation". As I was to point out to him later, he can't have watched very much *Star Trek*, which promoted a much more humane attitude towards alien life forms.

When I read Westall's article I wanted to defend Tolkien in *Signal* magazine, but I suspected that the editor would not wish to carry an article devoted to a book which had not been written for children. I jotted down my first impressions and sent them off to the editor anyway, who forwarded them to Westall. Soon I received four handwritten pages from Westall defending his views together with some personal information about his life, for example, that he was not a pacifist and did his National Service in 1954. Other information, and my advance reading of Tolkien's *Letters* in summer 1981, gave me cause for hope that I could modify his views by reference to the *Letters* – given time – but this would be a matter for private correspondence.

Meanwhile another children's book critic, Neil Philip, had published a letter in defence of Tolkien in *Signal*, May 1981, and Westall had right of reply in the same issue, whereupon the correspondence was closed, leaving me to respond privately to Westall about his letter as well as his article. How can I boil down about forty pages of correspondence into a few pages of this conference paper?

I agreed with Westall about the dangers of stereotyped literature when read by immature readers, but I argued that *The Lord of the Rings* was in a different class from Sven Hassel's war novels – though I would be concerned if young readers *were* misreading Tolkien. I argued that we were not meant to identify any one race in the real world with the orc.

Orcish tendencies are twofold: to vandalism and crude violence, and to blind fanaticism. Orcs follow their leaders because they have been brainwashed. Tolkien symbolises in the orc all mindless crowds who chant slogans and are ready to kill other people because their leader tells them so. When Westall wrote that he disliked the message "hate the alien; destroy the deviant" he was close to Tolkien; but it is the orcs, not the Westerners, who are filled with unreasoning hate for others who are different. In distancing the orcs from his other created races, Tolkien indicated that they symbolised human tendencies – and surely it cannot be denied that what is recorded of humans is far worse than what Tolkien describes of orcish behaviour. Several years ago I read Martin Gilbert's massive history, *The Holocaust* (Gilbert, 1986), and in great sorrow established for myself the truth of that assertion.

I sent Westall a copy of Nan Scott's fine article "War and Pacifism in *The Lord of the Rings*" (Scott, 1972), and urged him to read Tolkien's *Letters* (Tolkien, 1981) to discover that Tolkien and he felt exactly the same way about aerial bombing, Dresden and Hiroshima. I disagreed with Westall about Gollum's fate: Tolkien had declined to say whether Gollum had been consigned to eternal damnation.

I then turned to Neil Philip's letter in defence of Tolkien, and Westall's reply, which I found far easier to refute, it having probably been written at rather short notice. Neil Philip started a new hare, which ran for several years, by denying that *The Lord of the Rings* was a "Nazi tract", a fascist book. In fact Westall had not said that the book was "Fascist" – "racialist", yes, but he had used the term "fascist" to describe another popular author, in his words, "Dennis Wheatley . . . *the* hunt-for-evil man, a leading fascist of the 1950s, with his clichéd horrors of sinister 'negroes' and the international Communist plot." Even here, Westall was using the term very loosely: Dennis Wheatley supported the Allies as a patriotic Briton, writing thrillers throughout and after World War II which denounced German aggression.

But returning to Neil Philip, I quote from his defence of Tolkien:

> The complex triangle defined by Frodo, Sam and Gollum gives the lie to any view of the book as a Nazi tract . . . while *The Lord of the Rings* is in no sense a coherent religious allegory, Frodo and Aragorn are both to a certain extent types of Christ . . . They are not S.S. officers . . . what is the Ring? Power rooted in cruelty and tyranny, not love and service; power taken but not earned; power without responsibility; fascism . . . does Robert Westall see no significance in Frodo's rejection of violence in "The Scouring of the Shire"? . . . Tolkien's achievement has been to sensitize a generation to the nature and appeal of heroic literature, not to feed a new fascism . . .

(and so on)

I will now quote from Westall's riposte, inserting my own comments as I go, the gist of which I sent to Westall in a long letter of June 1981.

> I think Neil Philip hits the nail on the head when he writes "Middle Earth . . . is an ordered, 'whole' universe, and ours is a fragmented, morally unsettled age which desires above all things order and moral clarity".
>
> That's the one drug we must not offer people . . . It wasn't adulterers, drunkards or speculators who burnt 20,000 witches in Toulouse in the 16th century, or promoted the Albigensian crusade. It was the Holy Catholic Church in search of order and moral clarity. Hitler, too, promised a "New Order" and *great* moral clarity.
>
> Was there ever a time of "order" that did not thrive on the mute helpless suffering of vast numbers of the submerged masses?

Westall went on to cite the dwarves in C.S. Lewis's *The Last Battle*, who refused to join "our heroes" and preferred to mind their own business. "Needless to say Lewis swiftly condemns the dwarves. We must all take part in his Last Battle – which is the same as the War of the Ring – both are 'holy' wars, and a 'holy' war is the worst war of all."

I replied that I objected to the constant references to modern events which either Tolkien wasn't aware of, or, if he was, he probably held the same opinions as Westall about them anyway. I'll allow that Tolkien doesn't say anything about witch-hunts, but if anyone exemplifies the attitudes of witch-hunters, it is the orc. It was Saruman who spoke of a new Order when he tempted Gandalf, Saruman who stands for the politician who leads people into revolution, promising a better future.

Westall's phrase about the suffering of the masses is actually a very good description of Sauron's kingdom of slaves, or what the Shire would have been under Saruman – and Tolkien, of course, attacks both. Westall expresses sympathy for minority groups such as African peasant women – but just so do the hobbits represent ordinary, powerless people. The unemployed and the under-privileged are both victims of the profit motive – the spirit of Saruman. Frodo went to Mordor for the sake of the Shirefolk, not to seek personal glory.

I disagree with Westall's concept of "holy" war. Westall had agreed with me that Britain's role in World War II was necessary. Now, in Middle-earth, Sauron and Saruman are the aggressors, so war against them must be a "just", not a "holy" war. In each conflict described in the book, the good characters are usually, if not always, attacked, and always outnumbered.

As for Narnia, surely the Calormenes have invaded it, and have been told that they are fighting for their god Tash against the evil lion Aslan: thus the "holy" war is waged by the Calormenes against the Narnians. Moreover, as we read in Tolkien's *Letters* (Tolkien, 1981, no. 183, p. 243) "Sauron desired to be a God-King and was held to be this by his servants", so the War of the Ring could also be seen as a "holy" war waged by Sauron and his orcs against the West. Thus Lewis and Tolkien would have agreed with Westall about the evils of "holy" war!

Returning to Westall's critique: "And if Tolkien's achievement has been to 'sensitize a generation to the nature and appeal of heroic literature' isn't it time we asked exactly what 'heroic' literature consists of? Do the heroes of heroic literature cure people, teach people, wash people's feet, ask very awkward questions of entrenched hereditary rulers . . . or do they simply have a divine right to ordain things 'evil' without consultation or negotiation, kill people who get in the way, and summon up innocent bystanders to die painfully and unquestioningly?"

These points are easy to refute. There are two contrasted heroes in *The Fellowship of the Ring* – boastful Boromir, conscious of his rank as heir to Gondor, and discreet Aragorn. Look how Aragorn does not "pull rank" during the journey South: although he automatically assumes the leadership after Gandalf falls in Moria, he never orders Boromir about, and always behaves courteously to him. Aragorn *does* cure people: it is a sign of his kingship. He also *teaches* the hobbits some of the history of Middle-earth. He would also have posed a very awkward question to an entrenched hereditary ruler (Denethor) if that ruler had still been alive when Aragorn entered Minas Tirith. And Frodo also overthrows an entrenched ruler, Sauron.

As for killing people who get in the way, and summoning up innocent bystanders to die, this is a very good description of Sauron and Saruman. Finally, if we look at scenes where Aragorn takes a new step forward, we note that he always asks his companions if they want to come with him, for example on the Paths of the Dead and the last march to Mordor.

Faramir is a different kind of hero. He accepts war as his duty and is skilled in fighting and strategy, but would not choose it as his life's work.

Westall continued:

> of course, Frodo and Aragorn are not S.S. officers. They are British officers, pre-war vintage. They would never put Jews in camps (though they might exclude them from golf clubs). Like good British officers, they have a great concern for the welfare of ponies. However, they have no more concern for the flesh and blood of orcs than British officers had for the civilian populations of Hamburg and Dresden. As for their attitude towards coloured or eastern races, is it any coincidence that the only coloured or eastern people in *The Lord of the Rings* are "the cruel dark men of Harad" who play an ignominious part on the side of the *Dark* Lord?

First to the point about excluding Jews from golf clubs – an analogy which is fairly irrelevant to Tolkien's own life. We can see from Tolkien's *Letters* that he was disgusted with Nazi persecution of the Jews, and on page 229 he says that he had modelled his dwarves on Jewish culture. In Book Two of *The Fellowship of the Ring* and onwards, in the character of Gimli we see a figure who is constantly subject to snide remarks and discrimination from the people the Companions meet – from the Elves, from Treebeard, and from the Riders of Rohan who begrudge him a horse. When the Companions enter Lórien the Elves want to blindfold Gimli, who protests. Aragorn solves the impasse by agreeing to be blindfolded as well, with all the Company. How could such a man be the type to ban Jews from a golf club!

Especially considering Aragorn's position: betrothed to Arwen Half-elven, granddaughter of the rulers of Lórien, he yet risks Galadriel's displeasure by bringing a dwarf, their hereditary enemy, into their secret kingdom.

Tolkien's opinions on race relations are best seen through his treatment of the conflict between dwarves and elves. In *The Silmarillion*, as in the First World War, we see a futile struggle which should never have happened. As for the bombing of Hamburg and Dresden, as I said earlier, Tolkien's views are clear from his *Letters*, as they are on Hiroshima (Tolkien, 1981, no. 102, p. 116) and British nuclear tests (Tolkien, 1981, no. 135, p. 165).

The coloured and eastern races are recruited to Sauron's side because they are geographically close to Mordor, not because Tolkien was colour-prejudiced in the traditional sense. They are offered peace after Barad-dûr falls. Sam pities the dead Southron.

Westall continued: ". . . I cannot rejoice in the death even of orcs. The only death I could ever rejoice in is 'That a man lay down his life for his friends'."

Apart from the deaths of orcs – which should really be laid at Sauron's door (or Morgoth's) because it was he who corrupted their ancestors, and we may mourn their wasted potential if we like – there are in fact many deaths and near-deaths where leading characters risk their lives for their friends: Boromir, Théoden, Dáin and Háma die; near-deaths include Gandalf, Éowyn, Faramir, Pippin, Merry, Frodo and Sam. Surely this pattern of sacrifice must inspire some positive ethical response in young people, whose moral education concerns Westall so strongly.

Westall concluded:

> And I still love the book, because I am a *very* corrupt person. As Professor Berne says . . . "Every human being seems to have a little fascist in his head . . . in civilised people it is usually deeply buried beneath a platform of social ideals and training, but with proper permissions and directives, as history has shown again and again, it can be liberated into full bloom . . . a fascist may be defined as a person who has no respect for living tissue and regards it as his prey . . ."
>
> I am increasingly afraid that *Lord of the Rings* along with *Starsky and Hutch* is issuing our children with just such permissions and directives.

That was Westall's last word on Tolkien (apart from comments he has since made in the occasional interview), and the last word in *Signal*, for I never wrote a defence of Tolkien in those pages. Westall duly received a blockbusting letter from me, and responded most generously, conceding some points and holding to others. He wrote to me:

> I do admit being unfair to Tolkien . . . Many of the sins I accused him of were not his own personal sins, but sins of his culture, sins of his times . . . I did under-estimate the peace-loving propensities of the Hobbits . . . I always looked on the Hobbits as being the "light relief" rather than the true carriers of the message . . . I didn't take into account the fact that the

West was always on the defensive . . . However, where I am not prepared to give way is on the nature of the Orcs . . . I do free Tolkien from the charge of preaching "holy war".

So we parted friends, and kept up an occasional correspondence. In 1985 I sent him the articles in Tolkien Society fanzines inspired by his pieces in *Signal*, and he replied to say that he had read Tolkien's *Letters* (Tolkien, 1981) and had changed some of his opinions about him, especially finding him not guilty of fascism.

However, the association with fascism has persisted, not only via Westall, but other critics who have independently attached the label to Tolkien. I turn now to E.P. Thompson's misgivings about Tolkien, another mini-controversy of 1981. The critics I have already cited – Tom Davis, Stibbs, Westall – have all had at the back of their minds some notion that for young people to read the "wrong" books at a susceptible age is somehow a threat to world peace. Young people might grow up with racialist attitudes; it might be easier to persuade them of the inevitability of war, and even that nuclear war might be a good thing, according to the old slogan "Better dead than red". These ideas came into focus when the historian and peace campaigner E.P. Thompson accused some aggressive American defence analysts of having been influenced by *The Lord of the Rings* towards more hostile attitudes to the USSR. Thompson had once been a communist, had left the British Communist Party when the Russians invaded Hungary in 1956, and since then had been a member of the British Labour Party.

In 1980 there was a tremendous upsurge of concern over the escalation of Anglo-American nuclear weapons, after Margaret Thatcher led the Conservative Party to election victory in 1979 and became Prime Minister. She made public the modernisation of Polaris missiles which had been approved by the Labour Government a few years before, and announced that Britain was to buy Cruise missiles and Trident submarines from the United States. The debate about civil defence in the face of nuclear weapons was revived, and Thompson wrote a best-selling pamphlet *Protest and Survive* (Thompson, 1980), in its title a parody of the government's official booklet *Protect and Survive*.

With his pamphlet Thompson succeeded in making thousands of young people very worried about the dangers of World War III. He also tended towards presenting the USA and USSR as parallel threats to humanity, in contrast with an anti-American element in the British Campaign for Nuclear Disarmament which had tended to belittle the "Soviet threat" and as a result discredited the British peace movement, which was seen as the dupe, or even the tool, of Moscow in its secret plan to take over Western Europe – one way or another.

I became a great admirer of E.P. Thompson after reading this pamphlet and other writings, and was taken aback to read in the *New Statesman* (Bird, 1981) that he had revised his pamphlet for American readers and published it as a special issue of *Nation* magazine under the new title *America's Europe: A Hobbit Among Gandalfs* (Thompson 1981a). Throughout his introductory paragraphs he interspersed references to *The Lord of the Rings* to suggest that the warmongering postures he detected among American defence analysts and Ronald Reagan's advisers derived from their having read Tolkien in youth, with the result that they saw the USSR as Mordor.

Taking issue with the Winter 1981 issue of *Daedalus*, the journal of the American Academy of Arts and Sciences, which was mainly devoted to articles on "U.S. Defense Policy in the 1980s" written from a hawkish point of view, Thompson described this special issue as "chapters of bad advice from Satan's Kingdom", and offered this opinion of the authors:

> The expertise of the authors – for they are, all of them, undoubtedly very great experts – is contained within an infantile political view of the world, derived, I suppose, from too much early reading of Tolkien's *Lord of the Rings*. The evil kingdom of Mordor lies there, and there it ever will lie, while on our side lies the nice republic of Eriador, inhabited by confused liberal hobbits who are rescued from time to time by the genial white wizardry of Gandalf-figures such as Henry Kissinger, Zbigniew Brzezinski or, maybe, Richard Allen.
>
> That is an overstatement, for in fact the contributors to this issue say little about politics at all. A manichaean, black-white, world view is assumed, and the rest is politically null. That is, perhaps, what a top-flight "defense expert" is: a person with a hole in the head where politics and morality ought to be, who can then get along all the better with moving around the acronyms, in a vocabulary of throw-weight, delivery-systems, megatons and the extrapolation of ever-more-tenuous worst-case scenarios.

It is ironic that although Thompson is suspicious of Tolkien's influence on American military policy, in his own attack on this policy, he uses Tolkienian metaphor. Having described the volume of *Daedalus* as "chapters of bad advice from Satan's Kingdom", he entitled the third part of his own essay "Overthrowing the Satanic Kingdom" (by which he means not only U.S. militarism but also Russian super-power domination), and in his final exhortation he seems to have adopted a Tolkienian world-view:

> I doubt whether we can succeed: nothing less than a worldwide spiritual revulsion against the Satanic Kingdom would give us any chance of bringing the military riders down.

Doesn't that summon up the image of hobbits being menaced by Black Riders?

Thompson's suggestion that American defence analysts had been over-influenced by Tolkien, having been reported in the *New Statesman*, was requoted with glee by Robert Giddings when reviewing the BBC Radio 4 dramatisation of *The Lord of the Rings* in *Tribune* (Giddings, 1981). This view of Tolkien as a cold warrior was on the way to becoming commonplace in British political life, and since Tolkien would have been horrified at such a misuse of his work, to fuel the cold war instead of negotiating peace, I felt that there was something I could do.

I wrote letters to the *New Statesman* and *The Nation* in refutation of Thompson's suggestions, quoting Tolkien's revised Foreword to the second edition, and offering a new interpretation of *The Lord of the Rings* from the viewpoint of a novice peace campaigner – myself – who had found Tolkien an inspiration, not a handicap. My letters were not printed and so, a couple of months later, having received a copy of *The Nation* from an American Tolkien fan, I sent Thompson a two-page letter arguing for a different interpretation of Tolkien's book. By this time I had read the *Letters* (Tolkien, 1981) in proof, so could let him know Tolkien's views on aerial bombing and Hiroshima. I suggested that as the American Tolkien cult was active in the latter '60s, the mass of Tolkien fans would (in 1981) be in their early 30s, but that President Reagan's military advisers would belong to an earlier generation, that had had its attitudes to the Soviet Union and Communism moulded by the experience of the Korean War, not by reading Tolkien.

I reminded him of how the text of *The Lord of the Rings* contained many warnings about how, if the leaders of the West had used the Ring, they would conquer Sauron, but replace him with another evil. Emphasis was placed on the rightness of fighting one's enemy face to face. It was always Sauron or Saruman who initiated superior technology in the battle scenes.

I quoted Tolkien's words from the revised Foreword, a comment on the real-life cold war: "In that conflict both sides would have held hobbits in hatred and contempt: they would not long have survived even as slaves." I added to that, Frodo's question to Faramir, which might suggest nuclear holocaust to the modern reader:

> Shall there be two cities of Minas Morgul, grinning at each other across a dead land filled with rottenness?
> (Tolkien, 1967b, p. 302)

In another newspaper article Thompson had recently identified the enemy of peace as "the military and political establishments of both blocs", and so I offered him an alternative application of *The Lord of the Rings* for 1981:

Hobbits –	ordinary people everywhere, in the East, West or Third World;
Gandalfs –	leaders of the peace movement, for example, Thompson himself;
Saurons –	World leaders, sabre-rattlers – Mrs. Thatcher, President Reagan, President Brezhnev, plus their military advisers;
Saruman –	Economic imperialism: the power of the USA, USSR, nuclear power;
Orcs –	anyone who takes advantage of their uniform to inflict physical pain on another, could be a soldier, policeman, thug, neo-Nazi, doctor in psychiatric hospital, guard in labour camp;
The Ring –	Weapons of mass destruction and indoctrination; ideologies based on the ideas prominent in Orwell's *Nineteen Eighty-Four* that your enemy is totally evil – as Thompson wrote in *Protest and Survive* and *The Nation*:

> We *think* others to death as we define them as the Other: the enemy: Asians: Marxists: non-people. The deformed human mind is the ultimate doomsday weapon – it is out of the human mind that the missiles and the neutron warheads come.

I didn't expect a reply – but I did receive a postcard reading "Thank you for your Tolkien letter which I will inwardly digest – Edward Thompson". Since then I believe that he has only once used Tolkien to provide a metaphor for military aggression, and otherwise turned to cinematic sources for his allusions, such as *Star Wars* and *Rambo*.

However, the quotation printed in the *New Statesman* survived to be utilised among the various political critiques of Tolkien collected by Robert Giddings in his commissioned anthology *This Far Land* (Giddings, 1983). Giddings recalled Thompson in his Introduction, which attempted to set Tolkien in the context of spy and conspiracy literature and films.

I will return to *This Far Land* after looking at an earlier critique of Tolkien by one of Giddings's contributors, Fred Inglis, at that time an academic at Bristol University, and now at Warwick University. He first came to my attention with his critical study of children's literature, *The Promise of Happiness* (Inglis, 1981). Inglis is not primarily a children's book critic, and brings to that discipline the perspective of a socialist intellectual, an educationalist and critic of adult literature, and a parent concerned about transmitting his cultural heritage and guiding his children safely to responsible adulthood. "Novels for children" he writes, "are adult messages, bidding the children farewell into the future" (Inglis, 1981, pp. 44-5), and again, "If it is not a duty, it is surely a necessary virtue in children's novelists to offer their readers confidence and hope in the future" (Inglis, 1981, p. 297).

Inglis believes that children who have read the best books grow up to be better people, and like Westall he is concerned about popular fiction in comics, television and the cinema. "Only a monster," he writes, "would not want to give a child books she will delight in, which will teach her to be good" (Inglis, 1981, p. 4). For him, the best books are *The Wind in the Willows*, *The Secret Garden*, the *Alice* books, *The Railway Children*, and books by Arthur Ransome, Rosemary Sutcliff and William Mayne – he also has good words for *The Hobbit* and *A Wizard of Earthsea*.

But when he turns to *The Lord of the Rings* it is in chapter 8, "Cult and culture", a chapter comprising a study of Enid Blyton, Tolkien and *Watership Down*. I want to look at three aspects of Inglis's attack on *The Lord of the Rings*: his inconsistency as I see it; his abuse of what he knows of Tolkien's biography; and his association of Tolkien's epic with fascism.

Recalling his own youth as a reader in the 1950s, Inglis speaks warmly of Buchan, Sapper, Kipling and Haggard, though admitting in the first two cases their "snobbery . . . incipient Fascism, their arrogance and brutality" (Inglis, 1981, p. 52). He feels he was not tainted by their bad qualities, but inspired by their appeal to patriotism which "remains a strong potential for good" (Inglis, 1981, p. 58). Elsewhere he laments the way that the modern novel has lost its public dimension, whereas children's novelists still accept the duty "to show the way the world goes, and how [children] should act in it" (Inglia, 1981, p. 297). And apropos of great fiction, with the examples of *Watership Down*, *Treasure Island*, *The Jungle Book*, *Right Ho, Jeeves*, and "the best *Dr. Who* stories", he writes that their relation to our world is that of "metaphor to reality . . . they permit us to carry their scheme of interpretation back to the real world and to use it to see that world as potentially different" (Inglis, 1981, p. 155).

Had *The Lord of the Rings* also formed part of Inglis's beloved reading as an adolescent (he went to boarding-school in 1950, when he would have been aged 13, so his school library is unlikely to have acquired the three-volume set, published between 1954 and 1955, before he left school aged 18 or 19) – had he read it, as well as his beloved Kipling and Buchan, I think he would have been more enthusiastic about it, and fitted it into his approved reading-list of books which appeal to patriotism, courage and the desire for heroism, and which relate to our world as "metaphor to reality". Instead of which, he praises a sportsman in a boys' comic for his "chivalrous and knightly" qualities (Inglis, 1981, p. 49), but criticises Tolkien for his "literary, bookish and stilted" diction (Inglis, 1981, p. 193). He allows Tolkien "insistent heroic uplift" and "knightly high-mindedness", but balances this with "the vulgar simplicity of his ethics" and "a thinness of moral and physical substance, a lack of experienced content, which complement much of the insubstantiality of modern life" (Inglis, 1981, pp. 192-3).

Now for Inglis's ridicule of Tolkien's fans and home life:

> [Tolkien's] cult status is diminishing now (in 1980) but until very recently was signalled not only by the apparatus of quasi-marketing which followed his books in the form of calendars, lapel-buttons, posters, records . . . even dictionaries, but also by Middle-Earth societies on a hundred Midwest campuses and by bony, bearded thirty-five-year-olds careening along on Esalen and Meditation, and calling themselves Gandalf.
> (Inglis, 1981, pp. 191-2)

And of Tolkien himself:

> Tolkien, as his biographer tells us Auden said, lived in a "ghastly house". The Branksome Chine suburban lived in a house with switch-on logs and fubsy fittings. While you can hardly judge a man by pelmets and lampshades alone . . .
> (Inglis, 1981, p. 192)

Would it have been any use to point out that the house furnishings were conventional middle-class of the period, chosen by Tolkien's wife, and that Tolkien didn't move to Branksome Chine until 1968, not only because relentless fans drove him away from Oxford, but also because his concern for his wife's health and happiness prompted the move to a bungalow in Bournemouth? Auden visited Tolkien's house in Headington, Oxford, not Bournemouth: Inglis has confused the two.

I decided not to respond to Inglis, as the reviewers dealt with him quite satisfactorily, and any letter from a Tolkien fan might have afforded further ammunition for future attacks. In particular I was pleased to see his reference to Fascism taken up by a reviewer. Here is Inglis:

> for once it makes sense to use that much-abused adjective, and call Tolkien a Fascist. Can the word be used, just momentarily, in a quite non-hostile sense? Fascism . . . speaks up for "the individual against the machine", and . . . his tribal structures . . . his yeoman hero and freeman servant, his rituals and ceremonies and fealties, all belong to the hornbooks of a non-historical, romantic Fascism . . . the hills of Mordor and Mount Doom look very like the headquarters of the dirty, rough-spoken, brutal proletariat, just as Gandalf whisked away from one corner of the battle by the great eagle, Gwaihir the Windlord, reminds us irresistibly of a US marine general in his Cobra helicopter. Sometimes the rotund prose and heady chivalry look as though they are called to put down modern Socialism rather than the Last Enemy.
>
> *The Lord of the Rings* is a heady book . . . The child who reads it will be puzzled and stirred, and that is right. The adult who turns it into cult has shut himself in a rather grander version of Mistletoe Farm, and is trapped accordingly. Tolkien offers no key to the way out.
> (Inglis, 1981, p. 197)

(N.B. The allusion to Mistletoe Farm is a reference to Enid Blyton, the most popular and prolific children's author of the twentieth century, whose qualities and defects Inglis (pretty accurately, in my opinion) discusses just before turning to Tolkien.)

The critic Claude Rawson denied Inglis the possibility of using the term "Fascism" in a complimentary sense, though without, sadly, defending Tolkien against more of Inglis's charges. He spoke of Fascism in general, noting that the reason why the individual is held to be superior to the machine is because the well-tuned machine extended "man's speed and force and power to destroy". I would also like to emphasise Claude Rawson's warning about the misuse of the term "Fascism": "It's a foolish and imprecise term outside its precise political sense" (Rawson, 1981, p. 838)

Despite his pleasure in scoring cheap points, Inglis is still an honourable critic, and in his second critique of Tolkien, in *This Far Land*, he footnoted an acknowledgement to Rawson for setting him right about Fascism, and concluded his article with "Tolkien is no Fascist, but his great myth may be said, as Wagner's was, to prefigure the genuine ideals and nobilities of which Fascism is the dark negation" (Giddings, 1983, p. 40).

I shall not deal with *This Far Land* in detail, as I assume most serious students of Tolkien will have a copy; I shall make a few observations and pass on. Fred Inglis yet again plays the game of describing the typical Tolkien fan: this time it is an ex-teacher setting up in England's West Country to sell water-colour paintings while his wife serves cream teas to tourists! But Tolkien fans may also be cold warriors: the peace movement headed by E.P. Thompson was underway, and several contributors introduced the threat of nuclear war into their critiques of Tolkien, including Giddings, who quoted Thompson's speculations in *The Nation* two years earlier.

Here is Kenneth McLeish in *This Far Land*:

> ... carrying a Ring to dump into a volcano against all odds ... is a very poor allegory for how we should run our century ... it was precisely this Edwardianly cosy view of human affairs in real life that cost Britain its Empire, cost Europe millions upon millions of its young men, and, unless we abandon it right now, will quite possibly cost us this planet and everything on it.
> (Giddings, 1983, p. 133)

> ... we live in a nasty, dangerous and brutal world, and dressing up in elven-cloaks, baking lembas and writing poems in Entish, though a commendable and delightful game, is a way of avoiding, not finding, the truth of life.
> (Giddings, 1983, p. 134)

Other contributors, however, appear themselves to be avoiding "the truth of life", by the way they belittle military aggression such as Hitler's or Stalin's. McLeish accuses Tolkien of ignoring "Dachau, Hiroshima and the closing of the Iron Curtain" (Giddings, 1983, p. 133), but still holds, in his allusion to nuclear war, that that is the only war the world has to fear. He and the other contributors do not seem to believe in war caused by a warlord's evil aggression, or communal violence (as in the Partition of India) caused not, I believe, by psychopaths, but tragically from fear that the other side, the ethnic aliens, must be removed from the territory altogether, or they would threaten one's own tribe out of revenge for previous violence.

So Derek Robinson writes, "It is assumed that the Enemy has no plan or purpose except enslavement, exploitation and a permanent diet of woe" (Giddings, 1983, p. 124). Would it not be better if he asked himself why the Chinese are oppressing the Tibetans, and why the atrocities in Cambodia and East Timor took place: then he would realise that Tolkien only hints at the reality of man's inhumanity to man (and woman and child). I have only found one allusion to orcs wreaking atrocities on civilians: Théoden to Saruman: "... what will you say of your torches in Westfold and the children that lie dead there?" (Tolkien, 1967b, p. 185).

Leaving now *This Far Land*, I have had the situation in the former Yugoslavia much in mind while preparing my talk and then in the months following the Conference. It is ironic that some liberal voices have found it necessary to justify their denunciation of the Serbs by calling them "fascist" and "racist" (Letters to *The Guardian*, 5th and 13th August 1992): we do not need these labels to condemn the evils we have heard about, provided that the reports are, sadly, true.

The President of Serbia rose to power through the Communist Party, so technically should not be labelled as a fascist; this goes to show that a leader doesn't have to be a card-carrying fascist to carry out territorial expansion and racial persecution, though some political activists on the Left would hold that racism and genocide are entirely the product of right-wing political regimes.

As I type this, more examples arrive. *The Sunday Times*, a newspaper on the political Right in Britain, attacks the British government for its inaction over Bosnia, using terms to shame the Left for its past silences over evils committed by communist regimes: "a new fascist regime is on the march ... genocidal onslaughts ... stop the holocaust now". In other words, it doesn't matter about the political affiliation of the murderers: it is what they do which defines them, not their Party cards.

Martin Jacques, the former editor of *Marxism Today*, writes about the Balkan tragedy in the same issue of *The Sunday Times*. This left-wing intellectual has come to terms with the fact that genocidal atrocities can be committed by the heirs of a communist regime: "Milosevic ... has engaged in the most horrific acts of racist slaughter Europe has seen since Nazi Germany ... redolent of the experience of fascism in the 1930s ... Communism has been replaced by nationalism ... the Muslims are being threatened with genocide by the Serbs" (Jacques, 1993).

These contemporary events and comments illuminate, though in the most tragic context, the debate about Tolkien and fascism which took place in several Tolkien-related fanzines in the early 1980s, a debate begun by Iwan Rhys Morus of the Cambridge University Tolkien Society, who had read Westall's article in *Signal* and wanted to refute it from his own political perspective, one of being a Marxist himself, and a member of the Young Communist League.

In *Anor* 3, published in 1983, Morus's article "Tolkien the Fascist?" was published. First of all he told us that certain "liberal" critics had accused Tolkien "of being a Fascist and of subjecting young people to right-wing propaganda in his works." Morus then went on to refute a number of Westall's accusations, such as that characters in Tolkien's works are either good or evil with nothing in between. Then, looking particularly at the chapter "The Scouring of the Shire", Morus proved to his own satisfaction that since Tolkien presented hobbit society as an "ideal society; a rural community based on a great deal of mutual co-operation and very little governmental restriction", this shows both that Tolkien was no fascist, and also

> much nearer to Marxist Communism than he knew. Not of course that Tolkien was a Marxist: the few times he mentions such things in his letters make it obvious that Tolkien knew very little of Communism, and that what he knew was mostly mistaken ... The nature of the takeover of the Shire ... is unmistakably Fascist.
> (Morus, 1983)

In *Anor* 4 (late 1983) Brin Dunsire commented on Morus's article. Tolkien, he believed, was more of a conservative, and disliked forms of state control. He questioned whether Westall had actually used the term "Fascist", and whether anyone else had. He pointed out that Westall *did* use the term "racialist", and justified this use because commentators on children's books genuinely fear that the misreading of Tolkien by juveniles may lead them into stereotyping, and the equating of Russians and Black people with Orcs.

Dunsire further discussed whether the characters in *The Lord of the Rings* are "black or white" (metaphorically speaking) and questioned Morus's assertions about Tolkien's affinity to Marxism. He agreed that the Sharkey regime resembled Fascism, and was "undeniably evil".

In *Anor* 5 Morus supplied three paragraphs to close the correspondence. He returned to Westall's article, suggesting that Westall believed that the seeming prejudice and stereotyping he perceived in Tolkien were not the result of misreading, but were the author's deliberate intention. Then he admitted that Westall did not use the term "Fascist", and that it was Westall's term "racialist" which Morus equated with "Fascist". Finally, he reiterated his view that Tolkien's beliefs were close to Marxist Communism.

We have already established the usage of "fascist" in the *Signal* articles: Westall used it of Dennis Wheatley; Neil Philip picked up the allusion hoping to refute Westall, with the phrases "gives the lie to any view of the book as a Nazi tract" and "not to feed a new fascism". Finally, Westall quoted Professor Berne on the fascist inside every human being. So both Philip and Morus jumped to conclusions over whether Westall explicitly called Tolkien a fascist – he didn't. Morus would have done better to have looked at Inglis as well; in a report in *Amon Hen* 52 (Yates, 1981a) entitled "Tolkien: corrupter of youth" I summarised the views of John Carey (reviewing the BBC radio serial), E.P. Thompson, Westall and Inglis, and referred to Inglis's use of the term "Fascist".

I concluded my long letter to Westall by commending the Berne quotation as a good description of tendencies to orcishness, to Sauron- and Saruman-hood: exactly the evil which Tolkien was describing. Reading him aright, we ought to identify and reject such attitudes as stemming from Mordor, I said. And, as I have already written, after Westall read Tolkien's *Letters* (Tolkien, 1981) and received copies of the *Anor* articles, and my response to them, he wrote to me to exonerate Tolkien of charges of fascism.

My response to Morus, entitled "Tolkien: the anti-totalitarian" was published in Brin Dunsire's fanzine *Laurinquë* 5, March 1985. I conclude this paper with an adaptation of my text for *Laurinquë*. My theme was the irrelevance of the term "fascism", when there have been, and are today, evil regimes on the political Left which have also committed atrocities.

It is not as if the critics who attack Tolkien do themselves deny the existence of evil. They have their own picture of evil, and assert that Tolkien's picture is wrong. Yet when one finds them, for instance, denouncing Fascism, they use extreme rhetoric, condemning whole countries for their government's policies, and have little sympathy for the ordinary soldier, possibly a conscript and unaware, because uneducated or subject to censorship, of the moral issues involved in what he does. Yet these same critics, as we have seen with Westall, denounce Tolkien for creating the character of an evil warlord, out to conquer the whole world and in command of an unstoppable army – as if nothing like that ever happened in the real world!

In *The Lord of the Rings* Tolkien raises the issue of how one should act, if faced with the fact that such evil things are happening that it is one's Christian duty to intervene, and even to use force to save the innocent. His answer is that one might have to fight evil, face to face, but without using the ultimate weapon which would ensure one's victory – but at the cost of one's integrity. It should be clear from the *Letters* (Tolkien, 1981) that it was Tolkien's Christian beliefs, together with his reading of history and his life-time's experience of politics, which moulded his personal philosophy, and Morus does not consider how the Catholic doctrine of Original Sin contributed to Tolkien's view of good and evil.

With regard to the use of the term "fascism", I cannot agree entirely with the statement in *Anor* 3 that "The nature of the takeover of the Shire by Saruman's Ruffians is unmistakeably Fascist", despite the evidence of the article "The Scouring of the Shire: Tolkien's view of Fascism" by Robert Plank (Plank, 1975), an article which was not mentioned by the *Anor* contributors. Nor can I agree with the way "Fascism" is equated by Morus and Westall with Evil in the real world, as if no other system brought with it the seeds of evil. Every religion and ideology is run by fallible human beings, and evil deeds may be committed in their names.

Whereas the Concise Oxford English Dictionary sticks to the historical definitions of Fascism, as first of all describing Mussolini's regime; then similar regimes elsewhere; and finally "system of extreme right-wing or authoritarian views", the definitions given in *Anor* 3 and 5 are so wide that they could apply to other political systems altogether and could lead simply to the use of the word as a term of abuse. *Anor* 3 has:

> Fascism as a philosophy . . . is based on the right of one small group or class of society to absolute power and authority. All opposition is silenced brutally and without any regard to justice.

While *Anor* 5 has: -

> Loosely defined, a fascist is one who believes that the supposed superiority (moral, intellectual, cultural, etc.) of one particular class or race gives sufficient grounds for that class or race to impose its will on others with no loss of moral integrity. If that definition is accepted then the term "racialist" quite clearly implies "fascist".

Surely many nations throughout history have behaved in domineering, belligerent ways. During the Reformation and Counter-Reformation, Tudor monarchs persecuted Catholic and Protestant "heretics", and the Spanish Inquisition was even more notorious. The phrase "Reign of Terror" derives from the French Revolution, an uprising which ended by executing its own leaders. All these persecutions and massacres – and why not include the African slave trade, and the murder and dispossession of native Americans and Australians – were evil, but why do we have to go through the intermediate stage of defining such behaviour as "fascist" before we condemn it for being evil? Can't we just call it evil and rest our case? The *Anor* definitions ought, in my opinion, to be applied not to "fascism", but to my preferred term, "totalitarian evil". The concept of evil is narrowed by suggesting that only fascist states can be thus, and that only those states feature small dominant groups tyrannising the rest of the population!

The use of the term "fascism" as a synonym for evil camouflages the absolutely identical evil committed by so-called "socialist" states. If a ruling power assumes the right to dominate its citizens by terror, and to persecute ethnic, cultural, religious and intellectual minorities in the name of its "superior" ideology, then whether that ideology be Christian, Marxist, or Islamic, then by the *Anor* definitions that ruling power must be Fascist. And if a "revolutionary socialist state" assumes the right to dominate other countries in order to spread the revolution, then it too must be Fascist.

The editorial in my professional journal, *The Library Association Record*, for September 1980 (Usherwood, 1980, p. 393), stated, "Book burning, as history tells us, is a Fascist activity", but I have collected examples of book-burning by pressure groups in the USA as well as this country, and in "socialist" regimes such as that of the Khmer Rouge in Cambodia. Imprisonment of authors, and the banning of their books, has been commonplace in Eastern Bloc countries. One practical and relevant test might be to determine in which countries *The Lord of the Rings*, either in the original text or (better) in translation, is available to ordinary purchasers. One might then ask whether countries which do not feature Tolkien in their bookshops might be defined as "Fascist"?

I would prefer not to use that term, but to describe, say, both the Hitler and Stalin regimes as "totalitarian", with the refinement of "Stalinism" (not "Communism") for Stalin's regime alone, under which as many civilians were murdered as under Hitler. Then for the modern USSR until 1991, either "totalitarian" again, or its own technical term "Marxist-Leninist". "Communism/ist" (used in *Anor*) has been so widely used and abused that I prefer to avoid it, for it suggests that people whom I knew well, sincere members of the British Communist Party for instance, could have something in common with the Soviet regime under Stalin.

Finally I would reserve "socialism" only for those cases where I am sure I am describing the genuine article – which means it is more likely to be used for utopian socialism than for a real-life regime. It is significant that the 1984 Institute of Contemporary Arts exhibition (in London) on William Morris did not display any photographs from the Eastern Bloc, to show either the triumph or betrayal of Morris's ideals. Instead they had photographs from the new socialist state of Nicaragua!

It must be clear now that I totally disagree with the statement in *Anor* 3 that what Tolkien knew of Communism was "mostly mistaken". Here is that ambiguous word "Communism". If it means "theoretical Marxism", yes, certainly Tolkien wouldn't have read much of that, beyond some acquaintance with William Morris's non-fiction. But "Communism" can also mean "socialism-in-practice", and how can anyone suggest that Tolkien was mistaken when he wrote that Josef Stalin was a "bloodthirsty old murderer" (Tolkien, 1981, No 53, p. 65).

But if Tolkien's opinion of Stalin *was* unreliable, what about Orwell's? He knew Socialist theory, he was a committed Socialist, and he was utterly scathing about Stalin's betrayal of Socialism in his two novels *Animal Farm* and *Nineteen Eighty-Four*.

So, to conclude, back to Saruman and "The Scouring of the Shire": is this chapter really an indictment of Fascism? The character of Saruman has "clear modern relevance", as Tom Shippey indicates in *The Road to Middle-earth* (Shippey, 1982, p. 129). After his allusion to *Animal Farm* itself "an age which has seen many pigs become farmers" (Shippey, 1982, p. 104), Shippey links Saruman with Socialism on page 129:

> Saruman nevertheless does have one distinctively modern trait, which is his association with Socialism. His men *say* they are gathering things "for fair distribution", though nobody believes them – a particularly strange compromise of evil with morality, for Middle-earth, where vice rarely troubles to be hypocritical.

However, Saruman also stands for "technological man", for capitalism and industrialism, and as the *Anor* contributors agree, for the Nazi occupation of Europe. But Saruman's association with technology is surely not specifically a "fascist" trait – as Plank points out, industrialisation is a vice of the democratic West, while we have heard much in the last few years of the horrors of environmental pollution in the Eastern Bloc (for example Millinship, 1992).

In his revised Foreword to *The Lord of the Rings* Tolkien says that if he *had* written an allegory of the real war, then "Saruman . . . would . . . have found in Mordor the missing links in his own researches into Ring-lore, and before long he would have made a Great Ring of his own", i.e. like Stalin, whose scientists produced nuclear weapons after the War[1].

People tend to forget that although Western Europe was liberated from the Nazis, Eastern Europe was only "liberated" by the Russians, and countries which had hoped for independent freedom were once again enslaved by the regime which claimed to have freed them. Tolkien's grave in Wolvercote Cemetery is set among the graves of Polish Catholics who came to Oxford during the War. Why did they not return to Poland after the War, since Fascism had been defeated? Could it be that they, like Tolkien, rejected all forms of totalitarian evil?

I conclude my paper as I did my original article in 1985, though I must of course note that the Eastern Bloc countries have moved away from totalitarianism, and that, sadly, new tyrannies have arisen. A love of *The Lord of the Rings* is incompatible with tyranny, and Tolkien fans should condemn totalitarianism wherever and whenever it occurs.

---

[1] See Shippey, 1982, note 12 to chapter 5, p. 238.

References

Benchley, Peter and Gottlieb, Carl. 1975. *Jaws*, film. Zanuck-Brown.

Bird, Kai. 1981. "Diary" in *New Statesman*, 24th April 1981, p. 15.

Blinn, William (created by). 1975-9. *Starsky and Hutch*, television series. A Spelling-Goldberg Production for ABC, 1975-9.

Broomhead, Susantony. 1973. Letter in *The Listener*, 29th November 1973, p. 748.

Burrow, J.W. 1973. "Tolkien lives?" in *The Listener*, 8th November 1973, pp. 634-6.

Calder-Marshall, Arthur. 1955. "Talking of Books". British Broadcasting Corporation, Home Service, 30th October 1955.

Critics' Forum. 1981. Gillian Reynolds (chair), John Carey, Chris Dunkley and Stuart Hood (discussion of BBC Radio 4 production of *The Lord of the Rings*). BBC Radio 3, 4 April 1981.

Daedalus. Winter 1981, journal of the American Academy of Arts and Sciences.

Davis, Tom. 1973a. "Tolkien lives?" in *The Listener*, 22nd November 1973, p. 704.

Davis, Tom. 1973b. "Tolkien lives?" in *The Listener*, 6th December 1973, p. 780.

Dunsire, Brin. 1983. "Tolkien and Fascism" in *Anor* 4 (late 1983).

Giddings, Robert. 1981. "Conspiracy theories" in *Tribune*, 15th May 1981.

Giddings, Robert (ed.). 1983. *This Far Land*. London: Vision Press, 1983; Totowa, NJ: Barnes & Noble.

Gilbert, Martin. 1986. *The Holocaust*. London: Macmillan.

Home Office, The. 1980. *Protect and Survive*, various editions, reissue. London: Her Majesty's Stationery Office, May 1980.

Inglis, Fred. 1981. *The Promise of Happiness*. Cambridge: Cambridge University Press.

Jacques, Martin. 1993. "Timely clarion call puts the Balkans on moral high ground" in *The Sunday Times News Review*, 18 April 1993.

Koestler, Arthur. 1940. *Darkness at Noon*. London: Jonathan Cape.

Lewis, C.S. 1956. *The Last Battle*. London: Bodley Head.

Lucas, George. 1977. *Star Wars*, film. Lucasfilms.

Millinship, William. 1992. "Mother Russia's poisoned legacy" in *The Observer Review*, 31st May 1992, pp. 49-50.

Morus, Iwan Rhys. 1983. "Tolkien the Fascist?" *Anor* 3, 1983, pp. 8-9.

Morus, Iwan Rhys. 1984. "Tolkien the Fascist?" in *Anor* 5, Spring 1984, pp. 14-15.

Orwell, George. 1945. *Animal Farm*. London: Secker and Warburg.

Orwell, George. 1949. *Nineteen Eighty-Four*. London: Secker and Warburg.

Philip, Neil. 1981. Letter in *Signal* 35, May 1981, pp. 126-7.

Plank, Robert. 1975. "'The Scouring of the Shire': Tolkien's View of Fascism", in ed. Jared Lobdell, *A Tolkien Compass*. La Salle, IL: Open Court, pp. 107-15.

Rawson, Claude. 1981. "The exaltation of childhood" in *Times Literary Supplement* (Children's Books Supplement), 24th July 1981, pp. 837-8.

Reed, Diana. 1973. Letter in *The Listener*, 29th November 1973, p. 748.

Roddenberry, Gene (created by). 1966-69. *Star Trek*, television series. Desilu/A Norway Production/Paramount Television.

Scott, Nan C. 1972. "War and Pacifism in *The Lord of the Rings*" in *Tolkien Journal* 15, Summer 1972, pp. 23-25, 27-30.

Shippey, T.A. 1982. *The Road to Middle-earth*. London: Allen and Unwin.

Stallone, Sylvester and Cameron, James. 1985. *Rambo: First Blood Part Two*, film. Anabasis Investments NV/Buzz Feitshans.

Stibbs, Andrew. 1980. "For Realism in Children's Fiction" in *Use of English*, Autumn 1980, pp. 18-24.

Stibbs, Andrew. 1981. "Unrealism and Fantasy" in *Use of English*, Autumn 1981, pp. 65-67.

Sunday Times, The. 1993. "The shame and the slaughter", leader in the *News Review*, 18th April 1993.

Thompson, E.P. 1980. "*Protest and Survive* Campaign for Nuclear Disarmament, 1980" in eds. E.P. Thompson and Dan Smith, *Protest and Survive*. Harmondsworth: Penguin.

Thompson, E.P. 1981a. "America's Europe: A Hobbit Among Gandalfs" in *Nation*, 24th January 1981, pp. 68-93.

Thompson, E.P. 1981b. "Can Europe halt the next world war?" in *The Sunday Times*, 9th August 1981.

Tolkien, J.R.R. 1967a. *The Fellowship of the Ring*. London: George Allen & Unwin.

Tolkien, J.R.R. 1967b. *The Two Towers*. London: George Allen & Unwin.

Tolkien, J.R.R. 1967c. *The Return of the King*. London: George Allen & Unwin.

Tolkien, J.R.R. 1981. *Letters of J.R.R. Tolkien*, ed. Humphrey Carpenter. London: George Allen & Unwin.

Usherwood, Bob. 1980. "War and peace" in *Library Association Record*, September 1980, p. 393.

Westall, Robert. 1975. *The Machine-Gunners*. London: Macmillan.

Westall, Robert. 1978. *The Devil on the Road*. London: Macmillan.

Westall, Robert. 1981a. "The Hunt for Evil" in *Signal* 34, January 1981, pp. 3-13.

Westall, Robert. 1981b. Letter in *Signal* 35, May 1981, pp. 127-9.

Yates, Jessica. 1981a. "Tolkien: corrupter of youth" in *Amon Hen* 52, October 1981, pp. 9-10.

Yates, Jessica. 1981b. "In defence of fantasy" in *Use of English*, Summer 1981, pp. 70-73.

Yates, Jessica. 1984. "In Defence of Fantasy" in *Mallorn* 21, 1984, pp. 23-8.

Yates, Jessica. 1985. "Tolkien: the anti-totalitarian" in *Laurinquë* 5, March 1985, pp. 3-7.

Section seven

Tolkien Studies

Good Guys, Bad Guys, Fantasy and Reality

Helen Armstrong

Abstract: This paper begins by considering the nature of some of the stylised "evil" and "good" character types employed by J.R.R. Tolkien in his Middle-earth works, and their relationship both with folklore and with related character types appearing in the contemporary world (in Tolkien's time and in our own).

The paper then goes on to consider the role of women in Tolkien's fictional world, with particular reference to their status as mothers (particularly as absent mothers), and as heroic figures, and looks at the victimisation of the woman/wife/mother in the Biblical tradition of the Book of Genesis, and its possible relation to Tolkien's own situation.

The paper then relates these areas, particularly the latter, to the underlying stress in all the Middle-earth writings between a longing for certainty and permanence, and the recognition that there is no certain path to these desirable states.

Keywords: conventional hero-figures, dark side of human consciousness, demons, fairy-tale villains, orcs, personal hope and doubt in Tolkien's writing, real-world heroism, Tolkien's ability to transcend doctrine and convention with the personal, war (contemporary), wives (lack of) and mothers (dead) in Tolkien, women as hero-figures in Tolkien, women as scapegoat in "Fall" stories

J.R.R. Tolkien's *The Lord of the Rings* is a fairy-tale. A fairy-tale is expected to be ephemeral in its effect if not in its appeal, but Tolkien's writing has a quality of myth. The author spent his life writing *The Silmarillion* and its offshoots, and *The Lord of the Rings* is the cactus-flower of that work, unexpected, brilliant, organised, and seedbearing.

Tolkien's legendary peoples had two beginnings. One was in the *Lost Tales* (Tolkien, 1983 & 1984). The other was *The Hobbit*, where, beside the echoes of older and more conventional stories, we first encounter Bilbo Baggins, Gollum, and three cockney trolls. Compared to these, Thorin and his "Eddic dwarves" have a thoroughly respectable air.

The Hobbit is an outright fairy-tale, but the goblins sing and crack whips, and the elves sing, crack bad jokes, get drunk, and clap people in irons for interrupting their parties. There is an uncompromising quality about *The Hobbit*.

Goblins are traditionally on the malevolent side of fairyland. "Orc" is an Old English word meaning "infernal regions"; an *orc-thyrs* is a hell-devil, a demon (Bosworth & Toller, 1989). The goblins of *The Hobbit* are fairy-tale goblins; but there is a hint of more:

> Hammers, axes, swords, daggers, pickaxes, tongs, and also instruments of torture, they make very well, or get other people to make . . . prisoners and slaves that have to work till they die for want of air and light . . . It is not unlikely that they invented some of the machines that have since troubled the world, especially the ingenious devices for killing large numbers of people at once . . .

(Tolkien, 1966d, pp. 57-8)

Tolkien, as a traditional Catholic, knew about demons, and knew only too well that it is not devils or goblins that manufacture instruments of torture, but mankind.

The orcs of the *Lost Tales* were made originally by the demonic god Melkor. By the time of *The Silmarillion*, they were said to have been bred from captive elves. In this latter scenario, Melkor can corrupt life, but not create it.

But the orcs began their life in Tolkien's creation as automatons, something which continues to inform their behaviour right through the later works. Orcs don't reform or change sides. They seem to be essentially without free will, the vital characteristic of created souls. They personify the malevolent will of the Prince of Darkness, not as servants or followers, but as tools and cannon-fodder, disposable instruments of mass destruction.

But if orcs are the goblins that haunt Tolkien's darker dreams, they cannot be completely separated from the evil that Men do. Nightmares may take the form of bogles or goblins, but they mainly draw upon human experiences for their terror. It was inevitable, therefore, that orcs would take on some of the characteristics of men.

Devils lead souls astray, snare them, and turn them loose to wander the world in living captivity. But they do not snatch hobbits, bandage and feed them, beat them up, or send their luggage to head office for analysis. These are human activities.

It is clear that Tolkien has humans at least partly in mind when he writes about orcs. They have individual self-interest. They enjoy inflicting damage and cruelty, but can hold back in the pursuit of other goals. They would like to be self-employed. The inhabitants of fairyland are the denizens of our dreams, but we dream mainly of what we already know. Orcs are rather like humans because humans can be rather like orcs.

Yet orcs also behave like automatons. If characters in any of Tolkien's works encounter an orc, they do not ask whether it is friend or foe; they either run, hide, or attempt to kill it. They know that, unless they pursue one of these three options, they can themselves expect to be killed, or worse.

This is not how we would want to treat another human being, or be treated by one, yet the behaviour patterns are recognisable to us.

Professor Tolkien fought in the First World War, and lived through the Second World War. It would be impossible for any reasonably aware person living at that time not to have received an image of real evil active in the real world.

We hope that we are too enlightened to typecast members of another tribe, religion, or neighbouring country as demonic. We acknowledge that we are human and they are human; that they are like us, and we are like them.

But there comes a point when one human is not like another. When a soldier machine-guns a family of civilians, or when a gang kicks or knifes an unarmed victim to death, they are not sharing their likeness. When a child, or an old person, is abused, raped or killed, the common humanity between abuser and victim must seem very remote. Reports have been coming, throughout this year, from the wars in the former Yugoslavia, and Azerbaijan – of men starving, interned, sometimes massacred and mutilated; civilians, old people, unarmed women and children shot in the street or in their homes; teenage girls, as young as twelve and thirteen, taken from their families and systematically raped; some thrown back in a traumatised state, often pregnant; others kept in captivity as sex slaves.

All of this behaviour is cruel; much of it goes far beyond anything that can be explained as a necessity of war. This is not the time to tell the victims that the people who did this are "like them". They may have been once, they may be again; they may themselves have been abused; they may one day be old, or vulnerable. But there still exists that place where one human being can look at another and encounter something utterly alien, cruel, implacable and terrifying. All our darkest images come from this source.

Living people may regret and make amends, where that possibility remains. But the fact and the memory of atrocity also remain, and cannot simply be banished or denied.

There is no evidence that humankind can entirely exorcise the darker side from its consciousness. We can fight cruelty, hate and envy in ourselves as individuals; but to deny that they manifest themselves, horribly, in human experience is to create an illusion which is itself dangerous.

The Lord of the Rings is a straight battle between good and evil, but it is also a battle on several levels. There are the ugly, cruel personifications of our fears, and there are also living people.

Tolkien treats the "Mannish" enemy very differently from the goblin one. We hear remarks about cruel Haradrim, and fierce Easterlings, but we never meet them in the process of being cruel, and only briefly fierce. In *The Silmarillion*, one tribe of treacherous Easterlings is mentioned, but the other tribe from the dark-shrouded east remains loyal to its western allies. Even unlovely people – such as Wormtongue in *The Lord of the Rings* – were not born "bad", but turned bad; usually out of the process of seeking personal power or gain.

Tolkien distinguishes, constantly, between "bad" arising from fear and ignorance, and "bad" motivated by greed and jealousy.

The worst behaviour of all is attributed to the "chosen race" of the Númenóreans. The Mouth of Sauron – "more cruel than any orc" – is a renegade Númenórean. The downfall of Númenor is caused by its own people; Sauron only plays upon their pride and fear. Those who are privileged are given greater responsibility, and made to fall further when they become greedy and cruel.

Although advice, mutual support and loyalty are stressed throughout *The Lord of the Rings*, it is individual choice and action which are most significant in the creation of good as well as of evil, even when it goes against the grain. Both Éomer and Éowyn defy orders to take actions which save the lives of others. Beregond kills a colleague in attempting to rescue Faramir from the funeral pyre.

Even so, the heroes of *The Lord of the Rings* are conventional. They have a fairly clear idea of what they need to do, and they follow it through unswervingly; not without pain and doubt, but usually in uncertainty of method rather than of purpose.

These heroes are never found drunk on duty, in the chamber of a colleague's wife, or doing a dirty arms deal. They are old-fashioned heroes. There are such people, and society tends to value them most when its conscience is bothering it. Most, of course, are not kings and princes, but fairy-tale convention (which often rewards virtue by conferring kingship) also allows for shoemakers.

The Lord of the Rings, like *The Silmarillion*, is mainly a chronicle of war. This was a situation that Tolkien had experienced personally. In time of war, people become heroes as often as they become villains.

Where do we find these heroes otherwise?

In the last two or three years, two stories have stayed in my mind. One was of a Liverpool councillor who turned against council corruption. The other was of a Londoner who discovered a council-housing payola scheme in his neighbourhood, an area of high homelessness. He appealed for help to the council, and then to the police and the press.

Both men, predictably, had their homes vandalised and their lives and families threatened. Both could have turned their backs on the situation, but chose deliberately to follow it through, out of a mixture of principle and a sense of identification with their communities.

Stories like this may not rival in scale the saving of the Universe from the forces of Darkness, but the potential cost to the participants is as high as that to any god or hero faced with any imminent world-ending. And though they are not commonplace, they recur constantly, in every community.

The heroes of *The Lord of the Rings*, under their universalising and mythologising wizards' hats and enchanted swords, are of this kind. Aragorn is the leader of a declining people fighting for survival. Gandalf could have stayed in the office, but chose to go out into the field. Frodo leaves the Shire partly out of fear and partly out of genuine concern for his friends and neighbours. He takes on the bigger task because he is too conscientious to refuse it in front of those who have been kind to him. These are three types of individual who might, in the end, become heroic.

Incidentally, one of many studies undertaken on the effects of television on its audience reported in 1992 that the cult of the attractive villain seems to be communicating not that attractive people can be villains, but that villainy is attractive.

We should perhaps admit that we are vulnerable to appearances. The tall hero in the white hat may become acceptable at respectable dinner tables after all.

One extraordinary thing about the heroes of *The Lord of the Rings* is that so many of them, regardless of age group or status, have no wife. Many people postpone marriage in dangerous times, but others marry precisely because they know that time might be short. Tolkien himself was one of these (Carpenter, 1977, p.78).

Yet some of Tolkien's greatest heroes are women; most by virtue of being someone's wife or mother, but a considerable minority in their own right.

Nevertheless, a tally of major characters in *The Lord of the Rings* who have dead or otherwise absent mothers or wives produces startling results. An initial count produces ten: Bilbo (his mother, Belladonna, was apparently dead by the time of *The Hobbit*, although Bilbo was still then a youngish man); Frodo; Sam; Éowyn and Éomer; Théoden's son Théodred, whose mother died when he was born; Faramir and Boromir, whose mother died when they were young; Arwen Evenstar; Aragorn. The mothers or wives of other heroes are rarely or never mentioned. Even Gimli the Dwarf never raises an oath on his old mother's beard.

Moving into *Silmarillion* territory, we have Elrond: separated from his mother at the age of (approximately) three-and-a-half in the assault on Sirion; his mother Elwing: mother and father killed when she's about seven; Fingon: sends his young son away from home for safety, but no mention of his wife; Fingolfin: wife (and daughter) seen briefly getting lost in an early version (the daughter re-surfaces in the published text, where she survives long enough to produce a son and be murdered by her husband); Idril Celebrindal: mother died in the crossing of the Helcaraxë; seven sons of Fëanor: their mother estranged from their father early in the story. They stay with their father. At least one had an offspring (Celebrimbor), who was "estranged from his father", but not a single wife is mentioned; Finduilas beloved of Túrin: we meet her father — two fathers, in fact (the kind of thing we might expect from somebody who gets involved with Túrin) — but not even one mother; Finrod Felagund: his beloved stayed behind in the Land of the Valar, presumably out of a keen sense of self-preservation.

In *The Silmarillion*, the female survival rate is slightly better among the human races. Túrin's mother Morwen is a survivor, but there is a tension in that relationship, a mixture of coldness and intensity, which becomes self-destructive.

Despite the honours accorded to heroic women, the only part that most others have to play is as memories. Natural causes and war don't adequately account, particularly in *The Lord of the Rings*, for the differing survival rates of male and female parents.

Tolkien himself lost his father, and later his mother, while he was still young. He regarded his mother as "heroic" for the hardship she suffered supporting him and his brother. His wife Edith, also, never knew her father, and lost her mother while in her teens.

Tolkien would have learned about day-to-day relationships without the help of a complete family. I suspect he learned much about friendship from his peers, but did not have the same opportunity with women. His friendships with the women he knew seem to have been good-natured. But there is definitely an uneasiness about the part a woman may play in a man's life, as emerges most strongly in the story of *The Mariner's Wife* (Tolkien, 1980, pp. 173-217). But an analysis of that story is beyond the reference of this paper.

The lack of live mothers in *The Lord of the Rings* and *The Silmarillion* means much motherlessness, which is poignant, but also places the women concerned largely beyond the reckoning of the story.

A notable exception is Míriel, mother of Fëanor. Her husband Finwë, indeed, has turned out to have an excess of wives rather than a shortage, and yet, perhaps not unexpectedly, as more material comes to light, this story too moves ever further towards unreconciled loneliness. Míriel dies when Fëanor is a baby, but this does not entirely place her beyond the reckoning of the story. Her passing is seen as partly voluntary. She lies down in the garden of Lórien, and becomes, to all intents and purposes, dead. The Valar seem to agree, for in time they give Finwë permission to marry again. He and his second wife, Indis, have two sons. Fëanor grows up to be a gifted and self-centred man. He snubs his stepmother and half-brothers, is fiercely possessive of his devoted father, and centres his life on his achievements, gradually, to the exclusion of all else. He hates the demonic Melkor, but he is a man looking for trouble, and when Melkor creates it, he is quick to embrace it.

Before she dies, Míriel says to Finwë: "Hold me blameless in this, and in all that may come after." These words might be a fitting memorial to every woman who succumbs to fear, sickness or death, and is remembered afterwards only as "not there when she was needed".

But does Míriel's author hold her blameless? There is a very old resonance here, which I am following. *The Silmarillion* is mythic in tone. Myth carries part of the truth when the whole truth becomes too much to grasp in one piece. But it must tell the truth, and we must try to understand what part of the truth it is telling.

In the *Letters of J.R.R. Tolkien*, having described Men's attempt to defy their mortal nature as "a supreme folly and wickedness", Tolkien calls Míriel "An elf that tried to *die*, which had disastrous results, leading to the 'Fall' of the High-elves" (Tolkien, 1981, p. 286).

No doubt Míriel's absence did nothing to ease Fëanor's sensitive nature. But, even leaving aside that her illness was not of her making or choosing, how is it that Míriel can be blamed for the fall of the High Elves? What about Melkor? What about the many other factors and personalities involved? What about Fëanor himself?

Part of becoming adult is realising that our parents are not gods or demons, put here to answer our desires or take the blame for our own bad behaviour; and that our children are not put here to fulfil our own dreams and carry out our designs. Parents are an enormous influence on children, but each soul remains individual with no ownership rights over others, up or down the generations.

Fëanor also allowed his children to be tied up in his oath-swearing. Tolkien clearly disapproves of Fëanor and his actions, but, faced with Míriel's absence, he allows himself for a moment to forget that Fëanor is an adult, responsible for his own choices. It would be interesting to know to what part of the child/parent relationship Tolkien would trace, for instance, the behaviour of the Biblical Satan.

But what concerns me more is that old, old resonance; it's in the Book of Genesis. There is a man, and a woman, and trouble, and the same thing happens. The trouble belongs to everyone, but the finger of accusation swings steadily round until it points to the smaller participant, and the cry goes up again: "It was all her fault. She dunnit. She made me do it."

This does not sound to me like a myth out of fairyland; not even out of Tolkien's fairyland. This is a myth of Men.

Male-centred philosophy has had considerable currency for a long time. It's in the Bible. Tolkien's friend C.S. Lewis, following hotfoot, created a world in which the first male was "always older" than the first female (Lewis, 1943). Told that, biologically, male is derived from female, somebody in that circle – and I regret that I cannot trace the source, but the comment is commonplace enough – replied that, in that case, the male was obviously the improved version.

If you want a creed of convenience, and you have the means to do so, you can create one. When beliefs of this kind are written into the creed to which you have devoted your life – and are by no means inconvenient – it becomes unlikely that you will turn readily away from them.

However, when Tolkien himself develops female personalities in his writings, his tendency is to admire, even to exalt them. Many of the women he writes about are heroes.

I use the word hero advisedly as well as by preference. We are told – mainly in the later writings – how tall and strong these women are. Idril, "well nigh of warrior's stature" (Tolkien, 1988, p. 148); Galadriel, who was called Nerwen, "man-maiden" (Tolkien, 1980, p. 229); Éowyn, slender but as a steel blade; and tall Nienor; Beren's mother Emeldir the Manhearted; and the tribal chieftainess Haleth (which is an Old English word simply meaning warrior or hero).

Idril Celebrindal best balances the role of wife and mother with that of initiator and fighter. She orders the tunnel by which her family escapes from Gondolin; she fights for her life and her son's life against Maeglin; arms herself and goes around rescuing people. *The Silmarillion* takes the unusual step of referring the reader back to "The Fall of Gondolin" (*The Book of Lost Tales, part 2*) for this part of the story.

As Tolkien's mythology developed, its overall content and movement became truer, as he worked more deeply into it, and maybe also as he saw it through the eyes of his readership.

Tolkien had a personal point of view, beliefs and prejudices like anyone else. Some of them will seem alien to some of us. But despite the undercurrents which I have picked on in this paper, he kept his mythology startlingly free of personal and religious doctrinairism, while mirroring deep layers of personal belief, hope and fear, doubt and determination.

Despite the conventionally, even doctrinally, male-centred aspects of Tolkien's world, he also bucked that same system: by creating active heroines; by allowing himself to look towards faerie at all; by not preaching doctrines; and by allowing his imagination freedom to work, even in the context of his doctrinal beliefs.

I am not talking so much about the imagination as it tells a story, but the mythic imagination as it operates by itself and touches everything in our experience, especially the most personal, resonant, poignant and important things. And while many people seem serenely (or turbulently) unaware of the process in their lives, I believe that it has great force, whether or not we are mythopoeically inclined. Many a plain person, for instance, had recognised the likenesses between love, war and religion long before C.G. Jung arrived to reclassify the operations of the archetype.

Galadriel became more and more powerful as Tolkien's idea of her developed. Late in the day, he called her, "The greatest of the Noldor, except Fëanor maybe, though she was wiser . . ." and further: "These two kinsfolk, the greatest of the Eldar of Valinor, were unfriends for ever." She fights Fëanor's people physically at Alqualondë (Tolkien, 1980, pp. 229, 230 & 232). There are the beginnings here of a duality, an opposition between the less powerful but inherently wiser Galadriel and the destructive Fëanor.

I have not touched on the story of Éowyn in this paper, for abundance of other material. I will only add that I found it largely convincing when I first read it, as a teenager, in the 1970s, and now, twenty years later, I find it completely convincing.

There is a movement in these heroines towards a synthesis of "manly" and "womanly" qualities, as they are often understood: the woman who has virtuous male qualities as well as virtuous female ones. But there is no escaping that this movement is never allowed to take the opposite form. Gentleness in men is admired – in Faramir in particular – but this is never identified with any "female" quality. While certain "manly" qualities (without entering into any discussion on the justice of such attributions) are taken to be good enough for both men and women, "womanly" qualities are very definitely only for women. There is a profound imbalance here. It is part of our culture, and I doubt we will ever be rid of it. That is not to say that we should accept it.

Lúthien, however, is different again. She is one of the root characters in the cycle, and though she developed and changed, she was from the start the spirited dancer who challenged a demonic god for love of her lover. There is nothing of the warrior about her. She is a half-divine singer and dancer, innately powerful. She does not aspire to discover or conquer, but she outfaces both Morgoth and Sauron. She outfaces Mandos himself. Beren puts his best hand forward, and if it were possible to demonstrate worthiness of such a love, he does so — but ultimately he is helpless without her. But worth, as such, is never mentioned. He does his bit. She does hers. Then they die and go off together, leaving her relations mourning and not a little puzzled.

This is not the end of the story. This is what we have to believe, anyway. This is what Tolkien had to believe. He said that *The Lord of the Rings* was about death. I recall a television programme, *Tolkien in Oxford*, long ago, which I have only seen repeated as a handful of "quotes" in an as-yet-unbroadcast documentary made in the U.K. for the Centenary year. In this (if I remember rightly) he called death "the greatest insult" to a human being. One of the great pleasures of seeing these snatches of interview again was realising that he attributed the quotation to Simone de Beauvoir.

Despite the "supreme folly and wickedness" (as he described it) of trying to capture worldly immortality, Tolkien was himself wrestling with the Gift of Men. The whole of his work is a plea for life to be preserved somewhere, as pure and unchanging as it can be, beyond the reach of time and human frailty. He looks with yearning to the traditions that such a place existed; his mariners search for the land of the young. Of Lórien, an early version says that the travellers saw no fungus or other signs of decay there (Tolkien, 1992, p. 241 fn. 36). This was later altered to "no stain." But in the world we live in, if nothing decays, nothing can grow, either.

Our hope must be that it is the physical which changes, falls to pieces and dies, and not the heart and the spirit.

The western isles are only a mythic form, but a mythic form for something he hoped for, longed for, and doubted. His mariners get lost or find nothing. Eriol finds lovely isles and kind people, but their stories are full of doom and disaster. Eärendel, in the early versions of his story, comes to Eldamar — and finds it empty. Not temporarily empty because the elves are away at a festival, but completely empty — they have gone.

In "The Sea Bell" (Tolkien, 1962, p.57) — quite erroneously subtitled *Frodos Dreme*, as the oldest published version (called, incidentally, "Looney") (Tolkien, 1934, p. 340) is much older than Frodo — the mariner comes to a far, green country, but nobody will speak to him, and he sees no-one. He hears them running from him. Eventually he finds the sea again, and sails home. No-one will speak to him there, either.

This is a dark dream by any standards. It has the same motifs as his other western-isle poems and stories, but it concentrates despair with alarming intensity. What I do not detect, though, is any sign that the traveller regrets the journey, despite its uncertain outcome.

Tolkien spoke more often of his other dark dream, apparently a literal one — the green wave rising and overwhelming the land (Carpenter, 1977, p. 170): Atlantis falling, the Golden Age crashing in ruins. It seems to have had a stronger grip on his imagination than any other mythical image from any source, and appears in more diverse and more complete forms (I am excluding transitional drafts) than anything else he wrote.

The underlying tension is always there, between the wickedness and folly of longing for life, free from change and decay, and the continued presence of that longing.

Myth and fairy-tale traditionally encompass the extremes of longing and beauty, terror and ugliness in the human imagination. If it often appears that the beauty and hope go somewhat beyond the real world, while much of the horror only skims the surface of what humans have achieved, consider that we can only produce from our imaginations what we are capable in some degree of experiencing. It makes a certain amount of sense that literature should stress hope, even in the face of experience, while confronting horror in some form that is overwhelming but not completely and irreparably so.

The gap between life and story is mainly in the longing for permanence: that something felt and seen for a moment can become crystallised into something indestructible, as embodied in the classic ending: "And they lived happy ever after." But only the major religions and the simplest fairy-tales dare to claim this ending for themselves.

Tolkien's strength is that he has taken the material and language of folklore and folk-memory, and impressed on it a personal reality of hopes and fears, animating the images and figures that he uses, relating his dreams in a way that can be shared on a number of levels, and making no easy promises.

References

The Jerusalem Bible. 1966. Standard edition. London: Darton, Longman & Todd; New York: Doubleday & Co.

Bosworth, J. and Toller, T. Northcote. 1898. *An Anglo-Saxon Dictionary*. Oxford: Oxford University Press.

Carpenter, H. 1977. *J.R.R. Tolkien: A biography*. London: George Allen & Unwin.

Lewis, C.S. 1943. *Voyage to Venus (Perelandra)*. London: Bodley Head/John Lane.

Tolkien, J.R.R. 1934. "Looney", in *The Oxford Magazine*. Vol. LII, No. 9, 18 January 1934, p. 340.

Tolkien, J.R.R. 1962. "The Sea-bell", in *The Adventures of Tom Bombadil*. London: George Allen & Unwin, pp. 57-60.

Tolkien, J.R.R. 1966a. *The Fellowship of the Ring*, second edition. London: George Allen & Unwin.

Tolkien, J.R.R. 1966b. *The Two Towers*, second edition. London: George Allen & Unwin.

Tolkien, J.R.R. 1966c. *The Return of the King*, second edition. London: George Allen & Unwin.

Tolkien, J.R.R. 1966d. *The Hobbit*, third edition. London: George Allen & Unwin.

Tolkien, J.R.R. 1977. *The Silmarillion*, ed. Christopher Tolkien. London: George Allen & Unwin.

Tolkien, J.R.R. 1980. *Unfinished Tales*. London: George Allen & Unwin.

Tolkien, J.R.R. 1981. *Letters of J.R.R. Tolkien*, ed. H. Carpenter with C. Tolkien. London: George Allen & Unwin.

Tolkien, J.R.R. 1983. *The Book of Lost Tales*, part one, ed. Christopher Tolkien. London: George Allen & Unwin.

Tolkien, J.R.R. 1984. *The Book of Lost Tales*, part two, ed. Christopher Tolkien. London: George Allen & Unwin.

Tolkien, J.R.R. 1988. *The Shaping of Middle-earth*, ed. Christopher Tolkien. London: Unwin Paperbacks.

Tolkien, J.R.R. 1992. *The Treason of Isengard*, ed. Christopher Tolkien. London: Grafton Paperbacks.

The Realm of Faërie

Christine Barkley

Abstract: Middle-earth is not the only glimpse we get of Tolkien's view of Faërie. This paper examines his definition of Faërie and how it applies to Niggle's Parish and to the forest in *Smith of Wootton Major*. Once we are aware of certain aspects of Faërie (for example the double vision possible), we can appreciate them in Middle-earth.

Keywords: Faërie, fairies, fantasy, nature, peril, space, time, wonder

> Still round the corner there may wait
> A new road or a secret gate,
> And though we pass them by today,
> Tomorrow we may come this way
> And take the hidden paths that run
> Towards the Moon or to the Sun.
> (Tolkien, 1991, p. 91)

In Tolkien's work, Faërie can be just around the corner, at least to anyone privileged enough and perceptive enough to recognize it. It will look just like the Natural world, yet contain wonders almost unimaginable. What is the Realm of Faërie? Where can it be found? What can be found in it? And what is its purpose? First we should turn to "On Fairy-Stories" to see what Tolkien himself said about the purpose of Faërie. And then I would like to explore a few different realms of Faërie, some that aren't referred to as much as Middle-earth itself: that found in *Smith of Wootton Major* and Niggle's Parish from "Leaf by Niggle".

Tolkien was less concerned with "fairies" themselves than with Faërie, the place. I should like first to mention a few general misconceptions about fantasy or faërie worlds: that they are places where magic is prevalent and which defy the natural laws, that in them fairies play tricks but not life-threatening ones on humans, or that they are wishes-can-come-true places. Certainly actions which defy our laws of time and biology, such as the immediate growth and blooming of flowers at the feet of a dancing Faery Queen, will seem magical to us. Yet though this is present in Tolkien's Faërie, it is by no means the focus. Of more importance are works of nature such as the King's Tree or the willow in *Smith of Wootton Major* or Niggle's tree, the Forest, or the Mountains in "Leaf by Niggle". Another misconception about Faërie is that it is thought of only as a place of goodness and light, and in Tolkien's Faërie certainly wonders almost beyond belief are found, beauty and joy are present, but it is hardly the entire story; there is also much that is dangerous and even evil. Tolkien called it "a perilous land" containing "pitfalls for the unwary and dungeons for the overbold". What did he mean by "perilous"? There is physical peril, certainly, in all reality, and this is true in Faërie as well. Niggle never really suffers from danger, though his illness, he believes, hastened the day of his departure on his Journey. Smith encounters physical danger from the Mariners near the Sea of Windless Storm and also peril from physical forces such as the wild Wind near the lake in the Outer Mountains. While travelling in Faërie, Smith learns of many weapons that would cause great devastation in his world, yet he chooses never to reproduce any of these, though as a smith he might well have had the skill, or even to bring back knowledge of such weapons to his own world.

> Though in time he could have forged weapons that in his own world would have had power enough to become the matter of great tales and be worth a King's ransom, he knew that in Faery they would have been of small account. So among all the things that he made it is not remembered that he ever forged a sword or a spear or an arrow-head.
> (Tolkien, 1967, pp. 24, 26)

As Gimli pointed out when the Fellowship left Lothlórien, however, the greatest dangers are often not physical. Surely Tolkien realized, as did Shakespeare before him, that for joy to be more poignant, the possibility and sometimes the reality of sorrow must also be strong. Thus one of the pitfalls, something that made this a perilous realm, is that its joys are enhanced, but so are its sorrows and the grief at the loss of such joy. Thus even the poignancy of the joy Niggle feels when he encounters his tree or Smith feels while dancing with the Faery Queen make the realm of Faërie a more perilous place. Were there nothing but dangers in Faërie, leaving it would not be difficult. The loss of joy is a far more powerful grief.

To Tolkien the realm of Faërie is a place where one can satisfy

> certain primordial human desires. One of these desires is to survey the depths of space and time. Another is . . . to hold communion with other living things.
> (Tolkien, 1966b, p. 13)

Certainly the realms of Faërie in *Smith of Wootton Major* and Niggle's Parish in "Leaf by Niggle" function this way. How can one "survey the depths of space and time"? As with everything, one misses the wonder of a thing unless one "recovers" it, that is, sees it in a new way, not unlike Tolkien's example of "mooreeffoc" or coffeeroom spelled backwards. Both Smith and Niggle see space and time differently while in Faërie. In the Vale of Evermorn, Smith sees across space, that

> the air is so lucid that eyes can see the red tongues of birds as they sing on the trees upon the far side of the valley, though that is very wide and the birds are no greater than wrens.
> (Tolkien, 1967, p. 31)

After Smith is given the white flower by the Faery Queen, when he gets it home and his wife Nell looks at in her hand,

> it seemed like a thing seen from a great distance, yet there it was, and a light came from it that cast shadows on the walls of the room, now growing dark in the evening.
> (Tolkien, 1967, p. 35)

Not only is there a dual view of the flower – far away and up close – but another of its characteristics is shown: its ability to glow brightly.

Niggle also saw space with a new perspective when he got to the landscape which had been the inspiration for his painting and began to walk toward the Forest in the background of the painting.

> As he walked away, he discovered an odd thing: the Forest, of course, was a distant Forest, yet he could approach it, even enter it, without its losing that particular charm. He had never before been able to walk into the distance without turning it into mere surroundings.
> (Tolkien, 1966a, pp. 104-5)

For both Smith and Niggle the recovery of space and time involved a juxtaposition of two views of an object or place seen simultaneously: the flower or the birds seen from a distance and yet up close; the Forest remaining a distant Forest even up close.

In the two short stories I am examining, there is not as much holding of "communion with other living things" as we can see in *The Lord of the Rings* with the ents, dwarves, elves, hobbits, Istari and men working together against orcs, wargs, balrogs, and spiders. We do get a glimpse of the entire mating cycle of the birds in Niggle's Parish as

> they were mating, hatching, growing wings, and flying away singing into the Forest, even while he looked at them.
> (Tolkien, 1966a, p. 104)

Smith has meetings, though no words, with Mariners beside the Sea of Windless Storm and with dancing maidens. He encounters a young birch tree to which he clings when driven by the wild Wind. This encounter proves disastrous to the birch, for it is stripped of its leaves and left in sorrow. Also, both heroes encounter some sort of authority figures who seem supernatural: the First and Second Voice in "Leaf by Niggle" and the King and Queen of Faery in *Smith of Wootton Major*.

Not all encounters in Faërie are filled with happiness and joy. Thus it contradicts the fact that some critics have associated both Niggle's Parish and Smith's Faery with Heaven. Jane Nitzsche claimed:

> All secondary worlds, all realms of Faërie in such fairy-stories ultimately are modelled upon Heaven. Entering Paradise remains the deepest fantasy of man because it constitutes the most important escape from death and from the stranglehold of this world on his life.
> (Nitzsche, 1979, p. 53)

In agreeing with a Richard Purtill article in *Mythlore*, Eric Graff states that Niggle's Parish "can only be associated with Heaven" (1992, p. 16). Purtill, however, did make the distinction that Niggle's journey into the mountains was "Tolkien's metaphor for 'exploration into God'" (1979, p. 5). However, later Purtill claims "the country beyond the journey . . . can be taken as a metaphor . . . for an image of Heaven" (p. 5). Though all three writers are willing to establish Niggle's Parish as Tolkien's view of Heaven, I believe Purtill was closer to the truth when he suggested it was the mountains beyond that are more closely aligned with Heaven if we were to read the story as an allegory. After all, Niggle's Parish is said to be the "best introduction to the Mountains" (Tolkien, 1966a, p. 112). Once Niggle's work was done, he accompanied the shepherd to explore the "high pasturages, and look at a wider sky, and walk ever further and further towards the Mountains, always uphill" (Tolkien, 1966a, p. 109). It would be more in keeping with Tolkien's own modesty to suggest that the Mountains might represent Heaven (if one were to choose to interpret the story allegorically, which, of course, Tolkien disavowed). The concept of the Mountains as Heaven is reinforced when Smith is leaving Faërie and "far off he heard the echo of a trumpet in the mountains" (Tolkien, 1967, p. 39) as he was headed back to his real world. Faërie, then, is an introduction to the Mountains (to Heaven) but is not Heaven itself.

So beyond its role as a way to re-evaluate time and space and interact with other living beings, what is the purpose of Faërie? It is clearly a more enchanted place than our humdrum world, yet I would say it does not represent Tolkien's view of Heaven, though it might help to prepare us for that wonder. Yet, as well because of the "perilous" quality of Faërie, it also prepares us for loss, for bereavement. Tolkien's view is that not all is either joy *or* sorrow, but that both emotions are juxtaposed, most strongly in Faërie itself. It is the combination of the two which best allows us to recover or better appreciate the joy. As Smith gets ready to leave Faery for the last time, he encounters once again the Faery Queen.

> Then he knelt, and she stooped and laid her hand on his head, and a great stillness came upon him; and he seemed to be both in the World and in Faery, and also outside them and surveying them, so that he was at once in bereavement, and in ownership, and in peace.
> (Tolkien, 1966b, p. 38)

The great joy of a place can be measured by our own sorrow at its loss, yet also by our willingness to suffer that loss for the sake of the joy. Lúthien and Arwen both chose death, "the gift [or the doom] of Ilúvatar," over separation from the one loved. Sam's last line in *Return of the King*, "Well, I'm back" (Tolkien, 1991, p. 1069), is fraught with the same kind of juxtaposed sorrow and joy that I always feel at finishing my umpteenth reading of the tale. Smith's loss of the star, the willow tree's loss, even Atkins' recognition that the community had lost something of value when it ceased to respect the need for art in "Leaf by Niggle," all these show a reiteration and recovery of the value of the joy, or of nature, or of art, through an awareness of our sorrow at its loss.

Faërie then becomes a place to recover strong emotions, to realize that sorrow and joy are a yin and yang that must be combined to be understood fully. The realm of Faërie to Tolkien is also a wondrous place in which to see the value of nature, of trees and birds; also, through Niggle's painting, we see that art itself, though often an inaccurate or at least incomplete vision of Faërie, can be an introduction to it. We discover or recover Faërie by seeing a double view of nature, a juxtaposed view of the thing as it is and as it would be in Faërie. Thus we might see its true nature (the splendour of a tree), its complete existence (the life cycle of the wrens), or its emotional nature (the sorrow of the willow). This is not unlike the Renaissance view of earthly or human beauty and Heavenly or Ideal beauty. But rather than separating the two, Tolkien suggests the need to juxtapose them.

I have shown that Tolkien's shorter works — "Leaf by Niggle" and *Smith of Wootton Major* — illustrate quite well the theories about Faërie which he stated in "On Fairy Stories," notably that Faërie provides an opportunity to satisfy "certain primordial human desires": to understand time and space and other living things more clearly. I have gone beyond what Tolkien stated as the purpose of Faërie to suggest that nature itself and works of art could be considered a part of a wider and more mysterious world, part of the realm of Faërie itself, if we can look at them and rediscover through them the wonder of our own world. By implication, then, as we recover or become aware of the wonders of time and space, of communion with other living beings, of nature, and of art, we enter the world of Faërie. Thus in answer to the question of "Where is Faërie?" our answer could be "anywhere". We can expect to find Faërie around each corner, down a new road, through a secret gate, on a hidden path anywhere in our own world if we look with the eyes of wonder.

References

Graff, Eric S. 1992. "The Three Faces of Faërie in Tolkien's Shorter Fiction", *Mythlore* 69 (Summer 1992), pp. 15-19.

Nitzsche, Jane Chance. 1979. *Tolkien's Art*. New York: St. Martin's.

Purtill, Richard L. 1979. "Heaven and Other Perilous Realms", *Mythlore* 22 (Fall 1979), pp. 3-6.

Tolkien, J. R. R. 1966a. "Leaf By Niggle" in *The Tolkien Reader*. New York: Ballantine. pp. 85-112.

Tolkien, J. R. R. 1966b. "On Fairy Stories" in *The Tolkien Reader*. New York: Ballantine. pp. 3-84.

Tolkien, J. R. R. 1967. *Smith of Wootton Major*. London: George Allen and Unwin.

Tolkien, J. R. R. 1991. *The Lord of the Rings*. Boston: Houghton Mifflin.

Point of View in Tolkien

Christine Barkley

Abstract: Many stories are told by more than one teller in Tolkien's works. This paper compares different versions to see what areas of interest or emphasis arise, and what differences might be explained by the specific interests or culture of the teller. The paper also evaluates which kinds of stories are told most often by which tellers.

Keywords: *The Hobbit*, *The Lord of the Rings*, narrators, points of view, *The Silmarillion*, *Unfinished Tales*

Peter Pan is a very different story told from the point of view of Captain Hook rather than Wendy, as in Steven Spielberg's *Hook*. John Gardner's *Grendel* changes our perspective of *Beowulf*. A story from the point of view of Javert (as opposed to Jean Valjean) in *Les Misérables* or from the point of view of the Sheriff of Nottingham rather than Robin Hood would not only change our sympathies somewhat but also our perceptions about the world, what is right and wrong. Point of view is extremely important in a story. It affects our moral sense and our understanding of the secondary world of the tale. It provides us with our world view which suggests that the perceptions and judgments made by the omniscient narrator are absolute truth and right thinking. Even this, however, can be thought of as the author's point of view. And if the tale is told by a character or even by a narrator limiting his main perceptions to those of a single character, or only one character at a time (as does Tolkien), then more can be learned than from just plot, dialogue, or action of the story. For characters, by what they notice, report, comment upon, or find worthy of attention and by what they *fail* to notice, can reveal much about their own characters and world views than mere actions or dialogue.

Most criticism of literature asks us to look beyond *what* is being said by the author to examine also *how* it is presented. A closer look at J.R.R. Tolkien's technique of using a limited or omniscient point of view in his stories may reveal much to us. The diagram below illustrates several levels of interpretation possible for any work of literature. This represents various levels at which a work may be interpreted. It is based on a model by Hazard Adams from the University of Washington.

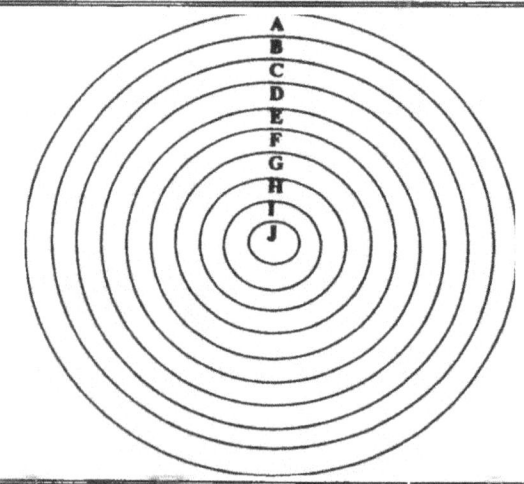

A) Context of Story, of author

B) Author, his canon or "fictive reader"

C) Title, introduction, preface

D) Theme(s), issues

E) Narrator(s) omniscient or limited

F) Visual tableaus – what we are only shown

G) Verbal tableaus – what we are only told about

H) Characters/events

I) Plot/story inferred

The centre of interpretation, of course, is the plot or the story itself. Our awareness of the particular character traits or personalities of the characters can colour our evaluation of the plot. These next two levels I added when I was writing a paper on *Hamlet* and may apply better to plays than to novels, but are still relevant here, I believe. What other characters tell us about (which I call verbal tableaus) or just show us (which I call visual tableaus) can also add to our understanding of the events. One example in Tolkien of this level comes in the "Council of Elrond" chapter of *The Lord of the Rings* when each participant at the council *tells* his own story, but we also *see* much of Boromir's personality coming forth when he is willing to interrupt Elrond's plan to get his own say in. However, it is on the fifth level, level E, the level of point of view of the narrator(s) that I wish to concentrate at present. But first let me continue to explain the other levels. Themes may be stated by the author, by characters, or implied by the action and resolution of the plot. Certainly the issues which the author is interested in will become known by the situations in which he or she placed the characters. Above the level of the tale itself, additional meaning can sometimes be inferred through the use of the title or from an introduction (often by the author himself). Tolkien's "Prologue" to *The Lord of the Rings* is a perfect example of this, as the entire frame tale which authenticates the story as having come from the "Red Book of Westmarch", a history of Hobbits which included the story of *The Hobbit*, also provides a larger context for the present tale and gives away the "happy ending" by mentioning some history of the characters after the events of the present tale. This level is useful to compare with the point of view in *The Hobbit*, as well, since the narrator then paraphrased Bilbo's account, revealing his own bias. Tolkien's "Foreword", in this case, is yet another level removed from his "Prologue". The "Prologue" deals mainly with hobbits and the tale of *The Lord of the Rings*; the "Foreword" refers to Tolkien's creative process in writing *The Lord of the Rings*. Beyond just one work lies an entire canon of a particular author. Knowing that, for Tolkien, *The Silmarillion* came first and was the major opus he kept returning to, adding to, and revising would also affect our interpretations of the other works. Sometimes themes become more evident when we see them repeated over and over in other works, or we get variations on a theme in other works. The last level of possible interpretation of a work (that I use) is the contextual level. Here not only the time period in which the author is writing, but also his particular interests and even the events which have shaped his life become important.

There are schools of criticism, such as deconstructuralism, which also include reference to our own paradigms, the contexts of the reader's life which might colour an interpretation of the work, but I have deliberately kept my focus on the text itself and its many levels of possible meaning. An evaluation of the reader's bias would, of course, be broader than my A level as would Marxist criticism which tries to tie power and finance into creativity by suggesting the political situation could dictate which works could get published. But this is not my concern. Another school would focus more particularly on the word or sentence level (in more detail than my level I, sort of on the J, K, or L level). Here the author's choice of vocabulary, sentence structure or the flow of the sentences, the division into paragraphs or chapters would be examined, but this is more detailed than I choose to be at this time. One might even doubt my own last level, arguing that a work of literature can stand on its own without need for knowledge about the author's life or likes, but in light of so many excellent critical articles published about Tolkien which illustrate his sources and influences, I doubt that anyone would begrudge me that level.

This paper will focus on level E, then, and compare three different sets of works to show how a change in narrator can change the focus of the tale itself. First I want to evaluate Bilbo as the narrator of *The Hobbit* and compare this to Gandalf's version of the first part of that story found in "The Quest of Erebor" in *Unfinished Tales*. For this I will also refer to the summary from Tolkien's "Prologue" to *The Lord of the Rings*. Then I would like to compare Aragorn's version of the Beren and Lúthien tale to that found in *The Silmarillion* with some reference to "The Tale of Aragorn and Arwen" from Appendix A. And finally I will look at Bilbo's telling of Eärendil's tale in the halls of Elrond to the version provided in *The Silmarillion*. Other such examples are possible but these should illustrate my points. I hope to show that hobbits, men, Istari, a historian/scholar or a scribe, and the omniscient narrator of *The Silmarillion* focus on different aspects of a tale due to their own personalities, interests, or concerns. Naturally the interests of the hobbits or men might be more limited than those of a God-like narrator.

Let me begin with a definition of the different kinds of narrator possible. A first-person narrator is the most limited because he can only report what he thinks, sees, says, hears, does, or is told about by another character. *The Hobbit* uses a third-person/limited narrator which is very similar. It also purports to have been written after the conclusion of the adventure from a journal kept by Bilbo on his travels; thus the subtitle "There and Back Again" reveals the ending. It also brings us the issue of memory and the trustworthiness of the recollection. *The Lord of the Rings* uses a similar third-person limited point of view with some variations. Its point of view is limited to one character at a time, but it is not always the same character: for example, it is Gimli's point of view we get on the Paths of the Dead, and more importantly Sam's in Mordor. But Tolkien usually chooses a less powerful, less "in charge" character for his point of view. However, there are even a few exceptions in *The Lord of the Rings*, for example the seeming omniscient reporting of the dreams each of the hobbits (except Sam) has in Tom Bombadil's house. But even this supposed exception could be explained by having each of the hobbits tell his dream to Frodo who eventually compiles the entire story. But this does not explain the fox's point of view as he wonders at seeing three hobbits travelling through the woods, but this is one of the few exceptions to Tolkien's use of third-person/limited point of view as opposed to omniscient in *The Hobbit* and *The Lord of the Rings*. This third-person/limited viewpoint narrows our focus to what that character is aware of or interested in. The choice of this character determines what details we will have, and how those details will be weighted or interpreted for us. Since the limit is on what the character already knows and then sees, hears, and does, there is often much dialogue, and even minor actions are reported. This tends to limit the story in time and space as well, but to expand it in detail.

The Silmarillion and *Unfinished Tales* often use a different narrator. It has been said that *The Silmarillion* was like Tolkien's Bible as it is the history of an entire race of beings and thus the scope is much vaster. Each tale is like reducing *The Lord of the Rings* to a 15-page summary, and connecting it to all other significant happenings of that age. The connections to other tales, to the larger history in *The Silmarillion*, become more important than the limited individual actions, dialogue, or observations. This provides us with a larger sense of purpose but less personal involvement. So there are advantages and disadvantages to each type of narrator. But that is not the point here. I simply want to illustrate how the choice of narrator affects our interpretation of the tale.

Let me begin with *The Hobbit*, "The Quest of Erebor" (which is Gandalf's version of the beginning of that tale), and the narrator from the Prologue to *The Lord of the Rings*. I will assume more familiarity on the part of the audience with *The Hobbit* and *The Lord of the Rings*, so I will focus more on the other works to show contrast. Bilbo, as has been pointed out, was very concerned about eating and drinking, creature comforts, and things familiar to himself (like riddles), so his version focused often on what meals he was enjoying or was deprived of, etc. At the beginning of the tale Bilbo has no plan to seek adventures – the designs seem to be either Thorin's or Gandalf's, and it is mainly Bilbo's confusion and limited understanding we see through the narrative. His interests are limited to dirty dishes and forgotten handkerchiefs. "The Quest of Erebor" shows a different focus on the tale itself and the choice of Bilbo to accompany Thorin and Company.

But first let me comment that "The Quest of Erebor" is complicated by yet another level of interpretation as to its narrator for it purports to be Frodo's recollection of a conversation with Gandalf in Minas Tirith after the coronation of King Elessar. So technically it is Frodo who is the narrator, but almost the entire tale is a quoted passage of Gandalf speaking, so perhaps we could trust to Frodo's memory and his accurate representation of Gandalf's words and intent. Therefore I will refer to this as Gandalf's point of view, despite the fact that Frodo admits, "I cannot remember all the tale now" (Tolkien, 1980, p. 321). So we know we do not have the entire story the exact way Gandalf told it. Frodo interprets Gandalf's interests and motives a bit when he says, "we gathered that to begin with Gandalf was thinking only of the defence of the West against the Shadow" (Tolkien, 1980, p. 321). This would make Gandalf's point of view broader, certainly more so than Bilbo's or even Thorin's, and more like that of the omniscient narrator in *The Silmarillion*. And yet the quoted material, supposedly Gandalf's own words, does not entirely bear out the claim that Gandalf was *only* concerned with Middle-earth itself. However, Frodo's claims predispose the reader towards a particular interpretation of the events which an examination of the text does not clearly prove true. But this just shows us the power of the narrator. In the text, Gandalf first admits to going to the Shire himself for some rest and to reason out the problem that Sauron posed to the West (not yet to act, in other words). Gandalf focuses much on the concept of fate. He claims when he met Thorin, "it was at that moment that the tide began to turn" (Tolkien, 1980, p. 322). He talks of his possession of the map and key as "another strange chance" (Tolkien, 1980, p. 323). Apparently an earlier version also suggested the older Gandalf was "no longer trammelled by the burden of Middle-earth as I was then" (Tolkien, 1980, p. 329). So the most recent version of "The Quest of Erebor" shows more awareness of the broader perspective of happenings in Middle-earth (beyond the scope of the concern of the dwarves or of the hobbit Bilbo) and at least in retrospect a belief in and trusting in fate – a faith in the concept of the overarching universe with some sort of plan beyond the individual's. Gandalf's point of view gives us a breadth of space, a larger view of Middle-earth, which includes the Necromancer/Sauron and his plans as well as the desires of the dwarves (and possibly one hobbit's desire for adventure). It gives us a larger space but not the same depth in time we would get in *The Silmarillion*. Nor does the quoted material support Frodo's claim for totally unselfish motives on Gandalf's part.

Gandalf's version provides another point of interest or comparison, for at one point he interprets Bilbo's motivations.

> I guessed that he wanted to remain "unattached" for some reason deep down which he did not understand himself – or would not acknowledge, for it alarmed him. He wanted, all the same, to be free to go when the chance came, or he had made up his courage.
>
> (Tolkien, 1980, p. 331)

Nowhere in Bilbo's version does he ascribe such motives to himself for his unmarried state. Thus a different narrator can give us a different psychological view of a character. This passage again reveals Gandalf's interest and belief in fate, which we don't find in Bilbo's account. Bilbo talks about *luck* and *chance* but not *fate*.

Gandalf himself recognized and acknowledged the truth that different narrators tell slightly different tales about the same events. "The Quest of Erebor" really only attempts to explain why Bilbo was included in the dwarves' plans at Gandalf's suggestion. Gandalf then said, "the rest of the story is well known to you – from Bilbo's point of view. If I had written the account, it would have sounded rather different" (Tolkien, 1980, p. 335). Later Frodo says,

> "Well, I am glad to have heard the full tale. If it is full. I do not really suppose that even now you are telling us all you know."
>
> "Of course not," said Gandalf.
>
> (Tolkien, 1980, p. 336)

And also we might remember that Frodo admitted that he had forgotten some of the tale when he went to set it down. Thus another truth about the point-of-view of the narrator is that it is always a partial story, not a complete version of the tale, which would require not only perfect memory, but also a point-of-view account from each of the characters. Ironically Tolkien's omniscient narrator in *The Silmarillion* is often the scantiest with details, though the limits of memory, or awareness of the thoughts, actions, dialogue, and perceptions of several characters are available to him. In other words, he should have access to more detail but he chooses not to include them. Instead the focus for the omniscient narrator is broader in purpose or theme. But he's still controlling to what the reader will be exposed.

The result of Gandalf's addition to the tale, however, is to broaden *The Hobbit* to include actions more directly connected with the larger picture provided by *The Lord of the Rings*. The actions of the dwarves and Bilbo are thus connected to Gandalf's battle with the Necromancer/Sauron and its repercussions for all of Middle-earth. No longer could Sauron enlist the aid of a dragon in the north; Sauron does not choose to attack Rivendell or Lothlórien but instead flees to Mordor; and finally fate decrees that the One Ring will be found again, thus precipitating the events in *The Lord of the Rings*. Gandalf as narrator broadens our perspectives and concerns over space, he shows us a larger map.

The "Prologue" to *The Lord of the Rings* provides a frame tale of the discovery of the "Red Book of Westmarch" telling tales of *days gone by* in the Third Age. Thus a perspective of time is introduced. The narrator at one point says, "Those days, the Third Age of Middle-earth, are now long past, and the shape of all lands has been changed" (Tolkien, 1991, p. 14). This narrator is complex, of course, because he is a "modern" historian/scholar who has uncovered an old manuscript and will interpret it for us. He is not involved in the tale nor affected by it. But through the perspective of time and with hindsight, he can focus on the most important events. Thus in his version of Bilbo's tale, his concern is not Bilbo's confusion or interest with food or a dry bed, nor Gandalf's designs and motivations. He summarizes in one paragraph the entire tale and then comments that this "adventure" was only important because of the "accident" of Bilbo's finding of the Ring. He then recounts in much more detail the "Riddles of the Dark" chapter from *The Hobbit*.

As a historian/scholar his interest also lies in the different versions of Bilbo's tale – the lie he first told the dwarves and set down in his memoirs and the true account which this narrator subscribes to Frodo or Sam rather than Bilbo. Our narrator from the Prologue, the historian/scholar, also analyses Bilbo's choice of calling the Ring a "present" as being suggested by Gollum's naming it his "birthday present." The historian/scholar not only has Gandalf's spacial perspective but also a temporal view from safely in the Fourth Age. However, unlike the omniscient narrator of *The Silmarillion*, he is limited to the text itself. He can interpret the author of the text's use of a specific word like "present" but has no other knowledge than that provided in his version of the "Red Book of Westmarch". And though he tries to claim its authenticity, he also admits his own limitations. This is not the original; "the original Red Book has not been preserved, but many copies were made" (Tolkien, 1991, p. 26). He traces his copy to one written in Gondor, "an exact copy in all details of the Thain's Book in Minas Tirith" (Tolkien, 1991, p. 27) which "was a copy, made at the request of King Elessar, of the Red Book of the Periannath" (Tolkien, 1991, p. 27). Thus even this narrator admits that he has only that portion of the tale which was preserved in his version.

Of the next two comparisons I wish to make, the tale of Beren and Lúthien is perhaps the best known though for my purposes the most obvious and therefore the less interesting. I am comparing Aragorn's telling of that story at Weathertop with *The Silmarillion*'s version. As I do this I will also refer to "The Tale of Aragorn and Arwen" from Appendix A of *The Lord of the Rings*. Most of Strider's entire poem or chant (eight of nine stanzas) deals with Lúthien and recounts her meeting with Beren. The only exception is a line that refers to Beren's fate: "Enchantment healed his weary feet / That over hills were doomed to roam" (Tolkien, 1991, p. 208). But this version does not tell us over which hills, why he was doomed, or where he roamed to and why. It does not require a great stretch of the critical faculties to suppose that Aragorn is reminded of his own meeting with Arwen and how he mistook her for Lúthien Tinúviel, and that this determines his focus on the tale that he tells the hobbits. Only the last stanza deals with the adventures Beren and Lúthien shared.

> Long was the way that fate them bore,
>   O'er stony mountains cold and grey,
> Through halls of iron and darkling door,
>   And woods of nightshade morrowless.
> The Sundering Seas between them lay,
>   And yet at last they met once more,
> And long ago they passed away
>   In the forest singing sorrowless.
> (Tolkien, 1991, p. 209)

And even this stanza mentions the romantic idea that even death could not keep them apart. But more importantly, the entire passage does not mention the Silmarils at all. Strider does admit that this is only part of the tale, and he summarizes part of the rest for the hobbits. He tells of the slaying of Barahir, Beren's father, and Beren's escape over the Mountains of Terror to Thingol's kingdom (Beren's early experiences here, by the way, do coincide a bit with Aragorn's own history of losing his own father at age two and going with his mother to live with Elrond under a hidden identity to keep Sauron from discovering his whereabouts, so again there is a personal connection). Thus there was more to the story *before* the part that Aragorn chose to relate. And there was more after:

> Many sorrows befell them afterwards, and they were parted long. Tinúviel rescued Beren from the dungeons of Sauron, and together they passed through great dangers, and cast down even the Great Enemy from his throne, and took from his iron crown one of the three Silmarils, brightest of all jewels, to be the bride-price of Lúthien to Thingol her father. Yet at the last Beren was slain by the Wolf that came from the gates of Angband, and he died in the arms of Tinúviel. But she chose mortality, and to die from the world, so that she might follow him.
> (Tolkien, 1991, p. 210)

Here at least we have a wider glimpse of the significance of the story but he also focuses still on the romance – Tinúviel's choice to become mortal, as Arwen will. Aragorn then relates the lineage of Lúthien and Beren, connecting both Elrond of Rivendell and the kings of Númenor (himself, though he does not claim this at the time). This part isn't in *The Silmarillion*, but it would certainly be of interest to Aragorn especially since he had just discovered it prior to meeting Arwen. Aragorn himself admits that he must of necessity omit part of the tale "for it is a long tale, of which the end is not known; and there are none now, except Elrond, that remember it aright as it was told of old" (Tolkien, 1991, p. 208). So his choices of what part of the tale to tell, what to summarize, and what to quote from the song "in a mode that is called *ann-thennath*" (Tolkien, 1991, p. 210) become even more significant. In addition this is supposedly a translation into the Common Speech and has by implication *lost* something in the translation, as Aragorn says, "this is but a rough echo of it" (Tolkien, 1991, p. 210).

But again, as I said before, this is a relatively simple comparison because Aragorn puts almost the entire emphasis on the romance of the tale, the meeting between Beren and Lúthien which is so closely related to his own meeting with Arwen. "The Tale of Aragorn and Arwen" (or actually a part of that tale as it is labelled in Appendix A of *The Lord of the Rings*) creates for us another problem with identifying the narrator. It is included as per the "Prologue" as part of the "Red Book of Westmarch". But according to our historian/scholar the "abbreviated version of those parts of *The Tale of Aragorn and Arwen* which lie outside the account of the War" (Tolkien, 1991, p. 27) was added later in Minas Tirith. Thus we cannot assume Frodo or any hobbit translated, transcribed, or wrote from memory this tale. The entire passage is in quotes which could be accounted for by the fact that it is only a part of a larger tale. But I prefer to think that it was written, dictated, or related by Aragorn himself. Certainly dialogue is included between Aragorn and his mother Gilraen, between Aragorn and Elrond, and even between Aragorn and Arwen which only he would know. The story also refers to Aragorn's solitude. Yet it often subtly praises him as well, for example, "he seemed to Men worthy of honour" (Tolkien, 1991, p. 1097) and this would suggest that a scribe or court writer might well have recorded the tale. And also the story continues beyond the death of Aragorn to that of Arwen as well, so the court scribe as narrator seems more likely but I will refer to Aragorn as the narrator in the same way I called Gandalf the narrator of "The Quest of Erebor" since (other than a little harmless flattery of Aragorn) the scribe does not seem to interject his own world view or observations.

In "The Tale of Aragorn and Arwen" we learn that indeed Aragorn had been singing part of the "Lay of Lúthien" about the meeting between Beren and Lúthien (perhaps the very same passage he quoted to the hobbits) when he first saw Arwen. So we know that Aragorn has a personal connection to and fondness for the part of the story he chose to relate. As I said, in *The Fellowship of the Ring*, the story focuses almost entirely on the romance. Very little was said of the long way "which fate them bore" or the dangers or indeed even the successes or the glories either. In "The Tale of Aragorn and Arwen" an older Aragorn with an awareness of how his own tale worked out (in retrospect) more clearly connects his life quest with Beren's when he relates his conversation with Elrond: " I see that I have turned my eyes to a treasure no less dear than the treasure of Thingol that Beren once desired. Such is my fate" (Tolkien, 1991, p. 1096). Both Gandalf and Aragorn (after the fact, with the quest successfully completed) do focus more on fate than they did earlier. Yet even "The Tale of Aragorn and Arwen" still emphasizes the romantic story, not Aragorn's role in the political events of Middle-earth, except that becoming King of both Gondor and Arnor was a condition upon which he could claim Arwen.

So we see, through Aragorn as a narrator, that his focus is more narrow even than Gandalf's. He is, of course, deeply involved in the War of the Ring, the battle against Sauron, but he limits his own concerns to those of men, to fight to defend Minas Tirith before attacking the Dark Lord directly, to claim his kingship and his bride, to govern well, and to choose the hour of his own death rather than to "fall from my high seat unmanned and witless" (Tolkien, 1991, p. 1100). And the primary motivating factor for him is his love for Arwen. This is revealed partly in his choice of which portion of the Beren and Lúthien tale to tell.

The narrator of *The Silmarillion*, on the other hand, has a much vaster focus of interest. He is telling the tale of the entire First Age, of which the tale of Beren and Lúthien is only a small, but important, part. His interests, though, will be in connecting this tale to the larger political and social history. In *The Silmarillion* the story is told in prose rather than poetry (either in the Common Speech as is Aragorn's translation, or in its original Elvish). This choice alone on the part of *The Silmarillion*'s narrator affects the reader. The narrator does use poetry to quote the battle between Finrod Felagund and Sauron in songs of power, and also quotes the Song of Parting which figures prominently in the plot. But he relates all the rest, even Lúthien's songs to Morgoth or to Mandos, in prose. Thus this version reads more like summary of a tale than the tale itself. We sometimes feel deprived of the dialogue, the psychological or physical detail, the report of the songs themselves.

I won't recount the entire tale of Beren and Lúthien from *The Silmarillion*, but I would like to point out that the emphasis is on the political interactions between the various groups of elves and how Beren's and Lúthien's actions affected those political relationships. The narrator often veers the tale away from Beren or Lúthien to reveal the political shenanigans of the sons of Fëanor – Celegorm and Curufin – or to reveal Sauron's or Morgoth's plots to defeat Huan, or to discuss the machinations of Thingol. The love between Beren and Lúthien is not as much the focus as the repercussions of that love on the other elves. Melian tells Thingol that the quest he has devised for Beren will bring doom and draw Doriath "within the fate of a mightier realm" (Tolkien, 1992, p. 168). Fate again is an important theme. And the perspective of this narrator is on the entire fate or history of the elves, how every action, every character, is interconnected with the others. It is broader in both space and time than Aragorn's view. Thus it seems weightier in theme, though scantier in detail.

My last example, I believe, will show much the same thing, as I compare Bilbo's version of the story of Eärendil to that given in *The Silmarillion*. Actually, the poem Bilbo recited, though composed mostly by himself, was also amended, edited, or added to by Aragorn. Bilbo claims that it should be easy to tell which is the narrator. To Lindir, a listening elf, he says, "if you can't distinguish between a Man and a Hobbit, your judgement is poorer than I imagined. They're as different as peas and apples" (Tolkien, 1991, p. 253). Lindir claims all mortals sound alike. Bilbo tells Frodo that Aragorn's addition was mostly the reference to a green stone (probably the line "upon his breast an emerald"). Aragorn's own name, "Elfstone", foretold to him even before he received the stone, might suggest his interest in such a talisman. And assuming Aragorn's interest in romance, there could easily have been more detail in the poem about Elwing and her love and help for her husband in his trials were Aragorn truly a co-author. Since there is not and also for other reasons (for one Aragorn had only been around three days and had doubtless had important business other than composing poems to attend to), and also because of the style and point of view in the poem, I will assume most of the version is Bilbo's and refer to him as the narrator, but I will eventually show how his interests and perceptions as revealed by the poem might also coincide with Aragorn's, so that it is appropriate that both are judged to be the author/narrator.

First, the choice of subject matter is always of interest – why does Bilbo choose Eärendil? Aragorn seems to think it a bit cheeky for him to do so in Elrond's own house. Bilbo could have done so to try to flatter Elrond but nothing in the poem suggests flattery (certainly not in the same way that the scribe of Minas Tirith seemed to flatter Aragorn in "The Tale of Aragorn and Arwen"). If this theory can be dismissed, then it seems likely that Bilbo's interest in Eärendil is personal, that he feels some kinship of spirit with the restless Elf (or half-Elf) who wanted adventure, yet later yearned for home, who took the plea for help from men and elves to the shores of Valinor itself, and who was eventually exiled from the earth into the heavens with the Silmaril on his brow. At the end Bilbo writes of Eärendil "But on him mighty doom was laid . . . [and he could] tarry never more on Hither Shores where mortals are" (Tolkien, 1991, p. 253). He is forever on an errand, never to rest or go home. At this point in his life, of course, Bilbo is in self-imposed exile from the Shire. He has done his wandering and merely settled in Rivendell because it seemed the best place to be – yet it isn't home and he is without his kin and loved ones (most notably Frodo). Aragorn as well has had little rest from wandering and thus it is appropriate that the poem be partly ascribed to him as well.

Bilbo does give elaborate detail of the makings of the ship, the wardrobe of Eärendil, his flight into the heavens. Bilbo is interested in the details of the story which personalize it to one man, one ship (actually two), more so than its political import. There is no mention of the political necessity for Eärendil's journey to Valinor, nor of the coming of the Valar to Middle-earth to fight with men and elves in the final battle between the Host of the West and Morgoth in which Morgoth is defeated and exiled to the void, nor of the part played by the sons of Fëanor when the other two Silmarils from the Iron Crown are recovered or how they are lost again. None of the vaster political or social ramifications of Eärendil's tale are referred to by Bilbo. This broader perspective is only seen through the point of view of the narrator of *The Silmarillion*.

The omniscient narrator in *The Silmarillion* has another advantage: he can provide for us motivation or emotion for several characters. He can tell us of Elwing that "she sat in sorrow by the mouths of Sirion" (Tolkien, 1992, p. 246) or that Maedhros was tormented by knowledge of his unfulfilled oath or that Eärendil turned in despair at seeing the ruins of Sirion. These details provide the logical connections, the cause-and-effect logic, to explain the actions of the characters on that grander scale, but also might divide the reader's interest or sense of loyalty. The limited third-person narrative focuses attention more on one character.

We've examined several kinds of narrators: Bilbo, Aragorn, Gandalf, the historian/scholar who discovered the "Red Book of Westmarch", the scribe in Minas Tirith who recorded Aragorn's story, and the omniscient narrator in *The Silmarillion*. As I said earlier, there are advantages and disadvantages to each kind of narrator – the more limited point of view is less broad in scope or theme, but at least in Tolkien more detailed in description, dialogue, poetry, song, etc. The omniscient narrator has a broader purpose but loses the ability to involve his readers with a greater wealth of detail and focus. He can still involve them with the power of the story or the theme or purpose itself. I do not presume to choose one as better than the other, though since we already have *The Silmarillion* to provide the scope, I would love to read a three-volume version of the Beren and Lúthien story or of the Fall of Gondolin in the same detail as *The Lord of the Rings*.

But hopefully I have demonstrated how the awareness and observations, the interests, the world view and concerns of the narrator can affect the telling of the tale. We never really get to read a definitive tale. It is always a summary or presentation by some narrator. If there were an ur-Tale or an Ideal Tale, it would have to encompass the points of view, awareness, and biases of all the characters as well as the scope of vision and the depth of space and time possible with an omniscient narrator. Not only would such redundancy be boring, but even that could not be without its bias as then the *order* of the presentation of the various points of view would suggest their relative importance.

So each author must choose *how* to present the tale. Looking at the circles again – an omniscient narrator tends to focus on the theme or issue level (D); a more limited narrator's interest stays more on the plot, action, character levels (I, H). This is not to say the limited narrator does not reveal theme, but it takes longer; the omniscient narrator does discuss plot and character but perhaps in less detail. But *any* narrator, whether limited or omniscient, still gives only a partial rendering of the tale. And therefore, the narrator by his choice of what aspects of the tale he presents or emphasizes can reveal as much about himself as he does about the tale. A gifted author, like Tolkien, would keep this in mind in *his* choice of narrator. This kind of evaluation, of course, focusing on point of view, going back to the circles again, is only one layer of analysis, but examination of the tale at this level should make our appreciation of the tale that much richer. It should also make us very appreciative of the other versions of Tolkien's tales which have come out as then we can better see the choices the narrator has made.

References

Tolkien, J. R. R. 1980. *Unfinished Tales*. Ed. Christopher Tolkien. Boston: Houghton Mifflin.

Tolkien, J. R. R. 1991. *The Lord of the Rings*. Boston: Houghton Mifflin.

Tolkien, J. R. R. 1992. *The Silmarillion*. Ed. Christopher Tolkien. London: HarperCollins.

J.R.R. Tolkien and the Clerihew

Joe R. Christopher

Abstract: The clerihew, a form of light verse, is part of Tolkien's *oeuvre*. This study offers (1) a brief history and an elaborate definition of the genre, (2) a discussion of the clerihews that have been written about Tolkien or his works, and (3) an analysis of the clerihews that Tolkien wrote.

Keywords: Owen Barfield, Edmund Clerihew Bentley, G.K. Chesterton, clerihew, Nevill Coghill, Grimalkin, Dr. Robert E. Havard, Sir Robert Helpmann, C.S. Lewis, Fr. Gervase Mathew, J.R.R. Tolkien, Charles Williams.

I. The Generic Background

When Edmund Clerihew Bentley (1875-1949) was sixteen, according to his autobiography, or possibly seventeen or eighteen, he wrote

> Sir Humphrey [sic] Davy
> Was not fond of gravy[.]
> He lived in the odium
> Of having discovered sodium.

At the time, Bentley was attending St. Paul's School in London. His school friends – G.K. Chesterton, L.R.F. Oldershaw, W.P.H. d'Avigdor and Maurice Solomon – as well as Chesterton's father, contributed verses of the same sort to the notebook, which is dated September 1893. This notebook has since been published as *The First Clerihews*.

Before the form is defined, an artistic point may be made. When Bentley collected his first verse in *Biography for Beginners* in 1905, the second line was revised to "Abominated gravy." Then, when he quoted the verse in his autobiography, *Those Days* (1940), the second line reads "Detested gravy." These are improvements. "Was not fond of" is acceptable as a litote, but it is a group of monosyllables, which makes for a weak line. "Abominated" is more forceful, but it does not tie into the rest of the quatrain. "Detested" alliterates on its weak, first syllable with "Davy" and with the unaccented, first syllable of "discovered". The only weakness of "Detested" as compared to "Abominated" is that it has the same metrical pattern as the first line (an iamb – X / – and an amphibrach – X / X – in each). As is apparent from a reading of Bentley's clerihews, no repeated metrics are intended.

The books of Bentley's clerihews are these:
> *Biography for Beginners* (1905),
> *More Biography* (1929),
> *Baseless Biography* (1939)
> *Clerihews Complete* (1951)
> *The Complete Clerihews of E. Clerihew Bentley* (1981, rev. 1983).

Clerihews Complete, compiled by Bentley's editor after Bentley's death, lacked over thirty published verses. With the revision, *The Complete Clerihews* is complete, except for ninety of Bentley's early attempts which he did not remember, or wish to print, from that early notebook:
> *The First Clerihews* (1982).

The other authors' contributions to this volume remind a reader that there have been many imitations of Bentley's works; the most easily available collection (and probably the best) is an anthology edited by Gavin Ewart:
> *Other People's Clerihews* (1983).

A very pleasant survey of these books is William A.S. Sarjeant's "E.C. Bentley, G.K. Chesterton, and the Clerihew".

Perhaps two other clerihews, set beside that on Sir Humpry Davy, will be enough to establish the type. Then the rules can be given. The first appeared in *Biography for Beginners*:
> The people of Spain think Cervantes
> Equal to half a dozen Dantes:
> An opinion resented most bitterly
> By the people of Italy.

And then one from *Baseless Biography*:
> Lewis Carroll
> Bought sumptuous apparel
> And built an enormous palace
> Out of the profits of *Alice*.

The first of these two (which, by the way, *The First Clerihews* shows was written in its first version by G.K. Chesterton) is built on rhetorical parallelism: "The people of Spain . . . the people of Italy." It also uses an off-rhyme in *bitterly* and *Italy*. The most likely stress pattern in the verse suggests the lines have, respectively, three, four, three, and two stresses. The second is notable for its alliteration: the two verbs – *bought* and *built* – being emphasised by their plosive *b*'s; the *p*'s of the stressed syllables in *apparel*, *palace*, and *profits* tying together the last three lines; the near-alliteration of *out* and *Alice* in the last line helping the emphatic close.

At this point the rules of the verse form may be identified:

(1) The clerihew, named after E.C. Bentley's middle name, is a type of light verse.

(2) The verse form is that of a quatrain with two rhyming (or occasionally off-rhyming) couplets. Jaques

Barzun, in his poem on the clerihew titled "The Muse is Speaking", sums up this aspect this way:

> [The] strange but rigorous rhymes in pairs
> Impress the memory unawares.

Both the couplets and the four lines are important. *Other People's Clerihews*, in a section at the rear, has some five- and six-line sports; but they are obviously not what Bentley intended (even though some of them are by his son Nicholas). Bentley himself wrote two monorhyming clerihews, but one of those he suppressed when collecting *Baseless Biography*.

(3) The metre is essentially that of prose rhythms, although Bentley's examples suggest that fairly short lines, of two to four stresses, are normative. Some of the verse in *Other People's Clerihews*, in their extremely short or long lines, suggest a "sophistication" of the clerihew – a Silver Age to follow the Golden. In general, the repetition of the *same* meter (not the number of stresses, which is a different thing) is to be avoided. Further, Bentley's examples suggest that having the same number of stresses in all four lines is to be avoided. (The clerihew on Lewis Carroll, above, seems to have two, three, three and three stresses, respectively, in its four lines.) Barzun sums the meter up this way:

> In clerihews it is the norm
> For rhythmic anarchy to reign.

(4) The matter is biographical. This is evident from the first three titles by Bentley. It is striking that *The Complete Clerihews* does not repeat each of the first three volumes individually, but instead rearranges their contents into an alphabetical sequence by the persons discussed. Anthony Hecht and John Hollander have written that the clerihew "does for the personal name what Lear's form of the limerick . . . does for the place-name or attribute" (quoted by Gavin Ewart in his introduction to *Other People's Clerihews*). Barzun also comments on the biographical basis:

> This Bentley, then, (E. C. for short)
> Believed that it would be good sport
> To ransack history and descant
> On persons dead or still extant.

However, it is true that Bentley wrote a few semi-clerihews without names as introductions to or jacket blurbs for his volumes: just as a senryu is a haiku without a seasonal reference, so these verses cannot be accounted true clerihews. Perhaps they should be called bentleys. (This means that those verses in the "Mavericks and Sequences" section of *Other People's Clerihews* which begin with newspaper, magazine, and holiday-resort names, etc., etc., are deeply suspect. *Some* of W.A.S. Sarjeant's "Geological Clerihews" have such other material in the line with the name as to be also suspect.)

(5) The rhetorical form most commonly seen has the biographical name in the first line, although it occasionally appears in the second, as in this beginning from *More Biography*: "A man in the position / Of the Emperor Domitian . . ." Further, unlike the use of the name in a double dactyl, it need not fill a whole line by itself, although about half the time in Bentley's examples, it does. The example about Cervantes, quoted above, shows this non-full-line use of a name. Other examples show various uses of titles and other cognomen extenders: "Alexander of Macedon" (originally in *Baseless Biography*), "Mr. Hilaire Belloc" (*Biography for Beginners*), "Sir (then Mr.) Walter Besant" (*Biography for Beginners*), "President Coolidge" (*More Biography*), "Edward the Confessor" (*Biography for Beginners*), and so on.

Barzun gives a fuller description of the four lines, although he seems to believe only the first line can contain the name:

> One line invokes a well-known name,
> Three more disclose, for praise or blame
> In words that make one want to quote
> A single vivid anecdote.
> . . . .
> Line Two is factual and curt,
> The Third is planned to disconcert –
> A "sprung" or "contrapuntal" stab;
> The varying [L]ast may clinch or jab[.]

Actually, although the Davy clerihew has a disconcerting third line (the introduction of "odium"), the Carroll clerihew does not seem to turn on that line. And the present writer does not find a common punch-line emphasis ("jab") to the fourth line in Bentley's clerihews. (Of the three models, only the one on Carroll comes close; the others' fourth lines presumably "clinch".)

(6) The tone of the clerihew, says Gavin Ewart in his introduction to *The Complete Clerihews*, is "civilised and dotty". More specifically, Bentley does not use the clerihew for satire or erotic jokes (although both appear in *Other People's Clerihews*). He suppressed one clerihew which was too biographically accurate, which suggests the title of *Baseless Biography* is to be taken seriously. (Lewis Carroll did not, in fact, spend his money frivolously, despite the above clerihew.) What Ewart meant by calling the clerihew "civilized" was that its readership should know enough of history, enough about significant biographies, to recognize the extent of fantasy in the verse. It is the audience, even more than the verse, which is civilised. Barzun sums up this question in this manner:

> Debate has freely ranged as to
> The needs that such reports be true.
> . . . .
> We may conclude that on the whole
> . . . .
> It's now maintained by very few
> That *ben trovata* will not do.

Indeed, it is best to say that the clerihew is a variety of nonsense verse; it is often anachronistic ("Archbishop Laud / Saw nothing to admire in *Maud*" – *Baseless Biography*); at most, it may be said to reveal the folly of humanity – occasionally, of the historical individual named. On the other hand, it would be nice if there was *some* historical accuracy in the verse – Sir Humphry Davy *did* first obtain sodium in its metallic state; Lewis Carroll *did* make money from his *Alice* volumes. But it cannot be said that even this modicum of accuracy is *necessary* to the genre. At most, it is the normative state. As stated above, the clerihew's readership should be civilized enough to recognise the extent of the fantasy.

Perhaps, as a comment on the sixth rule, it may be worthwhile to quote a verse which Ewart missed when collecting *Other People's Clerihews*. In his introduction to an edition of Bentley's best mystery novel, *Trent's Last Case* (1913), Aaron Marc Stein writes:

> Edmund Clerihew Bentley
> Made mock of his world, but gently.
> He gave us, in pursuit of his creative bent,
> Philip Trent.

How accurate that is! Indeed the main flaw the quatrain has as a clerihew is its accuracy. It is civilized but not dotty.

(7) None of Bentley's clerihews are given individual titles, outside of those semi-clerihews used as book introductions. In contrast, four by Edmund Wilson reprinted in the back of *Other People's Clerihews* (one is a five-line sport) have titles. Perhaps this is a trivial rule, but it does seem that Bentley did not intend for clerihews to receive individual titles. (Limericks, for the most part, are not individually titled; double dactyls normally are. One might think this the distinction between a folk art, the limerick — even if probably that of an educated folk — and an invented verse form, the double dactyl; but the clerihew indicates this is not a valid distinction.)

(8) Finally, the most trivial rule of all: Bentley's is old-fashioned verse with the first word of each line capitalized. In his introduction to *The Complete Clerihews*, Ewart quotes one of his own clerihews which does not follow this practice.

This introduction on the genre has been long and perhaps laborious, but most readers (outside of light-verse enthusiasts) do not seem to know what clerihews are. It will be the thesis of the last section that J.R.R. Tolkien did understand the genre. But first, a digression.

II. Celebrations of Tolkien

Before a consideration is given to Tolkien's own clerihews, perhaps those clerihews mentioning or alluding to Tolkien should be considered; after all, they too fit the title of this paper. At least four have been published, three of them preserved in *Other People's Clerihews*. One of these is by Robin Skelton:

> William Cobbett
> Never discovered a hobbit,
> Although he tried
> On every Rural Ride.

The "dotty" element, of course, is the introduction of hobbits into Cobbett's world; the "civilised" element is the reference to that minor but enduring work of English literature, *Rural Rides* (newspaper, 1820-30; book, 1830). The stress pattern of the syllables in the clerihew can best be shown here and later in this essay by a diagram — with X's for unstressed syllables, /'s for stressed, and occasional \'s for secondary stresses — which a reader can, if he or she wishes, compare to the verse. The pattern which matches the above verse is

/ X / X
/ X X / X X / X
X / X /
X / X [X] / X /

The stress pattern — two, three, two, three — is perhaps too regular; but the lines are varied with the feminine endings of the first couplet and the masculine of the second. The meter is trochaic in the first line, irregular in the second (a trochee, and iamb and a third-class pæon), and iambic in the last two. Those who pronounce *every* with three syllables will make the last line an iamb, an anapest and another iamb. There is alliteration on *k* in the first two lines (*Cob-* and *-cov-*); the *r*'s of "Rural Ride" are quietly prepared for in the nearly buried *r*'s of *tried* and *every* (and perhaps earlier, in the *r*'s of the off-rhyme of "Never discovered"). In short, Skelton's verse is an excellent clerihew.

Another of the verses in *Other People's Clerihews* is this one by Joanne Hill:

> J.R.R. Tolkien
> Was not, on the whole, keen
> On trolls made of plastic,
> But he thought gnomes were fantastic.

The meter is nicely irregular, and the first line with its three initials is uncertain in scansion (which is probably a virtue). No doubt different readers will stress that first line differently. Here is one version:

\ / \ / \
X / X X / /
X / X X / X
X X / / X X / X

This can be described in metrical terms, but it seems not worth doing. For example, to say that the first line consists of a "heavy" iamb and a "heavy" amphibrach is accurate enough as the above markings go; but the markings show the pattern already. The main point to be made is that the pattern is irregular. The second and the third lines are the closest in pattern, but they are framed with less regular lines. Surprisingly, the main stress pattern to the lines is not as irregular as the meters: two, three, two, three.

If Hill thought that Tolkien pronounced his name TOLE-keen, then she was attempting a pure rhyme in the first couplet. *Trolls* in line three would then echo the stressed syllable of the rhyme as well as alliterate with *Tol-*. But, since Tolkien did not pronounce his name that way, the first two lines must be considered an off-rhyme.

The fantasy element in Hill's clerihew involves shifting Tolkien's trolls (as in *The Hobbit*) and dwarves (one meaning of *gnomes*) into a modern form — plastic. (Are these supposed to be yard decorations? small figurines for whatnot shelves? or what? Whatever they are, the word *plastic* is the operative term.) The assertion of Tolkien's attitudes is sheer invention, of course — that is, it is part of the fantasy element.

Hill's clerihew is not as good as Skelton's, for she has essentially written a joke (the last line is a punch line). Jokes are not whimsical biographies. A glance through *The Complete Clerihews* shows that Bentley usually makes the last two lines (not the last line) into a complete clause. Hill's grammatical structure reveals her verse's limits. (Jaques Barzun's similar confusion was discussed in the first section.)

The third, and last, of these clerihews in Ewart's anthology is by Tess van Summers, appearing in a section titled

"Australians" in the back of the book:

> Helpmann (Sir Robert)
> Is *not* a hobbit.
> A hobbit is a species of fairy,
> And its feet are not small and neat but large and hairy.

A number of nice things could be said about the mechanics of this verse (including the internal rhyme of *feet* and *neat* in the last line, although the line itself is longer than Bentley's models), but two comments about the content are more significant here. First, is the third line the deliberate "dotty" element, or is it simply a mistake on the part of the author? Since that is a question of intention, it would need contact with van Summers to answer. But the line does not have the *feel* of dottiness. One suspects that the whimsical element in the verse is simply the introduction of hobbits, beginning in the second line, into the comparison. The third line, on the other hand, is simply wrong (within Tolkien's literary universe, at any rate; perhaps not in the popular mind). Hobbits, in Middle-earth, are a species of human beings – analogous to the non-fictional pygmies in Africa. (In order not to seem naive, one may note that van Summers may be *denying* that Helpman, despite the reputation of his profession, is a homosexual; in that case, the confusion of hobbits and fairies is deliberate, for a non-Tolkienesque point.)

Second, the choice of Sir Robert Helpmann raises the question of obscurity. He is presumably the Australian-born dancer, choreographer, and actor, best known in America for his work as choreographer and main male dancer in the movie *The Red Shoes*. In *Biography for Beginners* appears a verse about Mr Alfred Beit, whom Ewart in his introduction does not identify beyond what G.K. Chesterton's drawing suggests. Marie Smith, in a note to "An Alphabet" in Chesterton's *Collected Nonsense and Light Verse* (1987), identifies Beit as "a Hamburg-born financier (reputably the world's richest man) whose wealth came from South Africa" (123). It is impressive that the world's richest man is remembered today mainly because Chesterton disliked him. There are several other clerihews by Bentley that celebrate forgotten men – although not most of his. More analogous to Helpmann than to Beit is a series of clerihews by Esther M. Friesner: "A Short Slew of SF Clerihews", "More SF Clerihews", and "Yet More SF Clerihews" – all in one issue of a science-fiction magazine. (Technically she writes nine clerihews and one "bentley".) As in Australia Helpmann is common knowledge, so in the SF community, Isaac Asimov, Robert Heinlein, Frank Herbert, L. Ron Hubbard, Anne McCaffrey, Larry Niven, Ursula K. Le Guin and Marion Z. Bradley (together in one verse), Arthur C. Clarke, and James Tiptree, Jr., are well known. But this is no guarantee, even if most of these authors' names are currently familiar to American SF readers, that all of them will mean much in eighty years (it has been eighty years since *Biography for Beginners*) – let alone to any general readership. In short, it would be nice if clerihews were written about people more significant to the western tradition than, say, the governors of Oklahoma. (Tolkien's clerihews are mostly limited in this way – but, then, he did not publish them. Clerihews in manuscript for the private amusement of a group of friends are not subject to this complaint.)

The fourth of these clerihews about Tolkien was written by the present author and published, with an accidentally omitted letter, in a small journal, under the title "A Secret Vice (A Clerihew)":

> John Ronal[d] Reuel Tolkien
> Listen to the Gælic (more properly, Brythonic) of a Welsh colleen
> And muttered, "The beauty of her glottology is not my imagination hinderin' –
> Aha! Sindarin!"

Perhaps a few comments can be offered about this verse without, of course – since it would be inappropriate for the present writer – any judgement about its literary worth. (One reader of the original publication raised a question about the accentuation of *Sindarin* – was it not on the second syllable instead instead of the first? The reader was arguing from a Welsh basis of the language; the writer replied that he had followed the accentuation as given in James D. Allan's *An Introduction to Elvish*.)

The use of a title is not standard with a clerihew, but this one functions in two ways. "The Secret Vice" is an essay by Tolkien, discussing the invention of private languages. Tolkien's title is suggestive, of course; presumably deliberately so. The clerihew title therefore sets up these two strains. A created private language, by Tolkien, inspired by Welsh, as indicated above, is Sindarin, one of the elvish tongues in *The Lord of the Rings*. A vice (secret or not) tied to a young woman, with a man muttering about her beauty and an unhindered imagination, should lead most readers up a garden path of mistaken associations. (The woman's "glottology" should be outside of most readers' vocabulary, so it will not affect the sexual misreading.) Whether or not it is appropriate for clerihews to play this sort of game is a different question.

The technical aspects of this verse need not be dwelt on. The rhymes are imperfect, but off-rhymes were used, occasionally, in Bentley's verses. The parenthesis in the second line perhaps gives a scholarly flavour, appropriate enough for a verse about a linguist. *Colleen* may be inexact, Irish rather than Welsh; but perhaps (again *perhaps*) it may be acceptable for the sake of the rhyme. And the long lines – the second and the third – show more of an Ogden Nash influence than one of E.C. Bentley.

Is the verse dotty enough? Certainly Tolkien was not inspired by a young woman speaking the Welsh tongue. According to Humphrey Carpenter's biography, he first became aware of the language in words printed on sides of coal-cars ("coal-trucks") of trains (p. 26). But the real question is much like that about van Summers: is the material too limited to be worth writing and/or publishing? How many readers, even of Tolkien's books, worry about his languages? (The few who do, if one judges by their publications, worry – if that is the correct word – very much.) The literary journal which published this verse was one of the small-circulation fantasy journals, one with more of a mythopoeic orientation than Gothic. (There are a number of small Gothic magazines, whatever that says about the reading and writing public; and very few mythic ones.) Thus, it was essentially an in-group publication.

Of these four clerihews about Tolkien or involving his Middle-earth creation, certainly the best as a traditional, pure clerihew is the first, that by Robin Skelton.

III. Tolkien's Contributions

Off hand, a reader might assume that the author of a three-volume romance is not likely also to be the author of four-line light verses. Surely a writer's imagination is likely to work at one scale or the other – not both? Whatever the likelihood, Tolkien wrote both *The Lord of the Rings* and at least six clerihews.

A reader might notice also that a number of Tolkien's verses in his major works are light verses – though not clerihews. For example, Frodo's song about the cow jumping over the moon (an "explanation" of the nursery rhyme) is not a type of serious poetry (*The Lord of Rings*, Bk. 1, Ch. 9). Thus, among Tolkien's variety of styles and modes, light verse is one type.

Six clerihews were mentioned above; but there is in addition one bentley, or quasi-bentley, which makes a good place to begin. When *The Lord of the Rings* was published, the reviews tended to be either high praise or equally high condemnation. Tolkien summed it up in a quatrain which Humphrey Carpenter quotes in his biography (p. 223):

The Lord of the Rings
is one of those things:
if you like it you do:
if you don't, then you boo!

Whether or not Tolkien intended a bentley (a clerihew with, in this case, a book title instead of a person's name) is not certain. This verse violates three rules: (3) the meter is too regular, (6) the tone, while light, is not dotty enough, and (8) the first words of the second through fourth lines are not capitalized. All four lines have two beats each:

X / X X /
X / X X /
X X / X X /
X X / X X /

Obviously, the rhythm of the first two lines is identical, as is that of the latter two; except for the addition of an unstressed syllable at the first of the latter two, the stress pattern of the whole poem is the same. The only variation is that the cæsuræ fall differently in the second couplet: after the fourth syllable in the third line and after the third in the fourth. It seems dubious that a difference in placement of cæsuræ is a sufficient substitute for accentual rhythms, although it does affect how the lines sound, of course.

The light tone of this quatrain is due to the colloquial language: "one of those things" and "boo!" But there is nothing dotty here. The split reaction to Tolkien was a fact. Tolkien sums up the facts lightly but objectively.

If Tolkien's quatrain is a dubious bentley, at least it is worth considering. But there is no doubt about Tolkien's six clerihews. Four of these are quoted by Carpenter in *The Inklings* – appropriately enough, for Tolkien wrote his series of clerihews about his friends in that literary circle.

The first printed by Carpenter (p. 177) is on Doctor Robert E. Havard:

Dr U.Q. Humphrey
Made poultices of comfrey.
If you didn't pay his bills
He gave you doses of squills.

Carpenter gives the background of the pseudonym earlier in his book:

For some reason Havard . . . always attracted nicknames from the Inklings . . . he was once referred to by Hugo Dyson as "Humphrey", either in pure error or because it alliterated with his surname. [Lewis in 1943 used *Humphrey* for a doctor in Ch. 2 of *Perelandra*.] Some time later, Warnie Lewis was irritated one evening by Havard's failure to turn up with a car and give him a promised lift home, and dubbed the doctor "a useless quack"; and "The Useless Quack" or "U.Q." Havard . . . remained.
(p. 130)

("The Red Admiral" was another nickname [p. 177], though not significant here.) Typical of these clerihews but more extreme than the others, the above verse is an in-group comment. The sixth rule about the "civilized" aspects said that the audience needed to know enough history to recognise the dottiness of the clerihew: but there is no way for a reader to know about a pseudonymous minor doctor, significant mainly for his membership in the Inklings and for his note on a doctor's view of pain in Lewis's *The Problem of Pain* (1940). As was said about the Helpmann clerihews in the second section, the subject of a clerihew needs to be someone recognisable. (As was also said, Tolkien did not publish his clerihews, so *he* cannot be blamed for their flaw; but a critic must point out that the verse itself is limited in comparison to the better clerihews.)

The diction about Humphrey is interesting. What is *comfrey*? What are *squills*? It is typical of Tolkien's vocabulary that these are actual words. *Comfrey*, which may suggest a humorous version of *comfort*, actually refers to a plant (of the borage family) with coarse, hairy leaves. All of a sudden the medicine seems less appetising. The squills are equally interesting, for Tolkien seems to be making a double reference here. This plant, also called a sea onion, has bulbs which are sometimes dried and sliced – and used medicinally as a heart stimulant, as an expectorant, and as a diuretic. More sinister is the use of a red variety of squills as a rat poison. Tolkien's use of *dose* suggests the diuretic, but one cannot be *certain* which variety he meant.

The meter of this clerihew is acceptable: three of the four lines seem to have, three (major) stresses, and the other line, two stresses.

/ X / \ / X
X / X X X / X
X X / X / X /
X / X / X X /

There will be some variation simply from individual readings, of course. Does *Q* receive only a secondary stress? Will someone give a secondary stress to the last syllable of *poultices*? Will someone else stress *If*? A rather British reading has been assumed here, with minor syllables (*-ces, If*) swallowed.

Another technique, alliteration, ties the verse together, although it does not seem thematically significant: *Doctor, didn't, doses*; *poultices, pay*.

The second clerihew, since all of these are about members of the Inklings, picks another:

>Mr Owen Barfield's
>Habit of turning cartwheels
>Made some say: "He's been drinking!"
>It was only "conscientious thinking".

Barfield is better known than Havard, since Barfield has published a number of philosophic and/or anthroposophic books; but he can hardly be said to be widely known.

Carpenter explains the background of this clerihew:

>The cartwheels were of an intellectual sort, and "conscientious thinking" was one of Barfield's terms for the thought processes related to Anthroposophy.
>(1979, p. 177)

Would intellectual cartwheels cause people to think the thinker was drunk? Maybe. On the other hand, physical cartwheels would be more certain to excite viewers. It may be significant that Barfield, in his younger years, "thought at one time of earning his living as a dancer" (Carpenter, 1979, p. 33). Perhaps he had turned cartwheels then and the fact came up at an Inkling's meeting. (A person *might* celebrate Anthroposophy with cartwheels, Tolkien can be imagined as assuming.) But both Carpenter's interpretation and the present writer's quibbles are taking the clerihew seriously. Perhaps it would be best to take the cartwheels as the dotty aspect of the verse. Barfield is imagined as doing something that he, as a London solicitor, would not be doing (The "*Habit* of . . . cartwheel[ing]", if taken seriously, could only be an intellectual habit; if taken dottily, it is at the level of Edward Lear's Old Man of Whitehaven who danced a quadrille with a raven.)

This clerihew has little significant alliteration: *Owen* and *only*, but three lines apart; *Habit* and *It* under medieval rules of vowel alliteration, but dubious to the modern ear. "[S]ome say" causes the uncertainty of the meter in the third line; tied together by alliteration, the two syllables sound like a spondee – but what are they in the context of the line? Five monosyllables in a row at the first of the line allow for several readings.

The meter is varied:

/ X / X / X
/ X X / X / X
X / X / X / X
X X / X / X \ X / X

The first line is a trochaic trimeter; the second line is close to the same, but with a dactyl for the first trochee; the third line has all those single-syllable words but it is here scanned as two iambs and an amphibrach; the fourth line has a couple of uncertainties – some readers may add a stress on *It*, some may drop the secondary accent on *-ent-*, but it is here marked as an anapest, two iambs (the second a "light" iamb), and an amphibrach. The number of stresses in this scansion runs three, three, three, and four.

The third clerihew is also about a lesser Inkling (better known than Havard but less well known than Barfield):

>The Rev. Mathew (Gervase)
>Made inaudible surveys
>Of little-read sages
>In the dark Middle Ages.
>(Carpenter, 1979, p. 186)

Carpenter writes about this one that "This was entirely true, for Gervase Mathew was an expert on English medieval history . . ." Also he

>talked in a kind of breathless mutter, speaking at such speed that even Tolkien, until then the champion among the Inklings for haste and inaudibility, was left far behind.
>(p. 186)

Of course, what Carpenter does not seem to realise is that the statement "This [is] entirely true" is damning when applied to a clerihew. (If there is any wit or whimsey in the verse, it lies in the mixing of the Dark Ages and Middle Ages in "dark Middle Ages"; Tolkien would have known the distinction, of course.)

Again, the technique is satisfactory. The alliteration is more elaborate than in the last clerihew – *Reverend, read*; *Mathew, Made, Middle*; *-audible, Ages*; *surveys, sages*. In fact, the only stressed syllables that do not alliterate are the first of *little*, *In* (if it is stressed), and *dark*. The weakness of the verse is in Tolkien's tendency to trimeter lines:

X / X X / X / X
/ X / X X / X
X / X / / X
X X / / X / X

(In this scansion the *In* of the fourth line is not stressed.) It is possible, however to read "little-read sage-" as / X X / and "dark Middle Age-" as an identical / X X /, instead of / X / / and / / X /, respectively, as here; that would give two trimeter lines and two dimeter lines.

This clerihew has a historically interesting background. Those of Tolkien's readers who only know his works through such books as *The Inklings* and those by Tolkien himself do not tend to think of the original situation of Tolkien in Oxford, for example, reciting his verses to friends. To the Inklings, of course; but surely, the readers think, they were nearly isolated. However, evidence exists that this verse got into the oral culture of Oxford. Luke Rigby, O.S.B., in an essay titled "A Solid Man" (1979), repeats a clerihew he heard while a student there:

>Father Gervase
>Makes inaudible surveys
>On little-known sages
>Of the Middle Ages.
>(p. 40)

One notable characteristic of the oral tradition is apparent here: the verse has been simplified. The reversal of the name in the first line is eliminated; the second line is made present tense; the phrasing of the third line is shifted from the unexpected "little-read" to the more common "little-known"; and the fourth line loses its clever adjective *dark*.

But what is amusing about this example is that it is attributed not to Tolkien but to C.S. Lewis. Rigby's essay appears in James T. Como's anthology *"C.S. Lewis at the Breakfast Table" and Other Reminiscences*. Rigby introduces the clerihew with these words, "It is one of those quirks of memory that I recall a clerihew said to have been Mr. Lewis's on Father Gervase" (p. 40). If his memory is right about the attribution, it may be that Lewis heard the verse from Tolkien and quoted it in some public situation – and it was thereafter repeated as by him. (But anyone can invent other possible scenarios for the mistaken attribute – including just someone's poor memory.) Whatever the origin, this is a case in which – unlike that of some folk ballads – the oral transmission has not improved the poem as a poem.

There is a fourth clerihew about one of the lesser Inklings – Nevill Coghill – who is best known for his verse translation of Chaucer. This one was quoted by Tolkien himself in a letter to W.H. Auden. "The only thing I have ever written about Neville [*sic*] was:

> Mr Neville [*sic*] Judson Coghill
> Wrote a deal of dangerous doggerill [*sic*].
> Practical, progressive men
> Called him Little Poison-pen."
> (Tolkien, 1981, p. 359, No. 275)

Tolkien explains the content in his letter:

> That was at a time when under the name of Judson he was writing what I thought very good and funny verses lampooning forward-looking men like [Sir Cyril] Norwood [, President] of St John's [College, Oxford, and author of a then-significant report on education].
> (p. 359)

Despite Tolkien's difficulties in spelling *Nevill* and *doggerel*, there is nothing in the clerihew which seems dotty. "Judson" is added to Coghill's name, but that (while typical of the Inklings' liking for nicknames) seems to have been Coghill's own invention. Probably Coghill being called "Little Poison-pen" is Tolkien's creation; but the lampoons, as the above comment affirms, were factual – and a lampooner or a satirist may well be described in the cliché *poison pen*. In short, the clerihew is too factual to be first rate.

The form is acceptably irregular:

/ X / X / X / X
/ X / X / X X / X X
/ X X X / X /
/ X / X / X /

The stresses are four, four, three, four.

In addition to the interesting off-rhyme of *Coghill* and *doggerel*, the verse has some nice alliterative syllables: *deal*, *dan[j]-*, and *dog-* in the second line, and *Prac-*, *po-*, and *pen* in the third and fourth lines, with *pro-* in an unstressed syllable. (The framing alliteration of *Cog-* and *called* is probably too far apart for anyone's ear.) The "liquid" *l*'s, usually in unstressed syllables, also help the verse's flow: *Nevill*, *Coghill*, *doggerel*, *practical*, *called*, and *Little*. These aspects seem much better than the factuality.

The next clerihew cannot be blamed for having factuality:

> The sales of Charles Williams
> Leapt up by millions,
> When a reviewer surmised
> He was only Lewis disguised.
> (Carpenter, 1979, p. 187)

Indeed, with names of both Williams and C.S. Lewis, this clerihew cannot be blamed for being on minor figures like the earlier ones, either. (It is surprising that Tolkien seems to have not written a clerihew just about Lewis – his best friend among the Inklings – but perhaps this one was supposed to be sufficient. Or perhaps his clerihew on Lewis has not been published.)

Carpenter seems to take the wrong attitude on the factuality. He described the impulse for the verse:

> In the summer of 1943 Williams's book on Dante and Romantic Theology, *The Figure of Beatrice,* was published. Tolkien wrote [the above clerihew, the contents of which were] deliberate nonsense, for the book did not sell vastly and it did not remotely resemble anything Lewis had written.
> (1979, p. 187)

The clerihew should be celebrated for its "deliberate nonsense," its whimsy, its dottiness, not explained away.

The form of the verse is good. The lines are varied in meter, if not so certainly in number of accents.

X / X / / X
/ / X / X
X X X / X X /
X X / X / X X /

Some readers will probably stress the *When* in the third line and so produce four lines of trimeters, instead of three, as here. Or perhaps the *When* should have a secondary accent, and so the line should be \ X X / X X /. The only weakness in the meter (as contrasted to the number of stresses) is that both the third and fourth lines end with anapests. (There is almost no alliteration tying the stresses together – *-mil-* and *-mised*; the vowel pattern of *up*, *He*, and *on-*.)

The final clerihew appeared in another letter – and, as Tolkien writes it there, it violates the eighth rule about capitalization. More significantly, it is on the third significant Inkling, Tolkien himself:

> J.R.R. Tolkien
> had a cat called Grimalkin:
> once a familiar of Herr Grimm
> now he spoke the law to him.
> (Tolkien, 1981, p. 398)

Since Tolkien simply adds it as a postscript to one of his letters (No. 309), there is no context available; but a few things may be said about it.

The rhyme of the first two lines is not perfect: TALL-keen and -MAEL-kin or -MOL-kin. But it is close enough for Tolkien's purposes. The choice of this name is what is interesting. The name derives from *grey* + *malkin*. *Malkin* itself usually means a woman, being a variety of *Matilda* or *Maud*. But *grimalkin* usually refers to a cat, especially a she-cat, although occasionally a woman. (Tolkien uses the masculine pronoun for this cat in his fourth line.)

Since this cat is a supernatural being – a familiar – it is notable that the first discovered use of a form of *grimalkin* is in Shakespeare's *Macbeth* (1605), "I come, Gray-Malkin", where the line refers to a fiend. Of course, Tolkien, a devout Roman Catholic, does not mean anything serous by saying that he and Jakob Grimm before him had the same familiar – that is the dotty or whimsical aspect of this clerihew. (It is possible that Tolkien's interest in Grimalkin was aroused by John Masefield's *The Midnight Folk*, a children's book of 1927, where there are two evil cats – who reform at the end of the book – named Blackmalkin and Greymalkin. ". . . Greymalkin, that mysterious cat, who was so seldom seen" (p. 160), has the lesser role, probably because *black* suggests a greater evil. However, Tolkien's spelling of *Grimalkin* shows that he is not limited to Masefield and Shakespeare.)

The law that is spoken could be taken as some sort of supernatural rule or simply the stubbornness of cats demanding food, for example; but the actual reference no doubt is to a philological rule about the changes in the Indo-European language when German developed out of it (such as the initial IE *p* becoming a *f*, as in the Latin *pisces* and the English *fish*, or *pater* and *father*). This rule is known as Grimm's Law.

Did the familiar inspire Grimm with the law, or did Grimm teach it to his cat? Given the ambiguous pronouns, did Grimalkin recite the Law to Tolkien or *vice versa*? (Under the general rule of thumb that a pronoun refers back to the most immediate noun, presumably the former – but it is not quite certain.)

The clerihew has an uncertain meter in the first two lines. As has been said of an earlier clerihew, it is difficult to know how one should read those opening initials. Here is one version of the four lines:

```
 \ / \ / \
X X / \ X / X
\ X X / X X / /
 / X / X / X /
```

So the major stresses are varied: two, two, three, four – and the rhythms are equally varied.

In addition to the one alliteration noted above, there is a consonance tying together the second and third lines. -*mal*- and -*mil*-, and an alliteration connecting the third and fourth lines, *Herr* and *him*. In this poem, one unstressed syllable is important: the *gr* of *Grimalkin* echoes the sound in the stressed syllable *Grimm*. This alliteration not only ties lines together but connects two of the important terms. (Perhaps, since the first of these names comes from *grey-malkin* – presumable an anti-bacchius – *gri*- has a secondary accent here, not being an ordinary unaccented syllable.)

This final clerihew is obviously an interesting one, since a major romance writer (and expert philologist) composes it about himself; the use of a cat as a familiar seems almost too strong a supernatural note to just be dottiness, but it is reduced (for most readers) by the shift to a philological law as the basis for the conversation between the familiar and the – so to speak – wizard.

What may be said ultimately about Tolkien as a clerihew writer? Perhaps four things. First, as has been said, Tolkien's clerihews are too much of an in-group production to be great. Dr. Havard, Fr. Mathew, and Nevill Coghill are not significant historical figures. Owen Barfield is marginal: there are those who think he is of major importance in the history of ideas, but he certainly is not widely known to the public. Charles Williams, C.S. Lewis, and J.R.R. Tolkien himself are significant enough to meet the criterion of the clerihew being civilized – the reader should be able to read the verse and recognise the dottiness.

Second, these clerihews show Tolkien's sense of humour. The author himself wrote in a letter, "I . . . have a very simple sense of humour (which even my appreciative critics find tiresome)" (1981, p. 289). Perhaps the dottiness of these six verses, at the best, is not the same as the simplicity he mentions here – which may refer to obvious peripeteiæ. If not, these clerihews at least indicate one extension of Tolkien's sense of humour.

Third, these six verses show Tolkien's delight in poetic genres and forms. Perhaps this is not Tolkien's reputation because he does not write sonnets, blank verse, terza rima, sestinas, or rime royal. But many of these forms were French or Italian in origin, and it is no surprise that Tolkien does not touch those. But his use of verse genres is extensive; a few examples: (a) the verse of the Rohirrim (*The Lord of the Rings*, Bk. V., Chs. 5-6), as has often been said, is based on Anglo-Saxon alliterative verse; (b) the ballad of the troll (*The Lord of the Rings*, Bk. I., Ch. 12) is written to the English folk tune of "The Fox and the Hens", as was first pointed out by George Sayer; (c) the octosyllabic couplets of "The Lay of Leithian" are a standard romance form in medieval England, as in "Sir Orfeo" (they were also used in France, by Chrétien de Troyes, for example, but Tolkien would not have been influenced by that); (d) "Namárië (*The Lord of the Rings*, Bk. II., Ch. 8) was sung by Tolkien to a Gregorian chant, and this was written down by Donald Swann for his *The Road Goes Ever On: A Song Cycle* (1967). All of these are medieval forms: but Tolkien was obviously not against a modern English form – the clerihew. His use of this light-verse form does not extend his reputation as a poet, but it does as a versifier.

Fourth and finally, two of Tolkien's clerihews, as has been said, are significant in the genre. But also they, and indeed the one on Barfield in addition, are amusing – which is one purpose of light verse. This assertion, of course, cannot be proved, for it is a matter of taste. But Barfield, a London solicitor, turning cartwheels, is a traditional example of humour; the verse on Williams and Lewis may be taken either as nonsense (as it was presented earlier) or as a satire on the ineptitude of London reviewers – its ambivalence, between either sheer humour or ironic humour, may be part of its appeal; and the verse on the author himself is perhaps too mysterious to be a good clerihew, but the play with Grimm's law produces a surprising shift from witchcraft to philology and in that sense may be humorous.

In short, Tolkien's contribution to Edmund Clerihew Bentley's genre may not be great; but they are at least interesting for what they say about Tolkien's sensibilities, for what they reveal (in two cases) as good examples of the genre, and for what they contribute (in three cases) toward the reader's amusement.

Appendix: The Rules of the Clerihew

The following rules (as given in the first section of this essay) are based on E.C. Bentley's practices.

1. The clerihew, named after E.C. Bentley's middle name, is a type of light verse.
2. The verse form is that of a quatrain written with two rhyming (or occasionally off-rhyming) couplets.
3. The meter is essentially that of prose rhythms, although Bentley's practices suggest that fairly short lines, of two to four stresses, are normative.
4. The matter is biographical. This author proposes the name of "bentleys" for non-biographical clerihews.
5. The rhetorical form most commonly seen has the biographical name (with or without modification) in the first line, although it occasionally appears in the second; the fourth line is not normally a punch-line – indeed, the third and fourth lines are normally one clause.
6. The tone of the clerihew, says Gavin Ewart, is "civilised and dotty"; more specifically, the clerihew is not used for satire or erotic jokes ("civilized"), and the biographical information is not to be completely accurate – that is, the clerihew is a variety of nonsense verse ("dotty").
7. None of Bentley's clerihews are given individual titles, outside of a few semi-clerihews – "bentleys" – used as book introductions.
8. The most trivial rule of all: the first word of each line is to be capitalized.

References

Allan, Jim et al. 1978. *An Introduction to Elvish*. Hayes, Middlesex: Bran's Head Books.

Barzun, Jacques. 1985. "The Muse is Speaking" in *The Clerihews of Paul Horgan*. Middletown, Connecticut: Wesleyan University Press. Reprinted in *The Chesterton Review* 13:4 (November 1987) pp. 549-50.

Bentley, E. Clerihew, et al. 1982. *The First Clerihews*. Illus. G.K. Chesterton. Various prefatory material. Oxford: Oxford University Press.

Bentley, E. Clerihew. 1983. *The Complete Clerihews of E. Clerihew Bentley*. Rev. ed. Intro. Gavin Ewart. Illus. by Nicholas Bentley et al. Oxford: Oxford University Press.

Carpenter, Humphrey. 1977. *Tolkien: A biography*. Boston: Houghton Mifflin.

Carpenter, Humphrey. 1979. *The Inklings: C.S. Lewis, J.R.R. Tolkien, Charles Williams, and their friends*. Boston: Houghton Mifflin.

Chesterton, G.K. 1987. "An Alphabet" in *Collected Nonsense and Light Verse*. Ed. Marie Smith. London: Xanadu Publications, pp. 122-23.

Christopher, Joe R. 1987. "A Secret Vice (A Clerihew)" in *The Mythic Circle*. No. 3, Late Summer 1987, p.27.

Ewart, Gavin, ed. 1983. *Other People's Clerihews*. Illus. Nicola Jennings. Oxford: Oxford University Press.

Friesner, Esther M. 1986. "A Short Slew of SF Clerihews", "More SF Clerihews" and "Yet More SF Clerihews" in *Amazing Science Fiction Stories*. 60:2/526 (January 1986): pp. 100, 105, 129, respectively.

Masefield, John. 1927. *The Midnight Folk*. Reprinted, New York: Dell, 1985.

Rigby, Luke, O. B. S. 1979. "A Solid Man" in *"C.S. Lewis at the Breakfast Table" and Other Reminiscences*. Ed. James T. Como. New York: Macmillan, pp 38-40.

Sarjeant, William A.S. 1983. "The Geological Clerihew" in *Geolog* 12:4 (1983), pp. 38-40.

Sarjeant, William A.S. 1984. "A Mélange of Geological Clerihews" in *Geolog* 13:4 (1984), pp. 34-36.

Sarjeant, William A.S. 1985. "Clerihews" in *Geolog* 14:4 (1985), pp. 32-33.

Sarjeant, William A.S. 1987. "E.C. Bentley, G.K. Chesterton and the Clerihew" in *The Chesterton Review*. 13:2 (May 1987), pp. 176-191.

> Letters in subsequent issues discussing his essay: Kevin Dean, "A David Jones Special Issue?" 13:3 (August 1987), pp. 421-22; Eric Yates, "More Clerihews", p. 422; Darlene Kelly "Chesterton and 'Doctor Parker'" 13:4 (November 1987), pp. 559-560; William A.S. Sarjeant, [untitled], 14:2 (May 1988), 310-14; Canon Dr. M.W. Dewar, p. 314; Professor John Ferguson, p. 315.

Sarjeant, William A.S. 1989. "The Jurassic Clerihew" in *Stuifmail* 7:3 (Dec. 1989), p. 52. (Largely a reprint of Sarjeant, 1985.)

Sayer, George. 1975. [untitled note on the record jacket] *J.R.R. Tolkien reads and sings his The Hobbit and The Fellowship of the Ring*. Caedmon Records, No. TC 1477.

Stein, Aaron Mark. 1977. "Introduction" in *Trent's Last Case* by E.C. Bentley. Illus. Darrel Millsap. Various editorial material. San Diego: University Extension, University of California at San Diego, in co-operation with Del Mar: Publisher's Inc., pp. ix-xxv.

Tolkien, J.R.R. 1981. *The Letters of J.R.R. Tolkien*. Ed. Humphrey Carpenter, with Christopher Tolkien. Boston: Houghton Mifflin.

Tolkien, J.R.R. 1984. "A Secret Vice" in *The Monsters and the Critics and Other Essays*. Ed. Christopher Tolkien. Boston: Houghton Mifflin, pp. 198-223.

Power in Arda: Sources, Uses and Misuses

Edith L. Crowe

Abstract: Power and renunciation of power has long been recognised as an important theme in the works of J.R.R. Tolkien. This paper will examine the issue of power with particular attention to Riane Eisler's dominator/partnership model of power relations and the power within/power over dichotomy. It will consider the sources of various types of power: spiritual, political, physical; and how these are wielded by the various peoples and individuals of Middle-earth.

Keywords: feminism, gender, *The Lord of the Rings*, power, *Unfinished Tales*

A fine American cartoonist, Nicole Hollander, titled one of her collections *Ma, Can I Be a Feminist and Still Like Men?* Her punchline wasn't too encouraging: "Sure, just like you can be a vegetarian and like fried chicken." (We must remember humour often exaggerates for its effects.) The question I'm here to answer is a similar one: "Ma, can I be a feminist and still like Tolkien?" Obviously my answer is going to be a more positive one, since I am, and do. To be very practical about it, fantasy readers of my generation would have had precious little to read in the beginning if we had limited ourselves to works fully in tune with our feminist principles.

Females of a later generation are often less forgiving. The reaction of a friend's daughter, age five, upon hearing *The Hobbit* for the first time, was: "Mommy, aren't there any girls in this story?" Her mother was forced to admit that, by and large, there weren't. The most problematic aspect of Tolkien is indeed the disappointingly low percentage of females that appear in his best-known and best-loved works, *The Hobbit* and *The Lord of the Rings*. I don't intend to castigate Tolkien for this, though I certainly regret it, since he was only reflecting his sources and his times. Neither am I going to claim he was a hidden feminist – not the man who, in 1943, viewed with such alarm the possibility of a postwar world overrun with such horrors as "American sanitation, morale-pep, feminism, and mass production" (Tolkien, 1981, p. 65).

I would dearly love to know what he had against American sanitation, and how he defined it. I would also like to know how he defined feminism, since my experience has been that no two people mean the same thing by that rather charged word. However, to say that Tolkien's work is completely incompatible with feminism is to accept not only too limited a view of Tolkien's writings, but too narrow a definition of feminism. Tolkien's work is much richer than that, particularly if we include *The Silmarillion*, *Unfinished Tales*, and his other posthumous works. There are many interpretations of feminism, and some aspects are more compatible with Tolkien than others.

For instance, there is difference of opinion between what we might term "social constructionists" and "essentialists." The former claim that an individual's identity as "male" or "female" is almost purely a result of learning, of nurture if you will, both within the family and in the larger context of the world outside it. "Essentialists" feel that there is indeed a basic difference between men and women beyond the biologically obvious, and that the problem is that the natures of each sex are not equally valued. I suspect the truth, as it does in most things, lies somewhere in between.

At first, the main concern of feminists was to increase the participation and influence of women in society as it was – in politics, in professions historically closed to women, in education, etc. In a later stage, one begins to ask larger questions about the basic values of the society itself. A good example is the thorny question of women in the military –should one be working to increase the numbers of women in the military, or to change one's society in a more fundamental way and abolish or diminish the military?

We now come close to the place where Tolkien and feminism, while coming from very different places, grapple with some of the same issues. Many of those issues centre around power – where it comes from, who has it, the different ways in which it is utilized, and what constitutes legitimate or illegitimate use. It is my contention that in Middle-earth, Tolkien exhibits attitudes toward power that are quite compatible with, if not identical to, the attitudes of many who define themselves as feminists.

The first thing to look at is the ultimate source of power in Middle-earth. That source is theological, because it resides in Eru. Of all the beings that we meet in Tolkien's subcreated universe, only Eru is omnipotent. Only he possesses the Flame Imperishable, and is therefore capable of creation of the Ainur *ex nihilo*. And as he tells Melkor, "no theme may be played that hath not its uttermost source in me, nor can any alter the music in my despite." (Tolkien, 1977, p. 17). Although many other beings have the ability to alter Arda in major and minor ways, for good or ill, only Eru has the power to completely transcend it as he does when Númenor is destroyed and Valinor removed from the circles of the world. In addition, only Eru is omniscient: "to none but himself has Ilúvatar revealed all that he has in store" (Tolkien, 1977, p. 18), not even to the Ainur.

Eru is also portrayed as male, in a manner very reminiscent of Yahweh, of "God the Father" in the Judeo-Christian tradition. In that tradition,

> although the Hebrew word Elohim has both feminine and masculine roots (incidentally explaining how in the first creation story in Genesis both woman and man could be created in Elohim's image), all the other appellations of the deity, such as King, Lord, Father, and Shepherd, are specifically male.
>
> (Eisler, 1988, p. 94)

So Eru – or Ilúvatar, "Father of All" in Quenya – is firmly within a familiar patriarchal religious tradition. However, Eru seems to be much better at delegating authority than Yahweh, because, with the exception mentioned above, he does not interfere directly in the further creation and operation of Arda. Here we begin to part company with the Judeo-Christian model in ways that Tolkien found acceptable within his religious tradition but also give some satisfaction to the many within and without that tradition who hunger for a female conception of deity.

In his subcreation of the Valar, Tolkien has managed to incorporate female power at the penultimate level at least. At this point, he seems to reveal himself as an essentialist where male and female natures are concerned:

> But when they desire to clothe themselves the Valar take upon them forms some as of male and some as of female; for that difference of temper they had even from their beginning, and it is but bodied forth in the choice of each, not made by the choice.
>
> (Tolkien, 1977, p. 21)

Although he may give pride of place to the male, Tolkien has also given us a number of powerful female characters among the Valar. Varda, for example, although technically second to Manwë, actually has a greater presence in Middle-earth, especially in *The Lord of the Rings*, due to the reverence in which the Elves hold her and their tendency to call upon her. She is the closest thing Arda has to a goddess. Although Tolkien's religious beliefs would not allow him to conceptualize her as such, her creation of the stars suggests the Queen of Heaven, an appellation not only of Mary, the mother of Jesus, but of Isis, the great goddess of the ancient world to whom Mary owes many of her attributes. A suggestion of her power and significance is the intriguing fact that Melkor "feared her more than all others whom Eru made" (Tolkien, 1977, p. 26).

If Varda suggests the Great Goddess, the goddess as Creatrix, the other female Valar – the Valier – encompass other aspects of the Goddess. Yavanna is very much the Earth Mother: her Eldarin surname, Kementári, means Queen of the Earth; her role as the source of growing things is suggestive of Ceres or Demeter. The maiden aspect of the Goddess (although neither are technically maidens) is found in Nessa, the sister of Oromë the hunter, who is fleet of foot and loves deer (like Artemis), and in Vána, younger sister of Yavanna, who causes flowers to open if she looks at them and birds to sing at her coming. She is like a Persephone who need never fear that a Hades will carry her off.

The Valier associated with giving rest and healing to the hurt and weary (Estë) or with the Halls of Mandos where the dead wait (Nienna and Vairë) suggest the aspect of Goddess as Crone, that aspect associated with the end of life rather than its beginning. Therefore, although Eru is definitely portrayed as male, that is the only level of being at which a strong female presence is absent. Although one only familiar with *The Hobbit* and *The Lord of the Rings* might be forgiven for concluding that Tolkien was lacking in recognition of the importance of the feminine, the Valier alone should contradict that conclusion. Although the ultimate deity is male, spiritual power, as embodied in the Valar, is almost equally the province of male and female.

Already this is an improvement over the Primary World, since its major religions are not oversupplied with images of female spiritual power. As we move to the level of the Children of Ilúvatar, Elves and Men, another significant difference appears. In Judeo-Christian (and to some extent Islamic) traditions, woman, in the person of Eve, "has been blamed for nothing less than our fall from paradise." (Eisler, 1988, p. 190). Considering how often that belief has been used to justify the subordination and persecution of women, it is extremely refreshing to encounter a secondary world where the Fall of both Elves and Men is a male's fault. Interestingly enough, in both cases the action which brings about the Fall is preceded by an insufficiency of the "feminine principle," as in Fëanor's case, or in active damage to it, as in Ar-Pharazôn's.

In her excellent *Mythlore* article on "The Feminine Principle in Tolkien," Melanie Rawls (1984, p. 5) points out that

> Through *The Silmarillion* runs this theme: in Arda and in the Heavens, the Feminine and the Masculine are present; when they are in equilibrium and in harmony there is Good, but Evil is the result of an insufficiency or a disharmony of the attributes of one or the other of the genders.

Another important point she makes is that this equilibrium and harmony can be achieved either by the balance of masculine and feminine qualities within an individual, or by a less integrated being who has "access to the nature of the other gender, usually in the form of a spouse, a sibling, or a mentor" (Rawls, 1984, p. 5). Fëanor can hardly be blamed for the absence of his mother, but he is culpable for ignoring the advice of his wiser and more patient wife. Tolkien tells us that Nerdanel "restrained [Fëanor] when the fire of his heart grew too hot" (Tolkien, 1977, p. 64). This female restraint of male misuse of power has a precedent among the Maiar: Uinen, Lady of the Seas, not only "can lay calm upon the waves, restraining the wildness of Ossë" her spouse, but even kept Ossë from succumbing to the temptation of Melkor (Tolkien, 1977, p. 30). Fëanor, alas, was not so wise.

This theme permeates Tolkien's work – the absolute necessity of both male and female elements, however defined, for the proper functioning of both individuals and societies. More importantly, he recognizes the interdependence of male and female, and suggests repeatedly that to ignore one at the expense of the other is a grave mistake which at the very least diminishes the individual and at the worst can lead to disaster for both the individual and the society. Not only are Manwë and Varda the supreme powers among the Valar, but they enhance each other's power:

> When Manwë . . . ascends his throne and looks forth, if Varda is beside him, he sees further than all other eyes . . . And if Manwë is with her, Varda hears more clearly than all other ears . . .
> (Tolkien, 1977, p. 26)

Although the presence of the Valier and the absence of an Eve figure provide a strong sense of female spiritual power, Middle-earth still exhibits an almost invariably patriarchal and patrilineal political and social organization. Manwë clearly possesses the highest authority among the Valar, and among the peoples of Middle-earth, the norm in both government and the family is that the highest authority is male. This follows from the position of Eru, since in the primary world,

> Religions in which the most powerful or only deity is male tend to reflect a social order in which descent is patrilinear . . . and domicile is patrilocal . . . religions in which the most powerful or sole deity is female tend to reflect a social order in which descent is matrilinear . . . and domicile is likewise matrilocal.
> (Eisler, 1988, p. 24)

We now move to the level of temporal power, although among the Eldar and Edain, at least, spiritual and temporal power are to some extent interwoven. There are many varieties of temporal power, from many sources. Two of the more "outer-directed" are physical strength/skill; or power based in formal authority and/or the possession of tangible resources – that is, political/economic power. Power can also arise from "personal magnetism, attractiveness, or charisma" or from "access to information, particularly information that others do not have or cannot understand . . ." (Lips, 1985, pp. 5-6). Although the latter two types are more evenly distributed between men and women, physical and political power does seem to be associated rarely with women.

It does, however, exist, especially among the Eldar. Aredhel (Ar-Feiniel, the White Lady of the Noldor), "was tall and strong, and loved much to ride and hunt in the forests." (Tolkien, 1977, p. 60). The Galadriel that we see in *The Lord of the Rings* is clearly a great power, but in that work we see only the tip of the iceberg. Galadriel seemed to hold a particular fascination for Tolkien, since he continued to work on her character and history until the end of his life. In a letter written only a month before his death she is clearly much on his mind (Tolkien, 1981, p. 431).

After first meeting her in *The Lord of the Rings*, it is fascinating to read descriptions of her in the First Age which indicate a previously unstressed physical ability. We learn that her mother's name for her was Nerwen, or "manmaiden:" that "she grew to be tall beyond the measure even of the women of the Noldor; she was strong of body, mind, and will." Her depth of knowledge comes as no surprise, but we also learn that she was "a match for both the loremasters and the athletes of the Eldar . . ." (Tolkien, 1980, p. 229).

Her physical strength and courage are not limited to athletics. In one version of the Noldorian rebellion, Galadriel was at Alqualondë considering departure from Middle-earth for her own reasons, and "fought fiercely against Fëanor in defence of her mother's kin" during the Kinslaying (Tolkien, 1980, p. 230). In such a context, one can only assume a fight of the physical sort. In another version of the revolt, Fëanor leaves Fingolfin's people stranded in the Northern Waste, and Galadriel is among the small band who lead their people overland to Middle-earth. "Few of the deeds of the Noldor thereafter surpassed that desperate crossing in hardihood or woe" (Tolkien, 1977, p. 90).

There are a enough women in Middle-earth who possess both physical courage and political leadership ability to suggest that Tolkien did not believe that lack of these qualities was an essential aspect of femaleness. Why then are examples not more frequent? Part of the reason is, as noted above, a patriarchal social structure derived from a spiritual hierarchy with Eru on top. Another part of the reason may be the fact that for so many of the peoples of Middle-earth, having to fight almost constant battles against Melkor, Sauron, or their minions, the political leader of the group was also the military leader. Although the women of the Eldar and Edain are certainly capable of fighting in many instances, it tends to be in last-ditch defence of their homes and children, rather than organized warfare taken outside their territory.

In an extensive cross-cultural study of Primary World societies, Peggy Sanday discovered that women seldom engage in warfare, not necessarily because their culture views them as incapable of it, but because this is seen as inappropriate or too risky. Even in cultures where women have power and authority, they may believe

> . . . it is more efficient for women to delegate than to monopolize power. Since women are the potential bearers of new additions to the population, it would scarcely be expedient to place them on the front line at the hunt and in warfare . . ."
> (Sanday, 1981, p. 115)

This common belief may explain the rarity of female political leaders in Middle-earth. On the other hand, it may be a result of the Primary World attitude, especially prevalent since the Industrial Revolution, that the woman's domain is the domestic and private sphere, and the public world of commerce and politics the man's – an attitude particularly pervasive in nineteenth-century Britain and America, and still influential in Tolkien's formative years.

There are actually a number of interesting examples of women warriors in Middle-earth who fit this model of defenders of the home. One of the most interesting women of the Edain is Haleth, "a woman of great heart and strength." When her father and brother were killed by Orcs, "Haleth held the people together, though they were without hope" for seven days, until rescued by a force led by the Elf Caranthir. She was not only valiant in arms, but must have been an exceptional political leader. The people "took Haleth for their chief" and they "were ever after known to Elves and

Men as the People of Haleth." She kept her people moving west through difficult circumstances, "constraining them to go forward by the strength of her will" (Tolkien, 1977, p. 146).

In another description of the people of Haleth Tolkien states:

> One of the strange practices spoken of was that many of their warriors were women, though few of these went abroad to fight in the great battles. This custom was evidently ancient; for their chieftainess Haleth was a renowned Amazon with a picked bodyguard of women. (Tolkien, 1980, p. 377)

Another rather Amazonian figure is Emeldir the Manhearted, wife of Barahir and mother of Beren. Although she would have preferred "to fight beside her son and her husband than to flee" she "gathered together all the women and children that were left, and gave arms to those that would bear them; and she led them into the mountains . . ." (Tolkien, 1977, p. 155). Clearly Beren inherited his heroism from both sides.

In the late 1800s of the Third Age, the Wainriders warred against Rohan and Gondor. Left behind to defend the home front were youths, old men – and young women "who in that people were also trained in arms and fought fiercely in defence of their homes and their children" (Tolkien, 1980, p. 290). Éowyn is also presumably trained in arms, although it is never explained in detail what being a shieldmaiden of the Rohirrim entails. She is a skilled enough rider to be part of the difficult ride to Gondor, and a sufficiently skilled fighter to acquit herself well in the Battle of the Pelennor fields even before she dispatches the greatest of the Ringwraiths – with a little help from prophecy and a halfling. She is also not without a measure of political power: the suggestion that Éowyn serve as "Lord" of the Eorlingas in the absence of Théoden and Éomer comes from her own people, and is another example of the woman warrior's role as defender of the homestead. It is also an example of something we see in other peoples – that lineage and family are often more important than gender in legitimizing female political power. In Éowyn's case, being a member of the House of Eorl is apparently more important than her sex. That also may be the explanation that the eldest child of the Númenórean monarch should wear the crown, not the eldest son (although Tolkien was inconsistent on this point) (Tolkien, 1967, p. 316; Tolkien, 1980, pp. 208-9, 225-6).

Women of the Eldar can be formidable in battle as well, but the nature of their power is harder to categorize. Lúthien certainly shows physical courage in her travels with Beren to confront Sauron and later Morgoth (not to mention considerable intelligence and initiative in getting away from her father, in a tale which reads like a feminist retelling of Rapunzel). But her greatest power is that of Elven "magic," for lack of a better term, which is essentially a spiritual power:

> Then Lúthien stood upon the bridge, and declared her power: and the spell was loosed that bound stone to stone, and the gates were thrown down, and the walls opened, and the pits laid bare . . .
> (Tolkien, 1977, p. 15)

The recovery of the Silmaril utilizes this same "magic," with a bit of that charismatic power of attractiveness thrown in. Morgoth makes the mistake of leaving Lúthien free at first so he can ogle her, giving her the opportunity to sing him and his entire court to sleep so Beren can take a Silmaril. Levelling fortresses is a talent possessed by Galadriel also; the appendix to *The Lord of the Rings* tells us that after the fall of Sauron, Celeborn leads the people of Lórien on an assault against Dol Guldur. When they were successful, "Galadriel threw down its walls and laid bare its pits . . ." (Tolkien, 1967, p. 375).

We have considered the source of power, and seen that it is primarily theological or spiritual. The creatures of Arda may be able to use that power directly, such as the Valar and Maiar; they may be capable of a "magic" that derives from it; or they may inherit political power that derives from it – the rulers of Númenor are priest-kings (and occasionally -queens) and their later descendents divine-right monarchs. All these types of power are available to both males and females, though not equally.

The power of males in Middle-earth is manifested more frequently in those areas which are more obvious and which the culture of our primary world considers more important: warfare, commerce, the holding of political office. However, although Arda is hardly a feminist utopia (whatever that might be) it has its share of powerful and renowned females, and a spiritual tradition which includes a strong female dimension.

There is one more aspect of power we need to consider, however: its use and misuse. Tolkien's attitudes toward the proper and improper use of power permeate all his writings. More than anything else, his beliefs on this point toward a society which, in its ideal form, shares many traits with a society envisioned by some feminists.

Riane Eisler, in *The Chalice and the Blade* (1988), reviews a vast amount of archeological and other evidence which suggests that Neolithic societies that worshipped a female deity or deities were not matriarchies, as turn-of-the-century scholars mistakenly concluded, but egalitarian societies which were supplanted by Indo-European invaders who associated power with the ability to destroy rather than nurture. From her study of these various cultures, Eisler derives two basic models of society:

> The first, which I call the *dominator model*, is what is popularly termed either patriarchy or matriarchy – the *ranking* of one half of humanity over the other. The second, in which social relations are primarily based on the principle of *linking* rather than ranking, may best be described as the *partnership* model. In this model – beginning with the most fundamental difference . . . between male and female – diversity is not equated with either inferiority or superiority.
> (p. xvii)

In many ways, this could serve as a good description for Arda.

Although from Eru's realm down to the humblest hobbit-hole this universe is hierarchically structured, Eisler does not view hierarchy as automatically negative. She distinguishes "domination hierarchies, based on force or the express or implied threat of force" from "actualization hierarchies" which are "found in progressions from lower to higher orders of functioning" — like those in biological systems, for example (p. 106). Many of the hierarchies in Middle-earth arise not because because Tolkien thinks one group is inherently better than another, but because peoples develop differently due to choices that were made.

Throughout *Splintered Light*, Verlyn Flieger seems to suggest a spiritual hierarchy in Arda based on a group's distance from the light of Valinor, that is, from the spiritual. Thus the preeminent position of the Eldar among the Elves and the Númenóreans among Men is based on the choices they made to move closer to the light, the spiritual, and their long dwelling within its influence. Tolkien's treatment of such groups as the Easterlings and the Southrons has unfortunate overtones of racism to the modern ear. I doubt Tolkien intended it that way; his ringing denunciation of German racial attitudes prior to World War II suggests otherwise (Tolkien, 1981, pp. 37-8), as does a letter sent to Christopher while he was serving in South Africa (p. 73). The evil of the Easterlings, Southrons, Wainriders, etc., lies not in any inherent quality, but in the fact that they succumbed to the temptations of the Shadow. Other Men not of the Edain (Woses, Dunlendings) are good but lesser beings who never went to Númenor, but did resist Melkor and Sauron.

Tolkien certainly seems to feel that men and women have different, and sometimes contradictory, talents, interests, and attitudes. By and large, women are associated with the domestic and family sphere rather than the outer world; with insight and wisdom rather than physical prowess; with nature, especially in its domesticated form, rather than crafts of the more technological sort. However, Tolkien is not consistent in this, and the more we learn of his work the less essentialist he appears.

For example, in such couples as Tom Bombadil and Goldberry, or the Ents and the Entwives, the females seem to be associated with domesticated nature and the males with nature "in the raw." But is this really true? Tom and Fangorn are not hunters, but husbandmen. Their relationship to nature is not so different from their female counterparts as it first appears, indeed, more a difference in degree than in kind. And in the tale of "Aldarion and Erendis" from *Unfinished Tales*, it is Erendis who values the trees for themselves, in their natural state, and Aldarion who is more concerned with their "domestication" for human use. Whatever Tolkien's personal feelings might have been — and in deference to his well-known dislike for criticism via biography I do not intend to address that — his work exhibits a more complicated attitude toward appropriate male and female roles than is immediately apparent.

The more important point is not the fixity of the boundaries between male and female spheres, but the fact that their relationship is one of linking, not ranking. To quote Melanie Rawls again:

There is no war between the sexes in Tolkien's subcreation. Complementary and mutually augmenting positive feminine and masculine qualities are set against enantiodromic, negative feminine and masculine qualities. Feminine and masculine are diverse — not subordinate or antagonistic to one another. (p. 13)

Not only is that a fair assessment of Tolkien's work, it's a good description of what Eisler would call a partnership society.

Another important characteristic of Tolkien's universe is the refreshing absence of violence against women *as women*. In a dominator society, this a basic characteristic. Middle-earth certainly contains violence against women, but the perpetrators are those who are equally violent against everybody (Orcs, for example). Mutual violence and antagonism in Middle-earth depend on what people one belongs to, not which sex, and usually have their roots in some past event (such as the long-standing feud between Elves and Dwarves) or some action of Morgoth or Sauron (special hatred of Orcs for Elves explained by the possibility that the former were bred from the latter).

The most flagrant examples of violence against women are the two forced marriages of Númenórean kings in their spiritual decline — that of Gimilzôr to the Lady Inzilbêth, and later Ar-Pharazôn's treatment of Tar-Míriel. Not only did he usurp her throne but forced her into an incestuous marriage which, under the circumstances, can be viewed as nothing less than rape. This terrible and uncharacteristic (for Númenóreans in general) treatment of a woman is symbolic of the magnitude of Ar-Pharazôn's evil. Generally, men (or Elves) who treat women poorly come to a bad end. Eöl's marriage to Aredhel results as much from deceit as from force, but he comes to a bad end as well.

An apparent example of oppressive behaviour toward women is the tendency of Elven fathers to restrict their daughters' freedom to marry. Thingol is the most blatant example, since he actually resorts at one point to imprisoning Lúthien, but Elrond also forbids the marriage of Arwen and Aragorn, at least until certain demanding conditions are met. But is this type of behaviour only directed against women? Would an Elven father act the same way if his son wanted to make what he considered an inappropriate marriage? I don't think there's enough evidence to reach a judgement. Thingol aside, it's possible such prohibitions owe their power more to the reverence and love Elven daughters (and sons) seem to have for their fathers than to any belief such prohibitions would be otherwise enforced.

Eisler describes the power she symbolizes by the blade as "[t]he power to dominate and destroy" as opposed to that of the chalice, "the view of power as the capacity to support and nurture life . . ." (p. 53), and points out that "many women and men are frontally challenging de/structive [sic] myths, such as the hero as killer" (pp. 188-9). I think Tolkien can be counted among them. One of the most pervasive themes in his work is the association of the dominating power of the blade with evil and the nurturing power of the chalice with good. The whole point of *The Lord of the Rings* is, after all, the renunciation of the power of domination, whereas "The

Enemy in successive forms is always 'naturally' concerned with sheer Domination" (Tolkien, 1981, p. 146).

Tolkien's heroes may kill, but they are by no means the hero as killer. When they kill without need, such as Fëanor did at the Kinslaying, this is portrayed as a great wrong, and its negative consequences reverberate throughout the ages in Middle-earth. There is a great deal of killing, particularly in *The Silmarillion*, but it is either in self-defence, or evil if it is not, and attributed to the baleful influence of Melkor or Sauron, a symptom of Arda Marred. The heroes of Middle-earth go to war reluctantly, and only when their only other choice is to succumb to the greater evil of domination by the Shadow.

In fact, some of the greatest heroes of Middle-earth are those whose decision not to kill proves to have important consequences: if Faramir had not stayed his hand against Frodo and Sam; if Aragorn and the Wood-elves and Frodo had not spared Gollum, Sauron would have been triumphant. One of the things that sets *The Lord of the Rings* apart from most other works of contemporary fantasy – besides its sheer quality and richness – is this theme of the renunciation of power. Those on the side of good in Middle-earth are certainly capable of wielding the Ring, but recognize in their wisdom that to use that power – the power of the blade – would lead to the destruction of their essential selves.

Creative, life-affirming and nurturing powers are those associated with good in Middle-earth, and are found in both male and female. For example, Lúthien and Aragorn are healers. In fact, it is the ability to heal, rather than any military prowess, that marks Aragorn as the True King. Faramir, Gandalf, Galadriel, Bilbo and Frodo show reverence for the art and learning of the past; Bombadil, Goldberry, Ents and Entwives, Elves, Men and Hobbits reverence and care for the natural world in their different ways. Tolkien's ecological consciousness was ahead of its time, and in many ways worthy of a contemporary ecofeminist. The nurturing values of home and hearth may be more frequently ascribed to females, but they are given great importance and respect, not denigrated as they are so often in the Primary World.

This, then, is why I conclude that a person of feminist persuasion, while not necessarily agreeing with Tolkien's attitudes *in toto*, can find much to appreciate in his work. Arda is a world in which females share power in spiritual and temporal realms, although not always to the degree one might wish. More importantly, it is a world in which attitudes and values associated in the Primary World with the feminine are highly valued. Indeed, these "feminine" values triumph at the end of the Third Age, though not always incarnate in female bodies. Though Tolkien's road was his interpretation of Christianity, and Eisler's (and mine) our interpretation of feminism, the destination seems to have a great deal in common. Our mutual task in the Fourth Age is to resist the temptation to divide and dominate, whether we characterize this misuse of power as that of the Blade or the Ring. May Varda look with favour upon our efforts.

References

Eisler, Riane. 1988. *The Chalice and the Blade*. San Francisco: Perennial Library-Harper & Row.

Flieger, Verlyn. 1983. *Splintered Light: Logos and Language in Tolkien's World*. Grand Rapids, MI: Wm. B. Eerdmans.

Lips, Hilary M. 1981. *Women, Men, and the Psychology of Power*. Englewood Cliffs, N. J.: Prentice-Hall.

Rawls, Melanie. 1984. "The Feminine Principle in Tolkien." *Mythlore* 10.4 (1984), pp. 5-13.

Sanday, Peggy Reeves. 1981. *Female Power and Male Dominance*. Cambridge: Cambridge University Press.

Tolkien, J.R.R. 1967. *The Return of the King*, second edition. Boston: Houghton Mifflin.

Tolkien, J.R.R. 1977. *The Silmarillion*. Ed. Christopher Tolkien. Boston: Houghton Mifflin.

Tolkien, J.R.R. 1980. *Unfinished Tales*. Ed. Christopher Tolkien. Boston: Houghton Mifflin.

Tolkien, J.R.R. 1981. *The Letters of J.R.R. Tolkien*. Ed. Humphrey Carpenter. Boston: Houghton Mifflin.

Tolkien and Englishness

Chris Hopkins

Abstract: This paper discusses ways in which Tolkien draws upon various ideas of Englishness in order to construct his epic fictional world. In particular, Tolkien's combinations of different periods and traditions of Englishness – Anglo-Saxon, nineteenth-century – are explored.

Keywords: Anglo-Saxons, First World War, Englishness, "The Lady of Shalott", nationalism, Tennyson, trenches

The literary critical establishment has, on the whole, never been willing to place Tolkien's works within the context of serious English literature, or to discuss his place in English culture. Yet his works are particularly rich and complex expressions of various kinds of Englishness, which draw on both nineteenth- and twentieth-century ideas about English national identities. In this paper I will try to show some of the ways in which *The Lord of The Rings* can be related to English history, ideas and ideologies, and to suggest some of the ways in which it uses such conceptions within its fictional world.

Any paper interpreting Tolkien with reference to a real world should probably start by looking at his disclaimers about its references to particular events. In the "Foreword" to *The Lord of The Rings* Tolkien wrote,

> As for any inner meaning or "message", it has in the intention of the author none. It is neither allegorical nor topical.
> (Tolkien, 1979a, p. 11)

However: he also added

> An author cannot of course remain wholly unaffected by his experience, but the ways in which a story-germ uses the soil of experience are extremely complex, and attempts to define the process are at best guesses from evidence that is inadequate and ambiguous.

I certainly would not want to claim that the motives or energies of Tolkien's fiction can be entirely pinned down, but it is possible to trace some of the network of specifically English references and ideas through which it is constructed. These are of a number of different kinds.

Some are relatively straightforward references to periods of English history, particularly, of course, the Anglo-Saxon period. Thus it is clear that the mounds of the Barrow-wights are to an extent based on excavations of Anglo-Saxon burial mounds, and that the Rohirrim are to a large degree based on ideas of Anglo-Saxon society in an early heroic period. Even these references, though, in fact tend to be focused through English literary traditions or specific texts. Thus the rather ritualised approach of Aragorn, Gimli, Legolas and Gandalf to Théoden's Hall is very closely based on passages in *Beowulf* where strangers enter a king's hall after exchanging ritual speeches with a Doorward; and the evil counsellor Wormtongue has a clear relationship to the character of similar sort called Unferth.

Though *The Lord of the Rings* has many Anglo-Saxon sources, there is also a marked contribution from another period and type of English literature, that of nineteenth-century romanticism. It's notable that references to periods of literature in between this very early one and that of the one on which Tolkien was presumably brought up are much less frequent. Thus, I think that Tennyson in particular has a much stronger presence in Tolkien's work than Chaucer or Shakespeare. Much of Tolkien's poetry (for example that collected in *The Lays of Beleriand*, as well as many of the Elven songs) is distinctly Tennysonian in flavour. Some illustration of this can be given by comparing verses from *The Gest of Beren and Lúthien* and from "The Lady of Shalott".

In fact, I think there is a particular set of associations for Tolkien which are focused through a rather nineteenth-century sense of "faery" and perhaps specifically through "The Lady of Shallot". Tennyson's "faery lady" is mysterious, magical, linked to an idea of feminine creativity, rooted in a romantic past and subject to a fatal curse which will bring death in place of immortality if she strays from her magical web and looks out into the real world. These qualities are very much interlinked in much nineteenth-century thought: the Lady is a symbol of much that is valuable, and her fragility further enhances that value by guaranteeing that it is a value far from the vulgar modern values of the world. Her value is given strength and emotional power by her failure to survive, and this criterion for value is created in opposition to other strands of nineteenth- century ideology which stressed the value of success and progress. Like Tolkien's Elves – and particularly his Elvish women who clearly take precedence over Elvish men in *The Lord of The Rings* – it is notable that the Lady of Shalott, while based in a world of romance, is seen as being more mysterious, more romantic even than her framing romance. One could also note that part of the mystery of Tennyson's poem is created by the allusions to a narrative which is never explicitly stated. Thus we never know exactly what the terms of the curse are. Though *The Lord of The Rings* as an extended prose work tells us much more about the past history of the Elves than does Tennyson's poem about the Lady, there is often a similar allusiveness which implies an unfathomable recession into the past, and a sense both of mystery and value. The final passing beyond the seas of the elves at the end of the Third Age is, of course, the ultimate example of the fading away of a set of values beyond human understanding, and of a guarantee that such values will always retain their status as unknowable, and therefore supremely valuable.

With these kinds of complex literary references or influences we are already approaching a kind of Englishness which is more than a matter of specific references either historical or literary. For Victorian ideas about the past and its relation to the modern world are important aspects of major ideologies of Englishness. I want next to look at how the Shire and its Hobbitry might relate to some of these ideas of Englishness, and then finish the paper by looking at the impact on these notions of a particularly traumatic event in modern English history.

If one nineteenth-century literary tradition tried to constitute an alternative set of values to those of the modern world through a medievalising romance, another strategy with related elements of nostalgia was to imagine or refer to an England seen as essentially rural. In fact even before the end of the nineteenth century the majority of England's population probably lived in environments which were not rural ones; nevertheless, the idea of England and English values as essentially rural was a strong one. One example of this is William Morris's *News From Nowhere* (1891) which creates an image of social harmony by envisaging a return to an England of villages and a machineless rural economy. Another example might be the recruiting poster from the Great War, which showed fields and a plough team, and had the caption: "It's Your Country – Fight For It".

This has much to do with the Shire. There are in the Prologue to *The Fellowship of the Ring* various hints which might lead us to see a connection between the hobbits and the English. They are, for example, divided into three original peoples, the Harfoots, the Stoors and the Fallohides, who may be equivalent to the Angles, the Saxons and the Jutes. Just as two brothers, Hengist and Horsa, are among the first Angles to come to Britain, so the hobbits are led across the Brandywine by two brothers, Marcho and Blanco. However, even were there not these specific hints, there is a great deal said about hobbit identity which can be connected with ideas of rural England. When hobbits first came to the Shire (itself, of course, a quintessentially English name), we are told, "the land was rich and kindly, and though it had long been deserted . . . it had before been well tilled: and there the king had once had many farms, cornlands, vineyards, and woods" (Tolkien, 1979a, p. 22).

From this down to earth but idyllic rural setting many of the hobbits' characteristics seem to spring. Thus:

> The Shire at this time had hardly any "government". Families for the most part managed their own affairs. Growing food and eating it occupied most of their time. In other matters they were, as a rule, generous and not greedy, but contented and moderate, so that estates, farms, workshops, and small trades tended to remain unchanged for generations.
> (Tolkien, 1979a, p. 28)

Their concern with the basic needs and pleasures of growing and consuming makes them modest people who preserve tradition, do not initiate needless change, who are essentially peaceful, and perhaps a little inward looking. All of these qualities have been assigned to the English and there was a particular belief throughout the Victorian period that the English were essentially law-abiding and peace-loving (hence, unlike the French, they had not been involved in any recent revolution). Despite this idea of peacefulness and moderation, however, there was, I think, also a sense that if national need arose then the English would do their duty. This is the notion of the English yeoman – by choice a peaceful farmer, but if stirred a doughty fighter. There is a very similar qualification to the hobbits' peacefulness.

> At no time had Hobbits of any kind been warlike, and they had never fought among themselves . . . Nonetheless, ease and peace had left this people still curiously tough. They were, if it came to it, difficult to daunt or to kill; and they were, perhaps, so unwearyingly fond of good things not least because they could, when put to it, do without them.
> (Tolkien, 1979a, p. 23)

Another related quality of the hobbits is their rather parochial outlook – an example of which is Rosie's comic comment to Sam on his return to the Shire, "If you've been looking after Mr. Frodo all this while, what d'you want to leave him for, as soon as things look dangerous ?" (Tolkien, 1979c, p. 349). This is in many ways treated as an admirable (if comic) virtue, but there is a strand of criticism of it too. Such mixed feelings about the excitement of adventure and the comforts of home are already present in *The Hobbit* of course. But in *The Lord of The Rings* this criticism is also linked to a specific set of ideas about the English which arose because of this very parocial and peaceful model of identity which has been discussed.

This anxiety surfaces from the beginning of the twentieth century, and is present particularly in various kinds of spy thrillers, such as those of John Buchan. The worry is that England is so self-satisfied and content that it will not even notice external threats which may destroy that way of life. This anxiety was perhaps particularly stimulated by fears of potential German aggression (though in some early fictions, anxieties are focused on French aggression). Such thrillers usually set out to show – partly for reasons of fictional pleasure and partly as an increasingly popular political critique – that beneath the surface, or on the fringes of peaceful, everyday life, there are secret conspiracies designed to destroy England. The conspiracies are opposed only by a select few who, unknown to the majority, defend them in secret and desperate adventures.

All this sounds very reminiscent of some aspects of *The Lord of the Rings*. One might particularly recall the many references throughout to the secret labours of those who have watched over the Shire, such as the Rangers, who are regarded by unknowing hobbits with great suspicion. One such reference is made in the Prologue itself: "They forgot or ignored what little they had ever known of the Guardians, and of the labours of those that made possible the long peace of the Shire. They were, in fact, sheltered, but they had ceased to remember it" (Tolkien, 1979a, p. 23). The portrayals of the Shirriffs are also part of this idea; they are the equivalent of the fictional rural British policeman: slightly comic, able to deal with simple matters of property and stray beasts, but with no real idea of the true evils outside.

These aspects of Englishness come from a pre-Great War stratum, but that war, and its effect on various ideas of Englishness, is also very important in Tolkien's work. In his Foreword, Tolkien, denying that *The Lord of The Rings* was primarily about the Second World War, suggested that the First World War might be much more central to its genesis:

> as the years go by it seems now often forgotten that to be caught in youth by 1914 was no less hideous an experience than to be involved in 1939 and the following years. By 1918 all but one of my close friends were dead.
> (Tolkien, 1979a, p. 12)

This seems absolutely the case: many (though not all) aspects of the War of the Ring seem to have their source in that cataclysm.

The imagery of trench warfare has often been seen as having a widespread effect on post-war literature, and this seems true here. The Dead Marshes and the wasteland surrounding Mordor may both have part of their origin in the trenches. In the journey through the Dead Marshes (where Gollum says a great war was once fought) we get a description of horrific, sticky mud and pools which contain corpses:

> Sam tripped . . . fell and came heavily on his hands, which sank deep into sticky ooze, so that his face was brought close to the surface of the dark mere . . . "There are dead things, dead faces in the water," he said with horror. "Dead faces!".
> (Tolkien, 1979b, p. 291)

As Frodo and Sam approach Mount Doom from far off, they see a landscape which seems to draw on scenes of life in the area just behind the trenches:

> Frodo and Sam gazed out in mingled loathing and wonder on this hateful land. Between them and the smoking mountain . . . all seemed ruinous and dead, a desert burned and choked. They wondered how the Lord of this realm maintained and fed his slaves and his armies. Yet armies he had. As far as their eyes could reach . . . there were camps, some of tents, some ordered like small towns. One of the largest of these was right below them. Barely a mile out into the plain it clustered like some huge nest of insects, with straight dreary streets of huts and long low drab buildings.
> (Tolkien, 1979c, p. 239)

Such a landscape is, of course, notably opposed to the ordered fertile agricultural landscape of the Shire, and each is associated with its own set of utterly opposed values. Similarly, there was a stark contrast between the myths (and in some sense actualities) of the English countryside which contributed to English patriotic feeling, and the experience of the first "modern" war.

One other aspect of *The Lord of the Rings* may also have a partial origin in the First World War. It is very noticeable that the orcs, who provide the armies of The Enemy, are rarely portrayed as evil in quite the same way as the Ringwraiths or some other forces of evil are. They are brutal and brutalised, but their ways of talking and their motivations are often (indeed nearly always) sources of comedy to some extent – even if it is sometimes very black comedy. Thus we get the following kind of conversation:

> "Garn! You don't even know what you're looking for."
> "Whose blame's that?" said the soldier. "Not mine. That comes from Higher Up. First they say it's a great Elf in bright armour, then it's a sort of small dwarf-man, then it must be a pack of rebel Uruk-hai; or maybe it's all the lot together."
> (Tolkien, 1979c, p. 241)

It seems likely that this conversation – and the many similar orc conversations – is to some extent based on an idea of the kind of grumbling, jokey idioms allegedly used by "other ranks" during the War. It could even be said that this is another aspect of modern urban life – an urban working-class dialect which is opposed to the more rural dialect of Sam and many other of the hobbits.

As Tolkien himself said, an author cannot remain entirely unaffected by his experiences, and it seems to me that *The Lord of the Rings* is very deeply influenced by a whole range of ideas of and about Englishness, which it both contains and reinvents for its own purposes.

References

Tolkien, J. R. R. 1979a. *The Fellowship of the Ring*. London: Unwin Paperbacks.

Tolkien, J. R. R. 1979b. *The Two Towers*. London: Unwin Paperbacks.

Tolkien, J. R. R. 1979c. *The Return of the King*. London: Unwin Paperbacks.

Tolkien, J. R. R. 1985. "The Gest of Beren and Lúthien", in J. R. R. Tolkien ed. Christopher Tolkien *The Lays of Beleriand*. London: George Allen & Unwin. pp 154-308.

A Mythology for England

Carl F. Hostetter and Arden R. Smith

Abstract: As J.R.R. Tolkien developed a mythology for his invented languages to dwell and grow in, he found himself increasingly drawn to satisfy for himself his desire for a true English epic. Tolkien thus encompassed elements of English geography, language, and mythology within his geography, languages, and mythology, as demonstrated through an examination of five figures of Tolkien's mythology, Eärendil, Ermon and Elmir, Ælfwine, and Ingwë.

Keywords: Ælfwine, Anglo-Saxon, Aryaman, Askr, Eärendel, Eärendil, Elmir, Elvish, Embla, England, Eremon, Ermon, Germanic, Gnomish, Hengest, Ing, Ingwë, language, mythology, Ōhthere, Old English, philology, Quenya

Sometime late in 1951 J.R.R. Tolkien wrote a letter to Milton Waldman, an editor with the London publisher Collins, whom Tolkien hoped would publish *The Silmarillion* in conjunction with *The Lord of the Rings*. In the course of this remarkable letter, the full text of which is said to be some ten thousand words long, Tolkien wrote:

> I was from early days grieved by the poverty of my own beloved country: it had no stories of its own (bound up with its tongue and soil), not of the quality that I sought, and found (as an ingredient) in legends of other lands. There was Greek, and Celtic, and Romance, Germanic, Scandinavian, and Finnish (which greatly affected me); but nothing English, save impoverished chap-book stuff. Of course there was and is all the Arthurian world, but powerful as it is, it is imperfectly naturalized, associated with the soil of Britain but not with English; and does not replace what I felt to be missing.
> (Tolkien, 1981, p. 144).

The distinction that Tolkien draws between things British and things English is important. While there is a considerable body of legend concerning Britain, the Land of the Britons, there is virtually nothing of the proper quality that expresses the genius of England, *Englalond* of the Anglo-Saxons, "the Land of the people of the Angle". There is no English epic associated with both the soil *and* the tongue of England, no Anglo-Saxon *Mabinogion*, no *Iliad* or *Táin* or *Aeneid*, no *Nibelungenlied* or *Edda* or *Kalevala*.

It may be surprising at first that Tolkien excludes from this discussion the Anglo-Saxon poem *Beowulf*, whose study he had revolutionized some fifteen years earlier with his essay *Beowulf: The Monsters and the Critics*[1]. To be sure, *Beowulf* comes very close to the sort of epic that Tolkien desired for England. Tolkien notes at the conclusion of *Monsters and the Critics* that the English poet of *Beowulf* achieves an individual character for the poem by

> using the materials (then still plentiful) preserved from a day already changing and passing, a time that has now for ever vanished, swallowed in oblivion; using them for a new purpose, with a wider sweep of imagination, if with a less bitter and concentrated force.
> (Tolkien, 1984c, p. 33).

Thus the *Beowulf*-poet took the "materials" of an inherited Germanic mythology and used "for a new purpose, with a wider sweep of imagination", the mythology of the mysterious Scēaf and his son Scyld, the *gōd cyning*; of Eormenrīc, king of the Goths; and of Frōda and his fortunate son Ingeld. And certainly Tolkien finds the poem's individual character to be unmistakably English, for:

> it is in fact written in a language that after many centuries has still essential kinship with our own, it was made in this land, and moves in our northern world beneath our northern sky, and for those who are native to that tongue and land, it must ever call with a profound appeal – until the dragon comes.
> (Tolkien, 1984c, pp. 33-4)

Yet even *Beowulf* fails to meet Tolkien's criteria for a truly English epic, for though it was composed in Old English, and makes a new and characteristically English use of Germanic mythological elements, nevertheless no part of it is set in England; and so though the poem moves beneath northern skies, those skies are nevertheless not English. But while *Beowulf* is thus not a true English epic, English in both "tongue and soil", it does demonstrate that the Anglo-Saxons had a mythology from which such an epic could be formed. If anything, this hint of what might have been, this tantalizing near-satisfaction that *Beowulf* provides, must have served only to make Tolkien's longing more intense.

It is certainly no surprise then that as Tolkien developed a mythology for his invented languages to dwell and grow in,[2]

---
[1] Reprinted in Tolkien, 1984c, pp. 5-48.
[2] As Tolkienian linguists, we are compelled to point out that Tolkien's invention of languages did indeed precede his invention of a

he found himself increasingly drawn to satisfy for himself his desire for a true English epic. After explaining this desire to Milton Waldman, Tolkien continues:

> Do not laugh! But once upon a time (my crest has long since fallen) I had a mind to make a body of more or less connected legend, ranging from the large and cosmogonic, to the level of romantic fairy-story – the larger founded on the lesser in contact with the earth, the lesser drawing splendour from the vast backcloths – which I could dedicate simply to: to England; to my country.
> (Tolkien, 1981, p. 144)

By his own criteria, Tolkien could create a mythology for England only by setting it on English soil, writing it in Old English, and featuring figures from English or at least Germanic mythology; or at any rate by encompassing elements of English geography, language, and mythology within his own. And that is exactly what he did. Through an examination of five figures of Tolkien's mythology, Eärendil, Ermon and Elmir, Ælfwine, and Ingwë, we will see that English geography, language, and mythology are all incorporated into Tolkien's creation. Thus even as Tolkien developed a mythology for his Elvish languages, he encompassed in it a mythology for England.

Eärendil

We will begin with Eärendil, who was in fact the first figure of English mythology that Tolkien incorporated into his own. It has long been recognized that Tolkien's mariner and messenger is derived from English and Germanic mythology, in particular from the Anglo-Saxon poem *Crīst*:

> Ēalā Ēarendel   engla beorhtast,
> ofer middangeard   monnum sended
> ond sōðfæsta   sunnan lēoma,
> torht ofer tunglas
> "Hail Earendel, brightest of angels,
> over middle-earth sent unto men,
> and true gleam of the sun,
> radiant above the stars"[3]

In fact, in a letter from 1967, Tolkien describes how, upon encountering the Anglo-Saxon *Ēarendel* in 1913, he was "struck by the great beauty of this word (or name), entirely coherent with the normal style of [Anglo-Saxon], but euphonic to a peculiar degree in that pleasing but not 'delectable' language," and that he "adopted" him into his mythology, which he had already been forming for some years (Tolkien, 1981, p. 385). So taken was Tolkien with this figure of English mythology, in fact, that by the end of 1915 he had written no less than fourteen versions of four different poems concerning Eärendel, each of which contains explicit references to his mythology (Tolkien, 1984b, pp. 267-76).

One of the authors of this paper has elsewhere examined at some length the philological puzzle that the Anglo-Saxon *Ēarendel* presents (Hostetter, 1991), and shown that the major aspects of Tolkien's Eärendil, the Star, the Messenger, the Eagle, the Mariner, and the Herald, were all suggested to Tolkien either by the role of the remarkably wide-spread mythological "cognates" of *Ēarendel* in the various Germanic traditions, or by an exploration of the linguistic cognates of Ēarendel in the various Germanic languages. Thus for example the aspects of Star, Messenger, and Herald are found in the *Crīst*, among other sources, while those of Eagle and Mariner were perhaps suggested by Old English *earn* "eagle" and *ēar* "sea, ocean" respectively.

In adopting Ēarendel into his mythology, the Anglo-Saxon word exerted an influence on Tolkien's own languages, since as he points out:

> the name [Ēarendel] could not be adopted just like that: it had to be accommodated to the Elvish linguistic situation, at the same time as a place for this person was made in legend. From this, far back in the history of "Elvish", which was beginning, after many tentative starts in boyhood, to take definite shape at the time of the name's adoption, arose eventually (a) the [Common Eldarin] stem *AYAR "Sea" . . . and (b) the element, or verbal base (N)DIL, "to love, be devoted to" . . .
> (Tolkien, 1981, pp. 385-6)

Thus Tolkien's own languages were shaped by an Old English word, in order to provide a fictional origin and explanation for the name of a figure taken from the mythology of England. In the same way, Tolkien's mythology was shaped by the aspects of Ēarendel that he found in his philological inquiries, in order to recover for England something of the great Story of Ēarendel that must once have been told, a story that already by the time of the *Crīst* was, in the words of Tolkien's minstrel

> . . . but shreds one remembers
> Of golden imaginings fashioned in sleep,
> A whispered tale told by the withering embers
> Of old things far off that but few hearts keep.
> (Tolkien, 1984b, p. 271)

Ermon and Elmir

Like most mythologies, Tolkien's mythology gives accounts of the creation of the universe and the creatures living therein. A most interesting, albeit subtle, link between Tolkien's mythology and that of the English and Germanic peoples, indeed of all the Indo-Europeans, can be seen in an early version of the tale of the awakening of Men appearing in the outlines to "Gilfanon's Tale" in *The Book of Lost Tales*:

> The wizard Túvo told Nuin that the sleepers he had found were the new Children of Ilúvatar, and that they were waiting for light. He forbade any of the Elves to wake them or to visit those places, being frightened of the wrath of Ilúvatar; but despite this Nuin went there often and watched, sitting on a rock. Once he stumbled against a sleeper, who stirred but did not wake. At last,

---

mythology. Tolkien notes in a letter from 1967 (Tolkien, 1981, p. 375) that he created his "imaginary histories" because he "discovered, as others have who carry out [the invention of languages] to any degree of completion, that a language requires a suitable habitation, and a history in which it can develop."

[3] Lines 104-7; my translation – CFH.

overcome by curiosity, he awakened two, named Ermon and Elmir; they were dumb and very much afraid, but he taught them much of the Ilkorin tongue, for which reason he is called Nuin Father of Speech. Then came the First Dawn; and Ermon and Elmir alone of Men saw the first Sun rise in the West and come over to the Eastward Haven.

(Tolkien, 1984a, pp. 235-6 and cf. p. 237).

The most striking aspect of this version of the tale is the inclusion of the names of the first Men, which appear nowhere else. The only further textual information we have concerning Ermon and Elmir is that the people of Ermon alone of Men fought beside the fairies in the Battle of Palisor (Tolkien, 1984a, pp. 236-7), that an embassy was sent by Melko to Túvo, Tinwelint, and Ermon before the Battle of Unnumbered Tears (Tolkien, 1984a, pp. 238-9), and that Ermon (or both Ermon and Elmir) was the ancestor of Ing, King of Luthany (Tolkien, 1984b, p. 305).

Although Christopher Tolkien does not give etymologies for the names, he does give a very informative note:

> Above *Ermon* is written, to all appearance, the Old English word *Æsc* ("ash"). It seems conceivable that this is an anglicizing of Old Norse *Askr* ("ash"), in the northern mythology the name of the first man, who with the first woman (*Embla*) were made by the Gods out of two trees that they found on the seashore
> (Tolkien, 1984a, p. 245, n. 9).

The story of Askr and Embla is told in strophes 17 and 18 of *Vǫluspá*:

> Unz þrí(a)r kvámu   ór því liði
> ǫflgir ok ástgir   Æsir at húsi;
> fundu á landi   lítt megandi
> Ask ok Emblu,   ørlǫglausa.
> Ǫnd þau né áttu,   óð þau né hǫfðu,
> lá né læti   né litu góða;
> ond gaf Óðinn,   óð gaf Hænir,
> lá gaf Lóðurr   ok litu góða.
>
> To the coast then came, kind and mighty,
> from the gathered gods three great Æsir;
> on the land they found, of little strength,
> Ask and Embla, unfated yet.
> Sense they possessed not, soul they had not,
> being nor bearing, nor blooming hue;
> soul gave Óthin, sense gave Hænir,
> being, Lóthur, and blooming hue.
> (Nordal, 1980, pp. 32-5; translation Hollander, 1962, p. 3)

Askr and Embla are apparently names of trees. Askr at any rate denotes the ash tree (*Fraxinus excelsior*) or something made from its wood, such as a spear, a small ship, or a small wooden vessel (Loewenthal, 1922, p. 275, Jóhannesson, 1956, pp. 90-1, Cleasby/Vigfusson, 1957, p. 25, de Vries, 1962, p. 15), and furthermore has the poetic meanings "leader, man" and also "horse" (Holthausen, 1948, p. 3)[4]. OE *æsc* and its Germanic cognates are derived from the Indo-European root *ōsi-s* "ash"[5]. All scholars appear to agree on the connection between the name of the first man in *Vǫluspá* and this root.

The meaning of the name *Embla*, however, has been the topic of much debate. Jacob Grimm states that *embla* denotes a "busy woman"[6], and thus does not connect it to a plant name of any kind. Sophus Bugge notes, however, that "The man's name, 'ash,' shows that the woman's must also be that of a tree. I believe *Embla* to have arisen from Danish *Elmbla*, a diminutive of *almr*, 'elm.'" (1899, p. xxviii). Hans Sperber disagrees with Bugge on the basis of the loss of *l* in stressed position and his inadequate explanation of the epenthetic *b*, and suggests instead that it comes from a Germanic *ambilōn related to Gk. ἄμπελος "vine" and perhaps also to Gallic *amella* "honeysuckle" (Sperber, 1910, pp. 219-22). He gives as supporting evidence the manner in which the Indo-Europeans made fire, namely by boring a stick of a hardwood such as ash into a piece of softer wood, preferably that of some sort of climbing plant (pp. 220-1). The sexual connotations of this are clear, and the name "vine" for the first woman is thus appropriate. Loewenthal variously derives it from IE *āmliiā́, which he interprets as denoting some species of rowan (mountain-ash, genus *Sorbus*) (1922, pp. 275-8), or from IE *améla "yellow-wood" via Gmc. *amilōn "alder" (1924, pp. 80-1). The various etymological dictionaries tend to be noncommittal (e.g. Holthausen, 1948, p. 3; Jóhannesson, 1956, pp. 22, 88; de Vries, 1962, pp. 101-2), whereas translators of the Eddas tend to prefer "elm" (e.g. Bray, 1908, p. 283, Auden/Taylor, 1981, p. 247) or "vine"(e.g. Hollander, 1962, p. 3).

Now that we have examined the etymologies of Askr and Embla, what can we say about the etymologies of *Ermon* and *Elmir*? No derivations are given in *The Book of Lost Tales*, but the name *Elmir* is remarkably similar to *elm*, one of the candidates for the meaning of *Embla*. It should also be noted that when Tolkien was writing this version of the creation myth, Bugge's hypothesis that *Embla* means "elm" had been around for about a decade and a half in a book published in England in an English translation, whereas the other theories mentioned above, if in existence by that time at all, appeared in German in German journals. We might assume, therefore, that "elm" was the prevailing interpretation of *Embla* in England at that time and thus the meaning that Tolkien intended for *Elmir*. Not only does the name resemble the English word *elm*, but also Elvish words with that meaning: Qenya *alalmë* (whence *Alalminórë* "Land of Elms"), Gnomish *lalm* or *larm*, and *lalmir* (Tolkien, 1984a, p. 249).

On the other hand, while *Ermon*, as indicated by Tolkien's gloss, is clearly equivalent to *Æsc*, the first man of English

---

[4] This is most likely due to metonymy, with the material of the warrior's weapon or vehicle being used to denote the warrior, cf. ON *askmaðr* "viking, pirate", OE *æscmann*, both literally "ash-man" (Cleasby/Vigfusson, 1957, p. 25, de Vries, 1962, p. 15).
[5] Whence also a number of cognates in other Indo-European languages, including Lat. *ornus* "mountain ash, spear", Gk. ὀξύη "copper-beech, lance", OSl. *jasenu* "beech", OIr. *uinnius* "ash", Lith. *úosis* "ash", Alb. *ah* "beech", and Arm. *haçi* "ash" (Jóhannesson, 1956, pp. 90-1, de Vries, 1962, p. 15).
[6] "Ein geschäftiges weib", from *am(b)r*, *am(b)l* "labor assiduus", whence also the heroic name *Amala* (Grimm, 1875, p. I, 475).

mythology, his name bears no similarity to *ash* or its cognates. Furthermore, there do not appear to be any tree names in the Elvish languages with a form similar to this name. How then does *Ermon* fit into this schema and correspond to *Askr*? In strophe 19 of *Vǫluspá*, immediately following the Askr and Embla story, we have another occurrence of the word *askr*:

Ask veit ek standa, heitir Yggdrasill,
hár baðmr, ausinn hvíta auri;
þaðan koma dǫggvar, þærs í dala falla,
stendr æ yfir grœnn Urðarbrunni.

"An ash I know, hight Yggdrasil,
the mighty tree moist with white dews;
thence come the floods that fall adown;
evergreen o'ertops Urth's well this tree."
(Nordal, 1980, p. 36; translation Hollander, 1962, p.4)

This ash, Yggdrasill, is the World Tree of Norse mythology, the center of the universe, linking the nine worlds (Davidson, 1964, pp. 190-6). This notion of a World Tree was widespread among the Indo-European and Finno-Ugric peoples, by whom such a tree was revered. Sacred trees and (similarly) sacred posts and pillars were not uncommon among these peoples (Meringer, 1904, pp. 165-6 and 1907, pp. 296-306, de Vries, 1952, pp. 19-20, Turville-Petre, 1962, p. 242, Davidson, 1964, pp. 190-1). In fact, Old Norse *áss*, *ǫ́ss* means both "beam, girder" and "god, one of the Æsir", and Meringer gives numerous examples of the widespread worship of wooden blocks, stakes, and pillars among the various branches of the Indo-European family (Meringer, 1907, pp. 296-306). Among the revered posts that he mentions is the Greek *Herme* (anglicized as *herm*) (Fox, 1916), which he derives from ἕρμα "Balken" ("beam, girder") and regards as something of an intermediate stage between a bare pole and an anthropomorphic idol (Meringer, 1904, pp. 165-6 and 1907, p. 299). The herm, according to Fox, is a "developed fetish-form of Hermes" which "consists of a tall square column with stumps of arms and a phallos, and is surmounted by a bearded head . . ." (Fox, 1916, p. 195) Is *Ermon* then connected with *Hermes*? We will return to this question shortly.

Another venerated pillar mentioned by Meringer is the *Irminsûl* (Meringer, 1907, p. 300). In his *Translatio S. Alexandri* (A.D. 851) (Pertz, 1976ff., p. II.676), Ruodolf of Fulda writes that the Saxons worshipped a wooden pillar which they called *Irminsul*, meaning "column of the universe, supporting all things". A pillar with this name, a center of the religion of the Saxons, was located near Heresburg (modern-day Stadtbergen) in Westphalia[7]. As noted by Grimm, the idea of such a World Pillar is very closely related to the Yggdrasill of the Scandinavian myths (Grimm, 1875, p. II.667). For example, Yggdrasill's roots stretched out in three directions, whereas the *Irminsûl* was the hub from which three or four roads emanated. There is also the obvious parallel in their common function of supporting the universe.

The element *irmin-* in *Irminsûl* is certainly nearer in form to Tolkien's *Ermon* than is *Herme(s)*, since it shares all three consonants. That the vowels do not show an exact correspondence is not surprising, since the vocalism of this element within the Germanic cognates is rather variable; the word *Irminsûl* alone has a number of variant spellings in the old documents, including *irmansûl*, *yrmensûl*, *ermensul*, and *hirmensul* (Grimm, 1875, pp. I.95-8). The first element *irmin* and its cognates in other Germanic dialects display an even wider variety of vowels. (Voltaire is said to have observed that etymology is a science in which the consonants count for very little, and the vowels for nothing at all.)

But what does *Irminsûl* mean? The element *sûl*[8] is the predecessor of modern German *Säule* "pillar"[9] and *irmansûl* is rendered as *colossus* or *altissima columna* "very high column" in various Old High German glosses (Grimm, 1875, pp. I.95-6). The element *irmin* is therefore taken by Grimm to have an augmentative effect on the nouns with which it is compounded (Grimm, 1875, p. I.97); thus *irmingot* (the highest god, the god of all), *irminman* (an elevated term for "man"), *irminthiod* (the human race), and so on.

This element is present in all the old Germanic languages. Holthausen gives the reconstructed Gothic forms **aírman-s*, **aírmin-s* = "great, mighty" for the element, present in such personal names *Ermanaricus* (*Erminaricus*) and *Ermanagildus* (*Erminagildus*), and relates this vocable to Old Icelandic *jǫrmun-*, seen in such forms as *Jǫrmunrekr*, the cognate form of *Ermanaricus*, king of the Goths, *jǫrmungrund* "the wide earth", and *Jǫrmungandr*, the name of the serpent that surrounds the world (Holthausen, 1934, p. 4, 1963, p. 92). He also relates it to Anglo-Saxon *eormen-*, seen in such forms as *eormencyn(n)* "mankind", which occurs in *Beowulf*; and to Old Saxon *irmin-*, seen in such forms as *irminthiod* "the people of the earth", which occurs in the *Hêliand*[10]. Cleasby

---

[7] According to numerous chronicle entries for the year 772, Charlemagne, in the course of converting the Saxons to Christianity, destroyed this symbol of heathendom (Grimm, 1875, p. I.96, Davidson, 1964, p. 196). Thus we have in the Annals written by Einhard of Fulda in the early ninth century (Pertz, 1976ff., p. I.348), for example: "Karolus Saxoniam bello aggressus, Eresburgum castrum cepit, et idolum Saxonum quod vocabitur Irminsul destruit" (see Grimm, 1875, pp. I.96-7; cf. Pertz, 1976ff., pp. I.16, I.30, I.88, I.117, I.150-1, I.228, I.295, I.557, II.376, III.37, etc.).

[8] Which we may note here is remarkably similar to the Adûnaic word *sulum* "mast" (Tolkien, 1992, p. 419).

[9] Grimm (1875, pp. I.98, II.667, III.45) in fact uses the modernized forms *Irmanseul* and *Irmenseule*.

[10] Holthausen (1934, p. 4, 1963, p. 92) further lists as cognates Greek ὄρμενο-ς "hoch" [="high"]; Old Slavic *raměnŭ* "stark, gewaltig" [="strong, mighty"]; Lithuanian *erma-s* "Ungeheuer" [="monster"], *ermi-s* "übergroß" [="overlarge"], *erminga-s* "unförmlich" [="informal"]; Albanian *jerm* "rasend" [="raving"]; Armenian *arman* "Wunder" [="wonder"]. He later (1948, p. 146) relates these to the copulative stem seen in Old English *eart* "art" (2. sg. pres.) and *earon* "are" (pl. pres.) and to the stem seen in Latin *orior* "I rise", and in this connection it is interesting to note the Eldarin base ORO- "up; rise; high", whence Old Noldorin *orie*, Noldorin *erio* "rise", and the related base ÓR-NI- "high tree". Walde (1927-32, pp. I.136-9) gives Germanic **ermana-*, **irmino-* = "great" as a derivative of an Indo-European

and Vigfusson define Old Icelandic *jǫrmun-* as "a prefix in a few old mythical words, implying something huge, vast, superhuman" (Cleasby/Vigfusson, 1957, p. 328). Bosworth defines the Old English forms *eormen*, *eorman* as "Universal, immense, whole, general" and *irmen* as "A word occurring mostly as a prefix with the idea of greatness, universality" (Bosworth, 1882, pp. 254, 599). Bearing this aspect of universality in mind, it is quite interesting to note that a word *irmin* with a similar sense appears in Tolkien's *Qenya Lexicon*, which is contemporary with the *Lost Tales* and thus with the story of Ermon and Elmir. *Irmin* is listed in the *Qenya Lexicon* under the root IŘI "dwell ?" and is glossed "the inhabited world – the whole of the created world not only earth."[11]

This explains how the Germanic element *irmin* links with the Elvish word *irmin*, but how do these connect with our primordial man, *Ermon*? We have already seen how Germanic *irmin-* could be used as an augmentative prefix. But *Irmin* also appears in a proper name in its own right.

In chapter 12 of his *Res Gestae Saxonicae* (c.968), the monk Widukind wrote that the Saxons, after having triumphed over the Thuringians in the year 830, erected an altar at the eastern gateway of the town they had captured. This altar, according to Widukind, was in the form of a column imitating Hercules, positioned with respect to the sun (Apollo) and bearing the name of the god Mars, which appeared as *Hirmin*, a form of the Greek name *Hermis* (*Hermes*): "quia Hirmin vel Hermis graece Mars dicitur" (Pertz, 1976ff, p. III.423, de Vries, 1952, p. 18, Grimm, 1875, pp. I.292-3). The column is thus clearly an *Irminsûl*, but Widukind has the Greco-Roman gods confused: Mars corresponds to Ares, and Mercury corresponds to Hermes. Grimm believes that this is an indication that the Saxon *Hirmin* was a mixture of both Mars and Mercury, who is equated with the Germanic god **Wôðanaz* (Old Saxon *Wôdan*, Old Norse *Óðinn*; cf. Old English *Wôdnesdæg* for *Dies Mercurii*) (Grimm, 1875, p. I.293 and Dumézil, 1973, p. 19). Further evidence of a correlation between (H)irmin and Mercury/Wôdan can be seen in a twelfth-century chronicle: "*ûf einer yrmensûle stuont ein abgot ungehiure, den hiezen sie ir koufman*" ("upon an *irminsûl* stood a monstrous idol, whom they called their merchant"), since Mercury/Wôdan was the patron god of merchants (Fox, 1916, pp. 194-5, Davidson, 1964, pp. 56, 140-1). Perhaps the most telling evidence can be seen in the name *Jǫrmunr*, which is a sobriquet of the Norse god Óðinn (Jóhannesson, 1956, p. 64, Cleasby/Vigfusson, 1957, p. 328, de Vries, 1962, p. 295), whom many Germanic tribes claimed as their progenitor.

The name of *Irmin* also appears in the name of specific Germanic peoples. Tacitus tells us in his *Germania* that the three main branches of the Germanic people, the *Ingaevones*, *Herminones*, and *Istaevones*, were named after the three sons of *Mannus* "man" (Much, 1967, pp. 44, 51-60, also Much, 1900, pp. 72-3 and Grimm, 1875, pp. I.285-94, III.398-401). Grimm connects *Herminones* with a progenitor *Irmin*, saying: "The ancestor of the Herminones was without a doubt named *Hermin*, i.e. *Irmin*, whom later legend knows as a divine hero" (Grimm, 1875, pp. I.291-5, III.399)[12]. Grimm further claims that *Istaevones* should be read as *Iscaevones* (Grimm, 1875, pp. I.289-90, III.399), with its eponymous founder, *Iscvio* or *Isco*, corresponding to the Old Norse *Askr* and Old English *Æsc*, whom as we have seen Tolkien equates with Ermon. *Irmin* may even be present in the name *Germani* itself. According to one of the several etymologies for this name listed by Elston, it is a compound of a prefix **ga-* and the Germanic stem **ermena-*, and thus the name *Germani* may indicate some such idea as "the members of a great people" (Elston, 1934, p. 24).

It is clear then that English and Germanic mythology maintained a tradition of a progenitor whose name was a cognate of *Irmin*, which was also used adjectivally to mean "great, large" or "universal". But in fact this tradition is far older than the common Germanic period, extending in all likelihood back to the proto-Indo-Europeans. There is, for instance, an Indo-Iranian god *Aryaman* whom Georges Dumézil, in *Le Troisième Souverain* (1949), interprets as a god of the "third function", i.e. of the agricultural class, as opposed to priests and warriors, and thus connected with the well-being of the common people, their crops, and their livestock[13]. Dumézil also demonstrates the correspondences in name, function, and mythical deeds between the Indic *Aryaman* and a figure of Irish mythology, *Eremon*, who became the first king of Ireland after its conquest by the sons of Mile (Dumézil, 1949, pp. 163-85 and d'Arbois de Jubainville, 1903, p. 147). According to Dumézil:

> [Eremon] is king with the same title as those of Mitra and Varuna; he joins them functionally since he plays the same role, that of *introducing a new peopling* . . . Finally, jointly and separately without doubt from the word *aire* (**aryak-*), this Eremon is the *chief of the*

---

root 3. *er-* = "set into motion, excite, exalt", whence also such words as those mentioned by Holthausen, as well as Old English *rinnan* "flow, run" and *ears* "arse".

[11] In the *Gnomish Lexicon* from the same time appear the related forms *Idhru*, *Isbar*, and *Idhrubar*, all glossed as "the world, all the regions inhab[ited] by Men, Elves and Gods. (Cp. Qenya *irmin*)" (Tolkien, 1984b, p. 343). Citations from the *Qenya Lexicon* and the *Gnomish Lexicon* are taken from correspondence with Christopher Tolkien, and differ somewhat from those published in *The Book of Lost Tales*.

[12] My translation – ARS.

[13] See Dumézil, 1973, pp. ix-xviii for an overview of the Dumézilian tripartite framework. Jan de Vries (1952, pp. 26-7, my translation – ARS) provides a useful summary of Dumézil's argument:

> Aryaman is a derivation from *arya-*, the designation of the Aryan people, or more exactly of the people as a "social corps". Aryaman would have been the god of that body, in which the mutual, social bonds existing between the members of an Aryan community are concentrated and sublimated . . . Thus *arya* "is applied to each man, god, or thing belonging to that community or corresponding to that type, above all in opposition to the barbarians." The protector-god of that community, Aryaman, the third sovereign according to Georges Dumézil's expression, is the associate of the other gods of sovereignty: Mitra and Varuna.

ancestors of the present-day airig, *of the present-day Irish masses* and not of those prehistoric Irish, which were the gods, the Tuatha dê Danann.
(Dumézil, 1949, pp. 170-1)[14]

The Irish Eremon's connection with Tolkien's Ermon is thus clear: both mark the beginning of a new race, the race of Men[15].

We are not claiming that all of these figures and concepts were in Tolkien's mind when he decided to name his first human Ermon. Nevertheless, it can hardly be a mere coincidence that Tolkien's name for the first human should resemble so many names of founders of dynasties and eponymous gods and heroes. It is clear that Tolkien consciously chose the names *Ermon* and *Elmir* for the first Men in order to connect his mythology with English and Germanic tradition.

Ælfwine

No discussion of Tolkien's creation of a mythology for England would be complete without at least a cursory discussion of the story of Ælfwine, which is without a doubt its fullest, most complex, and most remarkable expression. Though the details of the role and significance of Ælfwine varied considerably as Tolkien developed and refined his mythology (in fact, in the earliest version, he was not even named Ælfwine), he serves throughout as an ambassador between Tolkien's mythology and English legend, the agent through whom the English receive, in Anglo-Saxon, what Tolkien calls "the true tradition of the fairies", a tradition "more true than anything to be found in Celtic lands" (Tolkien, 1984b, p. 290). Ælfwine's ambassadorship spans the whole *History of Middle-earth* series to date, from the earliest workings in *The Book of Lost Tales* of c.1916 through *The Lost Road* of 1937 to the *Notion Club Papers* of c.1945 in the most recent volume, *Sauron Defeated*.

Unfortunately, for us to fully explore the significance of Ælfwine to Tolkien's creation of a mythology for England would require an examination many times the length of the present discussion. In any event, the significance is so manifest and so thoroughly discussed by Christopher Tolkien in the course of the various volumes of *The History of Middle-earth*, in particular in *The History of Eriol or Ælfwine* in *The Book of Lost Tales Part II* (pp. 278-334), that it would be pointless here to do more than merely summarize the most important features of the story of Ælfwine, and add a few observations of our own along the way.

In the earliest version of what would become the story of Ælfwine (esp. Tolkien, 1984a, pp. 23-4, Tolkien, 1984b, pp. 289-94), the mortal mariner who comes to Tol Eressëa, the Lonely Isle of the Elves in the middle of the Great Sea, is named Ottor Wæfre "Ottor the Restless". Ottor, whom the Gnomes name *Eriol* "One who dreams alone", is the compiler of the *Parma Kuluinen*, the "Golden Book", whose tales he records in the Eressëan village of Tavrobel, the "Great Haywood", after hearing them recited by the Gnomes in *Mar Vanwa Tyaliéva*, the "Cottage of Lost Play" in Kortirion, the chief town of Alalminórë, the "Land of Elms". The most remarkable fact of this stage of the mythology is that Tol Eressëa *is* Britain; that is, Tol Eressëa is drawn east by the Vala Ulmo and the great whale Uin into the geographical position of England, and Ireland is formed when the god Ossë attempts to thwart Ulmo's efforts and breaks off the western half of the island. Thus Kortirion is not simply *modelled* on Tolkien's beloved Warwick, it *is* Warwick, both geographically and etymologically; and Tavrobel is the village of Great Haywood in Staffordshire (Tolkien, 1984b, pp. 291-2).

Of course, since Ottor Wæfre is thus in effect the first mortal "discoverer" of England, he could not himself be English. This is indeed the case, as we learn from the fact that Ottor took the name *Angol* "after the regions of his home" which, as Christopher Tolkien notes, "certainly refers to the ancient homeland of the 'English' before their migration across the North Sea to Britain: Old English *Angel* . . . the region of the Danish peninsula between the Flensburg fjord and the river Schlei, south of the modern Danish frontier" (Tolkien, 1984a, p. 24). We learn more about the pre-Eressëan life of Ottor in jottings by Tolkien titled "Story of Eriol's Life" (1984b, pp. 289-90), where it is told that "Ottor Wæfre settled on the island of Heligoland in the North Sea, and wedded a woman named Cwén; they had two sons named Hengest and Horsa . . ."

We see here the forging of an explicit link between Tolkien's legends and English history, for Hengest and Horsa are of course the first Saxon chieftains to wrest a solid foothold in England from the Britons. According to Gildas' *De Exicidio Britanniae* ("On the Ruin of Britain") about the year 450 the British king Vortigern invited Saxons, led by

---

[14] My translation – ARS. Jan de Vries, in his 1952 article "La valeur religieuse du mot germanique *Irmin*", extends Dumézil's hypothesis into the Germanic realm, arguing against the meaning "large" normally assigned to the element *irmin* and drawing instead on an idea that it implied a sense of affinity, similar to that in the Sanskrit *arya*: "The prefix *ermuna-*, *ermina-* . . . corresponds to a completely different idea than that of 'great, universal', it circumscribes in a very special manner the community of one people" (de Vries, 1952, p. 24, my translation – ARS). Thus, according to de Vries (1952, pp. 24-5), *irmintheod* does not merely designate "people of the world", but rather "our people", Ermanarik is not only "the mighty king" but also "our own king". Similarly, "the idea of affinity can be condensed into that of a divinity, a guarantor of the order of life, into which we find ourselves placed. A god *Erminaz* seems to be the quasi-necessary complement of the word *ermenaz* that we just defined" (de Vries, 1952, p. 26).

[15] The analogues of *irmin* among various Indo-European peoples may be even more widespread. This element may even be present in the name of the Armenian people. Ananikian (1964, p. 66) says of the legendary hero Armenak, the son of Hayk, that he is undoubtedly an eponymous hero of the Armenians and adds, "It is quite possible that Armenak is the same as the Teutonic Irmin and the Vedic Aryaman." He notes further (1964, p. 389) that "Patrubani explains *Armenus* [a Latinized form of the name] as *Arya-Manah*, 'Aryan (noble?)-minded.' The Vedic Aryaman seems to mean 'friend,' 'comrade.'" Thus we see again de Vries' notion of affinity and Dumézil's *Aryan* element in the name.

Hengest and Horsa, to cross the North Sea and settle in Britain as auxiliary troops. When Vortigern was unable to provide adequate supplies for the unexpectedly large host that accepted his invitation, the Saxons revolted and eventually established a kingdom in Kent under Hengest's rule.

There may also be an historical basis for Ottor Wǽfre himself. Incorporated by King Ælfred (A.D. 849-99) into his translation of Paulus Orosius' *Historiae adversum paganos* is an eyewitness account of the lands and peoples of Scandinavia and the Baltic regions by an intrepid Norse mariner named *Ōhthere*. The name *Ōhthere* is an Old English adaptation from Old Norse *Óttarr*, and thus is simply a variant of the attested Old English name *Ottor*. Ōhthere tells Ælfred that he dwells *ealra Norðmonna norþmest* "northmost of all Northmen" in a district called *Hālgoland* corresponding to the modern Norwegian Helgeland on the northwest coast of the Scandinavian peninsula. Ōhthere also gives a brief description of the *Cwēnas*, who harried the Norwegians from their homeland directly eastward across the Scandinavian peninsula from Hālgoland. The *Cwēnas* were a Lappish people, known in their own tongue as the *Kainulaiset*, whose name as rendered into Old English was equivalent to the word for "woman", and indeed Gwyn Jones notes that *Cwēnaland* "acquired notes of a *terra feminarum*", and was thus a sort of northern Amazonia (Jones, 1986, p. 253). It would of course be difficult to assert that Tolkien's Ottor is the same person as Ōhthere: Ottor's home is said to be the island Heligoland, which is not the same as the Norwegian district of Hālgoland; that his wife is named *Cwén* may indeed have no more significance than that it is an Anglo-Saxon word meaning "woman"; and since Ottor is the father of Hengest and Horsa, who invaded England c.A.D. 450, he lived some four centuries before Ōhthere, who would have flourished c.A.D. 875. But by noting that Ottor's draught of *limpë* is said to have made him young again (Tolkien, 1984b, p. 290), and may have granted him an extraordinary lifespan, as it did for Ing of Luthany (Tolkien, 1984b, p. 306), we can at least remove time's objection to equating Ottor with Ōhthere. In any event, the correspondence of Ōhthere – Hālgoland – Cwēnas with Ottor – Heligoland – Cwén is remarkable, and must have some significance in Tolkien's creation of the character and history of Ottor.

As Christopher Tolkien notes, the name *Ælfwine*, replacing the earlier Ottor Wǽfre, enters with "a new conception" of the mythology, "*subsequent to* the writing of the *Lost Tales*" (Tolkien, 1984b, p. 301). In this new conception, Tolkien abandons the identification of Tol Eressëa with England, which instead exists in its own right as a land named *Luthany* by the Elves who for a time dwelt there under the rule of Ing, a mysterious figure about whom we will have much more to say momentarily. Because England has a separate existence from Tol Eressëa, Ælfwine is now made a man of eleventh-century Wessex who is driven from England over the sea to Tol Eressëa in flight from the Norman invaders.

Little more need be said here of the subsequent course of the figure of Ælfwine Eriol in the volumes of *The History of Middle-earth* published to date, since, although he plays a role in all of the subsequent material of the Elder Days (except for the brief gap of *The Lays of Beleriand*), his role is simply that of the chronicler or, in the case of *The Lost Road* and *The Notion Club Papers*, the *receiver* of the legends of the Elves. Thus he appears in *The Shaping of Middle-earth* only as the author or translator of the *Qenta Noldorinwa* (Tolkien, 1986, pp. 76-218), Tolkien's 1930 version of his mythology, and of the various attendant *Annals* of Valinor (pp. 262-93) and Beleriand (pp. 294-341), portions of which are also given in Ælfwine's "original" Anglo-Saxon versions (pp. 205-8, 337-41). The Elven-sage Rúmil of Tûn recites the earliest version of the *Ainulindalë* to Ælfwine (Tolkien, 1987, pp. 155-66), and Ælfwine attests to various statements of the *Lhammas*, the "Account of Tongues" which he learned in Tol Eressëa (pp. 167-98); and he is the faithful translator of the first version of the *Quenta Silmarillion* (pp. 199-338). In both *The Lost Road* (Tolkien, 1987, pp. 36-104) and *The Notion Club Papers* (Tolkien, 1992, pp. 269-82) he is the son of Éadwine, just one of several father-son pairs throughout time – such as the present-day Edwin and Alwin, or Oswin and Alboin, and the Númenóreans Amandil and Elendil – whose names mean "Bliss-friend" and "Elf-friend", and who witness, either in person or through a vision, the Downfall of Númenor.

But simply because Ælfwine's role in Tolkien's subsequent mythology becomes less prominent than in *The Book of Lost Tales* is not to say that Ælfwine's significance to an examination of Tolkien's development of a mythology for England was ended. The mere fact that it is a man of Anglo-Saxon England who throughout receives the "true tradition" of the Elves demonstrates that Tolkien did not completely abandon his ambition of creating a mythology for England. Moreover, while English geographical and mythological elements are manifest in the story of Ælfwine, the role of Ælfwine as translator into Old English of the Elvish legends shows that the crucial third element of Tolkien's criteria for a true English mythology, the linguistic element, is also present, since it demonstrates that Old English and the Elvish tongues coexisted in Tolkien's mythology.

But in incorporating Old English into his mythology, one would expect Tolkien to explain how it and other languages of the Primary World fit in with his invented languages; and in fact he does just that. In §10 of the *Lhammas*, the "Account of Tongues" that was learned and, presumably, translated by Ælfwine in Tol Eressëa, we are told that:

> The languages of Men . . . were for the most part derived remotely from the language of the Valar. For the Dark-elves . . . befriended wandering Men in sundry times and places in the most ancient days, and taught them such things as they knew . . . Now the language of [the folk of Bëor and Haleth and Hádor] was greatly influenced by the Green-elves, and it was of old named *Taliska* . . . Yet other Men there were, it seems, that remained east of Eredlindon, who held to their speech, and from this, closely akin to Taliska, are come after many ages of change languages that live still

in the North of the earth.
(Tolkien, 1987, pp. 179).

The significance of this passage cannot be overstated. Here Ælfwine, an Anglo-Saxon mariner, reports that "languages that live still in the North of the earth", which can hardly be other than the Indo-European languages, and which must surely include Ælfwine's own language, are ultimately descended from the languages of the Dark-elves. Thus Ælfwine himself makes it clear that Old English and the Elvish tongues not only coexisted but, far more importantly, that they are cognate languages; that is, they are sprung from a common source[16].

Ingwë

We conclude with a discussion of Ingwë, or rather, of the *two* Ingwës, for there are two seemingly distinct figures of Tolkien's mythology that bear this name. We will first discuss Ingwë King of Luthany, who appears in *The History of Eriol or Ælfwine* in *The Book of Lost Tales, Part II*, and who is often called by the Gnomish form of his name, Ing, as we shall call him here in order to distinguish the pair.

From *The History of Ælfwine* (Tolkien, 1984b, pp. 300-310) we learn that Ing, apparently a mortal man, was the ruler of Luthany (that is, England) when the Elves retreated there from the Great Lands on their way back to Tol Eressëa. At this time, Ing was given a draught of *limpë*, the Elvish nectar, which endowed him with great longevity, if not immortality. After many ages of rule in Luthany, Ing set sail to rejoin the Elves in Tol Eressëa, but his ship was driven far east by Ossë and wrecked on the shores of the East Danes, where he became a "half-divine king" of the peoples collectively named the *Ingwaiwar*. After a sojourn among the Ingwaiwar, Ing departs once again for Tol Eressëa. Meanwhile, Luthany was made into an island by the remaining Elves for their defence, but they are nonetheless subjected to seven successive invasions, including that of the *Rúmhoth*, which is the Gnomish name for the Romans. The final invasion is by the *Ingwaiwar*, who because they have been instructed by Ing, are kindly disposed to the remaining Elves. After many years, Ælfwine, a descendant of Ing, is born and when grown sails to Tol Eressëa.

We have already mentioned Tacitus' threefold division of the Germanic tribes into *Ingaevones*, (properly the *Inguaeones*), *Herminones*, and *Istaevones* (*Germania* 2). Tacitus describes the Inguaeones as dwelling "nearest the Ocean", indicating the Baltic maritime peoples that were the parent nations of the Anglo-Saxons, including the Angles, the Saxons, the Jutes, and the Frisians. There can be no doubt that Tolkien's *Ingwaiwar* are to be identified with the Inguaeones, a fact made manifest by the apparently Quenya names for the peoples that the Ingwaiwar comprised: the *Angali, Saksani, Euti*, and *Firisandi*.

It will certainly come as no surprise, then, that the Inguaeones are named for a semi-divine figure of Germanic legend known to the Anglo-Saxons as Ing. As Christopher Tolkien notes (Tolkien, 1984b, p. 305), there is a very brief story of Ing in the Anglo-Saxon *Rune Poem*:

[Ing] wæs ærest   mid Eastdenum
gesewen secgun,   oþ he siððan eft
ofer wæg gewat,   wæn æfter ran;
ðus heardingas   ðone hæle nemdun.

Ing was first among the East-danes
seen by men, until he afterwards again
departed over the waves, the wagon ran after;
thus the brave-ones named that hero.[17]

It can be seen that Tolkien's account of the sojourn of his Ing among the East Danes agrees in all particulars with that of the Ing of the *Rune Poem*, which is, notably, unique to the Anglo-Saxons. It should also be noted that a name for the Danes in Anglo-Saxon poetry, notably in *Beowulf*, is *Ingwine*, literally the "friends of Ing".

The identity of Tolkien's Ing or Ingwë of Luthany with the Ing of the Anglo-Saxon *Rune Poem* is obvious, and in fact would not even require discussion here beyond Christopher Tolkien's own treatment, were it not for the fact that there is another figure of Tolkien's mythology named Ingwë, who also shares a remarkable association with a figure of Germanic mythology.

In his commentary in *Sauron Defeated* on the various versions of *The Drowning of Anadûnê*, Christopher Tolkien includes a remarkable set of notes by his father titled *The theory of the work*. In these notes are among the most explicit statements made by Tolkien demonstrating the intended geographical, historical, and mythological unity of Middle-earth with "our" earth. He states, for instance, that "Men 'awoke' first in the midst of the Great Middle Earth (Europe and Asia), and Asia was first thinly inhabited, before the Dark Ages of great cold" (Tolkien, 1992, p. 398). In fact, in the first sketch of this passage he was even more specific, writing that "Men awoke in Mesopotamia" (Tolkien, 1992, p. 410 n. 2).

In this same passage, Tolkien continues with an explanation of the relationship of Men and Elves, who are here called the *Eledāi*:

Even before that time Men had spread westward (and eastward) as far as the shores of the Sea. The Eledāi withdrew into waste places or retreated westward.

The Men who journeyed westward were in general those who remained in closest touch with the true Eledāi, and for the most part they were drawn west by the rumour of a land in or beyond the Western Sea which was beautiful, and was the home of the Eledāi where all things were fair and ordered to beauty . . .

Thus it is that the more beautiful legends (containing truths) arose, of oreads, dryads, and nymphs; and of the *Ljós-alfar*.

(Tolkien, 1992, p. 398)

As Christopher Tolkien notes, *Ljós-alfar* is an Old Norse

---

[16] The ramifications of this for the study of Tolkien's invented languages are enormous, and form the basis of the column *Words and Devices* by Carl Hostetter and Patrick Wynne that appears regularly in *Vinyar Tengwar*, a journal of the Elvish Linguistic Fellowship, to which interested persons are directed.

[17] My translation — CFH.

word meaning "Light-elves". (Tolkien, 1992, p. 410 n.3) The *Ljós-alfar* "Light-elves" are named in the Prose Edda of Snorri Sturluson, where they are described as "fairer than the sun to look upon", and they are said to dwell in a land named *Álfheim* "Elf-home" (Young, 1954, p. 46). The lord of Álfheim is Freyr of the Vanir, an elder race of gods, who was given Álfheim as a "tooth-fee", a custom in which an infant was given a gift upon cutting his first tooth (Hollander, 1962, p. 55).

It is clear from this passage that the *Ljós-alfar* of Norse myth are to be seen as a legend of Western Men inspired by their close contact with the Eledāi, the Elves of Tolkien's mythology. And when it is remarked that the name *Freyr* is literally "Lord", and thus simply a title of the deity who is also named *Yngvi-Freyr* or simply *Yngvi*, it becomes equally clear that Yngvi-Freyr of the Vanir, Lord of the *Ljós-alfar* "Light-elves", who dwells in *Álfheim* "Elf-home", is to be seen as a memory of *Ingwë* of the *Vanyar*, Lord of the *Calaquendi* "Light-elves", who dwells in *Eldamar* "Elvenhome". Thus just as Tolkien incorporated Irmin and Embla into his mythology as the first Men, so too did he incorporate a figure of Germanic mythology as the first and foremost of the Elves.

* * *

We have shown that several significant figures of Tolkien's mythology — Eärendil, the saviour of Elves and Men and bearer of the only surviving Silmaril; Ermon and Elmir, the first Men; Ælfwine, the Anglo-Saxon chronicler of Elvish mythology; and Ingwë, both the Lord of the Light-elves and the King of Luthany — are all derived from English and Germanic mythology, so that Tolkien could in some measure satisfy his desire for a mythology for England, a mythology that is English in both tongue and soil. By incorporating elements of English and Germanic mythology into his own mythology, Tolkien enriched both, providing a fictive unified background for the former, a continuity and heightened relevance for the latter, and a deepened significance for both. The effect of this on Tolkien's works is expressed best by Tolkien himself, though he was speaking of *Beowulf*:

> its maker was telling of things already old and weighted with regret, and he expended his art in making keen that touch upon the heart which sorrows have that are both poignant and remote. If the funeral of Beowulf moved once like the echo of an ancient dirge, far-off and hopeless, it is to us as a memory brought over the hills, an echo of an echo. There is not much poetry in the world like this . . .

(Tolkien, 1984c, p. 33).

Indeed, there is not.

In describing to Milton Waldman his ambition to create a vast, unified mythology for England, Tolkien concluded that he had wanted to

> draw some of the great tales in fullness, and leave many only placed in the scheme, and sketched. The cycles should be linked to a majestic whole, and yet leave scope for other minds and hands, wielding paint and music and drama. Absurd.

(Tolkien, 1981, p. 145)

Absurd? To us who have come together from around the world to celebrate in England the Centenary of its greatest mythologer, Tolkien's ambition is far from absurd. Indeed, it is realized in us, for we are those other minds and hands, wielding paint and music and drama, and words, within a majestic whole.

References

Ananikian, Mardiros H. 1964. "Armenian" in *The Mythology of All Races*. Edited by John Arnott MacCulloch. Volume VII. New York: Cooper Square.

Auden, W. H. and Taylor, Paul B. (ed. and transl.). 1981. *Norse Poems*. London: Faber and Faber.

Bosworth, Joseph. 1882. *An Anglo-Saxon Dictionary*. Edited and enlarged by T. Northcote Toller. Oxford: Clarendon Press.

Bray, Olive (ed. and transl.). 1908. *The Elder or Poetic Edda, commonly known as Sæmund's Edda*. Part I: The Mythological Poems. (Viking Club Translation Series, 2.) London: Viking Club.

Bugge, Sophus. 1899. *The Home of the Eddic Poems*. Revised edition. Translated by William Henry Schofield. London: David Nutt.

Cassidy, F. G. and Ringler, Richard N (eds.). 1971. *Bright's Old English Grammar and Reader*. Third edition second corrected printing. New York: Holt, Rinehart and Winston, Inc.

Clark-Hall, J.R. 1984. *A Concise Anglo-Saxon Dictionary*. With a supplement by Herbert D. Meritt. Fourth edition. Toronto: Univ. of Toronto Press.

Cleasby, Richard and Vigfusson, Gudbrand. 1957. *An Icelandic-English Dictionary*. Second edition with a supplement by Sir William A. Craigie. Oxford: Clarendon Press.

Cook, Albert S. 1900. *The Christ of Cynewulf*. New York: Books for Libraries Press.

d'Arbois de Jubainville, H. 1903. *The Irish Mythological Cycle and Celtic Mythology*. Translated by Richard Irvine Best. Dublin: O'Donoghue and Co./M. H. Gill and Son.

Davidson, H. R. Ellis. 1964. *Gods and Myths of Northern Europe*. Harmondsworth: Penguin Books.

de Vries, Jan. 1952. "La valeur religieuse du mot germanique *Irmin*" in *Cahiers du Sud* 36. pp. 18-27.

de Vries, Jan. 1962. *Altnordisches etymologisches Wörterbuch*. Second edition. Leiden: E. J. Brill.

Dumézil, Georges. 1949. *Le Troisième Souverain.* (Les dieux et les hommes, 3.) Paris: G. P. Maisonneuve.

Dumézil, Georges. 1973. *Gods of the Ancient Northmen.* Edited by Einar Haugen. Berkeley/Los Angeles/London: University of California Press.

Elston, Charles Sidney. 1934. *The earliest relations between Celts and Germans.* London: Methuen & Co.

Foster, Robert. 1978. *The Complete Guide to Middle-Earth.* New York: Ballantine Books.

Fox, William Sherwood. 1916. "Greek and Roman" in *The Mythology of All Races.* Edited by Louis Herbert Gray. Volume I. Boston: Marshall Jones.

Grimm, Jacob. 1875. *Deutsche Mythologie.* Fourth edition. Berlin: Ferd. Dümmler.

Hollander, Lee M. (ed. and transl.). 1962. *The Poetic Edda.* Second edition. Austin: University of Texas Press.

Holthausen, Ferdinand. 1934. *Gotisches etymologisches Wörterbuch.* Heidelberg: Carl Winter.

Holthausen, Ferdinand. 1948. *Vergleichendes und etymologisches Wörterbuch des Altwestnordischen.* Göttingen: Vandenhoeck & Ruprecht.

Holthausen, Ferdinand. 1963. *Altenglisches etymologisches Wörterbuch.* Second edition. Heidelberg: Carl Winter.

Hostetter, Carl F. 1991. "Over Middle-earth Sent Unto Men: on the Philological Origins of Tolkien's *Eärendel* Myth" *Mythlore* 65 pp. 5-10.

Jóhannesson, Alexander. 1956. *Isländisches etymologisches Wörterbuch.* Bern: Francke Verlag.

Jones, Gwyn. 1986. *The Norse Atlantic Saga.* Second edition. Oxford: Oxford Univ. Press.

Klaeber, Fr. (ed.). 1950. *Beowulf and the Fight at Finnsburg.* Third edition with first and second supplements. Lexington, MA: D.C. Heath and Co.

Loewenthal, John. 1915-16. "Zur germanischen Wortkunde" in *Arkiv för Nordisk Filologi* (ny följd) 28 (1915-16). pp. 270-301.

Loewenthal, John. 1922. "Germanische Culturaltertümer" in *Beiträge zur Geschichte der deutschen Sprache und Literatur* 47 (1922). pp. 261-89.

Loewenthal, John. 1924. "Culturgeschichtliche Fragen" in *Beiträge zur Geschichte der deutschen Sprache und Literatur* 49 (1924). pp. 63-88.

Meringer, Rudolf. 1904. "Wörter und Sachen. II" in *Indogermanische Forschungen* 17 (1904). pp. 100-66.

Meringer, Rudolf. 1907. "Wörter und Sachen. V" in *Indogermanische Forschungen* 21 (1907). pp. 277-314.

Much, Rudolf. 1900. *Deutsche Stammeskunde.* Leipzig: G. J. Göschen.

Much, Rudolf (ed.). 1967. *Die Germania des Tacitus.* Third edition, with Herbert Jankuhn, edited by Wolfgang Lange. Heidelberg: Carl Winter.

Nordal, Sigurður (ed.). 1980. *Vǫluspá.* Translated by B. S. Benedikz and John McKinnell. Corrected reprint. (Durham and St. Andrews Medieval Texts, 1.) Durham: The University.

Pertz, Georgius Heinricus (ed.). 1976ff. *Monumenta Germaniae Historica: Scriptores.* Stuttgart: Anton Hiersemann.

Sperber, Hans. 1910. "Embla" in *Beiträge zur Geschichte der deutschen Sprache und Literatur* 36 (1910). pp. 219-22.

Tolkien, J.R.R. 1977. *The Silmarillion.* Edited by Christopher Tolkien. Boston: Houghton Mifflin.

Tolkien, J.R.R. 1980. *Unfinished Tales.* Edited by Christopher Tolkien. Boston: Houghton Mifflin.

Tolkien, J.R.R. 1981. *The Letters of J.R.R. Tolkien.* Edited by Humphrey Carpenter. Boston: Houghton Mifflin.

Tolkien, J.R.R. 1984a. *The Book of Lost Tales, Part I.* Edited by Christopher Tolkien. Boston: Houghton Mifflin.

Tolkien, J.R.R. 1984b. *The Book of Lost Tales, Part II.* Edited by Christopher Tolkien. Boston: Houghton Mifflin.

Tolkien, J.R.R. 1984c. *The Monsters and the Critics and Other Essays.* Edited by Christopher Tolkien. Boston: Houghton Mifflin.

Tolkien, J.R.R. 1985. *The Lays of Beleriand.* Edited by Christopher Tolkien. Boston: Houghton Mifflin.

Tolkien, J.R.R. 1986. *The Shaping of Middle-earth.* Edited by Christopher Tolkien. Boston: Houghton Mifflin.

Tolkien, J.R.R. 1987. *The Lost Road and Other Writings.* Edited by Christopher Tolkien. Boston: Houghton Mifflin.

Tolkien, J.R.R. 1992. *Sauron Defeated.* Edited by Christopher Tolkien. London: HarperCollins.

Turville-Petre, G. 1962. "Thurstable" in *English and Medieval Studies Presented to J. R. R. Tolkien on the Occasion of his Seventieth Birthday.* Edited by Norman Davis and C. L. Wrenn. London: George Allen & Unwin.

Vinyar Tengwar. Edited by Carl F. Hostetter. Crofton, Maryland.

Walde, Alois. 1927-32. *Vergleichendes Wörterbuch der indogermanischen Sprachen.* Edited by Julius Pokorny. Berlin and Leipzig: Walter de Gruyter.

Young, Jean I. 1954. *The Prose Edda of Snorri Sturluson.* Berkeley: University of California Press.

A Tolkien Chronology

Nancy Martsch

Abstract: Premise: A writer's professional and personal life affect his creative writing. A knowledge of what Tolkien was doing, and when, may give insight into his Mythology, or creative writing on Middle-earth. Outlines Tolkien's life, giving dates of important events, professional and personal life, status of writing. Divides creative output into three Periods, Early, Middle, and Late, plus an *Ur*-Period (youth) before the Mythology was formed. Describes thematic and linguistic characteristics of each Period.

Conclusion: Although the substance of Tolkien's Mythology was not much influenced by outside events, except during the *Ur*-period, outside events greatly affected its composition, focus, and to a lesser degree its emotional content.

Keywords: Tolkien biography, influences on Tolkien, development of Mythology

Part I: Tolkien's Life

The personal and professional aspects of a writer's life influence his creative writing. One does not create in a vacuum. Therefore a knowledge of what J.R.R. Tolkien was doing, and when, during the composition of the Mythology, may give us some understanding of that work.

Perhaps "influence" with regard to the writing of J.R.R. Tolkien is too strong a word – he was not much *influenced* by anything except in the early years of his life. His Middle-earth creation, his Mythology, was his own. (I use the term "Mythology" in lieu of "Middle-earth" because it extends beyond the bounds of Middle-earth proper.) But Tolkien was certainly *affected* by outside events. On the most mundane level, his professional work dictated how much free time he had to write. Disparagement from colleagues or family pressures, discouraged him from writing. Praise, encouragement from friends or family, inspired him to creativity. A request from his publisher might call forth a round of revisions or direct his interest to a certain area. Finals exams put a stop to writing altogether. The freedom of vacation released a burst of activity, often in the form of poems and art.

One may also detect possible cross-fertilization among projects, as for instance a cluster of vaguely "Arthurian" works in the early 1930s ("The Fall of Arthur", *Farmer Giles of Ham*, his student Simonne d'Ardenne's *The Life and Passion of St. Juliene*). Another example may be a Quenya variant using a pronoun prefix instead of the pronoun suffix, written at about the same time that Adûnaic, with its pronoun prefixes, was being developed. (This exemplifies a characteristic of Tolkien's writing: the re-use of ideas. Pronoun prefixes had been employed before, but their use in Adûnaic might have caused them to be recalled at this time.)

A knowledge of what Tolkien was writing, and when, can be used to date unascribed pieces. This is particularly helpful with languages, where contemporary works may yield clues to the meaning of unknown words. For example, some of the poems in "A Secret Vice" contain ideas found in the early works, and probably belong with them.

Finally, a study of Tolkien chronology tells us more about the man.

Tolkien's mythology can be divided into three periods, which I shall call "Early", "Middle", and "Late". There is also an "*Ur*-period", before the actual Mythology was written, in which many important ideas were formed. These periods can be tied to events in Tolkien's life, and are recognisable in the Mythology by subject matter, style, and Elvish linguistics. The periods overlap somewhat, as Tolkien often began one project before ending another. The *Ur*-period encompasses Tolkien's youth, the most formative period of his life, from his birth in 1892 until about 1912. The Early Period dates from roughly 1912 to 1920, and is characterised by *The Book of Lost Tales* and the Qenya and Gnomish Lexicons. The Middle Period, 1920 to about 1949, or the "completed" *Lord of the Rings* before it was accepted for publication, is characterised by *The Hobbit*, the early *Lord of the Rings*, "The Lost Road" and "Etymologies". The Late Period, 1948 to Tolkien's death in 1973, is characterised by *The Lord of the Rings* as published and the posthumous *The Silmarillion*. Dates for the Late Period are tentative, as working papers from this period have not yet been published.

The Periods themselves can be subdivided: the *Ur*-period, into the houses where Tolkien lived, the schools he attended, his vacation trips, his courses of study. The Early Period divides into University, War, and work for the Oxford English Dictionary. The Middle Period, the most fertile part of Tolkien's life (both professionally and with regard to the

Mythology), is composed of Leeds (1920-25), the Silmarillion[1] material, *The Hobbit* (and other children's writing), "The Lost Road" and the "Etymologies", and *The Lord of the Rings*. The Late Period contains the completed *Lord of the Rings*, and bursts of Silmarillion activity in the 1950s, Númenórean work in the 1960s, and Silmarillion studies in the late 1960s and early 1970s.

In the *Ur*-period most of the ideas behind the Mythology were formed. The Early Period saw the development of a Finnish-based and a Welsh-based language, Qenya and Gnomish, and all of the major themes of the First Age. In the Middle Period the First Age material was refined, and stories relating to the Third Age (*The Hobbit*) and the Second Age (Númenor) developed; all were tied together in *The Lord of the Rings*. The Late Period saw further development of the Third Age and refinement of the First: how Tolkien would have told the tale is unknown, because he was unable to finish it. *The Silmarillion* was assembled by his son Christopher Tolkien from a compilation of his father's writings.

The *Ur*-period

J.R.R. Tolkien was born in Bloemfontein, South Africa, on January 3, 1892. His mother took John Tolkien and his younger brother Hilary to England in 1895 to visit her parents; while they were away their father died. Mabel then took a house in Sarehole, in the country outside of Birmingham, where the boys lived from 1896 to 1900. Sarehole and its mill formed the basis for the Shire. Mabel tutored her sons in language, natural history, art. Tolkien also ascribed his "Atlantis dream", which gave rise to Númenor, to his childhood. In 1900 the boys were sent to King Edward's School in Birmingham, and the family had to move to the city. Here Tolkien studied Latin. Mabel Tolkien converted to Roman Catholicism in 1900 and was ostracized by her family, thus providing Tolkien with an early lesson in prejudice and financial hardship. In 1901 the family moved to a house near the railroad, where Tolkien was fascinated by the Welsh names on trains. In 1902 Mabel discovered the Birmingham Oratory church, and its rector, Father Francis Morgan (who became a lifelong friend). The boys were sent to the cheaper St. Philips Grammar school for a while, then withdrawn when it proved to be not sufficiently challenging, and Tolkien returned to King Edward's. Here he was introduced to Old English, the love of his life. In 1903 Mabel became ill with diabetes; the following summer (1904) she moved to a cottage at the Birmingham Oratory Retreat in Rednal (on the outskirts of Birmingham), where she died November 14, 1904. Tolkien was 13. Father Morgan became the boys' guardian; the boys lived with their aunt Beatrice Suffield. Now Tolkien was studying Old Norse and Gothic at school, and inventing languages on his own. In 1908 the boys moved to Mrs. Faulkner's boarding-house. Here Tolkien met Edith Bratt, another orphan, and fell in love. Father Francis discovered the affair in 1909 and moved Tolkien to another house. Forbidden to see Edith, Tolkien began to write poetry.

Some of this contained themes later used in the Mythology: woodland fairies, for instance. Tolkien also read the *Kalevala* and identified with the luckless Kullervo – the inspiration for the story of Túrin. He became close friends with three other boys, a fellowship which was to last until the death of two of its members in World War I, and profoundly influenced the Mythology. Tolkien won a scholarship to Oxford in 1910 and left King Edward's in 1911. That summer he took a trip to Switzerland, which would result in the Misty Mountains and Gandalf. On his first Christmas vacation at Oxford (1911) Tolkien visited his friends at King Edward's School and was inspired to write a poem, thus establishing a pattern of vacation composition which was to continue throughout his life. In 1912 he took up the study of Welsh and comparative philology, discovered Finnish, and began to create a Finnish-based language – Qenya.

On his twenty-first birthday, the day of his majority – no longer bound by Father Morgan's wishes – Tolkien wrote to Edith, and they were re-united. She would give up a fiancé and convert to Catholicism to marry him, a sacrifice Tolkien remembered in the tales of Lúthien and Arwen. In September of 1914, on holiday, Tolkien wrote "Éala Éarendel engla beorhtast", said to be the origin of the Mythology. (The Christmas holiday produced "Goblin Feet".) The language of the Mythology had begun two years before, but was not at first identified with the Elves. So the *Ur*-period can be said to last until 1912 or 1914.

The Early Period

On August 4, 1914 England entered World War I. Tolkien enlisted, but was permitted to finish his studies. He graduated from Oxford in June 1915, then began military training. In 1915, while he was still in college, the material that was to become *The Book of Lost Tales* began to take shape, with the poem "You and Me and The Cottage of Lost Play" and the "Qenya Lexicon". Late autumn produced a spate of elegiac poetry, "Kortirion among the Trees" and the like; not surprisingly, for his old happy life at school had ended and he soon would be sent overseas to fight, perhaps to die. This melancholy poetry ended abruptly or March 22, 1916, when Tolkien and Edith were married.

Tolkien was sent to France June 4, 1916. On July 1 his boyhood friend R.Q. Gilson was killed on the Somme; Tolkien saw action there on July 14. He came down with trench fever in October and was sent home; he would be in and out of hospitals for the remainder of the War. Another friend, G.B. Smith, was killed December 3. The death of his friends impelled Tolkien to record his Mythology, lest all that they had shared be lost. Most of *The Book of Lost Tales* and the "Gnomish Lexicon" was written in periods of convalescence between 1916-1917. A child was conceived: John Francis Reuel Tolkien was born on November 16, 1917. World War I ended on November 11, 1918.

At the war's end Tolkien got a job at Oxford, on the *Oxford English Dictionary*. His work was largely on etymology, with some definitions for the nouns; his

---

[1] In this essay, *The Silmarillion*, italicised, refers to the book of that title; the Silmarillion, not italicised, to writing on the subject.

employer was less certain of his verbs (years later, in his invented languages, Tolkien usually spent the most time on etymology, developed the noun, and fizzled out on the verb). From the time of his employment until 1920, when he moved to Leeds, there was little work on *The Book of Lost Tales*, and he never returned to it. At about the same time Tolkien began a poem in alliterative verse, "The Lay of Húrin". Another child was conceived; Michael Hilary Reuel Tolkien was born on October 22, 1920. In the summer of 1920 Tolkien accepted the job of Reader in English Language at Leeds University. Edith rejoined him in early 1921.

The Early period can be said to come to an end with *The Book of Lost Tales*, and the Middle to begin with "The Lay of Húrin", though they overlap a bit, 1918-1920.

Middle Period

The Middle Period begins when Tolkien moved to Leeds in 1920, or perhaps when he joined the *Oxford English Dictionary* in 1918. At the Leeds Christmas party someone impersonated Father Christmas: that same year (1920) Tolkien wrote a Father Christmas Letter to his children, a practice which continued until 1941, when his youngest child reached 12. This was a fruitful period professionally: Tolkien began work on "Pearl", and "A Middle English Vocabulary"; in 1922 E.V. Gordon joined Leeds, and they collaborated on *Sir Gawain and the Green Knight*. Sinclair Lewis' *Babbit* was also published in 1922. Tolkien published on English every year from 1922 through 1928. In 1924 Tolkien was promoted to Professor of English Language, bought a house, and conceived another child: Christopher Reuel Tolkien, born November 21, 1924. (All these autumn births hint at fertility rites during Easter break.) Tolkien also told stories to his children, some of which ("Roverandom", 1925ff.) were written down. But in the summer of 1925 he got a job as Professor of Anglo-Saxon at Oxford, and the Leeds phase ended.

Tolkien returned to Oxford in the fall of 1925. Again Edith did not arrive until after the birth of her child, in early 1926. "The Lay of Leithian", in rhymed couplets, was begun at Oxford, and "The Lay of Húrin" ceased. In the spring of 1926 Tolkien met C.S. Lewis. He sent "Leithian" to Lewis to read, and wrote the "Sketch of The Mythology" to explain it. On vacation in the summer of 1927, and again in 1928, Tolkien drew pictures for the Silmarillion. The wonderful (in Tolkien's opinion) children's book *The Marvellous Land of the Snergs* was published in 1927.

But there were also marital problems between 1928 and 1929. A daughter, Priscilla Tolkien, was born in 1929. Tolkien was spending a lot of time with Lewis. Lewis had high praise for "Leithian", and encouraged it. Tolkien began other works: the "Annals of Beleriand" (1929), the "Qenta Noldorinwa", the "Annals of Valinor", and the "Aotrou and Itroun" (1930). Professional work fell off; between 1928 and 1940 Tolkien published on the average of once every three years. Perhaps, had he remained at Leeds with Gordon, Tolkien would have written more philology; as it was, he became friends with Lewis and wrote the Mythology instead.

Tolkien continued to tell stories to his children. *The Hobbit* may have begun in oral form around 1929; by 1931 it was certainly being written. In 1930 the Tolkien family moved to a larger house on 20 Northmoor Road, where they lived until 1947. In 1930 also Charles Williams' *War in Heaven* was published, a work which greatly influenced Lewis (Tolkien disliked it). Tolkien was active in academic life, proposed a revision of the English School Syllabus, which he got passed in 1931. "A Secret Vice" – no doubt hinting at what he had been doing – was read in 1931. On September 19, 1931, after a long conversation with Tolkien, C.S. Lewis converted to Christianity, an event which Tolkien recorded in his poem "Mythopoeia".

In 1932 Tolkien bought a car, which produced *Mr. Bliss*. The Inklings club was formed in 1933, and met mornings at the Eagle and Child pub. Lewis wrote his first book on religion, *Pilgrim's Regress*, in 1932 (published 1933). This irritated Tolkien, who may have felt that Lewis, a recent convert, was too hasty to rush into print. In the mid-1930s Tolkien also wrote "Errantry", "The Fall of Arthur", and *Farmer Giles of Ham*. Beginning around 1933-4 more Silmarillion material was written, the "Lhammas", "Quenta Silmarillion", "Ambarkanta". *The Hobbit* was nearing completion; it was essentially "complete" by 1935.

Tolkien's sons were now in their teens, and away at school. *The Hobbit* manuscript was read, submitted to publisher Allen & Unwin, and finally finished on October 3, 1936. (*Mr. Bliss* was also offered, but the colour pictures proved too difficult to print.) "Beowulf: The Monsters and the Critics" was presented on November 25. Lewis proposed a space/time trilogy: Tolkien promptly began work on "The Lost Road", which lead to "The Fall of Númenor" and "Etymologies"; Lewis wrote *Out of the Silent Planet* (published 1938). *The Hobbit* was published September 21, 1937. Then Allen & Unwin requested more, so Tolkien revised and submitted *Farmer Giles*, "Leithian", "Quenta Silmarillion", "The Lost Road", and others. They were rejected: Allen & Unwin wanted more Hobbit material. So between December 16 and December 19, 1937, Tolkien began *The Lord of the Rings*. And all work on Númenor and the Silmarillion ceased.

Professional publication pretty much ceased, too: Tolkien produced a preface for *Beowulf and the Finnesburg Fragment* in 1940, then nothing until 1947. (This does not mean Tolkien was idle: he was teaching and busy with academic work. There was the grind of examinations, and frequent illness. And he revised *Sir Gawain*, taught and collaborated with his students on their research projects, some of which contained his ideas. But he published nothing under his own name.)

Tolkien worked steadily on *The Lord of the Rings* until the spring of 1938, stopping when 15-year-old Christopher became ill. (At this time John was studying theology in Rome, Michael attending Trinity College in Oxford.) The Inklings now met twice weekly, in the pub and Thursday evenings at Lewis' rooms in Magdalen College. That July E.V. Gordon died. "On Fairy Stories" was also written that summer – Tolkien was trying to define his fantasy work; it was presented the following March (1939). Work on *The*

Lord of the Rings was not resumed until summer holiday (1938), after Christopher had recovered; it continued until September. That fall Tolkien revised it; by the following year (1939) he stopped altogether. In summer he was considering starting over. Edith was ill that summer and fall (1939), feared at first to be cancer, but fortunately not.

World War II began on September 1, 1939. It caused an upheaval in the lives of all concerned. John Tolkien rushed back to England, Michael tried to join the army, was told to wait one year, Priscilla stayed home. Charles Williams moved to Oxford and joined the Inklings. Tolkien gave up his car, and became an air-raid warden; Lewis joined the Home Guard, Lewis' brother and fellow-Inkling Warnie was on active service. (It should be remembered that, after the initial flurry, the first months of World War II in England were quiet.) Edith was recovering. Tolkien was able to continue *The Lord of the Rings* and, at his publisher's insistence, produced the preface to *Beowulf*.

He stopped again sometime in late 1939 or 1940, "stuck at Balin's tomb". But this was not the only reason. In spring fighting began in earnest; Germany invaded France (Dunkirk, May 24-June 4), England's back was to the wall, Churchill offered "blood, toil, tears, and sweat", the bombs rained down on London. Michael was an anti-aircraft gunner in the Battle of Britain (July 1940-May 1941). There were marital problems again, this time about religion. Tolkien was spending a great deal of time with the Inklings, who now met three times a week, and was jealous of Lewis' friendship with Williams. Tolkien did not resume work on *The Lord of the Rings* until 1941, by which time the situation had calmed somewhat. He also worked on "Sir Orfeo" and "Pearl". Michael Tolkien was married.

Meanwhile Lewis was publishing one or two books a year, Williams was publishing, there was a religious revival in Oxford and Lewis gave radio talks on Christianity. And Tolkien was still plodding along on *The Lord of the Rings*. He read E.R. Eddison's fantasy novels in 1942, and Eddison later visited the Inklings. Tolkien's first grandson, Michael George Tolkien, was born in 1942. In 1943 fellow Inkling Dr. Havard was called up (though Tolkien later got him transferred to Oxford – he seems to have had a talent for intrigue). Tolkien was stuck again in the summer of 1943, and Christopher joined the Royal Air Force. He expressed his feelings in "Leaf by Niggle" (triggered when a neighbour butchered her tree). Lewis persuaded Tolkien to start again in the spring of 1944: Tolkien wrote in a great rush of inspiration, sending his work to Christopher in South Africa to read, finally stopping in October. Then the work lay idle for nearly two years, while he contemplated finishing "The Lost Road" (Lewis' *Perelandra* was published in 1943) or collaborating with Lewis on a book on language.

World War II ended May 9, 1945; on May 15 Charles Williams died. Eddison also died that year. Lewis' *That Hideous Strength* (published 1945) showed Williams' influence: Tolkien disliked it. A second grandson, John Tolkien was born. Tolkien was appointed Merton Professor of English Language and Literature, a step up and new duties. He wrote "Imram", and had begun *Beorhtnoth*.

Christopher returned to Oxford in the fall of 1945, and joined the Inklings. The Inklings by now had become an institution, and were attracting members of the second generation. Thursday evenings were sometimes enlivened by ham dinners, the main course being sent by an American admirer. During Christmas vacation of 1945 Tolkien began "The Notion Club Papers", which spawned "The Drowning of Anadûnê" and the Adûnaic language. John Tolkien became a priest.

The friendship with Lewis began to cool. In the summer of 1946, at the insistence of his publisher, Tolkien reluctantly resumed work on *The Lord of the Rings*, abandoning the Númenórean material; it was read to the Inklings by Christopher. Money being tight, Tolkien sold his house on 20 Northmoor Road (now too large since the children had left), and moved to a smaller one on Manor Road (spring 1947). Inkling Hugo Dyson did not like *The Lord of the Rings* and in October 1947 Christopher ceased to read from it. (Lewis' *Narnia* stories – which Tolkien did not care for – were never read to the Inklings, either.) In 1947 Tolkien rewrote the "Riddles in the Dark" chapter of *The Hobbit*.

The Lord of the Rings was "finished" in 1948. Freed from this burden, Tolkien was able to resume professional writing, publishing in 1947 and 1948. He became embroiled in a debate with his publisher over illustrations for *Farmer Giles*. Also in 1948 Lewis was soundly trounced (by a woman!) in an Oxford debate on Christianity, a bitter blow; he did not try to "prove" Christianity by logic again for some time. And he was hurt by Tolkien's criticism of his professional book *English Literature in the Sixteenth Century*. In 1949 Tolkien typed *The Lord of the Rings*. Christopher graduated from Oxford; the last Inklings evening was held October 20, 1949 (though some friends continued to meet at the pub). *Farmer Giles* was finally published. Tolkien returned to the Silmarillion. The Middle Period came to an end, *circa* 1949.

Late Period

The house on Manor Road was too small, so Tolkien moved to another house, on Holywell Street, in March 1950 (probably over Easter break – many of his moves seem to have taken place at this time of year). Now filled with enthusiasm for the Silmarillion (he had begun a second version of "The Lay of Leithian" and perhaps the "Narn i Chîn Húrin"), he felt that the Silmarillion should be published with *The Lord of the Rings*. In February 1950 Milton Waldman of Collins expressed interest in it, so Tolkien contrived a quarrel with Allen & Unwin (demanding that they publish both or nothing; they said nothing) and offered the manuscript to Collins. Time passed. In 1951 a third grandchild (Judith Tolkien) was born. Lewis' long time companion Mrs. Moore died. Tolkien was involved in academic work, travelling to Ireland and to Belgium; his failure to support Lewis on a proposed change in the English curriculum or in the latter's bid for Professor of Poetry chilled their relationship still further. Tolkien gave "A Secret Vice" again, worked on the "Annals of Aman" and the "Grey Annals". The second edition of *The Hobbit* was published.

In the spring of 1952 Tolkien issued an ultimatum to

Collins: all or nothing, at which point Collins turned down both works. Feeling despondent, he visited his friend George Sayer. In an attempt to cheer him up, Sayer suggested that Tolkien read *The Lord of the Rings* into his (Sayer's) tape recorder. The therapy worked; the recordings would later be marketed by Caedmon Records, and Tolkien bought a tape recorder for himself when he returned home. (He later recorded *Beorhtnoth*, perhaps in 1954). On June 22, 1952, he offered *The Lord of the Rings* to Allen & Unwin; they snapped it up, sending Rayner Unwin to pick up the manuscript in person on September 9. The contract was signed on November 10, 1952. Work on the Silmarillion had to stop, for now *The Lord of the Rings* must be completed and proofs checked. Tolkien continued to revise at this late date, even after it was set in type. Many familiar works date from this time. Tolkien found his house too noisy, and Edith, lame with arthritis, was bothered by the stairs, so they moved again to Sandfield Road, in Headington, in March 1953. Volume I was finished in April, Volume II soon after, Christopher did the maps, Tolkien started on Volume III and bogged down on the Appendices. He was able to publish some professional work: *Beorhtnoth* and a philological essay; gave a lecture on *Sir Gawain* in August, and was working on *Ancrene Wisse*. *Sir Gawain* was broadcast on the BBC in 1953 and *Beorhtnoth* the following year (1954). On July 5, 1954, Tolkien received an Honorary Doctorate from the Catholic University of Dublin, and in October an Honorary doctorate from the University of Liège. On July 29 *The Fellowship of the Ring* was published. *The Two Towers* followed on November 11. Lewis became a Professor at Cambridge and left Oxford; the farewell dinner was held December 9. He continued to visit his friends at the pub on Mondays, but Tolkien no longer came. Lewis was also romantically involved with an American admirer, Joy Davidman.

Tolkien finally finished the Appendices on May 20, 1955 (they had produced such ancillary works as "The Istari" and "The Hunt for the Ring"). He went to Italy on holiday. He may also have resumed work on the Silmarillion. The lecture "English and Welsh" was presented October 21, the day after *The Return of the King* was published. *Ancrene Wisse* was completed, a preface (to *The Ancrene Riwle*) published. Lewis secretly married Joy (without telling Tolkien) on January 3, 1956; this caused the final breach between them. In 1956 Tolkien received his first payment for *The Lord of the Rings*, the handsome sum of £3,500. Marquette University (Milwaukee, Wisconsin) offered to purchase the manuscripts to *The Lord of the Rings* for £1,250 ($5,000) in 1957; they were delivered the following year. There was talk of a *The Lord of the Rings* film, too, but nothing came of it. Tolkien visited Holland in the spring of 1958. Christopher was married, and lecturing at Oxford. Lewis' wife Joy became ill with cancer.

Tolkien retired from teaching in June, 1959, at age 67. He brought his books back from the college and converted his garage into an office-library. He also hired a part-time secretary, for he had begun to receive fan mail for *The Lord of the Rings*. Christopher's son Simon was born. Tolkien worked on the Silmarillion, the proofs of *Ancrene Wisse* (which for various reasons, including a printer's strike, was not published until 1962), then *Sir Gawain*. Edith Tolkien became ill; she and Joy were in the hospital together in May 1960. This brought a reconciliation between Tolkien and Lewis. Joy died on July 13, 1960.

In 1961 Tolkien's aunt Jane Neave asked him for "a small book", which resulted in *The Adventures of Tom Bombadil*, published in November 1962. *Ancrene Wisse* was finally published. Edith was in poor health. Tolkien worked on the Númenórean material, produced newspaper doodles. The final version of "The Last Ark" may date from this time. In 1962 he revised some of his early poems, "The Cottage of Lost Play", "Kortirion". He also wrote "The Bovadium Fragments", a satire on Oxford. Jane Neave died in 1963, age 91; that summer Lewis suffered a heart attack and retired. Tolkien was given an Honorary Fellowship to Exeter College, and an Emeritus Fellowship of Merton. He revised *Sir Gawain*, "Pearl", "On Fairy-Stories". The mid-1960s saw another burst of creative activity, "A Description of Númenor", "Aldarion and Erendis", "The Quest for Erebor".

On November 22, 1963, C.S. Lewis died. Allen & Unwin expressed interest in the Silmarillion. *Tree and Leaf* was published in 1964. In 1965 Tolkien was asked to write a preface for George MacDonald's *The Golden Key*; it became *Smith of Wootton Major* (1967). Tolkien's oldest grandchild, Michael George Tolkien, was studying at St. Andrews University.

In 1965 Ace brought out an unauthorised edition of *The Lord of the Rings*, taking advantage of a loophole in copyright law. Allen & Unwin asked Tolkien for revisions to *The Lord of the Rings* so that it could again be copyrighted. He responded by revising *The Hobbit* in the spring, and making an analysis of "Namárië" for *The Road Goes Ever On* in June, finally finishing *The Lord of the Rings* in August. Work on the Númenórean material and *Sir Gawain* probably ceased. The Ballantine *Hobbit* (unrevised) came out in August 1965, *The Lord of the Rings* in October, and the Tolkien craze was on.

Tolkien societies were formed: Tolkien, pestered by fans, needed a secretary for fan mail. His last professional work, for *The Jerusalem Bible* (Jonah), was published in 1966 (he was unable to finish *Sir Gawain* and "Pearl"; they were published posthumously). Tolkien and Edith celebrated their Golden Wedding Anniversary March 22, 1966. They went on holidays to Bournemouth. Tolkien continued to produce essays on *The Lord of the Rings*: "The Palantíri"; "The Disaster of the Gladden Fields", "Cirion and Eorl", "Fords of Isen", "The Drúedain", and linguistic works. That summer Prof. Clyde S. Kilby, of Wheaton College, Illinois, came to assist him on The Silmarillion. Christopher and his wife had separated.

Edith suffered greatly from arthritis. The two-story house on Sandfield Road became too much for her to manage; it was also noisy and far from the centre of town. And Tolkien was increasingly bothered by fans. So in June 1968 the Tolkiens moved to Bournemouth, where they had spent their vacations. Unfortunately Tolkien fell and injured his leg, so was unable to supervise the move: as a result his papers were badly packed, which troubled him greatly. Nevertheless he continued to work on the Silmarillion. Edith, though in declining health, was happy. Tolkien was ill himself (July 1969). Christopher had remarried, and was teaching English at New College, Oxford. One grandchild and two great-grandchildren were born in 1969, another grandchild in 1971. Edith died November 29, 1971, after a short illness.

Tolkien returned to Oxford in 1972, to live in a house belonging to Merton College. He was awarded an honorary Doctor of Letters in Philology from Oxford, a CBE which was confirmed by the Queen March 28, 1972, and an Honorary Degree from the University of Edinburgh in June 1973. He did not do much writing. Tolkien died on a visit to Bournemouth on September 2, 1973.

It can be seen that although the substance of Tolkien's Mythology was not much influenced by outside events, except during the *Ur*-period, outside events greatly affected its composition, focus and to a lesser degree emotional content.

Part II: Themes and Linguistics

As has been already been noted above, the foundation of the Mythology was laid early in Tolkien's life. The Mythology proper grew from two created languages, one based on Finnish and the other on Welsh. The Finnish-based language (among other things) borrows from Finnish phonetics and noun case system; the Welsh-based language uses Welsh phonetics, noun plurals, and initial mutation (lenition). Stories developed about the speakers of these languages, the Elves. In the Early Period all of the major themes of the First Ages were invented, though sometimes differing in form (such as the tale of Lúthien). This was to be a "mythology for England", as the Elves were the ancestors of the English fairies. The tales were heard by an English traveller who sailed to the Lonely Isle, and bits of the stories were recorded in Old English. In some versions the Lonely Isle *was* England, and Elvish sites were identified with actual locales in England. The tales began with the Cottage of Lost Play, where the children of Men had travelled to fairyland in dreams; perhaps an explanation of how Tolkien felt he had acquired the stories. The Valar or Gods are described in lively fashion; they intrigue among themselves and make magic; Melko is more like Loki than Lucifer. Troops of sprites and fairies patter about the land. Less is told about the Elves and Men. Eärendel is the Eternal Wanderer. The love stories are permeated by a sense of loss; boy loses girl, perhaps a reflection of the uncertain state of Tolkien's own life at the time. There is a certain pettiness, a lack of nobility – as when Tinwelint (Thingol) cheats the Dwarves out of their wages. (And later Faramir would not tell a falsehood to an Orc!) The Three Kindreds of Elves are called Teleri, Noldoli, Solosimpi. The Elves of the Blessed Realms named their city Kôr, so they are called Korins and the Elves of Middle-earth (not those of Kôr), Ilkorins.

The Finnish-based language is Qenya, spoken in the Blessed Lands; the Welsh-based language is Gnomish or Goldogrin, evolved from the speech of the Noldoli (Gnomes) during their long thralldom under Melko in Beleriand. Other dialects are only hinted at. Men awakened mute, and were taught to speak by the Dark Elves. The tongues of Men and Dwarves are not developed.

Middle Period

In the Middle Period the tales of the First Age quickly approached their final (published *Silmarillion*) form, though many details still differed. The Cottage of Lost Play, the English locales, the pattering troops of fairies were eliminated. The mariner who travels to the Lonely Isle gradually fades out, though the tales are still ascribed to various authors, and some are in Old English.

What began as a children's story, *The Hobbit*, grew to become a part of the Mythology, a history of the Third Age. The time travel story "The Lost Road" brought forth Númenor and the Second Age. These were linked together by *The Lord of the Rings*, which set forth the Three Ages of Arda. Galadriel enters the Mythology. The Three Kindreds of Elves are called Lindar, Noldor (Gnomes), and Teleri. The city of the Noldor is Tûn (or Túna), upon the hill of Kôr; the Elves are first Koreldar and Ilkorindi (Ilkorins), later Kalaqendi (Elves of Light [of the Two Trees]) and Moriqendi (Elves of Darkness).

The Elvish languages underwent an explosion, a veritable Darwin's-finches speciation of evolution, that resulted in many dialects for both Undying Lands and Middle-earth ("Lhammas", "Etymologies"). The Finnish-based language became Qenya, the Common Speech of the Undying Lands: it had a colloquial and a written version. The Welsh-based language divided into three groups, with sub-groups: the language of the Noldor (Noldorin), of the Elves of Beleriand (Doriathrin); of the Elves east of the Blue Mountains (Danian). Men are either taught or influenced by Elves; the Men who journey westward speak a Danian-influenced language called Taliskan, which seems intended as a link between Elvish and Indo-European. The later development of Adûnaic may have invalidated this concept; at least, Taliskan is no longer named. The inclusion of *The Hobbit*, with its Northern European names, into the Mythology necessitated some explanation: in *The Lord of the Rings* they are said to be "translations" of Westron, the Common Speech, a derivative of Adûnaic (and Elvish). These "translations" also provide a history for the tongues of Men. Khuzdul and Orkish are developed, and Sauron invents the Black Speech.

Late Period

The Silmarillion, the history of the First Age, was published after Tolkien's death, assembled by his son Christopher from a mass of uncompleted manuscripts. As much of the Late writing on this subject has yet to be published, we can only deduce what it contains from that in *The Silmarillion* which differs from earlier versions. Christopher, under pressure to complete his father's work, and for an audience that expected another *Lord of the Rings*, decided to omit the mariner and various authors (whose importance had been diminishing anyway) and to present the tales themselves. We do not know if Tolkien would have done so. We are told (*Unfinished Tales*) that Tolkien's view of the role of Galadriel had expanded, that she was to become the female counterpart of Fëanor, but as the tales themselves were inchoate, Christopher was forced to fall back on earlier, more complete, versions. During the Late Period Tolkien also elaborated upon the Third Age and Númenor.

The sense of nobility, of wisdom, which infuses *The Lord of the Rings* (and to a lesser extent *The Silmarillion*) dates for the most part from the latter part of Tolkien's life. It is this moral depth which makes *The Lord of the Rings* a great work of literature and sets it apart from the earlier stories. First evident in *The Hobbit*, it grows as the series progresses. The Valar are now remote, lofty gods, and Melkor is akin to Lucifer. The three Kindreds of Elves are Vanyar, Noldor (now called Wise or Deep Elves, not Gnomes), and Teleri; the Calaquendi and the Moriquendi.

The Lord of the Rings and *The Silmarillion* don't discuss language very much, and the Late linguistic essays have yet to be published. So we don't know many details. The language of the Undying Lands is Quenya, the situation in Beleriand is greatly simplified, with the Welsh-based language now called Sindarin, the language of the Grey Elves (Sindar) of Beleriand, and it is adopted, not evolved, by the Noldor. There are two Welsh-based groups, Sindarin and Silvan, the language of the Elves east of the Blue Mountains. How these were to be equated with the languages described in "Etymologies" is not explained, though no doubt Tolkien knew. Again there are hints of dialects, but few published details. Foreign loan-words are described, and for the first time words from other languages are said to be taken into Elvish.

Men are described as having been influenced by Elves, dialects among Houses of Men are mentioned, and a new race, the Drúedain or Woses, appears. The history of Westron is set forth in *The Lord of the Rings* and elsewhere.

References

Carpenter, Humphrey. 1977. *J.R.R. Tolkien*. London: George Allen & Unwin.

Carpenter, Humphrey. 1978. *The Inklings*. London: George Allen & Unwin.

Tolkien, J.R.R. 1977. *The Silmarillion*. Ed. Christopher Tolkien. London: George Allen & Unwin.

Tolkien, J.R.R. 1979. *Pictures by J.R.R. Tolkien*. Ed. Christopher Tolkien. London: George Allen & Unwin.

Tolkien, J.R.R. 1980. *Unfinished Tales*. Ed. Christopher Tolkien. London: George Allen & Unwin.

Tolkien, J.R.R. 1981. *Letters of J.R.R. Tolkien*. Ed. Humphrey Carpenter with Christopher Tolkien. London: George Allen & Unwin.

Tolkien, J.R.R. 1983. *The Book of Lost Tales, Part One*. Ed. Christopher Tolkien. London: George Allen & Unwin.

Tolkien, J.R.R. 1984. *The Book of Lost Tales, Part Two*. Ed. Christopher Tolkien. London: George Allen & Unwin.

Tolkien, J.R.R. 1985. *The Lays of Beleriand*. Ed. Christopher Tolkien. London: George Allen & Unwin.

Tolkien, J.R.R. 1986. *The Shaping of Middle-earth*. Ed. Christopher Tolkien. London: George Allen & Unwin.

Tolkien, J.R.R. 1987. *The Lost Road*. Ed. Christopher Tolkien. London: George Allen & Unwin.

Tolkien, J.R.R. 1988. *The Return of the Shadow*. Christopher Tolkien. London: Unwin Hyman.

Tolkien, J.R.R. 1989. *The Treason of Isengard*. Christopher Tolkien. London: Unwin Hyman.

Tolkien, J.R.R. 1990. *The War of the Ring*. Christopher Tolkien. London: Unwin Hyman.

Tolkien, J.R.R. 1992. *Sauron Defeated*. Ed. Christopher Tolkien. London: HarperCollins.

Evil and the Evil One in Tolkien's Theology

Tadeusz Andrzej Olszański

Translated from the Polish by Agnieszka Sylwanowicz

Abstract: This paper analyses Tolkien's theological theory of evil: first its cosmological aspect (especially the relation between Eru and Melkor), then the place of evil in the structure of the world, the question of salvation, and finally, the question of the End and the second "Doom of Mandos" announcing Morgoth's fall.

Keywords: evil, God, mythology, theology

What is the essence of evil and where does evil come from? Was evil first as one of the principles of the world, or was it the Evil One, the being consciously creating evil? Humankind has worried about these questions since its very beginnings. Inasmuch as the existence of God and His nature as a good entity is obvious – at least from a certain stage in civilizational and moral development, it is in relation to the existence of God that evil is a phenomenon difficult, if not impossible, to explain. Throughout the ages many ideas of theodicy were formed, however none of them is free from insoluble contradictions. This may be the proof that the answer to the question of evil does not lie within the possibilities of the human mind.

Tolkien knew about it when he wrote in "Mythopoeia": ". . . and of Evil this /alone is dreadly certain: Evil is." However, creating the world of Eä with its elaborate theological structure, he could not ignore the question of the origin of evil and its relation to God. I shall try to answer it today.

First of all let us sketch the necessary theological background. In European religious thought there are two clearly differing views on theodicy. The first one, Semitic, is consistently monistic and first agrees to the indifferent character of God capable both of good and evil (this is especially striking in the earlier books of the Old Testament) and then explains that evil is the result of resistance to God's will. It also introduces the person of the evil-doer, the Tempter, who, however, is a creature and thus implicitly subject to God. This line of reflection reached its limits in the Book of Job, the conclusion of which amounts to the lack of a comprehensible answer to the questions about evil.

The other tradition is Indo-European, dualistic, and it reached its final stages in Manichaeism. According to it there are two equal god-creators, the good and the evil one, and in some approaches they are the sons of the absolute seen as god, who limits himself to giving the world its first spark and leaves it for his demiurge sons, who are its proper creators.

Christianity emerged from the pool of Semitic ideas. Christ is the answer to Job's question, but Christ does not give the answer. In Him evil is defeated, but not explained; on the contrary – the suffering of the Son of God (i.e. God Himself, which the Semites understood perfectly well) is a continuing insult to the human mind looking for the explanation, although this explanation is not necessary for belief. However, Christianity was in principle rejected by the Semitic peoples and developed by the Indo-Europeans, from whom it took over many elements of dualistic theodicy. Satan all too often grows to the rank of the adversary almost equivalent to the Son of God, who in turn is easily understood as different from God Himself. But this attempt at a synthesis of two opposing ideas is not satisfactory and forces one looking for a rational answer to new efforts.

The discussion of Tolkien's theodicy must start with cosmogony. Before the Ainur were created there was not only God, but also the Void. It was not merely an "absence" of God as the only being, but a nothingness existing in time and space, since Melkor could roam it before the music began. The Void was not created – it is impossible to create a nonentity – but it was real. Neither was it evil in its nature since nonentity as such cannot be evil. However, the fact of the Void's reality in some independence from God created a specific "space" where objection to God, a seed of evil, could appear and develop.

It is obvious to me that such an idea of the Void is rooted in the Bible, when in the Book of Genesis 1:4 we read that separating light from darkness God did not recognise darkness, as light is the only reality mentioned there as good ("And God saw the light, that it was good: and God divided the light from the darkness"). I think that this passage, extremely difficult to interpret, is the original source of the whole of Tolkien's theodicy.

The first creatures are the Ainur, the personified thoughts or rather features of Eru. It is not accidental that God's image emerging from the analysis of the Ainur's features is not univocal – God, being the original unity, must contain at least in the initial forms everything that is possible. And everything also means evil. We cannot comprehend and even more so we cannot say how good can contain the seeds of evil. However, some approximation can be reached in common observation that, for example, creative passion not being evil in itself, all too often leads to evil, and so must contain its origins.

Among the Ainur Melkor is the first one. He is also endowed with the greatest gifts of them all. He is not evil in the beginning – if it were so, we would have to say that evil as such originates in God, and this is impossible. However, the omniscient God has the abstract knowledge of the possibility of evil as a possibility of an opposition to his own will. And it is this knowledge that Melkor must have taken over. From the beginning he was independent and conceited, which soon lead him to impatience, disobedience and pride. Thus Melkor turns out to be prone to evil from the very beginning, i.e. he is prone to evil of his very own nature.

However, what does this mean? If Melkor, with his features, comes from the mind – i.e. from the essence – of Eru, it follows that the tendency to evil also comes from God. This is an unsettling conclusion, but it is confirmed by Ilúvatar himself when he says that in the end Melkor will turn out to be only a tool of his. Moreover, a disposition towards evil is not evil so long as it is not expressed in evil deeds. Are not other of the Valar proud? Do they not experience the passion of creation, exceeding the limits set to them? Do they not, in different ways, desire power?

Melkor, however, has not repented and humbled himself like Aulë or Ossë. Cherishing the Void – i.e. what is outside God – he has broken loose from Eru's control, at first unconsciously. Varda noticed future evil in him already at that point. Then he introduced discord into the Music, disturbing not only its development, but also the development of the future world. Most probably this was done in good faith, in pure competition with the others, which seems to be confirmed by Ilúvatar's words after the Music was finished – but it could already be in competition with God himself, an attempt at independent creation.

The further evolution of Melkor is a constant sliding into evil: envy of his brother, Manwë; rejection of Eru's rebuke (which probably was a decisive moment); destruction of the other Valars' work (although this was predetermined in the Music); refusal to mend his ways; the tempting of the Noldor; the destruction of the Trees; and finally the murder of Finwë – the point of no return. The disobedient, but still not evil, Melkor turned into Morgoth, evil to the roots and subject to fear. Nothing, however, justifies the view that Melkor's sin, rebellion and obduracy were inevitable or predetermined. If it were so, the Valar would not wonder at all if he repented, after having been imprisoned for centuries.

Evil therefore is unmistakably the work of the Evil One, introduced by him into an integrally good world. But once it happens, evil turns out to be irreversible. Admittedly, the Satanic forces cannot in the end be victorious and in every confrontation are defeated. However, the wounds inflicted on the world by evil and fighting itself can be healed only to a small extent and the victorious good is weakened. And no amount of victories is able to eradicate evil in Arda. This is why the Last Battle, Dagor Dagorath, is necessary.

As Eru said after the finishing of the Music, all deeds, even Melkor's, will at the end turn to the One's glory. This does not mean that they are foreseen. And it follows from the very nature of God as an indivisibly good entity that everything that exists must be turned to good. When Melkor's discord, incompatible with Eru's plan, destroyed the first version of the Music, it was immediately incorporated into this plan and Ilúvatar derived the fruits of beauty and good even from this. Could the love of Beren and Lúthien, Finrod's dedication, and Frodo's sacrifice, exist without Melkor's rebellion?

The common, practical belief of all free peoples is the belief in the inevitability of fate, i.e. – let us note – in the fundamental sense of the world. But this fate does not represent doom, a curse that it is impossible and improper to resist. On the contrary – fate, although inevitable, remains unknown even to the Valar and is realised through the free actions of Men and – to a lesser extent – other creatures, more fully determined. That future events depend on such actions follows clearly from Gandalf's words at the Council of Elrond and Galadriel's words at the Mirror, as well as from the statement that if the first reply of Fëanor to Yavanna's request for the Silmarils had been different, the future course of events would also have differed in many respects.

Standing on Caras Galadhon, Galadriel described the Elves' effort with the words: "we have fought the long defeat." A similar phrase was used by Tolkien in one of his letters (No. 195) when he said that from the Christian point of view history is a "long defeat", although it may contain glimpses of the final victory. The final victory does not, however, belong to Men, unable to defeat demonic evil – it belongs to God Himself.

Evil in the world is powerful, too powerful for the forces of the free peoples to resist it without supernatural assistance. Even Frodo breaks under the strain of temptation at the last moment and his whole mission would have been futile if not for Gollum, a wretched, deceitful creature saved for this hour perhaps by Eru himself.

Ilúvatar's children were helpless and were crying out for salvation, or more precisely – for a Saviour. They did not, however, have any Messianic hope and had to replace it with efforts of self-salvation. Thus in every age of the world we can see great missions aimed at obtaining supernatural help or reaching a supernatural goal. Eärendil's mission was first, then came Amandil, who could not succeed, and finally Frodo. It is characteristic that none of them were Elves (Eärendil chose the fate of a First-born under Elwing's influence, but he himself leaned rather towards the Younger Children).

We know the world will have an end that will be concurrent with the annihilation of evil. The only text on this is the Second Prophecy of Mandos, being a part of the *legendarium* from the very beginning, but omitted from the "canonical" version of *The Silmarillion*. I shall not discuss it here in detail and will only say that when both the world and the Valar grow old, Morgoth will return and on the fields of Valinor there will be fought Dagor Dagorath, the Last Battle.

In this battle immortal Morgoth the Vala will be slain by Túrin Turambar, which can only be understood as a special decree of Ilúvatar, as only he has the unlimited power of remaking everything that he has created. After this there will be the Renewal of the World, which will become flat again and steeped in the light of the Two Trees. Perhaps there will be no place for Men in this world since the Prophesy does not mention them – maybe the Last Battle will put an end to human life on earth.

How is it possible, however, for an immortal, pure spirit to be slain? In one of his letters (No. 211) Tolkien explained why Eru did not annihilate Sauron together with Numénor, and wrote about the indestructibility of spirits endowed with free will. However, omnipotence cannot have limits other than the self-imposed ones, and all rules of Creation are valid only within the created world. Thus when the Time of the End and Renewal, which is different from the Time of the World, comes, those old rules will lose their validity. It will be possible then for a mortal man slain a long time ago to kill an immortal angel, in this way to revenge all his brothers and finally to clear himself of his terrible guilt.

The reconciliation of Dagor Dagorath with the Second Music mentioned in "Ainulindalë" is possible, although difficult. The participation of Men in the Second Music does not mean that they have to be physically present on Arda or anywhere else. Moreover, this Music is to come after the end of Days and so it will not be as much the Music of the End as the Music of Duration, whose reality is different from the reality of Creation, perhaps fully independent from the fact of Arda's existence. The Second Music is to be the completion of God's plan, enriched with all the good that arose during the course of the World's history. Therefore it cannot occur until this history comes to an end.

The fulfilment of God's plan would be incomplete if any of the deeds were lost. We may be fairly sure that Morgoth's servants will be forgiven. True, they were seduced and corrupted, but Orcs (after all, descendants of the First-born), Men and spirits healed of evil will find a place among the choirs of the Second Music.

But what about Morgoth, doer of all evil, once an Ainu closest to the One? Will he be healed and will his death – for no death is final to God – become his salvation and the gateway to forgiveness? Or, on the contrary, will he be thrown into the eternity of the "Second Death" and will he be the only entity in the world to really die? This we do not and shall never know.

The theory of final, universal salvation (*apokatastasis*) is centuries old, but it always remains in the not wholly orthodox margins of theological thought. Judging from Tolkien's letters, he was not one of its followers. However, I think that the idea of the Remaking of the World and especially of the Second Music incorporates this ideal explicitly enough to accept it, regardless of the Author's views expressed in the texts outside the *legendarium*. They (mainly the letters) may be treated as the Author's comments and opinions on the reality of Sub-creation, not necessarily compatible with this reality contained in the texts which make up the *legendarium*.

What then is Tolkien's answer to the question of evil? It is perhaps most fully contained in the fragment of "Mythopoeia" quoted at the beginning. And Arda's theodicy has features of both systems previously discussed, with a marked domination of Manichaean views. Eru is the One God, the only creator of all reality, but he is also "the distant God" (*Deus otiosus*) who after the act of creation stopped being interested in the world and turned it over to the demiurges in spite of the fact that the most powerful of them had already rebelled before the act of creation. The source of evil in the world is this Evil One, the fallen angel – but not a god – doing and instigating evil in the world, although from a certain time only indirectly. Evil results from resisting the Creator, from a desire for independence from Him, and especially from laying down one's own laws for ruling the world, and also from conceit. Evil is always the result of a choice or a giving in to temptation, which is also a choice.

However, Men remain in a special relationship with Eru. After death they do not go to the immanent netherworld in the halls of the Valar, but to God's halls beyond the Created World (Eä). And when the Númenóreans rebelled against the Valar, the Valar could not defeat the Men and God had to intervene directly. The consequences were dramatic: both cosmologically (the earth becomes spherical and the netherworld is separated from the world) and theological. For from this moment Eru is no longer a distant god. In the Third Age we witness not the actions of the Valar but of Providence gradually clearing the ground for the future Revelation mentioned in "Akallabêth", which is to reveal to Men – and only to them – the secret of their final destiny. And knowing that Middle-earth represents the mystic past of the world we live in and knowing the religious opinions of Tolkien we cannot doubt that he meant the Christian Revelation.

References

Tolkien, J.R.R. 1988. *Tree and Leaf*, second edition. London: Unwin Hyman.

Tolkien's Exceptional Visit to Holland: A Reconstruction[1]

René van Rossenberg

Abstract: In March 1958 Tolkien was the guest of honour at a "Hobbit Meal" in Rotterdam, Holland. He had never before accepted such an invitation and never did again. By interviewing the organisers and many people who met Tolkien, the visit has been reconstructed, and many, often funny anecdotes have come to light.

Keywords: Hobbit dinner, Holland, The Netherlands, Cees Ouboter, Jo van Rosmalen, Rotterdam, speech, Voorhoeve & Dietrich

In March 1958 Her Majesty Queen Elizabeth II of Great Britain paid a state visit to the Netherlands. After her coronation in 1953 she went to a number of states which were considered "friendly nations", and despite the four wars the Dutch and English had waged against each other, the Netherlands were included in the list of the good guys.

On Thursday 27 March the royal party was in Rotterdam. Rotterdam is the largest port in the world, and is situated in the south of Holland, the coastal areas of the Netherlands. The British and Dutch royal families made a tour through the city and paid a visit to a -- no doubt -- typically Dutch family. After all this the British royal family returned to the royal yacht *Britannia*. With an official banquet on board the *Britannia* that night, the state visit came to an end. Early the next morning, Friday the 28th, the *Britannia* set sail for England. Just outside Dutch territorial waters the royal yacht crossed the path of the *SS Duke of York*, the ferry between Harwich and the Hook of Holland. On board the *Duke of York* was J.R.R. Tolkien; Ronald and Elizabeth, ships that passed in the night . . .

At about half past nine on a dreary, cold morning in March Tolkien stepped on the quay of the Hook of Holland. From the Hook of Holland he took the train to Rotterdam Central Station, where he was met by Cees Ouboter, an employee of the Rotterdam bookseller Voorhoeve & Dietrich. Tolkien would have had no problems in recognising Ouboter, for the man was enthusiastically waving his copy of *The Fellowship of the Ring*. Ouboter handed Tolkien over to Mr. Jo van Rosmalen, head of the publicity department of the Dutch Tolkien publishers Het Spectrum, for Mr. Ouboter had to return to Voorhoeve & Dietrich to go to work.

With this I have mentioned the two principal players (Ouboter and van Rosmalen) and the two institutions responsible for the organisation of this exceptional visit by Tolkien to Holland: bookseller Voorhoeve & Dietrich and publisher Het Spectrum. Let us pay some attention to them.

Voorhoeve & Dietrich was not just a bookshop. It was the leading bookseller in Rotterdam and in turnover one of the biggest in the Netherlands. They were also an old-fashioned bookshop, with knowledgeable employees who could recommend books to their clients. Among those clients was the intellectual and administrative elite of the city, such as professors from the university, the burgomaster and company executives. Also Voorhoeve & Dietrich was the cultural centre of Rotterdam. For instance, they organized meetings with authors in which they clearly followed the example of the London bookseller Foyles. The authors gave speeches and signed books, usually in the shop itself or in the church next door. Sometimes the meeting took the form of a banquet, a "literary luncheon" as they called it. In all these activities Cees Ouboter was the driving force. He was an erudite, intelligent and well-read man who gave lectures on literature, wrote articles and had a talent for organising.

Het Spectrum was a Catholic publishing house which overcame the hardships of the Second World War in the fifties by publishing cheap pocketbooks, dictionaries and a range of low-price scientific books. Due to an enthusiastic reviewer, who was a good friend of the chief editor of Het Spectrum, *The Lord of the Rings* came to the attention of the publishing firm. After considerable persuasion, the proprietor of Het Spectrum agreed to publish a Dutch translation of this massive work.

In 1956, only one year after the publication of *The Lord of the Rings* in Britain, part one of *In de Ban van de Ring* (meaning "Under the Spell of the Ring"), entitled *De Reisgenoten* hit the bookshops. The Dutch translation was the first translation of *The Lord of the Rings* that was published; the next one -- the Swedish translation -- dates from 1960.

---

[1] This paper is dedicated to Priscilla Tolkien for it was her enthusiastic reminiscences of her father's visit to Holland, which she told me the first time we met, that gave me the idea to write this paper.

The translator, Max Schuchart, had to work in haste, but made a very good job of it. In fact he received an important award for his translation. It is a pity that some mistakes were made by the publisher; for instance they managed to misspell Tolkien's name on the dust-jacket (J.J.R. instead of J.R.R.).

The Sales Director of Het Spectrum, a gentleman called Costa Yocarini, and his staff went round the Dutch bookshops offering *In de Ban van de Ring* to the booksellers, and they encountered serious problems in selling Tolkien for a number of reasons.

Tolkien was a totally unknown author (*The Hobbit* had not yet been translated into Dutch), writing in a genre we now call fantasy, but which was an unknown entity in the fifties. When Yocarini tried to typecast the novel with sentences like "a fairy-tale for grown-ups", that did not cut much ice with the sober Dutch booksellers. The 40% first-offer discount appealed more to them. Another problem was that *In de Ban van de Ring* was an expensive book. Its sheer size of well over 500,000 words forced Het Spectrum to publish the novel in three thick volumes. To limit the financial risks, Het Spectrum had decided on a low print-run of 3000 sets (which is relatively large if you compare it with the 3500 British print-run of *The Fellowship of the Ring*) and a de luxe binding and format to make a higher price more acceptable. The result was that each volume had a retail price of 12.50 Dutch guilders, while an average hardback at that time would cost 6.95 Dutch guilders.

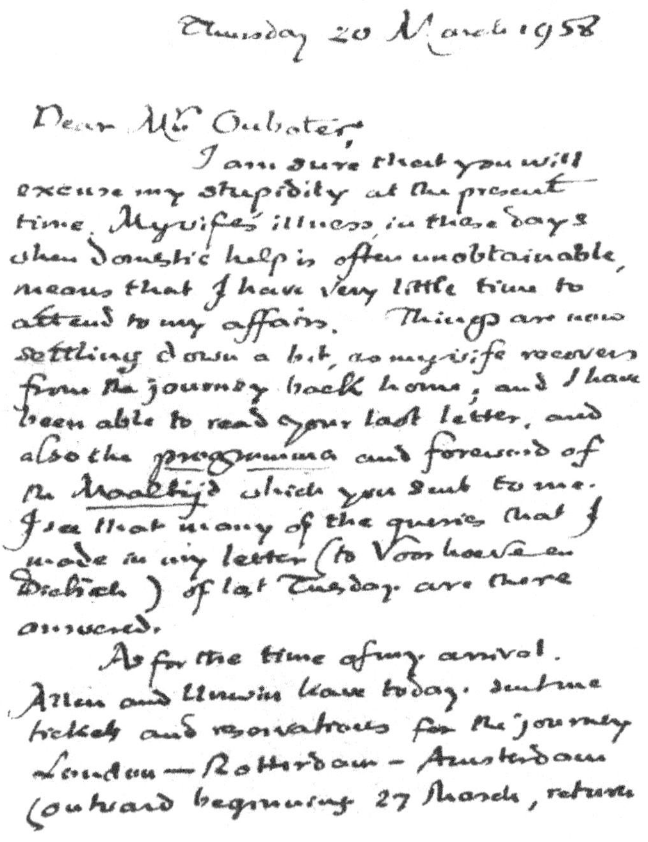
Thursday 20 March 1958

Dear Mr Ouboter,
I am sure that you will excuse my stupidity at the present time. My wife's illness in these days when domestic help is often unobtainable, means that I have very little time to attend to my affairs. Things are now settling down a bit, as my wife recovers from the journey back home, and I have been able to read your last letter, and also the programma and foreword of the Maaltijd which you sent to me. I see that many of the queries that I made in my letter (to Voorhoeve en Dietrich) of last Tuesday are there answered.
As for the time of my arrival. Allen and Unwin have today sent me tickets and reservations for the journey London – Rotterdam – Amsterdam (outward beginning 27 March, return

Figure 1. First page of a letter from J.R.R. Tolkien to Cees Ouboter, 20 March 1958. Private collection. Text © The Tolkien Trust, 1995.

Not surprisingly Mr. Yocarini and his colleagues received luke-warm receptions from the booksellers. Even large bookstores would not buy more than five or six, and after some persuasion perhaps ten sets. The big exception was Voorhoeve & Dietrich. When Yocarini came there he was welcomed with open arms. They had been quite successful in selling the original for well over a year, and the whole staff of Voorhoeve & Dietrich, and in particular Cees Ouboter, who simply loved the book, were very pleased that there was now a Dutch translation. The Rotterdam bookshop immediately ordered fifty sets.

But they were the exception and sales did not go that well, for the general public had not discovered Tolkien. Yet Cees Ouboter had an almost missionary zeal to promote Tolkien. For instance he gave to his regular customers a copy of *De Reisgenoten* to take home and read, with the warning that the first fifty pages were a bit dry, but that the story took off after that. If the customer did not like the book, he could give it back free of charge, and otherwise he would have to buy it. This was a clever trick, with hardly any risk for the bookshop. Even the returned well-read copies were no loss, for Voorhoeve & Dietrich supplied all the books for the libraries on board the ships of the Holland-America line. The HAL insisted that all books – even the brand-new ones – had to be re-bound, which gave Voorhoeve & Dietrich an excellent opportunity to sell second-hand books for the full cover-price.

Not surprisingly, Ouboter also got the idea to get Tolkien to Holland for one of Voorhoeve & Dietrich's famous literary luncheons. And to reflect the spirit of the novel the visit should have the form of a banquet, a "Hobbit dinner". In the second half of 1957 he contacted Het Spectrum about the idea. They loved it. Het Spectrum could use a good publicity stunt to boost sales. So, with the blessing of the publisher and the promise of financial support Cees Ouboter wrote Tolkien a letter via Rayner Unwin. In the middle of December, he received Tolkien's reply.

Tolkien explained that his poor health and that of his wife Edith had prevented him from writing sooner. He had been about to decline the invitation for he could not come to Holland in January, as Ouboter apparently had suggested. Yet before Tolkien could answer, Ouboter himself had postponed the date because they could not get the organisation ready for January. In his letter Tolkien could not give a definite yes or no, but he said: "I should like very much to come; I will do my best to do so."[2]

He continued by saying that a period between 24 March and 2 April would suit him best. Incidentally, in the second paragraph he mentioned that he was supposed to be visiting Sweden in March "though this is now highly improbable". Perhaps somebody from a Swedish Tolkien society can find out the background to this cancelled visit? After quite some correspondence between Tolkien and Ouboter[3] – in which Tolkien showed considerable anxiety about travelling alone – a date was set and confirmed: Friday, 28 March.

I left the story at Rotterdam Central Station, so let us speedily return to Tolkien and the nervous Jo van Rosmalen. Van Rosmalen was nervous, for he was faced with the for him daunting task of entertaining an Oxford don for the whole day, a man whom he had never met before. But, as Mr. van Rosmalen told me when I interviewed him, Tolkien was an amiable man who had a talent for making you feel at ease.

The first thing Jo van Rosmalen did was to take Tolkien to a restaurant, for he assumed that his guest would like a cup of coffee as it was about 11 o'clock. But Tolkien surprised him by ordering "Dutch cold beer". After Tolkien drank about four glasses they continued. Van Rosmalen clearly remembered that the alcohol did not affect Tolkien much. His back was a bit straighter and he walked a bit faster, to the dismay of the chubby van Rosmalen who had difficulties keeping up with Tolkien. Like this, they walked for hours through Rotterdam, for Tolkien wanted to see everything. Most of what he saw he did not like, for the city clearly bore the scars of the Second World War.

On 10 May, 1940, German troops invaded the Netherlands. The Nazis wanted to push through the Netherlands and Belgium to cut off the British Expeditionary Force and attack the French army from two sides. Yet the Dutch army put up a fiercer resistance than expected, and after four days the Germans were bogged down. To force an end to the war in Holland the Luftwaffe extensively bombed Rotterdam and the Germans delivered an ultimatum to the Dutch Military Command: surrender or Utrecht will be next. Faced with such barbarism the Dutch army capitulated.

Before the bombardment Rotterdam looked very much like Amsterdam; a combination of beautiful old buildings, canals and elegant bridges which is so appreciated by the millions of tourists who visit the Netherlands each year. The bombardment completely flattened a large part of the city and cut out the heart of Rotterdam. At the end of the fifties the effects of the bombardment were still visible. There were a lot of open spaces, partially filled with fast and cheaply built and extremely ugly high-rise flats. The town centre looked like a large building site: a lot of office blocks under construction, wide streets and much traffic. None of this appealed to Tolkien. As he wrote to Rayner Unwin on 8 April:

I . . . saw a good deal of the depressing world of ruined and half-rebuilt Rotterdam. I think it is largely the breach between this comfortless world, with its gigantic and largely dehumanised reconstruction, and the natural and ancestral tastes of the Dutch, that has (as it seems) made them, in R[otterdam] especially, almost intoxicated with *hobbits*!

(Tolkien, 1981, p. 265, No 206)

Tolkien did like the many parks of Rotterdam. He showed great interest in, and knowledge of the vegetation. He knew the Latin and English names and kept on asking van Rosmalen the Dutch names of trees and flowers. If Mr. Rosmalen did not know, Tolkien would translate the Latin or English name into Dutch to see if this would ring a bell with van Rosmalen. Tolkien had, not surprisingly for a philologist, some knowledge of Dutch, a point which he proved again, as well as his sense of humour, during his visit to Voorhoeve & Dietrich.

At about one o'clock Tolkien and van Rosmalen came to the bookshop to have something to eat. Tolkien talked with the staff and with some customers and during his stay he noticed a small Dutch pocketbook by Herbert Pollack entitled *Word slank en blijf gezond*. Tolkien took it from the shelves, wrote his translation of the title, "get slim and stay in trim", on the title-page, signed it and gave it as a present to the fat and by this time no doubt tired and out of breath Jo van Rosmalen. Mind you, Tolkien did not pay for the book . . .

After about an hour and a half, Tolkien asked van Rosmalen to take him to his hotel, for Tolkien wanted to take his usual half-hour midday nap. He requested that van Rosmalen would collect him precisely half an hour later. Van Rosmalen did so and they walked again for two hours through the streets and parks of Rotterdam. At about 5 o'clock van Rosmalen brought Tolkien to the location where the "official" program of the visit, the "Hobbit dinner", would take place.

Let us take another break from the story to tell something about the organization of the visit.

A press release was issued by Voorhoeve & Dietrich, which was also handed out to the customers. Very cleverly the press-release was in English to get the message across that the whole affair would be conducted in that language, and that you would not enjoy it very much if you did not understand English. It stated that the visit was organised on the occasion of the state visit of Queen Elizabeth, but that was a little lie for publicity's sake, for, as mentioned before, Tolkien's visit was first planned for January. Of course Cees Ouboter, who wrote the release, gave some information on Tolkien and his work, for Tolkien was unknown to the general public. To give an impression of what Ouboter wrote here are some quotes:

The hobbits are a race of small, near-human creatures who have not found their place in history.

Their story is known only to Mr. J.R.R. Tolkien, Professor at Oxford University, who has access to

---
[2] Letter of J.R.R. Tolkien to C. Ouboter, 19 December 1957.
[3] Six letters from Tolkien to Ouboter have been traced, but Ouboter's son remembers clearly that there were eight.

special sources which have enabled him to record their ups and downs in his beautiful books, especially in his trilogy: *The Lord of the Rings* . . .

Antiquarians dare not rank him among the experts of prehistory. But there are more and more enthusiastic people – some even call them zealots – who place him in the foremost ranks of those who have a thorough knowledge of the human soul.

All critics agree that Mr. Tolkien is an excellent story-teller but many a reader wonders what the meaning is of the fascinating story. They are looking for a hidden significance but they are at a loss as to what it might be. People who have a special weakness for the uncanny, as well as those who like adventure or humour, will be satisfied.

Especially to inform the press further Ouboter gave a lecture on *The Lord of the Rings* a week before the visit, as was announced in the last paragraph of the press release. This speech has also been published and is one of the first serious studies on Tolkien which appeared in the Dutch language (Ouboter, 1958). The benefit of Ouboter's trouble is clearly visible in the many newspaper articles on Tolkien which appeared in the local and national press before and after the visit.[4] What all these articles have in common is a sense of wonder for this "peculiar trilogy" and praise for Tolkien as a story-teller and for his remarkable imagination. But many journalists could hardly disguise the fact that they just did not know what to make of it all. Yet it brought Tolkien and his forthcoming visit to Rotterdam widely under the attention of the public in Holland in general and in Rotterdam in particular.

Publicity was also gained by the glossy invitations (as four-page leaflets) Het Spectrum had printed and which Voorhoeve & Dietrich distributed amongst their regular customers. It contained the program of the evening, the menu, the text of the press-release (but this time in Dutch) and proudly stated on the cover that on the occasion of the visit by H.M. Queen Elizabeth II of Great-Britain a Hobbit dinner ("Hobbit-maaltijd" in Dutch) would take place on Friday, 28 March 1958, from 17.30 hours onwards at the Flevo-restaurant in Rotterdam. In fact the Flevo-restaurant was not a restaurant at all; the Flevo-hall was part of the "Twaalf Provinciën Huis", a multi-functional building. The hall was also used for concerts, exhibitions and even as a cinema. Nobody I spoke to liked the hall, for it was barren, without style or attractiveness, and had no windows. Because it was not a restaurant, they had to use outside caterers. Printed in the invitation leaflet was also the list of the "Ere-Comité", the Committee of Honour. To give more standing to the visit and to get more publicity Voorhoeve & Dietrich and Het Spectrum established a committee of honour. Moreover, protocol demands that there be such a committee. With all its connections in Rotterdam high society, it was no wonder that Voorhoeve & Dietrich could find a number of people of substance to take a place in this committee: the burgomaster of Rotterdam, the alderman responsible for

Figure 2. The invitation to the "Hobbit dinner". Photograph by and © the Royal Library, The Hague.

culture, two representatives of the British embassy and five professors, including Tolkien's friend and colleague from the University of Amsterdam, Professor Piet Harting, constituted the "Ere-Comité".

Normal mortals who wished to attend the "Hobbit-maaltijd" had to make this known by filling out a card and paying Dfl. 7.50. Voorhoeve & Dietrich used this money to pay for the meal and the hall. To complete the financial picture: George Allen & Unwin paid Tolkien's travelling expenses, while Het Spectrum took care of the hotel bill and the additional costs. Tolkien did not get a fee for his troubles. After Voorhoeve & Dietrich had received your card and payment they mailed you your entrance ticket (a dinner-card) and, if you wanted to, Ouboter's introductory speech which was printed as a booklet. There was room for 200 guests, but well over that amount of reservations were made. Although a local, Rotterdam happening, the very first Dutch Tolkien-fans came from all over the country to Rotterdam to meet Tolkien.

---

[4] I have tracked down fifteen of such articles, but there are probably a few more.

Now let us return to Tolkien at the "Twaalf Provinciën Huis". At 6 o'clock the guests were asked to take their seats. Once everybody was seated Tolkien and the other special guests entered and took their places at the high table. Cees Baars, managing director of Voorhoeve & Dietrich, opened the proceedings by saying:

> Prof. Tolkien, Members of the Committee of Honour, Ladies and Gentlemen,
>
> Speaking on behalf of the organizers I take great pleasure in extending to you a warm welcome at this Hobbit dinner. This festivity – for a dinner is a festivity for every hobbit – is meant as a homage to Professor Tolkien and his creation. I hope – and now I am quoting old Mr. Bilbo – that you will all enjoy yourselves as much as I shall. May I introduce to you all Mr. Sötemann, who will be in the chair this evening.

Guus Sötemann (who later became Professor of Dutch Language and Literature at the University of Utrecht) was the reviewer who had brought *The Lord of the Rings* to the attention of Het Spectrum. He had helped in the organization of the visit and as chairman of the evening it was his job to introduce the speakers and to make sure that no speech lasted longer than five minutes. The program for the evening consisted only of speeches: in total nine were given.[5]

The first one was from the well-known Dutch author Hella Haasse. No doubt Tolkien was not very pleased with the fact that she immediately started to talk about the hidden meaning of *The Lord of the Rings*, *The Lord of the Rings* as an allegory, a theme which recurred several times that evening. Hella Haasse addressed the point as follows:

> It seems to me that all great literature is more or less openly allegorically, especially so in times, when one mode of thinking gives way to another, when the world is changing before human eyes, and human experience has not yet found the words to express the full scope of what is happening. Like all great literature your book is mythical and allegorical and at the same time it has all the sounds and colours and scents, all the glow and movement and density of real life on earth.
>
> Like all great literature it can be read many ways, it has many different layers of meaning, ranging from a delightful fairy-tale to a drama of cosmic order. Mr. Tolkien, it seems to me that one of the reasons, perhaps the most important reason, why your book makes such a deep and lasting impression on so many people, is this: that you have been able to make a composition, a structure, out of the broken fragments of reality, and that, within this composition, you have put the figure of the "hero" our time is so badly in need of and never yet has been able to conceive: a hero who in no way resembles the great epic figures of the past, a hero who is literally of small stature, who is at the same time rather comical and endearing, pathetic and yet somebody to be proud of, and even in his moments of doubt and hopelessness full of a definitely awe-inspiring kind of dignity . . .
>
> For having given us [a] symbol of ourselves, so charged with meaning that it will keep us company through the long hours of our own struggle, and for having given us this symbol in the disguise of a completely absorbing, poetic tale that keeps the reader spellbound from the first to the last word – for this, Mr. Tolkien, I want to thank you with all my heart.

After her spoke the editor of Het Spectrum, Daniël de Lange and then, according to the published program, publisher P.H. Bogaard. But he chickened out and left it to poor Jo van Rosmalen to give a speech on his behalf. Van Rosmalen spoke tongue-in-cheek about Tolkien's supposedly Dutch forefathers. "In the year 1480 there lived in Utrecht a man named Rutger Tulleken, also called Tolken. Of course he was of noble descent . . . Professor Tolkien, after five centuries, I give you a hearty welcome home. We are proud of your Dutch origins!" Tolkien's old friend Professor Piet Harting spoke, as well as three customers of Voorhoeve & Dietrich and of course Cees Ouboter. Ouboter's speech was different in the sense that he spoke about the negative criticism he had heard from some of his customers to whom he had given a "free" copy of *In de Ban van de Ring*. "In their opinion your story is too fantastic. They refuse to believe in fairy-tales. Elves were created for children only, to say nothing of orcs and trolls. One customer could not find the Hobbits in the *Encyclopedia Britannica*. This was such a strong argument against your creation that he returned the books." Others complained about the lack of women, the fact that love and marriage are scarcely mentioned or that the story was too violent. Ouboter classified those who liked *The Lord of the Rings* in two categories: those who liked it as an adventurous and even humorous story and those who wanted to emphasise the message in it. He concluded his speech as follows:

> Summarizing my speech, I must admit that I have spoken more about the negative than about the positive reactions to your work. I find the same thing in your book. The power of Evil is more impressive there than that of its opposers. But goodness prevails. And so will your work, the story of the fight of humility and humour in an ever-continuing strife against the seemingly overwhelming Power of Evil. We are grateful to you for writing this story, lest we forget . . .

All the speeches were full of praise, as one could expect of course, without being fawning. As Tolkien later wrote: "In the event they were all in English; and all but one quite sensible (if one deducts the high pitch of the eulogy, which was rather embarrassing)" (Tolkien, 1981, p. 266, No. 206). On the two photographs taken of the high table during Hella Haasse's speech you can clearly see that Tolkien was embarrassed; he rests his weary head on both fists. The one non-sensible speech was given, according to Tolkien, by a "lunatic *phycholog*".[6] A psychologist, Mr. L. Deen, did

---

[5] I have found the text of five of the speeches. Of the sixth there is no text, for the speaker made it up as he went along and never put it down on paper.
[6] Tolkien meant "psycholoog", which is Dutch for psychologist. This is probably a transcribing mistake.

address Tolkien, but there is nothing odd about his speech. I give you some sentences from Deen's speech:

> I shall take the story as it is, without attempting profound interpretations. Why not leave it to the individual purchaser to enjoy the book and to accept the story as he chooses? Is it not sufficient to enjoy wonderful scenery without trying to discover its meaning?
>
> Professor Tolkien's fascinating story, told in his own magnificent manner takes the reader outside the human and inhuman realities of everyday life, and gives him the reality of a creative fantasy, the privilege of a rich personal imagination . . .
>
> There are many reasons why we should thank Professor Tolkien for his marvellous story, every page of which is full of wonderful scenes, ideas and thoughts. May Professor Tolkien's creatures live long in our hearts.

I assume that Tolkien would have agreed to all this. However, another speaker, a Mr. P.A. Hekstra, said some peculiar things. Mr. Hekstra was a graphologist, which is close enough to psychology for Tolkien to make the mistake. Hekstra was a critic who reviewed books on national radio, and as such was invited to speak. He said about *The Lord of the Rings* that it was "a history of Elves and fairies, earthmen, cobolds and gnomes", and he summarised the novel as follows: "The story deals with brave knights, shrewd gnomes, bloodthirsty mercenaries and powermongers, who at one moment help each other, and the next moment are each others, mortal enemies." No wonder Tolkien said to Mrs. Sötemann, who was sitting next to him: "Either he did not see anything, or did not like what he saw."

The evening was announced as a Hobbit dinner, so food was provided. The intention was that between courses the speeches be given. This proved to be a small disaster, for many speeches were too long, so that the food was cold by the time the speech was finished. Only one person did not wait for the speaker to finish: Tolkien immediately dug in when something was set before him and thus proved that he was a real hobbit.

Nicely decorated menu cards were printed by Het Spectrum. Every course had a Tolkienesque name, such as "Egg-salad à la Barliman Butterbur", "Vegetables of Goldberry" and "Ice and Fruits of Gildor". Some confusion amongst the guests was caused by "Maggotsoup"; people feared the contents of the soup. But to everybody's relief it was of – course – mushroom. Also, meat was served ("Fricandeau à la Gimli") which was a problem, for it was Friday and Tolkien was a Roman Catholic. Catholics are not allowed to eat meat on Friday. But the organizers had thought of that and had asked – and received – dispensation from the diocese of Rotterdam. Sötemann had a little card from the deacon in his pocket, proving that dispensation was given in case Tolkien asked. He did not, and interestingly enough Sötemann said to me that Tolkien did not strike him as a man who would be concerned with a thing like that.

Of course no "Hobbit-maaltijd" could be complete without pipe-smoking. The Dutch tobacco company Van Rossum had supplied free tobacco in beautiful Delft blue porcelain jars and old-fashioned clay pipes to all the gentlemen present (of course not to the ladies, perish the thought, this is the fifties you know!). In the Flevo-hall hung several posters of Van Rossum's, advertising "Pipe-weed for Hobbits: In three qualities: *Longbottom Leaf, Old Toby* and *Southern Star*".

Besides eating, drinking, smoking and listening to all the speeches, Tolkien had to give autographs. A lady told me that she came to the "Hobbit-maaltijd" with her father to get her book autographed, but she did not speak any English. This was no problem for Tolkien; he signed his name and wrote down "Elen síla lúmenn, omentielvo" in Tengwar (which she could not read either, but that's beside the point).

At the end of the banquet came the high point of the evening, the reason why people from all over the Netherlands had come to Rotterdam, the ninth and final speech: Tolkien's speech.

Tolkien surprised his audience by starting with the Dutch greeting "beste luitjes" (dear folks). The speech he gave was a parody of the farewell speech of Bilbo Baggins at the beginning of *The Lord of the Rings*, and it was laced with jokes and small bits in Dutch and Elvish. It went down very well with the Rotterdam audience. Beforehand, Tolkien was afraid that his non-English audience would not understand him, but that fear was unfounded. It was another example of Tolkien's insecurity, his fear not to do justice to the occasion. Professor H. W. Lambers, one of the customers of Voorhoeve & Dietrich who had given a speech, told me that you could clearly notice that Tolkien was a very experienced teacher; he knew how to get a message across, how to address a large non-understanding audience, like a group of students.

It is amusing to notice that there has been some myth-forming around Tolkien's speech. It has been suggested that Tolkien was standing on his chair – like Bilbo did – during his speech. I have interviewed about a dozen people present at the Hobbit dinner and as is the case with eyewitnesses, some said yes, some said no, most did not know. But on the photograph taken of Tolkien while he is addressing the audience you can see that he was not standing on a chair.

Another nice anecdote – and one that did happen – occurred during the question time after Tolkien's speech. A lady argued elaborately that such a large work of literature surely must have a deeper meaning, a message. Are we, for instance, supposed to see the Soviet Union in Mordor, and is Sauron based on Stalin, and is Gandalf the personification of Christian ethics who leads ordinary people (the hobbits) on a crusade against injustice, communism and heresy? In short, my dear professor, what are you trying to say with this novel?

Tolkien had listened thoughtfully to the lady, rose from his chair, walked to the microphone, and said: "Absolutely nothing, madam", and took his chair again.

Tolkien always refuted the opinion that *The Lord of the Rings* was an allegory, yet the question of that lady was understandable. Especially because Tolkien had finished his speech in the following manner:

> It is now exactly twenty years since I began in

Figure 5. Tolkien giving autographs. From left to right Mrs. Sötemann, Mr. W.B.P.J. Blokhuis (holding a copy of *De Reisgenoten*), Mr. Cees Baars and Tolkien. Photograph by and © C.M. Tholens.

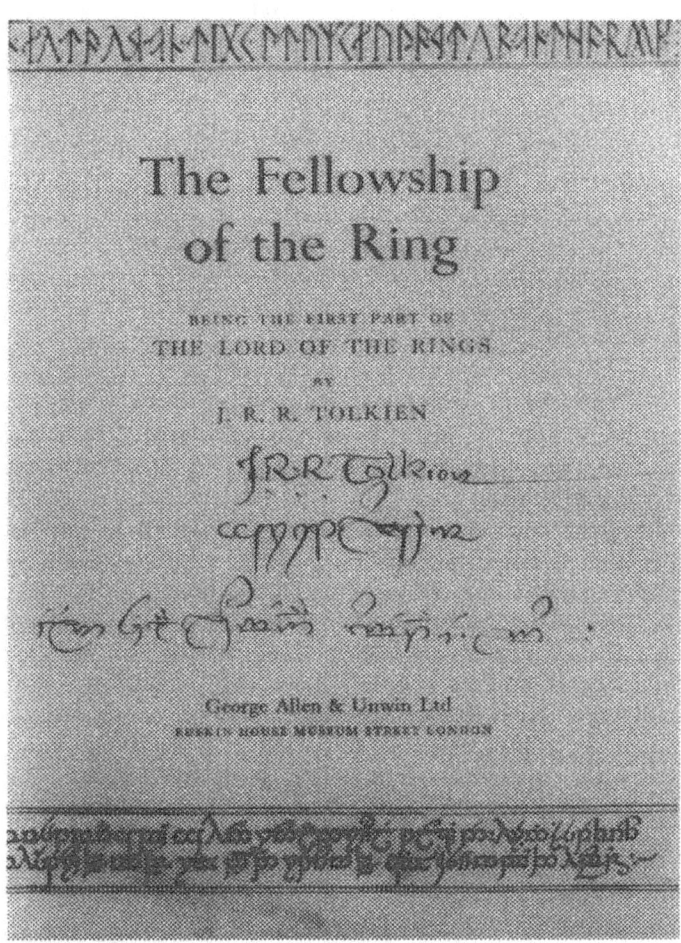

Figure 6. An autograph with inscription by Tolkien given at the Hobbit dinner. Private collection. Text © The Tolkien Trust, 1995.

earnest to complete the history of our revered hobbit-ancestors of the Third Age. I look East, West, North, South, and I do not see Sauron; but I see that Saruman has many descendants. We Hobbits have against them no magic weapons. Yet, my gentlehobbits, I give you this toast: To the Hobbits. May they outlast the Sarumans and see spring again in the trees.
(Carpenter, 1977, pp. 225-226)[7]

Of course his Dutch audience, with the Cold War at a freezing low point, took this as a warning against both expansionist empires: the one of the Soviets and the one of the Americans. Surely Tolkien meant politicians were the descendants of Saruman?

With the question time the "Hobbit-maaltijd" came to an end. Everybody I spoke to had had the best of times and still have fond memories of the occasion. If you ask them how they would describe Tolkien you get remarks like: amiable, friendly, open, witty, a real hobbit. Not to turn this into a hagiography let me also quote the one negative remark I heard: "He drank too much," but that too is in true hobbit-fashion.

A few people remained behind in the Flevo-hall to talk some more with Tolkien, among them Professor Lambers.

In his speech Lambers had praised Tolkien for his extremely vivid descriptions of nature and his excellent choice of words. Lambers shared Tolkien's love for trees; as a child he always wondered what the trees were gossiping about him. This struck a chord with Tolkien, even so much that they made plans for Tolkien to come to Holland again in the course of 1958, this time with Edith, to stay at the Lambers, illness of Tolkien's wife prevented this. Of his conversation with Tolkien, Lambers clearly remembers that he continued on the question the lady had asked during the question time.

---

[7] I would like to thank Mr. Christopher Tolkien for his search of his father's papers to find the text of the Rotterdam speech. Unfortunately it seems to be lost. Addendum, July 1993: Recently I have found a reel-to-reel tape with Tolkien's speech on it.

Figure 7. Tolkien giving his speech. Photograph by and © C.M. Tholens.

"Is there really no deeper meaning in *The Lord of the Rings*?", asked Lambers.

"It's just a story, it's just a story", reacted Tolkien passionately.

"Yes, but a story with a message", continued Lambers, and he argued the moral background of *The Lord of the Rings*. As an example he took that impressive scene on the border of Mordor, when Gollum bends over the sleeping Frodo, torn between Gollum's love for the Ring and Sméagol's word of honour to Frodo not to take it. The crucial element in this scene, according to Lambers, is "distrust" which causes Good to act as Evil. Gollum is mollified by the vulnerability of the sleeping hobbit and is at the point of redemption. But Sam, misguided by the love for his master, intervenes and thus prevents the rebirth of Sméagol. Sam's goodness makes the goodness of Gollum impossible. And Tolkien answered: "I wept when I wrote that."

Tolkien returned to his hotel, and the next day Piet Harting took him on a sight-seeing trip through The Hague and Amsterdam where he saw, as he wrote later, many beautiful pictures, meaning no doubt that he visited the Rijksmuseum. He spent the night in Amsterdam and on Sunday returned to Oxford.

And so his exceptional visit to Holland came to an end. It was exceptional because it was the first time, and also the last time, that Tolkien had accepted such an invitation. One should not conclude from his abstention from further trips that Tolkien had had an awful time in Holland. He wrote on 2 April to Cees Ouboter:

> I still find it hard to believe that all this really happened to me! It was a most marvellous and memorable event . . . I shall not, of course, ever forget the Hobbit-maaltijd, and the graciousness of all to me. The sooner I see your country again the better pleased I shall be. It seems clear to me that (as it suggests in the book) the English hobbits are really the migrant colonists, and their original home-land is "across the sea".

Of course the Dutch Tolkien-fans always knew that we are the only true hobbits.

References

Carpenter, Humphrey. 1977. *J.R.R. Tolkien. A biography*. London: George Allen & Unwin.

Tolkien, J.R.R. 1981. *Letters of J.R.R. Tolkien*, ed. Humphrey Carpenter. London: George Allen and Unwin.

Ouboter, C. 1958. "Een merkwaardige strijd om de macht" in *Ontmoeting. Letterkundig en algemeen cultureel maandblad* Volume 11 (March 1958) nr. 6. pp. 193-201.

A Mythology? For England?

Anders Stenström

Abstract: It is well known that J.R.R. Tolkien said that he wanted to make "a mythology for England". Well known, but not true. This paper investigates how Tolkien really used the word *mythology*, and also looks at the relation with England.

Keywords: Humphrey Carpenter's *J.R.R. Tolkien: A biography*, England, languages, legend, mythology

For many years it has been a received truth that what Tolkien wanted to make was (or was initially) "a mythology for England", a phrase which is always put within quotation marks and never provided with a source. As far as I have found, the true tale runs so: on p. 59 in *J.R.R. Tolkien: A biography* Carpenter (1977) wrote of the young Tolkien's appreciation of the *Kalevala*, quoting his wish for "something of the same sort that belonged to the English", and commented "perhaps he was already thinking of creating that mythology for England himself". Evidently satisfied with his phrase, Carpenter titled Part Three of his book "1917-1925: The making of a mythology" and opened it with stating Tolkien's "desire to create a mythology *for England*" (p. 89) (italics original). And thus it chanced that the phrase found its way into the biography's Index, where under Tolkien, John Ronald Reuel (1892-1973)[1] you find WRITINGS – PRINCIPAL BOOKS, starting with *The Silmarillion*, which has a secondary entry "a mythology for England", within single quotation marks (in the original) like the names from Tolkien's works, and the one actual quotation ("out of the leaf-mould of the mind"), to be found in the Index. This is where the quotation marks come from.

In context, the desirable "something of the same sort" refers to "that very primitive undergrowth" found in "[t]hese mythological ballads", the *Kalevala* (Carpenter, 1977, p. 59). This does not exactly equal *mythology*, though it might be difficult to find a one-word equivalent. It is more curious that in the later passage (p. 89) Carpenter supports his statement with a long quotation from the Waldman letter, where the original project described by Tolkien is not to make a mythology for England, but to make "a body of more or less connected legend" to be dedicated "to England; to my country" (Tolkien, 1981, number 131, paragraph 5). Like the quotation marks, this spurious connection has fixed itself in the mind of Tolkien students: during my search for the source of the quotation I was repeatedly and unhesitatingly referred to the Waldman letter.

At last I have now found a probable derivation. There are a number of places where Tolkien uses *mythology* about his own work, and in one of them he is not far from *a mythology for England*. One of the letters begins like this:

Thank you very much for your kind and encouraging letter. Having set myself a task, the arrogance of which I fully recognised and trembled at: being precisely to restore to the English an epic tradition and present them with a mythology of their own: it is a wonderful thing to be told that I have succeeded, at least with those who have still the undarkened heart and mind.
(Tolkien, 1981, number 180, paragraph 1)

The published text is a draft for a letter to an unidentified Mr. Thompson, so Carpenter probably saw it while he worked on the biography, and associated it with the "something . . . that belonged to the English" from Tolkien's *Kalevala* paper, and the dedication "to England" from the Waldman letter, These clearly express comparable thoughts, but the Author actually spoke of different things: in the earliest instance it was the fruitful "primitive undergrowth" in language and tradition, in the second instance his own projected *legendarium*; and the "successful mythology" in the Thompson letter was *The Lord of the Rings*, or elements of *The Lord of the Rings*. As the words *being precisely* in the quotation above seem to show, it was Mr. Thompson who had called it that; and that Tolkien, while accepting the term (cf. his acceptance in Tolkien, 1981, number 163, paragraph 1, answering W. H. Auden, another early admirer of *The Lord of the Rings*, of the term *Trilogy*) explained in paragraph 4 that behind the success there existed *The Silmarillion*, shows that Mr. Thompson had not been aware of the unpublished work. The Author's account of his project and his usage of *mythology* will both be examined below, but first I want to consider the critical tradition built on Carpenter's conflation *a mythology for England* (*a mythology* probably from the Thompson letter, *England* from the Waldman letter, and *for* chosen to join them), and his assertion that this was what Tolkien wished to create.

The word *mythology* certainly is capable of a wide sweep of meanings. Used broadly it may mean nothing more specific

---
[1] That is the entry, despite the note at the head of the Index.

than "a body of stories, epic corpus". The Author for instance employs this meaning in his footnote to letter number 211, paragraph 13, where "our 'mythological' Middle-Ages" means "the Middle-Ages as they are in our stories". A little further on in the same letter (paragraph 22) he mentions "the new and fascinating semi-scientific mythology of the 'Prehistoric'", using the word in a related broad sense, "a conceptual construction with imaginative power". Obviously Tolkien has indeed created a mythology in both these senses, and obviously the phrase *a mythology for England* seems to say something more specific and significant, and has commonly been taken to do so.[2] At the same time, though many critics have piously spoken the password it has not awarded much insight, though it might make an introduction or conclusion more evocative. The truth is of course that "a mythology" (in a more specific sense than those mentioned) is not what Tolkien's oeuvre is, and not what he set out to make. There is both "mythology" and "a mythology" in *The Book of Lost Tales*, but itself is neither "mythology" nor "a mythology", if *mythology* is used in its central current sense, involving such notions as the primordial, the cosmic, the divine, the sacred, the patterns for life, society and nature. A painting of a tree may to a large extent consist of painted sky, but this does not make it a painting of sky. There is a distinction between the subject matter and the background. In *The Book of Lost Tales* the mythology forms a background (though it might come in everywhere, like the sky glimpsed between the leaves).

Critics thoughtful and philological have associated the presupposed desire to create a mythology for England with the many instances where Tolkien in his stories "reconstructed"[3] a context for ancient English or Northern mythological fragments: Earendel is the most prominent case. (We may note that this interpretation in any case comes closer to the above-quoted dictum on *The Lord of the Rings*: in these "reconstructions" the Author is restoring something that belonged to the English, presenting them with their own mythology, rather than creating something for England.) In his article in the recent *Arda* one such philologist, T. A. Shippey, accordingly observed how Tolkien contrived "to fit in all the bits and pieces which philologists during the 19th and 20th centuries had uncovered from the English stories which would have made a mythology for England, if only it had not all got lost" (Shippey, 1992, p. 24), explicating: "Tolkien was trying to reach back to an old past, as it were the lost English equivalent of what had almost survived in Norse. He was looking back to try and find what we might call an asterisk-mythology" (Shippey, 1992, p. 26). The observation is true, but the explication only gets hold of what Tolkien was doing when he "reconstructed", not what Tolkien was doing. The painter may be using ochres, but that is not what he his doing, he is painting his tree: if every concerned element, down to the last repercussion of the *Edda*, of the mythological vestiges in English words and names, and so on, in *The Book of Lost Tales* were listed, we would still get only a list of scattered points, by which the cycle as it is would not be comprehended.[4] Important though some of the elements are, "reconstruction" is incidental to the work. Also, the reconstructive effort embraced not only mythological fragments like Earendel and Wade: the Man in the Moon might perhaps pass as "mythological", but not the nursery-rhyme porridge served to him; it could have been "reconstructed" as mythology, but was not. What the Author was concerned to cultivate the remnants of was not "mythology" but the whole "primitive undergrowth" of tradition and language, ranging from the serious to the curious.[5]

Most obviously, the asterisk-mythology view fails in that neither the Lost Tales in general nor their mythology in especial can sincerely be regarded as very like anything that might have been told among the ancient English. Tolkien's legends are (even in their earliest stage) undisguisedly idiosyncratic, and I will not be persuaded that this is the result of a glorious failure, that the Author in fact strove to reproduce the lost English mythology as he conceived it to have been.

There is a further difficulty which encumbers the idea of making *a mythology for England*, reconstruction or not. It may be less obvious, but was lucidly exposed by Shippey. I quote summarily:

> So if Tolkien thought he was going to make a mythology for England, this meant . . . trying to give people something which was so evidently missing that they would not believe it if you gave it to them . . . So I think that public acceptance would never have been very likely. I think Tolkien knew that . . . He tried a

---

[2] Quite possibly it was not meant very specifically. Where Carpenter (1977) on p. 6 says of Tolkien "Once more he refers to his own mythology", the back-reference is *The Lord of the Rings*.

It is of course absolutely legitimate to use *mythology* in the broad "imaginary invention"-sense – Tolkien himself did so, as we have seen and will return to below. Apart from the erroneous quotation marks, which may be the publisher's fault, there is no blame on the biography, which was not meant as a revealing literary analysis. My argument is that when *mythology* is used as a definition of Tolkien's project a highly-charged sense is assumed, which obscures a quintessential quality of his works.

[3] I adopt this term from T. A. Shippey (1982).

[4] What I mean is not that the rendering would be fragmentary: the list would be a mere assemblage, and as such no rendering at all. A list of all the Latin-derived words in this article would preserve nothing of it. Granted, that would be true even if the text were indeed precisely an exercise in writing Latin-derived words; but that they are prevalent and often important is no indication that it is one.

[5] "There has been been much debate concerning the relations of these things, of *folk-tale* and *myth*", the Author noted in "On Fairy-Stories" (1964), Origins, paragraph 6. In the following paragraphs (7-12) he argued that "the higher aristocracy of mythology" and the characters of "folk-tales, Märchen, fairy-stories – nursery-tales" live by the same life, the life of Faërie, derived from sub-creative man; there is "no fundamental distinction between the higher and lower mythologies", and, moreover, neither is prior to the other. According to Tolkien a pure mythology (in the current sense) has never existed and would be totally artificial: the intrinsic place of mythology is the marches of Faërie, related to its "Mystical [face] towards the Supernatural".

line of descent in English; he tried borrowing also from Norse. Neither of these, I think, would have been successful tactics.

(Shippey, 1992, pp. 23, 23-24, 25, 27)

In other words: could Tolkien ever have thought that the English would accept his writings as their mythology? (This is in effect a criticism of *for* in Carpenter's formula.)

The question is rhetorical and need not be pondered; the Author has with sufficient clarity described what he set out to do. The most comprehensive exposition is that in the justly famous Waldman letter (Tolkien, 1981, number 131). Picking the crucial points from the crucial paragraphs (2, 3, 5 and 6), what Tolkien says is this;

> 2. "[T]his stuff began with me . . . I mean, I do not remember a time when I was not building it. Many children make up, or begin to make up, imaginary languages. I have been at it since I could write. But I have never stopped."
>
> 3. "But an equally basic passion of mine *ab initio* was for myth (not allegory!) and for fairy-story, and above all for heroic legend on the brink of fairy-tale and history, of which there is far too little in the world (accessible to me) for my appetite. I was an undergraduate before thought and experience revealed to me that these were not divergent interests – opposite poles of science and romance – but integrally related . . . Also I was from early days grieved by the poverty of my own beloved county: it had no stories of its own (bound up with its tongue and soil)." Much of what is said in those two paragraphs reappears in letter 163, paragraphs 4-10:
>
>> It was an inevitable, though conditionable, evolvement of the birth-given. It has been always with me: the sensibility to linguistic pattern which affects me emotionally like colour or music; and the passionate love of growing things;[6] and the deep response to legends (for want of a better word) that have what I would call the North-western temper and temperature . . . I discovered . . . the acute aesthetic pleasure derived from a language for its own sake . . . – it is not quite the same as the mere perception of beauty: I feel the beauty of say Italian or for that matter of modern English (which is very remote from my personal taste): it is more like the appetite for a needed food . . . All this only as background to the stories, though languages and names are for me inextricable from the stories. They are and were so to speak an attempt to give a background or a world in which my expressions of linguistic taste could have a function.

To synthesize: a) Tolkien had a specific linguistic appetite which he satisfied partly by inventing languages of his own. b) He had also an appetite for myth and for stories on the brink of fairy-tale and history, for which *legends* was the best word he could find. c) He was especially responsive to legends of the North-western temper, and regretted that there were none bound up with the English tongue and soil. d) He discovered that language and legends were integrally related; his own invented languages and legends each reinforce the other. The last point is driven home in letter 180, the Thompson letter, paragraph 2:

> I made the discovery that "legends" depend on the language to which they belong; but a living language depends equally on the "legends" which it conveys by tradition . . . So though . . . I began with language, I found myself involved in inventing "legends" of the same "taste".

5. "Do not laugh! But once upon a time (my crest has long since fallen) I had a mind to make a body of more or less connected legend, ranging from the large and cosmogonic, to the level of romantic fairy-story – the larger founded on the lesser in contact with the earth, the lesser drawing splendour from the vast backcloths – which I could dedicate simply to: to England; to my country. It should possess the tone and quality that I desired, somewhat cool and clear, be redolent of our 'air' (the clime and soil of the North West, meaning Britain and the hither parts of Europe . . .) . . . The cycles should be linked to a majestic whole, and yet leave scope for other minds and hands, wielding paint and music and drama. Absurd." That his crest had by 1951 fallen apparently means that he no longer absurdly envisaged his opus as a majestic matter for elaboration in other arts, and that he would not pathetically dedicate it to England. In any case, he was still engaged on *a body of legend,* for this label is a gloss on the term *legendarium* or *legendary* which he had begun to use the year before (the earliest instance I have found is in letter 124, paragraph 6) about *The Silmarillion*, and which is also so used in paragraph 15 of the present letter. *The Silmarillion* (or what had acquired that overall title), then, was shaped to a) have the desired quality of the North-western clime and soil, and b) range from vast cosmogonic backcloths to the level of romantic fairy-story. The subsequent exposition in the letter turns on the latter fact; it was this inherent range which found its appropriate extension in the later works – *The Hobbit* "proved to be the discovery of the completion of the whole, its mode of descent to earth, and merging into 'history'" (paragraph 7; the Author had, as we now know, previously tried various modes of merging the high romance into history without finding what he wanted). The contents of *The Silmarillion* are also described in terms of the same gradation: "The cycles begin with a cosmogonical myth: the *Music of the Ainur*" (paragraph 10); "It moves then swiftly to the *History of the Elves,* or the *Silmarillion* proper . . . in a still half-mythical mode" (paragraph 11); "As the stories become less mythical, and more like stories and romances, Men are interwoven . . . The chief of the stories of the *Silmarillion*, and the one most fully treated is the *Story of Beren and Lúthien the Elfmaiden* . . . the story is (I think beautiful and powerful) heroic-fairy-romance" (paragraphs 16, 17).

6. "Of course, such an overweening purpose did not develop all at once. The mere stories were the thing. They arose in my mind as "given" things, and as they came, separately, so too the links grew." Letter 257, paragraph 4,

---

[6] Regrettably, Tolkien did not expand on the "inevitable evolvement" of this element into literary creation.

contains a fuller account:

> The germ of my attempt to write legends of my own to fit my private languages was the tragic tale of the hapless Kullervo in the Finnish *Kalevala*. It remains a major matter in the legends of the First Age (which I hope to publish as *The Silmarillion*), though as "The Children of Húrin" it is entirely changed . . . The second point was the writing, "out of my head", of the "Fall of Gondolin", the story of Idril and Eärendel . . . and the original version of the "Tale of Lúthien Tinúviel and Beren" later . . . I carried on with this construction after escaping from the army . . . In Oxford I wrote a cosmogonical myth, "The Music of the Ainur" . . .

Some of the leaves caught in the wind became a tree, and the tree required a sky behind it. The stories required the splendid mythological backcloths; the larger was founded on the lesser.[7] *The mere stories were the thing.*

Thus has Tolkien recounted the formation of his project. Against that background I have investigated his usage of *mythology* in his published letters. I have found 54 instances, distributed in 22 letters, where *mythology* (*-ies*, *-ical*, *-ically*) relates to his own works.[8] Schematically, the usage has three elements:

1) As I have already indicated, Tolkien not seldom used *mythology* broadly for "invention: nexus of imaginary tales, epic corpus; construction", as in letter 165, paragraph 12 (the first of the three attached paragraphs), where the tale of Lúthien and Beren is called "the kernel of the mythology", or in letter 229, paragraph 13, where the placing of Mordor is a "narrative and geographical necessity, within my 'mythology'". (It was apparently in this sense that the word was used by Mr. Thompson and paraphrased in Tolkien's answer.)

2) Again, he often used it strictly, connoting "the large and cosmogonic" (the earlier-mentioned notions adjoining): letters 156, 181, and 200 contain good examples.

3) It might also be used more loosely to connote, as it were, "an aura of mythology"; in especial, when he was speaking, as often, and for instance in letter 163, with the enlarged "legendarium, of which the Trilogy is part (the conclusion)" (paragraph 12) in view, he sometimes used *mythology* about the earlier past as a block, as in "the background mythology" (paragraph 17), leaving out of account that progressively within that block "the matter becomes 'storial' and not mythical" (Tolkien, 1981, number 212, footnote to paragraph 6).[9]

Senses 1 and 2 are clearly discriminable, but sense 3 overlaps both and has hardly any room of its own. Especially it overlaps sense 1: should the quoted "the kernel of the mythology" be taken simply as "the kernel of the nexus of stories" or as "the kernel of the nexus of notably mythical stories" – even though the same story is explicitly reckoned among the "less mythical" ones in a passage quoted above, and implicitly among the "not mythical" ones in another? Would the quoted "the background mythology" be better taken as a mere variation on "the greater construction" four paragraphs earlier in that letter? But sense 3 grows naturally out of sense 2: the lesser that draws splendour from the mythology behind may from a distance melt into it.

The lesson of that is not that the *legendarium*, or *The Silmarillion*, or the original project may after all be seen as "a mythology" – if they may be so seen it is when reduced (or raised) to the background of something else. The lesson is that when you are there, in the actual stories, the stage is always set in front of the vast backcloths, where things are becoming less mythical and more storial, passing into history. Tolkien desired, as we have seen, legends "on the brink of fairy-tale and history", and the transition is going on throughout the whole *legendarium*.[10]

To sum up, what Tolkien set out to make was languages to his taste. Because he made languages to his taste he found himself writing stories to his taste. Writing stories to his taste meant giving them the splendour of background mythology and a merging into history. That is what he was doing. The

---

[7] This is not to say that the mythology was added *ex nihilo*. The existence of such a background was already implied in the stories.

[8] I have also noted twelve occurrences of *mythology* with other references. However, when the sense is not independently indicated by the context it cannot be defined without circular argument (the same is true about the use in "A Secret Vice", paragraph 36). To the extent that the context does suggest the sense, the usage seems congruent to that in the examined cases.

The Thompson case shows that when *mythology* does refer to Tolkien's works, he may not always have chosen it wholly of his own accord. I have not included the occurrence in what is marked as a quotation from Lord Halsbury, in Tolkien, 1981, number 204, paragraph 1.

[9] To ascribe a given occurrence of *mythology* to sense 1, 2 or 3 is necessarily a matter of interpretation, but on my reading there are 17 instances of sense 1, 27 instances of sense 2, and 10 instances of sense 3. The adjectival and adverbial forms are found only in senses 2 and 3.

There are at least twenty-five letters where the Author characterizes his works without recourse to the word *mythology*, and is peripheral in some of the letters where he did use it. The term most frequently relied on is *legend* (derivatives included). Composite expressions are usual, like *legends and stories, legendary and history, mythical history, Elvish histories, fabulous history, Elvish legends, stories and romances, legends and annals*, etc. There is thus nothing like a settled and consistent terminology, which no doubt shows that, like *legend*, all the terms were used "for lack of a better word".

[10] This "brink of fairy-tale and history" is presumably the brink between the two; but in context it might conceivably mean the brink between on the one hand fairy-tale and history and on the other heroic legend, or possibly myth. From the ensuing exposition in letter 131 all the interpretations can be justified.

In all the stories there is an awareness of an exalted past, and with it intimations of the eternity whence it sprang. Glimpses from beyond the walls of the world come into the everyday in this historical, mediate, mode as well as in a fairy-story, immediate, mode, the eucatastrophe. The "brink" is thus really a complex borderland of three regimes: the mythical, the mundane and the miraculous.

stories were the thing. Not a mythology: a body of legend.

Tolkien was creating "for England", Carpenter said. What the Author himself spoke of was, we saw, presenting his work "to England", "to the English". His statements are not much elaborated. He said, as we read above, that England lacked stories "bound up with its tongue and soil", and he decided to make a legendarium redolent of its "clime and soil". What about the tongue? The Author always stressed that his stories are bound up with his own languages, and that "*mythically* these tales are Elf-centred" (Tolkien, 1981, number 212, paragraph 6; italics original). Yet of course he wrote in English, and while he never translated any longer passage into Elvish he did translate parts into Old English. Tolkien wished for a body of legends "bound up" with English by immemorial tradition, and he could not really create that. But Elvish and its legends have the Northwestern temper and therefore fit England's soil. And when they are presented to the English, the English might become Elf-friends. As these legends are written in English, the English have the birthright to them, not Celts or Scandinavians.

Where I broke the previous quotation from him, Shippey goes on to say:

> If he had succeeded, he would have run into another problem – one which should be considered some other time –: what is a "myth"? There are many definitions of "myth", but I would have thought that a myth was something that you believed in. But can you, then, present something to be believed in when you have invented it yourself? About that I am very doubtful. And if he had succeeded in doing it, there would have been a deep problem of belief. The myth that he created would have been a rival to Faith, and I think Tolkien would have found that particularly difficult if it had really appeared as a challenge.
> (Shippey, 1992, p. 27)

Tolkien, I think, would not have said that a myth is something you believe in.[11] But he was wary: "humility and an awareness of peril is required . . . Great harm can be done, of course, by this potent mode of 'myth'" (Tolkien, 1981, number 153, paragraphs 16-17). Creating an Elvish mythology for the legendary, one which becomes to the reader an awesome and edifying "mythology once removed", was a less problematic enterprise than it would have been to create a mythology for England.

References

Carpenter, Humphrey. 1977. *J.R.R. Tolkien: A biography*. London: Allen & Unwin.

Shippey, T.A. 1982. *The Road to Middle-earth*. London: George Allen & Unwin.

Shippey, T.A. 1992. "Long Evolution: *The History of Middle-earth* and Its Merits" in *Arda* 1987 (published 1992), pp. 18-43.

Tolkien, J.R.R. 1964. "On Fairy-Stories" in *Tree and Leaf*. London: George Allen & Unwin.

Tolkien, J.R.R. 1981. *Letters of J.R.R. Tolkien*, ed. Humphrey Carpenter. London: George Allen & Unwin.

---

[11] See for instance letter 211, paragraph 25, where he says that "all this is 'mythical', and not any kind of new religion or vision". In "On Fairy-Stories" (Tolkien, 1964), Origins, paragraphs 11-12, mythology and religion are described as two entangled but different things (though possibly fundamentally connected).

Tolkien's Elvish Craft

Dwayne Thorpe

Abstract: This paper examines "fusion", the basis of artistry, in the works of J.R.R. Tolkien. Fusion takes place in descriptive passages, in the characters' perception and in the language Tolkien uses. Fusion works toward the purpose of Tolkien's fiction, which is to be found in the Christian views of earth and escapism, especially as expressed by sea-longing.

Keywords: abstraction, aesthetics, fantasy, fusion, landscape, names, reality, perception, sea-longing, J.R.R. Tolkien: aims, artistry

Tolkien's readers all have the same impression: they have walked or ridden every inch of Middle-earth in all its weathers. It is a curious impression, this experience of an imaginary place, and one difficult to create, as Tolkien noted. "To make a Secondary World," he wrote, "commanding Secondary Belief, will probably require labour and thought, and will certainly demand a special skill, a kind of elvish craft" (Tolkien, 1984b, p. 140). It would require similar skill to explain that craft, though perhaps gnomish rather than elvish. That may be the reason why Tolkien's artistry has not been much studied. After the initial storm of reviews, both attacks and defences, we have had many studies of his relevance, themes, sources, bibliography, biography, and so on, but only an occasional comment on aesthetics. And that cannot be right. Given its international role in the literature of our century, the aesthetics of fantasy should be a major subject of analysis; and Tolkien's role in the turn from realism to fantasy is undisputed. He is too important to become the property of enthusiasts and too fine to shrivel into thematics. The power of his work, as he said and we should recognize, lies not in the message but in the telling. We are first caught by artistry, then led to concepts.

I want to say a little about Tolkien's artistry. Not that I propose a full explanation. That, like some name in Treebeard's language, would be too long and mouth-filling for hasty humans. I intend to examine only one tool in Tolkien's workshop, giving it the name of "fusion".

By way of illustration, let me begin with two paragraphs of description: the first a delight for those who enjoy seasons, country walks, and Wordsworth; the second a delight for Tolkien readers.

> After stumbling along for some way along the stream, they came quite suddenly out of the gloom. As if through a gate they saw the sunlight before them. Coming to the opening they found that they had made their way down through a cleft in a high steep bank, almost a cliff. At its feet was a wide space of grass and reeds; and in the distance could be glimpsed another bank almost as steep. A golden afternoon of late sunshine lay warm and drowsy upon the hidden land between. In the midst of it there wound lazily a dark river of brown water, bordered with ancient willows, arched over with willows, blocked with fallen willows, and flecked with thousands of faded willow-leaves. The air was thick with them, fluttering yellow from the branches; for there was a warm and gentle breeze blowing softly in the valley, and the reeds were rustling, and the willow-boughs were creaking.
> (Tolkien, 1965a, p. 126)

Many of you recognize that this passage describes not England but part of Tolkien's fantasy world: the Old Forest outside the Hedge. And the walkers are not Wordsworth, Dorothy, and Coleridge, but hobbits. Nevertheless, I would ask why the paragraph can't be called realistic: pure mimesis? Might this not be a place Tolkien had seen? Everything in it is actual. The interplay of light and shadow; angles of vision; season, weather, breeze, colour, motion: all mark the familiar, witnessed fact. Near the end of September, in the sunshine of late afternoon, river-banks really are thick with willow leaves that turn the air gold. This is the way realists use words: not as permission to dream, but as stand-ins for reality.

Nevertheless, this is a fantasy paragraph, though only context reveals it. It marks a crucial moment in the attempt of the hobbits to slip out of the Shire, setting the scene for Old Man Willow and Tom Bombadil. The hobbits have been forced down to the Withywindle, and the reader knows there is something hostile about the Old Forest. The gully opens like a gateway placed by some picturesque artist. But its beauty is a hook for an ancient willow who is using the golden day to fish for hobbits. In less than two pages Pippin vanishes; so does Merry (except for his legs); and Frodo nearly drowns, hypnotized by Old Man Willow's song. Tolkien's realistic treatment of willows, and especially his incessant repetition of that word "willow," are foreshadowings. We cannot, of course, know this on a first reading. But in retrospect the paragraph is a piece of deft fantasy-creation quietly doing its work.

Here now is the second passage, Frodo's first glimpse of Lothlórien as his blindfold is removed. As in the first paragraph, a hobbit emerging from darkness catches a vision of beauty.

> When his eyes were in turn uncovered, Frodo looked up and caught his breath. They were standing in an open space. To the left stood a great mound, covered with a sward of grass as green as Spring-time in the Elder days. Upon it, as a double crown, grew two circles of trees: the outer had bark of snowy white, and were leafless but beautiful in their shapely nakedness; the inner were mallorn-trees of great height, still arrayed in pale gold. High amid the branches of a towering tree that stood in the centre of all there gleamed a white flet. At the feet of the trees, and all about the green hillsides the grass was studded with small golden flowers shaped like stars. Among them, nodding on slender stalks, were other flowers, white and palest green: they glimmered as a mist amid the rich hue of the grass. Over all the sky was blue, and the sun of afternoon glowed upon the hill and cast long green shadows beneath the trees.
> (Tolkien, 1965a, pp. 364-365)

Again I would ask: why might this not be a real place? This time the question is more pressing, for the Withywindle only borders Faerie, but Lothlórien is its heart. All remember it with something like Sam's wonder at "going to see elves and all." Lothlórien is a haunting experience. Yet, nearly everything here might be found in a great landscape garden. Of course there are exotic touches: the reference to the "Elder days," or the unfamiliar words "mallorn" and "flet" (to be joined in the next paragraph by other names with an elven air – Cerin Amroth, *elanor*, *niphredil*, Galadrim). But as with the description of the Withywindle, most of the fantasy is in the context: the disaster at Khazad-Dûm which lies only one chapter back; dangers from orcs; the presence of elves; and Caras Galadon, the City of the Trees, which follows. The context provides a frame – not picturesque but enchanted – which creates the sense of beauty. And beauty is of the essence in Tolkien's fantasy. As he put it:

> We should look at green again, and be startled anew (but not blinded) by blue and yellow and red . . . We need . . . to clean our windows; so that the things seen clearly may be freed from the drab blur of triteness or familiarity.
> (Tolkien, 1984b, p. 146)

The Lord of the Rings, of course, contains much fantasy which is fantasy and nothing but fantasy: singing willows, a city of gigantic trees and sylvan immortals; intelligent tree-herds. But that fantasy is effective because it grows from paragraphs like these two. And these paragraphs represent Tolkien's dominant method, which typically makes the impossible believable by placing the exotic inside the familiar. Fusion blurs the line between reality and fantasy, enhancing the common while lending credence to the fantastic. This is not just a matter of landscape. Perception receives the same treatment. Here, for example, are Frodo's reactions to Cerin Amroth:

> It seemed to him that he had stepped through a high window that looked on a vanished world. A light was upon it for which his language had no name . . . He saw no colour but those he knew, gold and white and blue and green, but they were fresh and poignant, as if he had at that moment first perceived them and made for them names new and wonderful. In winter here no heart could mourn for summer or for spring. No blemish or sickness or deformity could be seen in anything that grew upon the earth. On the land of Lórien there was no stain.
> (Tolkien, 1965a, p. 365)

The experience fuses the mundane and transcendent. So does Tolkien's style, fusing two kinds of verbal signs: names for familiar things and words which point toward the nameless.

Soon after, Frodo has a second experience of the same kind, tactile rather than visual.

> He laid his hand upon the tree beside the ladder: never before had he been so suddenly and so keenly aware of the feel and texture of a tree's skin and of the life within it. He felt a delight in wood and the touch of it, neither as forester nor as carpenter; it was the delight of the living tree itself.
> (Tolkien, 1965a, p. 366)

These are elvish moments. Yet most people have had similar experiences of seeing ordinary things, such as colours, with the film of familiarity wiped away; or of suddenly realizing just how alive living things are: visions of a world with the sheen of wonder restored. The bark of a beech tree really is alive. But we do not always notice. And we never call it "skin." Tolkien's fusion wraps the surprising inside the ordinary, causing us to look. Thereafter we see trees in a new way. Mallorns, Ents, and ordinary elms become our delight. We feel we have seen deeply, like Merry and Pippin looking into the eyes of Treebeard:

> One felt as if there was an enormous well behind them, filled up with ages of memory and long, slow, steady thinking; but their surface was sparkling with the present: like sun shimmering on the outer leaves of a vast tree, or on the ripples of a very deep lake. I don't know, but it felt as if something that grew in the ground – asleep, you might say, or just feeling itself as something between root-tip and leaf-tip, between deep earth and sky had suddenly waked up, and was considering you with the same slow care that it had given to its own inside affairs for endless years.
> (Tolkien, 1965b, pp. 66-67)

This is the kind of thing Tolkien's fantasy does. But to what end? My subject is Tolkien's craft, of course – not his meaning. But one cannot understand a craftsman's methods without knowing what he is trying to do, so I must give some attention to Tolkien's aim as I see it.

The Lord of the Rings seems to me founded on the rock-bottom Christian belief that this world is not our home. Tolkien's elves singing of exile in "the world of woven trees," remembering "starlight on the Western Seas" (Tolkien, 1965a, pp. 88-89), give elven tongue to his own sense that the human world is a prison. In his lecture, "On Fairy-Stories," written as he was moving into *The Lord of the Rings*, he defended fairy-stories as legitimate reactions to that prison. "Why should a man be scorned, if, finding himself in prison, he tries to get out and go home? Or if, when he cannot do so, he thinks and talks about other topics than jailers and prison-walls?" (Tolkien, 1984b, p. 148). Of course this particular prison denies that it is a prison – or that there is any home to go to. It calls itself "the world." But its proper name is "culture." It would restrict all attention to itself. But Tolkien seizes on the desire for home as evidence that the prison is a prison.

Some readers, anxious about charges of escapism, ignore Tolkien's declaration that escape is a primary value of his sort of literature. But escape and escapism are not much alike. Escapism is by definition illegitimate, but escape may be not only legitimate but necessary: even a duty. At the very least, the desire to escape shows that some part of the prisoner is not imprisoned. It is a mark of humanity. Of course many desires are simply personal; but literary fantasy directs itself toward desires which are primordial and universal. A biographer, looking at Tolkien's life, has many reasons to see *The Lord of the Rings* as an orphan's book. It is certainly rooted in yearnings for mother, family, and belonging. That he began creating his elven world soon after the deaths of his two closest friends, while himself recuperating from trench fever, speaks for itself. But biography reads backward. It may explain the circumstance which caused Tolkien to turn down the road to Minas Tirith, but it does not explain what we really need to know: why we follow. Tolkien understood literary fantasy not as an uncontrollable overflow but as a painstaking art which arouses the very desire it intends to satisfy by creating a "secondary belief": one not equivalent to belief in the mundane world but taken seriously while the tale is told. That secondary belief is a hacksaw hidden inside a fruit pie. No belief, no saw. No saw, no escape. "Such stories," Tolkien said, "open a door on Other Time, and if we pass through, though only for a moment, we stand outside our own time, outside Time itself, maybe" (Tolkien, 1984b, pp. 128-129).

"The Monsters and the Critics," his 1936 address on *Beowulf*, describes an allegorical tower which says something about the *Beowulf*-poet but much more about Tolkien and Other Time.

> A man inherited a field in which was an accumulation of old stone, part of an older hall. Of the old stone some had already been used in building the house in which he actually lived, not far from the old house of his fathers. Of the rest he took some and built a tower. But his friends coming perceived at once (without troubling to climb the steps) that these stones had formerly belonged to a more ancient building. So they pushed the tower over, with no little labour, in order to look for hidden carvings and inscriptions, or to discover whence the man's distant forefathers had obtained their building material . . . They all said: "This tower is most interesting." But they also said (after pushing it over): "What a muddle it is in!" And even the man's own descendants . . . were heard to murmur: "He is such an odd fellow! Imagine his using these old stones just to build a nonsensical tower! Why did not he restore the old house? He had no sense of proportion." But from the top of that tower the man had been able to look out upon the sea.
> (Tolkien, 1984a, pp. 7-8)

The application to Tolkien is obvious. And the elven towers in *The Fellowship of the Ring* look back to that allegory.

> Three Elf-towers of immemorial age were still to be seen beyond the western marches. They shone far off in the moonlight. The tallest was furthest away, standing alone upon a green hill. The Hobbits of the Westfarthing said that one could see the Sea from the top of that tower; but no Hobbit had ever been known to climb it . . . They spoke less and less with the Elves, and grew afraid of them, and distrustful of those that had dealings with them; and the Sea became a word of fear among them, and a token of death, and they turned their faces away from the hills in the west.
> (Tolkien, 1965a, p. 17)

Sea-longing haunts Tolkien's characters. The earliest of them, Tuor, feels it at Vinyamar. All elves are driven by it, soon or late, like Legolas after he has ridden the Paths of the Dead. Frodo too at Cerin Amroth hears "far off great seas upon beaches that had long ago been washed away, and sea-birds crying whose race had perished from the earth" (Tolkien, 1965a, p. 366). *The Lord of the Rings* ends with the major characters taking ship at the Grey Havens. And an epilogue, only recently published, ends as that longing comes upon an ostensibly comfortable Sam, long after Frodo's departure. "He heard suddenly, deep and unstilled, the sigh and murmur of the Sea upon the shores of Middle-earth" (Tolkien, 1992, p. 128).

This sea-longing carries traditional significance: the rivers of time flow through Middle-earth to the sea, wherein lies the lost eternal world of the Eldar. But it also expresses Tolkien's motive for writing. Like his *Beowulf* poet Tolkien built from philology not only a house – his research and courses – but also a tower of fiction, which gave a glimpse of eternity beyond the modern prison and its intellectual systems based on conflict: Capitalism, Marxism, Fascism, Freudianism, Darwinism. *The Lord of the Rings* is a message from the Prisoners' Relief Society: a message of community. It begins with Bilbo's adoption of Frodo; extends to Frodo's devotion to the Shire; expands to include the members of the Fellowship, then their various peoples; and at last encompasses all Middle-earth. Evil is self-regarding and isolated. But from hobbits to elves, those on the side of good are moved by a sense of belonging to a larger thing. Sam's gardening, Frodo's affection for the Shire, the loyalty of the Fellowship, are really one thing. To be rooted is a drive shared by hobbits, elves, dwarves, men, trees, and even mountains: to be rooted in affection, yet desire the unknown sea.

Of such is the kingdom of heaven.

Having said this much about Tolkien's aim, let me return to his craft of fusion. I have already shown how he weds fantasy and realism to produce Middle-earth, but fusion is not limited to that combination. It produces many kinds of mixtures, using many kinds of materials. But all bear the same mark: qualities removed from their normal contexts and blended artfully to make a new thing. Neither it nor Middle-earth depend on magic, which Tolkien disliked. It depends on solid, patient, careful craft.

> I do not know what you mean by that [an elf responds when asked if elven-cloaks are magic] . . . They are elvish robes certainly, if that is what you mean. Leaf and branch, water and stone: they have the hue and beauty of all these things under the twilight of Lórien that we love; for we put the thought of all that we love into all that we make.
>
> (Tolkien, 1965a, p. 386)

The magic in Tolkien's world is, as Sam says, "right down deep, where . . . you can't see nobody working it" (Tolkien, 1965a, p. 376). Its effects are obvious but its operations nearly invisible.

Tolkien was a craftsman, therefore crafty. He was like a woodworker who makes a block of walnut seem flexible as caramel, or joins two pieces so cunningly that only the expert eye finds a seam. So his craft usually does its work without being noticed. But he did not keep his workshop locked. He led the reader through it in "On Fairy-Stories." There, he explained fantasy as a product of the same process which produces the adjective: the mind's ability to abstract. A mind which can remove green from grass, treating it as a separate quality, can also place it, at will, on a face, or a ceiling, or the sun. The mind has an innate ability to split wholes and abstract parts. The adjective, that common, unregarded aspect of language, is the key to the power of fantasy, which combines imagination (simple image-making) with art to achieve "the inner consistency of reality" (Tolkien, 1984b, p. 139). The combination is not necessarily significant. It is often frivolous, decorative, or fanciful. "Anyone inheriting the fantastic device of human language can say *the green sun*. Many can then imagine or picture it. But that is not enough" (Tolkien, 1984b, p. 140). Elvish craft "produces a Secondary World into which both designer and spectator can enter" (Tolkien, 1984b, p. 143).

Moria and Lórien, the realms of dwarf and elf, show the method, intertwining natural and human qualities and imposing the fusion on places. The beauties Tolkien associates with trees – grace, beauty, delight, longevity – he bestows on elves. At the same time, the human capacity to feel and respond, to deserve individual names, he bestows on trees. Mixing these things, he exchanges and fuses the human, the natural, and the fantastic till they are inseparable. "Whether they've made the land, or the land's made them, it's hard to say" (Tolkien, 1965a, p. 376). Dwarves, similarly, are the humanized forms of mineral qualities: hard, grim, enduring, unyielding; while places of stone and earth, such as Khazad-Dûm or Caradhras, have human qualities and make moral choices. Elves and dwarves are drawn partly from tradition, of course. But Tolkien uses the same process to make his own inventions: ents who are as ancient as their immemorial forest, and who boom and mutter about history and tales and the growth of words like a certain prominent philologist; the regal, civilized men of Gondor with their complex system of law, seven-volumed history, and seven-tiered city; the horsey riders of Rohan, their humanized horses, and the rolling horse-meadows which create both; and Hobbits, their furry toes, inns, six meals a day, and absorption in family trees drawn from the comfortable associations of rural Oxfordshire and the habits of Inklings. He was ingenious at abstracting qualities from their normal locations and fusing them with his own inventions to produce cultures, geography, languages, creatures.

Shelob is one of the best examples of fusion, joining the abstract, the physical, and the imaginary. She is "an evil thing in spider-form," Tolkien says at once (Tolkien, 1965b, p. 332), emphasizing abstraction. Yet, she is overwhelmingly physical: "Great horns she had, and behind her short stalk-like neck was her huge swollen body, a vast bloated bag, swaying and sagging between her legs" (Tolkien, 1965b, p. 334). She is arachnoid, of course, but not a spider so much as a fusion of many quite different spiders. Tunnelling spiders, for instance, are not web spinners; and neither chases prey, as Shelob chases Frodo. But Shelob's most marked features are fabulous: her mythic size and age. She is ancient beyond telling, one:

> such as Beren fought in the Mountains of Terror in Doriath, and so came to Lúthien upon the green sward amid the hemlocks in the moonlight long ago. How Shelob came there, flying from ruin, no tale tells, for out of the Dark Years few tales have come. But still she was there, who was there before Sauron, and before the first stone of Barad-dûr . . . Far and wide her lesser broods . . . spread from glen to glen, from the Ephel Dúath to the eastern hills, to Dol Guldur and the fastnesses of Mirkwood. But none could rival her, Shelob the Great, last child of Ungoliant to trouble the unhappy world.
>
> (Tolkien, 1965b, p. 332)

A lineage longer than Aragorn's, names from the mythic past, places covering half a continent, all weave her into Middle-earth, giving solidity and reality to the fabulous. The tactic is ingenious, for these specified places and names are inventions every bit as much as Shelob herself. But it is a rare reader who pauses to think so, much less to disentangle the web. The technique does its work by intertwining the conventions of realism and fantasy, creating a real-seeming dream whose parts are syllables. This careful specifying of mythic times, places, and people is a technique Tolkien made uniquely his own. He called his work "feigned history," a paradox which should make us pause. The tale is an account of the end of the Third Age, buttressed by chronologies, maps, and the sort of historical material we find in "Prologue: Concerning Hobbits." The carefully constructed network of topography, geography, history, cultures, and languages which makes Middle-earth all but tangible is the most obvious and frequently recognized aspect of *The Lord of the Rings* and needs no further comment. But Tolkien does not simply pile up false facts to gain verisimilitude. He is more subtle and artful than that. No one is taken in by Tolkien's history, any more than by his feigned role as editor and translator of the "Red Book of Westmarch". These things cater, rather, to our desire to believe. The fusion of feigning and history arouses a desire to enter the fantasy and promotes the illusion that we can. The way we read the maps and chronologies mimics conventional ways of treating space and time as Tolkien fuses recognized conventions of representation with invented space and time. Much of our conviction that his fantasy can be entered comes from redundancy: a judicious amount of material which goes beyond the requirements of story. Most of the places on the map of the Shire are gratuitous, like Brockenborings in the East Farthing or Needlehole in the West. They never appear in the story but remain names. Many events in the chronology of kings also lie outside the story: Rómendacil I's death in battle in 541; or the inauguration of Falastur in 830. Tolkien's place names too change according to the observed laws of actual language. Linguistic corruption has made "Brandywine" out of "Baranduin," and the Baranduin River is clearly related to the Anduin further east. Like real languages, Tolkien's are also consistent, as in the use of roots and suffixes: Forodwaith, Enedwaith, Haradwaith.

T.A. Shippey has analysed the varied styles of speech of Tolkien's characters. But that pattern is only one aspect of a larger stylistic strategy which allows Tolkien to fuse levels of diction, from high rhetoric to realistic description to satire, shifting so smoothly that one rarely notices. Everyone feels the comic incongruity when Pippin responds to Théoden King by whispering to Merry, "So that is the King of Rohan! A fine old fellow. Very polite" (Tolkien, 1965b, p. 164). But not one reader in a thousand sees the shifts in Tolkien's narrative voice. All seems perfectly natural while it is going on, but to take up three different passages is to almost feel one is looking at three different books. The playful style of the beginning does not balk at coy coinages like "eleventy-first birthday," or "*tweens*, as the hobbits called the irresponsible twenties" (Tolkien, 1965a, p. 29). The swift, straightforward voice of the action scenes is quite different. "The sun was already westering as they rode from Edoras, and the light of it was in their eyes, turning all the rolling fields of Rohan to a golden haze" (Tolkien, 1965b, p. 131). And neither of those styles is much like Tolkien's poetic prose.

> His golden shield was uncovered, and lo! it shone like an image of the Sun, and the grass flamed into green about the white feet of his steed. For morning came, morning and a wind from the sea; and darkness was removed, and the hosts of Mordor wailed, and terror took them, and they fled, and died, and the hoofs of wrath rode over them.

(Tolkien, 1965c, pp. 112-113)

Individuals may, of course, prefer one style to another. But it is a remarkable feat to bind them together so cunningly that not a single fuss about "stylistic inconsistency" has been heard for almost forty years. The reader experiences not a combination of styles but a fusion: a seamless unity.

Tolkien's flexibility extends even to himself. As narrator, he is a major presence at the beginning of the book; but he is quietly removed thereafter. In the "Foreword," he is the author, though a little uncertain about that role. At moments, he writes as if he has made this book; at others as if he has discovered it; at still others leans in both directions simultaneously. Part editor of the Red Book of Westmarch, part gentle satirist, part irritable critic of his critics, he is a fusion: a voice inviting us into the book. In the "Prologue," he is a scholar providing a helpful selection of information about hobbits. Particularly ingenious is his revised account of Bilbo's discovery of the One Ring, which he treats not as a revision but as a lie revealed, showing the effects of the Ring on its bearer. By "Chapter I" he has been reduced to a jovial presence in parenthetical asides and playful comments. And that is the last we hear of him. By the second chapter, the book has become mimetic, as thoroughly dramatized as any late nineteenth-century novel. With no audible narrative voice, the words as words fade, so that we seem to experience events. The elements of language which call attention to itself, or to the author as stylist, are avoided. Anglo-Saxon words dominate; sentences are normally short or mid-length, in that loose order which makes comprehension effortless for the modern reader: subject, followed by predicate, followed by objects and modifiers. The main principles of organization are time and space, other kinds of subordination used sparingly. An almost exclusive focus on actions and the senses promotes the illusion of sensory experience rather than a tale told. For example, in Moria:

> He raised his staff, and for a brief instant there was blaze like a flash of lightning. Great shadows sprang up and fled, and for a second they saw a vast roof far above their heads upheld by many mighty pillars hewn of stone. Before them and on either side stretched a huge empty hall; its black walls, polished and smooth as glass, flashed and glittered. Three other entrances they saw, dark black arches: one straight before them eastwards, and one on either side. Then the light went out.

(Tolkien, 1965a, pp. 328-329)

But Tolkien is not Conrad. The strategy does not simply aim to make the reader see. Like the realistic description of willows with which I began, it has one aim: to make the imaginary believable. And the more fantastic the events, the more tightly Tolkien screws down his style. About eighty percent of "The White Rider," for instance, consists of dialogue. All the rest describes action. But "The White Rider" contains the greatest risk and most astounding passage in *The Lord of the Rings*, Gandalf's return from the dead.

Tolkien showed his keen awareness of language as strategy in a letter to Hugh Brogan, a former student who had called the dialogue in "The King of the Golden Hall" fustian. Tolkien replied that he ought to distinguish between fustian and actual antiquarian language, which he had used because "many of [the] things said could not be said in our slack and often frivolous idiom" (Tolkien, 1981, pp. 225). His point was that language ought to be appropriate to particular ways of thinking rather than simply follow contemporary usage. It is a mistake to trick out a counterfeit warrior in modern words. Tolkien knew how cultures use language to form thought. But he also knew that the fantasist, by virtue of being a fantasist, can escape those "cookie-cutter sentences, all alike" which, just like grey uniforms, are prison-issue. Doing so, however, was not a simple matter of inserting antique language into his book. He needed to invent a style fusing his knowledge of archaic words and modern prose. Théoden's dialogue, the target of Brogan's objection, is a case in point. Here is the moment, in "Helm's Deep," which justifies character and speech.

> "The end will not be long," said the king. "But I will not end here, taken like an old badger in a trap. Snowmane and Hasufel and the horses of my guard are in the inner court. When dawn comes, I will bid men sound Helm's horn, and I will ride forth. Will you ride with me then, son of Arathorn? Maybe we shall cleave a road, or make such an end as will be worth a song – if any be left to sing of us hereafter."
> "I will ride with you," said Aragorn.
> (Tolkien, 1965b, pp. 144-145)

No modern speaker could say, "The end will not be long" without feeling stagey or archaic. No ancient speaker could say, "I will not end here, taken like an old badger in a trap," at all. Yet the reader experiences the speech not as two clashing styles but as one, proper to Théoden and no one else. The fusion, and the triumph of Tolkien's approach to style, are complete.

Tolkien's approach to language as strategy is, finally, only one aspect, though a large one, of his ideas about words, and especially word-making, which produced such a brilliant horse-name as Hasufel. There is neither time nor space here to take up the expansive subject of Tolkien's relationship to language. But I can point to Tolkien's lifelong attempt to wed things, thoughts, and sounds as a final example of fusion and at least one key to his poetics.

Not just Théoden but all Middle-earth is preoccupied with song. And in many ways *The Lord of the Rings* is about language as an escape from time and conflict into love and delight. In Middle-earth words – simple sounds – have power. And words – simple sounds – have power over Tolkien's readers. The realm of Faerie, Tolkien said, includes "ourselves, mortal men, when we are enchanted" (Tolkien, 1984b, p. 113): literally, brought inside song. One thinks of Sam rubbing his eyes in the light of Lothlórien and saying, "this is more elvish than anything I ever heard tell of. I feel as if I was *inside* a song, if you take my meaning" (Tolkien, 1965a, p. 365). That is the essential experience of Tolkien's readers. He works magic with sound, creating a poetry of names: Galadriel, Palantír, Rohirrim, Mordor. The effect of these fantasy names is one of the splendours of *The Lord of the Rings*. The names are so familiar now that we almost forget they were ever new – the pleasure with which we first heard of Legolas, Gimli, Gandalf, Frodo, Bilbo – and our sense that they had the same kind of rightness as names like Ebenezer Scrooge, Tom Jones, Robinson Crusoe. Tolkien makes names that never were, and the cultures which produced them, seem as natural as the sun. Names like Cerin Amroth, Michel Delving, Meduseld, Moria, Minas Tirith create whole peoples. It is not simply that each invented tongue adds to the vision beyond the prison. Naming is itself a way of breaching walls. If there ever was a time (as Owen Barfield believed, apparently with Tolkien's support) when language had semantic unity, making one thing of body and spirit, inner and outer, that time is lost in prehistory. Language, especially poetic language, tries to join inner perception and outer reality. But the language we know, and that Tolkien knew, cannot succeed in doing so because words are social products, evolved through long historical backgrounds. We are always using someone else's words – words rubbed and thumbed-over and smudged until even our most intimate expressions are palimpsests. So language is never quite on the mark. And above all, as an historical linguist like Tolkien well knew, it never stops changing. Of all things we make, words are the most human: the most us. But Tolkien resisted the idea that words are made only by cultures or that the fusion of sound, sense, and object is entirely beyond our craft. In Middle-earth, at least, all language is elvish. "Elves made all the old words: they began it," says Treebeard/Tolkien (Tolkien, 1965b, p. 68). That implies a good deal, for elvish language has wondrous effects. The hobbits, hearing an elvish song, "partly understood" it, without knowing the language. "The sound blending with the melody seemed to shape itself in their thought into words" (Tolkien, 1965a, p. 88). That happens again at Rivendell and once more in Lothlórien, when Galadriel sings a Quenya song that Frodo does not understand but which is so engraved in memory that he later translates it. Tolkien clearly believed language is more than a social phenomenon, for he created fourteen languages with no social function at all. Sense lies deeper than culture. Language can express meaning independent of history or culture: not nouns which mark known objects but sea-sounds which mark the yearnings of the heart and the something for which it yearns. That perception of the relationship of sound to meaning may be anathema to most contemporary linguists, but it is a commonplace among musicians. And it runs long roots through Tolkien's work, where language is music, meaning is everywhere, and even things speak. This is true fantasy: Tolkien's version, in truth, of one of the deepest human desires: that the world should make sense.

Frodo, in a passage I have already quoted, reacts to Lothlórien as Tolkien might, experiencing familiar yet unknown colours "as if he had at that moment first perceived them and made for them names new and wonderful." Perceiving the unfamiliar is not particularly Tolkienian. But making names new and wonderful is. And his practice issues a challenge to linguists. No theory which omits the capacity of language to give airy shape to our longings can be complete or convincing. Cultural theories of language allow us to reconstruct former realities, but only a theory which includes the capacity of language to articulate the nameless allows for the Word in its Christian sense, the *logos*. "In the beginning was the Word," begins the philological text Tolkien placed most faith in. "And the Word was with God;

and the Word was God." It is an almost-forgotten ideal which the twentieth century, dominated by political and social ideologues, has rejected. But Tolkien had not forgotten it. He made the elven tongues because the human heart wants a language where sound, sense, and beauty converge. Much has been said about the roots of his invented words and names in Welsh, Finnish, Old Norse, Icelandic, Anglo-Saxon. But a search into his sources, like one into his biography, seems to me to read backward. It is not his sources we want but his elvish craft, his glimpse of the sea, Galadriel singing to the hobbits as they glide away on the river of time:

Namárië! Nai hiruvalyë Valimar.
Nai elyë hiruva. Namárië!

References

Tolkien, J.R.R. 1965a. *The Fellowship of the Ring*. Boston: Houghton Mifflin.

Tolkien, J.R.R. 1965b. *The Two Towers*. Boston: Houghton Mifflin.

Tolkien, J.R.R. 1965c. *The Return of the King*. Boston: Houghton Mifflin.

Tolkien, J.R.R. 1981. *The Letters of J.R.R. Tolkien*, ed. Humphrey Carpenter. Boston: Houghton Mifflin.

Tolkien, J.R.R. 1984a. "Beowulf: The Monsters and the Critics" in *The Monsters and the Critics and Other Essays*, pp. 5-48. Boston: Houghton Mifflin.

Tolkien, J.R.R. 1984b. "On Fairy-Stories" in *The Monsters and the Critics and Other Essays*, pp. 109-161. Boston: Houghton Mifflin.

Tolkien, J.R.R. 1992. *Sauron Defeated*, ed. Christopher Tolkien. London: HarperCollins.

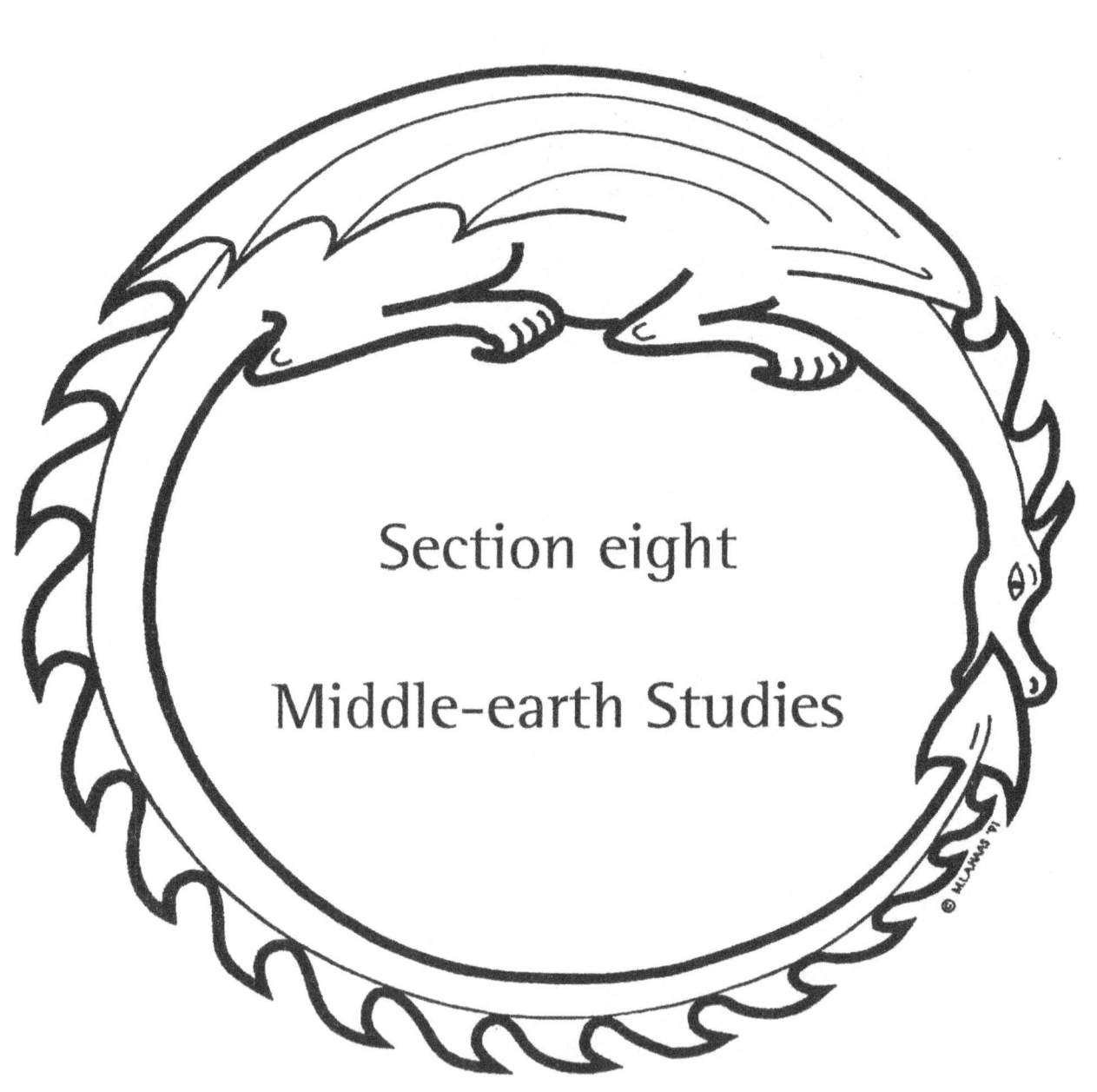

Section eight

Middle-earth Studies

A Physics of Middle-earth

Jenny Coombs and Marc Read (delivered by Marc Read)

Abstract: This paper takes a light-hearted look at how far one can go in applying primary world science to Middle-earth. Tolkien purists and physics purists may wish to pass over this!

Keywords: foresight, genetics, palantíri, physics, sight, swords, technology

Tolkien wrote in Letter 210 that "I dislike . . . any pull towards 'scientification' . . . No analysis in any laboratory would discover chemical properties of *lembas* that made it superior to other cakes of wheat-meal." However, he also wrote, in Letter 131, that his works should "leave scope for other minds and hands, wielding paint and music and drama." Yes; and why not science?

There seem to be at least two ways of going about a scientific analysis of the various features that make Middle-earth different from the world that we inhabit today. We can attempt to explain away magic by showing how the seemingly magical effects could, in fact, be produced by the operation of the physical laws that we all know and love. This is the approach which is favoured by my co-author. The other way is merely to provide new scientific laws to govern Middle-earth: and if these clash with the ones that we use, well, so much for the idea that Middle-earth and our world are one and the same. Perhaps there is a middle way, and this is the one that I prefer. Under this approach we can explain those things which fit neatly with our science, and plead lack of information instead of explaining the others – lack of information either about physics, or about Middle-earth. It is into this mould that this paper most easily falls. We shall discuss the worth of this whole scheme later in the paper.

We can put some of these principles into operation by looking more closely at the information that we are given about the various races of Middle-earth, and this is what we intend to do to in this paper. Elves, dwarves, hobbits and men each have their own peculiarities. Here we shall be looking at some quirks of biology, science and technology in Middle-earth. It is true that our title claims to examine physics, but titles of papers often prove deceptive. Anyway, "Science is either physics or stamp-collecting," in the words of Rutherford, and neither of us indulges in philately.

Elves are strange. Even the most cursory reading of the works will lead anyone to that conclusion, especially if we think about the Elves of *The Hobbit* (which I suspect that we would rather not do). They can intermarry with men and produce fertile offspring, and thus they are the same species, by definition. I rather fancy that any man attempting to inform Elves about this matter of definition would reduce his life-expectancy dramatically. However, they have physical differences from us, the most obvious being that they do not die. However strange this may at first appear, it is much more confusing why other races *do* age and die than why the First-born do not. Our cells gradually stop renewing themselves: the Elves' just stay as good as new. More surprising is the total immunity of the elves to disease. It seems that one or the other of these factors can be inherited in those of mixed blood, who are longer-lived than their purely human contemporaries. It is a debatable point whether this longevity is due to a resistance to disease or an extension of the time until cell renewal begins to break down, or both. The tolerance of various races to disease is highly questionable, since we don't seem to have any records of individuals' (as opposed to entire populations') falling prey to natural illnesses. But back to Elves.

Elven eyesight is known to be very good. Legolas can spot an orc-host at twelve leagues, and give fairly detailed descriptions of Éomer's éored at a distance of five leagues. This is remarkable, and highly embarrassing for Aragorn, though Gimli refuses to be impressed. Resolving power depends on the width of the aperture and the wavelength of the light observed. A back-of-the-envelope calculation (always the best sort) established that if Legolas used only visible light, he would have been a bug-eyed monster, to the extent of having eyes on stalks in order to fit in a human-shaped face. Rather than force all known Tolkien illustrators to redraw their life's work, we concluded that Elves have more of the high-frequency spectrum available to them. Assuming resolution of half a metre at fifteen miles, and a roughly human-sized pupil, we find that their visible spectrum extends to about 170nm, or 2000 THz – impossibly high energy. Maybe the tale grew in the telling, but this does not affect our main point: that Elves could see well at least into the ultra-violet – and this is not really so improbable. Many insects can see UV; as indeed could humans if only their lenses were removed (our receptors respond to high frequencies but they are blocked by our lenses). All that is required therefore is for Elven lenses to transmit high energy electromagnetic waves. Increased resolution also requires higher-density retinal receptors – but this is a purely physiological point and therefore not significant.

Something else is remarkable about Legolas's sighting of the riders. He can see that there are 105 men galloping across the plains (possibly including Éomer). It is possible that he was merely counting very quickly (and even this would be a considerable feat), but a more attractive explanation would be that he has just seen that there are this many, as I might see directly that there are two or three objects in front of me without having to count them. I find personally that I can only see twos, threes and possibly fours in this manner – larger groups are broken up into these and then summed. I don't know if this is typical of humans generally; but it seems inconceivable that 105 could be grasped "just like that" by any normal man. Feats such as these can be performed by some autistic people, which indicates that they are not entirely alien to the human brain, though. Elves would probably be the annoying types who know their Log tables by heart and could do any sort of mental arithmetic. Pure Maths seems to be the sort of field attractive to folk who have at best a tenuous connection with everyday affairs, and we can imagine Fermat's Last Theorem's having no terrors for the Eldar.

We know a further difference between Elves and Men, and this is related to their metabolism. During the pursuit of the orc-hoards across Rohan, we are told of Legolas that "in the waybread of the Elves he found all the sustenance that he needed." Now we shall perform the banned chemical analysis of lembas. It certainly could not have contained much (if any) Vitamin C, for that chemical decomposes rapidly. It is highly unlikely that Elves did not require this vitamin, and so we may conclude that they synthesised their own, like all primary-world animals save guinea-pigs, monkeys and men. The others, certainly, are worn down more quickly on the chase, and we attribute a certain part of this to malnutrition; lack of vitamin C, as well as leading eventually to scurvy, also causes anæmia, since it is required for the absorption of iron into the body.

We notice that the gene for beardlessness is transmitted from Elves to Half-Elves, and is to be found in those with even the slightest blood relation to the eldar. Círdan is a bearded mutant. A highly debatable theory is that he was sporting a false beard in homage to the Istari, or as a sign of solidarity with the dwarves of the Ered Luin. My co-author is tempted to hazard that Njal, as in the *Saga of Burnt*, has elven blood: at least he displays the typically Elven characteristics, of wisdom, prescience and beardlessness. Possibly there were Númenórean descendents among the Norsemen; this would account for their skill in sea-faring and also their predilection for killing anyone who disagreed with them. Talk of beards naturally leads to talk of the Khazâd. In *The Hobbit*, they are resplendent in beards of white, yellow and (surprisingly) blue. This is however, a possible result of small amounts of black pigment – we do not need to assume that Dwalin was making a fashion statement.

We move on to a consideration of the Dwarves. Mike Percival wrote a good article in *Mallorn* a few years ago about the draining of Moria (1988, pp. 30-32), and it seems reasonable to suppose that they had access to geothermal technology at the height of their civilization. I hope that I do not offend either engineers or Dwarves by saying that the Dwarves were the engineers of Middle-earth. On a related theme, it was encouraging to see in *The Treason of Isengard* that Tolkien toyed with the idea of Saruman's holding a Dwarven ring: certainly the wizard's technological aspirations fit in with the dwarves' racial characteristics. In their heyday, the Dwarves supplied armour and weaponry to the Elves. In return the Elves heaped abuse on their valiant but short comrades, whom they charmingly nick-named 'Naugrim', or 'Stunted Ones'. But this is not the place to pursue the pro-Dwarven sentiments of Taruithorn. The dwarves also appear to have been less isolationist than the First-born, freely trading their technology with, say, the hobbits.

The technology of the Edain didn't regain the heights of the Númenóreans until well after the end of the Third Age. One fragment in *The Lost Road* even refers to flying ships in the years immediately following the Akallabêth. This leads us into the murky waters of reliability of sources, which we shall return to before too long. It is tempting to think flying ships a legend that sprang up because of the incredible achievements of the Dúnedain, much as in later years the Palantíri were transformed into legends of bird-like spirits bringing messages to the King. We must be careful, though, in deciding which technologies to discard in this matter. Flying ships we can discount, as being removed from all later versions of the story.

It has often been asked why the technological level of the survivors of the Downfall was so low, and why what technology they did have had so many seeming lacunæ. As one example, there seems to be no reference to printing. However, this is quite a straightforward technology, certainly within the grasp of those who made steel bows, and is one of those inventions which is relatively simple to develop once someone has had the initial idea. There are, we suggest, two reasons for this phenomenon. The first is that the technology of Númenor was artificially accelerated by a certain Annatar, Lord of Gifts. And what possible gift other than knowledge could he give, given his situation? It would then hardly be strange to find the considerable resources of the race being concentrated on weapons research. But even so, this would not explain such obvious gaps.

To do this, we must consider the position of the Faithful. They were opposed to everything that Sauron stood for, and would, we suggest, have seen any advanced technologies as being the works of the devil. It was unfortunate from a technological point of view that Middle-earth was colonised by intolerably proud Luddites, technophobes who would use not Númenórean technology but the sword and the bow. The surviving artefacts, such as the Palantíri, were Elven made. The fear of a second Akallabêth obviously scared the Faithful and their descendants away from developing anything much of their own accord. Even at the end of the Third Age, we still have the office of King's Scribe in Gondor.

Nevertheless, the Faithful brought with them some truly powerful items: the Palantíri. We have here the benefit of a remarkably full description of their powers and operation, in the chapter "The Palantíri" in *Unfinished Tales*. The trouble is that they do not seem to operate by any known physical laws. However, it is indisputable that they do operate according to some sort of strict laws. The lesser stones, at any rate, must be oriented correctly in order for them to be used; and using the stones, a "surveyor" could see things many miles away, unless the location he was scrying was dark. Telepathic conversations could be held between the operators of two stones; and the Osgiliath stone could eavesdrop on any of these conversations. Just to complicate the matter still further, the stone at Emyn Beraid looked only Westward to the stone at Avallónë and was not connected to the other stones in any way. Indeed, the mention of a Stone in the Far West is surprising: presumably communication could have been set up between the Faithful (who had control of the stones) and Valinor. This could explain a lot, including the Faithful's knowledge of the plan of Ar-Pharazôn and their preparations for fleeing the Downfall.

So how could these things operate? Given that they can see through mountains, one might imagine that they "saw" by means of some sort of radiation that isn't blocked easily, like neutrinos, but in that case why should they reflect off the target? And why can't the stones see into dark places? That suggests some sort of visible electromagnetic radiation, unless "dark" is being used metaphorically. This, though, seems unlikely, and light isn't noted for its tendency to go through mountains. Possibly the light is bounced off something; but what? A satellite? It seems unlikely that Eärendil is sitting there with a mirror, even though he may be described as the Flammifer of Westernesse. It's at this stage that we could mutter sagely, "Hmm. Insufficient data." Even Terry Pratchett's standard cop-out, "it's quantum, innit?", doesn't help us here.

If we wish to press on in this matter, we must invoke a scientific principle which has long been the domain of authors wishing to lend an air of spurious verisimilitude to an otherwise bald and unconvincing narrative. Yes, folks, it's time for Hyperspace. Some of you may have read an article by a certain Marc Read in *Amon Hen* (1989, pp. 17-18) many years ago, attempting to explain the globing of the world and the removal of the Valar as a change from a Euclidean topology of space to a Minkowski topology of space-time. Perhaps extra physical dimensions are the single most useful tool in today's science for the Pseudo-Scientist. When we read about superstring theory requiring a number of physical dimensions which runs well into double figures, perhaps we feel that our explanations aren't so silly after all. But the counter-intuitive nature of modern science, fascinating though it is, is only a digression. Let us return to our hyperspatial Palantíri.

The way in which the vision of the Stone is not blocked, and yet is restricted to the light illuminating the actual scene being observed, goes to suggest that the scene is not being transmitted to the Stone by any radiation. Rather, it would seem that the scene is directly observed by the Surveyor. It is as if the Surveyor were actually there. Or, to put it another way, it is as if the light from the scene travelled directly to the Palantír. What better way for this to happen than for the light to travel down a "wormhole", a hyperspatial tunnel, it need only be a tiny size. Any light entering this volume would then travel directly to the stone. The various ways of controlling the palantír then translate to various ways of controlling the motion of this camera-space. The light takes a short-cut through another physical dimension. The standard analogy formed by removing one dimension may come in handy here – instead of looking around the surface of a sphere, we look from one point on the surface to another through the space in the middle. Of course, this is perfectly ridiculous. Although it is a nice picture, it would end up with, in effect, faster-than-light travel. Admittedly, the only thing travelling faster than light would be light itself, which mercifully rules out the possibility of Elven, Palantír-powered, jump-driven starships, but this is still enough to make causality a headache for anyone. Although this is a drawback from the scientific point of view, it might well be seen as a bonus from the textual point of view; after all, Palantíri can also see backwards and forwards in time, and that really could result in causality migraines.

Even this pseudo-explanation doesn't tie in with all the facts that we are given about the Stones. How could Osgiliath eavesdrop? A repeater station located in hyperspace? Surely such a thing is beyond the realm of possibility, unless one is E.E. 'Doc' Smith. And how are thoughts transmitted between two Palantíri in the same network? As Jenny sums up the whole matter of hyperspatial communications, "Aaaaaaaaaargh!"

The whole question of foreseeing the future is a vexed one. The Mirror of Galadriel shows possible futures, including things that may not come to pass. Such an intrusion of probability reminds us instantly of the field of Quantum Mechanics. A fascinating *Horizon* programme on television about a month ago (1992) revealed that theoretical physicists are coming to accept the so-called Many Worlds interpretation, and some other serious and possibly sober theoreticians are starting to suggest that time travel, of a sort, is a possibility. The "of a sort" is very important here and I shall discuss it now. The main objection to time travel is that it would seem to be open to the Grandfather paradox – what would happen if I killed my grandfather before my father was born?

The solution to this lies in the Many Worlds theory. This is an interpretation of quantum mechanics which suggests that every possible quantum event actually occurs. If (as is usually the case) two or more events are contradictory – the wave function collapses into one state or another – then the Universe splits. In one branch event "A" happens, in another it does not. In the classic thought-experiment, we may say that in one branch, Berúthiel's cat is killed, and the in other it remains alive. For many years this was seen to be the most flagrant breach of Occam's Razor imaginable: we're inventing untold universes just to avoid letting probability in. Jenny points out that it is impossible to breach a razor, but let that pass. Now I have been reliably informed that cosmologists, being depressed about dealing with only one universe, think that the other Many worlds have at least as much claim to existence as ours. Weird.

The most interesting thought that comes with this ontological nightmare is that perhaps some sort of communication between the parallel worlds (for want of a better term) is possible. Thus, it has been argued, we could have the equivalent of time travel so long as we stepped "sideways" in time, and across to a parallel world, so keeping all time-lines unmuddled. Any science fiction author who tried to get away with this would probably be laughed at, but it's just another example of Haldane's law in action: "The Universe is not only queerer than we suppose, it is queerer than we can suppose."

Anyhow, it now seems that we could explain Galadriel's Mirror as being a way of looking into the various parallel worlds. The time difference could be explained away by having worlds which developed at slightly different rates. After all, there is going to be a vast number of worlds out there. Indeed, J. Danforth Quayle's famous quantity comes in handy here – "nearly infinite". This explanation seems vaguely unsatisfactory but I am horribly afraid that it could be backed up by science. Any theoretical physicists out there are invited to do the maths, and let us know the results; perhaps by the Bicentenary conference. The question is basically, would such a device violate any physical laws? As Gell-Mann said, "Whatever is not forbidden is compulsory." Suffice to say that this is an area of real interest in modern research, especially for science fiction fans and rationalising pseudo-scientists.

We can now look at some of the powers of the Rings. I think that it is fair to say that they can be seen as the products of the various effects mentioned here and in our earlier paper (Coombs & Read, 1991). The ability to locate the other wearers and, perhaps, know their thoughts seems closely related to the functions of the Palantír. Amon Hen seems to act as a natural amplifier for the power of vision; it is terrifying to think what might happen to a ring wearer on Amon Lhaw. The problems of invisibility we have implicitly handled in our earlier paper, "Valaquanta". They also seem to amplify the wielder's natural ability – another idea closely tied in with our earlier work.

My co-author has turned her attention to two different examples of "magic" in Arda, and treated each in a different way. First, the Silmarils. These are bright, but not blinding to look at; it is unlikely that their luminosity exceeds that of a 100W light-bulb. Yet we are told that a silmaril became the morning-star. The obvious explanation, if explanation we seek, is that this is mythology, a story told by an ancient people; in reality, of course, Eärendil is Venus, the poisonous, sulphurous second planet. It is entertaining, however, to imagine for a moment that we are in a universe where the morning-star is a Silmaril, a few miles above the earth. The problem then arises of how the silmaril is still visible, and so bright; similar problems occur with the story of the Sun and Moon. In *The Book of Lost Tales* (Tolkien, 1983, p. 201), the Sun increases in heat and brilliance after its launching, so that, as Christopher Tolkien comments "the reflection rises less readily that if the Sun that brilliantly illumines the whole Earth was but one fruit of Laurelin then Valinor must have been painfully bright and hot in the days of the Trees"! But in Tolkien's later writing there is no mention of any such increase in luminosity. So why do the heavenly bodies still look bright? Or rather, why do we feel that they *ought* to look dimmer?

Well, that may be because we all have an instinctive feeling for the inverse-square law, which governs how distant objects appear to dim. So, we could either question the assumption that the Morning-Star is just a silmaril, without maintaining that it is a planet, or we could see what would happen if the inverse-square law did not hold. Let's consider the second case first.

The inverse-square law is simply derived for the case of an isotropic light-source emitting at constant power, P. The brightness as seen by an observer at a distance, r, away from the source depends on the power density at the location of the observer, which is $P/4\pi r^2$ since the light spreads out equally over the surface of a sphere. Hence the brightness falls off at $1/r^2$ – the inverse-square law.

We shall now consider the two-dimensional case. Consider a light-source on a plane, which emits a "light-circle" instead of a light-sphere. The brightness presumably depends on power per unit length, instead of power per unit area. The brightness to an observer at a distance r from the source would therefore be $P/2\pi r^2$. But this formula could be readily be changed if the light, instead of travelling in a plane, were to travel on some more complicated two-dimensional curve. Imagine, for instance, that the light-source, the observer and the light are all constrained to move on the surface of a sphere of radius a. Then elementary geometry shows that the brightness falls off not as $1/r$, but as the reciprocal of $a.\sin(r/a)$. If Arda were the three-dimensional surface of a suitable four-dimensional object, the desired function of brightness against distance could be obtained; that is to say, one in which light sources appear much brighter when they are further away. The problem is that of finding such a strange object. Jenny has devoted much thought to this, but, despite constructing many three-dimensional diagrams out of paper and mutilated satsumas, has had to give up. Is there an n-dimensional topologist in the house?

There are other possibilities concerning Eärendil. What was Vingilot made of? After all, we can see certain artificial satellites from reflected light. But what light could it reflect? This raises the whole problem of the Sun, as mentioned earlier. Perhaps some layer of the atmosphere acted as a natural photomultiplier, solving all our problems at a single stroke. I am attached to this explanation but can think of no justification for it whatsoever. Still, when has that ever got in the way of a good theory? Anyway, we shall now turn to the other area which Jenny has been investigating.

As we stated at the start of this paper, there is another way of going about things, which is to maintain that Middle-earth is *our* earth, and that therefore all its physical laws must be compatible with ours. Let us pursue this line of thought for a while. Our principle weapon will be source criticism. The various histories and legends of Arda exist as many different documents, in a great variety of styles, and are often flatly contradictory. Consider the difference, for example, in stye as well as plot, between the playful "Tale of Tinúviel" in *Lost Tales* (Tolkien, 1984, pp. 3-48), and the sombre "Lay of Leithian" (Tolkien, 1985, pp. 150-308). Clearly these can be regarded as Tolkien's successive reworks and adaptations of the myths.

It is more rewarding, however, to consider them as equally valid in the secondary world, but as representing different traditions, from different ages and cultures, of the same facts or legends. And, just as with primary-world historical sources, one must consider not only the material but its author: when he lived, what his culture was, how close he was to the events he describes, how he gathered his information. Many of the documents we have are songs or lays; has the poet adapted his material for dramatic effect, or for some other reason? To understand *The Æneid* one must consider Maecenas, who commissioned the work, as well as Virgil who wrote it. When discussing the portrayal of Orcs, one must remember that history is written by the victors. The racist, misanthropic tone of *The Silmarillion* betrays its Elven origin; and the constant reference to the great height of the heroes of the War of the Ring makes sense when we remember that the Red Book was written by hobbits.

So what is the relevance of this to a discussion of science? It is that one need not take every statement at face-value, as we have already shown. Exaggeration, confusion, and misunderstanding all play their part in the description of technological artefacts, especially when such artefacts belong to a civilization other than the narrator's, and to a technology he does not understand. An example is the Elven swords, Orcrist, Glamdring, and Sting, which magically glow in the dark to indicate the proximity of Orcs.

Whereas Jenny can accept the Palantíri as products of some far-advanced science, she baulks at luminous ironmongery. This seems to be "magic" pure and simple. She prefers to say that the reports that the swords glow when Orcs approached are untrue: they are based on rumour, exaggeration, and superstitious belief in the omnipotence of the ancient Elven science that produced them. Rather than being actually self-luminous, the swords were in fact only highly reflective. In dark surroundings, they reflected what available light there was, and so still seemed bright, just as white clothing shows up more at night. Over time this was distorted into the legend that the swords emitted their own light, and eventually that they glowed to indicate the presence of enemies.

Elven swords are in fact repeatedly referred to as "bright"; though how far this is merely a rhetorical adjective is hard to say. The ancient Elven swords are also prized for their strength. Both of these could be explained if the Noldor at the height of their civilisation were capable of manufacturing large single crystals of metal. This is a technology which we are just beginning to master. Normal metal consists of many small grains, or crystals, of metal atoms bonded in grain structures. Fracture occurs at grain boundaries; the size of the grains affects the strength of the metal; techniques such as tempering and work-hardening depend on this. If a sword consisted of monocrystalline iron, it would be very resistant to many forms of stress. It would also, due to its uniform surface, be highly reflective.

Now, I would be quite happy to accept monocrystalline swords, and of course the general point about source analysis. In this case, though, I think that reports of glowing swords are not greatly exaggerated. The sources that we have are relatively reliable; presumably the translated version of the Red Book was the annotated copy of Findegil, only two copies removed from the original. Bilbo could well be forgiven for making up some of the excesses of *There and Back Again*, but the Red Book was destined to be read by the great and the wise. The whole question is simply one of where to draw the lines between magic, legend and science.

This is much harder than it may sound. Clarke's Law is often cited in this context: that "any sufficiently advanced technology would be indistinguishable from magic." I suppose that most people would accept this; the disagreements start when someone tries to argue, fallaciously, from this to the idea that anything that is indistinguishable from magic must be advanced technology. Logically, this is the fallacy of affirming the consequent; to make the latter claim is to say far more than is stated by Clarke's Law, which is unobjectionable in itself.

It will be useful for the purpose of this discussion to set up two hypothetical Tolkien fans, the Scientist and the Magician. I hasten to add that both of these are caricatures; we are leaving the final decision to you. None of you will be surprised to hear that we're on the side of the Scientist in this argument. Perhaps the difference between Jenny and myself is that she is a little constant in her views while I waver with the natural indecision of the philosophy student.

The Magician really can't see the point of a paper like this. Almost certainly, he's not interested in science much in the primary world. Even if he is, he doesn't see why any of it should apply to Middle-earth. The Scientist makes him feel vaguely angry, and he feels a great temptation to jump up and down shouting, "He that breaks a thing to find out what it is has left the path of wisdom." He feels cheated if Magic is explained away: something precious has been lost, in his estimation. Perhaps the reason that he likes Tolkien so much is that he can find in Middle-earth the mysteries which are so elusive in today's over-scientific age.

The Scientist thinks that if man didn't break things from time to time we'd still be sitting in caves. He's probably got at least some scientific training. He really cannot understand the irrational technophobia of the Magician. He probably likes Middle-earth because of its inner consistency and logic. For him, the whole logic of that world breaks down if it cannot be codified and regulated somehow.

The Magician cannot help but admire the passage in Keats:
There was an awful rainbow once in heaven:
We know her woof, her texture; she is given
In the dull catalogue of common things.
Philosophy will clip an angel's wings.

The touch of science is for him the kiss of death. He draws support from Tolkien's seemingly anti-technological views.

But the Scientist is at a loss as to what to say in reply. Surely, he thinks, a rainbow is all the more beautiful for knowing the laws that govern it, not less! The simplest object is, to the Scientist, a source of limitless wonder. His ear strains ever after the music of the spheres. What though Tolkien seems to disapprove of his pursuits? Tolkien seems to have disliked every subject apart from his own field at one stage or another in his career.

It is because they have so little in common that their disagreements arise. If the Magician could only realise that the Scientist is not attempting to destroy the mystery, but to push it back even deeper to the mysteries that perplex modern science, then he might be more respectful. Similarly, the Scientist should not dismiss the Magician out of hand. For heaven's sake, this is meant as an enjoyable pastime, not a war. And here we reach the nub of the matter. For the Scientist, such analyses are fun. Jenny and I enjoyed writing this paper immensely, and we hope that you're finding it interesting and, perhaps, amusing.

I'm sure that the argument as to whether or not it is in the spirit of Middle-earth to analyse things from the scientific point of view is one that will go on for a long time. I'm aware that this paper is rapidly beginning to sound serious, and so I must do something – people who know me often suspect things are deeply wrong when my Tolkienian writing turns serious. So I shall close this section with a presentation of my own view, which might offend some "purists". If so, I'm sorry; but it's the only view I know well enough to explain. Then I shall present a few last mad ideas for future scientific enquiries into Middle-earth. We'd be thrilled if any of these were to stimulate any of you into writing something similar.

So, why do I enjoy this pseudo-scientific approach to the writings of J.R.R. Tolkien? Well, for me, giving a full scientific account of a seemingly magical phenomenon gives rise to the same sort of intellectual satisfaction as finishing the *Times* crossword. The analogy is good, in that at my present state of knowledge I have precious little chance of doing either satisfactorily. It's a challenging intellectual pursuit which draws together most of the things that I'm really interested in. Above all, it's a great game to treat the writings of Tolkien as if they were historical records, and see what sense we can make of them. It's a game which I think all Tolkien fans enjoy. In the back of my mind the whole time is the nagging thought that "after all, they are only works of fiction." But this doubt is pushed aside when discussing such themes as are dealt with in this paper. It is quite ironic, then, that we take the opposite approach "one level down", as it were, and introduce the obvious doubts about bias of the author only when we analyse the corpus as being secondary-world history. No wonder critics of Tolkien get confused!

"But it's only fantasy!" Well, yes, it is fantastic; but Middle-earth is the result of a genuinely sub-creative process. It's my belief that any conceivable world which isn't going to break apart under the stress of internal contradictions will have to have certain properties found in the primary world: for example, it must have causality of a sort. There is at least a good case for saying that the most fundamental laws of physics must hold as well. But this is leading us into the murky waters of modal logic and counterfactuals. Maybe this is a subject for another paper, one indulging my philosophical whims instead of my scientific ones. But on that note I shall leave this serious theme. Jenny's answer to this whole problem is slightly different from mine: but I just wanted to show that at least we've thought about what we're doing.

And now I turn with relief to a few ideas which the pseudo-scientific approach to Middle-earth could yield. As I mentioned earlier these are some areas we think could be developed much further.

i. An economic analysis of Middle-earth. This project has already been started by Mark Poles of Taruithorn in his excellent and amusing "Exchange Rates in Middle-earth".

ii. An investigation of the neuropsychology of Elves. Just how could they perform all those extraordinary mental feats?

iii. The whole matter of telepathy. This would be very problematic but could take comfort from the wonderfully pseudo-scientific and ramshackle way parapsychology has proceeded in the primary world.

iv. A genetic approach to beards. Why were dwarven females bearded? What was the genetic difference between the branches of hobbits? How often would Boromir have needed to shave?

v. What about mithril? Presumably a natural alloy, but of what? It seems to be just about the perfect material for most purposes. I suppose that it was a pity that the Dwarves seem to have mined it all well before our age began.

vi. Then there's the problem of how one could start with Elves and end up with Orcs, quite apart from the whole matter of Orcish immortality or otherwise. Is this straightforward genetic engineering? Or perhaps a programme of what has happily been called "dysgenics"?

vii Exactly what technologies were developed by the end of the Third Age? It would be very useful if someone could undertake the tedious task of indexing all mentions of artefacts in the books. Especially welcome would be a listing of the incredibly patchy technology of the Shire. Need we take seriously hobbit umbrellas? And surely only an advanced civilisation could be decent enough to produce waistcoats. Next we'll be hearing of hobbits in bow-ties. Whatever is Middle-earth coming to?

And on that happy note we shall draw this short paper to a close. We both hope that some of you will have understood what we've been saying, and, more importantly, the reasons why we say it.

References

Coombs, Jennifer and Read, Marc. 1991. "Valaquanta: Of the Energy of the Valar" in *Mallorn* No. **28**, pp. 29-35.

Percival, Michael. 1988. "The Draining of Moria" in *Mallorn* No. **25**, pp. 30-32.

Read, Marc. 1989. "The Einstein Connection or Cosmological implications of the Akallabêth" in *Amon Hen* No. 99, pp. 17-18. September 1989.

Tolkien, J.R.R. 1981. *Letters of J.R.R. Tolkien*. Ed. Humphrey Carpenter with Christopher Tolkien. London: George Allen & Unwin.

Tolkien, J.R.R. 1983. *The Book of Lost Tales Part 1*. Ed. Christopher Tolkien. London: George Allen & Unwin.

Tolkien, J.R.R. 1984. *The Book of Lost Tales Part II*. Ed. Christopher Tolkien. London: George Allen & Unwin.

Tolkien, J.R.R. 1985. *The Lays of Beleriand*. Ed. Christopher Tolkien. London: George Allen & Unwin.

Explorations into the Psyche of Dwarves

David A. Funk

Abstract: An attempt to explain the characters of the roles played by, and the major reasons for the creation of, Dwarves as presented in Tolkien's three major works of fiction concerning Middle-earth. The argument is heavily biased in favour of Dwarves' indispensability.

Keywords: beauty, crafts, creativity, Dwarves, mithril, perception, smiths

Preface
Before I begin reading I must acknowledge a debt of gratitude to my mother Grace for her encouragement and constructive criticism. Without her assistance I would not have come to Oxford and without access to her library I could not have made this presentation. My paper owes much to numerous authors who paved the way for me, in particular David Day who wrote *A Tolkien Bestiary* and J.E.A. Tyler who compiled *The Tolkien Companion*. Most of all I am indebted to Christopher Tolkien for his tireless efforts in editing and publishing the many posthumous volumes of his father's works. Let me stress that I approached this paper from a reader's point of view.

Foreword
> When we build, let us think that we build forever. Let it not be for present delight nor for present use alone. Let it be such work as our descendants will thank us for; and let us think, as we lay stone on stone, that a time is to come when these stones will be held sacred because our hands have touched them, and that men will say, as they look upon the labour and wrought substance of them, "See! This our father did for us." – John Ruskin

Introduction
First of all I must describe the way in which I was introduced to Dwarves. My mother narrated *The Hobbit* to an older brother and me before I could read. Later she read aloud to us *The Lord of the Rings* chapter by chapter as the volumes became available at the local library. I didn't consume these stories in one sustained gulp as I often do now. I had time to mull over the action and absorb it. The characters were alive for me; as real as English history, as close as the pioneers of colonialism. It was almost a year before I realized (and pointed out) that there was no 'r' in Gandalf. 'G' for 'grand' – remember the words of the hobbit children?

The events in these tales seemed so natural. Dwarves provided a link from prosaic everyday life to adventures filled with wonder and terror. The fireworks that Gandalf brought to Shire celebrations were accompanied by Dwarves, characters that Tolkien used because his protagonist and the reader could easily accept them. Dwarves are down-to-earth; understandable. Bilbo was familiar with Dwarves before he actually had a lot to do with them. In his younger days Bilbo had often met and discoursed with travellers before he became sedentary and set in his ways. Dwarves lived near the borders of the Shire and there was commerce between the two races.

No doubt Bilbo knew more of them than other inhabitants of his peaceful little country. They were regarded as makers of clever toys, smiths, taciturn wanderers on their way to or from the colony at the Blue Mountains. To quote T.A. Shippey,

> . . . men [Hobbits] dealt with dwarves in a way they could not with elves, on an equal basis marred often by hostility.
> (Shippey, 1982, p. 47)

The reader learns, as does Bilbo, more about Dwarves and their importance as the story progresses. But *The Hobbit* is basically a children's story, supplying only glimpses of the grand history concerning Dwarves.

Dwarves provide a counter-point to the elegance and nobility of Elves. They supply an underlying strength. One gets the feeling in times of crisis (the Battle of Helm's Deep for example) that all cannot be lost if the Dwarves or Dwarf, in the person of Gimli, are still in the thick of the fight. In fact, Tolkien uses this feeling to great effect when during the battle we almost believe the good guys could lose. Gimli has been lost temporarily and the situation looks very desperate.

Nature of Dwarves
Dwarves are practical and pragmatic; not easily swayed by high-flown rhetoric. The remark that Gimli made in response to Saruman's wily persuasions, "The words of this wizard stand on their heads" (Tolkien, 1965a, p. 235), was exactly the blunt grating tone of voice needed to remind the Riders just how badly their forces had been mauled in the recent struggles.

Even Sauron found them "untameable" despite the gift of Seven Rings. A quote from Appendix A reveals:

> Though they could be slain or broken, they could not be reduced to shadows enslaved to another will; and for the same reason their lives were not affected by any Ring, to live either longer or shorter because of it. All

the more did Sauron hate the possessors [of the Rings] and desire to dispossess them.
(Tolkien, 1965b, p. 446)

No doubt their powers of resistance are attributable to the virtues instilled in them at their creation.

The most significant clues to the existence of Dwarves are in a somewhat lengthy passage from the Valaquenta:

> Aulë has might little less than Ulmo. His lordship is over all the substances of which Arda is made. In the beginning he wrought much in fellowship with Manwë and Ulmo; and the fashioning of all lands was his labour. He is a smith and a master of all crafts[1], and he delights in works of skill, however small, as much as in the mighty building of old. His are the gems that lie deep in the Earth and the gold that is fair in the hand, no less than the walls of the mountains and the basins of the sea. The Noldor learned most of him, and he was ever their friend. Melkor was jealous of him, for Aulë was most like himself in thought and powers; and there was long strife between them, in which Melkor ever marred or undid the works of Aulë, and Aulë grew weary in repairing the tumults and disorders of Melkor. Both, also, desired to make things of their own that should be new and unthought of by others, and delighted in the praise of their skill. But Aulë remained faithful to Eru and submitted all that he did to his will; and he did not envy the works of others, but sought and gave counsel. Whereas Melkor spent his spirit in envy and hate, until at last he could make nothing save in mockery of the thought of others, and all their works he destroyed if he could.
> (Tolkien, 1977, p. 27)

This explains the animosity between them and their creatures that had its roots even at the creation of Arda. A further quotation taken from Chapter 2 of *The Silmarillion* (Tolkien, 1977, pp. 43-44) gives Aulë's reasoning in the making of Dwarves.

> . . . And Aulë made the Dwarves even as they still are, because the forms of the Children who were to come were unclear to his mind, and because the power of Melkor was yet over the Earth; and he wished therefore that they should be strong and unyielding . . . Since they were to come in the days of Melkor, Aulë made the Dwarves strong to endure. Therefore they are stone-hard, stubborn, fast in friendship, and in enmity, and they suffer toil and hunger and hurt of body more hardily than all other speaking peoples . . .

It seems clear that Aulë anticipated the need for such a sturdy race to aid in the travails of the First-born and of Men in the ages to come. Though there were tragic tales of woe between these peoples the fiercest hatreds were always reserved for the creatures of Morgoth, the Dark Enemy.

The quotations explain the reasons for Dwarves within the context of the story. What about Tolkien himself? A strong argument can be made supporting the theory that the author had a high regard for craftsmanship and esteemed the role of artisan. The progress of all the races is closely linked to their skills at building. They built ships, fortresses, great houses, extensive caverns, roads and bridges. The theme is (human) manipulation of the environment. If Hobbits embody the English farmer then surely Dwarves represent the English craftsman.

But why Dwarves specifically? Would some variation or evolution of Elves have done as well? Dwarves were not initially part of Tolkien's stories. *The Book of Lost Tales* makes no reference to them as such. The idea of them was present instead as Gnomes or Noldoli who had much the same relationship as in later versions but were not the "Children of Aulë". Dwarfs and dwarf-lore are an integral part of European mythology. Tolkien cleaned them up and generally made them more appealing just as he revised the modern image of Elves to distinguish them from sprites and fairies. In a letter drafted in response to comments by Robert Murray, S.J. (1954), Tolkien says this:

> Even the dwarfs are not really Germanic "dwarfs" . . . and I call them "dwarves" to mark that. They are not naturally evil, not necessarily hostile, and not a kind of maggot-folk bred in stone; but a variety of incarnate rational creature. (Tolkien, 1981, p. 207)

Someone had to do the dirty work, so to speak. Dwarves were miners, engineers, metalworkers. It was Dwarves who tunnelled under mountains unearthing rare minerals, jewels and the materials of work-a-day life. Iron and other minerals were essential commodities. Men and Elves did some of their own mining but it is with Dwarves that we associate labour underground. Indeed, as a people they preferred caverns to open plains, carving through rock as readily as might the settlers of Rohan cut sod to roof their buildings.

It was Dwarves who were reckoned cunning smiths and great engineers. Given their propensity for travel who knows what influence Dwarf masons may have had on the builders of Man's great cities?

Very little of legend or mythology exposes a psychology that is truly alien to human thought. Dwarves had essentially human personalities as did all Tolkien's people. They identify for us (the reader) the attributes of stoicism, courage, perseverance, physical and mental toughness and a love of crafts. They also reveal less endearing traits: stubbornness, avarice, secretiveness and a reluctance to admit to the competence of others, at least in the areas of Dwarvish expertise. As Gandalf explains to Gimli and the hobbits in a conversation at Minas Tirith after the climax of *The Lord of the Rings*,

> This Dwarvish conceit that no one can have or make anything "of value" save themselves, and that all fine things in other hands must have been got, if not stolen, from the Dwarves at some time, was more than I could stand at that moment
> (Tolkien, 1980, p. 334),

thereby precipitating the inclusion of Bilbo on the Quest of

---

[1] Originally the term "smith" was applied to anyone who made anything. The large family of Smiths are honourably descended from people who in early times had accomplished something notable.

Erebor.

But Dwarves have an importance to the story that goes beyond being instrumental in the finding of the Ring. They are the agents of Smaug's destruction and a crucial element in re-arming (re-populating) the region of the Lonely Mountain in time to divert or engage some of Sauron's forces who might otherwise have laid waste to many precious places left undefended while the war raged in Gondor. Gimli's presence at the Council of Elrond was no accident. As the men of Dale were approached by emissaries of Sauron, so were the Dwarves of Erebor. The choice was not whose side they were on but whether to get involved. Hence the need to consult with Elrond. They became part of the alliance yet remained on the edges of the main narrative. Given the malice and power of Sauron and his forerunners, the forces for "Good" against "Evil" needed all the help they could get. Dwarves were staunch allies, undaunted in the face of overwhelming odds, historically (within the context of the stories) credited as withstanding even the onslaught of the great fire-drakes at the Battle of Unnumbered Tears[2]. As smelters and refiners of ore they were accustomed to great heat and had invented protective gear. But as worthy as their armour was their strength of spirit.

Joy of Making

An aspect of dwarvish character I will focus on is what I term "the joy of making". Tolkien was a craftsman – a wordsmith. The evidence is the multitude of versions he produced for almost every piece of writing. He gave his work the care and attention to detail that he admired in the work of good craftsmen. He spent most of his life surrounded by the results of men's efforts that had lasted centuries. Certainly his own labours in fiction and non-fiction will stand the test of time.

Was Tolkien a crafty wanna-be or did he have the knack of getting inside the heart (head) of people he wrote about? Where does the concept "the joy of making" come from? The very first reference is (as one might expect) at the beginning of all things, when Eru made the world according to the Music of the Ainur. *The Silmarillion* (Tolkien, 1977, p. 19) describes their wonderment at the substances of which Arda was formed and goes on to say: "but the delight and pride of Aulë is in the deed of making, and in the thing made . . ." It is a phrase that strikes me as indicative of the author's attitude.

The joy of making as I know it is very real; a powerful incentive. The drive to create something: a toy, a tool, a tower of stone, is compelling. Not only is the urge a strong one, but as one's skills improve the created object must become more refined. Tolkien understood this, being a perfectionist in his own right. The finished product is only part of the satisfaction.

The use of the device "mithril" explains this more fully. As a material it was valued above all others – including gold. In the words of Gandalf to Sam:

The wealth of Moria was not in gold and jewels, the toys of the Dwarves; nor in iron, their servant . . . For here alone in the world was found Moria-silver, or true-silver as some have called it: *mithril* is the Elvish name . . . Its worth was ten times that of gold, and now it is beyond price . . .
(Tolkien, 1971, p. 331)

Note that Dwarves placed their highest values on a substance not only pleasant to look at but also rewarding to work with. Its virtues were strength, ductility, toughness and incorruptibility. It was rare but worth the energy required to find it. They dug for the ore because the process of finding it was part of the joy of working with it. It was part of an ingrained need to create things and so enrich their lives.

Unfortunately it was also their downfall. Tolkien writes in his letters to his son Christopher about a development of the human condition he refers to as "the machine". His particular point is about the (impersonal) destructive capabilities of aircraft but he says it shows a human failing to recognize that the worst destruction is to their own nature (spirit). A parallel can be observed in the actions of Dwarves (who exhibit human characteristics) when their desires to manipulate the fabric of the earth degenerate into excessive pride. They delved too deep in search of mithril and awakened an ancient evil which destroyed their greatest creation – the city of Khazad-dûm. Was this hubris? Tolkien kindly allows the possibility that the Balrog may already have been aware and the Dwarves merely unleashed it from imprisonment (1965b, p. 439). The example does imply that there is a danger in allowing the desire to create to become an obsession. Dwarves had a tendency towards possessiveness as well; a further perversion of the joy, demonstrating that Dwarves showed faults of a human kind. At any rate the joy of making is incontrovertibly a part of Dwarf nature.

Indeed, there are "Dwarves" alive and kicking in the world today. Who among us does not know of at least one person whose passion reflects "an almost dwarvish obsession with craft"[3] Not the painter or the sculptor but the talented amateur who labours countless hours reproducing classic furniture in meticulous detail or the mechanic who restores a vintage automobile to original condition.

The value of a Dwarf is the willingness to go beyond discomfort, inconvenience or simple utility. A diamond is after all only a rock, no matter how large or flawless. It has its uses as a very hard material and in the right setting can attain great beauty in human (dwarvish) eyes. The ability to recognize and utilize the potential of a material is a Dwarvish trait.

Hidden Beauty

The other aspect of Dwarves that describes their essential nature is what I will term "hidden beauty". Tolkien declined to use flattering physical descriptives for Dwarves. They were not considered handsome or fair to look upon; "unlovely" was more apt. What does this reveal about the

---

[2] Nirnaeth Arnoediad "Tears Unnumbered", the fifth battle in the Wars of Beleriand near the end of the First Age.
[3] An expression used to describe Celebrimbor, Lord of Eregion, an elven smith of renown *circa* 750 to 1697 of the Second Age.

author's thoughts on surface appearances? Unlovely exteriors could conceal admirable inner qualities. Dwarves perhaps best embodied this idea. Of particular relevance is the position that Dwarves occupied in Middle-Earth. Some Elves made long and perilous migrations (in rebellion) but Dwarves had always inhabited the world, indeed passed centuries with little or no contact with others. They were not "the Chosen" or First-born; had no quarrel with their Creator and did not have the same personal relationship with the Valar as did the Eldar. Having spent hundreds of years left to their own devices – left to evolve their own culture – perhaps made them insular; a little shy of revealing too much.

A prime example concerns Mîm the Petty-dwarf's sack of roots during his encounter with Túrin and his band of outlaws. "'They are of great worth,' he said. 'More than gold in the hungry winter.'"

And earlier is written:
> But when they were cooked these roots proved good to eat, somewhat like bread; and the outlaws were glad of them . . . "Wild Elves know them not; Grey-elves have not found them; the proud ones from over the Sea are too proud to delve," said Mîm.
> (Tolkien, 1980, p. 103)

The roots looked like nothing more than lumps of rock when harvested yet in the midst of winter famine had more to offer than precious metals. Considering that Dwarves generally disdained farming, preferring to trade for such goods, the quiet secret of a readily available, sustaining tuber seems very Dwarvish. Remember also the opening line of Tolkien's second most famous verse: "All that is gold does not glitter". The One Ring itself seemed only to be a plain gold band with no hint of its powers.

Dwarves are long-lived; not interested in transitory beauty. They made things to last. While not beautiful in themselves they appreciated beauty and were capable of great depths of feeling. One reason for Gimli's fascination with Galadriel was her timelessness, going beyond her physical appearance. Her poise and grace were acquired through ages of turmoil. The other reason was this: Galadriel is one of the central figures in the struggle against evil in Middle-earth. Of all the Eldar it was she who had the most wisdom regarding Dwarves. This played a part in the overwhelming impression she had on Gimli. To quote *Unfinished Tales*:
> In any case, Galadriel was more far-sighted in this than Celeborn; and she perceived from the beginning that Middle-earth could not be saved from "the residue of evil" that Morgoth had left behind him save by a union of all the peoples who were in their way and in their measure opposed to him. She looked upon the Dwarves also with the eye of a commander, seeing in them the finest warriors to pit against the Orcs. Moreover Galadriel was a Noldo, and she had a natural sympathy with their minds and their passionate love of crafts of hand[4], a sympathy much greater than that found among many of the Eldar: the Dwarves were "the Children of Aulë", and Galadriel, like others of the Noldor, had been a pupil of Aulë and Yavanna in Valinor.
> (Tolkien, 1980, p. 235)

Gimli's conversion to an appreciation of all things Elvish – a result of being smitten – is not surprising. Reverence for the beauty of Creation is common to all humans. Gimli was inspired to depict the underground wonders of Helm's Deep (another instance of hidden beauty) in words that moved even Legolas to comment. Elves exhibit joy in existence. Dwarves exhibit joy in the fabric and manipulation of material substance.

Conclusion

Aulë created Dwarves "in his own image"; skilled at crafts and imbued with a need to use those skills. Their capacity for vengeance and their martial powers had to be triggered. They were not empire-builders nor did they seek to impose their will on others. They were most content when left in peace. However it should be noted that they reached their highest attainments during the Second Age through collaboration with the Noldorin Elves of Eregion. It was Sauron who eventually shattered that accord, beginning the long chain of events that culminated in the War of the Ring. The reign of peace that followed its conclusion allowed for a return to the true nature of Dwarves and as noted in Appendix A regarding Durin's Folk:
> After the fall of Sauron, Gimli brought south a part of the Dwarf-folk of Erebor, and he became Lord of the Glittering Caves. He and his people did great works in Gondor and Rohan.
> (Tolkien, 1965b, p. 451)

So as Middle-earth began a new age, the need for craftsmen, appreciation of beauty, willingness and patience for hard labour – all the best qualities of Dwarves – still had a place, both to repair the ravages of conflict and to explore new territories of splendour. "Hidden beauty" describes what they (Dwarves) are and "the joy of making" describes what they do.

References

Shippey, T. A. 1982. *The Road to Middle-earth*. London: George Allen & Unwin.

Tolkien, J. R. R. 1971. *The Fellowship of the Ring*. Toronto: Methuen Publications.

Tolkien, J. R. R. 1965a. *The Two Towers*. New York: Ballantine Books.

Tolkien, J. R. R. 1965b. *The Return of the King*. New York: Ballantine Books.

Tolkien, J. R. R. 1977. *The Silmarillion*, ed. Christopher Tolkien. London: George Allen & Unwin.

Tolkien, J. R. R. 1980. *Unfinished Tales*, ed. Christopher Tolkien. London: George Allen & Unwin.

Tolkien, J. R. R. 1981. *Letters of J.R.R. Tolkien*, ed. Humphrey Carpenter. London: George Allen & Unwin.

---

[4] Recall the cloaks woven by Galadriel and her maidens given to the Company upon leaving Lórien (writer's note).

The Geology of Middle-earth

William Antony Swithin Sarjeant

Abstract: A preliminary reconstruction of the geology of Middle-earth is attempted, utilizing data presented in text, maps and illustrations by its arch-explorer J.R.R. Tolkien. The tectonic reconstruction is developed from earlier findings by R.C. Reynolds (1974). Six plates are now recognized, whose motions and collisions have created the mountains of Middle-earth and the rift structure down which the River Anduin flows. The stresses involved in the plate collisions have produced patterns of faults, whose lines have determined the courses of the other rivers and the occurrence of the richest ore deposits. However, the time of Bilbo and Frodo is a period of tectonic quiescence. Volcanic activity is at a minimum and confined to four "hot-spots", all at some distance from plate margins, while seismic activity is minor. Tolkien's paintings, in particular, show how glacial and riverine erosion have shaped Middle-earth's topography.

Keywords: earthquakes, erosion, faulting, Middle-earth geology, tectonics, topography, volcanic eruptions

The period of the rise of geology, in the late eighteenth and early nineteenth centuries, coincided with the epoch during which this Earth of ours was being fully explored for the first time. Most of its explorers were able to furnish quite accurate accounts of the geography of the lands they had visited, but few were trained geologists. The geological information those explorers brought back tended therefore to be incidental and imprecise. Even so, the geologists of their homeland did their best to utilize these scraps of data, to begin formulating a picture of geology on a global scale.

In seeking to elucidate the geology of Middle-earth, our task is similar. We have a good general picture of its topography, drawn by Christopher Tolkien on the basis of the information furnished by his father, as prime explorer of that special world. We have also the excellent paintings done by the explorer himself, representing his vision of Middle-earth and published in the 1973 and 1977 Tolkien calendars and subsequent compilations. In addition, we have the scraps of geological information to be found in *The Hobbit* and *The Lord of the Rings* – incidental observations only, but nevertheless helpful.

In contrast, the supplementary material brought together in the successive volumes of *The History of Middle-earth* must be viewed as the equivalent of a geologist's field notes – unrevised and not to be trusted; so this must be discounted. (In any case, the additional geological information to be found therein is quite remarkably meagre.) Moreover, though it is possible to determine the sequence of tectonic events, lack of information concerning fossils precludes any precise determination of the sequence of strata and geochronology.

The first person to attempt a geological history of Middle-earth was Margaret Howes (1967), in her survey of "The Elder Ages and the Later Glaciations Of the Pleistocene Epoch". In this, she strove to trace the successive geographies from the overthrow of Morgoth to a period beyond the time of Aragorn's rule in Gondor – indeed, into the late Pleistocene Epoch, when the geography of Middle-earth had been reshaped into present-day Eurasia and north Africa. Her work was original and imaginative, but it strayed far from Tolkien, utilizing data of such questionable authenticity that, in the last analysis, her conclusions must be set aside.

The truly seminal work on Middle-earth geology was written by Robert C. Reynolds for *The Swansea Geographer* in 1974. Though entitled "The Geomorphology of Middle-earth", it is much more than that, for it applies the concepts of plate tectonics then current to the whole geography of Middle-earth (Figure 1).

Four plates were recognized – the Eriador Plate in the west, the Rhovanion Plate in the north, and the Harad and Mordor Plates in the south. The River Anduin was considered as flowing through what was then styled an aulacogen and would now be regarded as a rift valley. Reynolds viewed the bounding faults as being transform faults, i.e. faults along which movement had been essentially lateral but occurring at different times in contrary directions. He considered the region south of the Emyn Muil and north of the line of the White Mountains to be a tectonic basin, the Nindalf Basin, while Rohan constituted a stable block of ancient rocks – a craton.

It is Reynolds' work that forms the basis for my own analysis of the geology of Middle-earth. However, our

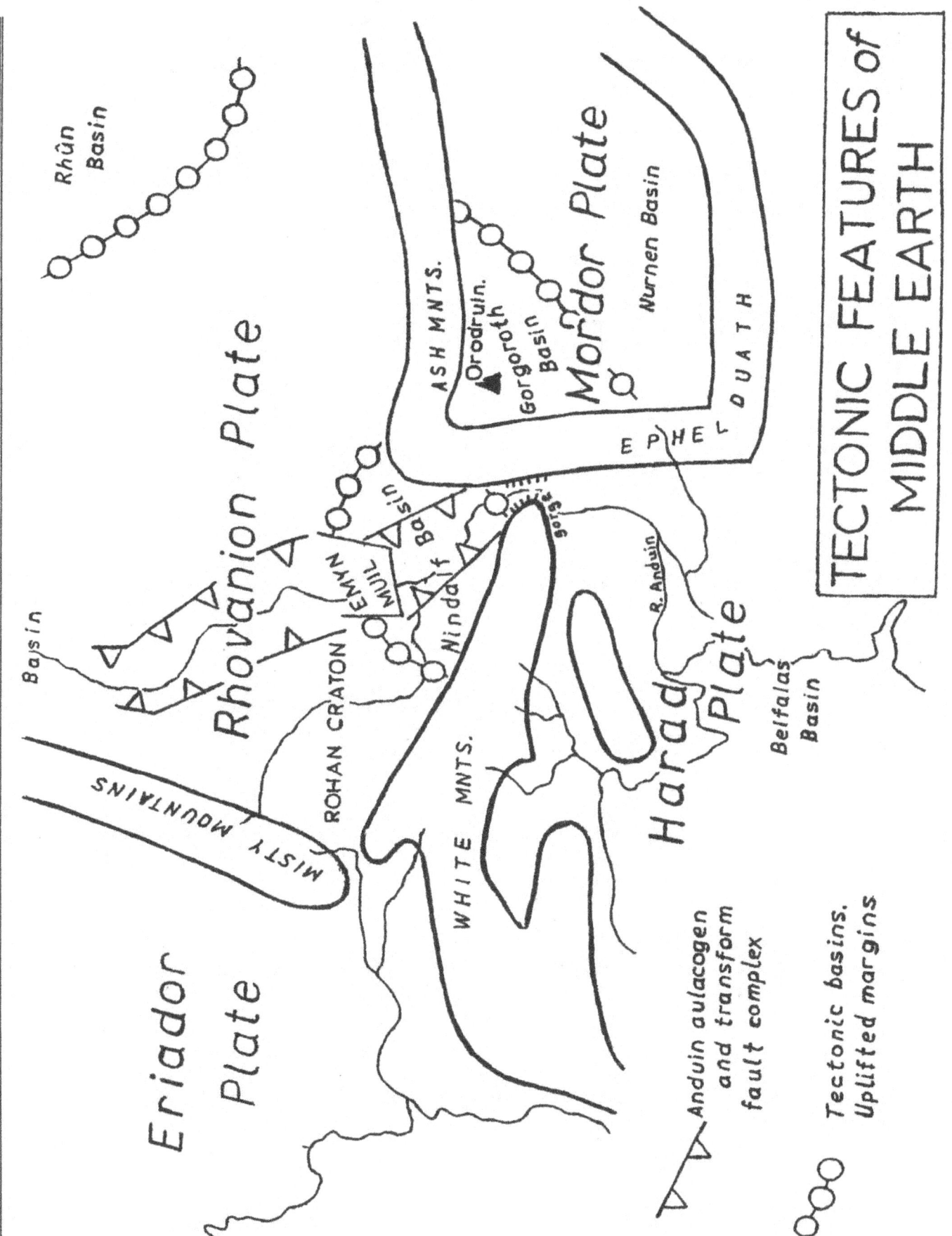

Figure 1: Reynolds' reconstruction of the tectonic features of Middle-earth. Modified after Reynolds, 1974.

knowledge of plate tectonics has grown, and the concepts have changed greatly, since Reynolds' work was published.[1] Moreover, in my view he pays too small a regard to the north and north-west of Middle-earth and to the many major faults, most of them normal faults with a trend from south-west to north-east – usually, indeed, from west-south-west to east-north-east – that control so much of Middle-earth geography.

My modified concepts (Figure 2) recognise not four, but six plates (or in modern terminology, as applied to American Cordilleran tectonics, six terrans) as being involved in the shaping of Middle-earth geography. The most ancient of these are the Forlindon Plate and the Eriador Plate, whose collision caused the orogeny – the mountain-building phase – that produced the Ered Luin or Blue Mountains. Since that time, the Forlindon Plate has been largely subsumed; that is, drawn down into a subduction zone at the continental margin, its materials reincorporated into the earth's mantle. Indeed, only two blocks west of the Ered Luin – the regions of Forlindon and Harlindon – still persist. Moreover, both plates have moved north, producing the many strike-slip faults that have furnished courses for westward-flowing rivers.

The collision of the Eriador Plate with two other plates, the Rhovanion Plate to eastward and the Harad Plate to southward, caused two further orogenies that, no doubt, overlapped in time. Between the Eriador and Rhovanion Plates, there arose the Misty Mountains and between the Eriador and Harad Plates, the White Mountains, the three plates forming a triple junction against the stable basement rocks of the Rohan Craton.

A second triple junction was formed by the collision of the Eriador and Rhovanion Plates with the Forodwaith Plate. The consequent orogeny produced the Ered Mithrin, the Grey Mountains, together with their westward extension through the region of Angmar toward the Ice-Bay of Forochel; Mount Gundabad surely represents a rotated block of erosion-resistant rocks at the exact position of the junction. Unfortunately, we know too little of the geology of these mountains to speculate further.

The most recent major tectonic event has been the collision of the rapidly moving Mordor Plate with the northern part of the Harad Plate and the southernmost part of the Rhovanion Plate. The Mordor Plate is bounded on north and south by transform faults, their motion at first westward and then, more prolongedly, eastward. A major consequence has been the formation of the Anduin Rift Valley, caused by the resultant tearing-apart of the crust. Despite the claims of Reynolds (1974), this rift is bounded not by transform but by normal faults. At its southern end, it has buckled against the stable Harondor Craton and has been turned westward.

Essentially this rift is, of course, a region of subsidence, most markedly in its northern portion – the "Gladden Basin" of Reynolds – and in the triangle between the Emyn Muil, the White Mountains and the Ephel Dúath – the Nindalf Basin. As Reynolds noted, the marshy nature of the Nindalf Basin – it incorporates the Dead Marshes, the Wetwang and the many mouths of the Entwash – indicates that this basin once contained a lake, since silted up.

However, the complex interaction of the plates has also produced three horsts (fault-bounded, elevated blocks) within the rift. Two of these – the Emyn Muil and Emyn Arnon – respectively determine the northern and southern limits of the Nindalf Basin; they control the Anduin's course and character, producing such dramatic features as Tol Brandir, with its "grey faces" of stone (Tolkien, 1954a, p. 412) and the Rauros Falls. The third occurs at the rift's southwesternmost end, forming the mountainous island of Tolfalas, beyond the depression marked by the many mouths of the Anduin.

Though no doubt there was much volcanic activity during the earlier orogenies, the only recently active region was associated with the crumpling of the Mordor Plate after collision, causing fissure vulcanism and some explosive activity around its rims. The spoiling of the landscape that so distressed Frodo and Sam was, I suspect, largely a consequence of the initial vulcanism and not just of the spoil-heaps produced by mining. (The solfatara fields around Namafjall, Iceland, afford just as grim a prospect.) It is likely that the Udûn Basin of northwesternmost Mordor is an enormous crater, a caldera, the product of a cataclysmic eruption like that of Krakatoa in 1883. (Reynolds' alternative suggestion, that it is an independent small plate, seems much less probable in view of its position and shape.) However, the only volcano recently active in this region is Mount Doom – Mount Orodruin – which, by its great height in proportion to its basal diameter (cal., 1977), must have been built up rapidly by basic lava, scoria and ash.

Mount Doom is indeed one of four isolated volcanoes, each representing a "hotspot" at some distance from a plate margin and all of them associated with evil-doing – Dol Goldur in Mirkwood, Orthanc in Isengard and Erebor, the Lonely Mountain. Isengard, with its black rocks (Tolkien, 1954b, pp. 159-160), was certainly a vast volcanic crater, while Orthanc itself (cal., 1977) must have been an aiguille – a column of solidified lava thrust up from the vent in a last spasm of an eruption within the crater of Isengard, to be afterward shaped by human hand or magic. (The so-called "spine" produced in the last phases of the eruption of Mont Pelée, Martinique, is comparable.) The Lonely Mountain, from its shape and with its "grey and silent cliffs" (Tolkien, 1951, p. 215) within a landscape "bleak and barren", was certainly a volcano (see cal., 1977); there are many present volcanoes of closely similar outline, e.g. La Tungar, Argentina. The huge cave in which the dragon piled his ill-gotten gains within the Lonely Mountain was surely a lava-tube ere the dwarves reshaped it, and so must have been the smaller tunnel down which Bilbo unwillingly went to seek the dragon. (A comparable structure is the Thurston lava tube of Kilauea Volcano, Hawaii.)

Yet of these recent volcanoes, only Mount Doom was still

---

[1] The later study by Pat McIntosh (1973) treats only surface outcrops, while the short papers by Duncan McLaren (1985) and Mike Percival (1985) deal with Númenor.

THE GEOLOGY OF MIDDLE-EARTH

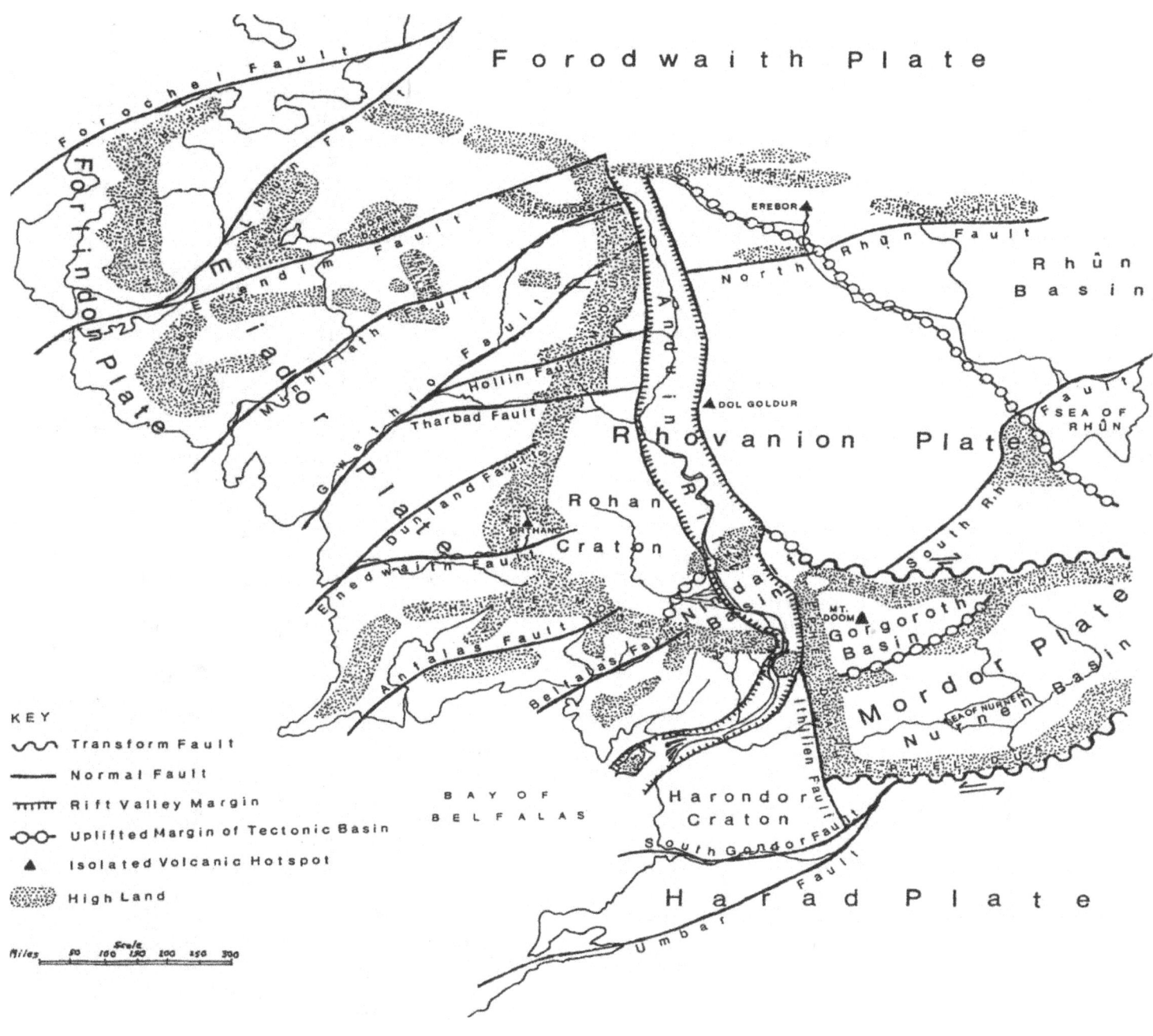

Figure 2: The principal tectonic features of Middle-earth: a new interpretation.

active in the time of Bilbo and Frodo. Moreover, the only "seismic events" recorded in the chronicles are those caused Gandalf's throwing-down of the balrog (Tolkien, 1954b) and Gollum's fall with the ring into the fires of Mount Doom (Tolkien, 1955). Of other earthquakes, we have no record. All in all, this time must have been one of unusual tectonic quiescence.

However, in the present topography of Middle-earth, the effects of earlier tectonic events are patent. Rivendell, for example, is positioned where the Misty Mountain foothills are intersected by the great Gwathlo Fault. The entry to the valley (see cal., 1977) is through a canyon reminiscent of the Black Canyon of the Gunnison River, Colorado, but the valley broadens beyond (cals., 1973, 1977). Helm's Deep (cal., 1977) must also be a canyon, within a terrain essentially of limestones; its situation and fortifications are comparable to those of the castle of Aigle, Switzerland. The troll-haunted Ettenmoors are a block of resistant rocks displaced between the Evendim and Minhiriath Faults. The rich mineral veins of Moria, with their priceless mithril, were developed where the Tharbad and Hollin Faults intersected the Misty Mountains. (Mithril itself, crystallizing out at so high a temperature that it is only found in veins at great depths, may well be a naturally-occurring alloy of platinum and another metal, perhaps palladium.) The almost equally rich mineralization of the Mordor Plate resulted from the fault movements along its rims, while the much less rich mineral deposits of the Iron Hills, worked by Dáin and his dwarves, are associated with the North Rhûn Fault.

Elsewhere, economic deposits are not common. There is iron in the Ered Luin; coal somewhere in the Shire (see Sarjeant, 1993, p. 64); limestone to be quarried for the buildings of Gondor in the White Mountains, chalk to be had in the Shire's White Downs and good building stones of other kinds in Arnor, Hollin and many other regions. (As Gimli said (Tolkien, 1954b, p. 137): "This country has tough bones.") Of the occurrences of precious stones, we have no details; perhaps the dwarves have kept that information to themselves!

The shaping of the landscape is, of course, dependent on the interplay of structure and rock type with erosion. It is glacial erosion that has shaped the northern mountains and the highest mountains of the south. The varied rocks of the Misty Mountains, as seen by Gandalf, Bilbo and the dwarves from the eagles' eyrie (cals., 1973, 1977), are strikingly comparable to the Nepal Himalayas of today. The volcanic Ephel Dúath, the Ash Mountains, as seen from near Shelob's Lair by Frodo and Sam (cal., 1977), have also been reshaped; the result is quite comparable to the Grand Tetons of Wyoming, even though their rocks are dissimilar. Moreover, the effects of glaciation have also modified the lowlands. As Reynolds (1974, p. 70) pointed out:

> . . . large areas of Rhovanion east of the Anduin . . . have been sculptured by these processes for considerable periods: the Iron Hills may be monadnock remnants of a former higher land surface, as may also be the hills near the Sea of Rhûn. Dagorlad, from its veneer of quartzitic regolith, could be a fossilised gravel-covered pediplaned surface (Tolkien, 1954b, p. 232). Extensive piedmont glaciation of the lowlands in the south seems unlikely from their latitude, but valley glaciation in the White Mountains has been very important. Over-deepened glacial troughs abound – Morgul Valley (Tolkien, 1954b, p. 319), Morthond Vale (Tolkien, 1955, p. 62), Harrowdale (Tolkien, 1955, p. 64); with overflow channels (Tarlang's Neck; Tolkien, 1955, p. 63) from one trough to another, and other classical glacial features such as arêtes and pyramidal peaks (Starkhorn and Irensaga; Tolkien, 1955, p. 68). Periglacial conditions are suggested in the lowlands and mountain fringes from unconsolidated materials incorporating coarse regolith (Tolkien, 1954b, p. 258). Northwards, glacial processes become more severe. Piedmont glaciers fed from the Misty Mountains stripped large areas of Eriador, producing its bleak ill-drained and stoney landscape (Tolkien, 1954a, pp. 294, 313) with ungraded tumbling streams (Tolkien, 1954a, pp. 295, 299). Caradhras is a fine pyramidal peak at the head of a U-trough whose snows still feed an icy stream, and the lake Mirrormere is an ice-scooped hollow (Tolkien, 1954a, p. 296) . . .

Reynolds noted also that the Long Lake on the River Running (Tolkien, 1951, p. 194), Lake Evendim and the hollow occupied by the Midgewater Marshes are probably of glacial origin. He considered that the extensive fluvio-glacial sands and gravels of the Shire (Tolkien, 1955, p. 296 and cal., 1973) were deposited under periglacial conditions and with localised lowering of groundwater base-level, consequent upon erosion by the Gwathló and Baranduin valley ice-tongues. The erosional deepening of the valleys on the chalk downs of the Shire (Tolkien, 1954a, pp. 126, 147) was another consequence. In addition, as he remarked (p. 70):

> Post-glacial eustatic changes have affected the whole coast, creating rias and small fjords and flooding low-lying basins (Belfalas) although delta formation by the Anduin has kept pace with this. Alluviation by the rivers has also occurred; the peats and clays of the Baranduin . . . being famous for turnips but especially mushrooms (Tolkien, 1954a, p. 100), as also is the Marish (Tolkien, 1954a, p. 112).
>
> In the north, areas of lithologically controlled high relief occur abutting glacially stripped lowlands (Tolkien, 1954a, pp. 211-212) occupied by bogs (Midgewater Marshes; Tolkien, 1954a, p. 194) and mis-fit streams in glacially enlarged valleys (Tolkien, 1954a, p. 212). The Weather Hills (Tolkien, 1954a, p. 197) are a rugged escarpment and the Trollshaws (Tolkien, 1954a, p. 213) a deeply dissected upland which includes rocks of probably red-bed facies (Tolkien, 1954a, p. 225).

The Carrock, by which Beorn once dwelt (Tolkien, 1951, p. 125), is surely an especially massive erratic block transported to its present position by a since-vanished glacier Elsewhere, riverine erosion has predominated. Subsurface erosion has produced the troll-hole in the Trollshaws

(Tolkien, 1951, p. 53), the "goblin-holes" in the Misty Mountains where Gandalf, Bilbo and the dwarves encountered trouble (Tolkien, 1951, p. 70), and the cave that serves as palace for the King of the Wood-elves (Tolkien, 1951, p. 178). Striking products are the underground lake once haunted by Gollum (Tolkien, 1951, p. 82), very like that underlying Australia's Nullarbor Plain today, and the Glittering Caves of Aglarond that so much delighted Gimli (Tolkien, 1954b, pp. 152-154) and would put even the Carlsbad Caverns to shame.

Many other deductions are possible. The West Gate of Moria appears, from the illustration (cals., 1973, 1977), to have been cut through a massive volcanic sill – a sheet of lava intruded between strata underground, to be brought to the surface by earth movements and exposed by erosion. (The Great Whin Sill of northern England is an example.) The staircase below the East Gate (cal., 1973) surely traverses a series of beds dipping westward at a low angle like steps, producing the Stair Falls (Tolkien, 1954a, p. 314). Bree-hill, "tall and brown" (Tolkien, 1954a, p. 193), and bleak Weathertop appear to be monadnocks, isolated hills within a landscape reduced by prolonged river action almost to the condition of a peneplain. Bree-hill is lower and formed probably of sandstone, Weathertop much higher and formed of more ancient indurated rocks, perhaps slates.

All in all, in geological terms, Tolkien's descriptions and pictures of Middle-earth are of a world that, geologically at least, is very like our own.

Acknowledgements

I am deeply indebted to my colleague Dr. Mel R. Stauffer (University of Saskatchewan) for his ideas on the application of plate tectonics to Middle-earth geology. Dr. John Senior (University of Saskatchewan) and an anonymous participant in the Tolkien Centenary Conference at Keble College, Oxford, made helpful suggestions concerning the probable nature of mithril.

References

References to Tolkien's illustrations, appearing initially in calendars, are cited as "cal., 1973" or "cal., 1977"; all have been subsequently published elsewhere.

cal. 1973. *The J.R.R. Tolkien Calendar 1973*. New York: Ballantine Books, 1972.

cal. 1977. *The Lord of the Rings 1977 Calendar*, illustrations by J.R.R. Tolkien. London: George Allen & Unwin, 1976.

Howes, Margaret M. 1967. "The Elder Ages and the later glaciations of the Pleistocene Epoch" in *Tolkien Journal*, vol. 3, no. 2, pp. 3-15, figs. 1-6.

McIntosh, Pat. 1973. "The geology of Middle-earth" in *Mallorn*, no. 7, pp. 3-7, 1 fig.

McLaren, Duncan. 1985. "Geographical observations on Númenor" in *Anor*, no. 7, pp. 2-4.

Percival, Mike. 1985. "On Númenor" in *Anor*, no. 8, pp. 4-6, figs. 1-2.

Reynolds, Robert C. 1974. "The geomorphology of Middle-earth" in *The Swansea Geographer*, vol. 11, pp. 67-71, 1 map.

Sarjeant, William A. S. 1992. "Where did the dwarves come from?" in *Mythlore* Vol. 19 No. 1 (Winter 1993), pp. 43,64.

Tolkien, J. R. R. 1951. *The Hobbit: or, There and Back Again*, second edition. London: Allen & Unwin.

Tolkien, J. R. R. 1954a. *The Fellowship of the Ring*. London: Allen & Unwin.

Tolkien, J. R. R. 1954b. *The Two Tower*. London: Allen & Unwin.

Tolkien, J. R. R. 1955. *The Return of the King*. London: Allen & Unwin.

Writing and Allied Technologies in Middle-earth

Lester E. Simons

Abstract: This paper discusses the possible (and probable) methods by which the inhabitants of Middle-earth at the end of the Third Age kept permanent records. A number of concepts are introduced and defined: *substrate*, *medium*, *implement*, *glyphs* and last, but not least, *scribe*! Suggestions regarding the possibility of the existence, late in the Third Age, of printing will be presented.

Keywords: binding, glyph, ink, medium, paper, pen, printing, scribe, substrate, vellum, writing

The various Speaking Peoples of Middle-earth had, by the end of the Third Age, developed a range of writing technologies, some of which they shared with others, some of which remained unique to the devisers.

The concept of writing, the committing of thoughts and ideas to a permanent medium, requires the development of several variously-linked procedures. It is not the purpose of this paper to discuss the origin, in Middle-earth or elsewhere, of the actual concept of writing, just the various aspects of it as presented in the late Third Age.

These can be expressed in general terms as "substrate", the material on which the writing is to be carried; "medium", in which the writing is expressed; "implement", used to perform the writing; and "glyphs", the signs, pictures and so on which are used to carry the meaning.

Substrates

Considering Middle-earth, even just as presented in *The Lord of the Rings*, there is a wide variety of substrates, not necessarily divided by usage according to People.

Hobbits used paper, in sheets (for correspondence) and bound in book form (for diaries, family records and so on); they also had thicker material (card) which would have appeared to be traditionally used for formal invitations (with or without gilded edges); the earliest Shire records would seem to be inscribed on vellum, a substrate which in European history has been used for the most formal and permanent documents; the so-called "Yellowskin" document of the Thain's library may indeed be vellum, if the name is any guide to the material.

Even at the beginning of the Fourth Age, the Hobbits were still using scrolls (also, it might be supposed, of vellum); for example, following the Battle of Bywater, "the names of all those who took part were made into a Roll." (Tolkien, 1954-5, Book 6, Chapter VIII [1])

However, collections of paper leaves may be gathered, sewn together along their top edges and then rolled into a cylindrical form. This is a simpler method of maintaining paper than the other method (book-binding), which is discussed elsewhere in this paper.

The Elves, however, may have relied on their memories for most of their long-term information storage, although Elrond's house did have a library ("Bilbo . . . had used all the sources available to him in Rivendell, both living and written." (Tolkien, 1954-5, Prologue "Note on the Shire Records"[2]). He did, after all, translate the Books of Lore as part of the Red Book). Again, paper and vellum were used by the Elves, as well as various metals: the Doors of Moria, although constructed by the Dwarves, had been engraved to a design by the Elves (possibly one of the last acts of cöoperation between those two Peoples for many a long year). Whether Celebrimbor of Hollin drew the signs himself directly on the mithril, or provided the designs for a Dwarf-engraver, is open to debate.

The Dwarves employed the skills of the stone-mason in carving their runes, as demonstrated on the Tomb of Balin in Moria. The existence of Thorin's Treasure Map, with its obvious cartography and rather-less obvious moon-runes, bespeaks a certain familiarity with the techniques of writing (as opposed to engraving), as does the Book of Mazarbûl; although the map was not likely to have been one of a series, the record of the Dwarf-colony in Khazad-dûm was intended for continuance. It may be worth considering that even though the enmity between the Elves and Dwarves was well established, the Dwarf-scribe still used the tengwar occasionally ("He could write well and speedily, and often used the Elvish characters." Tolkien, 1954-5, Book 2, Chapter V).

Ents may have relied even more strongly than the Elves on their memories. The thought of Ents using paper raises a

---

[1] Page numbers are not given because of the wide variation of pagination in different editions in existence.
[2] The "Note on the Shire Records" is in the Prologue of the Second Edition (1966).

number of interesting problems, not the least of which being whether they would call each sheet a "leaf"!

We shall assume that the city-state of Gondor had an established bureaucracy with its attendant requirement for record-keeping and the likely use of paper for this purpose. The Ruling Stewards kept a library of antiquarian records, but they were not accessible to the general public; even Gandalf had some difficulty in obtaining access to them ("grudgingly he permitted me to search among his hoarded scrolls and books." Tolkien, 1954-5, Book 2, Chapter II).

Cloth can be used for carrying information, woven or painted, but whether Middle-earth knew the use of silk is unsure; however, fine linen can be used instead, probably in locations such as Rivendell and Minas Tirith. The banners and tapestries of Rohan, though not "written", still convey meaning and can thus be considered as a form of writing.

We are not certain about the method of production of these woven items; whether the Rohirrim had progressed from the floor-standing loom, which may be little more than a rectangular frame, to a sophisticated loom with multiple "heddles" (or "healds") operated by a complex mechanism of levers and pulleys is outside the scope of this paper. (This matter may well be the subject of another paper in the future.)

Small items, of mainly decorative or commemorative purpose, made of carven and engraved mûmak ivory would have commanded a high price anywhere in Middle-earth, although any traveller's description of the animal from which the item was derived might have been disbelieved, especially in the Shire!

Metal engraving was known (the Doors of Moria, for example) but little is recorded of the craft. It is debatable whether the creation of the Letters of Fire on the One Ring represent an Elven skill or one peculiar to Sauron. In either case, the letters themselves are the Elven tengwar, somewhat stylised to reflect the nature of the process required to reveal them (fire).

As a digression, it can be supposed that Sauron may have been annoyed, frustrated or even angered because the Ruling Ring was engraved with the script of his arch-enemies and he being unable to rectify that particular annoyance. In the one-volume India paper edition of *The Lord of the Rings* the Ring-inscription is printed in bright red ink (Tolkien, 1954-5, Book 1, Chapter II) to enhance the contrast between the ordinariness of the hobbit-home and the power contained within the Ring.

Media

These varied almost as much as the substrates. "By no means all Hobbits were lettered, but those who were wrote constantly . . ." (Tolkien, 1954-5, Prologue. Section 3: "Of the Ordering of the Shire"). They appeared to use black ink for preference, but they used red ink for the signatures of witnesses to wills. This may simply indicate a long-established custom unique to testaments or a standard practice for any legal document.

There are three main natural sources of black for the ink: oak-gall, which, although initially black fades in time to a dark-brown colour and is in any case expensive; squid-ink, unlikely for Hobbits, although the seaboard Elves may have manufactured some for sale inland; lamp-black, which although permanent, requires a vehicle (the liquid in which the material is carried) with certain characteristics: it must be sufficiently fluid to permit the use of various implements (to be discussed later); it must not be so thin as to present problems of the substrate wrinkling or a very long drying time; and it must provide some adhesive properties. Mediæval scribes used a variety of materials (flour size, thinned egg white, animal glue) so we should be safe in assuming that the Hobbits used the same variety.

The red ink (beloved, it seems, of Shire bureaucrats) poses problems, as it is likely to have been a mineral (for permanence) and this would have had to have been imported, most probably from the Dwarves. Naturally-occurring red dyes, such as madder, may have been possible, but vegetable dyes can be fugitive and it would not be logical to assume that the hobbit scribes would use temporary pigments for permanent records.

We also know that the more wealthy (or eccentric) Hobbits used metal-based inks – Bilbo's invitation to the Sackville-Bagginses, written in gold ink, is a classic example. In this case, the metal would indeed have been gold itself, although the technique would be the same with a non-precious metal. A block of the metal is filed (and the finer the file, the better the result) and the filings suspended in a suitable vehicle. This will have to have a somewhat stronger adhesive power than the one for ordinary pigments, as un-bound metal filings might well loosen in time and flake off the substrate. If the Hobbit scribes made their own inks for daily use, I think that the production of the metal inks would have been left to the Dwarves – with the interesting implication that even the Elves would have had to transact some business with them if they required those materials.

Implements

The range of implements is almost as wide as the choice of substrates and inks. The simplest pen would have been the cut reed (easily obtained and cheap), although such pens do require more attention to retain a sharp edge to the nib and provide a clear impression. Reeds are, of course, aquatic plants, which would cause the Hobbits some concern, as the care and maintenance of reed-beds cannot be carried out exclusively from dry land – a boat is essential, even if only a shallow-draft vessel little more than a ferry-style platform, and that securely tethered to the bank.

After the reed comes the quill, less easy to cut but retaining the sharpness for longer (given a well-prepared substrate and a careful scribe, of course). Quill cutting needs a very sharp blade, so it is possible that, at some stage, the "pen-knife" made its appearance in Middle-earth.

Quills are time-consuming to prepare, as they have to be dried completely, then have the membrane sheathing the shaft removed. The usual way now is to embed the relevant part of the quill in hot sand and there is no reason to believe that the practice in Middle-earth would have been any different.

Another problem with quills is the obtaining of them. Feathers which are loose and fall away from birds are unlikely to be of the best quality, thus there would be a need for quills plucked from birds. Geese are the most likely source of "domestic" quills, although there were swans on the Brandywine and almost certainly in Lothlórien and perhaps a few colonies on the Anduin. Would swans have been a "royal" bird as they were (and indeed still are) in England? If so, the prerogative may well have been adopted by the Oldbucks, being (or at least claiming to be) the most senior of the Hobbit families. The idea of Hobbits attempting the practice of "swan-upping" brings certain hazards to mind; an irate cob-swan can break a full-size man's leg with a blow from its wing, so the Hobbits would certainly have treated the birds with respect!

This problem would not affect the other Speaking (and Writing) Peoples, so we can assume that Elves and Men (and even, perhaps, Dwarves, if any swans used the lakes round the Lonely Mountain) had access to the quills of their choice. The Dwarves could even have imported the quills they needed from Laketown; feathers are used in archery (the fletchings on an arrow provide stability and reliability in flight) so the raw material is present.

It would have been the Dwarves, the Middle-earth metallurgists, who developed the metal-nibbed pen; the quality of the metal must be fine, the nib flexible at need and hard enough to retain an even edge while not destroying the surface being used. Today, gold nibs tipped with iridium are among the most long-lasting: would Middle-earth nibs have been tipped with mithril?

Nibs and inks must be matched for their purpose; a reed pen would not be much use with the heavy gold or silver inks and even the standard quill requires careful handling to obtain a pleasing result.

No consideration of writing would be proper without adding the most important element of the list: the scribe (him-, her- or itself).

The various Councils mentioned in Middle-earth (for example, those of Elrond, Denethor and the Istari) might presumably have had to keep some written records, requiring a scribe or scribes to keep up with the flow of words, although there seems to be no mention of such an occupation; perhaps only the human councils required external "off-line" storage – the Elves and Istari, being excused the Gift of Mortality, might have developed mnemonic techniques; indeed, they may have needed them simply to remain sane over thousands of years! This may even apply to the long-lived, though mortal, Númenóreans and their descendants.

It is recorded that "by no means all Hobbits were lettered but those who were wrote constantly" (Tolkien, 1954-5, Prologue, Section 3: "Of the Ordering of the Shire") although there seems to have been no apparent need for Hobbit-minutes to have been kept, there being no obvious Hobbit-council to generate such things.

There were a number of copyists in Middle-earth, especially those in the Restored Kingdom: "Findegil, King's Writer" (Tolkien, 1954-5, Prologue: "Note on the Shire Records") has a formal title, which implies an officially appointed post, possibly as a successor to the Scribe of the Ruling Stewards, and, presumably, the Hobbits had a number of suitably-skilled individuals: their existence is implied by the statement "The original Red Book has not been preserved, but many copies were made, especially of the first volume . . ." (Tolkien, 1954-5, Prologue: "Note on the Shire Records"). It would be a monumental task for one scribe to produce "many copies", so a Hobbitic scriptorium should not be seen as an impossibility.

Glyphs

There were two main types of glyphs used in the Third Age. The tengwar in the various modes (Quenya, Sindarin, Beleriand and Westron) had the wider distribution, while the cirth did seem to be used almost exclusively by the Dwarves.

This is not, however, as clear-cut a division as it might seem, because the fireworks brought by Gandalf for the Long-expected Party were "each labelled with a large red G [tengwa 'ungwe'] and the elf-rune, [g – name unknown]" and the hobbit-children seem to have recognised one or both of them "'G for Grand!' they shouted . . ." (Tolkien, 1954-5, Book 1, Chapter I).

Other means of communication existed: ideograms, or ordinary pictures, used as badges (the Eye, the Red Hand, the White Horse); physical objects, most notably the Red Arrow (Tolkien, 1954-5, Book 5, Chapter III) and, of course, "seven stars, and seven stones, and one white tree".

Once the written material is produced, there is the problem of preservation. Scrolls are easier to keep, as they can simply be rolled up and slipped into protective tubes, which may be made of cloth, wood, leather, metal or even other pieces of parchment, or simply slid into a lattice-work shelf (rather like a wine-rack).

Parchment leaves, or paper, are more susceptible to damage, so they require collection and protection. There is evidence of book-binding – Bilbo's Diary, which seems to be more of a notebook, "a big book with plain red leather covers" (Tolkien, 1954-5, Book 6, Chapter IX). Given the likely thickness of this tome ("Chapter 80 was unfinished", Tolkien, 1954-5, Book 6, Chapter IX) it must surely have been constructed in the manner of books which have lasted well in our world, with the sheets collected into "signatures", sewn together using a strong waxed thread and the signatures bound with ribbon laced through the stitches at the fold of each signature, as is shown in the sample [produced at the presentation of this paper].

It is well within the abilities of the Hobbits to make such sturdy and long-lasting volumes, although the dye used on the leather (not to mention the production of the leather itself) poses a few questions.

The art of printing seems not to be mentioned in Middle-earth, though it would surely not have taxed the ingenuity of the Dwarves to devise a moveable-type system. The tengwar pose a problem, with the use of diacritics above and below various letters and carriers. I believe that the Middle-earth typesetters would not have tried to produce blocks with every combination of tengwa and tehta, but would have arranged the tengwa block so that there was space above and below the body for an inserted tehta.

When the Travellers returned to the Shire, they found their room at the Inn contained Rules – indeed all the rooms had such notices. We can theorise that although the Hobbits themselves had not devised the printing-press, such would have been well within the ability of Saruman ("a mind of metal and wheels", Tolkien, 1954-5, Book 3, Chapter IV), and the publication of the Rules, to be placed in every room of every inn, bespeaks either a massive scribal copying establishment or a printing-press. It is a purely personal impression, but I visualise the Rules as being poorly-printed on cheap paper, the ink smudgy and "feathering" (leaking into the paper because of a surface not adequately prepared) and the letters themselves not well-designed – all of which contrasts with the (presumed) elegance of the Elvish books in Rivendell and the sturdiness of the Book of Mazarbûl. The mere fact of the Rules being printed at all would be reason enough for Meriadoc or Peregrin to consider them an affront to a properly-raised Hobbit!

References

Tolkien, J.R.R. 1954-5. *The Lord of the Rings*, three volumes. London: George Allen & Unwin, 1954, 1954, 1955.

Section nine

The Inklings

Hermetic Imagination: The Effect of The Golden Dawn on Fantasy Literature

Charles A. Coulombe

Abstract: The Hermetic Order of the Golden Dawn was an English expression of the Nineteenth-Century occult revival in Europe. Dedicated to such practices as ceremonial magic and divination, it valued these more as gateways to true understanding of reality than for their intrinsic merit. The Golden Dawn's essentially Neoplatonic world-view is reflected in the writings of such some-time members as W.B. Yeats, Arthur Machen and Charles Williams.

Keywords: Golden Dawn, Hermeticism, Arthur Machen, Magic, Charles Williams, W.B. Yeats

Beyond these fields and this borderland there lies the legendary wonder-world of theurgy, so called, of Magic and Sorcery, a world of fascination or terror, as the mind which regards it is tempered, but in any case the antithesis of admitted possibility. There all paradoxes seem to obtain actually, contradictions coexist logically, the effect is greater than the cause and the shadow more than the substance. Therein the visible melts into the unseen, the invisible is manifested openly, motion from place to place is accomplished without traversing the intervening distance, matter passes through matter. There two straight lines may enclose a space; space has a fourth dimension, and untrodden fields beyond it; without metaphor and without evasion, the circle is mathematically squared. There life is prolonged, youth renewed, physical immortality secured. There earth becomes gold, and gold earth. There words and wishes possess creative power, thoughts are things, desire realises its object. There, also, the dead live and the hierarchies of extra-mundane intelligence are within easy communication, and become ministers or tormentors, guides or destroyers of man. There the Law of Continuity is suspended by the interference of the higher Law of Fantasia.
(Waite, 1961, pp. 3-4)

This rather lengthy quotation serves well as an introduction to the Hermetic or Magical world-view. It is in complete contradiction, needless to say, to the more or less materialistic perspective our education and upbringing have bestowed on us modern Europeans, North Americans, and Australasians. Since at least the Enlightenment, educated opinion has insisted on what we call the scientific method. Relying on the purely measurable, it has provided us with the technology necessary to provide us with all the conveniences we possess — surely a telling argument in any case. But to understand the world-view of W.B. Yeats, Arthur Machen, and Charles Williams, as well as that of the Hermetic Order of the golden Dawn to which they all belonged, we must first pick up a little of its history.

While the Magical world-view may not be popular among us today, it is an integral part of practically all pre-industrial societies. In Europe, the country-folk from time immemorial to this century (and in some out-of-the-way places even yet) saw this everyday life of ours as interpenetrated with beings and actions from other worlds co-existent with this one:

> Often they are described as distant realms, but almost as frequently they are imagined to lie so close alongside normal space that transition from one to the other is only too easy, in both directions. Certain places and times facilitate the transition. Supernatural powers break through into the normal (or can be summoned to it) at turning points of time: midnight, midday, New Year's Eve, Halloween, May Eve, Midsummer Night. Similarly with space; it is at boundaries, thresholds, crossroads, fords, bridges, and where verticality intersects the horizontal, as on top of mounds, down wells, under trees, that Otherworlds are accessible . . .
> One key is ambiguity, the concept both/and and neither/nor. If a man stands exactly on the boundary where three parishes meet, at the stroke of midnight, in which parish is he, and what date is it? He has cut loose from normal space and time. He has also reversed normal human conduct by going outside at night, the time when supernatural beings are active, but humans should be asleep. In such circumstances, he places himself in contact with "the other"; he can reach, or be reached by, fairies, ghosts, or demons.
> (Simpson, 1985, p. 34)

While the same views may be found in all the world's folklore and mythology (as, for example, the Australian aboriginal "dream-time", so often invoked today), in Europe the influence of Christian doctrine made a great impact. Even as Faerie was conceived in terms like those just quoted, so too were Heaven, Hell, and Purgatory, which realms also erupted into our own in various ways. Churches were seen as outposts of the celestial, brought down at the Sacrifice of the Mass and other Sacraments. Purgatory, through the medium of ghosts (*á la* Hamlet's father) played its part. Hell too, through its demons, those of Faerie who were evil (the "unseelie court", as the Scots put it), Werewolves, Vampires, and so on, made its presence felt. Human beings too could align with the infernal in return for supernatural power; these were of course the Witches of song and story. (To those who would claim that this sort of witchery was the invention of Church officials, it should be pointed out that to this day, supposed witches are burned, tortured, and hung in non-Christian places like China, Africa, and remoter Australia; it is this writer's contention that the origins of today's "Wicca" or neo-Paganism lie elsewhere.)

At any rate, the village wise-folk who trafficked with the unseen, the Anne Jeffries sorts of people who stumbled into it, and the generality of villagers who treasured up tales, charms, and beliefs of these kinds were for the most part merely reacting in a half-instinctual manner to the realities they perceived around them. There was perhaps little of a developed theory behind all of this (although this assertion may not be readily defensible – oral cultures can be richer and more complex than we moderns suspect).

Unlike today, however, the learned of earlier days held much the same world-view, albeit in a more reasoned and articulated manner. The Pre-Socratic philosophers "did not oppose matter to mind, soul to body, or subject to object, but had a tendency to approach nature with a nondualistic, noncategorical attitude. In such a view, all being is concrete." (Faivre, 1987a)

Socrates' pupil, Plato, developed the idea of the types or universals – such as "Man", "Horse", "King", and so on – of which their concrete representations which we experience (and we ourselves) are mere shadows. These realities reside in some supernatural realm from whence they cast their shadows upon the Earth. While this theory could lend itself to a real dualism, its effect on philosophers whose psychology was influenced by Pre-Socratic attitudes often led such to consider reality as an interconnecting web of coherences and correspondences, the seen operating upon the unseen, and vice versa. Obviously, such an intellectual context lent itself to any number of religious and mystical beliefs; the obscurest maxims of the Hellenistic Mystery Schools could be considered expressions of wisdom by the most rigorous thinkers of antiquity.

Into this philosophico-religious mix entered, in the first few centuries AD, the Alexandrian writings attributed to Hermes Trismegistus. Codifying the whole system of analogies which had grown up by the phrase "as above, so below", Hermeticism gave to philosophers and thinkers a model of dealing with the unseen. Neoplatonic Universals came in time to meet Hermetic Analogy. Thus was born the approach to reality our opening quote epitomises; thus was given to age-old magical practise a philosophical basis.

Just as Christianity affected and was in turn affected by the folk-beliefs of its humbler converts, so too did it and was it by the philosophies of its more educated neophytes. From this encounter emerged many of the ideas of the Church Fathers: St. Dionysius the Areopagite, St. Justin the Martyr, St. Clement of Alexandria, Origen, and St. Augustine are prime examples of this process. Similarly, the emerging traditional liturgies of East and West were much affected by ritual commonplaces in contemporary theurgy and prayers to higher spirits. To the sceptic, this interconnexion would doubtless relativise even further the value of Christian doctrine and practise; to the believer, it would simply be a demonstration of his Faith encompassing within itself all truths, revealed or otherwise. From Tertullian's maxim that "the soul is naturally Christian", such a believer would draw the Hermetic analogy that so too is reality as a whole. Thus the demons, angels, and so on spoken of in Neoplatonic theurgy would not be mere pagan engraftings onto Christianity, but simply pre-Christian acknowledgements of actual beings.

The dualism implicit in Neoplatonism, which provided its main distinction from Hermeticism, was lacking in the Christian Neoplatonism of the Church Fathers. For them, as for later Christian philosophers, the Universals did not exist independently, but in the mind of God. This concept gave philosophical comprehensibility to various difficult doctrines. The Fall of Man, for instance, could be seen in terms of the falling of the whole Universal "Man", in the persons of its then only two extant concrete representatives – Adam and Eve. This point of view, which saw the Universals as real and as the pattern from whence come all perceived physical things, is called "Ultra-Realism". Under its influence were composed the Catholic and Orthodox liturgies, most pre-13th Century theological works, and the writings of Mystics of the same period. It is a mark of Ultra-Realism, in fact, that Mysticism (with its concomitant physical phenomena, bilocation, the stigmata, etc.,) and Theology – that is, the practise and the study of unity with God – were then considered inseparable. By the same token, astrology (with the proviso that "the stars impel, they do not compel"), alchemy, the Jewish Qabbalah, and the like were taken seriously by devout writers like John Scotus Eriugena, Pope Sylvester II, Bl. Raymond Lully, Roger Bacon, St. Hildegarde of Bingen, St. Thomas Aquinas, and so on. The acceptance of the reality of the spiritual, and the possibility of exploring it by analogy from the natural, were accepted by all early Medieval Christian thinkers:

> In that which concerns speculative philosophy or metaphysics, the same role is reserved there for analogy. All conclusions of a metaphysical nature are based only on the analogy of man, Nature, and the intelligible or metaphysical world. Thus the two principal authorities of the most methodical and most disciplined philosophy – medieval Scholastic philosophy – St. Thomas Aquinas and St. Bonaventure (of whom one represents Aristotelianism and the other Platonism in Christian Philosophy) not only make use of analogy but also assign it a very important theoretical role in their doctrines themselves. St. Thomas advances the doctrine of *analogia entis*, the

analogy of being, which is the principle key to his philosophy. St. Bonaventure, in his doctrine of *signatura rerum*, interprets the entire visible world as the symbol of the invisible world. For him, the visible world is only another Holy Scripture, another revelation alongside that which is contained in Holy Scripture . . .
(Tonberg, 1991, p. 17)

Given this sort of world-view, it is not too surprising that during the Middle Ages sympathetic magic, based upon natural correspondences, and theurgy, based upon invocation of angels and elementals, flourished (so too, alas, did goetia, with its invocation of demons, and necromancy, with its consultation of the dead. Needless to say, the latter two were particularly discouraged by the Church). But SS. Thomas Aquinas and Bonaventure, in their own lives and careers, foreshadow the rise of modern philosophy.

St. Bonaventure was a traditional Ultra-Realist. St. Thomas, on the other hand, picked up the Aristotelian view that the Universals derive their reality from the sum total of their concrete expressions: that is, that rather than Men deriving their Mannishness from the Universal Man, said Universal is only identifiable from the shared Mannishness of individual Men. This may sound an arcane distinction, but it was in reality the first chink through which a tide of Aristotelian materialism would in the end divorce theology and the supernatural entirely from philosophy and the physical. "The Platonist sees things in God; the Aristotelian sees God at the summit of things" (Bettoni, 1964, p. 20). As St. Bonaventure was a disciple of St. Francis, first of the 400 attested stigmatics to have been marked down to our own day, it is no suprise that he should have been a Platonist. Indeed, for those who believe in it, the Stigmata might be seen as a concrete proof of Ultra-Realism.

However that may be, Moderate Realism produced over the course of the Middle ages Conceptualism, which saw the Universals as being only human concepts, and Nominalism, which saw them as mere names having no reality at all. It would not be unfair to say that most Modern Philosophy is Nominalism on a spree.

What these philosophical developments meant concretely was the progressive separation of Christian Theology from Philosophy. There was, it is true, during the Humanist movement of the Renaissance something of a recapturing of Neoplatonism and Hermeticism. This produced such figures as Cardinal Bessarion, Nicholas of Cusa, Pico Della Mirandola, Reuchlin, and Aeneas Sylvius Piccolomini (Pope Pius II). All of these and their ideological kin were also intensely interested in Qabbalah, Alchemy, etc. – in a strictly Christian and Catholic context.

The Reformation, spearheaded by the Nominalist Martin Luther, put an end to all such developments. While the next few centuries would produce a few figures like Jakob Böhme and Claude de St. Martin, for the most part materialism and "modern" scientific method grew in their monopoly of Europe's intellectual life. The Enlightenment was the fruition of this process. Then came the French and Industrial Revolutions, which idolised the materialistic. Almost inevitably, there came a reaction – Romanticism.

Romanticism encompassed many allied themes. To the Materialist assumption of the all-importance of the body and the group, it opposed the individual. To the mechanistic view of nature it replied with a *Naturphilosophie* which again saw nature as at once veiling and representing spiritual realities. To the cult of progress, the Romantics also opposed a love of the Medieval past and the Peasant or Exotic present. Perhaps the greatest of the Romantic philosophers was the incomparable Franz von Baader, who later inspired Vladimir Soloviev.

From the outpouring of all of this throughout the 19th Century, interest arose in much of the literate European public in fantasy literature, spiritualism, and the occult:

The industrial revolution naturally gave rise to an increasingly marked interest in the "miracles" of science. It promoted the invasion of daily life by utilitarian and socioeconomic preoccupations of all kinds. Along with the smoking factory chimneys came both the literature of the fantastic and the new phenomenon of spiritualism. These two possess a common characteristic: each takes the real world in its most concrete form as its point of departure, and then postulates the existence of another, supernatural world, separated from the first by a more or less impermeable partition. Fantasy literature then plays upon the effect of surprise that is provided by the irruption of the supernatural into the daily life which it describes in a realistic fashion . . . It is interesting that occultism in its modern form – that of the nineteenth century – appeared at the same time as fantastic literature and spiritualism. The French term *occultisme* was perhaps first used by Eliphas Lévi (1810-1875), whose work is sometimes somewhat misleadingly identified with the beginnings of occultism itself . . . Like the fantastic and the quasi religion of spiritualism, nineteenth century occultism showed a marked interest in supernatural phenomena, that is to say, in the diverse modes of passage from one world to the other.
(Faivre, "Occultism", 1987b).

Not too surprisingly the Occult revival in France which featured men like Lévi, Papus, Peladan, Grillot de Givry, and many others, was parallelled by a similar movement in French literature featuring such names as Barbey d'Aurevilly, Villiers de l'Isle Adam, and Huysmans. While many of these considered themselves loyal Catholics, the standard theologians of the time, much under Neo-Thomist influence, regarded them suspiciously.

This phenomenon was not restricted to the continent. In 1875, Helena Blavatsky founded the Theosophical Society in New York, which soon spread throughout the English-speaking world. Originally very Western in emphasis, studying such topics as alchemy and the writings of Paracelsus, the Society took on a strongly Oriental tone after Mme. Blavatsky took a voyage to India, and claimed to have made contact with various Tibetan "Ascended Masters". A number of members took issue with this (among whom was Rudolf Steiner, who eventually founded his own Anthroposophical Society in Germany). A further objection to the course of the Theosophical Society was that its membership were encouraged only to study occult doctrine, not to practise it – that is, not to practise Magic. But an organisation formed in 1888 soon attracted many Theosophists who wished either a more Western teaching or Magical practise, or both: The Hermetic Order of the Golden Dawn.

The Golden Dawn

This society was formed as a result of the discovery in a bookstall of a cypher MS by one Rev. A.F.A. Woodford. Supposedly, this manuscript was written by a German Rosicrucian lady, and invited anyone interested in setting up a similar organisation to contact her. In concert with Macgregor Mathers, a Scottish student of the Occult, and Dr. W. Wynn Westcott, the Golden Dawn was accordingly organised.

From the very beginning, its membership fell roughly into two categories: those who were of a Western-Theosophical bent (many of whom, as just noted, had left the Theosophical Society for that particular reason), and those of a more explicitly Christian orientation. This uneasy mix would erupt later into open conflict; but at the very beginning both camps were united in declaring that "to establish closer and more personal relations with the Lord Jesus, the Master of Masters, is and ever must be the ultimate object of all the teachings of our order." Unexceptional as this goal was, the Order's means of reaching it were quite unusual.

The Golden Dawn aspired to be not merely a complete academy of occult knowledge (as indeed the Theosophical Society had claimed to be) but also a forum for Mystico-Magical practise – which Magic was seen as being like that of Eliphas Lévi. In the words of Stephan Hoeller, Magic in this sense is "an umbrella term for the growth or expansion of consciousness by way of symbolic modalities." To impart both knowledge and practise, an elaborate system of grades was established; as the student ascended these grades, he or she learned ever more esoteric skills.

These latter included knowledge of Qabbalah (which Hebrew system's model of all reality – the "Tree of Life" – provided the Golden Dawn with its basic ideational framework); Tarot; Geomancy; Astrology; Alchemy; and ritual Magic. The workings of the last-named included making of sigils and talismans, communing with Elementals, evocation of Demons, and invocation of Angels. As well, the Golden Dawn initiate was taught "skrying", which included both clairvoyance and astral travel.

From its beginning, the Golden Dawn attracted a highly literary membership. In addition to the three whom we shall consider, Algernon Blackwood, Dion Fortune, Sax Rohmer, actress Florence Farr, Maud Gonne, E. Nesbit, and Evelyn Underhill were all members at one time or another, either of the Golden Dawn itself or of one of the splinter groups which survived the Order's disruption in 1900. With the publication of the Order's rituals by Israel Regardie, we are now in a better position to gauge the ideology of the Golden Dawn than were earlier writers on the topic.

Concurrent with its Western-Theosophic and Qabbalistic viewpoint (themselves manifestations of Hermeticism and Neo-Platonism) the Golden Dawn also reflected in its rituals the Christian emphasis earlier referred to. While subsequent authorities (notably Regardie) have sought to minimise this in accordance with their own biases, it is still evident from an examination of the material. Indeed, it is alleged that many of the first members of the Anglican Community of the Resurrection (the Mirfield Fathers) were members, although this would be hard to substantiate. Still, there can be no doubt that many Golden Dawn Fratres and Sorores achieved in their own devotional lives the same synthesis between Hermeticism/Neoplatonism and Sacramental Christianity that characterised Medieval Ultra-Realists, Renaissance Humanists, and (in a much less conscious way) European folk-culture members. In a word, their Christianity, while tied to the dogmas of Revelation, saw the world as both a symbol and concealment of higher realities, contact with which was obtainable both through magic and divination, and, on a purer and greater level, through the Sacraments.

Most representative of these was perhaps the Catholic A.E. Waite, who formed a separate, more explicitly Christian Mysticism-oriented Golden Dawn group in 1903. Commenting on Claude de St. Martin's works, Waite wrote: "It is difficult to agree that a system which includes institutions of such efficacy [the Sacraments], and apparently of divine origin, can at the same time transmit nothing. It becomes more apparent . . . that the failure in transmission is not in the Church, but in the ministers. The Church assists us towards regeneration by operating divers effects at divers seasons" (1970, p. 331). He goes on to say ". . . I think the Church Catholic is preferable to the most exotic plant of Lutheranism . . ." (1970, p. 333). A good understanding of Waite's position is important, because Yeats, Machen, and Williams all elected to follow him, and his view of matters esoteric is the strand of Golden Dawn tradition which informs their work. He wrote of the Golden Dawn itself: "It is not in competition with the external Christian Churches, and yet it is a Church of the Elect, a Hidden and Holy Assembly . . . It is a House of the Holy Graal in the sanctity of a High Symbolism, where the sacred intent of the Order is sealed upon Bread and Wine" (quoted in Carpenter, 1979, p. 82).

Odd though Waite's views may appear to many today, they were not unechoed on either side of the channel. In her 1963 foreword to Waite's similarly-viewed French contemporary Grillot de Givry's *Sorcery, Magic, and Alchemy*, Cynthia Magriel informs us that:

> De Givry lived in a moment in history and in France when his views, though strange to most Catholics, could be tolerated. They were shared in part by a number of Catholics who were considered no worse than eccentrics.
>
> Thus the Baron de Sarachaga, a Basque and a nephew of St. Teresa [of Avila], for forty years headed the Institut des Fastes; this school was approved by Popes Pius IX and Leo XIII. Pierre Dujois, a learned hermetist, wrote of this school in 1912: "There exists in Paray-le-Monial [the centre of devotion to the Sacred

Heart of Jesus] a mysterious Cabalic centre, sincerely Catholic it seems, and where the bizarre orthodoxy is nevertheless accepted and even encouraged by the Church . . ."
(p. 5)

So the mixture of orthodoxy and magic we encounter in the writings of our three authors, deriving from the Golden Dawn and particularly from Waite, was not without contemporary as well as past parallels. This is an important point, because for varying reasons Christian and non-Christian writers alike have attempted to set up a dichotomy between the Christian and occult elements in the three's work where there is in fact a synthesis – a synthesis which in these particular cases is the direct result of their membership in the Golden Dawn. Let us look now at each of them.

William Butler Yeats

Of the three, Yeats' connection with the Golden Dawn is the best known and documented. In his *Autobiography*, pp. 341-342, he discusses his involvement with the Golden Dawn and its history, calling it "the Hermetic Students", but giving Mathers and Westcott their proper names. His *Memoirs*, published posthumously, are full of bits of gossip about the Golden Dawn and its members. Of the Order, he says therein, "I . . . value a ritual full of the symbolism of the Middle Ages and the Renaissance . . ." (p. 27). He had come to the Golden Dawn after having been expelled from the Theosophical Society by Madame Blavatsky for actually practising Magic. Yet even before his entrance into the Theosophical Society, he and a number of other Dublin Anglo-Irish youths had formed a "Dublin Hermetic Society" for the study of European Magic and Mysticism, and to a degree of Eastern religion. Why? "All were parched by the desiccated religion which the Church of Ireland and the Presbyterian Church, now purged of their old evangelicalism, provided." (Richard Ellmann, 1964, p. 41). Certainly Yeats' exposure to the folk and fairy lore of the Irish played its part also.

Yeats entered into the Golden Dawn with great gusto in 1890. He followed its practises, and claimed to have particularly benefited from clairvoyance. For Yeats Magic and Poetry were near synonymous. When in 1892 a friend wrote to him questioning the "healthiness" of his Golden Dawn activity, he wrote back:

> Now as to Magic. It is surely absurd to hold me "weak" or otherwise because I chose to persist in a study which I decided deliberately four or five years ago to make, next to my Poetry, the most important pursuit of my life. Whether it be, or be not, bad for my health can only be decided by one who knows what Magic is and not at all by any amateur. If I had not made Magic my constant study I could not have written a single word of my Blake book, nor would *The Countess Kathleen* have ever come to exist. The Mystical life is the centre of all that I do and all that I think and all that I write.
> (Yeats in Wade 1954, p. 210).

In 1897, Yeats published *Rosa Alchemica*, an allegory of his studies with the Golden Dawn. But in practically everything he wrote, the world-view enunciated in the opening quote was evident. Whether he was dealing with fairy-lore or mystic visions, the conviction that this world both symbolises and conceals greater realities was ever obvious in his work. In 1915, he wrote a poem for initiation into the highest grade of the Golden Dawn's outer order:

FOR INITIATION OF 7 = 4
We are weighed down by the blood & the heavy weight of the bones
We are bound by flowers, & our feet are entangled in the green
And there is deceit in the singing of birds.
It is time to be done with it all
The stars call & all the planets
And the purging fire of the moon
And yonder is the cold silence of cleansing night
May the dawn break, & gates of day be set wide open.

It were useless to belabour the point much further. But what is not so well-known is the degree to which Waite (whom Yeats followed in the 1903 split) must have influenced Yeats' views of Christianity in general and Catholicism in particular. There can be no doubt of Yeats' disenchantment with both the Protestantism of his youth, and with the Irish Catholic hierarchy. He complained in 1907 of the "ingratiating manner . . . of certain well-educated Catholic priests, a manner one does not think compatible with deep spiritual experience" (Yeats, 1953, p. 282). Two years later he wrote in his diary: "Catholic secondary education destroys, I think, much that the Catholic religion gives. Provincialism destroys the nobility of the Middle Ages" (Yeats, 1953, p. 304).

Certainly, at first glance, such anti-clericalism, read in the light of his comment in *Rosa Alchemica* that ". . . I knew a Christian's ecstasy without his slavery to custom", would imply a Mysticism completely unChristian. But this would be a superficial reading indeed. In fact, it would appear that his view of the central Christian dogma of the Incarnation, while reminiscent of orthodoxy, was given the esoteric emphasis familiar to readers of Waite's work:

> Western civilisation, religion, and magic insist on power and therefore on body, and hence these three doctrines – efficient rule – the Incarnation – thaumaturgy. Eastern thoughts answer to these with indifference to rule, scorn of the flesh, contemplation of the formless. Western minds who follow the Eastern way become weak and vapoury, because unfit for the work forced upon them by Western life. Every symbol is an invocation which produces its equivalent expression in all worlds. the Incarnation invoked modern science and modern efficiency, and individualised emotion. It produced a solidification of all those things that grow from individual will.
> (Yeats, 1953, pp. 292-293)

In one sweep, we see that the causes for Yeats' break with the Theosophical Society (Mme. Blavatsky's eastern interests and her dislike of practical magic experimentation) he believed to be linked directly to the Incarnation.

There are other examples of Yeats' specifically Christian

esotericism, derived from the Golden Dawn and Waite. One must suffice, however. In his essay "Ceremonial Union" (in Waite, 1987, pp. 189-194), Waite describes the unity existing between Order members, a unity which permits them to share, via their ritual connexion, each other's pains and difficulties, and so lessen them. Compare Yeats:

> A French miracle-working priest once said to Maud Gonne and myself and to an English Catholic who had come with us, that a certain holy woman had been the "victim" for his village, and that another holy woman who had been "victim" for all France, had given him her Crucifix, because he, too, was doomed to become a "victim".
>
> French psychical research has offered evidence to support the historical proofs that such saints as Lydwine of Schiedam, whose life suggested to Paul Claudel his *L'Annonce faite à Marie*, did really cure disease by taking it upon themselves. As disease was considered the consequence of sin, to take it upon themselves was to copy Christ.
>
> (Yeats, 1953, p. 199)

Thus it was that a few years later, in 1917, he would write comparing the contemporary French Poets like Jammes and Peguy to those of his youth like Mallarmé:

> Nothing remained the same but the preoccupation with religion, for these poets submitted everything to the Pope, and all, even Claudel, a proud oratorical man, affirmed that they saw the world with the eyes of vine-dressers and charcoal-burners. it was no longer the soul, self-moving and self-teaching – the magical soul – but Mother France and Mother Church.
>
> Have not my thoughts run a like round, though I have not found my tradition in the Catholic Church, which was not the Church of my childhood, but where the tradition is, as I believe, more universal and more ancient?
>
> (1980, pp. 368-369)

It would appear that as Yeats grew older, he did, at least with one part of his complex psyche, ever more closely synthesise esotericism and mystical Christianity. But he would never be a conventional parishioner – nor did he ever settle publicly into any denomination. He would, until his death, remain critical of clerics of every denomination. Yet it may well be that his final word on the matter might be summed up in an editorial he ghost-wrote for the short-lived artistic journal *To-Morrow* in 1924:

> TO ALL ARTISTS AND WRITERS
>
> We are Catholics, but of the school of Pope Julius the Second and of the Medician Popes, who ordered Michael-Angelo and Raphael to paint upon the walls of the Vatican, and upon the ceiling of the Sistine Chapel, the doctrine of the Platonic Academy of Florence, the reconciliation of Galilee and Parnassus. We proclaim Michaelangelo the most orthodox of men, because he set upon the tomb of the Medici "Dawn" and "Night", vast forms shadowing the strength of antediluvian Patriarchs and the lust of the goat, the whole handiwork of God, even the abounding horn.
>
> We proclaim that we can forgive the sinner, but abhor the atheist, and that we count among atheists bad writers and Bishops of all denominations. "The Holy spirit is an intellectual fountain", and did the Bishops believe that, the Holy Spirit would show itself in decoration and architecture, in daily manners and written style. What devout man can read the Pastorals of our Hierarchy without horror at a style rancid, coarse and vague, like that of the daily papers? We condemn the art and literature of modern Europe. No man can create, as did Shakespeare, Homer, Sophocles, who does not believe, with all his blood and nerve, that man's soul is immortal, for the evidence lies plain to all men that where that belief has declined, men have turned from creation to photography. We condemn, though not without sympathy, those who would escape from banal mechanism through technical investigation and experiment. We proclaim that these bring no escape, for new form comes from new subject matter, and new subject matter must flow from the human soul restored to all its courage, to all its audacity. We dismiss all demagogues and call back the soul to its ancient sovereignty, and declare that it can do whatever it please, being made, as antiquity affirmed, from the imperishable substance of the stars.
>
> (Ellmann, 1964, pp. 246-247)

We are close here to Grillot de Givry's desire to build at Lourdes "a gothic jewel", which would "teach the clergy a lesson in architecture which they need", and Waite's gleeful repetition of St. Martin's maxim "The Church should be the Priest, but the Priest seeks to be the Church." It is just such surface anti-clericalism, concealing a desire to reintegrate the Christian Mysteries into Man's Art and conception of reality – whence they had been sundered by the Enlightenment and the Industrial and French Revolutions – which constituted the quest of that segment of the Golden Dawn with which Yeats, Machen, and Williams had affiliated.

This writer has seen in one source an indication that Yeats' first burial at Roquebrune in 1939 was conducted with Catholic rites. Should this be true, it would mean that he must have been received into that Church on his deathbed; such a reconciliation would not have been with the clergy he regarded as being in the main rationalist, but with the Sacramental and Mystical system they represented. It would mean that he had achieved at his death the Hermetic conjunction he at times approached in his work.

Arthur Machen

Where Yeats' attachment to Christianity is tenuous, there is no such ambiguity with Arthur Machen. As Ireland did for Yeats, so Wales cast its glamour over Machen. H.P. Lovecraft wrote of him that: "He has absorbed the mediaeval mystery of dark woods and ancient customs, and is a champion of the Middle Ages in all things – including the Catholic faith" (1973, p. 88). Unlike Yeats, Machen was never estranged from the faith of his youth. But the lore of the neighbourhood of Caerleon upon Usk, one of Arthur's cities, so it was said, worked powerfully upon his imagination. From this early experience he evolved the credo that "Man is made of mystery and exists for mysteries and visions." This view of life turned him early to writing of the fantastic. In "The Novel of the White Powder", he wrote: "The whole universe, my friend, is a tremendous sacrament; a mystic, ineffable force and energy, veiled by an outward form of matter; and man, and the sun, and the other stars, and the flower of the grass, and the crystal in the test tube, are each and every one as spiritual, as material, and subject to an inner working" (1964, p. 57). On his own, with just his admittedly mystical religion and his Celtic imagination, he had arrived at the same conclusions as the Hermeticists, Neoplatonists, and Ultra-Realists. He expressed much of the same viewpoint in "The Great God Pan":

> Look about you, Clarke. You see the mountain, and hill following after hill, as wave on wave, you see the woods and orchards, the fields of ripe corn, and the meadows reaching to the reed beds by the river. You see me standing here beside you, and hear my voice; but I tell you that all these things – yes, from the star that has just shone out in the sky to the solid ground beneath our feet – I say that all these are but dreams and shadows: the shadows that hide the real world from our eyes. There *is* a real world, but it is beyond this glamour and this vision, beyond these "chases in Arras, dreams in a career", beyond them all as beyond a veil.
> (1964, p. 62)

These two stories were written in 1895 and 1896. At the time that Machen wrote them, while he was perhaps temperamentally oriented in the direction of such beliefs, he was not inclined to give them much credence in the workaday world – in any case they were hazy, being based upon general impressions of life rather than experience of Magic. This changed with his entrance into the Golden Dawn in 1898. There he gained practical knowledge of what he had guessed. In an 1899 letter written to French novelist Paul-Jean Touletin, he declared:

> When I was writing *Pan* and *The White Powder*, I did not believe that such strange things had ever happened in real life, or could ever have happened. Since then, and quite recently, I have had certain experiences in my own life which have entirely changed my point of view in these matters. Henceforward I am quite convinced that nothing is impossible on this Earth. I need scarcely add, I suppose, that none of the experiences I have had has any connexion whatever with such impostures as spiritualism or theosophy. But I believe we are living in a world of the greatest mystery full of unsuspected and quite astonishing things.
> (Pauwels and Bergier, 1964, pp. 212-213)

In the 1903 split, Machen also followed Waite, whose more Christianised esotericism he apparently found congenial. Three years later, a new collection of his fiction appeared. While it included both of his older pieces, new material was included, in which obtains a certain shift of tone. In the first two works, he had been very vague about the shape of things, as we have seen. There is in part an almost Manichean quality to his description of reality – as well as a certain tentativeness. But the post-Golden Dawn material is at once more strictly in line with Christian dogma, and more authoritative. So he commences "The White People" with "Sorcery and sanctity . . . these are the only realities. Each is an ecstasy, a withdrawal from the common life" (Machen, 1964, p. 116). After declaring that real sin is an obscene alteration of reality, he writes, "Holiness requires as great, or almost as great, an effort; but holiness works on lines that *were* natural once; it is an effort to regain the ecstasy that was before the Fall. But sin is an effort to gain the ecstasy and the knowledge that pertain alone to angels, and in making this effort man becomes a demon" (p. 119). Similarly, a character in "The Red Hand" remarks "There are Sacraments of evil as well as good about us, and we live and move to my belief in an unknown world, a place where there are caves and shadows and dwellers in twilight" (Machen, 1961, pp. 170-171).

As for Waite, so too for Machen, the Holy Grail was an important theme. Symbolising at once the Eucharist, the Crucifixion, and the ecstasy Machen believed was the heart of Christianity, he returned to it again and again. In "The Great Return", he described the Grail's coming to a remote Welsh village during World War I, and the veil it removes during its short stay from the world around us:

> . . . if there be paradise in meat and in drink, so much the more is there paradise in the scent of the green leaves at evening and in the appearance of the sea and in the redness of the sky; and there came to me a certain vision of a real world about us all the while, of a language that was only secret because we would not take the trouble to listen to it and to discern it.
> (Machen, 1964, p. 222)

The presence of the Grail causes not only miracles but clarity of vision:

> Old men felt young again, eyes that had been growing dim now saw clearly, and saw a world that was like paradise, the same world, it is true, but a world rectified and glowing, as if an inner flame shone in all things, and behind all things.
>
> And the difficulty in recording this state is this, that it is so rare an experience that no set language to express it is in existence. A shadow of its raptures and ecstasies is found in the highest poetry; there are phrases in ancient books telling of the Celtic saints that dimly hint at it; some of the old Italian masters of painting had known it, for the light of it shines in their skies and about the battlements of their cities that are founded on magic hills. But these are but broken hints.
> (Machen, 1964, p. 237)

This union of the Catholic with the Hermetic, of the Christian with the Esoteric, would, it must be again repeated, have made perfect sense to the Ultra-Realist, the Humanist, or the peasant. For Arthur Machen, it required whatever experiences he gained in the Golden Dawn to transmute the iron of impression into the gold of conviction. What began as instinct on his part was, through the medium of his time in the Golden Dawn, made into experience. This in turn gives his later works the feeling of one who *knows* whereof he speaks. Yet it also presents those of us comfortable with neat compartments marked "religion", "magic", and "literature", with tremendous problems of classification.

So it is that Gunnar Urang in *Shadows of Heaven* is quite perplexed by Machen's definitions of literature in his *Hieroglyphics*, which he quotes on p. 150:

> If we, being wondrous, journey through a wonderful world, if all our joys are from above, from the other world where the Shadowy Companion walks, then no mere making of the likeness of the external shape will be our art, no veracious document will be our truth; but to us, initiated, the Symbol will be offered, and we shall take the Sign and adore, beneath the outward and perhaps unlovely accidents, the very Presence and eternal indwelling of God.

"But", Urang grumbles in reply, "he proposes another, quite different test: 'literature is the expression, through the artistic medium of words, of the dogmas of the Catholic Church, and that which in any way is out of harmony with these dogmas is not literature;' for 'Catholic dogma is merely the witness, under a special symbolism of the enduring facts of human nature and the universe.'"

For Machen, however, as for Yeats (at least, for Yeats when he was in the mood in which he wrote the earlier referred-to *To-Morrow* editorial), these two tests are not different; rather they are the same. This synthesis between Christianity and ecstasy and the Hermetic would have been well recognised by Bl. Raymond Lully or Pico della Mirandola. That it is not to us tells us much about the avenues in which religious and literary thought have flowed since then. But Machen was able to see the synthesis — precisely because of his experience with the Golden Dawn.

Charles Williams

Charles Williams stands out among the three both because of his overtly theological *oeuvre*, and because of his close connexion with C.S. Lewis and J.R.R. Tolkien. He joined the Golden Dawn in 1917, and was active for at least five years thereafter. He too was attached to Waite's group, and, as we shall see, some major themes in his work may be derived from that source.

There can be no doubt that Williams' novels owed their themes to areas studied by the Golden Dawn. *Shadows of Ecstasy* pulsates with the Hermetic dictum, "as above, so below". *War in Heaven* concerns the Grail, *Many Dimensions* the Philosopher's Stone, and *The Place of the Lion* the Platonic archetypes. We are confronted with the Tarot deck in *The Greater Trumps*, necromancy in *All Hallow's Eve*, and ghosts, witchcraft, and damnation in *Descent into Hell*.

Despite this, it is usual to downplay Williams' membership in the Golden Dawn as a factor in his artistic vision. His close friend, Alice Hadfield, remarks:

> In the end, what did Waite's Golden Dawn mean to him? Surely his outlook and philosophy were not generated, or indeed much affected, by it. He was thirty-one when he joined and his mind was already well-based, developed and directed. His three following works, *Divorce*, *Windows of Night*, and *Outlines of Romantic Theology*, scatter the shadows of such a suggestion. Referring long afterwards to the making of a magical circle against the dangers of the Dark, he wrote that he still felt the darkness, though it is "known to be merely untrue."

(1983, p. 30)

This is a view echoed by many other Williams scholars. The distinguished critic Thomas Howard declares:

> Williams was not interested in the occult at all except during a brief period in his early life. One might be pardoned for forming the impression from his novels that he was quite caught up in the occult, but this would be a mistake. His imagination was aroused by certain ideas that crop up in occult lore, but he remained a plain Anglican churchman all his life. He accepted the taboos that rule out forays into the occult.

(1983, p. 9)

While both of these statements reflect a very commonly held view, emphasising separation between the esoteric and Christianity, it is in this case based upon a false understanding of what the Golden Dawn was all about. The activities of its best known non-primarily-literary member, Aleister Crowley, have served to bring upon the Order enormous discredit, despite the fact of his early expulsion therefrom. As has been observed the whole point of the Order was, in essence, to reveal experientially to its members the subtler realities of the cosmos. Assuming Christianity to be literally true, such experimentation could only reveal this. We are very far here from the kind of opportunistic evocation castigated by Williams in *Many Dimensions*, *The Greater Trumps*, and *All Hallow's Eve*.

It is doubtless true that Williams came to the Golden Dawn with a fully formed world-view; so too did Machen and Yeats, for only such would be interested in joining this kind of a group anyway. What the Golden Dawn offered to these men and their colleagues was (a) a coherent philosophy of the esoteric; and (b) some type of actual experience which they, at any rate, accepted as objective factual confirmation of this philosophy (obviously, the exact nature of such confirmation is open to question).

Carpenter admits that "Waite himself discouraged the Order of the Golden Dawn from practising 'Magia', the Renaissance term for white magic, and certainly he was opposed to any meddling in 'Goetia' or black magic" (1979, p. 82). Neither Williams, Yeats, nor Machen appear to have done much vis-a-vis evocation of demons, in keeping with Waite's strictures. Presumably the ritual, meditation, clairvoyance, and divination that was practised was sufficient to confirm the Order's teachings to them. The result has been described by Urang:

> Charles Williams, in short, is a thoroughgoing supernaturalist. He predicates modes of existence other than those perceived by the senses and known by reason and takes for granted that the natural order proceeds from and is dependent upon a reality which is invisible and which operates by laws transcending those

discoverable in the physical world. He is eager to insist, however, that the supernatural is not divorced from the natural; one is not to escape from sensory illusion into spiritual reality. It is rather the true form of the natural, so that one knows the supernatural through images within the natural. Shakespeare, says Williams, conceived the whole supernatural life in terms of the natural, and his work should stand as a rebuke to "arrogant supernaturalists".
(1971, p. 56)

This is as true of Machen and Yeats as it is of Williams; it is an outlook directly traceable to the influence of the Golden Dawn.

There are many specific instances one could cite of particular traces of the Golden Dawn in Williams' work. For example, his conception in *Taliessin through Logres* of the Map of Europe corresponding to the human body is obviously connected with the sephiroth of the Qabalistic tree of life. But it is Williams' central doctrines of co-inherence, exchange, and substitution which figure in and inform all his prose fiction which most point up his Hermetic legacy. Alice Hadfield defines them thusly:

Co-inherence. Christ gave his life for us, and his risen life is in each one if we will to accept it. Simply as men and women, without being self-conscious or portentous, we can share in this life within the divine co-inherence of the Trinity, and in so doing live as members one of another. In our degrees of power, intelligence, love, or suffering, we are not divided from God or each other, for Christ's nature is not divided.

Exchange. The whole natural and social life of the world works as a process of living by and with each other, for good or bad. We cannot be born without physical exchange, nor can we live without it. But we can each day choose or grudge it, in personal contacts, in neighbourhood, and in our society under the law. To practise this approach to co-inherence we can find strength in the risen power of Christ linking all men.

Substitution. Another way of approach to co-inherence is by compact to bear another's burden. One can take by love the worry of another, or hold a terror, as one member of Christ's life helping, through that life, another member in trouble.

Williams saw these three principles as operating not only between the living in space and time, but also between the living and the dead — or the unborn.
(Hadfield, 1983, p. 32)

Here we see a proposal strikingly like Waite's in "Ceremonial Union", and reminiscent of Yeats' observations regarding "victims". This is deeply esoteric matter here. Yet it is also profoundly Christian, being a restatement of the idea of the "Mystical Body of Christ", exemplified by St. Paul: "We being many are one bread, one body; for we all partake of the one bread" (I Cor., x, 17). Here we see at once the identification of the Church with her founder, with the Sacraments, particularly the Eucharist, binding all together.

In time, Williams felt the need to give some kind of structure to like-minded friends. He founded in 1939 a loosely organised "Order of the Companions of the Co-inherence". To its membership were given seven guidelines. One of these advocated the study "of the Co-inherence of the Holy and Blessed Trinity, of the Two Natures in the Single Person, of the Mother and Son, of the communicated Eucharist, and of the whole Catholic Church" (Hadfield, 1983, p. 174). Another set down the Order's four feasts: the Annunciation, Trinity Sunday, the Transfiguration, and All Souls (Hadfield, 1983, p. 174). All of this is extremely reminiscent of Waite's version of the Golden Dawn. It is interesting to note that the Golden Dawn observed five feasts; these were the four solstices and equinoxes, and their high festival, the feast of Corpus Christi.

All of these concepts, applied to Christianity, may seem peculiar — particularly as expressed in Williams' fiction. Dr. Howard tells us, ". . . his religious vision was not idiosyncratic. It was a matter of traditional Christian orthodoxy. But his way of *picturing* it all was emphatically idiosyncratic" (1983, p. 17). But it is only idiosyncratic if one. is referring to Aristotelian and/or post-Reformation forms of Christianity. Urang (p. 156) tells us that, for Williams, "Particularity must submit to the Idea, individual experience to dogma." Further, "the unity he celebrates is one attained by including the natural within the supernatural. He focuses upon the structures of the natural and derives an 'ontology of love'; but he locates and interprets these structures by means of the insights available in the supernaturalist frame of reference." The Double Truth (the idea that what is true in theology may be false in philosophy) which has undergirded much of Western Christianity for a long time is indeed alien to all of this. But the Fathers, the Ultra-Realists, the Classical Humanists, and the orthodox Romantics would all have recognised this concept. However Williams initially arrived at it, there can be no doubt that he saw it codified and demonstrated while a member of the Golden Dawn.

Conclusion

One may legitimately wonder what influence the Golden Dawn had on Lewis and Tolkien via Williams. Certainly *That Hideous Strength* is universally acknowledged to have been greatly affected by Lewis' acquaintance with Williams. Its description of the Company of St. Anne's is certainly evocative of Williams' Companions of the Co-inherence; from afar off it carries therefore also the mark of the Golden Dawn.

Ithell Colquhoun, a relative of Golden Dawn co-founder MacGregor Mathers, opines that "*The Lord of the Rings* has a tinge of the Golden Dawn though this may be filtered through E.R. Eddison rather than Williams, since passages near the beginning of *The Worm Ouroboros* (1922) are so pervaded by the Golden Dawn atmosphere as to make one speculate on its author's esoteric background" (Colquhoun, 1975, p. 234). But the well-known suspicion J.R.R. Tolkien had for Williams' ideas in this area leads one to suspect a rather different source for the "tinge" Colquhoun detects. Tolkien was a cultural Catholic, deeply read in both folk-lore and in pre-Reformation literature. These were themselves suffused, albeit more or less unconsciously, with the magical or Hermetic world-view, of which, after all, the Golden Dawn was only one exponent.

Through it, however, and more particularly through the influence of Yeats, Machen, and Williams (to say nothing of Blackwood, Nesbit, etc.), the Hermetic/Neoplatonic worldview has come to be commonplace throughout fantasy literature. Exiled from mainstream Christian theology, academic philosophy, and the sciences, it has nevertheless subsisted, and even thrived – at least among readers of such literature.

But developments in such areas as Depth Psychology and the New Physics suggest that it may indeed have a validity beyond the pages of fiction. The popularity of the New Age might notify Christianity of a hunger unfed by either social activism or doctrinal rationalism.

The Christian Hermeticism encompassed by the Golden Dawn, like all such Hermeticism, might well be symbolised by a scene in the Medieval *Quest of the Holy Grail* (Matarasso, 1986, p. 275), wherein Joseph of Arimathea

> took from the Vessel a host made in the likeness of bread. As he raised it aloft there descended from above a figure like to a child, whose countenance glowed and blazed as bright as fire; and he entered into the bread, which quite distinctly took on human form before the eyes of those assembled there. When Josephus had stood for some while holding his burden up to view, he replaced it in the Holy Vessel.

In a real sense, the whole conundrum regarding an authentic understanding of the Golden Dawn's teaching may be symbolised by the Ace of Cups in the Tarot Deck. Considered merely as a fortune telling device, it can mean plans or latent thoughts, ready to be put into action but whose meaning is still hidden. On a higher level it is said to mean psychic protection and knowledge.

But its appearance suggests a world of meaning. For it shows a chalice held by a hand descending from a cloud. The Dove of the Holy Ghost conveys directly into it a wafer bearing a cross, and out from the chalice pour into the sea streams of pure and living water. We have at once a representation of the Sacramental system (the Eucharist and Baptism), and of the Holy Grail. Two mysteries, one attainable only at the end of a long quest, and the other so near as to be taken for granted. Yet they are in fact one.

This is deepest Christian Hermeticism indeed. It is to the honour of the Golden Dawn that the Order both developed an authentic strand of such Hermeticism, and attracted members of the calibre necessary to convey such to a world not without need of it.

References

Bettoni, Efrem. 1964. *St. Bonaventure* trans. Angelus Combatese. Notre Dame, Indiana: University of Notre Dame Press.

Carpenter, Humphrey. 1979. *The Inklings*. Boston: Houghton Mifflin.

Colquhoun, Ithell. 1975. *The Sword of Wisdom*. London: Neville Spearman.

Ellmann, Richard. 1964. *Yeats: The Man and The Mask*. New York: E.P. Dutton.

Faivre, Antoine. 1987a. "NATURE: Religious and Philosophical Speculations", in *Encyclopedia of Religion*, volume 10. Ed. Mircea Eliade. New York: Macmillan.

Faivre, Antoine. 1987b. "OCCULTISM", in *Encyclopedia of Religion*, volume 11. Ed. Mircea Eliade. New York: Macmillan.

Hadfield, Alice Mary. 1983. *Charles Williams*. New York and Oxford: Oxford University Press.

Howard, Thomas T. 1983. *The Novels of Charles Williams*. New York and Oxford: Oxford University Press.

Lovecraft, H.P. 1973. *Supernatural Horror in Literature*. New York: Dover Pubs.

Machen, Arthur. 1961. *The Strange World of Arthur Machen*. New York: Juniper Press.

Machen, Arthur. 1964. *Tales of Horror and the Supernatural*. London: John Baker.

Matarasso, Pauline (trans.). 1986. *The Quest of the Holy Grail*. Harmondsworth: Penguin Books.

Pauwels, Louis and Bergier, Jaques. 1964. *The Morning of the Magicians*. New York: Stein & Day.

Regardie, Israel. 1971. *The Golden Dawn: An Account of the Teachings, Rites and Ceremonies*. 2 vols. Enlarged edition. St. Paul: Llewellyn Publications.

Regardie, Israel. 1987. *The Complete Golden Dawn System of Magic*. Santa Monica, CA: Falcon Press.

Simpson, Jacqueline. 1987. *European Mythology*. New York: Peter Bedrick Books.

Tonberg, Valentine. 1991. *Meditations on the Tarot*. Rockport: Element.

Urang, Gunnar. 1971. *Shadows of Heaven*. Philadelphia: Pilgrim Press.

Wade, Allen (ed.). 1954. *The Letters of W.B. Yeats*. New York: Macmillan.

Waite, A.E. 1961. *The Book of Ceremonial Magic*. New York: University Books.

Waite, A.E. 1970. *The Unknown Philosopher*. Blauvelt, NY: Rudolf Steiner Pubs.

Waite, A.E. 1987. *Hermetic Papers*. Wellingborough, Northants.: Aquarian Press.

Williams, Charles. 1970. *Many Dimensions*. Grand Rapids: Wm. B. Eerdmans.

Williams, Charles. 1987. *The Greater Trumps*. Grand Rapids: Wm. B. Eerdmans.

Yeats, W.B. 1953. *Autobiography*. New York: Macmillan.

Yeats, W.B. 1973. *Memoirs*. Ed. Denis Donoghue. New York: Macmillan.

Yeats, W.B. 1980. *Mythologies*. New York: Collier Books.

Tolkien, Sayers, Sex and Gender

David Doughan

Abstract: Tolkien's expressed "loathing" for Dorothy Sayers and her novels *Gaudy Night* and *Busman's Honeymoon* is remarkable considering that Sayers is generally considered to belong to the same milieu as the Inklings. Possible reasons for this are the contrast between the orthodox Catholic Tolkien's view of male sexuality as inherently sinful, requiring "great mortification", and Sayers's frankly hedonistic approach. Another reason may be Sayers's depiction of an independent Oxford women's college getting by successfully without men, and her representation of marriage as a source of intellectual frustration for creative women.

Keywords: Gender, Oxford, Dorothy L. Sayers, Sex, Sin

> I could not stand Gaudy Night. I followed P. Wimsey from his attractive beginnings so far, by which time I conceived a loathing for him (and his creatrix) not surpassed by any other character in literature known to me, unless by his Harriet. The honeymoon one (Busman's H.?) was worse. I was sick . . .
> (Tolkien, 1981, p. 82, letter no. 71)

Dorothy Leigh Sayers is occasionally referred to as being a sort of honorary Inkling[1]. She certainly was in frequent correspondence with both C.S. Lewis and Charles Williams, and the writings of the latter especially influenced her to begin her translation of Dante's *Commedia*. So such an expression of distaste by a potential sympathiser is somewhat remarkable. The reasons for this have never been explicitly stated, but certain marked differences of style and emphasis (to say nothing of taste) have already been pointed out (Vink, 1990, p. 43) – Sayers's Anglicanism, her French studies, her involvement in and writing of drama, and her enthusiasm for Dante. However, none of this applies directly to the above quotation, which is concerned with Sayers's popular detective fiction featuring Lord Peter Wimsey, and especially the two novels *Gaudy Night* and *Busman's Honeymoon*. Tolkien was certainly far from averse to what is nowadays known as "genre" fiction, such as science fiction and crime stories, and initially he obviously found Wimsey an appealing character. What might have changed his view?

Personal antipathy can probably be ruled out, since Tolkien and Sayers most likely never met, at least in the belief of C.S. Lewis (1988, p. 481). Lewis himself knew and corresponded with her in a fairly friendly fashion, though he too disliked *Gaudy Night* (Carpenter, 1978, p. 189). As already mentioned, her acquaintanceship and correspondence with Charles Williams was far more extensive. They shared a similarity of outlook in many ways; indeed, parts of *Murder must advertise* (the least "realistic" of the Wimsey novels) almost read like a Williams story. Thus, Tolkien's distinctly wary attitude towards Williams might suggest a certain mistrust of his associates. However, not only does this not explain the strength of Tolkien's objection, but it does not take into account the fact that it was inspired by two in particular of the Wimsey books.

Lord Peter Wimsey is a preposterous creation, even by the standards of romantic crime fiction. Sayers, who mainly earned her living from him, created him with a shrewd calculation of the qualities that a gentleman sleuth should possess. He is in a position to work closely with the police: Inspector Charles Parker is not only a personal friend, but eventually marries Wimsey's sister. In detective stories generally, the tedious business of calling in expert opinions in support of plot details can hold up the narrative; therefore, to obviate the necessity of involving outsiders, Wimsey is made to be a gifted amateur criminologist. He also speaks half-a-dozen languages fluently, is an expert bibliophile, a virtuoso pianist, a brilliant cricketer, a *fin gourmet* and a connoisseur of wine, women and song. His wealth and leisure enable him to drop everything in order to dash round the world, if need be, in search of a vital piece of evidence. He speaks with kings, yet, when necessary, has the common touch, is highly proficient at physical combat, and has a shining war record. In short, "he was to show from the beginning what God could have done if only He'd had the money" (Heilbrun in Sandoe 1972, p. 462).

Sayers's relationship with her money-spinning hero is somewhat ambivalent. She certainly referred to the Wimsey novels as mere potboilers, and when she seemed to have earned enough from Lord Peter to concentrate on other matters, she prepared to marry him off – which is why he so unaccountably falls for Harriet Vane in *Strong Poison*. However, at this point she suffered a severe financial downturn, which meant that the Wimsey hymenaeals would have to be postponed until his author had seen off the creditors. As already indicated, Lord Peter does indeed have

---

[1] For one example out of many, see Brabazon, 1981, p. 235.

many hallmarks of a cynical commercial formulation; also, he is to a large extent a conscious parody, with something of Wodehouse's Bertie Wooster (comparisons between their respective impeccable menservants are illuminating), but rather more of Max Beerbohm's Duke of Dorset in *Zuleika Dobson*. However, this is by no means all there is to him. One of the qualities for which Sayers consciously strove was that his character should be capable of development; "this she certainly accomplished even if the change from the Wooster-like, monocled, man-about-Town of *Whose body?* to the sensitive guilt-oppressed scholar sobbing in his wife's lap at the end of *Busman's honeymoon* is less a development than a metamorphosis" (James in Brabazon, 1981, p. xiv) – though even as early as *Whose body?* he is already consulting psychiatrists about war-generated neuroses. Certainly over the years he becomes less of a two-dimensional parody and more of a wish-fulfilment fantasy of his creatrix's ideal man – and lover.

Of course, this could be one reason for Tolkien's growing aversion. Wimsey's increasingly un-"masculine" and often neurotic sensitivity might well have tried the patience of one who had actually been through the War, and caused him to wonder ever more testily, for example, why one who was so riven by guilt over the death penalty should be so zealous in seeking out candidates for it. Still, this by itself would hardly explain the strength of his reaction – and other more likely explanations are not far to seek; for example, in Tolkien's ideas about women.

Tolkien believed that women:
> are instinctively, when uncorrupt, monogamous. *Men are not* . . . . . No good pretending. Men just ain't, not by their animal nature. Monogamy [. . .] is for us men a piece of 'revealed' ethic, according to faith and not to the flesh [. . .]. It is a fallen world, and there is no consonance between our bodies, minds and souls.
>
> However, the essence of a *fallen* world is that the *best* cannot be attained by free enjoyment, or by what is called 'self-realization' (usually a nice name for self-indulgence, wholly inimical to the realization of other selves); but by denial, by suffering. Faithfulness in Christian marriage entails that: great mortification. Marriage may help to sanctify & direct to its proper object his sexual desires [. . .] but [. . .] it will not satisfy him – as hunger may be kept off by regular meals. It will offer as many difficulties to the purity proper to that state, as it provides easements.
>
> (Tolkien, 1981, p. 51)

Sayers, being a woman herself, had somewhat different ideas on sexuality, especially the male variety, and she regaled Charles Williams with some of them in a "discourse upon BEDWORTHINESS", in the course of which she asserted that "on the strength of his literary output alone . . . any woman of sense would decline to tackle D.H. Lawrence at £1,000 a night", before setting forth "the distinguishing marks of True Bedworthiness in the Male", which she found:

> to consist in the presence of Three Grand Assumptions . . . :
> 1. That the primary aim and object of Bed is that a good time should be had *by all*.
> 2. That (other things being equal) it is the business of the Male to make it so.
> 3. That he knows his business.
>
> The first Assumption rules out at once all . . . sadists, connoisseurs in rape, egotists, and superstitious believers in female reluctance, as well as Catholic (replenish-the-earth) utilitarians and stockbreeders.
>
> The second Assumption rules out the hasty, the clumsy [. . .], the untimely and (in most cases) the *routinier* – though one would not wish to be too hard on Mr. Shandy, senior, since Mrs. Shandy may have been as orderly-minded as himself and possibly preferred it that way – and those . . . who are without skill in the management of bed-furniture or wind the whole combination into toppling and insecure complications of pillows and blankets or (in extreme circumstances) bang their partner's head against the wall . . .
>
> (Letter of 18.10.1944 to Charles Williams, quoted in Brabazon, 1981, p. 112)

This view of male sexuality is a very long way indeed from "great mortification", which is not a concept which ever seems to have occurred to Lord Peter. His omnicompetence is indicated with increasing explicitness in the later books to extend to the bedroom – above all in *Busman's Honeymoon*, where not only is it clear that neither of the newlyweds are virgins, but where the reader is treated to a moderately suggestive (by 1937 standards of commercial fiction) epithalamium. Any question of Lord Peter's sexual experience had indeed already been conclusively settled in the biographical addendum to *Gaudy Night*, where his ageing but nonetheless dissolute Uncle Paul Delagardie related how he had taken his charge's sentimental education in hand: ". . . at the age of seventeen, Peter came to see me of his own accord. He was old for his age, and eminently reasonable, and I treated him as a man of the world. I established him in trustworthy hands in Paris, instructing him to keep his affairs upon a sound business footing and to see that they terminated with goodwill on both sides and generosity on his. He fully justified my confidence. I believe that no woman has ever found cause to complain of Peter's treatment; and two at least of them have since married royalties (rather obscure royalties, I admit, but royalty of a sort)[. . . H]owever good the material one has to work on, it is ridiculous to leave any young man's social education to chance" (Sayers, 1970, pp. 442-3).

This is moderately hot stuff for the time; for example, Queenie Leavis, that great fan of D.H. Lawrence and all his works, revealingly found that Sayers's "deliberate indecency is not shocking or amusing, it is odious merely as so much Restoration Comedy is" (Leavis, 1937, p. 336)[2]. Indeed, as

---

[2] Incidentally, it is interesting that the chief reason Leavis gives for denouncing *Gaudy Night* is its approval of a supposedly sterile academic way of working, the kind of scholarship that "never gears in with life". Her biggest denunciation is that of the "philological" approach: her final contemptuous dismissal of Sayers reads: "Miss Sayers, who might evidently have been an academic herself, is probably

distinct from the equally amorous heroes of D.H. Lawrence, Lord Peter's attitude to sex was not a matter of literary principle but of aesthetic pleasure, comparable with a discerning taste for good wine and incunables. The devoutly Catholic Tolkien was even less likely than D.H. Lawrence or Q.D. Leavis to put sex in the same category as a Dow '96 or a Wynkyn de Worde, and it can easily be imagined that Sayers's frankly hedonistic attitude towards it would indeed "make him sick". He certainly would have been likely to put it in the category of "self indulgence", if nothing worse.

And yet, Tolkien's original objection was to *Gaudy Night*. Disregarding the appended epilogue referred to above, there is little or nothing of the "sexually libertine" in this work which might have offended his ascetic Catholic sensibilities. What then was it that provoked his especial antipathy to this particular work, "and its creatrix"? An examination of some of the themes of *Gaudy Night* may illuminate this point.

First, locations. Sayers is usually very precise with her locations. At the beginning of *Gaudy Night*, when Harriet Vane is looking out over Mecklenburgh Square, WC1, her perspective may well be that of a room in London House, a sort of hostel for transatlantic academics, and at that time an entirely male establishment. Malice is frequently aforethought in her choice of locations; when Harriet eventually marries Lord Peter, their London pied-à-terre is at No.2 Audley Square, then and now the address of the very posh (but chronically hard-up) University Women's Club. And, only a few years after Virginia Woolf was shooed off a Cambridge quadrangle by an outraged Beadle (Woolf, 1929, p. 9) for being of the Wrong Gender, Sayers, in a mock-apologetic Author's Note to *Gaudy Night*, boasts of planting her idealised version of Somerville College upon the "spacious and sacred cricket ground" of Balliol College, the *sanctum sanctorum* of the male academic Establishment, and the English upper classes in general (Sayers, 1970, p. 6). In fine, this is a very pointed instance of claiming an egregiously male space for women, and it immediately establishes a theme which runs throughout the novel. Its location is certainly very different from the exclusively male Clubland of the earliest Wimsey books – the bachelor (or pseudo-bachelor) world inhabited by the characters of Haggard, Chesterton and Graham, for example, to say nothing of the all-male ambience of the Notion Club.

We may well disregard the location of Shrewsbury College as being merely a red rag (of one sort or another) waved at various Oxonian bulls – but Tolkien was subtler than to charge directly. His own attitudes to women and learning do, indeed seem to have been rather mixed; he certainly had female students, none of whom seem to have accused him of sexual discrimination. However, his own expressed views were that "it is [women's] gift to be receptive, stimulated, fertilized (in many other matters than the physical) by the male. Every teacher knows that. How quickly an intelligent woman can be taught, grasp his ideas, see his point – and how (with rare exceptions) they can go no further, when they leave his hand, or when they cease to take a *personal* interest in *him*." (Tolkien, 1981, p. 49, no. 43). Sayers's attitude, again like that of most prominent Somervilleans, is somewhat at odds with this conception of female nature. *Gaudy Night*, among other things, depicts a women's college full of female dons who are as eccentric, as querulous, as antipathetic *and* as scholarly as any fictional depiction of male dons (for example, compare the SCR at Shrewsbury with the SCR at Bracton in C.S. Lewis's *That Hideous Strength* – I aver that the former is a far more sympathetic, and probably a more scholarly, company). Meanwhile, the female students are shown to be about as silly as male students – no less, no more. Most of the action takes place in an Oxford college in which it is *men* who are the outsiders, either as visitors or as servants – the reverse of the conventional situation. Furthermore, most of the women academics portrayed in *Gaudy Night* appear as fulfilled as most men; indeed, the subversive dénouement reveals that the twisted culprit turns out to be not a frustrated lesbian academic but a "decent" wife and mother who is Standing By Her Man – and earlier, the most frustrated and disappointed of the returning Old Girls, Harriet Vane's contemporaries, is again the one among them who has tried to follow the conventional married rôle as delineated by Tolkien in Letter number 43. The final stages of Wimsey's courtship are shown to involve a danger for Harriet Vane: that in marriage she would be diminished as her fellow-alumna has been diminished, and excluded from the life of the mind – something which may have found uncomfortable resonances with Tolkien's own home life. And despite the fact that it is Lord Peter who has finally to be called in to unravel the mystery, the overall impression left is that of a self-sufficient community of women who in the main are doing very nicely without men, thank you. The men who work in the college are obviously uncomfortable with their rôle, to the extent of approving of 'Itler's measures to "keep the girls at home" (Sayers, 1970, p. 114), and the young men who stray in (Saint George, Pomfret) are depicted as being immature, silly and spoilt (albeit charming). How Tolkien might have taken this we may gather from the tale of *Aldarion and Erendis*, where his disapproval of the early all-woman education of Ancalimë is evident. In this attitude he was far from alone, and far from extreme – and, as has been shown recently, Oxford still does as much as it can to undermine autonomous women's colleges, by means already outlined by both Woolf and Sayers: money. The heavily pointed contrast between the plain living at Shrewsbury and the everyday luxury of menus at The House would probably not be welcomed by male academics then or now, though the continuing difference has recently been underlined by the final capitulation of Somerville under financial pressure. Dorothy, thou shouldst be living in this hour / Somerville hath need of thee.

Of course, the question of single-sex versus mixed colleges is a fraught and complex one, as is any question to do with sexuality or gender. Although in general I find Sayers's sentiments closer to my own, even so I should like to say that

---

quite sound on the philological side" (Leavis, 1937, p. 340).

I do not claim that Sayers had got these issues completely right, while Tolkien was absolutely wrong. As usual, the issue is more complicated than that. As I have mentioned, there is no record of Tolkien being anything but helpful to his women students, some of whom have gone on to be among his greatest admirers. There remains, however, the strength of Tolkien's stated objection to Sayers, which does not altogether seem to be justified even by the foregoing. I suspect that it may be another example of Tolkien making extravagant statements about his dislikes which, when challenged, he would at least seriously modify, if not retract altogether – for example, the case of Dante; and his well-advertised loathing of France and all things French blatantly did not prevent him from knowing a good Burgundy when he saw it (Tolkien, 1981, p. 405, no. 317). So he may have in this instance also intemperately overstated his case. However, on these issues Tolkien and Sayers were at least theoretically a long way apart in ways which have some significance for us now and here, in Oxford in 1992.

Afterword

This paper was presented in a session together with Lisa Hopkins's paper on Tolkien's heroines, which amply demonstrates that in his "sub-creation" Tolkien was far from averse to depicting positively strong, resourceful and independent women (if not in any great numbers). A fuller account of Tolkien's attitudes to sex and gender should take into account not only the above, but also the pertinent observation made by Len Sanford that both Sayers and Tolkien accept unquestioningly the "rampant" model of innate male sexuality. For further enlightenment on this topic I recommend Lesley Hall's *Hidden anxieties* (Polity, 1991), a study of attitudes to male sexuality in the early 20th century.

References

Brabazon, James. 1981. *Dorothy L. Sayers*. London: Gollancz.

Carpenter, Humphrey. 1978. *The Inklings*. London: Allen & Unwin.

Hall, Lesley. 1991. *Hidden anxieties*. London: Polity.

Leavis, Q.D. 1937. "The case of Miss Dorothy Sayers" in *Scrutiny*, v. 6 no. 3 (December 1937), pp. 334-340.

Lewis, W. H. (ed.). 1988. *Letters of C.S. Lewis* (rev. W. Hooper). London: Collins.

Sandoe, James (ed.). 1972. *Lord Peter*. New York: Harper & Row.

Sayers, D.L. 1970. *Gaudy night* (New English Library) new edition. London: Hodder & Stoughton.

Tolkien, J.R.R. 1981. *Letters of J.R.R. Tolkien* ed. Humphrey Carpenter. London: Allen & Unwin.

Vink, Renée. 1990. "The image of the maker" in *Elrond's holy round table*, pp. 43-59. Leiden: Unquendor.

Woolf, Virginia. 1929. *A Room of one's own*. London: Hogarth.

Tolkien and the Other Inklings

Colin Duriez

Abstract: This paper looks at Tolkien's relationship with the other Inklings, especially Lewis, Williams and Barfield, in particular studying the affinities and differences between them and what Tolkien owes to them. "The Notion Club Papers" is discussed as an idealized portrait of the Inklings.

Keywords: Owen Barfield, Christianity, friendship, Inklings, C.S. Lewis, J.R.R. Tolkien: influences, Charles Williams

The Inklings

The group did not have any consistent documentation such as the careful minuting of the fictional Notion Club, Tolkien's portrait of an Inklings-type group of friends, set in the future. Humphrey Carpenter's excellent study, *The Inklings*, draws on the key sources: the diaries of Major Warren Lewis, C.S. Lewis's letters to his brother in the early months of the Second World War, Tolkien's long letters to his son Christopher while in South Africa with the RAF in that war, Lewis's introduction to *Essays presented to Charles Williams*, and reminiscences by Inklings such as John Wain, Commander Jim Dundas-Grant, Christopher Tolkien and others. The Inklings expanded, I believe, from the deep friendship between Tolkien and Lewis, a remarkable association comparable to that between Wordsworth and Coleridge in literary significance. Lewis, in his book, *The Four Loves* explains the process by which friendship expands (the least jealous of loves, at least according to Lewis):

> In each of my friends there is something that only some other friend can fully bring out. By myself I am not large enough to call the whole man into activity; I want other lights than my own to show all his facets. Now that Charles is dead, I shall never again see Ronald's reaction to a specifically Caroline joke. Far from having more of Ronald, having him "to myself" now that Charles is away, I have less of Ronald. Hence true Friendship is the least jealous of loves. Two friends delight to be joined by a third, and three by a fourth, if only the newcomer is qualified to become a real friend . . . Of course the scarcity of kindred souls – not to mention practical considerations about the size of rooms and the audibility of voices – set limits to the enlargement of the circle; but within those limits we possess each friend not less but more as the number of those with whom we share him increases.

(Lewis, 1977a, pp. 58, 59)

In his book Humphrey Carpenter lists the various Inklings in a long list – but, in a letter to Bede Griffiths in December 1941, Lewis has quite a short list. He is explaining his dedication to The Inklings in his recently published *The Problem of Pain*. He lists Charles Williams, Dyson of Reading (H.V.D. "Hugo" Dyson), Warren Lewis, Tolkien, and Dr. "Humphrey" Havard. He explains Tolkien and Dyson as the "immediate human causes of my own conversion" to Christianity. Remarkably, the name of Owen Barfield does not appear. In fact, Barfield rarely was able to visit. On one occasion, Lewis grumbles that Barfield is visiting on a Thursday, which means he'll attend The Inklings and Lewis will have less time to himself with him! It was later that The Inklings swelled further to include Colin Hardie, Lord David Cecil, John Wain and others. Christopher Tolkien attended as soon as he was back from South Africa, and became a significant member. It was upon this larger group that Tolkien drew inspiration for "The Notion Club Papers", and it is likely that he read it all to them. Warren Lewis records in his diary, Thursday 22nd August, 1946, about "Tollers" reading "a magnificent myth which is to knit up and concludes his Papers of the Notions Club". This would have been "The Drowning of Anadûnê" (now published with "The Notion Club Papers" in *Sauron Defeated*). A further complexity of The Inklings is that there were two patterns of meetings: Tuesday mornings in the Bird and Baby pub (The Eagle and Child, St. Giles) – except when Lewis took the Chair in Cambridge, when Monday mornings were more suitable – and Thursday evenings, usually in Lewis' rooms in Magdalen, but often in Tolkien's in Merton College. The Thursday evenings were of more literary interest, as here members would read to each other work in progress, receiving criticism and encouragement. Much of the "new Hobbit", i.e. *The Lord of the Rings*, was read in this way, sometimes by Christopher instead of Tolkien senior. After 1951 the term, The Inklings, no longer appears in Warren's diaries and it is probable that about two years before the Thursday meetings dried up, though the Tuesday meetings (or Monday ones) continued until 1962. The key years of The Inklings, in terms of their literary significance, are probably therefore from, let's say, the mid nineteen-thirties until near the end of 1949. The death of Charles Williams was a great blow to the group, particularly Lewis, and the fifties marked a gradual cooling of the friendship between Lewis and Tolkien which I believe was the heart around which the Inklings formed and grew. The situation was not helped by "Hugo" Dyson exercising a veto against Tolkien reading from the unfinished *The Lord of the Rings* at Inklings meetings. A further complexity was introduced by Lewis's at first only intellectual friendship with Joy Davidman, but that is another story. It is valuable to look at some of The Inklings in relation to Tolkien. Not all Lewis's friends appealed to Tolkien, or at least not to the same extent, as in the case of Charles Williams.

1. Tolkien and C.S. Lewis

The friendship between the two men goes back to the time when Tolkien moved to Oxford from Leeds in 1926. The two met at an English Faculty meeting and it was not long after that that they discovered they shared similar worlds and their association began, often talking far into the night. Lewis remarked that

> friendship with [Tolkien] marked the breakdown of two old prejudices. At my first coming into the world I had been (implicitly) warned never to trust a Papist, and at my first coming into the English Faculty (explicitly) never to trust a philologist. Tolkien was both.
> (Lewis, 1977b, p. 173)

Let's first look briefly at the influence of Tolkien on Lewis, then the importance of Lewis to Tolkien.

1. There is firstly the influence of Tolkien's Christianity. Lewis was originally an atheist and Tolkien helped him to come to faith. The pattern of his persuasion is vividly captured in the poem, "Mythopoeia", published in the new edition of *Tree and Leaf*.

2. The second, related, element of Tolkien's influence is his view of the relation of myth and fact. The view can be seen as a theology of story. Tolkien had worked out a complex picture of the relation of story and myth to reality. This involved a view of how language itself relates to reality, as story and language were, for Tolkien, part of one human inventive process. He says that it dawned on him, as an undergraduate, that story and language were "integrally related". Tolkien saw the Gospel narratives — a story created by God himself in the real events of history — as having broken into the "seamless web of story". Story — whether preceding or subsequent to the Gospel events — is joyfully alive with God's presence. The importance of story became central to C.S. Lewis, expressed for example in his seminal *An Experiment in Criticism* (1961).

3. The third element, also related, is Tolkien's distinctive doctrine of sub-creation, the view that the highest function of art is the creation of convincing secondary or other worlds. Without the impact of Tolkien's view of sub-creation on Lewis we may not have had Malacandra, Perelandra, or Glome, particularly Perelandra, one of his most successful creations, or even Narnia.

Turning the other way, what was Lewis' importance to Tolkien? Lewis clearly didn't influence Tolkien's writing in the way Tolkien influenced his. In Lewis, rather, Tolkien found a ready listener and appreciator. This listening was institutionalized in The Inklings' Thursday night gatherings, where much of *The Lord of the Rings* was read. In fact, Tolkien confesses that without Lewis' encouragement it is unlikely that he would have finished *The Lord of the Rings*! We might speculate that if the Thursday meetings had continued, with the associated dynamic of Tolkien and Lewis's friendship, there would exist today tellings of the tales of Beren and Lúthien, and perhaps also of Túrin Turambar, and other key stories of the First Age, nearer the scale of *The Lord of the Rings*. The two friends had a great number of shared beliefs that transcend what Tolkien had in common with other Inklings friends, such as Barfield and Williams. These convictions derived from shared tastes, and particularly from their common faith, which though Orthodox, had an original cast, to say the least. For me, in considering the remarkable Inklings, Lewis and Tolkien always steal the show.

a. They saw the imagination as the organ of meaning rather than of truth (which made their romanticism distinctive). Imaginative invention was justifiable in its own right — it did not have to serve in a didactic medium, and didn't have the burden of carrying conceptual truths. Though Lewis was more allegorical and explicit than Tolkien, both writers valued a symbolic perception of reality. A further central preoccupation of Lewis and Tolkien is imaginative invention (most obviously expressed in Tolkien's concept of sub-creation). This was related to their view of the function of imagination as the organ of meaning rather than of truth. Products of the imagination were a form of knowledge, but knowledge discovered by making, essentially not accessible in any other way.

b. They also shared a sense of the value of otherness — or otherworldliness. Great stories take us outside of the prison of our own selves and our presuppositions about reality. In so far as stories reflect the divine maker, they help us face the ultimate Other — God himself, distinct as creator from all else, including ourselves. The very well of fantasy and imaginative invention is every person's direct knowledge of the Other. Lewis writes:

> To construct plausible and moving "other worlds" you must draw on the only real "other world" we know, that of the spirit.
> (Lewis, 1982, pp. 35-36).

Imaginative worlds, he says somewhere, are "regions of the spirit".

c. For both men, this all-pervasive sense of the other is focused in a quality of the numinous. Both successfully embodied this quality in their fiction.[1]

d. Also important to both men was a desire to embody a quality of joy in their work. Though associated with Lewis (e.g. through his autobiography, *Surprised by Joy*), joy is distinctive too in Tolkien's fiction, and supremely valued by him, as his essay "On Fairy-Stories" makes clear.

e. Both Tolkien and Lewis were preoccupied with pre-Christian paganism, particularly what might be called enlightened paganism. Most of Tolkien's fiction is set in a pre-Christian world, as was his great model, *Beowulf*,

---

[1] I explore the theme of the numinous further in my *The Tolkien and Middle-earth Handbook* (1992), pp. 192-194.

according to his own interpretation of that poem. Similarly, Lewis explored a pagan world in his fine novel, *Till We Have Faces*. Even while an atheist, Lewis was attracted by pagan myths of the North, and the idea of a dying god. In one of his *Latin Letters*, Lewis speculates that some modern people may need to be brought to pre-Christian pagan insights in preparation for more adequately receiving the Christian Gospel. Tolkien undoubtedly shared this view of pre-evangelism.

To point out these shared concerns is not to downplay important differences, often of emphasis, between Tolkien and Lewis. Their differences gave a dynamic to their friendship.

2. Tolkien and Charles Williams

The relationship between Williams and Tolkien has been superbly explored by Humphrey Carpenter in his biography and in his study of The Inklings. Late in his life Tolkien recalled that he and Williams liked one another, but had little to say to each other at a deeper level. While Williams appreciated Tolkien's chapters of *The Lord of the Rings* which were read to The Inklings, Tolkien found he had little taste for Williams' writing, though he made an effort to savour them. There seems to have been some jealously on Tolkien's part about Lewis's friendship for Williams, which had distracted from their own association. Also he felt that Williams had been an only partly digested influence on Lewis's writings, particularly on the third science-fiction story, *That Hideous Strength*. Williams' play, *The House of the Octopus*, is mentioned in "The Notion Club Papers", where it is clear that Tolkien believed, no doubt with some sadness, that Williams' work would fall into disfavour with future readers. Tolkien recognized his own limitations in failing to appreciate Williams, respecting him, and valuing his perceptive comments on chapters of *The Lord of the Rings* as they were read. He contributed his essay "On Fairy-Stories" to the posthumous tribute, *Essays Presented to Charles Williams*. At one stage he wrote an affectionate poem to Williams, complaining of his difficulty in understanding his writings, but valuing his person nonetheless:

> When your fag is wagging and spectacles are twinkling,
> when tea is brewing or the glasses tinkling,
> then of your meaning often I've an inkling,
> your virtues and your wisdom glimpse . . .[2]

Williams is important for his encouragement of Tolkien at a time when he particularly needed it, as he slogged away at finishing *The Lord of the Rings*. He is also important in helping Tolkien to be aware of his own imaginative limitations as he struggled with Williams' work, work of a person he admired. It also helps the modern reader to put Tolkien in perspective in comparison with Williams' richly imaginative work. Tolkien was struggling with his then private mythology and could see the artistic struggles of Williams, who could not succeed in making his work accessible to contemporary readers. At least, Tolkien didn't believe he was succeeding, and few will deny the obscurity of Williams' work. Williams was at the other end of the spectrum from Lewis, whose work Tolkien felt was often too obvious.

3. Tolkien and Barfield

I have already pointed out the paradox that Owen Barfield is considered one of the core Inklings, even though he rarely attended Inklings meetings. He contributed a chapter to *Essays Presented to Charles Williams* that was approved by the Inklings, including Tolkien. His influence on the Inklings was mainly through his book, *Poetic Diction* (1928), and through the many discussions between Barfield and Lewis from undergraduate days until Barfield left Oxford to become a solicitor. Tolkien seems to have accepted Barfield's basic thesis as thoroughly as Lewis did. Verlyn Flieger has demonstrated Barfield's importance to Tolkien's thought and fiction in her study of Tolkien, *Splintered Light* (1983). Barfield took up writing again after his retirement but it was his early work that was of central importance to Tolkien and Lewis. His essay in the Williams volume clarifies his basic position. The fact that Barfield is widely considered to be a core Inkling, though he rarely attended meetings, underlines his great impact on Lewis and Tolkien. An example of affinity between basic ideas of Barfield and Tolkien can starkly be seen in an appendix to *Poetic Diction*, where Barfield writes of allegory and myth:

> Allegory [is] a more or less conscious hypostatization of ideas, followed by a synthesis of them, and myth the true child of Meaning, begotten on imagination.
> (Barfield, 1952, p. 201)

Barfield speaks of Greek philosophers *contaminating* their original myths with allegory. A modern poet creates a new myth, or makes a true use of an old one, according to Barfield, if he or she succeeds in directly embodying concrete experience, rather than his or her idea of that experience. If the poet only deals with ideas, he or she has only invented an allegory, or has made allegorical use of a myth. Barfield's distinction between allegory and myth rings true of Tolkien's perception, leading to his dislike of allegory, and his concern, for example, about Lewis's fondness for allegory. We can also find Tolkien-like concepts in Barfield's view of prehistoric human consciousness, which he saw as unitary, not fragmented into subject and object. It was "a kind of thinking which is at the same time perceiving – a picture-thinking, a figurative, or imaginative, consciousness, which we can only grasp today by true analogy with the imagery of our poets, and, to some extent, with our own dreams." Such an attention to dreams, and to shifts in consciousness with developments in language, is typical also of Tolkien, and brings us to his unfinished "Notion Club Papers".

4. "The Notion Club Papers"

The Papers are a second attempt (the first being *The Lost*

---

[2] The whole poem is quoted in Carpenter, 1978, pp. 123-126.

Road) at time-travel, in response to a challenge that Lewis and Tolkien set themselves to write a time- or space-travel story. (Lewis's response was the first of his space trilogy.) According to Humphrey Carpenter, *The Lost Road* has elements of an idealized portrait of the father-son relationship between Tolkien and his son Christopher. Similarly, "The Notion Club Papers" idealizes the Inklings. Neither contains direct biography or autobiography. Both however concern the discovery of clues to the lost world of Númenor through strange words seemingly discovered rather than invented by Tolkien-like people exceptionally sensitive to language. The later work appreciates the value of a group or community of people in building up together an imaginative picture of the past. The insights into the past achieved imaginatively are in a curious way as objective as the seemingly hard facts of traditional history. This objectivity is demonstrated by the intrusion of a great storm in late twentieth-century Oxford which derives from the calamity which befell Númenor – perhaps a rare Charles Williams touch in Tolkien's writings! As well as language, the Inklings-like discussions of the Notion Club concern the status of dreams, and time- and space-travel via that medium. Behind it is an exciting exploration of the place imagination has in putting us in contact with objective reality, resisting the view that imagination is purely subjective and individualistic. Christopher Tolkien – who was a member of The Inklings at the time Tolkien created this idealized picture of them – assures us from his intimate knowledge that there is no direct correspondence between characters in the Notion Club and actual Inklings. However, there are hints of actual characters, e.g. parallels between Dolbear and Dr. Humphrey Havard, and between Dyson and Arry Lowdham. The extent that the picture is idealized can be discovered by comparing "The Notion Club Papers" with Humphrey Carpenter's powerful reconstruction of an Inklings evening in his study of *The Inklings* (Part 3, Chapter 3). Discussion (as is revealed in Warren Lewis' diary) ranges far and wide, which was very much to C.S. Lewis' taste. The Notion Club discussions are very much more focused around linguistic and dream issues, more to Tolkien's own taste (not that Lewis and others wouldn't have been interested in these issues – in fact the Papers were read to The Inklings, as I mentioned above). However, despite being idealized, they do acknowledge the value of a community of like-minded thinking and imagining. There is not the isolation of *The Lost Road*, with only the father and son.

5. Christopher Tolkien

I have already referred to the importance of Christopher Tolkien in understanding "The Notion Club Papers", as he was an Inkling at the period on which the Papers are based (though of course set in the future). It mustn't be overlooked that Christopher Tolkien was a key member of The Inklings. His insights into the group illuminate his commentary on the development of *The Silmarillion* and *The Lord of the Rings*. Furthermore, he was an essential element of Tolkien's original audience during the composition of his works, so important in encouraging him to continue. Humphrey Carpenter points out that, in the early 1930s, it was only Christopher Tolkien and C.S. Lewis that knew of the existence of *The Silmarillion* as such, and had parts of it read or told to them. As I said, Carpenter believes that Tolkien's relationship with Christopher is idealized in *The Lost Road*. He helped his father, furthermore, with the construction of maps of Middle-earth. His absence in South Africa during the Second World War was a further incentive for his father to write and to send instalments of *The Lord of the Rings*. Finally, this surviving Inkling has dedicated very many years to editing and publishing his father's unfinished work, not least achieving some kind of final order to the published *The Silmarillion*.

Conclusion

In all too short a time, I have tried to take a look at Tolkien's relation to the other Inklings, especially C.S. Lewis, Williams, and Barfield, particularly looking at affinities and differences between them, and what he owed to them. I have also looked at the importance of Christopher Tolkien to Tolkien's work. "The Notion Club Papers" has been briefly discussed as an idealized portrait of The Inklings.

References

Barfield, Owen. 1952. *Poetic Diction*, second Edition. London: Faber and Faber.

Carpenter, Humphrey. 1978. *The Inklings*. London: George Allen and Unwin.

Duriez, Colin. 1992. *The Tolkien and Middle-earth Handbook*. Tonbridge: Monarch. (in the USA published as *The J.R.R. Tolkien Handbook*. Grand Rapids: Baker Book House).

Lewis, C.S. 1977a. *The Four Loves*. London: Collins Fount.

Lewis, C.S. 1977b. *Surprised by Joy*. London: Collins Fount.

Lewis, C.S. 1982. "On Stories" in *Of This and Other Worlds*. London: Collins.

Female Authority Figures in the Works of Tolkien, C.S. Lewis and Charles Williams

Lisa Hopkins

Abstract: The powerful, learned woman is a figure of fear in the works of Williams, seen as transgressing her proper role. In Lewis, legitimate authority figures are male, illegitimate ones are female, and gender roles are strictly demarcated. Tolkien, however, not only creates powerful and heroic women, but also suggests that the combination of authority and femininity can be particularly potent and talismanic.

Keywords: Galadriel, gender, C.S. Lewis, Lucy, women

I intend in this paper to touch only briefly on Williams, look in slightly more detail at Lewis and to concentrate on Tolkien. In the work of Williams and of Lewis, to have an authority figure who is female is seen as being at best a contradiction in terms, at worst a fear of nightmare proportions. This is clearly illustrated in Williams' work by the case of the unfortunate Damaris, the heroine of *The Place of the Lion*, whose pretensions to scholarship are duly put in their place by a surprise visit from a pterodactyl, much to the approval of her fiancé Anthony and, it is fairly clearly indicated, the author. The fates that await Lewis' powerful women are less spectacular, but they are nevertheless unpleasant: the White Witch and the Lady of the Green Kirtle in the Narnia books are both destroyed by the forces of righteousness, as is Fairy Hardcastle in *That Hideous Strength*. Clearly these women will find few mourners, for they are all, in their various ways, virtually personifications of malignity, irrationality and selfishness. Throughout Lewis' work, however, we come across female figures who are far less demonstrably evil than these three, yet who are nevertheless sources of trouble and unease.

The Lady of Perelandra is an obvious example of this phenomenon. She is the second Eve, and even though she has not yet fallen she carries some of Eve's stigma with her: she is perceived instinctively by both the good Ransom and the bad Weston as the vulnerable point, innately corruptible apparently through the very fact of her feminine gender. For all her nobility and innocence, she is still tainted: like the evil witch of *The Silver Chair*, she is green – the colour, in popular iconography, of the serpent in the Garden of Eden, so that, like Milton's Eve, she has a strange bond with Satan inherent in her very nature. The overwhelming message of the book is that only in the safe grip of masculine control can she be made safe, just as Jane in *That Hideous Strength* needs firm handling by her husband Mark to restore her to the role of wife which she has forsaken and the role of mother which she has, disastrously for Logres, never attempted. The autonomous woman is seen as a terrifying and unnatural figure.

Even the virtuous and admirable female characters in Lewis' work have a troubling air of ambiguity around them. Lucy is, of course, the youngest and most favoured of the four Pevensie Children: she finds Narnia first, and always enjoys the closest relationship with Aslan. Her privileged status could however, be said to be purchased in effect at the expense of her femininity. Despite Father Christmas' dictum that "battles are ugly when women fight" (Lewis, 1959, p. 100), in *The Horse and His Boy*, Lucy, now Queen Lucy, does fight as an archer against the Calormenes, and she is conspicuously detached in that book from the love-intrigues surrounding her sister Susan. Unlike the real Lucy who was the dedicatee of *The Lion, The Witch and The Wardrobe*, Lucy Pevensie never disappoints Lewis by the attainment of mature femininity. Susan, on the other hand, does, and is punished for it by exclusion both from the books and from the family circle, being the only member of the Pevensie clan not to die and enter Aslan's country at the end of *The Last Battle*. Susan's interest in nylons and lipstick, foreshadowed by her initial blindness to Rabadash's unworthiness in *The Horse and His Boy*, clearly count as a far greater betrayal than Edmund's flight to the White Witch, for whereas he is forgiven and readmitted, she is exiled for ever.

For Lewis as for Williams, therefore, femininity is apparently perceived as problematic. He is of course aware of society's changing ideas on the subject: towards the beginning of *The Voyage of the Dawn Treader* Eustace, complaining in his private diary that Lucy has been given a better cabin than he, remarks "C. says that's because she's a girl. I tried to make him see what Alberta says, that all that sort of thing is really lowering girls but he was too dense" (1965c, p. 32). We of course are by no means too dense to pick up the implication that this sentiment is thoroughly to be distrusted, since it is expressed by the obnoxious Eustace and originates from his equally loathsome mother (so that a woman's voice is in fact used here to discredit notions of women's equality). It will also not be lost on us that the totally unsuitable head of Experiment House, Eustace and Jill's school, is a woman, who eventually has to be confined in an asylum after her encounter with the animals sent by Aslan. In the world of Lewis' books, while girls – like Lucy, Jill, Polly and the young Susan – may be likeable and even admirable characters, the transition into womanhood invariably turns females into something much more worrying.

In the world of Tolkien, however, attitudes are rather different. His books are of course notable on one level for their paucity of female characters: of the fifteen assorted travellers who set off on the quest in *The Hobbit*, not one is female, and nor is any of the Nine Walkers in *The Lord of the Rings*. And of the various forms of life that we encounter in the course of the books, it is notable that several species seem simply not to have any women: we meet no female trolls, for instance, the Entwives are missing, and an appendix to *The Lord of the Rings* informs us that dwarf-women are remarkably few in number – we certainly encounter none in the stories. Of female hobbits, we hear briefly of Bilbo's mother and of Frodo's, and meet Lobelia Sackville-Baggins and Rosie Cotton, later Mrs. Sam Gamgee; of female inhabitants of Minas Tirith, we meet only Ioreth, of Rohan, only Éowyn, of Rivendell, only Arwen, of Lothlórien, only Galadriel, and of Gondolin, only Idril Celebrindal; the only female inhabitant of Mordor of whom we hear is Shelob, who lives on its borders. And yet this small number of women have a range of parts to play whose importance is remarkably disproportionate to their numbers. Their very scarcity seems to invest them with an air of uniqueness and of almost talismanic status, and in some cases their very femininity, seen as such a disadvantage in Lewis, is in Tolkien the very source of their strength – the chief Nazgûl, who is invulnerable to the hand of mortal man, is destroyed, through some *Macbeth*-like equivocation, by Éowyn.

Power in the works of Tolkien is often to be found in the hands of a woman. In the *Book of Lost Tales*, the land to which Eriol travels is ruled over by a woman, Meril-i-Turinqi, and it eventually became Númenórean custom that the eldest child of the king should succeed him regardless of gender. Galadriel is an even more obvious example: the Lady of the Golden Wood far eclipses her husband Celeborn. It is she, not he, who wears the Ring of Power, and who has access to the insight granted by the Mirror, and ultimately she even acts independently of Celeborn, when she leaves Middle-earth without him. A similar state of affairs prevailed in Doriath in earlier times, where the powerful Maia Melian encircled the land with a Girdle which kept out the power even of Morgoth, providing a considerably more potent protection than any which could have been afforded by her husband Thingol. Melian's daughter Lúthien inherited some at least of her mother's might: she and Beren go to Thangorodrim as equals, and he would undoubtedly never have survived his quest without her help. Thingol, by contrast, is seen as prone to greed and self-will when he will not accept the restraining influence of Melian. Far wiser is Tuor, who follows unquestioningly the advice of his wife Idril Celebrindal, and so manages to get himself and his family safely away from the sack of Gondolin; and other wise women are Aragorn's mother Gilraen, who sends her son to Rivendell, and Túrin's mother Morwen – though her plans for her family's safety are eventually horribly frustrated in ways she could never have foretold.

What is perhaps even more remarkable is that women in Tolkien are not portrayed solely in the light of their relationships to men. The traditional roles for women in epic narratives are very seriously limited: they can normally appear either to be wooed, to be rescued, or occasionally to be killed. In any of these events, their ultimate fate is decided entirely by the men around them. Classical epic provides clear examples of this: Polyxena is sacrificed on Achilles' grave, Andromache is the grieving widow, Helen the cause of the war, Dido the abandoned victim of Aeneas. It is this tradition that can be seen providing clear structural problems for Spenser when he attempted, in *The Faerie Queene*, to write an epic that was at least nominally woman-centred, and it is also this tradition that Tolkien inherits for the epic aspects of *The Lord of the Rings* and *The Silmarillion*. It is, therefore, interesting to find him adopting a device that had already been used by Spenser, that of having a heroine actually take part in the fighting by disguising herself as a man. To have a cross-dressed heroine is, of course, a common enough motif: Lewis does it in *The Horse and His Boy*, where Aravis makes her escape disguised in her brother's clothing, and a number of Shakespeare's comedies hinge on the use of such disguise. Éowyn's motivation is, however, unusual in that it is only tenuously related to questions of romance. The Shakespearean heroine is either already in active pursuit of her lover when she adopts male disguise, or soon becomes so; in either event, she avoids as much as she can doing any actual fighting. Éowyn, however, actively wants to be engaged in battle, seeing herself as a shieldmaiden rather than a nurse and longing to prove herself worthy of her descent from Eorl. Obviously her love for Aragorn plays a part in this: but ultimately it is a deeper sentiment, of family and personal loyalty and of integrity, which sends her into her confrontation with the Nazgûl. Although her story ends in romance, with her marriage to Faramir, Éowyn has received that rare distinction for a female character, serious investigation of her psychology and motivation rather than depiction solely as a love-object.

Much the same is true of Galadriel. Considerable parts of Galadriel's earlier history are of course filled in in *The Silmarillion*, but even in *The Lord of the Rings* it is sufficiently apparent that she and Celeborn are no conventional husband-and-wife team of the sort that would have been familiar to Tolkien's contemporary readers. She lives with him, but at their first meeting with what survives of the Company it is obvious that she has access to information which he has not, and that they are accustomed to reach decisions separately rather than together. Moreover, for all her beauty and flowing golden hair, Galadriel is no conventional heroine of romance: she is not innocent but experienced, and although she rejects Frodo's offer of the Ring, she is astute enough to be able to perceive its superficial attractiveness. In creating the figure of Galadriel, Tolkien seems to benefit enormously from exploiting one particular aspect of his concept of Elves, their agelessness. The traditional older woman of fairy tale and romance is usually relegated to the roles of hag, witch or wicked stepmother; her child-bearing years long over, she retains no attractiveness for men, and her accumulated wisdom only turns her into a more effective threat to them. Galadriel, however, breaks this mould, for though certainly an older woman – she is in fact a grandmother – her Elven blood means that she also retains the beauty, vivacity and charm of a girl, able to enchant Gimli on sight.

Even Galadriel, however, has not been able to break quite free of some at least of the constraints of the female condition. It is notable that she is the only one of the leading characters opposed to Sauron, who suffers from a bad reputation: Boromir is reluctant even to enter Lothlórien, and Éomer is immediately suspicious of Aragorn, Gimli and Legolas on learning of their connection with it. What is more, both men directly cite Galadriel as the reason for their distrust. Even when Éomer learns better, his view of Galadriel is still an oddly limited one: he and Gimli enter the unwitting Galadriel and her granddaughter Arwen into what is in effect a beauty contest, with each deciding on a different winner. It is as if traditional categories of evaluating women and their behaviour are slow to be abandoned, even in the face of such untraditional behaviour as that of Galadriel.

Not all Tolkien's women, of course, are Galadriels. Several of them do indeed accord with the far more conventional pattern of including women in epic narrative simply as partners for men: Arwen, for instance, is a surprisingly shadowy figure, a re-run of Lúthien who takes no active part in her Beren's adventures, and seems only to exist to provide a suitable bride for Aragorn at the end of the story. Rosie Cotton performs a similar function for Sam, and Merry's and Pippin's wives do not even warrant naming. Even Éowyn eventually is brought back within the framework of convention by being paired off with Faramir in a marriage which may well appear to be born more of narrative convenience than of inspiration. It is notable, though, that considerable status is attributed to these women within their marriages. Many of the most notable heroes of Tolkien's world have their origins in marriages between Elves and mortals, and in these cases it is always the wife who is of Elven or Half-elven blood: Aragorn and Arwen, Tuor and Idril, Beren and Lúthien, or, in a parallel though not identical case, Thingol and Melian. Thus the role of woman as mother as well as wife is markedly stressed, just as we hear of the importance of Míriel to the young Fëanor. In an interesting contrast, it may be instructive to remember that all Lewis' powerful female figures are childless, often pointedly so: both the White Witch and the Lady of the Green Kirtle draw attention to this by their expressed desire to adopt children – and Jane in *That Hideous Strength* is expressly reprimanded by Merlin for her failure to reproduce. The stress in Tolkien on the fortunate motherhood of his dominant female figures is, however, notable, and in many ways sets the seal on the originality of his portrayal of them: not only politically active, not only romantically involved, they are also seen as progressing confidently and capably to the next stage of their lives, and as fully retaining the femininity which Lewis' girl heroines had had to sacrifice in order to render themselves acceptable. While aspects of Tolkien's vision of women may still remain within the realms of the conventional, in other ways his treatment of them shows a powerful clarity and novelty, unhampered by that crippling fear of femininity which besets the works of his fellow Inklings.

References

Lewis, C. S. 1945. *That Hideous Strength*. London: John Lane.

Lewis, C. S. 1959. *The Lion, The Witch and the Wardrobe*. Harmondsworth: Penguin.

Lewis, C. S. 1964. *The Last Battle*. Harmondsworth: Penguin.

Lewis, C. S. 1965a. *The Horse and his Boy*. Harmondsworth: Penguin.

Lewis, C. S. 1965b. *The Silver Chair*. Harmondsworth: Penguin.

Lewis, C. S. 1965c. *The Voyage of the Dawn Treader*. Harmondsworth: Penguin.

Spenser, Edmund. 1980. *The Faerie Queene*, ed. A.C. Hamilton. New York: Longman.

Tolkien, J.R.R. 1937. *The Hobbit*. London: George Allen & Unwin.

Tolkien, J.R.R. 1954-55. *The Lord of the Rings*. London: George Allen & Unwin.

Tolkien, J.R.R. 1977. *The Silmarillion*. London: George Allen & Unwin.

Williams, Charles. 1950. *The Place of the Lion*. Grand Rapids, MI: William B. Eerdmans.

More than a Bandersnatch: Tolkien as a Collaborative Writer

Diana Lynne Pavlac

Abstract: It is commonly argued that the Inklings had no influence on Tolkien. This paper will show that they had a profound influence, so much so, that Lewis and Williams should be considered co-architects of Middle-earth.

Keywords: influence, the Inklings, T.C.B.S.

Introduction: The Nature of Influence
There are many famous insults. Your mother wears army boots. When you were a kid, you were so ugly your mother tied a pork chop around your neck to get the dog to play with you.

Influence is a Dirty word
One of the worst insults in literary circles, worse than army boots or pork chops, is to accuse an author of influence. In literary circles, influence is a very dirty word.

Think about the language we use when we talk about literary influence. As Goran Hermeren has pointed out, the words themselves are value-laden. We say a writer borrows another's imagery, echoes another's phrases, overlaps another's interests. We use word like copies, follows, imitates, reflects, mirrors, derives from, and we use each of them in a negative sense. Hermeren notes that all of these terms are implied in accusations of some wrong-doing, such as lack of imagination, lack of originality, or even plagiarism.

In fact, the most common words used to describe influence use an economic metaphor: borrow, owe, debt, indebted, debtor, etc. Hermeren emphasizes "The economic metaphors used . . . have normative implications; at least, they do when used literally. If X owes 20 dollars to Y, then X ought to pay Y back 20 dollars" (Hermeren, 1975, p. 133). In other words, if Lewis borrows the term "Númenor" from Tolkien, then Lewis is in debt to Tolkien, and ought to pay Tolkien back what he owes him.

Tolkien certainly thought so. Tolkien wrote, "my only real desire is to publish 'The Silmarillion', . . . [e]specially as I find allusions and references to it creeping into Mr Lewis' work . . ." (Tolkien, 1981, p. 113). It annoyed Tolkien to see "echoes" of his unpublished work "creeping" into Lewis's published work: it annoyed him even more when readers noticed and wrote to ask him about it. In 1965, Tolkien wrote the following in a long letter to Dick Plotz:

> Lewis was, I think, impressed by "the Silmarillion and all that", and certainly retained some vague memories of it and its names in mind . . . since he had heard of it, before he composed or thought of *Out of the Silent Planet*, I imagine that *Eldil* is an echo of the *Eldar*; in *Perelandra* "*Tor and Tinidril*" are certainly an echo, since *Tuor and Idril*, parents of Eärendil, are major characters in "The Fall of Gondolin" . . .
> (Tolkien, 1981, p. 361)

Tolkien falls short of accusing Lewis of theft, but clearly he believes that some trespass has been committed, and that Lewis's accomplishment is the less because of it.

Studies of the Inklings, like studies of other writers and artists, have often been characterised by a similar suspicion of influence. It is almost humorous to hear various enthusiasts insist that their favourite Inkling was a unique and solitary genius. "My favourite Inkling was not sullied by the influence of others," they imply. "My favourite Inkling didn't need another's help."

Lois Lang-Sims, for example, has stated that Charles Williams is the most original of the Inklings and therefore the best:

> Nowadays the name of Charles Williams tends to be associated with those of J.R.R. Tolkien and C.S. Lewis . . . Neither Lewis nor Tolkien were *original* thinkers . . . Charles Williams will be remembered when they are forgotten . . . the association is misleading; and, in fact, when one looks around for his true companions, no name suggests itself. He stands *very much on his own* . . .
> (Lang-Sims, 1989, p. 16, emphasis added)

What makes Charles Williams stand head and shoulders above the rest? According to Lang-Sims, it is his independence and originality. According to Lang-Sims, Williams was free from influence. In a similar fashion, Humphrey Carpenter stubbornly insists that neither Tolkien nor Williams needed the other Inklings. "Tolkien and Williams owed almost nothing to the other Inklings, and would have written everything they wrote had they never heard of the group" (Carpenter, 1979, p. 160). I believe that such arguments, despite the sincerity of their proponents, have their basis in a faulty view of the nature of influence.

Influence Redeemed

No matter which of the Inklings is your personal favourite (but since this is the Tolkien Centenary Conference, I have a hunch which one it might be), I believe that the claims of originality and the accusations of influence are counterproductive ways to think about the accomplishments of these men. More importantly, I think this is a counterproductive way to think about influence. Harold Bloom has coined the phrase "the anxiety of influence", and in his book by that title he blames the Cartesian concept of the individual for creating it.

Such a possessive attitude toward ownership of texts and the value of individuality is, after all, an invention. Before the Enlightenment, Bloom explains, the prevailing attitude towards literary influence, even of the nature of authorship, was quite different from that taken for granted today. Ben Jonson, for example, defined imitation in art as "convert[ing] the substance or riches of another poet to his own use" (quoted in Bloom, 1973, p. 27). Similarly Goethe took the pervasiveness of influence utterly for granted: "As soon as we are born the world begins to influence us, and this goes on until we die" (quoted in Bloom, 1973, p. 52). Goethe continues,

> Do not all of the achievements of a poet's predecessors belong to him? Why should he shrink from picking flowers where he finds them? Only by making the riches of others our own do we bring anything great into being.
> (quoted in Bloom, 1973, p. 52)

Time does not me to quote Shelley, Blake, Wordsworth, Coleridge, Schopenhauer, Emerson and Baudelaire, who all agree, more or less, with this positive view of influence. I will quote one other writer, however, because he has been so influential in promoting a positive view of influence, and because he was well acquainted with the Inklings. That writer is T.S. Eliot.

Like Goethe, Eliot believed that literary influence is inevitable and that it is good. He goes further than Goethe, though, in stressing that good poets should actively seek the influence. The result will be a sense of tradition which compels the poet

> . . . to write not merely with is own generation in his bones, but with the feeling that the whole of the literature of Europe from Homer and within it the whole of the literature of his own country has a simultaneous existence and composes a simultaneous order.
> (Eliot, 1983, p. 784)

The poet who immerses himself in the literature of others, Eliot would say, writes not only for himself but for all of human kind. This is not far from Tolkien's own description of the writing process. Tolkien says that the stuff of his art does not arise fully-formed in his imagination, but

> . . . it grows like a seed in the dark out of the leaf-mould of the mind: out of all that has been seen or thought or read, that has long ago been forgotten, descending into the depths.
> (Carpenter, 1977, p. 126)

In his essay "On Fairy-Stories", Tolkien goes further in emphasising the continuity of the individual writer with all of the writers who have gone before, with writers who are his contemporaries, and with "all that have been seen or thought or read". He uses uses three great images: first, that of the "seamless web of story"; second, that of "the countless foliage of the Tree of Tales"; and third, that of the "Cauldron of Story". For Tolkien, literature is all of a piece, for there is only one web, one tree, one cauldron. In discussing the cauldron, Tolkien particularly emphasises the ongoing and inter-dependent nature of the creative process, for each individual author is merely adding his or her ingredients into a rich and timeless dish:

> Speaking of the history of stories and especially of fairy-stories we may say that the Pot of Soup, the Cauldron of Story, has always been boiling, and to it have continually been added new bits, dainty and undainty.
> (1947, p. 53)

As an antidote to a narrow and nasty view of influence, I would suggest we partake of this rich soup. As an alternative to a suspicious and anxiety-laden attitude towards influence, I would suggest we see it as an inherent part of the human creative process. As an alternative to drawing up a balance sheet of who owes what to whom, I would suggest that we take our cue from Michael Oakenshott, and see all writers as participants in the lively conversation of humankind, and welcoming the rich contribution of those who have gone before, and inviting the participation of contemporaries.

Influence on Tolkien

So far I have addressed three underlying assumptions that have guided my study of the Inklings: that all writers are influenced, that evidence of influence is not evidence of moral or literary failure.

I believe that the Inklings and others participated with Tolkien in his writing process, and that they influenced his work as a result. Now for some specifics: How was Tolkien influenced by those around him? If we put aside a negative view of influence, I believe we can identify many types of influence. For the sake of time, I will move quickly through two different aspects: Tolkien valued the encouragement of others, and he relied upon the suggestions of others.

Tolkien Relied on the Encouragement of Others

You have probably heard the statement made by C.S. Lewis that "No-one influenced Tolkien. You might as will try to influence a Bandersnatch." The title of this paper is a reference to that famous statement.

Another famous statement about influence comes from Tolkien. Listen carefully:

"The unpayable debt I owe to Lewis is not influence." The first thing I want you to notice from this statement is the use of an economic metaphor, the word "debt", as I discussed a little while ago. Influence is seen as a debt, a terrible debt

that is owed, in this case, an unpayable debt. It is negative, almost embarrassing to admit such a debt.

The second thing I want you to notice is that I have in fact just misquoted Tolkien. That is not what he said at all, but that is what we have often heard. Here is what he actually said:

> *The unpayable debt that I owe to Lewis is not influence as it is normally understood, but sheer encouragement.*

This statement is usually read as a denial of influence, quoted by Carpenter and others who argue that the Inklings did not influence Tolkien. It seems to me that this assertion demonstrates quite the opposite; Tolkien readily admits that he owes a great debt to Lewis, a debt of influence. What he seems to me to be pleading for is a broader view of influence. Influence as it is normally understood is inadequate, he says; we need a view of influence that includes encouragement.

I believe that the most important type of influence that took place in Tolkien's life was encouragement, as he himself acknowledged. As a result of his interaction with the Inklings, Tolkien became convinced that his "stuff" could be more than a hobby. He persisted in producing text long after his own energy and interest flagged.

Tolkien noted in a letter to his son, "[Lewis] is putting the screw on me to finish [*The Lord of the Rings*]", and there is a consensus that Tolkien would never have brought the project to a close if it had not been for the constant urging of his friends. I would argue further, that such encouragement, while not "influence as it is normally understood", is influence indeed. As LeFevre notes, "Certain acts of invention – or certain phases of inventive acts – are best understood if we think of them as being *made possible* by other people" (LeFevre, 1987, p. 64, emphasis added). Her wording is important, for these people do not merely help a project along, or quicken the pace; they become crucial participants in the fact of its existence.

Tolkien refers to Lewis and the Inklings as helpful, perceptive, and skilled critics. More than that, though, Tolkien expresses the conviction that his work could not have been completed apart from Lewis's input. "But for the encouragement of C.S.L.", he wrote, "I do not think that I should ever have completed or offered for publication *The Lord of the Rings*" (Tolkien, 1981, p. 366).

This remark was not made once, but over and over again. Just after reviews of *The Fellowship of the Rings* began to appear, in September of 1954, Tolkien wrote ". . . only by [Lewis's] support and friendship did I ever struggle to the end of the labour" (1981, p. 184). Several years later he again made a similar statement:

> . . . I owe to [Lewis's] encouragement the fact that in spite of obstacles (including the 1939 war!) I persevered and eventually finished *The Lord of the Rings*. He heard all of it, bit by bit, read aloud . . . (1981, p. 303)

And again, "But for [Lewis's] interest and unceasing eagerness for more I should never have brought *The L. of the R.* to a conclusion" (1981, p. 362). When we think about those who influence writers, we need to give credit to those who encourage and challenge a writer to produce a text in the first place.

Tolkien Followed the Specific Suggestions of Others

In addition to welcoming the encouragement of others, Tolkien also welcomed their advice. Following the suggestions of others is one of the most obvious kinds of influence, and yet it is often overlooked. Let me give you an example of how this works.

When we look for influence "as it is normally understood", we typically look for imitation. Let's say I am listening to a paper in a draughty lecture hall, and Lynn Maudlin is sitting next to me. She puts on her sweater, and I think, "Look at that. That's a great idea. I'll do the same." So I put on my sweater. That's one kind of influence.

That is the kind of influence we notice when we read *That Hideous Strength* and we say, "Wow, Lewis was really influenced by Charles Williams!" In the third book of the Space Trilogy Lewis apparently had observed Williams's approach to fiction, admired it, and imitated it in his own work.

Back to my sweater analogy. If I see Lynn put on her sweater and do likewise, that's influence. But let's say that we are sitting in that same lecture hall, and Lynn notices that I am shivering and says, "Why don't you put on your sweater?" That's influence, too, whether or not she puts on a sweater of her own.

Are there any instances where the Inklings gave Tolkien specific directions, where they told him what to do and he did it? Yes, there are.

One example is found in the manuscript of *The Lord of the Rings*. John Rateliff has noted that Tolkien made many changes in the text, "one might say there as many changes as there is manuscript" (1985, p. 279).

Rateliff points out that in the chapter where the character Treebeard is introduced, Tolkien originally gave Treebeard the line, "Crack my timbers, very odd." In the manuscript copy, the line is struck out, and underneath is written "queried by Charles Williams – root and twig". The published version bears this change. Rateliff observes that this is the only change in *The Lord of the Rings* that Tolkien ascribes to a specific source.

There are several things that are significant about this small detail. While some scholars have suggested that the Inklings found Tolkien's never ending manuscript tiresome to listen to and hard to follow, Williams apparently listened with enough attention to characterisation and phrasing that he noted that this small interjection seemed awkward.

In addition, it appears that very little pressure was used to provoke this change. Williams merely "queried" the appropriateness of the phrase: Tolkien promptly changed it.

Changing "Crack my timbers" to "Root and twig" is a very small change of wording. A larger, more pervasive change in the same manuscript occurred as a result of comments made first by Lewis, and later by Rayner Unwin. Both of them warned Tolkien that there was too much "hobbit talk" and not enough narration in the story. On June 4, 1938, Tolkien wrote,

I meant long ago to have thanked Rayner for bothering to read the tentative chapters, and for his excellent criticism. It agrees strikingly with Mr Lewis', which is therefore confirmed. I must bow to my two chief . . . critics.
(1981, p. 36)

Tolkien did not agree with Lewis or Unwin; he noted that he personally preferred "hobbit talk" to story telling. "The trouble is that 'hobbit talk' amuses me privately . . . more than adventures . . ." None the less, this so-called Bandersnatch did not argue, growl or fuss. He "bowed" to his critics, and expressed his intention to "curb this severely." Tolkien chopped dialogue and increased narrative in his draft, and increased the percentage of narrative in the new sections he wrote.

Another aspect of this same problem was Tolkien's tendency to abandon the text altogether in favour of refining his invented languages. Clyde Kilby noted this with obvious irritation during his stay with Tolkien; Tolkien sheepishly admits throughout his letters that if he had his way, he would devote his time to publishing the languages rather than telling the stories.

Here again, Tolkien curbed his preferences in deference to his audience. If he had not, the work would have been much different, for as he observed, "If I had considered my own pleasure more than the stomachs of a possible audience, there would have been a great deal more Elvish in the book" (1981, p. 216). In my opinion, there would have been a great deal more Elvish, and a great deal less book!

A third example of the interplay of detailed criticism and extended revision is a very early letter written by Lewis commenting on "The Lay of Leithian". In December of 1929, four years before the Inklings began to meet, Tolkien decided to show Lewis his narrative poem, "The Gest of Beren, son of Barahir, and Lúthien the Fay, called Tinúviel the Nightingale, or the Lay of Leithian, Release from Bondage". Lewis responded on December 7, 1929, with a brief and encouraging note:

> I can quite honestly say that it is ages since I have had an evening of such delight: and the personal interest of reading a friend's work had very little to do with it. I should have enjoyed it just as well as if I'd picked it up in a bookshop, by an unknown author.
> (quoted in Tolkien, 1985a, p. 151)

Early in 1930, Lewis responded to the poem again, this time with fourteen pages of detailed criticism. Most of this commentary is published in *The Lays of Beleriand*, volume three of the series *The History of Middle-earth*, edited by Christopher Tolkien. Lewis criticised the poem thoroughly, even suggesting new passages. According to Christopher Tolkien, Tolkien's revisions of this poem took into account "almost all" of Lewis 's comments. Christopher Tolkien writes:

> Almost all the verses which Lewis found wanting for one reason or another are marked for revision in the typescript B if not actually rewritten, and in many cases his proposed emendations, or modifications of them, are incorporated into the text.
> (Tolkien, 1985a, p. 151)

While it is clear that Tolkien took all of Lewis's comments seriously, and took most of them to heart, he did dispute a few of them. Lewis, for example, claimed that lines 629-630 made use of "half-hearted personification". Next to this comment in the letter, Tolkien wrote "Not so!!" and added the explanation, "The moon was dizzy and twisted because of the tears in his eyes." Christopher Tolkien notes that despite the objection, his father still struck the questioned lines from the manuscript.

In another case, Lewis wrote, "The chiasmus is suspiciously classical." In the margin Tolkien responded: "But classics did not invent chiasmus! – it is perfectly natural." No change was made in the text. Nor did Tolkien take Lewis's rather peculiar suggestion that the spelling of "labyrinth" in line 1075 of the poem be amended to "laborynth".

These exceptions aside, the degree to which Tolkien rewrote this text according to Lewis's suggestions is remarkable. According to Christopher Tolkien, J.R.R. Tolkien revised lines 563-592 of this poem more than a quarter of a century after it was written, and he rewrote it specifically along the lines that Lewis proposed (1985a, p. 322).

Let me give you a fourth example of a change that Tolkien made as a result of the advice of others. Tolkien wrote several versions of an epilogue for *The Lord of the Rings*, consisting of a bedtime conversation between Sam and his children. But *The Lord of the Rings* was published without the epilogue. Why? Tolkien admitted that he did it on the advice of his readers. He did it as a concession to those who read the manuscript.

> An epilogue giving a further glimpse (though of a rather exceptional family) has been so universally condemned that I shall not insert it. One must stop somewhere.
> (1981, p. 179)

I would not argue that *The Lord of the Rings* is a better book for Tolkien having followed the advice of those who "universally condemned" the epilogue. I will stress again, however, that the decision to leave it out offers further evidence of the very great extent to which Tolkien was influenced by those around him, even against his (and perhaps our) better judgement.

Tolkien's Life Demonstrates the Importance of Others

I have considered two ways that Tolkien was influenced: by the encouragement of those around him, and by the specific suggestions that others made. I might also look at factors like the effect of writing for a specific audience or his use of others as characters in his work, or the poems he wrote about many of the Inklings, or a number of other forms of influence. Instead I would like to shift my focus slightly in the time that remains. I have tried to demonstrate some of the ways Tolkien's work shows the direct influence of others. I would like to turn now to consider the importance or extent of that influence. I would like to consider two factors that I believe illustrate the central importance of others to Tolkien's own writing process: his life-long involvement in writing groups, and the collaborative projects that characterise his scholarly work.

Tolkien Had a Long History of Involvement in Groups

Humphrey Carpenter has said that Lewis and Williams needed the other Inklings, but that Tolkien would have written everything he did had he never heard of the group. I disagree. I think Tolkien was of central importance to the Inklings, and they to him. The importance of this group to Tolkien, and the evidence for the extent of their influence upon him, is underscored by the fact that participation in groups is a consistent feature of Tolkien's entire life.

The first group of which Tolkien was a founding member was the Tea Club and Barrovian Society, abbreviated T.C.B.S. The group began in 1911 when Tolkien was 19 years old and a student at King Edward's, an all-boys school. Three of the senior boys – John Ronald Tolkien, Christopher Wiseman, and R.Q. Gilson – worked in the school library and formed the nucleus of a clique which met in the library for tea.

The nature of the T.C.B.S. is suggested in a letter Tolkien received more than 60 yeas after the formation of the group. C.V.L. Lycett had been a classmate at King Edward's School. In 1973 he sent Tolkien the following note:

> As a boy you could not imagine how I looked up to you and admired and envied the wit of that select coterie of J.R.R.T., C.L. Wiseman, G.B. Smith, R.Q. Gilson, V. Trought, and Payton. I hovered on the outskirts to gather up the gems. You probably had no idea of this schoolboy worship.

(Tolkien, 1981, p. 429)

Tolkien did not view the group as a coterie, and certainly had not suspected that the meetings engendered awe and worship of others around them. Still, this glimpse of the group through Lycett's eyes shows something of the coherence and power that those outside the group attributed to it.

Bound together first and foremost by the difficulties of preparing and enjoying tea on the library premises, the fledgling T.C.B.S. took on an increasingly literary nature with the addition of Geoffrey Bache Smith to their ranks. Although Smith was a bit younger than the rest of the group, he wrote poetry. It was about this time that Tolkien tried his hand at poetry, too.

The initiation, then, of Tolkien's work as a poet and writer took place within the context of a small, enthusiastic group of young men. Before his involvement in this group, Tolkien was clearly both imaginative and literary. But unlike C.S. Lewis, who at the same age was writing tales of Animal-land (published in 1985 as *Boxen*), Tolkien's early creative expression consisted primarily in inventing languages. Learning foreign languages, inventing new languages, and creating alphabets to correspond to his languages occupied his creative energies until he helped form the T.C.B.S., and under their influence, he turned his energies to writing poetry[1].

In the fall of 1911, Tolkien began his studies at Oxford. Even though the four members of the T.C.B.S. were now separated geographically, they continued to exert a crucial influence over one another. In a letter to Edith Bratt dated November 26, 1915, Tolkien discusses his plans to send a copy of his poem "Kortirion" to the T.C.B.S. Despite the distance, members continued to exchange draft copies of work in progress, and comment upon one another's work.

All four members of the group assembled in London in December, 1914, for a weekend of conversation, which he referred to as the "Council of London". In a letter written in 1916 he indicated how significant it was:

> . . . I cannot abandon yet the hope and ambitions (inchoate and cloudy I know) that first became conscious at the Council of London. That council was as you know followed in my own case with my finding a voice for all kinds of pent up things and a tremendous opening up of everything for me: I have always laid that to the credit of the inspiration that even a few hours with the four always brought to all of us.

(Tolkien, 1981, p. 10)

This group gave impetus and focus to Tolkien's efforts as a young writer, "inspiration" as he puts it, a word that he used over and over again throughout his life in acknowledging the part that others played in his accomplishments. The T.C.B.S. provided the interested, sympathetic, and demanding readers that Tolkien relied on in all of his writing. In that sense, the T.C.B.S. can clearly be considered a precursor to the Inklings, and a first example of the key role that groups played in Tolkien's writing process.

Tolkien's participation in the T.C.B.S. did not prevent him from founding another group upon his arrival as an undergraduate at Oxford. He called the group Apolausticks and, according to Carpenter, ". . . it was chiefly composed of freshmen like himself. There were papers, discussions, and debates, and there were also large and extravagant dinners" (1977, p. 53). In addition, he and Colin Cullis started a group they called the Chequers, a small clique that met for dinner on Saturday nights.

While there is little evidence that the Apolausticks or the Chequers provided either audience or encouragement for Tolkien's writing, he joined yet another club which did, the college Essay Club. In a letter to Edith Bratt dated November 27, 1914, he reports that he read aloud his poem "The Voyage of Earendel the Evening Star", which was "well criticised". Just as his poetry had thrived at King Edward's School as he shared it with the members of the T.C.B.S., so now at Oxford his work continued to be produced within the context of interested readers, and continued to receive feedback which Tolkien apparently found not only welcome but necessary in order to continue to write.

In 1925 Tolkien and E.V. Gordon formed the Viking Club, a gathering of undergraduates devoted to reading sagas and

---

[1] I might add for the benefit of the elvish linguists among us, Paul Nolan Hyde, that I am not arguing that this shift from linguistics to poetry is an improvement, merely that it was stimulated by an external force.

translating songs and children's tale into Anglo-Saxon and Old Norse. In 1926 he began the *Kolbítar*, a group that consisted not of undergraduates but Oxford dons. Rather than translating material into Old Norse, this group read aloud from sagas in the original languages and translated them into English. C.S. Lewis became a member of the *Kolbítar*, and it is through this group that he and Tolkien established their friendship and began to read original works together.

I have argued that groups in general were important to Tolkien's written work, and that the T.C.B.S. in particular played a critical role: channelling his creative energy from languages into literature, modelling the behaviours of poets and story-tellers, providing critical feedback on his drafts in progress, developing his own critical faculties, recommending reading material that might support and shape his imagination, suggesting that certain pieces be started, reworded, completed, or submitted for publication. Ironically, it may be that the end of the T.C.B.S. provided for Tolkien the largest boost his writing career ever had, giving him another ingredient essential to his writing: a sense of mission.

Tolkien passed his final examination in English Language and Literature with First Class Honours in June of 1915. With the First World War in progress, he took up a commission as a second lieutenant. He trained for a year as a signaller, then was deployed in France.

Rob Gilson and G.B. Smith of the T.C.B.S. were similarly deployed, and on July 1, 1916, Rob Gilson was killed in battle. Five months later, G.B. Smith also died in battle. Tolkien felt devastated. With two of the four members gone, the T.C.B.S. was finished.

Before he died, Smith wrote the following assurance in a letter to Tolkien:

> My chief consolation is that if I am scuppered tonight – I am off on duty in a few minutes – there will still be left a member of the great T.C.B.S. to voice what I dreamed and what we all agreed upon.
> (Carpenter, 1977, p. 86)

Tolkien was fully convinced of the greatness of the T.C.B.S. With Smith's death, he became equally convinced that he had been spared in order to be a voice for ideas that the war had tried to silence. Smith's letter continued with a charge that is even more specific: "May God bless you, my dear John Ronald, and may you say the things I have tried to say long after I am not there to say them, if such be my lot" (Carpenter, p. 86).

After Smith and Gilson died, the other remaining member of the group, Christopher Wiseman, wrote to Tolkien in order to encourage him. Wiseman added, "You ought to start the epic."

Gilson had provided the vision, Smith the commission, and Wiseman the direction. Tolkien took them up, and began work on *The Silmarillion*, the work he considered his most important.

Tolkien's Scholarly Work is Clearly Collaborative

So far I have looked at Tolkien's literary work, his early work as a poet, and personal associations that inspired his mythological fiction. In these endeavours, Tolkien was strongly influenced by his involvement in writing groups. I would like to turn now to consideration of his scholarly work, and show that once again the input of other people made a critical difference. Following the Armistice on November 11, 1918, Tolkien took up his first professional writing task. He was hired by Henry Bradley to research and write etymologies for the *Oxford English Dictionary*.

He thoroughly enjoyed this work, partly because it was linguistic, and partly because he learned so much during this two year time. I believe that another reason for his great success in this venture was that he worked collaboratively as part of a team to contribute to this great work.

This is not the only major scholarly project in which Tolkien participated as a team member: much later he was one of the "principal collaborators" of the newly-translated Jerusalem Bible. He contributed to considerations of style, criticised the translation work of others, researched the translation of some large sections of text, and worked for five years to produce the translation for the book of Jonah. Unlike his enthusiasm about his contribution to the *O.E.D.*, however, Tolkien tended to understate his contribution to this translation.

Tolkien's first published book was also a collaborative project, a glossary to a Middle-English reader that had been edited by his former tutor, Kenneth Sisam. Once that was published in 1922, he began another collaboration, this time with colleague E.V. Gordon. They worked for three years on an edition of *Sir Gawain and the Green Knight*. They published it in 1925, and it remains a highly regarded work.

Gordon and Tolkien were a strong writing team: Gordon was aggressive, industrious, demanding, and energetic; Tolkien thorough, meticulous, and brilliant. Therefore, upon completion of *Gawain*, Gordon and Tolkien immediately planned additional projects; editions of the poems *Pearl*, *The Wanderer*, and *The Seafarer*. But when Tolkien was elected the Rawlinson and Bosworth Professor of Anglo-Saxon at Oxford, an honour he had achieved partly on the strength of the *Gawain* volume that he and Gordon had done, Tolkien left for Oxford, while Gordon remained on the faculty at Leeds.

The geographical separation proved too difficult to overcome. Each man continued researching for these books for almost thirteen years without further publication. After Gordon died suddenly in 1938, his widow, Ida Gordon, compiled her husband's research notes and finished the projects E.V. Gordon and Tolkien had begun.

Tolkien worked with another scholar in collaboration, and their story is nearly identical to that of Tolkien and Gordon. Tolkien began to work with Simonne d'Ardenne, a Belgian graduate student who had studied Middle English with him. Tolkien contributed significantly to d'Ardenne's *The Life and Passion of St. Juliene*, so much so, in fact, that the book has been said to reflect his views much more than hers. Tolkien and d'Ardenne planned to build on the success of this first volume with a second project, an edition of *Katerine*, another Western Middle English text. But distance and the war intervened, making communication difficult, and the work was never completed.

Tolkien's most important and most successful collaborator is his son Christopher Tolkien. The first posthumous collaboration between J.R.R. Tolkien and Christopher Tolkien is actually a Middle English work rather than a Middle-earth one. Tolkien's translation of *The Pearl* foundered on the publisher's desk for lack of an introduction. In 1975, two years after Tolkien's death, Allen and Unwin decided to issue Tolkien's translations of *Sir Gawain and the Green Knight*, *The Pearl*, and *Sir Orfeo* all in one volume. Christopher was called upon to write the introduction to that volume.

The publication of *The Silmarillion*, considered by Tolkien to be his most important work, offers yet another example of extensive collaboration. As Tolkien laboured on *The Lord of the Rings*, he often protested that his real work was *The Silmarillion*. The work was essentially drafted by 1924, although some parts admittedly were in outline form, and connecting material was scant. He made little more progress on it until his retirement, when he vowed to address his full attention to the work.

But he became overwhelmed by the task. He found himself easily distracted, and spent his days writing letters or playing solitaire. When he accepted Clyde Kilby's offer to come and help with the book, he still had trouble applying himself to the task. Kilby notes, "It would be satisfying to record that I always found [Tolkien] busy at his writing, but that is not true. I did find him sometimes working at his Elvish languages, an activity which seemed endlessly interesting to him" (1976, p. 26).

Kilby helped to impose a bit of order onto the disordered versions of the manuscripts, but was able to contribute little else to bring the book closer to publication. Tolkien had become increasingly isolated, and as a result he found himself increasingly unable to write.

Christopher Tolkien wrote, "On my father's death it fell to me to try to bring the work into publishable form" (Tolkien, 1977, p. 7). He decided that rather than present the different versions of the poems and stories, he should select among them, arrange them in the "most coherent and internally self-consistent" way, and compose connecting material. In this work, Christopher Tolkien not only collaborated with his father, but also with Guy Gavriel Kay, who worked with him on the project 1974-1975. *The Silmarillion* was published at last in 1977.

The Silmarillion was followed by *Unfinished Tales*, a collection of unfinished, unpublished works by Tolkien. And this was followed by Tolkien's longest published work, *The History of Middle-earth*. It spans nine volumes and more than 3,000 pages so far. The critical volumes, published after Tolkien's death and still in progress, represent an extensive collaborative effort between Tolkien's creative imagination and his son Christopher's persistent energy. I believe that the nine volumes of *The History of Middle-earth* are best understood as a collaborative effort.

In the absence of a present, active collaborator, Tolkien's progress on manuscripts was thwarted and his energies were dissipated. These are not the only examples of projects that were begun with abundant skill and enthusiasm, and later abandoned, incomplete. He began work on the Anglo-Saxon poem *Exodus*, but never finished. He did a translation of *The Pearl*, but never finished the introduction to the work and so publication was suspended.

Tolkien has argued that life events kept intervening: sick children, disruptive moves, etc. Carpenter has argued that Tolkien's "passion for perfection" is the cause (1977, p. 138). Others have pointed to procrastination, fear of criticism, overwork on his job and his passion for creating languages as the reasons for the large body of unfinished work Tolkien left when he died. While I agree that Tolkien exhibited these tendencies, I also feel that the occasions when he successfully overcame these obstacles have in common a single variable; the persistent motivation provided by other people taking an active, collaborative role.

Conclusion: Co-architects of Middle-earth

This discussion of the ways Tolkien was influenced by those around him is a small part of an ongoing study of the ways that the Inklings influenced each other. In looking at the Inklings, I am asking, what difference did it make that they wrote in association with each other? How did their relationship affect the amount of material that each man produced? What kind of feedback did they offer each other? What were the results of that feedback? What part did encouragement and discouragement play in the completion of texts? What impact did they have on the reception of their work by publishers and readers?

The Inklings met on an ongoing basis in order to discuss written works in progress. Like any successful writing group, they influenced each other and each other's writing. As a result of their interaction, Tolkien was influenced "more than a Bandersnatch". In fact, I see him a a model of life-long collaboration. Throughout his life Tolkien was surrounded and influenced by co-architects of Middle-earth.

References

Bloom, Harold. 1973. *The Anxiety of Influence*. London: Oxford University Press.

Carpenter, Humphrey. 1977. *J.R.R. Tolkien: A Biography*. Boston: Houghton Mifflin.

Carpenter, Humphrey. 1979. *The Inklings*. Boston: Houghton Mifflin.

Eliot, T.S. 1983 "Tradition and the Individual Talent" in *A World of Ideas*, ed. Lee A. Jacobus. New York: St. Martin's Press. pp. 599-614.

Hermeren, Goran. 1975. *Influence in Art and Literature*. Princeton: Princeton University Press.

Kilby, Clyde S. 1976. *Tolkien and The Silmarillion*. Wheaton: Harold Shaw Publishers.

Lang-Sims, Lois. 1989. *Letters to Lalage: The Letters of Charles William to Lois Lang-Sims* Kent: Kent State University Press.

LeFevre, Karen Burke. 1987. *Invention as a Social Act.* Carbondale: Southern Illinois University Press.

Lewis, C.S. 1985. *Boxen: The Imaginary World of the Young C.S. Lewis.* Ed. Walter Hooper. New York: Harcourt Brace Jovanovich.

Rateliff, John. 1985. "and Something Yet Remains to be Said – Tolkien and Williams" in *Proceedings of the Sixteenth Annual Convention of the Mythopoeic Society* Wheaton: Mythcon XVI. pp. 271-86.

Tolkien, J.R.R. 1947. "On Fairy Stories" in *Essays Presented to Charles Williams* Ed. C.S. Lewis. London: Oxford University Press. pp. 38-39.

Tolkien, J.R.R. 1977. *The Silmarillion* Boston: Houghton Mifflin Company.

Tolkien, J.R.R. 1981. *The Letters of J.R.R. Tolkien* Ed. Humphrey Carpenter. Boston: Houghton Mifflin Company.

Tolkien, J.R.R. 1985a. *The Lays of Beleriand* Ed. Christopher Tolkien. Boston: Houghton Mifflin Company.

Tolkien, J.R.R. (trans.). 1985b. *Sir Gawain and the Green Knight, Pearl, and Sir Orfeo.* Ed. Christopher Tolkien. Boston: Houghton Mifflin Company.

"A Pattern Which Our Nature Cries Out For": The Medieval Tradition of the Ordered Four in the Fiction of J.R.R. Tolkien

Stephen Yandell

Abstract: This paper considers the fiction of J.R.R. Tolkien and the other Inklings (specifically C.S. Lewis and Charles Williams) as being influenced by a set of shared ideas. First, Tolkien and the Inklings believed in a divine creator whose creation displays order. Every individual, they claimed, has been divinely called to be a "sub-creator" to create art so that this universal order might be reflected. And the Inklings' writings testify to the importance of this order in their lives (as displayed by six Medieval analogies: God as composer, choreographer, author, painter, player and guide).

Secondly, Tolkien and the Inklings were familiar with the primarily Medieval notion that the matter of the world is inherently divided into groups of "four." This division may be seen around humans (in Nature), among humans, within humans, and in human creations (Art). And every division of four may be seen to adhere to one of eight forms.

And finally, Tolkien and his colleagues perceived the process of creation, whether by God or humans, to be similar. There is a three-step process of 1) selecting parts with which to work, 2) creating a border within which to work, and 3) combining these separate pieces in a unique, ordered way so as to produce a harmonic whole.

The narrative structure of *The Lord of the Rings* represents the most effective application of these ideas. Tolkien's masterpiece makes use of a Medieval interlace structure which depends on the interaction of four narrative groups which exist after the breaking of the Fellowship. Weaving these four lines of narration is central to the "rhythm and ordering" of the tale and displays Tolkien's real skill. And not surprisingly, these four narrative groups can be better understood in the light of other creative divisions: the four elements, the four traditional classes of society, the four divisions of colour, the four parts of choral harmony, the four sections of an orchestra, etc.

Key words: divisions of the Four, the Inklings, interlace structure, C. S. Lewis, mediaeval analogies of order, narrative structure, process of creativity, Charles Williams

Despite their very distinct types of fiction, J.R.R. Tolkien and the other Inklings (namely C.S. Lewis and Charles Williams) shared a keen passion in the "stuff" of the universe – that is, those items in the world which an artist may choose as building blocks when creating new art. Tolkien and the others shared a core creative philosophy which was essentially threefold: first, they believed that the world is ordered – purposefully crafted by a divine creator. And they believed that as part of this creation, humans necessarily reflect the divine order when they create; it is through their artwork, in fact, that humans fulfil their call to become sub-creators (as Tolkien labelled himself). Secondly, they recognized a natural division of four in the "stuff" of the universe. This primarily (though not exclusively) Medieval notion dominated the works with which they were most familiar. And finally, Tolkien and the Inklings understood the act of creation (whether by God or humans) to be this: combining separate parts in a unique, ordered way so as to produce a harmonic whole.

Thus they possessed an ideology which was Christian in philosophy, Medieval in form, and Mythopoeic in nature. These beliefs affected their religious thought, directed their academic pursuits, and, as it relates to an understanding of their fiction, will be the focus of this paper. Each of these

The World Is Ordered

Finding ways to describe the divine creator is a task as old as humankind, but six particular analogies dominated Medieval thought: God as Composer, Choreographer, Author, Painter, Player and Guide. Not surprisingly, these are the same analogies which dominate the writings of Tolkien and two of the other Inklings, Lewis and Williams. All of these analogies are included in Figure 1, and should be very familiar, for they have been explored by writers for centuries. Tolkien's allusions to these analogies are listed above those of Lewis, Williams, and some of the more familiar non-Inkling authors. The references have been selected from letters, fiction and scholarly works and testify to the significance which the Medieval analogies held in every area of the Inklings' lives. And each of the entries confirms a core belief in an ordered, created world, and in creatures who are called to reflect this order by sub-creating.

Also central to each of these analogies is the relationship between the creator and creature. While the creator was traditionally depicted as maintaining a comprehensive view of the piece of art, the creature in the midst of the creation was believed to possess only a limited perspective. The image of The Divine Dance of the Universe is typical: although life's dance steps may seem chaotic to one down in the midst of the hurried frenzy, the divine one who has choreographed it all watches from above and understands how every measured step of the complicated pattern interacts with every other step. Several times Frodo and Sam discuss this feeling of being part of a divine order[1].

One of the best pieces of Tolkien criticism, T.A. Shippey's *The Road to Middle-earth*, discusses the analogy of humans as part of a created story:

> Events in the world, they say, appear chaotic and unplanned, appear so all but unmistakably. But however strong that impression is, it is a subjective one founded on the inevitably limited view of any individual.
> (Shippey, 1983, p. 124)

It is the creator's job to see that order exists on the grand scale, while allowing tensions to rise and fall in the midst of the created piece.

In *An Experiment in Criticism* Lewis discusses a human's role in creation:

> If the Poiema [something made], or the exercises, or the dance is devised by a master, the rests and movements, the quickenings and slowings, the easier and the more arduous passages, will come exactly as we need them . . . It would have been unbearable if it had ended a moment sooner or later or in any different way. Looking back on the performance, we shall feel that we have been led through a pattern or arrangement of activities which our nature cried out for.
> (Lewis, 1973a, pp. 133-4)

The Divisions of Four

Just as the Medieval analogies appealed to the Inklings, so did the Medieval patterns. Every number held some significance in the medieval mind, and "four" was believed to represent the temporal world. All of existence, in fact, was felt to be made up of four parts: the world was composed of the four elements; earth constantly underwent the cycle of the four seasons; distances were limited by the four corners of the earth (such references were still used, although only figuratively, in the Middle Ages). Four, they reasoned, was also one number away from the number of God — three, the Trinity. Added together, the numbers of God and humans came to seven, the number of perfection.

In his *Commentary of The Dream of Scipio*, Macrobius discusses the relationship between the creator and his medium, the four elements: "The creator of the universe bound the elements together with an unbearable chain . . . For thus, in spite of the utter diversity of these elements, the Creator harmonized them so skilfully that they could be readily united" (MacQueen, 1985, p. 61). The skill of the Creator, one sees again, is in bringing about harmony — specifically, through the ordering of four parts. John MacQueen's excellent text, *Numerology*, provides an important survey of the subject as it relates to medieval writers, and one of his conclusions is particularly valuable: "The harmony . . . of the four elements is derived from the harmonic, 'genial' properties of the number four." (MacQueen, 1985, p. 61).

These various divisions of four exist throughout the universe, as the four main categories in Figure 2 indicate: order around humans (Nature), among humans, within humans, and in human creations (Art). The idea of order and harmony is bound up intimately with the division of four. Four represents balance: the mixture of all four medieval humours, for example, was said to indicate balance in an individual's temperament. Four represents completion: the four seasons together represent a complete year; the combination of the four Gospel accounts provides a complete picture of Christ in his various roles (humanity, royalty, divinity and sacrifice). Four also represents harmony: the presence of all four choral parts, in Western music at least, defines musical harmony.

Figure 2 also includes examples of four found within Tolkien's, Lewis' and Williams' fiction. Every item in this figure is also accompanied by a symbol which describes the "form" of four which the item takes. In total, there are eight principal forms, and these are described in Figure 3. Figures 4, 5 and 6 focus on the individual items of Figure 3 in terms of their four component parts. Thus, Figures 2-6 testify to the fact that throughout history, the order of the world has been believed to be composed structurally by four, divided spatially by four, and rotated through cycles of four. Human

---

[1] Note in figure 1: Sam says he feels as if he were "inside a song" (Tolkien, 1986a, p. 455) and later realizes they are part of a great tale (Tolkien, 1986b, p. 408).

Order in the Universe: the Medieval analogies

created by S. Yandell, 1992

	The Music of the Spheres	The Divine Dance of the Universe	The Divine Story/Drama of Life	The Great Painting / Tapestry of Life	The Great Game of Life	The Great Journey of Life	(Also God as Sculptor, God as Architect, God as Chef)
	God as Composer/Conductor	God as Choreographer	God as Author/Playwright	God as Painter/Weaver	God as Player	God as Cartographer/Guide	
The Inklings: J.R.R. Tolkien	• Song of Eru/Music of the Ainur Sil 3-4, 8 • The song of Luthien released the bonds of winter, and the frozen waters spoke." Sil 199 • "I feel as if I was inside a song, if you take my meaning." Sam, FR 455 • "And I would not have it said of me in song only that I was always left behind!" Merry, RK 93 • "And now the songs have come down among us out of strange places and walk visible under the Sun." Theoden, TT 197	• "Luthien danced upon a green hill...and flowers sprang from the cold earth where her feet had passed." Sil 199	• "The Knowledge of the Creation Drama was incomplete." Lett 147 • "Someone else always has to carry on the story." Bilbo, FR 306 • "Do we walk in legends or on the green earth in the daylight?" "A Man may do both," said Aragorn. Eomer and Aragorn, TT 45 • "Don't the great tales never end?"..."The people in them come, and go when their part's ended." Sam and Frodo TT 407,8 • "Well, one can't be everywhere at once...But, I missed a lot, seemingly." Sam, RK 290	• "They lost the thread of his tale..." FR 182 • "There are children in your land who, out of the twisted threads of story, could pick the answer to your question." Gandalf to Theoden, TT 197 • Medusald's tapestries: "Many woven cloths were hung upon the walls, and over their wide spaces marched figures of ancient legend..." TT 148 • Niggle's painting: "All the leaves he had ever laboured on were there." Leaf By Niggle		• The Lost Road journey • "The road goes ever on and on...and I must follow, if I can..." FR 110 • "He used to say there was only one Road..."You step into the Road, and if you don't keep your feet, there is no knowing where you might be swept off to." Frodo about Bilbo, FR 110 • "There was once a little man called Niggle, who had a long journey to make..." Leaf By Niggle	
C.S. Lewis	• Music of the Universe Perelandra 214 • Song of creation/singing stars MN 98,99 • "We had the musicians up in the rigging playing flutes so that it sounded like music out of the sky." Lucy, PC 107 • "You must conceive yourself looking up at a world lighted, warmed, and resonant with music." (recommendation to readers of medieval literature) The Discarded Image 112 • "[the spaces] were perpetually filled with sweet, immeasurable sound. The vast hollow spheres, turning each at its proper interval inside its superior, gave out a blended harmony." Studies in Med. and Ren. Literature 52 • The melodies and silences of Heaven will be shouted down in the end." Screwtape Letters 114	• "Each one of us has got to enter that pattern, take his place in that dance." Mere Xianity 153 • Dance of the planets Perelandra 214, 217-219 • "The Company of St. Anne's 'taking their places places in the ordered rhythm of the universe.'" THS 325 • "The great lords of the upper sky know the steps of their dance too well for that." Cornelius, PC 45 • Dance of the trees: PC 134 • "I shall take my rising again...and once more tread the great dance." Ramandu, VDT 180 • The Great Snow Dance SC 193 • "The eternal dance" Prob Pain 153 • "If the dance is devised by a master, the rests and movements...will come exactly as we need them." Exp Crit 133 • "a subtler image of creation...would be the almost simultaneous mutual adaption in the movements of two expert dancing partners." Miracles Appendix B	• Spell for the Refreshment of the Spirit: "I will tell it to you for years and years." VDT 136 • Message in giant city: SC 133 • "Now at last they were beginning Chapter One in the Great Story." LB 184 • "I tell no-one any story but his own." HHB 159, 194 • "No-one is told what would've happened." PC 137, 136 • "But stranger, the sacred story is about...the things we do in the temple." TWHF 246 • "the very same story which is written across the whole world in letters too large for some of us to see." "Miracles" • "We do not even know whether we are in Act I or Act V...The Author knows." "The World's Last Night" 104,5 • "The whole...drama, or pattern of this life is to be played out in each one of us." Mere Xianity 153 • Novel analogy: Miracles Appendix B	• "And the sea in the mirror ...were in one sense just the same as the real ones; yet at the same time...different - deeper, more wonderful." LB 170 • A painting with several contributors: "The work done by every mass and color in the new patches will be affected through and through by the parts of the original...we should think of the total result, chemically rather than arithmetically." Discarded Image 209 • "He is the painter, we are only the picture." Mere Xianity 172 • "[Ransom] had been forced out of the frame, caught up into the larger pattern." Perelandra 147,8 • line drawing analogy: Miracles Appendix B	• "A mad chase began...It was such a romp as no one has ever had except in Narnia, and whether it was more like playing with a thunderstorm or...a kitten Lucy could never make up her mind." LWW 160,1 • The Great Snow Dance: "Of course it is a kind of game as well as a dance..." SC 193 • "But four babies playing a game can make a play-world which licks your real world hollow. That's why I'm going to stand by the play world." Puddleglum to the Lady of the Green Kirtle, SC 159 • "If a game is played, it must be possible to lose it." Prob of Pain 118 • "They did not know the first rule of the holy game..." Prob of Pain 153	• "He stole out by the back door and set his face to the West to seek for the Island." The Pilgrim's Regress 16	
Charles Williams	• Music of the chessboard: "There came a slight sound of music...perhaps the faint sound itself was but their harmonized movement upon their field." Greater Trumps 28	• Dance of the chessboard: "A number of little figures...were all in movement...as if to some complicated measure." GT 28 • "Imagine that everything which exists takes part in the movement of a great dance."GT 94,95	• "All things at all times and every where, rehearsed; some great art was in practice and the only business anyone had was to see that his part was perfect." DH 147	• "There she weaves by night and day...And moving through a mirror clear...Shadows of the world appear." "The Lady of Shalott" II. 37, 46-48, Tennyson • "The commonest room is a room in a poem when I turn to the glass." G Macdonald, Phantastes 66	• "The Divine chessboard: "The figures might have seemed like those in a game." GT 28		
Other Fiction / Myth	• Plato, Pythagoras, Kepler: musical harmony underlies the cosmos • Greece's eight sirens: eight single notes came together to form the concord of a single harmony. • "Where were you [at creation] when the morning stars sang together?" God to Job, Job 38:4,7	• Dante • Sir John Davies "Orchestra Or a Poeme of Daunsing" 1596 • Milton	• "All the world's a stage/And all the men and women merely players..." Jaques, As You Like It II.vii.134		• Game of the World being played by the Celtic gods	• Pilgrim's Progress, 1684 • Everyman - late 15th c	

Figure 1

Order in the Universe: the patterns

Order around humans – Nature

- ⊚ Celtic festivals
- ▯ Celtic regions
- ⊗ Creatures (5 sets)
- ⊚ Daily cycle
- ⊗ Daughters of God
- ▯ Directions of the World
- ▯ Elements
- ⊚ Elemental regions
- ⊗ Fate cycle
- ⊗ God, aspects of
- ⊗ Gospels
- ⊗ Greek gods, ruling
- ▯ Hell's rivers
- ⊗ Horsemen of the Apocalypse
- ▯ Jerusalem's walls
- ⊚ Jesus (dying/reviving god), cycle of life
- ⊗ Jesus, aspects of
- ⊚ Life cycle
- ⊛ Light
- ⊚ Lunar cycle
- ▯ Objects (4 sets)
- ⊗ Prophets, major
- ⊗ Qualities
- ⊗ Sacrificial forms
- ⊚ Season cycle
- ⊚ Spirits
- ⊚ Water cycle
- ▯ Winds
- ⊗ Zodiac, ruling

Order among humans

- ⊚ Classes of society

Order within humans

- ⊗ DNA
- ⊗ Personality types, modern
- ⊗ Psychological functions
- ⊗ Smell, sense of
- ⊗ Taste, sense of
- ⊗ Temperaments/humours
- ⊗ Touch, sense of
- ⊗ Virtues, cardinal

Order in human creations – Art

- ⊗ Choral setting
- ⊛ Pigments
- ⊗ Orchestra instrument families
- ⊛ Printing process colors

Four in Tolkien

- ⚔ Ages of Middle-earth
- ⊚ Middle-earth hierarchy
- ⊗ Narrative groups, LOTR
- ⊛ Races bound by the rings
- ▯ Shire Farthings
- ⊗ Steps in Creation of Ea

Four in Lewis

- ⊚ Deep Space hierarchy
- ⊚ Narnian hierarchy
- ⊗ Pevensie children
- ⊗ Spell for the Refreshment of the Spirit
- ▯ Thrones of Cair Paravel

Four in Williams

- ✳ Alternatives of the soul
- ⊗ Suits of the Divine Tarot
- ⊗ Virtues for writing poetry
- ⊛ Ways of Love

Figure 2

created by S. Yandell, 1992

The Forms of Four:

Four as Combination

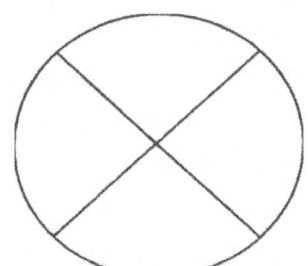

- Each part can mix with any other part

Four as Connection

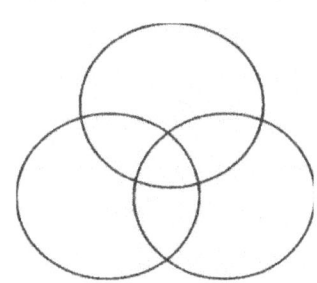

- Three parts are equally bound to a fourth, central part

Four as Cycle

- Related to the passing of time; a continuous repetition
- Each part leads into, and follows from, one other part

Four as Progression

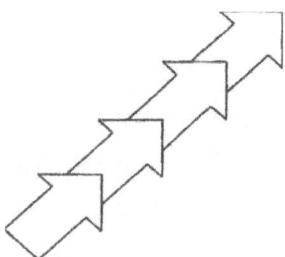

- Related to the passing of time, but does not repeat a cycle; the series may or may not lead to a climax
- Each part leads into, and/or follows from, one other part

Four as Boundary

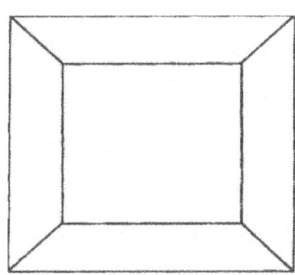

- Each part creates one side of a boundary
- Each part touches two others - one on each side

Four as Options

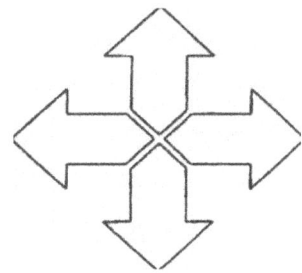

- Each part is an available, mutually-exclusive option

Four as Hierarchy

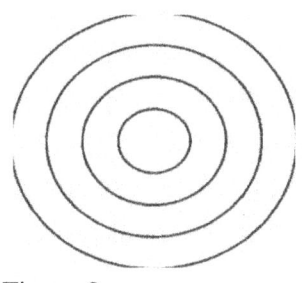

- Each part is embedded in a hierarchy where the parts get larger from the center
- Each part touches either one or two other parts

Four as Linear Hierarchy

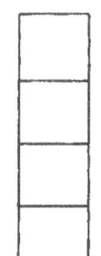

- Each part is embedded in a linear hierarchy where each part is of equal size
- Each part touches either one or two other parts

Figure 3

created by S. Yandell, 1992

Figure 4
created by S. Yandell, 1992

Four as Boundary

each part creates one side of a boundary and touches two other parts (one on each of its sides)

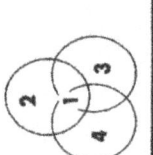

complete item	1	2	3	4	sources
Directions of the World	West	North	East	South	earliest cultures
Eden's rivers	Euphrates	Gihon	Tigris	Pishon	Judeo-Xian, Gen. 3:15
Hell's rivers, feed into Styx	Phlegethon	Lethe	Cocytus	Acheron	Greek, traditional
Jerusalem's walls	West wall	North wall	East wall	South wall	Judeo-Xian, Rev. 21:12
Celtic regions / main city	West/Connacht/Murias	North/Ulster/Falias	East/Leinster/Gorias	South/Munster/Finias	Celtic, traditional
Winds (Eos&Astraeus' sons)	Zephyrus, west wind	Boreas, north wind	Eurus, east wind	Notus, south wind	Greek, traditional

Four as Connection

Three parts are equally bound to a fourth, central part

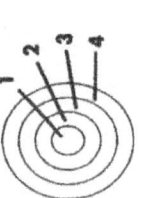

complete item	1	2	3	4	sources
Light	white - additive mix of light	red	green	blue-violet	Sir Isaac Newton, 17th c
Pigments	black - mixture	red - primary color	blue - primary color	yellow - primary color	early cultures, traditional
Printing process colors	black - "key" color	magenta	cyan	yellow	color printing, 18th c

Four as Hierarchy

Each part is embedded in a hierarchy; each part gets larger away from the center, and each part touches either one or two other parts

complete item	1	2	3	4	sources
Classes of society	priests	warriors	merchants	servants	India, traditional
Elemental regions	earth	water	air	fire	Greek, traditional

Four as Combination

Figure 5
created by S. Yandell, 1992

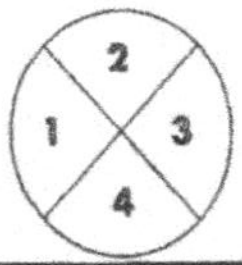

Each part can mix with any other part

complete item	1	2	3	4	sources
Choral setting	soprano	alto	tenor	bass	Western music, 12th c
Creatures (5 sets)					
Ezekiel's vision / Evangelists	man/angel, Matthew	lion, Mark	eagle, John	bull/calf/ox, Luke	Judeo-Xian, Ez. 1:10, Rev 4:7
Sumerian	peacock	lion	eagle	ox	Sumerian
Chinese	turtle	dragon	phoenix	unicorn	Chinese
Socratic	man	horse	cock	sheep	Socrates' followers, 5c BC
Egyptian gods of dead	man	dog/jackal	eagle	ape	Egyptian
DNA	adenine	guanine	thymine	cytosine	1950's Crick and Watson
Daughters of God	Truth (represents OT)	Righteousness (OT)	Peace (represents NT)	Mercy (NT)	Piers Plowman, 1380
Elements	fire	water	air	earth	Galen, 2nd c Greece
God, aspects of	creator	ruler	comforter/guide	servant	Judeo-Xian, Medieval
Gospels	Matthew	Mark	John	Luke	Judeo-Xian
Greek gods, ruling	Mars	Venus	Jupiter	Neptune	Greek, traditional
Horsemen of the Apocalypse	White - conquer/pestilence	Black - famine	Pale - death	Red - war	Judeo-Xian, Rev. 6:2-8
Jesus, aspects of	humanity (Matthew)	royalty (Mark)	divinity (John)	sacrificial (Luke)	Judeo-Xian, Medieval
Objects (4 sets)					
Archetypal symbols	sword	cup, drinking horn	lance, wand, tree, sceptre	dish, coin, circle, body, ship womb, egg, burial mound, hill	earliest fertility cults
Celtic gifts/Masters	sword / Uscias	cauldron / Semias	spear / Esras	stone / Morfessa	Celtic, traditional
Grail symbols	Sword of the Dolorous stroke	Grail, as cup of last supper	Lance of Longinius	Grail, as blood receptacle at cross; paten	Medieval (French, British)
Suits	swords (spades)	cups (hearts)	wands (diamonds)	coins, deniers (clubs)	Egyptian and after
Orchestra instrument families	brass	woodwinds	percussion	strings	modern form, 17th century
Personality types, modern	SP "Doers"	SJ "Keepers"	NT "Knowers"	NF "Growers"	Myers-Briggs, 20th c
Prophets, major	Ezekiel	Daniel	Jeremiah	Isaiah	Judeo-Xian, traditional
Psychological functions	intuition	sensation	thinking	feeling	Jung, early 20th c
Qualities	hot	wet	dry	cold	Greek, traditional
Sacrificial forms	cremation/death by fire	burial/death by earth	drowning/death by water	hanging/death by air	Celtic, traditional
Smell, sense of	fragrant	acid	rancid	burnt	science, 20th c
Spirits	salamanders	gnomes	undines/water nymphs	sylphs	early cultures, Rosicrucians
Taste, sense of	bitter	salt	sweet	sour	science, 20th c
Temperaments/humours	choleric/cholera	melancholic/black bile	phlegmatic/phlegm	sanguine/blood	Hippocrates, 4th c BC
Touch, sense of	contact	pressure	temperature	pain	science, 20th c
Virtues, cardinal	prudence	temperance	fortitude	justice	Judeo/Xian, Medieval
Zodiac, ruling	Aries/Leo/Sagittarius	Taurus/Virgo/Capricorn	Gemini/Libra/Aquarius	Cancer/Scorpio/Pisces	Greek, traditional

Four as Cycle

Figure 6
created by S. Yandell, 1992

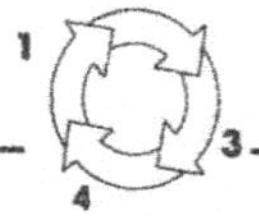

As time passes, each part leads into, and follows from, one other part, continuously repeating the order of parts

complete item	1	2	3	4	sources
Daily cycle	dawn/sunrise/morning 6am-noon	noon/afternoon noon-6pm	sunset/dusk/evening 6pm-midnight	night midnight-6am	earliest cultures
Fate cycle	Regnabo "I will rule"	Regno "I rule"	Regnavi "I have ruled"	Sum Sine Regno "I am without rule"	European, medieval
Jesus (dying/reviving god) cycle of life	incarnation/resurrection	ministry	passion	crucifixion/ascension	earliest cultures
Life cycle	birth/youth (0-20)	maturity (21-40)	adulthood (41-60)	seniority/death (61-80)	earliest cultures
Lunar cycle	new moon/waxing to half (day 1 - 7)	half moon/waxing to full (day 8 - 14)	full moon/waning to half (day 15 - 21)	half moon/waning to new (day 22 - 28)	earliest cultures
Season cycle	Spring (13 weeks/91 days)	Summer	Fall	Winter	earliest cultures
Water cycle	fountains	rivers	seas	rain, snow	earliest cultures
Celtic festivals	Vernal Equinox (March 22) Beltain (April 30)	Summer Solstice (June 21) Lughnasadh (July 31)	Autumnal Equinox (September 22) Samhain (October 31)	Winter Solstice (December 21) Oimelc (January 31)	Celtic, traditional

Four in Inkling fiction

complete item	1	2	3	4	sources
Ages of Middle-earth	First Age	Second Age	Third Age	Fourth Age	ME history
Middle-earth hierarchy	Eru	Valar	Maiar	races of Middle-earth	Middle-earth history
Narrative groups, LOTR	Gandalf, sometimes with Pippin	Aragorn, with Legolas and Gimli	Merry, sometimes with Pippin	Sam, with Frodo	LOTR
Races bound by the rings	Maiar - Sauron's one ring	Elves - three rings	Humans - nine rings	Dwarves - seven rings	Sil pp3-6
Shire Farthings	West farthing	North farthing	East farthing	South farthing	H, FR p30
Steps in Creation of Ea	first theme	second theme	third theme	silence/vision/creation	ME history
Deep Space hierarchy	The Old One and Maleldil	Oyarsa	Eldila	hnau and dumb animals	Space Trilogy
Narnian hierarchy	Emperor O.S. and Aslan	High King	nobility, humans	talking and dumb animals	Narnian Chronicles
Pevensie children	Peter	Edmund	Susan	Lucy	LWW
Spell for the Refreshment of the Spirit	cup	sword	tree	green hill	VDT p133
Thrones of Cair Paravel	High King's	King's	Queen's	Queen's	LWW p78
Alternatives of the soul	revolt	obey	compromise	deceive	Descent into Hell p185
Suits of the Divine Tarot	cup	sword	deniers	wands	Greater Trumps p44
Virtues for writing poetry	clarity	speed	humility	courage	Descent into Hell p63
Ways of Love	Almighty love	physical sensation - the play of love	pardon - the speed of love	action - the fact of love	Descent into Hell p147

societies have been seen as divided by four, as have been their bodies, the elements of their religions, and their artistic creations.

Again, these are truths which were embraced not only by Medieval authors, but also by Tolkien and the other Inklings. And their scientific validity was not at all a factor in their attractiveness to these authors; the notion of order was the vital concern. It is true, for example, that a fourth bodily fluid had to be invented by Galen just to conform to his elemental theories, but sociologists today still classify human personalities in four main groups although they are not named after the original temperaments. The senses are another good example of four that are recognized today; the primary way in which humans understand reality is through the senses, and yet science has discovered that humans can really only taste four types of tastes; one's smell receptors can only distinguish four different smells; and one only receives four types of touch information. It is the varied combination of all of these sensory inputs that allows a person to experience the diversity of the sensual world. Probably the best example of a modern division of four is the twentieth-century discovery of DNA. What Crick and Watson discovered was essentially a Medieval truth: all of life's complexities are constructed by combinations of four. The DNA sequencing is based on four base pairs of amino acids: adenine, guanine, thymine, and cytosine. It is their unique combination that produces all of life's diversity. The genetic code has been compared to an alphabet with only four letters, and yet every living thing possesses a unique genetic code.

It is also worth noting that numerous connections exist between the fifty sets of four which are listed in Figure 2, and different individuals and cultures have associated them differently. For example, in the Middle Ages, the four periods of the daily cycle were linked to the four humours. Throughout the day, one was said to be regulated more or less by a particular temperament. Similarly, the age of cathedrals saw artists enthralled with order being associated between musical harmonic patterns and architecture, while in more recent centuries, technology has allowed artists to create instruments like the colour organ which unites the parts of music with the parts of coloured light. As Calvin Johansson has observed: "Art in a sense is a reflective microcosm of the ordering of the world" (1986, p. 95).

Creativity is Combining

If God is in the unique position of creating something out of nothing, and matter be neither created nor destroyed, then how may humans fulfil their call to sub-create? After all, as Lewis recognized in *Miracles*, there is a finite amount of stuff in the universe: "We all live in second-hand suits and there are doubtless atoms in my chin which have served many another man, many a dog, many an eel, many a dinosaur" (1947, p. 181). Tolkien raises this same question and answers it:

> Who can design a new leaf? The patterns from bud to unfolding, and the colours from spring to autumn were all discovered by men long ago. But that is not true. The seed of the tree can be replanted in almost any soil. (Tolkien, 1984, p. 145)

In a letter to Sister Penelope, Lewis explains,

> We re-arrange elements He has provided. There is not a *vestige* of real creativity *de novo* in us. Try to imagine a new primary colour . . . or even a monster wh[ich] does not consist of bits of existing animals stuck together. Nothing happens.
> (Lewis, 1988, p. 371)

Rearranging elements in combination: this is the critical step in the creation process; but it is only the third of three steps which Tolkien and the Inklings saw as necessary in creating. First an artist must select carefully those parts with which he or she will be grappling. Second, the artist must construct a frame within which she or he will place these elements – a boundary with rules by which the artist must abide. And finally the artist must interweave these parts in a unique, ordered, harmonious manner.

The selection of parts is a unique task for every artist. A musician possesses well-defined elements with which to work: the musical scale, orchestra sections and choral parts; similarly, a painter has an existing palette of colours. The elements which a writer must combine may not be so easily named (themes, plot elements, archetypal images, character types, lines of narration, etc.), but it is the act of choosing which items to use from these limited sets which is of critical importance.

Medieval writers, for example, constantly chose the same themes to reuse in their works, and yet as Lewis points out in *The Discarded Image*, this showed no lack of creativity: "If you had asked Layamon or Chaucer 'Why do you not make up a brand-new story of your own?' I think they might have replied (in effect) 'Surely we are not yet reduced to that?'" (1984, p. 211). Even in modern English literature, authors have purposefully chosen the most worthwhile story elements, even if they have been used before: "Shakespeare takes a few bones from the novel's plot and flings the rest to a well-deserved oblivion" (Lewis, 1984, p. 209). In "On Fairy-Stories," Tolkien addresses the same selection process of an author: "But if we speak of a Cauldron [of mythic elements], we must not wholly forget the Cooks. There are many things in the Cauldron, but the Cooks do not dip in the ladle quite blindly. Their selection is important" (1984, p. 128). The selection, in fact, is the first, vital step in the creation of myth. Tolkien's decision to combine lines of narration is central to the structure of *The Lord of the Rings*, and will be considered shortly.

The construction of a "boundary" for any story is also an essential task according to Tolkien and the Inklings. In *The Last Battle*, Lewis uses the comparison between a mirror and a window to show how art – that is, the framed image – is related to, and different from, real life.

> And the sea in the mirror, or the valley in the mirror, were in one sense just the same as the real one: yet at the same time they were somehow different – deeper, more wonderful, more like places in a story: in a story you have never heard but very much want to know.
> (Lewis, 1973b, p. 170)

Tolkien also discusses the topic of framework in his essay "On Fairy-Stories":

> There is no true end to any fairy-tale... The verbal ending – usually held to be as typical of the end of fairy-stories as "once upon a time" is of the beginning – "and they lived happily ever after" is an artificial device. It does not deceive anybody... An enchanted forest requires a margin, even an elaborate border.
> (Tolkien, 1984, pp. 153, 160-161)

This border, then, is some construct of the author which determines how much art will be shown to a reader, since it is impossible to portray all of life everywhere.

Although each of the Arts possesses different sets of elements with which its artisans may work, these elements are available to all artists, and the talent of any one is determined by his or her skill in combining them in a unique way. And as permutation formulas will attest to, the number of ways in which the same elements may be recombined in unique ways is exponentially large. For this reason Tolkien warned artists against feeling frustrated at the limited number of usable materials: "We do not, or need not, despair of drawing because all lines must be either curved or straight, nor of painting because there are only three 'primary' colours" (1984, p. 145).

Tolkien believed that the unique, careful, harmonic combination of parts was the key to original art. First, the combination must be unique. Language is a good example of originality in combinations: provided with rudimentary vocabulary and basic knowledge of a language's syntax, even a child finds that he or she can use language in completely unique ways. It is true that most communication is usually more automatic than carefully considered, and yet that does not change the fact that every human has the ability to create unique utterances, simply because the linguistic elements allow unique combinations. Naturally, though, it is those in history who are careful in their language utterances that become great speakers and writers.

The artist's combinations must also be careful and ordered. Bad art, the Inklings believed, was not carefully constructed and did not produce harmony. Thus Screwtape claims, "We will make the whole universe a noise in the end" (Lewis, 1964, p. 114). And Tolkien wrote to his son of a trend in which music fails to do its job "well":

> Music will give place to jiving: which as far as I can make out means holding a "jam session" round a piano (an instrument properly intended to produce the sounds devised by, say, Chopin) and hitting it so hard that it breaks.
> (Tolkien, 1981, p. 89)

If an artist combines parts carefully in a unique way, he or she will not only create something new, and something harmonious, but also something more than a mere collection of the original parts. Lewis likens the experience to a painting with several contributors. "We should have to think of the total result chemically rather than arithmetically" (1984, p. 209). Of course, this is not at all a new idea, for Greek mythology expressed the same truth: "Each of the eight sirens... 'produced one sound, one note,' but the eight notes together produced a ninth feature, 'the concord of a single harmony'" (MacQueen, 1985, p. 30). It is this extra feature which Collins and Guetzkow have labelled the "assembly affect," by which the interaction of small groups produces a notably higher level of output than the mere combined work of individuals (Fisher and Ellis, 1990, p. 58).

The Valar discover that the beauty of the water cycle had been brought about after Melkor's attempts to disrupt the creation with changing temperatures:

> "[Melkor] hath bethought him of bitter cold immoderate, and yet hath not destroyed the beauty of thy fountains, nor of thy clear pools. Behold the snow, and the cunning work of frost! Melkor hath devised heats and fire without restraint... Behold rather the height and glory of the clouds, and the everchanging mists; and listen to the fall of rain upon the Earth!"
>
> Then Ulmo answered: "Truly, Water is become now fairer than my heart imagined, neither had my secret thought conceived the snowflake, nor... the falling of the rain."
> (Tolkien, 1982, p. 9)

The combination of each Valar's input, held together inside Eru's design, has produced something greater than a mere collection of their individual efforts.

Tolkien and *The Lord of the Rings*

The skill of creation may best be seen in *The Lord of the Rings*, for one can see skill used at every step of its creation: a careful choice of elements to combine (that is, four lines of narration); the establishment of a clear boundary in which to combine these elements (a limited-perspective narrator); and a harmonious, ordered combination of these parts handled through five narrative techniques. Each of these points will be dealt with in turn.

After the breaking of the Fellowship, Tolkien divides his characters into four separate narrative groups, each one "led" by a head character. Gandalf is the first character to be divided from the Fellowship and represents the first narrative group. He usually travels alone, but at one point he accompanies Aragorn, Legolas and Gimli – the second narrative group, headed by Aragorn. Merry and Pippin make up the third narrative group, headed by Merry. Pippin is a secondary character because he accompanies both Gandalf and Merry at separate times. These first three groups come in contact with each other and move away again at several times during the story, but this is not true of the isolated fourth group, Sam and Frodo. Sam is the head of this group because it is through his eyes that a reader most often peers, most notably when Frodo is captured in Cirith Ungol.

This principle of groups acting together and separating again is explained nicely when Merry and Pippin ask if Treebeard plans to do anything with them: "I am not going to do anything *with* you: not if you mean by that 'do something *to* you' without your leave. We might do some things together. I don't know about *sides*. I go my own way; but your way may go along with mine for a while" (Tolkien, 1986b, p. 86). And in fact, Treebeard's way does correspond with the Hobbits' for a time. They go to Isengard together, but due to the narrative perspective of the novel, the actions of the Ents are related only when they come in contact with members of the Fellowship.

This technique of splitting the focus of narration between separate groups is not at all new; in fact, Richard West has labelled it a reuse of a medieval narrative structure called the "interlace". "This was a narrative mode of such complexity and sophistication that, until recently, modern critics could not detect a coherent design in most medieval romances" (West, 1975, p. 78). By adopting the interlace form, Tolkien found himself having to combine carefully a large number of themes, characters, narrative groups, and sub-plots.

An understanding of Tolkien's division of four is essential to properly understanding the interlace structure. As Shippey explains, the plot undergoes "chronological 'leapfrogging'" (1983, p. 121), which makes its analysis difficult. As Peter Beagle has eloquently put it, "The structure of Tolkien's world is as dizzyingly complex and as natural as a snowflake or a spiderweb" (1986, p. xi). And for this reason Figure 7, a narrative timeline, was constructed. This timeline depicts only those events which take place after "The Breaking of the Fellowship". First, one should notice that not all events of Middle-earth are depicted, for the narrative itself is selective. Events outside the scope of the Fellowship are not shown (Faramir's and Éomer's various travels, for example). The timeline shows only the actions of the Fellowship members, for these are the only characters at whom the narrative "camera" is ever pointed. However, not even all of the events involving the Fellowship members are described in direct narrative. Some items are described in internal narrative after the event, or else only implied. Tolkien chose quite specifically what events he was going to show, and in what specific order, all to his best advantage. He described this to Rayner Unwin as "the rhythm or ordering of the narrative" (Tolkien, 1981, p. 170).

This "rhythm" lies at the heart of Tolkien's story-telling skills: the "natural" patterning of events, as West observed: "Such casual collisions of disparate people and events – in a manner familiar because it is the way in which things seem to us to happen in our own lives – knit the fabric of the story" (West, 1975, p. 83). And it is the interlace structure which allows this "rhythm" according to West:

> Interlace . . . seeks to mirror the perception of the flux of events in the world around us, where everything is happening at once. Its narrative line is digressive and cluttered, dividing our attention among an indefinite number of events, characters, and themes, any one of which may dominate at any given time.
>
> (West, 1975, pp. 78-9)

After Sam learns of all that has been going on while he was accompanying Frodo, especially the arrival of Oliphaunts, he is upset but realistic: "'Well, one can't be everywhere at once, I suppose,' he said. 'But I missed a lot, seemingly'" (Tolkien, 1986c, p. 290). Just like Sam, a reader cannot be "everywhere at once," for the art form of literature is uniquely like music in this respect: unlike a painting or sculpture or architecture, writing and music may only be experienced sequentially, at a pace and order determined by the artist.

And this "pace and order" Tolkien accomplished by combining, or rather "interweaving," his four lines of narrative. Of course, the position he places himself in is a difficult one for any author: for thirty-five of the novel's sixty-two chapters, his eight major characters are divided among four separate groups. By the end of Book Two, everything seems at its worst: Gandalf is dead; Boromir is dead; Merry and Pippin have been captured; and Frodo and Sam have foolishly gone on alone. And yet the image of an opening orchestra concert seems a more appropriate analogy than that of a funeral dirge. It is as if the individual instruments have been tuning up in the earlier chapters, and Tolkien has now begun his real performance. The laborious groundwork having been set, the author is anxious to break into song – and this is exactly what he does at the beginning of Book Three.

At first, Tolkien restrains himself by keeping the reader's eyes upon Aragorn, Legolas and Gimli. But it is not long before one discovers that not only are Merry, Pippin and Gandalf very much alive, but they are doing very important things for the plot. Likewise, one discovers that Sam and Frodo are not moving blindly toward Mordor; they have an important guide, Gollum. What Tolkien has essentially done is broken the plot into four-part harmony; or has taken the quiet, gentle murmur of tuning-up before a symphony piece and has suddenly brought out every instrument available to him, in perfect harmony.

The traditional view of music's four parts has been summarized by Giovanni de Bardi:

> Master bass, soberly dressed in semibreves and minims, stalks through the ground-floor rooms of his palace while Soprano, decked out in minims and semiminims, walks hurriedly about the terrace at a rapid pace and Messers Tenor and Alto, with various ornaments and in habits different from the others, stray through the rooms of the intervening floors.
>
> (Faulkner, 1986, p. 257)

This is also the way Tolkien would have understood traditional harmony. The Soprano line is that part of music which represents the highest performed notes, and is usually at the forefront of any listener's attention. It is also the part which tends to move around the scale most, taking the most risks range-wise, and usually contains the common, recognizable melody.

There is little doubt that Gandalf's actions clearly fit such a description. He is the prime mover of events according to Aragorn: "He has been the mover of all that has been accomplished, and this is his victory." (Tolkien, 1986c, p. 304). Whether he is moving to gather the scattered men of Rohan to lead them to Hornburg, flying with Gwaihir from Caradhras to Lothlórien, or racing over the countryside on Shadowfax to rescue or help defend, Gandalf is usually at the centre of attention. And this fits precisely into his plan of diverting Sauron's attention away from Mordor and Frodo's approach. The elements which Gandalf adds to the story are those which are most generally known to the other characters in Middle-earth, and which a reader most commonly

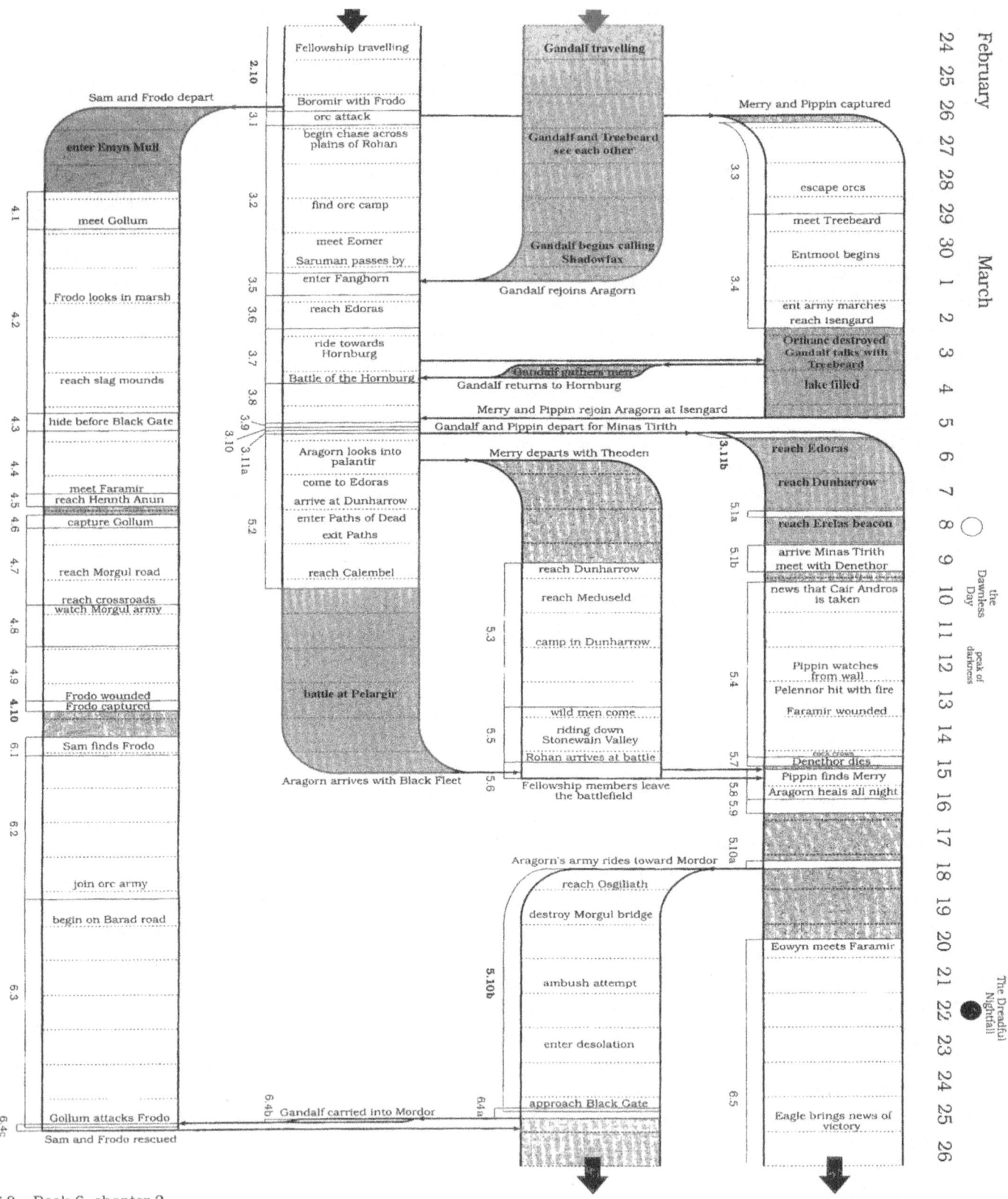

Figure 7

associates with the "action" of a story.

The Bass line, on the other hand, is commonly understood to be that part which is most stable, taking the least recognizable bounds; it is often slow and methodical, and yet usually sets the tone for the entire piece. And Sam and Frodo's march to Mount Doom is just that: often slow and methodical, with a tone of slight hope which sheds light on the whole work. Tolkien even emphasizes the long, drawn-out nature of their journey by separating its narration at only one point (after Frodo's capture), rather than the numerous narrative leapfrogging done between the other groups.

One's inability to always pick this part out from the others (none of the other Fellowship members have any idea as to how Sam and Frodo are progressing) is also entirely according to the divine power which leads them quietly into Mordor. The Bass line usually underlies any chord formed by all the other combined parts, and thus acts as a "harmonic anchor" within a piece. Similarly, Sam and Frodo's quest acts as the anchor around which all other sub-plots are taking place. Like the Soprano part of Baroque choral music, the Bass part is also called upon more frequently to perform solos.

The Tenor and Alto sections, as Giovanni's description implies, are generally much vaguer parts to define, but the Alto part shares the treble cleft with the Soprano line, while the Tenor line shares the Bass cleft. Thus, Aragorn is associated more closely with Gandalf, and can be compared to the Alto line (Pippin claims "I think they must be related" (Tolkien, 1986c, pp. 178-9)). The four Hobbits are also more closely associated, marking Merry's as the Tenor line.

The four-part organization of the orchestra is a traditional one which also aligns closely to the roles of these four narrative groups. In such a comparison, Gandalf would most naturally represent the String section. Norman Del Mar's *Anatomy of the Orchestra* helps explain why:

> The string body occupies a primary position in the constitution of the orchestra. This is not merely so in a visual sense – their position at the front of the concert platform – but because the very presence of multiple strings can be taken to determine whether a group of instruments should be described as an orchestra at all.
> (Del Mar, 1981, p. 29)

Similarly, Gandalf's presence as motivator defines the force opposing Sauron. And again, his actions are at the forefront of the "piece." The String instruments have been called the most "stirring" set of instruments, and according to how they are written into a piece, may inspire a listener to get up and move, or else quietly reflect. The soft techniques available to the Strings represent well the contemplative, patient side of Gandalf which we know he learned from Nienna (Tolkien, 1982, pp. 24-5). Gandalf's actions also display as wide a range as the Stringed instruments: as motivator he stirs men to action; he plays a violin-type lightness around the Hobbits when he is pleased, or else a cello/bass seriousness when things seem uncertain. Gandalf's actions add constant surprise to the piece: he rides off with Théoden's prized horse and goes off alone right before the Battle of the Hornburg.

The Percussion, or drum, section is reflected in Sam and Frodo's movements. Much like an orchestra's Percussion, Sam and Frodo work in the background of the piece, alone, setting a constant, methodical pace. And yet they are able to produce some of the largest sounds at need, as the eruption of Mount Doom testifies. Percussion also seems to pervade most of their journey, whether it is the approaching drumbeats of an Orc army (Tolkien, 1986b, p. 393), or else the warning bell piercing from the gates of Cirith Ungol (Tolkien, 1986c, p. 218). The sombre tone of Frodo's pessimism and the clear ring of Sam's continual hope may also be expressed within the range of Percussion instruments.

On the other hand, Merry seems to move into a situation with all the clamour and glory one might desire in a dramatic confrontation. The grandiose scale in which Isengard is overturned, or even the Rohirrim's entrance onto the Pelennor Fields, illustrates the type of blaring action which can be effectively represented by the brilliance of the Brass instruments. And of course it is Merry who blows the horn of Rohan to announce the beginning of the Shire battle against Saruman's men (Tolkien, 1986c, p. 353). Del Mar has described the Brass section in the following way: "Apart from its enormous power, one of the principal qualities of the brass is rhythmic incisiveness, which can have the edge on the entire orchestra . . . The upper end of the trumpet's register is so immensely striking that it imposes . . . the severest strain on human nerves and psychology in the entire orchestra" (Del Mar, 1981, pp. 3-4). This type of brass brilliance is reminiscent of how most of Merry's friends work: both the Ents and the Rohirrim.

The Woodwinds, while also being able to represent power, are used for colouring a piece and giving it a brighter quality. "One outstanding characteristic of the flute family is . . . [its] repertoire full of dazzling cascades of scales and arabesques that exploit this virtue [of agility] . . ." (Del Mar, 1981, p. 168). The Woodwinds are able to create a feeling of mysteriousness, respect and honour – all elements of Aragorn's character. Similarly, Aragorn displays his power by leading the Dead Riders, but this is a frighteningly surrealistic scene that only the Woodwind instruments could adequately capture. Usually placed centrally within an orchestra, the actions of the Woodwinds also act as stability for the other sections – much like Aragorn's actions do.

One of Tolkien's favourite analogies of creativity was that of light, and his understanding of its components is reflected in verse:

> Man, Sub-creator, the refracted Light
> through whom is splintered from a single White
> to many hues, and endlessly combined
> in living shapes that move from mind to mind.
> (Tolkien, 1984, p. 144)

The primary divisions of "splintered" light are red, green, blue-violet, and the combination of all of these, white. Gandalf's new role as the head of the White Council allows him to don the white robe of that position – garb which also matches the colour of his beard. Similarly his pure, selfless intentions and his angelic nature associate him with the flawless characteristics of white. Unlike his predecessor

Saruman the "many-coloured," Gandalf is not at all concerned with gaining personal status in Middle-earth. Rather, bringing about Eru's will and aiding Eru's creatures act as the prime motivations for his work. It is also his position as divine representative which places him morally and racially at the centre of the other three narrative groups.

The idea of associating "red" with Sam and Frodo's narrative line is not at all a random choice. It is this colour which predominates the settings of all their actions. Within one sequence of nine pages in *The Two Towers* (1986b), five references alone help establish a definite "hue" which dominates the scenes: "fire-flecked sky" (p. 387), "a dull red glare" (p. 390), a "fiery glow" (p. 390), "the Sun . . . falling in an ominous fire" (p. 394), "one large red eye in the midst of its forehead" (p. 395).

These are the days of travel in which they approach Mordor and the Crossroads of the West, but once Sam and Frodo enter Mordor, the theme of red becomes even more dominant. Numerous references are made to the "red glare of Mordor," the glowing red window in the tower of Cirith Ungol, the red-hued torches of the Orcs, and red blood (discovered after the Orc battle). Even the annoying flies, they notice, suggest the red eye insignia which is emblazoned upon all weapons and uniforms of Mordor: they were "marked like orcs with a red eye-shaped blotch . . ." (Tolkien, 1986c, p. 243). One of the better descriptions of Mount Doom itself is made as Sam peers from the Tower window: "A fresh turmoil was surging in its deep wells, and the rivers of fire blazed so fiercely that even at this distance of many miles the light of them lit the tower-top with a red glare" (Tolkien, 1986c, p. 221). It is this same volcano which spews forth in red, eruptional glory at the end of their quest. In fact, its name *Orodruin* means "mountain of red flame" in the Sindarin dialect of Elvish (Foster, 1979, p. 397).

The colour green, Tolkien explains, is a Hobbit favourite; but its particular association with Merry and Pippin is based on something even more significant. Their visit to Fangorn Forest — the last great green section of forest which once stretched all the way past the Shire — evokes an act of hospitality on Treebeard's part: "I can give you a drink that will keep you green and growing for a long, long while" (Tolkien, 1986b, p. 87). And Merry's travels through the forest on the slopes of the Ered Nimrais suggest this colour as well.

Finally, there exist some obvious ties between Aragorn and the colour of blue-violet. Aragorn's river approach to the Battle of Minas Tirith links him to blue water, but it is his genealogy which plays a greater role in this connection. Because of his direct Númenórean descent, his bond to the "land beneath the waves" should bring the blue deluge to mind; and his claim to the throne of Gondor makes one aware of his true royal nature. The blue-violet colour combination is actually considered a subdivision of "purple" according to many colour schemes; and it is purple which has been a symbol of royalty since the earliest societies found its dye most expensive.

Each of these four groups also seems to have clear ties with one of the four elements. As one of the Maiar, Gandalf is shown to travel most often by air. Gwaihir the eagle rescues him from atop Orthanc (Tolkien, 1986a, p. 343) and removes him from the top of Zirakzigil after his battle with the Balrog (Tolkien, 1986b, p. 135). This eagle is a symbol of Manwë's presence in Middle-earth and acts as the guardian for the Lord of Air (Tolkien, 1982, p. 44). Gandalf's other form of transport, the horse Shadowfax, is described as bearing its rider "swift as the flowing wind" (Tolkien, 1986a, p. 344).

Aragorn's lineage as a true Númenórean connects him logically with water, as do the sea-desires of his companion, Legolas. The earth nature of the Hobbits links Merry with the earth, as does his interaction with those natural creatures from earth's past: the Ents and the Woses. The goal of Sam and Frodo's quest, the fires of Mount Doom, associates them clearly with fire: "The fires below awoke in anger, the red light blazed, and all the cavern was filled with a great glare and heat" (Tolkien, 1986c p. 275).

Systems for structuring groups of humans have defined social classes since the earliest societies. It was, however, Indian society which declared every human to be part of one of four castes. These four existed because "mankind once comprised four races" (Birren, 1963, p. 43). Each of the four races was said to have come from a different part of the creator's body: from the mouth of the creator, the priests; from the arms, warriors; from the thighs, merchants; and from the feet, servants. These are the four varnas, *varna*, in Sanskrit, meaning "colour" (Birren, 1963, p. 43).

Not surprisingly, the four groups of Fellowship members also align with these cross-sections of society. The priests, as a sacred class, were to study, teach and act as divine representatives on earth, much like Gandalf. The warriors were responsible for governing and fighting the wars; Aragorn fills just such a role. Similarly, the other two members of Aragorn's group come from royal houses, and become members of the Fellowship to defend their races. The mercantile class were to cultivate their fields and engage in business and trade; Merry and Pippin fill such roles within the Shire.

And finally, the servile class obtained their livelihood by labouring for others. The character of Sam has always been of interest to scholars, for his rich delineation is a real tribute to Tolkien. As David Harvey observes in *The Song of Middle-earth*:

> Sam has been in service all along. As Frodo's gardener and as helper, servant and companion he doggedly attends to the practical needs and wants of the travellers and their pack animals . . . Sam's horizons are limited. He does not seek greater things or even greatness itself. He knows his place and he intends to stay there.
> (1985, p. 124)

These five sets of associations should provide adequate evidence for a careful selection of main characters on Tolkien's part.

Tolkien selected a boundary for his work very carefully: a single-narrator perspective which not only helps make *The Lord of the Rings* a unified piece, but also makes it quite distinct from Tolkien's other works. In fact, in *The Lord of the Rings*, the author's desire for a well-ordered novel with harmony between its complicated parts meant that the nature of the narrator was to be wholly different from the nature of *The Hobbit*'s. Just as the sub-plots were to be included, the complexity of the characters increased, and the geography expanded, the narrator was going to require immaculate accuracy in his adherence to self-made rules.

Tolkien discussed the rules of this narrator in a letter to Milton Waldman: "As the high Legends of the beginning are supposed to look at things through Elvish minds, so the middle tale of the Hobbit takes a virtually human point of view – and the last tale blends them" (Tolkien, 1981, p. 145). Once again we have a blending – a combining; in this case, a blending of perspectives. Tolkien was not to use the distant, lofty, omniscient narrator of *The Silmarillion* whose concerns were clearly Elven; nor the familiar story-teller narrator who spoke distinctly to children and concentrated on the actions of all the different races. As the title-pages indicate, the Hobbits' concerns were to be the centre of this story. And with this perspective in mind, Tolkien set two restrictions for his narrator.

First, this Hobbit perspective required that any events which neither involved, interested, nor directly affected the Hobbits were excluded, making room for the events which were very important to the Hobbits. Although the Battle of Bywater may have seemed trivial in comparison to the Battles of Lothlórien or the Battle of Pelargir, it is the former which receives an entire chapter of description. Likewise, the courtship of Sam and Rose receives more treatment than that of Aragorn and Arwen. Second, Tolkien dispensed with the omniscient freedom he had allowed himself in *The Silmarillion* and *The Hobbit*. Rather, he decided to only show scenes which had been seen by one of the Hobbits or else by one of their close friends in the Fellowship. The adoption of these narrator-restrictions is as much an aid to order and harmony in *The Lord of the Rings* as the strict guidelines of a sonnet are for a poet, or the time signatures for a composer.

The Lord of the Rings is quality art, finally, because the combination of the narrative parts is done in a skilled, harmonic way. This harmonic rhythm is produced with five techniques: 1) the order in which information is shown, 2) the length of time focus is placed on each narrative group, 3) the frequency of shifting between the various narratives, 4) the narrative breaks or cliffhangers, and 5) the inclusion of time-matches, cross-line communication and universal reference points.

When the tension of war rises with the approach of the Battle of Minas Tirith, Tolkien is able to reflect this in the narrative by switching more and more frequently between the various narrative groups (see Figure 7). Similarly, when Tolkien wants to heighten the effectiveness of any cliffhanger, he does so with the ordering of the narrative. He reveals pieces of information selectively so that a reader progresses with only the amount of information which will make the moments of tension most suspenseful. Aragorn's surprise arrival with the Black Fleet, for example, is dependent on a lack of knowledge of his earlier exploits, but the death of Denethor gains poignancy because it is described after the arrival, and the victory at Minas Tirith has been assured. One also knows, unlike Éomer, that Aragorn and the Grey Company have passed safely through the Paths of the Dead by the time the Rohirrim depart: "He is lost. We must ride without him, and our hope dwindles" (Tolkien, 1986c, p. 82). Understanding Éomer's despair is vital for understanding his character, and yet his pessimism takes on a deeper quality when one recognizes its unjustified nature.

It is for suspense purposes that Tolkien shows Aragorn, Legolas and Gimli chasing the Orc army over Rohan before showing Merry and Pippin covering the same ground. This allows for the introduction of a number of mysteries (i.e. how Pippin's broach was dropped, how the two escaped, etc.) before a reader is shown the actual scenes with the Hobbits. A rich piece of foreshadowing is also provided when Tolkien reveals Gandalf's resurrection (his appearance to Aragorn) after Merry and Pippin have told Treebeard of Gandalf's death (thus evoking a strange reaction from him since, as one learns later, Treebeard has spoken to Gandalf only two days earlier).

Tension is also aroused when Frodo's mithril coat is brought out to the army at Mordor's Gate, for the last thing a reader has seen of Frodo was his corpse being locked inside a Mordorian stronghold with Sam trapped outside. Tolkien plays the difficult situation for all its emotional impact, and Gandalf's sign of real despair here (one of the first) tops the effect magnificently. And just as urgency becomes the greatest element for achieving the quest, readers are forced to struggle through the disheartening passages of how, even after being rescued, Frodo and Sam's progress across Mordor is far from rapid: "The night seemed endless and timeless, minute after minute falling dead" (Tolkien, 1986c, p. 267).

Tolkien's emphasis upon the end of the quest and the reunion of the Fellowship members is made in a powerful way. Just after the Ring has been destroyed and Sauron's armies have poured from Mordor's Gate, Tolkien shows, for the first time, an overlapping of events in the narrative. Normally, if the narrative shifts from one of the groups, the narrator picks their story up again at the same moment or at a later point, but never back to events already described. The importance of this final eucatastrophe, however, warrants an exception. Twice a reader is with Gandalf when he cries, "The Eagles are coming! The Eagles are coming!" (Tolkien, 1986c, pp. 208, 278), and twice one hears Frodo say, "I am glad you are here with me. Here at the end of all things, Sam" (Tolkien, 1986c, pp. 277, 280).

Figures 8 and 9 list the three literary techniques which Tolkien employed to prevent cacophony as he wove his four groups. These time-matches, communications and universal reference points all provide lubrication within the narrative. The first of these, "time matches," are short references written into one line of narrative which merely remind a reader about the simultaneous actions taking place elsewhere in the story: "At last [Pippin] came out of shadow to the seventh gate . . . as Frodo walked in the glades of Ithilien . . ." (Tolkien, 1986c, p. 26). "But [Sam and Frodo] were alone . . . and Gandalf stood amid the ruin of

Maintaining harmony in
The Lord of the Rings:

1. References to other narrative lines (time matches)

No.	location	context (what's happening)	reference to simultaneous event	location
1.	4.1 TT274	Storm clouds pass Sam and Frodo in Emyn Muil	Riders of Rohan ride toward Meduseld after having passed Aragorn	(NPONL)
2.	4.3 TT318	Sam and Frodo hide before the Black Gate	"Aragorn was far away" and palantir crashes before Gandalf	3.10 TT241
3.	5.1 RK21	Pippin and Gandalf ride towards Minas Tirith	Sam and Frodo watch the full moonset at Henneth Annun	4.6 TT371
4.	5.1 RK26	Pippin ascends Minas Tirith	Frodo walks in the glades of Ithilien	4.7 TT386
5.	5.2 RK65	Aragorn and the Grey Company head for Edoras	Theoden travels "by slow paths in the hills"	(NSIDN)
6.	5.3 RK76	Theoden and Merry come out of the hills	Pippin watches Prince enter Minas Tirith	5.1 RK50
7.	5.4 RK97	Pippin on walls of Minas Tirith	Frodo sees sunset at Cross Roads	4.7 TT395
8.	5.4 RK126	Gandalf confronts nazgul at gate	Rohan's horns announce arrival	5.5 RK138
9.	5.7 RK160	Gandalf bearing Faramir to Houses of Healing	Nazgul shrieks as it dies	5.6 RK143
10.	6.1 RK212	Sam outside Cirith Ungol	Aragorn leading Black Fleet from Pelargir	(NSIDN)
11.	6.1 RK212	Sam outside Cirith Ungol	Merry and Theoden ride down Stonewain Valley	5.5 RK132
12.	6.1 RK212	Sam outside Cirith Ungol	Pippin watches madness grow in Denethor	5.4 RK120
13.	6.2 RK240	Sam and Frodo crossing Mordor	Theoden lays dying on Pelennor Fields	5.6 RK143
14.	6.2 RK240	Sam and Frodo crossing Mordor	Nazgul shrieks as it dies	5.6 RK143
15.	6.3 RK261	Sam and Frodo on road to Dark Tower	Aragorn passes Cross Roads and sets Minas Morgul aflame	5.10 RK197,8
16.	6.3 RK261	Sam and Frodo at the Dreadful Nightfall	Aragorn draws near to end of living lands	5.10 RK199
17.	6.3 RK270	Sam and Frodo crawling up Mount Doom	Aragorn and Company at the Black Gate	5.10 RK206
18.	6.3 RK275	Frodo puts on the ring	Sauron's army falters at the Black Gate	6.4 RK278
19.	6.5 RK297	Eowyn and Faramir at city walls	Barad-Dur is destroyed	6.3 RK276

(NPONL) = Not part of a narrative line   (NSIDN) = Not shown in direct narrative

2. Communication between narrative lines (through visions, dreams, unique sight)
(visions between non-narrative lines - i.e. those in palantir, Galadriel's mirror - are excluded)

No.	location	setting	person/method	sight	location
1.	1.7 FR177	At Tom Bombadil's	Frodo, in dream,	sees the past: Gandalf being rescued from Orthanc	(NSIDN - 2.2 FR343)
2.	2.10 FR519	On Amon Hen	Frodo, in vision,	hears Gandalf warning "Take off the ring!"	(NSIDN - 3.5 TT126)

Figure 8

created by S. Yandell, 1992

3. References to items outside the narrative lines (universal reference points)

Moon phases - full moon, Mar 10; new moon, Mar 22
1.	3.2 TT27	waxing moon at the start of the great chase
2.	3.2 TT35	young moon during the chase
3.	3.3 TT63	slim moon while hobbits are travelling with orcs
4.	3.6 TT140	waxing moon as Gandalf and Aragorn ride to Meduseld
5.	3.8 TT198	waxing moon as group approaches Isengard
6.	4.6 TT371	full moonset at Henneth Annun
7.	5.1 RK21	full moonset on Pippin's ride to Minas Tirith
8.	5.2 RK60	approaching full moon as Aragorn prepares to depart Hornburg
9.	5.3 RK78	recent full moon as Theoden reaches Harrowdale
10.	5.10 RK200	waxing moon four nights old as Aragorn approaches the Black Gate

Final sunset before the darkness - evening, Mar 9
1.	4.7 TT387	Sam, Frodo and Gollum see sunset
2.	5.3 RK76	Merry riding with Theoden
3.	5.1 RK50	Pippin on walls of Minas Tirith

The Dawnless Day opens - morning, Mar 10
1.	4.7 TT390	Sam, Frodo and Gollum awake to no dawn
2.	5.2 RK75	Aragorn and Dead Company see no dawn
3.	5.1/.4 RK52/95	Pippin with Gandalf
4.	5.3 RK88	Merry with Theoden

Sunset of the Dawnless Day - evening, Mar 10
1.	4.7 TT395	Frodo at the Cross Roads
2.	5.4 RK97	Pippin on walls of Minas Tirith

Rain begins in Gondor - afternoon, Mar 15
1.	5.6 RK147	Merry leaving the Pelennor Fields
2.	5.7 RK162	Gandalf and Pippin leaving the Houses of Healing

Winds change, Darkness passes - dawn, Mar 15
1.	5.5 RK135,7	Merry sees and feels the changes
2.	5.7 RK154	Gandalf and Pippin see and feel changes
3.	5.9 RK188	(indirect narrative only - Gimli describes how they observed changes)
4.	6.2 RK240	Sam and Frodo see and feel changes

Sullen, red sun - afternoon, Mar 25
1.	5.10 RK 206	Aragorn and Company see this at the Black Gate
2.	6.3 RK273	Sam and Frodo see this from Mount Doom

Figure 9

created by S. Yandell, 1992

Isengard and strove with Saruman, delayed by treason" (Tolkien, 1986b, p. 318).

Secondly, there are the rare occurrences when characters communicate between narrative lines. This does not include all visions and prophecies, but those times when one narrative line sees another during the time of the divided Fellowship. There are two examples of this: when Frodo sees Gandalf atop Orthanc, and Gandalf calls to Frodo on Amon Hen to take off the Ring. Thirdly, there are references to universal occurrences which are essential for letting a reader know the continuity of the events throughout Middle-earth. Most often these involve the description of some natural event which all group members are experiencing at the same time (such as a sunset, moonset, rain) or else an event of major importance which separate groups can experience from different locales (the arrival of the Rohirrim, the death of the Nazgûl king, morning of the Dawnless Day). About all such passages Shippey has noted:

These references and allusions tie the story together, we would say . . . They prove the author has the story under control, and are significant to any reader who has grasped the entire plot. However that is not how they appear to the characters, or to the reader whose attention has lapsed.
(Shippey, 1983, p. 123).

Thus, a reader experiences Tolkien's Middle-earth in the same way in which Tolkien and the Inklings experienced their own world: as an ordered creation which contains harmonic combinations of four parts. Tolkien's, Lewis's and Williams's fiction all attest to these ideas, but it is Tolkien's masterpiece, *The Lord of the Rings*, which appears to be the most effectively and impressively constructed answer to Lewis's call for art which makes one feel "that we have been led through a pattern or arrangement of activities which our nature cried out for."

References

Beagle, Peter. 1986. "Tolkien's Magic Ring" in *The Tolkien Reader*. New York: Ballantine Books.

Birren, Faber. 1963. *Color*. New Hyde Park: University Books Inc.

Del Mar, Norman. 1981. *Anatomy of the Orchestra*. Berkeley: Univ. of California Press.

Faulkner, Quentin. 1986. *Church Music: A History of Ideas*. unpublished course syllabus. Lincoln, Nebraska, c. 1986.

Fisher, Aubrey and Ellis, Donald G. 1990. *Small Group Decision Making*. New York: McGraw-Hill Publishing Co.

Foster, Robert. 1979. *The Complete Guide to Middle-earth*. New York: Ballantine Books.

Harvey, David. 1985. *The Song of Middle-earth*. London: George Allen & Unwin.

Johansson, Calvin M. 1986. *Music and Ministry*. Peabody, Mass.: Hendrickson Publishers Inc.

Lewis, C.S. 1947. *Miracles*. New York: Macmillan.

Lewis, C.S. 1964. *The Screwtape Letters*. New York: Macmillan Publishing Co.

Lewis, C.S. 1973a. *An Experiment in Criticism*. Cambridge: Cambridge Univ. Press.

Lewis, C.S. 1973b. *The Last Battle*. New York: Macmillan Publishing Co.

Lewis, C.S. 1984. *The Discarded Image*. Cambridge: Cambridge Univiversity Press.

Lewis, C.S. 1988. *Letters*. Collins, Fount Paperbacks.

MacQueen, John. 1985. *Numerology*. Edinburgh: Edinburgh Univ. Press.

Shippey, T.A. 1983. *The Road to Middle-earth*. Boston: Houghton Mifflin Co.

Tolkien, J.R.R. 1981. *The Letters of J.R.R. Tolkien*, ed. Humphrey Carpenter. Boston: Houghton Mifflin Co.

Tolkien, J.R.R. 1982. *The Silmarillion*, ed. Christopher Tolkien. New York: Ballantine Books.

Tolkien, J.R.R. 1984. "On Fairy-Stories" in *The Monsters and the Critics and Other Essays*, ed. Christopher Tolkien. Boston: Houghton Mifflin Co.

Tolkien, J.R.R. 1986a. *The Fellowship of the Ring*. New York: Ballantine Books.

Tolkien, J.R.R. 1986b. *The Two Towers*. New York: Ballantine Books.

Tolkien, J.R.R. 1986c. *The Return of the King*. New York: Ballantine Books.

West, Richard C. 1975. "The Interlace Structure of *The Lord of the Rings*" in *A Tolkien Compass*, ed. Jared Lobdell. La Salle, IL: Open Court.

Section ten

Flights of Fancy

Baggins Remembered

Reprinted from *The Hobbiton Advertiser*, for 15 Astron 1521 S.R.

John Ellison[1]

The events which are taking place all over the Shire during the Baggins Centenary Year will reach their peak during the month of Wedmath. This will be the Baggins Centenary Conference, to be held in Hobbiton for one week beginning on the 26 Wedmath. It is being jointly organised by the Baggins Society and the Mythopoeic Society of Tol Eressëa. Papers will be read by distinguished Baggins scholars and other aficionados, dealing with the lives and work of the late Bilbo and the late Frodo Baggins; their work as philologists, linguists and scholars of the early history and legends of Middle-earth will be covered, as well, of course, as the celebrated "fantasy" writings, the romances and stories which have made their names household words in the Shire, and spread their fame across the length and breadth of Middle-earth. A banquet will, obviously, feature as a principal highlight; and among the numerous other special events we may mention the pony tours being arranged to places, such as Crickhollow, which have special Baggins associations. The Mayor will, in addition, be hosting a number of "At Holes", in Bag End itself.

The Took and Thain, the Master of Buckland, and sundry other distinguished guests from near and far-off will be attending for all or part of the Conference; those who have registered for it, we are told, comprise not only Hobbits from the Shire and Bree, and Elves returning from the Uttermost West, but Men and Dwarves hailing from far-distant lands in Middle-earth, and even a few reformed Orcs as well. In this latter connection, we hear that the organisers found themselves facing a most awkward impasse presenting itself in the shape of the well-known edict of King Elessar, S.R. 1427, prohibiting Men from entering the Shire. However, officials of the King's civil service in Minas Tirith came to the rescue, it seems, at the eleventh hour, by devising a highly ingenious solution to the problem. As, owing to a curious legal anomaly no such prohibition affects those Orcs who have registered and propose to attend the Conference, all Men who declare their intention of coming are being sent an application form on receipt of their registration, whereby they can apply for temporary legal status as Orcs for the duration of the festivities. The provision of accommodation for the large number of guests expected to attend is, of course, the organising committee's principal headache, though one of many. We understand that the residential places at Keyhole which has been taken over for the duration of the Conference, are now almost fully booked.

It all began, of course, one warm summer afternoon as Bilbo Baggins sat in the garden at Bag End long ago, engaged in the tedious chore of marking student's examination papers in Elvish, and encountered, in the midst of them, a blank sheet of paper. What would he have thought, we ask ourselves, could he have foreseen the outcome of the simple sentence that he idly scribbled on the sheet: "In a college in Oxford there lived a don"?

"I didn't know who dons were, or where Oxford was", he later wrote, "so I thought I had better find out." And so, as everybody knows, he proceeded to write down, late in the long evenings at Bag End, as a diversion from his serious scholastic labours, the first of his Middle-earth-famous tales, *The Don*, set in an imaginary land called "Britain", most of whose inhabitants are Men, in the midst of whom dwell a race called "Dons", who wear square black caps, and dress in black robes called "gowns", and who live in a place called "Oxford", mostly in clusters of holes called "colleges". We have all read, or most of us have, the story of how a Don is visited one spring morning by a wizard, a wise Professor, who sends him off on an adventure far away from his comfortable college. The story goes on to tell of how he finds, with the Professor's aid, another colony of Dons inhabiting a remote clearing in the midst of the fens in the east of Britain, of how he and thirteen other Dons journey on to reach a perilous city called "London", where he enters a mysterious Garden and finds a magic Ring there which holds him trapped in the Garden for four days and nights, and of how a friendly Dragon he finds there helps him to escape with a share of the treasure in its cave, and of how he returns home – rich!

The Don was first read aloud by Mayor Samwise to his children – as a result of their favourable reviews of it, it was published, and the success of the venture led to the appearance of the three volumes of its successor, *The Fellowship of the Don*, *The Two Cultures* and *The Return of the Don*, (originally called *Hitler Defeated*). All these books have carried the name of Baggins far and wide over Middle-earth, and away over the Sea to the Uttermost West. They have been translated into Quenya, Sindarin and every other tongue known to Elves, Dwarves or Men. Persistent rumours of the existence of translations into the Black Speech have always been officially denied; the truth of the matter is

---

[1] First printed in *Oxonmoot 92 Programme Book*, The Tolkien Society and the Mythopoeic Society: Milton Keynes, 1992.

probably that the vocabulary of the B.S. is simply not large enough. Illustrations of the Baggins œuvre are, of course, a study in themselves, and an exhibition of book illustrations and dust-jackets will be one of the features of the Conference.

There have always been, of course, the few voices of dissent raised among hobbits- and elves-of-letters, the voices of those that question the relevance of the "Baggins cult", as they describe it, condemning it as "escapist fantasy, whose only consequence is to distract hobbits from the real concerns of life as they face it in today's Shire", and claiming that the books portray a morally simplistic world where the "goodies", merely fight it out with the "baddies", winning out, of course, in the end. It will be remembered that one of the earliest of these so-called "knocking" reviews entitled "Oo, these awful Nazis!", came from a critic called "Edmund", who claimed to be an Elf of Tol Eressëa. Some people have identified him with the recently late Edmund Sandyman, "Cap'n Ted", as he was known to his employees in his lifetime, who never ceased from excoriating "the Baggins cult" for its part, as he saw it, in retarding the industrial development of the Shire and stifling its entrepreneurial spirit. We shall no doubt hear somewhat less of this as a result of Cap'n Ted's demise following his unexplained disappearance from his private barge on the Brandywine river, and the subsequent revelations regarding the financial catastrophes overtaking his business enterprises inside and outside the Shire.

At least one business enterprise is very far from any such fate. This is the well-known publishing house of HarperBaggins, which today announces the publication of volume 10 of *The History of Britain* series; Frodo Baggins' scholarly reconstruction of the genesis and development of the whole legendarium of *The Matter of Britain*, from its first beginnings: this, the latest volume, is to have the original title, *Hitler Defeated*. This great enterprise provides the best answer to those colleagues of the late Bilbo and the late Frodo Baggins who complained that the time and energy they lavished on the writing of *The Don* and its successors, and the creation of *The Matter of Britain*, would have been better spent on the writing of learned articles and longer works on Elvish linguistics and related topics, and who disregarded or pooh-poohed the invention of the imaginary languages of "Greek", "Latin", "English", "French", "German", "Italian" and "Russian", which are such a prominent feature of their imaginary world. Clearly the material exists for many successful Baggins Conferences in future years, and is being added to year by year.

Short History of the Territorial Development of the Dwarves' Kingdoms in the Second and Third Ages of Middle-earth

Hubert Sawa   translated by Paulina Braiter

Abstract: This speculative paper, discusses the emergence of the kingdoms of the Dwarves, changes in their borders, and different factors influencing them (e.g. wars with Elves and Orcs). Their history recorded up to the beginning of the Fourth Age, when, after the fall of the enemy, the kingdoms flourished again. This fictional history is extrapolated from references to the Dwarves in the published works of J.R.R. Tolkien, to which much new material has been added by the paper's author.

Keywords: Adundor, Aglarond, Angrenril, Belegost, Blue Mountains, Forbelegost, Forgroth, Forodor, Gabilgathol, Grey Mountains, Hardum, Iron Hills, Khazad-dûm, Lithgoroth, Misty Mountains, Nogrod, Thorin Oakenshield, Sauron, Tumunzahar

The beginnings of the city-states of the Dwarves belong to the very distant past. As we know, the Seven Fathers of the Dwarves were the first intelligent beings created by the Gods. However, the Gods realised that the world was still too wild, and sent the Fathers to a well-hidden place, somewhere in Middle-earth. When the right moment came, the Fathers awakened and, together with them, their people. After several years of wandering across the whole of Middle-earth, one of them, named Durin, reached the Misty Mountains. In that place, under the mountain of Caradhras, he founded Khazad-dûm.

Khazad-dûm
From approximately 100 First Age to 1981 Third Age, from 2989 Third Age to 2994 Third Age and from 124 Fourth Age. (Maps I and II)

Khazad-dûm was the first and the most famous Kingdom of the Dwarves. At the beginning it comprised only the eastern slope of Caradhras. By the end of the First Age the Dwarves extended the mines under the Misty Mountains, seized the Dimrill Valley, built a watch-tower on the Redhorn Gate and drove a gate through the Mountains towards the west. After the down-fall of cities in the Blue Mountains, at the beginning of the Second Age an affluence of new strength occurred. About 40 Second Age the Sirannon Valley was taken. Next the Dwarves made their way to the south. By the year 90, they occupied most of the important valleys and mountain passes in the southern part of the Misty Mountains, and in the year 100 Second Age, they founded the city of Hardum, which was situated about 100 miles away from the Hollin Gate. When in 750 the Elves came from Eregion, the contemporary ruler of Khazad-dûm gave up the Sirannon Valley to them. In return the Dwarves started their expansion to the east. Around the year 800 they reached the Anduin River and by 1300 they had already occupied the territory from Lórien to the Gladden Fields. At that time the Khazad-fammos Haven was founded. This was the First Golden Age of Khazad-dûm. The Kingdom was placed on the chain of the Misty Mountains between Celebdil and Caradhras, on the eastern slopes of the Mountains, up to the southern springs of the Gladden River and to the banks of the Anduin River. In the south, between Khazad-dûm and Hardum, there stretched a belt of valleys and passes, controlled by the Dwarves. The kingdom of Khazad-dûm comprised 12,000 square miles in all. In the years 1695-1700 Sauron ravaged the land of the Dwarves, and their country was limited only to Khazad-dûm and the Dimrill Valley. But in the year of 1701 the old territories were recovered, except for the southern valleys in the Mountains, yet the Dwarves finally gave up the reconstruction of Hardum destroyed in 1699. That was when the Second Golden Age of Khazad-dûm began. The kingdom occupied the territory between Lórien and Gladden, Anduin and the eastern slopes of the Misty Mountains – altogether an area of 11,000 square miles. This state of affairs continued until the year 1981 Third Age, when the Balrog was awakened. He destroyed Khazad-dûm and drove away the Dwarves. Their state was restored when in 2989 Third Age Balin arrived there from Erebor. By the year 2891 he again occupied the majority of the area of the previous kingdom and even rebuilt Khazad-fammos. Now the kingdom took in a belt of land along Lórien up to Anduin and the east slopes of the Mountains, up to the springs of the Gladden River, that is about 8,000 square miles. However, Balin, later on, lost control over most of the area and at his death (2994) he only ruled Khazad-dûm. After the fall of Sauron, Durin VII restored the kingdom in 124 Fourth Age, again occupying the distant areas of the state's former prosperity. Hardum was restored, too.

Tumunzahar
(Nogrod)
From approximately 150 First Age until 1598 First Age.
(map II)

This was the second kingdom established by the Dwarves. It was founded on the northern edge of the southern range of the Blue Mountains. In 171, after founding Belegost the Dwarves passed the Mountains and took Askar Valley up to the Dolmed Mountains. Then they met the Elves, who had made it clear that they did not wish the Dwarves' presence on this side of the Mountains. Accordingly, settlements of the Dwarves started to expand along the eastern slopes, Belegost to the north, and Nogrod to the south. In about 100 years, the Dwarves took, without any difficulties, a belt of land about 200 miles long and 30 miles wide on the eastern slopes of the Blue Mountains. So by 250 First Age the borders were established. It is worth mentioning that the pass in the Mountains and the area on the western side were ruled together by the kings of Nogrod and Belegost. This situation lasted till 1598 First Age, when Elves, running away from Beleriand, ruined Nogrod and devastated its land.

Gabilgathol
(Belegost)
From 170 First Age until 1599 First Age.
(map II)

This was the third kingdom founded by the Dwarves. It was located on the southern end of the northern range of the Blue Mountains. In 171 together with Nogrod, it occupied the pass and the neighbouring lands around the Dolmed Mountain. Next the Dwarves made their way to the north. By 221 they explored and took the area which reached to the southern springs of the Lhûn River.

In 240 they passed the river springs and by 260 they already controlled the area around the northern springs of the Lhûn. All put together, the Dwarves occupied an area about 300 miles long and 30 miles wide. For many years the kingdom developed peacefully, for most of the wars were waged on the western side of the Mountains. This changed about the year 600, when the Orcs started to appear on the eastern side of them. In 630 Belegost lost the lands between the springs of Lhûn and did not regain the area till its last days. In the years 1597-1599 the lands of Belegost were ruined by the Elves running away from Beleriand, but the city itself was not conquered and in 1598 received the refugees from Nogrod. After the sea swallowed Beleriand and broke in two the ranges of Ered Luin, the Dwarves from Belegost founded Harbelegost and Forbelegost.

Forodor
From 200 First Age until 1800 Second Age.
(maps II, III and IV)

Forodor was the fourth kingdom of the Dwarves. It was founded at the springs of Anduin in the mountains, called at that time the Iron Mountains. Not being threatened by anyone, it flourished very quickly. By 250 the area from Gundabad Mountains to the springs of the Greylin River had been explored and settled. During the next 50 years the Dwarves took the Misty Mountains up to the springs of the Langwell River. In the year 400 the area lying between these two rivers was taken. The Dwarves made their way to the east, conquering the Iron Mountains up to the springs of the Forest River and in 450 they reached Greenwood the Great. They did not enter the Wood itself, but moving further south they took by the year 600 a whole belt of land between Greenwood the Great and the Iron Mountains. At the same time, they passed the point where the Misty and the Iron Mountains met. So in the year 600 First Age, Forodor was the most powerful kingdom of the Dwarves. It spread from the northern ends of the Misty Mountains, along the ridges of the Iron Mountains, about 400 miles to the east. To the south, it reached the Langwell River and Greenwood the Great. This was a territory of approximately 15,750 square miles. The Kingdom remained within these borders until the end of the First Age. In the Second Age, the ranges of the Iron Mountains, to the west of the Misty Mountains and far on towards the east collapsed, and in the central part some strong earthquakes were felt. What remained of the Iron Mountains now became known as the Ered Mithrin Mountains. These disasters considerably weakened the kingdom. The next blow came when about 30 Second Age, numerous tribes of Orcs approached from the north-west, and dragons invaded the land, fleeing the ruined Beleriand. As the result of wars in 40 Second Age, the Dwarves lost the region of the Gundabad Mountains, and in the years 60-70 the whole territory up to the springs of the Forest River. At the same time in the east, dragons forced the Dwarves out of the Grey Mountains, up to the Forest River. The Dwarves lost more than 6,750 square miles of land here. So about 100 Second Age the Forodor Kingdom shrank to the belt of land between the Anduin, the Forest River and Greenwood the Great. The wars with Orcs lasted until the end of the year 1000 Second Age, when Sauron, on his way through these lands to Mordor, concluded a peace-agreement with the ruler of Forodor. Under the agreement, the Dwarves started to deliver weapons to the Orcs from the Misty Mountains and they regained their territories east of the Forest River. But the Elves, who in the meantime settled in Greenwood the Great, almost immediately attacked Forodor and in 1200 captured the area between the Forest and the Mountains. The kingdom again shrunk to a belt of the southern slopes of the Grey Mountains and the triangle between Anduin and Greylin. In 1600 Second Age the Dwarves regained the land between Greylin and the Forest, but in 1702, after Sauron was evicted from Eriador, the Elves crossed the Greylin and in 1800 conquered and destroyed Forodor. This was the end of the kingdom, although scattered settlements survived until the end of the Third Age.

Lithgoroth
From 400 First Age until 3441 Second Age.
(map II)

In 375 First Age civil war broke out in the kingdom of

Forodor. It ended within twelve years with the exile of a group of Dwarves. They went south and established the kingdom of Lithgoroth on the northern slopes of the Ash Mountains. The only fact known about this kingdom is that it was situated near the western end of the range. Since 1000 Second Age these Dwarves had been allied with Sauron and in 3441 Second Age, after his defeat, they abandoned Lithgoroth and went east. Nobody has ever tried to search for that city.

Harbelegost
From 1 Second Age until 1692 Second Age.
(map V)

After the fall of Belegost and when the Blue Mountains split apart, the Dwarves divided into three groups. One of them set off to the east, another to the north, and the third went south. This last group settled on the eastern slopes of the southern range of the Mountains, about 110 miles from the mouth of the river Lhûn. There was an old mine once belonging to Tumunzahav here. The Dwarves took it in the first year of the Second Age and established the kingdom of Harbelegost. This land lay within the borders of Tumunzahav before. Striving to restore the kingdom to its former splendour, the Dwarves quickly took over the area between the main range of the mountains and their eastern spur. However, in 8 Second Age the development of the kingdom was checked by the Elves. They established some settlements around the mouth of the river Lhûn and claimed their right to the whole of the Blue Mountains and surrounding lands. Skirmishes with the Elves lasted for two years, until in 10 Second Age the first group of Dwarves returned from Khazad-dûm and Eriador. They fought a battle with the Elves on the area between the Blue Mountains and Tower Hills. As a result the Elves were forced to conclude a peace treaty and were obliged to give the Dwarves' kingdoms access to Brandywine and Lhûn. According to this treaty in 12 Second Age the Dwarves from Harbelegost owned the land between the eastern spur of the mountains and the Brandywine. The kingdom was developing so well that in 40 some surplus population was sent to Khazad-dûm, and in 50 a new city of Erlad was established at the southern end of the mountain range. The kingdom's prosperity lasted until 1693 Second Age, when the Elves began the war with Sauron. Out of stern necessity the Dwarves took the Elves' side and in 1695 marched against Sauron. As a result Sauron's armies captured and destroyed Erlad in 1697. The Dwarves lost their southern lands, but Sauron did not stop at that and in 1699 his armies captured and destroyed Harbelegost as well. The kingdom fell.

Forbelegost
From 1 Second Age.
(map VI)

The second group of Belegost Dwarves went north. 75 miles from the mouth of the Lhûn they found a mine formerly belonging to Gabilgathol. They established a settlement there called Forbelegost. The Dwarves were nearer to the Elves than Harbelegost, so they could not even dream of regaining the former lands of Belegost. However, when they concluded an agreement with the Elves, they took over the lands between the Blue Mountains and the junction of the rivers Lhûn and Evendim up to the southern springs of Lhûn. During the war of Sauron and the Elves Forbelegost, in 1698, lost the Lhûn valley, but succeeded in keeping the hills and the springs of Lhûn. After Sauron had been driven out in 1702 only a part of the valley was regained by the Dwarves, the rest of it being taken over by the Elves. From that time they started to exert pressure on the kingdom, which resulted in the Dwarves moving the Forbelegost settlement near the south springs of the Lhûn and, closely following, losing control over the southern part of the Blue Mountains. In 3430, when The Last Alliance was forged, the Elves returned the taken lands to the Dwarves and Forbelegost again expanded to its borders from the year 10 T.A. However, about 1000 Third Age the Elves again began to exert pressure on Forbelegost. As a result in 1558 Third Age the Dwarves lost the hills and kept only the Mountains. In 2120 the Dwarves lost all the lands and were left with only the city of Forbelegost. This state continued until the end of the Third Age, when the Elves got weaker and in 98 Fourth Age Forbelegost yet again regained its former territories.

Erebor
From 1999 Third Age until 2190 Third Age; from 2590 Third Age until 2770 Third Age; from 2941 Third Age.
(map VII)

In 1999 Third Age a group of Dwarves from Forbelegost and Khazad-dûm came to the Lonely Mountain and established the kingdom of Erebor there. The kingdom was developing slowly and in 2100 included only the Mountain and the surrounding fields. It was then that an expedition was sent to the Grey Mountains to explore them and take over some deserted mines formerly belonging to Forodor. The discovery of rich mineral lodes made the Dwarves leave Erebor in 2190. They moved to the Grey Mountains and established the kingdom of Forgroth there. After the invasion of dragons the Dwarves returned to the Lonely Mountain and in 2590 the kingdom was restored. This time the development was faster. In 2600 Dale was built. The King under the Mountain gave the valley of the River Running to the city. The Dwarves took over a belt of land to the east, in 2683 establishing the border between Erebor and Angrenril in the middle of the road between the Lonely Mountain and the Iron Hills. This rapid development was brutally checked in 2770 Third Age when the dragon attacked the Lonely Mountain and laid waste to Erebor. Again the kingdom was totally wiped out. However, in 2941 Dwarves returned to the Mountain and after the dragon's death Thorin II Oakenshield crowned himself king. His kingdom contained only the inside of the Mountain and existed no longer than twenty days. After Thorin's death in the Battle of Five Armies Dáin from the Iron Hills took the throne of Erebor and established the kingdom of Angrenril and Erebor. In 2944 the city and kingdom of Dale was rebuilt and the Dwarves again took control over the lands between the Lonely Mountain and the

Iron Hills. In 2949 an expedition was sent to the Grey Mountains. The expedition took over the waste lands of Forgroth and announced the establishment of the Grey Mountains Province, subject to Erebor from 2950. For the next thirty years the lands between the Province and the Lonely Mountain were slowly settled until the borders touched and merged in 2980 Third Age. The Withered Heath was incorporated within the Province then. The new borders remained intact until 3019, when at the beginning of March the armies of Sauron's allies crossed the river Carnen. They defeated the army of Dwarves from the Iron Hills and devastated the lands between the River Running and the Carnen. In a three-day battle they also defeated the armies of the king of Dale and the Dwarves from Erebor. Dale was captured and the Lonely Mountain was besieged. The enemy armies occupied the land between the Lonely Mountain and the Iron Hills and cut off the Mountain from the Province. However, on 27 March, Men and Dwarves counterattacked and on 30 March the Easterlings were pushed back over the river. The kingdom of Angrenril and Erebor regained its former territories, and the land along the border with Dale was incorporated into Erebor.

Forgroth
From 2211 Third Age until 2589 Third Age; from 2950 Third Age.
(map VIII)

Around the year 2000 Third Age the Dwarves escaping from Khazad-dûm came to the Grey Mountains. They were scattered until 2100, when messengers from Erebor came and in the name of the king began to explore and take over deserted mines once belonging to Forodor. Due to the discovery of rich mineral lodes the Dwarves from under the Lonely Mountain moved to the Grey Mountains in 2190, and in 2211 King Thorin I himself came there and established the kingdom of Forgroth. At the beginning it comprised the vicinity of the springs of the Forest River and the territories between the Grey Mountains and Mirkwood along the river. The kingdom expanded to the east and in 2500 ruled over the southern slopes of the Mountains up to their eastern tip. In 2570 the Dwarves began to penetrate the Withered Heath and the north-eastern range of the Mountains, and it is then that trouble with the dragons began. In 2589 Forgroth was destroyed by them and the kingdom ceased to exist. In 2950 Third Age the area was established as the Grey Mountains Province by the ruler of Angrenril and Erebor.

Angrenril
From 2590 Third Age.
(map VIII)

Some of the Dwarves fleeing from the Grey Mountains savaged by the dragons came to the Iron Hills and established the kingdom of Angrenril there. Within twenty years it grew until it comprised the whole of the Hills and then expanded to the west. Up to 2683, when the border with Erebor was established, the kingdom acquired a belt of land to the west of the Hills and the valley of the Carnen, some 150 miles long. In 2775, after the destruction of Erebor by the dragon, the western territories of Angrenril were depopulated. Their inhabitants moved to the bank of the Carnen, and so did those who had lived on its eastern bank and now fled before the Easterlings. Thus in 2780 the kingdom of Angrenril comprised the Iron Hills, the west bank of the Carnen up to the mouth of the River Running and some sixty miles along the eastern bank. The western lands returned to the kingdom in 2944, after the establishment of the kingdom of Angrenril and Erebor. In 2980 a belt of land between the south-east range of the Grey Mountains and the west end of the Iron Hills, along the border with Erebor, was incorporated into Angrenril. During the March War in 3019 the Easterlings occupied all the lands of Angrenril except for the Iron Hills. After the driving-off of the enemy, within about ten years, the Dwarves incorporated into Angrenril some lands on the western bank of the Carnen and the northern bank of the River Running, up to the border with Dale.

Adundor
From 2775 Third Age.
(map IX)

After the destruction of Erebor by the dragon in 2770 Third Age, a group of Dwarves went to the Blue Mountains. Some of them moved on to Forbelegost, but the rest went south and reached the eastern ranges of the Mountains some 140 miles to the south-east of Mithlond. They took advantage of the protection of the Elves' kingdom and rebuilt the mine of Adundor, once belonging to Harbelegost. In 2775 the Dwarves' leader crowned himself king of Adundor. The kingdom developed rather quickly and when in 2801, after the end of the Great War with the Orcs, many Dwarves came from the east, it comprised the whole eastern range of the Blue Mountains. Unfortunately, the unfavourable attitude of the Elves put an end to further territorial development of the kingdom for some 220 years. Only at the beginning of the Fourth Age did the Elves understand that the Dwarves needed the access to the Brandywine. Some treaties were signed, according to which Adundor acquired a belt of land 50 miles long and 60 miles wide along the border with Arnor. The Dwarves also ruled over a part of the southern range of the Mountains.

Aglarond
From the 2nd year Fourth Age.
(map X)

During the War of the Ring Gimli son of Gloin for some time fought at the side of King Théoden of Rohan. He helped the King during the defence of Helm's Deep – the northernmost valley of the White Mountains. It was then that Gimli discovered at the end of the Deep, a chain of caves running deep into the mountains, under the massif of Thrihyrne. They reminded him of Khazad-dûm at the time of its glory. So when the War of the Ring ended, Gimli led a group of Dwarves from Erebor to Helm's Deep. They established a settlement and a mine there, and in 2 Fourth Age Gimli son of Gloin crowned himself king of Aglarond. According to the treaty with the King of Rohan and the

Marshal of Westfold, Aglarond comprised the caves and Helm's Deep up to the walls of the Hornburg, thus being the smallest, but also the most beautiful, of all the Dwarves' kingdoms. As the massif of Thrihyrne was not used by Rohan in any way, the Dwarves explored it and took it for their property in 17 F.A. In 20 Fourth Age a tunnel was pierced through the mountain to its southern side. Thanks to his skill as a diplomat and a negotiator King Gimli managed to buy from Rohan the western slopes of the White Mountains and the dale between Thrihyrne and the springs of the River Adorn in 40.

KEY TO MAPS

The maps are based on Karen Fonstad's *The Atlas of Middle-earth* (first edition).

Map I

- ■ Khazad-dûm, end I a.
- ||| land annexed in 40 y. II a. and given up to Elves in 175 y. II a.
- • • • land annexed before 100 y. II a.
- === land lost after 1700 y. II a.
- +++ borders of Khazad-dûm in 2891 y. III a.

Map II

- ■ Khazad-dûm, end I a.
- ✷ Nogrod and its land, 250 y. I a. - 1598 y. I a.
- △ Belegost and its land, 221 y. I a. - 1599 y. I a.
- • • • land annexed to Belegost in 260 y. and lost after 600 y. I a.
- ||| Forodor, end I a.
- L Lithgoroth

Map III

- ■ Erebor in year 250 I a.
- —— land annexed before 300 y.
- • • • land annexed before 350 y.
- +++ land annexed before 400 y.
- –•– land annexed before 450 y.
- –:– land annexed before 600 y. I a.

Map IV

- —— borders of Erebor at first II a.
- ||| land lost in 40 y.
- === land lost in years 60 - 100
- ### land lost in years 60 - 100 and regained in 1000 y. II a.
- \\\ land lost in 1200 y.
- XXX land lost in 1200 y. and regained in 1600 y.

Map V

- —— borders of Harbelegost in 8 y. II a.
- • • • land annexed in 12 y.
- +++ land annexed in 50 y.

Map VI

- —— borders of Forbelegost in 10 y. II a.
- • • • land annexed in 12 y.
- +++ land lost in 1698 y.
- ||| land regained in 1702 y.
- /// land lost after 2320 y.
- === land lost after 1558 y. III a.

Map VII

- —— borders of Erebor in 2100 y. III a.
- ■ land given up by the King of Dale in 2600 y.
- • • • land annexed before 2683 y.
- +++ Grey Mountains Province in 2950 y.
- –:– land annexed to Province and Erebor before 2980 y.
- – – – border between Province and Erebor
- /// land taken by the Easterlings during the March War (3019 y.)
- === land annexed after the March War

Map VIII

- —— borders of Forgroth in 2211 y. III a.
- – – – land annexed before 2500 y.
- • • • borders of Angrenril in 2610 y.
- +++ land annexed before 2683 y.
- ||| land lost after 2775 y.
- –•– land annexed in 2980 y.
- /// land taken by the Easterlings during the March War
- –:– land annexed in 3029 y.

Map IX

- —— borders of Adundor in 2801 y. III a.
- • • • land annexed in IV a.

Map X

- ■ Aglarond in 2 y. IV a.
- – – – borders in 20 y.
- • • • borders in 40 y.

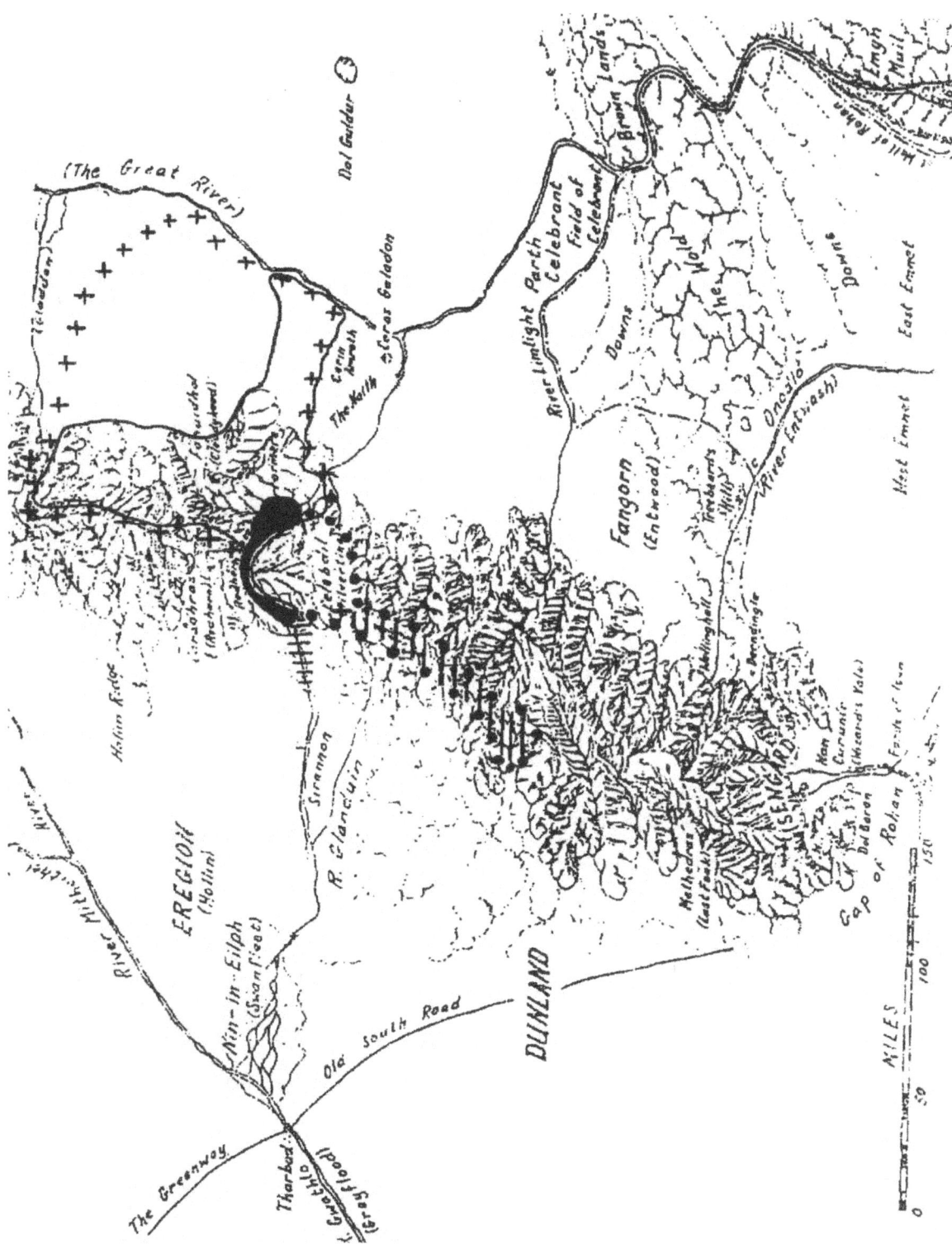

Map I

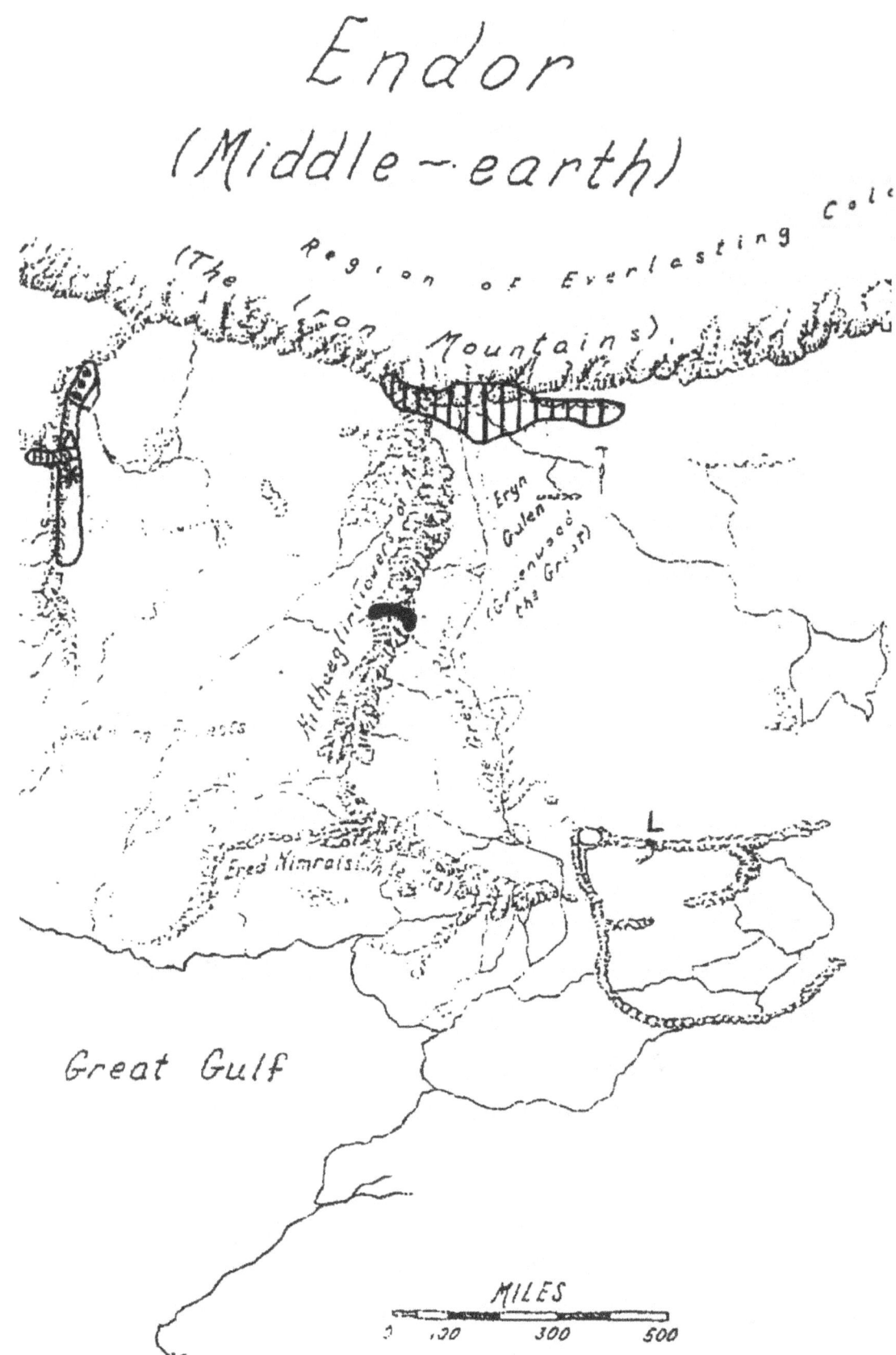

Map II

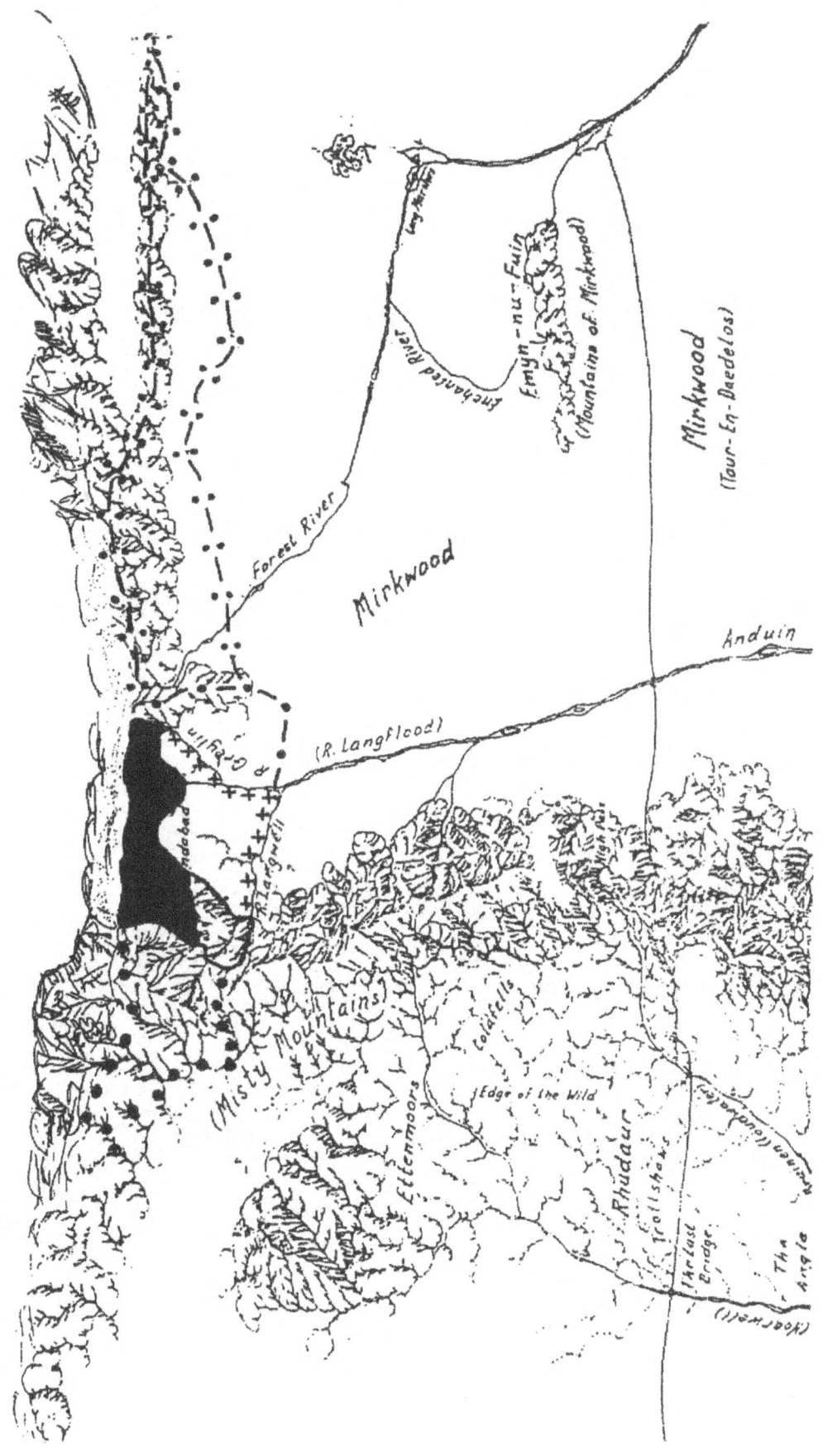

Map III

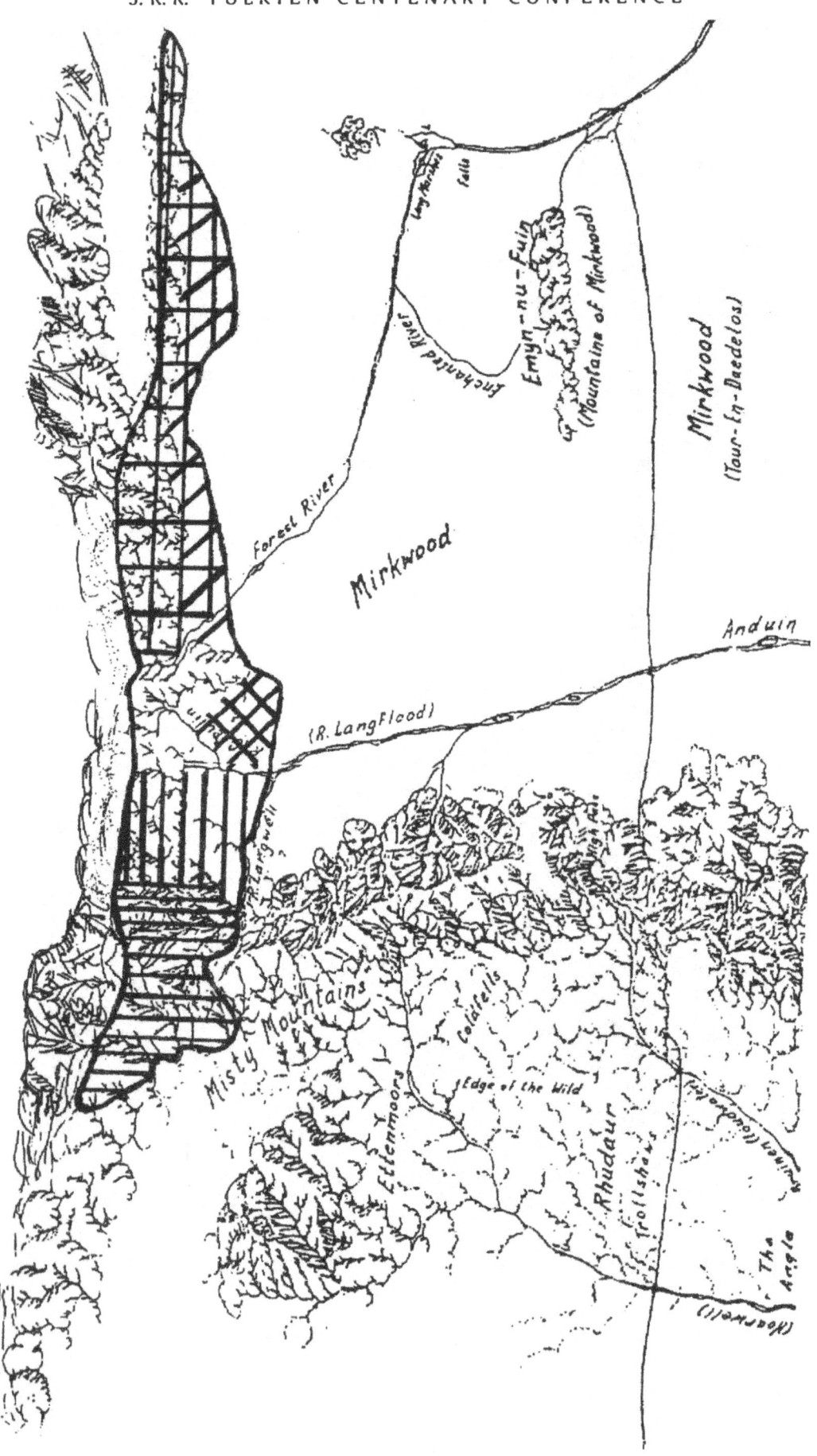

Map IV

TERRITORIAL DEVELOPMENT OF THE DWARVES' KINGDOMS

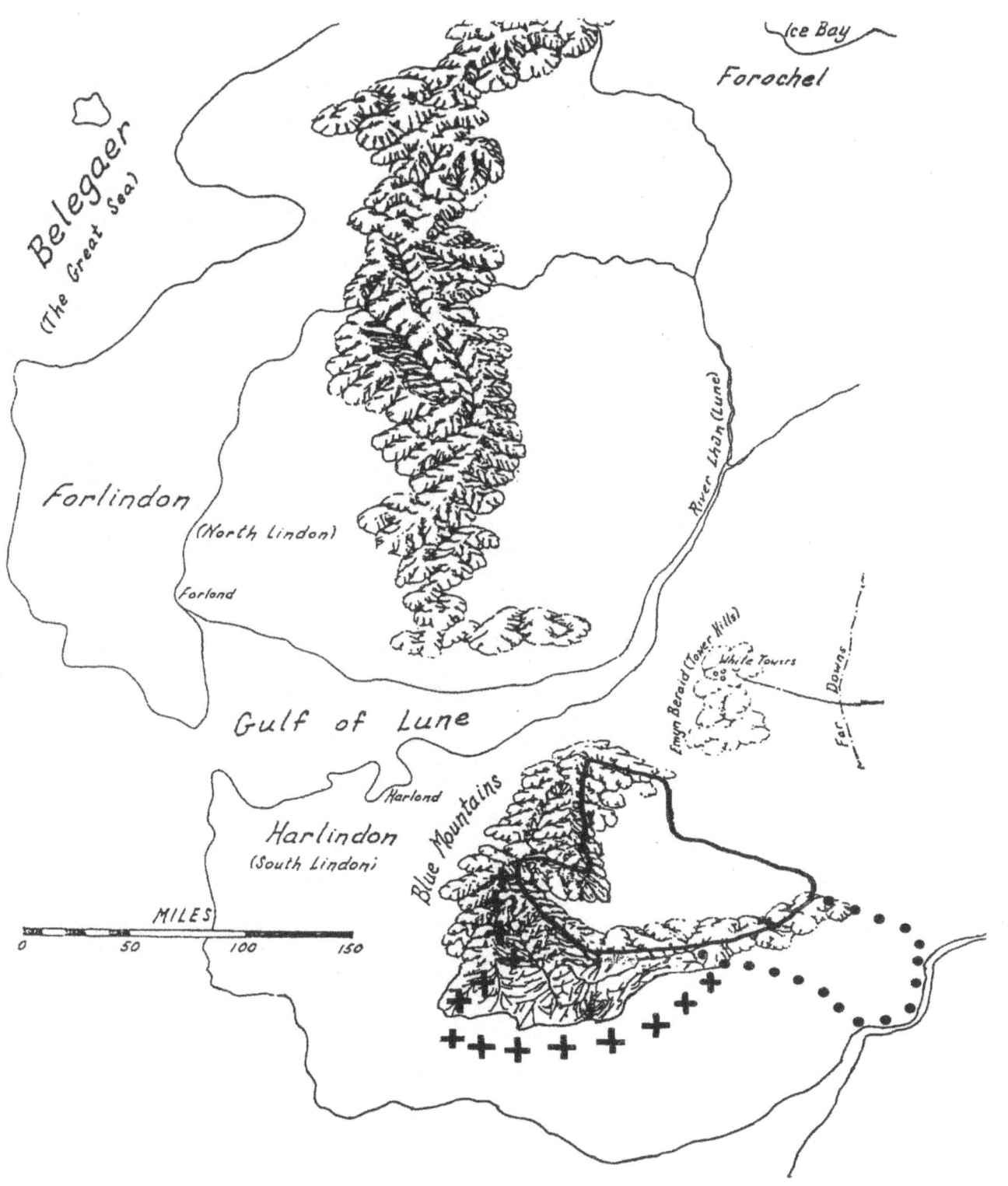

Map V

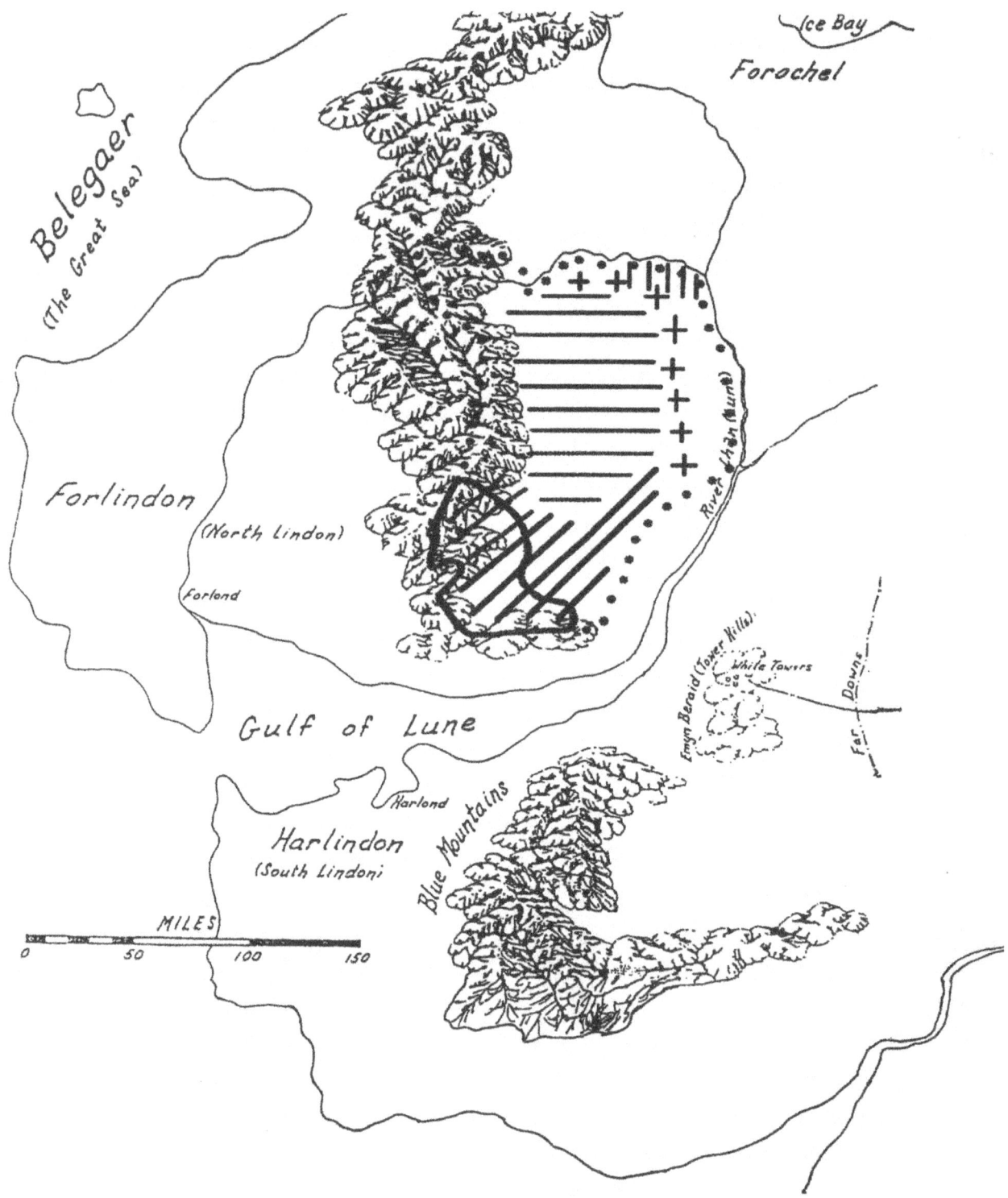

Map VI

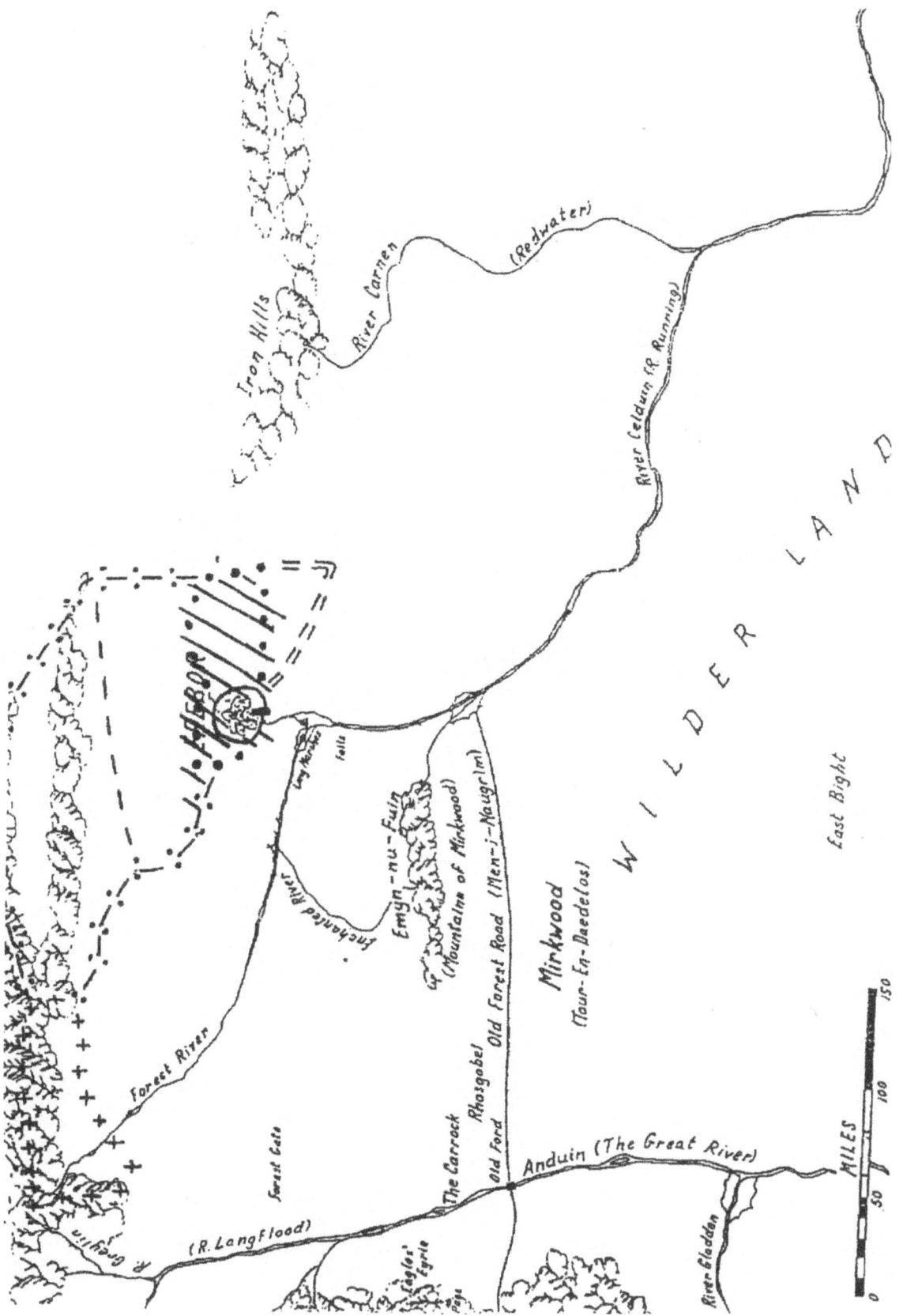

Map VII

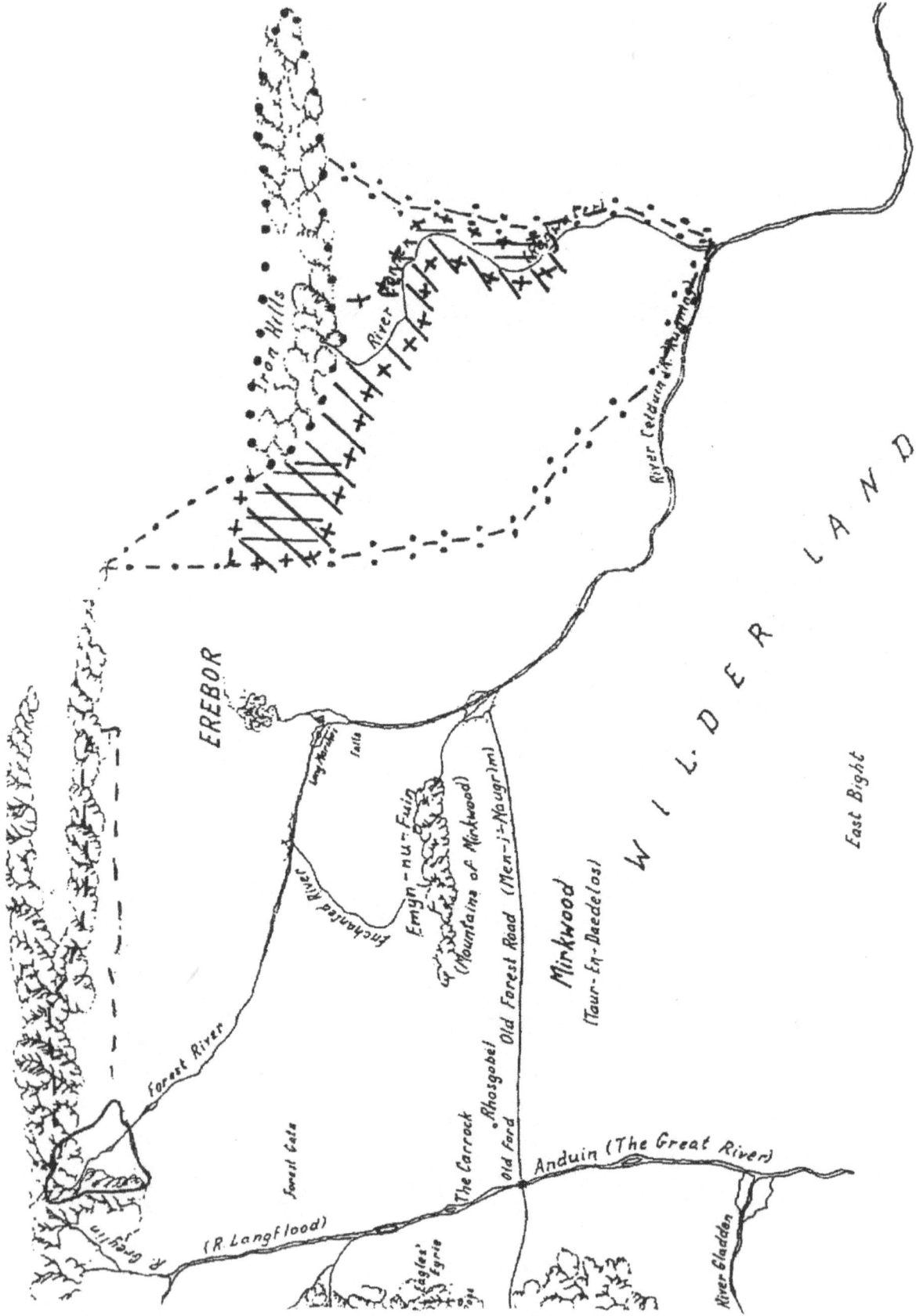

Map VIII

TERRITORIAL DEVELOPMENT OF THE DWARVES' KINGDOMS

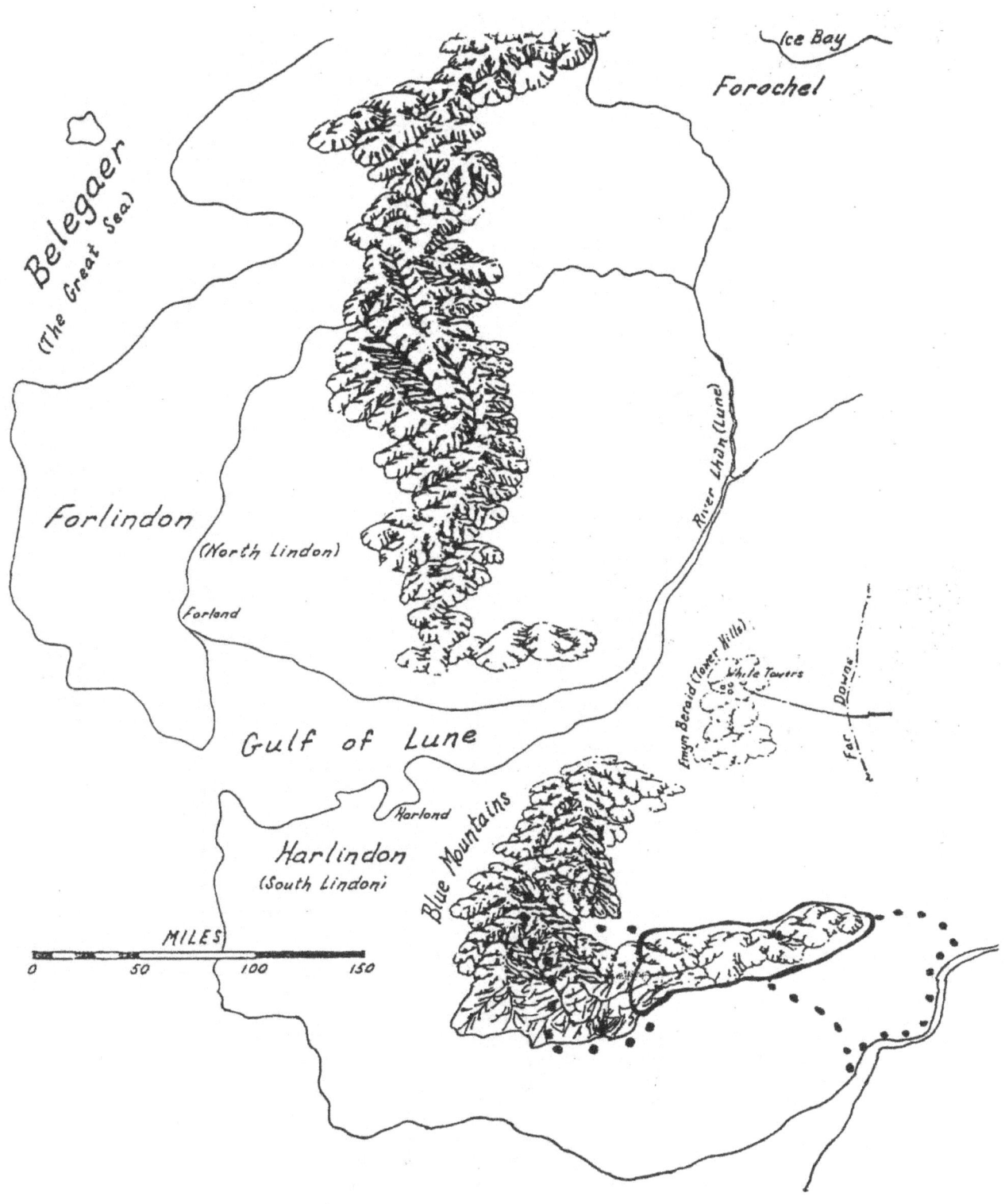

Map IX

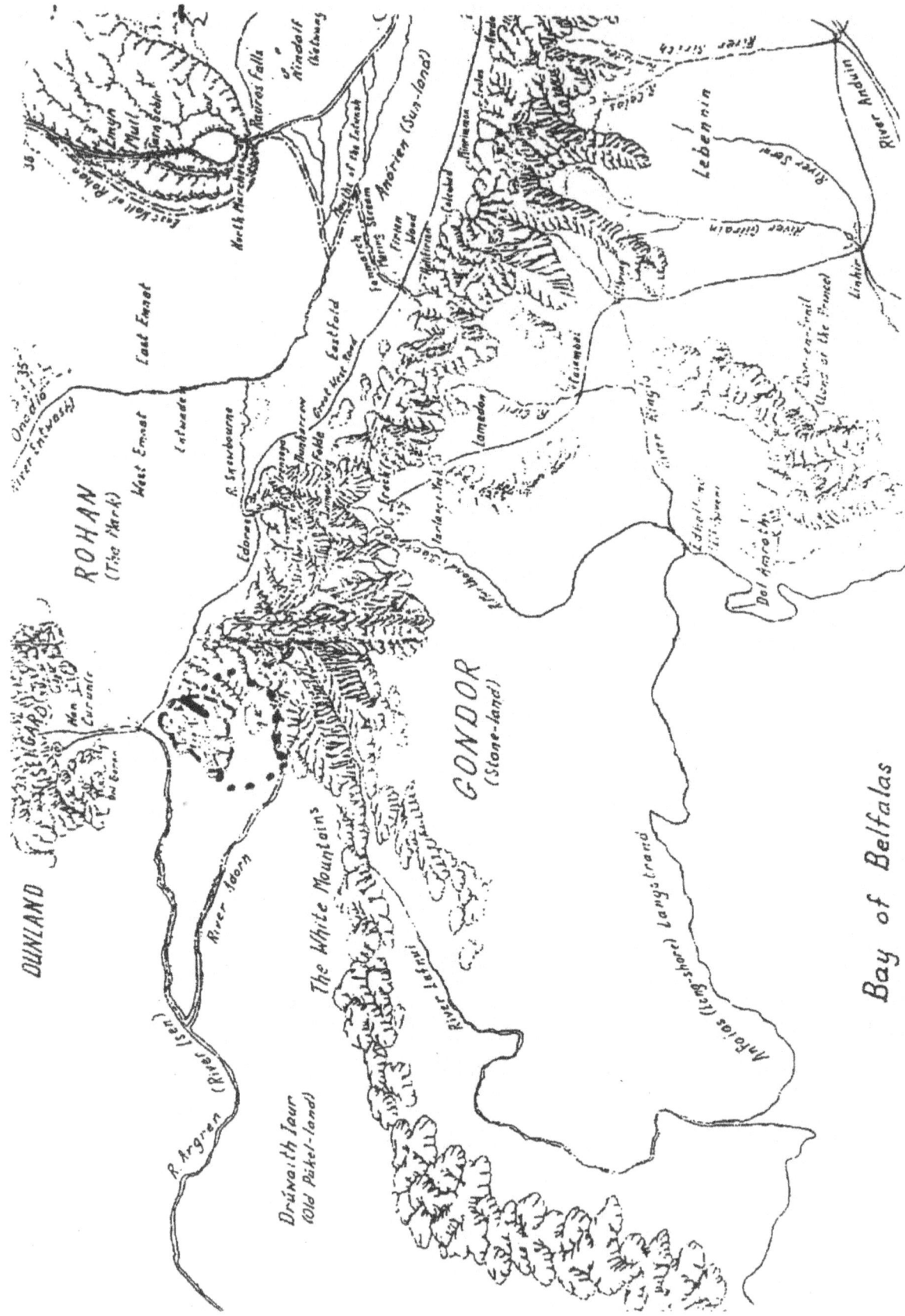

Map X

The Mechanics of Dragons: An Introduction to The Study of their 'Ologies

Angela Surtees and Steve Gardner[1]

Abstract: Dragons are found throughout the history of most civilisations, yet we appear to know little about them. This paper will present a (tongue-in-cheek) introductory analysis of dragons and their place in society, suggesting that perhaps they are not necessarily the terrible and evil creatures they are sometimes portrayed to be . . .

Keywords: dragons, hoards, leap years, treasure, virgins, wyverns

By the philosophers I am named Mercurius; my spouse is the (philosophic) gold, I am the old dragon found everywhere on the globe of the Earth, father and mother, young and old, very strong and very weak, death and resurrection, visible and invisible, hard and soft; I descend into the Earth and ascend to the heavens, I am the highest and the lowest, the lightest and the heaviest; often the order of nature is reversed in me, as regards colour, number, weight and measure; I contain the light of nature; I am dark and light; I come forth from Heaven and Earth; I am known yet do not exist at all; by virtue of the sun's rays all colours shine in me, and all metals.

Thomas Charnock (c.1524)

We would like to begin by following that prologue with the title of our paper, "The Mechanics of Dragons: An Introduction to the Study of Their 'Ologies". We must say "introduction" because, as Thomas Charnock pointed out over 450 years ago, we cannot hope to uncover all the dragon's secrets. Their "'ologies" is our short-hand way of covering alchemology, gemology and virginology. Our extensive research has uncovered many hitherto unrecorded facts detailing not only the different, more generally known, types of dragons, but also their social interactions and breeding habits. As may be expected, the only humans able to write with any authority on this subject were the mages and alchemists. Much of their work, by its very nature, was not written down but passed down through generations, garbled by the ignorant and left for the serious scholars to untangle. Let us begin our untangling with a look at the many and various types of this marvellous creature that man has sighted through the Ages.

Most people today seem to have an image in their minds of a ferocious creature with wings. However, the LUNG of the Chinese, the DRACON or DRAKOS of the Greeks, the DRACO of the Romans, the THANIN of the Hebrews, the DARKON of the Chaldees, the NAGA of the Sanskrit and the Egyptian dragon have no such limited signification. Indeed, we have found at least six main groupings for the supposedly mythical dragon. One myth about dragons we must first dispel. Dragons, like most dinosaurs, are not reptiles. They are a separate species descended from dinosaurs and have in fact retained the warm-blooded body of their dinosaur ancestors.

The most obvious to the European mind is the large, winged model with two large back legs, front legs, with a scaled skin and the ability to breath fire. These were generally the largest of the species and varied in total length from 10 - 15m. Above this size, flight probably becomes impossible and housing difficult to find. Smaug and Scatha were two examples of this type. Very occasionally a really ancient creature of high cunning can grow to 20m or even 30m long.

One such was the Dragon of Wantley. This wondrous beast was said to have "massive wings, a sting in its tail, long, long claws, 44 iron teeth, hide as tough as buff", and was partial to children, cattle and trees. It "smoked from the nose" and was over 90 feet long. This inoffensive creature was cruelly murdered by the knight More of Morehall, who, on the advice of a local witch, attached large iron spikes to the outside (being a smart chap!) of his armour. When the beast tried to squeeze him . . . ! This foul deed was recorded in 1699 and was said to be a recent event. This particular dragon was then very, very old. Maybe a little senile by then, to fall for such an old trick.

The next category is the large dragon, again with wings but without the ability to breath fire. One of the garbled tales mentioned earlier became a song referring to one of this type: *Puff the Magic Dragon* (Yerrow and Lipton, 1963) was popular a few years ago amongst children and those with an unsophisticated taste in music. These were generally between 6 and 12m long. There are many mentions of this type

---

[1] The illustrations in this paper are by Ruth Lacon.

Types –

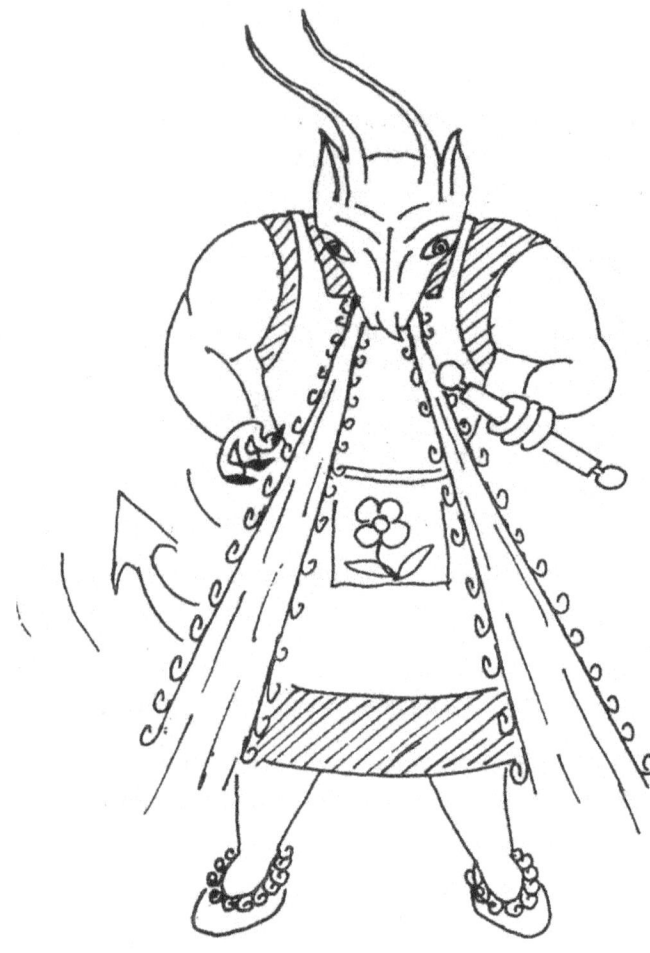

the Mother-in-law.

scales. It had two wings, blue above, but blood-coloured and yellow underneath; it was swifter than a horse, progressing partly by flight and partly by running.

(Gould *et al*, 1977, p. 41)

Recorded by Athanasius Kircher, being part of an account of the fight between a knight and a dragon on the island of Rhodes in 1349 AD.

The earliest reference we have come across was from the *Shan Hai King* or *Mountain and Sea Classic* (Gould *et al*, 1977, p. 71). This celebrated Chinese work is at least as old as the Chow dynasty as it is mentioned in contemporary manuscripts and is therefore pre- 1122 BC. It gives a description of the flying serpent of the Sien mountains. The words "drake" and "serpent" are often used in the classification of this particular type. The next variety are the true drakes of the dragon world. These are the wingless, fireless types often depicted as a snake-like creature. Eastern Mythology and art portray them as benign semi-deities. Western, Classical and Medieval dragons are portrayed differently so man has learned to fear them. They vary greatly in size and one of the largest recorded was Tolkien's Glaurung. In most mythologies these dragons possess and can confer immortality. More about the powers of dragons later.

There are smaller, younger dragons in this category that range from 1 – 4m. These were reputed to have guarded the olive trees in Greek mythology. The wyvern is another variation of this particular type, the difference being that the wyvern has no front legs.

Sea drakes had many features in common with their land-based cousins but a few major differences. Their front legs and their strong back legs developed into flippers and their tails became more muscular. They were wingless and, by necessity, fireless too. They were coastal by habit as they bred on land and were generally between 5 – 10m long. Several sightings have been made of much larger creatures though; notably by the captain of the *H.M.S. Daedalus* in 1847 who "watched a sea serpent more than sixty feet long for a full twenty minutes" (Cox and Attenborough, 1975, p. 31). At this late date in history he was derided for his report, but tales of sea monsters go back to the very earliest sea-faring days.

There are a few mentions of small land dragons that could breath fire, but these are very early sightings and we believe them to be the rare encounters with young dragons. This brings us neatly onto breeding. No, not virgins. Reproduction. In order to set the scene for the rare and dramatic coming together of sexually mature dragons, we will describe their physical and social surroundings and customs for your better understanding.

Dragons are territorial and isolationist. Their lairs are well away from built-up areas and the borders are carefully noted by other dragons. The older, more sophisticated ones will live near enough to landed gentry or royalty to periodically raid their dwellings for well-covered meals – cooks are particularly delectable – and to relieve men of the contents of their treasuries and armouries. Between raids sheep provide a

throughout history, and Aristotle, Herodotus and Cicero are not least amongst them. Pliny indeed talked of the "swarms of winged serpents about the Arabian marshes" (Gould *et al*, 1977, p. 27). Another is described thus:

> The monster is described as the bulk of a horse or ox, with long neck and serpent's head – tipped with mule's ears – the mouth widely gaping and furnished with sharp teeth, eyes sparkling as though they flashed fire, four feet provided with claws like a bear, a tail like a crocodile, the whole body being coated with hard

tasty meal and most dragons enjoy the occasional horse or goat. Also, stoats are a favourite snack amongst Western dragons.

The treasure is taken back to their lair which, wherever possible, is to be found in dry caves with plenty of airy tunnels leading to and from the main cavern. It is in this main hall that dragons of both sexes deposit their treasure.

> Wiglaf hastened into the earth-cavern, still wearing his corselet, his woven coat of mail. After the fierce warrior, flushed with victory, had walked past a daïs, he came upon the hoard – a hillock of precious stones and gold treasure on the ground. He saw wondrous wall-hangings; the lair of the serpent, the aged twilight flyer; and the stoups and vessels of a people long dead, now lacking a polisher, deprived of adornments. There were many old, rusty helmets, and many an armlet cunningly wrought. A treasure hoard, gold in the ground, will survive its owner easily, whosoever hides it!

(Crossley-Holland, 1987)

All pieces are mentally catalogued and current market values are always worked out. A dragon will always know the exact contents of his hoard. The bigger the dragon's hoard the more powerful he is. We know that size is not everything, but in the case of the ritual nesting of mature dragons – it sure is! Periodically the dragons that live on the borders of the most powerful dragon's domain will be invited to inspect the hoard. The sex of the most powerful and feared dragon is irrelevant. The owner of the richest nest of treasure will have first choice of suitors to begin the highly ritualistic and long courtship that will lead to the consummation in several month's time. "Come and see my chalices . . ." was a possible chat-up line.

The value of the hoard was mathematically correspondent to the size of the area over which the dragon had dominion. So, more treasure, more land, more choice of mate. If there was any discrepancy over the size and value of two hoards, then the rarely required code of practice would dictate the rules for engagement. Very occasionally would there be physical battle. The weaving of spells and the casting of riddles would usually establish a winner.

The female is very demanding of her prospective mate and things must be correct. He must bring gifts of food and minor treasures to her lair. It was often the case that the older, larger dragons were female as their treasures were increased by the mating rituals. The ones that men saw and encountered on raids were often marauding males looking for gifts for his mate, rather than give her something from his own hoard. Few things are so devastating to a dragon than to lose something from his hoard! When the female, or dragoness, is suitable courted and ready for the consummation of the temporary relationship she will indicate by rearing to meet the male. They mate eye to eye, belly to belly, showing complete trust by so exposing themselves.

The role of the male is then completely over and rarely will he see his young. Six weeks after fertilisation the dragoness lays her single egg into the carefully laid out treasure. The embryotic fluid in the egg has the ability to retain heat and

when the mother has to leave the lair to feed she buries the egg deep into the metals in the costly nest and warms them before she leaves.

The dragonet emerges from the egg a year and a day from the deposition. Over the next few months the mother will instruct junior in the rules for hunting and will find him a cave, not too near. She will allow him into her territory to hunt for a while, but will take the better pieces of any treasure acquired as payment. Once the dragonet is completely established in its own domain, however small, the mother is free to mate again.

Now that we have captured your interest by talking about sex, let us continue with a description of the physical and biological assets that enable dragons to be so unique in the animal world. We will concentrate on the largest species – the winged, fire-breathing dragons – and give a brief outline of their anatomical uniqueness. The wings would appear to be unable to support the weight of the fully grown creature. This is probably true. But it is worth pointing out that two fossils of flying dinosaurs have been found in the United States, the wingspans of which are nearly 50 feet (15 meters)! So the wings on their own were probably not capable of supporting the total weight in flight. What else was it about dragons that enabled some of them to fly? Firstly the bone-structure; the bones were not only hollow but built up of honey-combed blocks that are extremely light. Secondly the stomach is actually three chambers, similar to

Dragons and Flight

bovines. One is for digestion of food, one is for the production of special gases and the other is a storage chamber in which these gases are kept until needed. These hot gases are mainly by-products and variations on hydrogen- and sulphur-based compounds; such as Hydrogen Sulphide, Sulphur Dioxide, Sulphuric Acid, etc., and assist in both lift and fire. These gases are both the fuel for dragons' flames and the hidden element in their ability to fly. The wings are necessary for propulsion and manoeuvring — and fire served several purposes.

> As one, dragons swivelled their wedge-shaped heads to their riders for firestone. Great jaws macerated the hunks. The fragments were swallowed and more firestone was demanded. Inside the beasts, acids churned and the poisonous phosphines were readied. When the dragons belched forth gas, it would ignite in the air into ravening flame to sear the Threads from the sky.

(McCaffrey, 1970, pp. 177-178)

Any excess of gas could be used as a weapon during hunting or marauding. It was used during mating displays as a sign of strength. It was a useful way of dissuading the curious from cave entrances and was the ultimate mode of self-defence when challenged. The gases were ignited by a spark created in the back of the throat. Two small, but very tough muscles vibrated at great speed and produced a tiny electrical spark across the narrow gap. When the noxious gases were expelled, from the chamber within, a sheet of flame rushed from the dragon's mouth. When flame was not required the muscles contracted back into the sides of the throat and the only exhalation was the particularly revolting and distinctly sulphurous dragon's breath. Noxious products are sometimes named after this, for example Woodspring Smial's magazine and the condiment we showed at the presentation!

We cannot begin to cover the evolutionary growth of the dragons in this short time, but as a brief outline we can tell you this. The wings of the first drakes and dragons may have formed from the sail or fin of dinosaurs. Species such as Pelycosaurs refined and specialised their spinal sail into two parts. These developed into wings from the knuckle joint on the spine. There are indeed flying lizards alive today. Draco Volans ("flying dragon") has folds of skin supported by elongated ribs enabling it to glide between trees. There is a persisting legend about dragon blood, that it has mysterious properties. According to alchemists it contains a catalyst called "draconine" that makes the blood a deep purple colour, unique to dragons and other members of Royalty. It is also, apparently, very acidic like nitric acid. We only have the name for the catalyst but the alchemists of yore knew a way of extracting it from the blood and using the rest to create medicines and ingredients for expensive spells. Another lost art.

Fire-Breathing

From the vast amount of recorded material on the encounters with dragons in the past we have been able to make a list of the most common features that classify a dragon. They are very sharp-sighted. Their breath is poisonous. They are partial to virgins. They hoard gold. Land drakes dislike water. Water drakes dislike fire. They have dark, flat, hypnotic eyes. They have approximately 44 teeth. They are especially fond of milk. They have a strange stone (much sought after) in their forehead. They have wonderful scales.

These scales provide convincing camouflage as they often have the ability to blend into the surroundings. They are constructed in two layers. There is a translucent membrane over a metallic looking layer of flexible yet strong skin. As a dragon ages the scales become harder and very difficult to pierce. Young dragons are far more vulnerable to both accidents and attempted murder than their older counterparts. Those dragons that live in deep caverns have large ears because they have sonar capability. This is very necessary in deep, dark tunnels and caves. The ears can rotate to provide directional hearing, dragon hearing is very acute (ask Bilbo!). They also have an infrared capability which makes them formidable opposition underground.

The draconite is one of the rarest things on Earth. It is the precious "stone" that grows large in the forehead of the older, wilier, most "street-wise" dragons. It took many centuries to become fully mature and grew to become very beautiful. It was created by the dragoness marking her young, soon after birth, on the forehead with her sharp claw. This graze wept a waxy secretion that hardened and expanded the opening. As the dragon grew the draconite would grow new layers. As each layer solidified it created fascinating colours, edges and depths; so the beauty of the stone grew. It was said that there were as many colours of draconite as there are stars in the sky and it would appear to change colour within itself as the mood of the dragon changed. We believe it is likely that the "heart of the mountain" – the Arkenstone – was the draconite of one of Smaug's ancestors. The draconite was the centre of a dragon's soul and magic. A dragon's magic is the most wonderful thing that sets it apart from all other creatures, and we have selected a few examples and stories to illustrate this. A dragon's powers are both subtle and invidious. They can hypnotise and persuade with their voice, posture and eyes. The power comes from a strong psychic force that all dragons are born with, and the development of this is their highest goal.

The majority of dragons appreciate an adversary of some worth and a battle of wills is honour-bound by strict rules. It has been known for a hero or foe of high luck, or cunning, to sometimes get the better of a young or inexperienced dragon. Not often though. Bilbo was very different from any foe that Smaug had encountered before and much luck was with him, for as Tolkien says, "No dragon can resist the fascination of riddling talk" (Tolkien, 1966, p. 205). This enlarged sense of honour that makes a dragon stick to the rules can also mean that they can carry a grudge for many, many years. Some inherently wicked creatures take this to extremes. Glaurung,

Dragons and Magic.

for example, had a thing against the children of Húrin. His bewitching of Túrin and Nienor is a case in point and his conversations with Túrin say much about the finely-honed quality of his malice.

Many legends from many cultures have observed the power that a dragon can display with its magnetic eyes ". . . [Ged] almost stared into the dragon's eyes and was caught, for one cannot look into a dragon's eyes" (from Ursula Le Guin's *A Wizard of Earthsea*, 1971, p. 103).

A dragon's blood and teeth are also said to have extraordinary powers. It has been claimed that an unnamed substance in dragon's blood is the missing ingredient in the lost art of turning base metals into gold. Is this the "draconine" we mentioned earlier?

The draconite (the precious "stone" in the dragon's forehead) has also been much desired in this context as well. Obtaining all these was a very risky business. Another was attempting veterinary dentistry around dragons. The Greeks had a legend that when being routed if you planted dragon's teeth an army of immortal warriors would spring up in your defence. We have little proof of this one!

Because the various parts of the dragon's body were so rare and precious, on the rare occasion when a dead dragon or skeleton was found it was completely stripped clean by interested parties. There is no part of a dragon that did not have a use for somebody. A chair or throne of dragon's bones was beyond price – see Tad Williams (1988).

The staking of a live dragon was a task beyond most farmers but there is a basic analogy that the staking of a dragon was akin to staking the earth. Indeed in *The Lost Language of Symbolism* Harold Bayley (1912) says that "George", the most famous of all dragon slayers, could have lived up to the meaning of his name; "ge" meaning the earth and "urge" to encourage or stimulate the soil. It is not coincidence that St. George's Day, April 23rd, is the time of planting and fertilisation after the end of winter. Many of the tasks required for the planting of seeds and roots are redolent of "staking the dragon". The May Day celebrations to encourage growth and fertility are rooted in our deep past and even today symbolic dragons are used in many parts of the world to remind us of the immortality of both the dragon and of the seasons.

The consumption of a dragon's heart was guaranteed to confer immense bravery and prowess in war. The eyes were coveted by the alchemists and the local healers for being a vital ingredient in the production of a narcotic medicine used in the relief of pain. Such a medicine was beyond price in violent times and enriched its creators in man's eternal wars and battles. As well as the magic obtained from the dragon's physical form there are the more subtle powers that no other animal enjoys. At least not to any great extent; mankind has some limited mental skills but these pale into insignificance compared to the average drake's. One of a dragon's greatest abilities is the way in which he collects and collates information. The most obvious way is through hypnosis. Often information on the state of a nation, or neighbourhood, could be extracted from a passing minstrel or knight by straightforward mesmerisation.

On a more local level farmers would be persuaded (i.e. "You tell me what is going on or I will fry your barn, and how old is your daughter now?"), to be forthcoming about the others in their community. The underlying feeling about the basic information given would be picked up psychically, though. There was also a network of semi-minions such as crows and reptiles that the dragon could mentally extract emotions from. If a newcomer entered a dragon's territory, he could tell from the reactions of the other creatures whether the stranger was to be feared, ignored or investigated. A dragon always knows what is going on.

Another major asset to a dragon's vast repertoire is his Earth Knowledge. Using senses that other creatures do not understand, dragons use ley-lines extensively. The energy given off by these lines of power aid a dragon in flight, very much like thermal air currents. Very often the boundaries of a dragon's domain were along ley-lines and were as obvious as signposts to other dragons. Indeed, many of the major sightings of dragons in flight were made on known ley-lines and particularly on nodes where ley-lines meet: the dragons of Glastonbury Tor are a classic example.

There have been sightings of dragons all over the world and although characteristics vary, the similarities are enormous. Tales of knights, virgin daughters and treasure come from cultures and countries as varied as the Gauls, the Incas, the Chinese and the Tanzanians. The Bible mentions

dragons several times. Isaiah Ch.13 v.22 says: "And the wild beasts of the islands shall cry in their desolate houses and dragons in *their* pleasant palaces." In the Book of Revelations dragons and serpents are mentioned many times. The halls of long-dead kings were a favourite amongst Middle Eastern dragons, if they were high on a mountain, as sea level was far too hot for them. It is interesting to note that very few sightings of dragons have been made near the equator, too hot for dragons.

One of the most interesting tales for those at the Conference in Oxford is that a dragon was encountered locally in 1349 AD. This particular beast was unusual in that it was said to have two heads. Probably a bit of medieval exaggeration there. In Uffington, again not far from Oxford, was the unfortunate beast who had the bad luck to come across one of the St. Georges. In fact, if you look at the famous "Uffington Horse" chalk carving upside down it looks more like a dragon in flight than a horse.

The times, places, virgins and races that surround St. George vary considerably. One version involves our "hero" rescuing a princess from the monster (yawn) who is about to . . . devour her. Another tale relates how the dragon is standing guard over a spring and the country is in drought. St. George restores life to the land by extinguishing the bad dragon. There are so many Celtic and Slavonic fables along similar lines that one cannot blame the Christians for wanting one of their own.

Mind you, they did not stop at St. George. St. Romain of

Rouei killed "La Gargouille" which apparently went about ravaging and pillaging in the Middle Ages Seine region. St. Keyne of Cornwall gained renown by taking three days to kill his victim. Even the women got in on the action: St. Martha killed a terrible monster called "Tarasque" at Aix-la-Chapelle.

In the United Kingdom alone there have been over 70 written instances of dragons recorded for posterity. Add to this the considerable accounts in other parts of the world and the various depictions on coats-of-arms and crests, place names, pub names, etc., and you must seriously question the "mythical" nature of this wondrous animal.

One of the areas of "dragonology" that has not been investigated in any detail previously is the vexed question of the dragons' intent with regard to virgins, be they princesses or milkmaids. Unfortunately we do not have time to study this now, but we will tell you about an interesting effect dragons have had on our lives, associated with virgins: Leap Year. Every four years neighbouring dragons would meet on 1st March to check each other out and establish and confirm treasure hoards and thus pecking order within dragon society.

Dragons called it "Leet Year" in our tongue. This is an Old English word with two appropriate meaning – as we know, dragons loved puns and double meanings. It means a "meeting of the ways" and "counting", appropriate because the dragons would meet each other, do an elaborate dance in greeting and then check each other's hoards out.

Man misheard or misinterpreted this to be "Leap Year". "Leap" is a Middle English word meaning "a male animal copulating with a female animal". This confirmed man's interpretation of the meeting, as man could not tell the sexes of dragons apart easily. Therefore when two dragons met, did what looked like a courtship display and then disappeared into a cave together, man assumed they were breeding.

After any extensive activity dragons would love to feed, or drink their favourite food – milk. Man would see the dragons fly towards the farms and villages and chase and eat the cows, and milkmaids often got eaten as well.

This meant that whenever the 1st March of every fourth year came round it was recorded that dragons came hunting maids. So no young woman wanted to be known as a maid on that day. That is why on the day before, 29th February, any free woman would ask a man to marry her. And we still continue this ritual in modern times. It is no more possible to find the definitive dragon than it would be to frame a cloud formation. Dissect a flower and the beauty and magic of it are lost, but do what you will the beauty and magic of the dragon remain safe.

Thank you.

References

Bayley, Harold. 1912. *The Lost Language of Symbolism*. London: Williams & Norgate.

Cox, Molly and Attenborough, David. 1975. *David Attenborough's Fabulous Animals*. London: British Broadcasting Corporation.

Crossley-Holland, Kevin. 1987. *The Poetry of Legend: Classics of the Medieval World – Beowulf*. Woodbridge: Boydell.

Crossley-Holland, Kevin. 1990a. *Folk-Tales of the British Isles*. London: The Folio Society.

Crossley-Holland, Kevin. 1990b. *The Norse Myths*. London: The Folio Society.

Dickinson, Peter. 1979. *The Flight of Dragons*. London: Book Club Associates.

Gould, Charles et al. 1977. *The Dragon*, ed. Malcolm Smith. London: Wildwood House Ltd.

The Holy Bible (King James Version). 1611.

Hoult, Janet. 1987. *Dragons: Their History and Symbolism*. Glastonbury: Gothic Image Publications.

Le Guin, Ursula K. 1971. *A Wizard of Earthsea*. Harmondsworth: Puffin Books.

McCaffrey, Anne. 1970. *Dragonflight*. London: Corgi.

Miller, Hamish and Broadhurst, Paul. 1989. *The Sun and the Serpent*. Stuyvesant, NY: Pendragon Press.

The Oxford Universal Illustrated Dictionary, third edition, ed. C.T. Onions. London: The Caxton Publishing Co. Ltd.

Tolkien, J. R. R. 1966. *The Hobbit*. London: Unwin Books.

Tolkien, J. R. R. 1977. *The Silmarillion*. London: Guild Publishing.

Williams, Tad. 1988. *The Dragonbone Chair*. New York: Daw Books.

Yerrow, Paul and Lipton, Leonard. 1963. *Puff the Magic Dragon*. Blossom Music.

Section eleven

Other Writers

Tales of Wonder – Science Fiction and Fantasy in the Age of Jane Austen

Madawc Williams

Abstract: This paper challenges the accepted view that the works of writers such as Mrs. Radcliffe, "Monk" Lewis, Maturin and Mary Shelley are part of a Gothic tradition deriving from Horace Walpole's *Castle of Otranto*. The paper also studies the connection of Jane Austen to these writers and will try to unravel the errors of Brian Aldiss, whose ideas are taken from earlier authors.

Keywords: Brian Aldiss, *Arabian Nights*, Jane Austen, Coleridge, *Frankenstein*, genre fiction, Gothic, *Northanger Abbey*, *Otranto*, Mrs. Radcliffe, Science Fiction, Mary Shelley, terror-romance, Horace Walpole

As Tolkien enthusiasts, we all find ourselves in a peculiar limbo between SF and mainstream literature. The gap is less than it used to be, but it is still there. And there are plenty of *literati* who would love to apply a bit of "ethnic cleansing" to us, if they had the power to do so.

Undeniably, Tolkien's work does not belong to any recognised category. It is not a myth, not a joke, not SF, not a children's story. It is closer to SF than anything else, but very different in origin. It offends tidy-minded critics, who see it as an escaped children's story, badly needing to be expunged as a mistake of nature.

But how natural or valid are the standard categories? Do they represent fundamental rules that *The Lord of the Rings* improperly breaks? Or are they no more significant than the division of the files in a filing cabinet into *A to N* and *O to Z* (which was actually the origin of *The Marvelous Land of OZ*).

The received-standards view is that Science Fiction is an outgrowth of Gothic Terror, with Mary Shelley's *Frankenstein* as the connecting link (see figure 1).

This view is commonly associated with Mr. Brian Aldiss, who argued the case in 1973 in his *Billion Year Spree*. It actually goes back at least as far as 1907 and has been expressed by a large number of writers, including Muriel Spark in her 1951 biography of Mary Shelley. And also it's wrong.

The first thing to understand is that Mary Wollstonecraft Shelley's *Frankenstein* is not at all like the film and television versions of the myth. Mary's creature is highly intelligent, articulate and well-educated. He starts off full of benevolence, tries to do good, and only gradually turns to evil in the face of human rejection. The creature is not made of reconnected bits of miscellaneous dead bodies, and no mention is made in the text of electricity being the animating force. Victor Frankenstein is on one occasion described as working by the light of a candle. He is neither a baron nor a doctor, nor even a medical student.

Most of the familiar images come from the very remarkable and memorable 1931 film, which used or even invented many of the standard stock images of cinema science fiction, none of which are actually present in Mary Shelley's work. The 1931 American film has an understandable similarity to the early American SF of the same period. But all of these similarities are innovations, not found in the original.

The SF of Gernsback and Campbell derives from H.G. Wells, who in turn speaks of his "early, profound and lifelong admiration for Swift". Early SF, most SF up until the "New Wave" of the 1960s, has much in common with what is usually called the Augustan group of writers, Smollett, Goldsmith, Richardson, Sterne, Swift, and Defoe. Mary Shelley's work is something very different, an early example of the nineteenth-century romantic novel.

Quite apart from this, we have an odd situation if we uncritically accept the standard view. We have the Augustan Writers, all male and all very much products of the Age of Reason. Then we have female writers, expressing the vision of the Romantic Movement in novels. Between these two we have a group of men and women whose work includes both of these elements. The standard view classes them as "Gothic Fiction" and the "Novel of Doctrine". Gothic at least is said to have nothing to do with the development of proper literature. Yet all of these writers are intermediate in style and in ideas, as well as chronologically.

Figure 2 shows how the writers are conventionally grouped. Now let's look at the known influences.

The Gothic novel, as normally defined, begins in 1764 with Horace Walpole's *The Castle of Otranto: A Story*. Some reference works say 1765, which was the date printed on the first edition, but it is well established that it first went on sale in 1764. This first edition consisted of 500 copies, which was a fairly standard print run for those times. It sold well and

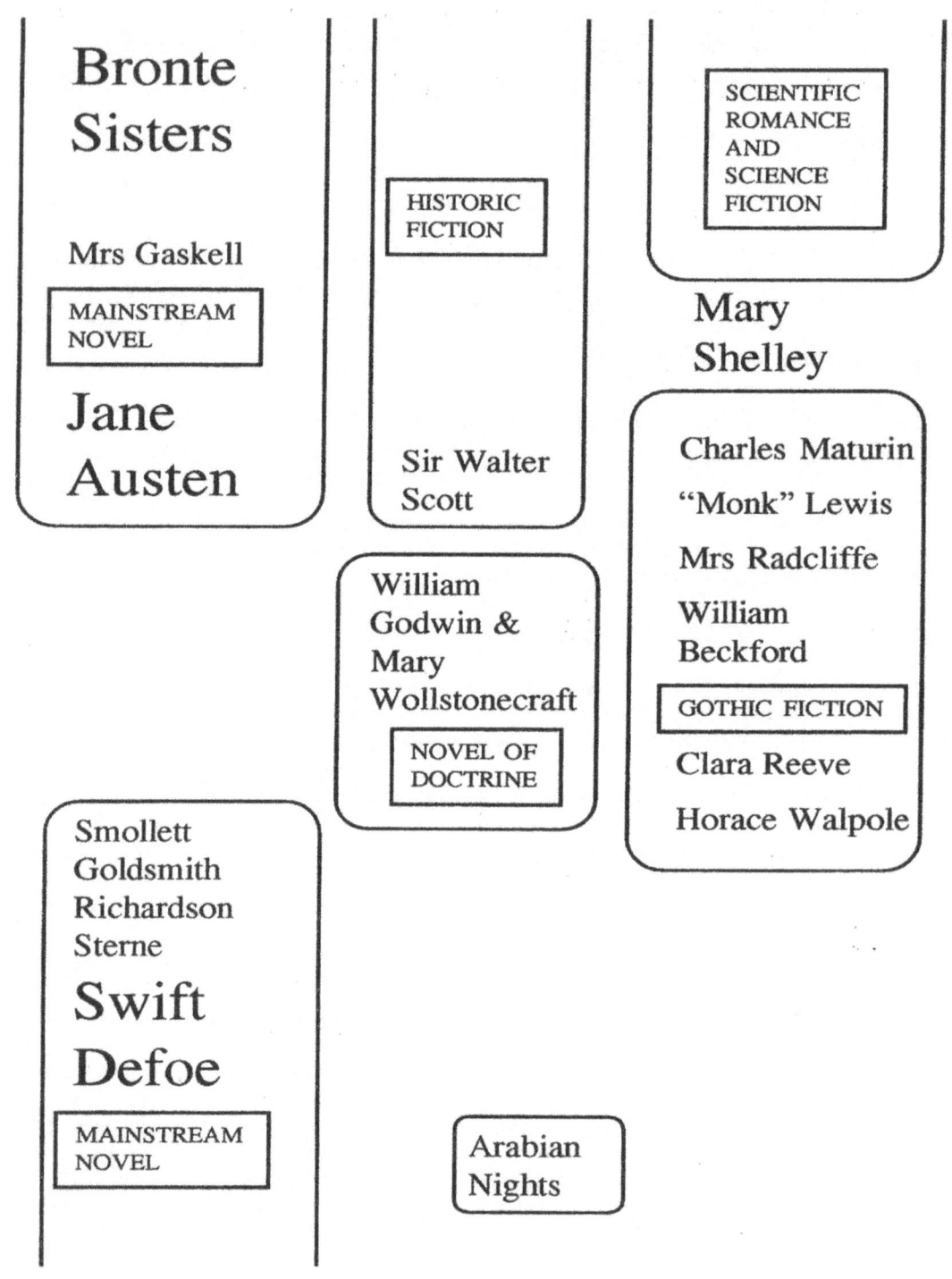

Figure 1.

was soon reprinted, and has in fact been a continuing influence right up to the present day.

Reading *Otranto*, I was struck by the similarity to some of the adventure tales in the *Arabian Nights*. Walpole knew this material – he coined the phrase *Serendipity*, the habit of making happy or chance finds, from *The Three Princes of Serendip* (Serendip is an old name for Sri Lanka or Ceylon, and actually means *Isle of Silk*). Also in 1757 Walpole had written *A Letter from Xo-Ho, a Chinese Philosopher at London*. Oliver Goldsmith improved on this theme in his book *The Citizen of the World*. Both used a Chinese visitor as a "rational observer", where people nowadays might use a Martian or a visitor from Canopus. Actual Chinese culture doesn't come into it.

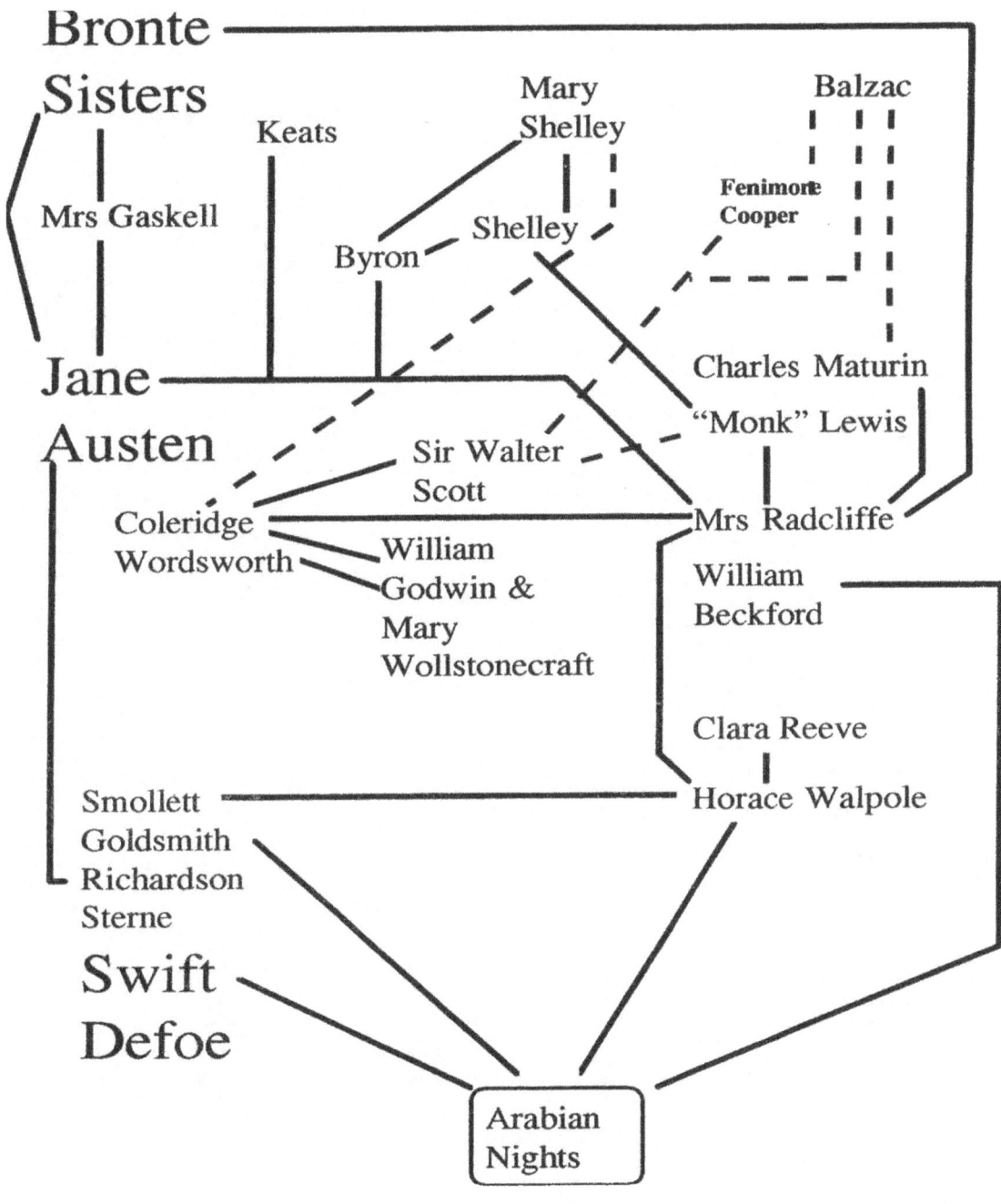

Figure 2.

Arabian Nights' influence goes even wider than that. You must also include Voltaire, influencing and influenced by English thought. His *Zadig*, written in 1747, is not only an oriental romance, but also pioneers the concept of a rational deductive detective – similar to both Sherlock Holmes and Poe's Chevalier Dupin. Poe is sometimes cited as the pioneer, but Voltaire was there more than 100 years earlier, and influenced by the oriental romance. And Smollett wrote *The History and Adventures of an Atom*, a parody of contemporary politics set in a fictional past era of Japan, with the narrator being a living and intelligent atom.

Walpole's *Otranto* seems to me to be an interesting hybrid of his two interests – oriental tales and the non-classical or Gothic tradition in Europe. It is a repackaging of the sort of adventure you find in the *Arabian Nights*' style, in the format of what was called the Gothic era, the period between the fall

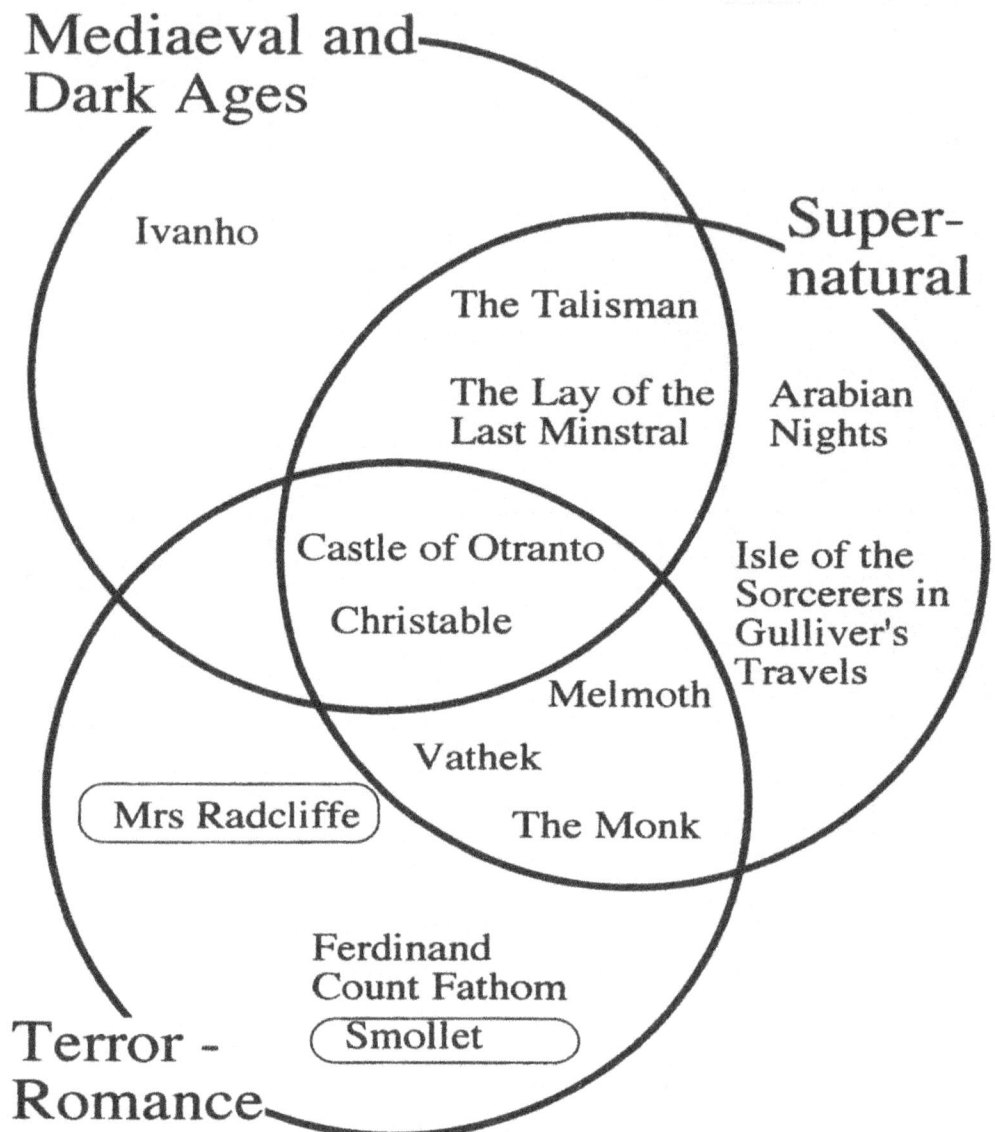

Figure 3.

of Rome and the Renaissance. Gothic is a misleading name, especially for Gothic architecture, which emerged long after the historic Goths had ceased to be a separate people. But it was then the standard term, and at that time had only the same overtones of magic or horror that the word "medieval" has today.

Burke's *Reflections on the Revolution in France* speaks approvingly of England's "*Gothic and monkish* education", and Burke was the best writer and orator of his day, with an exact knowledge of how every word was likely to affect his audience. Another writer even talks about "the cosy chair beside the Gothic fireplace . . ." This passage is cited in the full *Oxford English Dictionary*, which mentions Walpole's *Otranto* as one of the definitive texts for Gothic as medieval-romance.

It was actually only in the nineteenth century that the word "medieval" was coined and took over much of the eighteenth-century meaning of "gothic" (with "middleagism" briefly floated as an alternative). And Gothic in the literary context somehow lost its pre-Renaissance roots and became a general term for the terror-romance. The *Oxford Companion to English Literature* (5th Edition) (Drabble, 1985) confirms that a shift of meaning occurred, and claims that it happened in the late eighteenth-century. The fourth edition (Harvey, 1967) was less sure about when the shift happened, while the first three editions of the same work seem not to have heard of Gothic literature. Mrs. Radcliffe, "Monk" Lewis and the rest are all listed as individuals, but only Walpole is Gothic.

Puzzlingly, the full *Oxford English Dictionary*, which normally gives the first known usage of every word and every meaning of every word, is silent on Gothic in the sense of terror-romance. Only smaller versions of the dictionary mention this usage of Gothic, and with no clue to when this term came into use.

My own view, based on a lot of reading and checking old sources, is that the term Gothic for terror-romance is relatively recent, late nineteenth-century at the earliest. The first unambiguous case is 1907, and it doesn't really become widespread until the 1960s. I've found this by getting a whole set of old editions of the "Gothic" classics from the British Library and finding just how they were seen when published or republished.

In the process I discovered many other interesting matters, such as that Balzac had a very high opinion of Maturin, and even wrote a sequel to Maturin's *Melmoth the Wanderer*. This work seems never to have been translated into English, and modern editions of both Balzac and Maturin fail to mention the link. Balzac is literature and Maturin is Gothic and if the twain should somehow have met, there is no need to talk about the matter.

Somehow people got hold of the notion that Gothic was the proper term for a particular group of writers, whose work had nothing at all to do with proper literature. But the raw facts suggest that "Gothic" writers, though of no very large literary merit, were very much a part of the literary scene and the literary flow of ideas. They influenced later and better writers who created what we now call "mainstream", and in the nineteenth century this link was generally acknowledged. Confining all of these writers in a Gothic ghetto is a practice that spreads gradually from a few writers – Montague Summers is the best known of them, though I would not call him the best. Anyway, Gothic literature only gradually became established as a fact of literary knowledge, a *genre* that had existed ever since Walpole's day. As they used to say in the Soviet Union, you never know what is going to happen yesterday!

Look at the actual connections (see figure 2) – the material people actually read, the influences they themselves cited. Beckford and *Vathek* influenced Byron, who wrote quite a lot in both the oriental and terror-romantic mode. Byron considered that the best-ever tale of terror is the Biblical story of the Witch of Endor, in which the doomed King Saul confronts the ghost of the prophet Samuel. He even set it in verse:

> Is it thou, Oh King? Behold
> Bloodless are those limbs, and cold:
> Such are mine: and such shall be
> Thine, tomorrow, when with me . . .
> Crownless, breathless, headless fall,
> Son and sire, the house of Saul.

This comes form *Hebrew Melodies*, which appeared in 1815 – also the year of the first printed edition of *Beowulf*, as it happens. A lot of Byron's writing is in what we would now call a fantasy or science fiction mode.

I looked for an influence of Walpole on Beckford, or Beckford on Mrs. Radcliffe, and found no mention of any such link. Beckford was influenced by Walpole's notions of architecture, building a gothic mansion that latter fell down. But there is no sign of a *literary* connection. Beckford's *Vathek* is solidly in the tradition of the oriental romance. The so-called Gothic school does not look solid at all. Terror-romance in English prose writing begins with a chapter in Smollett's *Ferdinand, Count Fathom*, and also includes the Brontë sisters, and all in all is not a *genre* at all.

So where does SF come from? Broadly, the tale of wonder is as old as storytelling itself. In the twentieth century it was denied the stature of serious literature, unless it was by someone really famous like Shakespeare or Swift or Kafka or the Brontë sisters. Some of the rejected literature joined the newly established *genres* of ghost stories and horror stories. The rest crystallised around Gernsback's banner of Science fiction or Scientifiction, for want of anywhere else to go. But in the process SF itself expanded, becoming broader and deeper and more interesting.

Look again at the influence of *The Arabian Nights* – actually a collection of tales from many parts of Asia, with *Cinderella* probably originating in China. It was only in the early eighteenth century that this collection was translated into French, and then into other West European languages. I've speculated about a link from *The Arabian Nights* to Swift and *Gulliver's Travels*. The tales of *Sinbad the Sailor* have more in common with Swift's work than anything else that was around at the time, though Swift was certainly breaking new ground. The links from *The Arabian Nights* to Goldsmith, Smollett, Horace Walpole and William Beckford are not speculative at all. Each of them wrote "Easterns", what we now call *oriental romances*. So too did Byron and Shelley – the paper just didn't have room for any more links. Nor for other authors such as Washington Irving, who are also connected.

You could carry on the *Arabian Nights*' influence right up to the early twentieth century with *Weird Tales*, a mix of oriental romance, tales of imagination and tales of speculative science. The present-day *genre* of science fiction is more like an outgrowth of *Weird Tales* than Gernsback's notion, which was a narrow and technocratic version of what we now call "hard SF".

I said earlier that early SF had a lot in common with the Augustans, and was unlike the later Romantic Novels. There is a basic difference in method. You can write about people living in a spacecraft, or you can write about a spacecraft with people living in it. People in a situation, or a situation described by the people caught up in it. Myself, I like either sort of story when well done. And *Rendezvous with Rama*, a classic work in this second tradition, is by common consent much better than its sequels, which have a lot more about the individual personalities of the visitors.

SF up until the 1960s was generally about deeds, ideas and strange new possible worlds – as indeed are most of the works of the "Augustans", including *Gulliver's Travels*. You have a little bit about Mr. Lemuel Gulliver, and his personal disintegration as he fails to adjust to all of the strangeness he encounters. But this is maybe five or ten percent of the total.

Mary Shelley's *Frankenstein* is unambiguously a tale of personal interactions. Her work considers a bogey-man from the bogey-man's point of view. None of the film or television dramatisations really follow her in this, though the 1931 film has a little of it. The personality of the 1931 film monster is interesting, but is quite unlike the intelligent, well-intentioned and articulate being that Mary Shelley herself devised. But the central point to grasp is that a work that was originally very much in the Romantic tradition has been utterly transformed and brought into line with the "Augustan" tradition that was standard for SF tales in the 1930s. And none of the subsequent dramatizations have been wise enough to undo this change.

The Lord of the Rings itself has elements of both traditions, people in a situation or a situation described by those caught up in it. The two threads of the story, after the breaking of the Fellowship, follow rather different rules. With Frodo, Sam and Gollum, it is the personal interactions that are the prime focus, with various alarums and excursions playing a secondary role. With the other members of the Fellowship, kings and battle and heroic deeds are the prime focus. One might wish to know more about the personalities and private thoughts of people like Denethor, Éowyn, Aragorn and Gandalf. But that would spoil the grand design of the tale, the private ethical struggles of the Ringbearers set against the larger conflict that was going on all around them.

Incidentally, Tolkien and C.S. Lewis were well aware of Science Fiction, or rather of "Scientifiction", the original term used by Gernsback. Though Tolkien seems never to have thought of writing a tale of space travel, he could have written a very fine one, much better even than Lewis's. The early parts of the *Notion Club Papers* in *Sauron Defeated* show that he was ahead of the "hard SF" of his day, even at the level of speculations about what the solar system would actually be like. His voyager describes Venus as "a boiling whirl of wind and steam" and Mars as "a horrible network of deserts and chasms" – remarkably good predictions. Tolkien's forecast that the solar system would have no organic life expect on Earth also looks very probable, though Mars still has some possibilities, as do some of the outer worlds. But this is a large topic, so I'll cut the matter short for now.

To return to SF in the age of Jane Austen. Aldiss in his *Billion Year Spree* publicised a view of early SF that has become the received standard view – from Gothic, out of Mary Shelley. This view is repeated thirteen years later in his *Trillion Year Spree*, the revised, expanded, but sadly uncorrected reprint of the same work. Though Aldiss is undoubtedly a talented writer of fiction, he is not a useful or a reliable source on factual matters. His *Billion* did at least credit one of the previous exponents of the Gothic-origin theory, in an obscure footnote. His *Trillion* doesn't even have that. Perhaps his ego has undergone a thousand-fold expansion in the intervening years.

But there's also a nasty malignant side to what Aldiss says, which is why I'm fairly direct in criticising him. He is very rude about Tolkien, and very inaccurate. Yet this is preferable to his subtle dirtying of Mary Wollstonecraft Shelley's name. Aldiss says that when Mary Shelley wrote about the murder of Victor Frankenstein's little brother William, she was fantasising about murdering her own newborn child, who was also called William. He overlooks that Mary also had a younger brother called William, as well as being the daughter of William Godwin (see figure 4). She herself would have been William had she been born a boy.

Perhaps the fictional murder of Victor Frankenstein's brother expresses some subconscious resentment by Mary for her own younger half-brother William and against the restrictions that were placed on her as English society moved towards the Victorian era. But there is no justification for saying that she felt anything but love for her own little son, a tiny baby at the time, fated not even to live as long as William Frankenstein. One wonders if Aldiss even knows that Mary Shelley had a younger brother. He certainly confuses her half-sister Fanny Imlay with her step-sister Claire Clairmont, speaking of Claire as Mary's half-sister.

Aldiss finds *Frankenstein* similar to Modern SF. But read him carefully and you find that he hasn't clearly distinguished between Mary Shelley's work and the later forms of the myth, particularly the 1930s films. The first of the *Sprees* even describes Victor Frankenstein as a Baron, an odd distinction for a citizen of republican Geneva, particularly since Victor's father is still very much alive.

Scholarly research has discovered five immediate stimuli for *Frankenstein*, in the famous gathering of Byron, Percy Shelley, Mary Shelley, Claire Clairmont and Dr. Polidori on the shores of Lake Geneva. These were:

1st, a discussion of contemporary scientific notions as to how life might either be created artificially or restored to the dead.

2nd, the reading of what Mary Shelley refers to as "*some German ghost stories translated into French*" – actually a book called *Fantasmagoriana* (Eyriès, 1812).

3rd, a proposal by Byron that each of those present should write their own ghost story.

4th, a reading aloud of Coleridge's then unpublished poem *Christabel*, which Byron had in manuscript form. The malignant witch Geraldine had tricked Christabel into befriending her. While Christabel still suspects nothing, the narrator-voice of the poem has the following description of Geraldine:

> Behold! her bosom and half her side –
> Hideous, deformed, and pale of hue
> A sight to dream of, not to tell!
> O shield her! shield sweet Christabel!

The second line was suppressed in the published version of the poem.

5th, a waking nightmare that the poem sparked off in Shelley – a woman with eyes where her breasts should be.

You get these details from Dr. Polidori's diary, which Aldiss has obviously not read, or even read a decent summary of. (Dowden's nineteenth-century biography of Shelley, for instance, gives the essence of the matter.) Aldiss seems to rely on Mary Shelley's 1831 introduction to the tale, which is decidedly "economical with the truth". This account suppresses the reading of *Christabel* and Shelley's vision, as well as modestly concealing the fact that Mary was not at that time Percy Shelley's wife – not until later when his rejected first wife committed suicide. The fact that Mary Shelley fails to name the book as *Fantasmagoriana* is

Parents and children in the Godwin household

	Mary Woolstonecraft	Mary Jane Clairmont
Gilbert Imlay	Fanny Imlay	
Unknown		Charles Clairmont
Unknown, probably Swiss		Claire (Jane) Clairmont
William Godwin	Mary Wollstonecraft Shelley	William Godwin Junior

Figure 4.

probably due to a genuine lapse of memory – it seems to be a standard unexceptional work of terror-romance. Anyone interested can find a copy in the British Library, along with an English translation of 1813 called *Tales of the Dead* (Utterson), which seems to have had no influence on anyone.

Aldiss knows nothing of all this. Instead he suggests that the works that inspired the ghost-story composition might have included De Sade's *Justine*. He says "If Mary had read De Sade's novel *Justine*, as seems likely . . ." It's not likely at all. It's not even in line with what Mary Shelley says – De Sade was neither a German nor a writer of ghost stories. And I doubt if even Lord Byron himself would have given any of De Sade's books to young ladies, though he had read them himself.

Incidentally, Murial Spark knows no more than Aldiss about the genesis of *Frankenstein*. She makes much of a family legend that the Godwin children heard Coleridge reciting the *Rime of the Ancient Mariner*, which is indeed mentioned in *Frankenstein*. But the much more substantial link to *Christabel* is ignored. Yet it is most significant.

Coleridge in *Christabel* follows the conventional pattern in having the witch's hidden deformity a sure sign that she's evil. Mary Shelley makes a radical break with this tradition – the hideous artificial man has initial good intentions, and it is only rejection on account of his shocking ugliness that gradually makes him malicious. It has taken more than 150 years for such a perspective to become widespread, with films like *Mask* and *The Elephant Man*. No filmed version of

Frankenstein has included Mary's original insight. The 1931 film gets halfway there, more recent versions don't even manage that.

What of the wider context? Looking at the actual connections, one finds no sharp line between tales of the familiar, tales of the unfamiliar, and tales of wonder. You might say that it's the difference between the man on the Clapham omnibus, the ghost on the Clapham omnibus, the man from Clapham in a spacecraft, or the ghost in a spacecraft, or maybe haunting mysterious Elven ruins. Even the proverbial "man on the Clapham omnibus" is now outdated. To be modern, I suppose one should say "the person in the Clapham traffic jam". In a few years' time, the norm may be "the person on the Clapham electric-powered tram" – or even "the person wandering the radio-active ruins of Clapham." Anyway, I am again wandering off the subject, so I'll cut the matter short.

As well as contributing to *Frankenstein*, *Christabel* was also an inspiration for Walter Scott's *The Lay of the Last Minstrel*, his first really successful work. Scott had earlier been a literary assistant to "Monk" Lewis, who was at that time much better known, though four years younger than Scott. Lewis and Scott had, among other things, edited a collection called *Tales of Wonder*. But it was thanks to *Christabel* that Scott made his first breakthrough as a writer of narrative poems, allowing his later blossoming as a writer of historical novels.

Frankenstein, the other notable offspring of the virgin *Christabel*, has yet another neglected but important message. It is expressed by Victor Frankenstein at the end of Chapter 4:

> A human being in perfection ought always to preserve a calm and peaceful mind, and never to allow passion or a transitory desire to disturb his tranquillity.

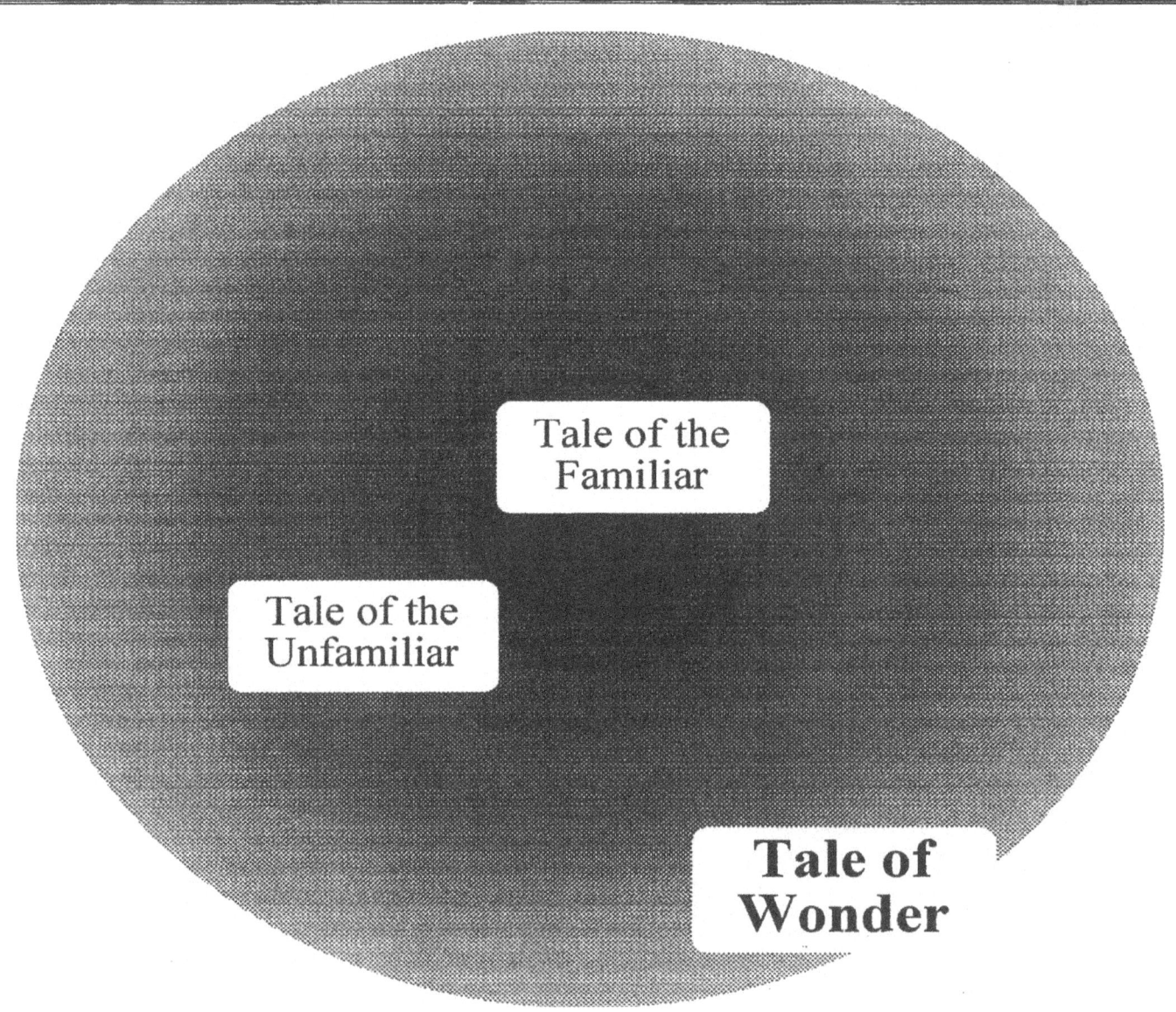

Figure 5.

I do not think that the pursuit of knowledge is an exception to this rule . . . If this rule were always observed . . . Greece had not been enslaved; Caesar would have spared his country; America would have been discovered more gradually; and the empires of Mexico and Peru had not been destroyed."

Victor Frankenstein recognises in himself an over-ambitious spirit that will do harm wherever it is applied. He does not single out pioneers of science for special blame. He does not ignore the politicians and generals who usually possess much more power and responsibility. Nor does he at any point behave like a scientist. Instead he acts like a magician in modern guise, keeping secret his special knowledge and discoveries, rather than publishing them for the benefit of anyone who may be interested, the scientific method in its proper form.

But none of this got through to the popular version of the myth. Victor has been turned into the prototype "mad scientist", isolated disrupter of an otherwise peaceful and tranquil society. Scientists get the blame for things that are mainly caused by much stronger, nastier and more aggressive social groups. It is of course much safer and easier to pick a fight with scientists than with businessmen, generals, farmers, anglers or fox-hunters.

To take just one instance, scientists are being blamed for the fact that genetic research is recognising some of the genetic factors in disease, which would allow employers and insurance companies to discriminate against such unfortunates. The sensible solution would be to get laws passed outlawing all such forms of discrimination. But that would mean taking on powerful vested interests. Denouncing science is a soft and easy alternative, and the name of "Dr." Frankenstein is often invoked in such a context. A proper understanding of Mary Shelley's original work would be a good corrective, particularly if you realised how different it is from the outlook of most works of Science Fiction and Fantasy. It includes many ideas that the bulk of society is only just now coming to terms with.

To return to the matter of SF origins. As far as I can tell, the idea that *Frankenstein* inspired Wells and the Scientific Romance originated with a man called Ernest A. Baker in his introduction to a 1907 edition of M.G. Lewis's *The Monk*. But in Baker's ten-volume *History of the English Novel*, he refers to "the rather absurd term 'Gothic'", without any explanation of how the term came to be attached to the non-medieval terror-romance. Indeed, he says:

> the usual assumption in studies of Gothic is that *The Castle of Otranto* inaugurated the genre which culminated in the novels of Mrs. Radcliffe. But it would be more reasonable to place the starting-point either earlier or later . . . the later Gothic romances were not like Walpole at all.

In Baker's work, Wells is linked to writers like Shaw, Lytton, Butler and Bellamy, rather than to a woman who died fifteen years before he was born.

Devendra P. Varma's book *The Gothic Flame*, often cited as the standard work on Gothic, sheds no light on the matter. He does mention Hans Möbius's 1902 dissertation *The Gothic Romance*, which is to be found in many of the bibliographies of serious writers on Gothic. It looked interesting, but was very hard to get hold of. I finally persuaded the British Library to borrow the University of Exeter's copy, and discovered that Möbius's work was written in German – a detail that none of those who cite it happen to mention.

Varma also cites Nathan Drake's *Literary Hours* as proof that "Gothic" meant "supernatural" as far back as 1798. Drake does indeed speak of Gothic in a way that sounds very much like the modern concept of Gothic-as-terror. But this is in an essay entitled *On Gothic Superstition* – a point that Varma omits. And Drake also says, "Next to Gothic, in point of sublimity and imagination, comes the Celtic . . ." (Varma, 1957, p. 108). That is to say, he uses the terms "the Gothic" or "the Celtic" to mean *Gothic superstition* or *Celtic superstition*.

Drake's idea of Gothic includes the Icelandic Eddas, the major source for the Norse mythology of Odin, Thor, etc., which is never included in the Gothic-as-terror tradition. He also speaks of Mrs. Radcliffe, but not as a Gothic writer. Instead he calls her "the Shakespeare of Romance Writers".

Mrs. Radcliffe deserves closer study. She is classed as a gothic writer, yet in all her important works the apparent supernatural happenings have some purely natural explanation. Nor was she a hack writer operating in some Gothic ghetto. Rather, she was a major, highly admired and highly influential figure in her own day. She published a Guide to the Lake District several years before Wordsworth, Coleridge and Southey became famous as the "Lake Poets". When she wrote, hardly anyone had heard of Wordsworth, and Coleridge and Southey had yet to visit that part of the world. Coleridge shows great respect for her when reviewing her "Gothic" novels (which he does not call Gothic). Keats refers to her as "Mother Radcliffe". Byron, who was no respecter of conventional ideas, and who sneered at Wordsworth, Coleridge and Southey, puts her in very exalted company in his description of Venice in *Childe Harold's Pilgrimage*:

> And Otway, Radcliffe, Schiller, Shakespeare's art
> Has stamp'd her image in me.
> (Canto IV. 18)

Mrs. Radcliffe was also a major influence on an unknown aspiring writer named Jane Austen.

To understand Jane Austen, we have to forget about her later fame and consider her in context – a young woman who had some aspirations to be a writer, in a period when Mrs. Radcliffe was both the most successful and the most widely admired role model. What was her picture of the world?

Figure 6, believe it or not, shows Jane Austen's sister's teenage impression of Henry the Fifth. She knew he was a famous solder, so she imagined him as a soldier of her own era. Her sister's vision of Queen Elizabeth is also very singular. Thankfully, when she came to write novels, she stuck very rigidly to things that she had direct knowledge of.

Most writers feel free to invent scenes and places in the familiar world which they have no direct experience of. Jane Austen was much more strict with her own imagining. For

Figure 6. Drawings by Cassandra E. Austen (Austen, 1922, p. 141): (a) Henry V, (b) Elizabeth I

instance she never writes about men talking when no ladies are present, because she would have no direct knowledge of such matters – and it would indeed have been quite different from what the men of that era would say when ladies were present. This is all part of the received standard view of Jane Austen, and I have no wish to disagree with it. I simply want to apply it to *Northanger Abbey*, the novel in which the link to Mrs. Radcliffe and the Terror-Romance is most visible.

I mentioned earlier that the link between Maturin and Balzac has been simply suppressed as an improper connection, turned into a non-fact of modern literature. One would not have expected Jane Austen to be guilty of an improper connection, yet her novel *Northanger Abbey* has a clear and obvious link to Mrs. Radcliffe and the terror-romance.

Northanger Abbey is too famous to become a non-fact. It was one of three novels that Jane Austen was working on for a very long time, with no certainty that they would ever be published. The other members of this trio were *Pride and Prejudice* and *Sense and Sensibility* – all three had various other titles at other times, but to be brief I'll ignore this complication. *Pride and Prejudice* was the first to be offered for publication, but it was rejected. *Northanger Abbey* was purchased by a publisher for £10, but was not then printed or published. *Sense and Sensibility* was the first to actually make it into print, and the publisher may have had some sort of subsidy or guarantee against loss. It was in fact a moderate success, so that *Pride and Prejudice* followed it, as well as other novels like *Mansfield Park*. *Northanger Abbey* was eventually re-purchased from the publisher who had paid £10 for it – since all of these works were anonymous, he had no idea that it was by a successful novelist. Jane Austen finally prepared it for a belated publication, with a note about the delay. It actually only appeared after her death, in 1818, the same year as *Frankenstein*.

Northanger Abbey is commonly described as a parody of Gothic. Some people even claim that it was suppressed because it might harm sales of the more popular Gothic tales. Yet parodies were common at the time, including *Christabess*, a vicious but clever parody of *Christabel*. And *Northanger Abbey* is not a parody. No one knows why it was not published after being purchased, but the publisher may have had second thoughts and refused to risk several hundred pounds printing and distributing a book that might not sell well. (This was in an age when a middle-class family could get by on an income of £200 a year.)

In *Northanger Abbey*, we have the tale of a young woman making a small entry into the fashionable society of early nineteenth-century Bath. The framework is a conventional tale of a true romance, with an unfortunate misunderstanding that spoils things and a final resolution with a happy marriage. The interesting part is that while all of this is happening, the heroine Catherine is imagining all sorts of things based on her reading of Mrs. Radcliffe and other writers of terror-romances. (One of these fantasies, incidentally, is about an imprisoned wife – surprisingly similar to the later plot of Charlotte Brontë's *Jane Eyre*.)

The narrator-voice of *Northanger Abbey* notes the ironic contrast between the silly terror-romance fantasies of the heroine and the cynical plotting that is actually controlling her fate. The difference between romance and reality is sharply pointed out. During Catherine's first trip to Bath, it is noted that "neither robbers not tempests befriended them, not one lucky overturn to introduce them to the hero". The resolution and the happy ending are combined with a realisation that terror-romance happenings are mere fantasies, at least in the context of early nineteenth-century England. Catherine's imagination comes into line with the actual world she lives in.

From where did Jane Austen get this ingenious idea? Note that she hardly ever worked without some real-life model – even some minor works of terror-romance mentioned in passing are real books. Also that the external aspects of Catherine's adventures are rather closer to Jane Austen's own life than the deeds of her other fictional heroines.

Is it not a reasonable hypothesis that the accounts of Catherine's terror-romantic imaginings are a slightly comical account of Jane Austen's own vivid imagination of her younger days? Might she not be making use of fantasies that she herself had had when she was Catherine's age and trying to make her way in the world, still hoping to get married and not resigned to being a spinster and novelist instead? Because for her, there was no happy resolution at a personal level. Instead she resolved and united two aspects of literature that had grown far apart: the rich emotional life of the terror-romantic fantasy with the realistic but limited framework of the Augustan novel of everyday life.

This unexpected influence on Jane Austen may have been Mrs. Radcliffe's main contribution to the development of the novel. Her popularity declined, though Henry James knew of her, and makes an oblique reference in *The Turn of the Screw*. Despite this, she ended up shut up in a Gothic ghetto, given a spurious link to Science Fiction, which she really had nothing to do with. Science Fiction in its "Golden Age" form comes from Swift via Wells, while the legacy of Mary Shelley remains to be developed in its full and proper form.

References

Aldiss, Brian. 1973. *Billion Year Spree*. London: Weidenfeld & Nicolson.

Aldiss, Brian. 1986. *Trillion Year Spree*. New York: Atheneum.

Austen, Jane. 1811. *Sense and Sensibility*. London: T. Egerton.

Austen, Jane. 1813. *Pride and Prejudice*. London: T. Egerton.

Austen, Jane. 1816. *Mansfield Park*, second edition. London: John Murray.

Austen, Jane. 1818. *Northanger Abbey*. London: John Murray.

Austen, Jane. 1922. "The History of England from the Reign of Henry the 4th to the Death of Charles the 1st by a Partial, Prejudiced, and Ignorant Historian" in *Love and Friendship and other Early Works*. London: Chatto & Windus, pp. 81-97 and 141.

Baker, Ernest A. 1924-39. *History of the English Novel*. London: H. F. & G. Witherby.

Baum, L. Frank. 1904. *The Marvelous Land of Oz*. Chicago: The Reilly & Briton Co.

Beckford, William. 1815. *Vathek*. London: Chez Clarke.

Brontë, Charlotte. 1847. *Jane Eyre*. London: Smith, Elder & Co.

Burke, Edmund. 1905. *Reflections on the Revolution in France*. London: Methuen.

Byron, George Gordon. 1812, 1816, 1818. *Childe Harold's Pilgrimage*. London: John Murray.

Byron, George Gordon. 1815. *Hebrew Melodies*. London: John Murray.

Clarke, Arthur C. 1973. *Rendezvous with Rama*. New York: Harcourt Brace Jovanovich.

Coleridge, Samuel Taylor. 1837. *The Rime of the Ancient Mariner*. Edinburgh: Alexander Hill.

Coleridge, Samuel Taylor. 1904. *Christabel*. London: John Dent & Co.

Dowden, Edward. 1886. *The Life of Percy Bysshe Shelley*. London: Kegan Paul & Co.

Drabble, Margaret (ed.). 1985. *The Oxford Companion to English Literature*, fifth edition. Oxford: Oxford University Press.

Drake, Nathan. 1798. *Literary Hours*. Sudbury.

Eyriès, Jean Baptiste Benoit (trans.). 1812. *Fantasmagoriana: ou, Recueil d'histoires, d'apparitions, des spectres, revenans fantômes*, [etc.]. Paris.

Goldsmith, Oliver. 1762. *The Citizen of the World; or Letters from a Chinese philosopher, residing in London, to his friends in the East*. London: Printed for the author.

Harvey, Sir Paul (ed.). 1967. *The Oxford Companion to English Literature*, fourth edition, revised by Dorothy Eagle. Oxford: Oxford University Press.

James, Henry. 1898. *Turn of the Screw*. London: W. Heinemann.

Lewis, M. G. 1796. *The Monk*. Waterford: J. Saunders.

Lewis, M. G. (ed.) and Scott, Walter (contrib.). 1800. *Tales of Wonder*. London.

Maturin, Charles Robert. 1820. *Melmoth the Wanderer*. Edinburgh: A. Constable & Co.

Möbius, Hans. 1902. *The Gothic Romance*. Leipzig: Buchdrucherei Grimme & Trömel.

Sade, Donatien Alphonse François de (Marquis de). 1791. *Justine, ou les malheurs de la vertu*. Paris.

Scott, Walter. 1805. *The Lay of the Last Minstrel*. London: Longman.

Shelley, Mary Wollstonecraft. 1818. *Frankenstein*. London: Lackington, Hughes, Harding, etc.

Smollett, Tobias George. 1753. *The Adventures of Ferdinand, Count Fathom*. London.

Smollett, Tobias George. 1769. *The History and Adventures of an Atom*. London: Robinson & Roberts, 1749 [1769].

Spark, Muriel. 1951. *Child of Light: A reassessment of Mary Wollstonecraft Shelley*. Hadleigh: Tower Bridge Publications.

Swift, Jonathan. 1726. *Travels into several remote nations of the World. By Capt. Lemuel Gulliver*, [commonly known as *Gulliver's Travels*]. London: B. Motte.

Tolkien, J.R.R. 1966a. *The Fellowship of the Ring*, second edition. London: George Allen & Unwin.

Tolkien, J.R.R. 1966b. *The Two Towers*, second edition. London: George Allen & Unwin.

Tolkien, J.R.R. 1966c. *The Return of the King*, second edition. London: George Allen & Unwin.

Tolkien, J.R.R. 1992. *Sauron Defeated*, ed. Christopher Tolkien. London: HarperCollins.

Utterson, Sarah Elizabeth Brown (trans.). 1813. *Tales of the Dead: principally translated from the French*. London: White Cochrane & Co.

Varma, Devendra P. 1957. *The Gothic Flame*. London: Arthur Barker.

Voltaire, Francois M. A. de. 1747. *Zadig*. London [Paris]: Pour la Compania.

Walpole, Horace. 1757. *A Letter from Xo-Ho, a Chinese Philosopher at London to his friend Lien Chi at Peking*. London: for Josiah Graham.

Walpole, Horace. 1764. *The Castle of Otranto: A Story*, pseud. Onophurio Muralto. London: T. Lownds, 1765 [1764].

Natural Mysticism in Kenneth Grahame's *The Wind in the Willows*

J.R. Wytenbroek

Abstract: This paper explores the use of Pan as the medium for an intense mystical experience in "The Piper at the Gates of Dawn", and how this mystical passage fits in with the rest of *The Wind in the Willows*. The author also explores possible influences on Grahame from writers of the nineteenth century who had mystical emphases in their books. The "Piper" is one of the most beautiful passages of natural mysticism in twentieth-century literature, but one rarely discussed: the author hopes this paper will begin to fill this critical gap.

Keywords: Kenneth Grahame, mysticism, Pan, romanticism, *The Wind in the Willows*

While many if not most of the great writers for children have clearly shown the influence of other children's authors on their writings, Kenneth Grahame seems to be an exception. While C.S. Lewis openly claims George MacDonald as an influence, while Burnett clearly borrows her description of the endless unused rooms in Misselthwaite Manor in *The Secret Garden* from MacDonald's descriptions of the Princess's house in *The Princess and the Goblin*, while Tolkien clearly bases Bilbo's hobbit hole in *The Hobbit* on Grahame's description of Badger's hole, and while these older authors obviously influence more recent writers, Grahame seems strangely removed from any influences by the children's authors he could have drawn from: Lewis Carroll, Edith Nesbit and his fellow Scotsman, George MacDonald, amongst others. In his *Wind in The Willows*, the reader gets a strong sense of Grahame's almost wistful love of the English countryside, filtered through a double filter of strictly adult influences: eighteenth-century Romanticism and nineteenth-century neo-paganism.

Neo-paganism, extolled and promoted by intellectuals such as Walter Pater, was a way out for the young person with spiritual tendencies who could no longer accept the seemingly outworn and certainly bowdlerized Christianity presented through either the Anglican or the Calvinist traditions. Grahame himself was thoroughly disenchanted by the strict and loveless Calvinism under which he had suffered as a child, later referring to it as "Scotch-Calvinist-devil worship" (in Green, 1957, p. 137). By the time of his writing the *Pagan Papers* (1893), he showed a strong sympathy for the neo-paganism embraced by many of the young intellectuals of his time.

Two elements seem to have been central to neo-paganism: a reverence for the Greek demi-god Pan and a pantheistic view of the universe (Green, 1957, p p. 140ff). The concept of pantheism was fairly unified. A concept of wholeness, with all things within the natural universe being seen as holy and imbued with the god and all things as part of the god, seems have to been the primary idea for many of the young, nineteenth-century pantheists. However, the role of Pan was seen in quite varies ways:

> For some he incarnated terror and cruelty, the rejected forces of nature taking their revenge . . . More often his sexual attributes are emphasized, the fierce unrestrained lechery free of all human conventions . . . [There is] a third aspect of Pan which the neo-pagans emphasized: his role as protector and healer of herds and country folk . . . this is the Pan on whom Grahame largely founds his own variant.
> (Green, 1957, pp. 141-42)

Pan appears early in Grahame's writings, in fact in the *Pagan Papers*, his first book of essays, many of which extol the beauties of the countryside and the desirability of a simple, rural life. These themes are to appear again and again in Grahame's writings, but nowhere as completely or coherently as in that portrait of idyllic country life, *The Wind in The Willows* (1908). In this novel, Grahame's only novel, Pan will become central to the natural mysticism expressed in the seventh chapter, "The Piper at The Gates of Dawn."

Pan, as part man and part animal, seems to signify that marriage of humanity and the natural world espoused by the pantheists of Grahame's time and so soundly rejected by the established Church. The Church, set as it was on the concept of a spiritual hierarchy with the animals and plants underneath humanity and therefore in subjection to it, had dominated western thought for centuries. This idea of subjection had led to a sense of superiority over nature and a belief in humanity's right to exploit nature in whatever way it wished. To those for whom nature was a source of solace, even enlightenment, and certainly pleasure, this position was untenable. The basis, then, of their pantheism

> is the oneness of creation – man as a natural force, differing in no essential way from plants and animals.

Then God is reduced to the same expression, and He and Man, and the Wind and Weather, Trees, Sheep, Love, Life, Death, Fear, all play their parts out and meet and merge, and mate and mingle . . .
(Hewlett in Green, 1957, p. 142)

This concept of oneness, wholeness, was not new with the neo-pantheists. Mystics throughout the centuries had espoused just such a vision of the universe, without the reductive quality mentioned by Hewlett. But even more concretely, all the English Romantic writers, including the two Christian Romantics Wordsworth and Coleridge, had also espoused such a vision of the universe.

And what if all of animated nature
Be but organic Harps diversely fram'd,
That tremble into thought, as o'er them sweeps
Plastic and vast, one intellectual breeze,
At once the Soul of each, and God of all?
(Coleridge, 1971, ll. 44-48)

. . . And I have felt
A presence that disturbs me with the joy
Of elevated thoughts; a sense sublime
Of something far more deeply interfused,
Whose dwelling is the light of setting suns,
And the round ocean and the living air,
And the blue sky, and in the mind of man:
A motion and a spirit, that impels
All thinking things, all objects of all thought,
And rolls through all things.
(Wordsworth, 1965, ll. 93-102)

These ideas permeate the Romantics' poetry again and again. They appear most clearly perhaps in Shelley's poetry. His Intellectual Beauty, praised so highly in his "Hymn to Intellectual Beauty," is surely the pantheistic god. And throughout his great elegy for Keats, "Adonais," the concept of the integration of all things within the god and the god within all things runs, cohering life and death as well as all that is and has been.

The great mystic vision of these three poets in particular is ultimately nature-based. The vision seems no more an incongruity for the Christian Wordsworth or Coleridge than it does for the agnostic Shelley. Although Coleridge himself shies away from the idea to some extent in "The Eolian Harp," he comes back to the idea again and again in his other poems, perhaps most strongly in "The Rhyme of The Ancient Mariner." But Wordsworth is unabashedly joyous in his embrasure of the holiness of all things, and the spirit that flows through all, linking all to that divinity within whom all things exist. Thus Walter Pater's insistence that, ultimately, paganism and Christianity are not opposed but are rather complementary seems a reasonable assertion if one looks at Wordsworth (Pater, 1961, pp. 56-58).

However, to the Churchmen of Grahame's day there was no link, so many of the young radicals rejecting Christianity could find an immediate home in paganism. In itself, nineteenth-century paganism had many forms, including many darker, occult manifestations. But Grahame's paganism was really a completely nature-oriented form of pantheism, with Pan as the symbol of the possibilities of the inherent spirituality within nature and therefore, although repressed, within humanity. In *Wind in The Willows*, this idea has its most perfect fulfillment of expression for Grahame, because in that novel he fundamentally discards human society, to which he had an increasing aversion during his life, and concentrates on the superior animal society. Although concerned almost exclusively with the lives of small animals, *The Wind in The Willows* presents two story lines that come together near the end of the novel. Many critics have discussed these two plots, some suggesting that it is an inherent weakness in the book, that Grahame could not make up his mind between the advantages of the life of adventure or the life of domestic bliss. Others insist that the book makes a coherent whole. I side with those who believe the "coherent whole" theory, partly because Grahame was too meticulous a craftsman to slap together two disparate stories and strain to bring them together into one novel and partly because of his intellectual committment to a sense of pantheistic wholeness. The only dissenting factor in Grahame's sense of wholeness was people, who had deliberately separated themselves off from the whole by their sense of superiority and their lack of sense of proportion. This part of his world view is borne out through the novel through the character of Toad, who is the only truly arrogant character in the novel, the only one who never seems to learn from his mistakes, and the only one who is devoted to a product of the technological age: the motor car. All these attributes seem to belong to Grahame's concept of humans in general, particularly industrial-age humans. As is evident in the *Pagan Papers*, Grahame hated technology and the destruction not only of the countryside that the railway and motor car brought, but of the rural way of life. He also seemed, like Pater, to dislike the materialism that accompanied the industrial-technological way of life, and this dislike too is revealed through the ostentatiously wealthy Toad, the only one who boasts of and parades possessions that are not immediately linked to basic comfort and survival (Paglia, 1990, p. 482).

On the other hand, the remainder of the novel is devoted to the more "natural" Ratty, Moly and Badger, who live in appropriate dwellings for their species (Toad lives in a manor house). Their pleasures are simple and all related to the natural world around them. Even Ratty's temptation to run away to sea in "Wayfarers All" springs from a longing for excitement related to another great place of nature, the sea. Never does he long for things mechanical such as those that have entranced Toad from time to time. As sensible animals, Ratty, Moly and Badger tend to steer clear of places where humans congregate. Therefore their lives remain simple and full of joy based on natural pleasures. There are adventures, not all of them comfortable, but they do not contain the elements of self-destructiveness that Toad's adventures do because they do not involve the human world of excess, imbalance and disregard for the natural order.

Thus throughout the novel, nature is extolled . In fact, frequently throughout the novel such natural objects as the river and the moon are personified, acting as conscious beings and therefore part of the holistic vision of nature presented here. However, Grahame is not so idealistic or simple-minded to believe that nature itself is always idyllic or safe. Moly's adventure in the Wild Wood indicates that, as does the take-over of Toad Hall by the weasels and stoats. Despite whatever satirical and social comments Grahame is making through these passages, he is also letting the reader know that nature is not the same thing as paradise. However, there is hope and balance and beauty shown in this novel through the "natural" animals that is quickly eroded in the Toad chapters, where police and prisons and hunger and danger proliferate at every turn.

In this novel, then, the human world is shown clearly to be a place where all real values have been replaced by the artificial values of the technological era. "Humanity" is rarely expressed amongst people; it remains for the animals to show true humanity and community. Grahame clearly believed that people have lost their sense of having an important and unique part to play in the wholeness that is the natural world, and the universe itself. By losing touch with their natural roots, they have lost touch with their true being and purpose, and therefore are spiritually adrift. The animals, however, are not. In *Willows*, their lives are full of purpose and meaning. They are fulfilled by simple things like the joys of a summer's evening, the warmth of a good fire on a cold day, the pleasures of food and companionship after an excursion or adventure. They do not require much but give a great deal. The discontented and bad-tempered bargewoman, the grasping, shifty gypsy, the warders at the prison all seem to be lacking in some fundamental way that the animals are not. Toad is presented negatively, not because his desire for adventure is bad, but because he cannot be content with what he has. He needs more and more things, and even when he has them, he is not truly content. His desires are excessive and therefore insatiable. In this way he represents the human adult who can never get enough of material things, who is never satisfied. The animals are more like children: easily satisfied and yet fulfilled in a way the human adults can never be.

Therefore the "Piper at The Gates of Dawn" chapter flows directly and consistently out of the vision that Grahame is presenting in this novel. At the beginning of the chapter, in an act of deep kindness and friendship, Ratty and Moly spend the night searching for young Portly, Otter's son, who has been missing for several days. Fearing the worst, they none the less search by moonlight both the river and its banks for any sign of the missing youngster. This act of kindness, together with their harmony with their natural world, leads them to an experience of Pan, the benevolent god who cares for and protects animals.

> Following music embued with divine beauty, they arrive at an island shrouded in awe and mystery and then, in that utter clearness of the imminent dawn, while nature, flushed with fullness of incredible colour, seemed to hold her breath for the event, [Mole] looked in the very eyes of the Friend and Helper; saw the backward sweep of the curved horns, gleaming in the growing daylight; saw the stern, hooked nose between the friendly eyes that were looking down on them humorously, while the bearded mouth broke into a half-smile at the corners; saw the rippling muscles on the arm that lay across the broad chest, the long supple hand still holding the pan-pipes only just fallen away from the parted lips; saw the splendid curves of the shaggy limbs disposed in majestic ease on the sward; saw, last of all, nestling between his very hooves, sleeping soundly in entire peace and contentment, the little, round, podgy, childish form of the baby otter. All this he saw, for one moment breathless and intense, vivid on the morning sky; and still, as he looked, he lived; and still, as he lived, he wondered.
> (Grahame, 1908, pp. 126-27)

Because of their kindness and harmony with their world, they have heard the call of the pipes that lead them to the god and the baby otter he is protecting. Because they answer that call, they see the god. "Transcendence of self and of the moment permits . . . the intensest consciousness of the immanent divine" (Gillin, 1988, p. 173). And because of the innate preciousness of their being, they are caused to forget.

> Lest the awful remembrance should remain and grow, and overshadow mirth and pleasure, and the great haunting memory should spoil all the after-lives of little animals helped out of difficulties, in order that they should be happy and light hearted as before.
> (Grahame, 1908, p. 127)

Here we have a natural order that, in its naturalness, allows the presence and action of the god and yet is made to forget its vision of the god so that it can remain truly itself.

In this view that Grahame is presenting, then, the being of each person is infinitely precious, and must remain truly itself to be able to participate fully in natural life. There is an awesome transcendency described in this chapter, yet that transcendency does not irrevocably alter the lives of those whom it touches. It aids, it touches, it moves on, leaving their lives fundamentally unchanged so that they can explore and develop themselves rather than becoming lost in the god, or in their experience of him. Surely this is the ultimate view of natural mysticism – a mysticism that in fact encourages only more naturalness, changing nothing of the essential nature of those it touches. This presentation of natural mysticism ties directly in with Grahame's view of nature as presented throughout the rest of the novel.

Yet, for all that, it is none-the-less a truly mystical experience that Ratty and Moly have. Through the agency of the god, and their own receptivity, they come face to face with the Friend and Helper. Through the power of his music they see the world through different eyes, colours and scents heightened, all of nature revealed in its truest splendour.

> On either side of them, as they glided onwards, the rich meadow-grass seemed that morning of a freshness and a greenness unsurpassable. Never had they noticed the roses so vivid, the willow-herb so riotous, the meadow-sweet so odorous and pervading.
> (Grahame, 1908, p., 125)

This vision is not one of imposed order, or of something beyond what is really there. It does not transcend their time and place. Rather, it reveals that place in its true glory, making plain the beauty inherent within each plant and flower they pass. The music and Pan himself, of course, are quite transcendental of the time and place. But what is revealed to the animals, and in them, is simply the deepest truths of the being of each. Ratty is revealed in this chapter truly as the poet he is. He is the first to hear the music; he is the one who hears the words in reeds that hold the last of the mystical melody. Moly is revealed as the deeply caring and intuitive creature that he is, as he is the first to decide they should seek for Portly and he feels the sadness of loss the longest after Pan has gone. Moly is the one to row them home, after Ratty falls asleep, exhausted from the experience they have had. Mole moves into a depth of character here that he has not revealed before, but which stays with him the chapters that follow. This movement is not a change so much as a release of what was already latent in him, glimpsed only occasionally in earlier chapters. Also during the chapter the comfortable and familiar diminutives, Ratty and Moly, are dropped for the more mature-sounding Rat and Mole, signifying that their truest and most essential selves have been touched through this experience of the god.

This mysticism is deeply spiritual but is completely natural, also. It reveals and augments what is already there in those who experience it. It does not alter them or demand of them. It simply reveals a greater reality both within the world at large and within them in particular.

This vision, then, is truly Romantic, truly pantheistic. The life they lead throughout the rest of the novel is, in some ways, a reflection of the essential harmony they have with the rest of their world, a harmony that exhibits the presence of the god in and of itself. Much has been made of this chapter as anachronistic in the context of the larger work: it is well-known that Grahame added this chapter and "Wayfarers All" to the book after he had written and compiled the rest. However, it seems that this chapter, rather than being an "addition," an "afterthought," is actually a coalescing, a summing up of the spiritual principles of natural harmony that inform all the other chapters. These principles permeate the whole book. The division between the Ratty and Moly chapters on the one hand and the Toad chapters on the other simply revolves round the fact that the former two animals live primarily within those principles while Toad, like most human beings, revolts against or, at the very best, ignores those principles. Thus in putting in the "Piper at The Gates of Dawn" chapter, Grahame has simply made explicit, in a passage of unparalleled beauty, his spiritual vision of the universe.

References

Coleridge, Samuel T. 1971. "The Eolian Harp" in *Samuel Taylor Coleridge: Selected Poetry and Prose*. Ed. Elizabeth Schneider. San Francisco: Rinehart. pp. 14-16.

Gillin, Richard. 1988. "Romantic Echoes in The Willows" in *Children's Literature*. Vol. 16. New Haven: Yale UP. pp. 169-74.

Grahame, Kenneth. 1893. *Pagan Papers*.

Grahame, Kenneth. 1908. *The Wind in The Willows*. New York: Charles Scribner's Sons.

Green, Peter. 1957. *Kenneth Grahame: A Biography*. London: John Murray.

Paglia, Camille. 1990. *Sexual Personae: Art and Decadence from Nefertiti to Emily Dickinson*. New Haven: Yale UP.

Pater, Walter. 1961. *The Renaissance*. Glasgow: Fontana.

Wordsworth, William. 1965. "Lines Composed A Few Miles above Tintern Abbey" in *Selected Poems and Prefaces*. Ed. Jack Stillinger. Boston: Houghton Mifflin. 108-11.

Cetacean Consciousness in Katz's *Whalesinger* and L'Engle's *A Ring of Endless Light*

J.R. Wytenbroek

Abstract: Both Canadian fantasist Welwyn Wilton Katz and American fantasist Madeleine L'Engle have written novels in which humans, in communicating with whales or dolphins, have been exposed to wholeness, harmony, unity, and pattern in the universe at large as perceived by cetaceans. While writing quite independently, these works show a remarkable similarity in their perception of cetacean consciousness. An exploration of these similarities shows the united mystical vision that writers from different backgrounds and beliefs can attain.

Keywords: communication, dolphins, Welwyn Wilton Katz, Madeleine L'Engle, perception, whales

Both Canadian fantasist Welwyn Katz and American science-fantasist Madeleine L'Engle have written about cetaceans in recent novels for young people. In Katz's *Whalesinger*, the author presents a vision of reality through the consciousness of a gray whale. In L'Engle's *A Ring of Endless Light*, the author presents a vision of the cosmos through the minds of dolphins. While these two novels are very different in many other particulars, including theme and general plot, there are two areas in which they are strangely similar. The first is the visions of reality that the authors present through the cetaceans, while the second is the type of characters whom they present in communication with the cetaceans.

The first comment that must be made about the presentation of cetacean consciousness in both novels is the inherent mysticism present in the cetacean vision. As Walter Stace defines it, true mystical consciousness

> involve[s] the apprehension of an ultimate nonsensuous unity in all things, a oneness or a One to which neither the sense nor the reason can penetrate. In other words, it entirely transcends our sensory-intellectual consciousness.
>
> (Stace, 1960, pp.14-15)

Fisher develops this idea when she says "concentrated on the transcendent moment of spiritual fusion with the deity or the universe, the mystic also 'loses' the self in wordless union with the Logos" (Fisher, 1990, p. 37). Consequently, authors of fantasy who try to write about the mystical experience "must continually make distinctions between what is and what can be described, between essences and their verbal approximations" (Fisher, 1990, p. 41). These statements can be applied to both L'Engle's and Katz's novels. In *A Ring of Endless Light*, the dolphins communicate the nature of the universal unity and of time to Vicky in a series of pictorial images, a device L'Engle uses for the mystic revelations in many of her novels. In *Whalesinger*, Katz's gray whale uses song and memory, also communicated through visual images, to explain her vision of a world unified into a coherent whole. Readers of these fantasies may be reminded of the writings of medieval mystics, particularly Hildegaard of Bingen, who communicated her experiences of mystical union with God through verbal images, paintings and music. Teresa of Avila, a much less "visual" person, gives far vaguer descriptions through words of her experiences with God than does Hildegaard, and frequently states that her experiences are inexpressible in language.

The visions of the universe communicated by the cetaceans in both books have very similar components, despite the different directions their authors are coming from. L'Engle, a somewhat theologically unorthodox Episcopalian, draws from a history of Christian mysticism, as well as from personal experience, to create the mystical passages that permeate her science fantasies for young people. In fact, she has said "[t]he fantasies are my theology" (L'Engle, 1979, p. 18). Katz has no particular religious affiliation. She says of herself that she is:

> not . . . a Churchy Christian. I love the ritual and the church building itself, because it is so laden with age and historical importance and myth. I do not, however, like the way the Church has used its power over the centuries, and I am not convinced in the least that it has a special pipeline to the divine.
>
> (Katz, pers. comm., p. 2)

This diversity of approach yielding similar perceptions of the mystical experience is not, however, unusual:

> There are several grounds for insisting that

intrinsically and in itself mystical experience is not a religious phenomenon at all and that its connection with religions is subsequent and even adventitious . . . [I]t is certainly the case that there can exist . . . a mystical experience naked and not clothed in any religious garb. (Stace, 1960, pp. 23-24)

The visions of reality presented in both novels revolve around two similar concerns. The first is the harmony or unity of all creatures, while the second is the non-linear nature of time. Both of these features are intrinsic to the true mystical experience (Stace, 1960, pp. 15ff, 25). In *Whalesinger*, the unity of all creatures on earth, from the beginning of time until the present, is part of the concept of the Song:

In the beginning, the Song sings, bright as the flashes of water-breathers in the deeps where few but we can see. We of the People listen to the Song and understand; we sing with the melody; we know what is and what is not. In this, we are alone. Listen now, Calfling. Hear the Song change. See what I see, the coming of the air-breathers that move about on two legs and have no wings. See them gather food in the shallows with their not-flippers-not-paws. Listen to them! They do not hear us; perhaps they cannot, but their minds can sing like ours. And we of the People, we listen to their singing, and almost we understand. But oh! Their songs are dark! Deep from the layers of the People's memory the mother sang these songs. The calf listened as the unadorned, easy melody of the Song thickened, losing itself in counterpoint and odd, dark tonalities. It was like the muddying of clear water by feeding. Confused, the calf moved closer to its mother. But there was more: later harmonies winding about the first, the Song growing stranger still, and darker.
(Katz, 1990, pp. 18-19)

The Song here is something which lies outside, beyond the whales. It is something which they alone can hear, of which they are a part. But all other things are a part of this Song too, even if they contribute only "dark" harmonies. In other passages within the novel, Katz refers to the singing of other creatures, either sky or sea creatures, and it is clear that such singing is all part of the great Song. "Harmony, Marty thought. A seamless, perfect join. The one Song played for once and for all the way it had been written" (Katz, 1990, p. 200). All things are part of the song, even the humans whose minds also sing as the whales' do but who do not hear the Song, and whose singing has "muddied" the song, causing the "odd, dark tonalities" that have appeared in the song. However, Katz's Song seems to be earthbound. There is not the same sense of cosmic harmony or unity here that permeates L'Engle's books. Instead, there is a strong sense that all things on Earth are part of a whole, a unity that goes beyond each but extends no further than the boundaries of our planet.

L'Engle's vision is very cosmic. Through her various science-fantasies, she has explored the unity of and within both the macrocosmic universe and the microcosmic. In her article "Subject to Change Without Notice," L'Engle identifies herself with astronomer Fred Hoyle when he says that she believes "in a total interrelation of all aspects of the universe, large or small" (L'Engle, 1982b, p. 334). In *A Ring of Endless Light*, she is more concerned with the macrocosmic, which she presents primarily through the dolphins' perception of the universe:

I rolled over onto my back and floated and Norberta moved her great body toward me until we were touching, and I was pressed against the beautiful resiliency of dolphin skin. And a whole series of pictures came flashing across the back of my eyes, in the dream part of my head.

The ocean.

Rain.

A rainbow, glittering with rain.

Snow, falling in great white blossoms to disappear as it touched the sea. And then the snow turned to stars, stars in the daytime, drenched in sunlight, becoming sunlight, and the sunlight was the swirling movement of a galaxy and the ocean caught the light and was part of the galaxy and the stars of the galaxies lifted butterfly wings and flew together, dancing.
(L'Engle, 1980, p. 276)

This description of unity begins with the earthbound but quickly moves into the universe at large and then flows back and forth from the Earth to the universe. It is as much in this pattern of verbal weaving as through the images that L'Engle communicates her sense of cosmic unity, a unity of which the dolphins are consciously and constantly aware, as Katz's gray whale is. As Vicky, the human character in communication with the dolphins in *A Ring of Endless Light* says, "Norberta was right. There was much she understood that was beyond anything I'd ever dreamed of" (L'Engle, 1980, p. 277).

The second aspect of mystic consciousness communicated through both novels is non-linear time. "The subconscious mind is uninhibited by linear time" (L'Engle, 1982a, p. 108). The mother whale in *Whalesinger* can tap into a subconscious, "racial" memory that goes back to the beginning of the existence of her species. (Gray whales are supposed to be "one of (if not the) oldest species of whale" in existence today.) (Katz, pers. comm., p. 2.) The simplicity of the Song at that point suggests a very early time, indeed. Therefore although she is aware of living in the present time, the whale has an unfettered access to all past times. Later, when she decides to stay in the bay to sing the repeating pattern of the Song that she sees shaping itself, she actively participates in the past revealed to her through memory, both repeating and shaping the Song herself. This ability to move within memory and to consciously recreate patterns of the Song long past suggests a non-linear concept of time. She does have a concept of the past, for she is aware that the previous pattern is a part of memory whereas her experience of the same pattern is part of her present life. However, the sense of pattern reaches beyond linear time into a much more circular concept of time – an inexpressible concept which is captured as elusively through Katz's whale as the concept remains elusive to ordinary human perception.

L'Engle's dolphins seem to exist primarily on an intuitive, almost subconscious plane as well. L'Engle argues in "Subject to Change" that until comparatively recently, we humans did not distinguish between the conscious and subconscious either, and so were more open to other realities.

> When Descartes wrote, "I think, therefore I am," he helped start us on a route where we extolled the intellect above the intuition, and thus created a chasm between the conscious and the creative subconscious mind.
> (L'Engle, 1982b, p. 333)

Because the dolphins have not divorced the conscious from the subconscious, their perception of time is different from ours. L'Engle is more explicit about the dolphin's perception of non-linear time than Katz. Because she believes that "[c]ontemporary physics is really mystical" (L'Engle, 1979, p. 19), she can use contemporary scientific terminology to express the otherwise inexpressible:

> "And then Norberta, with Njord echoing her, began making strange sounds, singing sounds . . . and they did something to my understanding of time so that I saw that it was quite different from the one-way road which was all I knew . . ."
>
> "She was trying to tell you about non-linear time . . . Time is like a river for most of us, flowing in only one direction . . . Physics isn't my strong point. But there's a possibility that time is less like a river than a tree, a tree with large branches from which small branches grow, and where they touch each other it might be possible to get from one branch of time to another."
>
> "Do you mean maybe for dolphins time is less — less restricted and limited than it is for us?"
> (L'Engle, 1980, pp. 276-78)

Typically, here L'Engle marries both the mystical perception of time and modern physics' explanation of the concept of time so that the second helps describe the first, at least in theoretical terms. In other books, such as *An Acceptable Time*, L'Engle shows the possibilities, both physical and mystical, that occur when two of those scientifically hypothetical "branches" of time touch each other.

One question arises directly from these authors' expositions of mystical perceptions. Why use cetacean consciousness to present these experiences? Amongst other reasons, both authors quite clearly state in their novels that humankind has chosen dark roads that have kept it unaware of its place in the greater pattern (except for a few notable exceptions). Katz speaks of our "dark tonalities" and dissonances, while L'Engle shows people as often selfish, greedy and corrupt, obviously set apart from an essentially loving universe. These traits effectively exclude most of us from communication with the world or cosmos at large, and other creatures in particular. However, as both writers also show, there are some of us who can still hear and understand other beings, if we listen with our spirits and respond with our intuitions, not our intellects. Essentially, then, even we dissonant humans belong to the unity and can overcome our dissonances to participate more consciously if we want to. As Gaudior the flying unicorn states in L'Engle's very mystical novel, *A Swiftly Tilting Planet*, "as long as there are even a few who belong to the Old Music, you are still our brothers and sisters" (L'Engle, 1978, p. 47). The two who are able to communicate best with the cetaceans in these novels are both teenaged girls who are strongly intuitive by nature. They react with intuition first, intellect later. They are both linked with teenaged boys who can also communicate with the cetaceans but are much more limited than the girls because their intellects are stronger than their intuition, but their intuition is still present to some degree. Both Vicky, the protagonist of *A Ring of Endless Light*, and Marty, one of the three protagonists of *Whalesinger*, are receptive to realities not strictly limited by intellectual concepts. Marty is particularly open, because she is a failure in school due to an unusual learning disability. In compensation, she has developed her facility for listening and receptivity to others to a point far in excess of the norm. Consequently she is at first the only one who can hear the whale's thoughts, although the whale can always hear the thoughts of human minds in her vicinity. Marty can, in fact, hear the whale from quite a distance away, and is not always sure of what she is hearing. She "hears" the whale's communication of memory to her calfling in her dreams, thus dreaming in images the centuries-old pattern which is being repeated in the bay. Later, as she begins to deliberately search the whales out and swim with them, she becomes aware of what she is hearing and is able to communicate directly to the mother whale, calling her, talking with her telepathically, glimpsing her bigger world and understanding it. "She could hear the one Song and know herself to be a part of it" (Katz, 1990, p. 168). In time Nick, her friend, is also able to hear the mother whale a little, but only when it is speaking directly to him, a rare event. He is also only able to hear the whale when he opens himself up to love, in a particularly deep way, with Marty.

Vicky is also able to communicate directly with the dolphins. She calls them, talks with them telepathically, glimpses their universe as Marty does with the whale. Both girls are aware throughout the novels of knowing certain things beyond knowledge, especially when they are in contact with the cetaceans. As Vicky tries to explain to her friend Adam when she knows something about the dolphins that she could not possibly know, "[i]t just came to me. As though Basil [the dolphin] had told me, in the language of knowing, not the language of words" (L'Engle, 1980, p. 175). This transcendental knowledge is often typical of mystical experiences. "The writers of mystical fantasy explore the acquisition of mystical knowledge" (Fisher, 1990, p. 46), which is exactly what both Marty and Vicky experience. This ability indicates their peculiar receptivity to the mystical experiences conveyed to them through their cetacean friends.

Further, both girls experience the "'melting away' into the Infinite of one's own individuality" (Stace, 1960, p. 24) so typical of mystics in their experiences of union with the One, or God, or the Infinite. When Marty swims with the whales she is completely in union with them. She is able to set herself aside completely, also, when she is with other people, and it is her intense concentrated listening that draws the needy Nick to her. "She made it happen by listening, listening with all of her being" (Katz, 1990, p. 164). Marty connects immediately and naturally with the whales because she already has a still and silent centre, open to hearing things beyond herself, beyond the immediate, beyond the expected. Her setting aside of self, an emptying of herself, in a way, makes her a natural candidate for the greater mystical experience of the dissolution of self that, in the long run, actually strengthens and develops the true being of the individual. The sense of melting is even more strongly described for Vicky, who is able to reach through to the other side of herself in an essentially mystical identification with nature:

> "And it's being part of everything, part of the rock and the sky and the sea and the wind and the rain and the sun and the stars . . ."
> "And you, Vicky? Are you still there?"
> "I'm there – but it's as though I'm out on the other side of myself – I'm not in the way."
> (L'Engle, 1980, p. 210)

Further, Vicky also gains a sense of herself through her mystical experiences with the dolphins. "I don't have a strong sense of my own centre, but when I'm with the dolphins, I do" (L'Engle, 1980, p. 202). She develops in her centredness and thus becomes more able to communicate with the dolphins, more open to mystical experiences. Thus by connecting with cetacean consciousness, both girls participate in mystical consciousness themselves, becoming connected with the universe in ways they were not before. For both of them, the cetaceans open up a universe of new possibilities of knowing, so that they are able to stretch and grow spiritually and as individuals. At the end of *Whalesinger*, the mother whale tells Marty

> [t]here are boundaries between us, little calf, but our songs meet. Whenever we listen we will hear each other, the soft harmony of two different singers looking at each other through clear water.
> (Katz, 1990, p. 200)

For a non-religious mystical approach, this statement becomes a promise of a deep communion with something greater than herself and humanity in general: the Song, which "is deep, it sings all things. All things add to it, though not all harmonically" (Katz, 1990, p. 200). This Song is essentially the same cosmic vision of unity that Vicky experiences through the dolphins, and which she is embraced by, at the end of *A Ring of Endless Light*: "we were both caught and lifted in the light" (L'Engle, 1980, p. 332), the same transcendental light that the dolphins have shown her, the same light her dying but spiritually powerful grandfather has called her to. Thus Song, dance, light all become part of the great mystic reality that the cetaceans are shown to be conscious participants in through both these novels, a reality that is available to those humans who will listen in silence and stillness, and who will respond to the universe, as the cetaceans do, with intuition and openness.

References

Fisher, Leona W. 1990. "Mystical Fantasy for Children: Silence and Community" in *The Lion and The Unicorn*, 14 (1990), pp. 37-57.

Katz, Welwyn Wilton. 1990. *Whalesinger*. Toronto: Douglas & MacIntyre.

Katz, Welwyn Wilton. Pers. comm. Letter to author, April 28th, 1992.

L'Engle, Madeleine. 1978. *A Swiftly Tilting Planet*. New York: Dell.

L'Engle, Madeleine. 1979. "Allegorical Fantasy: Mortal Dealings with Cosmic Questions" in *Christianity Today*, 8 June 1979. pp. 15-19.

L'Engle, Madeleine. 1980. *A Ring of Endless Light*. New York: Dell.

L'Engle, Madeleine. 1982a. "Childlike Wonder and The Truths of Science Fiction" in *Children's Literature*, 10 (1982), pp. 102-10.

L'Engle, Madeleine. 1982b. "Subject to Change without Notice" in *Theory into Practice*, XXI (Autumn 1982), pp. 332-36.

Stace, Walter T. 1960. *The Teachings of The Mystics*. New York: New American Library.

Index

Throughout this index Æ follows Z. The Greek and Cyrillic alphabets follow after the Latin alphabet. References to book titles will be found under the name of the authors. References to characters from books will be found under the characters' name. Names in bibliographic references are not indexed. The abbreviation ff. is used to indicate that references occur frequently throughout the remainder of the paper.

A

Abbott, Edwin A.: *Flatland*, 227
Abrazân: 43
Ace Books: 229, 295
Ace of Cups: 354
Achilles: 50, 365
Achyra: 102
Adam and Eve: 139, 162, 167, 171
Adams, Hazard: 256
Adams, Richard: *Watership Down*, 239-240
Adenine: 383
Adorn: 400
Adûnaic: 284, 291, 294, 296
Adundor: 399-400, 409
Adyan: 102
Aegnor: 159
Aeneas Sylvius Piccolomini: 347
Aeneid: see *Æneid, The*
Aerin: and Signy, 69-70
Africa: 334, 346
African tribesman: 53
Age of Reason, The: 419
Aging: of Elves, 323
Aglarond: 153, 339, 399-400, 410
Ah: 283
Ahania: 60
Aigle, Switzerland: 338
Ailin: 192
Ailinello: 192
Ailinisse: 191
Ailissen: 191
Ainu: 188-189
Ainur: 139, 141-142, 188-189, 272, 298-299
Aiqalin: 191
*aírman-s: 284
*aírmin-s: 284
Aix-la-Chapelle: 417
Akallabêth, The: 324
Alalmë: 283
Alalminórë: 283
Albanian: 284
Alboin: 40, 41, 43, 287
Alchemists: 414
Alchemy: 347-348
Alda: 188, 193
Aldar: 193
Aldarion: 276
Aldaron: 188, 192-193
Alder: 283
Aldiss, Brian: 425; *Billion Year Spree*, 419, 424; *Trillion Year Spree*, 424
Aldúya: 188
Alexander of Macedon: 264
Alfar: 95-96
Álfheim: 289
Alkar: 191
Alkarain: 191
Alkare: 191
*alkari: 191
Alkarissen: 191
All Souls: 353
Allan, James D.: *An Introduction to Elvish*, 266
Allen, Hugh, *Sir*: 13
Almr: 283
Alqalunte: 192
Alqalunten: 190, 192
Alqualondë: 161, 250
Altissima columna: 284
Alwin: 287
Amala: 283
Amandil: 40, 287, 299
Amazonia: 287
Ambaron: 193
Ambaróne: 193
Ambarónen: 193
Amberle: 100
*ambilōn: 283
Am(b)l: 283
Am(b)r: 283
*améla: 283
Amella: 283
Amelungenlied: 69
American Academy of Arts and Sciences: 238
American Cordilleran tectonics: 336
*amilōn: 283
Amino acids: 383
Amlach: 162
*āmlijá: 283
Amon Hen: 154, 326, 392
Amon Hen: 242, 325
Amon Lhaw: 326
Amras: 162
Amrod: 162
Amsterdam: 303, 309
Anarchism: 129
Ancrene Wisse: 295
Anderson, Poul: *The Broken Sword*, 96
André Deutsch: 14
Andreev, Daniil: *Roza Mira*, 223-224
Andromache: 365
Anduin: 319, 334, 336, 342, 396-397
Anduin Rift Valley: 336
Andúril: 146
Andvari: 64, 70
Angali: 288
Angamandi: 188
Angamandu: 188
Angband: 162-163
Angel: 286
Angels: 94-95, 348
Anglachel: 71, 165
Angles: 288
Anglican Community of the Resurrection: 348
Anglican traditions: 431
Anglo-Saxon: 282, 284, 286, 287, 288, 293, 321, 372-373
Anglo-Saxon burial mounds: 278
Anglo-Saxons: 279, 281
Angmar: 336
Angol: 286
Angrenril: 398-400, 408
Angrod: 159, 162
Anguirel: 165
Animism: in *The Lord of the Rings*, 134
Annatar: 324
Annunciation, The: 353
Anthroposophical Society: 347
Anæmia: 324
Apharesis: 196
Apokathastasis: 300
Apolausticks: 371
Appetite: in *The Lord of the Rings*, 108 ff.
Ar-Feiniel: 274
Ar-Pharazôn: 139, 168, 170, 273, 276, 325
Arabian Nights' Entertainments: 420-421, 423
Aragorn: 15, 65, 70, 109, 113, 122-123, 128, 137, 139, 142-143, 146-149, 153-156, 159, 161, 164, 170, 198, 203, 237, 249, 257, 259-261, 277-278, 318, 323, 334, 365-366, 384-385, 387-389, 424
Aravis: 365
Archbishop Cranby: 102
Archbishop Laud: 264
Archimagio: 49
Arda: 224, 272-273, 275-276, 299-300, 326, 331
Arda: 311
Arda Marred: 277
Aredhel: 159, 164-165, 274, 276
Ares: 285
Argentina: 10, 336
Ariosto, Ludovico: 227
Aristotelian Universals: 347
Aristotle: 412
Arkenstone, The: 415
Arman: 284
Armenak: 286
Armenian: 284
Armenians: 286
Armistice, The: 372
Armstrong, Helen: 9
Arnold, Matthew: "Forsaken Merman", 99
Arnor: 241-243
Arnor: 260, 338, 399
Artemis: 273
Arthur: 51; see also King Arthur
Arvalin: 190-191
Arwen: 99, 103, 128, 140, 143, 148, 153, 159, 161, 170, 249, 254, 257, 259-260, 276, 292, 365-366, 389
Arya: 286

Aryaman: 285-286
Asëa aranion: 198
Ash Mountains: 338
Ash tree: 283-284
Asimov, Isaac: 266
Askar Valley: 397
Askmaðr: 283
Askr: 283-285
Aslan: 236
Aslan: 364-365
Áss: 284
Astrology: 348
Atalantea: 190
Atalantië: 190
Athelas: 133, 156, 198
Atkins: 255
Atlantis: 134, 251
Atrocities: 248
Auden, W.H.: 90, 145, 207, 210, 228, 240, 269, 310
Audley Square, London W1: 358
Audoin: 41, 43
Augustan authors/novels: 419, 423-424, 429
Aulë: 160, 167, 299, 331-333; compariosn with Urthona, 59
Austen, Cassandra E.: 427-428
Austen, Jane: 424, 427-429; *Mansfield Park*, 428; *Northanger Abbey*, 428; *Pride and Prejudice*, 428; *Sense and Sensibility*, 428
Austin, Alfred: *Haunts of Ancient Peace*, 128
Austin, Vicky: 436-438
Australia: 10, 346
Austrian: 10
Authority Figures: in The Inklings' works, 364 ff.
Avallónë: 325
Azaghâl: 163
Azerbaijan: 248

B

Baal: 88
Baal-zebub: 88
Baars, Cees: 305, 308
Bacon, Roger: 346
Bad: in J.R.R. Tolkien's works, 247 ff.
Badger: 432
Bag End: 117, 119, 202, 204, 394
Baggins: 201
Baggins: 202
Baggins Society: 394
Baggins, Bilbo: 10, 15, 49, 61, 64, 66, 89, 116-119, 121-122, 126, 128, 133, 140-141, 145, 148-149, 152, 158-159, 161, 165, 196-197, 247, 249, 257-261, 277, 307, 317, 320, 330-331, 336, 338-339, 341-342, 365, 394-395, 415, 431; and mushrooms, 109-110, 112
Baggins, Drogo: 119
Baggins, Frodo: 15, 47, 49-50, 61-62, 64, 89, 90, 116-123, 127-128, 130-136, 141-146, 148-149, 151-152, 154-155, 159, 164, 198, 228, 236, 239, 249, 251, 257-261, 267, 277, 279-280, 299, 309, 315-318, 320, 336, 338, 365-366, 376, 384-385, 387-389, 392, 394-395, 424; and mushrooms, 109, 112-113
Bailey, Anthony: 228
Baker, Ernest A.: *History of the English Novel*, 427
Balder: 64
Balin: 396; Tomb of, 340
Ballantine Books: 229, 295
Balliol College, Oxford: 358
Balrogs: 112, 168, 332, 396
Balzac, Honoré de: 423
Bandersnatch: 368, 370
Banquet: 5
Banwaon tribe: 54
Baptism: 354
Barad-dûr: 237
Barahir: 259, 275
Baran: 162
Baranduin: 319
Baranduin ice-tongue: 338
Barbey d'Aurevilly: 347
Bardic Circle: 9
Barfield, Owen: 61, 268, 270, 320, 360; influence on J.R.R. Tolkien, 32, 37; *Poetic Diction*, 37, 74, 362; and J.R.R. Tolkien, 362-363;
Barrie, J.M.: 97, *Peter Pan*, 256
Barrow-wight: 121
Barzun, Jaques: 263-264
Basil: 437
Baths: 8
Battle of Britain: 294
Battle of Bywater: 340
Battle of Maldon, The: 209
Battle of Palisor: 283
Battle of Sudden Flame: 162
Baudelaire, Charles: 368
Baudino, Gael: *Strands of Starlight*, 102
Baum. L. Frank: *The Marvelous Land of OZ*, 419
Bawden, Nina: *Carrie's War*, 234
Bayley, Harold: *The Lost Language of Symbolism*, 416
BBC: 233, 295; Talks Department: 24
Be off: 196
Beagle, Peter: 385; *The Folk of the Air*, 101
Beardedness: and Genetics, 328
Beardlessness: and Elves, 324
Beckford, William: *Vathek*, 423
Bedworthiness: 357
Beerbohm, Max: *Zuleika Dobson*, 357
Behaviour: of Dragons, 411 ff.
Beit, Alfred: 266
Beleg: 71, 164
Belegost: 397-398, 400, 402
Beleriand: 296-297, 342, 397
Belgian: 10
Belgium: 294, 303
Bellamy, Edward: 427
Belle Dame sans Merci, The: Galadriel as, 97
Belloc, Hilaire: 264
Benchley, Peter: *Jaws*, 235
Bentley, Edmund Clerihew: 263 ff.; *Baseless Biography*, 263-264; *Biography for Beginners*, 263-264, 266; *The Complete Clerihews of E. Clerihew Bentley*, 263-265; *The First Clerihews*, 263; *More Biography*, 263-264; *Those Days*, 263; *Trent's Last Case*, 265
Bëor: 162
Beorn: 65, 108-110, 112, 338
Beowulf: 66, 90
Beowulf: 36, 63, 64, 68, 96, 133-134, 146-147, 209-210, 216, 256, 281, 284, 288-289, 294, 317, 362, 423
Beowulf-poet: 216, 218, 281, 317
Beregond: 155, 162, 248
Beren: 143, 159-160, 162-164, 169, 201, 224, 250-251, 257, 259, 261, 275, 299, 361, 365-366
Bergmann, Frank: 74
Bertenstam, Åke: 226-227
Berúthiel, *Queen*: 325
Besant, Walter: 264
Beulah: 59
Bias: in *The Silmarillion*, 158 ff.
Bible, The: 250, 416; as creative inspiration, 46
Bicentenary Tolkien Conference: 6
Bilbo: see Baggins, Bilbo
Bingo: 148-149
Biology: of Dragons, 411 ff.; in Middle-earth, 323
Bird and Baby, The: see Eagle and Child, The
Birmingham: 292
Birmingham Oratory: 292
Birmingham Oratory Retreat: 292
Birthday Party: 115 ff.
Bismarck: 85
Black Canyon: 338
Black Fleet, The: 389
Black Speech: 296, 394-395
Black-backed Gull: 175
Blackmalkin: 270
Blackwell's Bookshop: 5, 10
Blackwood, Algernon: 348, 354
Blair, Eric Arthur: 85, see Orwell, George
Blake, Leonard: holidays, 20-21
Blake, Maureen: holidays, 20-21
Blake, William: 45, 46, 49, 131, 368; *Book of Urizen*, 60; "Four Zoas", 59; *Jerusalem*, 61; C.S. Lewis' appreciation of, 62; *The Marriage of Heaven and Hell*, 60; mythology of, 59; parallels with J.R.R. Tolkien, 58 ff.; *Visions of the Daughters of Albion*, 60; Charles Williams' appreciation of, 62
Blanco: 279
Blavatsky, Helena: 347, 349
Blessed Realm: 140
Blessed Virgin Mary: 97
Blighter: 197
Blimey: 197

Blinking: 197
Bliss, Alan: 208, 210
Bloemfontein: 292
Blokhuis, W.B.P.J.: 307
Bloom, Harold: 368
Blue Mountains: 296-297, 330, 336, 397-399
Bluebeard: 217
Blunderbuss: 173, 195, 196
Blyton, Enid: 239-240
Bobir, Z.: 202
Bodleian Library: 173
Bogaard, P.H.: 305
Böhme, Jakob: 347
Bolger, Fredegar: 109
Bombadil, Tom: 49, 64, 112, 121, 125, 131, 143, 202-203, 257, 276-277, 315
Bonner, Nicholas: 101
Book of Mazarbûl: 340, 343
Book of Mormon: 230
Book Quenya: 187 ff.
Book-binding: in Middle-earth, 340
Boromir: 65, 89, 113, 127, 142, 147, 154, 156, 198, 237, 249, 256, 328, 366, 385
Bosnia and Herzegovina: 241
Bosworth, Joseph: 285
Bottom, Nick: 97
Boundaries: in J.R.R. Tolkien's works, 81
Bournemouth: 240, 295-296
Boyer, Elizabeth: *The Sword and the Satchel*, 96
Bracton: 358
Bradley, Henry: 173-175, 177-178, 181, 185, 195, 208, 372
Bradley, Marion: 102, 266; *The Mists of Avalon*, 100-101
Braiter, Paulina: 396
Brandir: 69, 71-72
Brandy Hall: 202
Brandybuck, Meriadoc: 15, 65, 66, 110, 112-113, 120-121, 146-147, 152, 154, 198, 218, 237, 315-316, 319, 343, 366, 384-385, 387-389
Brandybuck, Primula: 119
Brandywine: 119, 131, 279, 319, 342, 398-399
Branksome Chine: 240
Bratman, David: 9
Bratt, Edith: 292, 371; see also Tolkien, Edith
Bree: 55, 108, 112, 142, 152-153, 204, 339, 394
Brego: 147
Brezhnev, Leonid: 239
Brigade: 185
Brightness: of The Moon, 326; of Silmarils, 326; of The Sun, 326
Britannia, HMY: 301
British: 10
British Broadcasting Company: see BBC
British Communist Party: 238, 243
British Expeditionary Force: 303
British Library: 423, 425, 427
British royal family: 301

Brockenborings: 319
Brogan, Hugh: 319-320
Brontë sisters, The: 423
Brontë, Charlotte: *Jane Eyre*, 428
Brookhiser, Richard: 230
Brooks, Terry: *Elfstones of Shannara*, 100; *The Sword of Shannara*, 99; *Wishsong of Shannara*, 100
Browning, Robert: 123; "Abt Vogler", 20
Brynhild: 69
Brytta: 147
Buchan, John: 239-240, 279; *The Thirty-nine Steps*, 228
Buckhill: 204
Buckland: 151, 394
Bugge, Sophus: 283
Bugger: 196
Bulgakov, Mikhail: *The Master and Margarita*, 137
Burchfield, Robert: 195
Burgess, Anthony: 196, 229
Burgess, Guy: 91
Burgundy: 359
Burial customs: of Gondor and the North Sea, 64-65
Burke, Edmund: *Reflections on the Revolution in France*, 422
Burnett, Frances Hodgson: *The Secret Garden*, 239, 431
Burrow, J.W.: 233-234
Butler, Samuel: 427
Butterbur, Barliman: 112, 146, 152
Byron, George Gordon: 424; *Childe Harold's Pilgrimage*, 427; *Hebrew Melodies*, 423
Bywater: 389

C

Caedere: 131
Caedmon Records: 294
Caer Sidi: 101
Caerleon upon Usk: 350
Caith: 100
Calaquendi: 289, 297
Calder-Marshall, Arthur: 233
California, Southern: 5
Calma: 192
Calormenes: 236, 364
Calvinist traditions: 431
Cambodia: 241, 243
Cambridge: 295
Cambridge University Tolkien Society: 241
Camelot: 215
Cameron, James: *Rambo*, 239
Campaign for Nuclear Disarmament: see CND
Campbell, Amanda: 9
Campbell, Joseph: 137, 419
Canada: 10
Cannibalism: in Middle-earth, 110 ff.
Canopus: 420
Capitalism: 317
Captain Hook: 256
Caradhras: 66, 133, 318, 385, 396

Caranthir: 162, 274
Caras Galadhon: 130, 299, 316
Carcharoth: 163
Cardinal Bessarion: 347
Carey, John: 242
Carlsbad Caverns: 339
Carnen: 399
Carpenter, Humphrey: 48, 63, 168, 174, 207-208, 210, 213, 223, 267-269, 312, 314, 352, 362-363, 367, 369, 371, 373; *The Inklings*, 360, 226; *J.R.R. Tolkien: A biography*, 310
Carrock, The: 338
Carroll, Lewis: 39, 109, 263-264, 431; *Alice in Wonderland*, 227, 239, translations, 202; *Sylvie and Bruno*, 175
Carter, Angela: 130, 137
Carter, Douglas: 17
Cassirer, Ernst: influence on J.R.R. Tolkien, 32
Catholic liturgy: 346
Catholic University of Dublin: 295
Catholicism: and J.R.R. Tolkien, 23, 24, 31 ff., 53, 78, 217
Cecil, David: 360
Celebdil: 396
Celeborn: 65, 153, 156, 275, 365
Celebrían: 159
Celebrimbor: 249, 332, 340
Celegorm: 163-164, 260
Celtic fables: 416
Celts: 314
Ceres: 273
Cerin Amroth: 103, 136, 316-317, 320
Cervantes: 263-264
Cetacean Consciousness: 435 ff.
Chadwick, H.M.: 207
Chaldees: 411
Chance, Jane: 254
Chapman, George: *Homer*, 136
Chapman, Vera: *Blaedud the Birdman*, 14; *The Green Knight*, 14; *Judy and Julia*, 14; *King Arthur's Daughter*, 14; *The King's Damosel*, 14; *Miranty and the Alchemist*, 14; *The Wife of Bath*, 14
Charlemagne: 284
Charnock, Thomas: 411
Charrette, Robert N: *Never Deal with a Dragon*, 104; *Secrets of Power*, 104
Chaucer, Geoffrey: 46, 97, 214, 278, 383
Chequers: 371
Cherryh, C.J.: *Faery in Shadow*, 100
Cherubim: 94
Chesterton, G.K.: 74, 91, 263, 266, 358; *Collected Nonsense and Light Verse*, 266; influence on J.R.R. Tolkien, 32
Children: and the appreciation of J.R.R. Tolkien, 221
China: 346, 423
Chinese: 411, 416, 420
Chow dynasty: 412
Chrétien de Troyes: 270
Christ: 33, 112, 376
Christabess: 428

Christian Hermeticism: 354
Christian philosophy: 375
Christianity: and J.R.R. Tolkien, 53 ff.
Church of Ireland: 349
Church, The Established: 431
Cicero: 412
Circe: 99
Círdan: 165, 324
Cirith Ungol: 112, 143, 152, 384, 387-388
Cirya: 187, 189
Ciryai: 189
Ciryain: 191
Ciryainen: 192
Ciryais: 192
Ciryalin: 191
Ciryalínen: 192
Ciryalinna: 192
Ciryan: 188, 191
Ciryanen: 192
Ciryanna: 188, 192
Ciryar: 189
Ciryava: 188
Ciryö: 193
Clairmont, Claire: 424
Clapham omnibus, The: 426
Clark Hall, John R.: 209
Clarke's Law: 327
Clarke, Arthur C.: 266; *Rendezvous with Rama*, 423
Clarke, Lindsay: *The Chymical Wedding*, 137
Classical Humanists: 353
Classical thought: J.R.R. Tolkien and, 76, 77
Claude de St. Martin: 347-348
Cleasby, Richard: 284-285
Clerihew: J.R.R. Tolkien and, 263 ff.
CND: 238
Coalbiters, The: 63; see also Kolbítar
Cobbett, William: *Rural Rides*, 265
Cobweb: 97
Coghill, Nevill: 269-270; lectures, 21
Cold War, The: 234, 308
Coleridge, Samuel Taylor: 123, 315, 360, 368, 427, 432; *Christabel*, 99, 424-426, 428; "The Eolian Harp", 432; "The Rhyme of the Ancient Mariner", 432; *Rime of the Ancient Mariner*, 425; and Romanticism, 73 ff
Collins (publishers): 294
Colorado: 338
Colossus: 284
Colquhoun, Ithell: 353
Columbus, Christopher: 54
Comfrey: 267
Como, James T.: *C.S. Lewis at the Breakfast Table and Other Reminiscences*, 269
Companions of the Co-inherence: 353
Company of St. Anne's: 353
Conceptualism: 347
Conrad, Joseph: 124, 319
Consciousness: Cetacean, 435 ff.
Contextual levels: 257 ff.
Coolidge, Calvin *President*: 264

Coombs, Jenny: 325-326, 328
Corbet, Richard: "The Fairies' Farewell", 97
Cornwall: 417
Corpus: 109
Corpus Christi, feast of: 353
Cottage of Lost Play: 286, 296
Cotton MS. Nero A.X.: 213 ff.
Cotton, Rose: 389, 365-366
Counting: Elves and, 323-324
Craig, Amanda: 136
Craigie, William: 63, 173
Crankshaw, Edward: 28
Crawshaw, Christine: 9
Crawshaw, Richard: 9
Creation: Act of, 375
Creator, The: 376
Crick, Bernard: 85
Crick, Francis: 383
Crickhollow: 109, 202, 394
Crimea: 163
Critical response: J.R.R. Tolkien, 226 ff.
Crīst: 282
Crone: 273
Crossroads of the West, The: 388
Crowley, Aleister: 352
Crucifixion, The: 351
Crusoe, Robinson: 320
Cullis, Colin: 371
Cursing: in *The Lord of the Rings*, 196
Curufin: 163-165, 260
Cuyahoga: 131
Cwén: 286
Cwēnaland: 287
Cwēnas: 287
Cyberpunk: 103
Cytosine: 383
Czech: 10
Czech Republic: 9
Czech Tolkien Society: 10
Cædmon: 208

D

d'Ardenne, Simonne: 206, 210; *Þe Liflade ant te Passiun of Seinte Iuliene*, 291, 372
d'Artagnan: 104
d'Avigdor, W.P.H.: 263
d'Oyly Carte Company: 13
Daedalus: 238
Daedalus, HMS: 412
Daeron: 162
Dagnall, Susan: 26 ff.
Dagor Bragollach: 162-163
Dagor Dagorath: 299-300
Daily Telegraph, The: 130
Dain: 197
Dáin: 237, 338, 398
Dale: 201, 332, 398-399, 400, 404
Dance: 438
Dandies: 91
Danian: 296
Daniloth: 101
Danish: 283; J.R.R. Tolkien's knowledge of, 36

Dante: 39, 48, 140, 263, 359; *Commedia*, 356
Daoine Sidhe: 100
Dark-elves: 95-96, 102
Darkon: 411
Darling, Wendy: 256
Darwinism: 317
David and Goliath: 160
Davidman, Joy: 295
Davis, L.J.: 230
Davis, Norman: 213
Davis, Tom: 234, 238
Davy, Humphry: 263-264
Day, David: *A Tolkien Bestiary*, 330
de Givry, Gillot: 350; *Sorcery, Magic, and Alchemy*, 348
de la Mare, Walter: 97
de Lint, Charles: *Moonheart*, 103; *Spiritwalk*, 103
Dead Marshes: 336
Déagol: 119
Dean, Pamela: *Tam Lin*, 96
Deen, L.: 305, 307
Defoe, Daniel: 419
Del Mar, Norman: *Anatomy of the Orchestra*, 387
Delagardie, Paul: 357
Demeter: 273
Demons: 94, 348
Denethor (elf of Beleriand): 161
Denethor (Steward of Gondor): 49, 65, 111, 127, 140, 154-155, 342, 389, 424
Depth Psychology: 354
Deus otiosus: 300
Deverry: 102
Devils: 94-95
Dieulacres Abbey: 215
Dimrill Vale: 396
Dinosaurs: 411
Dior: 159-161
Disney, Walt: 133, 137
Divine Dance, The: 376
Divine order: 376
DNA: 383
Dr. Who: 240
Dodger: 104
Dol Goldur: 336
Dol Guldur: 275
Dolbear, Rupert: 363
Dolmed Mountains: 397
Dolores: 99
Dolphins: 435, 437-438
Dorethuriel: 104
Doriath: 161-162, 164, 168, 260, 365
Doriathrin: 296
Dorlas: 70
Dowden, Edward: 424
Drabble, Margaret: *The Oxford Companion to English Literature*, 422
Draco: 411
Draco Volans: 414
Dracon: 411
Dragons: Behaviour of, 411 ff.; Biology of, 411 ff.; Mechanics of, 411 ff.; Natural

History of, 411 ff.; in northern literature, 64
Drake, Nathan: *Literary Hours*, 427; *On Gothic Superstition*, 427
Drakos: 411
Drama: in J.R.R. Tolkien's writing, 79-80
Dranthon: 60
Drayton, Michael: 97
Dreped: 215-216, 218
Dresden: 236-237
Druadan: 154
Druadan Forest: 216
Drúedain: 55, 56, 297
Drûgs: 54, 55
Dryden, John: 46
Duane, Diane: *A Wizard Abroad*, 100
Dubhain: 100
Dublin Hermetic Society: 349
Duke of Dorset: 357
Duke of York, SS: 301
Dumézil, Georges: *Le Troisième Souverain*, 285
Duncan, Dave: *A Handful of Men*, 104; *A Man of His Word*, 104
Dundas-Grant, Jim: 360
Dúnedain: 151, 155, 324
Dunlendings: 54, 155, 276
Dunne, J.W.: *An Experiment with Time*, 39 ff.
Dunning, Tom: 210
Dunsire, Brin: 241-242
Dupin, Charles: 421
Durin: 204, 333, 396
Durrant, Anthony: 364
Dutch: 10, 301-305, 307-308
Dutch royal family: 301
Dwarfs: 94
Dwarves: 101, 110; and Jews, 237; Kingdoms of, 396 ff.; the Making of, 331, 333; in the "Narn i Hîn Húrin", 69, 70; in the *Poetic Edda*, 64; Psyche of, 330 ff.; in the *Volsunga Saga*, 69, 70
Dweomer: 102
Dying god: 362
Dyson, H.V.D. "Hugo": 294, 360-361, 363

E

Eä: 298, 300
Éadwine: 287
Eagle and Child, The: 293, 360
Ēar: 282
Earello: 192
Ēarendel: 282
Ēarendel: 282
Earendel: 311
Ēarendel: 251, 282, 296
Ēarendil: 56, 97, 134, 140-141, 143, 158-160, 164, 169, 224, 257, 260-261, 282, 289, 299, 325-326
Earn: 282
Earon: 284
Ears: 285
Eart: 284
Earth First!: 132

Earthly Paradise: in *The Lord of the Rings*, 139 ff.
Eärwen: 159
East Danes: 288
East Farthing: 319
East Timor: 241
Easterlings, The: 248, 276, 399-400, 408
Eastern mythology: 412
Eaton, Anne T.: 227
Ecocide: 131
Ecthelion: 162
Edain: 274, 276, 324
Eddison, E.R.: 39, 228, 294; *The Worm Ouroboros*, 353
Eden, 59, 139, 167, 364
Edoras: 319
Edward the Confessor: 264
Edwin: 287
Efreet: 94
Egil's Saga: 63, 65
Einhard of Fulda: 284
Eisler, Riane: *The Chalice and the Blade*, 275-276
Elaine: 101
Elanor: 316
Elbereth: 97, 102, 134, 140, 143
Elbereth Gilthoniel: 218
Elcryss: 100
Elcyion Lacar: 101-102
Eldaic: 134
Eldain: 191-192
Eldamar: 140, 188, 251, 289
Eldar: 189, 274, 276
Eledāi: 288-289
Elementals: 348
Elendil: 40, 41, 149, 224, 287
Eleni: 187
Elephant Man, The: 425
Elessar: 258-259, 394
Elf-human marriages: 95
Elfland: 96-97
Elijah: 123
Eliot, T.S.: 45, 123, 368
Elizabeth I, *Queen*: 51, 427-428
Elizabeth II, *Queen*: 301, 303-304
Elliot, R.W.V.: 215
Ellison, John: 8-9, 79
Elm: 204, 283
Elmbla: 283
Elmir: 282-283, 286, 289
Elrond: 66, 97, 131, 148, 153-154, 158-159, 161-165, 249, 256-257, 260-261, 276, 299, 332, 340, 342
Elston, Charles Sidney: 285
Elvea: 190
Elvenhome: 140
Elves: 54-56; Aging of, 323; and Beardlessness, 324; and Counting, 323-324; their Eyesight, 323; literary ideas about, 94 ff.; Neuropsychology of, 328; in northern literature, 64; role of, 81
Elvie: 190
Elvish: 8, 307, 314, 370, 388, 394, 395
Elvish Linguistic Fellowship: 288

Elvish mythology: 314
Elwë: 159-160
Elwes, Gervase: 13
Elwin: 40
Elwing: 158-159, 161, 164, 249, 261, 299
Embla: 283, 289
Emeldir: 250, 275
Emerson, Ralph: 368
Emyn Arnon: 336
Emyn Beraid: 325
Emyn Muil: 334, 336
Encyclopedia Britannica: 305
Enedwaith: 319
Engell, James: 75, 77
Englalond: 281
England: 9, 281, 286, 428, 301, 303, 395
English Faculty: 361
English mythology: 281 ff., 289, 311
English School Syllabus: 293
English syllabuses: Old English in, 206-207
English Yeoman: 279
Englishness: J.R.R. Tolkien and, 278 ff., J.R.R. Tolkien's view of, 126 ff.
Engraving: in Middle-earth, 341
Enitharmon: 60
Enlightenment, The: 345, 347, 368
Ennorath: 224
Enrof: 224
Enroth: 224
Ents: 156, 276, 277, 316, 340, 385, 387-388; and northern literature, 64
Entuthon Benython: 60
Entwash: 336
Entwives: 276-277, 365
Eöl: 71, 162, 164-165, 276
Eomer: 147
Éomer: 122, 147, 154-155, 156, 248-249, 275, 323, 366, 385, 389
Éomund: 147
Eönwë: 164
Eorl: 65, 275
Eorman: 285
Eormen: 285
Eormencyn(n): 284
Eormenrīc: 281
Eotenas: 216
Eowyn: 147
Éowyn: 15, 65, 66, 113, 127, 147, 198, 237, 248-250, 275, 365-366, 424
Ephel Dúath: 336, 338
Epiphanies: in *The Lord of the Rings*, 121 ff.
Episcopalian: 435
Erebor: 332, 336, 396, 398-400, 403-404, 404
Ered Luin: 324, 336, 338, 397
Ered Mithrin: 336, 397
Ered Nimrais: 388
Eregion: 332-333, 396
Eremon: 285-286
Erendis: 276
Eressëa: 59, 140
Erestor: 159
Erhan: 104

Eriador: 398
Eriador Plate: 334, 336
Erio: 284
Eriol: 40, 188, 251, 286-287, 365
Eriugena, John Scotus: 346
Erl-König: 99
Erlad: 398
Ermanagildus: 284
Ermanaricus: 284
Erma-s: 284
Ermenaz: 286
Ermensul: 284
Erminagildus: 284
Erminaricus: 284
*Erminaz: 286
Erminga-s: 284
Ermi-s: 284
Ermon: 282-286, 289
Errol: 40, 42
Eru: 44, 160-161, 272-275, 298-300, 332, 384, 388
Erúmëa: 190
Erúmear: 189
Escapism: 317
Esclairmonde, *Queen*: 98
Esgaroth: 149
Essay Club: 371
Established Church, The: 431
Estë: 273
Estolad: 162
Etayn: 216
Etaynes: 216
Eternal Man: in Blake, 60
Ethics: Norse, 65
Ettenmoors: 338
Eucatastrophe: 19-20, 73
Eucharist, The: 351, 353-354
Euclidean topology: 325
Eurasia: 334
Euti: 288
Evangelium: 19-20, 32, 73, 82
Evans, Robley: 200
Eve: 273, 364; see also Adam and Eve
Evendim: 398
Evendim fault: 338
Evil: in *The Lord of the Rings*, 222-224; in J.R.R. Tolkien's works, 88-89, 247 ff., 298 ff.
Ewart, Gavin: 266, 271; *Other People's Clerihews*, 263-265
Exeter College, Oxford: 295
Exodus: 210, 373
Experiment House: 365
Extinction: of fungi, 132
Eye of Sauron: 127, 146
Eyrbyggia Saga: 63, 65
Eyriès, Jean Baptiste Benoit: *Fantasmagoriana*, 424

F

Faërie: 311, 316, 320, 345-346; in J.R.R. Tolkien's works, 253 ff.
Fafnir: 64; and Glaurung, 69-71
Fairies: 94

Fairy-tales: *The Hobbit* as, 247 ff.; *The Lord of the Rings* as, 247 ff.
Falastanéro: 192
Falastur: 319
Fall, The: in the Silmarillion, 167 ff.
Fallohides: 151, 203, 279
Falmalinnar: 188
Falmari: 192
Fangorn: 140, 276, 388
Fantasy: as art form, 77-81; Nineteenth-century, 419 ff.
Fantasy Fiction: J.R.R. Tolkien's influence on, 99 ff.
Fantasy tradition: J.R.R. Tolkien and, 94 ff.
Faramir: 15, 65, 90, 109, 112-113, 140-141, 147-148, 154-156, 237, 239, 248-250, 277, 296, 365-366, 385
Farnell, *Mrs.*: 13
Farr, Florence: 348
FASA: *Shadowrun*, 103
Fascism: 317; and J.R.R. Tolkien, 236-243
Father Christmas: 293, 364
Faulkner, *Mrs.*: 292
Fëanor: 104, 158-165, 224, 249-250, 260-261, 273-274, 277, 296, 299, 366
Felaróf: 65
Female Authority Figures: in The Inklings' works, 364 ff.
Feminists: J.R.R. Tolkien and, 272, 274
Fermat's Last Theorem: 324
Ferny, Bill: 66
Fettes, C.D.: 226
Filostrato: 87-88
Finarfin: 158-159, 161-162
Findegil: 327, 342
Finduilas: 69, 72, 249
Fingolfin: 158-163, 249, 274
Fingon: 159, 162-163, 249
Finnish: 10, 292, 296, 321
Finrod: 159, 162, 249, 260, 299
Finwë: 159, 161, 249, 299
Fireworks: 330, 342
Fíriel: 59
Fírima: 189
Fírimar: 189
*fírimo: 191
Fírimoin: 191
Firisandi: 288
Fisher, Leona: 435
Flame Imperishable: 272
Flash brook: 215
Flensburg fjord: 286
Flet: 316
Flevo-hall: 304, 306-308
Flevo-restaurant: 304
Flieger, Verlyn: 88; *Splintered Light*, 276, 362
Flora: in the Lord of the Rings, 130
Fluvio-glacial sands and gravels: 338
Fonstad, Karen: *The Atlas of Middle-earth*, 400
Food: in *The Hobbit*, 108 ff.; in *The Lord of the Rings*, 108 ff.
Football: 217

Forbelegost: 397-398, 400, 406
Ford, Ford Madox: *The Heart of the Country*, 128
Fords of Bruinen: 142
Forest River, The: 397
Forgroth: 398-400, 408
Forlindon Plate: 336
Form: Medieval, 375
Forochel: 336
Forodor: 397-398, 400, 402
Forodwaith: 319
Forster, E.M.: 86
Fortune, Dion: 348
Foster, Robert: 170
Foucault, Michel: 116, 131; post-Enlightenment and, 115; *Power/Knowledge: Selected Interviews and Other Writings*, 115
Fouqué, La Motte: "Sigurd der Schlangentödter", 69; "Undine", 99
Four: significance of, 375-376, 383, 385, 388
Fowles, John: 132; *The Mantissa*, 127
Foyles Bookshop: 301
France: 359
Frankenstein, Victor: 419, 424, 426-427
Frankenstein, William: 424
French: 395, 423
French Revolution: 242
Freudianism: 317
Frey: compared with Radagast, 64
Freyr: 289
Friesner, Esther: 266; *Majyk By Accident*, 104; *Majyk By Design*, 104; *Majyk By Hook Or Crook*, 104
Frisians: 288
Fróda: 281
Frodo: see Baggins, Frodo
Frye, Northrop: 125
Fuck: 196
Fuller, Edmund: 226, 229
Fúmella: 188
Fumellar: 188
Fungi: extinction of, 132
Funk, Grace: 330
Furth, Charles: 26 ff., 145
Fussell, Paul: *The Great War and Modern Memory*, 86

G

Gabilgathol: 396, 398
*galadā: 187, 193
Galadhremmin ennorath: 218
Galadriel: 51, 65, 71, 90, 96-97, 109, 112-113, 121, 127, 135, 140-142, 146, 153-154, 156, 159-160, 162, 165, 187-188, 237, 250, 274-275, 277, 299, 320-321, 333, 365-366; as the Belle Dame sans Merci, 97
Galadrim: 316
Galdor: 131, 202
Galen, Claudius: 383
Galvorn: 165
Gamgee: 202

Gamgee, Gaffer: 117-119, 151
Gamgee, Samwise: 15, 49, 50, 56, 62, 98, 101, 110, 112, 120-124, 130-133, 135-136, 143, 152, 155, 197, 203-204, 237, 249, 254, 257, 259, 277, 279-280, 309, 316-318, 320, 332, 336, 338, 366, 376, 384-385, 387-388, 389, 394, 424
Gandalf: 49, 64, 66, 90, 101, 109, 111-113, 116, 118, 122-123, 131, 133-134, 136, 142, 145-149, 151-152, 155-156, 159, 196-198, 203-204, 236-237, 249, 257-261, 277-278, 292, 299, 307, 320, 330-332, 338-339, 341-342, 384-385, 387-389, 392, 424; Analogue, 239; as Ring-Lord, 60
Garden of Eden: 364
Gardner, Angela: 9
Gardner, John: 229; *Grendel*, 256
Gargouille, La: 417
Garner, Alan: *Stone Book Quartet*, 234
Gaudior: 437
Gauls: 416
Gawain-poet: 213 ff.
Geese: 342
Gell-Mann, Murray: 326
Genesis: 32, 250, 298
Genetics: Beardedness and, 328
Geneva: 424
Geochronology: 334
Geology: of Middle-earth, 334 ff.
Geomancy: 348
George Allen & Unwin: 84, 293-295, 304; correspondence with J.R.R. Tolkien, 26 ff.
Geraldine: 99, 424
German: 10, 395, 425, 427
Germani: 285
Germanic: 283
Germanic mythology: 281 ff., 288-289
Germanic tribes: 285, 288
Germans: 303
Germany: 347
Gernsback, Hugo: 419, 423-424
Ghân-buri-Ghân: 55, 56, 154
Ghosts: 95
Giddings, Robert: 238, 241; *This Far Land*, 239-240
Gilbert, Martin: *Holocaust, The*, 236
Gildas: *De Exicidio Britanniae*, 286
Gildor: 130, 141, 142-143, 153
Gilgalad: 149
Gilliver, Peter: 195
Gilraen: 260, 365
Gilson, Rob: 292, 371-372
Gimilzôr: 276
Gimli: 122, 128, 132, 145, 147, 153, 218, 237, 249, 253, 257, 278, 320, 323, 330-333, 338, 366, 384-385, 389, 399
Giovanni de Bardi: 385, 387
Gippus, E.: 201
Gladden Basin: 336
Gladden Fields: 396
Glamdring: 197; Luminosity of, 327
Glastonbury: 100

Glastonbury Tor: 416
Glaurung: 162-163, 412, 415; and Fafnir, 69-71
Glittering Caves of Aglarond: 339
Gloin: 197, 399
Glóin: 153
Glome: 361
Glorfindel: 142, 153, 158, 202
Gnomes: 296-297, 331
Gnomish: 283, 288, 292, 296
Go away: 196
Goat: 413
Goblins: 247-248
God: 298-300, 361, 375-376, 383, 435, 437
Godwin, William: 424
Goethe, Johann: 99, 368
Goldberry: 47, 48, 64, 276-277
Golden Dawn, Order of: see Hermetic Order of the Golden Dawn
Golden Walter: 99
Goldilocks: 108
Golding, William: "Envoy Extrordinary", 88; "Fable", 88; *The Inheritors*, 88; *Lord of the Flies*, 84, 85, 88, 91; *Pincher Martin*, 85; as a post-War writer, 84 ff.; *The Scorpion God*, 88
Goldogrin: 296
Goldsmith, Oliver: 419, 423; *The Citizen of the World*, 420
Goldstein: 86-87
Golgonooza: 60
Gollum: 61, 62, 66, 108-111, 113, 116, 118-119, 121-123, 127, 142, 148-149, 152-153, 155, 197, 202, 236, 247, 259, 277, 280, 299, 309, 338-339, 385, 424
Gondolin: 158-163, 165, 250, 261, 365
Gondor: 54, 56-57, 112, 152, 154-155, 237, 259, 260, 275, 318, 324, 332, 334, 338, 341, 388; burial customs in, 64-65; practices of Northern Countries in, 65
Gonne, Maud: 348
Good: in *The Lord of the Rings*, 222-225; in J.R.R. Tolkien's works, 247 ff.
GoodKnight, Glen: 8-9
Gopman, V.: 224
Gorbag: 111
Gordon, E.V.: 63, 213-215, 218, 293, 371, 372
Gordon, Ida L.: 213, 218, 372
Gorgoroth: 147
Gospel: 376
Gothic: 23, 292, 422-424, 427, 429
Gothic architecture: 422
Gothic fiction: 419
Gothic novel, The: 419
Gothic tradition: 421
Goths: 281
Gottlieb, Carl: *Jaws*, 235
Graff, Eric: 254
Grahame, Kenneth: 9, 109; *Pagan Papers*, 431-432; *The Wind in the Willows*, 227-228, 239, 431 ff.
Gram: 69, 71
Grammar: of Quenya, 187 ff.

Gramsci: 129
Grand Tetons of Wyoming: 338
Grassmann's Law: 181
Gray whale: 435-436
Great Haywood: 286
Great Whin Sill: 339
Greek: 395
Greek mythology: 412
Greeks: 411, 415
Green Chapel, The: 217
Green Knight, The: 90, 214, 216
Green, Martin: *Children of the Sun: a narrative of "decadence" in England after 1918*, 91-92
Greene, Deirdre: 80
Greenfield, Stanley B.: 209
Greenwood the Green: 397
Grendel: 66, 90
Grey Company, The: 389
Grey Havens: 103, 317
Grey Mountains: 336, 397-399, 400, 404
Greyfax: 146
Greylin: 397
Griffiths, Bede: 360
Griffiths, Marty: 437-438
Grigorieva, N.: 202-204
Grillot de Givry: 347
Gríma: 147
Grimalkin: 269-270
Grimm Brothers: 206
Grimm, Jacob: 283, 284-285, 269-270
Grimm, Wilhelm: *Deutsche Heldensage*, 69
Grishnakh: 111
Grundtvig, Nikolaj Frederik Severin: *Bjovulf's Drape*, 35; influence on J.R.R. Tolkien, 32 ff.; theology of, 32 ff.
Grushetskiy, V.: 202-204
Guanine: 383
Gudrun: 69
Guenevere: 87
Guerolt, Denis: 9
Guildford, Nicholas: 42, 43, 44
Guinea-pigs: 324
Guinevere: 90
Gulf War: 160
Gulliver, Lemuel: 423
Gundabad: 336, 397
Gunnar: 65, 69
Gunnison River, Colorado: 338
Gurthang: 71
Gutthorm: 69
Gwaihir: 385, 388
Gwathló Fault: 338
Gwathló ice-tongue: 338
Gwindor: 69

H

Haasse, Hella: 305-306
Haçi: 283
Hadfield, Alice: 352-353
Haggard, Henry Rider: 239, 358
Hague, The: 309
Haigh, Walter E.: *Glossary of the Dialect of the Huddersfield District*, 214-215

Haiku: 264
Haladin: 162
Halbarad: 146
Haldane's law: 326
Haldir: 153
Haleth: 162, 250, 274-275
Halflings: 202
Hālgoland: 287
Hall, Lesley: *Hidden anxieties*, 359
Hallgerd: 65
Halls of Mandos: 95
Háma: 237
Hamburg: 237
Hammond, Christina: 9
Hammond, Wayne: 9-10
Hansel and Gretel: 108
Harad Plate: 336
Haradrim: 56, 57, 127, 248
Haradwaith: 319
Harbelegost: 397-399, 400, 405
Hardcastle, Fairy: 364
Hardie, Colin: 360
Hardum: 396-397
Harfoots: 151, 203, 279
Harlindon: 336
Harondor Craton: 336
HarperBaggins: 395
Harrison, Fraser: 129, 132, 135
Harrison, Robert Pogue: 132
Harting, Piet: 304-306, 309
Harvey, David: 128; *The Song of Middle-earth*, 388
Harvey, Gabriel: 46
Harwalin: 190
Harwich: 301
Hassel, Sven: 235
Hasufel: 320
Havard, Robert E. "Humphrey": 267-268, 270, 294, 360, 363; holidays, 20-21, 24
Hawai'i: 336
Hayk: 286
Hayley, William: 61
Headington, Oxford: 240, 295
Heaney, Seamus: 123
Heath-Stubbs, John: 127
Heaton, R.: 9
Heaven: 346; J.R.R. Tolkien's view of, 254-255
Hebrew: 348
Hebrews: 411
Hecht, Anthony: 264
Hector: 50
Heimdall: 64
Heimskringla: 63
Heinlein, Robert: 266
Hekstra, P.A.: 307
Helcaraxë: 249
Helgeland: 287
Hêliand: 284
Heligoland: 286
Hell: 96, 346
Hellenistic Mystery Schools: 346
Helm of Awe: 71
Helm of Hador: 71

Helm's Deep: 330, 338, 399
Helms, Randel: 74, 200; "Orc: the Id in Blake and Tolkien", 59
Helpmann, Robert: 266-267
hem: 185
Hemingway, Ernest: 124
Hengest: 210, 286-287, 279
Henry V, *King*: 427-428
Herbert, Frank: 266
Hercules: 285
Herendil: 40, 41
Heresburg: 284
Herme: 284
Hermeren, Goran: 367
Hermes Trismegistus: 346
Hermetic Analogy: 346
Hermetic Order of the Golden Dawn: 345, 348-354
Hermetic world-view: 345
Hermeticism: 345 ff.
Herminones: 285, 288
Hermis: 285
Herodotus: 412
Heroines: in J.R.R. Tolkien's works, 252
Het Spectrum: 301-302, 304-305
Hewlett, Maurice: 432; *Song of the Plough*, 128
Hickman, Tracy: 103
High Elves: 141
High Fantasy: 95
Hildegaard of Bingen: 435
Hildórien: 162
Hill, Joanne: 265
Himalayas: 338
Hirmensul: 284
Hirmin: 285
Hiroshima: 234, 236-237, 239
Hīse: 192
Hīsen: 192-193
Hitler, Adolf: 241, 243
Hoards: 413
Hoban, Russell: *Riddley Walker*, 137
"Hobbit dinner": 302-304, 306, 308
Hobbit Games: 222
"Hobbiton": 10
Hobbiton: 394
Hobbiton Advertiser, The: 394
Hobbits: 95; Analogues, 239; compared with Icelanders, 64; prejudice and, 151
Hoeller, Stephan: 348
Hogg, James: 99
Holdstock, Robert: *Lavondyss*, 102; *Mythago Wood*, 102
Holland: 295; J.R.R. Tolkien's visit to, 301 ff.
Holland-America Line: 302
Hollander, John: 264
Hollander, Nicole: *Ma, Can I Be a Feminist and Still Like Men?*, 272
Hollin: 338, 340
Hollin fault: 338
Hollin Gate: 396
Holmes, Sherlock: 421
Holst, Gustav: *Hymn of Jesus*, 13

Holy Ghost, The: 354
Holy Grail, The: 351-352, 354
Holy Mother Vivien: 100
Holywell Street, Oxford: 294
Home Guard: 294
Homo ferox: 87
Homo sapiens: 87
Honeysuckle: 283
Honir: 70
Hood, Robin: see Robin Hood
Hook of Holland: 301
Hopkins, Gerard Manley: 123
Hopkins, Lisa: 359
Horizon: 325
Hornburg: 203, 385, 387, 400
Horsa: 279, 286-287
Hoskins, W.G.: 130
Hostetter, Carl: 288
Hott: 64
Housden, Valerie: 230
House of Beorn: 49
Howard, Thomas: 352
Howes, Margaret: "The Elder Ages and the Later Glaciations of the Pleistocene Epoch", 334
Hoyle, Fred: 436
Hreidmar: 70
Hrethel: 65
Hubbard, Ron L.: 266
Hudson Review: 228
Hughes, Richard: 29, 228
Hugo, Victor: *Les Misérables*, 256
Humours: 383
Hungary: 238
Huon, *King*: 98
Huor: 163
Húrin: 69, 71, 160, 162-164, 169, 415
Hussein, Saddam: 160
Huxley, Francis: 229
Huysmans: 347
Hy Braseal: 99, 103
Hyde, Paul Nolan: 371
Hydrogen Sulphide: 414
Hyperspace: 325
Hypnotism: 415

I

i-suffix: 188-190
Iceland: 336
Icelanders: compared with Hobbits, 64
Icelandic: 321, 427
Idhru: 285
Idhrubar: 285
Idril: 158-159, 165, 249-250, 365-366
Iliad: 281
Ilkorindi: 296
Ilkorins: 296
Illinois: 295
Ilmarin: 140
Ilúvatar: 96, 139, 141, 161, 164, 167-168, 193, 254, 273, 299-300
Ilúvatáren: 193
Imlay, Fanny: 424
Incarnation, The: J.R.R. Tolkien's view of,

82
Incas: 416
India: 347
Indis: 158, 249
Indo-European invaders: 275
Influence: of The Inklings on J.R.R. Tolkien, 367 ff.
Ing: 283, 287-288
Ingaevones: 285, 288
Inglis, Fred: *The Promise of Happiness*, 239-240, 242
Inguaeones: 288
Ingwaiwar: 288
Ingwë: 282, 288-289
Ingwine: 288
Ink: use of in Middle-earth, 341
Inklings, The: 63, 267-269, 293, 318, 356, 366, 368-371, 373, 375-376, 383-384, 392; their influence on J.R.R. Tolkien, 367 ff.; in Malvern, 20-21; and J.R.R. Tolkien, 360 ff.; walking, 22
Institute of Contemporary Arts: 243
Intellectual Beauty: 432
Interracial marriages: 128
Inverse-square law: 326
Inzilbêth: 276
Ioreth: 365
Iötnar: 216
Iötunn: 216
Ireland: 285-286, 294
Írima: 189
Irish mythology: 285
Irish Republic: 85
Irish Times: 230
Irmanseul: 284
Irmansûl: 284
Irmen: 285
Irmenseule: 284
Irmensûl: 284
Irmin: 284-286, 289
Irmingot: 284
Irminman: 284
Irminsul: 284
Irminsûl: 284-285
Irmintheod: 286
Irminthiod: 284
Iron Hills: 338, 398-399
Iron Mountains: 397
Irving, Washington: 423
Isaacs, Neil D.: 226, 230
Isaiah: 416
Isbar: 285
Iscaevones: 285
Isco: 285
Iscvio: 285
Isengard: 147, 336, 392
Isildor: 149
Isildur: 149, 155
Isis: 273
Istaevones: 285, 288
Istari, The: 324, 342
Italian: 395
Ithilien: 49, 152
Ivan-durak: 203
Ivan-tsarevich: 203

Ivy Bush, The: 151
Iynisin: 102-103

J

Jackson, Rosemary: 81
Jacques, Martin: 241
Jakobsen, Jakob: *Færøske Folkesagn og æventyr*, 36
James, Henry: 39; *The Turn of the Screw*, 429
Jammes: 350
Japanese: 10
Jasenu: 283
Javert: 256
Jeffery, Richard: 188
Jeffries, Anne: 346
Jeremy, Wilfred: 43
Jerm: 284
Jerusalem Bible, The: 295, 372
Jespersen, Otto: *Modersmålet fonetik*, 37
Jesus: 123, 273; and parables, 17 ff.
Jewish Qabbalah: 346
Jewish Scriptures: 123
Jews: and Dwarves, 237
Job: 298
Johansson, Calvin: 383
Johnson, Judith A.: 226
Johnson, Samuel: 60, 195
Jonah: 295, 372
Jones, David: 46
Jones, Diana Wynne: 235; *Fire and Hemlock*, 96
Jones, Gwyn: 287
Jones, Tom: 320
Jonson, Ben: 368
Jordanova, Ludmilla: 132
Jǫrmungandr: 284
Jǫrmungrund: 284
Jǫrmunr: 285
Jǫrmunrekr: 284
Joseph of Arimathea: 354
Joyce, James: 45; *Dubliners*, 123-124
Jung, C.G.: 250
Jutes: 288

K

Kafka, Franz: 423
Kainulaiset: 287
Kalaqendi: 296
Kalevala: 68, 281, 292, 310
Kalma: 192
*kalmali: 192
Kanuva: 190
Karneambarai: 189
Katerine: 372
Katz, Welwyn Wilton: 9; *Whalesinger*, 435 ff.
Kay: 88
Kay, Guy Gavriel: 230, 373; *The Darkest Road*, 101; *Fionavar Tapestry*, 101; *The Wandering Fire*, 101
Keats, John: 136, 427; "Adonais", 432; "Endymion", 99; "La Belle Dame Sans Merci", 99; "Ode on Melancholy", 99

Keble College, Oxford: 8, 339
Ker, W.P.: 213
Kerr, Katherine: 99; *Daggerspell*, 101; *Darkspell*, 101; *Dawnspell: The Bristling Wood*, 101; *Dragonspell: The Southern Sea*, 101
Khazâd: 324
Khazad-dûm: 316, 318, 332, 340, 396, 398-402
Khimiya i zhizn: 201
Khmer Rouge: 243
Khobbitskie Igrishcha: 222
Khuzdul: 296
Kilauea Volcano, Hawaii: 336
Kilby, Clyde S.: 127, 128, 295, 370, 373
Kilmeny: 99
Kilyanna: 192
King Arthur: 87, 156
King Edward's School: 292, 371
King, Francis: 229
Kingdoms: of Dwarves, 396 ff.
Kingsfoil: 198
-kins: 185
Kipling, Rudyard: 128, 239-240; "Cold Iron", 102; *Jungle Book, The*, 240; *Puck of Pook's Hill*, 97; *Rewards and Fairies*, 97, 99
Kircher, Athanasius: 412
Kiryasse: 191
Kiryo: 193
Kistyakovskiĭ, A.: 201-202
Knight's Low: 215
Knight, Gareth: 74
Koi: 189
Koire: 189
Kolbítar: 372; see also Coalbiters, The
Kōpas: 192
Kôr: 296
Korean War: 239
Koreldar: 296
Korins: 296
Korn, Eric: 229
Kortirion: 286
Koshelev, S.: 201, 222
Krakatoa: 336
Kuaknom: 103
Kullervo: 292
Kulukalmalínen: 192
Kuluvai: 189
Kwakiutl: 56

L

L'Engle, Madeleine: 9; *A Ring of Endless Light*, 435 ff.; *A Swiftly Tilting Planet*, 437
La Tungar, Argentina: 336
Labour Party: 238
Lacon, Ruth: 411
Lady Esclairmonde: 102
Lady Margaret Hall: 12
Lady of Shalott: 101
Lady of the Green Kirtle, The: 364, 366
Laiqa: 191
Laiqali: 191

Laiquendi: 103
Lake District: 427
Lake Evendim: 338
Lake Geneva: 424
Lake Núrnen: 155
Lalm: 283
Lalmir: 283
Lambers, H.W.: 306-309
Lamia: 99
Lammasethen: 187
Lamp-black: , 341
Lancashire Fusiliers: 85
Lancelot: 101; see also Sir Lancelot
Landar: 189
Landnamabok: 65
Lang-Sims, Lois: 367
Lange, Daniël de: 305
Langland, William: 46
Language: 384
Language (noun): 196, 198
Languages: Tree of, 187
Langwell: 397
Larm: 283
Larus marinus: 175
Lasse: 187, 189-190
Lasselin: 191
Lasselínen: 192
Lasselī: 187
Lassen: 191
Lassenen: 192
Lasser: 190
Lasset: 187
Lassi: 189-190
Lassin: 191
Lassínen: 192
Lassī: 187
Latin: 284, 292, 303, 311, 395
Laurelin: 326
Laurinquë: 242
Lawrence, D.H.: 357-358
Laxdale Saga: 63, 65
Layamon: 383
Le Guin, Ursula K.: 235, 266; *A Wizard of Earthsea*, 239, 415
Leah, Menion: see Menion Leah
Leap Year: 417
Lear, Edward: 264
Leavis, F.R.: 45
Leavis, Queenie H.: 357-358
Leeds: 291-293, 361
Leeds University: 293
Leek: 215
Leet: 417
LeFevre, Karen Burke: 369
Legendarium: 310 ff.
Legolas: 122, 128, 132, 142-143, 145, 147, 153, 168, 203, 278, 317, 320, 323-324, 366, 384-385, 388-389
Leif Erikson: 64
Lembas: 112, 323; chemical analysis of, 324
Lenéme: 188
Lévi, Eliphas: 347-348
Levi, Peter: and visionary poetry, 45, 46

Lewis, Alex: 76
Lewis, C.S.: 74, 145, 222, 224, 226-228, 233, 250, 269-270, 293-295, 352-353, 356, 360-361, 365-372, 375-376, 384, 392, 431; appreciation of Blake, 62; *Boxen*, 371; *The Discarded Image*, 383; *English Literature in the Sixteenth Century*, 294; *Essays presented to Charles Williams*, 360, 362; *An Experiment in Criticism*, 361, 376; Female Authority Figures in his works, 364 ff.; *The Four Loves*, 360; holidays, 20-21; *The Horse and His Boy*, 364-365; *The Last Battle*, 236, 364, 383; *Latin Letters*, 362; lectures, 21; *The Lion, the Witch and the Wardrobe*, 98, 364; *Miracles*, 383; on morals, 66; *Out of the Silent Planet*, 85, 87, 293; *Perelandra*, 294; *Pilgrim's Regress*, 293; post-Enlightenment and, 115; as a post-War writer, 84 ff.; *The Problem of Pain*, 360; Science Fiction, awareness of, 424; *The Silver Chair*, 364; *Suprised by Joy*, 361; *That Hideous Strength*, 84-87, 90, 294, 353, 358, 362, 364, 366, 369; *Till We Have Faces*, 362; and J.R.R. Tolkien, 25, 361-362 *The Voyage of the Dawn Treader*, 364; *Voyage to Venus*, 86, 89, 90; "What Chaucer really did to *Il Filostrato*", 87
Lewis, Matthew Gregory "Monk": 422, 426; *Monk, The*, 427; *Tales of Wonder*, 426
Lewis, Sinclair: *Babbit*, 293
Lewis, Warren "Warnie": 294, 360, 363; holidays, 20-21
Ley-lines: 416
Leyse: 101
Lhammas: 187
Lhûn: 397-398
li-suffix: 188
Library Association Record: 243
Lied vom Hürnen Seyfrid, Das: 69
Light: 438
Light Brigade, The: 163
Light-elves: 95-96, 102, 289
Lilith: 99
Lily Maid of Astolat: 101
Limericks: 265
Limpë: 287-288
Lindar: 296
Lindir: 261
Lindsay, David: *Voyage to Arcturus*, 137
Lintuilindova: 188
Lios-alfar: 95, 101
Lipton, Leonard: *Puff the Magic Dragon*, 411
Lírinen: 192
Lisse-miruvóreva: 188
Listener, The: 230, 233
Lithgoroth: 397-398, 400, 402
Lithuanian: 284
Little Red Riding Hood: 108
Liverpool City Council: 248
Ljós-alfar: 288-289

Lobdell, Jared: *A Tolkien Compass*, 200
Locke, John: 77
Loewenthal, John: 283
Logres: 364
Loki: 70, 296; compared with Saruman, 64
London: 358, 371
Lonely Mountain, The: 332, 336, 398-399
Long Lake, The: 338
Longbottom Leaf: 307
Lórien: 71, 96, 102, 132, 142-143, 153, 156, 159, 237, 249, 251, 275, 318, 333, 396
Los: and his spectre, 62
Lótefalmarínen: 192
Lothlórien: 49, 112, 121, 130, 136, 142, 153, 202, 253, 259, 315-316, 320, 342, 385, 389, 365-366
Lovecraft, H.P.: 350
Lowdham, Arundel: 42, 43, 44, 363
Lucas, George: *Star Wars*, 137, 239
Lucifer: 170-171, 296, 297
Luddites: 324
Luftwaffe: 303
Lully, Raymond, Bl.: 346, 352
Luminosity: of Glamdring, 327; of Orcrist, 327; of Sting, 327
Lung: 411
Lungane: 192
Luthany: 283, 287-288
Luther, Martin: 347
Lúthien: 143, 158-161, 163, 201, 204, 251, 254, 257, 259-261, 275-277, 292, 299, 361, 365-366
Luvah: compariosn with Melkor, 59, 60
Lycett, C.V.L.: 371
Lyngbye, Hans Christian: *Færøiske Qvæder om Sigurd Fofnersbane og hans Æt*, 36
Lyonya: 103
Lytton, Edward George: 427

M

Mabey, Richard: 132, 135
Mabinogion, The: 99, 281
Mablung: 162
MacDonald, George: 74, 99, 227-228; *The Golden Key*, 295; influence on J.R.R. Tolkien, 32; *The Princess and the Goblin*, 431Machen, Arthur: "The Great God Pan", 351
Machen, Arthur: 345, 350-354; *Hieroglyphics*, 352; "The Novel of the White Powder", 351; "The White People", 351
MacLean, Donald: 91
Macpherson, James: 60
MacQueen, John: *Numerology*, 376
Macrobius: *Commentary of The Dream of Scipio*, 376
Madder: , 341
Maecenas: 327
Maedhros: 161-164, 261
Maeglin: 160, 162-165, 250
Magdalen Bridge: 13
Magdalen College, Oxford: 293, 360

Maggot, *Farmer*: 119, 151
Magic: Ritual, 348
Magical world-view: 345
Maglor: 164
Magriel, Cynthia: 348
Maiar: 365, 388
Malacandra: 361
Malina: 189
Malinai: 189, 191
Mallarmé: 350
Mallorn: 5, 8, 234-235, 324
Mallom: 316
Mallory, Thomas: 89, 227; *Morte d'Arthur*, 198
Malvern: and The Inklings, 21-22
Mampadayag: 54
Man in the Moon, The: 311
Manat: 196
Mandel, Jerome: 209
Mandos: 162, 169-170, 251, 260, 273, 299
Manichaeism: 298, 300
Manor Road, Oxford: 294
Manwë: 139, 273, 274, 299, 388; compariosn with Urizen, 59
Manyu: 102
Mar: 190
Marcho: 279
Marquette University: 295
Marriages: elf-human, 95
Mars: 285, 424
Martian: 420
Martinique: 336
Marxism: 317
Marxism Today: 241
Máryat: 188
Masefield, John: *The Midnight Folk*, 270
Mask: 425
Masson, David: 89, 90, 228
Materialism: 347
Mathers, Macgregor, *Dr.*: 348, 353
Mathew, Gervase: 268-270
Matorina, V.: 202, 204
Maturin, Charles Robert: 423
Maudlin, Lynn: 9, 369
May Day: 416
Mayne, William: 239
McCaffrey, Anne: 266
McIntosh, Pat: 336
McLaren, Duncan: 336
McLeish, Kenneth: 241
McNeile, H.C.: see Sapper
Mechanics: of Dragons, 411 ff.
Mecklenburgh Square, London WC1: 358
Medieval: 422
Medieval analogies: 376
Medieval authors: 383
Medieval form: 375
Medieval patterns: 376
Medieval writers: 383
Meduseld: 320
Melian: 71-72, 158-160, 162, 165, 260, 365-366
Melko: 19, 282, 296
Melkor: 139, 160-161, 167-170, 247, 249-250, 272-274, 276-277, 297-299, 384; comparison with Luvah, 59
Melville, Herman: *Moby Dick*, 137
Menegroth: 153, 163
Menion Leah: 99
Mephistopheles: 90
Mercury: 285
Mereth Aderthad: 162
Meril-i-Turinqi: 365
Meringer, Rudolf: 284
Merlin: 103, 366
Merlyn: 87-88
Mermaids: 94
Merry: see Brandybuck, Meriadoc
Merton College, Oxford: 295-296, 360
Merton Professor of English Language and Literature: 206-207
Mesopotamia: 288
Messianic hope: 299
Michel Delving: 320
Middle Ages: 376, 383, 417
Middle English: 372-373
Middle-earth: Biology in, 323; Bookbinding in, 340; Engraving in, 341; Geology of, 334 ff.; Ink, use and production of in, 341; Paper, use of in, 340-342; Parchment, use of in, 342; Pens, use of in, 341-342; Physics of, 323 ff.; Printing in, 324, 342-343; Science in, 323; Scribes in, 342; Scrolls, use of in, 340, 342; Silk, use of in, 341; Technology in, 323; Tectonics in, 334 ff.; Vellum, use of in, 340; Vulcanism in, 336; Writing technologies in, 340 ff.
Middle-earth studies: 8
Midgewater Marshes: 338
Milton, John: 45-47, 49-51, 364; "L'Allegro", 97; *Comus*, 49; *Paradise Lost*, 89-90
Milwaukee: 295
Mîm: 70, 72, 160-161
Minas Morgul: 121
Minas Tirith: 123, 133, 154-156, 237, 258-261, 317, 320, 331, 341, 365, 388-389, 394
Minhiriath fault: 338
Minkowski topology: 325
Mir: 192
Mirfield Fathers, The: 348
Miriam: 102
Míriel: 249-250, 366
Mirkwood: 110, 149, 202, 336
Mirror of Galadriel, The: 325-326
Miruvóreva: 188, 192
Misselthwaite Manor: 431
Mistletoe Farm: 240
Misty Mountains: 292, 336, 338-339, 396-397
Mitchison, Naomi: 89, 155, 228-229
Mithlond: 399
Mithril: 328, 332, 338
Möbius, Hans: *The Gothic Romance*, 427
Mole: 434, 432-434
Mont Pelée, Martinique: 336

Moon, Elizabeth: *The Deed of Paksenarrion*, 102
Moon, The: Brightness of, 326
Moorcock, Michael: 211
Moore, *Mrs.*: 294
Moorman, Charles: 63
Morannon: 110
Mordor: 49, 57, 59, 62, 110, 112-113, 115-116, 122, 124, 127, 129, 131, 133, 135, 143-144, 150, 155-156, 234, 236, 238, 242-243, 257, 259, 280, 307, 309, 320, 336, 365, 385, 388-389
Mordor Plate: 334, 336, 338
More of Morehall: 411
Morgaine: 100
Morgan le Fay: 100-101, 104
Morgan, Francis *Father*: 292
Morgoth: 57, 70, 71, 95-96, 143, 161-164, 169-170, 224, 237, 251, 260-261, 275-276, 299-300, 334, 365
Moria: 122, 142-143, 237, 318, 320, 324, 338-339-341
Moriqendi: 296
Moriquendi: 160, 297
Morland, Catherine: 428-429
Morna: 190
mornai: 190
Morne: 190
Morning Star, The: 326
Morris, William: 128, 227, 243; *News From Nowhere*, 279; *Wood Beyond the World, The*, 99
Morus, Iwan Rhys: 241-242
Morwen: 70, 71, 164, 249, 365
Moses: 123
Moth: 97
Mount Doom: 123, 280, 336, 338, 387-388
Mountain and Sea Classic: 412
Mugabe, Robert: 235
Muir, Edwin: 89-91, 211
Mûmak: 141
Murav'ëv, V.: 200-204, 223; "Tolkien i kritiki", 200
Murray, Gilbert: 13
Murray, James: 173
Murray, Robert, SJ: 331
Music of the Ainur: 59
Mussolini, Benito: 242
Mustardseed: 97
Mycenae: 156
Myratana: 60
Mysti: 104
Mysticism: 346; Natural, 431 ff.
Mythcon: 9, 10
Mythlore: 5-6, 15, 273
Mythology: Eastern, 412; English, 281 ff.; Germanic, 281 ff.; Greek, 412; J.R.R. Tolkien's use of the word, 310 ff.
Mythopoeic Conferences: 5
Mythopoeic nature: 375
Mythopoeic Society, The: 5, 8-9, 15, 394

N

Naga: 411

Nagibin, Yu.: 201
Naiads: 94
Naifs: 91-92
Namafjall, Iceland: 336
Namárië: 188
Nandin: 188
Nandini: 188
Nargothrond: 161, 164
Narnia: 236, 361, 364
Narqelion: 188-191, 193
Narrative levels: 256 ff.
Narrator: the voice of the, 80
Nash, Ogden: 266
Nathan, the prophet: 17
Nation: 228, 238-239
National Review: 230
Natural History: of Dragons, 411 ff.
Natural Mysticism: 431 ff.
Naturphilosophie: 347
Nauglamír: 164
Naugrim: 161, 324
Nayda: 102
Nazgûl: 113, 133, 143, 168, 198, 365, 392
Nazis: 303, 395
Neave, Jane: 295
Needlehole: 319
Néka: 190
*nékai: 190
Néké: 190
Nell: 253
Neo-Paganism: 346, 431
Neo-pantheists: 432
Neo-Platonism: 346-348
Neo-Platonist: J.R.R. Tolkien as, 80
Neolithic societies: 275
Neoplatonic Universals: 346
Nepal: 338
Nerdanel: 273
Nerwen: 274
Nesbit, Edith: 348, 354, 431; *The Railway Children*, 239
Nessa: 273
Ne·súme: 188
Netherlands, The: 301, 303
Neuropsychology: of Elves, 328
Nevyn: 101
New College, Oxford: 295
New Physics: 354
New Republic: 230
New Statesman: 228, 238-239
New Testament: 123
New Year's Day: 8
New York: 347
New York Times Book Review: 227-229
New Zealand: 10
Newbolt, Henry: *The Old Country*, 128
Newby, Vivas: 24
Nibelungenlied: 68, 69, 71, 281
Nibs: , 341-342
Nicaragua: 243
N.I.C.E.: 86-87
Nicholas of Cusa: 347
Nichols, Ashton: *The Poetics of Epiphany: Nineteenth-Century Origins of the Modern Literary Movement*, 123
Nienna: 164, 273, 387
Nienor: 69, 71, 250, 415
Nier: 188
Nierme: 188
Nigerian: 10
Niggle: 201, 253-255
Niggle's Parish: 253-254
Nimruzīr: 43
Nin: 190
Nindalf Basin: 334, 336
Nineteenth-century: Fantasy and Science Fiction, 419 ff.
Níniel: 68
Ninque: 190
Ninqui: 190
Niphredil: 316
Nirnaeth: 160, 165
Nirnaeth Arnoediad: 169, 332
Nitzsche, Jane: see Chance, Jane
Niven, Larry: 266
Njal: 324
Njal's Saga: and *The Lord of the Rings*, 63 ff.
Noad, Charles: 9
Nogrod: 397, 400, 402
Noldo: 188
Noldoli: 188-189 191, 296, 331
Noldor: 103, 189, 274, 296-297, 299
Noldorin: 284
Nominalism: 347
Nont: 214, 216
Norman: 287
Norse ethics: 65
Norse Mythology: 427
Norsemen: 324
North Rhûn Fault: 338
Northern Tolkien Festival: 10
Northern Venture, A: 174
Northmoor Road, Oxford: 294
Norwegian: 10, 287
Notion Club: 358, 360, 363
Novel of Doctrine, The: 419
Nowell, Lawrence: 216
Nuallan: 100
Númenna: 192
Númenor: 134, 170, 248, 272, 275-276, 287, 292-293, 296, 300, 336, 363, 367

O

O'Brien: 86-88
Oak-gall: , 341
Oakenshott, Michael: 368
Oberon: 96-97
Observer: 229
Occam's Razor: 325
Odain Saker: 99
Odin: 64, 69, 70, 427
Óðinn: 285
Oedipus: 68-69
Ōhthere: 287
Oikos: 131
Oilima: 191
Oilimain: 191
Oilimaisen: 191-192
Oithona: 60
Oklahoma: 266
Old English: 282, 284-288, 292, 296, 314; in English syllabuses, 206-207
Old English Studies: J.R.R. Tolkien and, 206 ff.
Old Forest, The: 315
Old Gorbadoc: 119
Old High German: 284
Old Hobden: 98
Old Icelandic: 284
Old Man Willow: 64, 66, 110, 130, 204, 315
Old Music: 437
Old Noakes: 119
Old Noldorin: 284
Old Norse: 284-285, 287-288, 292, 321, 372
Old Slavic: 284
Old Testament: 298
Old Toby: 307
Oldbucks, The: 342
Oldershaw, L.R.F.: 263
Olwë: 159, 162
Ondoisen: 191
*ondoissen: 191
Ondoli: 191
Ondolissen: 191
One Ring, The: 341; analogues of, 239
Onions, Charles: 173, 182
Oothoon: 60
Opening Ceremonies: 5
Oppenheimer, Robert J: 116
Orang-utans: 105
Orc: in Blake and Tolkien, 59
Orc-thyrs: 247
Orcrist: 197; Luminosity of, 327
Orcs: 96, 247-248; Analogues, 239; portrayal of, 327
Order: 383
Ordered Four: in J.R.R. Tolkien's fiction, 375 ff.
Ordnance Survey: 215
Ōre: 191
Oregon: 104
Ōresse: 191
Orie: 284
Orienta; romances: 423
Origen: 346
Orior: 284
Orkish: 296
Orks: 104
Ornus: 283
Orodreth: 159
Orodruin: 49, 336, 388
Oromë: 141, 273
Orosius, Paulus: *Historiae adversum paganos*, 287
Orthanc: 49, 156, 159, 198, 336, 388, 392
Orthodox liturgy: 346
Orwell, George: 128-129; *Animal Farm*, 84, 85, 88, 90, 243; *Nineteen Eighty-Four*, 84, 86, 92, 234, 239, 243; as a post-War

writer, 84 ff.
Osgiliath: 155, 325
*ōsi-s: 283
Oslava zničení Prstenu: 10
Óss: 284
Ossë: 273, 286, 288, 299
Ossian: 60
Oswin: 40, 41, 287
Othanc: 65
Otr: 64
Óttarr: 287
Otter: 70
Ottor: 287
Ottor Wǣfre: 286-287
Ouboter, Cees: 301-305, 309
Out: 196
Oxford: 8, 10, 292-296, 309, 330, 339, 358-363, 371-372, 394, 416; conference in, 5; reminiscences, 12 ff.
Oxford Bach Choir: 13
Oxford Companion to English Literature, The: 422
Oxford English Dictionary: 173 ff., 291-293, 372, 422; influence on J.R.R. Tolkien's work, 195 ff.; style of entries, 195 ff.; J.R.R. Tolkien's work on, 68
Oxford English School, The: 207
Oxford Union, The: 90
Oxfordshire: 318
Oxleas Wood: 129
Oxonmoot: 10

P

Palamabron: 60
Palantíri: 159, 198, 320, 326; operation of, 324-325
Palladium: 338
Pan: 431-434
Paper: use of in Middle-earth, 340-342
Papus: 347
Parables: 17 ff.
Paradise: in *The Lord of the Rings*, 139 ff.
Parchment: use of in Middle-earth, 342
Parker, Charles: 356
Parker, Dorothy: 136
Parker, Douglass: 228
Parks, Henry: 74
Parousia: 196
Parson's Pleasure: 13
Pater, Walter: 431-432
Paths of the Dead, The: 389
Patience: 213
Peake, Mervyn: "Gormenghast Trilogy", 137
Pearl: 213-214, 218, 293-294, 372-373
Peaseblossom: 97
Peguy: 350
Peladan: 347
Pelargir: 132, 389
Pelennor Fields: 387
Pens: use of in Middle-earth, 341-342
Percival, Mike: 324, 336
Perelandra: 361, 364
Perestroika: 201
Periglacial conditions: 338
Persephone: 273
Petrushka: 203
Pevensie, Edmund: 364
Pevensie, Lucy: 364-365
Pevensie, Susan: 364-365
Philby, H.A.R. "Kim": 91
Philip, Neil: 235-236, 242
Philological Society: 173
Philologist: J.R.R. Tolkien as , 84
Philosopher's Stone: 352
Philosophy: Christian, 375
Physical laws: 323
Physics: of Middle-earth, 323 ff.
Pico Della Mirandola: 347, 352
Pigwiggen: 97
Pior: 188
Pippin: see Took, Peregrin
Pius II, *Pope*: 347
Plate tectonics: 334
Platinum: 338
Plato: 346
Platonic understanding: 46 ff.
Pleistocene Epoch: 334
Pliny: 412
Plotz, Richard: 187, 367
Plummer, Polly: 365
Poe, Edgar Allan: 421
Poetic Edda: 63-64, 68-69, 427
Point of view: in J.R.R. Tolkien's works, 256 ff.
Poland: 9
Pole, Jill: 365
Poles, Mark: 328
Polidori, *Dr.*: 424
Polish: 10, 298
Pollack, Herbert: *Word slank en bliff gezond*, 303
Polytheism: in *The Lord of the Rings*, 134
Polyxena: 365
Pope, Alexander: 97
Portly: 433-434
Post-Enlightenment: 115
Post-War writers: 84 ff.
Potter, Dennis: *Blackeyes*, 127
Power: in J.R.R. Tolkien's works, 272 ff.
Prancing Pony: 146
Pratchett, Terry: 325; *Lords and Ladies*, 104-105
Pre-Christian paganism: 361-362
Pre-Socratic philosophy: 346
Prejudice: and Hobbits, 151; in *The Lord of the Rings*, 151 ff.
Presbyterian Church: 349
Printing: in Middle-earth, 324, 342-343
Private Eye: 136
Professor Laverty: 104
Prose Edda: 63, 68-69, 281, 289, 311, 427
Protect and Survive: 238
Proto-elves: 102
"Proto-Frodo": 111
Prussian Guard: 85
Pseudo-scientific approach to J.R.R. Tolkien's works: 328
Psyche: 99
Pterodactyl: 364
Puck: 97-98, 102
Puns: in *The Hobbit*, 196
Pure Mathematics: 324
Purgatory: 346
Purity: 213, 218
Purtill, Richard: 134, 254
Pyle, Howard: 228

Q

Qabbalah: 346-348
Qabbalistic tree of life: 353
Qenya: 283, 292, 296
Quantum Mechanics: 325
Quayle, J. Danforth: 326
quell: 184
Quendi: 102
Quenya: 288, 297, 320, 342, 394; ban on, 165; grammar of, 187 ff.
Quest of the Holy Grail: 354
Quills: , 341-342

R

r-suffix: 188-189
Rabadash: 364
Racism: and J.R.R. Tolkien, 56, 236
Radagast: compared with Frey, 64
Radcliffe, Ann, *Mrs.*: 422-423, 427, 429
RAF: 294, 360
Ragnarǫk: 140
Ragnarök: 66
Rakhmanova, N.: 201
Rakoth Maugrim: 101
Raleigh, Walter: 13
Rámali: 191
Rámar: 187-188
Ramĕnŭ: 284
Ramer, Michael: 42, 43, 44, 173
Rána: 192-193
Ránar: 192
Ransom: 364
Ransome, Arthur: 239; opinion of *The Hobbit*, 28
Rapunzel: 275
Rateliff, John: 369
Ratty: 432-434
Rauros Falls: 336
Rawlinson and Bosworth Professor of Anglo-Saxon: 206-207, 372
Rawls, Melanie: 276; "The Feminine Principle in Tolkien", 273
Rawson, Claude: 240
Read, Marc: 325
Reagan, Ronald: 239
Red Arrow, The: 342
Red Cross Knight: 49
Redhorn Gate: 396
Rednal: 292
Reed, Diana: 234
Reeds: use as pens, 341
Regardie, Israel: 348
Regin: 64, 70-71
Reilly, Robert: 76

Reminiscences: of Oxford, 12 ff.
Renaissance thought: J.R.R. Tolkien and, 76
Renaissance, The: 422
Reuchlin: 347
Rex Collings: 14
Reynolds, Robert C.: 335-336, 338; "The Geomorphology of Middle-earth", 334
Reynolds, Trevor: 9
Rhovanion Plate: 334, 336
Richardson, Maurice: 229
Richardson, Samuel: 419
Riddles: 110
Rigby, Luke: 268-269
Ring, The: 341; analogues, 239
Ringil: 163
Ringwraiths: 88, 89
Rinnan: 285
Rivendell: 49, 121, 135, 142, 152-153, 158-159, 201, 259, 261, 338, 340-341, 343, 365
River Dane: 215-216
River Running, The: 338, 398-399
Rijksmuseum: 309
Roaches, The: 215
Robin Hood: 256
Robinson, Derek: 241
Robinson, Fred C.: 209
Roddenberry, Gene: *Star Trek*, 235
Rogues: 91
Rohan: 147, 152, 154-155, 203, 275, 318-319, 324, 331, 334, 341, 365, 385, 387, 389, 399-400; practices of Northern Countries in, 65
Rohan Craton: 336
Rohirrim: 54-56, 96, 153-156, 275, 278, 320, 341, 387, 389, 392
Rohmer, Sax: 348
Role playing games: 202
Romans: 288, 411
Romantic Movement, The: 419
Romantic novels: 423
Romantic tradition: 424
Romanticism: 347, 431; and Samuel Taylor Coleridge, 73 ff.; and J.R.R. Tolkien, 73 ff.
Rome: 422
Rómendacil: 319
Romney Marsh: 98
Rood-wold: 184
Rosmalen, Jo van: 301, 303, 305
Rosmall: 178
Rosmhvalr: 178
Rossetti, Christina: "Goblin Market", 99
Rossetti, D.G.: 99
Rossome: 184
Rotterdam: 301-304, 307
Round Table, The: 89, 90
Rowan: 283
Royal Air Force: see RAF
Royal Navy: 85
Rúmhoth: 288
Rúmil: 188, 287
Rune Poem: 288

Ruodolf of Fulda: *Translatio S. Alexandri*, 284
Russia: 9
Russian: 10, 395; translating into, 200 ff.
Russians: and J.R.R. Tolkien, 221 ff.

S

Sackville-Baggins, Lobelia: 109, 111, 118-119, 151-152, 365
Sackville-Baggins, Lotho: 152
Sackville-Baggins, Otho: 118
Sackville-Bagginses, The: 66, 341
Sacraments, The: 346, 353
Sacrifice: in *The Hobbit*, 109; in *The Lord of the Rings*, 109
Sade, Donatien Alphonse François de: *Justine*, 425
Saeros: 69, 164
Saga of Grettir the Strong: 63, 65
Saga of King Heidrek: 63
Saga of King Hrolf: 64
Saga of the Jomsvikings: 63, 65
St. Andrews University: 295
St. Augustine: 346
St. Bonaventure: 347
St. Clement of Alexandria: 346
St. Dionysius the Areopagite: 346
St. Erkenwald: 213
St. Francis: 347
St. George: 47, 416-417
St. George's Day: 416
St. Hildegarde of Bingen: 346
St. Justin the Martyr: 346
St. Keyne: 417
St. Martha: 417
St. Martin: 350
St. Matthew: 123
St. Paul: 353
St. Paul's School: 263
St. Philips Grammar School: 292
St. Romain of Rouei: 417
St. Thomas Aquinas: 346-347
Saksani: 288
Sammath Naur: 88-90
Samuel: 423
Sanday, Peggy: 274
Sandfield Road, Headington: 24, 295
Sandyman, Edmund: 395
Sandyman, Ted: 117-118, 155
Sanford, Len: 359
Sangar: 190
Sanskrit: 286, 411
Sapey, Mark: 9
Sapper: 239
Sapsanta: 192
Sarehole: 292
Sarjeant, William A.S.: 263-264
Saruman: 49, 54, 110, 113, 115-116, 122, 147-149, 152, 156, 168, 198, 236-237, 239, 241, 242-243, 308, 330, 343, 387-389; Analogues, 239; compared with Loki, 64-66
Satan: 89-90, 250
Satanic forces: 299

Saule: 284
Sauron: 49, 54, 56, 60, 64, 66, 89, 90, 95-96, 109, 111, 113, 115, 117, 131, 133, 148, 153-154, 156, 163, 168, 170, 198, 236-237, 239, 242, 248, 251, 258-260, 274-277, 300, 307, 324, 330-332, 341, 366, 385, 387, 396, 398-399; Analogue, 239
Saussure, Ferdinande de: 84
Saxon chieftains: 286
Saxons: 286-288
Sayer, George: 270, 294
Sayer, Sheena: 21
Sayers, Dorothy Leigh: *Busman's Honeymoon*, 356-357; *Gaudy Night*, 356-358; *Murder must Advertise*, 356; sexuallity in her works, 356 ff.; *Strong Poison*, 356; J.R.R. Tolkien's opinion of her works, 356 ff.; *Whose body?*, 357
Scandinavians: 314
Scatha: 411
Scēaf: 281
Schiller, Johann: 53
Schlei: 286
Schliemann, Heinrich: 156
Schopenhauer, Arthur: 368
Schuchart, Max: 302, 306
Schumpeter, Joseph: 134
Schwaben Redoubt: 85
Science: in Middle-earth, 323
Science Fiction: 419, 423-424, 427; Nineteenth-century, 419 ff.
Scientific laws: 323
Scott, Nan: "War and Pacifism in *The Lord of the Rings*", 236
Scott, Walter: 182; *Tales of Wonder*, 426
Screwtape: 384
Scribes: in Middle-earth, 342
Scrolls: use of in Middle-earth, 340, 342
Scrooge, Ebenezer: 320
Scrubb, Alberta: 364
Scrubb, Eustace: 364-365
Scull, Christina: 8-9, 207
Scurvy: 324
Scyld: 281
Sea drakes: 412
Sea of Windless Storm: 254
Sea-longing: 317
Seafarer, The: 372
Seal, Basil: 91
Secondary Belief: 73, 78; in J.R.R. Tolkien's work, 315, 317
Seine: 417
Seismic events: 338
Semitic ideas: 298
Senecdoche: 196
Senior, John: 339
Senryu: 264
Sephiroth: 353
Seraphim: 94
Serbia: 241
Serendipity: 420
Sexuality: in Sayer's work, 356 ff.
Sexual purity: 47

Shadowfax: 146-147, 385, 388
Shagrat: 111
Shakespeare, William: 253, 278, 365, 383, 423, 427; *Hamlet*, 256; *Macbeth*, 270, 365; *A Midsummer Night's Dream*, 130, 96-97; *Richard the Third*, 160; *The Tempest*, 97
Shan Hai King: 412
Shaw, George Bernard: 87, 427
Shea: 100
Shee, The: 100
Sheldonian Theatre: 5, 12
Shelley, Mary Wollstonecraft: 419, 424, 427; *Frankenstein*, 419, 423, 425-426, 429
Shelley, Percy Bysshe: 123, 368, 423-424, 432; "The Witch of Atlas", 99
Shelob: 64, 66, 88, 102, 108-109, 111-112, 115-116, 127, 143, 318, 338, 365
Sheriff of Nottingham: 256
Shields, Wil E.: 101
Shippey, Tom: 126, 128, 131, 133, 135, 141, 149, 168-169, 311, 314, 319, 330, 385, 392; *The Road to Middle-earth*, 84, 89, 91, 146, 198, 214-216, 233, 243, 376
Shire, The: 338, 343, 394-395
Shklovsky, Viktor: 95
Shorter Oxford English Dictionary: 195-196
Shreider, Yu.: 201
Shrewsbury College: 358
Sibley, Brian: 230
Sidhe: 100
Siegfried: 69
Sien mountains: 412
Sievers, Eduard: "Ziele und Wege der Schallanalyse", 208-209
Sigelhearwan: 206
Sigmund: 69
Signal: 235, 237-238, 241-242
Signy: and Aerin, 69-70
Sigurd: 64, 68; and Túrin, 69-71
Silda: 189
Sildai: 189
Silk: use of in Middle-earth, 341
Silmaril: 189
Silmarille: 189
Silmarilli: 189
Silmarils, The: 158, 161-165, 168-169, 224, 259, 275, 289, 299; Brightness of, 326
Silvan: 297
Silverlode, The: 136
Simons, Lester: 9
Sinbad the Sailor: 423
Sinda: 189
Sinda-nóriello: 188
Sindacollo: 189
Sindar: 160, 189, 297
Sindarin: 297, 342, 388, 394
Sinome: 188
Sinqi: 188
Sinyi: 102-103
Sir Bertilak: 215
Sir Gareth: 87
Sir Gawain: 90, 214, 216-217
Sir Gawain and the Green Knight: 96, 213 ff., 293, 295, 372-373, green girdle in, 71
Sir Huon: 102
Sir Lancelot: 87, 90
Sir Orfeo: 214, 294, 373
Sir Orfeo: 270
Sirannon Valley: 396
Sirion: 249
Sisam, Kenneth: 210, 372
Sister Penelope: 383
Skelton, Robin: 265, 267
Skrying: 348
Slavonic fables: 416
Smaug: 64, 109-110, 196-197, 332, 411
Sméagol: 111, 116, 119, 309; see also Gollum
Smirkle: 175
Smith: 253-255
Smith, E.E. "Doc": 325
Smith, Geoffrey Bache: 292, 371-372
Smith, Marie: 266
Smith, Winston: 86, 234
Smollett, Tobias George: 419, 423; *Ferdinand, Count Fathom*, 423; *The History and Adventures of an Atom*, 421
Snaga: 111
Snorri Sturluson: 289
Snowmane: 141
Società Tolkieniana Italiana: 10
Socrates: 346
Sod: 196
Solfatara Fields: 336
Solomon, Maurice: 263
Solor: 192
Solosimpe: 188-189
Solosimpi: 188-189, 296
Solosse: 192
Soloviev, Vladimir: 347
Somerville College, Oxford: 358
Somerville-Large, Gillian: 230
Somme: 292
Song: 436, 438
Sonnenkinder: 91-92
Sötemann, Guus: 305-306
Sötemann, *Mrs.*: 306-308
Soulmonger, The: 101
South Africa: 292, 360, 363
South America: 10
Southern California: 5
Southern Star: 307
Southey, Robert: 427
Southrons: 276
Soviet Union: 307, 423
Spanish Civil War: 85
Spanish Inquisition: 242
Spark, Muriel: 425; *Child of Light*, 419
Spectres: in Blake, 60
Spenser, Edmund: 45-47, 49, 97, 227; *Faerie Queene*, 49-51, 198, 365
Sperber, Hans: 283
Spielberg, Steven: *Hook*, 256
Squid-ink: , 341
Stace, Walter: 435
Stadtbergen: 284
Stair Falls, The: 339
Stalin, Josef: 234, 241, 243, 307
Stallone, Sylvester: *Rambo*, 239
Stauffer, Mel R.: 339
Stein, Aaron Marc: 265
Steiner, Rudolf: 347
Sterne, Laurence: 419
Stevens, Wallace: 123
Stevenson, R.L.: *Treasure Island*, 240
Stewards, The: 341-342
Stewart, J.I.M.: 210
Stibbs, Andrew: 234-235, 238
Stimpson, Catherine R.: 127
Sting: Luminosity of, 327
Stoats: 413
Stoors: 151, 203, 279
Strata: 334
Strider: 112, 145-146, 152-153; see also Aragorn
Strope: 218
Studdock, Jane: 364, 366
Studdock, Mark: 364
Sturch, Sarah: 9
Sturlunga Saga: 65
Sub-creation: 73, 76, 80
Subjunctive: 196
Suffield, Beatrice: 292
Sulphur Dioxide: 414
Sulphuric Acid: 414
Sulum: 284
Summers, Montague: 423
Sun, The: Brightness of, 326
Sunday Telegraph: 229
Sunday Times, The: 241
Súrinen: 188, 192
Sutcliff, Rosemary: 239
Svart-alfar: 95
Svoloch: 203
Swann, Donald: *The Road Goes Ever On*, 270
Swans: 342
Swansea Geographer, The: 334
Swearing: in *The Lord of the Rings*, 196
Sweden: 303
Swedish: 10; J.R.R. Tolkien's knowledge of, 36
Swift, Jonathan: 419, 423, 429; *Gulliver's Travels*, 423
Swinburne, Algernon: 99
Swinfen, Ann: 76
Switzerland: 292, 338
Swythamley Park: 215
Sylvester II, *Pope*: 346
Sylwanowicz, Agnieszka: 298

T

Tacitus: *Germania*, 285, 288
Táin: 281
Taliskan: 296
Talking Books: 233
"Tam Lin": 96
Tanzanians: 416
Tar: 192
Tar-Míriel: 276
Tarambo: 189

Taran: 189
Tarasque: 417
Tarot: 348, 352, 354
Taruithorn (Smail of the Tolkien Society): 324, 328
Tasarinan: 140
Tash: 236
Tavrobel: 286
T.C.B.S.: 371-372
Tea Club and Barrovian Society: see T.C.B.S.
Technology: in Middle-earth, 323
Tectonic events: 334
Tectonic features: 335, 337
Teenagers: and the appreciation of J.R.R. Tolkien, 221
Tehta: 343
Telelle: 189
Telelli: 189
Teleology: 196
Telepathy: 328
Teler: 188
Teleri: 160, 162, 188-189, 296-297
Tengwar: 342-343
Tennyson, Alfred *Lord*: 99, 123; *English Idylls*, 128; "The Lady of Shalott", 278-279
Ter i-aldar: 188
Teresa of Avila: 435
Tereva: 190
Terror-romance: 422-423, 428-429
Thain's library: 340
Thangorodrim: 365
Thanin: 411
Tharbad fault: 338
Thargelion: 162
Tharmas: compariosn with Ulmo, 59, 60
Thatcher, Margaret: 129, 238-239
Théoden: 65, 66, 122, 141, 147, 154, 156, 198, 237, 241, 249, 275, 278, 319-320, 399
Théodred: 147, 249
Theosophical Society, The: 347-349
Thidreks Saga: 69
Thingol: 69, 71, 158-165, 201, 259, 276, 296, 365-366
"Thomas the Rhymer": 96
Thomas, Keith: 132
Thomas, R.S.: "The Kingdom", 20
Thomistic sense of imagination: 76
Thompson, *Mr.*: 310, 312
Thompson, E.P.: 238-239, 241; *Protest and Survive*, 238-239, 242
Thomson, George: 226
Thor: 64, 95, 98, 427
Thorin I: 399
Thorin Oakensheild: 64, 113, 168, 197, 247, 398
Thorin's Treasure Map: 340
Thrihyrne: 399-400
Thuringians: 285
Thurston lava tube: 336
Thymine: 383
Tibet: 241

Tighe, Damaris: 364
Timbermill, *Dr.*: 210
Time travel: 39 ff., 363
Times Literary Supplement: 227-229
Tinkerbell: 97-98
Tinwelint: 283, 296
Tinwi: 191
Tiptree, James: 266
Tir Nan Og: 99, 103
Tir Tairngire: 104
Tiriel: 59
Titania: 96-97
To-Morrow: 350, 352
Toad: 432-433
Toad Hall: 433
Tol Brandir: 336
Tol Eressea: 189
Tol Eressëa: 286-288, 394-395
Tolfalas: 336
Tolkien Centenary Conference: 10, 231, 339. 368
Tolkien in Oxford: 251
Tolkien scholarship: 5
Tolkien Society of America: 187
Tolkien Society, The: 5, 8-10, 238; foundation of, 14
Tolkien, Christopher: 24, 139-140, 146-149, 158, 162, 164, 188, 213, 227, 276, 283, 285-288, 292-296, 308, 326, 330, 332, 334, 360, 363, 369-370, 373; guest of honour, 5; illness, 27
Tolkien, Edith: 23-25, 249, 293, 295-296, 308; see also Bratt, Edith
Tolkien, Faith: 24
Tolkien, Gabriel: 24
Tolkien, Hilary: 292
Tolkien, J.R.R.: *The Adventures of Tom Bombadil*, 295, publication of, 70; "Ainulindalë", 287, 300; "Akallabêth", 300; "Aldarion and Erendis", 295, 358; and allegory, 18-21; "Ambarkanta", 293; "*Ancrene Wisse* and *Hali Meiðhad*", 213; "Annals of Aman", 294; "Annals of Beleriand", 293; "Annals of Valinor", 293; "Aotrou and Itroun", 293; his Artistry, 315; artwork, 27; Bad in his works, 247 ff.; and Owen Barfield, 362-363; "Beowulf: The Monsters and the Critics", 146, 209, 293; "Bombadil Goes Boating", 98; boundaries in his works, 81; "The Bovadium Fragments", 295; and Catholicism, 23, 24, 31 ff., 53. 78, 217; and christianity, 53 ff., 133-134; "Cirion and Eorl", 295; and Classical thought, 76; and the clerihew, 263 ff.; correspondence with George Allen and Unwin, 26 ff.; "The Cottage of Lost Play", 295; the cover, 27; his Craft, 316; critical response to, 226 ff.; "A Description of Númenor", 295; "The Disaster of the Gladden Fields", 295; Drama in his writing, 79-80; "The Drowning of Anadûnê", 288, 294, 360; "The Drúedain", 295; "Earendel", 191, 193; "English and Welsh", 295; and Englishness, 278 ff.; "Enigmata Saxonica Nuper Inventa Duo", 174; "Errantry", 293; and escapism, 16; "Etymologies", 293; Evil in his works, 88-89, 247 ff., 298 ff.; Faërie in his works, 253 ff.; "The Fall of Arthur", 291, 293; "The Fall of Númenor", 293; and fantasy tradition, 94 ff.; *Farmer Giles of Ham*, 293, blunderbuss in, 173, 195, submission of, 28, translations, 201; Fascism and, 236-243; Female Authority Figures in his works, 364 ff.; Feminists and, 272, 274; "Fords of Isen", 295; *The Geste of Beren and Lúthien*, submission of, 28; "Gilfanon's Tale", 282; "Gnomish Lexicon", 285, 291-292; "Goblin Feet", 292; Good in his works, 247 ff.; "Grey Annals", 294; Heaven, his view of, 254-255; Heroines in his works, 250; his Life, 291 ff.; "The History of Eriol", 286, 288; *The Hobbit*, 85, 293, appetite in, 108 ff., as fairy-tale, 247 ff., 50th anniversary, 5, Gollum in, 61, as literary artefacts, 126 ff., publication of, 26 ff., puns in, 196, Arthur Ransome's opinion of, 28, recordings of, 23, sacrifice in, 109, second edition, 294, translations of, 201, 221; holidays, 20-21; "Homecoming of Beorhtnoth, Beorhthelm's Son", 209; "The Hunt for the Ring", 295; illness, 27; "Imram", 294; *In de Ban van de Ring*, 301-302, 305; influence of Owen Barfield, 32, 37; influence of Ernst Cassirer, 32; influence of G.K. Chesterton, 32; influence of Nikolaj Grundtvig, 32 ff.; influence of George MacDonald, 32; influence of Dorothy L. Sayers, 32; influence on later fiction, 99 ff.; and the Inklings, 360 ff.; The Inklings influence on, 367 ff.; "The Istari", 295; knowledge of languages, 36; "Kortirion", 292, 295, 371; "The Last Ark", 295; "The Lay of Húrin", 293; "The Lay of Leithian", 293-294, 368; "The Lay of the Children of Húrin", 68; *Lay of the Fall of Gondolin*, 185; "Leaf by Niggle", 48; "Leaf by Niggle", 294, translations, 201; lectures, 21; and C.S. Lewis, 25, 361-362; lexicographical work, 173 ff.; "Lhammas", 287, 293; his library, 36; "Looney", 251; *The Lord of the Rings*, Appetite in, 108 ff., animism in, 134, and Blakes *The Book of Urizen*, 60, context of its publication, 84, cursing in, 196, Dutch translation, 301, earthly paradise in, 139 ff., evil in, 222-224, as fairy-tale, 247 ff., film, 295, Flora in, 130, Food in, 108 ff., good in, 222-225, as literary artefacts, 126 ff., and northern literature, 63 ff., peaceful zone in, 71, polytheism in, 134, prejudice in, 151 ff., reading, 15, recordings of, 23, Sacrifice in, 109, swearing in, 196, Swedish translation, 301, translating, 200 ff., translations of,

221, writing of, 22 ff.; *The Lost Road*, 40 ff., 287, 292-293, submission of, 28; love of parties, 21; Marriage, 292; *A Middle English Vocabulary*, 174, 185, 293; *Mr. Bliss*, 293, submission of, 28; Mythology, his use of the word, 310 ff.; mythology of, 59; "Mythopoeia", 293, 298, 300, 361; "Namárië", 192, 295; "Narn i Chîn Húrin", 294; "Narn i Hîn Húrin", 68 ff.; "Narqelion", 188; as a Neo-Platonist, 80; "Nieninque", 192; "The Notion Club Papers", 39 ff., 286-287, 294, 360, 362-363, 424; "Oilima Markirya", 190-192; and Old English Studies, 206 ff.; "On Fairy-Stories", 73-75, 79, 80, 295, 361-362, 368, 384; the Ordered Four in his fiction, 375 ff.; *Oxford English Dictionary*, influence of, 195 ff.; "The Palantíri", 295; and parables, 18-19; parallels with William Blake, 58 ff.; "Parma Kuluinen", 286; as philologist, 84, 88; Point of view in his works, 256 ff.; post-Enlightenment and, 115; as a post-War writer, 84 ff.; Power in his works, 272 ff.; and pubs, 22; "Qenta Noldorinwa", 287, 293; "Qenya Lexicon", 188, 285, 291-292; "Quenta Silmarillion", 293; "Quest for Erebor", 295; racism and, 56, 236; "Red Book of Westmarch", 319, 327, 342; *De Reisgenoten*, 301-302; and Renaissance thought, 76; as reviser, 145 ff.; *The Road Goes Ever On*, 295; and Romanticism, 73 ff.; "Roverandum", 293; Russian editions, 200 ff.; and Russians, 221 ff.; Science Fiction, awarness of, 424; "The Sea Bell", 251; Secondary Belief in his work, 315, 317; "A Secret Vice", 291, 293; sexuallity in her works, 356 ff.; *The Silmarillion*, bias in, 158 ff., the Fall in, 167 ff., Noldor bias in, 95, "Of Túrin Turambar" in, 68, translations, 202, writing of, 22-23, 25; "Sketch of Mythology", 293; *Smith of Wootton Major*, 48, translations, 201; "Story of Eriol's Life", 286; sub-creation theory, 31 ff.; time travel and, 39 ff.; and Totalitarianism, 233 ff.; "Tree of Tongues", 187; "The Trees of Kortirion", 188; "Turambar and the Foalókë", 68; *Unfinished Tales*, Galadriel and Celeborn in, 65; view of Englishness, 126 ff.; his view of the Incarnation, 82; view of sermons, 17; visit to Holland, 301 ff.; "The Voyage of Earendel the Evening Star", 371; walking with, 22; and Charles Williams, 362; women in his works, 272 ff.; work on the *Oxford English Dictionary*, 68, 173 ff.; "You and Me and the Cottage of Lost Play", 292

Tolkien, John: 24, 292, 294
Tolkien, Judith: 294
Tolkien, Mabel: 292
Tolkien, Michael: 293-294

Tolkien, Michael George: 294
Tolkien, Priscilla: 178, 195, 293-294, 301
Tolkien, Simon: 295
Tollalinta: 192
Took: 202
Took, Belladonna: 196, 249
Took, Peregrin: 65, 112-113, 120-121, 135, 152, 155, 198, 218, 237, 315-316, 319, 343, 366, 384-385, 387-389
Topology: Euclidean, 325; Minkowski, 325
Totalitarianism: and J.R.R. Tolkien, 233 ff.
Touletin, Paul-Jean: 351
Toynbee, Philip: 91-92, 127, 211, 226, 229
Transfiguration, The: 353
Translation: into Russian, 200 ff.
Translators: 8
Tree of Languages: 187
Treebeard: 112, 130, 151, 156, 198, 237, 316, 320, 369, 384, 388-389
Tribune: 238
Trinity College, Oxford: 293
Trinity Sunday: 353
Trolls: 110
Trollshaws, The: 338
Trotter: 145-146
Troy: 156
Truss: 196
TSR: 103
Tukalia: 190
Tulkas: 161, 193
Tulkassen: 193
Tulkatho: 193
Tulleken, Rutger: 305
Tumunzahar: 397-398
Tûn: 287, 296
Tûna: 296
Tuor: 47, 158-160, 164, 317, 365-366
Turgon: 158-163, 165
Túrin: 68, 160-161, 164-165, 249, 292, 300, 365, 415; and Sigurd, 69 ff.
Turville-Petre, Joan: 208, 210
Túvo: 283
Twaalf Provinciën Huis: 304-305
Twain, Mark: 39
Twyford Down: 129
Tyalie: 190
Tyaliéva: 190
Tyler, J.E.A.: *The Tolkien Companion*,
Tyulma: 191
Tyulmin: 191

U

Udûn Basin: 336
Uffington: 416
Uin: 286
Uinen: 273
Uinnius: 283
Ulmo: 47, 160, 162, 286; compariosn with Tharmas, 59
Ulro: 59, 60
Umbar: 155
Úmea: 190
Úmeai: 189-190
Underhill, Evelyn: 348

Ungoliant: 160
Unicorn, The (public house) : 22
Unicorns: 437
Union of Soviet Socialist Republics: see USSR
United Kingdom: 417
United States of America: 10
Unity: 436
Universe, The: 375-376
University of Amsterdam: 304
University of Edinburgh: 296
University of Exeter: 427
University of Liège: 295
University of Saskatchewan: 339
University of Utrecht: 305
University Women's Club: 358
Unn the Deep-minded: 65
Unwin, Rayner: 23, 145, 227, 229, 295, 302-303, 369-370, 385
Unwin, Stanley: 146; letter to, 42
Úosis: 283
Urang, Gunnar: *Shadows of Heaven*, 352
Urdli: 104
Úri: 193
Úrio: 193
Urizen: compariosn with Manwë, 59, 60
Urthona: compariosn with Aulë, 59-61
Uruk-hai: 88, 110-111
USA: see United States of America
Use of English: 234-235
Usova: 201
USSR: 234, 238, 243
Utrecht: 303, 305
Uttermost West: 103, 140
Utterson, Sarah Elizabeth Brown: *Tales of the Dead*, 425
Úvea: 190

V

Vairë: 273
Vala: 188, 191, 300; in Blake and Tolkien, 59
Valacar: 155
Valar: 133-134, 139-141, 160-161, 164, 167, 169, 188-189, 203, 249, 273-275, 296-297, 299-300, 325, 384
Valatar: 192
Valatáren: 192
Vale of Evermorn: 253
Vali: 189-190, 193
Valier: 273-274
Valimar: 97, 101, 134, 140
Valinor: 59, 134, 139-143, 160-162, 164-165, 168, 170-171, 187, 190, 261, 272, 299, 326
Valion: 193
Valjean, Jean: 256
Valkyries: 103
Vampires: 346
Van Morrison: 128
Van Rossum: 307
van Summers, Tess: 265-266
Vána: 273
Vane, Harriet: 356, 358

Vanima: 189
Vanimar: 189
Vanir: 289
Vanya: 189
Vanyar: 189, 289, 297
Varaigs of Khand: 56
Varda: 97, 140, 273-274, 277, 299
Vardo: 187
Varma, Devendra P.: *The Gothic Flame*, 427
Vatnsdale Saga: 65
Vea: 191
Vear: 188
Vector: 230
Vellum: use of in Middle-earth, 340
Venice: 427
Venus: 97, 134, 326, 424
Vigfusson, Gudbrand: 285
Viking Club: 371
Villiers de l'Isle Adam: 347
Vine: 283
Vingilot: Construction of, 326
Vinyamar: 159, 162, 317
Vinyar Tengwar: 288
Virgil: 327
Virgins: 412, 415-416, 426
"Vision of Mac Conglinne": 98
Vitamin C: 324
Vivien: 99
Volcanoes: 336
Volsunga Saga, The: 63, 68 ff.
Voltaire: *Zadig*, 421
Vǫluspá: 283-284
von Baader, Franz: 347
Vonnegut, Kurt: *Slaughterhouse-Five, or The Children's Crusade*, 86
Voorhoeve & Dietrich: 301-305
Voro: 190
Vortigern: 152, 286-287
Vulcanism: in Middle-earth, 336

W

Wade: 311
Waedle: 175
Wag: 196
Wag(g)el: 175, 185
Waggle: 175-176, 185
Waggly: 175, 185
Wagner, Richard: 68, 71, 127
Wain: 175, 177, 185
Wain, John: 360
Wain-house: 175
Wain-trees: 175
Wainriders: 275-276
Waist: 175, 185
Waist-cloth: 175, 185
Waist-rail: 177, 185
Waist-tree: 185
Waistband: 175, 185
Waistcoat: 175, 177, 185
Waistcoated: 185
Waistcoateer: 185
Waisted: 177, 185
Waister: 185
Waistless: 185
Wait: 177
Wait-a-bit: 177, 185
Waite, A.E.: 348-353
Waiter: 177, 185
Waiterage: 177
Waiterdom: 177
Waiterful: 177
Waiterhood: 177
Waitering: 177
Waitership: 185
Waith: 177
Waiting: 177, 185
Waiting-maid: 185
Waiting-man: 185
Waiting-room: 177, 185
Waiting-woman: 177, 185
Waitress: 185
Waive: 177
Wake: 177-178, 185
Wake-robin: 178, 185
Wake-wort: 185
Waldend: 185
Waldman, Milton: 145, 282, 289, 294, 310, 312, 389
Wallop: 178, 185
Walloper: 185
Walloping: 185
Walm: 178, 185
Walming: 185
Walnut: 178, 185
Walpole, Horace: 423; *The Castle of Otranto: A Story*, 419-422; *A Letter from Xo-Ho, a Chinese Philosopher at London*, 420; *The Three Princes of Serendip*, 420
Walrus: 178, 181, 184, 186
*walþus: 184
*walþuz: 182
Wampum: 178, 186
Wampumpeag: 178, 186
Wan: 178, 181, 186
Wander: 178, 181, 186
Wander-year: 186
Wanderable: 186
Wandered: 186
Wanderer: 186
Wanderer, The: 210, 372
Wandering: 181, 184, 186
Wanderment: 186
Wandreth: 181, 186
Wane: 178, 186
Want: 181, 186
Want-louse: 186
Wantley: 411
Wariangle: 182, 186
Warlock: 182
Warlockry: 186
Warm: , 174-175, 186
Wart: 87
Warwick: 286
Wasp: 175, 186
Water: 175, 186
Water drakes: 415
Watson, George: 226
Watson, James: 383
Waugh, Evelyn: *Brideshead Revisited*, 91; *Put Out More Flags*, 91
Weald: 182, 186
Wealden: 186
Wealding: 186
Weathertop: 154, 259, 339
Weber, Max: 53
Weiner, Martin: 128
Weird Tales: 423
Weis, Margaret: 103
Wele: 181
Welfies: 104
Wells, Andrew: 9
Wells, H.G.: 419, 427, 429; and his followers, 87; *The Outline of History*, 88; parodies of, 88; *The Time Machine*, 39
Welsh: 292, 296-297, 321
Welthe: 181
Wer: 181
Werewolves: 346
Wessex: 287
West, Richard: 226, 385
Westall, Robert: "The Hunt for Evil", 235-237, 241-242
Westcott, W. Wynn, *Dr.*: 348
Westfold, The: 400
Weston: 364
Westphalia: 284
Westron: 296-297, 342
Wetwang: 336
Whale: Grey, 435-436
Wheat-meal: 323
Wheatley, Dennis: 236, 242
Wheaton: conference in, 5
Wheaton College: 295
White Council, The: 387
White Downs: 338
White Mountains: 334, 336, 338, 399-400
White Witch, The: 364, 366
White, T.H.: *The Book of Merlyn*, 85, 87; *The Once and Future King*, 84-85, 87, 90-91, 98; as a post-War writer, 84 ff.; *The Sword in the Stone*, 85, 87
Whitgift, Mrs.: 98
Wicca: 346
Wick (lamp): 175, 186
Widukind: *Res Gestae Saxonicae*, 285
Wield: 182, 186
Wil: 100
Wild: 182, 184, 186
Wild Wood, The: 433
Wildboarclough: 215
Williams, Charles: 74, 226, 269-270, 294, 345, 350, 352-354, 356, 360-361, 363, 367, 371, 369, 375-376, 392; *All Hallow's Eve*, 352; appreciation of Blake, 62; *Descent into Hell*, 352; Female Authority Figures in his works, 364 ff.; *Greater Trumps, The*, 352; *The House of the Octopus*, 362; *Many Dimensions*, 352; *The Place of the Lion*, 352, 364 *Shadows of Ecstasy*, 352; *Taliessin through Logres*, 353; and J.R.R. Tolkien, 362; *War in*

Heaven, 293, 352
Williams, Raymond: *The Country and the City*, 128-129
Williams, Tad: 416
Wilson, Edmund: 91, 127, 211, 265; "Oo, Those Awful Orcs!", 228-229
*wilþijaz: 182
Wimsey, Peter, *Lord*: 356-358
Winged serpents: 412
Winnie-the-Pooh: 127
Winter: 175, 186
Wisconsin: 295
Wiseman, Christopher: 371-372
Witch of Endor: 423
Witchcraft: 352
Witches: 346
Withered Heath, The: 399
Withywindle: 315-316
Wōdan: 285
Wodehouse, P.G.: 357; *Right Ho, Jeeves*, 240
Wōdnesdæg: 285
wodwos: 216
*Wōðanaz: 285
Woe: 181
Wojcik, Jan: 74-76
Wold: 182, 184, 186
Wolfe, Gene: *Castleview*, 100
Wolvercote Cemetery: 243
Women: in J.R.R. Tolkien's works, 272 ff.
Wood, Robin: 98
Woodford, A.F.A., *Rev.*: 348
Woodspring Smial: 414
Woodwoses: 217
Woolf, Virginia: 45, 86, 358
Wooster, Bertie: 357
Wordsworth, Dorothy: 315
Wordsworth, William: 315, 360, 368, 427, 432
World War I: 84, 85, 90, 92, 237, 248, 280, 291-292, 351, 357, 372
World War II: 85, 88, 90, 92, 116, 236, 248, 276, 280, 294, 303, 360
World War III: 234, 238
Worldes riches: 181
Wormtongue: 111, 147-148, 156, 248
Woses: 216, 276, 297, 388
Wrake: 181
Wrede, Patricia: *Shadow Magic*, 100
Wrenn, C.L.: 209
Wright, Joseph: 13
Writing technologies: in Middle-earth, 340 ff.
Wudu-wása: 216
Wursien: 175
Wyke-Smith, E.A.: *The Marvellous Land of Snergs*, 293
Wynne, Patrick: 288
Wyoming: 338
Wyrd: 218
Wyrds: 100
Wyvern: 412
Wǣfre, Ottor: see Ottor Wǣfre

Y

Yahweh: 273
Yar: 192
Yassen: 188
Yates, Jessica: "In Defence of Fantasy", 235
Yavanna: 160-161, 273, 299
Year's Work in English Studies, The: 184
Yeats, William Butler: 46, 123, 345, 349-350, 352-354; *Autobiography*, 349; *Memoirs*, 349; *Rosa Alchemica*, 349
Yerrow, Paul: *Puff the Magic Dragon*, 411
Yggdrasil: 64, 284
Yngvi-Freyr: 289
Yocarini, Costa: 302
Young, Nick: 437-438
Yrmensûl: 284
Yugoslavia (former): 248; see also Bosnia and Serbia
Yulma: 187

Z

Zerkalov, A.: 223
Zimbabwe: 235
Zimbardo, Rose A.: 230
Zipes, Jack: 134
Zirakzigil: 388

Æ

Ælfred: 287
Ælfwine: 40, 43, 44, 282, 286-289
Æneas: 365
Æneid, The: 281, 327
Ænt: 214, 216
Æsc: 283, 285
Æscmann: 283

A

Ἄμπελος: 283

E

Ἕρμα: 284

O

Ὀξύη: 283
Ὄρμενο-ς: 284

Б

Беляки: 203
Брыль: 204

В

Всеславур: 202
Вэггинс: 201
Вяз: 204

Г

Горки: 204
Горнбург: 203
Горы: 204
Гаральд: 202
Гэндалв: 204
Гэндальф: 204

Д

Дарин: 204
Дурень: 204
Дьюрин: 204
Дэйл: 201

З

Зайгород: 202
Засумки: 204
Заяч: 202

К

Конунг: 203
Квет: 202
Квиток: 202
Крол: 202
Кроличья Балка: 202

Л

Лох: 204
Лапитупы: 203
Лутиэн: 204
Лучиэнь: 204
Лютость: 204
Лютик: 204
Лютиэн: 204

М

Мел: 201
Мелкий: 201
Мелкин: 201
Мустанг: 203
Мустангрим: 203

Н

Невысоклики: 202

П

Прелесть: 202
Привражье: 204
Пригорье: 204
Приречное Взгорье: 204
Приречье: 204

Р

Райвенделл: 201
Ристания: 203
Ристати: 203

С

Сенешаль: 203
Скоцка: 204
Скромби: 202
Старуха Ива: 204
Старый Лох: 204
Струсы: 203
Сумкина Горка: 204

Т

Торбинсы: 202
Торбы-на-Круче: 202, 204
Трусицка: 203

Ф

Фермер: 201

Х

Хоббитания: 202

Ц

Цвет: 202
Цветок: 202

The Mythopoeic Society & Mythlore

The Mythopoeic Society is an international literary and educational organization devoted to the study, discussion, and enjoyment of the works of J.R.R. Tolkien, C.S. Lewis, and Charles Williams. It believes these writers can be more completely understood and appreciated by studying the realm of myth; the genres of fantasy; and the literary, philosophical, and spiritual traditions which underlie their works, and from which they have drawn and enriched.

MYTHLORE is a quarterly journal actively interested in J.R.R. Tolkien, C.S. Lewis, Charles Williams, and the genres of Myth and Fantasy which they have drawn from and enriched. It features articles, reviews, and an annotated Inklings Bibliography, letters of comment, art, editorials, columns — including one on current modern fantasy, and general interest information. By combining the best features of a scholarly journal and a popular literary magazine, it is appreciated by a wide range of international readers.

MYTHLORE is a juried journal, and is indexed in the *Modern Languages Association International Bibliography*, the *American Humanities Index*, the *Arts and Humanities Citation Index*, *Abstracts of English Studies*, and *Current Contents*, as well as other indexes. It has published a Subject Index of the first 50 issues, found in issue 51, available for $4 for the issue (or available separately for $2).

Individual Society Members: $20 for 4 issues, or $40 for 8 issues. (This includes $5 per year for membership in The Mythopoeic Society. If you are already a Society member, the rates are $15 for 4 issues or $30 for 8 issues.) **Libraries/Institutions: $20 for 4 issues, or $40 for 8 issues.** $4 for a sample issue. Second class (surface) postage is included in the above rates. The following mailing options are also available. First Class Delivery for 4 issues: $8 additional in the USA, $9 additional for Canada. For 8 issues: $16 in the USA, $18 for Canada. Overseas Airmail for 4 issues: add $20 to Europe & Latin America, add $25 to Australia & Asia.

Since its beginning in 1969, *Mythlore* has been recognized as the leading publication in its areas of interest. Its 68 typeset double columned pages are 8.5 x 11". Questions concerning submissions should be sent to the Editor: Glen H. GoodKnight, Park View Estates, 245-F South Atlantic Blvd., Monterey Park, CA 91754 USA.

Origin and Development

The Mythopoeic Society was founded in 1967 by Glen H. GoodKnight. From its first meeting in Southern California, it has grown to be an international organization. In 1970 it held its first annual Mythopoeic Conference. In 1971 it incorporated as an educational and literary nonprofit, tax-exempt organization. In 1972 THE TOLKIEN SOCIETY OF AMERICA merged with it to create a larger and stronger framework. Today its members can be found in many nations around the world.

Definition

The word "mythopoeic" (pronounced myth-o-pē-ic) means "myth making" or "productive of myths." It is a word that fits well the fictional and mythic works of the three authors, who were prominent members of a unique informal literary circle know as the Inklings, which met in Oxford, England, during the late 1930s through the 1950s. While the writers' works are individually distinct, there are common values, parallel themes, and cross-influences to be found.

Membership

Membership in The Mythopoeic Society is open to individuals, and includes participational and voting rights. It is $5 per person per year. Two or more individuals residing at the same address may apply for joint membership, giving each full membership rights. But they will receive one copy of the publications they have paid for under their joint membership.

Those living outside the USA may pay for their membership, publications, back issues, and other items by using an International Money Order, personal check, or money order in another nation's currency. If foreign currency is used, 15% should be added to the current prevailing exchange rate at the time of ordering to cover conversion costs.

Membership costs, subscription rates, and prices for back issues of the publications and other items are listed on the Society Order Form, which is available on request.

The Mythopoeic Conference

Each year the Mythopoeic Society holds its Mythopoeic Conference, which usually lasts three to four days, providing a variety of activities. Papers, panels, discussions, a musical program, a masquerade, an art show, an auction of books and memorabilia, films, drama, and colorful pageantry are some of the usually scheduled events. Each year the Conference hosts one or more Guests of Honor, who address the Conference. Details of the Conference are printed in advance in *Mythlore* and *Mythprint*.

The Mythopoeic Fantasy and Scholarship Awards

Beginning with 1992, each year at the Mythopoeic Conference Banquet the Mythopoeic Society presents four awards: The Mythopoeic Fantasy Award for Literature for Adults, The Mythopoeic Fantasy Award for Literature for Children, The Mythopoeic Scholarship Award for Inklings Studies, and The Mythopoeic Scholarship Award for Myth and Fantasy Studies. The Fantasy Awards are given to works of fantasy published during the preceding year, whose outstanding merit best exemplifies "the spirit of the Inklings" for that year. The Scholarship Awards go to works published in the preceding three years that make a significant contribution to scholarship in their respective fields.

Discussion Groups

Some Society members participate in meetings of independent, affiliated Discussion Groups. The Society seeks to help these groups by being a clearinghouse of information, and by printing meeting times, dates, and topics in *Mythprint*. Information and assistance in forming a Discussion Group in your area are available on request.

Other Society Publications

MYTHPRINT is the Society's monthly newsletter featuring meeting information, news of the Society and its interests, reviews, editorials and discussion reports. 20 pages, 7" x 8.5". Prices for Society members: $7 for 12 issues, 3rd Class delivery in the USA and Canada; $10 for overseas surface mail; $10 First Class delivery in USA and Canada; $14 for overseas Air Mail.

MYTHIC CIRCLE is a fantasy fiction periodical, published three times a year, which also includes art, letters, and poems. 50 pages, 8.5 x 11". Prices: 3 issues for $13 for Society members $18 for non-members, or $6.50 for the current issue.

The Mythopoeic Society

P.O. Box 6707, Altadena, CA 91003, USA

"In a hole in the ground there lived a hobbit . . ."

Published in 1937, these words introduced a new world, Middle-earth, to us all.
They were written by J.R.R. Tolkien.

In 1969 the Tolkien Society was founded, its aim being to further interest in the life and works of J.R.R. Tolkien, OBE, the author of *The Hobbit*, *The Lord of the Rings*, *The Silmarillion* and other works of fiction and philological study. Based in the United Kingdom and registered as an independent, non-profit making charity, (registered charity number 273809), the society boasts an international membership.

The society helps to bring together those with like minds, both formally and informally, with gatherings throughout the year. There are three such events at a national level. The first is the Annual General Meeting and Annual Dinner, held in the spring in a different town or city in the UK each year. At the AGM various committee members are elected and the running of the Society is discussed whilst after the formal Dinner there is always a Guest Speaker, either someone who knew J.R.R. Tolkien or someone explaining how his works have effected them. The second event, the Seminar, takes place in the summer at which various talks are given on a Tolkien-related subject. These range from the serious through the tongue-in-cheek to the sublime and there is always something for everyone, no matter how intellectual they THINK they are. THE special event of the Tolkien Society year is Oxonmoot, held over a weekend in September in an Oxford University College. There are talks, slideshows, a costume party and a lunch hosted by Miss Priscilla Tolkien, daughter of the late Professor. It is a great time for making new friends in the Society.

Within the Society there are local groups spread throughout the UK called "Smials", after hobbit homes. Here both members and non-members gather to discuss Tolkien's works, as well as other writers and topics, often on a humorous level. Smials act as the social lifeline of the Society. There are also postal smials for those who live far from a local group, with regular newsletters and occasional meetings.
There are also Special Interest Groups, covering various topics.

There are two regular journals produced by the Society.

Amon Hen appears six times a year with Tolkien-related reviews, news, letters, artwork and articles, both humorous and serious. There is also *Mallorn*, annual and more academic in nature with longer critical articles and essays. Nearly all the material appearing in the journals is the work of society members, often giving them their first opportunity of presenting their work to a wider audience. There are also occasional booklets produced by the Society, Special Interest Groups, Smials and also individual members, dealing with Tolkien-related matters and often "filling in the gaps" of the Professor's works.

The Society has close and friendly links with the late Professor's family and publishers, also with fellow literary societies and other groups in all fictional fields.
The Society also maintains a varied library and fine archives, both of which are accessible to members and, in the latter case, to bona fide scholars who may be referred by the Society to private collections.

For further details please write to the Secretary:

> Annie Haward
> Flat 6
> 8 Staverton Road
> Oxford
> OX2 6XJ
> United Kingdom

The Tolkien Society, home for those who wander in Middle-earth.

". . . a perfect house, whether you like food or sleep, or story telling, or just sitting and thinking best, or a pleasant mixture of them all . . ."

Subscription rates in 1995 are:

United Kingdom:	£15.00
Surface (World-wide):	£17.50
European Air Rate:	£18.00
USA/Canada/Near East/ Africa Airmail:	£21.00
Australasia/Far East Airmail:	£22.00
Associate Members (no magazines):	£7.50

Library rates (publications only)

United Kingdom:	£17.00
Surface (World-wide):	£18.00
European Air Rate:	£19.50
USA/Canada/Near East/Africa Airmail:	£24.00
Australasia/Far East Airmail:	£24.00

Payment can be made by cheque, Eurocheque or International Money Order. If the cheque is not in British pounds (pounds sterling), or is drawn on an overseas bank, even if in pounds, please add £6.00 to cover conversion charges. Please pay in pounds, if possible. Payment by Credit Card (Master Card/Visa/Eurocard/Access) or Debit Card (Visa-Delta only) is also acceptable. If paying by credit card add 5% to cover our bank charges.

www.ingramcontent.com/pod-product-compliance
Lightning Source LLC
Chambersburg PA
CBHW081828170426
43199CB00017B/2678